Photo Courtesy of Judge Albert B. Maria

THE COURTHOUSE ON THE ISLAND OF TOBAGO*

"Can the Island of Tobago pass a law to bind the rights of the whole world?"
per Lord Ellenborough in Buchanan v. Rucker, page 42, infra.

*This is the courthouse referred to by Lord Ellenborough.
It has been replaced by a modern building.

UNIVERSITY CASEBOOK SERIES®

CONFLICT OF LAWS

PRIVATE INTERNATIONAL LAW

CASES AND MATERIALS

SIXTEENTH EDITION

PETER HAY
L.Q.C. Lamar Professor of Law Emeritus
Emory University
and
University Professor Emeritus
Technische Universität Dresden

PATRICK J. BORCHERS
Lillis Family Distinguished Professor of Law
Creighton University

RICHARD D. FREER
Charles Howard Candler Professor of Law
Emory University

FOUNDATION
PRESS

University Casebook Series is a trademark registered in the U.S. Patent and Trademark Office.

© 1936, 1941. 1951, 1957, 1964, 1971, 1978, 1984, 1990, 1996, 2000, 2004 FOUNDATION PRESS
© 2009 by THOMSON REUTERS/FOUNDATION PRESS
© 2013 LEG, Inc. d/b/a West Academic Publishing
© 2017 LEG, Inc. d/b/a West Academic
© 2021 LEG, Inc. d/b/a West Academic
    444 Cedar Street, Suite 700
    St. Paul, MN 55101
    1-877-888-1330

Printed in the United States of America

ISBN: 978-1-64708-599-5

To the memory of the scholars who authored
prior editions of this book.

Elliott Evans Cheatham

Noel T. Dowling

Herbert F. Goodrich

Erwin Nathaniel Griswold

Willis L.M. Reese

Maurice Rosenberg

Russell J. Weintraub

PREFACE

At no point in history has the subject of the Conflict of Laws (or Private International Law as it is also known) been more important than now. Even the most mundane of transactions often cross state, provincial, and national boundaries. A huge fraction of the population—aware or not—is likely subject to dozens of agreements (many created by hitting "I agree" on a dialog box on a computer screen) that have interstate and international dimensions. Routine purchases of foreign products create close jurisdictional questions if a dispute about the safety of the product arises. Even businesses of modest size are wise to take account how a dispute with a customer or another business will be resolved and whether the forum's judgment or arbitration award can be enforced. Marital dissolutions across state and international lines create complicated problems. And so on. As a result, few competent lawyers can ignore the subject.

The principal audience of this book is United States law students. In this edition we have gone to considerable efforts to ensure that the material is being presented to them in a comprehensible way. The first-year curriculum at most U.S. law schools is devoted entirely, or mostly, to U.S. law. Thus the prospect that a California court might apply French law may strike U.S. law students as strange, if not unimaginable. We have attempted to achieve a realistic balance between interstate and international matters. Some matters involve Illinois and Wisconsin; others involve New York and Hong Kong. In the Documentary Appendix we have reproduced some important European Union laws. In other places, we note non-U.S. and non-E.U. materials.

All three of the legs of the Conflicts tripod: jurisdiction, choice of law and judgment recognition are covered in detail. Recognizing in a three (or even four) hour course that even with the most brisk of coverage the entire book cannot be taught, we have arranged the material in a way that the instructor can easily pick and choose what he or she thinks is most crucial.

This is a book with a long history. Its first edition dates to 1936. Obviously a lot has changed since then. But many of the fundamentals have not. It is a much better book for having 85 years of earlier editions. The wisdom of our preceding editors infuses it still.

Thus, it is fitting that we dedicate this book to the eminent scholars who shaped previous editions.

PETER HAY
PATRICK J. BORCHERS
RICHARD D. FREER

March 2021

ACKNOWLEDGMENTS

We thank the American Law Institute for permission to quote from the Restatement (Second) of the Conflict of Laws (1971).

SUMMARY OF CONTENTS

TABLE OF CONTENTS

TABLE OF CASES

The principal cases are in bold type.

TABLE OF AUTHORITIES

CONFLICT OF LAWS

PRIVATE INTERNATIONAL LAW

CASES AND MATERIALS

SIXTEENTH EDITION

CHAPTER 1

INTRODUCTION

SECTION 1. THE SUBJECT MATTER

The conflict of laws is the study of how the answer to a legal problem is affected by the fact that the elements of the problem have contacts with more than one jurisdiction. In a world in which interstate and international transactions take place more frequently, no competent lawyer can ignore the subject. Knowledge of the conflict of laws is necessary not only for litigators and arbitrators, but also for all lawyers who give advice or draft documents relating to interstate and international activities.

In interstate and international transactions, there are three major topics that lawyers must address either in the planning or dispute resolution stage. (1) Where can the parties resolve a dispute by suit or other means, such as arbitration? (2) What law will a court or arbitrators apply to resolve the dispute? (3) What will be the effect of any judgment or award? An example may be helpful.

A group of Texas residents contracts with Texas Lines, a Texas bus company, for a vacation bus tour of Mexico. In their home city of Corpus Christi, they board a Texas Lines bus to Brownsville, a Texas city on the border with Mexico. In Brownsville, they board a bus owned by a Mexican bus company. While traveling in the Mexican State of Tamaulipas, the bus plunges off a bridge and all the occupants are fatally injured. Some die immediately, some a few days later. Now let us consider the three major conflict-of-laws issues in the context of this case.

Where can the parties resolve the dispute? The representatives of the decedents wish to bring wrongful death and survival suits against Texas Lines and the Mexican bus company. Because liability of Texas Lines is doubtful, the representatives especially wish to sue the Mexican bus company. If plaintiffs sue in Mexico, there is no doubt that there is personal jurisdiction over the Mexican defendant, but is there jurisdiction over Texas Lines? If plaintiffs sue in Texas, can they obtain personal jurisdiction over the Mexican company? If plaintiffs can obtain jurisdiction over the Mexican defendant in a Texas state court, will that defendant be able to remove to a federal court? Will a Texas state court dismiss suit under the doctrine of forum non conveniens? Will a federal court sitting in Texas apply Texas doctrines of jurisdiction and forum non conveniens?

What law will the court apply? Under the law of the Mexican state of Tamaulipas, there are low statutory caps on some elements of recovery, such as lost wages, and there is no compensation for pain and suffering. As a result, the average recovery per passenger would be about

$30,000. Under Texas law, there are no statutory caps on economic damages and there is recovery for several kinds of non-economic injury, including pain and suffering. Punitive damages may be available on these facts under Texas law, but are not available under Tamaulipas law. Not including punitive damages, the average recovery per passenger under Texas law would be about $1,000,000. If plaintiffs sue in Mexico, a Mexican court will apply Tamaulipas law because the fatal injuries occurred in Tamaulipas.[1] If plaintiffs sue in Texas, will a Texas state court apply Texas law?[2] Can plaintiffs sue in or defendants remove the case to a federal court sitting in Texas? If so, will the federal court apply the same law as would a Texas state court?

What will be the effect of any judgment? Because of the difference in damages under Tamaulipas and Texas law, and the likelihood that a Texas court will apply Texas law, it would be advantageous for the plaintiffs to sue in Texas. If plaintiffs obtain in a Texas court a judgment against the Mexican bus company, does that defendant have sufficient assets in Texas or other states of the United States for satisfaction of the judgment? If not, will a Mexican court recognize and enforce the Texas judgment?

These are the questions that all parties in the litigation arising out of the bus crash must carefully research. Moreover, they must do the research before taking any action. For example, whether a Mexican court will recognize and enforce a Texas judgment depends, in part, on the method used to serve process on the Mexican defendant.[3]

This illustration concerned an unintentional tort. Parties to commercial transactions should ask and research similar questions before they sign any contract. In commercial agreements, the parties can, by properly drafted provisions, exercise substantial control over the place where they can resolve the dispute, the method of dispute resolution, and the law that courts or arbitrators will apply.

SECTION 2. THE FUNCTIONS OF CONFLICTS AS A BODY OF LAW

For the first and third of the basic topics of conflict of laws, jurisdiction and judgments, it is obvious that a coherent body of rules is necessary. Within a federal nation, such as ours, these rules control the jurisdictional reach of state and federal courts and determine the respect that courts in the United States must give to sister-state and federal judgments. Internationally there are or should be standards to determine what bases for jurisdiction are legitimate and under what circumstances

---

[1]   Mexican Civil Code for the Federal District and Territories, art. 12.

[2]   Trailways, Inc. v. Clark, 794 S.W.2d 479 (Tex. App.—Corpus Christi 1990, writ denied), page 621, infra, a case similar to the illustration, applied Texas law to the Mexican bus company.

[3]   See Anderson, Transnational Litigation Involving Mexican Parties, 25 St. Mary's L.J. 1059 (1994).

courts will recognize and enforce judgments of another country. No country that believes a foreign court has improperly exercised jurisdiction will recognize that court's judgment. Lord Ellenborough's comment on the Island of Tobago, quoted in the caption of the frontispiece photograph, is an expression of this concept.

But what of choice of law? Here the need for rules has been more frequently questioned. Why not have every court simply apply the law of its own jurisdiction? This would certainly be simpler than entertaining complex arguments concerning what law applies and then, if the court chooses foreign law, attempting to apply without distortion the law of another state or country.

Ernst Rabel, a great scholar of comparative conflict of laws, wrote "it has been customary to regard the attainment of uniform solutions as the chief purpose of" choice-of-law rules.[4] But surely there must be other reasons for rules concerning choice of law than an attempt to insulate the result from the selection of the forum.[5] Rabel himself quickly translated the need for "uniform solutions" into protection of "the legitimate expectations of the parties."[6] In the last half century there was an increased acceptance of the contention that one purpose for choosing law is to give effect to the policies underlying the diverse domestic rules of the jurisdictions that have contacts with the parties or the transaction. This period is commonly known as "The Conflicts Revolution." But recently, the American Law Institute has embarked on the project of creating a Third Conflicts Restatement, to succeed the Second, which was promulgated in 1971. The Conflicts Revolution clearly succeeded in breaking courts out of some overly mechanistic rules, but with increasing frequency courts and scholars are debating whether the Revolution's excesses came at too high of a cost in terms of predictability of result. The debate is certain to continue.

SECTION 3. HISTORY

Our debt to England is here not as large as in other fields, for conflict of laws had an arrested development in English jurisprudence. The early centralization of power in the king and the establishment of a common law for the whole realm put an end to the conflicting laws inside the kingdom and eliminated the intra-national conflict of laws, which

---

[4]   E. Rabel, 1 The Conflict of Laws: A Comparative Study 94 (2d ed. by Drobnig 1958).

[5]   The "primitive idea that jurisdiction implies the applicable law, or in other words that a court can apply only the rules prescribed by its hierarchic superior, universally prevailed in ancient times, until about 1200 the general equitable conception was introduced that the more convenient and useful law should furnish the rule of decision conformably to the nature of the case." Yntema, The Objectives of Private International Law, 35 Can.Bar.Rev. 721–22 (1957).

[6]   Rabel, supra Note 4, at 94. See also Kegel, The Crisis of Conflict of Laws, Hague Academy of International Law, 112 Collected Courses 91, 188 (1964-II) ("since every state has to insure the achievement of justice on its own, these interests [in international uniformity of result] are, despite widespread opinion to the contrary, rather sharply delimited.").

elsewhere stimulated the development of the subject. A principle of venue kept international conflict of laws cases out of the common law courts. Because trial required a jury of the vicinage, the courts felt themselves unable to adjudicate cases arising in other countries. International cases had to go into special courts—the merchants courts and the court of admiralty. In time the common law courts used a fiction to surmount the difficulty of venue. Courts refused to admit any evidence to rebut the false allegation that the foreign location of the events in dispute was in England—"to wit, in the Parish of St. Mary le Bow, in the Ward of Cheap."[7] The idea persisted that an English court must decide a case under English law. Not until the nineteenth and twentieth centuries did England develop a body of conflict-of-laws rules. By that time developments on this side of the ocean had taken their own course.

Very early on the continent of Europe, scholars recognized the need for principles of conflict of laws, at first in Italy and later in France. The development of the principles of conflict of laws began in the Italian universities in the 1200s and 1300s during the revival of the study of Roman law. Conditions demanded it. Northern Italy consisted of a number of city states. While these states were a part of the Holy Roman Empire and regarded Roman law as a common law applicable to all of them, each had its local laws governing many matters. Trade was brisk between these city states and conflicts between their local laws arose with some frequency. A Bologna-Padua case or a Florence-Perugia case was apt to involve conflicting laws. In time, commentators developed principles to resolve these conflicts. "Statuta" was the term for the local laws of the city states. The statuta or statute theory became the basic method for choosing law. Some American cases discuss the theory.[8]

Afterwards, France and then the Netherlands developed conflicts theories that were in a sense intra-national, reflecting the diversity of legal systems among their constituent provinces. The writings of a Dutch jurist, Huber, proved highly influential in America, for his conception of territorial sovereignty made a deep impact on a great, early theorist in American conflicts law, Justice Joseph Story. In 1834 Story published his Commentaries on the Conflict of Laws, the first comprehensive treatment in English on the subject. He relied on continental theorists, particularly on Huber's concept of territorial sovereignty as the foundation for developing rules.

The Story-Huber approach shaped the course of growth in the next century. Harvard Law School professor Joseph H. Beale embraced the theory's major premises. Professor Beale had an enormous influence through his teachings, commentaries, and, ultimately, his work as Reporter for the American Law Institute's first Restatement of Conflict of Laws, published in 1934.

[7] See Friedman, Legal Rules and the Process of Social Change, 19 Stan.L.Rev. 786 (1967).
[8] See Milkovich v. Saari, 166, 203 N.W.2d 408, 414 (Minn.1973), p.584, infra.

SECTION 4. THE CONFLICT OF LAWS TODAY

Judicial Jurisdiction. The due process clauses of the Fifth and Fourteenth Amendments limit the jurisdiction of state and federal courts. International Shoe Co. v. State of Washington[9] displaced a power theory of jurisdiction with the requirement that the defendant "have certain minimum contacts with [the forum] such that maintenance of the suit does not offend 'traditional notions of fair play and substantial justice.' " This opinion appeared to free our courts to exercise jurisdiction within broad boundaries of civilized reasonableness. Instead, in its attempt to give more concrete meaning to the general standard of International Shoe, the Supreme Court of the United States has added layer upon layer of complexity to the task of determining when the exercise of jurisdiction is constitutionally permissible. Approximately five hundred reported cases a year focus on personal jurisdiction, and these are a small fraction of the unreported cases in which parties argue the issue. One reason for this amount of litigation concerning jurisdiction is that prediction of the result is difficult. It is a truism that the determination of jurisdiction is fact driven; minor changes in circumstances can affect the result. The task is even more formidable than this would suggest, because in many instances, our courts cannot agree on what facts are relevant.

Choice of Law. Here there has been revolutionary change. In 1960, every United States court would have chosen Tamaulipas law to apply to the bus accident discussed previously. This was because Tamaulipas was the place of injury. Forty states plus the District of Columbia and Puerto Rico,[10] would choose law by a rule or method that took into account the content and purposes of the Tamaulipas and Texas laws. Similar changes in conflicts rules have also occurred in other countries.

The abandonment of territorial conflicts rules, such as place of injury, has ameliorated some problems, but has generated new difficulties. Richard Posner has listed the change in choice-of-law method among the "legal reforms [that] have miscarried [resulting in] the destruction of certainty in the field of conflict of laws as a result of the replacement of the mechanical common law rules by 'interest analysis.' "[11] The choice-of-law materials in this book focus on the issues of whether this criticism is justified and whether there is a desirable via

---

[9] 326 U.S. 310, 66 S.Ct. 154, 90 L.Ed. 95 (1945), p. 65, infra.

[10] See Symeonides, Choice of Law in the American Courts in 2006, 54 Am.J.Comp.L. 697.

[11] R. Posner, The Problems of Jurisprudence 429–30 (1990). But cf. Judge Richard Posner in Kamelgard v. Macura, 585 F.3d 334 (7th Cir.2009): "The theory of the old rule (if it can be dignified with the word theory), *lex loci delicti*, as explained in the Holmes and Cardozo opinions that we cited, is that the right to a tort remedy vests upon injury; the existence and scope of the right therefore depend on the law of the place of injury; and the vested right, viewed as a piece of property acquired in the place of injury, is carried by the plaintiff, like the turtle's shell, to wherever he decides to sue.

"The old rule came to seem too rigid, mainly because of such anomalies as suits between citizens of the same state when it was not the state where the accident had occurred. Id. at 341."

media between territorial rules that select law without regard to its content, and methods that result in ad hoc chaos.

Judgments. Within the United States, docket pressures have greatly increased the ability of non-parties to utilize a judgment to preclude relitigation of issues decided. Internationally, the United States is not a signatory of any bilateral or multinational treaty for the recognition of judgments. All our states grant broad comity to foreign judgments. Except for punitive or multiple damages, many foreign courts enforce American money judgments.

SECTION 5. THE FUTURE OF CONFLICTS

Jurisdiction. Domestically, the challenge is to stem the flood of cases that contest this threshold issue and to improve predictability. Perhaps comparative study of how others, such as the European Union, have formulated jurisdictional rules, would facilitate the task. Internationally, we must respond to the charge that some of our bases for jurisdiction over foreigners are exorbitant, a task in which the U.S. Supreme Court has showed renewed interest since 2011.

Choice of Law and Judgments. Courts and legislatures will continue their attempts to fashion rules that avoid mechanical approaches yet provide reasonable predictability.[12] The Louisiana codification[13] is an attempt to do this. One method of eliminating conflicts between state rules is to substitute federal law. In the past, attempts to do this for issues such as products liability and airplane accidents have failed, but the efforts are likely to continue. Some scholars have argued that we cannot trust the states to decide when their law applies and that either Congress or federal courts should impose rules under the aegis of such clauses of the United States Constitution as due process, full faith and credit, commerce, and equal protection. As the materials in this book indicate, for a time in the early decades of the twentieth century, the United States Supreme Court did appear to raise some territorial choice-of-law rules to constitutional status. More recently, the Court has allowed the states to do pretty much what they will with choice of law.

Internationally, there are many treaties in force affecting choice of law. One that the United States was instrumental in drafting and has ratified is The United Nations Convention on Contracts for the International Sale of Goods. Instead of choice-of-law rules, the Convention sets out uniform law to cover certain aspects of international sales. The United Nations, The Hague Conference on Private International Law, The International Bank for Reconstruction and Development, and regional organizations such as the European Union

---

[12] For a survey of contemporary approaches, see Hay, Flexibility Versus Predictability and Uniformity in Choice of Law, Hague Academy of International Law, 226 Collected Courses 281–412 (1991-I).

[13] La.Civ.Code Ann.arts. 3515–3549.

and the Organization of American States, have produced multinational conventions and regulations covering the major topics of the conflict of laws. This book makes frequent reference to these conventions and regulations as part of its pervasive comparative coverage. The future will see many more such international collaborative efforts.

As Niels Bohr and Yogi Berra have stated, "prediction is very difficult, especially about the future." One certainty is that the growing number of transactions that cross borders gives added importance to satisfactory resolution of problems in the conflict of laws.

CHAPTER 2

DOMICILE

INTRODUCTORY NOTE

For many purposes, the law looks to a persistent relationship between an individual and a geographic area. In Anglo-American common law, this relationship is captured by the concept of "domicile." Thus, the law of one's domicile may govern various matters, including aspects of family law and the distribution of (at least some) assets at death. A domiciliary of a state may be entitled to privileges, such as voting and education benefits. She may also be subjected to taxation and to be subject to general personal jurisdiction in the courts of that state.

Because the need to identify a person with a geographic area arises in so many contexts, the cases present different theories on how one acquires and changes domicile. Notwithstanding this flexibility in application, two general tenets of the common law must be borne in mind: (1) every natural person has a domicile, and (2) no natural person has more than one domicile at a time.

SECTION 1. INTESTATE SUCCESSION TO MOVABLES

In re Estate of Jones
Supreme Court of Iowa, 1921.
192 Iowa 78, 182 N.W. 227.

Plaintiff claims that she is the illegitimate child of the decedent, Evan Jones, and as such is his sole heir and entitled to his entire estate. The administrator of the estate is made a party and also the brothers and sisters of the said decedent, who claim that the estate of the decedent descends to them. The court denied the plaintiff the relief sought, and she prosecutes this appeal. Reversed.

■ FAVILLE, J. The decedent, Evan Jones, was a native of Wales. When he was about 33 years of age, he came to America as an immigrant. This was in 1883. He came over on the same ship with the wife and children of one David P. Jones. At that time, David P. Jones was living in Oskaloosa, Iowa, to which place the decedent went. After the death of David P. Jones, the decedent married his widow, who subsequently died in January, 1914. The decedent, Evan Jones, was a coal miner, an industrious, hard-working, thrifty Welshman, who accumulated a considerable amount of property. In 1896, he was naturalized in the district court of Wapello county, Iowa, and thereafter voted at elections. The reason for his leaving Wales at the time he did was because of bastardy proceedings which had been instituted against him by the mother of the appellant. In 1915, the decedent disposed of his property, which then consisted of two farms and some city real estate. He was advised by his banker to leave the greater part of his money in a bank at Ottumwa until he got to Wales, and did so deposit it. He purchased a draft for about $2,000 and left some $20,000 on deposit in the bank, and also a note and mortgage for collection, and left with the banker the address of a sister in Wales, stating that he intended to live with said sister. He sailed from New York on May 1, 1915, on the ill-fated Lusitania, and was drowned when the boat was sunk by a German submarine on May 7, 1915. The Lusitania was a vessel of the Cunard line, flying the British flag. . . .

I.   The question for our determination in this case is whether or not, under the facts stated, the domicile of the decedent at the time of his death was in Wapello county, Iowa, or in Wales. If his domicile at the time that the Lusitania sank was legally in Wales, then it is conceded by all the parties that, under the laws of the British Empire, the appellant, as his illegitimate child, would have no interest in his estate. On the other hand, if the decedent at said time legally had his domicile in Wapello county, Iowa, then the property passed to the appellant as his sole heir under the laws of this state.

For the purposes of the present discussion, it may be conceded that the evidence is sufficient to justify a finding that the appellant was the child of the decedent and had been so recognized and declared to such an extent as to satisfy the requirements of Code, § 3385.

It may also be conceded, for present purposes, that it is established by the evidence in the case that the decedent had by acts and declarations evidenced a purpose to leave his home in Iowa permanently and to return to his native country, Wales, for the purpose of living there the remainder of his life. . . .

It is well settled that every person, under all circumstances and conditions, must have a domicile somewhere.

There are different kinds of domiciles recognized by the law. It is generally held that the subject may be divided into three general classes:

(1)   Domicile of origin.

(2)   Domicile of choice.

(3)   Domicile by operation of law.

The "domicile of origin" of every person is the domicile of his parents at the time of his birth. In Prentiss v. Barton, 19 Fed.Cas. 1276, No. 11384, Circuit Justice Marshall said: "By the general laws of the civilized world, the domicile of the parents at the time of birth, or what is termed 'the domicile of origin', constitutes the domicile of an infant, and continues, until abandoned, or until the acquisition of a new domicile, in a different place."

The "domicile of choice" is the place that a person has elected and chosen for himself to displace his previous domicile.

"Domicile by operation of law" is that domicile which the law attributes to a person independent of his own intention or action of residence. This results generally from the domestic relations of husband and wife, or parent and child.

In the instant case, we have to deal only with the first two kinds of domicile; that is, domicile of origin and domicile of choice. Applying these general definitions to the facts of this case, the domicile of origin of Evan Jones was in Wales, where he was born, and the domicile of choice was Wapello county, Iowa. The question that concerns us is: Where was his domicile for the purpose of descent of personal property on the 7th day of May, 1915, when the Lusitania was sunk off the coast of the British Isles?

The matter of the determination of any person's domicile arises in different ways and is construed by the courts for a variety of different purposes. Apparent inconsistencies occur in the authorities because of the failure to clearly preserve the distinctions to be made by reason of the purpose for which the determination of one's domicile is being legally ascertained. The question frequently arises where it becomes important to determine the domicile for the purpose of taxation, or for the purpose of attachment, or for the levy of execution, or for the exercising of the privilege of voting, or in determining the statute of limitations, or in ascertaining liability for the support of paupers, and perhaps other purposes. Definitions given in regard to the method of ascertaining the domicile for one purpose are not always applicable in ascertaining the domicile for another purpose. . . .

In the instant case, we are concerned only in the matter of the domicile of the decedent, Evan Jones, as it affects the question of the descent of his personal estate. . . . [D]ecedent's intention was to abandon his domicile of choice and return to his domicile of origin. He died in itinere. It is needless for us to cite the vast number of cases announcing the general rule that the acquisition of a new domicile must have been completely perfected, and hence there must have been a concurrence both of the fact of removal and the intent to remain in the new locality before the former domicile can be considered lost. . . .

At the outset, it is obvious that under the circumstances of the instant case the domicile of the decedent at the time of his death must in any event be determined by the assumption of a fiction. All will agree that the decedent did not have a domicile on the Lusitania. In order to determine his domicile, then, one of two fictions must be assumed, either that he retained the Iowa domicile until one was acquired in Wales, or that he acquired a domicile in Wales the instant he abandoned the Iowa domicile and started for Wales, with the intent and purpose of residing there. Which one of these fictions shall we assume for the purpose of determining the disposition of his personal property? This question first came before the courts at an early day, long before our present easy and extensive methods of transportation, and at a time before the present ready movement from one country to another. At that time men left

Europe for the Western Continent or elsewhere largely for purposes of adventure or in search of an opportunity for the promotion of commerce. It was at a time before the invention of the steamboat and before the era of the oceanic cable. Men left their native land knowing that they would be gone for long periods of time, and that means of communication with their home land were infrequent, difficult, and slow. The traditions of their native country were strong with these men. In the event of death, while absent, they desired that their property should descend in accordance with the laws of the land of their birth. . . .

These reasons, which were, to an extent at least, historical and patriotic, found early expression in the decisions of the courts on the question of domicile. The general rule was declared to be that a domicile is retained until a new domicile has been actually acquired. At an early time, however, an exception was ingrafted upon this rule to the effect that, *for the purposes of succession,* a party abandoning a domicile of *choice,* with the intent to return to his domicile of *origin,* regains the latter the instant that the former domicile is abandoned. . . .

The leading and most frequently cited English case is that of Udny v. Udny, L.R. 1 H.L. (Sc.) 441. In this case the question arose as to the domicile of one Udny, who was born in Scotland and who afterward resided in England and in France. The Lord Chancellor declared: "But the domicile of origin is a matter wholly irrespective of any animus on the part of its subject. He acquires a certain status civilis, which subjects him and his property to the municipal jurisdiction of a country which he may never even have seen and in which he may never reside during the whole course of his life, his domicile being simply determined by that of his father."

It is further said: "It seems reasonable to say that if the choice of a new abode and actual settlement there constitute a change of the original domicile, then the exact converse of such a procedure, viz., the intention to abandon the new domicile, and an actual abandonment of it, ought to be equally effective to destroy the new domicile. . . . Why should not the domicile of origin cast on him by no choice of his own, and changed for a time, be the state to which he naturally falls back when his first choice has been abandoned animo et facto, and whilst he is deliberating before he makes a second choice." . . .

It is true that the question of domicile is not to be determined by the question of citizenship, but when we are assuming the fiction that the domicile of origin reverts immediately upon the abandonment of a domicile of choice and assume that fiction, because of native allegiance, to the land of one's birth, then the basis for the fiction and assumption is destroyed when it appears that the party has renounced his native allegiance and has secured citizenship in the land of his domicile of choice. The reason for the rule having failed, the rule fails also. . . .

One reason that is persuasive why such a rule should not be adopted is that a person who in these days abandons his domicile of origin and acquires a legal domicile in another jurisdiction, presumably, at least, is familiar with the laws, of the jurisdiction of the latter domicile, and there is to say the least, as strong a presumption that he desires his estate to be administered according to the laws of that jurisdiction as of the jurisdiction of the domicile of origin. While there may have been a good reason for the establishment of the English rule at the time and under the conditions under which it was announced, we do not believe that any good reason exists for the recognition of such a rule under the circumstances disclosed in this case. The general rule that a domicile once legally acquired is retained until a new domicile is secured, and that, in the acquisition of such new domicile, both the fact and the intention must concur, it seems to us is a rule of universal and general application and that there is neither good logic nor substantial reason for the application of [an] exception to that rule in the case where the party is in itinere toward the domicile of origin. . . .

[Judgment of the trial court reversed and the estate ordered distributed under Iowa law to the decedent's child as his sole heir.]

WHITE V. TENNANT, 31 W.Va. 790, 8 S.E. 596 (1888). Michael White, until a month before his death, had been a life-long domiciliary of West Virginia, where his wife, brothers, and sisters were also domiciled. His mother, brothers, and sisters lived in the mansion-house of the family farm, which was on the West Virginia-Pennsylvania border and extended into both states. Michael White and his wife occupied a separate farm fifteen miles away in West Virginia. He sold that farm and made an agreement with his mother and siblings to occupy a house on part of the family farm that was in Pennsylvania. The day he left his farm intending not to return, he stopped off at the Pennsylvania house to unload household goods and turn livestock loose. His wife was not feeling well and on the invitation of his family, Michael and his wife stayed that night at the mansion-house in West Virginia. His wife was found to have typhoid fever. She recovered, but Michael also contracted the fever and died intestate before ever living in the Pennsylvania house. Under West Virginia intestacy law, Michael's entire estate would go to his widow, but under Pennsylvania law, half went to his siblings and half to his widow. The court decided that Michael died domiciled in Pennsylvania and that therefore the distribution of his estate was governed by Pennsylvania law. The court reasoned that he had the intention of making the Pennsylvania house "his residence for an indefinite time [and] when he and his wife arrived at his new home, it become eo instanti his domicile. . . ."

NOTES

1.   The English case of Udny v. Udny, L.R. 1 H.L. 441 (1869), quoted in *Estate of Jones*, set forth the "doctrine of reverter." Under this doctrine, one's domicile

of origin is revived as soon as the person abandons a domicile of choice. Thus, if the person dies in transit to a new domicile (either the domicile of origin or a new domicile of choice), the domicile of origin springs back into application. Id. at 448, 454, 460–61.

The American rule, applied in *Estate of Jones*, is that one retains her domicile (whether of origin or of choice) until she establishes presence in the new domicile. Thus, when one abandons a domicile, it continues to apply until she affirmatively establishes a new one.

The doctrine of reverter has been abolished in Australia and New Zealand. Aust. Acts of Parliament, Domicile Act of 1982 § 7; New Zealand Domicile Act § 11. The English and Scottish Law Commissions have proposed similar legislation (The Law of Domicile, Law.Com. No. 168 ¶ 5.25), but there is as yet no implementing legislation.

2.   The court in *Estate of Jones* states "[a]ll will agree that the decedent did not have a domicile on the Lusitania." The issue was whether Jones had acquired a domicile in Wales. The Restatement takes the position that if domicile of choice in a state is the issue, a person meets the physical presence part of the requirement by "presence anywhere in the state." Restatement, Second, Conflict of Laws § 16 cmt. a (1971). Wales and England share the same legal system. Marshall v. Murgatroyd, 6 Q.B. 31 (1870), involving application of a bastardy statute limited in its operation to England and Wales, declared: "It is part of the common law and of the law of nations, that a ship on the high seas is a part of the territory of that state to which she belongs; and therefore an English ship is deemed to be part of England. The child having been born on board an English ship, the statute applies." Id. at 33–34. Should the siblings of Evan Jones have made an argument that the Lusitania was part of the jurisdiction in which he had a present intention to acquire a domicile?

3.   The Iowa court suggests that selecting the law of domicile at death for intestate succession is likely to accord with the intention of the decedent who "presumably, at least, is familiar with" its laws. There is at least some evidence that this presumption is not realistic. A 1978 survey of Iowa citizens indicated that in various hypothetical situations, most would want their property distributed in a manner different from that provided by Iowa intestacy law. Note, A Comparison of Iowans' Dispositive Preferences with Select Provisions of the Iowa and Uniform Probate Codes, 63 Iowa L. Rev. 1041, 1077, 1091, 1146 (1978). As the Court said in Trimble v. Gordon, 430 U.S. 762, 775 n.16 (1977): "With respect to any individual, the argument of knowledge and approval of the state law [on intestate succession] is sheer fiction."

4.   Is the domicile at death the state that will usually bear the social consequences of the method of intestate distribution? Was that true in either *Estate of Jones* or *White v. Tennant*? The record in *Estate of Jones* reveals that all of the contestants (the illegitimate daughter and the brothers and sisters of the decedent) were residents of Great Britain and, with the exception of one sister who had sojourned in the United States, had been so all their lives. Appellant's Abstract of Record, pp. 2, 11, 114–15, 128–30.

Section 2 of the Inheritance (Provision for Family and Dependants) Act 1975 allows an English court to order a decedent's estate to make a further payment to the dependents of the deceased if the deceased's will did not "make reasonable financial provision" for the dependants. Section 1 limited section 2 to a decedent who "dies domiciled in England and Wales."

5. *Declarations of intention.* In Fritzshall v. Board of Police Commissioners, 886 S.W.2d 20, 27–28 (Mo.App.1994), a man declared on many occasions that he resided in Kansas City, Missouri. The court noted, however: "While a declaration of residence is entitled to some deference, it may be overcome by evidence of strong circumstances to the contrary. Behavior may speak louder than words."

Courts appear to conclude that the relevant intention is not specifically directed to change of domicile, but to the intention to reside in a place for an unlimited time. Consider the advice of a lawyer to Dr. John T. Dorrance. The lawyer said that maintaining Dr. Dorrance's domicile in New Jersey "was largely a matter of intention." Dr. Dorrance planned to purchase a mansion in Pennsylvania and move there with his family, but to avoid Pennsylvania taxes during his life and for various estate planning reasons, he wished to maintain his domicile in New Jersey. After moving to Pennsylvania, he and his family spent a few weeks each year at their former New Jersey residence, he made many formal and informal declarations that he was domiciled in New Jersey, and he kept many contacts with New Jersey such as church membership and car registration.

Nevertheless, the Pennsylvania Supreme Court found that Dr. Dorrance had acquired a domicile in Pennsylvania. This finding subjected stocks and bonds in his estate to Pennsylvania estate and personal property taxes. The court dismissed his declarations and his New Jersey contacts as "things which he did to avoid the appearance of identifying himself with the community in which he resided with his family." New Jersey courts, however, determined that Dorrance never intended to change his New Jersey domicile. Thus New Jersey also levied an estate tax on the stocks and bonds. In re Estate of Dorrance, 170 A. 601, 172 A. 503 (N.J.Prerogative Ct.1934), aff'd, 176 A. 902 (N.J.App.1935), 184 A. 743 (N.J.1936), cert. denied, 298 U.S. 678, 56 S.Ct. 949 (1936).

On the other hand, Mrs. Newcomb was successful in having a New York probate court give effect to her formal declarations that she elected to make New Orleans, Louisiana her "place of domicile and permanent home." She had been domiciled in New York and spent time at homes in both New York and Louisiana. She wished to change her domicile to Louisiana to ensure that probate jurisdiction over her estate would be there and her relatives would have more difficulty contesting her will (which left substantially all her property to Tulane University in New Orleans). In rejecting jurisdiction over probate proceedings in New York, the Court of Appeals of that state said: "While acts speak louder than words, the words are to be heard for what they are worth." In re Newcomb's Estate, 84 N.E. 950 (N.Y.1908).

The "Reporter's Note" to Restatement, Second, Conflict of Laws § 18 suggests that statements of domiciliary desire should be accorded more weight "in areas where normally the desires of the person concerned are supreme, such as in matters relating to the distribution of property upon death," but the

Note states that there is "little evidence that such distinctions have been drawn by the courts."

In Schill v. Cincinnati Ins. Co., 24 N.E.3d 1138, 2014 WL 5285445 (Ohio 2014), an Ohio domiciliary moved to Florida, intending to retire there. He "flunked retirement," however, and returned to Ohio for approximately two weeks of each month to engage in the business from which he thought he was retiring. In Ohio, he stayed at his son's house. In Florida, he lived in his wife's house. He maintained an automobile in Ohio, but it was registered in Florida. While recognizing that statements of intent are relevant to, but not dispositive of, a determination of domicile, the Ohio Supreme Court concluded that the erstwhile retiree was a domiciliary of Florida. The decision dealt with domicile for purposes of insurance coverage, and not succession, but includes a helpful discussion of factors relating to the establishment of domicile.

6.   *Domicile of wives and children.* The court in *Estate of Jones* noted that domicile by operation of law "results generally from the domestic relations of husband and wife, or parent and child." The common law rule was that a married woman was incapable of determining her own domicile; thus, she was ascribed the same domicile as her husband. In the United States, the rule concerning domicile of a wife gradually evolved from (1) she may acquire a separate domicile if she has justifiably left her husband, to (2) she may acquire a separate domicile if in fact she is separated from her husband, to the present rule, (3) that the domicile of each spouse is determined by his or her individual intentions and actions. The notion of such "derivative domicile" has never been struck down by the Supreme Court, however, and "there is some evidence that the derivative domicile rule frequently still functions in a gendered way, even today." Keffy Abrams, *Citizen Spouse,* 101 Cal. L. Rev. 407, 424–45 (2013).

By legislation, the United Kingdom, Australia, and New Zealand, have abolished the rule that a wife must have her husband's domicile. U.K. Domicile & Matrimonial Proceedings Act § 1 (1973); Aust. Family Law Act 1975 § 4(3); N.Z. Domicile Act § 5(1) (1976). Previously, English courts had held that even though the marital domicile had been in England, if the husband deserted the wife and moved abroad, the wife could not obtain a divorce in England although she continued to reside there, because she was no longer "domiciled" there. Herd v. Herd [1936] P. 205.

Emancipation is the process by which a minor is released from the control and authority of the minor's parents. Emancipation occurs when (1) the minor reaches the age of discretion and (2) the parents expressly or impliedly renounce their parental duties and all rights to the minor's services. A minor who contracts a valid marriage is thereby emancipated. In some states, emancipation is controlled by statute, but in others by judge-made rules. See Restatement, Second, Conflict of Laws § 22 cmt. f (1971). Until emancipated, a legitimate child's domicile is that of the parents and, if the parents are separated, that of the parent with whom the child is living. Restatement, Second, Conflict of Laws § 22 (1971) discusses rules to determine the domicile of an unemancipated minor who is illegitimate or does not live with a parent.

7. *Estate tax on intangible property.* At the time of the Dorrance litigation, discussed in Note 5, only the domicile at death had the constitutional power to levy an estate tax on intangible property, such as stocks and bonds. Unless the taxing authorities of the two or more states claiming the power to tax could be brought into the same court, there was danger of multiple taxation, as in Dorrance. In Texas v. Florida, 306 U.S. 398, 59 S.Ct. 563 (1939), the situation for the estate was so bad that it was good. In that case the Court accepted original jurisdiction of a dispute among four states as to where Edward Green, son of the legendary Wall Street investor Hetty Green, was domiciled at death. The combined state and federal estate taxes would have exceeded the value of the estate. The Court confirmed a master's finding that Green had died domiciled in Massachusetts.

Soon after Texas v. Florida, the Supreme Court abrogated the doctrine that only the domicile at death could tax intangibles. Curry v. McCanless, 307 U.S. 357, 59 S.Ct. 900 (1939), decided that Alabama and Tennessee may each impose death taxes upon intangibles held in trust by an Alabama trustee but passing under the will of a beneficiary decedent domiciled in Tennessee. State Tax Comm'n of Utah v. Aldrich, 316 U.S. 174, 62 S.Ct. 1008 (1942), held that Utah may impose an estate tax on stock in a Utah corporation, even though the stock was owned by a person who died domiciled in New York. In rejecting domicile at death as the sole constitutional nexus for death taxes on intangibles, the Court said: "Another State which has extended benefits or protection, or which can demonstrate 'the practical fact of its power' or sovereignty as respects the shares may likewise constitutionally make its exaction."

Despite this change in doctrine, California v. Texas, 457 U.S. 164, 102 S.Ct. 2335 (1982), again granted leave to file a complaint under the Court's original jurisdiction when federal and state death taxes threatened to exceed the value of the Howard Hughes estate. In a previous proceeding in the matter, the Court had denied the complaint. California v. Texas, 437 U.S. 601, 98 S.Ct. 3107 (1978). Justice Stewart, concurring in this denial, suggested that the estate bring an interpleader action in federal district court against the tax officials of each state. Under the Federal Interpleader Act, 28 U.S.C.A. §§ 1335, 1397, 2361, federal district courts have nationwide jurisdiction.

Justice Stewart premised this interpleader suggestion on the rule that "intangible personal property may, at least theoretically, be taxed only at the place of the owner's domicile." For this proposition, Justice Stewart cited First National Bank v. Maine, 284 U.S. 312, 52 S.Ct. 174 (1932). He failed to note, however, that that case had been overruled by State Tax Comm'n v. Aldrich (cited above in this Note). The administrator of the Hughes estate filed an interpleader proceeding, but the Supreme Court ultimately held that it was barred by the Eleventh Amendment. Cory v. White, 457 U.S. 85, 102 S.Ct. 2325 (1982). The second and successful invocation of the Court's original jurisdiction then followed. A special master was appointed to hear the case, but the matter was settled before the master ruled.

In view of the fact that both California and Texas probably had sufficient nexus with the Hughes estate to levy a tax on its intangible property, was original jurisdiction prudently granted? Were California and Texas free to construe their residence-based estate statutes as encompassing any contacts that were constitutionally sufficient to tax intangibles?

The Uniform Interstate Compromise of Death Taxes Act (1943), withdrawn by the Uniform Law Commission in 2005, remains vital in several states. It authorizes the taxing authorities of the states involved and the estate representative to make a written compromise of tax claims. The Uniform Interstate Arbitration of Death Taxes Act (1943), also withdrawn in 2005, is also effective in some states. It authorizes binding arbitration to "determine the domicile of the decedent at the time of his death."

Long ago, a commentator suggested that while due process permits more than one state to levy an estate tax on intangibles, it may also compel each state to tax only a fair share of the property. Farange, Multiple Domiciles and Multiple Inheritance Taxes—A Possible Solution, 9 Geo.Wash.L. Rev. 375, 379, 383 (1941), suggests that although the due process clause permits more than one state to levy an estate tax on intangibles, it may compel each state to tax only a fair share of the intangibles.

8. *"Habitual Residence."* European law often employs the concept of habitual residence instead of domicile. For example, conventions of the Hague Conference on Private International Law generally employs habitual residence as the relevant factor connecting a person to a state. At least in part, use of the term reflects the fact (demonstrated in *Estate of Jones*) that domicile bears different meanings in English and American law. For a discussion of habitual residence and whether it might have a useful role to play in American law, see Cavers, "Habitual Residence": A Useful Concept? 21 Am.U.L.Rev. 475 (1972).

The distinction between the two is demonstrated in Agulian v. Cyganik, [2006] EWCA Civ. 129, which was decided by the English Court of Appeal. In this case, the decedent was born in Cyprus. He fled to England at age 18, fearing for his safety because he had broken an engagement to be married. He resided in England for 43 years between returns to Cyprus. In England, he lived with a woman as husband and wife for ten years immediately preceding his death.

The decedent's net estate at death was £6,527,362, but his will left only £50,000 to the woman with whom he lived and to whom he was engaged to be married. The woman brought proceedings under the Inheritance (Provision for Family and Dependants) Act 1975, seeking increased payment from the estate. That law, as discussed above in Note 4, permits a court to make an increased provision for a decedent's dependent, but applies only if the decedent died while domiciled in England or Wales. The court concluded that the decedent died domiciled in Cyprus and thus ordered the action dismissed for want of jurisdiction. One justice, in concurring with the result, said:

> I find it rather surprising that the somewhat antiquated notion of domicile should govern the question whether the estate of a person, who was, on any view, habitually resident in England should make provision for his dependants. Now that many family matters are decided by reference to habitual residence, there may,

perhaps, be something to be said for reconsidering the terms of section 1 of the Inheritance (Provision for Family and Dependants) Act 1975.

The Hague Convention on the Civil Aspects of International Child Abduction, 1343 U.N.T.S. 98. provides for return of a child to the country of the child's "habitual residence" if the child was wrongfully removed from that country or wrongfully retained elsewhere. The removal or retention is wrongful if it was in breach of custody rights under the law of the habitual residence. United States courts have differed in determining "habitual residence." Robert v. Tesson, 507 F.3d 981 (6th Cir.2007), disagreed with Mozes v. Mozes, 239 F.3d 1067 (9th Cir.1999), which emphasized the intentions of the parents. The court stated that in determining the child's habitual residence, the focus is "solely on the past experiences of the child, not the intentions of the parents." Id. at 991.

The leading English case interpreting the term "habitual residence" is In re J. The parents, United Kingdom citizens, emigrated to Australia where they met, cohabited, had a child, but did not wed. Over two years after the child, J, was born, the mother left Australia without notifying the father. She took the child with her to England where she intended to reside indefinitely and not return to Australia. Twenty-two days after the mother had left Australia, the father obtained an order from an Australian Family Court judge awarding the father sole custody of the child. An English court dismissed the father's application for return of the child under the Convention and the Court of Appeal and the House of Lords affirmed. The opinion in the House of Lords held that the removal of the child from Australia was not wrongful because under Australian law, until the father obtained the custody order, the sole right of custody of the illegitimate child was in the mother. The retention of the child in England after the Australian custody order was not wrongful because by that time Australia was no longer the child's "habitual residence." On this last point, the opinion stated:

> [T]here is a significant difference between a person ceasing to be habitually resident in country A, and his subsequently becoming habitually resident in country B. A person may cease to be habitually resident in country A in a single day if he or she leaves it with a settled intention not to return to it but to take up long-term residence in country B instead. Such a person cannot, however, become habitually resident in country B in a single day. An appreciable period of time and a settled intention will be necessary to enable him or her to become so. During that appreciable period of time the person will have ceased to be habitually resident in country A but not yet have become habitually resident in country B. * * * [W]here a child of J's age is in the sole lawful custody of the mother, his situation with regard to habitual residence will necessarily be the same as hers.

9. *Residence.* Many statutes refer to "residence" rather than "domicile." In most contexts, "residence" is used as a synonym for "domicile," but at times the word has different meanings. For example, "residence" has been held to differ from "domicile" in focusing primarily upon physical presence and discounting the element of intent. Given the differing contexts in which it appears, a court construing the word "residence" should give it a meaning that fits the particular context. For a dated but thorough discussion, see Reese & Green, That Elusive Word, "Residence," 6 Vand.L.Rev. 561 (1953). See also Hay, Borchers & Symeonides, Conflict of Laws §§ 4.13–4.14 (6th ed. 2018); Restatement, Second, Conflict of Laws § 11 cmt. k (1971).

Following the divorce of his parents, a child spent weekends with his father and the rest of the time with his mother. Miller v. United States Fidelity and Guaranty Co., 127 N.J.Super. 37, 316 A.2d 51 (1974), held that the child was a resident of the "household" of each parent and hence covered by each parent's "homeowner policy." Accordingly, each insurer was held liable for the damage caused by a fire that the child had set. The court declared that "[w]hile a person may have only one true domicile, he may have more than one residence."

10. *Nationality as a connecting factor.* Sometimes in continental countries, nationality is used as the "connecting factor," for determining the governing law for certain personal rights. For a consideration of the relative advantages and disadvantages of nationality and domicile for this purpose, see Hay, Borchers & Symeonides, Conflict of Laws §§ 4.11–4.12 (5th ed.2010).

11. The impropriety of a person's motive in coming to a place does not prevent his acquisition there of a domicile of choice. In Gasper v. Wales, 223 App.Div. 89, 227 N.Y.S. 421 (1st Dep't 1928), the court had the problem of a man with two places of abode. The family home was in Connecticut. Relations with his wife were strained. The court concluded that his real home was in New York, where he had lived with another woman for many years. Proskauer, J., said: "While the furtiveness of this New York home is one of the facts to be considered in deciding whether he intended it to be his legal domicil[e], it is not controlling. . . . The [trial judge] seems to have assumed that [one] could not have a legal residence for an illegal purpose. Legal residence, however, does not depend upon the legality of the object of the residence; it rests upon physical presence in a dwelling coupled with an intent to make that dwelling one's home."

As discussed in Section 3 of this Chapter, an American citizen is considered a citizen of the U.S. state in which she is domiciled, and her motive in changing domicile (even if it is to create diversity jurisdiction) is irrelevant.

SECTION 2. VALIDITY OF A WILL

In re Estate of Clark

Court of Appeals of New York, 1968.
21 N.Y.2d 478, 288 N.Y.S.2d 993, 236 N.E.2d 152.

■ FULD, CHIEF JUDGE.

This appeal poses an interesting and important question concerning a widow's right of election to take against her husband's will. More particularly, may her husband, domiciled in a foreign state, by selecting New York law to regulate his testamentary dispositions, cut off or otherwise affect the more favorable right given his widow to elect by the law of their domicile?

In the case before us, Robert V. Clark, Jr., died in October of 1964, domiciled in Virginia, and there his widow continues to reside. His estate, consisting of property in Virginia and in New York, had an aggregate value of more than $23,000,000—the bulk of which consisted of securities on deposit with a New York bank. His will, made in 1962, contained a provision that "this Will and the testamentary dispositions in it and the trusts set up shall be construed, regulated and determined by the laws of the State of New York." It devised the Clark residence in Virginia, together with its contents, to the widow and created for her benefit a preresiduary marital deduction trust—under which she would receive the income for life, with a general testamentary power of appointment over the principal of the trust. The residue of the estate, after payment of estate taxes, was placed in trust for the testator's mother. There has been a bi-state administration of the estate. The New York executors who are administering the major portion of the estate—consisting, as noted, of securities held in New York during Mr. Clark's lifetime—and the Virginia executors are administering the balance, including the real and tangible personal property located in Virginia.

The testamentary trust for the widow's benefit would satisfy the requirements of section 18 of our Decedent Estate Law, Consol.Laws, c. 13 [and defeat her right to elect against the will]. However, it is conceded that, under the statutes of Virginia, the widow has an absolute and unconditional right to renounce her husband's will and take her intestate share (in the absence of issue, one half) of his estate outright (Virginia Code, § 64–16). Timely notice of the widow's election having been given, the New York executors initiated this special proceeding in the Surrogate's Court. . . . The executors contend that, by declaring that his testamentary dispositions should be construed by the laws of New York, the testator meant to bar his widow from exercising her Virginia right of election and that section 47 of the Decedent Estate Law requires that we give effect to his purpose. That section—replaced, since the testator's death, by a very similar provision (EPTL 3—5.1, subd. (h))—provided, in essence, that, when a nondomiciliary testator recites in his will that he elects that his *testamentary dispositions*" [of property in New York] shall be construed and regulated by the laws of New York, "the validity and effect of *such dispositions* shall be determined by such laws."

The Surrogate upheld the executor's position. On appeal, the Appellate Division reversed, deciding that the widow's right to take in opposition to the will must be determined by the law of the domicile of the parties. Section 47—which relates solely to the decedent's "testamentary dispositions" and their validity and effect—was inapplicable, the court concluded, because "the right of a widow to inherit despite the will is not a 'testamentary disposition' in any sense" but is, on the contrary, "a restriction on the right to make a testamentary disposition." (28 A.D.2d 55, 57, 281 N.Y.S.2d 180, 183.)

We thoroughly agree with the Appellate Division's construction of the statute and with the conclusion it reached. . . .

A moment's reflection is all that is necessary to establish the difference between statutes which have to do with restrictions placed on the decedent's testamentary power—for instance, to disinherit his spouse or other members of his family—and those which bear on discerning and carrying out the testator's wishes and desires. Section 47 is an example of the latter sort of legislation. Its earliest version (Code Civ.Proc., § 2694 (L.1880, ch. 178)) simply reflected the traditional choice of law rules, referring dispositions of personal property to the law of the decedent's domicile. It provided that the "validity and effect * * * of a testamentary disposition" of real property were to be regulated by the law of the situs and those of personalty by the law of the domicile; no exception was made for a case in which the testator might express a contrary intent. . . .

Moreover, consideration of general principles of choice of law serve to confirm the conclusion, at which we have arrived, that it is the law of Virginia as to the widow's right of election, not that of New York, which here controls. As between two states, the law of that one which has the predominant, if not the sole, interest in the protection and regulation of the rights of the person or persons involved should, of course, be invoked. . . .

While Virginia, as well as New York, has demonstrated concern for surviving spouses, the two states have done so in substantially different ways. A right to the income of a trust, sufficient under our law, is by no means the equivalent of taking the principal outright as would be the widow's right upon her election under Virginia law. Whether the widow in the case before us would be adequately provided for under the will or on our own law is irrelevant, for the same principles must apply to an estate of $23,000 as to one of $23,000,000, and we reject the notion that New York ought to impose upon its sister states its own views as to the adequacy of a surviving spouse's share. . . .

■ BURKE, SCILEPPI, BERGAN, BREITEL and JASEN, JJ., concur.

■ KEATING, J., taking no part.

Order affirmed.

NOTES

1.   The "very similar provision" mentioned in the opinion, EPTL § 3–5.1(h), which replaced § 47 of the Decedent Estate Law, refers to "disposition of property situated in this state" and the "validity . . . of any such disposition," rather than, as did § 47, to "testamentary dispositions." This change proved decisive in In re Estate of Renard, 439 N.E.2d 341 (N.Y.1982), which construed the successor provision as choosing New York law to prevent a son's election under French law against his mother's will. The son, although a citizen of both

France and the United States, was domiciled in the United States. His mother died domiciled in France.

2. *Estate of Clark* refers to "traditional choice of law rules," which apply the law of the testator's domicile at death to the validity of testamentary dispositions of personal property and the law of the situs to dispositions of realty.

The Convention on the Law Applicable to Succession to the Estates of Deceased Persons, promulgated under the auspices of the Hague Conference on Private International Law in 1988, departs from both of these rules. For testate and intestate succession of either personalty or realty, the Convention refers to the country in which the decedent was "habitually resident" at death, with alternative references under some circumstances to the law of the decedent's nationality. Habitual residence was discussed in Note 8, p. 18, supra.

A survey of countries that are members of the Conference revealed two major differences in the law applicable to estates. One difference was that some countries applied the same law to both personal and real property (unity principle) and some applied the law of the situs to realty and some other law to personalty (scission principle). The other difference was the law applied to all property in the "unity principle" countries, and the law applied to personalty in the "scission principle" countries. Here, the division was between countries that applied the law of the domicile at death and those that applied the law of the decedent's nationality. The scission principle and reference to domicile rather than nationality prevailed primarily, but not exclusively, in common law countries. Droz, Commentary on the Questionnaire on Succession in Private International Law, and Van Loon, Update of the Commentary, in Proceedings of the Sixteenth Session of the Hague Conference on Private International Law.

KANZ V. WILSON, 703 So.2d 1331 (La.App. 1st Cir.1997). Ms. Kanz was born in Texas, lived in Illinois most of her adult life, and after she became infirm, lived in a Louisiana nursing home for the last five years of her life. While living in Illinois, Ms. Kanz opened accounts in Illinois banks. When Ms. Kanz moved to Louisiana, she left the bank accounts in Illinois and opened two new accounts in Louisiana banks. She then executed signature cards purporting to give Mrs. Wilson a survivorship in all the bank accounts. If Louisiana law applied, the gifts were not valid because they were not evidenced by a notarized document executed before two witnesses. The court held that Louisiana law applied and that the gifts were not valid.

The court applied Louisiana Civil Code art. 3515, the "general and residual rule" of the conflict-of-laws provisions. Art. 3515 states: "an issue in a case having contacts with other states is governed by the law of the state whose policies would be most seriously impaired if its law were not applied to that issue." The court decided that Ms. Kanz died domiciled in Louisiana, despite her residence in a nursing home and her expressed desire to move to a retirement community in Texas. The court then declared that "this case is governed by Louisiana's law because it is the state whose policies would be most seriously impaired if its law were not applied."

NOTE ON DEVOLUTION OF REAL PROPERTY

The rule that devolution at death is governed by the law of the decedent's domicile applies only regarding personal property. When the question is inheritance of realty, courts generally apply the law of the situs of the property to determine the validity of testamentary dispositions.

In In re Estate of Boyd, 321 P.3d 1001, 1005–06 (Okla.App.2014), a Texas testator died, leaving all property to one of her four children; the other three were pretermitted. A Texas probate court entered judgment in favor of the sole named beneficiary, holding that he was "the sole devisee" under the will. This judgment was not entitled to full faith and credit in Oklahoma, however, which was the situs of mineral rights. The Oklahoma Court of Appeals held that the Texas judgment was *coram non judice* as to the validity and interpretation of wills concerning real property interests situated in Oklahoma. Under Oklahoma law, the four children were entitled to equal shares in the Oklahoma property.

Similarly, Mohr v. Langerman, 2014 WL 5243364 at *3 (Iowa App. Oct. 15, 2014), involved an inheritance dispute over Iowa land between a citizen of Arizona and a citizen of California. The testator was a citizen of Arizona at his death. The Iowa Court of Appeals held "the descent of real property is governed by the laws of the state wherein the land is situated, regardless of the domicile of the deceased."

SECTION 3. DIVERSITY OF CITIZENSHIP JURISDICTION

Rodriguez-Diaz v. Sierra-Martinez
United States Court of Appeals, First Circuit, 1988.
853 F.2d 1027.

■ Before CAMPBELL, CHIEF JUDGE, and TORRUELLA and SELYA, CIRCUIT JUDGES.

■ LEVIN H. CAMPBELL, CHIEF JUDGE.

Plaintiff Wilfredo Rodriguez Diaz (Rodriguez Diaz) appeals from an order of the United States District Court for the District of Puerto Rico dismissing his complaint for negligence and medical malpractice for lack of diversity jurisdiction. Rodriguez Diaz brought this action in the district court following a motor vehicle accident in Puerto Rico when he was 17 years of age. All the defendants reside in Puerto Rico. However, between the time of the accident and the commencement of this action, Rodriguez Diaz moved from his family's home in Puerto Rico to New York, and attained his 18th birthday. He then sued in the United States District Court for the District of Puerto Rico, on his own behalf and through his parents as next friends, alleging that he is a citizen of New York and that there is diversity of citizenship under 28 U.S.C. § 1332 (1982).

I

The facts relevant to the jurisdictional issue are these: On November 21, 1984, Rodriguez Diaz, while operating a motorcycle in Caguas, Puerto Rico, was in a collision with an automobile driven by Marcelo Sierra Martinez. Rodriguez Diaz suffered bodily injuries. He was immediately taken to the Hospital Regional de Caguas, from where he was transferred to the Centro Medico for emergency treatment. Rodriguez Diaz alleges in the present complaint that the treatment he received at the Centro Medico caused him to suffer a massive bone infection and aggravation of a leg injury. From Centro Medico he was transferred to Hospital General San Carlos where he alleges he also received improper treatment. Sometime later, Rodriguez Diaz was transferred to a hospital in New York City. He alleges he was living in New York at the time he brought this action in the United States District Court for the District of Puerto Rico. He further alleges in his complaint that he intends to remain in New York and make it his permanent home, and that he is now domiciled there. Rodriguez Diaz had turned 18 [the age of majority in New York] by the time he brought this action. His parents were and still are residents and domiciliaries of Puerto Rico, where the age of majority is 21.

The defendants in the action brought by Rodriguez Diaz were the driver of the automobile, Sierra Martinez, and two Puerto Rico hospitals, all of whom are residents and domiciliaries of Puerto Rico. The defendants moved in the United States District Court for the District of Puerto Rico where the action was brought to dismiss the complaint for lack of diversity jurisdiction. The district court concluded that, under Puerto Rico law, Rodriguez Diaz is a minor, and, therefore, his domicile is that of his parents. 665 F.Supp. 96 (D.P.R.1987). Ruling that as a matter of law Rodriguez Diaz's domicile at the time of the filing of this action was Puerto Rico, the court dismissed the complaint for lack of diversity. This appeal followed.

In its decision, the district court observed that, for purposes of diversity jurisdiction under 28 U.S.C. § 1332(a)(1), state citizenship and domicile are equivalents. The court also noted that in a diversity case the capacity of a person to sue or be sued is determined by the law of the state of the litigant's domicile. Fed.R.Civ.P. 17(b). The court then made certain observations crucial to its analysis. These were that the citizenship of a minor was the citizenship of his parents, and that the latter's domicile determined whether the minor had become emancipated so that he could establish a domicile of choice elsewhere. 665 F.Supp. at 98–99. On the basis of the foregoing, the district court concluded that the law of Puerto Rico—the home of Rodriguez Diaz's parents—controlled the issue of Rodriguez Diaz's present domicile. As under Puerto Rico law plaintiff was still a minor, being under 21 at the time of suit, and as he was unemancipated under Puerto Rico law, he could not establish a domicile of choice outside Puerto Rico. It followed that he was still a domiciliary of Puerto Rico, and that, therefore, there was no diversity of citizenship. Id.

II

While the case is close, we disagree with the district court's conclusion that the domicile of Rodriguez Diaz's parents—Puerto Rico—is the jurisdiction whose law must necessarily determine his capacity to acquire a domicile of choice.

We begin with certain generally accepted principles: As the lower court correctly noted, state citizenship for diversity purposes is ordinarily equated with domicile. . . . It is the domicile at the time suit is filed which controls, and the fact that the plaintiff has changed his domicile with the purpose of bringing a diversity action in federal court is irrelevant. Thus, except for the possible effect of his being a minor under Puerto Rico law, plaintiff's settling in New York with the requisite domiciliary intent would make him a citizen of New York and entitle him to pursue this action. . . .

We shall assume for purposes of resolving the legal issue raised in this appeal that New York is plaintiff's "true, fixed home." The question before us is whether this is enough for plaintiff to have acquired a New York domicile for diversity jurisdiction purposes.

The parties and the district court have framed the issue as one of choice of law: which law is applicable, Puerto Rico law or New York law.

It is a general principle of common law, recognized also in Puerto Rico, that the domicile of an unemancipated minor is ordinarily that of his parents. . . . Depending on which law is applied, the argument goes, Rodriguez Diaz will be treated as an adult or as a minor, with the capacity or lack of capacity to establish his own independent domicile. Plaintiff argues that we have to apply New York law, because that was his "domicile" at the time the action was filed. Not surprisingly, defendants argued, and the district court agreed, that whether Rodriguez Diaz was an adult with capacity to establish his domicile of choice is governed by Puerto Rico law.

As we see it, resolution of the issue before us does not and should not turn solely upon a conflicts of laws analysis. Although federal courts have to apply the choice of law rules of the forum to determine the substantive law in diversity cases, the "determination of litigant's state citizenship for purposes of section 1332(a)(1) is controlled by federal common law, not by the law of any state." Kantor v. Wellesley Galleries, Ltd., 704 F.2d 1088, 1090 (9th Cir. 1983). . . . That does not mean that state law and state conflicts rules regarding domicile should be ignored. At very least, they are "useful in providing basic working definitions." Stifel v. Hopkins, 477 F.2d 1116, 1120 (6th Cir. 1973). However, as the Sixth Circuit pointed out in Stifel, the considerations undergirding state choice-of-law rules have often been "developed in such diverse contexts as probate jurisdiction, taxation of incomes or intangibles, or divorce laws." Id. Choice-of-law formulae, therefore, cannot be the sole guideposts when determining, for federal diversity purposes, whether a party is domiciled in one or another state. Id. at 1126. The ultimate decision must be such as will best serve the aims of the federal diversity statute and the perspectives of a nationwide judicial system.

III

In the case at bar, the district court noted that in a suit brought by the next friend, the minor's domicile was controlling for diversity purposes. The court went on to state: "Under the common law, the citizenship of a minor is the citizenship of his parents, and to determine whether the minor has become emancipated so that he may establish a domicile of choice, we look to the law of the state of the citizenship of the parents." . . .

The difficulty with this rationale, as we see it, lies in the court's basic premise that the law of Puerto Rico controls. If Rodriguez Diaz were clearly a minor (under, say, both New York and Puerto Rico law), the court's analysis would be hard to fault. . . .

The problem here, however, is that the question is not whether, as a minor, plaintiff was emancipated, but whether he is a minor. That, in turn, depends upon a determination of where he is domiciled, the ultimate question. We do not, therefore, find the district court's analysis persuasive. . . .

The fact is, there is no purely logical way out of the dilemma. We cannot decide whether plaintiff is a minor under Puerto Rico law or an adult pursuant to New York law, without first determining where he is domiciled. On the other hand, we cannot make a determination whether he has the capacity to establish his own domicile without first knowing if he has reached the age of majority. We have, therefore, come full circle. To know if he has the legal capacity to establish his domicile of choice we need to know if he is an adult. But to determine whether he is an adult or a minor we first have to know where he is domiciled. There is, to be sure, a possible way out of this circle under formal conflict of laws principles. We could apply forum law to determine Rodriguez Diaz's legal capacity. Restatement of the Law, Conflicts of Law (Second), §§ 13 and 15(a) (1971).[5] This might be a proper resolution had the question of plaintiff's domicile arisen in a Commonwealth of Puerto Rico court, where the question of domicile is likely to implicate local matters over which Puerto Rico has the final say. But we do not think the lex forum provides a satisfactory resolution where the overriding and ultimate question is plaintiff's citizenship for purposes of federal diversity jurisdiction. Federal district courts sit throughout the nation. While it is unlikely a tort action like this, based on an accident in Puerto Rico, with all defendants residing there, could be pursued elsewhere than in the District of Puerto Rico, plaintiff could be involved in other federal diversity cases in other federal district

---

[5] "[A] person cannot acquire a domicile of choice unless he has legal capacity to do so. Whether such legal capacity exists will be determined by the law of the forum." Restatement of the Law, Conflicts of Law (Second) § 13, comment d.

courts, including the district courts located in New York. Were we to apply the rule of lex forum, Rodriguez Diaz could be viewed at one and the same time, and within the same judicial system, as both a citizen of New York and a citizen of Puerto Rico. That this is even theoretically possible suggests the unsatisfactoriness of determining state citizenship here, for federal diversity purposes, on the basis of lex forum. Rodriguez Diaz, we think, must be a "citizen" of one or the other state—not of both simultaneously.

We do not, moreover, see any compelling reasons of policy for adopting the law of the forum here. As pointed out already, while Puerto Rico doubtless has legitimate reasons for regulating persons such as plaintiff in respect to the making of contracts, property dispositions, support, and the like in Puerto Rico, it has little if any interest, based simply on the continuing presence of his parents in Puerto Rico, in denying to Rodriguez Diaz, while physically residing in New York, the right to sue under the diversity jurisdiction in a federal district court whether in Puerto Rico or elsewhere. While not crucial to our result, we also note that even plaintiff's parents have joined him in bringing this action: thus the parents' separate interests provide no reason to deny him the right to sue in a federal court. . . .

IV

Since neither pure logic nor conflict rules provide a meaningful solution, we feel free to make the choice we think fits best with the aims of the diversity statute and the national character of the federal judicial system. We hold that Rodriguez Diaz is a domiciliary of the State of New York—or, rather, that, if he can satisfy the district court that he meets the requisite factors of physical presence and intent, he is entitled to be a New York domiciliary for diversity purposes notwithstanding his minority status under Puerto Rico law. In reaching this result, we focus upon the physical and mental aspects of plaintiff's own situation, rather than imposing upon him a disability foreign to the law of the state where he now resides and having little meaning in this situation even to the place— Puerto Rico—whose law calls for it. To hold that one who meets all the domiciliary requirements (including capacity) of the state where he currently resides is a citizen of that state, seems clearly the most reasonable result here. . . .

In the present case, there are perhaps no urgent reasons of federal diversity policy. . . . Since Rodriguez Diaz is recently from Puerto Rico, and his parents reside there, it is unlikely he would encounter prejudice were he forced to sue in Puerto Rico's own courts. The more realistic comparison, however, may be between the relative unfairness of denying a federal forum to Rodriguez Diaz while granting it to another young Puerto Rican of similar age whose parents moved to New York with him. Federal diversity jurisdiction exists as a matter of right for those who meet the statutory criteria, whether or not the plaintiff would actually encounter prejudice in the courts of another state. Federal courts should not, therefore, deny the right on the basis of pointless technicalities. In this case, if Rodriguez Diaz, being physically present in New York, qualifies under regular domiciliary rules as a domiciliary of New York, we do not think the difference in law between his former domicile, Puerto Rico, and New York concerning the age of majority should deny him the right to sue as a citizen of New York in federal court. . . .

Vacated and remanded for further proceedings not inconsistent herewith.

■ TORRUELLA, CIRCUIT JUDGE (dissenting). . . .

Since there is no case in which a change in domicile has taken place without, at the very least, a physical departure from the place of original domicile, and it is legally impossible to acquire a new domicile without first losing the old one, we must determine the legal significance of such action in that jurisdiction; i.e., Puerto Rico. The issue thus is what, if any, is the legal significance, for change of domicile purposes, of an 18 year old resident of Puerto Rico leaving that jurisdiction.

The answer under Puerto Rican law is clear: none. . . .

That a state has a paramount interest in protecting, regulating and controlling its minor citizens is beyond cavil. . . .

Because this is, as it should be, an area highly reflective of local attitudes, values and mores, it is particularly unsuited to federalized tinkering. Thus, the majority is mistaken in placing emphasis on the "right of access to a federal court" as the central issue raised by this appeal. . . .

Diversity jurisdiction, particularly in this day and age, is not in need of unnatural expansion, and especially not at the expense of important, non-selective local interests. . . .

The majority also implicitly rejects without explanation the only precedent directly on point, cited by the district court. In Spurgeon v. Mission State Bank, 151 F.2d 702 (8th Cir. 1945), the court determined whether an eighteen-year-old minor who moved to Kansas from his parents' home in Missouri was "capable of acquiring a domicile of his choice" for purposes of diversity jurisdiction. The court determined that the appellant had acquired a domicile in Kansas by first ruling that "[w]hether the appellant was an emancipated minor at the time of his departure from the home of his parents is a question controlled by Missouri law." Id. at 703. That is, for purposes of determining whether an eighteen-year-old had the capacity to acquire a domicile of choice, the court looked to the law of the jurisdiction from which the youth had departed.

Admittedly, the above cited authority can be read to support an alternative rule of law, a rule implicitly applied by at least one court but also rejected by my brothers. In Appelt v. Whitty, 286 F.2d 135 (7th Cir. 1961), the court denied diversity jurisdiction after it used Illinois law to determine that the minor plaintiff, who had moved from Michigan to Illinois, was emancipated. Although the court gave no reason why it applied Illinois rather than Michigan law (nor did it suggest that the outcome would have been different), it appears to have used the principle of lex loci, since the case came on appeal from the District Court of the Northern District of Illinois. The lex loci approach to capacity is also the suggested approach of the Restatement, Second, Conflict of Laws (1971), as stated in comment d to its section 13, for determining capacity to acquire a domicile of choice.[11]

Appellant is not looking to federal court for protection from bias and parochialism but rather is forum shopping by filing in the federal jurisdiction in Puerto Rico where he is entitled to a civil jury trial. . . .

Assuming there is a federal policy to make federal courts more widely available to litigants and to not "deny the right [to federal court] on the basis of pointless technicalities," the majority's approach does not satisfy even this goal. For example, if any individual in appellant's situation now wanted to file a diversity suit against a New York citizen in New York (a forum much more likely to be unfriendly), he would be barred from access to federal court due to lack of diversity. Thus, the majority's approach provides neither greater access nor eliminates "pointless technicalities" as a barrier to federal court. . . .

NOTES

1. *Compare Rodriguez-Diaz* with Mitchell v. Mackey, 915 F.Supp. 388 (M.D.Ga.1996), which placed the diversity citizenship of a majority-aged college student with her parents, notwithstanding the fact that her parents had moved to a new abode during the student's college attendance and the student had not as of yet visited her parents at their new home. The court emphasized that the student suffered from physical disabilities, making her unusually dependent on her parents, and referred to the requirement that a party actually "set foot" in the new domicile as a "needless formality."

2. The plaintiff in *Rodriguez-Dias* attempted to establish domicile (and therefore citizenship) in New York for the purpose of invoking diversity of citizenship jurisdiction. If the change of domicile was effected, this motivation does not make it improper. As Justice Holmes said in Williamson v. Osenton, 232 U.S. 619, 625, 34 S.Ct. 442 (1914): "the motive for the change was immaterial; . . . the plaintiff had a right to select her domicil for any reason that seemed good to her."

GALVA FOUNDRY CO. V. HEIDEN, 924 F.2d 729 (7th Cir.1991). An Illinois company sued its former president for fraud. The plaintiff

---

[11] A preference for the lex loci approach is also suggested by rule 17(b) of the Federal Rules of Civil Procedure which, while stating that the "capacity of an individual . . . shall be determined by the law of his domicile," also states that "[i]n all other cases [not concerning a corporation or an entity whose capacity is determined by federal law] capacity . . . shall be determined by the law of the state in which the district court is held. . . ." The rules, therefore, suggest that when domicile is not determinative, capacity should be determined according to the law of the forum.

attempted to invoke diversity jurisdiction on the ground that the defendant had acquired a domicile in Florida. Defendant had a vacation home in Florida and took several steps to indicate his change of domicile to Florida, including registering to vote, acquiring a driver's license, and listing the Florida address on his federal tax return. The defendant had sold his stock in the plaintiff and if he were domiciled in Florida, he would avoid Illinois taxes on the profit from this sale. The district court dismissed the case for lack of diversity, and the Seventh Circuit affirmed:

> Unfortunately, in this age of second homes and speedy transportation, picking out a single state to be an individual's domicile can be a difficult, even a rather arbitrary, undertaking. Domicile is not a thing, like a rabbit or a carrot, but a legal conclusion, though treated as a factual determination for purposes of demarcating the scope of appellate review. And in drawing legal conclusions it is always helpful to have in mind the purpose for which the conclusion is being drawn. The purpose here is to determine whether a suit can be maintained under the diversity jurisdiction, a jurisdiction whose main contemporary rationale is to protect nonresidents from the possible prejudice that they might encounter in local courts. This argues for finding the defendant, Mr. Heiden, to be a domiciliary of the same state as the plaintiff, Galva—that is, Illinois. Heiden is a long-time resident of Illinois and unlikely therefore to encounter hostility in its state courts. And anyway he does not want to be in federal court. It is Galva that wants to be in federal court. Yet Galva is indisputably a citizen of Illinois. . . .

> Heiden intended no change in the manner or style of his life, the center of gravity of which was and remains in Peoria[, Illinois], but only a change in his tax rate. The aura of fraud that surrounds his maneuverings in 1988 [to acquire indicia of Florida citizenship] would help Galva if citizenship for diversity purposes could be acquired by estoppel—which Galva does not argue, and rightly so, for such an argument would be inconsistent with the rule that diversity is a jurisdictional requirement, which a defendant cannot, therefore, waive. But since citizenship cannot be acquired by estoppel, the aura of fraud hurts Galva. It shows that Heiden did not want to change his domicile. He just wanted to fool the taxing authorities in Florida and particularly Illinois (for it was Illinois taxes that he was trying to escape) into thinking he did. This is shady business but it cannot convert a suit between two residents of Illinois into a suit against a Floridian.

PALAZZO V. CORIO, 232 F.3d 38 (2d Cir.2000), affirms the granting of defendant's motion to dismiss for lack of diversity jurisdiction. The district court found that both parties were New York citizens because defendant had not changed his domicile to Pennsylvania when he moved there to live with his grandparents. Defendant continued to attend school in New York, left most of his personal effects at his parent's house in New York, and testified that he regarded his parents' house as his home and his move to Pennsylvania as temporary. The Second Circuit states: "The district court's factual findings as to whether there has been a change of residence and whether that move was effected with the requisite intent of permanence may be overturned on appeal only if they are 'clearly erroneous'. . . . [T]he factual questions that inform a determination as to a federal jurisdiction need not be submitted to a jury and may be resolved by the court."

Federal courts of appeals disagree as to whether for the purposes of diversity jurisdiction an incompetent's guardian can change the incompetent's domicile. See Acridge v. The Evangelical Lutheran Good Samaritan Society, 334 F.3d 444 (5th Cir.2003), collecting authority and holding that the guardian effects a change of domicile if acting in the incompetent's best interest.

SECTION 4. JUDICIAL JURISDICTION

Alvord & Alvord v. Patenotre

Supreme Court of New York, Special Term, New York County, 1949.
196 Misc. 524, 92 N.Y.S.2d 514.

Action by Alvord & Alvord against Raymond Patenotre and Eleanor Patenotre, wherein defendants moved to vacate order for substituted service and the service made pursuant thereto.

■ MILLER, J. . . .

The order for substituted service was obtained on October 5, 1949 and service pursuant thereto was made by affixing to the door of the moving defendant's apartment a copy of the summons, complaint and order on the same day and by depositing a copy of the papers in the mails at 1:05 A.M. on the next day, October 6th.

Concededly the moving defendant did not arrive in France until October 5th. The affidavit of his attorney submitted in support of the present motion states that the movant "departed from this country for the purpose of establishing his domicile in Switzerland and with the intent and purpose to change his domicile in this country which had existed in or about the years 1946 and 1947". No claim is made that at the time service was effected pursuant to the order for substituted service the movant had already arrived in Switzerland. It is thus clear that his presence in France was merely a temporary stopover en route to Switzerland. In view of the admission of movant's attorney that the movant's domicile had been in this country up to the time he left, it is clear that the domicile was still in this country at the time service was made, for the movant had not yet arrived in Switzerland, his allegedly intended new domicile. "The existing domicile, whether of origin or selection, continues until a new one is acquired." Rawstorne v. Maguire, 265 N.Y. 204, 208, 192 N.E. 294, 295. . . .

In the court's opinion the moving defendant, concededly domiciled here at the time of the service, may not obtain vacatur of the order for substituted service and the service made pursuant thereto merely because he had just left this state for the purpose of avoiding service. . . .

[Motion denied.]

NOTES

1. It is not clear from the opinion in *Alvord & Alvord* whether the claim asserted arose in the forum state. The question may be irrelevant, however, because American courts historically have held that one's domicile in a state subjects the person to "general personal jurisdiction," which is sometimes called "all-purpose personal jurisdiction." As discussed in detail in Chapter 3, Section 2, general jurisdiction means that the defendant may be sued in the forum for a claim arising anywhere in the world.

2. The Supreme Court has been active recently in addressing the scope of general jurisdiction. In Daimler AG v. Bauman, 571 U.S. 117, 134 S.Ct. 746 (2014), which is a principal case p. 126, infra and Goodyear Dunlop Tires Operations, S.A. v. Brown, 564 U.S. 915, 131 S.Ct. 2846 (2011), the Court recognizes general jurisdiction in cases in which the defendant is "at home" or "essentially at home" in the forum. The decisions focus on what constitutes "at home" for purposes of corporations, but state that the archetypal example of "at home" is an individual's domicile.

3. Why is it usually reasonable to exercise general jurisdiction over a domiciliary of the forum? Was that justification present in *Alvord & Alvord*?

4. RESTATEMENT, SECOND, CONFLICT OF LAWS § 29 originally read: "A state has power to exercise judicial jurisdiction over an individual who is domiciled in the state." In 1988, the American Law Institute revised the section to read: "A state has power to exercise judicial jurisdiction over an individual who is domiciled in the state, except in the highly unusual case where the individual's relationship to the state is so attenuated as to make the exercise of such jurisdiction unreasonable."

Council Regulation on Jurisdiction and Enforcement of Judgments in Civil and Commercial Matters, in force in the European Union, Art. 2(1) states: "Subject to this Regulation, persons domiciled in a Member State shall, whatever their nationality, be sued in the courts of that Member State." For further discussion of this Article, see p. 1137, et seq. infra.

If a New York court could not exercise jurisdiction over the defendant in *Alvord* based on his technical retention of domicile, does that mean that the defendant could not be subject to general jurisdiction in another state until he had acquired a new domicile? What about jurisdiction arising from or related to the defendant's conduct? With a few exceptions, such as damage caused by motorists, it was not until 1963 that New York had a statute that conferred jurisdiction over nonresidents based on in-state acts or effects.

SECTION 5. SPECIAL SITUATIONS

A. REFUGEES

The domicile of refugees is likely to raise peculiar problems. An example is Roboz v. Kennedy, 219 F.Supp. 892 (D.D.C.1963) which involved a suit for the return of property vested in the Attorney General under the International Claims Settlement Act (22 U.S.C.A. § 1631). By the terms of that Act, the vesting of plaintiffs' property would have been proper if the plaintiffs had been "domiciled" in Hungary after March 13, 1941. The plaintiffs were mother and son. They and the father were nationals of Hungary and had lived in that country all their lives up to the crucial date. At that time, they were all in Hungary, the father in a Nazi prison and the mother engaged in seeking his release.

"In view of the increasing Nazi orientation of the Hungarian Government," the plaintiffs and the father had planned to leave Hungary since 1939. In 1940, the plaintiffs obtained United States visas. They did not leave at that time because of the imprisonment of the father and only reached the United States in 1947 "resolved never to return to Hungary under any circumstances." Held for the plaintiffs. "The facts ... demonstrate conclusively that plaintiffs had a firm and continuing intent to leave Hungary forever before March 13, 1941 ... Clearly, they were involuntarily in Hungary. They therefore cannot be considered ... domiciled in ... Hungary" within the meaning of the statute. "Congress could not have intended so inequitable a result. ..."

NOTES

1.   In Gaudin v. Remis, 379 F.3d 631 (9th Cir.2004), Father removed two children from Canada to Hawaii. Mother, a Canadian citizen, traveled to Hawaii as a "nonimmigrant alien" and filed a petition to have the children returned to Canada pursuant to the Hague Convention on the Civil Aspects of International Child Abduction. The court had previously ruled that the petition was moot if the mother had moved permanently to Hawaii. Now the court noted that the statutory definition of "nonimmigrant alien" is a person who has no intention of abandoning the alien's residence in a foreign country. Applying "the federal common law of domicile" the court held that the mother "is barred by law from possessing the requisite intent to establish domicile in Hawaii. Because she cannot lawfully have moved permanently to Hawaii, the case is not moot, and the [district] court erred in so holding." Id. at 638.

Mark v. Mark, [2005] 3 All E.R. 912 (H.L.2005). A Nigerian national began divorce proceedings in England. At that time she had overstayed her visa and her presence in England was unlawful. The husband contested the English court's jurisdiction on the ground that the wife did not have the requisite domicile in England. Baroness Hale of Richmond wrote the opinion for the House of Lords upholding jurisdiction to divorce: "[T]here is no reason in principle why a person whose presence here is unlawful cannot acquire a domicile of choice in this country. Although her presence here is a criminal offence, it is by no means clear that she will be required to leave if the position is discovered." Id. at 930.

At times, a person has been found to have a domicile in the United States although present here only on a temporary basis or after the person's visa had expired. Rzeszotarski v. Rzeszotarski, 296 A.2d 431 (D.C.App.1972) (expired temporary visa—divorce); Seren v. Douglas, 30 Colo. App. 110, 489 P.2d 601 (1971) (expired student visa—in-state tuition benefits); Williams v. Williams, 328 F.Supp. 1380 (D.V.I.1971) (temporary worker visa—divorce and adoption); Bustamante v. Bustamante, 645 P.2d 40 (Utah 1982) (tourist visa—divorce). Contra: Gosschalk v. Gosschalk, 48 N.J.Super. 566, 138 A.2d 774 (1958), aff'd, 28 N.J. 73, 145 A.2d 327 (1958) (alien on temporary visa held incapable of acquiring domicile for divorce).

2.   *Illegal entrants.* In Cabral v. State Board of Control, 112 Cal.App.3d 1012, 169 Cal.Rptr. 604 (1980), aliens who had entered the United States illegally were held capable of acquiring a domicile in California for purposes of recovering under that state's Victims of Violent Crimes Act. However, in Buscema v. Buscema, 20 N.J.Super. 114, 89 A.2d 279 (1952), an alien, who was released on his own recognizance while awaiting a deportation hearing for having illegally entered the United States, was held incapable of acquiring a domicile for divorce purposes. See also St. Joseph's Hosp. v. Maricopa County, 142 Ariz. 94, 688 P.2d 986 (1984). Illegal aliens were held to be domiciled in the county where they were receiving emergency medical care for purposes of the statutes determining eligibility for such care. See also Pilkington, Illegal Residence and the Acquisition of a Domicile of Choice, 33 Int'l & Comp.L.Q. 885 (1984).

B. STUDENTS

A student will usually not acquire a domicile of choice in the place where the school or college is located. The tendency of most students to continue to regard their parents' dwelling as "home" and the relative shortness of the intended stay at the school or college work against regarding the school's situs as home.

The situation is different, however, if the student has abandoned the parental home and has struck out to make an independent life, particularly if the student has married. It then becomes far more likely that the court will accept the claim that the location of the institution of learning is the student's "home" and constitutes a domicile of choice. See Robbins v. Chamberlain, 297 N.Y. 108, 75 N.E.2d 617 (1947).

C. MILITARY PERSONNEL

The United States Constitution limits the power of a state to impose rules that make it difficult for certain classes of persons, such as military personnel and students, to acquire a local domicile for purposes of voting.

In Carrington v. Rash, 380 U.S. 89 (1965), the Supreme Court struck down a Texas constitutional provision that precluded military personnel stationed in the state from acquiring a domicile there for voting purposes. With regard to students, Judge Friendly stated in Ramey v. Rockefeller, 348 F.Supp. 780 (E.D.N.Y.1972) that, although a state may insist that all applicants for the vote fulfill the requirements of bona fide residence:

> The only constitutionally permissible test is one which focuses on the individual's present intention and does not require him to pledge allegiance for an indefinite future. The objective is to determine the place which is the center of the individual's life now, the locus of his primary concern. The determination must be based on *all* relevant factors; it is not enough that a student, or any other former nondomiciliary, would find that the place of his presence is more convenient for voting or would enable him to take a more active part in political life. The state may insist on other indicia, including the important one of abandonment of a former home.

> We think therefore that, in determining bona fide residence for a person physically present, the state cannot constitutionally go further than the test set out in the Restatement (Second) of the Conflict of Laws § 18 (1971), namely, that he "must intend to make that place his home for the time at least."

In Newburger v. Peterson, 344 F.Supp. 559 (D.N.H.1972), the plaintiff, a Dartmouth student, asked the court to enjoin the use of a New Hampshire statute that disqualified a person from voting in a town if that person had a firm intention of leaving the town at a fixed time in the future. The court held that the statute violated the equal protection clause of the Fourteenth Amendment:

> In this day of widespread planning for change of scene and occupation we cannot see that a requirement of permanent or indefinite intention to stay in one place is relevant to responsible citizenship. . . .

> We are sensitive to the compelling need "to preserve the basic conception of a political community". . . . But the challenged New Hampshire law forces persons who are in every meaningful sense members of New Hampshire political communities to vote in communities elsewhere which they have long departed and with whose affairs they are no longer concerned, if indeed the former community still recognizes the right. . . .

NOTES

1.   Any person age eighteen years or older has the capacity to acquire a domicile of choice for voting purposes, and that capacity is not impaired by living in a college dormitory and receiving parental support. Hershkoff v. Board of Registrars of Voters of Worcester, 366 Mass. 570, 321 N.E.2d 656

(1974). See also Paulson v. Forest City Community School District, 238 N.W.2d 344 (Iowa 1976).

Frankel v. Board of Regents of the Univ. of Maryland System, 761 A.2d 324 (Md.2000), holds that a rule precluding in-state tuition status to any student whose primary monetary support comes from an out-of-state source discriminates against bona fide Maryland residents in violation of the equal protection clause of the state's constitution.

2. Wit v. Berman, 306 F.3d 1256 (2d Cir.2002), cert. denied, 538 U.S. 923, 123 S. Ct. 1574 (2003). Voters maintained residences in both New York City and the Hamptons on Long Island. They divided their time between these residences and asserted the right to vote in local elections in both places. New York Election Law bars them from voting in more than one place. The voting registrars permit persons with two or more principal residences in New York to choose one, but only one, as the voting residence. The voters challenged the law as unconstitutionally violating their rights to equal protection of the laws and to due process. Held: The law and practice are valid. "Legal bright lines will always be under- or over-inclusive, but chaos is hardly preferable." Id. at 1262.

3. Where the serviceman lives off the base and shows a clear intention to make his home where he lives, he may acquire a domicile there. See Sasse v. Sasse, 41 Wash.2d 363, 249 P.2d 380 (1952). A serviceman was found to be domiciled in the state in Slade v. Slade, 122 N.W.2d 160 (N.D.1963), even without such evidence. For a typical case refusing to find a soldier domiciled for purposes of divorce jurisdiction in the place where he was stationed, although he had testified that he intended to make that place his home following his discharge from the Army, see Hammerstein v. Hammerstein, 269 S.W.2d 591 (Tex.Civ.App.1954). A few courts have held that service personnel living on base have acquired a domicile in the state for divorce purposes. See Bezold v. Bezold, 95 Idaho 131, 504 P.2d 404 (1972); Marcus v. Marcus, 3 Wisc. App. 370, 475 P.2d 571 (1970).

4. More than a dozen states have statutes providing that persons in the armed services, living in the state for a specified period, shall be deemed a resident for purposes of divorce suits. See generally Leflar, Conflict of Laws and Family Law, 14 Ark.L.R. 47, 49 (1960); see also Hay, Borchers & Symeonides, Conflict of Laws § 4.26 and § 15.5 (5th ed.2010).

RESTATEMENT, SECOND, CONFLICT OF LAWS (1988 REVISIONS):

§ 17. Presence Under Compulsion

A person does not usually acquire a domicil of choice by his presence in a place under physical or legal compulsion. . . .

b. Inmates of prisons. Under the rule of this Section, it is difficult for a person to acquire a domicil of choice in the prison in which he is incarcerated. To enter prison, one must first be legally committed and thereby lose all power of choice over the place of one's abode. Under such circumstances it is highly unlikely that a person will form the attitude of mind toward the place of his incarceration that is requisite for the acquisition of a domicil of choice. If he were to form such an attitude of mind, however, he would there acquire a domicil.

   c.   *Members of armed services.* A member of the armed services who is ordered to a station to which he must go and live in quarters assigned to him will usually not acquire a domicil there though he lives in the assigned quarters with his family. He must obey orders and cannot choose to go elsewhere. On the other hand, if he is allowed to live with his family where he pleases provided it is near enough to his post to enable him to perform his duties, he retains some power of choice over the place of his abode and may acquire a domicil. To do so, however, he must regard the place where he lives as his home. Such an attitude on his part may be difficult to establish in view of the nomadic character of military life and particularly if he intends, upon the termination of his service, to move to some other place.

D. PRISON INMATES

   Stifel v. Hopkins, 477 F.2d 1116 (6th Cir.1973), held that a person who was domiciled in Ohio before he was incarcerated for life in a Pennsylvania prison was capable of acquiring Pennsylvania citizenship for the purpose of bringing a diversity action. He had refused a transfer to an Indiana prison and said in an affidavit that he considered Pennsylvania his home and intended to remain there indefinitely.

   Dane v. Board of Registrars, 374 Mass. 152, 371 N.E.2d 1358 (1978), held that persons incarcerated in Massachusetts jails had the capacity "to form the requisite intent to make . . . the place of their incarceration their domicile for voting purposes." The court stated: "We think that prisoners, like servicemen or students, should be able to 'rebut' the presumption that by reason of their involuntary presence at the place of incarceration, they have retained their former domicile."

   Would the result in these two cases have been the same if the issue had involved either succession or taxation?

Is Domicile a Unitary Concept?

   May a person (at the same time) have a domicile in one place for one purpose and a second domicile for some other purpose? Do the cases you have read up to now provide an answer to this question? Do you think it likely that a clear answer would be found in the cases? A famous debate on this question took place nearly a century ago between Professors Walter Wheeler Cook and Austin Wakeman Scott at an American Law Institute meeting. 3 The American Law Institute Proceedings 226–231 (1925). In the course of this debate, Professor Cook said:

> There is no doubt that what you might call the core of the concept is the same in all these situations; but as you get out towards what I like to call the twilight zone of the subject, I don't believe the scope remains exactly the same for all purposes. . . .

> The court has a concrete problem to solve. It is trying to decide whether the courts of the state should grant a divorce on constructive service; whether the man is sufficiently connected with the state to make that a reasonable thing to do. It may be reasonable to do that, but not reasonable to apply the same concept in the case involving the validity of the provisions of a will. The court has a will to consider, or a divorce, or the administration of an estate, or whatever it may be, and the exact point at which it draws the line is undoubtedly drawn with the concrete problem that they have before them in mind. . . .

> I do not believe we can make up our minds as to the exact scope [domicile] ought to have for a particular purpose without having that purpose in mind, and we ought to address ourselves to the question of whether it ought to have the same exact scope for all purposes. I do not believe it should. I am not talking about a theoretical thing, but what the courts actually do. What I think the courts should do and are actually doing is, that while they use the same word as if they had a single concept, actually you will find they have not. . . .

The Restatement, Second, Conflict of Laws § 11 comment o states that "in close cases, decision of a question of domicil may sometimes depend upon the purpose for which the domicil concept is used in the particular case."

NOTES

1. See Reese, Does Domicile Bear a Single Meaning, 55 Colum.L.Rev. 589 (1955). Professor Cook's last word is found in Cook, Logical and Legal Bases of the Conflict of Laws 194–210 (1942). Reiersen v. Commissioner of Revenue, 26 Mass. App. 124, 524 N.E.2d 857 (1988), held that Mr. Reiersen was domiciled in the Philippines for the purposes of determining his obligation to pay Massachusetts income tax. The court discussed approvingly the concept that a person could be domiciled in different places for different purposes.

2. Section 5 of the Canadian Divorce Act of 1968 (Stat.Can.1968, c. 24) provides that a provincial court is competent to grant a divorce if the petitioner is domiciled in Canada and if either the petitioner or the respondent has been "ordinarily resident" in the province for one year prior to the filing of the petition. As a result, a person can be domiciled in Canada for divorce purposes and domiciled in a province for another purpose. Da Costa, The Canadian Divorce Law of 1968 and its Provisions on Conflicts, 17 Am.J.Comp.L. 214

(1969). A somewhat similar situation prevails in Australia. Cowen and Da Costa, The Unity of Domicile, 78 L.Q.Rev. 92 (1962).

By What Law is the Meaning of Domicile Determined?

Rodriguez-Diaz v. Sierra-Martinez, 853 F.2d 1027 (1st Cir.1988), p. 24, supra, dealt with the issue of whether federal, Puerto Rican, or New York law applied to determine where the plaintiff was domiciled for purposes of bringing a diversity action. Another classic case in point is Torlonia v. Torlonia, 108 Conn. 292, 142 A. 843 (1928). A wife sought a divorce in Connecticut from her Italian husband, claiming that she was domiciled in Connecticut, and that accordingly that state had divorce jurisdiction. The husband argued that the action should be dismissed, since "as a matter of law, the plaintiff cannot have a domicile . . . other than that of her husband," because "under the law of Italy the husband is entitled to the control of the wife to the extent that she must follow him wherever he chooses to establish his residence, except as such control may be modified or affected by a decree of an Italian court of competent jurisdiction." The trial court granted the divorce and the Supreme Court of Errors of Connecticut affirmed:

> We hold, then, that a wife separated from her husband, . . . is not precluded from establishing an independent domicil in this State; indeed, we are convinced that this right has long been tacitly recognized and frequently given effect in divorce actions in our trial courts, although its existence has not, heretofore, been challenged on appeal.

> Since domicil, as well as the other questions upon which the granting of a divorce depends, is governed by the laws of the forum in which the action is pending, the Italian law, above stated, pertaining to control of the wife by the husband, does not preclude the plaintiff from acquiring an independent domicil in Connecticut.

CHAPTER 3

JURISDICTION OF COURTS

SECTION 1. INTRODUCTION AND GENERAL CONSIDERATIONS

"Jurisdiction" is a concept that appears in many legal contexts and bears diverse meanings depending upon the nature or purpose of the inquiry at hand. The meaning of the word jurisdiction that is in widest use and has been employed in compiling this book is: the power of a state to create or affect legal interests that will be recognized as valid in other states. See Restatement, Second, Conflict of Laws § 24. It is helpful to distinguish "jurisdiction to adjudicate" from "jurisdiction to prescribe." The latter concept refers to the circumstances under which a state or nation can apply its own law to a dispute. Section 9 of the Second Conflicts Restatement describes those circumstances as follows: "A court may not apply the local law of its own state to determine a particular issue unless such application of this law would be reasonable in the light of the relationship of the state and of other states to the person, thing or occurrence involved." Restatement, Second, Conflict of Laws § 9. The issue of jurisdiction to prescribe is discussed extensively in Chapter 9, Section 2.

In this chapter, we are concerned with jurisdiction to adjudicate. In the United States, there are three requirements for this type of jurisdiction. The first is "personal jurisdiction": that the state have some contact with the parties (jurisdiction in personam) or with property (jurisdiction in rem) that makes it reasonable for the court to exercise jurisdiction. Jurisdiction in personam deals with the power of a government (usually acting through its courts) to impose on a defendant "a personal liability or obligation in favor of the plaintiff." Restatement, Second, Conflict of Laws, ch. 3, Introductory Note at 103. Jurisdiction in rem deals with the power to adjudicate interests in property even though the court may not have jurisdiction in personam over all of those whose interests the court affects. Shaffer v. Heitner, p. 173, infra, ended the traditional use of in rem jurisdiction to litigate the merits of disputes unrelated to the property.

The second requirement for jurisdiction to adjudicate is notice. Notice questions deal with whether the method of informing the unwilling party is sufficient to allow that government to fairly determine the party's rights.

The third requirement for jurisdiction to adjudicate is subject matter jurisdiction, or, as it is often called, competence. Questions of subject matter jurisdiction usually deal with the internal allocation of business among a government's courts. Thus, for instance, in the United States the question of whether a case belongs in a state court or a federal court is one of subject matter jurisdiction. More mundane questions of competence can arise with regard to allocation of cases as between particular state courts. Questions of, say, whether a case belongs in a probate court or a general state trial court are usually thought of as issues of competence or subject matter jurisdiction.

Buchanan v. Rucker

Court of King's Bench, 1808.
9 East 192.

The plaintiff declared in assumpsit for 2000*l*. on a foreign judgment of the Island Court in Tobago; and at the trial before Lord Ellenborough, C.J., at Guildhall, produced a copy of the proceedings and judgment, certified under the hand-writing of the Chief Justice, and the seal of the island, which were proved; which, after containing an entry of the declaration, set out a summons to the defendant, therein described as "formerly of the city of Dunkirk, and now of the city of London, merchant," to appear at the ensuing court to answer the plaintiff's action; which summons was returned, "served, etc. by nailing up a copy of the declaration at the courthouse door," etc. on which judgment was afterwards given by default. Whereupon it was objected, that the judgment was obtained against the defendant, who never appeared to have been within the limits of the island, nor to have had any attorney there; nor to have been in any other way subject to the jurisdiction of the Court at the time; and was therefore a nullity. And of this opinion was Lord Ellenborough; though it was alleged, (of which however there was no other than parol proof,) that this mode of summoning absentees was warranted by a law of the island, and was commonly practised there: and the plaintiff was thereupon nonsuited. . . .

Taddy moved to set aside the nonsuit, and for a new trial, on an affidavit verifying the island law upon this subject; which stated "That every defendant against whom any action shall be entered, shall be served with a summons and an office copy of the declaration, with a copy of the account annexed, if any, at the same time by the Provost Marshal, etc. six days before the sitting of the next Court, etc.; and the Provost Marshal is required to serve the same on each defendant in person. But if such defendant cannot be found, and is not absent from the island, then it shall be deemed good service by leaving the summons, etc. at his most usual place of abode. And if the defendant be absent from the island, and hath a power of attorney recorded in the secretary's or registrar's office of Tobago, and the attorney be resident in the island, or any manager or overseer on his plantation in the island, the service shall be either upon such attorney personally, or by leaving it at his last place of abode, or upon such overseer or manager personally, or by leaving it at the house upon the defendant's plantation where the overseer or manager usually resides. But if no such attorney, overseer or manager; then the nailing up of a copy of the declaration and summons at the entrance of the court-house shall be held good service."

■ LORD ELLENBOROUGH, C.J. There is no foundation for this motion even upon the terms of the law disclosed in the affidavit. By persons absent from the island must necessarily be understood persons who have been present and within the jurisdiction, so as to have been subject to the process of the Court; but it can never be applied to a person who for aught appears never was present within or subject to the jurisdiction. Supposing however that the act had said in terms, that though a person sued in the island had never been present within the jurisdiction, yet that it should bind him upon proof of nailing up the summons at the court door: how could that be obligatory upon the subjects of other countries? Can the island of Tobago pass a law to bind the rights of the whole world? Would the world submit to such an assumed jurisdiction? The law itself, however, fairly construed, does not warrant such an inference: for "absent from the island" must be taken only to apply to persons who had been present there, and were subject to the jurisdiction of the Court out of which the process issued: and as nothing of that sort was in proof here to shew that the defendant was subject to the jurisdiction at the time of commencing the suit, there is no foundation for raising an assumpsit in law upon the judgment so obtained.

■ PER CURIAM, Rule refused.

SCHIBSBY V. WESTENHOLZ, L.R. 6 Q.B. 155 (Court of Queen's Bench, 1870): The plaintiff sought the recognition and enforcement of a French judgment in England. The French court had based jurisdiction on the plaintiff's French residence; the defendants were neither French nationals nor residents and had no property in France. It appeared that English statutory law likewise permitted the exercise of jurisdiction over foreigners under certain circumstances. Blackburn, J., however, drew the following distinction: "Should a foreigner be sued under the provisions of the statute referred to, and then come to the courts of this country and desire to be discharged, the only question which our courts could entertain would be whether the Acts of the British legislature, rightly construed, gave us jurisdiction over this foreigner, for we must obey them. But if, judgment being given against him in our courts, an action were brought upon it in the courts of the United States (where the law as to the enforcing foreign judgments is the same as our own), a further question would be open, viz., not only whether the British legislature had given the English courts jurisdiction over the defendant, but whether he was under any obligation which the American courts could recognize to submit to the jurisdiction thus created. This is precisely the question which we have now to determine with regard to a jurisdiction assumed by the French jurisprudence over foreigners." He concluded that, since the defendants were not French subjects or residents and had not otherwise submitted to French jurisdiction, "there existed nothing in the present case imposing on [them] any duty to obey the judgment of a French tribunal."

NOTE

Parties (usually defendants) wishing to challenge jurisdiction do so in one of two principal ways. The first is a direct attack on jurisdiction. A party making such an attack appears in the court in which the action is initially filed and contests the jurisdiction of that court (often known by the shorthand " F-1", an abbreviation for "forum one" or "first forum"). Appearances for the sole purpose of contesting jurisdiction are referred to in some states as "special appearances." The difference between a special appearance and a general appearance—i.e., an appearance to contest the merits of the case—is procedurally important, because a general appearance waives any jurisdictional objection and subjects the defendant to the court's in personam jurisdiction.

The federal courts, and many state courts, have abolished the distinction between a general and special appearance by allowing both jurisdictional and non-jurisdictional objections to be made at the same time. A defendant objecting to jurisdiction must, however, do so at the outset of the case or be held to have waived the objection. See F.R.C.P. 12(b), (g). For a party to make a successful direct attack on jurisdiction, that party must persuade F-1 that it lacks jurisdiction under the standards set forth in F-1's law. Direct attacks to jurisdiction have the practical advantage that a party making an unsuccessful challenge to jurisdiction still has the opportunity to contest the case on its merits.

The other principal route by which defendants challenge jurisdiction is collaterally. A defendant making a collateral attack does not appear before F-1, but instead allows F-1 to enter judgment against the defendant. When the plaintiff in whose favor the judgment was entered attempts to enforce the judgment in another proceeding, the defendant then appears before the court (known as F-2) and in that second proceeding contests jurisdiction.

Defendants sometime elect this route when they have no assets in the state in which F-1 sits. Such defendants know that this lack of assets within F-1's reach will require the plaintiff holding the judgment to try to enforce it in another court (F-2), which is located where the defendant has substantial assets.

A defendant making a collateral attack to jurisdiction can do so either on the grounds that F-1 lacked jurisdiction under its own standards or that F-1 did not acquire jurisdiction on a basis that would require F-2 to recognize the judgment. Other systems limit collateral attacks. See, e.g., Article 45 of the European Council Regulation No. 1215/2012 of 2012 on Jurisdiction and the Recognition of Judgments in Civil and Commercial Matters, O.J.L. 35/1/1 (the "Brussels Ia Regulation").

In the United States, as a result of the Due Process and Full Faith and Credit Clauses, the standards for direct and collateral challenges to jurisdiction are the same. In the case of Riverside & Dan River Cotton Mills v. Menefee, 237 U.S. 189 (1915), the Supreme Court held that the Due Process Clause gives a defendant being subjected to an unfair assertion of jurisdiction the right to directly attack that attempted assertion of jurisdiction on due process grounds. In the famous case of Pennoyer v. Neff, 95 U.S. 714 (1878), the Supreme Court suggested that the Due Process and Full Faith and Credit Clauses give defendants the right to collaterally attack unfair assertions of jurisdiction. The eventual merger of the due process and full faith and credit standards means that for cases in which F-1 and F-2 are both U.S. courts, a defendant can challenge jurisdiction either directly or collaterally on the grounds that F-1's attempted exercise of authority went beyond the bounds of due process. The unified standard also means that the converse is true, however: if F-1's assertion of jurisdiction was authorized and constitutional, F-2 must enforce F-1's judgment without reexamination. If the defendant appears in F-1 to contest jurisdiction and loses, the defendant must appeal this jurisdictional decision in order to get it reversed. Otherwise a sister state must give full faith and credit to F-1's jurisdictional ruling.

American practice is of considerable importance even in international litigation. For many reasons and perceived advantages of American substantive or procedural law (e.g., availability of jury trial, of damages for intangible harm, of punitive damages, and of discovery procedures) plaintiffs—including foreign plaintiffs—like to litigate in the United States. This country has become a magnet forum. When the defendant is foreign and perhaps the underlying facts also occurred mainly abroad, it is a frequent source of international tension and irritation that the defendant should be subject to jurisdiction in the United States (and its local assets put at risk) because it engages in general (but unrelated) business activity here. Exorbitant rules of jurisdiction of foreign countries in turn are an irritant to U.S. parties, although their impact is not so great in practice. See Articles 5(2), 76(2) of the European Council Regulation No. 1215/2012 of 2012 on Jurisdiction and the Recognition of Judgments in Civil and Commercial Matters, O.J.L. 35/1/1 (prohibiting the use of such bases of jurisdiction against the domiciliaries of a Member State), reproduced in the Documentary Appendix. See generally Symposium, Enforcing Judgments Abroad: The Global Challenge, 24 Brooklyn J.Int'l L. 1 (1998); Juenger, A Shoe Unfit for Globetrotting, 28 U.C.Davis L.Rev. 1027, 1041–45 (1995), with further references.

The text of the constitutional and federal statutory provisions most often invoked relative to U.S. jurisdiction is set forth here:

———

CONSTITUTION OF THE UNITED STATES

Full Faith and Credit Clause—Article IV, Section 1:

Full Faith and Credit shall be given in each State to the public Acts, Records, and judicial Proceedings of every other State. And the Congress may by general Laws prescribe the Manner in which such Acts, Records and Proceedings shall be proved, and the Effect thereof.

Privileges and Immunities Clause—Article IV, Section 2:

The Citizens of each State shall be entitled to all Privileges and Immunities of Citizens in the several States.

———

Supremacy Clause—Article VI:

This Constitution, and the Laws of the United States which shall be made in Pursuance thereof; and all Treaties made, or which shall be made, under the Authority of the United States, shall be the supreme Law of the Land; and the Judges in every State shall be bound thereby, any Thing in the Constitution or Laws of any State to the Contrary notwithstanding. . . .

Fifth Amendment:

No person shall . . . be deprived of life, liberty, or property, without due process of law; . . . .

Fourteenth Amendment:

Section 1. All persons born or naturalized in the United States, and subject to the jurisdiction thereof, are citizens of the United States and of the State wherein they reside. No State shall make or enforce any law which shall abridge the privileges or immunities of citizens of the United States; nor shall any State deprive any person of life, liberty, or property, without due process of law; nor deny to any person within its jurisdiction the equal protection of the laws.

Section 5. The Congress shall have power to enforce, by appropriate legislation, the provisions of this article.

STATUTORY PROVISION

Title 28, United States Code Annotated, § 1738 (approved June 25, 1948):

The Acts of the legislature of any State, Territory, or Possession of the United States, or copies thereof, shall be authenticated by affixing the seal of such State, Territory or Possession thereto.

The records and judicial proceedings of any court of any such State, Territory or Possession, or copies thereof, shall be proved or admitted in other courts within the United States and its Territories and Possessions by the attestation of the clerk and seal of the court annexed, if a seal exists, together with a certificate of a judge of the court that the said attestation is in proper form.

Such Acts, records and judicial proceedings or copies thereof, so authenticated, shall have the same full faith and credit in every court within the United States and its Territories and Possessions as they have by law or usage in the courts of such State, Territory or Possession from which they are taken.

In international litigation, however, the standards for direct and collateral challenges are often not the same. Look back at *Buchanan* and *Schibsby*, pp. 42 and 43, supra. Both are international cases that involve collateral, not direct, attacks on jurisdiction. Why is this?

In *Schibsby*, it was undeniable that F-1 (the French court) had jurisdiction under its own law, as a result of Article 14 of the French Civil Code, giving to French courts jurisdiction in cases in which the plaintiff is French. Why, then, does the English court (F-2) not enforce the French judgment?

In *Buchanan*, the question of whether F-1 (the court on the Island of Tobago) had jurisdiction under its own law was more difficult. Lord Ellenborough interpreted the Tobogan statute not to authorize jurisdiction in that case. Was that a fair interpretation of the statute? Suppose that instead of making a collateral attack on jurisdiction, the defendant in *Buchanan* had made a direct attack by specially appearing in the Tobogan court to argue that the statute did not allow for jurisdiction. Would a Tobogan court have interpreted its own statute in the way that Lord Ellenborough interpreted it?

The applicable indirect or collateral standard of jurisdiction in international litigation is called "jurisdiction in the international sense." Jurisdiction in the international sense may be established by agreement among nations or by a supra-national directive. Jurisdiction was once principally defined in Europe by the Brussels Convention among the member states of the European Union and the Lugano (Parallel) Convention between them and the remaining states of the European Free Trade Association. The Brussels Convention, however, has been substantially replaced by what is known as the "Brussels Ia Regulation." See European Council Regulation No. 1215/2012 of 2012 on Jurisdiction and the Recognition of Judgments in Civil and Commercial Matters, O.J.L. 35/1/1 reproduced in the Documentary Appendix. The Convention, however, still governs as to Denmark.

The Brussels Ia Regulation not only establishes the acceptable bases of jurisdiction but also lists, with reference to each member state, the bases of jurisdiction that may *not* be invoked in litigation with respect to parties or causes to which the Regulation applies. Such excluded bases of jurisdiction—generally any basis of jurisdiction that will not be accepted for purposes of granting recognition to an ensuing judgment—are known as "*exorbitant* bases of jurisdiction." In the European Union, these include, among others, service of process on a transiently present defendant under English and Irish law, the plaintiff's forum nationality under Belgian and French law (the provision invoked by the French court in *Schibsby*), and the presence of assets unrelated to the action, a basis allowed for by German law.

In the absence of agreement on acceptable bases of jurisdiction, each state defines "jurisdiction in the international sense" for itself. Usually a state will use its own standards, but some states—for example the United

Kingdom—will recognize judgments from countries with which it does not have a judgment-recognition treaty on fewer jurisdictional bases than it employs in its own courts.

In domestic litigation a failed direct attack on jurisdiction precludes a collateral attack on jurisdiction. In Baldwin v. Iowa State Traveling Men's Ass'n, 283 U.S. 522, 51 S.Ct. 517 (1931) the defendant appeared in F-1 and unsuccessfully challenged the court's jurisdiction. The defendant then defaulted and then attempted to again challenge F-1's jurisdiction when the judgment creditor sought to enforce the judgment in F-2. The Supreme Court held that the earlier attack on jurisdiction in F-1 precluded the later attack. In theory a different result should attain in international litigation because a foreign F-1 determining that it has jurisdiction under its own law cannot have determined whether jurisdiction is constitutional under U.S. standards.

In contrast, under Section 5(a)(2) of the Uniform Foreign Money Judgments Act a foreign F-1 has jurisdiction if the defendant appears "other than for the purpose . . . of contesting jurisdiction of the court over him." This has been interpreted literally so that if an American defendant contests the jurisdiction of a French court based on the French domicile of the plaintiff and loses and then proceeds to defend the case on the merits in the French court he cannot do so without losing his right to attack the judgment collaterally in a U.S. court. See CIBC Mellon Trust Co. v. Mora Hotel Corp., 792 N.E.2d 155 (N.Y. 2003). Is this approach fair to U.S. defendants?

SECTION 2. BASES OF JUDICIAL JURISDICTION OVER NATURAL AND LEGAL PERSONS

A. THE HISTORIC BASES: JURISDICTION THEORY BEFORE INTERNATIONAL SHOE

1. IN-STATE SERVICE OF PROCESS

Barrell v. Benjamin
Supreme Judicial Court of Massachusetts, 1819.
15 Mass. 354.

[T]he parties agreed on the following statement of facts:

Barrell, the plaintiff, is a native citizen of the United States, having been born within this commonwealth: but at the time when this action was commenced, and long before, he lived in the town of Norwich, in the state of Connecticut.

The defendant, Benjamin, is a native citizen of the state of Connecticut; but more than twenty years past has had, and still has, his domicile in Demerara; although, when this action was commenced, he was in Boston, on his way to Demerara; and the plaintiff's writ was served by arresting his body.

The plaintiff and defendant were partners in a [business] in Demerara, jointly carrying on commerce there as partners for many years before the year 1807, when their copartnership was dissolved. This action was commenced and prosecuted to recover the balance supposed to be due, from the defendant to the plaintiff, on settlement of their accounts. When the British took possession of the colony of Demerara, in the year 1803, the said Benjamin took an oath of allegiance to that government.

If the Court should be of opinion that they ought to hold jurisdiction of the action, it was agreed that the defendant should be holden to render his account, and that auditors should be appointed to audit the same. But if the Court should be of a different opinion, the plaintiff was to become nonsuit, and the defendant recover his costs. . . .

■ PARKER, C.J. delivered the opinion of the Court. Upon the facts agreed in this case, the defendant's counsel has argued against the jurisdiction of this Court, both from the nature of the contract, and the situation of the parties; and has cited some authorities in support of his argument. Upon examining them, however, and such others as can be found bearing upon the question, it does not appear that any direct decision has been had upon this subject. Indeed, it would seem, from the entire want of authorities in the English books, that the question has never been raised there; and the presumption is violent, that the jurisdiction of the common-law courts in such a case would not be doubted.

In the case of Melan vs. Duke de Fitzjames, 1 B & P 138, the point was not started. Both the parties were French subjects. The defendant had been arrested and held to special bail, on a contract made in France, and to be performed at his house there. All that was moved for was, that his bail bond might be discharged, and he permitted to enter a common appearance; because, by the laws of France, he was not liable to arrest upon such a contract. Both court and counsel take the ground that the action was maintainable. . . .

[T]he jurisdiction of this Court, as a court of common law, is unlimited; and all cases, cognizable by any of the courts of common law in England, are cognizable here.

Personal contracts are said to have no situs or locality, but follow the person of the debtor, wherever he may go; and there seems to be no good reason why courts of any country may not lend their aid to enforce such contracts; especially since it is a well-known principle that, in construing such contracts, the law of the place where they are made will be administered. So that the objection made, in this case, of the possible difference between the laws of Demerara and this commonwealth, can have no influence on the question.

It is true that the debtor may be put to inconvenience by being obliged to answer in a foreign country. But the creditor may also be put to inconvenience if he should be denied the privilege of suing in a foreign court; for the debtor may withdraw his person and effects from the place of his business; and if he cannot be pursued, may defraud his creditor of his due. . . .

According to the agreement of the parties, there must be judgment that the defendant account; and auditors must be appointed.

NOTES

1. The connection between the Commonwealth of Massachusetts and the dispute between Barrell and Benjamin was extremely slight. Neither party was at any relevant time a domiciliary of Massachusetts, none of the events leading up to the suit appeared to have any connection with the forum, and the court admitted that it would be required to apply foreign law to resolve the dispute. The only basis for jurisdiction was that "the plaintiff's writ was served by arresting [defendant's] body" while the defendant was temporarily in the forum state. The modern equivalent of an "arrest" in a civil case is service of process on—i.e., physically handing the complaint and summons to—the defendant while the defendant is physically located in the forum state. What authority does the court rely upon for allowing jurisdiction on the basis of such an attenuated connection? Are the court's practical justifications for the rule convincing?

2. *The Power Theory and In-State Service.* Jurisdiction based upon service of process on the defendant in the forum is sometimes called "transient" or "tag" jurisdiction. The conceptual justification for allowing tag jurisdiction is the power theory of jurisdiction. The state demonstrates its power over the defendant by the sovereign act of an arrest or service of process. The best-known exposition of that theory is the Supreme Court's opinion in Pennoyer v. Neff, 95 U.S. 714 (1878), which held that mere "constructive" service of an out-of-state defendant by publication of the summons in a newspaper rendered a state court judgment vulnerable to later collateral attack in federal court. *Pennoyer* is often associated with the power theory, and that theory continued to exercise a strong hold well after. Justice Holmes put it this way over a generation later: "The foundation of jurisdiction is physical power. . . ." McDonald v. Mabee, 243 U.S. 90, 91 (1917).

3. *The power theory and corporations:* The power theory proved more difficult to apply to corporations, which as fictional persons cannot be "arrested" in any obvious physical sense. The prevailing common-law rule was that in-state service of process of a corporate officer, even the corporation's president, did not by itself confer in personam jurisdiction over the corporation. See, e.g., Goldey v. Morning News, 156 U.S. 518 (1895). Some states did, however, allow for jurisdiction over corporations on the basis of in-state service of an officer or other authorized corporate representative. For instance, in Pope v. Terre Haute Car and Manufacturing Co., 87 N.Y. 137, 139 (1881), the New York Court of Appeals allowed for jurisdiction over a corporation with no connection to New York other than

that the corporate president had the bad luck to be served with process on the corporation while "on his way to a seaside resort" in the forum state. See also Jester v. Baltimore Steam Packet Co., 42 S.E. 447 (N.C.1902) (following New York rule). The Supreme Court eventually held that allowing jurisdiction over corporations solely on the basis of in-state service of an officer violates the Due Process Clause. See Riverside & Dan River Cotton Mills v. Menefee, 237 U.S. 189 (1915). For a discussion of *Menefee* and the *Pope* rule, see Borchers, Pennoyer's Limited Legacy: A Reply to Professor Oakley, 29 U.C.Davis L.Rev. 115, 138–48 (1995). See generally Jacobs, If Corporations Are People Why Can't They Play Tag?, 46 N.M.L.Rev. 1 (2015).

The inability of plaintiffs to obtain jurisdiction over corporations solely through in-state service required the development of alternative bases, or which the notion of "implied consent" was the most important. They are discussed infra.

4.   *The wisdom and constitutionality of the in-state service rule:* The wisdom and constitutionality of allowing in personam jurisdiction over individuals merely on the basis of in-state service have been debated widely. The classic treatment is Ehrenzweig, The Transient Rule of Personal Jurisdiction: The "Power" Myth and Forum Conveniens, 65 Yale L.J. 289 (1956). The justifications for the rule are at their weakest when the defendant's journey to the state is a casual one. The rule also presents special problems for foreign-national defendants. See Hay, Transient Jurisdiction, Especially Over International Defendants: Critical Comments on Burnham v. Superior Court, 1990 U.Ill.L.Rev. 593.

Many commentators and some courts thought that allowing jurisdiction solely on the basis of in-state service was unconstitutional in light of Shaffer v. Heitner, p. 173, infra. That case, treated extensively below, held that allowing jurisdiction solely on the basis of attachment of defendant's property within the forum's borders was unconstitutional. In ruling that such assertions of jurisdiction violate the Due Process Clause, the Court stated: "We therefore conclude that all assertions of state court jurisdiction [require minimum contacts between the defendant and the forum]." 433 U.S. at 212, 97 S.Ct. at 2584. That broad language, coupled with a footnote (n.39) purporting to overrule at least some aspects of *Pennoyer*, led many to conclude that allowing tag jurisdiction over a defendant who has no meaningful connection to the forum violates due process.

The Supreme Court directly addressed that constitutional question in the following case.

Burnham v. Superior Court of California

Supreme Court of the United States, 1990.
495 U.S. 604, 110 S.Ct. 2105, 109 L.Ed.2d 631.

■ JUSTICE SCALIA announced the judgment of the Court.

The question presented is whether the Due Process Clause of the Fourteenth Amendment denies California courts jurisdiction over a nonresident, who was personally served with process while temporarily in that State, in a suit unrelated to his activities in the State.

I

Petitioner Dennis Burnham married Francie Burnham in 1976, in West Virginia. In 1977 the couple moved to New Jersey, where their two children were born. In July 1987 the Burnhams decided to separate. They agreed that Mrs. Burnham, who intended to move to California, would take custody of the children. Shortly before Mrs. Burnham departed for California that same month, she and petitioner agreed that she would file for divorce on grounds of "irreconcilable differences."

In October 1987, petitioner filed for divorce in New Jersey state court on grounds of "desertion." Petitioner did not, however, obtain an issuance of summons against his wife, and did not attempt to serve her with process. Mrs. Burnham, after unsuccessfully demanding that petitioner adhere to their prior agreement to submit to an "irreconcilable differences" divorce, brought suit for divorce in California state court in early January 1988.

In late January, petitioner visited southern California on business, after which he went north to visit his children in the San Francisco Bay area, where his wife resided. He took the older child to San Francisco for the weekend. Upon returning the child to Mrs. Burnham's home on January 24, 1988, petitioner was served with a California court summons and a copy of Mrs. Burnham's divorce petition. He then returned to New Jersey.

Later that year, petitioner made a special appearance in the California Superior Court, moving to quash the service of process on the ground that the court lacked personal jurisdiction over him because his only contacts with California were a few short visits to the State for the purpose of conducting business and visiting his children. The Superior Court denied the motion, and the California Court of Appeal denied mandamus relief, rejecting petitioner's contention that the Due Process Clause prohibited California courts from asserting jurisdiction over him because he lacked "minimum contacts" with the State.[1] The court held it to be "a valid jurisdictional predicate for in personam jurisdiction" that

---

[1] We have said that "[e]ven when the cause of action does not arise out of or relate to the foreign corporation's activities in the forum State, due process is not offended by a State's subjecting the corporation to its in personam jurisdiction when there are sufficient contacts between the State and the foreign corporation." Helicopteros Nacionales de Colombia v. Hall, 466 U.S., at 414. Our only holding supporting that statement, however, involved "regular service of summons upon [the corporation's] president while he was in [the forum State] acting in that capacity." See Perkins v. Benguet Consolidated Mining Co., 342 U.S. 437, 440 (1952). It may be that whatever special rule exists permitting "continuous and systematic" contacts, id., at 438, to support jurisdiction with respect to matters unrelated to activity in the forum applies only to corporations, which have never fitted comfortably in a jurisdictional regime based primarily upon "de facto power over the defendant's person." International Shoe Co. v. Washington, 326 U.S. 310, 316 (1945). We express no views on these matters—and, for simplicity's sake, omit reference to this aspect of "contacts"-based jurisdiction in our discussion.

the "defendant [was] present in the forum state and personally served with process." . . . We granted certiorari. 493 U.S. 807 (1989).

II

A

The proposition that the judgment of a court lacking jurisdiction is void traces back to the English Year Books, see Bowser v. Collins, Y.B.Mich. 22 Edw. IV, f. 30, pl. 11, 145 Eng.Rep. 97 (1482), and was made settled law by Lord Coke in Case of the Marshalsea, 10 Co.Rep. 68b, 77 Eng.Rep. 1027, 1041 (K.B.1612). Traditionally that proposition was embodied in the phrase coram non judice, "before a person not a judge"—meaning, in effect, that the proceeding in question was not a judicial proceeding because lawful judicial authority was not present, and could therefore not yield a judgment. American courts invalidated, or denied recognition to, judgments that violated this common-law principle long before the Fourteenth Amendment was adopted. See, e.g., Grumon v. Raymond, 1 Conn. 40 (1814); Picquet v. Swan, 19 F.Cas. 609 (No. 11,134) (CC Mass.1828); Dunn v. Dunn, 4 Paige 425 (N.Y.Ch.1834); Evans v. Instine, 7 Ohio 273 (1835); Steel v. Smith, 7 Watts & Serg. 447 (Pa.1844); Boswell's Lessee v. Otis, 50 U.S. 336, 350, 9 How. 336 (1850). In Pennoyer v. Neff, 95 U.S. 714, 732 (1878), we announced that the judgment of a court lacking personal jurisdiction violated the Due Process Clause of the Fourteenth Amendment as well.

To determine whether the assertion of personal jurisdiction is consistent with due process, we have long relied on the principles traditionally followed by American courts in marking out the territorial limits of each State's authority. . . . In what has become the classic expression of the criterion, we said in International Shoe Co. v. Washington, 326 U.S. 310 (1945), that a State court's assertion of personal jurisdiction satisfies the Due Process Clause if it does not violate " 'traditional notions of fair play and substantial justice.' " Id., at 36, quoting Milliken v. Meyer, 311 U.S. 457, 463 (1940). . . . Since International Shoe, we have only been called upon to decide whether these "traditional notions" permit States to exercise jurisdiction over absent defendants. . . . The question we must decide today is whether due process requires a similar connection between the litigation and the defendant's contacts with the State in cases where the defendant is physically present in the State at the time process is served upon him.

B

Among the most firmly established principles of personal jurisdiction in American tradition is that the courts of a State have jurisdiction over nonresidents who are physically present in the State. The view developed early that each State had the power to hale before its courts any individual who could be found within its borders, and that once having acquired jurisdiction over such a person by properly serving him with process, the State could retain jurisdiction to enter judgment against him, no matter how fleeting his visit. See, e.g., Potter v. Allin, 2 Root 63, 67 (Conn.1793); Barrell v. Benjamin, p. 48, supra. That view had antecedents in English common-law practice, which sometimes allowed "transitory" actions, arising out of events outside the country, to be maintained against seemingly nonresident defendants who were present in England. See, e.g., Mostyn v. Fabrigas, 98 Eng.Rep. 1021 (K.B.1774)....

This American jurisdictional practice is, moreover, not merely old; it is continuing.... We do not know of a single State or federal statute, or a single judicial decision resting upon State law, that has abandoned in-State service as a basis of jurisdiction. Many recent cases reaffirm it. See Hutto v. Plagens, 254 Ga. 512, 513, 330 S.E.2d 341, 342 (1985)....

C

Despite this formidable body of precedent, petitioner contends, in reliance on our decisions applying the International Shoe standard, that in the absence of "continuous and systematic" contacts with the forum, ... a nonresident defendant can be subjected to judgment only as to matters that arise out of or relate to his contacts with the forum. This argument rests on a thorough misunderstanding of our cases.

Nothing in International Shoe or the cases that have followed it ... offers support for the very different proposition petitioner seeks to establish today: that a defendant's presence in the forum is not only unnecessary to validate novel, nontraditional assertions of jurisdiction, but is itself no longer sufficient to establish jurisdiction. That proposition is unfaithful to both elementary logic and the foundations of our due process jurisprudence. The distinction between what is needed to support novel procedures and what is needed to sustain traditional ones is fundamental....

The short of the matter is that jurisdiction based on physical presence alone constitutes due process because it is one of the continuing traditions of our legal system that define the due process standard of "traditional notions of fair play and substantial justice." That standard was developed by analogy to "physical presence," and it would be perverse to say it could now be turned against that touchstone of jurisdiction.

D

It goes too far to say, as petitioner contends, that Shaffer [v. Heitner, 433 U.S. 186 (1977)] compels the conclusion that a State lacks jurisdiction over an individual unless the litigation arises out of his activities in the State. Shaffer, like International Shoe, involved jurisdiction over an absent defendant, and it stands for nothing more than the proposition that when the "minimum contact" that is a substitute for physical presence consists of property ownership it must, like other minimum contacts, be related to the litigation. Petitioner wrenches out of its context our statement in Shaffer that "all assertions of state-court jurisdiction must be evaluated according to the standards set forth in International Shoe and its progeny." 433 U.S., at 212. When read together with the two sentences that preceded it, the meaning of this statement becomes clear:

> "The fiction that an assertion of jurisdiction over property is anything but an assertion of jurisdiction over the owner of the property supports an ancient form without substantial modern justification. Its continued acceptance would serve only to allow state-court jurisdiction that is fundamentally unfair to the defendant."

> "We therefore conclude that all assertions of state-court jurisdiction must be evaluated according to the standards set forth in International Shoe and its progeny." Ibid. (emphasis added).

Shaffer was saying, in other words, not that all bases for the assertion of in personam jurisdiction (including, presumably, in-state service) must be treated alike and subjected to the "minimum contacts" analysis of International Shoe; but rather that quasi in rem jurisdiction, that fictional "ancient form," and in personam jurisdiction, are really one and the same and must be treated alike—leading to the conclusion that quasi in rem jurisdiction, i.e., that form of in personam jurisdiction based upon a "property ownership" contact and by definition unaccompanied by personal, in-state service, must satisfy the litigation-relatedness requirement of International Shoe. . . .

It is fair to say, however, that while our holding today does not contradict Shaffer, our basic approach to the due process question is different. We have conducted no independent inquiry into the desirability or fairness of the prevailing in-state service rule, leaving that judgment to the legislatures that are free to amend it; for our purposes, its validation is its pedigree. . . . Shaffer did conduct such an independent inquiry, asserting that " 'traditional notions of fair play and substantial justice' can be as readily offended by the perpetuation of ancient forms that are no longer justified as by the adoption of new procedures that are inconsistent with the basic values of our constitutional heritage." 433 U.S., at 212. Perhaps that assertion can be sustained when the "perpetuation of ancient forms" is engaged in by only a very small minority of the States. Where, however, as in the present case, a jurisdictional principle is both firmly approved by tradition and still favored, it is impossible to imagine what standard we could appeal to for the judgment that it is "no longer justified." While in no way receding from or casting doubt upon the holding of Shaffer or any other case, we reaffirm today our time-honored approach. . . . For new procedures, hitherto unknown, the Due Process Clause requires analysis to determine whether "traditional notions of fair play and substantial justice" have been offended. International Shoe, 326 U.S., at 316. But a doctrine of personal jurisdiction that dates back to the adoption of the

Fourteenth Amendment and is still generally observed unquestionably meets that standard.

III

A few words in response to Justice Brennan's concurrence:

The subjectivity, and hence inadequacy, of this approach [which uses "contemporary notions of due process"] becomes apparent when the concurrence tries to explain why the assertion of jurisdiction in the present case meets its standard of continuing-American-tradition-plus-innate-fairness. Justice Brennan lists the "benefits" Mr. Burnham derived from the State of California—the fact that, during the few days he was there, "his health and safety [were] guaranteed by the State's police, fire, and emergency medical services; he [was] free to travel on the State's roads and waterways; he likely enjoy[ed] the fruits of the State's economy." . . . Three days' worth of these benefits strike us as powerfully inadequate to establish, as an abstract matter, that it is "fair" for California to decree the ownership of all Mr. Burnham's worldly goods acquired during the ten years of his marriage, and the custody over his children. We dare say a contractual exchange swapping those benefits for that power would not survive the "unconscionability" provision of the Uniform Commercial Code. . . .

The difference between us and Justice Brennan has nothing to do with whether "further progress [is] to be made" in the "evolution of our legal system." . . . It has to do with whether changes are to be adopted as progressive by the American people or decreed as progressive by the Justices of this Court. Nothing we say today prevents individual States from limiting or entirely abandoning the in-state service basis of jurisdiction.

Because the Due Process Clause does not prohibit the California courts from exercising jurisdiction over petitioner based on the fact of in-state service of process, the judgment is Affirmed.

■ JUSTICE WHITE, concurring in part and concurring in the judgment.

I join Part I and Parts II-A, II-B, and II-C of Justice Scalia's opinion and concur in the judgment of affirmance. The rule allowing jurisdiction to be obtained over a non-resident by personal service in the forum state, without more, has been and is so widely accepted throughout this country that I could not possibly strike it down, either on its face or as applied in this case, on the ground that it denies due process of law guaranteed by the Fourteenth Amendment. Although the Court has the authority under the Amendment to examine even traditionally accepted procedures and declare them invalid, e.g., Shaffer v. Heitner, 433 U.S. 186 (1977), there has been no showing here or elsewhere that as a general proposition the rule is so arbitrary and lacking in common sense in so many instances that it should be held violative of Due Process in every case. Furthermore, until such a showing is made, which would be difficult indeed, claims in individual cases that the rule would operate unfairly as applied to the particular non-resident involved need not be entertained. At least this would be the case where presence in the forum state is intentional, which would almost always be the fact. Otherwise, there would be endless, fact-specific litigation in the trial and appellate courts, including this one. . . .

■ JUSTICE BRENNAN with whom JUSTICE MARSHALL, JUSTICE BLACKMUN, AND JUSTICE O'CONNOR join, concurring in the judgment.

I agree with Justice Scalia that the Due Process Clause of the Fourteenth Amendment generally permits a state court to exercise jurisdiction over a defendant if he is served with process while voluntarily present in the forum State. . . . I do not perceive the need, however, to decide that a jurisdictional rule that " 'has been immemorially the actual law of the land,' " . . . automatically comports with due process simply by virtue of its "pedigree." . . . Unlike Justice Scalia, I would undertake an "independent inquiry into the . . . fairness of the prevailing in-state service rule." . . .

I

I believe that the approach adopted by Justice Scalia's opinion today—reliance solely on historical pedigree—is foreclosed by our decisions in International Shoe Co. v. Washington, 326 U.S. 310 (1945), and Shaffer v. Heitner, 433 U.S. 186 (1977). In International Shoe, we held that a state court's assertion of personal jurisdiction does not violate the Due Process Clause if it is consistent with " 'traditional notions of fair play and substantial justice.' " 326 U.S., at 316, quoting Milliken v. Meyer, 311 U.S. 457, 463 (1940). In Shaffer, we stated that "all assertions of state-court jurisdiction must be evaluated according to the standards set forth in International Shoe and its progeny." 433 U.S., at 212 (emphasis added). The critical insight of Shaffer is that all rules of jurisdiction, even ancient ones, must satisfy contemporary notions of due process. No longer were we content to limit our jurisdictional analysis to pronouncements that "[t]he foundation of jurisdiction is physical power," McDonald v. Mabee, 243 U.S. 90, 91 (1917), and that "every State possesses exclusive jurisdiction and sovereignty over persons and property within its territory." Pennoyer v. Neff, 95 U.S. 714, 722 (1878). While acknowledging that "history must be considered as supporting the proposition that jurisdiction based solely on the presence of property satisfie[d] the demands of due process," we found that this factor could not be "decisive." 433 U.S., at 211–212. We recognized that " '[t]raditional notions of fair play and substantial justice' can be as readily offended by the perpetuation of ancient forms that are no longer justified as by the adoption of new procedures that are inconsistent with the basic values of our constitutional heritage." Id., at 212 (citations omitted). . . .

II

Tradition, though alone not dispositive, is of course relevant to the question whether the rule of transient jurisdiction is consistent with due process.

[H]owever murky the jurisprudential origins of transient jurisdiction, the fact that American courts have announced the rule for perhaps a century (first in dicta, more recently in holdings) provides a defendant voluntarily present in a particular State today "clear notice that [he] is subject to suit" in the forum. World-Wide Volkswagen Corp. v. Woodson, 444 U.S. 286, 297 (1980). . . .

By visiting the forum State, a transient defendant actually "avail[s]" himself, Burger King, [Corp. v. Rudzewicz, 471 U.S. 462, 476 (1985)] of significant benefits provided by the State. His health and safety are guaranteed by the State's police, fire, and emergency medical services; he is free to travel on the State's roads and waterways; he likely enjoys the fruits of the State's economy as well. Moreover, the Privileges and Immunities Clause of Article IV prevents a state government from discriminating against a transient defendant by denying him the protections of its law or the right of access to its courts. See Supreme Court of New Hampshire v. Piper, 470 U.S. 274, 281, n. 10 (1985); Baldwin v. Fish and Game Comm'n of Montana, 436 U.S. 371, 387 (1978); see also Supreme Court of Virginia v. Friedman, 487 U.S. 59, 64–65 (1988). Subject only to the doctrine of forum non conveniens, an out-of-state plaintiff may use state courts in all circumstances in which those courts would be available to state citizens. Without transient jurisdiction, an asymmetry would arise; a transient would have the full benefit of the power of the forum State's courts as a plaintiff while retaining immunity from their authority as a defendant. . . .

The potential burdens on a transient defendant are slight. " '[M]odern transportation and communications have made it much less burdensome for a party sued to defend himself' " in a State outside his place of residence. Burger King, 471 U.S., at 474, quoting McGee v. International Life Insurance Co., 355 U.S. 220, 223 (1957). That the defendant has already journeyed at least once before to the forum—as evidenced by the fact that he was served with process there—is an indication that suit in the forum likely would not be prohibitively inconvenient. Finally, any burdens that do arise can be ameliorated by a variety of procedural devices. For these reasons, as a rule the exercise of personal jurisdiction over a defendant based on his voluntary presence in the forum will satisfy the requirements of due process.

In this case, it is undisputed that petitioner was served with process while voluntarily and knowingly in the State of California. I therefore concur in the judgment.

■ JUSTICE STEVENS, concurring in the judgment.

As I explained in my separate writing, I did not join the Court's opinion in Shaffer v. Heitner, 433 U.S. 186 (1977), because I was concerned by its unnecessarily broad reach. Id., at 217–219 (opinion concurring in judgment). The same concern prevents me from joining either Justice Scalia's or Justice Brennan's opinion in this case. For me, it is sufficient to note that the historical evidence and consensus identified by Justice Scalia, the considerations of fairness identified by Justice Brennan, and the common sense displayed by Justice White, all combine to demonstrate that this is, indeed, a very easy case.* Accordingly, I agree that the judgment should be affirmed.

NOTES

1.   Justice Scalia specifically invoked *Barrell v. Benjamin*, p. 48, supra, as one of the leading cases establishing the "pedigree" of the rule allowing in personam jurisdiction based upon in-state service of process on the defendant. For Justice Scalia, the pedigree of the in-state service rule was sufficient to immunize it from due process attack, at least as long as the rule remains in wide use in the United States (as it does). Justice Brennan attached considerably less weight to the rule's traditional and current use. Nonetheless, he was willing to uphold jurisdiction over Mr. Burnham even for a claim unrelated to his contacts in California. Given that they agree on the result, why do the two principal opinions disagree so strenuously on methodology?

2.   The relevance of *Shaffer's* holding to the rule of in-state service was the subject of debate almost immediately from the issuance of that opinion in 1977. Most commentators took the position that Shaffer's "all assertions" language meant that allowing jurisdiction over a defendant who was served in the forum state, but had no other connection to the forum state, would be or should be unconstitutional. See, e.g., Bernstine, Shaffer v. Heitner: A Death Warrant for the Transient Rule of In Personam Jurisdiction?, 25 Vill. L.Rev. 61 (1979–80); Silberman, Shaffer v. Heitner: The End of an Era, 53 N.Y.U.L.Rev. 33, 75 (1978). Courts, however, were quite divided. It seems that most concluded that the rule of in-state service had survived *Shaffer*. Compare Amusement Equipment, Inc. v. Mordelt, 779 F.2d 264 (5th Cir. 1985) (in-state service a sufficient basis for jurisdiction notwithstanding *Shaffer*); Humphrey v. Langford, 246 Ga. 732, 273 S.E.2d 22 (1980) (same) with Nehemiah v. Athletics Congress of U.S.A., 765 F.2d 42 (3d Cir.1985) (in-state service alone not a constitutionally sufficient basis for jurisdiction).

3.   If the fact that the United States is one country should lend some support to the outcome in *Burnham*, should tag or transient jurisdiction also be available against foreign-country defendants casually present here on a fortnight's holiday at the time of service? See Restatement (Third), Foreign Relations Law of the United States § 421(2)(a) (1987): a state (country) has

---

*   Perhaps the adage about hard cases making bad law should be revised to cover easy cases.

jurisdiction to adjudicate if a "person or thing is present in the ... state, other than transitorily." Comment e to § 421 states that the exercise of jurisdiction based on transient presence "is not generally acceptable under international 'law.'" For an argument that *Burnham* should be restricted to interstate defendants, see Hay, Transient Jurisdiction, Especially Over International Defendants: Critical Comments on Burnham v. Superior Court, 1990 U.Ill.L.Rev. 593. Should the fact that European Community law specifically abolishes the in-state service basis as between member nations factor into the use of the rule as against foreign defendants?

4. Suppose a state interprets its own constitution as prohibiting use of "transient" presence as a basis for personal jurisdiction without some additional connection to the forum. How long a stay in the state by a non-resident converts presence there into something more than transient presence for jurisdictional purposes? If the sojourn is unrelated to the claim sued upon, does it make any difference whether it is for pleasure rather than business?

5. Under Justice Scalia's test, would service of process on a defendant in an airplane while flying over the state be sufficient for jurisdiction? Jurisdiction based upon such service was upheld in Grace v. MacArthur, 170 F.Supp. 442 (E.D.Ark.1959). Is it of any relevance to Justice Scalia's approach that air travel was unknown at the time of the ratification of the Fourteenth Amendment? Under Justice Brennan's approach, is a state flyover too scant a connection with the state to allow jurisdiction? What if the state is being overflown not because it is on the planned route of the flight, but rather because the airplane has been forced to alter course to avoid bad weather?

6. For extensive discussions of *Burnham*, see Symposium: The Future of Personal Jurisdiction, 22 Rutgers L.J. 559 (1991), with contributions by Brilmayer, Silberman, Stein, Weintraub, Kogan, Twitchell, Redish, and Maltz; see also Borchers, The Death of the Constitutional Law of Personal Jurisdiction: From Pennoyer to Burnham and Back Again, 24 U.C.Davis L.Rev. 19 (1990); Stempel, The Irrepressible Myth of Burnham and Its Increasing Indefensibility After Goodyear and Daimler, 15 Nev.L.J. 1203, 1208 (2015)("The argument against the continuing validity of service to establish personal jurisdiction is a powerful one—that mere service is not a very weighty contact with the forum state and should not, by itself, establish the requisite minimum contacts required by *International Shoe* . . . .").

In continental Europe, jurisdiction may not be based on service of process on the defendant during a brief sojourn. Upon their accession to the Brussels Convention Ireland and the United Kingdom therefore had to give up this "exorbitant" basis of jurisdiction in relation to defendants domiciled in the European Union. This is continued now that the Convention has been substantially replaced by the Brussels Ia Regulation.

2.   DOMICILE, RESIDENCE AND NATIONALITY

The sovereign's power also reaches the subject or citizen while temporarily outside the state's territory. In Blackmer v. United States, 284 U.S. 421, 52 S.Ct. 252 (1932), a citizen of the United States, domiciled in France, was required to appear as a witness at a criminal trial in the United States under a statute authorizing the service of a subpoena for that purpose. Such service was effected by a United States consul in France. When Blackmer failed to appear, he was fined for contempt. The Supreme Court rejected his objection that the trial court lacked jurisdiction. As a citizen, he was "bound to take notice of the laws that are applicable to him and to obey them." The decision is accepted as establishing the principle of jurisdiction on the basis of citizenship, even though it arose in the context of a subpoena in a criminal trial. Restatement, Second, Conflict of Laws § 31 now also so provides.

From a practical perspective, it is far more important to ask whether state court jurisdiction (or a federal court's jurisdiction in a diversity case) may be based on the defendant's affiliation with the forum state. In Milliken v. Meyer, 311 U.S. 457, 61 S.Ct. 339 (1940), the Supreme Court gave an affirmative answer. "As in case of the authority of the United States over its absent citizen [citing to *Blackmer*], the authority of a state over one of its citizens is not terminated by the mere fact of his absence from the state. The state which accords him privileges and affords protection to him and his property by virtue of his domicile may also exact reciprocal duties. . . . The responsibilities of [state] citizenship arise out of the relationship to the state which domicile creates." See also Skiriotes v. Florida, 313 U.S. 69, 61 S.Ct. 924 (1941), affirming a Florida state court conviction for illegal sponge taking outside Florida's three-mile limit: "if the United States may control the conduct of its citizens upon the high seas, we see no reason why the State of Florida may not likewise govern the conduct of its citizens" outside the state with respect to matters in which it has a legitimate interest.

The notion of state citizenship appears in the Federal Constitution: persons are citizens of the United States and of the state "wherein they reside." U.S. Const. Amend. XIV, § 1. The Restatement, Second, Conflict of Laws acknowledges jurisdiction on the basis of "nationality and citizenship" (§ 31), but also states: A state has power to exercise judicial jurisdiction over an individual who is a resident of the state unless the individual's relationship to the state is so attenuated as to make the exercise of such jurisdiction unreasonable. The *Milliken* decision was based on domicile. Does mere residence make for state citizenship in the Constitutional sense? Would mere residence of a presently absent defendant support jurisdiction in any event?

Article 4 of the Brussels Ia Regulation refers to "domicile," but European law ordinarily defines this as something less than domicile in the Anglo-American sense, but as more than casual residence. The Council of the European Union is considering a new convention that would substitute the term "habitually resident." See the discussion of domicile and "habitual residence", p. 18, supra. At the same time, "residence" in the European sense falls short of "domicile" in the Anglo-American sense. In order to accommodate the Brussels Convention and now the Regulation, Section 41 of the English Civil Jurisdiction and Judgments Act 1982 now provides that, for purposes of Art. 2 of the Convention and now Article 4 Regulation, an individual is domiciled in the United Kingdom if he is resident in, "and the nature and circumstances of his residence indicate that he has a substantial connection with the United Kingdom. . . ." See Dicey, Morris & Collins, Conflict of Laws 402–07 (15th ed.2006). Three months' residence raise a presumption of a "substantial connection." Id. at 337. Contrary to the usual common-law rule, the English provision now makes it possible for a person to have more than one domicile (for jurisdictional purposes). Id. at 338.

3.   APPEARANCE AND CONSENT IN ADVANCE

The Restatement, Second, Conflict of Laws summarizes the case law as follows for cases in which the defendant either appears in an action or consented to jurisdiction in advance:

RESTATEMENT, SECOND, CONFLICT OF LAWS:

§ 32. Consent

A state has power to exercise judicial jurisdiction over an individual who has consented to the exercise of such jurisdiction.

§ 33. Appearance as Defendant

A state has power to exercise judicial jurisdiction in an action over an individual who enters an appearance as defendant in that action.

§ 81. Special Appearance

A state will not exercise judicial jurisdiction over an individual who appears in the action for the sole purpose of objecting that there is no jurisdiction over him.

The leading Supreme Court case in which advance consent was upheld as a basis for jurisdiction in National Equipment Rental v. Szukhent, 375 U.S. 311, 84 S.Ct. 411, 11 L.Ed.2d 354 (1964). In that case, Michigan farmers signed an equipment lease that allowed the New York lessor to litigate disputes arising out of the lease in New York. The Supreme Court held that the clause was a sufficient basis for jurisdiction. The related problem of whether parties can, by contract, *limit* the available fora is considered p. 207, infra.

Courts vary somewhat as to the proper procedure for making a jurisdictional objection. Federal courts, and many state courts, allow a defendant to combine jurisdictional objections with objections that go to the merits of the case (such as the sufficiency of the complaint) as long as the jurisdictional objection is lodged in the defendant's initial appearance. See F.R.C.P. 12(b), (g), (h). Some states, however, still require a strict "special appearance," i.e., an appearance that raises only jurisdictional challenges. See, e.g., Alioto Fish Co. v. Alioto, 27 Cal.App.4th 1669, 34 Cal.Rptr.2d 244 (1994).

Does a nonresident who files suit in a forum that previously lacked any jurisdictional basis over him thereby become amenable to jurisdiction for a counterclaim? In Adam v. Saenger, 303 U.S. 59, 67–68, 58 S.Ct. 454 (1938), the Supreme Court said: "The plaintiff having, by his voluntary act in demanding justice from the defendant, submitted himself to the jurisdiction of the court, there is nothing arbitrary or unreasonable in treating him as being there for all purposes for which justice to the defendant requires his presence. It is the price which the state may exact as the condition of opening its courts to the plaintiff."

Apparently, however, not all efforts to seek the court's aid constitute consent to personal jurisdiction. In SEC v. Ross, 504 F.3d 1130 (9th Cir.2007), the court held that intervenor defendants had not waived their right to contest jurisdiction, venue and service simply by attempting to enter the case under FRCP 24(a). The intervenors were various individual salesmen who had received commissions on the sale of what the court had found to be unregistered securities. The receiver appointed for the company that had sold the securities brought a motion to "disgorge" the salesmen of their commissions. The salesmen intervened while simultaneously asserting jurisdictional defenses. The court, while recognizing that the result might differ under different facts, noted that the district court had essentially precluded them from litigating important issues that had been resolved prior to their entry into the case.

4.   JURISDICTION BASED UPON LOCAL ACTIVITY

Jurisdiction that emphasizes territoriality, sovereign power based on allegiance, or—absent these—the defendant's consent will prove inadequate for the needs of a society that is at once highly mobile and in which people interact in a variety of ways across state lines and through the Internet. For generations, out-of-state corporations ("foreign corporations") have been required to appoint resident agents or to consent to service of process on a governmental officer of the host state. When an agent was appointed, consent to jurisdiction might be implied. See Lafayette Insurance Co. v. French, 59 U.S. (18 How.) 404 (1856). In due course, however, the "implied consent" rationale was abandoned, and courts recognized that a state may exercise jurisdiction over a corporation that does business in the state, at least with respect to claims arising from the transaction of that business. Restatement, Second, Conflict of Laws § 47. The same evolution was seen regarding jurisdiction over non-incorporated business associations, including partnerships, which were required to register to do business in the forum state. Today, "registration" statutes, requiring out-of-state businesses to register to do business, fall into three general categories: (1) those that simply appoint an agent for service of process but do not subject the business to jurisdiction, (2) those that subject the business to jurisdiction for claims arising from activity in the forum, and (3) in a few instances, those that purport to subject the business to jurisdiction for all claims, even those that arise out of state.

What about jurisdiction over individuals who were not domiciled in the forum and who could not be served with process in the forum? Again, "implied consent" served as an early justification. The U.S. Supreme Court's influential decision in Hess v. Pawloski, 274 U.S. 352, 47 S.Ct. 632 (1927) upheld the constitutionality of a Massachusetts statute providing for the exercise of judicial jurisdiction over nonresident motorists. The statute granted jurisdiction, however, only with respect to claims arising from motor vehicle accidents in the state. By operating a motor vehicle in the state, the nonresident was deemed to have appointed a specified state official to be his agent for the service of process. The Supreme Court noted that "the difference between the formal and implied appointment is not substantial, as far as concerns the application of the due process clause of the Fourteenth Amendment." *Hess* supported not only nonresident motorist statutes, but was extended to statutes dealing with travel by air and sea. Today, every state in the United States has such a nonresident motorist statute.

Hess and cases like it seem a quite doubtful application of the term "consent" in any ordinary sense of the word. The driver in the *Hess* case could have, for instance, announced upon entering the state of Massachusetts that he in no way "consented" to the jurisdiction of the Massachusetts court, and it seems unlikely that the result in the case would have been altered. In reality, *Hess* and cases like it were the beginnings of the fairness standard alluded to in *Burnham*. As the cases below show, the Supreme Court's notion of jurisdictional fairness is one that has undergone a considerable evolution.

B. MODERN JURISDICTIONAL STANDARDS: THE ERA OF INTERNATIONAL SHOE, "MINIMUM CONTACTS," AND "FAIRNESS"

By the mid-twentieth century, the Supreme Court felt the need to restate jurisdictional doctrine. With the following case, it made clear that jurisdiction no longer had to be rooted in the traditional *Pennoyer* bases of the defendant's domicile, consent, or service of process in the forum.

1.   INTERNATIONAL SHOE AND ITS EARLY INTERPRETATION

International Shoe Co. v. State of Washington
Supreme Court of the United States, 1945.
326 U.S. 310, 66 S.Ct. 154, 90 L.Ed. 95, 161 A.L.R. 1057.

Appeal from the Supreme Court of Washington.

■ CHIEF JUSTICE STONE delivered the opinion of the Court.

The questions for decision are (1) whether, within the limitations of the due process clause of the Fourteenth Amendment, appellant, a Delaware corporation, has by its activities in the State of Washington rendered itself amenable to proceedings in the courts of that state to recover unpaid contributions to the state unemployment compensation fund exacted by state statutes, Washington Unemployment Compensation Act, Washington Revised Statutes, § 9998–103a through § 9998–123a, 1941 Supp., and (2) whether the state can exact those contributions consistently with the due process clause of the Fourteenth Amendment.

The statutes in question set up a comprehensive scheme of unemployment compensation, the costs of which are defrayed by contributions required to be made by employers to a state unemployment compensation fund. The contributions are a specified percentage of the wages payable annually by each employer for his employees' services in the state. . . .

In this case notice of assessment for the years in question was personally served upon a sales solicitor employed by appellant in the State of Washington, and a copy of the notice was mailed by registered mail to appellant at its address in St. Louis, Missouri. Appellant appeared specially before the office of unemployment and moved to set aside the order and notice of assessment on the ground that the service upon appellant's salesman was not proper service upon appellant; that appellant was not a corporation of the State of Washington and was not doing business within the state; that it had no agent within the state upon whom service could be made; and that appellant is not an employer and does not furnish employment within the meaning of the statute.

The motion was heard on evidence and a stipulation of facts by the appeal tribunal which denied the motion and ruled that respondent Commissioner was entitled to recover the unpaid contributions. That action was affirmed by the Commissioner; both the Superior Court and the Supreme Court affirmed. 22 Wash.2d 146, 154 P.2d 801. Appellant in each of these courts assailed the statute as applied, as a violation of the due process clause of the Fourteenth Amendment, and as imposing a constitutionally prohibited burden on interstate commerce. The cause comes here on appeal under § 237(a) of the Judicial Code, 28 U.S.C. § 344(a), appellant assigning as error that the challenged statutes as applied infringe the due process clause of the Fourteenth Amendment and the commerce clause.

The facts as found by the appeal tribunal and accepted by the state Superior Court and Supreme Court, are not in dispute. Appellant is a Delaware corporation, having its principal place of business in St. Louis, Missouri, and is engaged in the manufacture and sale of shoes and other footwear. It maintains places of business in several states, other than Washington, at which its manufacturing is carried on and from which its merchandise is distributed interstate through several sales units or branches located outside the State of Washington.

Appellant has no office in Washington and makes no contracts either for sale or purchase of merchandise there. It maintains no stock of merchandise in that state and makes there no deliveries of goods in intrastate commerce. During the years from 1937 to 1940, now in question, appellant employed eleven to thirteen salesmen under direct supervision and control of sales managers located in St. Louis. These salesmen resided in Washington; their principal activities were confined to that state; and they were compensated by commissions based upon the amount of their sales. The commissions for each year totaled more than $31,000. Appellant supplies its salesmen with a line of samples, each consisting of one shoe of a pair, which they display to prospective purchasers. On occasion they rent permanent sample rooms, for exhibiting samples, in business buildings, or rent rooms in hotels or business buildings temporarily for that purpose. The cost of such rentals is reimbursed by appellant.

The authority of the salesmen is limited to exhibiting their samples and soliciting orders from prospective buyers, at prices and on terms fixed by appellant. The salesmen transmit the orders to appellant's office in St. Louis for acceptance or rejection, and when accepted the merchandise for filling the orders is shipped f.o.b. from points outside Washington to the purchasers within the state. All the merchandise shipped into Washington is invoiced at the place of shipment from which collections are made. No salesman has authority to enter into contracts or to make collections.

[Here the opinion of the State court is summarized and the contention of appellant that the statute imposes an unconstitutional burden on interstate commerce rejected.]

Appellant also insists that its activities within the state were not sufficient to manifest its "presence" there and that in its absence the state courts were without jurisdiction, that consequently it was a denial of due process for the state to subject appellant to suit. It refers to those cases in which it was said that the mere solicitation of orders for the purchase of goods within a state, to be accepted without the state and filled by shipment of the purchased goods interstate, does not render the corporation seller amenable to suit within the state. . . . And appellant further argues that since it was not present within the state, it is a denial of due process to subject it to taxation or other money exaction. It thus denies the power of the state to lay the tax or to subject appellant to a suit for its collection.

Historically the jurisdiction of courts to render judgment in personam is grounded on their de facto power over the defendant's person. Hence his presence within the territorial jurisdiction of a court was prerequisite to its rendition of a judgment personally binding him. Pennoyer v. Neff, 95 U.S. 714, 733. But now that the capias ad respondendum has given way to personal service of summons or other form of notice, due process requires only that in order to subject a defendant to a judgment in personam, if he be not present within the territory of the forum, he have certain minimum contacts with it such that the maintenance of the suit does not offend "traditional notions of fair play and substantial justice." Milliken v. Meyer, 311 U.S. 457, 463. See Holmes, J., in McDonald v. Mabee, 243 U.S. 90, 91. Compare Hoopeston Canning Co. v. Cullen, 318 U.S. 313, 316, 319. See Blackmer v. United States, 284 U.S. 421; Hess v. Pawloski, 274 U.S. 352; Young v. Masci, 289 U.S. 253.

Since the corporate personality is a fiction, although a fiction intended to be acted upon as though it were a fact, Klein v. Board of Tax Supervisors, 282 U.S. 19, 24, it is clear that unlike an individual its "presence" without, as well as within, the state of its origin can be manifested only by activities carried on in its behalf by those who are authorized to act for it. To say that the corporation is so far "present" there as to satisfy due process requirements, for purposes of taxation or the maintenance of suits against it in the courts of the state, is to beg the question to be decided. For the terms "present" or "presence" are used merely to symbolize those activities of the corporation's agent within the state which courts will deem to be sufficient to satisfy the demands of due process. L. Hand, J., in Hutchinson v. Chase & Gilbert, 45 F.2d 139, 141. Those demands may be met by such contacts of the corporation with the state of the forum as make it reasonable, in the context of our federal system of government, to require the corporation to defend the particular suit which is brought there. An "estimate of the inconveniences" which would result to the corporation from a trial away from its "home" or principal place of business is relevant in this connection. Hutchinson v. Chase & Gilbert, supra.

"Presence" in the state in this sense has never been doubted when the activities of the corporation there have not only been continuous and systematic, but also give rise to the liabilities sued on, even though no consent to be sued or authorization to an agent to accept service of process has been given. . . . Conversely it has been generally recognized that the casual presence of the corporate agent or even his conduct of single or isolated items of activities in a state in the corporation's behalf are not enough to subject it to suit on causes of action unconnected with the activities there. . . . To require the corporation in such circumstances to defend the suit away from its home or other jurisdiction where it carries on more substantial activities has been thought to lay too great and unreasonable a burden on the corporation to comport with due process.

While it has been held in cases on which appellant relies that continuous activity of some sort within a state is not enough to support the demand that the corporation be amenable to suits unrelated to that activity, Old Wayne Mut. Life Ass'n v. McDonough [204 U.S. 8]; Green v. Chicago, Burlington & Quincy R. Co. [205 U.S. 530]; Simon v. Southern R. Co., 236 U.S. 115; People's Tobacco Co. v. American Tobacco Co. [246 U.S. 79]; cf. Davis v. Farmers' Co-operative Equity Co., 262 U.S. 312, 317, there have been instances in which the continuous corporate operations within a state were thought so substantial and of such a nature as to justify suit against it on causes of action arising from dealings entirely distinct from those activities. See Missouri, K. & T.R. Co. v. Reynolds, 255 U.S. 565; Tauza v. Susquehanna Coal Co., 220 N.Y. 259, 115 N.E. 915; cf. St. Louis S.W.R. Co. v. Alexander [227 U.S. 218].

Finally, although the commission of some single or occasional acts of the corporate agent in a state sufficient to impose an obligation or liability on the corporation has not been thought to confer upon the state authority to enforce it, Rosenberg Bros. & Co. v. Curtis Brown Co., 260 U.S. 516, other such acts, because of their nature and quality and the circumstances of their commission, may be deemed sufficient to render the corporation liable to suit. Cf. Kane v. New Jersey, 242 U.S. 160; Hess v. Pawloski, supra; Young v. Masci, supra. True, some of the decisions holding the corporation amenable to suit have been supported by resort to the legal fiction that it has given its consent to service and suit, consent being implied from its presence in the state through the acts of its authorized agents. . . . But more realistically it may be said that those authorized acts were of such a nature as to justify the fiction. Smolik v. Philadelphia & R.C. & I. Co., D.C., 222 F. 148, 151. Henderson, The Position of Foreign Corporations in American Constitutional Law, 94–95.

It is evident that the criteria by which we mark the boundary line between those activities which justify the subjection of a corporation to suit, and those which do not, cannot be simply mechanical or quantitative. The test is not merely, as has sometimes been suggested, whether the activity, which the corporation has seen fit to procure through its agents in another state, is a little more or a little less. St. Louis S.W.R. Co. v. Alexander [227 U.S. 228]; International Harvester Co. v. Kentucky [234 U.S. 587]. Whether due process is satisfied must depend rather upon the quality and nature of the activity in relation to the fair and orderly administration of the laws which it was the purpose of the due process clause to insure. That clause does not contemplate that a state may make binding a judgment in personam against an individual or corporate defendant with which the state has no contacts, ties, or relations. Cf. Pennoyer v. Neff, supra; Minnesota Commercial Men's Ass'n v. Benn, 261 U.S. 140.

But to the extent that a corporation exercises the privilege of conducting activities within a state, it enjoys the benefits and protection of the laws of that state. The exercise of that privilege may give rise to obligations; and, so far as those obligations arise out of or are connected with the activities within the state, a procedure which requires the corporation to respond to a suit brought to enforce them can, in most instances, hardly be said to be undue. . . .

Applying these standards, the activities carried on in behalf of appellant in the State of Washington were neither irregular nor casual. They were systematic and continuous throughout the years in question. They resulted in a large volume of interstate business, in the course of which appellant received the benefits and protection of the laws of the state, including the right to resort to the courts for the enforcement of its rights. The obligation which is here sued upon arose out of those very activities. It is evident that these operations establish sufficient contacts or ties with the state of the forum to make it reasonable and just according to our traditional conception of fair play and substantial justice to permit the state to enforce the obligations which appellant has incurred there. Hence we cannot say that the maintenance of the present suit in the State of Washington involves an unreasonable or undue procedure.

We are likewise unable to conclude that the service of the process within the state upon an agent whose activities establish appellant's "presence" there was not sufficient notice of the suit, or that the suit was so unrelated to those activities as to make the agent an inappropriate vehicle for communicating the notice. It is enough that appellant has established such contacts with the state that the particular form of substituted service adopted there gives reasonable assurance that the notice will be actual. . . . Nor can we say that the mailing of the notice of suit to appellant by registered mail at its home office was not reasonably calculated to apprise appellant of the suit. . . .

Only a word need be said of appellant's liability for the demanded contributions of the state unemployment fund. The Supreme Court of Washington, construing and applying the statute, has held that it imposes a tax on the privilege of employing appellant's salesmen within the state measured by a percentage of the wages, here the commissions payable to the salesmen. This construction we accept for purposes of determining the constitutional validity of the statute. The right to employ labor has been deemed an appropriate subject of taxation in this country and England, both before and since the adoption of the Constitution. Steward Machine Co. v. Davis, 301 U.S. 548, 579 et. seq. And such a tax imposed upon the employer for unemployment benefits is within the constitutional power of the states. Carmichael v. Southern Coal & Coke Co., 301 U.S. 495, 508 et seq.

Appellant having rendered itself amenable to suit upon obligations arising out of the activities of its salesmen in Washington, the state may maintain the present suit in personam to collect the tax laid upon the exercise of the privilege of employing appellant's salesmen within the state. For Washington has made one of those activities, which taken together establish appellant's "presence" there for purposes of suit, the taxable event by which the state brings appellant within the reach of its taxing power. The state thus has constitutional power to lay the tax and to subject appellant to a suit to recover it. The activities which establish its "presence" subject it alike to taxation by the state and to suit to recover the tax. . . .

Affirmed.

■ JUSTICE BLACK delivered the following opinion. . . .

I believe that the Federal Constitution leaves to each State, without any "ifs" or "buts", a power to tax and to open the doors of its courts for its citizens to sue corporations whose agents do business in those States. Believing that the Constitution gave the States that power, I think it a judicial deprivation to condition its exercise upon this Court's notion of "fair play", however appealing that term may be. Nor can I stretch the meaning of due process so far as to authorize this Court to deprive a State of the right to afford judicial protection to its citizens on the ground that it would be more "convenient" for the corporation to be sued somewhere else.

There is a strong emotional appeal in the words "fair play", "justice", and "reasonableness." But they were not chosen by those who wrote the original Constitution or the Fourteenth Amendment as a measuring rod for this Court to use in invalidating State or Federal laws passed by elected legislative representatives. . . . Superimposing the natural justice concept on the Constitution's specific prohibitions could operate as a drastic abridgment of democratic safeguards they embody, such as freedom of speech, press and religion, and the right to counsel. This has already happened. Betts v. Brady, 316 U.S. 455. Compare Feldman v. United States, 322 U.S. 487, 494–503. For application of this natural law concept, whether under the terms "reasonableness", "justice", or "fair play", makes judges the supreme arbiters of the country's laws and practices. . . . This result, I believe, alters the form of government our Constitution provides. I cannot agree. . . .

NOTES

1.   *International Shoe* is a landmark in the law of judicial jurisdiction. What test or tests of jurisdiction does it announce? What factors does it identify as determinative of whether a state's courts have jurisdiction in a given case? Should the existence of "minimum contacts" guarantee "fairness" or is "fairness" a separate standard that must be satisfied even when the defendant has minimum contacts with the forum state? Does the Court purport to replace the traditional bases of domicile, consent, and in-state

service? Or does the Court purport to add a new jurisdictional basis as an alternative to the traditional bases?

2. We refer later to the distinction between "general" and "specific" (i.e., claim-related) jurisdiction. p. 122 et seq., infra. Note that the Court in *International Shoe* recognized the possibility that a defendant's "systematic and continuous" business activity in the forum could support jurisdiction even for claims that arose outside the forum. This is "general" jurisdiction. On the facts of the case, the Court concluded that the International Shoe Company had such "systematic and continuous" contacts with Washington. Does this mean that Washington courts could have exercised general jurisdiction—say, for a tort committed by the company in Missouri? Or was it important that the claim in issue arose out of the Washington activities? If so, why would it matter that the activities were systematic and continuous?

3. In *International Shoe,* the Court upheld the State's power to impose tax obligations on the Missouri company. That power was established by the same factors that subjected the company to personal jurisdiction in Washington. Of course, that does not mean that the factors that suffice to subject a nonresident to judicial jurisdiction are always co-extensive with those that make it amenable to the State's law-making authority. See Phillips Petroleum Co. v. Shutts, p. 445, infra.

4. Justice Black's concurrence in *International Shoe* reads more like a dissent. He criticized the injection of open-ended terms such as "fair play and substantial justice" as "elastic standards" that would allow courts to *restrict* state-court exercise of personal jurisdiction. The next case is the Court's preeminent early decision concerning how *International Shoe* should be applied. Notice that Justice Black wrote the majority opinion. How does he treat the open-ended concepts of fair play and substantial justice?

McGee v. International Life Insurance Co.

Supreme Court of the United States, 1957.
355 U.S. 220, 78 S.Ct. 199, 2 L.Ed.2d 223.

■ Opinion of the Court by JUSTICE BLACK, announced by JUSTICE DOUGLAS.

Petitioner, Lulu B. McGee, recovered a judgment in a California state court against respondent, International Life Insurance Company, on a contract of insurance. Respondent was not served with process in California but by registered mail at its principal place of business in Texas. The California court based its jurisdiction on a state statute which subjects foreign corporations to suit in California on insurance contracts with residents of that State even though such corporations cannot be served with process within its borders.

Unable to collect the judgment in California petitioner went to Texas where she filed suit on the judgment in a Texas court. But the Texas courts refused to enforce her judgment holding it was void under the Fourteenth Amendment because service of process outside California could not give the courts of that State jurisdiction over respondent. 288 S.W.2d 579. It is not controverted that if the California court properly exercised jurisdiction over respondent the Texas courts erred in refusing to give its judgment full faith and credit. 28 U.S.C.A. § 1738.

The material facts are relatively simple. In 1944, Lowell Franklin, a resident of California, purchased a life insurance policy from the Empire Mutual Insurance Company, an Arizona corporation. In 1948 the respondent agreed with Empire Mutual to assume its insurance obligations. Respondent then mailed a reinsurance certificate to Franklin in California offering to insure him in accordance with the terms of the policy he held with Empire Mutual. He accepted this offer and from that time until his death in 1950 paid premiums by mail from his California home to respondent's Texas office. Petitioner, Franklin's mother, was the beneficiary under the policy. She sent proofs of his death to the respondent but it refused to pay claiming that he had committed suicide. It appears that neither Empire Mutual nor respondent has ever had any office or agent in California. And so far as the record before us shows, respondent has never solicited or done any insurance business in California apart from the policy involved here.

Since Pennoyer v. Neff, 95 U.S. 714, this Court has held that the Due Process Clause of the Fourteenth Amendment places some limit on the power of state courts to enter binding judgments against persons not served with process within their boundaries. But just where this line of limitation falls has been the subject of prolific controversy, particularly with respect to foreign corporations. In a continuing process of evolution this Court accepted and then abandoned "consent," "doing business," and "presence" as the standard for measuring the extent of state judicial power over such corporations. See Henderson, The Position of Foreign Corporations in American Constitutional Law, c. V. More recently in International Shoe Co. v. State of Washington, 326 U.S. 310, the Court decided that "due process requires only that in order to subject a defendant to a judgment in personam, if he be not present within the territory of the forum, he have certain minimum contacts with it such that the maintenance of the suit does not offend 'traditional notions of fair play and substantial justice.'" Id., 326 U.S. at page 316.

Looking back over this long history of litigation a trend is clearly discernible toward expanding the permissible scope of state jurisdiction over foreign corporations and other nonresidents. In part this is attributable to the fundamental transformation of our national economy over the years. Today many commercial transactions touch two or more States and may involve parties separated by the full continent. With this increasing nationalization of commerce has come a great increase in the amount of business conducted by mail across state lines. At the same time modern transportation and communication have made it much less burdensome for a party sued to defend himself in a State where he engages in economic activity.

Turning to this case we think it apparent that the Due Process Clause did not preclude the California court from entering a judgment binding on respondent. It is sufficient for purposes of due process that the suit was based on a contract which had substantial connection with that State. Cf. Hess v. Pawloski, 274 U.S. 352; Henry L. Doherty & Co. v. Goodman, 294 U.S. 623; Pennoyer v. Neff, 95 U.S. 714, 735. The contract was delivered in California, the premiums were mailed from there and the insured was a resident of that State when he died. It cannot be denied that California has a manifest interest in providing effective means of redress for its residents when their insurers refuse to pay claims. These residents would be at a severe disadvantage if they were forced to follow the insurance company to a distant State in order to hold it legally accountable. When claims were small or moderate individual claimants frequently could not afford the cost of bringing an action in a foreign forum—thus in effect making the company judgment proof. Often the crucial witnesses—as here on the company's defense of suicide—will be found in the insured's locality. Of course there may be inconvenience to the insurer if it is held amenable to suit in California where it had this contract but certainly nothing which amounts to a denial of due process. Cf. Travelers Health Ass'n v. Commonwealth of Virginia ex rel. State Corporation Comm., 339 U.S. 643. There is no contention that respondent did not have adequate notice of the suit or sufficient time to prepare its defenses and appear.

The California statute became law in 1949, after respondent had entered into the agreement with Franklin to assume Empire Mutual's obligation to him. Respondent contends that application of the statute to this existing contract improperly impairs the obligation of the contract. We believe that contention is devoid of merit. The statute was remedial, in the purest sense of that term, and neither enlarged nor impaired respondent's substantive rights or obligations under the contract. It did nothing more than to provide petitioner with a California forum to enforce whatever substantive rights she might have against respondent. At the same time respondent was given a reasonable time to appear and defend on the merits after being notified of the suit. Under such circumstances it had no vested right not to be sued in California. . . .

Judgment reversed and cause remanded with directions.

NOTES

1. On the facts of the *McGee* case, would Texas have had judicial jurisdiction to entertain an action brought by the insurance company against the insured for a declaration that it was not liable under the policy? The answer might well be no, based upon the Court's case-specific analysis of whether jurisdiction would be fair in light of such things as the relative wealth of the parties and the forum state's interest. In *McGee*, Justice Black took the opportunity to use the "elastic standards" of fair play and

substantial justice to *support* jurisdiction. He employed concepts of fairness to uphold the plaintiff's right to sue in a convenient forum.

2. Justice Black made no distinction between facts (1) that demonstrate that the defendant forged a contact with the forum and (2) facts relating to whether the forum is fair or convenient. Rather, in the paragraph beginning "Turning to this case," he lumped together the defendant's solicitation of business in California (contact) with considerations supporting the fairness of jurisdiction in that state, including the forum state's interest in providing a remedy and the difficulty that plaintiff would encounter if she were required to sue the insurance company in Texas. Justice Black had debuted this "mélange" approach—mixing considerations of contact with those of fairness—in Travelers Health Ass'n v. Virginia, 339 U.S. 643 (1950), 70 S.Ct. 927. That case upheld jurisdiction in Virginia over a Nebraska nonprofit health insurance company. The approach was clear from the first sentence of that opinion: "[T]he contacts and ties of appellants with Virginia residents, together with that state's interest in faithful observance of the [law requiring out-of-state businesses to appoint an agent for service of process], justify subjecting appellants" to jurisdiction. 339 U.S. at 648.

3. Many observers regard *McGee* as the high-water mark in the Supreme Court's progressive expansion of the permissible bases of a state's personal jurisdiction over nonresident defendants. Is its holding confined to insurance claims? Would it support the result in Hirsch v. Blue Cross, Blue Shield of Kansas City, 800 F.2d 1474 (9th Cir.1986)? There, a Kansas employer contracted for group health insurance in Kansas for its Kansas employees. The contract was entered into with a Kansas insurance carrier. The parties subsequently added three California employees to the coverage. The carrier issued membership cards to the California employees whose premiums were paid through Kansas payroll deductions. When the carrier subsequently failed to pay a Californian's claim, the insured employee sued in California. The defendant had no office, property, or employees in California, and did not solicit business there. Held: there was limited jurisdiction over the defendant with respect to this plaintiff's claim.

4. Is *McGee* a "consumer preference" case? Article 14(1) of the Brussels Ia Regulation contains a provision restricting insurance companies to bringing actions against policyholders and beneficiaries only in the state of the policyholder's or beneficiary's domicile. Article 9, however, allows policyholders and beneficiaries to bring actions either in their domicile or in the company's "domicile," which is defined in Article 60 to be either the company's place of registration, central administration or principal business. Thus, under the Regulation, the *McGee* case would come out the same way. However, in the "reverse" *McGee* case posited in Note 1, the International Life Insurance Company would have been required to bring such an action in Mrs. McGee's home state of California.

5. Justice Black's mélange approach to *International Shoe* was not to last, as the next case shows.

———————

HANSON V. DENCKLA, 357 U.S. 235, 76 S.Ct. 1228 (1958). While *McGee* emphasized the practicalities of litigation and the relative burdens on the parties, and in so doing de-emphasized the importance of state lines, *Hanson* reasserted the importance of state lines and the allocation of authority between states.

Hanson involved a protracted, multistate battle over the estate of Dora Donner. Donner, while living in Pennsylvania, created a trust, appointing a Delaware corporation as trustee, and leaving to two grandchildren the residue of the trust upon her death. The creation of the trust was apparently part of an overall plan for her estate, whereby she intended to leave her worldly possessions in thirds: one third each passing through a will to Donner's two living daughters, and the remaining third to pass via the trust created with the Delaware trustee to Donner's deceased daughter's two children (i.e., Donner's grandchildren).

Years after the trust was created, Donner retired to Florida, where she, in the words of the Supreme Court, continued to carry on "some bits of trust administration," but otherwise did little relative to the trust. When Donner died, her will was offered for probate in Florida. The two living daughters, apparently not satisfied with their already substantial shares, sued in Florida to invalidate the trust that Donner had created with the Delaware trustee. The effect of successful invalidation of the trust would have been to place the trust assets in the estate, where they would pass to the living daughters, leaving the children of Donner's deceased daughter (i.e., Donner's grandchildren) emptyhanded. The Florida courts—applying Florida law—invalidated the trust.

The case in the Supreme Court reduced to the question of whether the Florida courts had jurisdiction over the Delaware trustee. Without jurisdiction over the Delaware trustee, the Florida courts would be unable to proceed, as the trustee was an indispensable party. The Supreme Court ruled out *in rem* jurisdiction as a possibility, as the trust assets did not have their situs in Florida. This left *in personam* jurisdiction over the trustee as the only possibility. The only conceivable basis for *in personam* jurisdiction was that the trustee had "minimum contacts" with Florida by virtue of having maintained the trust after Donner became domiciled in Florida. The Supreme Court, however, concluded that allowing the Florida courts to take *in personam* jurisdiction over the trustee would be unconstitutional. Some of language in *Hanson* has proved enormously influential on the development of the minimum contacts test:

> "[T]he requirements for personal jurisdiction over nonresidents have evolved from the rigid rule of Pennoyer v. Neff, 95 U.S. 714 to the flexible standard of International Shoe Co. v. Washington, 326 U.S. 310. But it is a mistake to assume that this trend heralds the eventual demise of all restrictions on the personal jurisdiction of state courts. Those restrictions are more than a

guarantee of immunity from inconvenient or distant litigation. They are a consequence of territorial limitations on the power of the respective States. However minimal the burden of defending in a foreign tribunal, a defendant may not be called upon to do so unless he had the 'minimal contacts' with that State that are prerequisite to its exercise of power over him. . . .

"[T]he record discloses no instance in which the [Delaware] *trustee* performed any acts in Florida that bear the same relationship to the agreement as the solicitation [of insurance premiums] in *McGee.* . . .

"The unilateral activity of those who claim some relationship with a nonresident defendant cannot satisfy the requirement of contact with a forum State. The application of that rule will vary with the quality and nature of the defendant's activity, but it is essential in each case that there be some act by which the defendant purposefully avails itself of the privilege of conducting activities within the forum State, thus invoking the benefits and protections of its laws. . . ."

"It is urged that because the settlor and most of the appointees and beneficiaries were domiciled in Florida the courts of that State should be able to exercise personal jurisdiction over the nonresident trustees. This is a non sequitur. With personal jurisdiction over the executor, legatees, and appointees, there is nothing in federal law to prevent Florida from adjudicating concerning the respective rights and liabilities of those parties. But Florida has not chosen to do so. As we understand its law, the trustee is an indispensable party over whom the court must acquire jurisdiction before it is empowered to enter judgment in a proceeding affecting the validity of a trust. It does not acquire that jurisdiction by being the 'center of gravity' of the controversy, or the most convenient location for litigation. The issue is personal jurisdiction, not choice of law. It is resolved in this case by considering the acts of the trustee. As we have indicated, they are insufficient to sustain the jurisdiction."

NOTES

1.   *Hanson* marked a profound shift of emphasis—from the "mélange" approach of *McGee*, which considered factors of contact, fairness, state's interest, and relative means of the parties to a rigid, lock-step approach. The approach emphasizes first the contact between the defendant and the forum. Such contact must result from the defendant's "purposeful availment" of the forum. The suggestion seems to be that without such availment, fairness factors are not relevant in the jurisdictional assessment.

2.   In Kulko v. Superior Court of California, 436 U.S. 84, 98 S.Ct. 1690 (1978), a child custody and support action, the Supreme Court reversed a state's assertion of judicial jurisdiction over the nonresident father on the

ground that he had not purposefully availed himself of the benefits and protections of the forum state's law. In *Kulko*, the former spouses had resided in New York with their minor children. Upon their separation, the mother moved to California. A subsequent Haitian divorce obtained by her incorporated the New York separation agreement. It provided that the children were to live with the father during the school year and with the mother during vacations. The father made support payments while the children were in the mother's care. When the daughter requested permission to live with the mother, the father acquiesced and bought her a one-way ticket to California. She was subsequently joined by her younger brother. The mother then started an action in California against the father, seeking full custody, increased support payments and other relief. The California courts upheld personal jurisdiction. Held: reversed. "A father who agrees, in the interests of family harmony and his children's preferences, to allow them to spend more time in California than was required under a separation agreement can hardly be said to have 'purposefully availed himself' of the 'benefits and protections of California' laws. . . ." The fact that the father now had fewer expenses than before, the Court noted, was the result of the absence of the children from New York and not of their presence in California.

3.   Would it have been unfair to subject the father in *Kulko* to jurisdiction in California for the claim for support modification? In the European Union, there is judicial jurisdiction in the courts of the place where the person entitled to support is domiciled or habitually resident. Council Regulation (EC) No. 4/2009 on Jurisdiction, Applicable Law, and Enforcement of Decisions and Cooperation in Matters relating to Maintenance Obligations [2009] Official Journal L 7/1. Note that whether someone is entitled to support is in itself a conflicts question (i.e., a choice-of-law determination answers the jurisdictional question) and that "support" is not limited to child support. Jurisdiction at the residence of the claimant also is the rule in England, Sweden, Switzerland, and under the proposed Inter-American Convention on Support Obligations. Since 1992, Australia, another federal nation, has given its courts nationwide jurisdiction over any defendant served in the country, with the power to transfer the case to a more appropriate court if the defendant demonstrates unfairness in being required to defend in the forum. See Service and Execution of Process Act 1992 §§ 12, 130; Jurisdiction of Courts (Cross-Vesting) act 1987 § 5. This theme is also considered p. 369, infra.

In the United States, the Uniform Interstate Family Support Act provides for the continuing jurisdiction of the original court under certain circumstances, and federal law provides for interstate recognition of child support orders. *Kulko*, however, still determines when a court other than the original court has jurisdiction over an absent defendant to establish or to modify a support obligation.

Note, however, that status determinations (including custody, but not support, matters) are governed by special jurisdictional rules that usually allow the state in which the affected person is domiciled to exercise jurisdiction. Matters of status have been subject to their own jurisdictional rules at least since *Pennoyer,* in which the Court recognized jurisdiction for "every State . . . to determine the civil status and capabilities of all its inhabitants" (95 U.S. at 732). More recently, the Supreme Court said: "We do not suggest that jurisdictional doctrines . . . such as the particularized ruling governing status . . . are inconsistent with the standard of fairness. . . ." Shaffer v. Heitner, n. 30, p. 176, infra.

4.   In *Hanson,* the Court clearly separated the jurisdictional and choice-of-law inquiries. The majority was willing to concede, arguendo, that Florida could apply its law to the transaction, even if the nonresident trustee's contact were too insubstantial to warrant exercising personal jurisdiction over it. Does this separation make sense? Was it sensible for the Florida courts to apply their own law to determine the validity of Donner's trust given that the transaction had been completed long before Donner moved to Florida? If the validity of a trust depends upon where the settlor eventually takes up residence, is a company in the position of Donner's trustee in a position to ensure that the trusts it creates will be adjudged valid? Other legal systems tie judicial jurisdiction and choice of law more closely, at least in some circumstances. Order 11, rule 1(1)(d)(iii) of the Rules of the Supreme Court of Judicature of England, as amended, provides for the jurisdiction over a nonresident for breach of a contract which is to be "governed by English law." Dicey, Morris & Collins, Conflict of Laws 444–45 (15th ed.2012). The Brussels I Regulation, as well as the Lugano Convention, provide for general jurisdiction at the defendant's domicile or, if an enterprise, at its principal place of business, and for specific jurisdiction in a number of enumerated cases as well as on the basis of a written stipulation by the parties (forum selection clause). They do not confer jurisdiction by inference from the applicability of the forum's substantive law. With respect to its European partner states, this is now also the law in England. Dicey, Morris & Collins, supra. In the United States, the applicability of a particular state's law, even if as a result of a choice-of-law clause, does not ordinarily, without more, confer jurisdiction. Hay, Borchers, Symeonides & Whytock, Conflict of Laws § 18.1 n. 8 (6th ed.2018). However, a choice-of-law clause in a contract may be a "contact" and may also represent a party expectation which, together with other contacts, may serve to satisfy the *International Shoe* test: Burger King Corp. v. Rudzewicz, 471 U.S. 462, 105 S. Ct. 2174 (1985), p. 83, infra. Should a choice-of-law clause be deemed an ipso facto basis of jurisdiction? Conversely, should a forum-selection clause imply that the chosen forum's substantive law is to apply?

NOTE ON STATUTORY DEVELOPMENTS IN THE WAKE OF INTERNATIONAL SHOE

Before *International Shoe,* the constitutional limitations on jurisdiction corresponded closely with the common law bases. Thus, for jurisdiction to be constitutional, it had to fit within one of the traditional bases: in-state service, consent, appearance, domicile, nationality, etc. In some instances, as discussed above, doing so required stretching the ordinary sense of those bases, as the expanded use of "implied consent" in *Hess* made clear. Except for cases that involved statutes that made aggressive use of the implied consent basis, the question of affirmative, state-law authorization for jurisdiction did not often arise, because it was usually provided by the common law.

International Shoe, however, made clear that there is a large universe of cases beyond the traditional bases in which state-court assertion of jurisdiction will be constitutional. Rather than attempting to rely upon piecemeal jurisdictional statutes to take advantage of these broadened horizons, states passed general jurisdictional statutes, which became known as "long-arm statutes," in reference to the relatively long jurisdictional reach permissible after *International Shoe*.

In 1955, Illinois passed the first such statute. The Illinois legislation provided a detailed list of bases of jurisdiction, such as the "transaction of any business within this State" and "the commission of a tortious act" within the forum state. Illinois Code of Civil Procedure § 2–209. Illinois's statute became a model for many other states.

There are two generic types of long-arm statutes. One is the "laundry list," which, like the Illinois statute, provides that specific acts, events or occurrences will give rise to jurisdiction; these generally do not expressly purport to reach the constitutional limits of jurisdiction. New York has such a statute. The other type, exemplified by California, does not list actions that will lead to jurisdiction, but simply permits jurisdiction to the full extent allowed by the Constitution. These statutes are short, usually one sentence: jurisdiction is granted "on any basis not inconsistent" with the Constitution. Cal.Code Civ.Proc. § 410.10. In some laundry list states, the supreme court has interpreted the statute to grant jurisdiction to the constitutional limit. See, e.g., Hall v. Helicopteros Nacionales de Colombia, 638 S.W.2d 870 (Tex.), rev'd on other grounds, 466 U.S. 408, 104 S.Ct. 1868, 80 L.Ed.2d 404 (1984); Certain-Teed Prods. v. District Court, 87 Nev. 18, 23, 479 P.2d 781, 784 (1971). And some states, such as Illinois, replaced their laundry list statute with one of the California variety. See, e.g., Ill.Ann.Stat. ch. 735 Art. 5 § 2–209 (Smith-Hurd Supp. 1989). Today, over 30 states fall into the maximalist group, either because of an expressly maximalist statute or because their statutes have been so interpreted.

Both types of statutes have advantages and drawbacks. Detailed statutes give rise to their own questions of interpretation but are not vulnerable to the shifting sands of Supreme Court interpretation of the constitutional standards. For instance, in Ingraham v. Carroll, 687 N.E.2d 1293 (N.Y.1997), the New York Court of Appeals held that a Vermont doctor who took some New York patients was not operating in "interstate commerce" within the meaning of the New York long-arm statute, and thus was not subject to personal jurisdiction in New York on a claim that he had misdiagnosed the condition of one of his New York patients. The New York court thus never faced the difficult constitutional question of whether the doctor's activities constituted minimum contacts with New York. In Green v. Wilson, 455 Mich. 342, 565 N.W.2d 813 (Mich. 1997), the Michigan Supreme Court concluded that its long-arm statute did not reach a Canadian driver who, while allegedly drunk, collided with the plaintiffs' automobile. The collision occurred about 1000 yards on the Ontario side of the Michigan-

Ontario line, though the defendant-driver was alleged to have become intoxicated in a Michigan bar. The majority concluded that the defendant-driver could not be reached under the long-arm statute because the defendant's "act . . . resulting in an action for tort" occurred in Ontario, not in Michigan.

Maximalist statutes have the advantage that they avoid closing the door to claims that rationally ought be pursued in the forum state. They also bypass questions of statutory interpretation by requiring the court to proceed directly to the constitutional question. Such statutes do, however, reduce predictability somewhat, because application of the constitutional test is often uncertain.

In some respects, the problems arising under detailed long-arm statutes are similar to those presented under jurisdictional treaties. For instance, in the Article 5(3) of the Brussels Convention (now the Regulation) provides for specific jurisdiction at the place where the "harmful event occurred." An essentially identical provision appears in Article 5(3) of the Brussels I Regulation. In Handelskwekerij G.J. Bier B.V. v. Mines de Potasse d'Alsace S.A., (Case No. 21/76) 1976 E.C.R. 1735, 1 Common Mkt.L.R. 284 (1976), a Dutch horticulturist sued a French mining company alleging that upstream discharges of massive amounts of salt into the Rhine River required the plaintiff to take expensive measures to purify the water used at the plaintiff's nursery. In particular, the plaintiff alleged that the salty water damaged its seed beds and forced the plaintiff to take expensive measures to eliminate the damage. The European Court of Justice interpreted the treaty language broadly, and held that jurisdiction would lie either in the place of the tortious actions (France) or the injury (the Netherlands).

How does the European Court's treatment of the treaty language compare with the Michigan Supreme Court's interpretation of the statutory words "act . . . resulting in an action for tort"? As you read cases in this chapter, consider whether the European Court's holding would be constitutional had the case arisen in the United States.

2.   "SPECIFIC JURISDICTION": THE HEGEMONY OF CONTACT, 1980– 2014

As noted above, "specific jurisdiction" refers to a case in which the claim against the defendant arises from or relates to the defendant's contact with the forum. "General jurisdiction," in contrast, refers to a case in which the defendant is sued for a claim that has no connection with the forum. The overwhelming majority of Supreme Court interpretations of *International Shoe* involve specific jurisdiction. One important question lingering from the 1950s decisions was which approach—the mélange analysis of *McGee* or the two-step analysis of *Hanson*—was to prevail. The Court did not answer that question until 1980, when it left no doubt in the next case.

———————

WORLD-WIDE VOLKSWAGEN CORP. V. WOODSON, 444 U.S. 286, 100 S.Ct. 559 (1980). Plaintiffs were New York domiciliaries relocating to

Arizona. While en route, they were involved in an auto accident in Oklahoma. They brought a product liability suit in that state, arguing that the placement of the gas tank caused a fire when the car was struck from behind. They sued the manufacturer and the North American distributor of the vehicle, who did not challenge personal jurisdiction. They also sued the New York dealer from which they bought the car (Seaway) and the Northeast distributor of the auto (World-Wide).[14] The Court held that these two defendants were not subject to jurisdiction in Oklahoma. The majority opinion endeavored to give meaning to the phrase "fair play and substantial justice" from *International Shoe* by setting forth a catalogue of at least five "fairness factors":

> The protection against inconvenient litigation is typically described in terms of 'resonableness' or 'fairness.' . . . Implicit in this emphasis on reasonableness is the understanding that [1] the burden on the defendant, while always a primary concern, will in an appropriate case be considered in light of other relevant factors, including [2] the forum State's interest in adjudicating the dispute, see McGee [p. 71, infra]; [3] the plaintiff's interest in obtaining convenient and effective relief, see Kulko [p. 76, infra], at least when that interest is not adequately protected by the plaintiff's power to choose the forum . . . ; [4] the interstate judicial system's interest in obtaining the most efficient resolution of controversies; and [5] the shared interest of the several states in furthering fundamental substantive social policies. See Kulko.

On the facts of the case, however, the Court was not required to address whether jurisdiction in Oklahoma would have been fair or reasonable. There is an absolute prerequisite to the exercise of jurisdiction under *International Shoe*:

> [W]e have never accepted the proposition that state lines are irrelevant for jurisdictional purposes, nor could we, and remain faithful to the principles of interstate federalism embodied in the Constitution. The economic interdependence of the States was foreseen and desired by the Framers. . . . But the Framers also intended that the States retain many essential attributes of sovereignty, including, in particular, the sovereign

---

[14] The manufacturer and importer of the car did not pursue their jurisdictional objection and thus remained amenable to jurisdiction in Oklahoma. The careful reader may thus wonder why, with two deep-pocketed defendants subject to jurisdiction, the issue of jurisdiction over the two more local defendants was worth pursuing to the Supreme Court. The answer is that the defendants were hoping to create diversity jurisdiction and remove the case from state court to a more defense-friendly federal court. The defendants succeeded and won the case on the merits in federal court. See Adams, World-Wide Volkswagen v. Woodson—The Rest of the Story, 72 Neb.L.Rev. 1122 (1993). The tactical considerations would be somewhat different today, however, as 28 U.S.C. § 1446(b) provides that a defendant generally may not remove a case on the basis of diversity of citizenship more than one year after the commencement of the action. Even at the time of *World-Wide* there was authority that a case could not become removable without some voluntary act by the plaintiff to dismiss claims against the non-diverse defendants. See DeBry v. Transamerica Corp., 601 F.2d 480 (10th Cir.1979).

power to try causes in their courts. The sovereignty of each
State, in turn, implied a limitation on the sovereignty of all of
its sister States—a limitation express or implicit in both the
original scheme of the Constitution and the Fourteenth
Amendment.

... Thus, the Due Process Clause 'does not contemplate
that a state may make binding a judgment in personam against
an individual or corporate defendant with which the state has
no contacts, ties, or relations.' International Shoe. Even if the
defendant would suffer minimal or no inconvenience from being
forced to litigate before the tribunals of another State; even if
the forum State has a strong interest in applying its law to the
controversy; even if the forum State is the most convenient
location for litigation, the Due Process Clause, acting as an
instrument of interstate federalism[15] may sometimes act to
divest the State of its power to render a valid judgment in
person. Hanson v. Denckla.

NOTES

1.   *World-Wide Volkswagen* established that the rigid lock-step approach of
Hanson, p. 75, supra, prevailed over the mélange approach of *McGee*, supra
p. 71. Instead of assessing facts relating to contact and fairness together,
first there must be a relevant contact—one resulting from the defendant's
purposeful availment of the forum—before an assessment of fair play and
substantial justice come into play. Considerations of fairness and
convenience thus cannot alone establish jurisdiction.

2.   In *World-Wide Volkswagen,* the Court concluded that neither Seaway
nor World-Wide had availed itself of Oklahoma. Why? Because the car they
distributed and sold in New York got to Oklahoma not through their efforts,
but by the "unilateral act of a third party": the plaintiffs had driven it to
Oklahoma. Thus, neither of those defendants had forged a relevant contact
with Oklahoma.

3.   Most of the specific jurisdiction cases decided by the Court for the
remainder of the twentieth century reject jurisdiction on the basis that the
defendant had failed to forge a relevant contact with the forum state. The
next case, however, is one of the relatively rare cases in which the Court
upheld jurisdiction.

---

[15] The Court explained that the requirement of a relevant contact between the defendant
and the forum was rooted in "interstate federalism." Less than two years later, however, an
opinion by Justice White (the author of the majority opinion in *World-Wide*) stated: "The
restriction on state sovereign power described in *World-Wide Volkswagen Corp.*, however, must
be seen as ultimately a function of the individual liberty interest preserved by the Due Process
Clause. That Clause is the only source of the personal jurisdiction requirement and the Clause
itself makes no mention of federalism concerns." Insurance Corp. of Ireland, Ltd. v. Compagnie
des Bauxites de Guinee, 456 U.S. 694, 702, n.10, 102 S.Ct. 2099 (1982). This doctrinal shift does
not change the fact that, under *World-Wide*, overwhelming evidence that a forum is fair and
convenient will not overcome the lack of a relevant contact between the defendant and the
forum.

BURGER KING CORP. V. RUDZEWICZ, 471 U.S. 462, 105 S.Ct. 2174 (1985). Two individuals in Michigan entered into a franchise agreement with Burger King (BK), pursuant to which they would operate a franchise in Michigan for 20 years. The contract included a provision that Florida law would govern any dispute arising from the franchise relationship. A dispute arose and BK sued the two franchisees in federal court in Miami, Florida, where BK has its principal place of business.

The Court again adhered to the strict two-step approach outlined in *Hanson* and *World-Wide Volkswagen*: (1) defendant must have forged a relevant contact with the forum through purposeful availment, rendering it foreseeable that they could be sued there, and (2) if there was a contact, an assessment of whether jurisdiction would be fair or reasonable under the circumstances. The first issue was easy: the defendants had reached out to BK to form a 20-year arrangement with the Florida company, to be governed by Florida law. The decision focused on whether the exercise of jurisdiction in Florida was unconstitutionally inconvenient for the defendants. In an opinion by Justice Brennan, the Court upheld jurisdiction and set a high bar for any defendant who challenges jurisdiction on the basis of its being unreasonable. Such a defendant must show not simply that the forum is inconvenient, but unconstitutionally so, which means "so gravely difficult and inconvenient that a party unfairly is at a severe disadvantage in comparison to his opponent." 471 U.S. at 478, quoting The Bremen v. Zapata Off-Shore Co., 407 U.S. 1, 18, 92 S.Ct. 1907 (1972). Moreover, "[a]bsent compelling considerations, a defendant who has purposefully derived commercial benefit from his affiliations in a forum may not defeat jurisdiction there simply because of his adversary's greater wealth." Id. At 484 n.25. On the facts of the case, the defendants failed to show that BK had acted with fraud or that the contract was the product of overweening power. Thus, the Court upheld jurisdiction in Florida.

NOTES

1. *Burger King* is noteworthy for three reasons. First, was a contract dispute, rather than a tort; this fact, however, does not alter the analysis under *International Shoe*. Second, the issue of contact between the defendant and the forum was easy and obvious; as noted, the defendants' principal argument was that jurisdiction was not fair, not that there was no relevant contact. Third, the majority opinion was written by Justice Brennan. Brennan wrote more individual opinions concerning the application of *International Shoe* than any other Justice, but this is the only time he wrote for the majority. Typically, he dissented, and urged the Court to adopt the more fluid mélange approach set forth in *McGee*, p. 71, supra.

In *Burger King*, Justice Brennan adhered to the rigid two-step regime set up in *Hanson*, p. 75, supra, but with a nuance. After listing the five fairness factors seen in *World-Wide Volkswagen*, p. 80, supra, he said: "These considerations sometimes serve to establish the reasonableness of jurisdiction upon a lesser showing of minimum contacts than would otherwise be required." 471 U.S. at 477. He seemed to propose a sliding scale, under which a weak showing of contact would require the court to consider whether jurisdiction would be fair under the circumstances. This approach would make it more difficult to dismiss a case without at least considering the reasonableness of jurisdiction on the facts. If there were any semblance of a contact, the court must assess whether jurisdiction might be upheld because of the fairness factors—such as a strong forum state interest or if the burden on defendant would be light. See Richard Freer, Personal Jurisdiction in the Twenty-First Century: The Ironic Legacy of Justice Brennan, 63 S.C.L.Rev. 551, 569–72 (2012).

The Court has never implemented Justice Brennan's sliding scale approach. In several subsequent cases, as we shall see, the Court denied jurisdiction after finding a lack of purposeful contact, without assessing whether jurisdiction would fair under the circumstances of the case.

2.   The remainder of this section consists of cases addressing two fact patterns: the "stream of commerce" and "effects" jurisdiction. The Court struggled in each area to define what constitutes a relevant contact for purposes of *International Shoe*.

NOTE ON CONTACT AND THE "STREAM OF COMMERCE"

In *World-Wide Volkswagen*, p. 80, supra, the Court rejected jurisdiction over the New York defendants because they had played no role in sending the automobile that crashed in Oklahoma to Oklahoma. The car got to Oklahoma through the "unilateral act" of the plaintiffs, and thus could not serve as purposeful availment by the New York defendants.

In much-cited dicta in *World-Wide Volkswagen*, however, the Court stated: "The forum State does not exceed its powers under the Due Process Clause if it asserts personal jurisdiction over a corporation that delivers its products into the stream of commerce with the expectation that they will be purchased by consumers in the forum State. Cf. Gray v. American Radiator & Standard Sanitary Corp., 22 Ill. 2d 432, 176 N.E. 2d 761 (1961)." The citation to *Gray*, and the explicit reference to consumers purchasing products in the forum in the stream of commerce, seemed to draw a line between the predictable purchase of a product in the forum state and random use of the product in the forum state. In other words, the Court seemed to be saying that has the plaintiffs in *World-Wide* ordered the car and had it shipped to Oklahoma, where the transaction had been completed, they would have had a much better case for jurisdiction.

The notion of "stream of commerce" jurisdiction is usually thought to have originated with the Illinois decision in *Gray*. In that case, an allegedly defective valve on a water heater was manufactured in Ohio, then assembled into the finished product in Pennsylvania, and then sold to the plaintiff at her Illinois home, where it exploded and injured her. She sued in Illinois. The Ohio valve manufacturer objected to jurisdiction on the grounds that the sale of the valve that reached Illinois was too tenuous of a connection to satisfy due process. After all, the Ohio valve manufacturer had sold its product only into Ohio. The valve got into Illinois only through the action of the Ohio manufacturer of the finished product. The Illinois Supreme Court upheld jurisdiction, and concluded: "it is not unreasonable, where a cause of action arises from alleged defects in his product, to say that the use of such products in the ordinary course of commerce is sufficient contact with this State to justify a requirement that he defend here." 176 N.E.2d at 766. The Court's dictum in *World-Wide Volkswagen* appeared to accept the stream-of-commerce analysis of the Illinois court in *Gray*. The Court finally addressed a similar fact pattern in the following case.

ASAHI METAL INDUS. CO. V. SUPERIOR COURT, 480 U.S. 102, 107 S.Ct. 1026 (1987). In *Asahi*, the plaintiffs made a claim for compensation as the result of a motorcycle tire blowout that led to a collision in their home state of California. The plaintiffs brought a products liability action against the Taiwanese manufacturer of the allegedly defective tire tube, which the plaintiffs had purchased in California. Cheng Shin in turn made a claim for indemnity against the Japanese manufacturer of the tire valve, Asahi Metal Industry Co. Asahi sold its valves to Cheng Shin (as well as other manufacturers) who incorporated them into the finished tire tubes, which were then sold by Cheng Shin throughout the world, including in the forum state of California. Asahi's sales to Cheng Shin represented only about 1% of Asahi's total sales, although Cheng Shin's sales of tire tubes to California represented about 20% of its total U.S. sales, and the record showed that annual sales in California were approximately 100,000.

In an opinion that splintered on the rationale but not the result, the Court held that Asahi was not subject to personal jurisdiction in California. Four Justices, led by Justice O'Connor, concluded that all that had been shown was Asahi's "mere awareness" that its valves would reach California in the stream of commerce, and this was not sufficient to establish minimum contacts. The O'Connor opinion argued that to the necessary purposeful availment between Asahi and California required some "plus" factor, such as special design of the product for use in the forum, marketing in the forum, or providing customer support in the forum. Four Justices, led by Justice Brennan, however, concluded that Asahi did have minimum contacts with the forum. According to the Brennan opinion, "the regular and anticipated flow of products from manufacture, to distribution, to retail sale" in the forum established minimum contacts.

Justice Stevens refused to endorse either test. He did opine, however, that the substantial volume of sales in the forum should suffice to establish minimum contacts under either test. Thus, the Court failed to generate a majority opinion on what constitutes purposeful availment (and therefore a relevant contact under *International Shoe*) in the stream-of-commerce scenario.

Interestingly, however, all nine Justices concluded that California's attempted exercise of jurisdiction was unconstitutional. The unanimity of result came about because all five of the Justices (Justice Stevens and the four Justices to sign Justice Brennan's opinion) who concluded that Asahi had minimum contacts, agreed with Justice O'Connor that jurisdiction would be unreasonable even if Asahi did have minimum contacts with the forum. Picking up on the "fair play and substantial justice" language in *International Shoe*, the Court concluded that, at least in rare cases, generalized notions of reasonableness can defeat jurisdiction. The Court pointed to two main factors. One was that Asahi was a foreign defendant and being subjected to "the unique burdens . . . [of] a foreign legal system." A second was that the California plaintiffs no longer remained in the case. The plaintiffs had settled with Cheng Shin, leaving only the third party indemnity dispute between Asahi and Cheng Shin. As a result, the Court concluded, California's interest in deciding the case was greatly diminished.

With the Supreme Court divided four to four on the stream-of-commerce question, lower courts predictably split on the question. Some followed the O'Connor opinion, others followed the Brennan opinion, and others attempted to avoid the issue by concluding that jurisdiction could be established, or not, under either test.

In the following case, the Supreme Court revisited the stream-of-commerce scenario. After 24 years of uncertainty under *Asahi*, the profession hoped that the Court would give clear guidance regarding what constitutes purposeful availment in stream-of-commerce cases. The hope was in vain.

J. McIntyre Machinery, Ltd. v. Nicastro

Supreme Court of the United States, 2011.
564 U.S. 873, 131 S. Ct. 2870, 180 L.Ed.2d 765.

■ JUSTICE KENNEDY announced the judgment of the Court and delivered an opinion, in which THE CHIEF JUSTICE, JUSTICE SCALIA and JUSTICE THOMAS join.

Whether a person or entity is subject to the jurisdiction of a state court despite not having been present in the State either at the time of suit or at the time of the alleged injury, and despite not having consented to the exercise of jurisdiction, is a question that arises with great frequency in the routine course of litigation. The rules and standards for determining when a State does or does not have jurisdiction over an absent party have been unclear because of decades-old questions left open in Asahi Metal Industry Co. v. Superior Court of Cal., Solano Cty., 480 U.S. 102, 107 S. Ct. 1026, 94 L. Ed. 2d 92 (1987). Here, the Supreme Court of New Jersey, relying in part on Asahi, held that New Jersey's courts can exercise jurisdiction over a foreign manufacturer of a product so long as the manufacturer "knows or reasonably should know that its products are distributed through a nationwide distribution system that might lead to those products being sold in any of the fifty states." Nicastro v. McIntyre Machinery America, Ltd., 201 N. J. 48, 76, 77, 987 A.2d 575, 591, 592 (2010). Applying that test, the court concluded that a British manufacturer of scrap metal machines was subject to jurisdiction in New Jersey, even though at no time had it advertised in, sent goods to, or in any relevant sense targeted the State.

That decision cannot be sustained. Although the New Jersey Supreme Court issued an extensive opinion with careful attention to this Court's cases and to its own precedent, the "stream of commerce" metaphor carried the decision far afield. Due process protects the defendant's right not to be coerced except by lawful judicial power. As a general rule, the exercise of judicial power is not lawful unless the defendant "purposefully avails itself of the privilege of conducting activities within the forum State, thus invoking the benefits and protections of its laws." Hanson v. Denckla, 357 U.S. 235, 253, 78 S. Ct. 1228, 2 L. Ed. 2d 1283 (1958). There may be exceptions, say, for instance, in cases involving an intentional tort. But the general rule is applicable in this products-liability case, and the so-called "stream-of-commerce" doctrine cannot displace it.

I

This case arises from a products-liability suit filed in New Jersey state court. Robert Nicastro seriously injured his hand while using a metal-shearing machine manufactured by J. McIntyre Machinery, Ltd. (J. McIntyre). The accident occurred in New Jersey, but the machine was manufactured in England, where J. McIntyre is incorporated and operates. The question here is whether the New Jersey courts have jurisdiction over J. McIntyre, notwithstanding the fact that the company at no time either marketed goods in the State or shipped them there. Nicastro was a plaintiff in the New Jersey trial court and is the respondent here; J. McIntyre was a defendant and is now the petitioner.

At oral argument in this Court, Nicastro's counsel stressed three primary facts in defense of New Jersey's assertion of jurisdiction over J. McIntyre. See Tr. of Oral Arg. 29–30.

First, an independent company agreed to sell J. McIntyre's machines in the United States. J. McIntyre itself did not sell its machines to buyers in this country beyond the U.S. distributor, and there is no allegation that the distributor was under J. McIntyre's control.

Second, J. McIntyre officials attended annual conventions for the scrap recycling industry to advertise J. McIntyre's machines alongside the distributor. The conventions took place in various States, but never in New Jersey.

Third, no more than four machines (the record suggests only one), including the machine that caused the injuries that are the basis for this suit, ended up in New Jersey.

In addition to these facts emphasized by petitioner, the New Jersey Supreme Court noted that J. McIntyre held both United States and European patents on its recycling technology. . . .

Both the New Jersey Supreme Court's holding and its account of what it called "[t]he stream-of-commerce doctrine of jurisdiction," were incorrect, however. This Court's Asahi decision may be responsible in part for that court's error regarding the stream of commerce, and this case presents an opportunity to provide greater clarity.

II

The Due Process Clause protects an individual's right to be deprived of life, liberty, or property only by the exercise of lawful power. Cf. Giaccio v. Pennsylvania, 382 U.S. 399, 403, 86 S. Ct. 518, 15 L. Ed. 2d 447 (1966) (The Clause "protect[s] a person against having the Government impose burdens upon him except in accordance with the valid laws of the land"). This is no less true with respect to the power of a sovereign to resolve disputes through judicial process than with respect to the power of a sovereign to prescribe rules of conduct for those within its sphere. See Steel Co. v. Citizens for Better Environment, 523 U.S. 83, 94, 118 S. Ct. 1003, 140 L. Ed. 2d 210 (1998) ("Jurisdiction is power to declare the law"). As a general rule, neither statute nor judicial decree may bind strangers to the State. Cf. Burnham v. Superior Court of Cal., County of Marin, [p. 51, supra.] A court may subject a defendant to judgment only when the defendant has sufficient contacts with the sovereign "such that the maintenance of the suit does not offend 'traditional notions of fair play and substantial justice.' " International Shoe Co. v. Washington, [p. 65, supra]. Freeform notions of fundamental fairness divorced from traditional practice cannot transform a judgment rendered in the absence of authority into law. As a general rule, the sovereign's exercise of power requires some act by which the defendant "purposefully avails itself of the privilege of conducting activities within the forum State, thus invoking the benefits and protections of its laws," Hanson, 357 U.S., at 253, 78 S. Ct. 1228, 2 L. Ed. 2d 1283, though in some cases, as with an intentional tort, the defendant might well fall within the State's authority by reason of his attempt to obstruct its laws. In products-liability cases like this one, it is the defendant's purposeful availment that makes jurisdiction consistent with "traditional notions of fair play and substantial justice."

A person may submit to a State's authority in a number of ways. There is, of course, explicit consent. E.g., Insurance Corp. of Ireland v. Compagnie des Bauxites de Guinee, 456 U.S. 694, 703, 102 S. Ct. 2099, 72 L. Ed. 2d 492 (1982). Presence within a State at the time suit commences through service of process is another example. See Burnham, [supra.] Citizenship or domicile—or, by analogy, incorporation or principal place of business for corporations—also indicates general submission to a State's powers. Each of these examples reveals circumstances, or a course of conduct, from which it is proper to infer an intention to benefit from and thus an intention to submit to the laws of the forum State. Cf. Burger King Corp. v. Rudzewicz, [p. 83, infra.] These examples support exercise of the general jurisdiction of the State's courts and allow the State to resolve both matters that originate within the State and those based on activities and events elsewhere. Helicopteros Nacionales de Colombia, S. A. v. Hall, [p. 122, infra]. By contrast, those who live or operate primarily outside a State have a due process right not to be subjected to judgment in its courts as a general matter.

There is also a more limited form of submission to a State's authority for disputes that "arise out of or are connected with the activities within the state." International Shoe Co., [p. 65, supra.] Where a defendant "purposefully avails itself of the privilege of conducting activities within the forum State, thus invoking the benefits and protections of its laws," Hanson, supra, at 253, 78 S. Ct. 1228, 2 L. Ed. 2d 1283, it submits to the judicial power of an otherwise foreign sovereign to the extent that power is exercised in connection with the defendant's activities touching on the State. . . .

The imprecision arising from Asahi, for the most part, results from its statement of the relation between jurisdiction and the "stream of commerce." The stream of commerce, like other metaphors, has its deficiencies as well as its utility. It refers to the movement of goods from manufacturers through distributors to consumers, yet beyond that descriptive purpose its meaning is far from exact. This Court has stated that a defendant's placing goods into the stream of commerce "with the expectation that they will be purchased by consumers within the forum State" may indicate purposeful availment. World-Wide Volkswagen Corp. v. Woodson, 444 U.S. 286, 100 S. Ct. 559, 62 L. Ed. 2d 490 (1980) (finding that expectation lacking). But that statement does not amend the general rule of personal jurisdiction. It merely observes that a defendant may in an appropriate case be subject to jurisdiction without entering the forum—itself an unexceptional proposition—as where manufacturers or distributors "seek to serve" a given State's market. . . .

In Asahi, an opinion by Justice Brennan for four Justices outlined a different approach. It discarded the central concept of sovereign authority in favor of considerations of fairness and foreseeability. As that concurrence contended, "jurisdiction premised on the placement of a product into the stream of commerce [without more] is consistent with the Due Process Clause," for "[a]s long as a participant in this process is aware that the final product is being marketed in the forum State, the possibility of a lawsuit there cannot come as a surprise. It was the premise of the concurring opinion that the defendant's ability to anticipate suit renders the assertion of jurisdiction fair. In this way, the opinion made foreseeability the touchstone of jurisdiction.

The standard set forth in Justice Brennan's concurrence was rejected in an opinion written by Justice O'Connor; but the relevant part of that opinion, too, commanded the assent of only four Justices, not a majority of the Court. That opinion stated: "The 'substantial connection' between the defendant and the forum State necessary for a finding of minimum contacts must come about by an action of the defendant purposefully directed toward the forum State. The placement of a product into the stream of commerce, without more, is not an act of the defendant purposefully directed toward the forum State."

Since Asahi was decided, the courts have sought to reconcile the competing opinions. But Justice Brennan's concurrence, advocating a rule based on general notions of fairness and foreseeability, is inconsistent with the premises of lawful judicial power. This Court's precedents make clear that it is the defendant's actions, not his expectations, that empower a State's courts to subject him to judgment.

The conclusion that jurisdiction is in the first instance a question of authority rather than fairness explains, for example, why the principal opinion in Burnham "conducted no independent inquiry into the desirability or fairness" of the rule that service of process within a State suffices to establish jurisdiction over an otherwise foreign defendant. . . .

Two principles are implicit in the foregoing. First, personal jurisdiction requires a forum-by-forum, or sovereign-by-sovereign, analysis. . . . [W]hether a judicial judgment is lawful depends on whether the sovereign has authority to render it.

The second principle is a corollary of the first. Because the United States is a distinct sovereign, a defendant may in principle be subject to the jurisdiction of the courts of the United States but not of any particular State. . . . That would be an exceptional case, however. If the defendant is a domestic domiciliary, the courts of its home State are available and can exercise general jurisdiction. And if another State were to assert jurisdiction in an inappropriate case, it would upset the federal balance, which posits that each State has a sovereignty that is not subject to unlawful intrusion by other States. Furthermore, foreign corporations will often target or concentrate on particular States, subjecting them to specific jurisdiction in those forums.

It must be remembered, however, that although this case and Asahi both involve foreign manufacturers, the undesirable consequences of Justice Brennan's approach are no less significant for domestic producers. The owner of a small Florida farm might sell crops to a large nearby distributor, for example, who might then distribute them to grocers across the country. If foreseeability were the controlling criterion, the farmer could be sued in Alaska or any number of other States' courts without ever leaving town. And the issue of foreseeability may itself be contested so that significant expenses are incurred just on the preliminary issue of jurisdiction. Jurisdictional rules should avoid these costs whenever possible.

The conclusion that the authority to subject a defendant to judgment depends on purposeful availment, consistent with Justice O'Connor's opinion in Asahi, does not by itself resolve many difficult questions of jurisdiction that will arise in particular cases. The defendant's conduct and the economic realities of the market the defendant seeks to serve will differ across cases, and judicial exposition will, in common-law fashion, clarify the contours of that principle.

III

In this case, petitioner directed marketing and sales efforts at the United States. It may be that, assuming it were otherwise empowered to legislate on the subject, the Congress could authorize the exercise of jurisdiction in appropriate courts. That circumstance is not presented in this case, however, and it is neither necessary nor appropriate to address here any constitutional concerns that might be attendant to that exercise of power. See Asahi, 480 U.S., at 113 n. *, 107 S. Ct. 1026, 94 L. Ed. 2d 92. Nor is it necessary to determine what substantive law might apply were Congress to authorize jurisdiction in a federal court in New Jersey. See Hanson, 357 U.S., at 254, 78 S. Ct. 1228, 2 L. Ed. 2d 1283 ("The issue is personal jurisdiction, not choice of law"). A sovereign's legislative authority to regulate conduct may present considerations different from those presented by its authority to subject a defendant to judgment in its courts. Here the question concerns the authority of a New Jersey state court to exercise jurisdiction, so it is petitioner's purposeful contacts with New Jersey, not with the United States, that alone are relevant.

Respondent has not established that J. McIntyre engaged in conduct purposefully directed at New Jersey. Recall that respondent's claim of jurisdiction centers on three facts: The distributor agreed to sell J. McIntyre's machines in the United States; J. McIntyre officials attended trade shows in several States but not in New Jersey; and up to four machines ended up in New Jersey. The British manufacturer had no office in New Jersey; it neither paid taxes nor owned property there; and it neither advertised in, nor sent any employees to, the State. . . . These facts may reveal an intent to serve the U.S. market, but they do not show that J. McIntyre purposefully availed itself of the New Jersey market.

* * *

Due process protects petitioner's right to be subject only to lawful authority. At no time did petitioner engage in any activities in New Jersey that reveal an intent to invoke or benefit from the protection of its laws. New Jersey is without power to adjudge the rights and liabilities of J. McIntyre, and its exercise of jurisdiction would violate due process. The contrary judgment of the New Jersey Supreme Court is

Reversed.

■ JUSTICE BREYER, with whom JUSTICE ALITO joins, concurring in the judgment.

The Supreme Court of New Jersey adopted a broad understanding of the scope of personal jurisdiction based on its view that "[t]he increasingly fast-paced globalization of the world economy has removed national borders as barriers to trade." Nicastro v. McIntyre Machinery America, Ltd., 201 N. J. 48, 52, 987 A.2d 575, 577 (2010). I do not doubt that there have been many recent changes in commerce and communication, many of which are not anticipated by our precedents. But this case does not present any of those issues. So I think it unwise to announce a rule of broad applicability without full consideration of the modern-day consequences.

In my view, the outcome of this case is determined by our precedents. Based on the facts found by the New Jersey courts, respondent Robert Nicastro failed to meet his burden to demonstrate that it was constitutionally proper to exercise jurisdiction over petitioner J. McIntyre Machinery, Ltd. (British Manufacturer), a British firm that manufactures scrap-metal machines in Great Britain and sells them through an independent distributor in the United States (American Distributor). On that basis, I agree with the plurality that the contrary judgment of the Supreme Court of New Jersey should be reversed.

I

None of our precedents finds that a single isolated sale, even if accompanied by the kind of sales effort indicated here, is sufficient. Rather, this Court's previous holdings suggest the contrary. The Court has held that a single sale to a customer who takes an accident-causing product to a different State (where the accident takes place) is not a sufficient basis for asserting jurisdiction. See World-Wide Volkswagen Corp. v. Woodson, 444 U.S. 286, 100 S. Ct. 559, 62 L. Ed. 2d 490 (1980). And the Court, in separate opinions, has strongly suggested that a single sale of a product in a State does not constitute an adequate basis for asserting jurisdiction over an out-of-state defendant, even if that defendant places his goods in the stream of commerce, fully aware (and hoping) that such a sale will take place. See Asahi Metal Industry Co. v. Superior Court of Cal., Solano Cty., 480 U.S. 102, 111, 112, 107 S. Ct. 1026, 94 L. Ed. 2d 92 (1987) (opinion of O'Connor, J.) (requiring "something more" than simply placing "a product into the stream of commerce," even if defendant is "awar[e]" that the stream "may or will sweep the product into the forum State"); id., at 117, 107 S. Ct. 1026, 94 L. Ed. 2d 92 (Brennan, J., concurring in part and concurring in judgment) (jurisdiction should lie where a sale in a State is part of "the regular and anticipated flow" of commerce into the State, but not where that sale is only an "edd[y]," i.e., an isolated occurrence); id., at 122, 107 S. Ct. 1026, 94 L. Ed. 2d 92 (Stevens, J., concurring in part and concurring in judgment) (indicating that "the volume, the value, and the hazardous character" of a good may affect the jurisdictional inquiry and emphasizing Asahi's "regular course of dealing").

Here, the relevant facts found by the New Jersey Supreme Court show no "regular . . . flow" or "regular course" of sales in New Jersey; and there is no "something more," such as special state-related design, advertising, advice, marketing, or anything else. Mr. Nicastro, who here bears the burden of proving jurisdiction, has shown no specific effort by the British Manufacturer to sell in New Jersey. He has introduced no list of potential New Jersey customers who might, for example, have regularly attended trade shows. And he has not otherwise shown that the British Manufacturer "purposefully avail[ed] itself of the privilege of conducting activities" within New Jersey, or that it delivered its goods in the stream of commerce "with the expectation that they will be purchased" by New Jersey users. . . .

There may well have been other facts that Mr. Nicastro could have demonstrated in support of jurisdiction. And the dissent considers some of those facts. . . .

Accordingly, on the record present here, resolving this case requires no more than adhering to our precedents.

II

I would not go further. Because the incident at issue in this case does not implicate modern concerns, and because the factual record leaves many open questions, this is an unsuitable vehicle for making broad pronouncements that refashion basic jurisdictional rules.

A

The plurality seems to state strict rules that limit jurisdiction where a defendant does not "inten[d] to submit to the power of a sovereign" and cannot "be said to have targeted the forum." But what do those standards mean when a company targets the world by selling products from its Web site? And does it matter if, instead of shipping the products directly, a company consigns the products through an intermediary (say, Amazon.com) who then receives and fulfills the orders? And what if the company markets its products through popup advertisements that it knows will be viewed in a forum? Those issues have serious commercial consequences but are totally absent in this case.

B

But though I do not agree with the plurality's seemingly strict no-jurisdiction rule, I am not persuaded by the absolute approach adopted by the New Jersey Supreme Court and urged by respondent and his amici. Under that view, a producer is subject to jurisdiction for a products-liability action so long as it "knows or reasonably should know that its products are distributed through a nationwide distribution system that might lead to those products being sold in any of the fifty states." 201 N. J., at 76–77, 987 A. 2d, at 592 (emphasis added). In the context of this case, I cannot agree.

For one thing, to adopt this view would abandon the heretofore accepted inquiry of whether, focusing upon the relationship between "the defendant, the forum, and the litigation," it is fair, in light of the defendant's contacts with that forum, to subject the defendant to suit there. Shaffer v. Heitner, [p. 173, infra]. . . .

For another, I cannot reconcile so automatic a rule with the
constitutional demand for "minimum contacts" and "purposefu[l]
avail[ment]," each of which rest upon a particular notion of defendant-
focused fairness. . . . I know too little about the range of these or in-
between possibilities to abandon in favor of the more absolute rule what
has previously been this Court's less absolute approach.

Further, the fact that the defendant is a foreign, rather than a
domestic, manufacturer makes the basic fairness of an absolute rule yet
more uncertain. I am again less certain than is the New Jersey Supreme
Court that the nature of international commerce has changed so
significantly as to require a new approach to personal jurisdiction.

It may be that a larger firm can readily "alleviate the risk of
burdensome litigation by procuring insurance, passing the expected costs
on to customers, or, if the risks are too great, severing its connection with
the State." . . . But manufacturers come in many shapes and sizes. It may
be fundamentally unfair to require a small Egyptian shirt maker, a
Brazilian manufacturing cooperative, or a Kenyan coffee farmer, selling
its products through international distributors, to respond to products-
liability tort suits in virtually every State in the United States, even
those in respect to which the foreign firm has no connection at all but the
sale of a single (allegedly defective) good. And a rule like the New Jersey
Supreme Court suggests would require every product manufacturer,
large or small, selling to American distributors to understand not only
the tort law of every State, but also the wide variance in the way courts
within different States apply that law. See, e.g., Dept. of Justice, Bureau
of Justice Statistics Bulletin, Tort Trials and Verdicts in Large Counties,
2001, p. 11 (reporting percentage of plaintiff winners in tort trials among
46 populous counties, ranging from 17.9% (Worcester, Mass.) to 69.1%
(Milwaukee, Wis.)).

C

At a minimum, I would not work such a change to the law in the way
either the plurality or the New Jersey Supreme Court suggests without
a better understanding of the relevant contemporary commercial
circumstances. This case presents no such occasion, and so I again
reiterate that I would adhere strictly to our precedents and the limited
facts found by the New Jersey Supreme Court. And on those grounds, I
do not think we can find jurisdiction in this case. Accordingly, though I
agree with the plurality as to the outcome of this case, I concur only in
the judgment of that opinion and not its reasoning.

■ JUSTICE GINSBURG, with whom JUSTICE SOTOMAYOR and JUSTICE
KAGAN join, dissenting.

A foreign industrialist seeks to develop a market in the United
States for machines it manufactures. It hopes to derive substantial
revenue from sales it makes to United States purchasers. Where in the
United States buyers reside does not matter to this manufacturer. Its

goal is simply to sell as much as it can, wherever it can. It excludes no region or State from the market it wishes to reach. But, all things considered, it prefers to avoid products liability litigation in the United States. To that end, it engages a U.S. distributor to ship its machines stateside. Has it succeeded in escaping personal jurisdiction in a State where one of its products is sold and causes injury or even death to a local user?

Under this Court's pathmarking precedent in International Shoe Co. v. Washington, [p. 65, supra], and subsequent decisions, one would expect the answer to be unequivocally, "No." But instead, six Justices of this Court, in divergent opinions, tell us that the manufacturer has avoided the jurisdiction of our state courts, except perhaps in States where its products are sold in sizeable quantities. Inconceivable as it may have seemed yesterday, the splintered majority today "turn[s] the clock back to the days before modern long-arm statutes when a manufacturer, to avoid being haled into court where a user is injured, need only Pilate-like wash its hands of a product by having independent distributors market it." Weintraub, A Map Out of the Personal Jurisdiction Labyrinth, 28 U.C. Davis L. Rev. 531, 555 (1995).

I

On October 11, 2001, a three-ton metal shearing machine severed four fingers on Robert Nicastro's right hand. Established in 1872 as a United Kingdom corporation, and headquartered in Nottingham, England, McIntyre UK "designs, develops and manufactures a complete range of equipment for metal recycling." The company's product line, as advertised on McIntyre UK's Web site, includes "metal shears, balers, cable and can recycling equipment, furnaces, casting equipment and . . . the world's best aluminum dross processing and cooling system."

The machine that injured Nicastro, a "McIntyre Model 640 Shear," sold in the United States for $ 24,900 in 1995, and features a "massive cutting capacity[."] According to McIntyre UK's product brochure, the machine is "use[d] throughout the [w]orld." Ibid. McIntyre UK represented in the brochure that, by "incorporat[ing] off-the-shelf hydraulic parts from suppliers with international sales outlets," the 640 Shear's design guarantees serviceability "wherever [its customers] may be based." . . .

Nicastro operated the 640 Shear in the course of his employment at Curcio Scrap Metal (CSM) in Saddle Brook, New Jersey. Id., at 7a, 43a. "New Jersey has long been a hotbed of scrap-metal businesses . . . ."

CSM's owner, Frank Curcio, "first heard of [McIntyre UK's] machine while attending an Institute of Scrap Metal Industries [(ISRI)] convention in Las Vegas in 1994 or 1995, where [McIntyre UK] was an exhibitor."

In a November 23, 1999 letter to McIntyre America [a now bankrupt distributor of McIntrye UK], McIntyre UK's president spoke plainly about the manufacturer's objective in authorizing the exclusive distributorship: "All we wish to do is sell our products in the [United] States—and get paid!" Notably, McIntyre America was concerned about U.S. litigation involving McIntyre UK products, in which the distributor had been named as a defendant. McIntyre UK counseled McIntyre America to respond personally to the litigation, but reassured its distributor that "the product was built and designed by McIntyre Machinery in the UK and the buck stops here—if there's something wrong with the machine." . . .

In sum, McIntyre UK's regular attendance and exhibitions at ISRI conventions was surely a purposeful step to reach customers for its products "anywhere in the United States." At least as purposeful was McIntyre UK's engagement of McIntyre America as the conduit for sales of McIntyre UK's machines to buyers "throughout the United States." Given McIntyre UK's endeavors to reach and profit from the United States market as a whole, Nicastro's suit, I would hold, has been brought in a forum entirely appropriate for the adjudication of his claim.

II

A few points on which there should be no genuine debate bear statement at the outset. First, all agree, McIntyre UK surely is not subject to general (all-purpose) jurisdiction in New Jersey courts. . . .

Second, no issue of the fair and reasonable allocation of adjudicatory authority among States of the United States is present in this case. New Jersey's exercise of personal jurisdiction over a foreign manufacturer whose dangerous product caused a workplace injury in New Jersey does not tread on the domain, or diminish the sovereignty, of any sister State. . . .

Third, the constitutional limits on a state court's adjudicatory authority derive from considerations of due process, not state sovereignty. . . .

Finally, in International Shoe itself, and decisions thereafter, the Court has made plain that legal fictions, notably "presence" and "implied consent," should be discarded, for they conceal the actual bases on which jurisdiction rests. . . .

Whatever the state of academic debate over the role of consent in modern jurisdictional doctrines, the plurality's notion that consent is the animating concept draws no support from controlling decisions of this Court. . . .

III

This case is illustrative of marketing arrangements for sales in the United States common in today's commercial world. . . .

McIntyre UK dealt with the United States as a single market. Like most foreign manufacturers, it was concerned not with the prospect of suit in State X as opposed to State Y, but rather with its subjection to suit anywhere in the United States. See Hay, Judicial Jurisdiction Over Foreign-Country Corporate Defendants—Comments on Recent Case Law, 63 Ore. L. Rev. 431, 433 (1984) (hereinafter Hay). As a McIntyre UK officer wrote in an e-mail to McIntyre America: "American law—who needs it?!" App. 129a–130a (e-mail dated April 26, 1999 from Sally Johnson to Mary Gaither). If McIntyre UK is answerable in the United States at all, is it not "perfectly appropriate to permit the exercise of that jurisdiction . . . at the place of injury"? See Hay 435. . . .

IV

A

While this Court has not considered in any prior case the now-prevalent pattern presented here—a foreign-country manufacturer enlisting a U.S. distributor to develop a market in the United States for the manufacturer's products—none of the Court's decisions tug against the judgment made by the New Jersey Supreme Court. . . .

[The dissent then discussed the opinions in *World-Wide Volkswagen* and *Asahi.*]

Asahi arose out of a motorcycle accident in California. Plaintiff, a California resident injured in the accident, sued the Taiwanese manufacturer of the motorcycle's tire tubes, claiming that defects in its product caused the accident. The tube manufacturer cross-claimed against Asahi, the Japanese maker of the valve assembly, and Asahi contested the California courts' jurisdiction. By the time the case reached this Court, the injured plaintiff had settled his case and only the indemnity claim by the Taiwanese company against the Japanese valve-assembly manufacturer remained.

The decision was not a close call. The Court had before it a foreign plaintiff, the Taiwanese manufacturer, and a foreign defendant, the Japanese valve-assembly maker, and the indemnification dispute concerned a transaction between those parties that occurred abroad. All agreed on the bottom line: The Japanese valve-assembly manufacturer was not reasonably brought into the California courts to litigate a dispute with another foreign party over a transaction that took place outside the United States.

Given the confines of the controversy, the dueling opinions of Justice Brennan and Justice O'Connor were hardly necessary. How the Court would have "estimate[d] . . . the inconveniences," see International Shoe, 326 U.S., at 317, 66 S. Ct. 154, 90 L. Ed. 95 (internal quotation marks omitted), had the injured Californian originally sued Asahi is a debatable question. Would this Court have given the same weight to the burdens on the foreign defendant had those been counterbalanced by the burdens litigating in Japan imposed on the local California plaintiff? Cf. Calder v. Jones, 465 U.S. 783, 788, 104 S. Ct. 1482, 79 L. Ed. 2d 804 (1984) (a plaintiff's contacts with the forum "may be so manifold as to permit jurisdiction when it would not exist in their absence").

In any event, Asahi, unlike McIntyre UK, did not itself seek out customers in the United States, it engaged no distributor to promote its wares here, it appeared at no tradeshows in the United States, and, of course, it had no Web site advertising its products to the world. Moreover, Asahi was a component-part manufacturer with "little control over the final destination of its products once they were delivered into the stream of commerce." To hold that Asahi controls this case would, to put it bluntly, be dead wrong.

B

The Court's judgment also puts United States plaintiffs at a disadvantage in comparison to similarly situated complainants elsewhere in the world. Of particular note, within the European Union, in which the United Kingdom is a participant, the jurisdiction New Jersey would have exercised is not at all exceptional. The European Regulation on Jurisdiction and the Recognition and Enforcement of Judgments provides for the exercise of specific jurisdiction "in matters relating to tort . . . in the courts for the place where the harmful event occurred." Council Reg. 44/2001, Art. 5, 2001 O. J. (L. 12) 4. The European Court of Justice has interpreted this prescription to authorize jurisdiction either where the harmful act occurred or at the place of injury. See Handelskwekerij G.J. Bier B.V. v. Mines de Potasse d'Alsace S.A., 1976 E. C. R. 1735, 1748–1749.

V

The commentators who gave names to what we now call "general jurisdiction" and "specific jurisdiction" anticipated that when the latter achieves its full growth, considerations of litigational convenience and the respective situations of the parties would determine when it is appropriate to subject a defendant to trial in the plaintiff's community. See von Mehren & Trautman 1166–1179. Litigational considerations include "the convenience of witnesses and the ease of ascertaining the governing law." Id., at 1168–1169. As to the parties, courts would differently appraise two situations: (1) cases involving a substantially local plaintiff, like Nicastro, injured by the activity of a defendant engaged in interstate or international trade; and (2) cases in which the defendant is a natural or legal person whose economic activities and legal involvements are largely home-based, i.e., entities without designs to gain substantial revenue from sales in distant markets. See id., at 1167–1169. As the attached appendix of illustrative cases indicates, courts presented with von Mehren and Trautman's first scenario—a local plaintiff injured by the activity of a manufacturer seeking to exploit a multistate or global market—have repeatedly confirmed that jurisdiction is appropriately exercised by courts of the place where the product was sold and caused injury.

* * *

For the reasons stated, I would hold McIntyre UK answerable in New Jersey for the harm Nicastro suffered at his workplace in that State using McIntyre UK's shearing machine. While I dissent from the Court's judgment, I take heart that the plurality opinion does not speak for the Court, for that opinion would take a giant step away from the "notions of fair play and substantial justice" underlying International Shoe. 326 U.S., at 316, 66 S. Ct. 154, 90 L. Ed. 95 (internal quotation marks omitted).

[Appendix to dissent omitted.]

NOTES

1.   Does *J. McIntyre* resolve the split between Justices O'Connor and Brennan in *Asahi*?

2.   Is the plurality opinion's heavy emphasis on sovereignty and rejection of fairness consistent with *International Shoe's* holding minimum contacts are a proxy for notions of "fair play and substantial justice"?

3.   As a lower court judge in New Jersey, how would you resolve a case like *J. McIntyre* if the plaintiff were able to show that ten machines had been sold through a distributor directly to New Jersey but that—to obtain a better price—the plaintiff's employer had decided to purchase his machine from a New York distributor? Which of the three *Nicastro* opinions would you consider controlling? Would you continue to apply the independent reasonableness check on jurisdiction employed in *Asahi*?

4.   As Justice Ginsburg pointed out, had the facts of this case involved an E.U. country—as opposed to the United States—J. McIntyre would have been forced to defend in a court at the locus of the injury. Does it make sense to have a more restrictive rule in the U.S.?

5.   In Section II.B. of his concurrence, Justice Breyer worries that "a rule like the New Jersey Supreme Court suggests would require every product manufacturer, large or small, selling to American distributors to understand not only the tort law of every State. . . ." Does this not confuse jurisdiction and choice of law? In many nations, the presumption in tort cases is that the law of the place of the injury or the victim's home governs. New Jersey law would apply under the "Rome II" Regulation on the Law Applicable to Non-Contractual Obligations that governs in the E.U. See p. 1211, infra. Article 5(1)(a) of the Rome II Regulation provides that in product liability actions "the law of the country in which the person sustaining the damage had his or her habitual residence when the damage occurred, if the product is marketed in that country. . . ." Article 3 makes clear that this rule holds even when the law chosen by the other articles is not that of an E.U. country. Article 25 provides that subdivisions of a country, such as a state or province, are considered "countries" for purposes of the Regulation.

6.   In Soria v. Chrysler Canada, Inc., 958 N.E.2d 285 (Ill.App.2011), leave denied, 963 N.E.2d 250 (Ill.2012), the court found jurisdiction over the Canadian assembler of an allegedly defective minivan, which was sold to the U.S. sister corporation of the assembler, and then sold in Illinois. The court summarized all three J. McIntyre opinions at length but concluded that under any version of the stream-of-commerce theory the Canadian assembler was subject to jurisdiction in Illinois. The court noted that 82% of the Canadian assembler's market was in the United States, and distinguished J. McIntyre in part on the grounds that the Canadian assembler knew the final destination of each vehicle that it assembled. Does it make sense for jurisdiction to turn upon such fine factual distinctions? Would it have made a difference if the defendant could show that the vehicle in question had originally been shipped to an Indiana dealership but (as often happens) the Indiana dealership had traded the vehicle to the Illinois dealership that ultimately sold it?

7.   The *J. McIntyre* case, as well as its companion *Goodyear Dunlop Tire Operations, S.A. v. Brown,* p. 126, infra, generated considerable commentary. See, e.g., Borchers, J. McIntyre Machinery, Goodyear, and the Incoherence of the Minimum Contacts Test, 44 Creighton L.Rev. 1245 (2011), Symposium, Personal Jurisdiction in the Twenty-First Century: The Implications of McIntyre and Goodyear, 63 S.C.L.Rev. 436 (2012) (contributions by Miller, Steiman, Vail, Stein, Freer, Silberman, Brilmayer/Smith, Carrington, Citron, Feder, Peddle, Perdue and Stravitz); Rhodes, Nineteenth Century Personal Jurisdiction Doctrine in a Twenty-First Century World, 64 Fla.L.Rev. 387 (2012). Much of the commentary has been critical of the plurality opinion in *J. McIntyre.*

NOTE ON CONTACT AND "EFFECTS" JURISDICTION

Despite the holding in *J. McIntyre*, the Supreme Court has not ruled out the possibility of personal jurisdiction over a defendant based upon tortious acts committed outside the forum. In 1984, it decided two companion cases upholding personal jurisdiction for defamation claims.

In Calder v. Jones, 465 U.S. 783, 104 S.Ct. 1482 (1984), a California-domiciled actress (Academy-Award winner Shirley Jones) claimed she was libeled by an article in *The National Enquirer.* She sued in California, and the Supreme Court held that the writer and the editor of the article (who were domiciled outside California and whose activities regarding the article took place in Florida) had forged contacts with California and were subject to personal jurisdiction there. The Court concluded that the defendants' "intentional, and allegedly tortious, actions were expressly aimed at California" and that the plaintiff suffered the majority of her harm there, because she lived there and because the publication had its largest circulation in that state. "Jurisdiction . . . is therefore proper in California based on the 'effects' of [the defendants'] Florida conduct in California." 465 U.S. at 784. Courts and commentators refer to jurisdiction based upon the "*Calder* effects" test.

The companion case was Keeton v. Hustler Magazine, Inc., 465 U.S. 770, 104 S.Ct. 1473, 79 L.Ed.2d 790 (1984). In *Keeton*, a New York citizen sued a magazine publisher in New Hampshire, alleging that the magazine defamed her on five occasions in articles it published. The principal defendant was an Ohio corporation with its principal place of business in California. The plaintiff sued in New Hampshire solely because it was the only state in which the statute of limitations had not run. The suit sought damages for defamation caused nationwide, and not simply in New Hampshire. The claim was based upon the "single publication rule," which stands for the proposition that a single publication of a defamatory statement gives rise to one claim, allowing damages suffered in all states to be recovered in one suit. The defendant sold between 10,000 and 15,000 copies of the magazine in New Hampshire each month.

The Court upheld jurisdiction, and explained:

> The "single publication rule," New Hampshire's unusually long statute of limitations, and plaintiff's lack of contacts with the forum State do not defeat jurisdiction otherwise proper under both New Hampshire law and the Due Process Clause. In judging minimum contacts, a court properly focuses on "the relationship among the defendant, the forum, and the litigation." Shaffer v. Heitner, infra p. 173. Thus, it is certainly relevant to the jurisdictional inquiry that petitioner is seeking to recover damages suffered in all States in this one suit. The contacts between respondent and the forum must be judged in the light of that claim, rather than a claim only for damages sustained in New Hampshire. That is, the contacts between respondent and New Hampshire must be such that it is "fair" to compel respondent to defend a multistate lawsuit in New Hampshire seeking nationwide damages for all copies of the five issues in question, even though only a small portion of those copies were distributed in New Hampshire. The Court of Appeals expressed the view that New Hampshire's "interest" in asserting jurisdiction over plaintiff's multistate claim was minimal. We agree that the "fairness" of haling respondent into a New Hampshire court depends to some extent on whether respondent's activities relating to New Hampshire are such as to give that State a legitimate interest in holding respondent answerable on a claim related to those activities. See World-Wide Volkswagen Corp. v. Woodson, 444 U.S. 286 (1980); McGee v. International Life Ins. Co., p. 71, supra. But insofar as the State's "interest" in adjudicating the dispute is a part of the Fourteenth Amendment due process equation, as a surrogate for some of the factors already mentioned, see Insurance Corp. of Ireland v. Compagnie des Bauxites de Guinee, 456 U.S. 694, 702–703, n. 10 (1982), we think the interest is sufficient. The Court of Appeals acknowledged that petitioner was suing, at least in part, for damages suffered in *New Hampshire*. And it is beyond dispute that New Hampshire has a significant interest in redressing injuries that actually occur within the State. " 'A state has an especial interest in exercising judicial jurisdiction over those who commit torts within its territory. This is because

torts involve wrongful conduct which a state seeks to deter, and against which it attempts to afford protection, by providing that a tort-feasor shall be liable for damages which are the proximate result of his tort.' " Leeper v. Leeper, 114 N. H. 294, 298, 319 A. 2d 626, 629 (1974) (quoting Restatement (Second) of Conflict of Laws § 36, Comment c (1971)).

This interest extends to libel actions brought by nonresidents. False statements of fact harm both the subject of the falsehood and the readers of the statement. New Hampshire may rightly employ its libel laws to discourage the deception of its citizens. There is "no constitutional value in false statements of fact." Gertz v. Robert Welch, Inc., 418 U.S. 323, 340 (1974). New Hampshire may also extend its concern to the injury that in-state libel causes within New Hampshire to a nonresident. The tort of libel is generally held to occur wherever the offending material is circulated. Restatement (Second) of Torts § 577A, Comment a (1977). The reputation of the libel victim may suffer harm even in a State in which he has hitherto been anonymous. The communication of the libel may create a negative reputation among the residents of a jurisdiction where the plaintiff's previous reputation was, however small, at least unblemished.

New Hampshire has clearly expressed its interest in protecting such persons from libel, as well as in safeguarding its populace from falsehoods. Its criminal defamation statute bears no restriction to libels of which residents are the victim. Moreover, in 1971 New Hampshire specifically deleted from its long-arm statute the requirement that a tort be committed "against a resident of New Hampshire."

New Hampshire also has a substantial interest in cooperating with other States, through the "single publication rule," to provide a forum for efficiently litigating all issues and damages claims arising out of a libel in a unitary proceeding. . . .

The Court of Appeals also thought that there was an element of due process "unfairness" arising from the fact that the statutes of limitations in every jurisdiction except New Hampshire had run on the plaintiff's claim in this case.[10] Strictly speaking, however, any potential unfairness in applying

---

[10] Under traditional choice-of-law principles, the law of the forum State governs on matters of procedure. See Restatement (Second) of Conflict of Laws § 122 (1971). In New Hampshire, statutes of limitations are considered procedural. Gordon v. Gordon, 118 N. H. 356, 360, 387 A. 2d 339, 342 (1978); Barrett v. Boston & Maine R. Co., 104 N. H. 70, 178 A. 2d 291 (1962). There has been considerable academic criticism of the rule that permits a forum State to apply its own statute of limitations regardless of the significance of contacts between the forum State and the litigation. See, e. g., R. Weintraub, Commentary on the Conflict of Laws § 9.2B, p. 517 (2d ed. 1980); Martin, Constitutional Limitations on Choice of Law, 61 Cornell L. Rev. 185, 221 (1976); Comment, The Statute of Limitations and the Conflict of Laws, 28 Yale L.J. 492, 496–497 (1919). But we find it unnecessary to express an opinion at this time as to whether any arguable unfairness rises to the level of a due process violation.

New Hampshire's statute of limitations to all aspects of this nationwide suit has nothing to do with the jurisdiction of the court to adjudicate the claims. "The issue is personal jurisdiction, not choice of law." Hanson v. Denckla, [p. 75, infra]. The question of the applicability of New Hampshire's statute of limitations to claims for out-of-state damages presents itself in the course of litigation only after jurisdiction over respondent is established, and we do not think that such choice-of-law concerns should complicate or distort the jurisdictional inquiry.

The chance duration of statutes of limitations in nonforum jurisdictions has nothing to do with the contacts among respondent, New Hampshire, and this multistate libel action. Whether Ohio's limitations period is six months or six years does not alter the jurisdictional calculus in New Hampshire. Petitioner's successful search for a State with a lengthy statute of limitations is no different from the litigation strategy of countless plaintiffs who seek a forum with favorable substantive or procedural rules or sympathetic local populations.

The plaintiff's residence is not, of course, completely irrelevant to the jurisdictional inquiry. As noted, that inquiry focuses on the relations among the defendant, the forum, and the litigation. Plaintiff's residence may well play an important role in determining the propriety of entertaining a suit against the defendant in the forum. That is, plaintiff's residence in the forum may, because of defendant's relationship with the plaintiff, enhance defendant's contacts with the forum. Plaintiff's residence may be the focus of the activities of the defendant out of which the suit arises. See McGee v. International Life Ins. Co., p. 71, supra. But plaintiff's residence in the forum State is not a separate requirement, and lack of residence will not defeat jurisdiction established on the basis of defendant's contacts. It is undoubtedly true that the bulk of the harm done to petitioner occurred outside New Hampshire. But that will be true in almost every libel action brought somewhere other than the plaintiff's domicile. There is no justification for restricting libel actions to the plaintiff's home forum.[12] . . .

In his concurring opinion, Justice Brennan said:

I agree with the Court that "[respondent's] regular circulation of magazines in the forum State is sufficient to support an assertion of jurisdiction in a libel action based on the contents of the magazine." Ante, at 773–774. These contacts between the respondent and the forum State are sufficiently important and sufficiently related to the underlying cause of

---

[12] As noted in Calder v. Jones, we reject categorically the suggestion that invisible radiations from the First Amendment may defeat jurisdiction otherwise proper under the Due Process Clause.

action to foreclose any concern that the constitutional limits of the Due Process Clause are being violated. This is so, moreover, irrespective of the State's interest in enforcing its substantive libel laws or its unique statute of limitations. Indeed, as we recently explained in Insurance Corp. of Ireland v. Compagnie des Bauxites de Guinee, 456 U.S. 694 (1982), these interests of the State should be relevant only to the extent that they bear upon the liberty interests of the respondent that are protected by the Fourteenth Amendment. "The restriction on state sovereign power described in World-Wide Volkswagen Corp. . . . must be seen as ultimately a function of the individual liberty interest preserved by the Due Process Clause. That Clause is the only source of the personal jurisdiction requirement and the Clause itself makes no mention of federalism concerns."

NOTES

1. Was *Calder* or *Keeton* a better case for jurisdiction? In *Keeton*, the plaintiff had little connection with New Hampshire, and the Court held that her lack of connection was not fatal for jurisdictional purposes. But the plaintiff's connection to California was seen as quite important in *Calder*; it was highly relevant because it helped to localize the injury there. In *Calder*, the action was against the individual writer and editor. Suppose the plaintiff in *Calder* had sued *The National Enquirer* itself, and that that entity is neither incorporated nor headquartered in California. Would the California courts have had jurisdiction?

2. The "*Calder* effects" test is similar to the Brussels Ia Regulation test under Article 7(2), see Case C-68/93, Shevill v. Presse Alliance SA, [1995] 2 W.L.R. 499, [1995] EWS 165, [1995] ECR I-415 (under predecessor convention with similar language, jurisdiction in a libel case allowed in every state of publication, but only for the harm caused at the place of publication unless the plaintiff sues at the defendant's domicile), but broader than the approach taken in *World-Wide*. In *World-Wide*, the dealer's and the distributor's allegedly tortious sale of the Audi in New York had profound effects in Oklahoma, yet the Court held that jurisdiction was unconstitutional. Should intentional tort cases be treated differently from non-intentional tort cases? Should the *Calder* effects test apply to other species of intentional torts, such as fraud? See, e.g., Carteret Savings Bank v. Shushan, 954 F.2d 141 (3d Cir.1992) (minimum contacts established in the forum because defendant's fraudulent representations had a foreseeable effect in the plaintiff's home state).

3. *Calder* and *Keeton* do not resolve the question of whether jurisdiction will lie in a state based upon the distribution of a trivial number of a publication in the forum. There is no clear rule in such cases. Compare Gordy v. Daily News, 95 F.3d 829 (9th Cir.1996) (New York newspaper has minimum contacts in California based upon circulation of approximately 20 daily copies allegedly to have libeled the California-domiciled plaintiff) with Noonan v. The Winston Co., 135 F.3d 85 (1st Cir.1998) (French language publication does not have minimum contacts with the forum state even though several hundred publications were sold in the forum state; no showing that the defendant was aware of the sales).

Compare these decisions with a 1977 decision of the German Supreme Court. The defendants were the publisher and editor of a magazine published in Vienna, Austria. The German plaintiff, resident in Berlin, learned that a particular issue carried allegedly libelous material. He obtained a copy through a friend and subsequently placed an order for an additional copy with a dealer. The Court held that the tort of libel is committed, and jurisdiction exists to entertain claims arising from it, where the magazine is published and where it is distributed. "It does not suffice that an occasional issue, through third parties, reaches an area not usually served by the publisher's distribution system. . . . It also does not amount to 'distribution' when someone places a special order for a copy of an issue in order to establish his domicile as the place of the commission of the tort for jurisdictional purposes. . . . It is thus decisive for the jurisdictional determination . . . whether the magazine containing the article was distributed in Berlin. . . . If, upon remand, the [trial] court should find that copies of the particular issue . . . were sold commercially in Berlin or sent there to subscribers, it need not require that a particularly substantial number of copies was involved in order to find the 'distribution' requirement satisfied." Decision of May 3, 1977, [1977] Neue Juristische Wochenschrift 1590, eds.' transl.

4. *Calder* and *Keeton* also raise the problem of the relationship between individual and corporate defendants. In *Keeton*, the Court held that the individual publisher was not necessarily subject to jurisdiction in New Hampshire just because the corporation had minimum contacts there. Conversely, in *Calder* the Court held that the individual defendants' "status as employees does not somehow insulate them from jurisdiction." 465 U.S. at 789–90. Despite the Supreme Court's apparent summary dismissal of the idea, a fair number of courts developed the "fiduciary shield" doctrine, which held that individual defendants acting in their capacities as fiduciaries or employees of a corporate defendant could not be made subject to jurisdiction based upon those activities. See, e.g., Marine Midland Bank v. Miller, 664 F.2d 899 (2d Cir. 1981); Weller v. Cromwell Oil Co., 504 F.2d 927 (6th Cir.1974). While *Calder* makes clear that the doctrine is not a due process limitation on jurisdiction, it could exist as a statutory limitation, perhaps as an interpretation of a long-arm statute that does not go to the limits of due process.

5. A related question of great practical significance is whether one member of a corporate family can be reached (jurisdictionally) through another. In the typical case, the goal will be to get personal jurisdiction over the out-of-state parent corporation of an in-state subsidiary. If the claim relates to the subsidiary's activities, the case is one of vicarious liability, and the question becomes what standards should be applied to hold the party liable, for instance, for the tortious conduct of the subsidiary. An example is the Bhopal disaster case, infra at p. 239 The Indian Union Carbide subsidiary, where the disaster had occurred, was capital-poor. Suit against Union Carbide

Corporation, the parent, provided the solvent party. See Note, Developments in the Law—International Environmental Law, 104 Harv.L.Rev. 1484, 1620 (1991); Lowenfeld, International Litigation and Arbitration 276 (1993). American-owned maquiladoras, which are shell corporations in Mexico for the local assembly of goods from American-supplied components, present another example. See Vaznaugh, Extraterritorial Jurisdiction—Environmental Muscle for the North American Trade Agreement, 17 Hastings Int'l & Comp.L.Rev. 207 (1993).

"Enterprise theory" has long suggested that traditional principles of corporate separateness should yield to the needs of compensation when substantive liability is at stake. See Blumberg, The Corporate Personality in American Law, 38 Am.J.Comp.L. 49, 63–69 (Supplement 1990). The amount of control exercised by the parent over the subsidiary might be an appropriate standard for determining vicarious liability. See My Bread Baking Co. v. Cumberland Farms, Inc., 233 N.E.2d 748, 752 (Mass.1968). In the case of the tanker M/V Amoco Cadiz, whose breakup caused a vast oil spill off the coast of France, the court wrote: "As an integrated multinational corporation . . . , Standard is responsible for the tortious acts of its wholly owned subsidiaries and instrumentalities. . . ." In re Oil Spill by the Amoco Cadiz off the Coast of France on March 16, 1978, 1984 AMC 2123, 2194 (N.D.Ill.1984). For further discussion and illustrations, see Lowenfeld, International Litigation and the Quest for Reasonableness—General Course on Private International Law, Hague Academy, 245 Collected Courses 9, 129–152 (1994-I).

To get jurisdiction over the out-of-state parent, whether on claims relating to the subsidiary (vicarious liability) or for claims against itself, there must be jurisdiction over the subsidiary. Assume that the case involves a claim against an out-of-state manufacturer of a product which it distributes through separately incorporated, but wholly-owned, subsidiaries. When the product causes injury in the forum state, is the manufacturer subject to jurisdiction there? The discussion concerning "stream-of-commerce" based jurisdiction suggests that there is jurisdiction over the manufacturer, and that the presence of the subsidiary is not a necessary prerequisite for this conclusion. But what if the stream-of-commerce theory is not followed? Or what about general jurisdiction? In these circumstances, the question becomes important whether the activities of the local subsidiary can be attributed to the parent and the latter be subjected to jurisdiction on the basis of those contacts. The U.S. Supreme Court wrote in the *Schlunk* case, p. 200, infra: "In the only cases in which it has considered the question, this Court held that the activities of a subsidiary are not necessarily enough to render a parent subject to a court's jurisdiction, for service of process or otherwise. Cannon Mfg. Co. v. Cudahy Packing Co., 267 U.S. 333, 336–337 (1925)," *Schlunk*, 486 U.S. 694, 705 n. 1 (1988). *Cannon* and many other cases addressed the question whether mere stock ownership, even 100%, by the parent of the subsidiary subjected the former to jurisdiction. See also Restatement Second, Conflict of Laws § 52, comment b. But what about the activities of the subsidiary that it undertakes for and on behalf of the parent, perhaps even at its direction? What does "not necessarily" in *Schlunk* mean?

The court in Gallagher v. Mazda Motor of America, 781 F.Supp. 1079 (E.D.Pa.1992), reviewed the case law and adopted a broadly phrased test: "jurisdictional contacts of [a] subsidiary . . . should be imputed to . . . [the] parent, for purposes of service of process when [the] subsidiary is engaged in functions that, but for the existence of [the] subsidiary, [the] parent would have to undertake."

The foregoing comments do not differentiate, and neither does the U.S. Supreme Court in its n. 1 in the *Schlunk* decision, p. 200, infra, between the standard appropriate for holding the parent liable for the subsidiary's actions and for attributing the subsidiary's forum contacts to the parent for purposes of suing the parent for its wrongs. Is the standard necessarily the same? Does it depend on whether the issue is specific or general jurisdiction?

When courts subject the out-of-state parent to jurisdiction in the state in which the subsidiary acts or has acted, they may do so on agency principles or by disregarding the corporate separateness ("piercing the corporate veil"). If, as a result, of "piercing", the two are the same, service on the subsidiary is service on "the" company.

The Hague Convention on the Service Abroad of Judicial and Extrajudicial Documents in Civil and Commercial Matters, to which the United States is a party (20 U.S.T. 361, 28, U.S.C.A. Rule 4), provides specific and exclusive procedures for the transmission of documents to parties in foreign states. Does the Convention affect the problems discussed above?

6. Related questions can arise if the action is against defendants who do not do business in the corporate form. Extraterritorial enforcement of in personam judgments against partnerships and other unincorporated associations raises a few special points stemming from historical oddities in local law treatment of those entities. One question, for example, is whether personal service upon a partner gives jurisdiction to bind partnership property outside the state. If the firm were owned by an individual, his presence in the state would be a sufficient basis for a valid personal judgment that could be enforced against his firm's property elsewhere. On the other hand, if the nonresident firm were incorporated, mere presence on personal business of a shareholder, officer, or director would not furnish a basis for an in personam judgment against the corporation. See Riverside & Dan River Cotton Mills v. Menefee, 237 U.S. 189, 35 S.Ct. 579 (1915); Goldey v. Morning News of New Haven, 156 U.S. 518, 15 S.Ct. 559 (1895). Shall a partnership be treated as amenable in the manner of an individual, or not amenable by analogy to a corporation? Further, under what circumstances may the members of a partnership be bound as to their personal property by a judgment against the firm?

The Restatement, Second, Conflict of Laws, provides some guidance:

§ 40. Partnerships or Other Unincorporated Associations

(1) A state in which a partnership or other unincorporated association is subject to suit in the firm or common name has power to exercise judicial jurisdiction over the partnership or association if under the circumstances it could exercise judicial jurisdiction over an individual. . . .

(2) A valid judgment rendered against a partnership or association is a binding adjudication as to the liability of the partnership or association with respect to its assets in every state.

Comment: . . .

d. Effect of judgment. A valid judgment rendered against a partnership or other unincorporated association under the circumstances stated in Subsection (1) will be recognized and enforced in other states, and, as between States of the United States, this result is required by full faith and credit. An action to enforce the judgment may be maintained against the partnership or association in another state, provided that it is subject to the judicial jurisdiction of that state and by the local law of that state may be sued in its firm or common name. If by the local law of the second state the partnership or association is not subject to suit in its firm or common name, the action to enforce the judgment may be maintained against the members individually, but recovery will be permitted to be had only out of firm, as opposed to individual, property.

Lower federal courts and state courts have struggled to apply the *Calder* effects test generally, and especially regarding cases involving the Internet.

Baldwin v. Fischer-Smith

Court of Appeals of Missouri, 2010
315 S.W.3d 389.

■ DANIEL E. SCOTT, CHIEF JUDGE

People write lots of nasty stuff about each other and publish it on the Internet. Sometimes the targets of these publications sue for defamation. Usually the targets want to sue at home and most of the time the defendants live elsewhere. Those who then find themselves defending libel actions brought in other states often move to dismiss on the ground that the court lacks personal jurisdiction. This basic scenario has been played out in dozens of reported cases.

One might think that by now there would have emerged a clear rule on whether the target can sue at home or not. However, there is no clear rule; in fact, there is not even really a clear majority position. . . . More-over, the variables on which the outcome depends seem to vary from court to court and case to case.[1]

This describes the situation before us, which apparently presents issues of first impression in our state. In dismissing the underlying action, the trial court found that even if the nonresident defendants used a website to libel plaintiffs in Missouri, they lacked "the minimum

---

[1] Patrick J. Borchers, Internet Libel: the Consequences of a Non-Rule Approach to Personal Jurisdiction, 98 Nw. U. L. Rev. 473 (2004)(internal citation omitted).

contacts necessary under the due process clause to establish personal jurisdiction by the courts of Missouri." . . .

Facts and Background

Plaintiffs are Missouri residents doing business as "Whispering Lane Kennel" near Ava, Missouri. They breed and sell dogs, exhibit them at American Kennel Club shows, and board and show client dogs for pay. Plaintiffs work primarily with the Chinese Crested breed and have won various awards, including "Best of Breed" at the Westminster Dog Show in New York City. Defendants Fischer-Smith and Hall, who live in Arizona and Pennsylvania respectively, show and sell Chinese Cresteds in competition with plaintiffs.

The jurisdictional issue hinges on plaintiffs' allegations that defendants libeled them via an internet website: www.stop-whisperinglane.com ("the website"). Defendant Fischer-Smith bought the website name and, with defendant Hall's aid and assistance, created and used the website to malign and damage plaintiffs and their business.

The website could be viewed by anyone with internet access. Its homepage, titled "STOP-WHISPERING LANE KENNEL," said the kennel was in Ava, Missouri, and named three plaintiffs as owners. We need not further describe the website content since defendants have not cross-appealed the finding that plaintiffs' libel allegations are adequate.

Google searches for the name of plaintiffs' kennel returned links to the website, which received some 2,500 "hits" or visits from internet users in one year. At least 25 hits were by Missouri residents involved in the dog business as owners, breeders, and/or exhibitors.

Plaintiffs sued defendants in Missouri on libel and other tort theories. Defendants moved to dismiss for lack of personal jurisdiction. The trial court expressed doubt about the jurisdictional allegations and allowed plaintiffs to replead. Defendants again sought dismissal, which was granted. The trial court found the petition adequately alleged "that both defendants committed libel in Missouri," but not "the minimum contacts necessary under the due process clause" for long-arm jurisdiction.

Plaintiffs' appeal raises three points. Point II addresses their principal claims for reversal, which hinge primarily on what now is known as the "effects" test of Calder v. Jones, 465 U.S. 783, 104 S. Ct. 1482, 79 L. Ed. 2d 804 (1984), with its divergent and somewhat irreconcilable interpretations by lower courts. We consider it first.

Calder and the Effects Test

In Calder, actress Shirley Jones filed suit in California, where she lived, against the author and editor of an unsavory National Enquirer story. The defendants lived in Florida and moved to dismiss for lack of personal jurisdiction. The Supreme Court unanimously found that the defendants were "primary participants in an alleged wrongdoing intentionally directed at a California resident, and jurisdiction over them is proper on that basis." 465 U.S. at 790.

The allegedly libelous story concerned the California activities of a California resident. It impugned the professionalism of an entertainer whose television career was centered in California. The article was drawn from California sources, and the brunt of the harm, in terms both of respondent's emotional distress and the injury to her professional reputation, was suffered in California. In sum, California is the focal point both of the story and of the harm suffered. Jurisdiction over petitioners is therefore proper in California based on the "effects" of their Florida conduct in California. . . .

As the Seventh Circuit recently put it, "Calder thus suggests three requirements for personal jurisdiction in this context: (1) intentional conduct (or 'intentional and allegedly tortious' conduct); (2) expressly aimed at the forum state; (3) with the defendant's knowledge that the effects would be felt—that is, the plaintiff would be injured—in the forum state." Tamburo v. Dworkin, 601 F.3d 693, 703 (7th Cir. 2010). It is "reasonably straightforward" to extract these rules from Calder, but applying them to internet tort cases "is more challenging." Id.

Indeed, "the body of law surrounding Internet personal jurisdiction remains unquestionably vague." Teresa J. Cassidy, Civil Procedure— Effects of the "Effects Test": Problems of Personal Jurisdiction and the Internet; Dudnikov v. Chalk & Vermilion Fine Arts, Inc., 514 F.3d 1063 (10th Cir. 2008), 9 Wyo. L. Rev. 575, 594 (2009). Although cases invariably hinge on federal due process, the Supreme Court has never directly ruled on such a case. Kyle D. Johnson, Measuring Minimum Contacts over the Internet: How Courts Analyze Internet Communications to Acquire Personal Jurisdiction over the Out-of-State Person, 46 U. Louisville L. Rev. 313, 323 (2007). Many internet cases cite Calder, which was not an internet case, and the Supreme Court declined the chance to consider it in an internet setting. See Young v. New Haven Advocate, 315 F.3d 256, 262–64 (4th Cir. 2002), cert. denied, 538 U.S. 1035, 123 S. Ct. 2092, 155 L. Ed. 2d 1065 (2003).

Since we do not have definitive guidance or controlling authority, we read cases far and wide, federal and state, reported and unreported, especially the latest decisions. One thing we found is that cases rarely turn on the first or third elements described in Tamburo (i.e., that the defendants acted intentionally, knowing the plaintiffs would feel the effects in the forum state). The battle generally involves the second element—commonly called "express aiming" or "targeting"—and the same can be said for this case.

Express Aiming

Unfortunately, narrowing the fight to this issue hardly solves the problem since there are at least three judicial views about it. "To some courts, 'targeting' . . . only indicates an effort to reach an individual in the forum. To others, it may require a finding of intent to target the forum state itself. To still others, 'targeting' may only require foreseeability of effects within the forum, as based on other non-Internet connections." Cassidy, supra, 9 Wyo. L. Rev. at 592 (footnote references omitted).

Obviously, the test focuses on a defendant's purpose or intent, but what kind of purpose and what sort of intent? The Supreme Court's opinion in Calder gives very little guidance on this question. In holding that the individual defendants in that action "knew" that the brunt of the harm caused by their allegedly defamatory article would be felt by the plaintiff in California, the court did not clearly indicate whether a desire or purpose to harm the plaintiff in California was required, or whether it was sufficient that defendants merely were aware that such harm would occur there, or whether jurisdiction should be sustained if defendants merely should have been aware that the primary impact of their conduct would occur in California. Nor did the Court indicate whether purpose or knowledge that a particular plaintiff would suffer harm in the state was required, or whether it was sufficient that the defendants were or should have been aware that some industry or person might suffer predictable harm there as a result of their conduct.

These ambiguities have led to widespread divergence among the lower courts. Some courts have suggested that something close to a subjective purpose or desire to harm the plaintiff in the forum state is required. Most courts have focused on the defendants' awareness that their conduct would cause harm in the forum state—an interpretation that most closely corresponds with the Supreme Court's language in Calder. However, some courts have gone further by indicating that the critical issue is not whether the defendants were in fact aware that their tortious conduct would have effects in the forum, but only whether they should have been aware that it would.

And if awareness is the key, awareness of what? Is it sufficient that the defendants are or should be aware that the primary effects of their conduct would be felt by the plaintiff in a particular state? Many courts have stated that such awareness is not alone sufficient to satisfy Calder's express aiming requirement, and that something more must be required before the express aiming or targeting requirement is met. . . .

We choose not to discuss every viewpoint and judicial opinion— plaintiffs' initial brief in this court addressed some 70 cases on these issues alone—or weigh in on various proposals for a decisional model to fit all situations. Our more modest goal is to properly review the case before us and let others ponder the grand scheme of things.

For purposes of this opinion, therefore, we focus on Tamburo, which was decided three months ago and reflects views that we share. Interestingly enough, it also involved the dog breeding business.

Tamburo v. Dworkin

Tamburo lived and worked in Illinois. He designed software for dog breeders and incorporated data from the websites of breeders in Colorado, Michigan, and Ohio, who responded by posting statements on their websites "accusing Tamburo of 'theft,' 'hacking,' and 'selling stolen goods,' and calling on readers to boycott his products. They also posted Tamburo's Illinois address on their websites and urged readers to contact him to harass him and otherwise complain." 601 F.3d at 698. Tamburo sued in tort in an Illinois federal court, which dismissed for lack of personal jurisdiction. Citing "Calder's 'express aiming' test for personal jurisdiction in intentional-tort cases" (Id. at 697), the Seventh Circuit reversed, finding these defendants had purposely directed their conduct at Illinois. . . .

[L]ike our case, Tamburo "primarily concern[ed] the question whether the defendants 'purposefully directed' their conduct at the forum state." . . .

Yet the case law goes in all directions and we might have papered another result as easily. It is fair, therefore, to ask how and why we came to our conclusions. Here are five of the reasons.

First, we are not persuaded by the view that Calder cannot be satisfied, even by targeting a known forum resident and causing injury in the forum, unless the defendant also intended to target the forum state itself. This seems inconsistent with what the Supreme Court said in Burger King. . . .

Second, even if Calder does require targeting of both plaintiffs and Missouri, the website proclaimed that:

> MO has the most LAX laws when it comes to the safety and concern of animals being housed and kept for breeding. This is why MO is knows [sic] as the Puppy Mill capitol of the WORLD. Commercial dog breeders from other parts of the US often relocate to MO to make their living off of dogs and puppy sales as there are few laws to force them to raise the animals in a clean, healthy environment. There are more breeders in MO than in most other states combined! Because there are not enough state inspectors many breeders are able to breed and raise dogs in filthy, disgusting conditions.

If plaintiffs must show both targeting of this state and of themselves to establish jurisdiction (which we do not believe), these statements serve that purpose.

Third, we are not overwhelmed by the occasionally-expressed concern about internet activities exposing a defendant to jurisdiction in many forums.

> A tortfeasor who mails a thousand bombs to recipients in one state, and one to recipients in each of the other forty-nine states,

should not be relieved from geographic responsibility for the consequences of his actions in each of those states simply because he is subject to suit everywhere, or because his conduct has a uniquely intensive relationship with a single state. Floyd & Baradaran-Robison, supra, 81 Ind. L.J. at 659.

Fourth, our Missouri Supreme Court recently expressed a broad jurisdictional view of communication that gives rise to intentional tort claims. . . .

Fifth, to tweak an observation from Revell v. Lidov, 317 F.3d 467, 476 (5th Cir. 2002), if you pick a fight in Missouri, you can reasonably expect to settle it here.

Fair Play and Substantial Justice

Since defendants' contacts are constitutionally sufficient, jurisdiction is appropriate unless it offends traditional notions of fair play and substantial justice. Int'l Shoe, 326 U.S. at 316. This is a much easier call and requires no extended discussion. "An individual injured in California need not go to Florida to seek redress from persons who, though remaining in Florida, knowingly cause the injury in California." Calder, 465 U.S. at 790. This case is no different. Due process is not offended if Missouri exercises jurisdiction over defendants in this case.

Conclusion

. . . Reversal and remand on that basis means we need not address other claims of error. Finally, we reiterate that we have not sought to tease out any universal rule about personal jurisdiction in internet cases. We merely decided this case.

We reverse the judgment of dismissal and remand the case for further proceedings.

NOTES

1.   One can sympathize with the court's observation about the inconsistency in the authorities in this increasingly common fact pattern. Is an "express aiming" requirement necessary to establish jurisdiction? Recall that in *Keeton*, the plaintiff chose the New Hampshire forum because of its long statute of limitations, but had no pre-litigation link to that state.

2.   A variant of this question arose in Yahoo! Inc. v. La Ligue Contre Le Racisme, 433 F.3d 1199 (9th Cir.2006) (en banc). In that case, the plaintiff was a California-based provider of various Internet-related products, including an auction site. The defendant, a French entity, brought suit in the French courts to prevent the plaintiff from allowing the sale of Nazi memorabilia to French buyers, because to do so would violate various French laws. The defendant was successful in obtaining various orders from a French court that purported to impose substantial monetary penalties on Yahoo!. Yahoo! then brought a diversity action in a California federal court against the French entity for a declaration that the French decrees were unenforceable against it. A majority of the en banc judges Ninth Circuit ruled

that there was personal jurisdiction because the decrees were aimed a Yahoo! and caused it significant harm in California.

Should the fraction of the harm felt by the plaintiff in the forum be of constitutional significance? For discussion of other aspects of the Yahoo! litigation see p. 405, infra. Although a majority of the judges upheld personal jurisdiction over the French defendants, the three judges who ruled that there was no jurisdiction combined with three judges who held that the case was not ripe for decision. The bare majority of six judges remanded the case with the direction to dismiss without prejudice.

3.   Compare the court's approach in *Baldwin* with that of the courts of other nations. In Dow Jones & Co. v. Gutnick, [2002] HCA 56 (Austl.2002), the High Court of Australia held that a plaintiff resident in Victoria could sue Dow Jones there for defamation. Dow Jones maintained a subscription news site on the World Wide Web. Dow Jones uploaded the allegedly defamatory material on its servers in New Jersey. The plaintiff resided in Victoria, which was the center of his business and social activities. The court also held that the law of Victoria applied. The defamation law of Victoria is more favorable to the plaintiff than the law of any U.S. jurisdiction. Dow Jones has no office or assets in Australia. The plaintiff sued only for harm that he suffered in Victoria and undertook not to sue defendant anyplace else.

The Ontario Court of Appeal distinguished *Gutnick* in Bangoura v. The Washington Post, [2005] O.J. No. 3849, leave to appeal denied [2006] S.C.R. vi, on the basis that Mr. Gutnick had been a well-known businessman who resided in Victoria (Australia) at the time of publication of the alleged libel, while the present plaintiff had moved to Canada more recently and had lived abroad when the material was published. The court held that the trial court had misapplied the factors announced in Muscutt v. Courcelles, [202] O.R. 3d 20 (C.A.) for determining jurisdiction, among them: the connection between the forum and the plaintiff's claim, unfairness to the defendant in assuming jurisdiction, unfairness to the plaintiff in not assuming jurisdiction, whether the case is interprovincial or international in nature, as well as others. Given the factual differences between the *Gutnick* case and the present case (including also the far fewer copies of the offending material published in Canada), the court concluded that it was "not appropriate for the courts of Ontario to assume jurisdiction." Should the court in *Keeton*, supra at p. 100, have considered similar factors?

The German Supreme Court (BGH) similarly held that there was no jurisdiction in Germany for a libel action arising from an internet publication of offending material describing the plaintiff's conduct at a party in Russia, even though the internet site was in Germany and the plaintiff and "some others" had accessed the site there, because the publication was in Russian, accessed mainly in that country and presumably causing greater injury to plaintiff's reputation in Russia then in Germany. BGH, Judgment of March 29, 2011, Docket No. VI ZR 111/10, 2011 NJW 2059 (with anno. by Brand). Like the court in *Bangoura,* supra, the German court made a jurisdictional determination on essentially *forum non conveniens* grounds, although this common law doctrine is not part of German law.

4. Should the nature of the relief sought make any difference? Note that the plaintiff in the principal case sought money damages. In cases brought under the Anti-cybersquatting Consumer Protection Act, 15 U.S.C.A. § 1125(d) in which the plaintiff merely seeks cancellation of an offending internet domain name, but no other relief, the statute essentially gives the plaintiff-infringee a jurisdictional preference by allowing it to employ in rem jurisdiction by treating the domain name as property with a situs in the forum. Should the fact that even a successful suit by the plaintiff would put the defendant only to the minimal burden or removing the offending information from his website make a difference?

5. Should the "interactivity" of the website make any difference? In a well-known federal trial court case, Zippo Mfg. Co. v. Zippo DOT Com, Inc., 952 F. Supp. 1119 (W.D.Pa.1997), the court held that a merely "passive" website should not subject its creator to jurisdiction wherever the website could be viewed. On the other hand, "interactive" websites—in which the host uses the website to enter into commercial transactions—should render the host subject to jurisdiction in states in which he enters into those commercial transactions. Does that framework make sense in the context of Internet libel cases?

<hr>

Thirty years after *Calder*, the Supreme Court returned to the question of whether effects caused in the forum can support jurisdiction.

WALDEN V. FIORE, 571 U.S. 277, 134 S.Ct. 1115, 188 L.Ed.2d 12 (2014): Walden, a local police officer deputized to work for the Drug Enforcement Agency as an agent at the Atlanta airport, searched the plaintiffs' luggage after they had flown to Atlanta from the Caribbean and were waiting to board a flight to their home in Nevada. The search yielded cash of nearly $97,000, which Walden seized. The plaintiffs protested, explaining that they were professional gamblers returning home from a gambling trip. After the plaintiffs returned to Nevada, the officer helped draft an allegedly false affidavit to support probable cause for forfeiture of the cash. The affidavit was sent to the United States Attorney, who ultimately decided not to prosecute the plaintiffs; their cash was returned. The plaintiffs sued Walden in federal court in Nevada, asserting that he had violated their rights under the Fourth Amendment. (Whether a federal court would have personal jurisdiction over Walden depended upon whether a state court in Nevada would have had such jurisdiction. See Note on Personal Jurisdiction in Federal Court, p. 161, infra.) The Ninth Circuit, relying on *Calder*, upheld jurisdiction over Walden for "the false probable cause affidavit aspect of the case." It concluded that Walden had "expressly aimed" his submission of the affidavit knowing that it would affect persons who had a "significant connection" to Nevada. The Supreme Court reversed. Its unanimous opinion explained:

> [O]ur "minimum contacts" analysis looks to the defendant's contacts with the forum State itself, not the defendant's contacts

with persons who reside there. See, e.g., *International Shoe* (Due process "does not contemplate that a state may make binding a judgment *in personam* against an individual . . . with which the state has no contacts, ties, or relations"); *Hanson* ("However minimal the burden of defending in a foreign tribunal, a defendant may not be called upon to do so unless he has had the 'minimal contacts' with that State that are a prerequisite to its exercise of power over him"). Accordingly, we have upheld the assertion of jurisdiction over defendants who have purposefully "reach[ed] out beyond" their State and into another by, for example, entering a contractual relationship that "envisioned continuing and wide-reaching contacts" in the forum State, *Burger King*, or by circulating magazines to "deliberately exploi[t]" a market in the forum State, *Keeton*, And although physical presence in the forum is not a prerequisite to jurisdiction, . . . physical entry into the State—either by the defendant in person or through an agent, goods, mail, or some other means—is certainly a relevant contact. See, e.g., *Keeton*.

But the plaintiff cannot be the only link between the defendant and the forum. Rather, it is the defendant's conduct that must form the necessary connection with the forum State that is the basis for its jurisdiction over him. See *Burger King* ("If the question is whether an individual's contract with an out-of-state party *alone* can automatically establish sufficient minimum contacts in the other party's home forum, we believe the answer clearly is that it cannot"); *Kulko* (declining to "find personal jurisdiction in a State . . . merely because [the plaintiff in a child support action] was residing there"). To be sure, a defendant's contacts with the forum State may be intertwined with his transactions or interactions with the plaintiff or other parties. But a defendant's relationship with a plaintiff or third party, standing alone, is an insufficient basis for jurisdiction. Due process requires that a defendant be haled into court in a forum State based on his own affiliation with the State, not based on the "random, fortuitous, or attenuated" contacts he makes by interacting with other persons affiliated with the State. *Burger King*. . . .

These same principles apply when intentional torts are involved. In that context, it is likewise insufficient to rely on a defendant's "random, fortuitous, or attenuated contacts" or on the "unilateral activity" of a plaintiff. *Ibid.* A forum State's exercise of jurisdiction over an out-of-state intentional tortfeasor must be based on intentional conduct by the defendant that creates the necessary contacts with the forum.

Calder v. Jones, . . . , illustrates the application of these principles. In *Calder*, a California actress brought a libel suit in

California state court against a reporter and an editor, both of whom worked for the National Enquirer at its headquarters in Florida. The plaintiff's libel claims were based on an article written and edited by the defendants in Florida for publication in the National Enquirer, a national weekly newspaper with a California circulation of roughly 600,000.

We held that California's assertion of jurisdiction over the defendants was consistent with due process. Although we recognized that the defendants' activities "focus[ed]" on the plaintiff, our jurisdictional inquiry "focuse[d] on 'the relationship among the defendant, the forum, and the litigation.'" *Id.*, at 788. . . . Specifically, we examined the various contacts the defendants had created with California (and not just with the plaintiff) by writing the allegedly libelous story.

We found those forum contacts to be ample: The defendants relied on phone calls to "California sources" for the information in their article; they wrote the story about the plaintiff's activities in California; they caused reputational injury in California by writing an allegedly libelous article that was widely circulated in the State; and the "brunt" of that injury was suffered by the plaintiff in that State. In sum, California [wa]s the focal point both of the story and of the harm suffered." *Id.*, at 789. Jurisdiction over the defendants was "therefore proper in California based on the 'effects' of their Florida conduct in California." *Ibid.*

The crux of *Calder* was that the reputation-based "effects" of the alleged libel connected the defendants to California, not just to the plaintiff. The strength of that connection was largely a function of the nature of the libel tort. However scandalous a newspaper article might be, it can lead to a loss of reputation only if communicated to (and read and understood by) third persons. See Restatement (Second) of Torts § 577, Comment *b* (1976); see also *ibid.* ("[R]eputation is the estimation in which one's character is held by his neighbors or associates"). Accordingly, the reputational injury caused by the defendants' story would not have occurred but for the fact that the defendants wrote an article for publication in California that was read by a large number of California citizens. Indeed, because publication to third persons is a necessary element of libel, see *id.*, § 558, the defendants' intentional tort actually occurred *in* California. . . . In this way, the "effects" caused by the defendants' article—*i.e.*, the injury to the plaintiff's reputation in the estimation of the California public—connected the defendants' conduct to *California,* not just to a plaintiff who lived there. That connection, combined with the various facts that gave the article a California focus, sufficed to authorize the California court's exercise of jurisdiction.

Applying the foregoing principles, we conclude that petitioner lacks the "minimal contacts" with Nevada that are a prerequisite to the exercise of jurisdiction over him. It is undisputed that no part of petitioner's course of conduct occurred in Nevada. Petitioner approached, questioned, and searched respondents, and seized the cash at issue, in the Atlanta airport. It is alleged that petitioner later helped draft a "false probable cause affidavit" in Georgia and forwarded that affidavit to a United States Attorney's Office in Georgia to support a potential action for forfeiture of the seized funds. Petitioner never traveled to, conducted activities within, contacted anyone in, or sent anything or anyone to Nevada. In short, when viewed through the proper lens—whether the *defendant's* actions connect him to the *forum*—petitioner formed no jurisdictionally relevant contacts with Nevada.

The Court of Appeals reached a contrary conclusion by shifting the analytical focus from petitioner's contacts with the forum to his contacts with respondents. Rather than assessing petitioner's own contacts with Nevada, the Court of Appeals looked to petitioner's knowledge of respondents' "strong forum connections." 688 F.3d, at 577–579, 581. In the court's view, that knowledge, combined with its conclusion that respondents suffered foreseeable harm in Nevada, satisfied the "minimum contacts" inquiry. *Id.,* at 582.

This approach to the "minimum contacts" analysis impermissibly allows a plaintiff's contacts with the defendant and forum to drive the jurisdictional analysis. Petitioner's actions in Georgia did not create sufficient contacts with Nevada simply because he allegedly directed his conduct at plaintiffs whom he knew had Nevada connections. Such reasoning improperly attributes a plaintiff's forum connections to the defendant and makes those connections "decisive" in the jurisdictional analysis. It also obscures the reality that none of petitioner's challenged conduct had anything to do with Nevada itself.

Relying on *Calder,* respondents emphasize that they suffered the "injury" caused by petitioner's allegedly tortious conduct (*i.e.,* the delayed return of their gambling funds) while they were residing in the forum. Brief for Respondents 14. This emphasis is likewise misplaced. As previously noted, *Calder* made clear that mere injury to a forum resident is not a sufficient connection to the forum. Regardless of where a plaintiff lives or works, an injury is jurisdictionally relevant only insofar as it shows that the defendant has formed a contact with the forum State. The proper question is not where the plaintiff experienced a particular injury or effect but whether the defendant's conduct connects him to the forum in a meaningful way.

Respondents' claimed injury does not evince a connection between petitioner and Nevada. Even if we consider the continuation of the seizure in Georgia to be a distinct injury, it is not the sort of effect that is tethered to Nevada in any meaningful way. Respondents (and only respondents) lacked access to their funds in Nevada not because anything independently occurred there, but because Nevada is where respondents chose to be at a time when they desired to use the funds seized by petitioner. Respondents would have experienced this same lack of access in California, Mississippi, or wherever else they might have traveled and found themselves wanting more money than they had. Unlike the broad publication of the forum-focused story in *Calder,* the effects of petitioner's conduct on respondents are not connected to the forum State in a way that makes those effects a proper basis for jurisdiction.

NOTES

1. The Missouri Court of Appeals, when deciding *Baldwin,* did not have the guidance offered in *Walden.* Would *Baldwin* be decided differently after *Walden?*

2. To date, the Supreme Court has not taken a case presenting personal jurisdiction by Internet contact. Does *Walden* shed any light on how Internet cases should be approached?

3. In the European Union, there is specific jurisdiction at the place where the contractual "obligation in question" was or is to be performed. Brussels I Regulation Art. 5(1). With regard to contracts for the sale of goods or services, this is defined as the place where the goods and services were or should have been delivered or provided. Quite clearly, a single contract will support jurisdiction. For other contracts, the Regulation does not provide a definite rule and the trial court must determine the place of performance of "the obligation in question. The European Court, interpreting similar Convention language, has held that it is the contractual obligation in issue in the litigation that is relevant for the jurisdictional determination.

Thus, depending on who sues whom on what aspect of a contract, different courts may have specific jurisdiction (in addition to the court with general jurisdiction at the defendant's domicile). The matter is made more difficult still because the legal systems of the member states may differ as to where a particular contract obligation is to be performed (and it is the place of performance that has jurisdiction). Thus, the questions a court must ask are: what is the obligation in issue; where—as determined by my (the forum's) conflicts law—is the place of performance of such an obligation; if that should turn out to be another state, would it determine the "place-of-performance" issue the same way or, under its law, have looked to yet another state or referred back to me (for "renvoi", see p. 562, infra)? Only after all these questions have been answered, will the court know whether it or another court has specific jurisdiction to proceed to the merits. Is this system a useful way to give jurisdiction to the state with the closest connection to the issue or is it too complicated to make sense? For comment and further references, see Hill, Jurisdiction in Matters Relating to a Contract under the Brussels Convention, 44 Int'l & Comp.L.Q. 591 (1995). Also, what is a "matter relating to contract?" Does it include claims based on precontractual liability (as in German law) or these tort claims and therefore not part of this jurisdictional provision (as in the common law)? The question is important if a resulting judgment is later challenged in another state on the basis that the first court lacked jurisdiction (by the standards of the second court). For comment, see Hay and Rasmussen, Uniform Interpretation and Application of Brussels-I and Lugano, 2011 Eur.L.F. 105.

4. Buyers are often treated more gently than sellers in jurisdictional cases, on the theory that the buyer is more likely to be weaker financially than the seller, especially when consumer goods are involved. Thus, "with few exceptions, in those cases where jurisdiction is extended over a nonresident defendant purchaser, that purchaser has either initiated the relationship or actively participated in negotiations and plans for production (e.g., design specifications)." Vacu-Maid, Inc. v. Covington, 530 P.2d 137, 141, 143 (Okla.App.1974). See also Tube Turns Div. of Chemetron v. Patterson Co., 562 S.W.2d 99 (Ky.App.1978). When the buyer is not an individual but a large and sophisticated business, jurisdiction is more likely to be sustained. Nordberg Div. of Rex Chainbelt Inc. v. Hudson Eng. Corp., 361 F.Supp. 903 (E.D.Wis.1973).

5. Some courts have made the issue of jurisdiction turn on which party took the initiative in the transaction. Courts sometimes refer to this as the "aggressor" test. Under this approach, the "aggressor" is generally required to sue the "aggressee" in the aggressee's home state, but the aggressee can obtain jurisdiction over the aggressor in the aggressee's home state. See, e.g., TRWL v. Select Int'l Inc., 527 N.W.2d 573, 576 (Minn.App.1995). Is this a sensible test? Suppose an out-of-state, mail-order company mails thousands of identical catalogs to households in the forum state. A recipient of one of the catalogs calls the toll-free number provided in the catalog and orders a chair. The chair arrives and the consumer claims that it is defective. The mail-order company claims that the chair is not defective, refuses to grant a refund, and sues in its home state for the balance of the purchase price. Can the mail order company obtain jurisdiction over the consumer on the theory that the consumer is the aggressor in the transaction? If so, is this consistent with *Burger King*? with *McGee*?

Suppose the same facts apply, except that the catalog was sent by email and the order was made over the Internet. Same result?

6. Could problems like the one suggested in the previous note be solved by an express consumer exception to jurisdiction? If so, how should "consumer" be defined? Should it include, say, the Microsoft Corporation when it buys goods from another corporation? The Brussels I Regulation contains special jurisdictional provisions for consumer transactions. The consumer may be sued only in the state of his or her residence, while "the other party" may also be sued there as well as at its own domicile or business seat. Art. 16. Forum selection clauses that provide for jurisdiction elsewhere are permissible only in limited and specifically described circumstances, e.g., when the clause gives the consumer additional courts in which to sue the other party. Art. 17(2). Article 15 defines "consumer transactions" for purposes of these provisions (e.g., installment sales, loans and credit transactions, sales of personal property and the rendition of services when the contract was with a merchant who pursues commercial or professional activities in the consumer's state or directs such activities to the state).

7.   Concerning Internet auction sites, recall the *Yahoo!* litigation noted following *Keeton*. Another example is Dudnikov v. Chalk & Vermilion Fine Arts, Inc., 514 F.3d 1063 (10th Cir.2008) in which Colorado sellers over the popular site Ebay brought suit against an out-of-state corporation which had threatened the sellers with a lawsuit for copyright infringement and also had successfully persuaded Ebay to cancel their auction of certain items alleged to infringe on copyrights. The court concluded that the foreseeable harm to the sellers in Colorado was sufficient to allow them to gain jurisdiction there.

The Court of Justice of the European Union recently stated some guidelines for the determination of what constitutes "targeting" of a market and customers by internet in the consumer context. See Note 4, p. 1163, infra.

8.   A related issue that often arises in these fact patterns is the degree to which the activities of domestic subsidiaries can be attributed to foreign corporations. For example, in Stubbs v. Wyndham Nassau Resort, 447 F.3d 1357 (11th Cir.2006), the plaintiff was injured at a Bahamian resort but brought suit in Florida. The circuit court ruled that the Florida subsidiaries of the Bahamian corporate owner "conducted business solely for the nonresident corporation . . . and thus their activities could be imputed to the nonresident corporations." Id. at 1362. In light of this material should conducting business "solely" for a nonresident defendant be sufficient to impute the activities of a local subsidiary to the nonresident? What sort of information would you gather in discovery to attempt to prove or disprove a sufficient connection to meet this standard?

In Daimler AG v. Bauman, 571 U.S. 117, 134 S. Ct. 746, 758–60 (2014), p. 126, infra, the Supreme Court granted certiorari on the question of whether the forum activities of a subsidiary may be attributed to a parent corporation. The Ninth Circuit had used an "agency theory" to attribute the California contacts of Mercedes Benz USA to the parent corporation, the German entity Daimler AG. The Supreme Court expressed doubt about the theory as applied by the Ninth Circuit but refused to define the permissible scope of such corporate attribution. It was not necessary to reach the question, according to the Court, because California would lack general jurisdiction over Daimler AG even if the subsidiary's contacts with the forum were attributed to it. We turn to general jurisdiction now.

3. "GENERAL JURISDICTION"

With general jurisdiction, the defendant is sued for a claim that arose outside the forum, and not from the defendant's forum activities. Defendants may be subjected to general jurisdiction only in states with which they have considerable ties. Using language from *International Shoe*, p. 65, supra, courts for decades upheld general jurisdiction where the defendant has "continuous and systematic" connections.

PERKINS V. BENGUET CONSOLIDATED MINING CO., 342 U.S. 437, 72 S.Ct. 413 (1952). The president of the defendant, a Philippine corporation, was served with a process in Ohio for a case filed in an Ohio state court by a non-resident of Ohio. The cause of action did not arise in Ohio and did not relate to the corporation's activities there. The defendant owned mining properties in the Philippines, but its operations there halted during the Japanese occupation in World War 2. The main activities in Ohio were carried on by the president, who was also general manager and principal stockholder of the company, and included: maintaining the files, corresponding, paying salaries of employees out of the company's local bank accounts, holding directors' meetings, and supervising rehabilitation of the corporation after the occupation.

On motion, the Ohio courts quashed service and rejected jurisdiction. The Supreme Court reversed and upheld general jurisdiction. The company's activities in Ohio were sufficiently "continuous and systematic" as to permit general jurisdiction. (The Court also concluded that the due process clause of the Fourteenth Amendment did not *compel* Ohio to open its courts to the case.) On remand, the Ohio Supreme Court held that its courts should exercise jurisdiction. 158 Ohio St. 145, 107 N.E.2d 203 (1952).

HELICOPTEROS NACIONALES DE COLOMBIA, S.A. V. HALL, 466 U.S. 408, 104 S.Ct. 1968 (1984). Representatives of four persons killed in a helicopter crash in South America sued the Colombian business that operated the aircraft (Helicol). They filed suit in Texas. The parties stipulated that the claim did not arise from or relate to the defendant's contacts with Texas, which meant that if the court were to have jurisdiction, it had to be general jurisdiction. Indeed, the stipulation was taken as the plaintiffs' waiver of any basis for specific jurisdiction.

The Court rejected general jurisdiction. Helicol's contacts with Texas included: (1) its chief executive officer went to Texas to negotiate the contract by which the company provided transportation services to the company for which the decedents worked, (2) it received over $5,000,000 for such services, paid through a Texas bank, and (3) it purchased more than $4,000,000 worth of helicopters from Texas, which included the one that crashed. The majority opinion in *Helicopteros* simply concluded that these contacts were not "continuous and systematic."

Note a difference between this case and *Perkins*, p. 122, supra. In *Perkins*, the defendant corporation actually operated its business from Ohio, while in *Helicopteros*, the defendant mainly purchased products in Texas. In *Helicopteros*, the Court relied on an old case, Rosenberg Brothers v. Curtis Brown Co., 260 U.S. 516, 518 (1923), in which the Court held that general jurisdiction cannot be based upon the defendant's purchases in the forum, notwithstanding that the company's officers made regular visits to the forum to make those purchases.

The most interesting aspect of *Helicopteros* is the dissent by Justice Brennan. First, he disagreed regarding general jurisdiction, arguing, among other things, that the Court was wrong to rely on *Rosenberg Brothers*, which predated *International Shoe* by more than two decades. Second, and more importantly, Justice Brennan argued for an expansive view of specific jurisdiction. He focused on the distinction between a claim that "arises from" the defendant's contacts with the forum and one that "relates to" those contacts:

> [T]he contacts between petitioner Helicol and the State of Texas . . . are significantly related to the cause of action alleged in the original suit filed by the respondents. Accordingly, in my view, it is both fair and reasonable for the Texas courts to assert specific jurisdiction over Helicol in this case.
>
> By asserting that the present case does not implicate the specific jurisdiction of the Texas courts, . . . the Court necessarily removes its decision from the reality of the actual facts presented for our consideration. Moreover, the Court refuses to consider any distinction between contacts that are "related to" the underlying cause of action and contacts that "give rise" to the underlying cause of action. In my view, however, there is a substantial difference between these two standards for asserting specific jurisdiction. Thus, although I agree that the respondents' cause of action did not formally "arise out of" specific activities initiated by Helicol in the State of Texas, I believe that the wrongful death claim filed by the respondents is significantly related to the undisputed contacts between Helicol and the forum. On that basis, I would conclude that the Due Process Clause allows the Texas courts to assert specific jurisdiction over this particular action.
>
> The wrongful death action filed by the respondents was premised on a fatal helicopter crash that occurred in Peru. Helicol was joined as a defendant in the lawsuit because it provided transportation services, including the particular helicopter and pilot involved in the crash, to the joint venture that employed the decedents. Specifically, the respondents claimed in their original complaint that "Helicol is . . . legally responsible for its own negligence through its pilot employee." . . . Viewed in light of these allegations, the contacts between

Helicol and the State of Texas are directly and significantly related to the underlying claim filed by the respondents. The negotiations that took place in Texas led to the contract in which Helicol agreed to provide the precise transportation services that were being used at the time of the crash. Moreover, the helicopter involved in the crash was purchased by Helicol in Texas, and the pilot whose negligence was alleged to have caused the crash was actually trained in Texas. . . . This is simply not a case, therefore, in which a state court has asserted jurisdiction over a nonresident defendant on the basis of wholly unrelated contacts with the forum. Rather, the contacts between Helicol and the forum are directly related to the negligence that was alleged in the respondents' original complaint. Because Helicol should have expected to be amenable to suit in the Texas courts for claims directly related to these contacts, it is fair and reasonable to allow the assertion of jurisdiction in this case. . . .

Limiting the specific jurisdiction of a forum to cases in which the cause of action formally arose out of the defendant's contacts with the State would subject constitutional standards under the Due Process Clause to the vagaries of the substantive law or pleading requirements of each State. For example, the complaint filed against Helicol in this case alleged negligence based on pilot error. Even though the pilot was trained in Texas, the Court assumes that the Texas courts may not assert jurisdiction over the suit because the cause of action "did not 'arise out of,' and [is] not related to," that training. . . . If, however, the applicable substantive law required that negligent training of the pilot was a necessary element of a cause of action for pilot error, or if the respondents had simply added an allegation of negligence in the training provided for the Helicol pilot, then presumably the Court would concede that the specific jurisdiction of the Texas courts was applicable.

NOTES

1. In *International Shoe*, the Court stated that if a corporation carries on "continuous and systematic" activities within the forum, it may be subject to jurisdiction even on "causes of action arising from dealing entirely distinct for those activities." 326 U.S. at 317, 318. The distinction between general and specific jurisdiction is particularly sharp if specific jurisdiction requires that the claim "arise out of" the forum contact. The distinction is more fluid if, as Justice Brennan writes, a state may assert jurisdiction if the claim "relates" to the defendant's forum activities.

2. Does a sharp distinction between general and specific jurisdiction reflect the way business is done? Suppose that a foreign car manufacturer has its principal U.S. establishment in California. It has divided the country into regions. Each regional establishment supervises and directs retail outlets in a number of states. New Jersey parties, while vacationing in Florida, purchase a car from a local retailer. Because of a defect in the automobile, the purchasers are injured in an accident in North Carolina on their trip home. General jurisdiction presumably exists at the manufacturer's California U.S. headquarters. Specific jurisdiction over the same defendant will exist where the accident occurred, just as in *World-Wide Volkswagen* jurisdiction existed in Oklahoma over the manufacturer and the principal importer. Assuming, however, that the accident occurred neither in New Jersey nor in New York and that suit at the place of the accident or in California would be inconvenient, is there jurisdiction over the manufacturer in the New York regional center?

Arguably, New York may have general jurisdiction because the defendant carries on "continuous and systematic" business there. Perkins, p. 122, supra. Would the defendant also be subject to general jurisdiction in New Jersey on the theory that, having structured its business activity in the United States in a regional manner, the foreign enterprise should be subject to general jurisdiction not only at its headquarters and at the place where an office doing "continuous and systematic" business is physically located but also in any state of the region which it serves?

3.   The post-*International Shoe* general jurisdiction cases do nothing to resolve the question of what relationship is necessary between the contacts and the underlying theories in the lawsuit to create specific jurisdiction. In *Perkins* it was clear that the underlying theories of the lawsuit had little to do with the corporation's Ohio activities. In *Helicopteros*, the question was much closer, but the majority held that the issue had been waived by the parties' stipulation.

4.   *Practice exercise:* Suppose that you were the plaintiffs' attorney in the *Helicopteros* case, and that the question of specific jurisdiction has not been waived. What theories might you raise in the complaint to maximize the connection between the defendants' activities and Texas? How would you develop proof of the factual matters necessary to sustain these theories?

5.   The other large question that *Helicopteros* and *Perkins* did little to resolve is the quantum of contacts necessary to sustain general jurisdiction. *Perkins* was an easy case. According to the Court, to the extent the company was doing anything during World War 2, it was doing it in Ohio. *Helicopteros* held that mere purchases in the forum state were not. Certainly, a huge spectrum of economic activity exists between these poles. Substantial sales within the forum, the opening of stores or branch offices, substantial advertising and the acceptance of business from the forum state are all examples of activities that could be seen as more substantial than those found insufficient in *Helicopteros* but less substantial than those in *Perkins*. Moreover, in *Perkins* the plaintiff probably did not have a reasonable alternative forum. Whether jurisdiction can exist on a "necessity" theory remains uncertain; the Court alluded to such a possibility in *Helicopteros*, but did not endorse such a theory.

6.   European law has nothing comparable to our general jurisdiction on the basis of "doing business", no matter how "systematic and continuous" (in the

sense of *Perkins*, p. 122, supra) such business activity was. Under Article 2 of the Brussels I Regulation, general jurisdiction exists only at the domicile of a person. A "company or other legal person" is treated as being "domiciled at the place where it has its: (a) statutory seat, or (b) central administration, or (c) principal place of business."

Throughout the remainder of the twentieth century and into this century, courts assessing general jurisdiction largely invoked the phrase "continuous and systematic" and concluded, based upon the facts, that the standard either was or was not met. Despite the open-endedness of the concept, lawyers, judges, and businesspeople came to have a reasonable understanding of how much contact in a state was enough to subject a business to general jurisdiction. Then, starting in 2011, the Court embarked on a dramatic restriction of general jurisdiction, the reason for which remains unexplained.

GOODYEAR DUNLOP TIRES OPERATIONS, S.A. V. BROWN, 564 U.S. 915, 131 S.Ct. 2846, 180 L.Ed.2d 796 (2011). The result of this case—rejecting general jurisdiction over European tire manufacturers in North Carolina—was easy, because the defendants' contacts with the forum of North Carolina were nowhere near "continuous and systematic." In fact, the North Carolina court invoked general jurisdiction based upon minimal stream of commerce contacts. As studied at pp. 84–99, infra, stream of commerce is often not sufficient as a basis for *specific* jurisdiction, let alone general jurisdiction.

The remarkable part of *Goodyear* was its suggestion that general jurisdiction is proper only in a state in which a defendant's contacts so continuous and systematic as to render the defendant "essentially at home" in the forum. The unanimous Court listed two "paradigms" for where a corporation is "essentially at home": the state of its incorporation and the state of its principal place of business. In dictum, it noted that a natural person would be "essentially at home" in the state of her domicile. Lawyers and courts were not entirely sure whether *Goodyear* signaled a broad restriction of general jurisdiction. Any doubt on that score was removed, however, three years later:

Daimler AG v. Bauman

Supreme Court of United States, 2014.
571 U.S. 117, 134 S.Ct. 746, 187 L.Ed.2d 624.

■ JUSTICE GINSBURG delivered the opinion of the Court.

This case concerns the authority of a court in the United States to entertain a claim brought by foreign plaintiffs against a foreign defendant based on events occurring entirely outside the United States. The litigation commenced in 2004, when twenty-two Argentinian residents filed a complaint in the United States District Court for the Northern District of California against DaimlerChrysler

Aktiengesellschaft (Daimler), a German public stock company, headquartered in Stuttgart, that manufactures Mercedes-Benz vehicles in Germany. The complaint alleged that during Argentina's 1976–1983 "Dirty War," Daimler's Argentinian subsidiary, Mercedes-Benz Argentina (MB Argentina) collaborated with state security forces to kidnap, detain, torture, and kill certain MB Argentina workers, among them, plaintiffs or persons closely related to plaintiffs. Damages for the alleged human-rights violations were sought from Daimler under the laws of the United States, California, and Argentina. Jurisdiction over [Daimler] was predicated on the California contacts of Mercedes-Benz USA, LLC (MBUSA), a subsidiary of Daimler incorporated in Delaware with its principal place of business in New Jersey. MBUSA distributes Daimler-manufactured vehicles to independent dealerships throughout the United States, including California.

The question presented is whether the Due Process Clause of the Fourteenth Amendment precludes the District Court from exercising jurisdiction over Daimler in this case, given the absence of any California connection to the atrocities, perpetrators, or victims described in the complaint. Plaintiffs invoked the court's general or all-purpose jurisdiction. California, they urge, is a place where Daimler may be sued on any and all claims against it, wherever in the world the claims may arise. For example, as plaintiffs' counsel affirmed, under the proffered jurisdictional theory, if a Daimler-manufactured vehicle overturned in Poland, injuring a Polish driver and passenger, the injured parties could maintain a design defect suit in California.... Exercises of personal jurisdiction so exorbitant, we hold, are barred by due process constraints on the assertion of adjudicatory authority.

In *Goodyear Dunlop Tires Operations, S.A. v. Brown,* 564 U.S. 915, 131 S.Ct. 2846 (2011), we addressed the distinction between general or all-purpose jurisdiction, and specific or conduct-linked jurisdiction. As to the former, we held that a court may assert jurisdiction over a foreign corporation "to hear any and all claims against [it]" only when the corporation's affiliations with the State in which suit is brought are so constant and pervasive "as to render [it] essentially at home in the forum State." Instructed by *Goodyear*, we conclude Daimler is not "at home" in California, and cannot be sued there for injuries plaintiffs attribute to MB Argentina's conduct in Argentina.

I

In 2004, plaintiffs (respondents here) filed suit in the United States District Court for the Northern District of California, alleging that MB Argentina collaborated with Argentinian state security forces to kidnap, detain, torture, and kill plaintiffs and their relatives during the military dictatorship in place there from 1976 through 1983, a period known as Argentina's "Dirty War." Based on those allegations, plaintiffs asserted claims under the Alien Tort Statute, 28 U.S.C. § 1350, and the Torture Victim Protection Act of 1991, 106 Stat. 73, Note following 28 U.S.C.

§ 1350, as well as claims for wrongful death and intentional infliction of emotional distress under the laws of California and Argentina. . . . [N]o part of MB Argentina's alleged collaboration with Argentinian authorities took place in California or anywhere else in the United States.

Plaintiffs' operative complaint names only one corporate defendant: Daimler, the petitioner here. Plaintiffs seek to hold Daimler vicariously liable for MB Argentina's alleged malfeasance. Daimler is a German *Aktiengesellschaft* (public stock company) that manufactures Mercedes-Benz vehicles in Germany and has its headquarters in Stuttgart. At times relevant to this case, MB Argentina was a subsidiary wholly owned by Daimler's predecessor in interest.

Daimler moved to dismiss the action for want of personal jurisdiction. Opposing the motion, plaintiffs submitted declarations and exhibits purporting to demonstrate the presence of Daimler itself in California. Alternatively, plaintiffs maintained that jurisdiction over Daimler could be founded on the California contacts of MBUSA, a distinct corporate entity that, according to plaintiffs, should be treated as Daimler's agent for jurisdictional purposes.

MBUSA, an indirect subsidiary of Daimler, is a Delaware limited liability corporation. MBUSA serves as Daimler's exclusive importer and distributor in the United States, purchasing Mercedes-Benz automobiles from Daimler in Germany, then importing those vehicles, and ultimately distributing them to independent dealerships located throughout the Nation. Although MBUSA's principal place of business is in New Jersey, MBUSA has multiple California-based facilities, including a regional office in Costa Mesa, a Vehicle Preparation Center in Carson, and a Classic Center in Irvine. According to the record developed below, MBUSA is the largest supplier of luxury vehicles to the California market. In particular, over 10% of all sales of new vehicles in the United States take place in California, and MBUSA's California sales account for 2.4% of Daimler's worldwide sales.

The relationship between Daimler and MBUSA is delineated in a General Distributor Agreement, which sets forth requirements for MBUSA's distribution of Mercedes-Benz vehicles in the United States. That agreement established MBUSA as an "independent contracto[r]" that "buy[s] and sell[s] [vehicles] . . . as an independent business for [its] own account." The agreement "does not make [MBUSA] . . . a general or special agent, partner, joint venturer or employee of DAIMLERCHRYSLER or any DaimlerChrysler Group Company"; MBUSA "ha[s] no authority to make binding obligations for or act on behalf of DAIMLERCHRYSLER or any DaimlerChrysler Group Company."

[The district court granted Daimler's motion to dismiss. The Ninth Circuit initially affirmed but subsequently granted plaintiffs' petition for rehearing, withdrew its original opinion, and reversed the district court.]

* * *

We granted certiorari to decide whether, consistent with the Due Process Clause of the Fourteenth Amendment, Daimler is amenable to suit in California courts for claims involving only foreign plaintiffs and conduct occurring entirely abroad.

II

Federal courts ordinarily follow state law in determining the bounds of their jurisdiction over persons. See Fed. Rule Civ. Proc. 4(k)(1)(A) (service of process is effective to establish personal jurisdiction over a defendant "who is subject to the jurisdiction of a court of general jurisdiction in the state where the district court is located"). Under California's long-arm statute, California state courts may exercise personal jurisdiction "on any basis not inconsistent with the Constitution of this state or of the United States." Cal. Civ. Proc. Code § 410.10 (West 2004). California's long-arm statute allows the exercise of personal jurisdiction to the full extent permissible under the U.S. Constitution. We therefore inquire whether the Ninth Circuit's holding comports with the limits imposed by federal due process.

III

In *Pennoyer v. Neff,* decided shortly after the enactment of the Fourteenth Amendment, the Court held that a tribunal's jurisdiction over persons reaches no farther than the geographic bounds of the forum. In time, however, that strict territorial approach yielded to a less rigid understanding, spurred by "changes in the technology of transportation and communication, and the tremendous growth of interstate business activity." *Burnham v. Superior Court of Cal., County of Marin,* 495 U.S. 604, 617 (1990) (opinion of Scalia, J.).

"The canonical opinion in this area remains *International Shoe,* in which we held that a State may authorize its courts to exercise personal jurisdiction over an out-of-state defendant if the defendant has 'certain minimum contacts with [the State] such that the maintenance of the suit does not offend "traditional notions of fair play and substantial justice.' " *Goodyear* (quoting *International Shoe*). . . .

International Shoe's conception of "fair play and substantial justice" presaged the development of two categories of personal jurisdiction. The first category is represented by *International Shoe* itself, a case in which the in-state activities of the corporate defendant "ha[d] not only been continuous and systematic, but also g[a]ve rise to the liabilities sued on." . . . Adjudicatory authority of this order, in which the suit "aris[es] out of or relate[s] to the defendant's contacts with the forum," *Helicopteros Nacionales de Colombia, S.A. v. Hall,* 466 U.S. 408, 414, n. 8 (1984), is today called "specific jurisdiction." . . .

International Shoe distinguished between, on the one hand, exercises of specific jurisdiction, as just described, and on the other, situations where a foreign corporation's "continuous corporate operations within a state [are] so substantial and of such a nature as to justify suit against it on causes of action arising from dealings entirely distinct from those activities." As we have since explained [in *Goodyear*], "[a] court may assert general jurisdiction over foreign (sister-state or foreign-country) corporations to hear any and all claims against them when their affiliations with the State are so 'continuous and systematic' as to render them essentially at home in the forum State."

Since *International Shoe*, "specific jurisdiction has become the centerpiece of modern jurisdiction theory, while general jurisdiction [has played] a reduced role." . . .

Our post-*International Shoe* opinions on general jurisdiction, by comparison, are few. "[The Court's] 1952 decision in *Perkins v. Benguet Consol. Mining Co.* remains the textbook case of general jurisdiction appropriately exercised over a foreign corporation that has not consented to suit in the forum." *Goodyear*. The defendant in *Perkins*, Benguet, was a company incorporated under the laws of the Philippines, where it operated gold and silver mines. Benguet ceased its mining operations during the Japanese occupation of the Philippines in World War II; its president moved to Ohio, where he kept an office, maintained the company's files, and oversaw the company's activities. The plaintiff, an Ohio resident, sued Benguet on a claim that neither arose in Ohio nor related to the corporation's activities in that State. We held that the Ohio courts could exercise general jurisdiction over Benguet without offending due process. That was so, we later noted, because "Ohio was the corporation's principal, if temporary, place of business."[8]

[The Court next discussed *Helicopteros*, which appears p. 122, infra.]

Most recently, in *Goodyear*, we answered the question: "Are foreign subsidiaries of a United States parent corporation amenable to suit in state court on claims unrelated to any activity of the subsidiaries in the forum State?" . . . The complaint named as defendants not only The Goodyear Tire and Rubber Company (Goodyear), an Ohio corporation, but also Goodyear's Turkish, French, and Luxembourgian subsidiaries. Those foreign subsidiaries, which manufactured tires for sale in Europe and Asia, lacked any affiliation with North Carolina. A small percentage of tires manufactured by the foreign subsidiaries were distributed in North Carolina, however, and on that ground, the North Carolina Court of Appeals held the subsidiaries amenable to the general jurisdiction of North Carolina courts.

We reversed, observing that the North Carolina court's analysis "elided the essential difference between case-specific and all-purpose (general) jurisdiction." Although the placement of a product into the stream of commerce "may bolster an affiliation germane to *specific*

---

[8] * * * All of Benguet's activities were directed by the company's president from within Ohio. * * * Given the wartime circumstances, Ohio could be considered "a surrogate for the place of incorporation or head office." * * *

jurisdiction," we explained, such contacts "do not warrant a determination that, based on those ties, the forum has *general* jurisdiction over a defendant." As *International Shoe* itself teaches, a corporation's "continuous activity of some sorts within a state is not enough to support the demand that the corporation be amenable to suits unrelated to that activity." Because Goodyear's foreign subsidiaries were "in no sense at home in North Carolina," we held, those subsidiaries could not be required to submit to the general jurisdiction of that State's courts. . . .

As is evident from *Perkins, Helicopteros,* and *Goodyear,* general and specific jurisdiction have followed markedly different trajectories post-*International Shoe.* Specific jurisdiction has been cut loose from *Pennoyer*'s sway, but we have declined to stretch general jurisdiction beyond limits traditionally recognized. As this Court has increasingly trained on the "relationship among the defendant, the forum, and the litigation," *Shaffer, i.e.,* specific jurisdiction, general jurisdiction has come to occupy a less dominant place in the contemporary scheme.[11]

IV

. . .

A

In sustaining the exercise of general jurisdiction over Daimler, the Ninth Circuit relied on an agency theory, determining that MBUSA acted as Daimler's agent for jurisdictional purposes and then attributing MBUSA's California contacts to Daimler. The Ninth Circuit's agency analysis derived from Circuit precedent considering principally whether the subsidiary "performs services that are sufficiently important to the foreign corporation that if it did not have a representative to perform them, the corporation's own officials would undertake to perform substantially similar services."

[The Court here criticized the Ninth Circuit's agency theory for failing to recognize that the fact that one is an agent for one purpose does not mean that it is an agent for all purposes. Ultimately, the Court did not] pass judgment on invocation of an agency theory in the context of general jurisdiction, for in no event can the appeals court's analysis be sustained.

The Ninth Circuit's agency finding rested primarily on its observation that MBUSA's services were "important" to Daimler, as gauged by Daimler's hypothetical readiness to perform those services itself if MBUSA did not exist. Formulated this way, the inquiry into importance stacks the deck, for it will always yield a pro-jurisdiction answer: "Anything a corporation does through an independent contractor, subsidiary, or distributor is presumably something that the

[11] As the Court made plain in *Goodyear* and repeats here, general jurisdiction requires affiliations "so 'continuous and systematic' as to render [the foreign corporation] essentially at home in the forum State." *i.e.,* comparable to a domestic enterprise in that State.

corporation would do 'by other means' if the independent contractor, subsidiary, or distributor did not exist." The Ninth Circuit's agency theory thus appears to subject foreign corporations to general jurisdiction whenever they have an in-state subsidiary or affiliate, an outcome that would sweep beyond even the "sprawling view of general jurisdiction" we rejected in *Goodyear*.

B

Even if we were to assume that MBUSA is at home in California, and further to assume MBUSA's contacts are imputable to Daimler, there would still be no basis to subject Daimler to general jurisdiction in California, for Daimler's slim contacts with the State hardly render it at home there.

Goodyear made clear that only a limited set of affiliations with a forum will render a defendant amenable to all-purpose jurisdiction there. "For an individual, the paradigm forum for the exercise of general jurisdiction is the individual's domicile; for a corporation, it is an equivalent place, one in which the corporation is fairly regarded as at home." With respect to a corporation, the place of incorporation and principal place of business are "paradig[m] ... bases for general jurisdiction." Those affiliations have the virtue of being unique—that is, each ordinarily indicates only one place—as well as easily ascertainable. These bases afford plaintiffs recourse to at least one clear and certain forum in which a corporate defendant may be sued on any and all claims.

Goodyear did not hold that a corporation may be subject to general jurisdiction *only* in a forum where it is incorporated or has its principal place of business; it simply typed those places paradigm all-purpose forums. Plaintiffs would have us look beyond the exemplar bases *Goodyear* identified, and approve the exercise of general jurisdiction in every State in which a corporation "engages in a substantial, continuous, and systematic course of business." That formulation, we hold, is unacceptably grasping.

As noted, the words "continuous and systematic" were used in *International Shoe* to describe instances in which the exercise of *specific* jurisdiction would be appropriate. Turning to all-purpose jurisdiction, in contrast, *International Shoe* speaks of "instances in which the continuous corporate operations within a state [are] so substantial and of such a nature as to justify suit ... *on causes of action arising from dealings entirely distinct from those activities.*" Accordingly, the inquiry under *Goodyear* is not whether a foreign corporation's in-forum contacts can be said to be in some sense "continuous and systematic," it is whether that corporation's "affiliations with the State are so 'continuous and systematic' as to render [it] essentially at home in the forum State."[19]

---

[19] We do not foreclose the possibility that in an exceptional case, see, *e.g.*, *Perkins* [*v. Benquet Consolidated Mining Co.*] a corporation's operations in a forum other than its formal

Here, neither Daimler nor MBUSA is incorporated in California, nor does either entity have its principal place of business there. If Daimler's California activities sufficed to allow adjudication of this Argentina-rooted case in California, the same global reach would presumably be available in every other State in which MBUSA's sales are sizable. Such exorbitant exercises of all-purpose jurisdiction would scarcely permit out-of-state defendants "to structure their primary conduct with some minimum assurance as to where that conduct will and will not render them liable to suit." *Burger King Corp.*

It was therefore error for the Ninth Circuit to conclude that Daimler, even with MBUSA's contacts attributed to it, was at home in California, and hence subject to suit there on claims by foreign plaintiffs having nothing to do with anything that occurred or had its principal impact in California.[20]

C

Finally, the transnational context of this dispute bears attention.

* * *

---

place of incorporation or principal place of business may be so substantial and of such a nature as to render the corporation at home in that State. But this case presents no occasion to explore that question, because Daimler's activities in California plainly do not approach that level. It is one thing to hold a corporation answerable for operations in the forum State, quite another to expose it to suit on claims having no connection whatever to the forum State.

[20] To clarify in light of Justice SOTOMAYOR's opinion concurring in the judgment, the general jurisdiction inquiry does not "focu[s] solely on the magnitude of the defendant's in-state contacts." General jurisdiction instead calls for an appraisal of a corporation's activities in their entirety, nationwide and worldwide. A corporation that operates in many places can scarcely be deemed at home in all of them. Otherwise, "at home" would be synonymous with "doing business" tests framed before specific jurisdiction evolved in the United States. Nothing in *International Shoe* and its progeny suggests that "a particular quantum of local activity" should give a State authority over a "far larger quantum of . . . activity" having no connection to any in-state activity.

Justice SOTOMAYOR would reach the same result, but for a different reason. Rather than concluding that Daimler is not at home in California, Justice SOTOMAYOR would hold that the exercise of general jurisdiction over Daimler would be unreasonable "in the unique circumstances of this case." In other words, she favors a resolution fit for this day and case only. True, a multipronged reasonableness check was articulated in *Asahi,* but not as a free-floating test. Instead, the check was to be essayed when *specific* jurisdiction is at issue. See also *Burger King Corp. v. Rudzewicz.* First, a court is to determine whether the connection between the forum and the episode-in-suit could justify the exercise of specific jurisdiction. Then, in a second step, the court is to consider several additional factors to assess the reasonableness of entertaining the case. When a corporation is genuinely at home in the forum State, however, any second-step inquiry would be superfluous.

Justice SOTOMAYOR fears that our holding will "lead to greater unpredictability by radically expanding the scope of jurisdictional discovery." But it is hard to see why much in the way of discovery would be needed to determine where a corporation is at home. Justice SOTOMAYOR's proposal to import *Asahi's* "reasonableness" check into the general jurisdiction determination, on the other hand, would indeed compound the jurisdictional inquiry. The reasonableness factors identified in *Asahi* include "the burden on the defendant," "the interests of the forum State," "the plaintiff's interest in obtaining relief," "the interstate judicial system's interest in obtaining the most efficient resolution of controversies," "the shared interest of the several States in furthering fundamental substantive social policies," and, in the international context, "the procedural and substantive policies of other *nations* whose interests are affected by the assertion of jurisdiction." Imposing such a checklist in cases of general jurisdiction would hardly promote the efficient disposition of an issue that should be resolved expeditiously at the outset of litigation.

The Ninth Circuit, moreover, paid little heed to the risks to international comity its expansive view of general jurisdiction posed. Other nations do not share the uninhibited approach to personal jurisdiction advanced by the Court of Appeals in this case. In the European Union, for example, a corporation may generally be sued in the nation in which it is "domiciled," a term defined to refer only to the location of the corporation's "statutory seat," "central administration," or "principal place of business." The Solicitor General informs us, in this regard, that "foreign governments' objections to some domestic courts' expansive views of general jurisdiction have in the past impeded negotiations of international agreements on the reciprocal recognition and enforcement of judgments." Considerations of international rapport thus reinforce our determination that subjecting Daimler to the general jurisdiction of courts in California would not accord with the "fair play and substantial justice" due process demands. *International Shoe* (quoting *Milliken v. Meyer,* 311 U.S. 457, 463 (1940)).

* * *

For the reasons stated, the judgment of the United States Court of Appeals for the Ninth Circuit is

Reversed.

■ JUSTICE SOTOMAYOR, concurring in the judgment.

I agree with the Court's conclusion that the Due Process Clause prohibits the exercise of personal jurisdiction over Daimler in light of the unique circumstances of this case. I concur only in the judgment, however, because I cannot agree with the path the Court takes to arrive at that result.

The Court acknowledges that Mercedes-Benz USA, LLC (MBUSA), Daimler's wholly owned subsidiary, has considerable contacts with California. It has multiple facilities in the State, including a regional headquarters. Each year, it distributes in California tens of thousands of cars, the sale of which generated billions of dollars in the year this suit was brought. And it provides service and sales support to customers throughout the State. Daimler has conceded that California courts may exercise general jurisdiction over MBUSA on the basis of these contacts, and the Court assumes that MBUSA's contacts may be attributed to Daimler for the purpose of deciding whether Daimler is also subject to general jurisdiction.

Are these contacts sufficient to permit the exercise of general jurisdiction over Daimler? The Court holds that they are not, for a reason wholly foreign to our due process jurisprudence. The problem, the Court says, is not that Daimler's contacts with California are too few, but that its contacts with other forums are too many. In other words, the Court does not dispute that the presence of multiple offices, the direct distribution of thousands of products accounting for billions of dollars in sales, and continuous interaction with customers throughout a State would be enough to support the exercise of general jurisdiction over some businesses. Daimler is just not one of those businesses, the Court concludes, because its California contacts must be viewed in the context of its extensive "nationwide and worldwide" operations. In recent years, Americans have grown accustomed to the concept of multinational corporations that are supposedly "too big to fail"; today the Court deems Daimler "too big for general jurisdiction."

The Court's conclusion is wrong as a matter of both process and substance. As to process, the Court decides this case on a ground that was neither argued nor passed on below, and that Daimler raised for the first time in a footnote to its brief. As to substance, the Court's focus on Daimler's operations outside of California ignores the lodestar of our personal jurisdiction jurisprudence: A State may subject a defendant to the burden of suit if the defendant has sufficiently taken advantage of the State's laws and protections through its contacts in the State; whether the defendant has contacts elsewhere is immaterial.

Regrettably, these errors are unforced. The Court can and should decide this case on the far simpler ground that, no matter how extensive Daimler's contacts with California, that State's exercise of jurisdiction would be unreasonable given that the case involves foreign plaintiffs suing a foreign defendant based on foreign conduct, and given that a more appropriate forum is available. Because I would reverse the judgment below on this ground, I concur in the judgment only.

I

. . .

Our personal jurisdiction precedents call for a two-part analysis. The contacts prong asks whether the defendant has sufficient contacts with the forum State to support personal jurisdiction; the reasonableness prong asks whether the exercise of jurisdiction would be unreasonable under the circumstances. Burger King Corp. v. Rudzewicz, 471 U.S. 462–478 (1985). As the majority points out, all of the cases in which we have applied the reasonableness prong have involved specific as opposed to general jurisdiction. Whether the reasonableness prong should apply in the general jurisdiction context is therefore a question we have never decided,[1] and it is one on which I can appreciate the arguments on both sides. But it would be imprudent to decide that question in this case given that respondents have failed to argue against the application of the reasonableness prong during the entire 8-year history of this litigation. . . .

---

[1]   The Courts of Appeals have uniformly held that the reasonableness prong does in fact apply in the general jurisdiction context. [Citations to decisions from the First, Second, Fourth, Fifth Eighth, Ninth, Tenth Circuits.] Without the benefit of a single page of briefing on the issue, the majority casually adds each of these cases to the mounting list of decisions jettisoned as a consequence of today's ruling. See at 21, n. 20.

We identified the factors that bear on reasonableness in Asahi Metal Industry Co. v. Superior Court of Cal., Solano Cty., 480 U.S. 102 (1987): "the burden on the defendant, the interests of the forum State," "the plaintiff's interest in obtaining relief" in the forum State, and the interests of other sovereigns in resolving the dispute. Id., at 113–114. We held in Asahi that it would be "unreasonable and unfair" for a California court to exercise jurisdiction over a claim between a Taiwanese plaintiff and a Japanese defendant that arose out of a transaction in Taiwan, particularly where the Taiwanese plaintiff had not shown that it would be more convenient to litigate in California than in Taiwan or Japan. Id., at 114.

The same considerations resolve this case. It involves Argentine plaintiffs suing a German defendant for conduct that took place in Argentina. Like the plaintiffs in *Asahi*, respondents have failed to show that it would be more convenient to litigate in California than in Germany, a sovereign with a far greater interest in resolving the dispute. *Asahi* thus makes clear that it would be unreasonable for a court in California to subject Daimler to its jurisdiction.

II

The majority evidently agrees that, if the reasonableness prong were to apply, it would be unreasonable for California courts to exercise jurisdiction over Daimler in this case. See ante, at 20–21 (noting that it would be "exorbitant" for California courts to exercise general jurisdiction over Daimler, a German defendant, in this "Argentina-rooted case" brought by "foreign plaintiffs"). But instead of resolving the case on this uncontroversial basis, the majority reaches out to decide it on a ground neither argued nor decided below.

. . .

We granted certiorari on the question "whether it violates due process for a court to exercise general personal jurisdiction over a foreign corporation based solely on the fact that an indirect corporate subsidiary performs services on behalf of the defendant in the forum State." Pet. for Cert. i. At no point in Daimler's petition for certiorari did the company contend that, even if this attribution question were decided against it, its contacts in California would still be insufficient to support general jurisdiction. The parties' merits briefs accordingly focused on the attribution-of-contacts question, addressing the reasonableness inquiry (which had been litigated and decided below) in most of the space that remained. See Brief for Petitioner 17–37, 37–43; Brief for Respondents 18–47, 47–59.

In bypassing the question on which we granted certiorari to decide an issue not litigated below, the Court leaves respondents "without an unclouded opportunity to air the issue the Court today decides against them," Comcast Corp. v. Behrend, 569 U.S. ___, ___ (2013) (Ginsburg and Breyer, JJ., dissenting) (slip op., at 3). Doing so "does 'not reflect well on the processes of the Court.' " Ibid. (quoting Redrup v. New York, 386 U.S. 767, 772 (1967) (Harlan, J., dissenting)). "And by resolving a complex and fact-intensive question without the benefit of full briefing, the Court invites the error into which it has fallen." 569 U.S., at ___ (slip op., at 3).

The relevant facts are undeveloped because Daimler conceded at the start of this litigation that MBUSA is subject to general jurisdiction based on its California contacts. We therefore do not know the full extent of those contacts, though what little we do know suggests that Daimler was wise to concede what it did. MBUSA imports more than 200,000 vehicles into the United States and distributes many of them to independent dealerships in California, where they are sold. Declaration of Dr. Peter Waskönig in Bauman v. DaimlerChrysler Corp., No. 04-00194-RMW (ND Cal.), ¶ 10, p.2. MBUSA's California sales account for 2.4% of Daimler's worldwide sales, which were $192 billion in 2004. And 2.4% of $192 billion is $4.6 billion, a considerable sum by any measure. MBUSA also has multiple offices and facilities in California, including a regional headquarters.

But the record does not answer a number of other important questions. Are any of Daimler's key files maintained in MBUSA's California offices? How many employees work in those offices? Do those employees make important strategic decisions or oversee in any manner Daimler's activities? These questions could well affect whether Daimler is subject to general jurisdiction. After all, this Court upheld the exercise of general jurisdiction in Perkins v. Benguet Consol. Mining Co., 342 U.S. 437–448 (1952)—which the majority refers to as a "textbook case" of general jurisdiction—on the basis that the foreign defendant maintained an office in Ohio, kept corporate files there, and oversaw the company's activities from the State. California-based MBUSA employees may well have done similar things on Daimler's behalf. But because the Court decides the issue without a developed record, we will never know.

III

A

Until today, our precedents had established a straightforward test for general jurisdiction: Does the defendant have "continuous corporate operations within a state" that are "so substantial and of such a nature as to justify suit against it on causes of action arising from dealings entirely distinct from those activities"? International Shoe Co. v. Washington, 326 U.S. 310, 318 (1945); see also Helicopteros Nacionales de Colombia, S.A. v. Hall, 466 U.S. 408, 416 (1984) (asking whether defendant had "continuous and systematic general business contacts"). In every case where we have applied this test, we have focused solely on the magnitude of the defendant's in-state contacts, not the relative magnitude of those contacts in comparison to the defendant's contacts with other States.

In *Perkins*, for example, we found an Ohio court's exercise of general jurisdiction permissible where the president of the foreign defendant "maintained an office," "drew and distributed . . . salary checks," used "two active bank accounts," "supervised . . . the rehabilitation of the corporation's properties in the Philippines," and held "directors' meetings," in Ohio. 342 U.S., at 447–448. At no point did we attempt to catalog the company's contacts in forums other than Ohio or to compare them with its Ohio contacts. If anything, we intimated that the defendant's Ohio contacts were not substantial in comparison to its contacts elsewhere. See id., at 438 (noting that the defendant's Ohio contacts, while "continuous and systematic," were but a "limited . . . part of its general business").

We engaged in the same inquiry in *Helicopteros*. There, we held that a Colombian corporation was not subject to general jurisdiction in Texas simply because it occasionally sent its employees into the State, accepted checks drawn on a Texas bank, and purchased equipment and services from a Texas company. In no sense did our analysis turn on the extent of the company's operations beyond Texas.

Most recently, in Goodyear Dunlop Tires Operations, S.A. v. Brown, 564 U.S. ___ (2011), our analysis again focused on the defendant's in-state contacts. Goodyear involved a suit against foreign tire manufacturers by North Carolina residents whose children had died in a bus accident in France. We held that North Carolina courts could not exercise general jurisdiction over the foreign defendants. Just as in Perkins and Helicopteros, our opinion in Goodyear did not identify the defendants' contacts outside of the forum State, but focused instead on the defendants' lack of offices, employees, direct sales, and business operations within the State.

This approach follows from the touchstone principle of due process in this field, the concept of reciprocal fairness. When a corporation chooses to invoke the benefits and protections of a State in which it operates, the State acquires the authority to subject the company to suit in its courts. See International Shoe, 326 U.S., at 319 ("[T]o the extent that a corporation exercises the privilege of conducting activities within a state, it enjoys the benefits and protection of the laws of that state" such that an "obligatio[n] arise[s]" to respond there to suit); J. McIntyre Machinery, Ltd. v. Nicastro, 564 U.S. ___, ___ (2011) (plurality opinion) (slip op., at 5) (same principle for general jurisdiction). The majority's focus on the extent of a corporate defendant's out-of-forum contacts is untethered from this rationale. After all, the degree to which a company intentionally benefits from a forum State depends on its interactions with that State, not its interactions elsewhere. An article on which the majority relies (and on which *Goodyear* relied as well, 564 U.S., at ___ (slip op., at 7)) expresses the point well: "We should not treat defendants as less amenable to suit merely because they carry on more substantial business in other states . . . . [T]he amount of activity elsewhere seems virtually irrelevant to . . . the imposition of general jurisdiction over a defendant." Brilmayer et al., A General Look at General Jurisdiction, 66 Texas L. Rev. 721, 742 (1988).

Had the majority applied our settled approach, it would have had little trouble concluding that Daimler's California contacts rise to the requisite level, given the majority's assumption that MBUSA's contacts may be attributed to Daimler and given Daimler's concession that those contacts render MBUSA "at home" in California. Our cases have long stated the rule that a defendant's contacts with a forum State must be continuous, substantial, and systematic in order for the defendant to be subject to that State's general jurisdiction. See *Perkins*, 342 U.S., at 446. We offered additional guidance in *Goodyear*, adding the phrase "essentially at home" to our prior formulation of the rule. 564 U.S., at ___ (slip op., at 2) (a State may exercise general jurisdiction where a defendant's "affiliations with the State are so 'continuous and systematic' as to render [the defendant] essentially at home in the forum State"). We used the phrase "at home" to signify that in order for an out-of-state defendant to be subject to general jurisdiction, its continuous and substantial contacts with a forum State must be akin to those of a local enterprise that actually is "at home" in the State. See Brilmayer, supra, at 742.[8]

Under this standard, Daimler's concession that MBUSA is subject to general jurisdiction in California (a concession the Court accepts, ante, at 15, 17) should be dispositive. For if MBUSA's California contacts are so substantial and the resulting benefits to MBUSA so significant as to make MBUSA "at home" in California, the same must be true of Daimler when MBUSA's contacts and benefits are viewed as its own. Indeed, until a footnote in its brief before this Court, even Daimler did not dispute this conclusion for eight years of the litigation.

NOTES

1.   In *Goodyear*, the Court addressed only whether there was general jurisdiction over European tire manufacturers. One of the defendants in the case was Goodyear USA, which is incorporated in Ohio with its principal place of business in Ohio. It had three manufacturing plants and employed hundreds of people in North Carolina. Based on the law as it then stood, Goodyear USA assumed that it was subject to general jurisdiction in North Carolina because of its "continuous and systematic" contacts there. After *Goodyear* and *Daimler*, would Goodyear USA be subject to general jurisdiction in North Carolina? Is Mercedes Benz USA (chartered in

---

[8]   The majority views the phrase "at home" as serving a different purpose—that of requiring a comparison between a defendant's in-state and out-of-state contacts. That cannot be the correct understanding though, because among other things it would cast grave doubt on *Perkins*—a case that pointed to as an exemplar of general jurisdiction, 564 U.S., at ___ (slip op., at 11). For if had applied the majority's newly minted proportionality test, it would have come out the other way.

Delaware with its principal place of business in New Jersey) subject to general jurisdiction in California?

2.   As we have seen, the Court has employed a two-pronged approach to personal jurisdiction under *International Shoe*: first, there must be a relevant contact between the defendant and the forum and, second, the exercise of jurisdiction must be fair or reasonable. In her dissent in *J. McIntyre*, p. 86, supra, Justice Ginsburg criticized this mechanical two-step approach as overemphasizing contact and underemphasizing the assessment of whether jurisdiction would be reasonable on the facts of the case. Based upon footnote 20 in *Daimler*, did Justice Ginsburg (and the seven other Justices who signed her opinion) embrace the two-step approach?

3.   Remarkably, in footnote 20 of *Daimler*, the Court tells us that an assessment of "fair play and substantial justice" is irrelevant in general jurisdiction cases. In her concurring opinion, Justice Sotomayor excoriated the majority for making this change without having had the parties even brief the issue. After *Daimler*, then, once a court determines that the defendant is "essentially at home" in the forum, the jurisdictional assessment is complete; the "fairness factors" are not to be consulted. Stated another way, a fairness assessment is only relevant in specific jurisdiction cases. For an argument that the Court has limited personal jurisdiction more severely than the pre-*International Shoe* approach of implied consent, see Patrick Borchers, The Twilight of the Minimum Contacts Test, 11 Seton Hall Cir.Rev. 1 (2014).

4.   In footnote 19 of *Daimler*, the Court leaves open the possibility of finding a corporation subject to general jurisdiction based upon its activities (other than incorporation or keeping its principal place of business) in the forum. The only example it gives of such an "exceptional" case is *Perkins*, p. 122, supra. The Court characterizes *Perkins* as involving a corporation that was completely inactive except for some paperwork being done at the owner's Ohio residence. It is overwhelmingly likely that such a localized company—engaging in activities in only one state—would be incorporated or have its principal place of business (or both) in that state. How likely is it, then, that *Daimler* will support general jurisdiction in a third state—that is, a state in addition to the that of the corporation's charter and that of its principal place of business?

Justice Sotomayor, in her concurrence in *Daimler*, criticized the Court for mischaracterizing the facts from *Perkins*. She asserted that at the relevant time the Benguet Mining Company was engaged in mining in the Philippines (its place of incorporation) and that it was actively engaged in business in the state of its principal place of business, California). Justice Sotomayor thus argued that *Perkins* supports general jurisdiction in states of considerable corporate activity—even if those states are not where the company is incorporated or has its principal place of business.

5.   The possibility of finding that a corporation is "essentially at home" based upon contacts (other than incorporation or establishing its principal place of business) may have been scuttled by BNSF Railway Co. v. Tyrell, 137 S. Ct. 1549 (2017). There, the plaintiffs sued a railroad in Montana under

CHAPTER 3   JURISDICTION OF COURTS   141

the Federal Employer Liability Act (FELA), which permits railroad employees to sue their employers for injuries suffered on the job. The plaintiffs' claims arose entirely outside Montana.

The Montana Supreme Court upheld general jurisdiction, based upon the fact that the railroad had over 2,000 miles of track and 2,100 employees in the state. It refused to follow *Goodyear* and *Daimler* because neither of those cases involved claims under FELA. The Court rejected this contention, held that *Goodyear/Daimler* applied, and that under those cases Montana did not have general jurisdiction. The railroad was not incorporated there. It did not have its principal place of business there. And the level of activity there was comparable to that in several other states, so there could not be general jurisdiction based upon activities. It reiterated its phrase from *Daimler*: when a corporation operates in several states, it "can scarcely be deemed at home in all of them." 137 S.Ct. at 1559.

Justice Sotomayor dissented. She lamented that now "it is virtually inconceivable that [interstate] corporations will ever be subject to general jurisdiction in any location other than their principal places of business or incorporation." 137 S.Ct. at 1560 (Sotomayor, J., dissenting in part).

6. In *Daimler* the Court stated that the "paradigm" for where a natural person is "essentially at home" (and thus subject to general jurisdiction) is the state of her domicile. Why does it not also discuss the fact that a natural person, as in *Burnham*, p. 51, supra, usually is subject to general jurisdiction where she is served with process? Is that not at least as true a "paradigm" for the exercise of general jurisdiction?

7. Where are unincorporated businesses, such as partnerships and limited liability companies, "at home"? The Court said nothing about such associations in *Goodyear* or *Daimler*. Should the rule be the same as it is with corporations? (Remember that for purposes of diversity of citizenship jurisdiction, the citizenship of corporations and unincorporated businesses are assessed differently. Should that matter for determining personal jurisdiction?)

4.   RETURN TO SPECIFIC JURISDICTION: THE EMERGING IMPORTANCE OF "RELATEDNESS"

Goodyear, Daimler, and *BNSF Railway,* which we studied in the preceding section, have markedly restricted general jurisdiction over corporations. Instead of being subject to general jurisdiction in states in which it had "continuous and systematic" contacts, a corporation now is amenable to such jurisdiction in at most two states: where it incorporated and where it has its principal place of business. Courts now are encountering an increasing number of cases in which the defendant has substantial contact with the forum, but not enough to satisfy the new standard for general jurisdiction. In such cases, the plaintiff must attempt to invoke specific jurisdiction. The hurdle plaintiffs face is whether their claims are sufficiently connected with the defendant's forum contacts to satisfy specific jurisdiction—the requirement of "relatedness."

Bristol-Myers Squibb Co. v. Superior Court of California

Supreme Court of the United States, 2017.
137 S.Ct. 1773, 198 L.Ed.2d 395.

■ JUSTICE ALITO delivered the opinion of the Court.

More than 600 plaintiffs, most of whom are not California residents, filed this civil action in a California state court against Bristol-Myers Squibb Company (BMS), asserting a variety of state law claims based on injuries allegedly caused by a BMS drug called Plavix. The California Supreme Court held that the California courts have specific jurisdiction to entertain the nonresidents' claims. We now reverse.

I

A

BMS, a large pharmaceutical company, is incorporated in Delaware and headquartered in New York, and it maintains substantial operations in both New York and New Jersey. 1 Cal. 5th 783, 790, 377 P.3d 874, 879 (2016). Over 50 percent of BMS's work force in the United States is employed in those two States.

BMS also engages in business activities in other jurisdictions, including California. Five of the company's research and laboratory facilities, which employ a total of around 160 employees, are located there. *Ibid.* BMS also employs about 250 sales representatives in California and maintains a small state-government advocacy office in Sacramento.

One of the pharmaceuticals that BMS manufactures and sells is Plavix, a prescription drug that thins the blood and inhibits blood clotting. BMS did not develop Plavix in California, did not create a marketing strategy for Plavix in California, and did not manufacture, label, package, or work on the regulatory approval of the product in California. BMS instead engaged in all of these activities in either New York or New Jersey. But BMS does sell Plavix in California. Between 2006 and 2012, it sold almost 187 million Plavix pills in the State and took in more than $900 million from those sales. This amounts to a little over one percent of the company's nationwide sales revenue.

B

A group of plaintiffs—consisting of 86 California residents and 592 residents from 33 other States—filed eight separate complaints in California Superior Court, alleging that Plavix had damaged their health. All the complaints asserted 13 claims under California law, including products liability, negligent misrepresentation, and misleading advertising claims. The nonresident plaintiffs did not allege that they obtained Plavix through California physicians or from any other California source; nor did they claim that they were injured by Plavix or were treated for their injuries in California.

[BMS objected to personal jurisdiction regarding all claims by nonresidents of California. The California trial court, addressing the matter before the restriction of general jurisdiction in *Daimler*, held that it had general jurisdiction. The California Court of Appeal ultimately held that general jurisdiction was not possible under *Daimler*, but that California had specific jurisdiction. The California Supreme Court affirmed on the basis of a "sliding scale approach to specific jurisdiction."]

Under this approach, "the more wide ranging the defendant's forum contacts, the more readily is shown a connection between the forum contacts and the claim." Applying this test, the majority concluded that "BMS's extensive contacts with California" permitted the exercise of specific jurisdiction "based on a less direct connection between BMS's forum activities and plaintiffs' claims than might otherwise be required." This attenuated requirement was met, the majority found, because the claims of the nonresidents were similar in several ways to the claims of the California residents (as to which specific jurisdiction was uncontested). The court noted that "[b]oth the resident and nonresident plaintiffs' claims are based on the same allegedly defective product and the assertedly misleading marketing and promotion of that product." And while acknowledging that "there is no claim that Plavix itself was designed and developed in [BMS's California research facilities]," the court thought it significant that other research was done in the State.

. . .

We granted certiorari to decide whether the California courts' exercise of jurisdiction in this case violates the Due Process Clause of the Fourteenth Amendment.[16]

II

A

. . .

Since our seminal decision in *International Shoe*, our decisions have recognized two types of personal jurisdiction: "general" (sometimes called "all-purpose") jurisdiction and "specific" (sometimes called "case-linked") jurisdiction. . . . But "only a limited set of affiliations with a forum will render a defendant amenable to" general jurisdiction in that State.

Specific jurisdiction is very different. In order for a state court to exercise specific jurisdiction, "the suit" must "aris[e] out of or relat[e] to the defendant's contacts with the forum." In other words, there must be "an affiliation between the forum and the underlying controversy, principally, [an] activity or an occurrence that takes place in the forum State and is therefore subject to the State's regulation." For this reason,

---

[16] California law provides that its courts may exercise jurisdiction "on any basis not inconsistent with the Constitution . . . of the United States," Cal. Civ. Proc. Code Ann. §410.10 (West 2004).

"specific jurisdiction is confined to adjudication of issues deriving from, or connected with, the very controversy that establishes jurisdiction."

B

In determining whether personal jurisdiction is present, a court must consider a variety of interests. These include "the interests of the forum State and of the plaintiff in proceeding with the cause in the plaintiff's forum of choice." Kulko v. Superior Court [p. 76, supra]; . . . . But the "primary concern" is "the burden on the defendant." Assessing this burden obviously requires a court to consider the practical problems resulting from litigating in the forum, but it also encompasses the more abstract matter of submitting to the coercive power of a State that may have little legitimate interest in the claims in question. As we have put it, restrictions on personal jurisdiction "are more than a guarantee of immunity from inconvenient or distant litigation. They are a consequence of territorial limitations on the power of the respective States." Hanson v. Denckla, [p. 75, supra]. "[T]he States retain many essential attributes of sovereignty, including, in particular, the sovereign power to try causes in their courts. The sovereignty of each State . . . implie[s] a limitation on the sovereignty of all its sister States." World-Wide Volkswagen, p. 80, supra. And at times, this federalism interest may be decisive. As we explained in *WorldWide Volkswagen*, "[e]ven if the defendant would suffer minimal or no inconvenience from being forced to litigate before the tribunals of another State; even if the forum State has a strong interest in applying its law to the controversy; even if the forum State is the most convenient location for litigation, the Due Process Clause, acting as an instrument of interstate federalism, may sometimes act to divest the State of its power to render a valid judgment."

III

A

Our settled principles regarding specific jurisdiction control this case. In order for a court to exercise specific jurisdiction over a claim, there must be an "affiliation between the forum and the underlying controversy, principally, [an] activity or an occurrence that takes place in the forum State." *Goodyear*, [p. 126, supra]. When there is no such connection, specific jurisdiction is lacking regardless of the extent of a defendant's unconnected activities in the State. . . .

For this reason, the California Supreme Court's "sliding scale approach" is difficult to square with our precedents. Under the California approach, the strength of the requisite connection between the forum and the specific claims at issue is relaxed if the defendant has extensive forum contacts that are unrelated to those claims. Our cases provide no support for this approach, which resembles a loose and spurious form of general jurisdiction. For specific jurisdiction, a defendant's general connections with the forum are not enough. As we have said, "[a] corporation's continuous activity of some sorts within a state . . . is not enough to support the demand that the corporation be amenable to suits unrelated to that activity.' "

The present case illustrates the danger of the California approach. The State Supreme Court found that specific jurisdiction was present without identifying any adequate link between the State and the nonresidents' claims. As noted, the nonresidents were not prescribed Plavix in California, did not purchase Plavix in California, did not ingest Plavix in California, and were not injured by Plavix in California. The mere fact that other plaintiffs were prescribed, obtained, and ingested Plavix in California—and allegedly sustained the same injuries as did the nonresidents—does not allow the State to assert specific jurisdiction over the nonresidents' claims. As we have explained, "a defendant's relationship with a . . . third party, standing alone, is an insufficient basis for jurisdiction." Walden, [p. 115, supra] . . . . This remains true even when third parties (here, the plaintiffs who reside in California) can bring claims similar to those brought by the nonresidents. Nor is it sufficient—or even relevant—that BMS conducted research in California on matters unrelated to Plavix. What is needed—and what is missing here—is a connection between the forum and the specific claims at issue.

Our decision in *Walden*, supra, illustrates this requirement. In that case, Nevada plaintiffs sued an out-of-state defendant for conducting an allegedly unlawful search of the plaintiffs while they were in Georgia preparing to board a plane bound for Nevada. We held that the Nevada courts lacked specific jurisdiction even though the plaintiffs were Nevada residents and "suffered foreseeable harm in Nevada." Because the "relevant conduct occurred entirely in Georgi[a] . . . the mere fact that [this] conduct affected plaintiffs with connections to the forum State d[id] not suffice to authorize jurisdiction."

In today's case, the connection between the nonresidents' claims and the forum is even weaker. The relevant plaintiffs are not California residents and do not claim to have suffered harm in that State. In addition, as in *Walden*, all the conduct giving rise to the nonresidents' claims occurred elsewhere. It follows that the California courts cannot claim specific jurisdiction. See World Wide Volkswagen (finding no personal jurisdiction in Oklahoma because the defendant "carr[ied] on no activity whatsoever in Oklahoma" and dismissing "the fortuitous circumstance that a single Audi automobile, sold [by defendants] in New York to New York residents, happened to suffer an accident while passing through Oklahoma" as an "isolated occurrence").

B

The nonresidents maintain that two of our cases support the decision below, but they misinterpret those precedents.

. . .

The nonresident plaintiffs in this case point to our holding in *Keeton* that there was jurisdiction in New Hampshire to entertain the plaintiff 's request for damages suffered outside the State, but that holding concerned jurisdiction to determine the scope of a claim involving in-state injury and injury to residents of the State, not, as in this case, jurisdiction to entertain claims involving no instate injury and no injury to residents of the forum State. Keeton [p. 100, supra] held that there was jurisdiction in New Hampshire to consider the full measure of the plaintiff's claim, but whether she could actually recover out-of-state damages was a merits question governed by New Hampshire libel law.

. . .

C

In a last ditch contention, respondents contend that BMS's "decision to contract with a California company [McKesson] to distribute [Plavix] nationally" provides a sufficient basis for personal jurisdiction. But as we have explained, "[t]he requirements of *International Shoe* . . . must be met as to each defendant over whom a state court exercises jurisdiction." Rush v. Savchuk, 444 U.S. 320, 332 (1980); see Walden ("[A] defendant's relationship with a . . . third party, standing alone, is an insufficient basis for jurisdiction"). In this case, it is not alleged that BMS engaged in relevant acts together with McKesson in California. Nor is it alleged that BMS is derivatively liable for McKesson's conduct in California. And the nonresidents "have adduced no evidence to show how or by whom the Plavix they took was distributed to the pharmacies that dispensed it to them." 1 Cal. 5th, at 815 (Werdegar, J., dissenting). The bare fact that BMS contracted with a California distributor is not enough to establish personal jurisdiction in the State.

IV

Our straightforward application in this case of settled principles of personal jurisdiction will not result in the parade of horribles that respondents conjure up. See Brief for Respondents 38–47. Our decision does not prevent the California and out-of-state plaintiffs from joining together in a consolidated action in the States that have general jurisdiction over BMS. BMS concedes that such suits could be brought in either New York or Delaware. Alternatively, the plaintiffs who are residents of a particular State—for example, the 92 plaintiffs from Texas and the 71 from Ohio— could probably sue together in their home States. In addition, since our decision concerns the due process limits on the exercise of specific jurisdiction by a State, we leave open the question whether the Fifth Amendment imposes the same restrictions on the exercise of personal jurisdiction by a federal court. See Omni Capital Int'l, Ltd. v. Rudolf Wolff & Co., 484 U.S. 97, 102, n. 5 (1987).

. . .

The judgment of the California Supreme Court is reversed, and the case is remanded for further proceedings not inconsistent with this opinion.

It is so ordered.

■ JUSTICE SOTOMAYOR, dissenting.

Three years ago, the Court imposed substantial curbs on the exercise of general jurisdiction in its decision in Daimler AG v. Bauman, [p. 126, supra]. Today, the Court takes its first step toward a similar contraction of specific jurisdiction by holding that a corporation that engages in a nationwide course of conduct cannot be held accountable in a state court by a group of injured people unless all of those people were injured in the forum State.

I fear the consequences of the Court's decision today will be substantial. The majority's rule will make it difficult to aggregate the claims of plaintiffs across the country whose claims may be worth little alone. It will make it impossible to bring a nationwide mass action in state court against defendants who are "at home" in different States. And it will result in piecemeal litigation and the bifurcation of claims. None of this is necessary. A core concern in this Court's personal jurisdiction cases is fairness. And there is nothing unfair about subjecting a massive corporation to suit in a State for a nationwide course of conduct that injures both forum residents and nonresidents alike.

I

Bristol-Myers Squibb is a Fortune 500 pharmaceutical company incorporated in Delaware and headquartered in New York. It employs approximately 25,000 people worldwide and earns annual revenues of over $15 billion. In the late 1990's, Bristol-Myers began to market and sell a prescription blood thinner called Plavix. Plavix was advertised as an effective tool for reducing the risk of blood clotting for those vulnerable to heart attacks and to strokes. The ads worked: At the height of its popularity, Plavix was a blockbuster, earning Bristol-Myers billions of dollars in annual revenues.

Bristol-Myers' advertising and distribution efforts were national in scope. It conducted a single nationwide advertising campaign for Plavix, using television, magazine, and Internet ads to broadcast its message. A consumer in California heard the same advertisement as a consumer in Maine about the benefits of Plavix. Bristol-Myers' distribution of Plavix also proceeded through nationwide channels: Consistent with its usual practice, it relied on a small number of wholesalers to distribute Plavix throughout the country. One of those distributors, McKesson Corporation, was named as a defendant below; during the relevant time period, McKesson was responsible for almost a quarter of Bristol-Myers' revenue worldwide.

. . .

II

Viewed through this framework [of *International Shoe* and progeny], the California courts appropriately exercised specific jurisdiction over respondents' claims.

First, there is no dispute that Bristol-Myers "purposefully avail[ed] itself" of California and its substantial pharmaceutical market. Bristol-Myers employs over 400 people in California and maintains half a dozen facilities in the State engaged in research, development, and policymaking. It contracts with a California-based distributor, McKesson, whose sales account for a significant portion of its revenue. And it markets and sells its drugs, including Plavix, in California, resulting in total Plavix sales in that State of nearly $1 billion during the period relevant to this suit.

Second, respondents' claims "relate to" Bristol-Myers' instate conduct. A claim "relates to" a defendant's forum conduct if it has a "connect[ion] with" that conduct. International Shoe, 326 U.S., at 319. So respondents could not, for instance, hale Bristol-Myers into court in California for negligently maintaining the sidewalk outside its New York headquarters—a claim that has no connection to acts Bristol-Myers took in California. But respondents' claims against Bristol Myers look nothing like such a claim. Respondents' claims against Bristol-Myers concern conduct materially identical to acts the company took in California: its marketing and distribution of Plavix, which it undertook on a nationwide basis in all 50 States. That respondents were allegedly injured by this nationwide course of conduct in Indiana, Oklahoma, and Texas, and not California, does not mean that their claims do not "relate to" the advertising and distribution efforts that Bristol- Myers undertook in that State. All of the plaintiffs—residents and nonresidents alike—allege that they were injured by the same essential acts. Our cases require no connection more direct than that.

Finally, and importantly, there is no serious doubt that the exercise of jurisdiction over the nonresidents' claims is reasonable. Because Bristol-Myers already faces claims that are identical to the nonresidents' claims in this suit, it will not be harmed by having to defend against respondents' claims: Indeed, the alternative approach—litigating those claims in separate suits in as many as 34 different States—would prove far more burdensome. By contrast, the plaintiffs' "interest in obtaining convenient and effective relief," Burger King, [p. 78, supra], is obviously furthered by participating in a consolidated proceeding in one State under shared counsel, which allows them to minimize costs, share discovery, and maximize recoveries on claims that may be too small to bring on their own. . . .

Nothing in the Due Process Clause prohibits a California court from hearing respondents' claims—at least not in a case where they are joined to identical claims brought by California residents.

III

Bristol-Myers does not dispute that it has purposefully availed itself of California's markets, nor—remarkably—did it argue below that it would be "unreasonable" for a California court to hear respondents' claims. Instead, Bristol-Myers contends that respondents' claims do not "arise out of or relate to" its California conduct. The majority agrees, explaining that no "adequate link" exists "between the State and the nonresidents' claims"—a result that it says follows from "settled principles [of] specific jurisdiction." But our precedents do not require this result, and common sense says that it cannot be correct.

A

The majority casts its decision today as compelled by precedent. But our cases point in the other direction.

The majority argues at length that the exercise of specific jurisdiction in this case would conflict with our decision in Walden v. Fiore [p. 115, supra] That is plainly not true. *Walden* concerned the requirement that a defendant "purposefully avail" himself of a forum State or "purposefully direc[t]" his conduct toward that State, not the separate requirement that a plaintiff's claim "arise out of or relate to" a defendant's forum contacts. The lower court understood the case that way. The parties understood the case that way.... And courts and commentators have understood the case that way.... *Walden* teaches only that a defendant must have purposefully availed itself of the forum, and that a plaintiff cannot rely solely on a defendant's contacts with a forum resident to establish the necessary relationship. ("[T]he plaintiff cannot be the only link between the defendant and the forum"). But that holding has nothing to do with the dispute between the parties: Bristol-Myers has purposefully availed itself of California—to the tune of millions of dollars in annual revenue. Only if its language is taken out of context, can Walden be made to seem relevant to the case at hand.

By contrast, our decision in Keeton v. Hustler Magazine, Inc. [p. 100, supra], suggests that there should be no such barrier to the exercise of jurisdiction here. In *Keeton*, a New York resident brought suit against an Ohio corporation, a magazine, in New Hampshire for libel. She alleged that the magazine's nationwide course of conduct—its publication of defamatory statements—had injured her in every State, including New Hampshire. This Court unanimously rejected the defendant's argument that it should not be subject to "nationwide damages" when only a small portion of those damages arose in the forum State; exposure to such liability, the Court explained, was the consequence of having "continuously and deliberately exploited the New Hampshire market," .... The majority today dismisses *Keeton* on the ground that the defendant there faced one plaintiff's claim arising out of its nationwide course of conduct, whereas Bristol-Myers faces many more plaintiffs' claims. But this is a distinction without a difference: In either case, a defendant will face liability in a single State for a single course of conduct that has impact in many States. *Keeton* informs us that there is no unfairness in such a result.

The majority's animating concern, in the end, appears to be federalism: "[T]erritorial limitations on the power of the respective States," we are informed, may—and today do—trump even concerns about fairness to the parties. Indeed, the majority appears to concede that this is not, at bottom, a case about fairness but instead a case about power: one in which " 'the defendant would suffer minimal or no inconvenience from being forced to litigate before the tribunals of another State; . . . the forum State has a strong interest in applying its law to the controversy; [and] the forum State is the most convenient location for litigation' " but personal jurisdiction still will not lie. *Ante*, at 7 (quoting World-Wide Volkswagen [p. 80, supra]. But I see little reason to apply such a principle in a case brought against a large corporate defendant arising out of its nationwide conduct. What interest could any single State have in adjudicating respondents' claims that the other States do not share? I would measure jurisdiction first and foremost by the yardstick set out in *International Shoe*—"fair play and substantial justice," 326 U.S., at 316 (internal quotation marks omitted). The majority's opinion casts that settled principle aside.

B

I fear the consequences of the majority's decision today will be substantial. Even absent a rigid requirement that a defendant's in-state conduct must actually cause a plaintiff's claim,[3] the upshot of today's opinion is that plaintiffs cannot join their claims together and sue a defendant in a State in which only some of them have been injured. That rule is likely to have consequences far beyond this case.

First, and most prominently, the Court's opinion in this case will make it profoundly difficult for plaintiffs who are injured in different States by a defendant's nationwide course of conduct to sue that defendant in a single, consolidated action. The holding of today's opinion is that such an action cannot be brought in a State in which only some plaintiffs were injured. Not to worry, says the majority: The plaintiffs here could have sued Bristol-Myers in New York or Delaware; could "probably" have subdivided their separate claims into 34 lawsuits in the States in which they were injured; and might have been able to bring a single suit in federal court (an "open . . . question"). *Ante*, at 12. Even setting aside the majority's caveats, what is the purpose of such limitations? What interests are served by preventing the consolidation of claims and limiting the forums in which they can be consolidated? The effect of the Court's opinion today is to eliminate nationwide mass actions in any State other than those in which a defendant is " 'essentially at home.' " Such a rule hands one more tool to corporate defendants determined to prevent the aggregation of individual claims, and forces injured plaintiffs to bear the burden of bringing suit in what will often be far flung jurisdictions.

---

[3] Bristol-Myers urges such a rule upon us, but its adoption would have consequences far beyond those that follow from today's factbound opinion. Among other things, it might call into question whether even a plaintiff injured in a State by an item identical to those sold by a defendant in that State could avail himself of that State's courts to redress his injuries—a result specifically contemplated by *World-Wide Volkswagen Corp. v. Woodson*, 444 U.S. 286, 297 (1980). . . . That question, and others like it, appears to await another case.

[Second, Justice Sotomayor noted that in light of *Daimler's* limits on general jurisdiction and the holding in the present case, plaintiffs will find it impossible to bring a nationwide case against two defendants if those defendants are not incorporated in the same state or do not maintain their principal places of business in the same state. No state will have general jurisdiction over both defendants.]

It "does not offend 'traditional notions of fair play and substantial justice,'" *International Shoe*, 326 U.S., at 316, to permit plaintiffs to aggregate claims arising out of a single nationwide course of conduct in a single suit in a single State where some, but not all, were injured. But that is exactly what the Court holds today is barred by the Due Process Clause.

This is not a rule the Constitution has required before. I respectfully dissent.

NOTES

1.   In cases addressed in subsection 2 of this chapter, p. 80, supra, we saw the Supreme Court reject specific jurisdiction for lack of a relevant contact between the defendant and the forum. These cases included *Walden, J. McIntyre, World-Wide Volkswagen,* and *Hanson.* In *Bristol-Myers Squibb,* however, the problem is not contact; the defendant forged plenty of purposeful ties with California. The problem was relatedness for specific jurisdiction—the claims (by the non-California plaintiffs) did not arise out of or related to those contacts.

2.   It is likely that before the Court limited the reach of general jurisdiction in *Goodyear, Daimler and BNSF Railway*, p. 126 et seq., supra, California would have exercised general jurisdiction over BMS—based upon the company's "continuous and systematic" ties with California. Now, however, California lacks general jurisdiction because BMS was not incorporated in California and did not establish its principal place of business there.

3.   In his dissent in *Helicopteros*, p. 122, supra, Justice Brennan urged that specific jurisdiction should not require that the plaintiff's claims "arise out of" the defendant's contact with the forum. Rather, it should require only that the claims "relate to" those contacts. Linguistically, he noted, "relate to" would permit a broader exercise of specific jurisdiction than a requirement that the claim "arise out of" the contact. 444 U.S. at 425 (Brennan, J., dissenting). Did the majority in *Bristol-Myers Squibb* make such a distinction? What test does it employ? Did Justice Sotomayor make such a distinction?

4.   In light of Justice Ginsburg's dissent in *J. McIntyre*, p. 86, supra, which Justice Kagan joined, are you surprised that those two Justices signed the majority opinion in *Bristol-Myers Squibb*?

———

The following case was decided before *Bristol-Myers Squibb,* but remains an instructive discussion of relatedness.

Moki Mac River Expeditions v. Drugg

Supreme Court of Texas, 2007.
221 S.W.3d 569.

■ JUSTICE O'NEILL delivered the opinion of the Court, in which CHIEF JUSTICE JEFFERSON, JUSTICE HECHT, JUSTICE WAINWRIGHT, JUSTICE BRISTER, JUSTICE GREEN, and JUSTICE WILLETT joined.

A Texas court may assert specific jurisdiction over an out-of-state defendant if the defendant's contact with this state is purposeful and the injury arises from or relates to those contacts. In this wrongful-death case against a Utah-based river-rafting outfitter, the defendant contends the plaintiff's death on a Grand Canyon hiking trail did not arise from or relate to its in-state commercial activities so as to establish specific jurisdiction over it in Texas. We agree. Accordingly, we reverse and remand the case to the court of appeals to determine whether general jurisdiction exists.

I.   Background

Charles and Betsy Drugg's thirteen-year-old son, Andy, died on a June 2001, river-rafting trip in Arizona with Moki Mac River Expeditions, a Utah-based river-rafting outfitter. Moki Mac did not directly solicit the Druggs to participate in the trip. Instead, the Druggs learned about Moki Mac's excursions from a fellow Texas resident, Annie Seals, who had contacted the company regarding a rafting trip in the Grand Canyon. There was no space available for her at that time, but Seals's contact information was placed on Moki Mac's computerized mailing list so that she would automatically receive a brochure for the 2001 season when it became available. Moki Mac subsequently sent two brochures to Seals in Texas detailing pricing and schedules for upcoming excursions. Seals informed Moki Mac of the interest of several others in Texas with whom she shared the literature, including Andy and members of his family.

Betsy Drugg reviewed the brochures and information from Moki Mac's website. After corresponding with Moki Mac representatives from her home in Texas, Betsy ultimately decided to send Andy on the rafting trip. . . . As was its practice, Moki Mac sent a letter confirming payment to the Druggs' home in Texas along with an acknowledgment-of-risk and release form, which the company requires participants to sign as a prerequisite to attendance. Both Andy and his mother signed the form and returned it to Moki Mac.

The Druggs allege that on the second day of Andy's fourteen-day trip, Moki Mac guides led the group up an incline on a trail that narrowed around and was obstructed by a large boulder. The guides were positioned at the head and rear of the group, but no guide was present near the boulder. As Andy attempted to negotiate the boulder-blocked path, requiring him to lean back while attempting to cross a very narrow ledge, he fell backwards approximately fifty-five feet and was fatally injured.

The Druggs filed suit in Texas for wrongful death due to Moki Mac's negligence and for intentional and negligent misrepresentation. . . .

III. In Personam Jurisdiction

We have said that the [Texas] long-arm statute's broad doing-business language allows the statute to "reach as far as the federal constitutional requirements of due process will allow." . . .

Personal jurisdiction is proper when the nonresident defendant has established minimum contacts with the forum state, and the exercise of jurisdiction comports with "'traditional notions of fair play and substantial justice.'" Int'l Shoe Co. v. Washington, [p. 65, supra], 326 U.S. 310, 316, 66 S. Ct. 154, 90 L. Ed. 95 (1945) (quoting Milliken v. Meyer, 311 U.S. 457, 463, 61 S. Ct. 339, 85 L. Ed. 278 (1940)). . . .

. . . [W]hen specific jurisdiction is alleged, we focus the minimum-contacts analysis on the "relationship among the defendant, the forum[,] and the litigation." Specific jurisdiction is established if the defendant's alleged liability "aris[es] out of or [is] related to" an activity conducted within the forum. The United States Supreme Court has provided relatively little guidance on the "arise from or relate to" requirement, nor have we had occasion to examine the strength of the nexus required to establish specific jurisdiction.

IV. Jurisdictional Analysis

The Druggs assert that Moki Mac established sufficient minimum contacts with Texas by making material misrepresentations to them here, upon which they relied, regarding the nature of the services that would be provided on its trips. The wrongful death of their son, the Druggs argue, arose from or related to the fact that Moki Mac's services did not meet the standards it represented in Texas. Moki Mac's principal argument is that there is an insufficient nexus between any alleged misrepresentations that it made in Texas and Andy's wrongful death in Arizona to satisfy jurisdictional due process. According to Moki Mac, Andy's death might have arisen out of or related to alleged negligence that occurred in Arizona, but it had no meaningful connection to Moki Mac's alleged misrepresentations in Texas.

For a Texas forum to properly exercise specific jurisdiction in this case, (1) Moki Mac must have made minimum contacts with Texas by purposefully availing itself of the privilege of conducting activities here, and (2) Moki Mac's liability must have arisen from or related to those contacts . . .

A. Purposeful Availment

A nonresident defendant that directs marketing efforts to Texas in the hope of soliciting sales is subject to suit here for alleged liability arising from or relating to that business. . . .

The United States Supreme Court has recognized that a nonresident who places products into the "stream of commerce" with the expectation that they will be sold in the forum state is subject to the forum's jurisdiction. . . . Although the Court has also stated that a single contact can support jurisdiction if that contact creates a "substantial connection" with the forum, jurisdiction cannot be established where the contact creates only an " 'attenuated' affiliation with the forum." . . .

Thus, the mere sale of a product to a Texas resident will not generally suffice to confer specific jurisdiction upon our courts.

Moki Mac's efforts to solicit business in Texas, however, go further [than mere sales]. It solicited Texas residents through mass and targeted direct-marketing email campaigns. . . . In addition, Moki Mac established channels of regular communication with its customers in Texas. It was Moki Mac's practice to utilize particular customers, who would become de facto group leaders, to plan, organize, and promote its trips . . .

We conclude that Moki Mac had sufficient purposeful contact with Texas to satisfy the first prong of jurisdictional due process. But purposeful availment alone will not support an exercise of specific jurisdiction. Specific-jurisdiction analysis has two co-equal components. For specific-jurisdiction purposes, purposeful availment has no jurisdictional relevance unless the defendant's liability arises from or relates to the forum contacts. Moki Mac contends there was an insufficient nexus between Andy's injuries and Moki Mac's contacts with Texas to establish specific jurisdiction, an argument to which we now turn.

B. Relatedness Requirement

The "arise from or relate to" requirement lies at the heart of specific jurisdiction by defining the required nexus between the nonresident defendant, the litigation, and the forum. To support specific jurisdiction, the Supreme Court has given relatively little guidance as to how closely related a cause of action must be to the defendant's forum activities. In assessing the relationship between a nonresident's contacts and the litigation, most courts have focused on causation, but they have differed over the proper causative threshold. See Nowak v. Tak How Invs., Ltd., 94 F.3d 708, 714 (1st Cir. 1996) (discussing various causative approaches). Some courts have pursued an expansive but-for causative approach, others have adopted a restrictive relatedness view requiring forum contacts to be relevant to a necessary element of proof, and some have applied a sliding-scale analysis that attempts to strike a balance between the two. See Mark M. Maloney, Specific Jurisdiction and the "Arise From or Relate to" Requirement . . . What Does it Mean?, 50 Wash. & Lee L. Rev. 1265, 1276, 1299 (1993). Each approach has proponents and detractors, for the reasons we examine below.

1.   "But-For" Relatedness

In Helicopteros Nacionales de Colombia v. Hall, [p. 122, infra], the Supreme Court evaluated a Colombian corporation's limited contacts with Texas and decided they were not sufficiently continuous and systematic to support general jurisdiction over the defendant in Texas. 466 U.S. at 418–19. The Court did not reach specific jurisdiction because the parties had conceded that the plaintiffs' claims did not arise from or relate to the defendant's activities in Texas. Id. at 415–16. Justice Brennan, though, dissented, espousing a broad "but-for" approach to relatedness, and courts that have applied that test have generally relied on his view. Id. at 427–28.

Courts that support the but-for approach have said that a cause of action arises from or relates to a defendant's forum contacts when, but for those contacts, the cause of action would never have arisen. See Shute v. Carnival Cruise Lines, 897 F.2d 377, 385 (9th Cir. 1990), rev'd on other grounds, 499 U.S. 585, 111 S. Ct. 1522, 113 L. Ed. 2d 622 (1991); see also Prejean v. Sonatrach, Inc., 652 F.2d 1260, 1270 n.21 (5th Cir. 1981) (holding that a "contract [was] a but for causative factor" for the tort suit); cf. Lanier v. Am. Bd. of Endodontics, 843 F.2d 901, 909 (6th Cir. 1988) (interpreting "arising out of" language in Michigan's long-arm statute and concluding that alleged discrimination would not have occurred but for the defendants' contacts with the forum). Rather than considering only isolated contacts that relate to a specific element of proof or the proximate cause of injury, the but-for analysis considers jurisdictional contacts that occur over the "entire course of events" of the relationship between the defendant, the forum, and the litigation. See Shute, 897 F.2d at 384.

As the sole jurisdiction to explicitly adopt the but-for test, the Ninth Circuit Court of Appeals has been its staunchest advocate, and Shute's progeny have generally demonstrated the circuit's continuing support. . . .

Few courts beyond the Ninth Circuit have adopted the but-for approach to relatedness. Specifically, both the Fifth and Sixth Circuits have signaled a movement away from such a broad test. We agree with those courts and commentators who view the but-for test as too broad and judicially unmoored to satisfy due-process concerns.

2.   Substantive Relevance/Proximate Cause

Far more structured than the but-for approach is the restrictive view of relatedness known as "substantive relevance." As the name implies, this test requires forum-related contacts to be substantively relevant, or even necessary, to proof of the claim. See Tecre Co. v. Buttonpro, Inc., 387 F. Supp. 2d 927, 933 (E.D. Wis. 2005) (citing Marino v. Hyatt Corp., 793 F.2d 427, 430 (1st Cir. 1986)). One iteration of this standard is known as the "proximate cause" test, reasoning that a contact that is the proximate or legal cause of an injury is substantively relevant to a cause of action that arises from it. The First, Second, and Eighth Circuits appear to have followed this approach. See United Elec., Radio & Mach. Workers of Am. v. 163 Pleasant St. Corp., 960 F.2d 1080, 1089 (1st Cir. 1992); Pizarro v. Hoteles Concorde Int'l, C.A., 907 F.2d 1256, 1259–60 (1st Cir. 1990); Marino, 793 F.2d at 429–30; Morris v. Barkbuster, Inc., 923 F.2d 1277, 1281 (8th Cir. 1991); Pearrow v. Nat'l Life & Accident Ins. Co., 703 F.2d 1067, 1068–69 (8th Cir. 1983); Gelfand v. Tanner Motor Tours, 339 F.2d 317, 321–22 (2d Cir. 1964).

Proximate cause requires the defendant's conduct to be both the cause in fact and the foreseeable cause of injury. See Doe v. Boys Clubs of Greater Dallas, Inc., 907 S.W.2d 472, 477, 38 Tex. Sup. Ct. J. 732 (Tex. 1995). Under this more stringent relatedness standard, the purposeful contact that is a proximate cause of injury is an essential liability element and is thus substantively relevant to a plaintiff's claim of harm. . . .

. . . Moki Mac urges us to follow the substantive-relevance approach, we have generally eschewed pinning jurisdictional analysis on the type of claim alleged. . . .

3. "Sliding Scale" Relationship

Attempting to moderate the seemingly categorical effects of the but-for and substantive-relevance tests, some commentators have espoused, and a few courts have adopted, a "sliding scale" approach that examines the relationship between forum contacts and the litigation along a continuum. Under this view, as the extent of forum contacts goes up, the degree of relatedness to the litigation necessary to establish specific jurisdiction goes down, and vice versa. . . .

Although the sliding scale jurisdictional analysis studiously avoids the extremes that the other two relatedness tests present, it too presents a number of problems. Most significantly, deciding jurisdiction based on a sliding continuum blurs the distinction between general and specific jurisdiction that our judicial system has firmly embraced and that provides an established structure for courts to analyze questions of in personam jurisdiction. . . .

4. Substantial Connection to Operative Facts

As we have said, the but-for relatedness test is too broad and conceptually unlimited in scope, the substantive-relevance/proximate-cause test poses too narrow an inquiry, and the sliding-scale analysis conflates the fundamental distinction between general and specific jurisdiction that is firmly embedded in our jurisprudence. In light of these concerns, some courts have applied alternative approaches, requiring that a cause of action "lie in the wake of the [defendant's] commercial activities" in the forum, Deluxe Ice Cream Co. v. R.C.H. Tool Corp., 726 F.2d 1209, 1215–16 (7th Cir. 1984), or that the forum contacts be "critical steps in the chain of events that led to the [injury]," In re Oil Spill by Amoco Cadiz, 699 F.2d 909, 915–16 (7th Cir. 1983). . . .

Our limited jurisprudence similarly suggests a middle ground, more flexible than substantive relevance but more structured than but-for relatedness, in assessing the strength of the necessary connection between the defendant, the forum, and the litigation. . . . Considering our own jurisprudence and the Supreme Court's analysis . . . we believe that for a nonresident defendant's forum contacts to support an exercise of specific jurisdiction, there must be a substantial connection between those contacts and the operative facts of the litigation.

C.   Relatedness of Moki Mac's Contacts

Betsy Drugg alleges she was induced to send Andy on the rafting trip by Moki Mac's direct solicitation, which included statements made in Moki Mac's brochures and in the release it sent to the Druggs. Specifically, Andy's mother claims she made the decision to send Andy on the trip based on Moki Mac's assurances that "[y]ou don't need 'mountain man' camping skills to participate in one of our trips," children age twelve or above are suited to participate, and "Moki Mac has taken reasonable steps to provide you with appropriate equipment and/or skilled guides." But for these promises, the Druggs claim, they would not have sent Andy on the rafting trip and he would not have fallen on the hiking trail.

Certainly on a river rafting trip safety is a paramount concern, and we accept as true the Druggs' claim that Andy might not have gone on the trip were it not for Moki Mac's representations about safety. However, the operative facts of the Druggs' suit concern principally the guides' conduct of the hiking expedition and whether they exercised reasonable care in supervising Andy. The events on the trail and the guides' supervision of the hike will be the focus of the trial, will consume most if not all of the litigation's attention, and the overwhelming majority of the evidence will be directed to that question. Only after thoroughly considering the manner in which the hike was conducted will the jury be able to assess the Druggs' misrepresentation claim. . . .

[T]he injuries for which the Druggs seek recovery are based on Andy's death on the hiking trail in Arizona, and the relationship between the operative facts of the litigation and Moki Mac's promotional activities in Texas are simply too attenuated to satisfy specific jurisdiction's due-process concerns.

V.   Conclusion

We reverse the court of appeals' judgment and remand the case. . . .

JUSTICE JOHNSON filed a dissenting opinion, in which JUSTICE MEDINA joined.

Texas' long-arm jurisdiction over non residents reaches as far as the federal constitution allows. . . .

Moki Mac is a Utah company which has conducted guided tours in the Grand Canyon for many years. In addition to general advertising and maintaining a website for potential clients to access, Moki Mac's efforts to attract customers include targeting particular persons to whom it sends brochures describing Moki Mac's rafting and hiking trips. Its targeted audience includes persons who previously inquired about or have taken its trips. At and for several years prior to the time reservations were made for Andy's trip in 2001, Moki Mac's targeted audience included Texas residents. . . .

Participants on Moki Mac's guided rafting and hiking trips engage in activities and encounter conditions which Moki Mac recognizes pose risks of injury and death. . . .

The Druggs received Moki Mac's brochures from a Texas acquaintance. After reviewing the brochures and corresponding with Moki Mac from Texas, the Druggs decided to allow thirteen-year-old Andy to go on one of the trips. . . .

[C]ourts have developed a series of factors that bear on the fairness of subjecting a nonresident to a foreign tribunal . . . as follows: "(1) the defendant's burden of appearing, (2) the forum state's interest in adjudicating the dispute, (3) the plaintiff's interest in obtaining convenient and effective relief, (4) the judicial system's interest in obtaining the most effective resolution of the controversy, and (5) the common interests of all sovereigns in promoting substantive social policies." Such an approach properly focuses on and emphasizes the actions of a nonresident defendant that has purposefully directed actions at a forum's residents, and on the reasonable foreseeability to the defendant that its actions will make it amenable to suit in that forum.

While Moki Mac might have a strong forum non conveniens argument, the facts before us do not present a compelling case that Texas' exercise of jurisdiction over Moki Mac would be unreasonable. Moki Mac's conduct was particularly designed to and did increase the likelihood that Texas residents would respond favorably. Andy Drugg's death occurred while he was engaged in activities integral to the relationship Moki Mac induced by its efforts specifically directed toward Texas residents. Moki Mac should have reasonably foreseen that an injury to a client such as Andy while the client participated in activities integral to the relationship directly produced through Moki Mac's activities directed toward Texas residents would subject Moki Mac to being sued over the injury in Texas. There was a meaningful link between Moki Mac's actions directed toward Texas residents and the Druggs' suit. Accordingly, I would hold that the substance of the Druggs' suit is related to Moki Mac's activities which were purposefully directed toward Texas residents; the second prong of the due process inquiry is satisfied; it is not unreasonable or unfair to Moki Mac for Texas to exercise jurisdiction over Moki Mac as to the Druggs' suit; and subject to a "fair play and substantial justice" analysis, the exercise of jurisdiction by Texas in this case falls within the boundaries of federal constitutional due process requirements. . . .

NOTES

1. In this case, the Texas Supreme Court chronicles how lower courts have failed to forge consensus about what level of connection is required between a defendant's forum contacts and the plaintiff's claim to support specific jurisdiction. Did the Supreme Court's decision in *Bristol-Myers Squibb,* p. 142 supra, resolve the debate over the issue?

2. The most "pro-jurisdiction" of the tests discussed in *Moki Mac* is the "but for" test favored by the Ninth Circuit and applied most famously in Shute v. Carnival Cruise Lines, 897 F.2d 377, 385 (9th Cir.1990), rev'd on other grounds, 499 U.S. 585, 111 S.Ct. 1522, 113 L.Ed.2d 622 (1991). Under the *Shute* test, the contacts in the principal case clearly would have been related because without Moki Mac's efforts to obtain customers in Texas, the decedent never would have made the trip and suffered the fatal injury. Most of the cases that present the difficult issues involve the basic fact pattern of *Shute* and the principal case: a forum resident plaintiff is drawn to the defendant's location by the defendant's marketing activities and injured while on the defendant's commercial property or involved in the activity being marketed to forum residents. See, e.g., Pizarro v. Hoteles Concorde Int'l, 907 F.2d 1256 (1st Cir.1990) (hotel stay); Prejean v. Sonatrach, Inc., 652 F.2d 1260 (5th Cir.1981) (engineers killed at defendant's commercial site after being recruited to come there to provide technical assistance); Presbyterian Univ. Hosp. v. Wilson, 337 Md. 541, 654 A.2d 1324 (1995) (specialized medical care outside decedent's home state).

3. The other tests all require something more than a cause-in-fact relationship between the defendant's contacts and the liability-creating events. Professor Brilmayer argued for a test of "substantive relevance," which would require that the contacts be relevant to the substantive theories in the case before being treated as related. See Brilmayer, How Contacts Count: Due Process Limitations on State Court Jurisdiction, 1980 Sup.Ct.Rev. 77, 82. Does the Texas Supreme Court's "substantial connection to operative facts" test differ in any meaningful way from Professor Brilmayer's substantive relevance test?

4. Discussing the relatedness requirement in Compania de Inversiones Mercantiles, S.A. v. Grupo Cementos de Chihuahua S.A., 970 F.3d 1269, 1287–88 (10th Cir.2020), the court explained that the relatedness requirement functions to a balance between the defendant's invocation of benefits from the forum with that state's imposition of obligations. "[T]o do so, [the relatedness analysis] must keep the jurisdictional exposure that results from a contact tailored to that contact's accompanying substantive obligations. The causal connection can be somewhat looser than the tort concept of proximate causation, but it must nonetheless be intimate enough to keep the quid pro quo proportional and personal jurisdiction reasonably foreseeable." How helpful is this standard. The court noted that tort proximate causation is required when a defendant has limited contacts with the forum but not when the defendant's contacts are more substantial. Id. at 1287. Does that approach differ from the "sliding scale" rejected in *Bristol-Myers Squibb*?

5. How convincing is the majority's application of its own test in *Moki Mac*? Note that the court took as undisputed that the decedent and his mother specifically relied upon the defendant's assurances that the trip was appropriate for someone of the decedent's age and experience. If that reliance does not qualify as a "substantial connection to the operative facts" would it ever be possible to establish specific jurisdiction in a tort case in a state other than the one in which the injury took place?

NOTE ON THE THREE-STEP ANALYSIS OF JURISDICTION UNDER INTERNATIONAL SHOE

Cases such as *Bristol-Myers Squibb* and *Moki Mac* make clear that what the two-step *International Shoe* analysis set forth in *Hanson*, p. 75, supra, and *World-Wide Volkswagen*, p. 80, supra, is actually a three-step analysis.

First, there must be a relevant contact between the defendant and the forum—one forged by the defendant's purposeful availment of the forum.

Second, if there is such contact, the court must assess relatedness by asking whether the plaintiff's claim arises from or relates to the defendant's contact with the forum. If relatedness is not satisfied—if the plaintiff's claim does not relate to the defendant's contact—the case can proceed only under general jurisdiction. This, in turn, is possible if the defendant is "essentially at home" in the forum. If the defendant is not at home in the forum, that state cannot exercise personal jurisdiction. *Bristol-Myers Squibb* is an example of such a case: the lack of relatedness meant there was no specific jurisdiction California, and the defendant was not essentially at home in California, which mean that state lacked general jurisdiction.

Third, if the relatedness requirement is satisfied, the court proceeds to assess whether jurisdiction in the forum would be fair or reasonable, weighing the fairness factors catalogued in *World-Wide Volkswagen*, p. 80, supra.

NOTE ON THE FORD MOTOR COMPANY CASES

In October 2020, the Supreme Court heard oral argument on two consolidated cases, each against the Ford Motor Company. The Court likely will not decide the cases before this book goes to press.

Ford is incorporated in Delaware and has its principal place of business in Michigan. It manufactures motor vehicles, which it sells to independently owned dealers. In Ford Motor Co. v. Bandemer, 931 N.W.2d 744 (Minn. 2019), the plaintiff, a passenger in a 1994 Ford Crown Victoria, was injured when the driver rammed the car into a snow plow on a Minnesota road and the air bag failed to deploy. Ford had designed the car in Michigan and assembled it in Canada. It was sold and delivered to an independent Ford dealership in North Dakota. From there, the vehicle was bought and sold several times over two decades. Ford was not involved in any of these resales. The car's fifth owner registered the car in Minnesota and drove the car during the accident.

The plaintiff sued Ford and the driver in state court in Minnesota, asserting negligence, product liability, and breach of warranty claims. The Minnesota Supreme Court upheld specific jurisdiction over Ford. First, Ford had forged contacts with Minnesota by collecting data on vehicle performance, used the data to improve performance, sold more than 2000 Crown Victorias and over 20,000 vehicles of all types through independent dealerships, and conducted advertising and marketing in Minnesota. Second, regarding relatedness, the court held that the plaintiff's claim "related to" Ford's contacts with Minnesota. Unlike the court in *Moki Mac*, the Minnesota court did not require a causal relationship between Ford's contacts and the plaintiff's claim. Third, fairness factors, including the state's interest in adjudicating claims arising on a Minnesota road, supported the exercise of jurisdiction.

The companion case, Ford Motor Co. v. Montana Eighth Judicial District Court, 442 P.3d 407 (Mont.2019), involved the wreck of a 1996 Ford Explorer in Montana. Ford manufactured the vehicle in Kentucky and sold it to an independent dealership in Washington. The dealership sold the vehicle to an Oregon consumer, after which it was bought and resold several times, without Ford's involvement. The Montana Supreme Court found a sufficient nexus between the plaintiff's claim and Ford's "extensive" activities in that state.

In March 2021, as this book went to press, the Court decided the Ford cases, upholding jurisdiction in both. Specific jurisdiction was proper because the claim "related to" defendant's forum activities; causation was not required. An Update Memorandum to professors provides an edited version of the case.

NOTE ON PERSONAL JURISDICTION IN FEDERAL COURT

Ordinarily, federal courts have the same territorial reach than their state court counterparts. This is a consequence of Federal Rule of Civil Procedure 4(k)(1)(A), which provides that federal district courts have personal jurisdiction over a defendant "who could be subjected to the jurisdiction of a court of general jurisdiction in the state in which the district court is located. . . ."

There are exceptions, however, to the rule that federal courts and state courts have the same territorial reach. A fair number of federal statutes authorize either "nationwide" or even "worldwide" service of process, by which Congress apparently means to allow personal jurisdiction over defendants in certain cases without regard to state boundaries. Some examples are: 15 U.S.C.A. § 22 (authorizing service on Clayton Act defendants "wherever [defendant] may be found"); 18 U.S.C.A. § 1915(d) (RICO actions); 42 U.S.C.A. § 9613(P) (CERCLA actions); Bankr. R. 7004(f); 15 U.S.C.A. § 78aa (Section 27 of the 1934 Securities Act); 29 U.S.C.A. § 1132(e)(2) (ERISA actions).

Federal Rule of Civil Procedure 4 itself, in some circumstances, authorizes a broader territorial reach for federal courts. Federal Rule 4(k)(2) provides that "[i]f the exercise of jurisdiction is consistent with the

Constitution and the laws of the United States [district courts have jurisdiction], with respect to claims arising under federal law, . . . over the person of any defendant who is not subject to the courts of the general jurisdiction of any state." (An older and more modest provision in Rule 4 provides for personal jurisdiction over certain ancillary parties in federal actions who can be served within 100 miles of the federal courthouse. F.R.C.P. 4(k)(1)(B).)

Most courts conclude that the party resisting jurisdiction under Rule 4(k)(2) has the burden with regard to the question of "negation"—that is, whether any state would have jurisdiction. Thus it becomes that party's burden to point the court to some other state that might have jurisdiction so that the court can assess whether that state's long-arm statute and the Fourteenth Amendment test—i.e., "minimum contacts" with that state—is met. If the party resisting jurisdiction does not carry this burden, the court then proceeds to the question of whether the constitutional test mandated by Rule 4(k)(2)—i.e., the question of whether jurisdiction would comport with the Fifth Amendment is met. This burden-shifting mechanism avoids requiring the party asserting jurisdiction and the court to show state-by-state that no other state would have jurisdiction.

These various statutes and rules authorizing broader personal jurisdiction for federal courts in some circumstances raise the constitutional question noted, but not resolved, by the Supreme Court. The personal jurisdiction of state courts is limited by the Due Process Clause of the Fourteenth Amendment; for federal courts, however, the relevant Due Process Clause is the one found in the Fifth Amendment. These special statutes and rules are effective in authorizing broader jurisdiction for federal courts only if the Fifth Amendment's limitations on jurisdiction are more relaxed than the parallel Fourteenth Amendment limitations.

Essentially, courts and commentators have taken three positions on the question. The broadest is that the Fifth Amendment allows for personal jurisdiction under a theory of "national contacts." Under this theory a defendant can be subjected to jurisdiction if the defendant has minimum contacts with the United States taken as a whole. This theory was advanced by Justices Stewart and Brennan in their dissent in Stafford v. Briggs, 444 U.S. 527, 100 S.Ct. 774, 63 L.Ed.2d 1 (1980). The majority's disposition of that case made it unnecessary to address the national contacts theory. At the other extreme, the Fifth and Fourteenth Amendment standards might be treated as identical, each requiring minimum contacts with the forum state. Cf. Republic of Panama v. BCCI Holdings, S.A., 119 F.3d 935, 942 (11th Cir.1997) (summarizing the competing views).

An emerging middle view is that the existence of national contacts presumptively, but not conclusively, establishes jurisdiction under the Fifth Amendment. If the defendant has minimum contacts with the United States taken as a whole, it becomes the defendant's burden to show that the chosen forum is sufficiently inconvenient that it will materially disadvantage the defendant in the trial of the case. A good example of this middle approach is Republic of Panama, supra. In that case, the defendant was being sued under RICO, a federal statute with a special service provision. The district court was located in Florida. The defendant had few relevant contacts with Florida, but ample contacts with the United States taken as a whole. The court held that the defendant's extensive east coast operations were enough to show that trial of the action in Florida would not prejudice the defendant, and thus the Fifth Amendment did not render jurisdiction unconstitutional.

An interesting use of FRCP 4(k)(2) occurred in Odilla Mutaka Mwani v. Osama Bin Laden, 417 F.3d 1 (D.C.Cir.2005), in which the court concluded that bin Laden's aggregate contacts with the U.S. were sufficient to establish personal jurisdiction over him on claims by various Kenyan victims who were injured in the notorious bombing of the U.S. embassy there.

C. CONTINUANCE OF JURISDICTION

RESTATEMENT, SECOND, CONFLICT OF LAWS:

§ 26. Continuance of Jurisdiction

If a state obtains judicial jurisdiction over a party to an action, the jurisdiction continues throughout all subsequent proceedings which arise out of the original cause of action. Reasonable notice and reasonable opportunity to be heard must be given the party at each new step in the proceeding.

Michigan Trust Co. v. Ferry

Supreme Court of the United States, 1913.
228 U.S. 346, 33 S.Ct. 550, 57 L.Ed. 867.

■ JUSTICE HOLMES delivered the opinion of the court:

These are suits brought in the Circuit Court for the District of Utah upon decrees of the Probate Court of Ottawa, Michigan. The defendant demurred to the complaints, the Circuit Court sustained the demurrers and gave judgments for the defendant, and these judgments were affirmed by the Circuit Court of Appeals. . . .

William M. Ferry died in 1867 domiciled in Ottawa County, Michigan. His will was proved, and the defendant, Edward P. Ferry, was appointed executor by the Ottawa Probate Court, qualified and entered upon his duties. In 1878 he removed to Utah and becoming incompetent was put under the guardianship of two sons, W. Mont Ferry and Edward S. Ferry, in 1892. In 1903 residuary legatees and devisees petitioned the Michigan Probate Court that the defendant be removed from his office of executor, that he be ordered to account for the unadministered residue of the estate and that the Michigan Trust Company be appointed administrator de bonis non with the will annexed. Notice of the petition and time and place of the hearing was given by publication and also was given to the defendant and his guardians personally in Utah. The guardians by order of the Utah court appeared and asked for the appointment of a guardian ad litem, which was made . . . There were various proceedings the end of which was that the plaintiff was appointed administrator de bonis non . . . and it was decreed that the defendant was indebted to the estate for $1,220,473.41. The defendant being entitled to one-fourth of the above sum as residuary legatee, he was declared liable for $915,355.08 and ordered to pay it over within sixty days to the Michigan Trust Company. . . .

Ordinarily jurisdiction over a person is based on the power of the sovereign asserting it to seize that person and imprison him to await the sovereign's pleasure. But when that power exists and is asserted by service at the beginning of a cause, or if the party submits to the jurisdiction in whatever form may be required, we dispense with the necessity of maintaining the physical power and attribute the same force to the judgment or decree whether the party remain within the jurisdiction or not. This is one of the decencies of civilization that no one would dispute. . . . This is true not only of ordinary actions but of proceedings like the present. It is within the power of a State to make the whole administration of the estate a single proceeding, to provide that one who has undertaken it within the jurisdiction shall be subject to the order of the court in the matter until the administration is closed by distribution, and, on the same principle, that he shall be required to account for and distribute all that he receives, by the order of the Probate Court. . . .

It follows from what we have said that a petition to the Probate Court that the defendant be ordered to account covered all his receipts as executor and that notice of the petition was notice that the accounting would have that scope. The decree upon the account was made with full jurisdiction and . . . could be sued upon . . . and was entitled to full faith and credit elsewhere. . . .

Judgment reversed.

NOTES

1.   In Fitzsimmons v. Johnson, 90 Tenn. 416, 17 S.W. 100 (1891), a decree of an Ohio court against the defendant, as executor qualified in Ohio, was enforced in Tennessee, even though the proceedings to reverse the initial judgment of the Ohio court, approving the defendant's account and discharging him, were instituted more than twenty years after the entry of that judgment, and the only service of process on the defendant, a nonresident of Ohio, was by publication. See also Blumle v. Kramer, 14 Okla. 366, 79 P. 215 (1904), involving jurisdiction to enter a judgment for a deficiency following a mortgage foreclosure, and after the defendant had moved away from the state.

2.   In Ohlquist v. Nordstrom, 143 Misc. 502, 257 N.Y.S. 711 (1932), aff'd, 238 App.Div. 766, 261 N.Y.S. 1039 (1933), aff'd, 262 N.Y. 696, 188 N.E. 125 (1933), A recovered a judgment in New York against B and C as joint tortfeasors, whereupon C removed his residence to Pennsylvania. B paid the entire judgment and began the present suit for contribution, serving C's

attorneys in New York and C personally outside the state. The service was held effective. Cf. New York Life Insurance Co. v. Dunlevy, p. 173, infra.

3.   Continuing jurisdiction is of great practical importance in the family law area. For instance, a federal statute gives continuing jurisdiction to state courts to make custody determinations as long as that state continues to be the residence of one or more of the parties. 28 U.S.C.A. § 1738A(d).

SECTION 3. JURISDICTION OVER "THINGS"

RESTATEMENT, SECOND, CONFLICT OF LAWS:

Chapter 3, Introductory Note to Topic 2:

INTRODUCTORY NOTE

    . . . [E]very valid exercise of judicial jurisdiction affects the interests of persons. It is possible, however, to affect the interests of persons in different ways, and it is convenient to divide the subject of judicial jurisdiction into three main categories: jurisdiction over persons, jurisdiction over things and jurisdiction over status. . . . When one or more of . . . [the various bases for the exercise of judicial jurisdiction over persons] exists, a personal judgment may be rendered against the defendant. The effect of such a judgment, if it is one for money, is to make the defendant a judgment debtor of the plaintiff. This debt may be enforced against any property in the state subject to execution which the defendant then owns or subsequently acquires. An action to recover this debt may likewise be maintained against the defendant either in the same state or elsewhere. A personal judgment may also take the form of an equitable decree ordering the defendant either to do something or to refrain from action. In such a case, the defendant may be punished for contempt if he fails to obey the court's order.

    Even though personal jurisdiction over the defendant is lacking, the state may affect any interests he may have in things subject to its jurisdiction. A judgment rendered in such a proceeding binds only the defendant's interests in the specific thing at which it is directed and thus has a more limited effect than a judgment rendered against the defendant personally. All that a defendant risks in a proceeding directed against a particular thing, if he is at no time personally subject to the judicial jurisdiction of the state, is the loss of his interests therein. An in personam judgment, on the other hand, may be enforced against any and all of his property which is not exempt from execution.

    Where a thing is subject to the judicial jurisdiction of a state, an action may be brought to affect the interests in the thing of all persons in the world. Such an action is commonly referred to as a proceeding in rem. Or, as is usually the case, the action may be brought to affect the interests in the thing of particular persons only, in which case it is commonly referred to as a proceeding quasi in rem. . . .

    Proceedings quasi in rem are of two types. In the first type the plaintiff asserts an interest in a thing, and seeks to have his interest established against the claim of a designated person or persons. Of this type are actions to recover possession of land or to establish title to land, such as an action of ejectment, or one to quiet title or to remove a cloud on title, where the court has jurisdiction to give the relief asked because of its power over the land even though it has no power over the adverse claimant. Of this type also is an action to foreclose a mortgage.

In the second type of proceeding quasi in rem, the plaintiff does not assert that he has an interest in the thing, but asserts a claim against the defendant personally and seeks, by attachment or garnishment, to apply the thing to the satisfaction of his claim against the defendant.

A classic statement of the nature of a proceeding in rem was provided by Justice Holmes in Tyler v. Judges of the Court of Registration, 175 Mass. 71, 76, 55 N.E. 812, 814 (1900):

> "If . . . [the object of the suit] is to bar indifferently all who might be minded to make an objection of any sort against the right sought to be established, and if anyone in the world has a right to be heard on the strength of alleging facts which, if true, show an inconsistent interest, the proceeding is in rem. . . . All proceedings, like all rights, are really against persons. Whether they are proceedings or rights in rem depends on the number of persons affected."

The traditional concept of jurisdiction over land was based on the theory that only the state where the land was located had power to deal with it effectively; hence, only the situs state was thought to have jurisdiction to issue decrees "directly" affecting title to land. However, some courts permitted themselves to issue decrees ordering the defendant to pay damages with regard to foreign real estate, or even to convey interests in land outside the state. The most famous example of the latter is Penn v. Lord Baltimore, 1 Ves.Sr. 444, 27 Eng.Rep. 1132 (Ch. 1750). The principle was approved in Massie v. Watts, 10 U.S. (6 Cranch) 148 (1810), with Chief Justice Marshall declaring that where the defendant "is liable to the plaintiff, either in consequence of contract, or as trustee, or as the holder of a legal title acquired by any species of mala fides practiced on the plaintiff, the principles of equity give a court jurisdiction wherever the person may be found, and the circumstance, that a question of title may be involved in the inquiry, and may even constitute the essential point on which the case depends, does not seem sufficient to arrest that jurisdiction."

NOTES

1. Should the fact that a great many people (or even "all the world") will be bound by the judgment make it possible to employ a more wholesale type of notification of the suit than if only one person is defendant? For the type of notice to adverse claimants, known and unknown, required by registration statutes, see McKinney's N.Y. Real

Property Law § 385. Generally, as to notice, see Mullane v. Central Hanover Bank & Trust Co., 339 U.S. 306, 70 S.Ct. 652 (1950), p. 192, infra. The Supreme Court has upheld state statutes providing that title to real property within the state may be determined in a suit in which a non-resident defendant is served only by publication. See Arndt v. Griggs, 134 U.S. 316, 10 S.Ct. 557 (1890). But such decisions seem questionable in the light of more recent cases.

2.   A buyer of land is entitled to a decree for the conveyance of land in the state of the situs if the court has been made competent to grant such relief, even though the vendor is served outside the state. Garfein v. McInnis, 248 N.Y. 261, 162 N.E. 73 (1928).

3.   Even though a court cannot directly affect interests in foreign land, it may exercise its personal jurisdiction over the parties before it to order appropriate relief. Incident to a divorce proceeding, for instance, a court may award real property in another state and, in the exercise of its equitable powers, compel one party to convey to the other. See Dority v. Dority, 645 P.2d 56, 58 (Utah 1982); Miller v. Miller, 109 Misc.2d 982, 441 N.Y.S.2d 339 (1981); Anno., Power of Divorce Court to Deal with Real Property Located in Another State, 34 A.L.R.3d 962 (1970). See also Hay, The Situs Rule in European and American Conflicts Law—Comparative Notes, in: Hay and Hoeflich (eds.), Property Law and Legal Education— Essays in Honor of John E. Cribbet 109 (1988). See Chapter 5, Sec. 3 for discussion of whether equitable decrees affecting foreign land are entitled to recognition at the situs under Full Faith and Credit principles.

4.   A deed to land, executed by the owner in accordance with a decree of a foreign court, will be given effect as a valid conveyance in the state where the land lies. Deschenes v. Tallman, 248 N.Y. 33, 161 N.E. 321 (1928). Where a court, having jurisdiction over the defendant, orders a conveyance of foreign land, what effect will be given to the decree in the state where the land is located, if no conveyance is actually made? See *Fall v. Eastin*, p. 328, infra.

Combs v. Combs

Supreme Court of Kentucky, 1933.
249 Ky. 155, 60 S.W.2d 368, 89 A.L.R. 1095.

■ THOMAS, J. The appellant, A.T. Combs, who was one of the defendants below, became indebted to the appellees and plaintiffs below, in a considerable sum. A lien to secure it was created on a tract of land in Washington county, Ark. Plaintiffs were and are residents of Kentucky and of other states, and all of them were and are nonresidents of the state of Arkansas. Appellant's brother, who was a joint defendant with him, is a resident of this commonwealth, and this action was filed by plaintiffs in the Breathitt circuit court against appellant and his brother to obtain a personal judgment against them for the amount of the debt. Personal process could not [be] and was not served on appellant for a considerable time after he was proceeded against and made a defendant in the action. During that time he filed an equity action in the chancery court of Washington county, Ark., in which the land in lien was situated, against the plaintiffs in this action, and proceeded against them exclusively by constructive process in accordance with the prescribed practice of the Arkansas forum. In his petition in that court he set forth the facts creating the indebtedness, as well as the lien on his land to secure it, and stated that he had paid part of the debt, leaving a named sum as the balance due, and that the lien to secure it was a cloud on the title to his land which he desired released, and he asked that court to enter judgment fixing the amount of the balance due by him to plaintiffs in this action (but defendants in that one) and to permit him to pay that amount into that court to be followed by a decree canceling the lien on his land. The Arkansas practice for that kind of procedure was followed, and upon submission, without any of the defendants therein entering their appearance in any manner, that court adjudged that plaintiff therein, appellant herein, was indebted to the defendants in that action (plaintiffs herein) in the sum admitted in his petition, and ordered him to pay it to the master commissioner of that court which he did, and when done, that the lien on his land should be released. Appellant then procured a copy of that proceeding and filed his answer in this action relying upon the Arkansas judgment in bar of a recovery herein. The court disallowed that defense and rendered judgment against appellant for the amount it found to be due plaintiffs, and to reverse it defendant prosecutes this appeal.

The only argument made, and the only possible one that could be made, against the propriety of the judgment appealed from is that the Arkansas judgment, under the provisions of section 1 of article 4 of the Federal Constitution, is entitled to full faith and credit in this state the same as if it had been rendered by a court of competent jurisdiction in this state, and that, since it is argued that the Arkansas court had jurisdiction to render the judgment relied on as a defense herein, it is binding on plaintiffs, and that they may not impeach it in this collateral attack. In making that argument, counsel assumes the correctness of the crucial point in this case, and we think erroneously so. It is, that the Arkansas court had jurisdiction, upon constructive process alone, to finally and conclusively adjudge the amount of plaintiff's debt owed to them by defendant, and then to assume to collect it through its master commissioner, or, more appropriately, to direct plaintiff in the Arkansas judgment to discharge it by paying the amount found to be due to the court's master commissioner, and to thereby completely discharge defendant from all further liability to plaintiffs. The error in the assumption of counsel for defendant lies in their failure to appraise and comprehend the nature of the relief granted by the Arkansas judgment and relied on as a defense in this case; confusing it with the power and jurisdiction of that court to deal with and adjudicate concerning the res within its jurisdiction, which in this case was the land in lien for plaintiff's debt.

[The court first questioned, without deciding, whether, under the doctrines of equity, an appropriate case for a bill to remove a cloud on title was made out in the Arkansas proceeding, since the alleged cloud was created by the debtor himself.]

. . . [I]n this case, conceding that there was no doubt of the proper cloud upon defendant's title to his Arkansas land so as to authorize the action in that state to remove it, the judgment rendered by the Arkansas court would be obligatory on plaintiffs herein in so far as it released their lien upon the land in that state. But, when the court undertook to grant additional relief strictly in personam, it transgressed its jurisdiction so as to render such unauthorized additional relief of no force and effect whatever. That relief in this case was the adjudication that defendant herein had paid to plaintiffs herein any part of his debt and thereby discharged a part of his obligation to them, and that the court could and did fix the amount due from him to plaintiffs herein and directed its payment to the commissioner of that court. The rights so attempted to be adjudicated were and are strictly personal. It may be that the Arkansas court was vested with authority to lift the lien from the land involved, and for that purpose to incidentally determine the amount of the lien, and whether or not it had been paid, but the only binding effect of such adjudications would be that of releasing the lien as an incumbrance upon the title to the res. Such adjudications in so far as they affected the personal obligations and rights of the parties were and are not binding upon plaintiffs herein, nor do they operate as a res adjudicata estoppel in any future action. . . .

Wherefore the judgment is affirmed.

NOTES

1.   If the creditors, after the entry of the Arkansas judgment, sued the debtor in Arkansas for the balance alleged to be due, and the Arkansas court held the prior judgment to be res judicata of the plaintiff's rights, would this constitute a denial of due process? On the conclusiveness of a judgment quasi in rem, see Restatement, Second, Judgments §§ 30, 32 (1982).

2.   Freeman v. Alderson, 119 U.S. 185, 7 S.Ct. 165 (1886) determined that, in an action to try title to real estate and obtain a partition thereof against a non-resident defendant served only by publication, a personal judgment for costs could not be entered. Similarly, in State ex rel. Truitt v. District Court, 44 N.M. 16, 96 P.2d 710 (1939), a non-resident lessee of New Mexico land, sued by his sublessee for reformation of the lease, was held not subject to suit in New Mexico when notified by mail outside the state. Would there not have been jurisdiction over the non-resident in these cases under a modern statute taking advantage of all constitutionally permissible bases of personal jurisdiction, including "ownership, possession or use of real estate situated within the state?"

Harris v. Balk

Supreme Court of the United States, 1905.
198 U.S. 215, 25 S.Ct. 625, 49 L.Ed. 1023.

[Harris, a North Carolina domiciliary, was indebted to Balk, another North Carolina domiciliary, in the amount of $180. Balk in turn owed more than $300 to Epstein, who lived in Baltimore, Maryland. One day Harris came to Baltimore for a short visit and while there was served in hand by Epstein with a writ attaching the debt which Harris owed Balk. In addition, in accordance with the Maryland practice, process against Balk was delivered to a Baltimore sheriff and then placed at the court house door. Harris did not contest the garnishment action and consented to the entry against him of a payment for $180 which he paid. Thereafter in North Carolina, Balk sued Harris on his debt. A judgment in Balk's favor was affirmed by the North Carolina Supreme Court on the ground that Maryland had no jurisdiction to garnish the debt Harris owed Balk "because Harris was but temporarily in the state, and the situs of the debt was in North Carolina."]

■ JUSTICE PECKHAM . . . delivered the opinion of the Court.

. . . Attachment is the creature of the local law . . . If there be a law of the State providing for the attachment of the debt, then if the garnishee be found in that State, and process be personally served upon him therein, we think the court thereby acquires jurisdiction over him, and can garnish the debt due from him to the debtor of the plaintiff and condemn it, provided the garnishee could himself be sued by his creditor in that State. We do not see how the question of jurisdiction vel non can properly be made to depend upon the so-called original situs of the debt, or upon the character of the stay of the garnishee, whether temporary or permanent, in the State where the attachment is issued. Power over the person of the garnishee confers jurisdiction on the courts of the State where the writ issues. Blackstone v. Miller, 188 U.S. 189, 206. If, while temporarily there, his creditor might sue him there and recover the debt, then he is liable to process of garnishment, no matter where the situs of the debt was originally. . . . The obligation of the debtor to pay his debt clings to and accompanies him wherever he goes. He is as much bound to pay his debt in a foreign state when therein sued upon his obligation by his creditor, as he was in the state where the debt was contracted. We speak of ordinary debts, such as the one in this case. . . . [P]ossession cannot be taken of a debt or of the obligation to pay it, as tangible property might be taken possession of. Notice to the debtor (garnishee) of the commencement of the suit, and notice not to pay his creditor, is all that can be given, whether the garnishee be a mere casual and temporary comer, or a resident of the State where the attachment is laid. His obligation to pay to his creditor is thereby arrested and a lien created upon the debt itself. Cahoon v. Morgan, 38 Vermont 236; National Fire Ins. Co. v. Chambers, 53 N.J.Eq. 468, 483. We can see no reason why the attachment could not be thus laid, provided the creditor of the garnishee could himself sue in that State and its laws permitted the attachment. . . .

It . . . appears that Balk could have sued Harris in Maryland to recover his debt, notwithstanding the temporary character of Harris' stay there; it also appears that the municipal law of Maryland permits the debtor of the principal debtor to be garnished . . .

It seems to us, therefore, that the judgment against Harris in Maryland, condemning the $180 which he owed to Balk, was a valid judgment, because the court had jurisdiction over the garnishee by personal service of process within the State of Maryland.

It ought to be and it is the object of courts to prevent the payment of any debt twice over. Thus, . . . Harris . . . should have the right to plead his payment under the Maryland judgment. It is objected, however, that the payment by Harris to Epstein was not under legal compulsion. Harris in truth owed the debt to Balk, which was attached by Epstein. He had, therefore, as we have seen, no defense to set up against the attachment of the debt. Jurisdiction over him personally had been obtained by the Maryland court. As he was absolutely without defense, there was no reason why he should not consent to a judgment impounding the debt . . . There was no merely voluntary payment within the meaning of that phrase as applicable here.

[Justice Peckham went on to state that it is the garnishee's duty to take reasonable steps to notify his creditor of the pendency of the garnishment proceedings "so that the creditor may have the opportunity to defend himself against the claim of the person suing out the attachment." It did not appear that Harris had given Balk such notice and therefore his payment of the garnishment judgment would not under ordinary circumstances have constituted a defense to Balk's action against him. This was not true, however, in this particular case, because Balk did receive notice of the garnishment judgment shortly after its entry and under the peculiar Maryland practice had a year's time following such entry to establish that he was not indebted to Epstein in the amount claimed.]

The judgment of the Supreme Court of North Carolina must be reversed and the cause remanded for further proceedings not inconsistent with the opinion of this court.

Reversed.

■ JUSTICE HARLAN and JUSTICE DAY dissenting.

NOTES

1.   The reasoning and result *of Harris v. Balk* were severely questioned and perhaps overruled in *Shaffer v. Heitner*, n. 39, p. 173, infra. But its influence, if not its authority, endures. It gave constitutional approval to garnishment proceedings.

2. Garnishment proceedings present another constitutional issue related to due process. Garnishment, and other provisional remedies, implicate a defendant's property interests, and thus require minimally fair procedures relative to their imposition. The seminal Supreme Court case is Sniadach v. Family Finance Corp. of Bay View, 395 U.S. 337 (1969). In *Sniadach* the Supreme Court struck down as violative of due process provisions of the Wisconsin garnishment procedure under which wages are frozen when process in a garnishment action is served upon the employer of the alleged debtor and the latter "without any opportunity to be heard and to tender any defense he may have, whether it be fraud or otherwise" is thereby deprived of his earned wages until after the termination of the creditor's action against him. For essentially similar reasons the Georgia garnishment provisions were declared unconstitutional in North Georgia Finishing, Inc. v. Di-Chem, Inc., 419 U.S. 601 (1975).

In Connecticut v. Doehr, 501 U.S. 1 (1991), a tort plaintiff in a state court case obtained prejudgment attachment of $75,000 of the defendant's real estate through an ex parte proceeding. The proceeding, permitted by state statute, took place before the defendant had been given notice of the lawsuit. The defendant's remedy under the statute would have been a proceeding to attempt to set aside the attachment. A unanimous Court held that the Connecticut state was unconstitutional because the risk of an erroneous deprivation of the defendant's property interests was too high to allow for a post-deprivation, instead of a pre-deprivation, hearing. Four members of the Supreme Court also opined that the procedures such as the one authorized by the Connecticut statute would also require the defendant to be able to release his property by the posting of a bond. There was no majority opinion on this point, however, as two other justices thought that resolution of this question should await another case. In subsequent proceedings, however, the Second Circuit determined that Doehr was not entitled to recover damages for the unconstitutional attachment of his property, because he could not show that the constitutional violation was reckless or committed in bad faith. Pinsky v. Duncan, 79 F.3d 306 (2d Cir.1996).

Provisional remedies are also subject to non-constitutional limitations. In Grupo Mexicano de Desarrollo, S.A. v. Alliance Bond Fund, 527 U.S. 308 (1999), the Supreme Court, dividing five to four, held that a federal district court could not, in an action for money damages, issue a preliminary injunction to prevent the transfer of the assets of the defendant (a Mexican company). Although it seemed likely that the plaintiffs (American companies that had loaned the Mexican defendant millions of dollars) would not be able to recover anything without provisional relief to prevent the defendant's assets being paid to other creditors, the majority held that traditional principles of equity did not countenance such relief without a preexisting lien or equitable interest in the defendant's assets. Although *Grupo Mexicano de Desarrollo* held that federal courts have no independent power to grant prejudgment relief to protect assets in which the plaintiff does not claim a lien or equitable interest, Federal Rule of Civil Procedure 64 provides that "all remedies providing for seizure of person or property for the purpose of securing satisfaction of the judgment ultimately to be entered in the action are available under the circumstances and in the manner provided by the law of the state in which the district court is held. . . ."

3. Although the broad conception of "property" embraced by *Harris v. Balk* expanded quasi-in-rem jurisdiction, it did not solve all jurisdictional problems. Several years after *Harris*, in New York Life Insurance Co. v. Dunlevy, 241 U.S. 518, 36 S.Ct. 613 (1916), the Supreme Court held that an earlier garnishment proceeding could not bind an out-of-state rival claimant to an insurance policy, essentially exposing the insurance company to double liability on the policy, with no forum in which to bind both of the claimants. The difficulty encountered in obtaining jurisdiction over all claimants in state proceedings led to the adoption and gradual extension of federal interpleader proceedings.

The federal interpleader statutes are 28 U.S.C. §§ 1335, 1397, 2361. 28 U.S.C. § 1335 gives the federal district courts subject matter jurisdiction over interpleader actions in which $500 or more is at stake and two or more of the rival claimants have differing state citizenships. Interpleader actions usually begin with the stakeholder (often an insurance company) filing a complaint in interpleader to force the rival claimants to the "stake" (often an insurance policy) to litigate their rival claims in that forum. To avoid the problem, presented in *Dunlevy* and like cases, of obtaining personal jurisdiction over the claimants, 28 U.S.C. § 2361 allows district courts to have process served "where the claimants reside or may be found." These so-called "nationwide" service-of-process statutes, bring into play the more relaxed jurisdictional standards of the Fifth Amendment, and thus avoid the more confining requirement of minimum contacts with the forum state imposed by the Fourteenth Amendment. Federal Rule of Civil Procedure 22 also allows for interpleader actions, though Rule 22 interpleader actions are subject to the usual jurisdictional requirements of personal jurisdiction over all of the unwilling parties and full diversity of citizenship as between the stakeholder and the claimants. Rule 22's utility is primarily in handling cases in which the claimants are not of diverse citizenship (one of the requirements for statutory interpleader), but the claimants are of diverse citizenship with respect to the stakeholder.

Shaffer v. Heitner

Supreme Court of the United States, 1977.
433 U.S. 186, 97 S.Ct. 2569, 53 L.Ed.2d 683.

■ JUSTICE MARSHALL delivered the opinion of the Court.

The controversy in this case concerns the constitutionality of a Delaware statute that allows a court of that State to take jurisdiction of a lawsuit by sequestering any property of the defendant that happens to be located in Delaware. . . .

I

Appellee Heitner, a nonresident of Delaware, is the owner of one share of stock in the Greyhound Corporation, a business incorporated under the laws of Delaware with its principal place of business in Phoenix, Ariz. On May 22, 1974, he filed a shareholder's derivative suit in the Court of Chancery for New Castle County, Del., in which he named as defendants Greyhound, its wholly owned subsidiary Greyhound Lines, Inc., and 28 present or former officers or directors of one or both of the corporations. In essence, Heitner alleged that the individual defendants had violated their duties to Greyhound by causing it and its subsidiary to engage in actions that resulted in the corporations being held liable for substantial damages in a private antitrust suit and a large fine in a criminal contempt action. The activities which led to these penalties took place in Oregon.

Simultaneously with his complaint, Heitner filed a motion for an order of sequestration of the Delaware property of the individual defendants pursuant to 10 Del.C. § 366. . . . The requested sequestration order was signed the day the motion was filed. Pursuant to that order, the sequestrator "seized" approximately 82,000 shares of Greyhound common stock belonging to 19 of the defendants, and options belonging to another two defendants. . . . So far as the record shows, none of the certificates representing the seized property was physically present in Delaware. The stock was considered to be in Delaware, and so subject to seizure, by virtue of 8 Del.C. § 169, which makes Delaware the situs of ownership of all stock in Delaware corporations.

All 28 defendants were notified of the initiation of the suit by certified mail directed to their last known addresses and by publication in a New Castle County newspaper. The 21 defendants whose property was seized (hereafter referred to as appellants) responded by entering a special appearance [asserting] that under the rule of International Shoe Co. v. Washington, 326 U.S. 310 (1945), they did not have sufficient contacts with Delaware to sustain the jurisdiction of that State's courts. . . .

II

The Delaware courts rejected appellants' jurisdictional challenge by noting that this suit was brought as a quasi in rem proceeding. Since quasi in rem jurisdiction is traditionally based on attachment or seizure of property present in the jurisdiction, not on contacts between the defendant and the State, the courts considered appellants' claimed lack of contacts with Delaware to be unimportant. This categorical analysis assumes the continued soundness of the conceptual structure founded on the century-old case of Pennoyer v. Neff, 95 U.S. 714 (1877).

[Justice Marshall here discussed the *Pennoyer* case and noted that it based "authority to adjudicate . . . on the jurisdiction's power over either persons or property." He stated that with respect to judicial jurisdiction over persons the *Pennoyer* rule has been supplanted by the rule of *International Shoe*. He continued:]

No equally dramatic change has occurred in the law governing jurisdiction in rem. There have, however, been intimations that the collapse of the in personam wing of Pennoyer has not left that decision unweakened as a foundation for in rem jurisdiction. Well-reasoned lower court opinions have questioned the proposition that the presence of property in a State gives that State jurisdiction to adjudicate rights to the property regardless of the relationship of the underlying dispute and the property owner to the forum. [Citations omitted.]. The overwhelming majority of commentators have also rejected Pennoyer's premise that a proceeding "against" property is not a proceeding against the owners of that property. Accordingly, they urge that the "traditional notions of fair play and substantial justice" that govern a State's power to adjudicate in personam should also govern its power to adjudicate personal rights to property located in the State. [Citations omitted.] . . .

Although this Court has not addressed this argument directly, we have held that property cannot be subjected to a court's judgment unless reasonable and appropriate efforts have been made to give the property owners actual notice of the action. Schroeder v. City of New York, 371 U.S. 208 (1962); Walker v. City of Hutchinson, 352 U.S. 112 (1956); Mullane v. Central Hanover Bank & Trust Co., 339 U.S. 306 (1950). This conclusion recognizes, contrary to Pennoyer, that an adverse judgment in rem directly affects the property owner by divesting him of his rights in the property before the court. . . .

III

The case for applying to jurisdiction in rem the same test of "fair play and substantial justice" as governs assertions of jurisdiction in personam is simple and straightforward. It is premised on recognition that "[t]he phrase, 'judicial jurisdiction over a thing,' is a customary elliptical way of referring to jurisdiction over the interests of persons in a thing." Restatement (Second) of Conflict of Laws § 56, introductory note. This recognition leads to the conclusion that in order to justify an exercise of jurisdiction in rem, the basis for jurisdiction must be sufficient to justify exercising "jurisdiction over the interests of persons in a thing." The standard for determining whether an exercise of jurisdiction over the interests of persons is consistent with the Due Process Clause is the minimum contacts standard elucidated in International Shoe.

This argument, of course, does not ignore the fact that the presence of property in a State may bear on the existence of jurisdiction by providing contacts among the forum State, the defendant, and the litigation. For example, when claims to the property itself are the source of the underlying controversy between the plaintiff and the defendant, it would be unusual for the State where the property is located not to have jurisdiction. In such cases, the defendant's claim to property located in the State would normally indicate that he expected to benefit from the

State's protection of his interest. The State's strong interests in assuring the marketability of property within its borders and in providing a procedure for peaceful resolution of disputes about the possession of that property would also support jurisdiction, as would the likelihood that important records and witnesses will be found in the State.[28] The presence of property may also favor jurisdiction in cases, such as suits for injury suffered on the land of an absentee owner, where the defendant's ownership of the property is conceded but the cause of action is otherwise related to rights and duties growing out of that ownership.

It appears, therefore, that jurisdiction over many types of actions which now are or might be brought in rem would not be affected by a holding that any assertion of state court jurisdiction must satisfy the International Shoe standard.[30] For the type of *quasi in rem* action typified by Harris v. Balk and the present case, however, accepting the proposed analysis would result in significant change. These are cases where the property which now serves as the basis for state court jurisdiction is completely unrelated to the plaintiff's cause of action. Thus, although the presence of the defendant's property in a State might suggest the existence of other ties among the defendant, the State, and the litigation, the presence of the property alone would not support the State's jurisdiction. If those other ties did not exist, cases over which the State is now thought to have jurisdiction could not be brought in that forum.

Since acceptance of the International Shoe test would most affect this class of cases, we examine the arguments against adopting that standard as they relate to this category of litigation. Before doing so, however, we note that this type of case also presents the clearest illustration of the argument in favor of assessing assertions of jurisdiction by a single standard. For in cases such as *Harris* and this one, the only role played by the property is to provide the basis for bringing the defendant into court. Indeed, the express purpose of the Delaware sequestration procedure is to compel the defendant to enter a personal appearance. In such cases, if a direct assertion of personal jurisdiction over the defendant would violate the Constitution, it would seem that an indirect assertion of that jurisdiction should be equally impermissible.

The primary rationale for treating the presence of property as a sufficient basis for jurisdiction to adjudicate claims over which the State would not have jurisdiction if International Shoe applied is that a wrongdoer "should not be able to avoid payment of his obligations by the expedient of removing his assets to a place where he is not subject to an

---

[28] We do not suggest that these illustrations include all the factors that may affect the decision, nor that the factors we have mentioned are necessarily decisive.

[30] Smit, The Enduring Utility of In Rem Rules: A Lasting Legacy of Pennoyer v. Neff, 48 Brooklyn L.Rev. 600 (1977). We do not suggest that jurisdictional doctrines other than those discussed in text, such as the particularized rules governing adjudications of status, are inconsistent with the standard of fairness. . . .

in personam suit." Restatement (Second) of Conflicts § 66, comment a. . . . This justification, however, does not explain why jurisdiction should be recognized without regard to whether the property is present in the State because of an effort to avoid the owner's obligations. Nor does it support jurisdiction to adjudicate the underlying claim. At most, it suggests that a State in which property is located should have jurisdiction to attach that property, by use of proper procedures, as security for a judgment being sought in a forum where the litigation can be maintained consistently with International Shoe. . . . Moreover, we know of nothing to justify the assumption that a debtor can avoid paying his obligations by removing his property to a State in which his creditor cannot obtain personal jurisdiction over him. The Full Faith and Credit Clause, after all, makes the valid in personam judgment of one State enforceable in all other States.

It might also be suggested that allowing in rem jurisdiction avoids the uncertainty inherent in the International Shoe standard and assures a plaintiff of a forum.[37]. . . We believe, however, that the fairness standard of International Shoe can be easily applied in the vast majority of cases. Moreover, when the existence of jurisdiction in a particular forum under International Shoe is unclear, the cost of simplifying the litigation by avoiding the jurisdictional question may be the sacrifice of "fair play and substantial justice." That cost is too high. . . .

We are left, then, to consider the significance of the long history of jurisdiction based solely on the presence of property in a State. Although the theory that territorial power is both essential to and sufficient for jurisdiction has been undermined, we have never held that the presence of property in a State does not automatically confer jurisdiction over the owner's interest in that property. This history must be considered as supporting the proposition that jurisdiction based solely on the presence of property satisfies the demands of due process, . . . but it is not decisive. . . . The fiction that an assertion of jurisdiction over property is anything but an assertion of jurisdiction over the owner of the property supports an ancient form without substantial modern justification. Its continued acceptance would serve only to allow state court jurisdiction that is fundamentally unfair to the defendant.

We therefore conclude that all assertions of state court jurisdiction must be evaluated according to the standards set forth in International Shoe and its progeny.[39]

---

[37] This case does not raise, and we therefore do not consider, the question whether the presence of a defendant's property in a State is a sufficient basis for jurisdiction when no other forum is available to the plaintiff.

[39] It would not be fruitful for us to reexamine the facts of cases decided on the rationales of *Pennoyer* and *Harris* to determine whether jurisdiction might have been sustained under the standard we adopt today. To the extent that prior decisions are inconsistent with this standard, they are overruled.

IV

The Delaware courts based their assertion of jurisdiction in this case solely on the statutory presence of appellants' property in Delaware. Yet that property is not the subject matter of this litigation, nor is the underlying cause of action related to the property. Appellants' holdings in Greyhound do not, therefore, provide contacts with Delaware sufficient to support the jurisdiction of that State's courts over appellants. If it exists, that jurisdiction must have some other foundation.

Appellee Heitner did not allege and does not now claim that appellants have ever set foot in Delaware. Nor does he identify any act related to his cause of action as having taken place in Delaware. Nevertheless, he contends that appellants' positions as directors and officers of a corporation chartered in Delaware provide sufficient "contacts, ties, or relations," International Shoe Co. v. Washington, supra, at 319, with that State to give its courts jurisdiction over appellants in this stockholder's derivative action. This argument is based primarily on what Heitner asserts to be the strong interest of Delaware in supervising the management of a Delaware corporation. That interest is said to derive from the role of Delaware law in establishing the corporation and defining the obligations owed to it by its officers and directors. In order to protect this interest, appellee concludes, Delaware's courts must have jurisdiction over corporate fiduciaries such as appellants.

This argument is undercut by the failure of the Delaware Legislature to assert the state interest appellee finds so compelling. Delaware law bases jurisdiction not on appellants' status as corporate fiduciaries, but rather on the presence of their property in the State. Although the sequestration procedure used here may be most frequently used in derivative suits against officers and directors, . . . the authorizing statute evinces no specific concern with such actions. Sequestration can be used in any suit against a nonresident, . . . , and reaches corporate fiduciaries only if they happen to own interests in a Delaware corporation, or other property in the State. But as Heitner's failure to secure jurisdiction over seven of the defendants named in his complaint demonstrates, there is no necessary relationship between holding a position as a corporate fiduciary and owning stock or other interests in the corporation. If Delaware perceived its interest in securing jurisdiction over corporate fiduciaries to be as great as Heitner suggests, we would expect it to have enacted a statute more clearly designed to protect that interest.

Moreover, even if Heitner's assessment of the importance of Delaware's interest is accepted, his argument fails to demonstrate that Delaware is a fair forum for this litigation. The interest appellee has identified may support the application of Delaware law to resolve any controversy over appellants' actions in their capacities as officers and directors. But [in Hanson v. Denckla, p. 75, supra] we . . . rejected the argument that if a State's law can properly be applied to a dispute, its courts necessarily have jurisdiction over the parties to that dispute. . . .

Appellee suggests that by accepting positions as officers or directors of a Delaware corporation, appellants performed the acts required by Hanson v. Denckla. He notes that Delaware law provides substantial benefits to corporate officers and directors, and that these benefits were at least in part the incentive for appellants to assume their positions. It is, he says, "only fair and just" to require appellants, in return for these benefits, to respond in the State of Delaware when they are accused of misusing their powers. . . .

But like Heitner's first argument, this line of reasoning establishes only that it is appropriate for Delaware law to govern the obligations of appellants to Greyhound and its stockholders. It does not demonstrate that appellants have "purposefully avail[ed themselves] of the privilege of conducting activities within the forum State," Hanson v. Denckla, supra, at 253, in a way that would justify bringing them before a Delaware tribunal. Appellants have simply had nothing to do with the State of Delaware. Moreover, appellants had no reason to expect to be haled before a Delaware court. Delaware, unlike some States, has not enacted a statute that treats acceptance of a directorship as consent to jurisdiction in the State. . . . Appellants, who were not required to acquire interests in Greyhound in order to hold their positions, did not by acquiring those interests surrender their right to be brought to judgment only in States with which they had had "minimum contacts." . . .

. . . The judgment of the Delaware Supreme Court must, therefore, be reversed.

■ JUSTICE REHNQUIST took no part in the consideration or decision of this case.

■ JUSTICE POWELL, concurring.

I agree that the principles of International Shoe Co. v. Washington, 326 U.S. 310 (1945), should be extended to govern assertions of in rem as well as in personam jurisdiction in state court. I also agree that neither the statutory presence of appellants' stock in Delaware nor their positions as directors and officers of a Delaware corporation can provide sufficient contacts to support the Delaware courts' assertion of jurisdiction in this case.

I would explicitly reserve judgment, however, on whether the ownership of some forms of property whose situs is indisputably and permanently located within a State may, without more, provide the contacts necessary to subject a defendant to jurisdiction within the State to the extent of the value of the property. In the case of real property, in particular, preservation of the common law concept of quasi in rem jurisdiction arguably would avoid the uncertainty of the general International Shoe standard without significant cost to " 'traditional notions of fair play and substantial justice.' " . . .

Subject to that reservation, I join the opinion of the Court.

■ JUSTICE STEVENS, concurring in the judgment.

The Due Process Clause affords protection against "judgments without notice." . . . Throughout our history the acceptable exercise of in rem and quasi in rem jurisdiction has included a procedure giving reasonable assurance that actual notice of the particular claim will be conveyed to the defendant. Thus, publication, notice by registered mail, or extraterritorial personal service has been as essential ingredient of any procedure that serves as a substitute for personal service within the jurisdiction.

The requirement of fair notice also, I believe, includes fair warning that a particular activity may subject a person to the jurisdiction of a foreign sovereign. If I visit another State, or acquire real estate or open a bank account in it, I knowingly assume some risk that the State will exercise its power over my property or my person while there. My contact with the State, though minimal, gives rise to predictable risks.

Perhaps the same consequences should flow from the purchase of stock of a corporation organized under the laws of a foreign nation, because to some limited extent one's property and affairs then become subject to the laws of the nation of domicile of the corporation. As a matter of international law, that suggestion might be acceptable because a foreign investment is sufficiently unusual to make it appropriate to require the investor to study the ramifications of his decision. But a purchase of securities in the domestic market is an entirely different matter.

One who purchases shares of stock on the open market can hardly be expected to know that he has thereby become subject to suit in a forum remote from his residence and unrelated to the transaction. As a practical matter, the Delaware sequestration statute creates an unacceptable risk of judgment without notice. Unlike the 49 other States, Delaware treats the place of incorporation as the situs of the stock, even though both the owner and the custodian of the shares are elsewhere. Moreover, Delaware denies the defendant the opportunity to defend the merits of the suit unless he subjects himself to the unlimited jurisdiction of the court. Thus, it coerces a defendant either to submit to personal jurisdiction in a forum which could not otherwise obtain such jurisdiction or to lose the securities which have been attached. If its procedure were upheld, Delaware would, in effect, impose a duty of inquiry on every purchaser of securities in the national market. For unless the purchaser ascertains both the State of incorporation of the company whose shares he is buying, and also the idiosyncrasies of its law, he may be assuming an unknown risk of litigation. I therefore agree with the Court that on the record before us no adequate basis for jurisdiction exists and that the Delaware statute is unconstitutional on its face.

How the Court's opinion may be applied in other contexts is not entirely clear to me. . . . My uncertainty as to the reach of the opinion, and my fear that it purports to decide a great deal more than is necessary to dispose of this case, persuade me merely to concur in the judgment.

■ JUSTICE BRENNAN, concurring and dissenting.

I join Parts I–III of the Court's opinion. I fully agree that the minimum-contacts analysis developed in International Shoe Co. v. Washington, 326 U.S. 310 (1945), represents a far more sensible construct for the exercise of state court jurisdiction than the patchwork of legal and factual fictions that has been generated from the decision in Pennoyer v. Neff, 95 U.S. 714 (1877). It is precisely because the inquiry into minimum contacts is now of such overriding importance, however, that I must respectfully dissent from Part IV of the Court's opinion. . . .

. . . I am convinced that as a general rule a state forum has jurisdiction to adjudicate a shareholder derivative action centering on the conduct and policies of the directors and officers of a corporation chartered by that State. Unlike the Court, I therefore would not foreclose Delaware from asserting jurisdiction over appellants were it persuaded to do so on the basis of minimum contacts.

It is well settled that a derivative lawsuit as presented here does not inure primarily to the benefit of the named plaintiff. Rather, the primary beneficiaries are the corporation and its owners, the shareholders. . . .

Viewed in this light, the chartering State has an unusually powerful interest in insuring the availability of a convenient forum for litigating claims involving a possible multiplicity of defendant fiduciaries and for vindicating the State's substantive policies regarding the management of its domestic corporations. I believe that our cases fairly establish that the State's valid substantive interests are important considerations in assessing whether it constitutionally may claim jurisdiction over a given cause of action. . . .

To be sure, the Court is not blind to these considerations. It notes that the State's interests "may support the application of Delaware law to resolve any controversy over appellants' actions in their capacities as officers and directors." . . . But this, the Court argues, pertains to choice of law, not jurisdiction. I recognize that the jurisdictional and choice-of-law inquiries are not identical. Hanson v. Denckla, 357 U.S. 235, 254 (1958). But I would not compartmentalize thinking in this area quite so rigidly as it seems to me the Court does today, for both inquiries "are often closely related and to a substantial degree depend upon similar considerations." Id., at 258, 78 S.Ct., at 1242 (Black, J., dissenting). In either case an important linchpin is the extent of contacts between the controversy, the parties, and the forum state. While constitutional limitations on the choice of law are by no means settled, see, e.g., Home Ins. Co. v. Dick, 281 U.S. 397 (1930), important considerations certainly include the expectancies of the parties and the fairness of governing the defendants' acts and behavior by rules of conduct created by a given jurisdiction. See, e.g., Restatement (Second) Choice of Law § 6. These same factors bear upon the propriety of a State's exercising jurisdiction over a legal dispute. At the minimum, the decision that it is fair to bind a defendant by a State's laws and rules should prove to be highly relevant to the fairness of permitting that same State to accept jurisdiction for adjudicating the controversy.

Furthermore, I believe that practical considerations argue in favor of seeking to bridge the distance between the choice-of-law and jurisdictional inquiries. . . . [A] court will feel less knowledgeable and comfortable in interpretation, and less interested in fostering the policies of [a] foreign jurisdiction, than would the courts established by the State that provides the applicable law. . . . Obviously, . . . choice-of-law problems cannot entirely be avoided in a diverse legal system such as our own. Nonetheless, when a suitor seeks to lodge a suit in a State with a substantial interest in seeing its own law applied to the transaction in question, we could wisely act to minimize conflicts, confusion, and uncertainty by adopting a liberal view of jurisdiction, unless considerations of fairness or efficiency strongly point in the opposite direction.

This case is not one where, in my judgment, this preference for jurisdiction is adequately answered. Certainly nothing said by the Court persuades me that it would be unfair to subject appellants to suit in Delaware. The fact that the record does not reveal whether they "set foot" or committed "acts related to [the] cause of action" in Delaware . . . is not decisive, for jurisdiction can be based strictly on out-of-state acts having foreseeable effects in the forum state. E.g., McGee v. International Life Ins. Co., supra; Gray v. American Radiator & Standard Sanitary Corp., supra; Restatement (Second) Conflicts of Law § 37. . . . Further, I cannot understand how the existence of minimum contacts in a constitutional sense is at all affected by Delaware's failure statutorily to express an interest in controlling corporate fiduciaries. To me this simply demonstrates that Delaware did not elect to assert jurisdiction to the extent the Constitution would allow.

[I] . . . would approach the minimum contacts analysis differently than does the Court. Crucial to me is the fact that appellants voluntarily associated themselves with the State of Delaware, "invoking the benefits and protections of its laws," Hanson v. Denckla, [p. 75, supra]; International Shoe Co. v. Washington, [p. 65, supra], by entering into a long term and fragile relationship with one of its domestic corporations. They thereby elected to assume powers and to undertake responsibilities wholly derived from that State's rules and regulations, and to become eligible for those benefits that Delaware law makes available to its corporations' officials. . . .

NOTES

1. Despite its rejection of the theoretical underpinning of *Harris v. Balk*, the majority in *Shaffer* stopped short of explicitly overruling the decision. (See footnote 39.) Perhaps the Court was aware, as Professor Andreas F. Lowenfeld has observed, that the record in the Harris case shows that both Harris and Balk were customers of Epstein and that on the facts Balk probably would be subject to jurisdiction in Maryland by today's standards. See Lowenfeld, In Search of the Intangible: A Comment on Shaffer v. Heitner, 53 N.Y.U.L. Rev. 102, 103–107 (1978). Consider again *Combs v. Combs*, p. 167, supra. Could *in rem* jurisdiction have been sustained in that case in light of *Shaffer*? If both *in rem* and *in personam* jurisdiction were possible in that case under modern standards, what advantage would there have been to the plaintiffs in proceeding on an *in personam* basis?

2. Does the *Shaffer* decision spell the end of quasi-in-rem attachments for jurisdictional purposes? Since the plaintiff's judgment in an attachment-for-jurisdiction case will be limited to the value of the attached property and since the required contacts are likely to be no more exacting, the plaintiff would usually do better to use the defendant's contacts with the forum to assert in personam jurisdiction. See Silberman, Shaffer v. Heitner: The End of an Era, 53 N.Y.U.L.Rev. 33, 67–68 (1978).

One post-*Shaffer* exception to the general rule that *in personam* and *in rem* jurisdiction are co-extensive comes about in states, such as New York, in which the state's *in personam* long-arm statute stops short of the constitutional limit, but state law continues to authorize *in rem* jurisdiction. Such a case occurred in Banco Ambrosiano, S.P.A. v. Artoc Bank & Trust Ltd., 62 N.Y.2d 65, 476 N.Y.S.2d 64, 464 N.E.2d 432 (1984). The dispute was between two foreign banks involving a loan. The plaintiff proceeded by attaching the defendant's New York bank account. Although the defendant did not fall within any of the *in personam* bases under New York's long-arm statute, New York state law continued to authorize *in rem* jurisdiction, and the New York Court of Appeals found that the minimum contacts test was satisfied because the loan in question was paid through the seized account, making it a purposeful, related contact. At least one post-*Shaffer* opinion has upheld an assertion of *in rem* jurisdiction based upon the seizure of an unrelated bank account on the theory that the creation of a bank account is a voluntary affiliation with the forum state. See Feder v. Turkish Airlines, 441 F.Supp. 1273 (S.D.N.Y.1977).

Some suggestion of the correctness of this expansive jurisdictional view can be found in the Supreme Court's decision in Republic of Argentina v. Weltover, 504 U.S. 607 (1992). *Weltover* dealt with a claim of sovereign immunity by Argentina for that country's failure to pay on certain loan guarantees. The plaintiffs were two Panamanian corporations and a Swiss bank who were creditors on the defaulted notes. The plaintiffs had, as allowed for by the guarantees, designated New York as the place of repayment. When Argentina unilaterally rescheduled payment, the plaintiffs brought suit under the Foreign Sovereign Immunities Act ("FSIA"), 28 U.S.C. §§ 1602–11. The FSIA makes foreign governments amenable to suit "in connection with a commercial activity . . . that causes a direct effect in the United States." 28 U.S.C. § 1605(a)(2). The FSIA further requires that the commercial activity have "substantial contact with the United States." 28 U.S.C. § 1603(e). After deciding that Argentina's actions were commercial and not governmental, the Supreme Court also decided that the transaction had enough nexus with the United States to satisfy the FSIA. Although avoiding the question of whether foreign governments are "persons" for due process purposes, the Supreme Court held that Argentina had minimum contacts with New York by designating it as one of the places of repayment, and then failing to make the required repayment. 504 U.S. at 619.

3. A *"Mareva"* injunction (also called a "freezing injunction"), in English practice, enjoins a defendant from removing assets from the jurisdiction while an action is pending against it. Mareva Cia Naviera SA v. International Bulk Carriers SA, [1980] 1 All E.R. 213 (C.A.). As a result of English accession to the Brussels Convention and its replacement by the Brussels I Regulation, *Mareva* injunctions are now also granted in support of proceedings commenced in other E.U. countries. Republic of Haiti v. Duvalier, [1989] 1 All E.R. 456 (C.A.). *Mareva* injunctions may also issue to restrain a defendant over whom the court has personal jurisdiction from dealing with its assets worldwide. Republic of Haiti, supra; Derby & Co. Ltd. v. Weldon, [1989] 1 All E.R. 469 (C.A.). See Collins, The Territorial Reach of *Mareva* Injunctions, 105 L.Q.Rev. 262 (1989); Dicey, Morris & Collins, Conflict of Laws 263–64 (15th ed.2012). Would U.S. courts enforce a *Mareva* injunction against a defendant seeking to dispose of assets located in the United States? The "Babanaft proviso" in *Mareva* injunctions makes clear that "no person other than the defendants themselves shall . . . be affected" and that there is no intent to attempt to affect the foreign property directly. Babanaft International Co. SA v. Bassatne, [1989] 1 All E.R. 433 (C.A.).

Mareva injunctions may issue on the basis of information about the defendant's assets obtained by means of an *"Anton Piller* Order" (now called a "search order"). The order takes its name from Anton Piller KG v. Manufacturing Processes Ltd., [1976] Ch. 55, [1976] 1 All E.R. 779 (C.A.), and is now also part of discovery procedures in Australia and Canada. The order issues ex parte and permits the successful movant to search the opponent's premises to secure and safeguard evidence in danger of destruction or loss. During the search, however, the holder of the order may also discover bank account information and learn of the location of assets and then seek to freeze these by means of a *Mareva* injunction. See House of Spring Gardens Ltd. v. Waite, [1985] F.S.R. 173 (C.A.). See Dockray & Laddie, Piller Problems, 106 L.Q.Rev. 601 (1990); Collins, Anton Piller Orders and Fundamental Rights, id. at 173. Should recognition of a *Mareva* injunction depend on how the underlying information was obtained? The European Court of Human Rights has held that the ex parte nature and lack of a public hearing in *Anton Piller* Order cases does not violate the European Convention on Human Rights, of which the United Kingdom is a contracting state. Chappell v. United Kingdom, 1989 Eur. Court of Human Rights, Series A, No. 152-A. The European Court of Justice has held that protective orders and decisions that issue ex parte are not entitled to recognition in another member state. ECR 1980, 1553 (Denilauer).

4.   Compare footnote 37 in the *Shaffer* decision with footnote 13 in *Helicopteros*, p. 122, supra. Is it likely today that the Supreme Court would uphold jurisdiction based on the presence of property in the forum upon a showing that the defendant is not subject to personal jurisdiction anywhere else in the United States?

5.   After the Supreme Court's decision in *Shaffer*, the Delaware Code was amended (Del.Code Title 10, § 3114) to provide that "every nonresident of [Delaware] who after September 1, 1977, accepts election or appointment as a director, trustee or member of the governing body of a [Delaware] corporation, . . . or who after June 30, 1978 serves in such capacity . . . shall, by such acceptance or by such service, be deemed thereby to have consented to the appointment of the registered agent of such corporation (or, if there is none, the Secretary of State) as his agent upon whom service of process may be made in all civil actions or proceedings brought in this state, by or on behalf of, or against such corporation, in which such director, trustee or member is a necessary or proper party, or in any action or proceeding against such director, trustee or member for violation of his duty in such capacity. . . ."

Delaware's high court subsequently held that being appointed a director of a Delaware corporation is by itself a constitutionally sufficient basis for the application of this statute to a non-resident defendant. Armstrong v. Pomerance, 423 A.2d 174 (Del.1980).

6.   In Rush v. Savchuk, 444 U.S. 320, 100 S.Ct. 571, 62 L.Ed.2d 516 (1980), the Supreme Court made clear that *Shaffer* had the effect of abolishing a peculiar kind of quasi-in-rem jurisdiction invented by the New York courts in Seider v. Roth, 28 A.D.2d 698, 280 N.Y.S.2d 1005 (1967). So-called *Seider* jurisdiction allowed the plaintiff to attach the defendant's insurance policy in any state in which the insurance company did business, thus essentially creating nationwide jurisdiction over defendants who were insured by major insurance company. Minnesota and New York were the only states to fully embrace the theory of *Seider* jurisdiction. The Supreme Court held that such assertions of jurisdiction were unconstitutional unless the defendant himself (not merely his insurer) has minimum contacts with the forum state.

7.   A fascinating use of *in rem* jurisdiction arises under the Anticybersquatting Consumer Protection Act, ("ACPA") 15 U.S.C.A. § 1125(d), which took effect on November 29, 1999. "Cybersquatting" is the practice of registering internet domain names that potentially infringe on another's trademark. See, e.g., Caesars World, Inc. v. Caesars-Palace.Com, 112 F.Supp.2d 502 (E.D.Va.2000). Often, the person registering the domain name hopes to profit at the expense of the owner of the mark by either intercepting internet traffic intended for the owner's business or by selling the domain name to the mark's owner. The ACPA seeks to combat unfair practices of this sort.

15 U.S.C.A. § 1125(d)(1)(A) ("Cyberpiracy prevention") gives a civil cause of action against a registrant who "has a bad faith intention to profit

from that mark" and "registers, traffics in, or uses a domain name that"—with regard to so-called "famous marks"—"is identical or confusingly similar to or dilutive of that mark." Such a civil action allows for damages against the registrant as well as other remedies, including cancellation of the domain name registration. A major practical problem, however, is that domain name registration is done electronically and fairly often under aliases, making it difficult to find such registrants, let alone to serve and obtain personal jurisdiction over them.

Thus, as an alternative to *in personam* civil actions, the ACPA provides that "[t]he owner of a mark may file an *in rem* civil action against a domain name in the judicial district in which the domain name registrar, domain name registry, or other domain name authority . . . is located. . . ." 15 U.S.C.A. § 1125(d)(2). The remedies in such *in rem* actions "shall be limited to a court order for the forfeiture or cancellation of the domain name or the transfer of the domain name to the owner of the mark." 15 U.S.C.A. § 1125(d)(2)(D)(i). As a practical matter, however, this relief is often the best that the holder of the mark can expect, making an *in rem* proceeding the preferred vehicle for many mark owners. See, e.g., Heathmount A.E. Corp. v. Technodome.com, 106 F.Supp.2d 860, 863 (E.D.Va.2000). *In rem* proceedings are permitted, however, only if the mark owner "is not able to obtain *in personam* jurisdiction over [the registrant]" or "through due diligence was not able to find" the registrant. 15 U.S.C.A. § 1125(d)(2)(A)(ii). Interestingly, this provision thus puts a "reverse" incentive on the mark owner to show that the registrant does *not* have minimum contacts with the forum state. See, e.g., *Heathmount*, 106 F.Supp.2d at 862. Cf. Fed.R.Civ.Proc. 4(k)(2).

What about the constitutionality of this use of *in rem* jurisdiction? Does it violate *Shaffer*'s command that even *in rem* proceedings require that the property owner (here, the domain name registrant) have minimum contacts with the forum? The courts that have considered this issue thus far have rejected the constitutional challenge. One court considering expressly the *Shaffer* problem limited the Supreme Court's contacts requirement to "*in rem* proceedings where the underlying cause of action is unrelated to property which is located in the forum state." *See Caesars World*, 112 F.Supp.2d at 504. That court distinguished ACPA *in rem* actions from the derivative action involved in *Shaffer* because under the ACPA "the domain name . . . is not only related to the cause of action but is its entire subject matter." Id. Is this analysis convincing? Would a stronger argument be that by insisting that an *in personam* action be unavailable, Congress brought ACPA actions within the *Shaffer* court's dictum that *in rem* jurisdiction without contacts might be available based solely on "the presence of the defendant's property . . . when no other forum is available to the plaintiff."?

Under the ACPA, *in rem* actions must be brought in the district in which the domain-name authority or the entity registering the domain is located because this is the "situs" of the domain name. The Second Circuit summarized as follows:

"the ACPA's basic *in rem jurisdictional grant, contained in subsection (d)(2)(A), contemplates exclusively a judicial district*

> *within which the registrar or other domain-name authority is located. A plaintiff must initiate an* in rem *action by filing a complaint in that judicial district and no other. Upon receiving proper written notification that the complaint has been filed, the domain-name authority must deposit with the court documentation 'sufficient to establish the court's control and authority regarding the disposition of . . . the domain name,' as required by subsection (d)(2)(D). This combination of filing and depositing rules encompasses the basic, mandatory procedure for bringing and maintaining an* in rem *action under the ACPA."*

Mattel, Inc. v. Barbie-Club.com, 310 F.3d 293, 306 (2d Cir.2002).

8. *Shaffer* might open up the possibility of in rem jurisdiction without having the property in the forum as long as there are otherwise minimum contacts with the forum. Contents of Account Number 03001288 v. United States, 344 F.3d 399 (3d Cir.2003) involved an in rem civil forfeiture action brought by the U.S. government against bank accounts located in the United Arab Emirates. The government contended that the funds were proceeds of illegal narcotics trafficking. The owner of the accounts resisted jurisdiction on the grounds that the accounts were not located in the forum. The court, however, found that there was jurisdiction based upon 28 U.S.C.A. § 1355(b)(1)(A) which confers jurisdiction in such actions on the federal district court "for the district in which any of the acts or omissions giving rise to the forfeiture occurred." Another circuit, however, has concluded that this statute does not confer jurisdiction, but is merely a venue statute. See United States v. All Funds on Deposit in an Accounts Maintained in the Names of Meza, 63 F.3d 148 (2d Cir.1995). Assuming that section 1355 does confer "in rem" jurisdiction without the presence of the res in the forum, is there any meaningful distinction remaining with in personam jurisdiction?

9. In the principal case, footnote 36 states that an in personam judgment can be enforced wherever the defendant has property without the need for personal jurisdiction over the defendant in the enforcing state. Does this apply to foreign judgments and to foreign arbitral awards? Glencore Grain Rotterdam B.V. v. Shivnath Rai Harnarain Co., 284 F.3d 1114 (9th Cir.2002), invoked footnote 36 and stated that it would have enforced a United Kingdom arbitration award without jurisdiction over the award debtor, but affirmed dismissal because plaintiff had not identified any assets of the debtor in the jurisdiction. But cf. Lenchyshyn v. Pelko Electric, Inc., 281 A.D.2d 42, 723 N.Y.S.2d 285 (2001).

Contrary to *Glencore Grain*, Base Metal Trading, Ltd. v. OJSC "Novokuznetsky Aluminum Factory," 283 F.3d 208 (4th Cir.2002), cert. denied, 537 U.S. 822, 123 S.Ct. 101 (2002), affirmed district court rulings that dismissed a suit to enforce a Russian arbitral award and vacated an attachment of aluminum alleged to belong to the award debtor. The Fourth Circuit held that the plaintiff must have personal jurisdiction over the award debtor in order to enforce the award. The plaintiff did not cite footnote 36 to the court.

SECTION 4. COMPETENCE OF COURT AND NOTICE

RESTATEMENT, SECOND, CONFLICT OF LAWS:

§ 105. Judgment Rendered By Court Lacking Competence

A judgment rendered by a court lacking competence to render it and subject to collateral attack for that reason in the state of rendition will not be recognized or enforced in other states.

Thompson v. Whitman

Supreme Court of the United States, 1874.
85 U.S. (18 Wall.) 457, 21 L.Ed. 897.

■ JUSTICE BRADLEY delivered the opinion of the court:

This is an action of trespass for taking and carrying away goods, originally brought in the superior court of New York City, and removed by the defendant, now plaintiff in error, into the circuit court of the United States. The declaration charges that, on the 26th of September, 1862, the defendant, with force and arms on the high seas, in the outward vicinity of the Narrows of the Port of New York, and within the southern district of New York, seized and took the sloop Ann L. Whitman, with her tackle, furniture, etc., the property of the plaintiff, and carried away and converted the same. The defendant pleaded "Not guilty" and a special plea in bar. The latter plea justified the trespass by setting up that the plaintiff, a resident of New York, on the day of seizure was raking and gathering clams with said sloop in the waters of New Jersey, to wit: within the limits of the county of Monmouth, contrary to the law of that state; and that, by virtue of said law, the defendant, who was sheriff of said county, seized the sloop within the limits thereof, and informed against her before two justices of the peace of said county, by whom she was condemned and ordered to be sold. In answer to this plea the plaintiff took issue as to the place of seizure, denying that it was within the state of New Jersey or the county of Monmouth, thus challenging the jurisdiction of the justices, as well as the right of the defendant to make the seizure. On the trial conflicting testimony was given upon this point, but the defendant produced a record of the proceedings before the justices which stated the offense as having been committed and seizure as made within the county of Monmouth, with a history of the proceedings to the condemnation and order of sale. The defendant claimed that this record was conclusive, both as to the jurisdiction of the court and the merits of the case, and that it was a bar to the action, and requested the court so to charge the jury. But this was refused, and the court charged that the said record was only prima facie evidence of the facts therein stated, and threw upon the plaintiff the burden of proving the contrary. The defendant excepted, and the jury, under the direction of the court, found for the plaintiff generally, and in answer to certain questions framed by the court found specially: first, that the seizure was made within the state of New Jersey; second, that it was not made in the county of

Monmouth; third, that the plaintiff was not engaged on the day of the seizure in taking claims within the limits of the county of Monmouth. Judgment being rendered for the plaintiff, the case is brought here for review.

The main question in the cause is, whether the record produced by the defendant was conclusive of the jurisdictional facts therein contained. It stated, with due particularity, sufficient facts to give the justices jurisdiction under the law of New Jersey. Could that statement be questioned collaterally in another action brought in another State? If it could be, the ruling of the court was substantially correct. If not, there was error. . . .

Without that provision of the Constitution of the United States which declares that "full faith and credit shall be given in each State to the public acts, records, and judicial proceedings of every other State," and the act of Congress passed to carry it into effect, it is clear that the record in question would not be conclusive as to the facts necessary to give the justices of Monmouth County jurisdiction, whatever might be its effect in New Jersey. In any other State it would be regarded like any foreign judgment; and as to a foreign judgment it is perfectly well settled that the inquiry is always open, whether the court by which it was rendered had jurisdiction of the person or the thing. . . .

Justice Story, who pronounced the judgment in Mills v. Duryee [7 Cranch 484], in his Commentary on the Constitution (Sec. 1313), after stating the general doctrine established by that case with regard to the conclusive effect of judgments of one State in every other State, adds: "But this does not prevent an inquiry into the jurisdiction of the court in which the original judgment was given, to pronounce it; or the right of the State itself to exercise authority over the person or the subject-matter. The Constitution did not mean to confer [upon the States] a new power or jurisdiction, but simply to regulate the effect of the acknowledged jurisdiction over persons and things within their territory." . . .

But if it is once conceded that the validity of a judgment may be attacked collaterally by evidence showing that the court had no jurisdiction, it is not perceived how any allegation contained in the record itself, however strongly made, can affect the right so to question it. The very object of the evidence is to invalidate the paper as a record. If that can be successfully done no statements contained therein have any force. If any such statements could be used to prevent inquiry, a slight form of words might always be adopted so as effectually to nullify the right of such inquiry. Recitals of this kind must be regarded like asseverations of good faith in a deed, which avail nothing if the instrument is shown to be fraudulent. The records of the domestic tribunals of England and some of the States, it is true, are held to import absolute verity as well in relation to jurisdictional as to other facts, in all collateral proceedings. Public policy and the dignity of the courts are supposed to require that no averment shall be admitted to contradict the record. But, as we have seen, that rule has no extra-territorial force. . . .

On the whole, we think it clear that the jurisdiction of the court by which a judgment is rendered in any State may be questioned in a collateral proceeding in another State, notwithstanding the provision of the fourth article of the Constitution and the law of 1790, and notwithstanding the averments contained in the record of the judgment itself.

This is decisive of the case; for, according to the findings of the jury, the justices of Monmouth County could not have had any jurisdiction to condemn the sloop in question. It is true she was seized in the waters of New Jersey; but the express finding is, that the seizure was not made within the limits of the county of Monmouth, and that no clams were raked within the county on that day. The authority to make the seizure and to entertain cognizance thereof is given by the ninth section of the act, as follows:

> "It shall be the duty of all sheriffs and constables, and may be lawful for any other person or persons, to seize and secure any such canoe, flat, scow, boat, or other vessel as aforesaid, and immediately thereupon give information thereof to two justices of the peace of the county where such seizure shall have been made, who are hereby empowered and required to meet at such time and place as they shall appoint for the trial thereof, and hear and determine the same; and in case the same shall be condemned, it shall be sold by the order of and under the direction of the said justices, who, after deducting all legal costs and charges, shall pay one-half of the proceeds of said sale to the collector of the county in which such offense shall have been committed, and the other half to the person who shall have seized and prosecuted the same."

From this it appears that the seizure must be made in a county, and that the case can only be heard by justices of the county where it is made—"two justices of the peace of the county where such seizure shall have been made." The seizure in this case as specially found by the jury was not made in Monmouth County; but the justices who tried the case were justices of that county. Consequently the justices had no jurisdiction, and the record had no validity.

It is argued that the seizure was continuous in its character, and became a seizure in Monmouth County when the sloop was carried into that county. This position is untenable. Suppose the seizure had been made in Cumberland County, in Delaware Bay, could the sloop have been carried around to Monmouth County and there condemned, on the ground that the seizure was continuous, and became finally a seizure in Monmouth County? This would hardly be contended. But it is said that the seizure was made within the State, off the county of Monmouth, and not within the limits of any county; and, hence, that Monmouth County was the first county in which the seizure took place. If this had been true (as it undoubtedly was), and the jury had so found, still it would not have helped the case. The major proposition is not correct. A seizure is a single act, and not a continuous fact. Possession, which follows seizure, is continuous. It is the seizure which must be made within the county where the vessel is to be proceeded against and condemned. The case may have been a casus omissus in the law; it is certainly not included in it.

As this disposes of all the errors which have been assigned, the judgment must be

Affirmed.

NOTES

1.   In his assertion that "the justices [of Monmouth County] had no jurisdiction," what did Justice Bradley intend to convey by the word "jurisdiction"? Would "competence" have been an accurate word? Or should he have said the "venue" was incorrect? If the latter, should the New Jersey judgment have been vulnerable to collateral attack?

2.   In Pemberton v. Hughes, [1889] 1 Ch. 781, the validity of a Florida divorce decree was in question in an English court. The defendant asserted the decree was void because the return day of appearance in court was only nine days after the service of process, while under the rules of the Florida court the period should have been ten days. The court held that the divorce was valid, since the tests of "international jurisdiction" were met. What is the dividing line between a defect that can be corrected only by appeal and a defect that impairs jurisdiction?

3.   In Aldrich v. Aldrich, 378 U.S. 540, 84 S.Ct. 1687 (1964), a Florida alimony decree that purported to bind the estate of the obligor was entitled to recognition in West Virginia when the Florida Supreme Court, upon certification by the U.S. Supreme Court, responded that the decree, though entered without subject matter jurisdiction, "passed into verity, became final" for lack of appeal, and was no longer subject to collateral attack.

4.   The rule is the same if the question of subject matter jurisdiction is actually contested and litigated in F-1. Durfee v. Duke, 375 U.S. 106, 84 S.Ct. 242 (1963) involved a dispute over whether certain bottom land in the Missouri River was located in Nebraska or Missouri. The dispute turned on the resolution of a factual question as to whether the river had shifted course by accretion or avulsion. F-1, a Nebraska state court, had subject matter jurisdiction only if the land were located in Nebraska. The parties litigated the question and the Nebraska court found that the land was located in Nebraska, and entered judgment accordingly. A second suit was filed in the Missouri state courts. The U.S. Supreme Court held that the Full Faith and Credit Clause prevented the Missouri court from reexamining the question of the location of the land, as that issue had been litigated and determined in the earlier Nebraska proceeding.

Mullane v. Central Hanover Bank & Trust Co.

Supreme Court of the United States, 1950.
339 U.S. 306, 70 S.Ct. 652, 94 L.Ed. 865.

■ JUSTICE JACKSON delivered the opinion of the Court.

This controversy questions the constitutional sufficiency of notice to beneficiaries on judicial settlement of accounts by the trustee of a common trust fund established under the New York Banking Law. The New York Court of Appeals considered and overruled objections that the statutory notice contravenes requirements of the Fourteenth Amendment and that by allowance of the account beneficiaries were deprived of property without due process of law. . . .

Common trust fund legislation is addressed to a problem appropriate for state action. Mounting overheads have made administration of small trusts undesirable to corporate trustees. In order that donors and testators of moderately sized trusts may not be denied the service of corporate fiduciaries, the District of Columbia and some thirty states other than New York have permitted pooling small trust estates into one fund for investment administration. The income, capital gains, losses and expenses of the collective trust are shared by the constituent trusts in proportion to their contribution. By this plan, diversification of risk and economy of management can be extended to those whose capital standing alone would not obtain such advantage.

Statutory authorization for the establishment of such common trust funds is provided in the New York Banking Law, § 100–c (c. 687, L.1937, as amended by c. 602, L.1943 and c. 158, L.1944). Under this Act a trust company may, with approval of the State Banking Board, establish a common fund and, within prescribed limits, invest therein the assets of an unlimited number of estates, trusts or other funds of which it is trustee. Each participating trust shares ratably in the common fund, but exclusive management and control is in the trust company as trustee, and neither a fiduciary nor any beneficiary of a participating trust is deemed to have ownership in any particular asset or investment of this common fund. The trust company must keep fund assets separate from its own, and in its fiduciary capacity may not deal with itself or any affiliate. Provisions are made for accountings twelve to fifteen months after the establishment of a fund and triennially thereafter. The decree in each such judicial settlement of accounts is made binding and conclusive as to any matter set forth in the account upon everyone having any interest in the common fund or in any participating estate, trust or fund.

In January, 1946, Central Hanover Bank and Trust Company established a common trust fund in accordance with these provisions, and in March, 1947, it petitioned the Surrogate's Court for settlement of its first account as common trustee. During the accounting period a total of 113 trusts, approximately half inter vivos and half testamentary, participated in the common trust fund, the gross capital of which was nearly three million dollars. The record does not show the number or residence of the beneficiaries, but they were many and it is clear that some of them were not residents of the State of New York.

The only notice given beneficiaries of this specific application was by publication in a local newspaper in strict compliance with the minimum requirements of N.Y.Banking Law § 100–c(12): "After filing such petition (for judicial settlement of its account) the petitioner shall cause to be issued by the court in which the petition is filed and shall publish not less than once in each week for four successive weeks in a newspaper to be designated by the court a notice or citation addressed generally without naming them to all parties interested in such common trust fund and in such estates, trusts or funds mentioned in the petition, all of which may be described in the notice or citation only in the manner set forth in said petition and without setting forth the residence of any such decedent or donor of any such estate, trust or fund." Thus the only notice required, and the only one given, was by newspaper publication setting forth merely the name and address of the trust company, the name and the date of establishment of the common trust fund, and a list of all participating estates, trusts or funds.

At the time the first investment in the common fund was made on behalf of each participating estate, however, the trust company, pursuant to the requirements of § 100–c(9), had notified by mail each person of full age and sound mind whose name and address were then known to it and who was "entitled to share in the income therefrom . . . (or) . . . who would be entitled to share in the principal if the event upon which such estate, trust or fund will become distributable should have occurred at the time of sending such notice." Included in the notice was a copy of those provisions of the Act relating to the sending of the notice itself and to the judicial settlement of common trust fund accounts.

Upon the filing of the petition for the settlement of accounts, appellant was, by order of the court pursuant to § 100–c(12), appointed special guardian and attorney for all persons known or unknown not otherwise appearing who had or might thereafter have any interest in the income of the common trust fund; and appellee Vaughan was appointed to represent those similarly interested in the principal. There were no other appearances on behalf of anyone interested in either interest or principal.

Appellant appeared specially, objecting that notice and the statutory provisions for notice to beneficiaries were inadequate to afford due process under the Fourteenth Amendment, and therefore that the court was without jurisdiction to render a final and binding decree. Appellant's objections were entertained and overruled, the Surrogate holding that the notice required and given was sufficient. 75 N.Y.S.2d 397. A final decree accepting the accounts has been entered, affirmed by the Appellate Division of the Supreme Court, 275 App.Div. 769, 88 N.Y.S.2d

907, and by the Court of Appeals of the State of New York, 299 N.Y. 697, 87 N.E.2d 73.

The effect of this decree, as held below, is to settle "all questions respecting the management of the common fund." We understand that every right which beneficiaries would otherwise have against the trust company, either as trustee of the common fund or as trustee of any individual trust, for improper management of the common trust fund during the period covered by the accounting is sealed and wholly terminated by the decree. . . .

We are met at the outset with a challenge to the power of the State— the right of its courts to adjudicate at all as against those beneficiaries who reside without the State of New York. It is contended that the proceeding is one in personam in that the decree affects neither title to nor possession of any res, but adjudges only personal rights of the beneficiaries to surcharge their trustee for negligence or breach of trust. Accordingly, it is said, under the strict doctrine of Pennoyer v. Neff, 95 U.S. 714, the Surrogate is without jurisdiction as to nonresidents upon whom personal service of process was not made. . . .

Judicial proceedings to settle fiduciary accounts have been sometimes termed in rem, or more indefinitely quasi in rem, or more vaguely still, "in the nature of a proceeding in rem." It is not readily apparent how the courts of New York did or would classify the present proceeding, which has some characteristics and is wanting in some features of proceedings both in rem and in personam. But in any event we think that the requirements of the Fourteenth Amendment to the Federal Constitution do not depend upon a classification for which the standards are so elusive and confused generally and which, being primarily for state courts to define, may and do vary from state to state. Without disparaging the usefulness of distinctions between actions in rem and those in personam in many branches of law, or on other issues, or the reasoning which underlies them, we do not rest the power of the State to resort to constructive service in this proceeding upon how its courts or this Court may regard this historic antithesis. It is sufficient to observe that, whatever the technical definition of its chosen procedure, the interest of each state in providing means to close trusts that exist by the grace of its laws and are administered under the supervision of its courts is so insistent and rooted in custom as to establish beyond doubt the right of its courts to determine the interests of all claimants, resident or nonresident, provided its procedure accords full opportunity to appear and be heard.

Quite different from the question of a state's power to discharge trustees is that of the opportunity it must give beneficiaries to contest. Many controversies have raged about the cryptic and abstract words of the Due Process Clause but there can be no doubt that at a minimum they require that deprivation of life, liberty or property by adjudication be preceded by notice and opportunity for hearing appropriate to the nature of the case.

In two ways this proceeding does or may deprive beneficiaries of property. It may cut off their rights to have the trustee answer for negligent or illegal impairments of their interests. Also, their interests are presumably subject to diminution in the proceeding by allowance of fees and expenses to one who, in their names but without their knowledge, may conduct a fruitless or uncompensatory contest. Certainly the proceeding is one in which they may be deprived of property rights and hence notice and hearing must measure up to the standards of due process.

Personal service of written notice within the jurisdiction is the classic form of notice always adequate in any type of proceeding. But the vital interest of the State in bringing any issues as to its fiduciaries to a final settlement can be served only if interests or claims of individuals who are outside of the State can somehow be determined. A construction of the Due Process Clause which would place impossible or impractical obstacles in the way could not be justified.

Against this interest of the State we must balance the individual interest sought to be protected by the Fourteenth Amendment. This is defined by our holding that "The fundamental requisite of due process of law is the opportunity to be heard." Grannis v. Ordean, 234 U.S. 385, 394. This right to be heard has little reality or worth unless one is informed that the matter is pending and can choose for himself whether to appear or default, acquiesce or contest.

The Court has not committed itself to any formula achieving a balance between these interests in a particular proceeding or determining when constructive notice may be utilized or what test it must meet. Personal service has not in all circumstances been regarded as indispensable to the process due to residents, and it has more often been held unnecessary as to nonresidents. We disturb none of the established rules on these subjects. No decision constitutes a controlling or even a very illuminating precedent for the case before us. But a few general principles stand out in the books.

An elementary and fundamental requirement of due process in any proceeding which is to be accorded finality is notice reasonably calculated, under all the circumstances, to apprise interested parties of the pendency of the action and afford them an opportunity to present their objections. . . . The notice must be of such nature as reasonably to convey the required information . . . and it must afford a reasonable time for those interested to make their appearance. . . . But if with due regard for the practicalities and peculiarities of the case these conditions are reasonably met, the constitutional requirements are satisfied. "The criterion is not the possibility of conceivable injury but the just and reasonable character of the requirements, having reference to the subject with which the statute deals." American Land Co. v. Zeiss, 219 U.S. 47, 67; and see Blinn v. Nelson, 222 U.S. 1, 7.

But when notice is a person's due, process which is a mere gesture is not due process. The means employed must be such as one desirous of actually informing the absentee might reasonably adopt to accomplish it. The reasonableness and hence the constitutional validity of any chosen method may be defended on the ground that it is in itself reasonably certain to inform those affected, compare Hess v. Pawloski, 274 U.S. 352, with Wuchter v. Pizzutti, 276 U.S. 13,[17] or, where conditions do not reasonably permit such notice, that the form chosen is not substantially less likely to bring home notice than other of the feasible and customary substitutes.

It would be idle to pretend that publication alone, as prescribed here, is a reliable means of acquainting interested parties of the fact that their rights are before the courts. It is not an accident that the greater number of cases reaching this Court on the question of adequacy of notice have been concerned with actions founded on process constructively served through local newspapers. Chance alone brings to the attention of even a local resident an advertisement in small type inserted in the back pages of a newspaper, and if he makes his home outside the area of the newspaper's normal circulation the odds that the information will never reach him are large indeed. The chance of actual notice is further reduced when, as here, the notice required does not even name those whose attention it is supposed to attract, and does not inform acquaintances who might call it to attention. In weighing its sufficiency on the basis of equivalence with actual notice, we are unable to regard this as more than a feint.

Nor is publication here reinforced by steps likely to attract the parties' attention to the proceeding. It is true that publication traditionally has been acceptable as notification supplemental to other action which in itself may reasonably be expected to convey a warning. The ways of an owner with tangible property are such that he usually arranges means to learn of any direct attack upon his possessory or proprietary rights. Hence, libel of a ship, attachment of a chattel or entry upon real estate in the name of law may reasonably be expected to come promptly to the owner's attention. When the state within which the owner has located such property seizes it for some reason, publication or posting affords an additional measure of notification. . . .

This Court has not hesitated to approve of resort to publication as a customary substitute in another class of cases where it is not reasonably possible or practicable to give more adequate warning. Thus it has been

---

[17] In Wuchter v. Pizzutti, the defendant had received notice by personal service outside the state but was nevertheless allowed to attack successfully the New Jersey nonresident motorist statute on the ground that it did not require that anyone inform defendant of the commencement of suit in a way making it "reasonably probable" that he would receive actual notice. —eds.

recognized that, in the case of persons missing or unknown, employment of an indirect and even a probably futile means of notification is all that the situation permits and creates no constitutional bar to a final decree foreclosing their rights. . . .

Those beneficiaries represented by appellant whose interests or whereabouts could not with due diligence be ascertained come clearly within this category. As to them the statutory notice is sufficient. However great the odds that publication will never reach the eyes of such unknown parties, it is not in the typical case much more likely to fail than any of the choices open to legislators endeavoring to prescribe the best notice practicable.

Nor do we consider it unreasonable for the State to dispense with more certain notice to those beneficiaries whose interests are either conjectural or future or, although they could be discovered upon investigation, do not in due course of business come to knowledge of the common trustee. Whatever searches might be required in another situation under ordinary standards of diligence, in view of the character of the proceedings and the nature of the interests here involved we think them unnecessary. We recognize the practical difficulties and costs that would be attendant on frequent investigations into the status of great numbers of beneficiaries, many of whose interests in the common fund are so remote as to be ephemeral; and we have no doubt that such impracticable and extended searches are not required in the name of due process. The expense of keeping informed from day to day of substitutions among even current income beneficiaries and presumptive remaindermen, to say nothing of the far greater number of contingent beneficiaries, would impose a severe burden on the plan, and would likely dissipate its advantages. These are practical matters in which we should be reluctant to disturb the judgment of the state authorities.

Accordingly, we overrule appellant's constitutional objections to published notice insofar as they are urged on behalf of any beneficiaries whose interests or addresses are unknown to the trustee.

As to known present beneficiaries of known place of residence, however, notice by publication stands on a different footing. Exceptions in the name of necessity do not sweep away the rule that within the limits of practicability notice must be such as is reasonably calculated to reach interested parties. Where the names and postoffice addresses of those affected by a proceeding are at hand, the reasons disappear for resort to means less likely than the mails to apprise them of its pendency.

The trustee has on its books the names and addresses of the income beneficiaries represented by appellant, and we find no tenable ground for dispensing with a serious effort to inform them personally of the accounting, at least by ordinary mail to the record addresses. Cf. Wuchter v. Pizzutti, supra. Certainly sending them a copy of the statute months and perhaps years in advance does not answer this purpose. The trustee periodically remits their income to them, and we think that they might reasonably expect that with or apart from their remittances word might come to them personally that steps were being taken affecting their interests.

We need not weigh contentions that a requirement of personal service of citation on even the large number of known resident or nonresident beneficiaries would, by reasons of delay if not of expense, seriously interfere with the proper administration of the fund. Of course personal service even without the jurisdiction of the issuing authority serves the end of actual and personal notice, whatever power of compulsion it might lack. However, no such service is required under the circumstances. This type of trust presupposes a large number of small interests. The individual interest does not stand alone but is identical with that of a class. The rights of each in the integrity of the fund and the fidelity of the trustee are shared by many other beneficiaries. Therefore notice reasonably certain to reach most of those interested in objecting is likely to safeguard the interests of all, since any objection sustained would inure to the benefit of all. We think that under such circumstances reasonable risks that notice might not actually reach every beneficiary are justifiable. . . .

The statutory notice to known beneficiaries is inadequate, not because in fact it fails to reach everyone, but because under the circumstances it is not reasonably calculated to reach those who could easily be informed by other means at hand. However it may have been in former times, the mails today are recognized as an efficient and inexpensive means of communication. Moreover, the fact that the trust company has been able to give mailed notice to known beneficiaries at the time the common trust fund was established is persuasive that postal notification at the time of accounting would not seriously burden the plan.

In some situations the law requires greater precautions in its proceedings than the business world accepts for its own purposes. In few, if any, will it be satisfied with less. Certainly it is instructive, in determining the reasonableness of the impersonal broadcast notification here used, to ask whether it would satisfy a prudent man of business, counting his pennies but finding it in his interest to convey information to many persons whose names and addresses are in his files. We are not satisfied that it would. Publication may theoretically be available for all the world to see, but it is too much in our day to suppose that each or any individual beneficiary does or could examine all that is published to see if something may be tucked away in it that affects his property interests. We have before indicated in reference to notice by publication that, "Great caution should be used not to let fiction deny the fair play that can be secured only by a pretty close adhesion to fact." McDonald v. Mabee, 243 U.S. 90, 91.

We hold that the notice of judicial settlement of accounts required by the New York Banking Law § 100–c(12) is incompatible with the requirements of the Fourteenth Amendment as a basis for adjudication depriving known persons whose whereabouts are also known of substantial property rights. Accordingly the judgment is reversed and the cause remanded for further proceedings not inconsistent with this opinion.

Reversed.

[A dissenting opinion by JUSTICE BURTON is omitted.]

NOTES

1.   Does *Mullane* require any particular form of notice? See Federal Rule of Civil Procedure 4(e): service is to be effected either in accordance with the law of the state in which the federal district court sits or by delivery of the complaint to the individual personally or by leaving copies at his place of residence or with a "person of suitable age and discretion" there. See also Hanna v. Plumer, 380 U.S. 460 (1965), p. 711, infra.

In a series of cases the Supreme Court has held that publication in a newspaper, with or without posted notice, is insufficient to comply with the Mullane standards of due process. In Mennonite Board of Missions v. Adams, 462 U.S. 791 (1983), a notice of tax sale was posted in the county courthouse and published once a week for three weeks. This was held inadequate notice to a mortgagee of the property despite the dissenters' argument that the notification satisfied Mullane's "balancing" test. Similarly, in Tulsa Professional Collection Services, Inc. v. Pope, 485 U.S. 478 (1988), the Court required notice by a better method than publication to bar the creditor of a decedent's estate by a two month non-claim period. Cf. Schroeder v. City of New York, 371 U.S. 208, 83 S.Ct. 279 (1962) and Walker v. City of Hutchinson, 352 U.S. 112, 77 S.Ct. 200 (1956), invalidating newspaper and posted notices in condemnation cases where the owner's address was known to the city. In Greene v. Lindsey, 456 U.S. 444, 102 S.Ct. 1874 (1982), the court held that posting a summons on the tenant's apartment door was inadequate notice for a forcible entry and detainer.

2.   The common forms of notice in an action *in personam* are: handing the process to the person to be served; leaving it at his place of residence (with a person of a described class or affixed to the door, etc.); sending it by registered mail after service on a designated statutory agent, such as a registrar. Should registered mail alone always be sufficient? At least one case has held that first class mail alone does not satisfy due process. See Miserandino v. Resort Properties, Inc., 345 Md. 43, 691 A.2d 208 (Md.), cert. denied, 522 U.S. 953, 118 S.Ct. 376, 139 L.Ed.2d 292 (1997).

Dusenbery v. United States, 534 U.S. 161 (2002), held that notice of property forfeiture to a prisoner by certified mail was sufficient even though the prisoner did not receive the notice. A prison officer had signed for the mail. The five-justice majority found that the method used was reasonably calculated to give notice and rejected a requirement that the prisoner personally sign the receipt. Four dissenters viewed the notice as constitutionally deficient, because, quoting from *Mullane*, the method used was " 'substantially less likely to bring home notice' to prison inmates than a 'feasible . . . substitut[e].' "

In Jones v. Flowers, 547 U.S. 220, 126 S.Ct. 1708 (2006), the U.S. Supreme Court held that registered mail sent to a taxpayer at the property's address was insufficient notice for a tax sale of an $80,000 home where the letters had twice been returned undeliverable. The majority analogized the failure to follow up on the returned letters to seeing "the departing postman accidentally drop[ ] the letters down the storm drain." Id. at 229. Would follow-up measures be required if it were a matter of a $25 parking ticket rather than valuable real estate? For a suggestion that the constitutional standard would be less demanding in the case of a $25 parking ticket, see Borchers, Jones v. Flowers: An Essay on a Unified Theory of Procedural Due Process, 40 Creighton L.Rev. 343 (2007).

Are *Dusenbery* and *Jones* consistent with each other?

3.   Should the *Mullane* test be applied in cases in which the defendant is foreign, or should greater care be taken to ensure that a foreign defendant is actually apprised of the pendency of the U.S. proceeding? Consider that question in light of the next case.

Volkswagenwerk Aktiengesellschaft v. Schlunk

Supreme Court of the United States, 1988.
486 U.S. 694, 108 S.Ct. 2104, 100 L.Ed.2d 722.

■ JUSTICE O'CONNOR delivered the opinion of the Court. . . .

I

The parents of respondent Herwig Schlunk were killed in an automobile accident in 1983. Schlunk filed a wrongful death action on their behalf in the Circuit Court of Cook County, Illinois. Schlunk alleged that Volkswagen of America, Inc. (VWoA) had designed and sold the automobile that his parents were driving, and that defects in the automobile caused or contributed to their deaths. . . . Schlunk successfully served his complaint on VWoA, and VWoA filed an answer denying that it had designed or assembled the automobile in question. Schlunk then amended the complaint to add as a defendant Volkswagen Aktiengesellschaft (VWAG), which is the petitioner here. VWAG, a corporation established under the laws of the Federal Republic of Germany, has its place of business in that country. VWoA is a wholly-owned subsidiary of VWAG. Schlunk attempted to serve his amended complaint on VWAG by serving VWoA as VWAG's agent.

VWAG filed a special and limited appearance for the purpose of quashing service. VWAG asserted that it could be served only in accordance with the Hague Service Convention, and that Schlunk had not complied with the Convention's requirements. The Circuit Court denied VWAG's motion. It first observed that VWoA is registered to do business in Illinois and has a registered agent for receipt of process in Illinois. The Court then reasoned that VWoA and VWAG are so closely related that VWoA is VWAG's agent for service of process as a matter of law, notwithstanding VWAG's failure or refusal to appoint VWoA formally as an agent. The court relied on the facts that VWoA is a wholly-owned subsidiary of VWAG, that a majority of the members of the board of directors of VWoA are members of the board of directors of VWAG, and that VWoA is by contract the exclusive importer and distributor of VWAG products sold in the United States. The court concluded that, because service was accomplished within the United States, the Hague Service Convention did not apply. . . . [The Illinois Appellate Court affirmed, and the Illinois Supreme Court denied leave to appeal.]

We granted certiorari to address this issue . . . which has given rise to disagreement among the lower courts. . . .

II

The Hague Service Convention is a multilateral treaty . . . Thirty-two countries, including the United States and the Federal Republic of Germany, have ratified or acceded to the Convention. . . .

The primary innovation of the Convention is that it requires each state to establish a central authority to receive requests for service of documents from other countries. Once a central authority receives a request in the proper form, it must serve the documents by a method prescribed by the internal law of the receiving state or by a method designated by the requester and compatible with that law. . . .

Article 1 defines the scope of the Convention, which is the subject of controversy in this case. It says: "The present Convention shall apply in all cases, in civil or commercial matters, where there is occasion to transmit a judicial or extrajudicial document for service abroad." . . . By virtue of the Supremacy Clause, U.S. Const., Art. VI, the Convention preempts inconsistent methods of service prescribed by state law in all cases to which it applies. Schlunk does not purport to have served his complaint on VWAG in accordance with the Convention. Therefore, if service of process in this case falls within Article 1 of the Convention, the trial court should have granted VWAG's motion to quash. . . .

The Convention does not specify the circumstances in which there is "occasion to transmit" a complaint "for service abroad." But at least the term "service of process" has a well-established technical meaning. Service of process refers to a formal delivery of documents that is legally sufficient to charge the defendant with notice of a pending action. . . . The legal sufficiency of a formal delivery of documents must be measured against some standard. The Convention does not prescribe a standard, so we almost necessarily must refer to the internal law of the forum state. If the internal law of the forum state defines the applicable method of serving process as requiring the transmittal of documents abroad, then the Hague Service Convention applies. . . .

VWAG correctly maintains that the Convention also aims to ensure that there will be adequate notice in cases in which there is occasion to serve process abroad. Thus compliance with the Convention is mandatory in all cases to which it applies. . . . Our interpretation of the Convention does not necessarily advance this particular objective, inasmuch as it makes recourse to the Convention's means of service dependent on the forum's internal law. But we do not think that this country, or any other country, will draft its internal laws deliberately so as to circumvent the Convention in cases in which it would be appropriate to transmit judicial documents for service abroad. For example, there has been no question in this country of excepting foreign nationals from the protection of our Due Process Clause. Under that Clause, foreign nationals are assured of either personal service, which typically will require service abroad and trigger the Convention, or substituted service that provides "notice reasonably calculated, under all the circumstances, to apprise interested parties of the pendency of the action and afford them an opportunity to present their objections." Mullane v. Central Hanover Bank & Trust Co., 339 U.S. 306 (1950).*

Furthermore, nothing that we say today prevents compliance with the Convention even when the internal law of the forum does not so require. The Convention provides simple and certain means by which to serve process on a foreign national. Those who eschew its procedures risk discovering that the forum's internal law required transmittal of documents for service abroad, and that the Convention therefore provided the exclusive means of valid service. In addition, parties that comply with the Convention ultimately may find it easier to enforce their judgments abroad. . . . For these reasons, we anticipate that parties may resort to the Convention voluntarily, even in cases that fall outside the scope of its mandatory application.

III

In this case, the Illinois long-arm statute authorized Schlunk to serve VWAG by substituted service on VWoA, without sending documents to Germany. . . . VWAG has not petitioned for review of the Illinois Appellate Court's holding that service was proper as a matter of Illinois law. VWAG contends, however, that service on VWAG was not complete until VWoA transmitted the complaint to VWAG in Germany.

---

* The concurrence believes that our interpretation does not adequately guarantee timely notice, which it denominates the "primary" purpose of the Convention, albeit without authority. The concurrence instead proposes to impute a substantive standard to the words, "service abroad." Evidently, a method of service would be deemed to be "service abroad" within the meaning of Article 1 if it does not provide notice to the recipient "in due time." This due process notion cannot be squared with the plain meaning of the words, "service abroad." The contours of the concurrence's substantive standard are not defined and we note that it would create some uncertainty even on the facts of this case. If the substantive standard tracks the Due Process Clause of the Fourteenth Amendment, it is not self-evident that substituted service on a subsidiary is sufficient with respect to the parent. In the only cases in which it has considered the question, this Court held that the activities of a subsidiary are not necessarily enough to render a parent subject to a court's jurisdiction, for service of process or otherwise. Cannon Mfg. Co. v. Cudahy Packing Co., 267 U.S. 333, 336–337 (1925). . . .

According to VWAG, this transmission constituted service abroad under the Hague Service Convention. . . .

We reject this argument. Where service on a domestic agent is valid and complete under both state law and the Due Process Clause, our inquiry ends and the Convention has no further implications. . . .

Affirmed.

[Justice Brennan concurred in the judgment in an opinion joined by Justices Marshall and Blackmun.] Until the Convention was implemented, the contracting nations followed widely divergent practices for serving judicial documents across international borders, some of which did not ensure any notice, much less timely notice, and therefore often produced unfair default judgments. See generally International Co-Operation in Litigation: Europe (H. Smit ed. 1965); 3 1965 Conférence de la Haye de Droit International Privé, Actes et Documents de la Dixime Session (Notification) 11–12 (1965) (hereinafter 3 Actes et Documents). Particularly controversial was a procedure, common among civil-law countries, called "notification au parquet," which permitted delivery of process to a local official who was then ordinarily supposed to transmit the document abroad through diplomatic or other channels. See S.Exec.Rep. No. 6, 90th Cong., 1st Sess., 11–12, 14–16 (1967) (S.Exec.Rep. No. 6); S.Doc. C, 90th Cong., 1st Sess., 5–6, 21 (1967) (S.Exec.Doc. C). Typically, service was deemed complete upon delivery of the document to the official whether or not the official succeeded in transmitting it to the defendant and whether or not the defendant otherwise received notice of the pending lawsuit.[1]

The United States delegation to the Convention objected to notification au parquet as inconsistent with "the requirements of 'due process of law' under the Federal Constitution." 3 Actes et Documents 128 (citations omitted). . . .

In response to this and other concerns, the Convention prescribes the exclusive means for service of process emanating from one contracting nation and culminating in another. As the Court observes, the Convention applies only when the document is to be "transmit[ted]

---

[1] The head of the United States delegation to the Convention described *notification au parquet* as follows:

"This is a system which permits the entry of judgments in personam by default against a nonresident defendant without requiring adequate notice. There is also no real right to move to open the default judgment or to appeal, because the time to move to open judgment or to appeal will generally have expired before the defendant finds out about the judgment.

"Under this system of service, the process-server simply delivers a copy of the writ to a public official's office. The time for answer begins to run immediately. Some effort is supposed to be made through the Foreign Office and through diplomatic channels to give the defendant notice, but failure to do this has no effect on the validity of the service. . . .

"There are no . . . limitations and protections [comparable to due process or personal jurisdiction] under the *notification au parquet* system. Here jurisdiction lies merely if the plaintiff is a local national; nothing more is needed." S.Exec.Rep. No. 6, at 11–12 (statement by Philip W. Amram).

. . . for service abroad"; it covers not every transmission of judicial documents abroad, but only those transmissions abroad that constitute formal "service." See ante, at 700. It is common ground that the Convention governs when the procedure prescribed by the internal law of the forum nation or state provides that service is not complete until the document is transmitted abroad. That is not to say, however, as does the Court, that the forum nation may designate any type of service "domestic" and thereby avoid application of the Convention.

Admittedly, as the Court points out, ibid., the Convention's language does not prescribe a precise standard to distinguish between "domestic" service and "service abroad." But the Court's solution leaves contracting nations free to ignore its terms entirely, converting its command into exhortation. Under the Court's analysis, for example, a forum nation could prescribe direct mail service to any foreigner and deem service effective upon deposit in the mailbox, or could arbitrarily designate a domestic agent for any foreign defendant and deem service complete upon receipt domestically by the agent even though there is little likelihood that service would ever reach the defendant. In fact, so far as I can tell, the Court's interpretation permits any contracting nation to revive notification au parquet so long as the nation's internal law deems service complete domestically, but cf. ante, at 704, even though, as the Court concedes, "such methods of service are the least likely to provide a defendant with actual notice," and even though "[t]here is no question but that the Conference wanted to eliminate notification au parquet," ante, at 703 (citation omitted). . . .

The negotiating history and the uniform interpretation announced by our own negotiators confirm that the Convention limits a forum's ability to deem service "domestic," thereby avoiding the Convention's terms. Admittedly, the Convention does not precisely define the contours. But that imprecision does not absolve us of our responsibility to apply the Convention mandatorily, any more than imprecision permits us to discard the words "due process of law," U.S. Const., Amdt. 14, § 1. And however difficult it might be in some circumstances to discern the Convention's precise limits, it is remarkably easy to conclude that the Convention does not prohibit the type of service at issue here. Service on a wholly owned, closely controlled subsidiary is reasonably calculated to reach the parent "in due time" as the Convention requires. . . . That is, in fact, what our own Due Process Clause requires, see Mullane v. Central Hanover Bank & Trust Co., 339 U.S. 306, 314–315 (1950), and since long before the Convention's implementation our law has permitted such service, see, e.g., Perkins v. Benguet Consolidated Mining Co., 342 U.S. 437, 444–445 (1952); . . . This is significant because our own negotiators made clear to the Senate their understanding that the Convention would require no major changes in federal or state service-of-process rules. Thus, it is unsurprising that nothing in the negotiating history suggests that the contracting nations were dissatisfied with the practice at issue here, of which they were surely aware, much less that they intended to abolish it like they intended to abolish notification au parquet. And since notice served on a wholly owned domestic subsidiary is infinitely more likely to reach the foreign parent's attention than was notice served au parquet (or by any other procedure that the negotiators singled out for criticism) there is no reason to interpret the Convention to bar it. . . .

NOTES

1. In United Electrical, Radio & Machine Workers v. 163 Pleasant Street Corp., 960 F.2d 1080 (1st Cir.1992), the court declined to pierce the corporate veil between the Scottish parent and its Massachusetts subsidiary for service-of-process purposes when plaintiffs had not offered any proof that the separate corporations had been established for an improper purpose or that they had failed to maintain their separate corporate identities. In Vermeulen v. Renault, U.S.A. Inc., 965 F.2d 1014 (11th Cir.1992), the court employed an agency theory to uphold Georgia's assertion of jurisdiction over the French defendant car manufacturer on the basis of the activities of its wholly-owned distributor. The court held that the defendant purposefully availed itself of the American market by specifically designing cars for it, advertising in it, and setting the distribution system. However, after further appeals, the court concluded that jurisdiction—both subject matter and personal—were governed by a federal statute, the Foreign Sovereign Immunities Act, and that both kinds of jurisdiction existed. See Vermeulen v. Renault U.S.A., Inc., 975 F.2d 746 (11th Cir. 1992) and Vermeulen v. Renault, U.S.A., Inc., 985 F.2d 1534 (11th Cir.1993).

2. The *Schlunk* decision is equally relevant for an American defendant served with process for a suit in another country. See Ackermann v. Levine, 788 F.2d 830 (2d Cir.1986) (enforcing a German default judgment against a U.S. defendant over the latter's objection to service of process).

3. See also Voxman, Jurisdiction over a Parent Corporation in Its Subsidiary's State of Incorporation, 141 U.Pa.L.Rev. 327 (1992).

4. The Brussels Ia Regulation addresses only one aspect of the problems considered here: If litigation relates to the activities of a branch, agency or other establishment, (special) jurisdiction exists in the courts of the place where such a branch is located. Art. 7(5). Recall that there is no general jurisdiction under European law for "systematic and continuous" doing of business. Except for stream-of-commerce cases, in which the parent can be reached by means of the tort provisions, jurisdiction over the out-of-state parent in the state of the subsidiary in other cases would therefore require analytically that the two be regarded as one (piercing of the corporate veil) and that the parent/subsidiary then be subjected to specific jurisdiction for its/their activity. Disregard of the separate personality of parent and subsidiary for jurisdictional purposes is generally not part of European law. See also Hofstetter, Parent Responsibility for Subsidiary Corporations: Evaluating European Trends, 39 Int'l & Comp. L.Q. 576 (1990).

5.   Federal Rule 4(f), concerning service of process on an individual who is not found in any judicial district in the United States, provides in part that such service may be effected:

> (1)   by any internationally agreed means reasonably calculated to give notice, such as those authorized by the Hague Convention . . . ;
>
> (2)   if there is no internationally agreed means [in the manner prescribed by foreign law or by foreign authorities or, unless prohibited by foreign law, by personal delivery or by mail]; or
>
> (3)   by other means not prohibited by international agreement, as the court orders.

Does the new version of the Rule have any effect on the problems raised in *Schlunk*?

6.   Article 10(a) of the Hague Convention provides for "the freedom to send judicial documents, by postal channels, directly to persons abroad." In Menon v. Water Splash, Inc., 472 S.W.3d 28 (Tex. App. 2015), a Texas appellate court held that Article 10(a) applies to service of documents *other than* process, and not to service of process itself. At the request of the plaintiff, who had served process for the Texas suit by mail delivered to the defendant in Canada, the Supreme Court has agreed to hear the case. Water Splash, Inc. v. Menon, 137 S.Ct. 547 (Dec. 2, 2016). The precise question raised is: "Does the Hague Service Convention authorize service of process by mail?"

7.   Even if, as in *Schlunk*, the requirements of the Hague Convention can be avoided because service can be completed without transmitting the documents abroad, are there advantages to complying with the Convention? One advantage may be that compliance with the Convention may aid in the successful enforcement of the judgment in the courts of other signatory nations. See generally Weintraub, How Substantial is our Need for a Judgments-Recognition Convention and What Should we Bargain Away to Get It?, 28 Brooklyn J.Int'l L. 167, 170–71 (1998). A fair number of countries have service provisions that are not common in the U.S., and will not enforce U.S. judgments absent compliance with them. See Adler, If We Build it, Will They Come?—The Need for a Multilateral Convention on the Recognition and Enforcement of Civil Monetary Judgments, 26 Law & Policy of Int'l Bus. 79, 95 (1994) (listing South Korea, Japan, Mexico, Panama, Portugal, Panama, South Africa, Spain, Taiwan and Venezuela as among those countries that will not enforce U.S. judgments without compliance with their local service rules).

CHAPTER 4

LIMITATIONS ON THE EXERCISE OF JURISDICTION

INTRODUCTORY NOTE

This chapter examines situations where states choose not to exercise judicial jurisdiction they undoubtedly have. This may be the result of an agreement between the parties purporting to give exclusive jurisdiction to the courts of another state or because the court deems itself to be an inconvenient forum for the trial of the action or to be incapable of granting appropriate relief. A related question concerns what we call the "race to judgment": when the parties sue each other in different courts on essentially the same claim in the hope of obtaining a favorable judgment with which to bar the other action.

Another question treated in this chapter is whether, when a state seeks by statute to restrict to its own courts jurisdiction to entertain particular actions, the courts of other states will give effect to the former state's desires. On some occasions, a state which has judicial jurisdiction in the due process sense may be required by other provisions of the United States Constitution either to hear or to refrain from hearing a case.

SECTION 1. LIMITATIONS IMPOSED BY CONTRACT

A state has judicial jurisdiction over a defendant who appears or has consented in advance to the court's jurisdiction. Section 2 of the Model Choice of Forum Act, (since withdrawn) stated the conditions upon which courts will usually exercise jurisdiction when the parties have made a contractual choice of the local forum. The *conferral* of jurisdiction by means of a contractual choice-of-court clause is also known as *"prorogation."* Either by express stipulation or by interpretation of the clause, the parties may have intended the prorogation to be exclusive or an alternative choice of court. Suppose, however, that the plaintiff brings an action in a court other than the chosen forum and that it is now the defendant who seeks to enforce an exclusive choice-of-court stipulation: will the court dismiss for lack of jurisdiction or will it refrain from exercising the jurisdiction that it otherwise possesses? A jurisdiction-*limiting* effect of a choice-of-court clause is known as *"derogation."* The European Union law (Council Regulation No. 1215/2012), p. 1165, Note 6, infra, does not distinguish, in its Art. 25(1), between the prorogation and derogation effects of these clauses, but treats the latter to follow from the former ("... such [prorogated] jurisdiction shall be exclusive ..."). However, the provision generally proscribes the use of such clauses in certain transactions (Art. 25(5)). Other EU law provisions protect weaker parties (insureds, consumer, employees) against prorogation clauses that would deprive them of advantageous jurisdiction provisions (see Arts. 15, 19, 23). In contrast, American courts in the past often drew a distinction between prorogation and derogation, accepting jurisdiction conferred on them but disregarding the parties' choice of another forum on the ground that parties cannot, by private argument, "oust" a court of jurisdiction given it by law. Modern decisions usually give effect to these agreements except when it would be "unfair or unreasonable" to do so. Restatement, Second, Conflict of Laws § 80.

Section 3 of the Model Choice of Forum Act* stated more precisely the circumstances making it "unfair or unreasonable" to give effect to the parties' agreement.

Section 3. [*Action in Another Place by Agreement.*] If the parties have agreed in writing that an action shall on a controversy be brought only in another state and it is brought in a court of this state, the court will dismiss or stay the action, as appropriate, unless

(1) the court is required by statute to entertain the action;

(2) the plaintiff cannot secure effective relief in the other state, for reasons other than delay in bringing the action;

(3) the other state would be a substantially less convenient place for the trial of the action than this state;

(4) the agreement as to the place of the action was obtained by misrepresentation, duress, the abuse of economic power, or other unconscionable means; or

(5) it would for some other reason be unfair or unreasonable to enforce the agreement.

Comment

Clause (4): A significant factor to be considered in determining whether there was an "abuse of economic power or other unconscionable means" is whether the choice of forum agreement was contained in an adhesion, or "take-it-or-leave-it," contract.

The Hague Conference on Private International Law, of which the United States is a member, drafted a "Convention on Choice of Court Agreements" in 2005. It entered into force in 2015 for the member states of the European Union, except Denmark, and for Mexico and Singapore. 44 I.L.M. 1294 (2005). The United Kingdom subsequently withdrew but acceded again in January 2021. The United States has signed but has not yet ratified the Convention. Its text is similar to the Model Act, but expands upon the latter's provisions in Art. 3(2) and (5) by stating in its Art. 6(c) that the non-chosen court may disregard the agreement "if giving effect . . . would lead to a manifest injustice or would be manifestly

---

* After having been adopted in four states, this model act was withdrawn in 1975. (Handbook of the Conference of Commissioners on Uniform State Laws 351 (1976)).

contrary to the public policy of the [non-chosen] court [in which the action was brought]." As to unfairness, see also Note 5, p. 223, infra.

M/S Bremen v. Zapata Off-Shore Co.

Supreme Court of the United States, 1972.
407 U.S. 1, 92 S.Ct. 1907, 32 L.Ed.2d 513.

[The defendant, a German corporation, agreed to tow a drilling rig of Zapata, an American corporation, from Louisiana to a point off Ravenna, Italy. The contract provided that "any dispute arising must be treated before the London Court of Justice" and also contained two clauses purporting to exculpate the defendant from liability for damages to the rig. These latter provisions were valid under English law, and, according to the uncontradicted testimony of a British legal expert, would have been applied to exonerate the defendant if suit had been brought in England. On the other hand, these latter provisions were invalid under the law of the United States. The rig was damaged while being towed in the Gulf of Mexico. Suit to recover for this damage was brought in a federal district court in Florida. The lower courts refused to dismiss the action despite the fact that it had been brought in violation of the choice-of-forum clause. The Supreme Court reversed.]

■ CHIEF JUSTICE BURGER delivered the opinion of the Court.

. . . The expansion of American business and industry will hardly be encouraged if, notwithstanding solemn contracts, we insist on a parochial concept that all disputes must be resolved under our laws and in our courts. . . .

Forum-selection clauses have historically not been favored by American courts. Many courts, federal and state, have declined to enforce such clauses on the ground that they were "contrary to public policy," or that their effect was to "oust the jurisdiction" of the court. Although this view apparently still has considerable acceptance, other courts are tending to adopt a more hospitable attitude toward forum-selection clauses. This view . . . is that such clauses are prima facie valid and should be enforced unless enforcement is shown by the resisting party to be "unreasonable" under the circumstances. We believe this is the correct doctrine to be followed by federal district courts sitting in admiralty. . . . This approach is substantially that followed in other common-law countries including England. . . . It accords with ancient concepts of freedom of contract and reflects an appreciation of the expanding horizons of American contractors who seek business in all parts of the world. Not surprisingly, foreign businessmen prefer, as do we, to have disputes resolved in their own courts, but if that choice is not available, then in a neutral forum with expertise in the subject matter. Plainly, the courts of England meet the standards of neutrality and long experience in admiralty litigation. The choice of that forum was made in an arm's-length negotiation by experienced and sophisticated businessmen, and absent some compelling and countervailing reason it should be honored by the parties and enforced by the courts.

The argument that such clauses are improper because they tend to "oust" a court of jurisdiction is hardly more than a vestigial legal fiction. It appears to rest at core on historical judicial resistance to any attempt to reduce the power and business of a particular court and has little place in an era when all courts are overloaded and when businesses once essentially local now operate in world markets. It reflects something of a provincial attitude regarding the fairness of other tribunals. No one seriously contends in this case that the forum-selection clause "ousted" the District Court of jurisdiction over Zapata's action. The threshold question is whether that court should have exercised its jurisdiction to do more than give effect to the legitimate expectations of the parties, manifested in their freely negotiated agreement, by specifically enforcing the forum clause.

There are compelling reasons why a freely negotiated private international agreement, unaffected by fraud, undue influence, or overweening bargaining power, such as that involved here, should be given full effect.... Manifestly much uncertainty and possibly great inconvenience to both parties could arise if a suit could be maintained in any jurisdiction in which an accident might occur or if jurisdiction were left to any place where the *Bremen* or Unterweser might happen to be found. The elimination of all such uncertainties by agreeing in advance on a forum acceptable to both parties is an indispensable element in international trade, commerce, and contracting.

[I]t seems reasonably clear that the District Court and the Court of Appeals placed the burden on Unterweser to show that London would be a more convenient forum than Tampa, although the contract expressly resolved that issue. The correct approach would have been to enforce the forum clause specifically unless Zapata could clearly show that enforcement would be unreasonable and unjust, or that the clause was invalid for such reasons as fraud or overreaching. Accordingly, the case must be remanded for reconsideration.

We note, however, that there is nothing in the record presently before us that would support a refusal to enforce the forum clause. The Court of Appeals suggested that enforcement would be contrary to the public policy of the forum under Bisso v. Inland Waterways Corp., 349 U.S. 85 (1955), because of the prospect that the English courts would enforce the clauses of the towage contract purporting to exculpate Unterweser from liability for damages to the [rig]. A contractual choice-of-forum clause should be held unenforceable if enforcement would contravene a strong public policy of the forum in which suit is brought, whether declared by statute or by judicial decision. It is clear, however, that whatever the proper scope of the policy expressed in *Bisso,* it does not reach this case. *Bisso* rested on considerations with respect to the towage business strictly in American waters, and those considerations are not controlling in an international commercial agreement.

Courts have also suggested that a forum clause, even though it is freely bargained for and contravenes no important public policy of the forum, may nevertheless be "unreasonable" and unenforceable if the chosen forum is *seriously* inconvenient for the trial of the action. Of course, where it can be said with reasonable assurance that at the time they entered the contract, the parties to a freely negotiated private international commercial agreement contemplated the claimed inconvenience, it is difficult to see why any such claim of inconvenience should be heard to render the forum clause unenforceable. . . . [S]election of a remote forum to apply differing foreign law to an essentially American controversy might contravene an important public policy of the forum. For example, so long as *Bisso* governs American courts with respect to the towage business in American waters, it would quite arguably be improper to permit an American tower to avoid that policy by providing a foreign forum for resolution of his disputes with an American towee.

This case, however, involves a freely negotiated international commercial transaction between a German and an American corporation for towage of a vessel from the Gulf of Mexico to the Adriatic Sea.

[T]o allow Zapata opportunity to carry its heavy burden of showing not only that the balance of convenience is strongly in favor of trial in Tampa (that is, that it will be far more inconvenient for Zapata to litigate in London than it will be for Unterweser to litigate in Tampa), but also that a London trial will be so manifestly and gravely inconvenient to Zapata that it will be effectively deprived of a meaningful day in court, we remand for further proceedings.

[JUSTICE DOUGLAS dissented primarily on the ground that the parties should not be permitted to escape the strong policy expressed in the *Bisso* case by means of a choice-of-forum clause.]

NOTES

1. Objection to forum selection by the parties, mentioned by the Court in the case above, goes back to Nute v. Hamilton Mutual Ins. Co., 72 Mass. (6 Gray) 174, 181 (Mass. 1856): "[T]he remedy does not depend on contract but upon law . . . ," also using the verb "oust." The Restatement (Second), Conflict of Laws (1971) still states in its § 80 that the "parties' agreement . . . cannot oust a state of judicial jurisdiction . . . ."

2. So far as appears, England had no contact in the *Zapata* case with the parties or the transaction. Under these circumstances, would a choice-of-law clause calling for application of English law have been given effect? For the European Community approach, see the Rome-I Regulation on the Law Applicable to Contractual Obligations, p. 1192, infra, in which Art. 3 grants parties the freedom to choose applicable law, subject to Art. 9, which allows courts to disregard the parties' choice if it derogates from the forum's overriding mandatory rules. Can the parties, by means of a choice-of-forum clause, obtain application of a law which could not have been made applicable by a choice-of-law clause? See Chief Justice Burger's reference to "important public policy of the forum." *But see* Richards v. Lloyd's of London and the other cases in Note 3, infra.

3.   The needs of international trade were also emphasized in Scherk v. Alberto-Culver Co., 417 U.S. 506 (1974), where the Supreme Court enforced an arbitration clause in a contract calling for the purchase by an American manufacturer of foreign enterprises owned by a German citizen. This was done despite the fact that the Court had previously held that an arbitration clause in an analogous agreement with only United States contacts was unenforceable by reason of the Securities and Exchange Act. *Zapata* was cited as an important precedent in the *Alberto-Culver* opinion. Similarly, the Supreme Court held in Mitsubishi Motors Corp. v. Soler Chrysler-Plymouth, Inc., 473 U.S. 614, 629 (1985), that an antitrust claim was covered by the parties' agreement to arbitrate, even though such an agreement might not be enforceable in the interstate context: "[C]oncerns of international comity, respect for the capacities of foreign and international tribunals, and sensitivity to the need of the international commercial system for predictability in the resolution of disputes require that we enforce the parties' agreement, even assuming that a contrary result would be forthcoming in a domestic context."

Lower courts have wrestled with the joint operation of choice-of-law and choice-of-forum clauses where the effect of the two clauses is essentially to waive application of federal substantive law. In Richards v. Lloyd's of London, 107 F.3d 1422 (9th Cir.1997), the court, expressly disagreeing with other circuits, refused to enforce choice-of-law and choice-of-forum clauses pointing towards England in a dispute involving alleged violations of federal securities laws. The court distinguished *Scherk* as involving a conflict between two statutes—the Federal Arbitration Act and the securities laws—while the case at hand involved no such conflict. The court also distinguished *Scherk* as involving only slight contacts with the United States, while the case at hand involved recruitment of securities offerees in the United States as well as other contacts. On review by an eleven-judge, en banc panel, the Ninth Circuit withdrew its earlier opinion and held—consistent with other circuits—that choice-of-forum and choice-of-law clauses of this type do not violate the anti-waiver provisions of federal securities law. Richards v. Lloyd's of London, 135 F.3d 1289 (9th Cir.1998) (en banc), cert. denied, 525 U.S. 943 (1998).

4.   In extension of the policy expressed in *Scherk, Mitsubishi*, Note 3, supra, and other cases, federal courts have applied *M/S Bremen* to uphold choice-of-forum clauses in cases (e.g., involving personal injuries) arising out of contracts of maritime employment. See, e.g., Francisco v. M/T Stolt Achievement, 293 F.3d 270 (5th Cir. 2002), cert. denied, 537 U.S. 1030 (2002); Bautista v. Star Cruises, 396 F.3d 1289 (11th Cir.2005); Lim v. Offshore Specialty Fabricators, Inc., 404 F.3d 898 (5th Cir. 2005), cert. denied, 546 U.S. 826 (2005).

Carnival Cruise Lines, Inc. v. Shute

Supreme Court of the United States, 1991.
499 U.S. 585, 111 S.Ct. 1522, 113 L.Ed.2d 622.

[The Shutes, a Washington State couple, bought tickets for a cruise through a local travel agent from Carnival Cruise Lines, a Panamanian corporation with its principal place of business in Miami, Florida. Payment was forwarded to Miami; the tickets were issued there. They also constituted the Contract of Passage, which contained a forum-selection clause in favor of Florida. The cruise departed from Los Angeles. Mrs. Shute was injured as a result of a fall when the ship was in international waters. The Shutes sued in Washington. The Court of Appeals held that the forum-selection clause was unenforceable because it was not freely bargained for and because enforcement of the clause would deprive the Shutes of their day in court inasmuch as they were physically and financially unable to pursue litigation in Florida. The Court of Appeals also held that Carnival Cruise Lines' Washington contacts were sufficient for the exercise of specific jurisdiction.]

■ BLACKMUN, J., delivered the opinion of the Court, in which REHNQUIST, C.J., and WHITE, O'CONNOR, SCALIA, KENNEDY, and SOUTER, JJ., joined. STEVENS, J., filed a dissenting opinion, in which MARSHALL, J., joined.

[T]he Court of Appeals acknowledged that a court concerned with the enforceability of such a clause must begin its analysis with The Bremen v. Zapata Off-Shore Co., 407 U.S. 1 (1972), where this Court held that forum-selection clauses, although not "historically . . . favored," are "prima facie valid." The appellate court concluded that the forum clause should not be enforced because it "was not freely bargained for." As an "independent justification" for refusing to enforce the clause, the Court of Appeals noted that there was evidence in the record to indicate that "the Shutes are physically and financially incapable of pursuing this litigation in Florida" and that the enforcement of the clause would operate to deprive them of their day in court and thereby contravene this Court's holding in *The Bremen.*

We begin by noting the boundaries of our inquiry. First, this is a case in admiralty, and federal law governs the enforceability of the forum-selection clause we scrutinize. Second, we do not address the question whether respondents had sufficient notice of the forum clause before entering the contract for passage. Respondents essentially have conceded that they had notice of the forum-selection provision. Brief for Respondent 26 ("The respondents do not contest the incorporation of the provisions nor [sic] that the forum selection clause was reasonably communicated to the respondents, as much as three pages of fine print can be communicated."). Additionally, the Court of Appeals evaluated the enforceability of the forum clause under the assumption, although "doubtful," that respondents could be deemed to have had knowledge of the clause.

In evaluating the reasonableness of the forum clause at issue in this case, we must refine the analysis of *The Bremen* to account for the realities of form passage contracts. As an initial matter, we do not adopt the Court of Appeals' determination that a non-negotiated forum-selection clause in a form ticket contract is never enforceable simply because it is not the subject of bargaining. Including a reasonable forum clause in a form contract of this kind well may be permissible for several reasons: First, a cruise line has a special interest in limiting the fora in which it potentially could be subject to suit. Because a cruise ship typically carries passengers from many locales, it is not unlikely that a mishap on a cruise could subject the cruise line to litigation in several different fora. Additionally, a clause establishing *ex ante* the forum for dispute resolution has the salutary effect of dispelling any confusion about where suits arising from the contract must be brought and defended, sparing litigants the time and expense of pretrial motions to determine the correct forum, and conserving judicial resources that otherwise would be devoted to deciding those motions. Finally, it stands to reason that passengers who purchase tickets containing a forum clause like that at issue in this case benefit in the form of reduced fares reflecting the savings that the cruise line enjoys by limiting the fora in which it may be sued.

We also do not accept the Court of Appeals' "independent justification" for its conclusion that *The Bremen* dictates that the clause should not be enforced because "there is evidence in the record to indicate that the Shutes are physically and financially incapable of pursuing this litigation in Florida." We do not defer to the Court of Appeals' findings of fact. . . . The Court of Appeals' conclusory reference to the record provides no basis for this Court to validate the finding of inconvenience. Furthermore, the Court of Appeals did not place in proper context this Court's statement in *The Bremen* that "the serious inconvenience of the contractual forum to one or both of the parties might carry greater weight in determining the reasonableness of the forum clause." 407 U.S., at 17. The Court made this statement in evaluating a hypothetical "agreement between two Americans to resolve their essentially local disputes in a remote alien forum." Ibid. In the present case, Florida is not a "remote alien forum," nor—given the fact that Mrs. Shute's accident occurred off the coast of Mexico—is this dispute an essentially local one inherently more suited to resolution in the State of Washington than in Florida. In light of these distinctions, and because respondents do not claim lack of notice of the forum clause, we conclude that they have not satisfied the "heavy burden of proof" required to set aside the clause on grounds of inconvenience.

It bears emphasis that forum-selection clauses contained in form passage contracts are subject to judicial scrutiny for fundamental fairness. In this case, there is no indication that petitioner set Florida as the forum in which disputes were to be resolved as a means of discouraging cruise passengers from pursuing legitimate claims. Any suggestion of such a bad-faith motive is belied by two facts: petitioner has its principal place of business in Florida, and many of its cruises depart from and return to Florida ports. Similarly, there is no evidence that petitioner obtained respondents' accession to the forum clause by fraud or overreaching. Finally, respondents have conceded that they were given notice of the forum provision and, therefore, presumably retained the option of rejecting the contract with impunity. In the case before us, therefore, we conclude that the Court of Appeals erred in refusing to enforce the forum-selection clause.

[Reversed.]

■ JUSTICE STEVENS, joined by JUSTICE MARSHALL, dissented on the grounds inter alia that the Shutes did not have notice of the clause and that it was not freely bargained for.

CARNIVAL CRUISE LINES, INC. V. SUPERIOR COURT, 286 Cal.Rptr. 323 (Cal.App.1991). Two hundred thirty-eight cruise passengers sought damages for injuries sustained during a storm. The trial court refused to honor a forum-selection clause in favor of Florida, identical to the clause involved in the *Shute* case, and Carnival Cruise Lines petitioned for a writ of mandamus. The appellate court denied the writ on the basis of the considerations advanced by the Court of Appeals in *Shute*. The United States Supreme Court ultimately reversed and remanded for reconsideration in the light of its decision in *Shute*. On remand, held: "[T]he forum-selection clause is unenforceable as to any particular plaintiff if the [trial] court determines that such plaintiff did not have sufficient notice of the forum-selection clause prior to entering into the contract for passage. Absent such notice, the requisite mutual consent to that contractual term is lacking and no valid contract with respect to such clause thus exists. [Remanded to the trial court for a determination of this issue.]"

STOBAUGH V. NORWEGIAN CRUISE LINE LTD., 5 S.W.3d 232 (Tex.App. 1999). The court ruled as a matter of law that the forum-selection clause was not enforceable and remanded for a trial on the merits of a class action against a cruise line for injuries when the ship sailed into a hurricane. The court noted that not only were the passengers not informed of the forum-selection clause until after paying for the tickets, but also that they would not have received a full refund if they had tried to cancel after receiving their tickets.

NOTES

1.   Two-thirds of the plaintiffs in the California *Carnival Cruise* case were California residents, close to one half of the remaining plaintiffs were residents of Western states. Not a single plaintiff was from Florida, Carnival Cruise Lines' place of business. The court had originally stressed this fact to

emphasize the "unreasonableness" of the forum-selection clause. Obviously wishing to provide the plaintiffs with a local forum, the court seized on the notice issue that the United States Supreme Court had expressly left open. Is it not likely that the notice issue will swallow up the *Shute* decision's endorsement of forum-selection clauses in standard form contracts? Casavant v. Norwegian Cruise Line, Ltd., 829 N.E.2d 1171 (Mass.App.Ct.2005), cert. denied, 546 U.S. 773 (2006), refused to enforce a forum-selection clause in a cruise contract. The court held that the clause was not binding because the defendant did not deliver the contract to the plaintiffs until almost a year after the original booking and two months after full payment of the cruise price. The court summarized the view that federal courts have taken of the enforceability of forum clauses: "In the wake of *Carnival Cruise*, the Federal courts have decided a number of cases which establish that, for vacation cruise ticketing contracts, in order for the passenger to be bound by the forum selection clause under Federal maritime law, the private ticket cruise buyer must be given reasonable time within which to act and to reject the ticketing contract and forum selection clause, without incurring disproportionately unfair penalties for such a rejection." Id. at 1180.

Both the California *Carnival Cruise* opinion, supra, and the opinion in *Casavant*, this note, supra, focus on the party's notice of the forum-selection term. Recall that this is also a problem in the law of sales: the term-in-the-box, the shrink-wrap item with warranty limitations in the box that the buyer does not see until after subsequent inspection. In the leading decision on the subject, Hill v. Gateway 2000, 105 F.3d 1147 (7th Cir.1997), Judge Easterbrook contributed the idea of what became known as "rolling contract formation": the contract is not finally formed until the buyer has notice of the terms and has not objected (rejected them) within the time limit stipulated in them. The *Casavant* court puts its conclusion in similar terms: see the quote at the end of the previous paragraph.

2. If the forum-selection clause is unenforceable in the California case, the California court obviously has jurisdiction: the cruise in question departed from and was to end in Los Angeles. If the forum-selection clause had been unenforceable in *Shute,* would the Washington court have had jurisdiction? Carnival Cruise Lines had no offices and no exclusive agents in Washington, is not registered to do business there, and does not pay taxes there. It did advertise in local media, conducted promotional seminars, and paid commissions to local travel agents. It issued cruise tickets in Florida. The Court of Appeals held that these facts permitted the exercise of specific jurisdiction: ". . . Carnival's solicitation of business in Washington attracted the Shutes (through their travel agent) to the Carnival cruise. In the absence of Carnival's activity, the Shutes would not have taken the cruise, and Mrs. Shute's injury would not have occurred. It was Carnival's forum-related activities that put the parties within 'tortious striking distance' of one another." Shute v. Carnival Cruise Lines, 897 F.2d 377, 386 (9th Cir.1990). Is the court's "but for" test consistent with the United States Supreme Court's approach in *Helicopteros,* p. 122, supra, or the dissent at p. 123, and with *J. McIntyre,* supra p. 86? See *Moki Mac River Expeditions v. Drugg,* p.

152, supra. For an argument that a "but for" test would have provided specific jurisdiction in *Helicopteros,* see Seidelson, Recasting World-Wide Volkswagen as a Source of Longer Jurisdictional Reach, 19 Tulsa L.J. 1, 27 n.105 (1983). Wilson v. Humphreys (Cayman) Ltd., 916 F.2d 1239 (7th Cir.1990), cert. denied, 499 U.S. 947 (1991), upheld jurisdiction over a Cayman Island hotel without reaching the "arising out of" issue, perhaps assisted by the fact that the complaint pleaded not only negligence, but also breach of express and implied warranties, and breach of contract. Will all the uncertainty have been resolved by an U.S. Supreme Court decision in *Ford Motor Co. v. Montana* (see Note, p. 161, supra)?

What claims are governed by a particular forum-selection clause? "Usually courts have given clauses a transactional reading, meaning that all claims that are part of the same transaction are covered by the clause." Hay, Borchers, Symeonides, Whytock, Conflict of Laws § 11.6 (6th ed.2018), with references. In Quebecor World (USA), Inc. v. Harsha Associates, L.L.C., 455 F.Supp.2d 236, 238–39 (W.D.N.Y.2006), the court held that a forum selection in a guaranty did not carry over to the underlying contract because the two were not closely enough related. "Relevant factors include whether the two documents were executed contemporaneously, whether the guaranty is stated to have been an inducement or consideration for the contract or incorporates the contract by reference, and whether the two documents cover the identical subject matter."

3. In the *M/S Bremen v. Zapata* decision, the U.S. Supreme Court referred to the old objection to forum selection clauses as impermissibly trying to "oust" a court's jurisdiction (supra p. 209 and Note (1), p. 211). Does the decision now permit the parties to decide which court shall have jurisdiction or where alone venue is proper? Has the inquiry changed from civil procedure (jurisdiction and venue) to contract (and its validity)? Consider these questions as you read the following case.

Atlantic Marine Construction Co., Inc. v. U.S. Dist. Court for the Western District of Texas

Supreme Court of the United States, 2013.
571 U.S. 49, 134 S. Ct. 568, 187 L.Ed.2d 487.

[A Virginia contractor, Atlantic Marine, and a Texas subcontractor had included a forum selection stipulation in favor of a Virginia state or federal court. The Texas party brought suit for payment in Texas federal court and the Virginia party moved for transfer to Virginia on the basis of the forum selection clause. The district court denied the motion. The Virginia party petitioned the Court of Appeal for mandamus, which the court denied, holding that the district court had not abused its discretion in balancing the relevant private and parties interests in reaching its decision. The Supreme Court granted certiorari.]

■ JUSTICE ALITO delivered the opinion of the Court.

Atlantic Marine contends that a party may enforce a forum-selection clause by seeking dismissal of the suit under § 1406(a) and Rule 12(b)(3).

We disagree. Section 1406(a) and Rule 12(b)(3) allow dismissal only when venue is "wrong" or "improper." Whether venue is "wrong" or "improper" depends exclusively on whether the court in which the case was brought satisfies the requirements of federal venue laws, and those provisions say nothing about a forum-selection clause.

A

Section 1406(a) provides that "[t]he district court of a district in which is filed a case laying venue in the wrong division or district shall dismiss, or if it be in the interest of justice, transfer such case to any district or division in which it could have been brought." Rule 12(b)(3) states that a party may move to dismiss a case for "improper venue." These provisions therefore authorize dismissal only when venue is "wrong" or "improper" in the forum in which it was brought. [W]hether venue is "wrong" or "improper"—is generally governed by 28 U.S.C. § 1391. That provision states that "[e]xcept as otherwise provided by *law* . . . this section *shall* govern the venue of *all civil actions* brought in district courts of the United States." § 1391(a)(1) (emphasis added). . . . The conclusion that venue is proper so long as the requirements of § 1391(b) are met, irrespective of any forum-selection clause, also follows from our prior decisions construing the federal venue statutes.

Although a forum-selection clause does not render venue in a court "wrong" or "improper" within the meaning of § 1406(a) or Rule 12(b)(3), the clause may be enforced through a motion to transfer under § 1404(a). That provision states that "[f]or the convenience of parties and witnesses, in the interest of justice, a district court may transfer any civil action to any other district or division where it might have been brought or to any district or division to which all parties have consented." Unlike § 1406(a), § 1404(a) does not condition transfer on the initial forum's being "wrong." And it permits transfer to any district where venue is also proper (*i.e.,* "where [the case] might have been brought") or to any other district to which the parties have agreed by contract or stipulation. Section 1404(a) therefore provides a mechanism for enforcement of forum-selection clauses that point to a particular federal district. And for the reasons we address in Part III, *infra,* a proper application of § 1404(a) requires that a forum-selection clause be "given controlling weight in all but the most exceptional cases." [Citation omitted.]

Atlantic Marine argues that § 1404(a) is not a suitable mechanism to enforce forum-selection clauses because that provision cannot provide for transfer when a forum-selection clause specifies a state or foreign tribunal . . . , and we agree with Atlantic Marine that the Court of Appeals failed to provide a sound answer to this problem. . . . [T]he appropriate way to enforce a forum-selection clause pointing to a state or foreign forum is through the doctrine of *forum non conveniens.* Section 1404(a) is merely a codification of the doctrine of *forum non conveniens* for the subset of cases in which the transferee forum is within the federal court system; in such cases, Congress has replaced the traditional remedy of outright dismissal with transfer. See *Sinochem Int'l Co. v. Malaysia Int'l Shipping Corp.*, 549 U.S. 422, 430 . . . (2007) ("For the federal court system, Congress has codified the doctrine . . .") . . . . For the remaining set of cases calling for a nonfederal forum, § 1404(a) has no application, but the residual doctrine of *forum non conveniens* "has continuing application in federal courts." . . .

III

When the parties have agreed to a valid forum-selection clause, a district court should ordinarily transfer the case to the forum specified in that clause. Only under extraordinary circumstances unrelated to the convenience of the parties should a § 1404(a) motion be denied. And no such exceptional factors appear to be present in this case.

A

In the typical case not involving a forum-selection clause, a district court considering a § 1404(a) motion (or a *forum non conveniens* motion) must evaluate both the convenience of the parties and various public-interest considerations.[6] Ordinarily, the district court would weigh the relevant factors and decide whether, on balance, a transfer would serve "the convenience of parties and witnesses" and otherwise promote "the interest of justice." The calculus changes, however, when the parties' contract contains a valid forum-selection clause, which "represents the parties' agreement as to the most proper forum." The "enforcement of valid forum-selection clauses, bargained for by the parties, protects their legitimate expectations and furthers vital interests of the justice system. For that reason, and because the overarching consideration under § 1404(a) is whether a transfer would promote "the interest of justice," "a valid forum-selection clause [should be] given controlling weight in all but the most exceptional cases." (Citations omitted). The presence of a valid forum-selection clause requires district courts to adjust their usual analysis in three ways.

First, the plaintiff's choice of forum merits no weight. Rather, as the party defying the forum-selection clause, the plaintiff bears the burden of establishing that transfer to the forum for which the parties bargained is unwarranted. Because plaintiffs are ordinarily allowed to select whatever forum they consider most advantageous (consistent with jurisdictional and venue limitations), we have termed their selection the "plaintiff's venue privilege.". . . But when a plaintiff agrees by contract to

---

[6] Factors relating to the parties' private interests include "relative ease of access to sources of proof; availability of compulsory process for attendance of unwilling, and the cost of obtaining attendance of willing, witnesses; possibility of view of premises, if view would be appropriate to the action; and all other practical problems that make trial of a case easy, expeditious and inexpensive." *Piper Aircraft Co. v. Reyno*, 454 U.S. 235, 241, n. 6 ...(1981) (internal quotation marks omitted). Public-interest factors may include "the administrative difficulties flowing from court congestion; the local interest in having localized controversies decided at home; [and] the interest in having the trial of a diversity case in a forum that is at home with the law." *Ibid.*

bring suit only in a specified forum—presumably in exchange for other binding promises by the defendant—the plaintiff has effectively exercised its "venue privilege" before a dispute arises.

Second, a court evaluating a defendant's § 1404(a) motion to transfer based on a forum-selection clause should not consider arguments about the parties' private interests. When parties agree to a forum-selection clause, they waive the right to challenge the preselected forum as inconvenient or less convenient for themselves or their witnesses, or for their pursuit of the litigation. A court accordingly must deem the private-interest factors to weigh entirely in favor of the preselected forum. As a consequence, a district court may consider arguments about public-interest factors only. See n. 6, *supra*. Because those factors will rarely defeat a transfer motion, the practical result is that forum-selection clauses should control except in unusual cases. Although it is "conceivable in a particular case" that the district court "would refuse to transfer a case notwithstanding the counterweight of a forum-selection clause," such cases will not be common. [Citation omitted.]

Third, when a party bound by a forum-selection clause flouts its contractual obligation and files suit in a different forum, a transfer of venue will not carry with it the original venue's choice-of-law rules—a factor that in some circumstances may affect public-interest considerations. See *Piper Aircraft Co. v. Reyno*, 454 U.S. 235, 241 n. 6 . . . (1981) (listing a court's familiarity with the "law that must govern the action" as a potential factor). A federal court sitting in diversity ordinarily must follow the choice-of-law rules of the State in which it sits. *Klaxon* [infra p. 746]. However, we previously identified an exception to that principle for § 1404(a) transfers, requiring that the state law applicable in the original court also apply in the transferee court. See *Van Dusen* [infra p. 257] We deemed that exception necessary to prevent "defendants, properly subjected to suit in the transferor State," from "invok[ing] § 1404(a) to gain the benefits of the laws of another jurisdiction. . . ."; see *Ferens v. John Deere* [infra p. 751] (extending the *Van Dusen* rule to § 1404(a) motions by plaintiffs). . . . [This exception does not apply when a case is transferred on the basis of a forum selection clause in an action brought in breach of that clause. To hold otherwise would encourage forum shopping.]

B

The District Court's application of § 1404(a) in this case did not comport with these principles. The District Court improperly placed the burden on Atlantic Marine to prove that transfer to the parties' contractually preselected forum was appropriate. As the party acting in violation of the forum-selection clause, [the Texas subcontractor] must bear the burden of showing that public-interest factors overwhelmingly disfavor a transfer. [The decision of the Court of Appeals was reversed and the case remanded to the District Court for a determination of whether public interest factors justified denial of Atlantic Marine's motion.]

NOTES

1.   The Court instructs trial courts to enforce forum selection clauses, except in very limited, unusual cases. The court is not to weigh private and public interests as in the usual forum non conveniens cases, but to consider only the public interests that may call for denial of a transfer or dismissal. How much leeway does footnote 6 of the opinion give lower courts? In McGregor v. Tune Music Group, 2016 WL 8737941, *10 (S.D.Fl.2016) (magistrate's report), adopted 2016 WL 8809246 (S.D. Fl. 2016), the court concluded, citing footnote 6, that there was a "strong interest in having United States copyright law interpreted in the United States, rather than the United Kingdom" and that there was also a localized interest in having Plaintiff's controversy decided at home, where Plaintiff's music originated and is listened to." Was this a correct reading of footnote 6 in limiting the thrust of the Court's opinion.

2.   A contract between a German and an American company, the parties stipulated for exclusive jurisdiction of the court of Bonn, Germany, and also selected German law as the applicable law for their agreement. The American party sued the German company on a contract claim in federal court in Virginia. That court dismissed the suit in favor of the German court, enforcing the forum selection clause on the basis of forum non conveniens (for which see infra p. 246). In subsequent litigation in Germany, the German Supreme Court held that the American company's suit in Virginia constituted a breach of contract under German law (which had been stipulated as applicable), entitling the German party to recover as damages all expenses incurred in the United States (attorneys' fees, courts costs, and the like). Under German law, a forum selection clause—that is part of a valid contract—determines jurisdiction and venue. German Code of Civil Procedure § 38. The same is the case under the European Union's Brussels Ia Regulation Art. 25 (infra p. 1147). At the same time, the Court held, the stipulation is a contractual obligation like any other, breach of it entitles the aggrieved party to contract remedies (damages, even specific performance). That is the "dual nature" of the forum selection clause. German Supreme Court (*Bundesgerichtshof*) Judgment of October 17, 2019, Case III ZR 42/19, [2020] Neue Juristische Wochenschrift 399.

Now consider again the question supra in Note (3), p. 217: has American law changed from granting exceptions to the exercise of otherwise valid local jurisdiction to basing jurisdiction and venue on valid contractual obligations? In the latter approach, particular local concerns—for instance, consumer or other weaker party protection—would be achieved (as in European law) by prohibiting or restricting particular contracts or their provisions. For discussion of this issue, in light of the German decision, see Peter Hay, Forum Selection Clauses—Procedural Tools or Contractual Obligations?, 35 Emory Int'l L. Rev. 1 (2021). See also infra Note (5). For maintenance of the local jurisdiction oriented approach, see David Marcus, The Perils of

Contract Procedure: A Revised History of Forum Selection Clauses in the Federal Courts, 82 Tulane L. Rev. 973, 987, 1043, 1048 (2008).

3. Forum-selection clauses have won widespread approval. From among the extensive contributions to the literature, see Hay, Borchers, Symeonides, Whytock, Conflict of Laws § 11.3 (6th ed. 2018); Borchers, Forum Selection Agreements in the Federal Courts After Carnival Cruise: A Proposal for Congressional Reform, 67 Wash. L. Rev. 55 (1992); Coyle and Richardson, Enforcing Outbound Forum Selection Clauses, 9_ Indiana L. J. ___ (2021).

For general discussion of the effect given choice-of-forum clauses in the United States and in other countries, see Symeonides, Codifying Choice of Law Around the World: An International Comparative Analysis 388 et seq. (2014). For English practice see Torremans & Fawcett, Cheshire, North & Fawcett's Private International Law 229–43 (15th ed.2017).

4. In international contracts, the parties often combine forum-selection and choice-of-law clauses. In this way, they can be sure that the chosen court will apply a particular law rather than select one on the basis of its own conflicts rules. Since forum-selection and choice-of-law clauses could favor one party, contracts sometimes provide for alternatives—depending on who is the plaintiff and who is the defendant in a potential future dispute. Such a "floating" clause, for instance, may select the courts and the law at the defendant's principal place of business. For discussion, see Rasmussen-Bonne, Alternative Rechts- und Forumswahlklauseln (1999); Annotation, Enforceability of Floating Forum Selection Clauses, 39 A.L.R. 6th 629 (2008).

A different kind of "floating" forum-selection clause is employed both in domestic and international contracts when the contract looks to the place of a future, as-yet-undetermined assignee. In IFC Credit Corp. v. Aliano Bros. Gen. Contractors, 437 F.3d 606, 607 (7th Cir.2006), the stipulation read as follows: "This agreement shall be governed by, construed and enforced in accordance with the laws of the State in which the Rentor's principal offices are located or, if this Lease is assigned by the Rentor, the State in which the assignee's principal offices are located . . . and all legal actions relating to this Lease shall be venued exclusively in a state or federal court located within that State, such court to be chosen at Rentor['s] or Rentor's assignee's sole option." The court upheld the clause against the argument that it should be considered invalid because non-specific and therefore not providing sufficient notice to the lessee concerning possible places of suit. The court balanced the lessee's inconvenience against the inconvenience to assignees, the effect of the latter on the ready assignability of such leases and, with it, on prices to customers. Id. at 612–13. Other courts are split on the issue. See cases collected in Cross & Oxford, IV, "Floating" Forum Selection and Choice of Law Clauses, 48 S.Tex.L.Rev. 125, 139–41 (2006). Should it make a difference whether such a clause is part of a commercial equipment lease or is contained in a contract for personal, family, or household purposes? The provision involved in *Aliano* was "found in most of the 11,000 equipment rental agreements entered into by NorVergence, Inc. in connection with telecommunications service agreements . . . ." Id. at 135 n.67.

5. Choice-of-forum agreements have sometimes been denied effect. For instance, because it was "clearly and palpably unreasonable," the court in Calzavara v. Biehl & Co., 181 So.2d 809 (La.App.1966) ignored a provision purporting to give an Italian court exclusive jurisdiction over any action on a ticket for transportation from New Orleans to Italy. Plaintiff was a Louisiana resident and the defendant a Louisiana corporation. See also Kolendo v. Jerell, Inc., 489 F.Supp. 983 (S.D.W.Va.1980); Lulling v. Barnaby's Family Inns, Inc., 482 F.Supp. 318 (E.D.Wis.1980); Carefree Vacations, Inc. v. Brunner, 615 F.Supp. 211 (W.D.Tenn.1985) (choice of Texas forum in contract executed in Illinois and Tennessee held to be unreasonable). If one regards a forum selection provision as a contract clause like any other (see supra Note (2)), should a court ask whether it was "reasonable" or would that inject the court into making contracts for the parties? It is a different matter if certain kinds of contracts are not permitted in the first place: take for instance a contract that fixes prices and selects a country and its law where this would not violate antitrust laws. In such a case, American law prohibits the contract as such. American law is "mandatory" and cannot be evaded. Contract law may also hold certain adhesion contracts to be unenforceable. All this is quite different, however, from reviewing a particular forum selection for its reasonabless. Recall that, in *M/S Bremen v. Zapata*, supra p. 209, English law permitted exculpatory clauses while American law would not have upheld them: the forum selection was upheld nevertheless. On mandatory clauses, see Fazilatfar, Overriding Rules in International Arbitration 21 (2019).

6. Some states adhere to the older view that forum-selection clauses represent an attempt to oust a court of jurisdiction given it by law, and therefore violate public policy and are unenforceable. Professional Insurance Corp. v. Sutherland, 700 So.2d 347, 351 (Ala.1997) overruled prior cases and held that "a forum selection clause should be enforced so long as enforcing it is neither unfair nor unreasonable under the circumstances." The court noted that as a result of its change of heart "only Iowa, Idaho, and Montana appear to hold that . . . forum selection provisions [that choose a forum outside the state] are per se unenforceable, and the latter two states do so based on interpretations of state statutes." Id. at 349–50.

In Idaho, one of the three states that do not enforce choice-of-forum agreements, courts base this refusal on Idaho Code § 29–110(1), which provides: "Every stipulation or condition in a contract, by which any party thereto is restricted from enforcing his rights under the contract in Idaho tribunals, or which limits the time within which he may thus enforce his rights, is void." The Ninth Circuit construed this language as an expression of the state's public policy and therefore under the exception states in *M/S Bremen v. Zapata*, supra p. 209: the selection of a non-local forum was unenforceable. Gemini Technologies, Inc. v. Smith & Wesson Corp., 931 F.3d 911, 916 et seq. (9th Cir. 2019). The decision in *Gemini* was applied in Swank Enterprises, Inc. v. NGM Insurance Company, 2020 WL 1139607 (D. Mont. Mar. 9, 2020) with respect to Montana Code § 28–2–708. In addition, many states have laws protective of particular persons or groups, such as consumers, and preserving access to local courts for them (thereby prohibiting forum selection clauses that deprive these persons of that protection. For comprehensive analysis, see Cara Reichard, Keeping Litigation at Home: The Role of States in Preventing Unjust Choice of Forum, 129 Yale L.J. 866, 898 et seq. (2020), with detailed table of state laws at 909 et seq.

7.   Antisuit Injunctions. A court may also protect its jurisdiction by issuing an injunction prohibiting a party from suing elsewhere (antisuit injunction). This may be the case when a party threatens to sue elsewhere in violation of a local protective statute or of a forum selection clause in its (the local court's) favor, or when the local court had denied a motion to dismiss or to transfer. For recent comprehensive discussion of such injunctions, see KBC v. Pertamina, 500 F.3d 111 (2d Cir.2007), cert. denied, 554 U.S. 929, (2008); Lam Yeen Leng et al. v. Pinnacle Performance Ltd., 474 Fed.App'x 810 (2d Cir.2012); Jolen, Inc. v. Kundan Rice Mills, Ltd., 2019 WL 1559173 (S.D.N.Y., April 9, 2019). To protect its jurisdiction, the local court may not only enjoin litigation in another court, but enjoin the party to seek an antisuit injunction in the other court against litigation in the local court: this is an anti-antisuit injunction. For examples, see Laker Airways Ltd. v. Sabena, Belgian World Airlines, 731 F.2d 909 (D.C. Cir. 1984) (injunction enjoining pursuit of English antisuit injunction); Landgericht München, Germany, Case No. 21 0 9333/19, Oct. 2, 2019, [2019] Wirtschaft und Wettbewerb 661 (injunction against seeking an injunction in the United States). Are antisuit injunctions in domestic American (i.e. interstate) cases entitled to recognition? See James v. Grand Trunk Western Railroad Co., 152 N.E.2d 858 (Ill. 1958) (not entitled to recognition); Am. Star Ins. Co. v. Grice, 865 P.2d 507, 511 (Wash. 1994) (entitled to recognition). In Baker v. General Motors Corp., 522 U.S. 222, 235 (1998), Justice Ginsburg, writing for the Court, noted that "enforcement measures do not travel" and referred, at p. 236, to the hornbook statement suggesting that no recognition is required because antisuit injunction does not address substantive issues and therefore has no preclusive effect. That statement is now in Hay, Borchers, Symeonides, Whytock, Conflict of Laws § 24.21 at 1408 (6th ed. 2018). Justice Ginsburg's reference was not part of the holding in that decision. See Strong, Anti-Suit Injunctions in Judicial and Arbitral Procedures in the United States, 66 Am.J. Comp. L. 153 (2018).

8.   What law governs the interpretation of a forum-selection clause? For the view that it is the law chosen by the parties, see Yavuz v. 61 MM, Ltd., 465 F.3d 418, 427–28 (10th Cir.2006), concluding that Swiss law, which the parties chose, determines whether the forum-selection clause is mandatory or permissive and what parties and issues the clause covers. The clause is part of the contract and should be governed by the law applicable by it. See Clermont, Reconciling Forum-Selection and Choice-of-Law Clauses, 69 Am. U. L. Rev. F. 171 (2020). European law tends to view the contract, the choice-of-forum, and the choice-of-law agreements as—at least conceptually— separate contracts so that, occasionally, one might be valid under its applicable law, while another might not be. Regulation (EU) No. 1215/2012, Art. 25(5), p. 1147, infra. But cf. for U.S. law, Schwan's Sales Enterprises, Inc. v. SIG Pack, Inc., 476 F.3d 594 (8th Cir.2007) (forum law, not the law chosen in a choice-of-law provision, determines the effect of the provision; absent more express stipulation by the parties to the contrary, see infra this note, the provision does not cover prejudgment interest because the forum regards this issue as procedural). See also Abbott Laboratories v. Takeda Pharmaceutical Co., 476 F.3d 421 (7th Cir.2007), restated in IFC Credit Corp. v. United Bus. & Indus. Fed. Credit, 512 F.3d 989, 991 (7th Cir.2008): the validity of a forum-selection clause depends on the law of the jurisdiction that governs the dispute. See also Gita Sports Ltd. v. SG Sensortechnik GmbH & Co. KG, 560 F.Supp.2d 432 (W.D.N.C.2008). Can the parties designate in their choice-of-law agreement what law governs the interpretation of the forum-selection and choice-of-law provisions in the contract? See *Schwan's Sales*, 476 F.3d at 596: "If the parties wish for the application of another state's law concerning such procedural and remedial matters [prejudgment interest], they must expressly state it in their agreement."

9.   In the European Union, Art. 25 of Regulation (EU) No. 1215/2012, infra p. 1147, allows parties (one of whom must be habitually resident in a member state) to select, by agreement, a member state court for the resolution of a present or future dispute. The court so selected then has exclusive jurisdiction, even if it otherwise would not have. (Art. 25(1)). The provision applies to the prorogation of a Member State court. The domicile of the parties, even if not in the European Union, is not relevant, nor need the dispute be related to the European Union. Exceptions apply when the stipulation contravenes special provisions protective of consumers and insureds (see p. 1163, infra) or for an exclusive jurisdiction established by the Regulation (Art. 22). Prorogation agreements in favor of third states remain subject to the national law of the member states. What if the parties chose the court of a third (non-EU) state but the defendant has his/her domicile or principal place of domicile in the EU: may the defendant be sued at his/her domicile or principal place of business (Art. 4 or 62, respectively, Brussels-Ia Regulation) or must the suit be dismissed under former Art. 23 [now 25]? A (declaratory) Opinion of the EU Court of Justice concludes that the answer is "yes, the action may be maintained": The exclusivity character of former Art. 23 [now 25] works only in favor of an EU forum chosen by the parties; the choice of a third-country forum, however, is trumped by the Regulation's jurisdictional provisions defining the jurisdiction of courts within the EU. For the construction of a forum-selection clause as "exclusive" on the basis of former Art. 23 [now 25] by an American court, see *Gita Sports Ltd.*, Note 7, supra. For criticism of the non-exclusive treatment given forum-selection clauses in favor of a third country and for discussion of the availability of damages (under English law) for breach of such a forum-selection clause, see Merrett, The Enforcement of Jurisdiction Agreements Within the Brussels Regime, 55 Int'l & Comp.L.Q. 315 (2006).

Note on Stipulations Against Judicial Redress:
Mandatory Arbitration Clauses
in Consumer Transactions

In the *Carnival Cruise Lines* cases, pp. 213, 215, supra, the provider of services (the cruise line) sought to protect itself against lawsuits in all places where there might otherwise be jurisdiction by stipulating in its General Conditions its place of business as the only place where it could be sued. This was a contract provision like any other, subject to ordinary contract defenses, such lack of agreement, lack of consideration, and the like. The courts came to different results on the basis of these defenses. None dealt with public policy concerns, such as the protection of consumers against overreaching (adhesion contracts).

Another, more recent practice raises these public policy concerns more directly. It has become standard practice of sellers, providers of services, insurance companies, and others to stipulate in their General Conditions that the sole remedy for the resolution of disputes is *private individual arbitration*. Sometimes this provision binds both parties, sometimes it only binds the consumer, recipient of services, or other such party, sometimes the clause allows the provider to opt out of litigation within a specified time even after suit has been filed. In 2016, nearly three quarters of large U.S. retail banks included mandatory clauses for private arbitration in their contracts for checking and savings accounts. PEW Charitable Trust, Report: Consumers Want the Right to Resolve Bank Disputes in Court (August 2016). What are the advantages to the business party? There are several: no jury trial (reducing the danger of high awards and punitive damages), no class action (hence "private individual" arbitration), discovery rules do not apply, non-mutual collateral estoppel rules also do not apply (p. 324, infra), and arbitration decisions are rarely published.

While the Class Action Fairness Act limited the availability of class actions (especially in state courts), mandatory, often one-sided, arbitration clauses bar recourse to judicial redress altogether. The individual consumer is limited to individual arbitration, with even class arbitration precluded under the clause.

State legislative initiatives sought to provide greater consumer protection by limiting or proscribing the exclusion of access to judicial redress. They were overturned by the U.S. Supreme Court on the ground that the federal policy in favor of arbitration, as expressed in the Federal Arbitration Act, 9 U.S.C.A. §§ 1–16 (West 2020), preempts state legislative competence: Southland v. Keating, 465 U.S. 1 (1984); AT&T Mobility, L.L.C. v. Concepcion, 563 U.S. 333, 344 (2011), forcefully restated in DIRECTV, Inc. v. Imburgia, 577 U.S.47 (2015). On the compatibility of Fed.R.Civ.Pr. 23 (on class actions) with these cases, see also Freer, Front-Loading, Avoidance, and Other Features of the Recent Supreme Court Class Action Jurisprudence, 48 Akron L.Rev. 721, 742 et seq. (2015). As a result, only remedies available at common law or in equity are available to contest the validity of the contract provision. A number of bills introduced in Congress to overturn the result in *AT&T Mobility* never made it out of Committee. In a subsequent case, the issue was whether arbitration clauses in employment contracts violate employees' rights under the National Labor Relations Act (for instance, to engaged in "concerted" activities), thereby constituting unfair labor practices. The Supreme Court upheld the arbitration agreement. Epic Sys. Corp. v. Lewis, 138 S.Ct. 1612 (2018). An exception is a rule issued by an agency of the Department of Health and Human Services prohibiting federally funded long-term care facilities from entering into pre-dispute agreements for binding arbitration with residents and prescribing the content of any such agreement concluded after a dispute has arisen. 42 C.F.R. § 483.70(n) (2016). For critical and comparative comment, see Hay, One-Sided (Asymmetrical) Remedy Clauses and Weaker Party Protection in American Law, in R.A. Schütze et al. (eds.), Festschrift für Reinhold Geimer (II) 219 (2017). See also Briggs, One-Sided Jurisdiction Clauses: French Folly and Russian Menace, 2013 Lloyd's Mar. & Com.L.Q. 137; Fentiman, Unilateral Jurisdiction Agreements in Europe, 72 Camb.L.J. 24 (2013); Horton & Chandrasekher, After the Revolution: An Empirical Study of Consumer Arbitration. 104 Geo.L.J. 57, 124 (2015).

NOTES

1.   Severability: The agreement to arbitrate is regarded separately from the substantive contract of which it is part. See Buckeye Check Cashing, Inc. v. Cardegna, 546 U.S. 440 (2006). The court determines whether the parties validly concluded an arbitration agreement. If so, then all other issues fall within the jurisdiction of the arbitrator, particularly whether the substantive contract is valid (Williams v. Eaze Solutions, Inc., 417 F.Supp.3d 1233 (N.D.Cal.2019)) and what issues are arbitrable.

2.   In considering the validity of the (severable) arbitration agreement, the court may only entertain such defenses that were available "at law or in equity" at the time the Federal Arbitration Act was adopted. See 9 U.S.C. § 2. A narrow reading of this restriction underlies the U.S. Supreme Court's rejection of defenses based on newer state statutes, as reviewed in the main text above. A common law defense would be lack of notice and therefore lack of agreement. In Kindred Nursing Ctrs. Ltd. Partnership v. Clark, 137 S.Ct. 1421, 1427–29 (2017), the Supreme Court rejected Kentucky's "clear statement" rule as a defense because designed to hinder formation of arbitration agreements. For another narrow approach to a challenge to an arbitration clause, see Richardson v. Coverall North America, Inc., 811 Fed.Appx 100 (3d Cir. 2020).

SECTION 2. FRAUD, FORCE AND PRIVILEGE*

Terlizzi v. Brodie

Supreme Court, Appellate Division, Second Department, 1972.
38 A.D.2d 762, 329 N.Y.S.2d 589.

■ MEMORANDUM BY THE COURT. . . .

In May or June, 1968 defendants, New Jersey residents, were in an automobile collision in New Jersey which caused plaintiffs, New York residents, to sustain injuries. In February, 1971 defendants were called at home and told that they had been chosen to receive two tickets to a Broadway show as a promotional venture to get their opinion on a questionnaire of the new 7:30 P.M. curtain time. After the performance and while still in the theatre, defendants were served with a summons in this action by a man who had been sitting behind them. No questionnaire had been given them. Plaintiffs have presented no facts concerning the service to refute defendants' claim and have not submitted an affidavit of the investigator retained to effect service.

It has long been held that where a defendant has been lured into this jurisdiction by fraud or deceit in order that he may be served, the service so effected is invalid . . .

In our opinion, the service was invalid and the [defendants'] motion [to vacate service of process] should have been granted.

NOTES

1.   Where the defendant's presence in the state was obtained by fraudulent use of extradition procedure, it has been held that service on him is not effective to support a civil judgment against him. Klaiber v. Frank, 86 A.2d 679 (N.J.1952). However, the mere fact that the defendant is a non-resident and is under arrest for a criminal charge does not make him immune from the valid service of civil process. State ex rel. Sivnksty v. Duffield, 71 S.E.2d 113 (W.Va.1952).

2.   Suppose the defendant is kidnapped and brought into the state by force. If he is then served with civil process, does the state get jurisdiction over him? See Restatement, Second, Conflict of Laws, § 82, Comments *e–f* (1971).

3.   The Uniform Criminal Extradition Act, now enacted in 47 states, Puerto Rico and the U.S. Virgin Islands, (see 11 Uniform Laws Ann. 51) provides (in § 25) that where a person is brought into a state on extradition, or after waiver of extradition, he shall not be subject to service of process "in civil actions arising out of the same facts as the criminal proceedings . . . until he has been convicted in the criminal proceeding, or if acquitted, until he has had reasonable opportunity to return to the state from which he was extradited." In Bubar v. Dizdar, 60 N.W.2d 77 (Minn.1953), the defendant waived extradition, came into the state, and pleaded guilty. Later the same

---

*   See Restatement, Second, Conflict of Laws §§ 82–83.

day, but before sentence was imposed, he was served with process. It was held that this was after conviction, and valid.

4. In criminal cases, the Supreme Court has consistently held under the "Ker-Frisbie" doctrine that a state may exercise jurisdiction over a person even if the person was unlawfully extradited or brought into the jurisdiction by force. See Ker v. Illinois, 119 U.S. 436 (1886); Frisbie v. Collins, 342 U.S. 519 (1952) (upholding criminal jurisdiction even where the abduction violated the Federal Kidnapping Act); United States v. Alvarez-Machain, 504 U.S. 655 (1992) (upholding criminal jurisdiction, despite Mexico's objection, over a Mexican citizen abducted by federal agents in Mexico). See also United States v. Struckman, 611 F.3d 560 (9th Cir.2010). See also United States v. Khatallah, 160 F.Supp.3d 144 (D.D.C. 2016) (upholding jurisdiction, despite abduction from Libya in alleged violation of U.N. Charter and a non-self-executing provision of a treaty). See generally Scott, Criminal Jurisdiction of a State over a Defendant Based upon Presence Secured by Force or Fraud, 37 Minn.L.Rev. 91 (1953); Bush, How Did We Get Here? Foreign Abduction After Alvarez-Machain, 45 Stan.L.Rev. 939 (1993).

The question of criminal jurisdiction based on removing a person by force arose in dramatic form when the Nazi war criminal Adolf Eichmann was abducted from Argentina by Israeli agents, taken to Israel, there tried for war crimes and executed. Israel asserted that genocide and war crimes are subject to universal jurisdiction, and Argentina acquiesced. Attorney General v. Eichmann, 36 Int'l L.Rep. 18 (Dist.Ct.Israel 1961), aff'd, 36 Int'l L.Rep. 277 (Sup.Ct.Israel 1962). Section 404 of the Restatement, Third, Foreign Relations Law of the United States (1987) now also adopts this view. See also In re Demjanjuk, 603 F.Supp. 1468 (N.D.Ohio 1985), aff'd, 776 F.2d 571 (6th Cir.1985), cert. denied, 475 U.S. 1016 (1986) (approving Israeli request for extradition of person charged with murder alleged to have been committed in Nazi camps in Eastern Europe). After Demjanjuk's acquittal of charges in Israel, the Sixth Circuit Court of Appeals reopened the case and found prosecutorial misconduct in failing to disclose exculpatory information. Demjanjuk v. Petrovsky, 10 F.3d 338 (6th Cir.1993), cert. denied, 513 U.S. 914 (1994).

A number of cases have involved persons who were brought by force from foreign countries to the United States to stand trial on criminal charges. In these cases, jurisdiction to try the defendant was ultimately upheld even though it was alleged that the defendant had been forcefully abducted at the instigation of agents of the United States. United States v. Lira, 515 F.2d 68 (2d Cir.1975); United States v. Gengler, 510 F.2d 62 (2d Cir.1975); United States v. Cotten, 471 F.2d 744 (9th Cir.1973); United States v. Marzano, 388 F.Supp. 906 (N.D.Ill.1975); see Annot., 28 A.L.R.Fed. 685 (1976). In United States v. Toscanino, 500 F.2d 267 (2d Cir.1974), the court held that jurisdiction would be lacking and the defendant's conviction void if he could establish that he had not only been kidnapped but also tortured and interrogated abroad by U.S. agents and that the United States attorney was at all times aware of these activities. The court said that Frisbie v. Collins must be read in the light of such supervening Supreme Court decisions as Mapp, Miranda, etc. which hold that "due process not only requires a fair trial but also protects the accused against pretrial illegality by denying to the government the fruits of its exploitation of any deliberate and unnecessary lawlessness on its part." After remand to the District Court, however, Toscanino failed to establish that United States officials had participated in his abduction or torture. Accordingly, his motion to vacate his judgment of conviction was denied. United States v. Toscanino, 398 F.Supp. 916 (E.D.N.Y.1975). See LaFave, Search and Seizure § 1.9(a) (4th ed.2004); see also Kletter, 3 A.L.R. Fed.3d Art. 4 (2015) for the applicability of the 4th Amendment exclusionary rule to evidence obtained from searches conducted abroad by officials of foreign governments.

The Antiterrorist and Effective Death Penalty Act of 1996 (AEDPA), 110 Stat. 1214 (1996), among other things, amended the Foreign Sovereign Immunities Act (Note 5, infra), eliminating immunity for countries designated as supporters of terrorism. When there is a claim based, for instance, on the Alien Torts Statute, 28 U.S.C.A. §1350 (2020), the AEDPA provides for adjudicatory jurisdiction. See, e.g., Salazar v. Islamic Republic of Iran, 370 F.Supp.2d 105 (D.D.C.2005); Belkin v. Islamic Republic of Iran, 667 F.Supp.2d 8, 19 (D.D.C.2009); Spencer v. Islamic Republic of Iran, 2014 WL 12773915 (D.D.C. 2014). In application of (2012) Canadian legislation allowing victims of terrorism to sue foreign states for compensation, the Ontario Superior Court held that Iran was not entitled to immunity in an action to enforce an American judgment in favor of American victims of Iran-sponsored terrorist acts. Tracy v. The Iranian Ministry of Information and Security, 2016 ONSC 3759 (Ont.Super.Ct.(Commercial) June 9, 2016), additional reasons added, 2017 ONSC 943 (Feb. 8, 2017) (appeal pending).

5.   Privilege and Immunity. A foreign sovereign is generally immune from suit. Foreign Sovereign Immunities Act, 28 U.S.C.A. § 1604. There are exceptions, for instance when the foreign sovereign engages in commercial (non-governmental) activity. Foreign diplomats enjoy absolute immunity from criminal as well as civil and administrative jurisdiction. However, the sending state can waive the immunity of its envoys. Arts. 31, 32, para. 4, Vienna Convention on Diplomatic Relations, 23 U.S.T. 3227, T.I.A.S. No. 7502, 500 U.N.T.S. 95. See Fernandez v. Fernandez, 545 A.2d 1036 (Conn.1988), noted 102 Harv. L. Rev. 1403 (1989), interpreting partial waiver of immunity allowing the exercise of divorce jurisdiction to confer authority to entertain petitioner's claim for the marital residence.

6.   "It is customary for a state to grant immunity from service of process to non-residents whose presence it deems necessary for the proper conduct of a judicial proceeding. Such immunity is usually granted to witnesses and to lawyers and in some states to parties as well. The immunity ceases when the need for protection ends. It is lost, for example, when the person fails to leave the state within a reasonable time after his presence there has ceased to be necessary." Restatement, Second, Conflict of Laws § 83, Comment *b* (1971).

7.   Immunity from service of process in a civil action is usually granted to persons who enter the state, either voluntarily or under subpoena, for the purpose of appearing as a witness in a state or federal proceeding. See, e.g., Shapiro & Son Curtain Corp. v. Glass, 348 F.2d 460 (2d Cir.), cert. denied, 382 U.S. 942 (1965); Celanese Corporation v. Duplan Corporation, 502 F.2d

188 (4th Cir.1974), cert. denied, 420 U.S. 929 (1975); Viking Penguin, Inc. v. Janklow, 98 F.R.D. 763 (S.D.N.Y.1983); Glynn v. EDO Corp., 641 F.Supp.2d 476, 486 (D.Md.2009).

In Youpe v. Strasser, 113 F.Supp. 289 (D.D.C.1953), it was held that a witness subpoenaed to appear before a Congressional investigating committee was immune from service in a civil suit.

SECTION 3. FORUM NON CONVENIENS

American jurisdictional law provides plaintiffs with a wide choice of fora in which to sue. Individuals are subject to jurisdiction at their domicile and in any state where personal service can be effected. For a discussion of "transient" service, see p. 51, supra.

In addition, a state has jurisdiction when the nonresident defendant's contact with that state gave rise to the plaintiff's cause of action. For discussion of "specific" jurisdiction, see p. 64 et seq., supra. Similarly, a corporation may be subject to "general" jurisdiction where it does such substantial "continuous and systematic business" that it can be considered to be "at home" there, p. 163, supra, as well as to "specific" jurisdiction where its acts or contacts give rise to the cause of action, pp. 80, 100 supra.

A plaintiff thus has considerable opportunity to "shop around" for a forum. Reasons may include geographic convenience, but also advantages of the potentially applicable law. For instance, the forum may characterize as procedural an outcome-determinative rule, such as its longer statute of limitations, or may choose other law favorable to the plaintiff. See *Allstate*, p. 432, infra. The doctrine of *forum non conveniens* affords an avenue for relief in jurisdictionally hard cases.

The doctrine of *forum non conveniens* has by now been widely accepted throughout the common law world, from the doctrine's first recognition in Scotland in 1866. The United States Supreme Court accepted the use of *forum non conveniens* in 1947, in the lead case below.

However, the Supreme Court has limited the applicability of the doctrine, on the federal level, to situations where the alternative forum is not a federal district court. Where the parties' choices of fora are both federal district courts, on the other hand, the federal transfer statute (28 U.S.C.A. § 1404(a)), if applicable, provides the proper remedy. American Dredging Co. v. Miller, 510 U.S. 443 (1994); see p. 238, Note X, infra. Some decisions, however, still confuse the two. The doctrine still be properly applied when a forum-selection clause selected a state court or a foreign-country court.

Gulf Oil Corp. v. Gilbert

Supreme Court of the United States, 1947.
330 U.S. 501, 67 S.Ct. 839, 91 L.Ed. 1055.

[A resident of Virginia brought an action in a federal district court in New York against a Pennsylvania corporation. The cause of action was based on a fire in Virginia alleged to have resulted from the defendant's negligence. The defendant was qualified to do business in Virginia, and could have been sued there. The defendant moved to dismiss on grounds of forum non conveniens.

■   The opinion of the Court, by JUSTICE JACKSON, contains the following passages:]

I

It is conceded that the venue statutes of the United States permitted the plaintiff to commence his action in the Southern District of New York and empower that court to entertain it. But that does not settle the question whether it must do so. Indeed the doctrine of *forum non conveniens* can never apply if there is absence of jurisdiction or mistake of venue. . . . In all cases in which the doctrine of *forum non conveniens* comes into play, it presupposes at least two forums in which the defendant is amenable to process; the doctrine furnishes criteria for choice between them.

II

The principle of *forum non conveniens* is simply that a court may resist imposition upon its jurisdiction even when jurisdiction is authorized by the letter of a general venue statute. These statutes are drawn with a necessary generality and usually give a plaintiff a choice of courts, so that he may be quite sure of some place in which to pursue his remedy. But the open door may admit those who seek not simply justice but perhaps justice blended with some harassment. A plaintiff sometimes is under temptation to resort to a strategy of forcing the trial at a most inconvenient place for an adversary, even at some inconvenience to himself.

Many of the states have met misuse of venue by investing courts with a discretion to change the place of trial on various grounds, such as the convenience of witnesses and the ends of justice. The federal law contains no such express criteria to guide the district court in exercising its power. But the problem is a very old one affecting the administration of the courts as well as the rights of litigants, and both in England and in this country the common law worked out techniques and criteria for dealing with it.

Wisely, it has not been attempted to catalogue the circumstances which will justify or require either grant or denial of remedy. The doctrine leaves much to the discretion of the court to which plaintiff resorts, and experience has not shown a judicial tendency to renounce one's own jurisdiction so strong as to result in many abuses.

If the combination and weight of factors requisite to given results are difficult to forecast or state, those to be considered are not difficult to name. An interest to be considered, and the one likely to be most pressed, is the private interest of the litigant. Important considerations are the relative ease of access to sources of proof; availability of compulsory process for attendance of unwilling, and the cost of obtaining attendance of willing, witnesses; possibility of view of premises, if view would be appropriate to the action; and all other practical problems that make trial of a case easy, expeditious and inexpensive. There may also be questions as to the enforceability of a judgment if one is obtained. The court will weigh relative advantages and obstacles to fair trial. It is often said that the plaintiff may not, by choice of an inconvenient forum, "vex," "harass," or "oppress" the defendant by inflicting upon him expense or trouble not necessary to his own right to pursue his remedy. But unless the balance is strongly in favor of the defendant, the plaintiff's choice of forum should rarely be disturbed.

Factors of public interest also have place in applying the doctrine. Administrative difficulties follow for courts when litigation is piled up in congested centers instead of being handled at its origin. Jury duty is a burden that ought not to be imposed upon the people of a community which has no relation to the litigation. In cases which touch the affairs of many persons, there is reason for holding the trial in their view and reach rather than in remote parts of the country where they can learn of it by report only. There is a local interest in having localized controversies decided at home. There is an appropriateness, too, in having the trial of a diversity case in a forum that is at home with the state law that must govern the case, rather than having a court in some other forum untangle problems in conflict of laws, and in law foreign to itself.

The law of New York as to the discretion of a court to apply the doctrine of *forum non conveniens,* and as to the standards that guide discretion is, so far as here involved, the same as the federal rule. . . .

[The Court held that the district court had acted properly in dismissing the suit.]

Piper Aircraft Co. v. Reyno

Supreme Court of the United States, 1981.
454 U.S. 235, 102 S.Ct. 252, 70 L.Ed.2d 419.

[The appointed administratrix over the decedents' estates brought an action in California state court against the manufacturers of an aircraft and its propellers to recover for the wrongful death of persons killed in an airplane crash in Scotland. At the time of the crash, the plane was registered in Great Britain and was being operated by a Scottish air taxi service. All of the decedents were Scottish subjects and residents.

The plaintiff-administratrix of the decedents' estates was frank to admit that the suit had been brought in the United States because its laws regarding liability, capacity to sue, and damages were more favorable to her cause than those of Scotland. Defendants removed the case to California federal court, where one of the defendants, Hartzell, filed for dismissal for lack or personal jurisdiction, or alternatively, for transfer to Pennsylvania, where the plane was manufactured. In Pennsylvania, the trial court granted a dismissal on the grounds of forum non conveniens in favor of a Scottish Court. The Third Circuit reversed, holding that the trial court should not have granted a forum non conveniens dismissal when it would lead to the application of law less favorable to the plaintiff.]

■ MARSHALL, J., delivered the opinion of the Court. JUSTICE WHITE, concurred in part and dissented. JUSTICE STEVENS, with whom JUSTICE BRENNAN joined, dissented.

II.

The Court of Appeals erred in holding that plaintiffs may defeat a motion to dismiss on the ground of forum non conveniences merely by showing that the substantive law that would be applied in the alternative forum is less favorable to the plaintiffs than that of the present forum. The possibility of a change in substantive law should ordinarily not be given conclusive or even substantial weight in the *forum non conveniens* inquiry ... Under *Gilbert,* dismissal will ordinarily be appropriate where the trial in the plaintiff's chosen forum imposes a heavy burden on the defendant or the court, and where the plaintiff is unable to offer any specific reasons of convenience supporting his choice. If substantial weight were given to the possibility of an unfavorable change in law, however, dismissal might be barred even where trial in the chosen forum was plainly inconvenient. ...

In fact, if conclusive or substantial weight were given to the possibility of a change in law, the *forum non conveniens* doctrine would become virtually useless. Jurisdiction and venue requirements are often easily satisfied. As a result, many plaintiffs are able to choose from among several forums. Ordinarily, these plaintiffs will select that forum whose choice-of-law rules are most advantageous. Thus, if the possibility of an unfavorable change in substantive law is given substantial weight in the *forum non conveniens* inquiry, dismissal would rarely be proper. ...

The Court of Appeals' approach is not only inconsistent with the purpose of the *forum non conveniens* doctrine, but also poses substantial practical problems. If the possibility of a change in law were given substantial weight, deciding motions to dismiss would become quite difficult. Choice-of-law analysis would become extremely important, and the courts would frequently be required to interpret the law of foreign jurisdictions. First, the trial court would have to determine what law would apply if the case were tried in the chosen forum, and what law would apply if the case were tried in the alternative forum. It would then have to compare the rights, remedies, and procedures available under the law that would be applied in each forum. Dismissal would be appropriate only if the court concluded that the law applied by the alternative forum is as favorable to the plaintiff as that of the chosen forum. . . . The American courts, which are already extremely attractive to foreign plaintiffs,[18] would become even more attractive. The flow of litigation into the United States would increase and further congest already crowded courts.

The Court of Appeals based its decision, at least in part, on an analogy between dismissals on grounds of *forum non conveniens* and transfers between federal courts pursuant to § 1404(a). . . . Congress enacted § 1404(a) to permit change of venue between federal courts. Although the statute was drafted in accordance with the doctrine of *forum non conveniens,* it was intended to be a revision rather than a codification of the common law. . . . District courts were given more discretion to transfer under § 1404(a) than they had to dismiss on grounds of *forum non conveniens.* . . . Of course, if the remedy provided by the alternative forum is so clearly inadequate or unsatisfactory that it is no remedy at all, the unfavorable change in law may be given substantial weight; the district court may conclude that dismissal would not be in the interest of justice.

III.

The Court of Appeals also erred in rejecting the District Court's *Gilbert* analysis. . . . The District Court's distinction between resident or citizen plaintiffs and foreign plaintiffs is fully justified. . . . When the home forum has been chosen, it is reasonable to assume that this choice is convenient. When the plaintiff is foreign, however, this assumption is much less reasonable. Because the central purpose of any *forum non conveniens* inquiry is to ensure that the trial is convenient, a foreign plaintiff's choice deserves less deference.

[The Court then assessed the district court's *Gilbert* analysis and found no abuse of discretion.]

. . . [T]he judgment of the Court of Appeals is reversed.

---

[18] First, all but 6 of the 50 American States—Delaware, Massachusetts, Michigan, North Carolina, Virginia, and Wyoming—offer strict liability. . . . Rules roughly equivalent to American strict liability are effective in France, Belgium, and Luxembourg. West Germany and Japan have a strict liability statute for pharmaceuticals. However, strict liability remains primarily an American innovation. Second, the tort plaintiff may choose, at least potentially, from among 50 jurisdictions if he decides to file suit in the United States. Each of these jurisdictions applies its own set of malleable choice-of-law rules. Third, jury trials are almost always available in the United States, while they are never provided in civil law jurisdictions. . . . Even in the United Kingdom, most civil actions are not tried before a jury. . . . Fourth, unlike most foreign jurisdictions, American courts allow contingent attorney's fees, and do not tax losing parties with their opponents' attorney's fees. . . . Fifth, discovery is more extensive in American than in foreign courts.

NOTES

1. In Miles v. Illinois Central R.R., 315 U.S. 698 (1942), Justice Jackson, in a concurring opinion, stated: "An advantage which it is hoped will be reflected in a judgment is what makes plaintiffs leave home and incur burdens of expense and inconvenience that would be regarded as oppressive if forced upon them." Id. at 706. Will it be easy to determine when depriving plaintiffs of this advantage by a forum non conveniens dismissal will result in denial of "substantial justice"?

See Gemini Capital Group, Inc. v. Yap Fishing Corp., 150 F.3d 1088 (9th Cir.1998), where the court held that a California corporation's choice of a Hawaiian forum was entitled to "less deference" than if the corporation had sued in California and affirmed a forum non conveniens dismissal although the alternative forum was in a foreign country.

But see Iragorri v. United Technologies Corp., 274 F.3d 65, 73 (2d Cir.2001): "It is not a correct understanding of the rule to accord deference only when the suit is brought in the plaintiff's home district. Rather, the court must consider a plaintiff's likely motivations in light of all the relevant indications. We thus understand the Supreme Court's teachings on the deference due to plaintiff's forum choice as instructing that we give greater deference to a plaintiff's forum choice to the extent that it was motivated by legitimate reasons, including the plaintiff's convenience and the ability of a U.S. resident plaintiff to obtain jurisdiction over the defendant, and diminishing deference to a plaintiff's forum choice to the extent that it was motivated by tactical advantage." For an application, see Fredriksson v. H.R. Textron, Inc., 484 Fed.App'x 610 (2d Cir.2012).

In Guidi v. Inter-Continental Hotels Corp., 224 F.3d 142 (2d Cir.2000), the Court reversed a forum-non-conveniens dismissal in favor of Egypt, inter alia, because "the special circumstances presented by this case—specifically, the emotional burden on Plaintiffs of returning to the country where they or their loved ones were shot in an act of religious terrorism—provide additional weight for favoring Plaintiffs' choice of their home forum for this litigation." Id. at 145. Keep in mind that forum-non-conveniens dismissal is discretionary. Ask yourself, nonetheless, whether the court should consider individual emotional concerns.

2. In the Matter of the Arbitration Between Monegasque De Reassurances S.A.M. (Monde Re) v. Nak Naftogaz of Ukraine and State of Ukraine, 311 F.3d 488 (2d Cir.2002), the Court affirmed a dismissal in favor of the Ukraine on forum non conveniens grounds when the contract dispute between the Russian supplier of natural gas and a Ukrainian pipeline operator and distributor had no contact with the United States, except that all states, including the United States, were parties to the U.N. Convention on the Recognition and Enforcement of Arbitral Awards. The Russian plaintiff in the New York action had sought confirmation of a Moscow arbitral award in its favor. In reaching its conclusion, the Court had to decide whether the Convention's grounds for non-recognition of a member state's arbitral award were indeed exclusive, as provided in 9 U.S.C. § 207. It held that they were not, at least not so as to proscribe a forum non conveniens dismissal (id. at

496). It gave three principal reasons in support. A forum non conveniens dismissal does not deny recognition on substantive grounds, given the U.S. Supreme Court's classification of the doctrine as "procedural rather than substantive" (American Dredging Co. v. Miller, 510 U.S. 443, 453 (1994)), id. at 495; Convention states may therefore apply their own non-onerous procedures in enforcement proceedings. Furthermore, citing to *Gilbert*, p. 232, supra, at 507, the Court explained that the doctrine has its roots in the principle "that a court may resist imposition upon its jurisdiction even when jurisdiction is authorized by a general venue statute." Id. at 497, 500. Finally, since the doctrine may be applied "in domestic arbitration cases brought under provisions of the Federal Arbitration Act, ... it therefore may be applied under the provisions of the Convention", citing to one of its own earlier decisions.

Do these points convince you? For instance, national "procedures" may well have to do with the manner of enforcement, including filing requirements, time limitations, and the like, rather than to justify a refusal to entertain a case at all. In other words, the "substance/procedure" classification of traditional conflicts law may be inapposite in the context of a treaty obligation. Likewise, the Court's last point seems inapplicable in an international context: practices under domestic law do not define the obligation under a treaty. The Court's second point (the historic roots of the doctrine) likewise proceeds from domestic law. In that context, the Court also mentions that non-application would permit forum shopping in any number of courts that have no connection with the underlying transaction. This may be so. However, forum non conveniens dismissals are an unknown remedy outside of the common law world. Once again, the definition of a treaty obligation should not proceed from the perspective of domestic law.

The facts are not entirely clear but it is reasonable to assume that plaintiff indeed only sought "confirmation" of the Moscow arbitral award and not its "recognition and enforcement" against the defendant and its property (there seemed to be none) in the United States. An easier resolution of the case, with like outcome, would have been to hold the Convention and its limitation on permissible defenses against enforcement to be inapplicable to the case. In such circumstances, there would have been no problem with a forum non conveniens dismissal. But cf. Lenchyshyn v. Pelko Electric, Inc., 723 N.Y.S.2d 285 (N.Y.App.Div.2001), which recognized a Canadian judgment under the New York version of the Uniform Foreign Money-Judgments Recognition Act and held that there is no need for personal jurisdiction over defendants in New York. The defendants contended that they had no assets in New York. The court rejected this objection: "Moreover, even if defendants do not presently have assets in New York, plaintiffs nevertheless should be granted recognition of the foreign country money judgment pursuant to [the Uniform Act], and thereby should have the opportunity to pursue all such enforcement steps *in futuro*, whenever it might appear that defendants are maintaining assets in New York, including at any time during the initial life of the domesticated Ontario money judgment or any subsequent renewal period." Id. at 291.

Interestingly also, the Court was not bothered by the fact that the trial court had dismissed for forum non conveniens without having inquired first whether it had jurisdiction at all: "While such abstention may appear logically to rest on an assumption of jurisdiction, . . . it is as merits-free as finding no jurisdiction," quoting from In re Papandreou, 139 F.3d 247, 255–56 (D.C.Cir.1998). Does this make sense to you? See the statement in *Gilbert*: "the doctrine of *forum non conveniens* can never apply if there is absence of jurisdiction. . . ." It is on this basis that a number of courts had disagreed with *Monegasque de Reassurance*. See, e.g., Dominguez-Cota v. Cooper Tire & Rubber Co., 396 F.3d 650 (5th Cir.2005). However, in Sinochem Int'l Co. Ltd. v. Malaysia Int'l Shipping Corp., 549 U.S. 422 (2007), the U.S. Supreme Court distinguished away its statement in *Gilbert* and held unanimously that in cases in which jurisdiction "is difficult to determine, and forum non conveniens considerations weigh heavily in favor of dismissal, the court properly [may take] the less burdensome course." Id. at 1194. Assume that a forum non conveniens dismissal gives heavy weight to the court's finding that the law of the alternative forum will apply. Is this finding binding on the parties in the alternative forum? If so, is this a case in which a jurisdictional finding should come first?

3. Even aside from the forum non conveniens issue, *Piper* is a factually and procedurally complex case, and an example of clever lawyering. Is *Piper*'s bottom line that the party who controls forum selection controls the case's outcome? For discussion, see Freer, Refracting Domestic and Global Choice-Of-Forum Doctrine Through the Lens of a Single Case, 2007 B.Y.U.L.Rev. 959.

4. In American Dredging Co. v. Miller, 510 U.S. 443 (1994) the Supreme Court succinctly recognized, at Note 2, what was already implicitly understood: "the federal doctrine of forum non conveniens has continuing application only in cases where the alternative forum is abroad"; otherwise, the proper route is 28 U.S.C. § 1404(a). But note that the federal transfer statute also does not apply when a forum-selection clause selects a state court.

The development of forum non conveniens through the Court's decision in *Piper* has been criticized as allowing a simple reasonableness test, committed to the sound discretion of the trial court, to consider many factors, including, most noticeably, docket congestion. Consider pundits' detractions with respect to the following decision, controversial in many respects.

LUBBE V. CAPE PLC, [2000] 1 W. L.R. 1545 (H. L. appeal taken from Eng.). In a "group action," representatives of almost 4,000 South Africans brought claims against an English company for injuries and death suffered in South Africa because of asbestos fibers released into the air by the defendant's manufacturing and mining subsidiaries. The House of Lords reversed a forum non conveniens stay that had been granted by the High Court and affirmed by the Court of Appeal. The Lords found that because of the large number of claimants and the need for medical evidence, the defendant had met its burden to "show that England is not the natural or appropriate forum for the trial [and] establish that there is another available forum which is clearly or distinctly more appropriate than the English forum." Nevertheless, the Lords allowed the appeal (reversed) because plaintiffs had met their burden to "establish that substantial justice will not be done in the appropriate forum." The claimants would not receive substantial justice in a South African court because, unlike England, South Africa did not provide legal aid to finance investigation, to hire expert witnesses, and for other litigation expenses. The Lords also stated that "the principles on which the doctrine of forum non conveniens rest [sic] leave no room for considerations of public interest or public policy which cannot be related to the private interests of any of the parties or the ends of justice in the case which is before the court." In this regard, the court declined to follow the practice in the United States of considering public as well as private interests. The case also decided that Cape's agreement to submit to jurisdiction of the South African courts was "sufficient to satisfy the requirement that the alternative forum in South Africa was available."

NOTES

1. Lubbe v. Cape PLC rejects consideration of public interest factors that "cannot be related to the private interests of any of the parties or the ends of justice." Can any of the public interest factors listed by Justice Jackson in *Gulf Oil v. Gilbert* be so related?

2. Should a multinational enterprise be able to engage in reverse forum shopping by voluntarily submitting to jurisdiction in a host country and thereby buttress its argument that the claimants' suit in England should be dismissed on grounds of forum non conveniens? Should the court order defendant to reimburse plaintiff for plaintiff's costs in bringing suit in what was then the only available forum? For discussion, see Morse, Not In The Public Interest? Lubbe v. Cape PLC, 37 Texas Int'l L.J. 541 (2002); Derr, Striking a Better Public-Private Balance in Forum non Conveniens, 93 Cornell L.Rev. 819 (2008).

In re Union Carbide Corporation Gas Plant Disaster at Bhopal, India in December, 1984

United States District Court, S.D. New York, 1986.
634 F.Supp. 842.

[In the aftermath of the most devastating industrial catastrophe in history, some 145 actions by victims were started in federal courts in the United States against Union Carbide Corporation, a New York corporation. The disaster occurred when a lethal gas known as methyl isocyanate escaped from a chemical plant operated by Union Carbide India Limited (UCIL) in Bhopal, India. More than 2,000 people were killed and hundreds of thousands injured. A few months later the Union of India (UOI) enacted the Bhopal Gas Leak Disaster (Processing of

Claims) Act, granting the Indian government the exclusive right to represent the victims.

The Indian government, acting as *parens patriae,* filed a complaint in the federal court for the Southern District of New York on behalf of all victims of the Bhopal disaster, similar to the class action complaints filed by individuals in the United States. Under multi-district procedures, the Southern District of New York was designated the court for resolution of all the federal actions. UOI asserted it had to sue in the United States because the Indian courts did not have jurisdiction over UCC, which is the American parent of UCIL by virtue of ownership or control of 50.9% of its stock. Of the balance of UCIL's stock, 22% is in the hands of the government of India and the rest is owned by 23,500 members of the Indian public.]

"This Court is firmly convinced that the Indian legal system is in a far better position than the American courts to determine the cause of the tragic event and thereby fix liability. Further, the Indian courts have greater access to all the information needed to arrive at the amount of the compensation to be awarded the victims."

The presence in India of the overwhelming majority of the witnesses and evidence, both documentary and real, would by itself suggest that India is the most convenient forum for this consolidated case. The additional presence in India of all but the less than a handful of claimants underscores the convenience of holding trial in India. All of the private interest factors described in *Piper* and *Gilbert* weigh heavily toward dismissal of this case on the grounds of *forum non conveniens.*

The public interest factors set forth in *Piper* and *Gilbert* also favor dismissal. The administrative burden of this immense litigation would unfairly tax this or any American tribunal. The cost to American taxpayers of supporting the litigation in the United States would be excessive. When another, adequate and more convenient forum so clearly exists, there is no reason to press the United States judiciary to the limits of its capacity. No American interest in the outcome of this litigation outweighs the interest of India in applying Indian law and Indian values to the task of resolving this case.

The Bhopal plant was regulated by Indian agencies. The Union of India has a very strong interest in the aftermath of the accident which affected its citizens on its own soil. Perhaps Indian regulations were ignored or contravened. India may wish to determine whether the regulations imposed on the chemical industry within its boundaries were sufficiently stringent. The Indian interests far outweigh the interests of citizens of the United States in the litigation.

In re Union Carbide Corporation Gas Plant Disaster at Bhopal, India in December, 1984

United States Court of Appeals, Second Circuit, 1987.
809 F.2d 195, cert. denied, 484 U.S. 871, 108 S.Ct. 199, 98 L.Ed.2d 150 (1987).

[UCC moved to dismiss the complaints of the Indian plaintiffs and UOI on *forum non conveniens* and other grounds. The district judge granted the motion on condition that UCC:

(1) consent to the jurisdiction of the courts of India and continue to waive defenses based on the statute of limitations,

(2) agree to satisfy any judgment rendered by an Indian court against it and upheld on appeal, provided the judgment and affirmance "comport with minimal requirements of due process," and

(3) be subject to discovery under the Federal Rules of Civil Procedure of the United States.

Relying on the standards laid down in Piper Aircraft Co. v. Reyno, 454 U.S. 235 (1981), the Court of Appeals affirmed the dismissal, but modified two of the conditions.]

■ MANSFIELD, CIRCUIT JUDGE. The first condition, that UCC consent to the Indian court's personal jurisdiction over it and waive the statute of limitations as a defense, are not unusual and have been imposed in numerous cases where the foreign court would not provide an adequate alternative in the absence of such a condition. The remaining two conditions, however, pose problems.

In requiring that UCC consent to enforceability of an Indian judgment against it, the district court proceeded at least in part on the erroneous assumption that, absent such a requirement, the plaintiffs, if they should succeed in obtaining an Indian judgment against UCC, might not be able to enforce it against UCC in the United States. The law, however, is to the contrary. Under New York law, which governs actions brought in New York to enforce foreign judgments, see Island Territory of Curacao v. Solitron Devices, Inc., 489 F.2d 1313, 1318 (2d Cir. 1973), cert. denied 416 U.S. 986 (1974), a foreign-country judgment that is final, conclusive and enforceable where rendered must be recognized and will be enforced as "conclusive between the parties to the extent that it grants or denies recovery of a sum of money" except that it is not deemed to be conclusive if:

"1. the judgment was rendered under a system which does not provide impartial tribunals or procedures compatible with the requirements of due process of law;

"2. the foreign court did not have personal jurisdiction over the defendant."

Art. 53, Recognition of Foreign Country Money Judgments, 7B N.Y.Civ.Prac. L. & R. § 5301–09 (McKinney 1978). Although § 5304 further provides that under certain specified conditions a foreign country judgment need not be recognized, none of these conditions would apply to the present cases except for the possibility of failure to provide UCC with sufficient notice of proceedings or the existence of fraud in obtaining the judgment, which do not presently exist but conceivably could occur in the future.

UCC contends that Indian courts, while providing an adequate alternative forum, do not observe due process standards that would be required as a matter of course in this country. As evidence of this apprehension it points to the haste with which the Indian court in Bhopal issued a temporary order freezing its assets throughout the world and the possibility of serious prejudice to it if the UOI is permitted to have the double and conflicting status of both plaintiff and co-defendant in the Indian court proceedings. It argues that we should protect it against such denial of due process by authorizing Judge Keenan to retain the authority, after *forum non conveniens* dismissal of the cases here, to monitor the Indian court proceedings and be available on call to rectify in some undefined way any abuses of UCC's right to due process as they might occur in India.

UCC's proposed remedy is not only impractical but evidences an abysmal ignorance of basic jurisdiction principles, so much that it borders on the frivolous. The district court's jurisdiction is limited to proceedings before it in this country. Once it dismisses those proceedings on grounds of *forum non conveniens* it ceases to have any further jurisdiction over the matter unless and until a proceeding may some day be brought to enforce here a final and conclusive Indian money judgment. Nor could we, even if we attempted to retain some sort of supervisory jurisdiction, impose our due process requirements upon Indian courts, which are governed by their laws, not ours. The concept of shared jurisdictions is both illusory and unrealistic. The parties cannot simultaneously submit to both jurisdictions the resolution of the pre-trial and trial issues when there is only one consolidated case pending in one court. Any denial by the Indian courts of due process can be raised by UCC as a defense to the plaintiffs' later attempt to enforce a resulting judgment against UCC in this country.

We are concerned, however, that as it is written the district court's requirement that UCC consent to the enforcement of a final Indian judgment, which was imposed on the erroneous assumption that such a judgment might not otherwise be enforceable in the United States, may create misunderstandings and problems of construction. Although the order's provision that the judgment "comport with *minimal* requirements of due process" (emphasis supplied) probably is intended to refer to "due process" as used in the New York Foreign Country Money Judgments Law and others like it, there is the risk that it may also be interpreted as providing for a lesser standard than we would otherwise require. Since the court's condition with respect to enforceability of any final Indian judgment is predicated on an erroneous legal assumption and its "due process" language is ambiguous, and since the district court's purpose is fully served by New York's statute providing for recognition of foreign-country money judgments, it was error to impose this condition upon the parties.

We also believe that the district court erred in requiring UCC to consent (which UCC did under protest and subject to its right of appeal) to broad discovery of it by the plaintiffs under the Federal Rules of Civil Procedure when UCC is confined to the more limited discovery authorized under Indian law. We recognize that under some circumstances, such as when a moving defendant unconditionally consents thereto or no undiscovered evidence of consequence is believed to be under the control of a plaintiff or co-defendant, it may be appropriate to condition a *forum non conveniens* dismissal on the moving defendant's submission to discovery under the Federal Rules without requiring reciprocal discovery by it of the plaintiff. See, e.g., Piper Aircraft v. Reyno, supra, 454 U.S. at 257 n. 25 (suggesting that district courts can condition dismissal upon a defendant's agreeing to provide all relevant records); Ali v. Offshore Co., 753 F.2d 1327, 1334, n. 16 (5th Cir. 1985) (same); Boskoff v. Transportes Aereos Portugueses, 17 Av.Cas. (CCH) 18,613, at 18,616 (N.D.Ill. 1983) (accepting defendant's voluntary commitment to provide discovery in foreign forum according to Federal Rules). Basic justice dictates that both sides be treated equally, with each having equal access to the evidence in the possession or under the control of the other. Application of this fundamental principle in the present case is especially appropriate since the UOI, as the sovereign government of India, is expected to be a party to the Indian litigation, possibly on both sides.

For these reasons we direct that the condition with respect to the discovery of UCC under the Federal Rules of Civil Procedure be deleted without prejudice to the right of the parties to have reciprocal discovery of each other on equal terms under the Federal Rules, subject to such approval as may be required of the Indian court in which the cases will be pending. If, for instance, Indian authorities will permit mutual discovery pursuant to the Federal Rules, the district court's order, as modified in accordance with this opinion, should not be construed to bar such procedure. In the absence of such a court-sanctioned agreement, however, the parties will be limited by the applicable discovery rules of the Indian court in which the claims will be pending.

NOTES

1. Under the Indian Bhopal Gas Leak Disaster Act, enacted in 1985, the Government of India had the exclusive right to represent victims of the Bhopal disaster. The Government pursued claims in the courts of India until the Supreme Court of India approved a settlement in February of 1989. Under the terms of the settlement, Union Carbide India Limited and its

parent corporation agreed to pay $470 million to the Indian Government for the benefit of the victims of the disaster. The Supreme Court of India found the settlement just and reasonable, see Union Carbide Corp. v. Union of India, 1989 [Supp.] S.C.A. L.E. 89.

2. In support of the contention that a successful forum non conveniens motion may be the ultimate defense tactic, see Robertson, Forum Non Conveniens in America and England: "A Rather Fantastic Fiction," 103 L.Q.R. 398 (1987), and Robertson, The Federal Doctrine of Forum Non Conveniens, 29 Tex.Int'l L.J. 353 (1994). Robertson makes the point that the great majority of foreign plaintiffs who have their United States cases dismissed never pursue their claims abroad or settle for a fraction of what they would likely get in a United States court. Do these statistics give credence to the popular notion that the American jury is the forum shopper's prize? See also Michael J. Zezima, Jr., Letter to the Editor, *Carbide got off easy in Bhopal Disaster*, New York Times, Dec. 18, 1994, at E14. But see Whytock, The Evolving Forum Shopping System, 96 Cornell L.Rev. 481, 529 (2011), whose empirical study leads him to conclude that "the current system is unlikely to encourage transnational forum shopping into U.S. courts to the extent suggested by the conventional understanding." In particular, "one important form of transnational litigation—alienage litigation—actually has been decreasing." See also Whytock & Robertson, Forum Non Conveniens and the Enforcement of Foreign Judgments, 111 Colum.L.Rev. 1444 (2011).

Consider also whether the forum-non-conveniens dismissal perhaps averted an improper "piercing the corporate veil," i.e., placing liability for the subsidiary's actions at the feet of the parent. Query further whether the dismissal had the aforementioned effect: note that the settlement was ten times the value of the subsidiary and twenty times Union Carbide's share of the equity in the subsidiary.

Judge Mansfield dismissed the idea that the American court could hold the action in abeyance while litigation proceeded in India and, in a way, supervise how things were proceeding there. However, the American court might have retained the case in a lesser, non-supervisory fashion: see Cardiorentis AG v. IQVIA Ltd., 837 S.E.2d 873 (N.C. 2020) (local action stayed for six months while litigation proceeds in England, periodic reports required).

Forum Non Conveniens—In General

3. Most states now recognize some form of forum non conveniens in non-custodial matters. See Kedy v. A.W. Chesterton Co., 946 A.2d 1171, 1180 n.9 (R.I.2008) (authorities cited therein). In *Kedy*, the Rhode Island Supreme Court resolved a split among its lower courts and endorsed both the forum non conveniens doctrine and the federal *Piper* standard. Does this mean that state and federal courts in Rhode Island will now apply the same test? Consider Florida, which has adopted the federal standard. Esfeld v. Costa Crociere, SPA, 289 F.3d 1300 (11th Cir.2002), reversed and remanded the district court's forum non conveniens dismissal, which came after a Florida state court had ordered a forum non conveniens dismissal. The 11th Circuit stated that the Florida court only took into account Florida contacts in applying the *Piper* standard, but that the district court should take into account national contacts. It emphasized in a subsequent case that the trial court should also consider public factors, regardless of whether the private factors are in equipoise. Fresh Results, LLC v. ASF Holland, B.V., 921 F.3d 1043, 1051 (11th Cir.2019.

Of the three states that traditionally did not recognize the doctrine of forum non conveniens, none has yet expressly rejected it. In Oregon an appellate court assumed that the doctrine exists in the state. Espinoza v. Evergreen Helicopters, Inc., 337 P.3d 169 (Or.App.2014), aff'd, 376 P.3d 960 (Or. 2016). The Montana Supreme Court left the question open as a general matter, but held that Montana "does not recognized [the doctrine] in FELA actions." Rule v. Burlington Northern and Santa Fe Railway Co., 106 P.3d 533, 536 (Mont.2005). Idaho did not deal with the doctrine, even when deciding a case (on other grounds) in which the doctrine had been employed by a lower court. See, e.g., Marco Distributing, Inc. v. Biehl, 555 P.2d 393 (Idaho 1976). For a review of these cases and a statement setting forth the standards for the application of the doctrine in Rhode Island, see Kedy v. A.W. Chesterton Co., 946 A.2d at 1181.

4. A number of long-arm statutes expressly authorize the court to dismiss the case on forum non conveniens grounds. See, e.g., Wis.Stat.Ann. § 801.63(1). It makes "substantial justice" the standard for the exercise of the court's discretion in the area. It expressly provides that forum non conveniens may be invoked even where the defendant would not have been subject to jurisdiction in the more convenient forum, provided that the moving party (1) stipulates consent to jurisdiction in the new forum, and (2) waives any statute of limitations that may have run therein. Section 801.63(3) lists four criteria to be followed by the court: (a) amenability of the parties to personal jurisdiction in this and the other forum; (b) convenience of witnesses; (c) differences in conflict of laws rules; and (d) "any other factors having substantial bearing upon the selection of a convenient, reasonable, and fair place of trial."

Texas law permits a dismissal or stay for forum non conveniens when the plaintiff is a non-resident but forbids it when the plaintiff is a "legal resident" of Texas. Tex. Civ. Prac. & Rem. Code Ann. § 71.051(e) (Vernon's Stat. 2019). For an application, see In re Mahindra, USA Inc., 549 S.W.3d 541 (Tex.2018). Does this provision violate obligations undertaken by the United States in many bilateral treaties of Friendship, Commerce, and Navigation to afford citizens of the other treaty party national treatment with respect to access to courts? Does it violate U.S. obligations as a signatory of the International Covenant on Civil and Political Rights, which forbids discrimination against "all individuals within its territory" on the grounds of "race, colour, sex, language, religion, political or other opinion, national or social origin, property, birth or other status?" The question has been the subject of debate between Professor Weintraub (= no violation) and Professor Paust (= violation): Weintraub, International Litigation and Forum Non Conveniens, 29 Tex.Int'l L.J. 321, 349 (1994); Paust, "Equal Treaty Rights," Resident Status and Forum Non Conveniens, 26 Hou.J.Int'l L. 405, 409 (2004); Weintraub, "Equal Treaty Rights": A Response to

Professor Paust, 27 Hous.J.Int'l L. 241 (2005); Paust, Discrimination on the Basis of Resident Status and Denial of Equal Treatment: A Reply to Professor Weintraub's Response, 27 Hous.J.Int'l L. 253 (2005).

Should the court entertain a motion to dismiss on forum non conveniens grounds when the parties had executed a forum-selection clause in favor of the local forum? In England, the forum-selection clause is prima facie evidence that England is the convenient forum. See Torremans & Fawcett, Cheshire, North & Fawcett's Private International Law 251–57 (15th ed.2017). New York law goes further: a New York court may not dismiss for forum non conveniens in the face of a forum-selection clause in favor of New York when the case involves obligations of $1 million in the aggregate and when New York law has been chosen as the applicable law. N.Y. Gen.Oblig.Law § 5–1402 (McKinney 2020. See Credit Suisse Intern. v. URBI, Desarrollos Urbanos, S.A.B. de C.V., 971 N.Y.S.2d 177 (N.Y.Sup. 2012); Carlyle CIM Agent, L.L.C. v. Trey Resources I, LLC, 50 N.Y.S.3d 326 (N.Y.A.D. 2017). In New York, the legislative policy gives the parties the opportunity to select a sophisticated body of commercial law and a judicial system with substantial experience in administering it and thereby enhances the importance of New York as an international commercial center. 1984 McKinney's Sess. Law News A-689-A-690. Absent legislative directive, in what circumstances should a court disregard the forum-selection clause and dismiss or stay for reasons of forum non conveniens?

Atlantic Marine Construction Co., Inc. v. United States District Court for Western District of Texas

Supreme Court of the United States, 2013.
571 U.S. 49, 134 S. Ct. 568, 187 L.Ed.2d 487.

[The case appears at p. 217, supra]

NOTES

1.   Compare the weighing of private and public interest factors in *Piper* and *Lubbe*, supra. *Atlantic Marine* focuses on public interest factors in cases involving forum selection clauses: which interests prevailed in the other cases? In *McGregor*, supra p. 221, Note (1), did the Florida court follow *Atlantic Marine* or give weight to private interests? Does *Atlantic Marine* provide clear guidance? Does *Piper*?

2.   Lower courts had previously also addressed the venue question in other contexts: "[T]he *forum non conveniens* doctrine is a rule of venue, not a rule of decision." The trial court therefore did not transgress the limitations imposed by *Erie* when it applied the federal and not the Florida standard. See Sibaja v. Dow Chemical Co., 757 F.2d 1215, 1219 (11th Cir.1985). See also Hay, Borchers, Symeonides, Whytock, Conflict of Laws § 11.10 (6th ed.2018). Cf. Stewart Organization, Inc. v. Ricoh Corp., 487 U.S. 22 (1988), p. 224, supra.

3.   Suits have often been dismissed on forum non conveniens grounds in situations where the more convenient forum was a foreign country. See, e.g.,

Tjontveit v. Den Norske Bank ASA, 997 F.Supp. 799 (S.D.Tex.1998); Delgado
v. Shell Oil Co., 890 F.Supp. 1324 (S.D.Tex. 1995); Gonzalez v. Naviera
Neptuno A.A., 832 F.2d 876 (5th Cir.1987); Vaz Borralho v. Keydril Co., 696
F.2d 379 (5th Cir.1983); Vargas v. M/V Mini Lama, 709 F.Supp. 117
(E.D.La.1989). For an erudite and entertaining opinion, see Syndicate 420 at
Lloyd's London v. Early Am. Ins., 796 F.2d 821 (5th Cir.1986) (drawing on
Greek drama and mythology). For validity and propriety of conditions
imposed on a foreign court, see Thomas, 89 A. L.R.Fed. 238 (1988).

Dismissals have been ordered even when the plaintiff was a United
States citizen. See, e.g., Mercier v. Sheraton Intl., Inc., 981 F.2d 1345 (1st
Cir.1992); Penny v. United Fruit Co., 869 F.Supp. 122 (E.D.N.Y.1994); Pain
v. United Technologies Corp., 637 F.2d 775 (D.C.Cir.1980), cert. denied, 454
U.S. 1128 (1981); In re Air Crash Over Mid-Atlantic on June 1, 2009, 760
F.Supp.2d 832 (N.D.Cal.2010). See also Cardiorentis AG v. IQVIA Ltd., 837
S.E,2d 873 (N.C.2020) (memorandum affirming lower court's opinion in the
appendix: local action stayed for six months to allow action to proceed in
England). It has been said that the presumption in favor of the plaintiff's
chosen forum is "even stronger" when the plaintiff is an American citizen
and the alternative forum is a foreign country. Olympic Corp. v. Societe
Generale, 462 F.2d 376, 378 (2d Cir.1972); Complexions, Inc. v. Indus.
Outfitters, Inc., 2011 WL 13070424 (N.D.N.Y.2011), reh'g denied, 2011 WL
5007981 (N.D.N.Y.2011). The decision in *Pain*, supra, may now have to be
reexamined in the light of *Piper*, with greater weight given: Nemarian v. Fed.
Democratic Republic of Ethiopia, 315 F.3d 390 (D.C.Cir.2003) (per Chief
Judge Ginsburg) (inadequate remedy in foreign forum); *Pain* was followed,
on the basis of public interest factors, in Glen v. BP p.l.c. (In re BP p.l.c. Secs.
Litig.), 27 F.Supp.3d 755, 760 (Tex.2014).

When litigation is already pending in a foreign forum, an American
court may abstain from exercising jurisdiction and dismiss in favor of the
foreign forum. See Rolls Royce (Canada), Ltd. v. Cayman Airways, Ltd., 617
F.Supp. 17 (S.D.Fla.1985). But see American Home Assur. Co. v. Insurance
Corp. of Ireland, 603 F.Supp. 636 (S.D.N.Y.1984) (when the plaintiffs are
U.S. citizens or residents and trial in the United States is merely
inconvenient but not oppressive for the foreign defendant, the court may
decline to dismiss but instead enjoin the simultaneous prosecution of the
foreign litigation). See also China Trade and Development v. M.V. Choong
Yong, 837 F.2d 33 (2d Cir.1987). In English practice, multiplicity of
proceedings which may result from the pendency of litigation elsewhere ("lis
alibi pendens") now is also an important element to be taken into account in
ruling on forum non conveniens motions. See The Abidin Daver, [1984] AC
398, [1984] 1 All E.R. 470 (H. L.). In Canada, see Amchem Products Inc. v.
Worker's Comp. Bd., 102 D. L.R. (4th) 96 (1993). On "lis pendens", see textual
Note, infra.

Having to litigate in a foreign forum does not deprive the parties of all
advantages of American law. The Court of Appeals in the *Union Carbide* case
mentioned the problem of discovery under U.S. law. Note that 28 U.S.C.A.
§ 1782 provides that the "district court of the district in which a person
resides . . . may order him to give his testimony or statement or to produce

... other things for use in a foreign or international tribunal." For an application, see In re Letter Rogatory from Nedenes District Court, Norway, 216 F.R.D. 277 (S.D.N.Y.2003) (putative father compelled to give blood sample for use in Norwegian paternity proceeding); for extensive discussion, see Intel v. Advanced Micro Devices, Inc., 542 U.S. 241 (2004); Brandi-Dohrn v. IKB Deutsche Industriebank AG, 673 F.3d 76, 80 (2d Cir.2012); In re Tiberius Group AG, 2020 WL 1140784 (S.D.N.Y. 2020); In re Kidd, 2020 WL 2404928 (D.Conn. 2020). For discovery in France, Germany, the U.K., and other countries, see Alvarez, Conducting Discovery in Foreign Countries, in: D. Levy (ed.), International Litigation 275 (ABA Tort Trial and Insurance Practice Section, 2003); for Germany, see Meier, U.S. Discovery: A German Perspective, 2012 DAJV Newsletter 9; for an Austrian Perspective, see Klausegger & Fritz, id. at 12. See also Hilgard, Cross Border Data Transfer in E-Discoveries in the U.S. and the European and German Privacy Laws, 2010 Computer L.Rev. Int'l 13.

4.   Dismissals on forum non conveniens grounds have been denied in a variety of circumstances. Lake v. Richardson-Merrell, Inc., 538 F.Supp. 262 (N.D.Ohio 1982) (court believed that action would be dismissed in Québec on the ground of prescription, a defense that, under Québec law, could not be waived by the defendant); In re Air Crash Disaster Near Bombay, 531 F.Supp. 1175 (W.D.Wash.1982) (statute of limitations had run in India and there was a substantial possibility that the Bombay court would not accept defendant's waiver of the statute); Canadian Overseas Ores Limited v. Compania, 528 F.Supp. 1337 (S.D.N.Y.1982) (court feared that fair trial could not be had in Chile); Nemarian v. Fed. Democratic Republic of Ethiopia, supra Note 3. See also Note 6, infra.

5.   A factor that militates against dismissal of a case on forum non conveniens grounds is that the forum may be the only state where jurisdiction can be obtained over all defendants. See Watson v. Merrell Dow Pharmaceuticals, Inc., 769 F.2d 354, 356 (6th Cir.1985); Varkonyi v. S.A. Empresa De Viacao A.R.G., 239 N.E.2d 542 (N.Y.1968). Cf. Islamic Republic of Iran v. Pahlavi, 467 N.E.2d 245, 247 (N.Y.1984), cert. denied, 469 U.S. 1108 (1985). See also Pacific Employers Ins. Co. v. M/V Capt. W.D. Cargill, 751 F.2d 801 (5th Cir.1985); Madanes v. Madanes, 981 F.Supp. 241, 265 et seq. (S.D.N.Y.1997).

Availability of an Alternate Forum

6.   The availability of an alternate forum is "the essential predicate for dismissal": Liaw Su Teng v. Skaarup Shipping Corp., 743 F.2d 1140, 1147 (5th Cir.1984). This is an especially important question when the forum is asked to dismiss in favor of a foreign jurisdiction. The fact that the other forum would apply a different substantive law or that procedural advantages which the plaintiff would enjoy in the local forum are not available in the foreign court, or that the foreign legal system does not provide punitive damages should not defeat a dismissal for forum non conveniens that is otherwise indicated. See, e.g., Piper Aircraft Co. v. Reyno, 454 U.S. 235 (1981), p. 233, supra (no strict liability under Scottish law); Coakes v. Arabian American Oil Co., 831 F.2d 572 (5th Cir.1987) (no contingent-fee system in England); de Melo v. Lederle Laboratories, 801 F.2d 1058 (8th

Cir.1986) (no punitive damages in Brazil); Associação Braileira de Medicina de Grupo v. Stryker Corp., 891 F.3d 615 (6th Cir. 2018).

A common argument against a forum non conveniens dismissal is that the foreign legal system is corrupt and therefore does not serve as an adequate alternative forum. Challenges to the adequacy of the foreign legal system. In Stroitelstvo Bulgaria Ltd. v. Bulgarian-American Enterprise Fund, 589 F.3d 417 (7th Cir.2010), a dismissal on grounds of forum non conveniens was affirmed because allegations of corruption in the Bulgarian judicial system were too generalized to overcome the presumption that Bulgaria had an available and functioning civil justice system. The decision was followed in Zeevi Holdings Ltd. v. Republic of Bulgaria, 2011 WL 1345155 (S.D.N.Y.2011). See also Doe v. Ritz Carlton Hotel Company, LLC, 666 Fed.Appx. 180 (3d Cir. 2016) (United Kingdom and Cayman Islands); Nagy v. Náday, 2020 WL 1308191 (D.Mass. 2020) (Hungary). For a more stringent evaluation of foreign courts, see Fitt, Note, The Tragedy of Comity: Questioning the American Treatment of Inadequate Foreign Courts, 50 Va.J.Int'l L. 1021 (2010).

Alternate Forum and Foreign "Blocking Statutes"

7. In 1998, the Congress of Ecuador enacted Law No. 55, which provides: "[I]n case of international concurrent jurisdiction the plaintiff can freely choose to file a complaint in Ecuador or in another country. . . . In the case that the demand is filed outside of Ecuador, the national competence and the jurisdiction of the Ecuadorian Judges on the case will be terminated forever." Several Latin American countries (e.g., Costa Rica, Dominica, Guatemala, Nicaragua, and Panama) have similar statutes designed to discourage foreign forum non convenience dismissals that would send suits to them. Ecuador (its law has since been declared unconstitutional on formal grounds) and Guatemala based their blocking statutes on the Model Law on International Jurisdiction and Applicable Law to Tort Liability of 1958 (Dahl's Law Dictionary 242 (4th ed. 2006)). Art. 1 of the statute is intended to make "sure that . . . a foreign court with jurisdiction . . . will not be able to close the doors on [a Latin American plaintiff] as, for instance has been happening with the theory of forum non conveniens." Henry Saint Dahl, Forum Non Conveniens, Latin America, and Blocking Statutes, 35 U.Miami Inter-Amer. L.Rev. 21, 47 (2003). This type of legislation has a parallel in the civil law concept of lis alibi pendens but goes beyond it: lis pendens results in the stay (and ultimate dismissal) of the second proceeding in order to let the first-filed action go ahead and thereby to prevent parallel litigation. In contrast, the Latin American statutes close the second court altogether even when there is no parallel litigation elsewhere any longer. Another way to discourage American defendants from trying to move their suits abroad through a forum non conveniens dismissal in the U.S., accompanied by readiness to submit abroad, is legislation, for instance in Nicaragua and Dominica, imposing additional burdens on U.S. defendants, such as requiring deposits for security or the application of American discovery standards. See Weintraub, International Litigation and Arbitration 239–41 n.6 (6th ed.2011). If a blocking statute does bar a Latin American court from entertaining an action after a forum non conveniens dismissal in the United

States, should that circumstance preclude the American court from ordering such a dismissal on the ground that there is no alternative forum? For a decision reviewing the case law and concluding that a foreign law could not force the exercise of jurisdiction on an American court, see Del Istmo Assur. Corp. v. Platon et al., 2011 WL 5508641 (S.D.Fl. Nov. 9, 2011). Nonetheless, the court equivocated: its order dismissing the case without prejudice also stated that "Plaintiff may move to reopen this case if a court in Panama refuses jurisdiction over its claims." Id. at *9. Similarly: Mootilal Rambit & Sons Contracting Ltd. v. Farouk Mohammed, 2014 WL 3439742, *4 (S.D.Fla. Jul. 15, 2014). See also Heiser, Forum Non Conveniens and Retaliatory Legislation: The Impact on the Available Alternative Forum Inquiry and on the Desirability of Forum Non Conveniens as a Defense Tactic, 56 Kan. L. Rev. 609 (2008); Sold, Inappropriate Forum or Inappropriate Law? A Choice of Law Solution to the Jurisdictional Standoff Between the United States and Latin America, 60 Emory L.J. 1437 (2011). Consider in this context that the U.S. Supreme Court wrote in *Gilbert*, supra, that the forum non conveniens doctrine furnished a way to choose between "at least two forum [sic] in which the defendant is amenable to process" (330 U.S. 501, 506–07 (1947)) and that the *Piper* Court (p. 233, supra) noted in a footnote that the existence of an alternative forum must be determined "at the outset of any forum non conveniens inquiry" (454 U.S. 235, 254 n.22 (1981)). See also Rajeev Muttreja, Note, How to Fix the Inconsistent Application of Forum Non Conveniens to Latin American Jurisdiction—And Why Consistency May Not Be Enough, 83 N.Y.U.L.Rev. 1607, 1611 (2008); Whytock & Robertson, Forum BNon Conveniens and the Enforcement of Foreign Judgments, 111 Colum.L.Rev. 1444 (2011), and the response by Brand, Access-to-Justice Analysis On A Due Process Platform, 112 Colum.L.Rev. Sidebar 76 (2012).

One way to avoid application of a "blocking statute" would be not to use the forum non conveniens doctrine but to dismiss for lack of jurisdiction. Gordon, Forum Non Conveniens Misconstrued: A Response to Henry Saint Dahl, 38 U.Miami Inter-Am. L. Rev. 141, 151 n.61 (2006). One court did just that, finding that no facts supported assertion of jurisdiction by Texas: Johnston v. Multidata Systems Int'l Corp., 523 F.3d 602 (5th Cir.2008).

Forum Non Conveniens in Other Common Law Jurisdictions

8. The doctrine of forum non conveniens is widely recognized throughout the common law world. Of all countries, *Australia* likely recognizes the purest approach to forum non conveniens determinations, see Voth v. Manildra Flour Mills, [1990] 171 C. L.R. 538 (noting, with respect to public-interest factors, that Australian courts do not usually take account of local administrative problems, such as congested dockets, but that the applicability of forum law may be an important factor in the decision to retain or to dismiss). See also Puttick v. Tenon Ltd., [2008] HCA 54 (High Ct., Australia, 2008) (Supreme Court of Victoria not clearly an inappropriate forum, at No. 51.). But, see also Garsec Pty. Ltd. v. His Majesty The Sultan of Brunei [2008] NSWCA 211 (dismissing on forum non conveniens grounds although there was arguably no alternative forum). For *England,* see Spiliada Maritime Corp. v. Cansulex Ltd. (The Spiliada), [1986] 3 All ER (HL) 843; for *Canada,* see Amchem Products Inc. v. Worker's Comp. Bd., 102

D. L.R. (4th) 96 (1993); for *New Zealand,* see VanDyck v. VanDyck, [1990] 3 NZLR 624 (High Ct. Whangarei); for *South Africa,* see Great River Shipping Inc. v. Sunnyface Marine Ltd., 1992 (4) SA 291; for *Scotland,* see the original use of forum non conveniens in Clements v. Macauley, 4 Mac Pherson (Sess. Cas. 3rd Serv.) 583 (1866), and more recently, Shell UK v. Andrew Innes, 1994 Outer House Cases; for *Ireland,* see Doe and Dowling v. Armour Pharmaceutical Co., [1994] 1 ILRM 416; for *Northern Ireland,* see Macrete v. Guardian Royal Exchange Plc., [1988] NI 332; and for the *Philippines,* see Hong Kong & Shanghai Banking Corp. v. Sherman, 176 Sup.Ct.Rep.Ann. 331 (1989). For comparative treatment, see also Reus, Die "forum non conveniens-doctrine" in Großbritannien und den USA in Zukunft auch in Deutschland?, [1991] Recht der Internationalen Wirtschaft 542. For *Hong Kong* and some comparative treatment, see Svantesson, In Defence of the Doctrine for Forum Non Conveniens, 35 Hong Kong L.J. 395 (2005).

European Union

9.   European Union law (Council Regulation (EU) No. 1215/2012) contains detailed jurisdictional rules, as we have seen, and also deals with the problem of potential multiplicity of litigation. It does not provide for judicial discretion to decline to exercise jurisdiction. Forum non conveniens is generally unknown in civil-law systems. It is common ground that the doctrine is not part of European Union law. For a comprehensive international study of forum non conveniens and related doctrines, see James J. Fawcett (ed.), Declining Jurisdiction in Private International Law (1995). See also Torremans & Fawcett, Cheshire, North & Fawcett's Private International Law 388–89 (15th ed.2017); Kropholler and von Hein, Europäisches Zivilprozessrecht anno. 20 vor Art. 2 (9th ed.2011).

But what about England where the doctrine has a long tradition (Note 8, supra)? In Case C-281/02, Owusu v. Jackson, [2005] ECR 1–1383, [2005] 1 Lloyd's Rep. 452, [2005] 2 W.L.R. 942, the Court of Justice of the European Communities held that an English court could not grant a forum non conveniens stay of a suit brought by an English domiciliary against an English company and several Jamaican defendants to recovery for injuries suffered while the plaintiff was diving in the sea during a vacation in Jamaica. The Court ruled that the Brussels Convention precludes an EU court "from declining the jurisdiction conferred on it by Article 2 of that convention [now Article 2 of the Regulation] on the ground that a court of a non-Contracting State would be a more appropriate forum for the trial of the action even if the jurisdiction of no other Contracting State is in issue or the proceedings have no connecting factors to any other Contracting State." *Owusu* dealt a mortal blow to a prior English ruling, In re Harrods (Buenos Aires) Ltd., [1992] Ch.72 (C.A.), which had held that England's use of forum non conveniens was not contradictory to European Community law. In *Harrods,* the Court of Appeal decided that section 49 of the 1982 Civil Jurisdiction and Judgments Act was not inconsistent with European Community law (then the Brussels Convention) and that an English court could therefore dismiss, in favor of Argentina, an action against a defendant domiciled in England on forum non conveniens grounds. The House of Lords referred the question to the European Court of Justice which has jurisdiction to render binding decisions of interpretation of the Brussels Convention (and now of the Regulation). When the case was settled, the matter was removed from the Court's docket and no decision issued on the question submitted. *Owusu* now supplies the answer. Nevertheless, English scholars and some decisions take the position that forum non conveniens-dismissals are still permissible under English law in cases where litigation is already pending in a non-EU state or when the plaintiff has breached a choice-of-forum clause in favor of a non-EU state (i.e., in cases covered by Arts. 22 and 23 of the Brussels I Regulation for inter-EU cases): Dicey, Morris & Collins, Conflict of Laws 548 (15th ed.2012); J. Harris, The Brussels I Regulation and the Re-Emergence of the English Common Law, [2008–4] Eur.Legal F. I-181, 185.

As a departure from the rejection of the doctrine in European national law and in general European Community law, the doctrine has been adopted for child custody cases in the European Union. Regulation (EC) 2201/2003, ("Brussels IIa", see p. 1169, infra), Art. 15(1) provides that a court that otherwise has jurisdiction under the Regulation may stay a case to permit a proceeding elsewhere or request another court to assume jurisdiction when it considers that the court of the other state "with which the child has a particular connection, would be better placed to hear the case" and "where this is in the best interest of the child." Interestingly enough, it is not only a party that may request such action: the court may initiate it itself and even the other court—for instance, the court at a former or at the new habitual residence of the child (see Art. 15(3))—may make such a request.

The Forum Non Conveniens Doctrine Elsewhere

10. Outside the Common Law and Western European contexts, the forum-non-conveniens doctrine has been proposed for adoption in China. Art. 51 of the Model Law on Private International Law of the People's Republic of China (6th draft, 2000) expressly provides for application of the doctrine and does so on conditions essentially similar to American law. The Supreme Court of Japan has developed a doctrine similar to forum non conveniens. In Family Co. Ltd. v. Miyahara, [1998] H.J. (1626) 74, translation in Japanese Annual Int'l L. 117 (1998), the Supreme Court of Japan held that Japanese courts did not have jurisdiction of a Japanese company's suit to recover funds from an individual residing in Frankfurt. The company had given the Frankfurt resident the funds to purchase goods for the company. The court held that in international cases jurisdiction is based on rules of reason for maintaining impartiality, fairness, and speediness. The court then stated: "However, if we find some exceptional circumstances, where a trial in a Japanese court would result in contradicting the ideas of promoting fairness between the parties and equitable and prompt administration of justice, the international adjudicatory jurisdiction of the Japanese court should be denied." The court found such exceptional circumstances in this case. The contract between the parties was made in Germany, defendant had his home and principal place of business in Germany for more than 20 years, and much of the evidence relevant to the defense is in Germany. For a German Supreme Court decision deciding an essentially forum-non-conveniens case on jurisdictional grounds, see p. 114, supra.

The Race to a Judgment—the Defense of Lis Pendens

The Full Faith and Credit Clause of the Federal Constitution requires the interstate recognition of judgments rendered by courts of competent jurisdiction. Parallel litigation in a second forum may therefore be a means to obtain a quick determination of an issue in order to preclude further consideration of it in the first court or in other fora. It may be used by the plaintiff or, as a preemptive strike, by the defendant, in both cases often for perceived procedural or choice-of-law advantages. For obvious reasons, such tactics are often referred to as a "race to judgment," or "race to the courthouse."

In civil-law practice, statutes permit a defendant to move for dismissal or stay of the second action on the ground of *lis alibi pendens* (the action is already pending elsewhere), which we consider below in this Note. In U.S. *federal* practice and when the claim arises under federal law, most federal circuits follow a "first filed" rule: "[a]ll the issues are, or can be ... joined [in the first forum] and the balance of convenience appears to be in favor of that action. Moreover, it was the first suit brought, and absent the showing of balance of convenience in favor of the second action, it should have priority." Remington Products Corp. v. American Aerovap, 192 F.2d 872 (2d Cir.1951); Zide Sport Shop of Ohio, Inc. v. Ed Tobergte Assocs., Inc., 16 Fed.App'x 433, 437 (6th Cir.2001). "In deciding between competing jurisdictions, it has often been stated that the balancing of convenience should be left to the sound discretion of the district courts. . . . [An] example [of when departure from the 'first filed rule' is justified] is where forum shopping alone motivated the choice of the situs for the first suit," William Gluckin & Co. v. International Playtex Corp., 407 F.2d 177, 178 (2d Cir.1969). See also Meeropol v. Nizer, 505 F.2d 232, 235 (2d Cir.1974), and more recently, College Envy, LLC v. Dirty World, LLC, 2016 WL 70828 (M.D.Tenn.2016). Thus, the second-filed action may be entertained when the first-filed action was brought in anticipation of the second: non-application of the "first filed rule" in these circumstances protects the "real plaintiff," as it were, in his traditional right to choose a forum. Conversely, the first forum may seek to protect its jurisdiction by enjoining litigation elsewhere. See New York v. Exxon Corp., 932 F.2d 1020 (2d Cir.1991); AFA Dispensing Group B.V. v. Anheuser-Busch, Inc., 740 F.Supp.2d 465 (S.D.N.Y.2010).

When the pendency of a state-law action in another forum is invoked in *state* court or in a federal court exercising *diversity jurisdiction,* state law will determine whether the second action should be dismissed or stayed. In interstate cases, the common law "plea in abatement" has been broadened in some states to allow dismissal of an action when the cause is pending in the same or in another state. The effect is that of a "first-filed" rule. However, abatement remains discretionary. See A.E. Staley

Mfg. Co. v. Swift & Co., 419 N.E.2d 23 (Ill.1980); Glick v. Randle, 2012 IL App. (4th) 110497-U, 2012 WL 7017742 (Ill.App.2012), at ¶ 13.

When state courts enjoin parallel litigation in state or federal courts of other states, violation of the injunction may result in the imposition of penalties in the first state; however, recognition and enforcement by the second state does not seem to be required. James v. Grand Trunk Western Railroad Co., 152 N.E.2d 858 (Ill.1958). The Supreme Court has not had occasion to determine whether an injunction against suit in another state is entitled to full faith and credit. Usually courts have disregarded the sister state injunction and have permitted the action to proceed. The Illinois Supreme Court revisited the issue in 1992 and found that an injunction against suit in another state rested on the court's equitable power to "restrain a person over whom it has jurisdiction from instituting a suit or proceeding with a suit in a foreign state. . . . [However,] Courts do not, in such cases, pretend to direct or control the foreign court, but the decree acts solely on the party," Pfaff v. Chrysler Corp., 610 N.E.2d 51 (Ill.1992). See also Baker v. General Motors Corp., p. 333 infra, as well as next paragraph. For further discussion, see John Crane, Inc. v. Admiral Ins. Co., 910 N.E.2d 1168, 1175 (Ill.App.2009).

Antisuit Injunction

Preserving the jurisdiction a court by anti-suit injunction is the flip side of giving it up by means of a forum-non-conveniens dismissal in favor of another court. Likewise, a chosen court may issue an antisuit injunction to guard against a breach of a forum selection clause in its favor. Antisuit injunctions or the threat of one may prompt an anti-antisuit injunction. See p. 252 supra. In the European Union, the Court of Justice held that it is incompatible with the allocation of jurisdiction by the then EU's Brussels-I Regulation to decline jurisdiction on forum non conveniens grounds. See p. 251, Note supra. What about an order restraining a person from proceeding in another member state's court, for instance in violation of an arbitration agreement? Note that the Brussels-I Regulation does not "apply to" arbitration: Art. 1(2)(d), p. 1140, infra. The English House of Lords noted that there was considerable support in the literature both for and against extension of the Regulation to cover this question, but thought that the great practical importance of arbitration favored the ability to enforce arbitration agreements by injunctions against suit. In view of the split of opinion on this matter, the House of Lords referred the question to the EU Court of Justice for a preliminary ruling: West Tankers Inc. v. RAS Riunione Adriatica di Sicurta SpA and others, [2007] UKHL 4, [2007] 1 Lloyd's Rep. 391 (HL). The EU Court of Justice ruled that the Regulation precludes a national court from issuing an injunction to restrain a party from litigating in another Member State in breach of an agreement to arbitrate. [2009] ECRI-663 (Grand Chamber), 2009 WL 303723. Opinion of Advocate General Kokott, Allianz SpA (formerly Riunione Adriatica Di Sicurta SpA) and Others v. West Tankers Inc., Case C-185/07 (2009).

For preserving jurisdiction under a choice-of-court clause or for protecting the efficacy of a local judgment against litigation elsewhere by antisuit injunction, see p. 252, supra, and particularly KBC v. Pertamina, 500 F.3d 111 (2d Cir.2007), cert. denied, 554 U.S. 929 (2008). See also Baker v. General Motors Corp., p. 333, infra.

In *international* litigation, the balancing of litigants' and public interests is particularly difficult. The pendency of foreign litigation could be a factor in a forum-non-conveniens analysis, but the issue of whether to keep the case rarely arises in this fashion: in most cases, the issue is whether to stay the local action or, in contrast, to enjoin prosecution of the foreign action. See American Cyanamid Co. v. Picaso-Anstalt, 741 F.Supp. 1150 (D.N.J.1990) (French defendants, prior action pending in Paris); American Home Assurance Co. v. Insurance Corp. of Ireland, 603 F.Supp. 636 (S.D.N.Y.1984) (motion to dismiss or stay pending outcome of litigation in the United Kingdom denied, parties enjoined from pursuing simultaneous litigation abroad).

In Laker Airways v. Sabena, Belgian World Airlines, 731 F.2d 909 (D.C.Cir.1984), the court upheld an injunction in favor of an English plaintiff, restraining defendants from participating in an English action in turn designed to enjoin the plaintiff from pursuing the U.S. action. As part and parcel of the complexity of transnational litigation, the Laker court noted that "mere filing of a suit in one forum does not cut off the preexisting right of an independent forum to regulate matters subject to its prescriptive jurisdiction," so "injunctions are most often necessary to protect the jurisdiction of the enjoining court, or to prevent the litigant's evasion of the important public policies of the forum," at 927.

In Turner Entertainment Co. v. Degeto Film GmbH, 25 F.3d 1512 (11th Cir.1994), the Eleventh Circuit had still held that international comity *requires* a stay of the proceedings when a foreign action is pending, while other courts held that international comity *allows* dismissal of an action. The latter is the prevailing view, which the Eleventh Circuit now also seems to have adopted: Belize Telecom, Ltd. v. Gov't of Belize, 528 F.3d 1298, 1305 (11th Cir.2008); Cannon Latin America, Inc. v. Lantech (CR), S.A., 453 F.Supp.2d 1357 (S.D.Fla.2006) (enforcing a choice-of-court clause in favor of Florida by enjoining litigation in Costa Rica); St. Martinus University, NV v. Caribbean Health Holding, LLC, 2020 WL 956301 (S.D.Fl. 2020), See also Parrish, Duplicative Foreign Litigation, 78 Geo.Wash.L.Rev. 237, 248 et seq. (2010); N. Jansen Calamita, Rethinking Comity: Towards a Coherent Treatment of International Parallel Proceedings, 27 U.Pa.J.Int'l Econ L. 601, 680 (2006) (urging a "presumption in favor of deferring to the earlier-filed foreign action in comity-stay cases and a presumption against interfering with the foreign proceeding in anti-suit injunction cases"). See also Levy, Antisuit Injunctions in Multinational Cases, in D. Levy (ed.), International Litigation (ABA, Tort Trial and Insurance Practice Section, 2003).

In the European Union, as in civil law systems generally, specific provisions deal with the problem of "lis pendens." Regulation No. 1215/2012, Art. 29 requires a Member State court stay proceedings on "its own motion" if proceedings were already pending in another Member State court. The second court has discretion to stay its proceeding if the first court is one of a third (non-member) state, subject to conditions listed in Art. 33.

See also Juenger, What's Wrong with Forum Shopping?, 18 Sydney L.Rev. 5 (1994); Opeskin, The Price of Forum Shopping—A Reply to Professor Juenger, 18 Sydney L.Rev. 14 (1994); Juenger, Form Shopping: A Rejoinder, 18 Sydney L.Rev. 28 (1994); Herzog, Brussels and Lugano, Should You Race to the Courthouse or Race for a Judgment, 43 Am.J.Comp.L. 379 (1995); Whytock, The Evolving Forum Shopping System, 96 Cornell L.Rev. 481 (2011).

Federal Transfer

In 1948, Congress adopted a revision of the Judicial Code, known as Title 28, United States Code. Section 1404(a) of this Act provides, with respect to the Federal district courts:

> "For the convenience of parties and witnesses, in the interest of justice, a district court may transfer any civil action to any other district or division where it might have been brought."

This provision has been before the Supreme Court in a number of cases. In Norwood v. Kirkpatrick, 349 U.S. 29 (1955), the Court observed that under section 1404(a) the district court has "broader discretion in the application of the statute than under the doctrine of *forum non conveniens*." It pointed out that a transfer under section 1404(a) does not involve a dismissal of the proceeding, and it held that Congress, by enacting the transfer statute, "intended to permit courts to grant transfers upon a lesser showing of inconvenience." For applications see Pennwalt Corp. v. Purex Indus., Inc., 659 F.Supp. 287 (D.Del.1986); Round Rock Research LLC v. ASUSTeK Computer Inc., 967 F.Supp2d. 969 (D.Del.2013).

In Ex parte Collett, 337 U.S. 55 (1949), the Court held that a case brought under the Federal Employers' Liability Act could be transferred under § 1404(a) even though the original forum was appropriate under the special venue provision of the Act and dismissal would not be appropriate under the local state rule of forum non conveniens. See more recently In re Princeton Digital Image Corp., 496 Fed.App'x 73, 74 (Fed.Cir.2013).

In 2012, Section 1404(a) was amended by adding a new clause at the end of the sentence quoted above: "or any district or division to which all parties have consented." This amendment broadens prior law which restricted transfer to a district where venue normally would lie.

For discussion of transfer, dismissal for forum non conveniens, and honoring forum selection clauses in application of 28 U.S.A. §1404(a), see Atlantic Marine, p. 246, supra. See also Ferens v. John Deere Co., p. 751, infra.

NOTES

1. A federal court may not dismiss under forum non conveniens unless the only convenient forum is in a foreign country or is a state court. American Dredging Co. v. Miller, 510 U.S. 443 (1994).

2. Some decisions state that a plaintiff may obtain a transfer under § 1404(a) only if, after having brought the action, she then discovers good reason for the transfer. Philip Carey Manufacturing Co. v. Taylor, 286 F.2d 782 (6th Cir.1961), cert. denied, 366 U.S. 948 (1961). See also Andrews v. Encompass Home and Auto Ins. Co., 2015 WL 3631749 (E.D.Pa.2015). Contra: Cordis Corp. v. Siemens-Pacesetter, Inc., 682 F.Supp. 1200 (S.D.Fla.1987) (reviewing case law and concluding that there is no additional requirement of changed circumstances when the plaintiff is the moving party); Schoendorf v. RTH Mechanical Contractors, Inc., 2012 DNH 94, 2012 WL 1986508 (D.N.H.2012).

Many of the problems arising out of federal transfer under § 1404(a) were resolved by the Supreme Court in Van Dusen v. Barrack, 376 U.S. 612 (1964). That case arose out of an airplane accident which occurred in Boston, Massachusetts. The plane was scheduled to fly from Boston to Philadelphia. As a result more than 100 actions were brought against various defendants in the United States District Court for the District of Massachusetts, and more than 45 actions were brought in the United States District Court for the Eastern District of Pennsylvania. Most of the latter actions were brought by executors and administrators appointed in Pennsylvania, who were not qualified to act in Massachusetts.

The defendants moved in the Pennsylvania court that most of the actions be transferred to Massachusetts under § 1404(a). The Third Circuit held that the proceedings could not be transferred. It relied on the fact that since the plaintiffs in Pennsylvania were not qualified to act in Massachusetts, the actions were not ones which "might have been brought" in Massachusetts. Barrack v. Van Dusen, 309 F.2d 953 (3d Cir.1962), noted in 76 Harv.L.Rev. 1679 (1963).

The Supreme Court reversed. It held that the phrase "might have been brought" related to the suability of the defendant, and not to the capacity of the plaintiff. It also held that, "where the defendants seek transfer, the transferee district court must be obligated to apply the state law that would have been applied if there had been no change of venue.

A change of venue under § 1404(a) generally should be, with respect to state law, but a change of courtrooms." The Court added:

> ... we do not and need not consider whether in all cases § 1404(a) would require the application of the law of the transferor, as opposed to the transferee, State. We do not attempt to determine whether, for example, the same considerations would govern if a plaintiff sought transfer under § 1404(a) or if it was contended that the transferor State would simply have dismissed the action on the ground of *forum non conveniens. . . .*

The case was remanded to the Pennsylvania District Court to determine whether the facts justified a transfer to Massachusetts on the grounds of "convenience and fairness." On this point, the Court noted:

> ... it has long been recognized that: "There is an appropriateness ... in having the trial of a diversity case in a forum that is at home with the state law that must govern the case, rather than having a court in some other forum untangle problems in conflict of laws, and in law foreign to itself." Gulf Oil Corp. v. Gilbert, 330 U.S. 501, 509. Thus, to the extent that Pennsylvania laws are difficult or unclear and might not defer to Massachusetts laws, it may be advantageous to retain the actions in Pennsylvania where the judges possess a more ready familiarity with the local laws. ... We do not suggest that elements of uncertainty in transferor state law would alone justify a denial of transfer; but we do think that the uncertainty is one factor, among others, to be considered in assessing the desirability of transfer. . . .

Thus if a case were transferred from Pennsylvania to Massachusetts, the Massachusetts District Court, subject perhaps to a few rare exceptions, would sit as if it were a federal court in Pennsylvania. Under Erie Railroad v. Tompkins, 304 U.S. 64 (1938), it would be required to apply the law of Pennsylvania, including the conflict laws of Pennsylvania. Klaxon Co. v. Stentor Electric Manufacturing Co., Inc., 313 U.S. 487 (1941). This would mean that it would apply the Pennsylvania law to determine the qualification of the plaintiff, and thus the Pennsylvania executors and administrators would be competent to sue in the case transferred to Massachusetts. Whether the conflict laws of Pennsylvania would refer to the law of Massachusetts for the substantive rules applicable to the accident would have to be determined by the Massachusetts District Court sitting as if it were a District Court in Pennsylvania, and applying Pennsylvania law.

The Van Dusen decision thus was an exception to the result that follows from Erie (p. 257, infra) that a federal court, sitting in diversity, applies the law of the state in which it sits. When it is the plaintiff who seeks a transfer, this may result in forum shopping: a plaintiff sues in a court of the state the law of which he wants and then seeks transfer to another court, taking the transferor's law along. See Ferens v. John Deere, p. 751, infra. If the same rule applied when a federal court transfers an action to honor a forum selection clause, breaching of such clauses and applicable-law shopping would be encouraged (the breaching party would take dismissing court's law along). For that reason, the U.S. Supreme Court held in Atlantic Marine, p. 217, supra, that the Van Dusen exception to Erie does not apply in these cases: the transferee court, following Erie, applies the law of the state in which it sits.

NOTES

1. The rule of *Van Dusen*—that the law of the transferor forum should be applied—is a complicating factor in situations where a number of cases originally brought in various Federal districts in several states are consolidated for trial in a single district court under § 1407. See, e.g., In re Paris Air Crash of March 3, 1974, 399 F.Supp. 732 (C.D.Cal.1975); In re Air Crash Disaster at Boston, Mass., July 31, 1973, 399 F.Supp. 1106 (D.Mass.1975); Symposium: Conflict of Laws and Complex Litigation Issues in Mass Tort Litigation, Introduction, 1989 U.Ill.L.Rev. 35.

Boardman Petroleum, Inc. v. Federated Mutual Ins. Co., 135 F.3d 750 (11th Cir.1998) involved cases originally brought in two federal districts in different states with different choice-of-law rules but involving the same two parties and a single issue of insurance coverage. The court held that "in consolidated cases such as these, when the choice-of-law provisions governing each of the separate lawsuits require the application of differing state substantive laws, the court should balance the interest of each state in having its laws apply and apply the law of the state with the greater interests." Id. at 753. This choice-of-law approach differed from that of either of the two states in which the parties had sued and resulted in the application of Georgia law. The Georgia place-of-making choice-of-law rule would have chosen Georgia law. The cases had been consolidated in the Georgia district after the insurer's declaratory judgment action had been transferred to Georgia under § 1404(a). South Carolina's rule would have applied South Carolina law as the situs of the insured property. The loss was not covered under South Carolina law, but the insured claimed that it was covered under Georgia law. See also Eisenstadt v. Tel. Elecs. Corp., 2008 WL 4386993, 2008 WL 4452999 (N.D.Tex.2008); Driving Force Technologies, Inc. v. Panda Distribution, Inc., 2011 WL 1194348 (E.D.Tex.2011).

2. When the case raises issues of *federal* law, the transferee court follows its own circuit's interpretation of the federal law and not that of the transferor's circuit. In re Korean Air Lines Disaster of Sept. 1, 1983, 829 F.2d 1171 (D.C.Cir.1987), aff'd, 490 U.S. 122 (1989). See Marcus, Conflicts Among Circuits and Transfers Within the Federal Judicial System, 93 Yale L.J. 677, 686, 702, 721 (1984).

Where the case is initially brought in a court lacking proper venue, the case is governed by 28 U.S.C.A. § 1406(a), which provides that the district court "shall dismiss, or if it be in the interest of justice, transfer such case to any district in which it could have been brought." The courts are agreed that where the transferor forum lacks either jurisdiction or proper venue, the law of the transferee forum will be applied regardless of whether the plaintiff or the defendant sought the transfer. LaVay Corp. v. Dominion Federal Sav. & Loan Ass'n, 830 F.2d 522 (4th Cir.1987) cert. denied, 484 U.S. 1065 (1988); Manley v. Engram, 755 F.2d 1463 (11th Cir.1985). 28 U.S.C.A. § 1631, as interpreted, clarified that not only must the transferee court apply its own law, but that it must accept the date on which the action was removed as the filing date. Ross v. Colorado Outward Bound School, Inc., 822 F.2d 1524 (10th Cir.1987); W. Inv. Total Return Fund v. Bremner, 762 F.Supp.2d 339, 341 (D.Mass.2011). See also Federal Home Loan Bank of Boston v. Moody's Corp., 821 F.3d 102 (1st Cir.2016).

SECTION 4. OTHER LIMITATIONS IMPOSED BY THE FORUM

RESTATEMENT, SECOND, CONFLICT OF LAWS

§ 53. Decree to Be Carried Out in Another State

b.   *When jurisdiction exercised.* A person will be ordered to do an act in another state when this relief is required by the demands of justice and convenience. The reluctance of the courts to issue such orders stems primarily from (1) the fear of interfering unduly with the affairs of the other state and (2) the possible difficulty of enforcing obedience to an order that the defendant do an act in a place beyond the effective control of the court. Because of the first factor, the defendant will not, except on extremely rare occasions, be ordered to do an act which violates the law of the other state . . . there is greater likelihood of the defendant's being ordered to do an act in another state if the court has some means at its disposal of insuring compliance with the decree, such as by requiring the defendant to post a bond or to act in the other state through the medium of an agent. . . .

United States v. First National City Bank

United States Court of Appeals, Second Circuit, 1968.
396 F.2d 897.

[In aid of a grand jury investigation of suspected antitrust violations, a subpoena was served upon the First National City Bank (Citibank) requiring it to produce all documents in its office in Frankfurt, Germany, which involved certain of its customers. The Bank refused to comply on the ground that production of these documents would subject it to civil liability to these customers under German law. The District Court held the Bank liable for contempt, and it appealed.]

■ KAUFMAN, CIRCUIT JUDGE . . . It is no longer open to doubt that a federal court has the power to require the production of documents located in foreign countries if the court has *in personam* jurisdiction of the person in possession or control of the material. . . . Thus, the task before us, as Citibank concedes, is not one of defining power but of developing rules governing the proper exercise of power.... This problem is particularly acute where the documents are sought by an arm of a foreign government. The complexities of the world being what they are, it is not surprising to discover nations having diametrically opposed positions with respect to the disclosure of a wide range of information. It is not too difficult, therefore, to empathize with the party or witness subject to the jurisdiction of two sovereigns and confronted with conflicting commands. . . .

. . . Where, as here, the burden of resolution ultimately falls upon the federal courts, the difficulties are manifold because the courts must take care not to impinge upon the prerogatives and responsibilities of the political branches of the government in the extremely sensitive and delicate area of foreign affairs.... Mechanical or overbroad rules of thumb are of little value; what is required is a careful balancing of the interests involved and a precise understanding of the facts and circumstances of the particular case.

With these principles in mind, we turn to the specific issues presented by this appeal. Citibank concedes, as it must, that compliance with the subpoena does not require the violation of the criminal law of a foreign power ... or risk the imposition of sanctions that are the substantial equivalent of criminal penalties ... or even conflict with the public policy of a foreign state as expressed in legislation.... Instead, all that remains, as we see it, is a possible prospective civil liability flowing from an implied contractual obligation between Citibank and its customers that, we are informed, is considered implicit in the bank's license to do business in Germany.

. . . In the instant use, the obvious, albeit troublesome, requirement for us is to balance the national interests of the United States and Germany and to give appropriate weight to the hardship, if any, Citibank will suffer.

The important interest of the United States in the enforcement of the subpoena warrants little discussion.... [T]he antitrust laws ... have long been considered cornerstones of this nation's economic policies, have been vigorously enforced and the subject of frequent interpretation by our Supreme Court. We would have great reluctance, therefore, to countenance any device that would place relevant information beyond the reach of this duly impaneled Grand Jury or impede or delay its proceedings. . . .

We examine the importance of bank secrecy within the framework of German public policy with full recognition that it is often a subtle and difficult undertaking to determine the nature and scope of the law of a foreign jurisdiction. There is little merit, however, in Citibank's suggestion that the mere existence of a bank secrecy doctrine requires us to accept on its face the bank's assertion that compliance with the subpoena would violate an important public policy of Germany.... While we certainly do not intend to deprecate the importance of bank secrecy in the German scheme of things, neither can we blind ourselves to the doctrine's severe limitations as disclosed by the expert testimony. We have already made the assumption that the absence of criminal sanctions is not the whole answer to or finally determinative of the problem. But, it is surely of considerable significance that Germany considers bank secrecy simply a privilege that can be waived by the customer and is content to leave the matter of enforcement to the vagaries of private litigation. Indeed, bank secrecy is not even required by statute. . . . [Likewise, the Bank could not assert bank secrecy in a criminal investigation in Germany.]

In addition, it is noteworthy that neither the Department of State nor the German Government has expressed any view on this case or indicated that, under the circumstances present here, enforcement of the subpoena would violate German public policy or embarrass German-American relations. . . .

[Finally, the court turned to the hardship, if any, which the Bank would suffer if it complied with the subpoena. The Court found little merit in the contention that compliance by the Bank would result in the loss of foreign business or in economic reprisals by its customers. The Court further found that the chance of the Bank being held liable for civil damages under German law was "slight and speculative."]

Affirmed.

NOTE

On occasion, courts in this country have ordered a person to testify or to bring documents from a foreign country even though compliance with the order would violate the law of that country. In re Grand Jury Proceedings, 694 F.2d 1256 (11th Cir.1982) (attorney-client privilege); In re Grand Jury Proceedings, 691 F.2d 1384 (11th Cir.1982), cert. denied, 462 U.S. 1119 (1983) (bank secrecy law); In re Grand Jury Proceedings, 532 F.2d 404 (5th Cir.1976) (bank secrecy law). Cf. Civil Aeronautics Board v. Deutsche Lufthansa Aktiengesellschaft, 591 F.2d 951 (D.C.Cir.1979) (defendant ordered to use all good faith efforts to obtain government permission for release of documents). On other occasions, the courts have refused to issue an order that would require violation of the law of a foreign country. In re Westinghouse Electric Corp. Uranium Contracts Litig., 563 F.2d 992 (10th Cir.1977) (interests of the foreign country held to be more seriously involved than those of the United States); Application of Chase Manhattan Bank, 297 F.2d 611 (2d Cir.1962), distinguished and not applied in JW Olfield v. Commerzbank AG, 764 F.Supp.2d 587 (S.D.N.Y.2011). For a general discussion of the problem, see Note, Extraterritorial Discovery: An Analysis Based on Good Faith, 83 Colum.L.Rev. 1320 (1983). See also Connorton, Note, Tracking Terrorist Financing Through Swift: When U.S. Subpoenas and Foreign Privacy Law Collide, 76 Fordham L.Rev. 283 (2007).

The Restatement (Third) of Foreign Relations Law of the United States (1986), § 442(2), takes the following position: "If disclosure of information located outside the United States is prohibited by a law, regulation, or order of a court or other authority of the state in which the information or prospective witness is located, or of the state of which a prospective witness is a national, [and if the person cannot secure permission from foreign authorities for the production of the information sought], . . . (b) a court . . . should not ordinarily impose sanctions of contempt, dismissal, or default, except in cases of deliberate concealment or removal of information . . . ; (c) a court . . . may, in appropriate cases, make findings of fact adverse to a party that has failed to comply with the order for production, even if that party has made a good faith effort. . . ."

———————

The problem addressed by Section 53 of the Restatement, Second, and in *First National City Bank* today arises most frequently in the context of pretrial discovery in international cases. Foreign legal systems do not provide for extensive pretrial discovery, and foreign countries have therefore become increasingly sensitive about what they regard as intrusive and overreaching American discovery orders. In recent years, a number of foreign countries have adopted "blocking statutes" forbidding the production of documents located in their territories in response to foreign orders or requests. Examples include the English Protection of Trading Interests Act of 1980, the Canadian Foreign Extraterritorial Measures Act of 1985, and the Australian Foreign Proceedings (Excess of Jurisdiction) Act of 1984. In Société Nationale Industrielle Aerospatiale v. United States District Court for the Southern District of Iowa, 482 U.S. 522 (1987), the defendant resisted a pretrial discovery order for the production of documents located in France on the ground that the Hague Convention on the Taking of Evidence Abroad provided the exclusive, or at least the primary means for obtaining such documents. In support of its argument, the defendant also pointed to the existence of a French blocking statute. The Supreme Court rejected the argument: "It is well-settled that such statutes do not deprive an American court of the power to order a party subject to its jurisdiction to produce evidence even though the act of production may violate that statute. . . ." Extraterritorial assertions of jurisdiction are not one-sided. While the District Court's discovery orders arguably have some impact in France, the French blocking statute asserts similar authority over acts to take place in this country. . . . The blocking statute . . . is relevant to the court's particularized comity analysis only to the extent that its terms and its enforcement identify the nature of the sovereign interests in nondisclosure. . . . 482 U.S. at 544 n.29. For a differentiated application of this decision, see Tiffany (NJ) LLC v. Forbse, 2012 WL 1918866 (S.D.N.Y.2012) (inquiring whether the Hague Convention method was a reasonable alternative to the issuance of an American discovery order and concluding that this was questionable as to one of the defendants, but not at the others), affirmed in part and vacated and remanded in part, 589 Fed.App'x 550 (2d Cir.2014).

NOTES

1.   The subject is discussed further at p. 798–799, infra.

2.   See Note, A Comparative Study of U.S. and British Approaches to Discovery Conflicts: Achieving a Uniform System of Extraterritorial Discovery, 18 Fordham Int'l. L.J. 1340 (1995). For extensive and comparative discussion of discovery of documents and inspection of objects in civil litigation, see Hay, Informationsbeschaffung über schriftliche Unterlagen und Augenscheinsobjekte im Zivilprozess, 8 Veröffentlichungen der Wissenschaftlichen Vereinigung für Prozessrecht 1 (1996).

3.   For a discussion of the factors that should be considered by a court in a situation where two or more states have power to require a person to engage in inconsistent courses of conduct, see Restatement, Third, Foreign Relations Law of the United States § 403 and Reporters' Notes Nos. 6–7 (1987).

Slater v. Mexican National R. Co.

Supreme Court of the United States, 1904.
194 U.S. 120, 24 S.Ct. 581, 48 L.Ed. 900.

■ MR. JUSTICE HOLMES delivered the opinion of the court.

This is an action brought in the United States Circuit Court for the Northern District of Texas by citizens and residents of Texas against a Colorado corporation operating a railroad from Texas to the City of Mexico. The plaintiffs are the widow and children of William H. Slater, who was employed by the defendant as a switchman on its road and was killed through the defendant's negligence while coupling two freight cars at Nuevo Laredo, in Mexico. This action is to recover damages for the death. . . .

As Texas has statutes which give an action for wrongfully causing death, of course there is no general objection of policy to enforcing such a liability there, although it arose in another jurisdiction. Stewart v. Baltimore & Ohio R.R., 168 U.S. 445. But when such a liability is enforced in a jurisdiction foreign to the place of the wrongful act, obviously that does not mean that the act in any degree is subject to the lex fori, with regard to either its quality or its consequences. On the other hand, it equally little means that the law of the place of the act is operative outside its own territory. The theory of the foreign suit is that although the act complained of was subject to no law having force in the forum, it gave rise to an obligation, an *obligatio,* which, like other obligations, follows the person, and may be enforced wherever the person may be found . . . But as the only source of this obligation is the law of the place of the act, it follows that the law determines not merely the existence of the obligation, . . . but equally determines its extent. It seems to us unjust to allow a plaintiff to come here absolutely depending on the foreign law for the foundation of his case, and yet to deny the defendant the benefit of whatever limitations on his liability that law would impose. . . . As the cause of action relied upon is one which is supposed to have arisen in Mexico under Mexican laws, the place of the death and the domicile of the parties have no bearing upon the case.

By Article 318 [of the Penal Code of Mexico] civil responsibility for a wrongful homicide includes, besides the expenses of medical attendance and burial and damages to the property of the deceased, the expenses "of the support not only of the widow, descendants and ascendants of the deceased, who were being supported by him, he being under legal obligations to do so, but also to the posthumous descendants that he may leave." Then, by Art. 319, the obligation to support shall last during the time that the deceased might have lived, calculated by a given life table, but taking the state of his health before the homicide into consideration, but "the obligation shall cease: 1. At whatever time it shall not be absolutely necessary for the subsistence of those entitled to receive it. 2. When those beneficiaries get married. 3. When the minor children become of age. 4. In any other case in which, according to law, the deceased, if alive; would not be required to continue the support." It is unnecessary to set forth the detailed provisions as to support in other parts of the statutes. It is sufficiently obvious from what has been quoted that the decree contemplated by the Mexican law is a decree analogous to a decree for alimony in divorce proceedings—a decree which contemplates periodical payments and which is subject to modification from time to time as the circumstances change. See, also, Arts. 1376, 1377, of the Code of Procedure, and Penal Code, Bk. 2, Art. 363.

The present action is a suit at common law and the court has no power to make a decree of this kind contemplated by the Mexican statutes. What the Circuit Court did was to disregard the principles of the Mexican statute altogether and to follow the Texas statute. This clearly was wrong and was excepted to specifically. But we are of opinion further that justice to the defendant would not permit the substitution of a lump sum, however estimated, for the periodical payments which the Mexican statute required.

The case is not one demanding extreme measures like those where a tort is committed in an uncivilized country. The defendant always can be found in Mexico, on the other side of the river, and it is to be presumed that the courts there are open to the plaintiffs, if the statute conferred a right upon them notwithstanding their absence from the jurisdiction, as we assume that it did, for the purposes of this part of the case. See Mulhall v. Fallon, 176 Mass. 266. . . .

Judgment affirmed.

■ CHIEF JUSTICE FULLER dissented in an opinion, in which JUSTICE HARLAN and JUSTICE PECKHAM concurred.

NOTES

1.   The Supreme Court of Texas finally abolished "dissimilarity" as a basis for refusing to entertain cases applying Mexican personal injury law, Gutierrez v. Collins, 583 S.W.2d 312 (Tex.1979).

2.   Phrantzes v. Argenti, [1960] 2 Q.B. 19, [1960] 1 All Eng.R. 778, was a suit brought by a daughter, under Greek law, claiming a dowry from her father. The court refused to entertain the suit, saying that the Greek "machinery by way of remedies" was entirely different from the English machinery.

Other legal systems will entertain claims involving legal rights or interest under foreign law that are unknown to the forum. In such cases, the forum will seek to find and apply a functionally equivalent or similar rule of forum law. For Germany, see Hay and Rösler, Internationales Privat- und Zivilverfahrensrecht (PdW Series, 5th ed.2016).

3.   In a number of decisions, the United States Supreme Court addressed constitutional limitations on the power of states to refuse to entertain a case. In Mondou v. New York, New Haven & Hartford Railroad Co., 223 U.S. 1 (1912), the Court confirmed that a federal statute supersedes state law so that a state may not refuse to apply it on the ground that it contravenes its public policy. Similarly, a state may not refuse to apply a treble damage provision of a federal law on the ground that it is "penal." Testa v. Katt, 330 U.S. 386 (1947). See also Hughes v. Fetter, p. 413, infra. On the other hand, a state court is free to apply the forum non conveniens doctrine to claims arising under federal law. Missouri ex rel. Southern Railway Co. v. Mayfield, 340 U.S. 1 (1950).

SECTION 5. LIMITATIONS IMPOSED BY THE STATE OF THE TRANSACTION*

Buttron v. El Paso Northeastern Ry. Co.

Court of Civil Appeals of Texas, 1906.
93 S.W. 676.

Action by Louis Buttron against the El Paso Northeastern Railway Co. and others. From a judgment for defendants, plaintiff appeals.

■ JAMES, C.J. This action was brought by Buttron in the district court of El Paso county, Tex., against the above-named appellee and two other railway companies, to recover damages for injury alleged to have been caused him by their negligence. The court directed the jury to find for defendants, stating as its reason for so doing that defendants had introduced in evidence a valid and subsisting judgment of the Sixth judicial district court of the territory of New Mexico, adjudicating the issues involved. The said territorial judgment was rendered in a proceeding begun and prosecuted by the defendants herein against

---

*   See Restatement, Second, Conflict of Laws § 91 (1971).

Buttron, under the provisions of the second and fourth sections of the following act of the Legislature Assembly of the said territory (Laws 1903, p. 51, c. 33). . . .

There are peculiar and radical features in this law . . . These are stated by appellant to be: (1) It provides that no suit for personal injuries incurred within the territory shall be brought in another jurisdiction, provided the defendant can be served within the territory. (2) The right of action is taken away from the claimant, unless within ninety days after the injury, and thirty days before commencing his action he shall serve upon his adversary a sworn statement giving the details of his case and the names and addresses of his witnesses. (3) The suit must be brought in one year after the injury. (4) The party who has inflicted the injury can compel the one he has injured to come into the court for the district in which the wrongdoer lives and set up his claim there, and, in case he does not do it, then the court will try the case on the statement of the wrongdoer, and upon that statement of the claim render judgment, which shall be final. (5) On its appearing to the court that any such suit has been begun in a court outside the territory, the court in the territory where an action is pending, under the act, may try the latter case upon such short notice as the court may direct, and compel the parties to plead on such short day as the court may fix, and the institution of such suit outside the territory shall be construed by the court as a waiver of a jury in the case pending in the territorial court. (6) On showing made that a party injured contemplates bringing suit outside the territory, or has already instituted such a suit, the court may perpetually enjoin the claimant from prosecuting or maintaining his suit outside the territory. . . .

The Court gave effect to a judgment of the territorial court rendered under the provisions of section 2 of the act. . . . Section 2 allows the person or corporation inflicting the injury, or causing the death, to commence a proceeding against the injured party, in the district court for the county in the territory where it has its principal office, if a corporation, and requires the injured party to appear and litigate his claim. The defendants in the case resorted to such a proceeding, and plaintiff, a resident of the territory, was personally served with the prescribed summons. He failed to appear, and, the court proceeding in the prescribed manner, judgment was rendered against him in favor of these defendants on his cause of action, upon the hearing required by the act. The only point of objection which we perceive possible in reference to section 2 is that it gives to one who is accustomed to figure as a defendant, and who has heretofore invariably occupied that attitude in the courts, the right to anticipate the ordinary action, and to himself begin a proceeding requiring the injured party to appear and submit his cause of action to adjudication. Why is this not due exercise of power vested in a legislative body? It consisted in giving the person or corporation charged with committing a wrong remedy which it otherwise would not have had. Ordinarily such party would have had to await the bringing of the action by the claimant at his convenience, within the period of limitations. Such delay, it can readily be conceived, might often work a hardship on the former, by the loss of testimony. It is true there generally are statutes enabling a party to perpetuate testimony, but it is well known that written testimony is not always as effective as oral, which might not be obtainable in the course of time. Viewing the matter abstractly, what justice is there, after all, in forcing a party interested in the settlement of a controversy to await the pleasure of his adversary as to the time of its adjudication? Why should they not have equal right and opportunity to bring the matter to issue in the courts? There may be reasons of a substantial nature for such legislation. If they were sufficient in the minds of the legislators to dictate the wisdom of policy of a statute conferring on a prospective defendant such a remedy, it is for the courts to give effect to the will of the people thus expressed, though the wisdom and policy may be doubted by some. There is no obstacle of a constitutional nature, to the adoption of such a rule. It concerns merely procedure which is a proper subject of legislative action. Our courts are required to give full faith and credit to the judgment of the territorial court. Therefore we think the judgment appealed from should be affirmed.

Affirmed.

NOTES

1.   Compare Atchison, Topeka & Santa Fe Railway Co. v. Sowers, 213 U.S. 55 (1909), which involved Sec. 1 of the same New Mexico statute and is outlined in the opinion of the court in Tennessee Coal, Iron & Railroad Co. v. George, infra.

2.   A considerable number of states have adopted declaratory judgment acts. See 12 Uniform Laws Annotated 109 (1975). See also 28 U.S.C.A. § 2201. May the declaratory judgment acts be utilized by the alleged obligor to have a controversy tried (a) in the normal forum, or (b) in any forum selected by him that has jurisdiction over the alleged obligee? Will the courts exercise the same type of discretion in taking jurisdiction to render a declaratory judgment as they have done in other cases?

Tennessee Coal, Iron & Railroad Co. v. George

Supreme Court of the United States, 1914.
233 U.S. 354, 34 S.Ct. 587, 58 L.Ed. 997.

■ JUSTICE LAMAR delivered the opinion of the court.

Wiley George, the defendant in error, was an engineer employed by the Tennessee Coal, Iron and Railroad Company at its steel plant in Jefferson County, Alabama. While he was under a locomotive repairing the brakes, a defective throttle allowed steam to leak into the cylinder causing the engine to move forward automatically in consequence of which he was seriously injured. He brought suit by attachment, in the City Court of Atlanta, Georgia, founding his action on sec. 3910 of the Alabama Code of 1907, which makes the master liable to the employee when the injury is "caused by reason of any defect in the condition of the ways, works, machinery or plant connected with or used in the business of the master or employer."

The defendant filed a plea in abatement in which it was set out that sec. 6115 of that Code also provided that "all actions under said section 3910 must be brought in a court of competent jurisdiction within the State of Alabama and not elsewhere." The defendant thereupon prayed that the action be abated because "to continue said case on said statutory cause of action given by the statutes of Alabama and restricted by said statutes to the courts of Alabama, . . . would be a denial so far as the rights of this defendant are concerned, of full faith and credit to said public acts of the State of Alabama in the State of Georgia, contrary to the provisions of Art. 4, sec. 1 of the Constitution of the United States." A demurrer to the plea in abatement was sustained and the judgment for the plaintiff thereafter entered was affirmed by the Court of Appeals. The case was then brought to this court.

The record raises the single question as to whether the full faith and credit clause of the Constitution prohibited the courts of Georgia from enforcing a cause of action given by the Alabama Code, to the servant against the master, for injuries occasioned by defective machinery, when another section of the same Code provided that suits to enforce such liability "must be brought in a court of competent jurisdiction within the State of Alabama *and not elsewhere.*"

There are many cases where right and remedy are so united that the right cannot be enforced except in the manner and before the tribunal designated by the act. For the rule is well settled that "where the provision for the liability is coupled with a provision for a special remedy, that remedy, and that alone, must be employed." Pollard v. Bailey, 20 Wall. 520, 527. . . .

But that rule has no application to a case arising under the Alabama Code relating to suits for injuries caused by defective machinery. For, whether the statute be treated as prohibiting certain defenses, as removing common law restrictions or as imposing upon the master a new and larger liability, it is in either event evident that the place of bringing the suit is not part of the cause of action,—the right and the remedy are not so inseparably united as to make the right dependent upon its being enforced in a particular tribunal. The cause of action is transitory and like any other transitory action can be enforced "in any court of competent jurisdiction within the State of Alabama." . . .

The case here is controlled by the decision of this court in Atchison & C. Ry. v. Sowers, 213 U.S. 55, 59, 70, where the New Mexico statute, giving a right of action for personal injuries and providing that suits should be brought after certain form of notice in a particular district, was preceded by the recital that "it has become customary for persons claiming damages for personal injuries received in this Territory to institute and maintain suits for the recovery thereof in other States and Territories to the increased cost and annoyance and manifest injury and oppression of the business interests of this Territory and in derogation of the dignity of the courts thereof." Despite this statement of the public policy of the Territory, the judgment obtained by the plaintiff in Texas was affirmed by this court in an opinion wherein it was said that where an action is brought in "another jurisdiction based upon common law principles, although having certain statutory restrictions, such as are found in this [territorial] act as to the making of an affidavit and limiting the time of prosecuting the suit, full faith and credit is given to the law, when the recovery is permitted, subject to the restrictions upon the right of action imposed in the Territory enacting the statute. When it is shown that the court in the other jurisdiction observed such conditions, and that a recovery was permitted after such conditions had been complied with, the jurisdiction thus invoked is not defeated because of the provision of the statute" requiring the suit to be brought in the district where the plaintiff resides or where the defendant, if a corporation, has its principal place of business. . . .

In the present case the Georgia court gave full faith and credit to the Alabama act and its judgment is

Affirmed.

■ JUSTICE HOLMES dissents.

NOTES

1. The Supreme Court confirmed and applied *Tennessee Coal* in Marshall v. Marshall, 547 U.S. 293, 314 (2006). For a recent application, see Ralph v. Whetsell et al., 2014 WL 12284029 (N.D.Ga.2014).

If in the principal case the Georgia court had refused to entertain the plaintiff's action, would its refusal have been in violation of any provision of the Constitution? Would the Constitution require that the plaintiff's action be entertained in Georgia despite the wishes of both Alabama and Georgia, the only two states of interest? Compare Hughes v. Fetter, p. 413, infra

2. Note Justice Lamar's statement in the *George* case that "[t]he courts of the sister state trying the case would be bound to give full faith and credit to all those substantial provisions of the statute which inhered in the cause of action or which name conditions on which the right to sue depend." In connection with this statement, consider the following:

In Pearson v. Northeast Airlines, Inc., 309 F.2d 553 (2d Cir.1962), a majority of the court, sitting en banc, held it constitutional for a state to apply the wrongful death statute of a sister state to determine whether the defendant was liable for the death and at the same time refuse to apply the limitation contained in that statute as to the amount of recovery. Speaking for a minority of three, Judge Friendly wrote a dissent in which he said:

"An important reason why a forum state may not do this is that it thereby interferes with the proper freedom of action of the legislature of the sister state. The terms and conditions of a claim created by statute inevitably reflect the legislature's balancing of those considerations that favor and of those that oppose the imposition of liability. The legislature may be quite unwilling to create the claim on terms allowing it to be enforced without limit of amount as most common law rights can be, or for a period bounded only by statutes of limitations ordinarily applicable. The Full Faith and Credit Clause insures that, in making its choice, the legislature creating the claim need not have to weigh the risk that the courts of sister states looking to its 'public acts' as a source of rights will disregard substantial conditions which it has imposed. . . . This consideration is inapplicable to instances where the forum, looking solely to its own substantive law, wholly disregards that of the sister state. . . . True, conduct in the enacting state has been given consequences different from what the legislators of that state desired; but that is the inevitable result of the duplicate law-making jurisdiction that can never be wholly avoided even in our federal system. . . ."

3. Crider v. Zurich Insurance Co., 380 U.S. 39 (1965), involved an action brought in an Alabama court by a resident of that state to recover under the Georgia Workmen's Compensation Act for injuries suffered in Alabama. Georgia decisions had previously held that the remedy provided by the Georgia act is "an exclusive one which can be afforded only" by the Georgia Compensation Board. Nevertheless, the Supreme Court held that Alabama was not prohibited from entertaining the action. In the course of his majority opinion, Justice Douglas stated that the rule of the Georgia case "has been eroded" to the extent that it would limit the courts of a second state to the award of a "special remedy" that is "coupled" with the provision for liability on which the action is based.

4. Judge Friendly's dissent in *Pearson,* supra, expressed the concern that the majority was giving less than *full* faith and credit to the law of a sister state. Does *Crider* raise a different issue?

The Crider case is discussed in Greenspan, Crider v. Zurich Insurance Co.: Decline of Conceptualism in Conflict of Laws, 27 U.Pitt.L.Rev. 49 (1965). The question of whether it is a denial of full faith and credit to rely on a sister-state law as the basis for enforcing a claim while at the same time rejecting a limitation provided in that law is considered in Chapter 6, infra.

CHAPTER 5

FOREIGN JUDGMENTS

SECTION 1. POLICIES UNDERLYING THE RECOGNITION AND ENFORCEMENT OF FOREIGN JUDGMENTS

"Public policy dictates that there be an end of litigation; that those who have contested an issue shall be bound by the result of the contest, and that matters once tried shall be considered forever settled as between the parties."[1] This policy, embodied in the doctrine of res judicata, prevents the parties from relitigating issues that have been determined between them by a valid local judgment. It also forms the basis for the firmly established principle of Anglo-American law that foreign judgments, subject to only a few exceptions, are not open to reexamination on the merits when placed in issue before a local court. In the United States, however, this latter principle is frequently explained by the courts in terms other than that of res judicata. Thus, in cases which do not fall within the constitutional mandate of full faith and credit, American courts have often talked in terms of "comity,"[2] while those of England may also phrase their opinions in terms of the "legal obligation of foreign judgments."[3] These expressions merely state but do not explain the result; they are shorthand for the underlying policy of preclusion.

In the United States, an express constitutional mandate calls for the recognition and enforcement of state court judgments rendered in other states and territories of the Union. This mandate is embodied in the Full Faith and Credit Clause and its implementing statute, which, in the words of Chief Justice Stone, were designed to

"... establish throughout the federal system the salutary principle of the common law that a litigation once pursued to judgment shall be as conclusive of the rights of the parties in every other court as in that where the judgment was rendered. ... The full faith and credit clause like the commerce clause thus became a nationally unifying force. It altered the status of the several states as independent foreign sovereignties, each free to ignore rights and obligations created under the laws or established by the judicial proceedings of the others, by making each an integral part of a single nation, in which rights judicially established in any part are

---

[1] Roberts, J., in Baldwin v. Iowa State Traveling Men's Association, 283 U.S. 522, 525 (1931).

[2] See, e.g., Hilton v. Guyot, p. 275, infra.

[3] See, e.g., Godard v. Gray, L.R. 6 Q.B. 139 (1870). For a reference to "principles of judicial comity," see Regina v. Lyons and others, [2002] UKHL 447, [2003] 1 AC 976, [2002] 4 All ER 1028 (HL), at para. 107, affirming, [2002] 2 Cr App R 210 (Court of Appeal, Criminal Division), with respect to a judgment of the European Court of Human Rights.

given nation-wide application. Because there is a full faith and credit clause a defendant may not a second time challenge the validity of plaintiff's right which has ripened into a judgment and a plaintiff may not for his single cause of action secure a second or a greater recovery. . . ."[4] For federal judgments, see Note 4, infra.

NOTES

1. The Full Faith and Credit Clause and its implementing statute are quoted at p. 45, supra.

For general consideration of the problems of this Chapter, see Hay, Borchers, Symeonides & Whytock, Conflict of Laws ch. 24 (6th ed.2018); Weintraub, Commentary on the Conflict of Laws 773–98 (6th ed.2010).

2. Not all questions relating to the extraterritorial respect owed to federal and state judgments are governed by the Full Faith and Credit Clause and its implementing statute. There is still room for the occasional application by the states of their individual rules and policies. See, for example, p. 377, infra.

3. Is the implementing statute constitutional? Note that whereas the Full Faith and Credit Clause only requires extraterritorial respect for the acts, records, and judicial proceedings of the several states, the statute also includes within its scope those of every "Territory, or Possession of the United States." From what source, if any, did Congress derive power so to enact? See Embry v. Palmer, 107 U.S. 3 (1883).

4. *Federal judgments in state court.* It is well established that state courts must accord a federal judgment the same preclusive effect that the judgment has in federal court. Stoll v. Gottlieb, 305 U.S. 165 (1938); Hancock National Bank v. Farnum, 176 U.S. 640 (1900); Metcalf v. City of Watertown, 153 U.S. 671 (1894). Does the Full Faith and Credit Clause or 28 U.S.C.A. § 1738 require this? See Semtek International, Inc. v. Lockheed Martin Corp., 531 U.S. 497 (2001), p. 725, infra.

State court judgments in federal court. Federal courts are required by the implementing statute to give full faith and credit to the judgments of state and territorial courts. Kremer v. Chemical Construction Corp., 456 U.S. 461 (1982), p. 316, infra; Huron Holding Corp. v. Lincoln Mine Operating Co., 312 U.S. 183 (1941); Davis v. Davis, 305 U.S. 32 (1938). A Puerto Rican judgment is covered by the implementing statute. Americana of Puerto Rico, Inc. v. Kaplus, 368 F.2d 431 (3d Cir.1966).

5. *Exclusive federal jurisdiction.* The judicial power of the United States encompasses "Cases of admiralty and maritime jurisdiction." U.S. Const. art. III, Sect. 2. Federal courts therefore have subject matter jurisdiction for the recognition of foreign judgments on maritime claims." What law determines whether a foreign judgment involves a maritime claim, especially if it was not rendered by a court designated to be an admiralty court? Recent decisions have held that it is not the law of the rendering (foreign) jurisdiction but the law of the American recognizing court because the

---

[4]   Magnolia Petroleum Co. v. Hunt, 320 U.S. 430, 439–40 (1943).

question of enforceability of the judgment purportedly involving a maritime claim is itself a maritime matter. D'Amico Dry Ltd. v. Primera Maritime (Hellas) Ltd., 756 F.3d 151 (2d Cir.2014), after extensive subsequent litigation affirmed in 794 Fed.Appx 127 (2d Cir. 2020); Flame S.A. v. Freight Bulk Pte. Ltd., 762 F.3d 352 (4th Cir.2014). See generally Seismic Reservoir 2020, Inc. v. Paulsson, 785 F.3d 330, 335 (9th Cir. 2015).

6. What is a "judgment" for our present purposes? Is a workers' compensation award by a state board or commission established for this purpose equivalent to a judgment of a court? See *Thomas v. Washington Gas Light Co.*, p. 356 infra. Unlike the Full Faith and Credit Clause, European law contains a broad definition: "any judgment given by a court or tribunal . . . , whatever [it] may be called, including a decree, order, decision. . . ." Regulation (EU) No. 1215/2012, Art. 2(a), p. 1141 infra.

What about decrees that are not final, for instance modifiable support decrees? Older American case law required finality for the Constitution's recognition command to apply. This requirement has been considerably relaxed, e.g., for family law matters. See p. 1001, infra; for registration under federal law, see p. 1012, infra. For a similar development in *Canada*, see Janet Walker, Conflict of Laws—2016 Reissue, Halsbury's Laws of Canada 510 et seq. (2016). *European* law seems broader as a result of its expansive definition of a "judgment," supra. However, limits result from a strict view of when a court has jurisdiction in the first place. As to custody and support, for instance, see p. 983, infra.

Hilton v. Guyot

Supreme Court of the United States, 1895.
159 U.S. 113, 16 S.Ct. 139, 40 L.Ed. 95.

[Action in a circuit court of the United States upon a judgment of a French court against citizens of the United States, and in favor of a French firm, the plaintiffs in the French proceeding. The answer, setting forth the original dealings between the parties, alleged that the defendants were not indebted to the plaintiffs. The defendants also contended that the French judgment should not be enforced without an examination of the merits of the case, since the courts of France would examine anew the merits of a controversy if an American judgment against a French national were sued on in France. Other objections of the defendants are specified in the court's opinion. The circuit court entered a judgment and a decree for the French firm without examining the merits.]

■ JUSTICE GRAY, after stating the case, delivered the opinion of the Court. . . .

No law has any effect, of its own force, beyond the limits of the sovereignty from which its authority is derived. The extent to which the law of one nation, as put in force within its territory, whether by executive order, by legislative act, or by judicial decree, shall be allowed to operate within the dominion of another nation, depends upon what our greatest jurists have been content to call "the comity of nations." Although the phrase has been often criticized, no satisfactory substitute has been suggested.

"Comity," in the legal sense, is neither a matter of absolute obligation, on the one hand, nor of mere courtesy and good will, upon the other. But it is the recognition which one nation allows within its territory to the legislative, executive or judicial acts of another nation, having due regard both to international duty and convenience, and to the rights of its own citizens or of other persons who are under the protection of its laws. . . .

In order to appreciate the weight of the various authorities cited at the bar, it is important to distinguish different kinds of judgments. Every foreign judgment, of whatever nature, in order to be entitled to any effect, must have been rendered by a court having jurisdiction of the cause, and upon regular proceedings and due notice. In alluding to different kinds of judgments, therefore, such jurisdiction, proceedings and notice will be assumed. It will also be assumed that they are untainted by fraud, the effect of which will be considered later.

A judgment in rem, adjudicating the title to a ship or other movable property within the custody of the court, is treated as valid everywhere. . . . The most common illustrations of this are decrees of courts of admiralty and prize, which proceed upon principles of international law. . . . But the same rule applies to judgments in rem under municipal law.

A judgment affecting the status of persons, such as a decree confirming or dissolving a marriage, is recognized as valid in every country, unless contrary to the policy of its own law. . . .

Other judgments, not strictly in rem, under which a person has been compelled to pay money, are so far conclusive that the justice of the payment cannot be impeached in another country, so as to compel him to pay it again. For instance a judgment in foreign attachment is conclusive, as between the parties, of the right to the property or money attached. Story on Conflict of Laws (2d ed.), sec. 592a . . . .

The extraterritorial effect of judgments in personam, at law or in equity, may differ, according to the parties to the cause. A judgment of that kind between two citizens or residents of the country, and thereby subject to the jurisdiction, in which it is rendered, may be held conclusive as between them everywhere. So, if a foreigner invokes the jurisdiction by bringing an action against a citizen, both may be held bound by a judgment in favor of either. And if a citizen sues a foreigner, and judgment is rendered in favor of the latter, both may be held equally bound. . . .

The effect to which a judgment purely executory, rendered in favor of a citizen or resident of the country, in a suit there brought by him against a foreigner, may be entitled in an action thereon against the latter in his own country-as is the case now before us-presents a more difficult question, upon which there has been some diversity of opinion. . . . [The court reviewed the common-law cases.]

In view of all the authorities upon the subject, and of the trend of judicial opinion in this country and in England, following the lead of Kent and Story, we are satisfied that, where there has been opportunity for a full and fair trial abroad before a court of competent jurisdiction, conducting the trial upon regular proceedings, after due citation or voluntary appearance of the defendant, and under a system of jurisprudence likely to secure an impartial administration of justice between the citizens of its own country and those of other countries, and there is nothing to show either prejudice in the court or in the system of laws under which it was sitting, or fraud in procuring the judgment, or any other special reason why the comity of this nation should not allow it full effect, the merits of the case should not, in an action brought in this country upon the judgment, be tried afresh, as on a new trial or an appeal, upon the mere assertion of the party that the judgment was erroneous in law or in fact. The defendants, therefore, cannot be permitted, upon that general ground, to contest the validity or the effect of the judgment sued on.

But they have sought to impeach that judgment upon several other grounds, which require separate consideration.

It is objected that the appearance and litigation of the defendants in the French tribunals were not voluntary, but by legal compulsion, and therefore that the French courts never acquired such jurisdiction over the defendants, that they should be held bound by the judgment. . . . [The court found that the French court had acquired jurisdiction of the person of the defendants.]

It is next objected that in those courts one of the plaintiffs was permitted to testify not under oath, and was not subjected to cross-examination by the opposite party, and that the defendants were, therefore, deprived of safeguards which are by our law considered essential to secure honesty and to detect fraud in a witness; and also that documents and papers were admitted in evidence, with which the defendants had no connection, and which would not be admissible under our own system of jurisprudence. But it having been shown by the plaintiffs, and hardly denied by the defendants, that the practice followed and the method of examining witnesses were according to the laws of France, we are not prepared to hold that the fact that the procedure in these respects differed from that of our own courts is, of itself, a sufficient ground for impeaching the foreign judgment. . . .

When an action is brought in a court of this country, by a citizen of a foreign country against one of our own citizens, to recover a sum of money adjudged by a court of that country to be due from the defendant to the plaintiff, and the foreign judgment appears to have been rendered by a competent court, having jurisdiction of the cause and of the parties, and upon due allegations and proofs, and opportunity to defend against them, and its proceedings are according to the course of a civilized jurisprudence, and are stated in a clear and formal record, the judgment is prima facie evidence, at least, of the truth of the matter adjudged; and it should be held conclusive upon the merits tried in the foreign court, unless some special ground is shown for impeaching the judgment, as by showing that it was affected by fraud or prejudice, or that, by the principles of international law, and by the comity of our own country, it should not be given full credit and effect.

There is no doubt that both in this country, as appears by the authorities already cited, and in England, a foreign judgment may be impeached for fraud. . . .

But whether those decisions can be followed in regard to foreign judgments, consistently with our own decisions as to impeaching domestic judgments for fraud, it is unnecessary in this case to determine, because there is a distinct and independent ground upon which we are satisfied that the comity of our nation does not require us to give conclusive effect to the judgments of the courts of France; and that ground is, the want of reciprocity, on the part of France, as to the effect to be given to the judgments of this and other foreign countries. . . . [The court quoted the French statutes as to the effect of foreign judgments.]

The defendants, in their answer, cited the above provisions of the statutes of France, and alleged, and at the trial offered to prove, that, by the construction given to these statutes by the judicial tribunals of France, when the judgments of tribunals of foreign countries against the citizens of France are sued upon in the courts of France, the merits of the controversies upon which those judgments are based are examined anew, unless a treaty to the contrary effect exists between the Republic of France and the country in which such judgment is obtained, (which is not the case between the Republic of France and the United States,) and that the tribunals of the Republic of France give no force and effect, within the jurisdiction of that country, to the judgments duly rendered by courts of competent jurisdiction of the United States against citizens of France after proper personal service of the process of those courts has been made thereon in this country. We are of the opinion that this evidence should have been admitted. . . . [The court's lengthy review of the laws of many countries as to the enforcement of foreign judgments is omitted.]

It appears, therefore, that there is hardly a civilized nation on either continent, which, by its general law, allows conclusive effect to an executory foreign judgment for the recovery of money. In France, and in a few smaller States—Norway, Portugal, Greece, Monaco, and Haiti— the merits of the controversy are reviewed, as of course, allowing to the foreign judgment, at the most, no more effect than of being prima facie evidence of the justice of the claim. In the great majority of the countries on the continent of Europe—in Belgium, Holland, Denmark, Sweden, Germany, in many cantons of Switzerland, in Russia and Poland, in

Romania, in Austria and Hungary, (perhaps in Italy,) and in Spain—as well as in Egypt, in Mexico, and in a great part of South America, the judgment rendered in a foreign country is allowed the same effect only as the courts of that country allow to the judgments of the country in which the judgment in question is sought to be executed.

. . . [T]he rule of reciprocity has worked itself firmly into the structure of international jurisprudence.

The reasonable, if not the necessary, conclusion appears to us to be that judgments rendered in France, or in any other foreign country, by the laws of which our own judgments are reviewable upon the merits, are not entitled to full credit and conclusive effect when sued upon in this country, but are prima facie evidence only of the justice of the plaintiff's claim.

In holding such a judgment, for want of reciprocity, not to be conclusive evidence of the merits of the claim, we do not proceed upon any theory of retaliation upon one person by reason of injustice done to another; but upon the broad ground that international law is founded upon mutuality and reciprocity, and that by the principles of international law recognized in most civilized nations, and by the comity of our own country, which it is our judicial duty to know and to declare, the judgment is not entitled to be considered conclusive. . . .

[The judgment and the decree were reversed.]

■ CHIEF JUSTICE FULLER, with whom concurred JUSTICE HARLAN, JUSTICE BREWER, and JUSTICE JACKSON, dissenting.

I cannot yield my assent to the proposition that because by legislation and judicial decision in France that effect is not there given to judgments recovered in this country which, according to our jurisprudence, we think should be given to judgments wherever recovered, (subject, of course, to the recognized exceptions,) therefore we should pursue the same line of conduct as respects the judgments of French tribunals. The application of the doctrine of res judicata does not rest in discretion; and it is for the government, and not for its courts, to adopt the principle of retorsion, if deemed under any circumstances desirable or necessary.

As the court expressly abstains from deciding whether the judgment is impeachable on the ground of fraud, I refrain from any observations on that branch of the case.

NOTES

The Hilton *Decision*

1.   Apart from the question of reciprocity, what defenses, according to the principal case, can be raised in this country to a suit seeking the enforcement of a foreign country judgment?

2. In Ritchie v. McMullen, 159 U.S. 235 (1895), decided the same day as Hilton v. Guyot, the Supreme Court held that an Ontario judgment should be enforced without an examination of its merits, as Canada would give conclusive effect to a judgment rendered by a court in the United States.

3. The doctrine of *révision au fond* was first abandoned in France in matters relating to status. In Munzer v. Dame Munzer-Jacoby, decided by the Cour de Cassation on January 7, 1964, it was held that no such doctrine exists. See Nadelmann, French Courts Recognize Foreign Money-Judgments: One Down and More to Go, 13 Am.J.Comp.L. 72 (1964); Batiffol & Lagarde, Traité de droit international privé, vol. 2, 593–95 (7th ed.1983). In 2007, the Cour de Cassation, the highest French court for civil matters, expressly enunciated liberal conditions for judgment recognition. The rendering foreign court must have had jurisdiction, the judgment must not offend French public policy, and there must not have been a "fraude à la loi" in its procurement. Cornelissen v. Avianca Inc., [2007] Recueil Dalloz 1115. For discussion, see Gilles Cuniberti, The Liberalization of the French Law of Foreign Judgments, 56 Int'l & Comp.L.Q. 931 (2007).

Public Policy—Foreign Courts on Punitive Damages

4. In 1992, the German Supreme Court adopted a liberal view with respect to the recognition and enforcement of American money judgments in Germany. Judgment of June 4, 1992, [1992] Wertpapiermitteilungen 1451. It had previously been uncertain whether Germany would recognize awards for expenses not yet incurred (e.g., future medical expenses), awards for pain and suffering far in excess of what a German court would have awarded, and for punitive damages. In its decision, the Court accepted the first of these in recognition of the American rule that a plaintiff cannot split his cause of action. It also accepted the award of pain and suffering in an amount eleven times greater than a comparable domestic award, and declaring that German public policy is not offended by the application of California law and practice to a case that arose there, between parties domiciled there at the time; an interposition of German public policy concerns presupposes German "contacts," and they were lacking. However, the Court declined, in keeping with general Continental practice, to recognize the award of punitive damages. Punishment is within the province of the criminal justice system, which also affords defendants different rights and protections than obtained in civil litigation. The Court left open whether punitive damages would be recognized to the extent that they contain identifiable compensatory aspects, e.g., the plaintiff's attorney's contingent fee. For discussion see Hay, The Recognition and Enforcement of American Money-Judgments in Germany, 40 Am.J.Comp.L. 729 (1992); Hay, On Comity, Reciprocity, and Public Policy in U.S. and German Judgments Recognition Practice, in: Basedow et al. (eds.), Private Law in the International Arena—Liber Amicorum Kurt Siehr 237 (2000).

Because German courts regard punitive damages as contrary to public policy and therefore will not recognize and enforce American judgments awarding them, a defendant in an American suit seeking punitive damages sought to resist service of process in Germany under the Hague Convention. The defendant argued that exposing it to the possibility of such a judgment violated its constitutionally guaranteed right to personality (right to privacy). The German Constitutional Court disagreed and held that the defendant could be served. The Court reasoned that the American proceeding would move ahead with or without service because the defendant had a wholly owned American subsidiary and that the defendant would be better off being served, so that it would have full knowledge of the proceeding and would be able to defend. The defendant's rights were assumed to be adequately protected by the German policy of non-recognition of such judgments. Bundesverfassungsgericht, Decision of December 7, 1994, [1995] Neue Juristische Wochenschrift 649. In 2003, the Court distinguished its earlier decision and issued a preliminary injunction against service of process on the German media company Bertelsmann in a New York class action seeking $17 billion in damages from a number of defendants for copyright infringement ("Napster" litigation). The amount of damages sought was so disproportionate to the damage suffered, the Court reasoned, as to suggest that plaintiffs in reality sought to coerce a settlement. In the Court's view, this would constitute abuse of legal process and would violate German public policy. Bundesverfassungsgericht, Decision of July 25, 2003 (No. 2 BvR 1198/03), [2003] IPRax No. 5 at vii–x. The Court noted that Bertelsmann has two U.S. subsidiaries and that these had been served. Could there also be service on Bertelsmann by service on the subsidiaries as agents or by piercing the corporate veil? See Volkswagenwerk Aktiengesellschaft v. Schlunk, p. 200, supra. Would this be a matter of New York law? After the preliminary injunction in *Bertelsmann* had been extended three times but the petition had never been decided on the merits, Bertelsmann withdrew its complaint [see 2005 RIW No. 2, p. II] and the Bundesverfassungsgericht then lifted the preliminary injunction: Decision of November 9, 2005, 2 BvR 1198/03. The constitutional question therefore still remains unresolved. For detailed analysis, see Rasmussen-Bonne, Zum Stand der Rechtshilfepraxis bei Zustellungsersuchen von US-Schadensersatzklagen nach dem Beschluss des Bundesverfassungsgerichts vom 25. Juli 2003, in Rasmussen-Bonne, Freer, Lüke & Weitnauer (eds.), Balancing of Interests—Festschrift für Peter Hay 323 (2005). For a discussion of the subsequent litigation, see Jan von Hein, Recent German Jurisprudence on Cooperation with the United States in Civil and Commercial Matters, in: Eckart Gottschalk, Ralf Michaels, Giesela Rühl, Jan von Hein (eds.), Conflict of Laws in a Globalized World 101 (2007).

In a defamation action brought by Princess Caroline of Monaco against a German tabloid, the German Supreme Court held that she was entitled to have the defendant print a retraction, but that the extent and print size of such a retraction had to be determined by balancing her interests against the defendant's freedom-of-press rights to publish additional material on the front page. Because such a balancing might not adequately redress the plaintiff's injury, the award of damages should take into account what it would take to give her satisfaction for her injury, focus on the egregious nature of defendant's conduct of "marketing" the plaintiff's private life, and the need to deter such conduct by others in the future. The remedy, the court said, was not based on or an enlargement of § 847 of the Civil Code (damages for pain and suffering, now § 253 para. 2 of the Civil Code as revised in 2001) but is (judicially) derived from the constitutional guarantee of the right of personality (the right of privacy). Arts. 1, 21, German Constitution. German Federal Supreme Court (BGH). Judgment of Nov. 11, 1994, [1995] Neue Juristische Wochenschrift 861. Despite the court's narrow focus on the constitutional right of privacy and the express disclaimer of the applicability of its ruling in the general context of damages for pain and suffering, is this decision not an example of an award of punitive damages? If such an award becomes possible, albeit in limited and specified circumstances, can this type of relief, when awarded by an American court, still violate German public policy as a matter of principle?

In 1999, German conflicts law was codified further. A new provision (Art. 40(3) No. 2 EGBGB) precludes the court from entertaining damage claims under foreign law which "obviously serve purposes other than the provision of appropriate compensation. . . ." Bundesgesetzblatt 1999, I, 1026. Subsequent EU legislation replaced national conflicts rules for torts with EU-wide uniform rules, but rejection of punitive damages on public policy grounds was expressly left to national law. See p. 1214 (No. 32), infra. While the recognition of non-EU country judgments remains national law, it is therefore unlikely that German case law will change with respect to the recognition of American punitive damage awards. See also Note 5, infra.

Public Policy—American Constitutional Objections

5.   Differences in British procedural and substantive law that existed at the time (putting the burden of proof on the defendant in libel actions and, substantively, having a much narrower "public figure" defense than American law) led to "libel tourism": if the libel was published in England (among other places), plaintiffs would sue there and then seek recognition of their judgments wherever the defendant had assets, including in the United States. European Union defendants received some protection from the European Court's decision in Case C-68/93, Shevill v. Presse Alliance S.A., [1995] ECR 1–415, which limited recoveries against defendants not habitually resident in the state of suit to damages suffered in that country. Non-EU defendants did not have that protection; their liability potentially extended to damages suffered worldwide. See, e.g., Bin Mahfouz v. Ehrenfeld, [2005] EWHC 1156 (Q.B. 2005). With some limits, the rule seems to be the same in Canada: Janet Walker, p. 275, Note 6, supra, at 358–59.

In response, New York's Recognition of Foreign Money Judgments statute was amended to require U.S. constitutional protections in foreign defamation actions: NY CLS CPLR § 5304(b)(8) ("A foreign country judgment need not be recognized if . . . (8) the cause of action resulted in a defamation judgment obtained in a jurisdiction outside the United States, unless the court before which the matter is brought sitting in this state first determines that the defamation law applied in the foreign court's adjudication provided at least as much protection for freedom of speech and press in that case as would be provided by both the United States and New York constitutions").

California and several other states enacted similar legislation. Federal legislation followed: The SPEECH Act of 2010 now provides as follows:

28 U.S.C.A. § 4102. Recognition of foreign defamation judgments

(a) First Amendment considerations.

(1) In general.—Notwithstanding any other provision of Federal or State law, a domestic court shall not recognize or enforce a foreign judgment for defamation unless the domestic court determines that—

(A) the defamation law applied in the foreign court's adjudication provided at least as much protection for freedom of speech and press in that case as would be provided by the first amendment to the Constitution of the United States and by the constitution and law of the State in which the domestic court is located; or

(B) even if the defamation law applied in the foreign court's adjudication did not provide as much protection for freedom of speech and press as the first amendment to the Constitution of the United States and the constitution and law of the State, the party opposing recognition or enforcement of that foreign judgment would have been found liable for defamation by a domestic court applying the first amendment to the Constitution of the United States and the constitution and law of the State in which the domestic court is located.

(2) Burden of establishing application of defamation laws.—The party seeking recognition or enforcement of the foreign judgment shall bear the burden of making the showings required under subparagraph (A) or (B).

(b) Jurisdictional considerations.—

(1) In general.—Notwithstanding any other provision of Federal or State law, a domestic court shall not recognize or enforce a foreign judgment for defamation unless the domestic court determines that the exercise of personal jurisdiction by the foreign court comported with the due process requirements that are imposed on domestic courts by the Constitution of the United States.

(2) Burden of establishing exercise of jurisdiction.—The party seeking recognition or enforcement of the foreign judgment shall bear the burden of making the showing that the foreign court's exercise of personal jurisdiction comported with the due process requirements that are imposed on domestic courts by the Constitution of the United States.

(c) Judgment against provider of interactive computer service.—[provides similar protection]

(d) Appearances not a bar.—An appearance by a party in a foreign court rendering a foreign judgment to which this section applies shall not deprive such party of the right to oppose the recognition or enforcement of the judgment under this section, or represent a waiver of any jurisdictional claims.

NOTE

The SPEECH Act was applied in Trout Point Lodge, Ltd. v. Handshoe, 729 F.3d 481 (5th Cir.2013) (Canadian libel judgment denied recognition because not compatible with First Amendment protections), and in 2016 WL 3746742 (S.D.Miss.2016) (motion to vacate previous *Trout Point* judgment for lack of jurisdiction denied); Electronic Frontier Foundation v. Global Equity Management (SA) Pty Ltd., 290 F.Supp.3d 923 (N.D.Cal.2017) (Australian injunction ordering removal of article from publication violates petitioner's U.S. constitutional rights and is not entitled to recognition, declaratory relief granted). In Naoko Ohno v. Yuko Yasuma, 723 F.3d 984 at 1004 n.22 (9th Cir.2013), the court expressly declined to extend the public policy concerns underlying the SPEECH Act to judgments other than those for redress for defamation.

The reform of British libel law in 2013 (Defamation Act of 2013, c. 26, effective for England and Wales as of 2014) goes a long way toward meeting the objections that gave rise to the American SPEECH Act. These defenses are noteworthy: a statement is not defamatory unless it has or will cause serious harm to the plaintiff's reputation; a statement expressing "honest opinion" that anyone could have had or one in the "public interest" also is not actionable. Note that there is no American-type "public figure" defense unless the statement is also in the "public interest." Most important, however, from an American perspective might be the jurisdictional provision: if the defendant is not a U.K. or EU domiciliary (e.g., an American), the British courts do not have jurisdiction only on the basis of publication of the libel in the England or Wales; rather, of all places of publication, England and Wales must be the most appropriate for litigation. Special, detailed provisions apply to operators of websites.

The Northern Ireland Assembly did not approve the Defamation Act of 2013 so that, as to Northern Ireland, previous UK law continues to apply, potentially giving rise to "libel tourism" there. However, since 2016 efforts have been under way, but not yet adopted, to opt into the English law, albeit with some minor changes. The Scottish Law Commission also studied reform proposals for Scottish libel law and a bill to that effect was introduced in the Scottish Parliament late in 2019. A first reading of the Defamation and Malicious Publication (Scotland) Bill was approved on November 5, 2020.

Recognition Treaties

6.   In the European Union, Regulation (EU) No. 1215/2012, p. 1137, infra, governs the recognition and enforcement of judgments in civil and commercial matters rendered by courts of all Member States, except Denmark. Pursuant to an agreement between the European Community and Denmark signed on 19 October 2005, the Brussels Regulation applies between other European Community countries and Denmark. The Lugano Convention, p. 1135, infra, extends the Brussels Regulation system to Iceland, Norway, and Switzerland. As a result of the "Brexit," the Regulation (phrased in terms of a party domiciled or incorporated "in a member state") will no longer apply to the United Kingdom, unless it decides to opt into a Lugano-type of arrangement. From among the extensive contributions to the literature see Hartley, Civil Jurisdiction and Judgments (1984); Dicey, Morris & Collins, Conflict of Laws 663 et. seq. (15th ed.2012), & 185 et seq. 15th ed. Supplement 4th (2017). National law with respect to jurisdiction and the recognition and enforcement of judgments remains in force with respect to non-member states of the European Union. The Regulation and the Conventions expressly prohibit *révision au fond*, i.e., the review of the foreign judgment for its correctness, including correct application of conflicts law. Regulation Art. 52. With respect to the defense of lack of reciprocity, see Note 8, infra.

7.   In 1992, the United States proposed that the Hague Conference on Private International Law resume work on drafting a convention on the recognition and enforcement of judgments, which would be open for potentially worldwide acceptance. Because of considerable differences in national laws, it proved difficult to reach agreement and work on the project was abandoned for now. However, one part of the work survived and became the Hague Convention on Choice of Court Agreements of 2005 that was considered at p. 208, supra.

In 2019, the Hague Conference adopted the final text of a proposed a worldwide recognition and enforcement of judgments convention. The Convention is not yet in force, and has only been signed (and not yet ratified) by few countries, not including the United States. The Convention tracks EU law (p. 1137, infra) in many respects but, given the greater diversity of potential participants, is less prescriptive. For instance, it does not establish an exclusive list of permissible bases of jurisdiction, but declares judgments "eligible" for recognition and enforcement if they are based on the jurisdictional grounds it provides (Art. 5(1)). A number of subject matters are excluded (for instance, insolvency, arbitration, defamation, intellectual property, Art. 2), but contracting states are free to accord recognition under national law to judgments not covered or not "eligible" (Art. 15).

Its provisions for refusal of recognition, in contrast, are exclusive (Art. 7), but include a judgment's incompatibility with fundamental principles of procedural fairness of the recognizing state, in addition to the latter's objections on public policy grounds (Art. 7(1)(c)). Interestingly, the proposal adopts the American approach (p. 253, supra) to the *lis pendens* problem (Art. 7(2)). It is, of course, too early to predict whether the proposal or modifications of it will be successful. For comment see Brand, Jurisdiction and Judgments Recognition at the Hague Conference: Choices Made, Treaties Completed, and the Path Ahead, 67 Netherlands Int'l L. Rev, 3 (2020); Coco, Note: The Value of a New Judgments Convention for U.S. Litigants, 94 N.Y.U. L.Rev. 1209 (2019); Nielsen, The Hague 2019 Judgments Convention—From Failure to Success?, 16 J. Priv. Int'l L. 205 (2020).

Reciprocity Today

8.   The defense of lack of reciprocity has been widely discarded today. See, e.g., Somportex Limited v. Philadelphia Chewing Gum Corp., 453 F.2d 435

(3d Cir.1971); Nicol v. Tanner, 256 N.W.2d 796 (Minn.1976). But see Gross v. German Foundation Industrial Initiative, 456 F.3d 363, 393 (3d Cir.2006) ("Even in the context of a foreign court's judgment, we condition application of international comity on reciprocity" in a federal question case). Some states have adopted reciprocity requirements by statute. This is the case in the Florida, Maine, Massachusetts, Ohio, and Texas versions of the Uniform Foreign Money-Judgments Recognition Act: Fla.Stat.Ann. § 55.605(2)(g); 14 M.R.S § 8505(2)(G); Mass.Gen.Laws Ann. ch. 235, § 23A; Ohio Rev.Code Ann. § 2329.92(B); V.T.C.A., Civ.Prac. & Rem.Code § 36.005(b)(7). Colorado, Georgia, Idaho, North Carolina, and Oregon had statutory reciprocity requirements that have been repealed. See also N.H.Rev.Stat.Ann. § 524:11 (with respect to Canadian judgments). In Texas, the defense of lack of reciprocity failed in the context of Canadian and English judgments. See Norkan Lodge Co. Ltd. v. Gillum, 587 F.Supp. 1457 (N.D.Tex.1984) (Canada); Hunt v. BP Exploration Co. (Libya) Ltd., 580 F.Supp. 304 (N.D.Tex.1984); recognition now governed by Uniform Act, p. 400, infra: The Society of Lloyd's v. Price, 2004 WL 2550590 (W.D.Tex.2004). See also Hay, On Comity, Reciprocity, and Public Policy in U.S. and German Judgments Recognition Practice, in: Basedow et al. (eds.), Private Law in the International Arena-Liber Amicorum Kurt Siehr 237 (2000). Colorado, Idaho, and North Carolina adopted the 2005 amendments to the Foreign Money-Judgments Recognition Act, which repealed their reciprocity provisions.

German law retains a reciprocity requirement for the recognition of non-EU country judgments. Code of Civil Procedure (ZPO) § 328(1) No. 5. In keeping with general German recognition practice (see No. 4, supra), this requirement has been construed in a pro-recognition fashion. Thus, in a German-American recognition case, the German judgment debtor resisted recognition because the successful American claimants (plaintiffs in the original action, now judgment creditors) would recover their court and attorneys' costs of the enforcement proceeding under applicable German law, while German claimants in reverse cases in American courts bear their own costs. Since a German judgment creditor would thus recover less than the full value of his or her German judgment in the United States (i.e., judgment less costs and fees), so the argument went, reciprocity in judgment recognition is not assured with respect to the United States. This argument of course overlooks that the German creditor, having been awarded his or her costs in all antecedent German proceedings, may recover these in the United States as part of the judgment, while the reverse is not true. Without addressing the last point, the German Supreme Court pointed to an earlier decision, in which it had held that the " 'American rule of costs' violates neither basic rights of the parties nor general principles of the rule of law [due process]," and held that reciprocity with respect to the United States is assured, "at least in those cases in which the amount to be recognized and enforced [in Germany] . . . exceeds the attorneys' fees [in the United States]." Bundesgerichtshof (BGH), Decision of October 20, 2005, SGL Acotec v. American Ins. Co., Dock No. IX ZR 246/03, at No. 5; briefly noted by M. Stürner, jurisPR-BGHZivilR 51/2005, anno. 3. See Schack, Internationales Zivilverfahrensrecht p. 359 et seq. (7th ed. 2017).

In the United States, the American Law Institute adopted a proposal for a federal "Foreign Judgments and Enforcement Act" in 2005. It was intended to achieve what the earlier Hague Conference effort, p. 285, Note 7, supra, had failed to do The drafters noted that American courts had gone in different directions after *Hilton*, with most having adopted the dissenting view, and that it was desirable that "state as well as federal courts [be] held to a uniform national standard, thus both avoiding forum-shopping in enforcing foreign-country judgments and affording to foreign courts [for the reverse case] a clear picture of practice in the United States." ALI, Proposed Foreign Judgments Recognition and Enforcement Act (2005), § 7, comment *a*. These goals could be achieved either by adopting or by rejecting a reciprocity requirement as a matter of national law. The proposed act opts for the former: "A foreign judgment shall not be recognized or enforced in a court in the United States if the court finds that comparable judgments of courts of the United States would not be recognized or enforced in the courts of the state of origin." § 7(a). Subsection (e) contemplates agreements between the United States and foreign states, "setting forth reciprocal practices." By opting in favor of a reciprocity requirement, the proponents seek "to create an incentive to foreign countries to commit to recognition and enforcement of judgments rendered in the United States." § 7, comment *b*. The proposal thus favors a public interest goal over a private party's interest in the recognition and enforcement of a foreign judgment that is otherwise free of jurisdictional or procedural defects. For a different view of the appropriate respective roles of public and private interests, see—in the context of *forum non conveniens*—the House of Lords' decision in Lubbe v. Cape Plc, p. 238, supra, and accompanying notes. Further: in the absence of agreements, such as envisioned by subsection (e) of the proposed provision, will adoption of a reciprocity requirement by the United States be likely to contribute to pro-recognition practices on the part of foreign courts—such as in the case of the German Supreme Court's decision reported in the preceding paragraph—or will it invite a harder look at United States practice? A comprehensive historical review of the reciprocity requirement, which also comments on the ALI proposal, addresses the intersection of private and public international law and the question whether governments do or should have and promote a "public" interest in private litigation. For discussion of the American Law Institute proposal, see S.I. Strong, Recognition and Enforcement of Foreign Judgments in U.S. Courts: Problems and Possibilities, 33 Rev.Litig. 45, 92 et seq. (2014). The ALI proposal for a federal statute went nowhere. The issues it raised, however, continue to be important, particularly in light of the new Hague Conference proposal of a worldwide Jurisdiction and Judgments Convention, p. 285, Note 7, supra.

COWANS V. TICONDEROGA PULP & PAPER CO., 219 App.Div. 120, 219 N.Y.S. 284 (1927), affirmed on opinion below, 246 N.Y. 603, 159 N.E. 669 (1927): Action brought in a New York court to enforce a money judgment recovered in the Province of Québec, Canada. Plaintiffs appealed from an order of the trial court denying their motion for judgment on the pleadings. Held, reversed. Van Kirk, J. . . . "The question presented here is whether this Québec judgment is in our court merely prima facie proof of liability, against which any defense which could have been used at the trial in the Québec court is available to defeat recovery here, or is it conclusive, subject only to the recognized exceptions. The respondent's proposition is that the judgment is only prima facie evidence, because, under the Québec law (Code Civ.Proc. of Québec § 210): 'Any defense which was or might have been set up to the original action may be pleaded to an action brought upon a judgment rendered out of Canada' . . ."

"The force and effect which is to be given to a foreign judgment is for each sovereign power to determine for itself. . . . The general rule in this State is settled as follows: A judgment recovered in a foreign country, when sued upon in the courts of this State, is conclusive so far as to preclude a retrial of the merits of the case, subject, however, to certain well-recognized exceptions, namely, where the judgment is tainted with fraud, or with an offense against the public policy of the State, or the foreign court had no jurisdiction."

". . . The respondent does not question the general rule as above stated, but urges that the denial of reciprocity in the Province of Québec furnishes a further exception to the general rule. It rests its contention confidently on the decision in Hilton v. Guyot. . . ."

". . . Our Court of Appeals [in Johnston v. Compagnie Generale Transatlantique, 242 N.Y. 381, 152 N.E. 121 (1926)] has we think definitely refused to accept that holding as the policy of this State; and, without reciprocity, would give to the foreign judgment the full effect to which its persuasiveness entitles it. The decision in the Hilton case would deprive a party of the private rights he has acquired by reason of a foreign judgment because the country in whose courts that judgment was rendered has a rule of evidence different from that which we have and does not give the same effect as this State gives to a foreign judgment."

"We think the general rule as above stated must be applied to this case, and that the proposition which the respondent would maintain is in conflict with the policy and law of this State. . . ."

NOTES

1. What law determines the effect to be given the judgments of foreign countries by American courts? Is this a question of national law or one to be decided by the conflict of laws rules of the individual states? The consensus today is that state law controls. Somportex Ltd. v. Philadelphia Chewing Gum Corp., 453 F.2d 435 (3d Cir.1971), cert. denied, 405 U.S. 1017 (1972); Toronto-Dominion Bank v. Hall, 367 F.Supp. 1009 (E.D.Ark.1973). See also, Banque Libanaise Pour Le Commerce v. Khreich, 915 F.2d 1000 (5th Cir.1990); Derr v. Swank, 766 F.3d 430, 436 (5th Cir. 2014); In re Carmona, 580 B.R. 690, 707 (S.D. Tex. 2018). Accordingly, if the question presented in the *Hilton* case were to arise today in a New York federal court exercising diversity jurisdiction, the court would presumably follow Cowans v.

Ticonderoga Pulp and Paper Co. rather than *Hilton*. In Evans Cabinet Corp. v. Kitchen Intern., Inc., 593 F.3d 135, 140 et seq. (1st Circ. 2010), the court expressly left the question open, noting that several courts and commentators advocated the application of a federal standard so that the United States would deal in a uniform way with foreign country judgments. The court, for other reasons, applied Massachusetts state law. Consider, however, Banco Nacional de Cuba v. Sabbatino, 376 U.S. 398 (1964), p. 783, infra. In federal question cases, federal courts apply federal judgment-recognition doctrine. See, e.g., Gordon & Breach Science Publishers v. Amer. Inst. of Physics, 905 F.Supp. 169, 178–79 (S.D.N.Y.1995) (concerning the question whether Swiss and German judgments precluded a Lanham Act claim); In re Sino-Forest Corp., 501 B.R. 655 (Bkr.S.D.N.Y.2013). See Brand, Enforcement of Foreign Money-Judgments in the United States: In Search of Uniformity and International Acceptance, 67 Notre Dame L.Rev. 253 (1991); For an extensive bibliography, see Ebke & Parker, Foreign Country Money-Judgments and Arbitral Awards and the Restatement (Third) of the Foreign Relations Law of the United States: A Conventional Approach, 24 Int'l Law 21 (1990).

2. For a comparison of the effects accorded in this country to sister state and foreign country judgments, see p. 398, infra. For a general discussion of the recognition and enforcement of foreign country judgments, see Weintraub, Commentary on the Conflict of Laws 746–59 (6th ed.2010); Hay, Borchers, Symeonides & Whytock, Conflict of Laws ch. 24 (6th ed.2018).

3. In Chevron Corp. v. Naranjo, 667 F.3d 232 (2d Cir.2012), cert. denied, 133 S.Ct. 423 (2012), the court considered the latest chapter in a long-running battle over the enforceability of an Ecuadorian judgment for $ 8.646 billion. The plaintiffs in the Ecuadorian suit were residents of the Lago Agrio region of the Ecuadorian Amazon. The plaintiffs claimed that Chevron's predecessor Texaco extensively polluted the Lago Agrio region, causing massive environmental damage. The plaintiffs and their U.S. lawyer originally attempted to file the action in U.S. courts, but the case was dismissed on forum non conveniens grounds in favor of the Ecuadorian courts. This turned out to be a tactical mistake by Chevron, as the Ecuadorian courts entered the huge judgment against Chevron. Chevron claims that the foreign judgment is tainted by fraud and was the product of collusion between the U.S. plaintiffs' attorney and the court, rendering it unenforceable. Anticipating potential enforcement of the judgment in New York, Chevron sought, under New York's version of the Uniform Act (see N.Y.C.P.L.R. §§ 5301–09) an injunction against enforcement of the judgment in any court as well as a declaration that the judgment was unenforceable. The District Court granted Chevron the requested injunction, but the Second Circuit reversed holding that anticipatory relief against enforcement was not available under the Uniform Act. In a subsequent action against members of the law firm and others Chevron sought and was granted an injunction against enforcement of the Ecuadorian judgment anywhere in the United States, imposition of a constructive trust on any assets already received or to be received in the future in connection with that judgment and $800,000 in damages for RICO violations committed by the defendants in obtaining the judgment. Chevron Corporation v. Donziger, 833 F.3d 74 (2d Cir. 2016), cert. denied 137 S.Ct. 228 (2017). When the damages awarded were not paid and other requirements not fulfilled, the district court held the defendants in civil contempt, agreed to compensatory damages as well as to the award of attorneys' fees. Chevron Corporation v. Donziger, 384 F.Supp.3d 465 (S.D.N.Y.2019), appeal docketed, No. 19-1584 (2d Cir.May 28, 2019).

4.   *Judgments in foreign currency.* A foreign money judgment presumably will be expressed in the foreign currency. May the judgment creditor seek recognition and enforcement in the United States in the foreign currency? If the foreign judgment is to be converted into dollars, is the relevant time for the conversion the time of breach, the time the foreign judgment was rendered, the time of recognition, or some other time? It is debatable whether a United States court can render a judgment in foreign currency. Section 890 of the Restatement (Fourth) of the Foreign Relations Law of the United States (2018) states that United States courts may express judgments enforcing foreign judgments in the foreign currency or in United States dollars, "unless State law requires otherwise." See N.Y. Jud. Law § 27(b) (McKinney 2019); In re Oil Spill by the Amoco Cadiz Off the Coast of France on March 16, 1978, 954 F.2d 1279 (7th Cir.1992), ordered entry of a judgment in francs; Waterside Ocean Navigation Co., Inc. v. International Navigation Ltd., 737 F.2d 150 (2d Cir.1984) (enforcing foreign arbitral award partly in dollars and partly in English pounds); Liberty Media Corp. v. Vivendi Universal, S.A., 2013 WL 105776, *3 (S.D. N.Y. 2013) (judgment entered in euro).

        Rendering U.S. judgments in foreign currency would not, however, solve the conversion date problem. As a practical matter, unless a complex double conversion were used, a U.S. judgment in foreign currency would result in a judgment day conversion and, if one adopts the position of the Foreign Relations Restatement (Third) § 823 that losses resulting from shifts in the relative value of currencies should be treated as foreseeable consequential damages, would be unfair to the foreign creditor if the dollar has appreciated since breach day. The Restatement recognized this and stated that the judgment should be in foreign currency only when judgment day conversion would be proper. The Restatement (Fourth) of 2018 has now modified this rule (see previous paragraph). The UNIDROIT Principles, in 6.1.9(1) and (4) take a position on currency conversion that is essentially the same as that of the Restatement (Third). There is no flexibility in the Uniform and New York statutes. For adverse criticism on this ground of the Uniform Foreign-Money Claims Acts, see Brand, Note 1, supra, and Westerheim, The Uniform Foreign-Money Claims Act: No Solution to an Old Problem, 69 Tex.L.Rev. 1203 (1991).

        For the view that the Restatement's rule for shifts in the value of currencies "introduces into a purely procedural rule an element of substantive justice" and that compensation for delay and ensuing loss due to currency fluctuations should therefore be left to the law applicable to the claim or judgment, see F.A. Mann, The Legal Aspect of Money 351 (5th ed.1992); Hay, Fremdwährungsanprüche und -urteile nach dem US-amerikanischen Uniform Act, [1995] Recht der Internationalen Wirtschaft 113, 115 n.35, 118 n.66.

SECTION 2. RECOGNITION AND ENFORCEMENT IN GENERAL

In this section and the one immediately succeeding, we examine the effects which a state or federal judgment carries in the state of rendition and those, which under full faith and credit, must be accorded it in other states. Here, consideration is given to a judgment's basic effects as res judicata and to methods of enforcing a foreign judgment. In Section 3, attention is directed to other questions relating to the parties and issues concluded by a judgment and to various special matters.

A. IN PERSONAM JUDGMENTS

In the state of rendition, an in personam judgment for a sum certain can normally be enforced by a levy of execution against any local property of the defendant. All in personam judgments also have one or more of the following effects: (1) *Merger,* by which the plaintiff's original claim (cause of action) is merged in a judgment for a sum certain, so that the original claim is extinguished and a claim on the judgment takes its place.[5] (2) *Bar,* by which a judgment for the defendant extinguishes the original claim. (3) *Issue preclusion,*[6] by which issues of fact and perhaps of law actually litigated in the action are conclusively determined in subsequent proceedings in which the same issues arise, even though the claim may be different. If the subsequent proceedings are on the same claim, this is sometimes known as direct estoppel. If the question arises in connection with another claim, this has commonly been called collateral estoppel. Further reference to the problem of issue preclusion is made at pp. 323 et seq., infra.

The rule was concisely put in Mendez v. Bowie, 118 F.2d 435, 440 (1st Cir.1941) as follows:

> "The effect of a judgment or decree as res judicata depends upon whether the second action or suit is upon the same or a different cause of action. If upon the same cause of action, the judgment or decree upon the merits in the first case is an absolute bar to

---

[5] It has been held, however, that the rule of merger does not apply to a judgment of a foreign country. Eastern Townships Bank v. H.S. Beebe & Co., 53 Vt. 177 (1880). The Restatement, Second, Conflict of Laws § 95, cmt. (c)(1) retains this view. The rule has been changed in England: unless the foreign judgment is not entitled to recognition in England, a plaintiff who obtained a valid judgment in his favor abroad may not bring another action on the same claim in England. Civil Jurisdiction and Judgments Act (1982) § 34. See Dicey, Morris & Collins, Conflict of Laws 673 et seq. (15th ed.2012) & 187 (15th ed. Supp. 4th 2017). For criticism of the American non-merger rule, see Scoles, Interstate and International Distinctions in Conflict of Laws in the United States, 54 Calif.L.Rev. 1599, 1607 (1966); Hay, Borchers, Symeonides & Whytock, Conflict of Laws § 24.3 (6th ed.2018).

[6] This is the terminology adopted by the Restatement, Second, Judgments § 17, now widely accepted in American law.

the subsequent action or suit between the same parties or those in privity with them, not only in respect of every matter which was actually offered and received to sustain the demand or to make out a defense, but also as to every ground of recovery or defense which might have been presented. . . . But if the second case be upon a different cause of action, the prior judgment or decree operates as an estoppel only as to matters actually in issue or points controverted, upon the determination of which the judgment or decree was rendered, and not as to matters or points which might have been litigated and determined."

Obviously, much depends on whether the term "claim" (cause of action) is given a broad or a narrow definition. See Restatement, Second, Judgments 24–26 (1982); James, Hazard & Leubsdorf, Civil Procedure 578–641 (4th ed.1992); Rosenberg, Collateral Estoppel in New York, 44 St. John's L.Rev. 165 (1969). The broader the definition, the more a plaintiff will be required to seek relief in a single action for his various complaints against the defendant. The present trend, according to Section 24, comment *a.*, of the Restatement of Judgments, Second, is to define "claim" to embrace all the remedial rights of the plaintiff against the defendant growing out of the relevant transaction or series of connected transactions.

An important problem is whether the definition of claim is to be sought in the law of F-1 or of F-2. Should a distinction be made in this connection between a judgment rendered in a state of the United States and one rendered in a foreign country?

<h1 style="text-align:center">Lynde v. Lynde</h1>
Supreme Court of the United States, 1901.
181 U.S. 183, 21 S.Ct. 555, 45 L.Ed. 810.

[In 1892 Mrs. Lynde filed a bill in New Jersey asking for a divorce on the ground of desertion and for reasonable alimony. Service was had by publication. The decree of divorce was granted but no provision for alimony was made. In 1896 Mrs. Lynde asked that the decree be amended to provide for alimony, alleging an oversight on the part of her attorney in failing to include such a provision in the original decree. In the interim her divorced husband had married again in New York but he now appeared generally in the proceeding and contested the alimony request. The court, however, awarded the wife $7,840 back alimony and further alimony at the rate of $80 a week. A receiver of the husband's New Jersey property was appointed but was able to find no property in New Jersey. The second New Jersey decree also provided for security, which the husband failed to give, and for an injunction against disposal of property to evade the decree. (Lynde v. Lynde, 54 N.J.Eq. 473.)

The wife then brought suit in New York asking for past due alimony, counsel fees, and $80 weekly as allowed her by the New Jersey court. She also asked that her ex-husband be directed to give security, and that the order provide for sequestration, receivership, and an injunction. The New York court (Lynde v. Lynde, 162 N.Y. 405) conceded the New Jersey court's jurisdiction to grant an in personam decree against the husband for alimony because of his general appearance in the later New Jersey proceedings. The judgment was enforced only as to counsel fees and past due alimony; since future alimony remained subject to modification in the discretion of the New Jersey chancellor, the judgment on that point was not final and could not be enforced in New York. The collateral means of enforcement provided in the New Jersey decree and asked for by the plaintiff were also denied since the Constitution does not require such action to be taken, being a mode of effectuating the decree and not part of the decree itself.

Each party to the New York proceeding then sued out a writ of error from the Supreme Court of the United States, which rendered the following opinion.]

■ GRAY, J. The husband, as the record shows, having appeared generally in answer to the petition for alimony in the Court of Chancery in New Jersey, the decree of that court for alimony was binding upon him. . . . The court of New York having so ruled, thereby deciding in favor of the full faith and credit claimed for that decree under the Constitution and laws of the United States, its judgment on that question cannot be reviewed by this court on writ of error. . . . The husband having appeared and been heard in the proceeding for alimony, there is no color for his present contention that he was deprived of his property without due process of law. . . . His writ of error, therefore, must be dismissed.

By the Constitution and the act of Congress, requiring the faith and credit to be given to a judgment of the court of another State that it has in the State where it was rendered, it was long ago declared by this court: "The judgment is made a debt of record, not examinable upon its merits; but it does not carry with it, into another State, the efficacy of a judgment upon property or persons, to be enforced by execution. To give it the force of a judgment in another State, it must be made a judgment there; and can only be executed in the latter as its laws may permit." McElmoyle v. Cohen, 13 Pet. 312, 325; Thompson v. Whitman, 18 Wall. 457, 463. . . .

The decree of the Court of Chancery of New Jersey, on which this suit is brought, provides, first, for the payment of $7840 for alimony already due, and $1000 counsel fee; second, for the payment of alimony since the date of the decree at the rate of $80 per week; and third, for the giving of a bond to secure the payment of these sums, and, on default of payment or of giving bond, for leave to apply for a writ of sequestration, or a receiver and injunction.

The decree for the payment of $8840 was for a fixed sum already due, and the judgment of the court below was properly restricted to that. The provision of the payment for alimony in the future was subject to the discretion of the Court of Chancery of New Jersey, which might at any time alter it, and was not a final judgment for a fixed sum. The provisions for bond, sequestration, receiver and injunction, being in the nature of execution, and not of judgment, could have no extraterritorial operation; but the action of the courts of New York in these respects depended on the local statutes and practice of the State, and involved no Federal question.

On the writ of error of the wife, therefore, the judgment is affirmed.

NOTE

For the recognition and enforcement of out-of-state equity decrees, see also Baker v. General Motors Corp., 522 U.S. 222, p. 333, infra.

NOTE ON METHODS OF ENFORCEMENT

In this country, the original method of enforcing an F-1 judgment was to bring an action in the nature of debt upon the judgment in F-2. That method has persisted. Only after a new judgment has been obtained in F-2 can execution there be had against the property of the defendant. This requirement is time-consuming; it also results in the efficacy of a judgment being greatly decreased when enforcement is sought in other states. For example, although a foreign judgment, since it establishes the existence of a debt, may be filed as a claim against an insolvent estate, it does not have the priority over simple contract debts in the distribution of assets which it had in F-1 or which F-2 gives to domestic judgments. Trionics Research Sales Corp. v. Nautec Corp., 237 N.E.2d 68 (N.Y.1968). To acquire such a priority, the judgment creditor must obtain a new judgment in F-2 in the manner set forth above.

The problems and burdens presented by this method of enforcement are mitigated by the availability in the great majority of states of summary judgment procedures for the enforcement of foreign judgments. See p. 296, infra.

In 1948, Congress provided for the registration in any federal district court of a judgment rendered in any other district. This statute (28 U.S.C.A. § 1963, as amended) reads as follows:

"A judgment in an action for the recovery of money or property entered in any court of appeals, district court, bankruptcy court, or in the Court of International Trade may be registered by filing a certified copy of the judgment in any other district or, with respect to the Court of International Trade, in any judicial district, when the judgment has become final by appeal or expiration of the time for appeal or when ordered by the court that entered the judgment for good cause shown. Such a judgment entered in favor of the United States may be so registered any time after judgment is entered. A judgment so registered shall have the same effect as a judgment of the district court of the district where registered and may be enforced in like manner.

"A certified copy of the satisfaction of any judgment in whole or in part may be registered in like manner in any district in which the judgment is a lien."

Congress has likewise provided that a judgment entered in the United States Court of Federal Claims in favor of the United States may be registered and enforced in any district court. 28 U.S.C.A. § 2508.

NOTES

1. Section 1963 applies only to judgments in "an action for the recovery of money or property." In Stiller v. Hardman, 324 F.2d 626 (2d Cir.1963), the court held that a judgment for money could be registered, even though it was rendered on a counterclaim in a suit originally brought for a declaratory judgment. See also Cianbro Corp. v. Georgia H. Dean, Inc., 749 F.Supp.2d 1 (D.Me.2010). The *Stiller* court also held that the judgment could not be registered insofar as it involved an injunction. It pointed out that "The mandate of an injunction issued by a Federal district court runs throughout the United States. Leman v. Krentler-Arnold Hinge Last Co., 284 U.S. 448, 52 S.Ct. 238 (1932)." Thus there is no need to register judgments of district courts in so far as they involve injunctions.

2. Originally § 1963 only applied to judgments that had become final by appeal or expiration of the time for appeal. A 1988 revision added an exception. When a judgment is pending on appeal or was issued by default and the judgment debt has insufficient local assets for its satisfaction but does have assets elsewhere, the rendering court may permit the registration of the judgment in those other locations when "good cause shown." On what constitutes "good cause" see Cheminova A/S v. Griffin L.L.C., 182 F.Supp.2d 68 (D.D.C.2002); Non-Dietary Exposure Task Force v. Tagros Chemicals, India, Ltd., 309 F.R.D. 66 (D.D.C.2015); Pharmacy Corporation of America v. Concord Healthcare Group, LLC, 2017 WL 10221198 (W.D.Ky. 2017).

3. A judgment registered in a second federal district under § 1963 becomes in effect a new F-2 judgment subject to the rules of F-2. So the judgment will be subject to the F-2 statute of limitations rather than to that of F-1. Matanuska Valley Lines, Inc. v. Molitor, 365 F.2d 358 (9th Cir.1966); Stanford v. Utley, 341 F.2d 265 (8th Cir.1965). Similarly, the law of F-2 will be applied to determine the circumstances under which the judgment may be stayed. United States ex rel. Hi-Way Elec. Co. v. Home Indem. Co., 549 F.2d 10 (7th Cir.1977); Deep v. Boies, 2009 WL 10675920, *5 (N.D.N.Y.2009). The F-2 court can take any action to protect the judgment that the F-1 court could have taken, including an anti-suit injunction if appropriate. Karaha Bodas Co., L.L.C. v. Perusahaan Pertambangan Minyak Dan Gas Bumi Negara, 500 F.3d 111 (2d Cir.2007), cert. denied, 554 U.S. 929 (2008). See also Lam Yeen Leng v. Pinnacle Performance Ltd., 474 Fed.App'x 810 (2d Cir.2012); AU New Haven, LLC v. YKK Corporation, 2018 WL 2128373 (S.D.N.Y. 2018) . For antisuit injunctions, see also p. 254, supra.

4. Just as a judgment registered under § 1963 becomes an F-2 judgment subject to F-2 rules, a judgment registered in a state under the Uniform Enforcement of Foreign Judgments Act, below, may be treated as a local judgment. In National Bank of Arizona v. Moore, 122 P.3d 1265 (N.M.App.2005), cert. denied, 122 P.3d 1263 (N.M.2005), the bank recovered a judgment in Arizona against an Arizona husband. Arizona and New Mexico are both community property states. The judgment was for husband's separate debt, not a community debt. The bank registered the judgment in New Mexico under the Uniform Act. Under Arizona law but not New Mexico law a judgment for a spouse's separate debt cannot be enforced against community property. Held: the registered judgment may be enforced against a New Mexico bank account that is community property. "Once the Arizona judgment was converted into a New Mexico judgment, New Mexico law was applicable to the enforcement of that judgment." 122 P.3d at 1267. "To the extent Husband argues that the law applicable to the enforcement of the judgment against him depends on whether the bank account is Arizona community property as opposed to New Mexico community property, Husband did not make this argument below. We therefore decline to address this contention." Id. at 1268. See similarly Wells Fargo Equipment Finance, Inc. v. Asterbadi, 841 F.3d 237, 243–45 (4th Cir.2016); Medical Provider Financial Corporation II v. San Diego Center for Women's Health, 2017 WL 1711053 (S.D.Cal. 2017). See also Levin v. Islamic Republic of Iran, 2018 WL 10638333 (S.D.N.Y.2018) (judgment creditor who registered judgment retains right to sue on original judgment; this reflects the rule that judgments do not merge, see p. 291).

Uniform Enforcement of Foreign Judgments Act (Revised 1964 Act)

13 Uniform Laws Ann. 149 (1986).

§ 1. Definition. In this Act "foreign judgment" means any judgment, decree, or order of a court of the United States or of any other court which is entitled to full faith and credit in this state.

§ 2. Filing and Status of Foreign Judgments. A copy of any foreign judgment authenticated in accordance with the act of Congress or the statutes of this state may be filed in the office of the Clerk of any [District Court of any city or county] of this state. The Clerk shall treat the foreign judgment in the same manner as a judgment of the [District Court of any city or county] of this state. A judgment so filed has the same effect and is subject to the same procedures, defenses and proceedings for reopening, vacating, or staying as a judgment of a [District Court of any city or county] of this state and may be enforced or satisfied in like manner.

§ 3. Notice of Filing. (a) At the time of the filing of the foreign judgment, the judgment creditor or his lawyer shall make and file with the Clerk of Court an affidavit setting forth the name and last known post office address of the judgment debtor, and the judgment creditor.

(b) Promptly upon the filing of the foreign judgment and the affidavit, the Clerk shall mail notice of the filing of the foreign judgment to the judgment debtor at the address given and shall make a note of the mailing in the docket. The notice shall include the name and post office address of the judgment creditor and the judgment creditor's lawyer, if any, in this state. In addition, the judgment creditor may mail a notice of the filing of the judgment to the judgment debtor and may file proof of mailing with the Clerk. Lack of mailing notice of filing by the Clerk shall not affect the enforcement proceedings if proof of mailing by the judgment creditor has been filed.

[(c) No execution or other process for enforcement of a foreign judgment filed hereunder shall issue until [ ] days after the date the judgment is filed.]

§ 4. Stay. (a) If the judgment debtor shows the [District Court of any city or county] that an appeal from the foreign judgment is pending or will be taken, or that a stay of execution has been granted, the court shall stay enforcement of the foreign judgment until the appeal is concluded, the time for appeal expires, or the stay of execution expires or is vacated, upon proof that the judgment debtor has furnished the security for the satisfaction of the judgment required by the state in which it was rendered.

(b) If the judgment debtor shows the [District Court of any city or county] any ground upon which enforcement of a judgment of any [District Court of any city or county] of this state would be stayed, the court shall stay enforcement of the foreign judgment for an appropriate period, upon requiring the same security for satisfaction of the judgment which is required in this state.

§ 6. Optional Procedure. The right of a judgment creditor to bring an action to enforce his judgment instead of proceeding under this Act remains unimpaired.

NOTES

1. As of 2021, the 1964 Revision of the Uniform Act had been adopted in 48 states, the District of Columbia, and the Virgin Islands; it had been introduced in Massachusetts. It is discussed in Homburger, Recognition and Enforcement of Foreign Judgments, 18 Am.J.Comp.L. 367 (1970). See also Brand, Enforcement of Judgments in the United States and Europe, 13 J.L. & Com. 193 (1994); Brand, Enforcement of Foreign Money-Judgments in the United States: In Search of Uniformity and International Acceptance, 67 Notre Dame L.Rev. 253 (1991); Zitter, Annotation, 88 A.L.R.5th 545 (2001).

2. Undoubtedly, Congress has power to provide in the case of sister state judgments for a system of registration under which a duly registered judgment could be enforced just like a domestic judgment. See Note, Constitutionality of a Uniform Reciprocal Registration of Judgments Statute, 36 N.Y.U.L.Rev. 488 (1961); Cook, The Powers of Congress under the Full Faith and Credit Clause, 28 Yale L.J. 421 (1919).

3. *Australia*, which has a federal system much like our own, has provided by an act of its Parliament for the registration throughout the

Commonwealth of local state judgments. This act applies not only to judgments for money but also to those which order or forbid the doing of acts. Service and Execution of Process Act, 1901–1963 (11 Commonwealth Acts 359 (1901–1963)). See also Foreign Judgments Act 1991 (Cth.), as applied in Jenton Overseas Investment Pty. Ltd. v. Townsing, [2008] VSC 470 (S.Ct.Victoria). In *Canada*, the Enforcement of Canadian Judgments Act, enacted by several, but nor all, Canadian Provinces, likewise provides for registration. Janet Walker, Conflict of Laws—reissue 2016, Halsbury's Laws of Canada 549–52 (2016). See also Weintraub, Recognition and Enforcement of Judgments and Child Support Obligations in United States and Canadian Courts, 34 Texas Int'l L.J. 361 (1999). In the *United Kingdom*, statutes provide for a similar system of registration in the case of judgments rendered in any division of the United Kingdom and also, where the court thinks it "just and convenient," in the case of those rendered in Commonwealth countries. Administration of Justice Act, 1920, 10 & 11 Geo. 5, c. 81. Moreover, the Foreign Judgments (Reciprocal Enforcement) Act, 1933, 23 Geo. 5, c. 13, authorizes the extension by Order in Council of the registration system to money judgments rendered in foreign countries which are prepared to give substantial reciprocity of treatment to judgments originally handed down in the United Kingdom.[7] Thus, the enforcement of intra-Commonwealth and, in some cases, of international judgments in the United Kingdom is easier than the method that generally prevails in this country for the enforcement of sister state judgments. See also, Private International Law (Miscellaneous Provisions) Act 1995 (c. 42).

For a discussion of the British statutory system of registration, see Torremans & Fawcett, Cheshire, North & Fawcett's Private International Law 591–601 (15th ed.2017); Graveson, Conflict of Laws 235–45 (7th ed.1974); Dicey, Morris & Collins, Conflict of Laws 745 et seq. (15th ed.2012) & 194 et seq. (15th ed. Supp. 4th 2017).

B. JUDGMENTS BASED ON JURISDICTION OVER THINGS OR OVER STATUS

Judgments of this sort do not impose a personal obligation upon the defendant and hence, unlike in personam judgments, cannot be enforced by a personal action in other states. Their basic effects in the state of rendition are set forth in the Restatement, Second, Judgments:

§ 30. Judgments Based on Jurisdiction to Determine Interests in Things

A valid and final judgment in an action based only on jurisdiction to determine interests in a thing:

(1) Is conclusive as to those interests with regard to all persons, if the judgment purports to have that effect

---

[7] A number of countries have been so specified: Australian capital territory, Austria, France, Germany, Guernsey, India, Isle of Man, Israel, Jersey, The Netherlands, Norway, and Pakistan. The provisions of the Foreign Judgments Act, 1933, have been extended to apply to judgments of the supreme courts of these countries. Judgments of American courts do not benefit from the registration procedure.

(traditionally described as "in rem"), or with regard to the named parties, if the judgment purports to have that effect (traditionally described as "quasi in rem"); and

(2) Does not bind anyone with respect to a personal liability; and

(3) Is conclusive between parties, in accordance with the rules of issue preclusion, as to any issues actually litigated by them and determined in the action.

Sec. 31 states an analogous rule with respect to judgments determining status.

These being the basic effects of such judgments in F-1, to what extent, if at all, do they differ when the judgment is placed in issue in F-2?

Combs v. Combs
Supreme Court of Kentucky, 1933.
249 Ky. 155, 60 S.W.2d 368.

[The case appears p. 167, supra.]

Harnischfeger Sales Corp. v. Sternberg Dredging Co.
Supreme Court of Mississippi, 1939.
189 Miss. 73, 191 So. 94.

[Harnischfeger Sales Corporation sold a dredge to Sternberg Dredging Company, taking notes secured by a chattel mortgage for a part of the purchase price. Thereafter, Harnischfeger started a suit in Louisiana to enforce the chattel mortgage, and prayed a personal judgment for $16,000 on the notes. Sternberg appeared and moved to dismiss for want of jurisdiction. This plea was overruled. Sternberg then pleaded that the dredge was defective and did not meet warranties which were given at the time of sale. The trial court in Louisiana, after a full trial on the merits of this question, entered a decree that the machine be sold and also rendered a personal judgment against Sternberg for the amount due on the notes. The Supreme Court of Louisiana affirmed the judgment enforcing the lien of the chattel mortgage, but held that the trial court did not have jurisdiction to enter a personal judgment and reversed that part of its judgment. See Harnischfeger Sale Corp. v. Sternberg Co., 179 La. 317, 154 So. 10 (1934).

Harnischfeger then started the present suit in Mississippi, where it obtained personal jurisdiction over Sternberg. The suit in Mississippi was to recover the balance due on the notes after making allowance for the amount obtained through the sale of the dredge in the Louisiana proceedings. Sternberg defended on the ground of breach of warranty and fraud, and Harnischfeger replied that that issue was res judicata as a result of the Louisiana judgment. The trial court struck out the plea of res judicata, and on the merits held in favor of Sternberg on the defense of breach of warranty. Harnischfeger then appealed.]

■ MCGOWAN, JUSTICE. . . . At the outset we will state that the effect of the estoppel by the final decree of the Supreme Court of Louisiana is to be determined by the laws of that state where the decree was rendered, and this seems to be an accepted and universal rule. . . .

. . . The ultimate facts as to whether or not a debt existed that would authorize the enforcement of a lien are the same in both the Louisiana and the Mississippi courts. The litigation was between the same parties, the same subject, the only difference in the pleas and proof in the two courts being a change in the name of the pleading. The same cause of action was alleged in the Louisiana Court as was interposed and allowed by the lower court in this state, and that cause of action was, when the case is stripped to the bone, that the machine delivered would not and did not carry a two-yard bucket, and by this we understand it to mean that the machine was not capacitated to be filled with two yards of earth and successfully dumped therefrom. . . .

It is said that the Louisiana decree cannot operate as res adjudicata or estoppel because the Supreme Court held that the proceeding was in rem. 179 La. 317, 154 So. 10. The appellant, Harnischfeger Sales Corporation, is not seeking here to bring a suit on the contention that the Louisiana judgment and action of that court, on the defense thereto, operated as a judgment which concluded the parties as to the amount of the judgment. The contention of the appellant is, as we understand it, that the Sternberg Dredging Company interposed the same defense in the Louisiana court as it interposed in the case at bar, and as to that defense the doctrine of res adjudicata is interposed and effective to conclude it, even though the proceedings in Louisiana to enforce a chattel mortgage on the thing mortgaged in that state were in rem. The appellee had its option to stand on the want of jurisdiction of the Court, but it did not do so. It appeared there. Sternberg, the main witness in both trials, testified to the same salient facts as to this defense in the Louisiana Court as was testified by him in the Mississippi Court in the case at bar. We are of the opinion that the defense was adjudged and concluded as to that defense and that every court everywhere would be bound to so hold. . . .

When the Sternberg Dredging Company decided and elected to resist the entry of any decree in rem against the machine and to interpose the breach-of-warranty defense, it thereby concluded itself irrevocably. Suppose the Louisiana Court had taken the opposite view and had determined in the court of last resort that the defense was valid in that it extinguished the debt? By that decree it would have retained the machine free from the lien; and, certainly where both parties appeared and contested the issue, debt or no debt, because of a breach of warranty, that decree would be final and conclusive on that issue actually litigated, and we think under the statute controlling in Louisiana would be res adjudicata. Such statute is as follows: "The authority of the thing adjudged takes place only with respect to what was the object of the judgment. The thing demanded must be the same; the demand must be founded on the same cause of action; the demand must be between the same parties, and formed by them against each other in the same quality." Art. 2286, Louisiana Civil Code. . . .

We are, therefore, of the opinion that the court below erred in striking the plea of res adjudicata and declining to allow it as an estoppel to the defense here involved. . . .

Reversed, and judgment for appellant.

NOTES

1. In a further opinion in 195 So. 322 (Miss.1940), the court refused to modify this opinion against the contention that the issue raised in the Louisiana proceeding was breach of warranty, while in the Mississippi suit the defendant relied on fraud. The court held that the same evidence bore on the questions of fraud and breach of warranty, and that the two defenses were really the same though "here the name given the counterclaim is different from that given it in the Louisiana court."

2. What accounts for the different effect given the judgment of F-1 (Arkansas) in the *Combs* case, p. 167, supra, and the judgment of F-1 (Louisiana) in the *Harnischfeger* case?

3. The defendant is faced with a dilemma when suit is brought in a state whose sole basis of jurisdiction is the presence there of the defendant's property. If the defendant does not appear and defend on the merits, he stands a strong risk of losing the property. He will not be bound, however, under principles of res judicata by any finding of fact that the court may have made. On the other hand, if he enters a defense on the merits, he runs the risk that the findings made by the court will be binding upon him everywhere. It has been argued that to place the defendant in such a position is so unfair as to violate due process. Taintor, Foreign Judgments in Rem: Full Faith and Credit v. Res Judicata in Personam, 8 U.Pitt.L.Rev. 223, 226 (1942). For a decision following *Harnischfeger*, see Paris v. Cooper, 279 S.E.2d 507 (Ga.App.1981); for critical discussion of the case law and literature, see Minichiello v. Rosenberg, 410 F.2d 106, 111–13 (2d Cir.1968).

To mitigate this problem, a fair number of courts permit the defendant to make a so-called limited appearance. By means of this device, the defendant can appear and resist on the merits and yet be protected from the entry of a personal judgment against him. In some states, he may further be protected from being collaterally bound as to issues actually litigated. It seems probable that the practical significance of a limited appearance has been diminished substantially by the ruling of the Supreme Court in Shaffer v. Heitner, 433 U.S. 186 (1977), p. 173, supra. This is because the property owner may now invoke the principles of *International Shoe* (p. 65, supra) in an attempt to have the action wholly terminated. Restatement, Second, Judgments 8, comment *g*.

The problem also arises in other legal systems. In 1981, the European Court of Justice had to answer the question whether contesting jurisdiction constituted an "appearance" under the (then) Brussels Convention (now Brussels-Ia Regulation Art. 26) when the defendant also made submissions on the merits. The Court held that it did not, so long as the defendant made it clear from the beginning that he or she was contesting jurisdiction and did not just raise this point as an afterthought, having already addressed the merits. Elefanten Schuh GmbH v. Jacqmain, [1981] ECR 1671.

SECTION 3. PARTICULAR EFFECTS

A. PERSONS AFFECTED[*]

NOTES

1.   RESTATEMENT, SECOND, CONFLICT OF LAWS

§ 94. Persons Affected

What persons are bound by a valid judgment is determined, subject to constitutional limitations, by the local law of the State where the judgment was rendered.

Comment:

. . .

d.   Privies. Subject to constitutional limitations (see Comment b), the local law of the State where the judgment was rendered determines which persons are in privity with the parties to the action and hence are bound by and entitled to the benefits of the rules of res judicata. This law determines whether the judgment was rendered in a class action and, if so, which persons are members of the class and the extent to which the interests of these persons are affected by the judgment. This law likewise determines, for example, whether the term "privies" includes those who control an action although not parties to it, those whose interests are represented by a party to the action and those who are successors in interest to a party to the action. . . .

2.   The various situations where privity is commonly found to exist in local law are set forth in Restatement, Second, Judgments § 41.

---

[*]   See generally Restatement, Judgments, Second §§ 34–63.

Riley v. New York Trust Co.

Supreme Court of the United States, 1942.
315 U.S. 343, 62 S.Ct. 608, 86 L.Ed. 885.

Certiorari to the Supreme Court of Delaware.

■ JUSTICE REED delivered the opinion of the Court.

Coca-Cola International Corporation, incorporated in Delaware, filed a bill of interpleader in a Delaware Court of Chancery against Julian Riley and Hughes Spalding, petitioners here, the Executors of Mrs. Julia M. Hungerford, with letters testamentary issued by the Court of Ordinary of Fulton County, Georgia, and against the New York Trust Company, the respondent, a New York corporation, as temporary administrator (afterward administrator c.t.a.) of the same decedent, appointed by the Surrogate's Court for New York County, New York.

The Georgia executors and the New York administrator each claim the right to have transferred to them, in their representative capacity, stock in the Coca-Cola Corporation now on its books in the name of the decedent. The outstanding certificates are in Georgia, in the hands of the Georgia executors. The parties are agreed, and it is therefore assumed, that Delaware is the situs of the stock. In accordance with the prayer of the bill, the Delaware court directed the adversary claimants to interplead between themselves as to their respective claims.

The Georgia executors assert that original domiciliary probate of Mrs. Hungerford's will in solemn form was obtained by them in Georgia, with all beneficiaries and heirs at law of testatrix, including her husband, Robert Hungerford, actual parties by personal service. These, it is conceded, were all the parties under the law of Georgia entitled to be heard on the probate of the will. The respondent administrator c.t.a. was not a party. The record of probate includes a determination by special finding, over the objection of the caveator, the husband, that the testatrix was domiciled in Georgia. The special finding was specifically approved as an essential fact to determine the jurisdiction of the Court of Ordinary by the highest court of Georgia in its affirmance of the probate. Hungerford v. Spalding, 183 Ga. 547, 189 S.E. 2. . . .

From the facts alleged, petitioners inferred the conclusive establishment of the place for domiciliary distribution against "all persons," and prayed the issue to them of new certificates. An offer was made to pay all Delaware taxes or charges on the stock.

Respondent admitted that all parties entitled under the law of Georgia to be heard in opposition to probate were actually before the Georgia courts. It denied that Mrs. Hungerford was domiciled in Georgia or that the Georgia judgment of domicile and probate was binding on it, and averred testatrix's domicile at death was New York. It further averred that there were New York creditors of the estate interested in the proper and lawful administration of the estate, and that New York had certain claims for inheritance and estate taxes. Its own subsequent appointment by the Surrogate's Court of New York County, New York, on the suggestion of testatrix's husband and the State Tax Commission, was pleaded with applicable provisions of New York probate and estate tax law. By stipulation it was established that petitioners and the heirs and beneficiaries of testatrix, except her husband, who was an actual party, were notified of the New York proceedings for probate only by publication or substituted service of the citation in Georgia, and did not appear. As a domiciliary administrator c.t.a., the respondent prayed the issue to it of new certificates for the stock in controversy.

The trial court concluded from the evidence adduced at the hearings that the testatrix was domiciled in Georgia. It was therefore, as the court stated, unnecessary for it to consider the binding effect of the Georgia judgment. The Supreme Court of Delaware reversed this finding of fact, determined that New York was testatrix's domicile and denied petitioners' contention that Article IV, 1, of the Constitution required the award of the certificates of stock to the Georgia executors. The Coca-Cola Corporation was directed to issue its stock certificate to the respondent, the New York administrator c.t.a. New York Trust Co. v. Riley, 16 A.2d 772. . . .

The constitutional effect of the Georgia decree on a claim in his own name in another state by a party to the Georgia proceedings is not here involved. The question we are to decide is whether this Georgia judgment on domicile conclusively establishes the right of the Georgia executors to demand delivery to them of personal assets of their testatrix which another state is willing to surrender to the domiciliary personal representative, when another representative, appointed by a third state, asserts a similar domiciliary right. For the purpose of this review, the conclusion of Delaware that the testatrix was in fact domiciled in New York is accepted. The answer to the question lies in the extent to which Article IV, § 1, of the Constitution, as made applicable by R.S. § 905, nevertheless controls Delaware's action.

This clause of the Constitution brings to our Union a useful means for ending litigation. Matters once decided between adverse parties in any state or territory are at rest. Were it not for this full faith and credit provision, so far as the Constitution controls the matter, adversaries could wage again their legal battles whenever they met in other jurisdictions. Each state could control its own courts but itself could not project the effect of its decisions beyond its own boundaries. Cf. Pennoyer v. Neff, 95 U.S. 714, 722. That clause compels that controversies be stilled, so that, where a state court has jurisdiction of the parties and subject matter, its judgment controls in other states to the same extent as it does in the state where rendered. Roche v. McDonald, 275 U.S. 449, 451. . . . By the Constitutional provision for full faith and credit, the local doctrines of *res judicata*, speaking generally, become a part of national jurisprudence, and therefore federal questions cognizable here.

. . . The full faith and credit clause allows Delaware, in disposing of local assets, to determine the question of domicile anew for any interested party who is not bound by participation in the Georgia proceeding [Citing cases.] It must be admitted that this re-examination may result in conflicting decisions upon domicile, but that is an inevitable consequence of the existing federal system, which endows its citizens with the freedom to choose the state or states within which they desire to carry on business, enjoy their leisure or establish their residences. Worcester County Co. v. Riley, 302 U.S. 292, 299. But, while allowing Delaware to determine domicile for itself, where any interested party is not bound by the Georgia proceedings, the full faith and credit clause and R.S. § 905, do require that Delaware shall give Georgia judgments such faith and credit "as they have by law or usage" in Georgia. . . .

We find nothing in [Tant v. Wigfall, 65 Ga. 412 (1880), and Wash v. Dickson, 147 Ga. 540, 94 S.E. 1009 (1918)] which would lead to the conclusion that, in Georgia, the New York administrator c.t.a. was in privity, so far as the sequestration of assets for the payment of death taxes or indebtedness of decedent or her estate is concerned, with any parties before the Georgia court, or that the New York representative could not take steps in Georgia courts which might result in its getting possession of any assets which under the Georgia law of administration would be properly deliverable to a foreign domiciliary administrator. . . . Hence, if the Georgia judgment is to bind the New York administrator, it can be considered to do so only *in rem*.

. . . It may be assumed that the judgment of probate and domicile is a judgment *in rem* . . . But this does not bar litigation anew by a stranger, of facts upon which the decree *in rem* is based. . . . While the Georgia judgment is to have the same faith and credit in Delaware as it does in Georgia, that requirement does not give the Georgia judgment extra-territorial effect upon assets in other states. So far as the assets in Georgia are concerned, the Georgia judgment of probate is *in rem;* so far as it affects personalty beyond the state, it is *in personam* and can bind only parties thereto or their privies. This is the result of the ruling in Baker v. Baker, Eccles & Co., 242 U.S. 394, 400.[13] Phrased somewhat

---

[13] Illustrative state cases.

A will is admitted to original domiciliary probate in state A. Thereafter an ancillary proceeding is commenced in state B based upon the domiciliary determination of A. At that point a beneficiary, a stranger to the proceeding in A, appears and asserts that the decedent was domiciled in B. The determination of domicile by state A will not be recognized by state B, but state B will take evidence and redetermine the issue of domicile. Estate of Clark, 148 Cal. 108, 82 P. 760. . . .

If the objector was privy to the proceeding in state A, state B will not redetermine the issue of domicile. Willetts' Appeal, 50 Conn. 330. . . .

Where the proceeding in state B is by a stranger to the proceedings for original domiciliary probate in state A upon the theory that the domicile is actually B, state B will determine domicile for itself. Scripps v. Wayne Probate Judge, 131 Mich. 265, 90 N.W. 1061. . . .

Where the person seeking to establish domicile in state B, and to have original domiciliary probate there, was a party to the proceeding in state A, state B will not redetermine domicile.

differently, if the effect of a probate decree in Georgia *in personam* was to bar a stranger to the decree from later asserting his rights, such a holding would deny procedural due process.

It seems quite obvious that the administrator c.t.a., appears in Delaware as an agency of the State of New York, and not as the *alter ego* of the beneficiaries of the Hungerford estate. In its answer to the petitioners' statement of claim, it established its status by alleging that not merely the beneficiaries but creditors residing in New York and the State of New York were interested in the estate, that its appointment as temporary administrator had been sought by the New York Tax Commissioner "to protect the claim of the State of New York to inheritance and succession taxes," that the State of New York was asserting such claims in substantial amount on the theory that the domicile was New York. . . .

Georgia and New York might each assert its right to administer the estates of its domiciliaries to protect its sovereign interests, and Delaware was free to decide for itself which claimant is entitled to receive the portion of Mrs. Hungerford's personalty within Delaware's borders.

Affirmed.

■ CHIEF JUSTICE STONE: I concur upon the single ground that the New York administrator was not bound by the Georgia judgment. He was not a party to the Georgia proceedings, nor was he represented by any of those who were parties. As administrator appointed under the New York statutes, he was charged with the duty of administering the estate of the decedent and paying inheritance taxes upon it. His interest so far as he owes duties to the state is therefore adverse to that of the husband and the next of kin, who alone were parties to the Georgia proceeding. To have bound him by representation of those so adverse in interest would have been a denial of due process. Hansberry v. Lee, 311 U.S. 32. A judgment so obtained is not entitled to full faith and credit with respect to those not parties. . . . Any other conclusion would foreclose New York from litigating its right to collect taxes lawfully due, by the simple expedient of a probate by the next of kin of the will of the decedent as the domiciled resident of another state, without notice to any representative of New York or opportunity to be heard.

It is unnecessary to consider the other questions discussed by the opinion.

■ JUSTICE FRANKFURTER and JUSTICE JACKSON concur in this opinion.

Hopper v. Nicholas, 106 Ohio St. 292, 140 N.E. 186. . . . [Footnote by the Court. Other footnotes omitted.]

Taylor v. Sturgell

Supreme Court of the United States, 2008.
553 U.S. 880, 128 S.Ct. 2161, 171 L.Ed.2d 155.

■ JUSTICE GINSBURG delivered the opinion of the Court.

"It a principle of general application in Anglo-American jurisprudence that one is not bound by a judgment in personam in a litigation in which he is not designated as a party or to which he has not been made a party by service of process." Hansberry v. Lee, 311 U.S. 32 (1940). Several exceptions, recognized in this Court's decisions, temper this basic rule. In a class action, for example, a person not named as a party may be bound by a judgment on the merits of the action, if she was adequately represented by a party who actively participated in the litigation. See id., at 41. In this case, we consider for the first time whether there is a "virtual representation" exception to the general rule against precluding nonparties. Adopted by a number of courts, including the courts below in the case now before us, the exception so styled is broader than any we have so far approved.

The virtual representation question we examine in this opinion arises in the following context. Petitioner Brent Taylor filed a lawsuit under the Freedom of Information Act seeking certain documents from the Federal Aviation Administration. Greg Herrick, Taylor's friend, had previously brought an unsuccessful suit seeking the same records. The two men have no legal relationship, and there is no evidence that Taylor controlled, financed, participated in, or even had notice of Herrick's earlier suit. Nevertheless, the D.C. Circuit held Taylor's suit precluded by the judgment against Herrick because, in that court's assessment, Herrick qualified as Taylor's "virtual representative."

We disapprove the doctrine of preclusion by "virtual representation," and hold, based on the record as it now stands, that the judgment against Herrick does not bar Taylor from maintaining this suit.

I

The Freedom of Information Act (FOIA) accords "any person" a right to request any records held by a federal agency. 5 U.S.C. § 552(a)(3)(A) (2006 ed.). No reason need be given for a FOIA request, and unless the requested materials fall within one of the Act's enumerated exemptions, see § 552(a)(3)(E), (b), the agency must "make the records promptly available" to the requester, § 552(a)(3)(A). If an agency refuses to furnish the requested records, the requester may file suit in federal court and obtain an injunction "order[ing] the production of any agency records improperly withheld." § 552(a)(4)(B).

The courts below held the instant FOIA suit barred by the judgment in earlier litigation seeking the same records.

* * * [The opinion's extensive account of the history of the prior and of the present case is omitted.]

II

The preclusive effect of a federal-court judgment is determined by federal common law. See Semtek Int'l Inc. v. Lockheed Martin Corp., 531 U.S. 497, 507–508, 121 S.Ct. 1021, 149 L.Ed.2d 32 (2001). For judgments in federal-question cases—for example, Herrick's FOIA suit—federal courts participate in developing "uniform federal rule[s]" of res judicata, which this Court has ultimate authority to determine and declare. Id., at 508, 121 S.Ct. 1021.[4] The federal common law of preclusion is, of course, subject to due process limitations. See Richards v. Jefferson County, 517 U.S. 793, 797, 116 S. Ct. 1761, 135 L. Ed. 2d 76 (1996).

Taylor's case presents an issue of first impression in this sense: Until now, we have never addressed the doctrine of "virtual representation" adopted (in varying forms) by several Circuits and relied upon by the courts below. Our inquiry, however, is guided by well-established precedent regarding the propriety of nonparty preclusion. We review that precedent before taking up directly the issue of virtual representation.

A

The preclusive effect of a judgment is defined by claim preclusion and issue preclusion, which are collectively referred to as "res judicata."[5] Under the doctrine of claim preclusion, a final judgment forecloses "successive litigation of the very same claim, whether or not relitigation of the claim raises the same issues as the earlier suit." New Hampshire v. Maine, 532 U.S. 742, 748, 121 S.Ct. 1808, 149 L.Ed.2d 968 (2001). Issue preclusion, in contrast, bars "successive litigation of an issue of fact or law actually litigated and resolved in a valid court determination essential to the prior judgment," even if the issue recurs in the context of a different claim. Id., at 748–749, 121 S.Ct. 1808, 149 L.Ed.2d 968. By "preclud[ing] parties from contesting matters that they have had a full and fair opportunity to litigate," these two doctrines protect against "the expense and vexation attending multiple lawsuits, conserv[e] judicial resources, and foste[r] reliance on judicial action by minimizing the possibility of inconsistent decisions." Montana v. United States, 440 U.S. 147, 153–154, 99 S.Ct. 970, 59 L.Ed.2d 210 (1979).

A person who was not a party to a suit generally has not had a "full and fair opportunity to litigate" the claims and issues settled in that suit. The application of claim and issue preclusion to nonparties thus runs up against the "deep-rooted historic tradition that everyone should have his own day in court." Richards, 517 U.S., at 798, 116 S.Ct. 1761, 135 L.Ed.2d 76 (internal quotation marks omitted). Indicating the strength of that

---

[4]   For judgments in diversity cases, federal law incorporates the rules of preclusion applied by the State in which the rendering court sits. See Semtek Int'l Inc. v. Lockheed Martin Corp., 531 U.S. 497, 508, 121 S.Ct. 1021, 149 L.Ed.2d 32 (2001).

[5]   These terms have replaced a more confusing lexicon. Claim preclusion describes the rules formerly known as "merger" and "bar," while issue preclusion encompasses the doctrines once known as "collateral estoppel" and "direct estoppel." See Migra v. Warren City School Dist. Bd. of Ed., 465 U.S. 75, 77, n. 1, 104 S.Ct. 892, 79 L.Ed.2d 56 (1984).

tradition, we have often repeated the general rule that "one is not bound by a judgment in personam in a litigation in which he is not designated as a party or to which he has not been made a party by service of process." Hansberry, 311 U.S., at 40.

B

Though hardly in doubt, the rule against nonparty preclusion is subject to exceptions. For present purposes, the recognized exceptions can be grouped into six categories.[6]

First, "[a] person who agrees to be bound by the determination of issues in an action between others is bound in accordance with the terms of his agreement." 1 Restatement (Second) of Judgments § 40, p. 390 (1980) (hereinafter Restatement). For example, "if separate actions involving the same transaction are brought by different plaintiffs against the same defendant, all the parties to all the actions may agree that the question of the defendant's liability will be definitely determined, one way or the other, in a 'test case.' " D. Shapiro, Civil Procedure: Preclusion in Civil Actions 77–78 (2001) (hereinafter Shapiro).[7]

Second, nonparty preclusion may be justified based on a variety of pre-existing "substantive legal relationship[s]" between the person to be bound and a party to the judgment. Shapiro 78. See also Richards, 517 U.S., at 798, 116 S.Ct. 1761, 135 L.Ed.2d 76. Qualifying relationships include, but are not limited to, preceding and succeeding owners of property, bailee and bailor, and assignee and assignor. See 2 Restatement §§ 43–44, 52, 55. These exceptions originated "as much from the needs of property law as from the values of preclusion by judgment." 18A C. Wright, A. Miller, & E. Cooper, Federal Practice and Procedure § 4448, p. 329 (2d ed.2002) (hereinafter Wright & Miller).[8]

Third, we have confirmed that, "in certain limited circumstances," a nonparty may be bound by a judgment because she was "adequately represented by someone with the same interests who [wa]s a party" to the suit. Richards, 517 U.S., at 798, 116 S.Ct. 1761 (internal quotation marks omitted). Representative suits with preclusive effect on nonparties include properly conducted class actions, see Martin, 490 U.S., at 762, n.

---

[6] The established grounds for nonparty preclusion could be organized differently. See, e.g., 1 & 2 Restatement (Second) of Judgments §§ 39–62 (1980) (hereinafter Restatement); D. Shapiro, Civil Procedure: Preclusion in Civil Actions 75–92 (2001); 18A C. Wright, A. Miller, & E. Cooper, Federal Practice and Procedure § 4448, pp. 327–329 (2d ed. 2002) (hereinafter Wright & Miller). The list that follows is meant only to provide a framework for our consideration of virtual representation, not to establish a definitive taxonomy.

[7] The Restatement observes that a nonparty may be bound not only by express or implied agreement, but also through conduct inducing reliance by others. See 2 Restatement §§ 62. See also 18A Wright & Miller § 4453, pp. 425–429. We have never had occasion to consider this ground for nonparty preclusion, and we express no view on it here.

[8] The substantive legal relationships justifying preclusion are sometimes collectively referred to as "privity." See, e.g., Richards v. Jefferson County, 517 U.S. 793, 798, 116 S.Ct. 1761, 135 L.Ed.2d 76 (1996); 2 Restatement § 62, Comment a. The term "privity," however, has also come to be used more broadly, as a way to express the conclusion that nonparty preclusion is appropriate on any ground. See 18A Wright & Miller § 4449, pp. 351–353, and n. 33 (collecting cases). To ward off confusion, we avoid using the term "privity" in this opinion.

2, 109 S.Ct. 2180 (citing Fed. Rule Civ. Proc. 23), and suits brought by trustees, guardians, and other fiduciaries, see Sea-Land Services, Inc. v. Gaudet, 414 U.S. 573, 593, 94 S.Ct. 806, 39 L.Ed.2d 9 (1974). See also 1 Restatement § 41.

Fourth, a nonparty is bound by a judgment if she "assume[d] control" over the litigation in which that judgment was rendered. Montana, 440 U.S., at 154, 99 S. Ct. 970. See also Schnell v. Peter Eckrich & Sons, Inc., 365 U.S. 260, 262, n. 4, 81 S. Ct. 557, 5 L. Ed. 2d 546 (1961); 1 Restatement § 39. Because such a person has had "the opportunity to present proofs and argument," he has already "had his day in court" even though he was not a formal party to the litigation. Id., Comment *a*, p. 382.

Fifth, a party bound by a judgment may not avoid its preclusive force by relitigating through a proxy. Preclusion is thus in order when a person who did not participate in a litigation later brings suit as the designated representative of a person who was a party to the prior adjudication. See Chicago, R. I. & P. R. Co. v. Schendel, 270 U.S. 611, 620, 623, 46 S. Ct. 420, 70 L. Ed. 757 (1926); 18A Wright & Miller § 4454, pp. 433–434. And although our decisions have not addressed the issue directly, it also seems clear that preclusion is appropriate when a nonparty later brings suit as an agent for a party who is bound by a judgment. See id., § 4449, p. 335.

Sixth, in certain circumstances a special statutory scheme may "expressly foreclos[e] successive litigation by nonlitigants . . . if the scheme is otherwise consistent with due process." Martin, 490 U.S., at 762, n. 2, 109 S. Ct. 2180. Examples of such schemes include bankruptcy and probate proceedings, see ibid., and quo warranto actions or other suits that, "under [the governing] law, [may] be brought only on behalf of the public at large," Richards, 517 U.S., at 804, 116 S.Ct. 1761.

III

Reaching beyond these six established categories, some lower courts have recognized a "virtual representation" exception to the rule against nonparty preclusion. Decisions of these courts, however, have been far from consistent. Some Circuits use the label, but define "virtual representation" so that it is no broader than the recognized exception for adequate representation. . . . But other courts, including the Eighth, Ninth, and D.C. Circuits, apply multifactor tests for virtual representation that permit nonparty preclusion in cases that do not fit within any of the established exceptions. . . .

A

The D.C. Circuit purported to ground its virtual representation doctrine in this Court's decisions stating that, in some circumstances, a person may be bound by a judgment if she was adequately represented by a party to the proceeding yielding that judgment. See 490 F.3d at 970–

971. But the D. C. Circuit's definition of "adequate representation" strayed from the meaning our decisions have attributed to that term.

In Richards, we reviewed a decision by the Alabama Supreme Court holding that a challenge to a tax was barred by a judgment upholding the same tax in a suit filed by different taxpayers. 517 U.S., at 795–797, 116 S.Ct. 1761. The plaintiffs in the first suit "did not sue on behalf of a class," their complaint "did not purport to assert any claim against or on behalf of any nonparties," and the judgment "did not purport to bind" nonparties. Id., at 801, 116 S.Ct. 1761. There was no indication, we emphasized, that the court in the first suit "took care to protect the interests" of absent parties, or that the parties to that litigation "understood their suit to be on behalf of absent [parties]." Id., at 802, 116 S.Ct. 1761. In these circumstances, we held, the application of claim preclusion was inconsistent with "the due process of law guaranteed by the Fourteenth Amendment." Id., at 797, 116 S.Ct. 1761.

The D.C. Circuit stated, without elaboration, that it did not "read Richards to hold a nonparty . . . adequately represented only if special procedures were followed [to protect the nonparty] or the party to the prior suit understood it was representing the nonparty." 490 F.3d at 971. As the D.C. Circuit saw this case, Herrick adequately represented Taylor for two principal reasons: Herrick had a strong incentive to litigate; and Taylor later hired Herrick's lawyer, suggesting Taylor's "satisfaction with the attorney's performance in the prior case." Id., at 975.

The D.C. Circuit misapprehended Richards. As just recounted, our holding that the Alabama Supreme Court's application of res judicata to nonparties violated due process turned on the lack of either special procedures to protect the nonparties' interests or an understanding by the concerned parties that the first suit was brought in a representative capacity. See Richards, 517 U.S., at 801–802, 116 S.Ct. 1761. Richards thus established that representation is "adequate" for purposes of nonparty preclusion only if (at a minimum) one of these two circumstances is present. . .

Our decisions recognizing that a nonparty may be bound by a judgment if she was adequately represented by a party to the earlier suit thus provide no support for the D. C. Circuit's broad theory of virtual representation.

B

[Respondents] ask us to abandon the attempt to delineate discrete grounds and clear rules altogether. Preclusion is in order, they contend, whenever "the relationship between a party and a non-party is 'close enough' to bring the second litigant within the judgment." . . . Courts should make the "close enough" determination, they urge, through a "heavily fact-driven" and "equitable" inquiry.

We reject this argument for three reasons. First, our decisions emphasize the fundamental nature of the general rule that a litigant is not bound by a judgment to which she was not a party. . . . Respondents' amorphous balancing test is at odds with the constrained approach to nonparty preclusion our decisions advance. . . .

Our second reason for rejecting a broad doctrine of virtual representation rests on the limitations attending nonparty preclusion based on adequate representation. A party's representation of a nonparty is "adequate" for preclusion purposes only if, at a minimum: (1) the interests of the nonparty and her representative are aligned, see Hansberry, 311 U.S., at 43 and (2) either the party understood herself to be acting in representative capacity or the original court took care to protect the interests of the nonparty, see Richards, 517 U.S., at 801–802 . . . In addition, adequate representation sometimes requires (3) notice of the original suit to the persons alleged to have been represented, see Richards. In the class-action context, these limitations are implemented by the procedural safeguards contained in Federal Rule of Civil Procedure 23.

An expansive doctrine of virtual representation, however, would "recogniz[e], in effect, a common-law kind of class action." Tice, 162 F.3d at 972 (internal quotation marks omitted). That is, virtual representation would authorize preclusion based on identity of interests and some kind of relationship between parties and nonparties, shorn of the procedural protections prescribed in Hansberry, Richards, and Rule 23. These protections, grounded in due process, could be circumvented were we to approve a virtual representation doctrine that allowed courts to "create de facto class actions at will." Tice, 162 F.3d at 973.

Third, a diffuse balancing approach to nonparty preclusion would likely create more headaches than it relieves. Most obviously, it could significantly complicate the task of district courts faced in the first instance with preclusion questions. An all-things-considered balancing approach might spark wide-ranging, time-consuming, and expensive discovery tracking factors potentially relevant under seven-or five-prong tests. And after the relevant facts are established, district judges would be called upon to evaluate them under a standard that provides no firm guidance. . . .

C

Finally, relying on the Eighth Circuit's decision in Tyus, 93 F.3d at 456, the FAA maintains that nonparty preclusion should apply more broadly in "public-law" litigation than in "private-law" controversies. . . . [O]ur decision in Richards acknowledges that, in certain cases, the plaintiff has a reduced interest in controlling the litigation "because of the public nature of the right at issue." Brief for Respondent FAA 28. When a taxpayer challenges "an alleged misuse of public funds" or "other public action," we observed in Richards, the suit "has only an indirect impact on [the plaintiff's] interests." 517 U.S., at 803, 116 S. Ct. 1761. In actions of this character, the Court said, "we may assume that the States have wide latitude to establish procedures . . . to limit the number of judicial proceedings that may be entertained." Ibid.

Taylor's FOIA action falls within the category described in Richards, the FAA contends, because "the duty to disclose under FOIA is owed to the public generally." . . . [I]n contrast to the public-law litigation contemplated in Richards, [however,] a successful FOIA action results in a grant of relief to the individual plaintiff, not a decree benefiting the public at large.

Furthermore, we said in Richards only that, for the type of public-law claims there envisioned, States are free to adopt procedures limiting repetitive litigation. See 517 U.S., at 803 . . . In this regard, we referred to instances in which the first judgment foreclosed successive litigation by other plaintiffs because, "under state law, [the suit] could be brought only on behalf of the public at large." Id., at 804 . . . Richards spoke of state legislation, but it appears equally evident that Congress, in providing for actions vindicating a public interest, may "limit the number of judicial proceedings that may be entertained." Id., at 803. . . . It hardly follows, however, that this Court should proscribe or confine successive FOIA suits by different requesters. Indeed, Congress' provision for FOIA suits with no statutory constraint on successive actions counsels against judicial imposition of constraints through extraordinary application of the common law of preclusion. . . .

IV

For the foregoing reasons, we disapprove the theory of virtual representation on which the decision below rested. The preclusive effects of a judgment in a federal-question case decided by a federal court should instead be determined according to the established grounds for nonparty preclusion described in this opinion. See Part II-B, supra.

Although references to "virtual representation" have proliferated in the lower courts, our decision is unlikely to occasion any great shift in actual practice.

Many opinions use the term "virtual representation" in reaching results at least arguably defensible on established grounds. See 18A Wright & Miller § 4457, pp. 535–539, and n. 38 (collecting cases). In these cases, dropping the "virtual representation" label would lead to clearer analysis with little, if any, change in outcomes. See Tice, 162 F.3d at 971. ("[T]he term 'virtual representation' has cast more shadows than light on the problem [of nonparty preclusion].").

In some cases, however, lower courts have relied on virtual representation to extend nonparty preclusion beyond the latter doctrine's proper bounds. We now turn back to Taylor's action to determine whether his suit is such a case, or whether the result reached by the courts below can be justified on one of the recognized grounds for nonparty preclusion.

A

It is uncontested that four of the six grounds for nonparty preclusion have no application here: There is no indication that Taylor agreed to be bound by Herrick's litigation, that Taylor and Herrick have any legal relationship, that Taylor exercised any control over Herrick's suit, or that this suit implicates any special statutory scheme limiting relitigation. . . .

It is equally clear that preclusion cannot be justified on the theory that Taylor was adequately represented in Herrick's suit. . . .

That leaves only the fifth category: preclusion because a nonparty to an earlier litigation has brought suit as a representative or agent of a party who is bound by the prior adjudication. Taylor is not Herrick's legal representative and he has not purported to sue in a representative capacity. He concedes, however, that preclusion would be appropriate if respondents could demonstrate that he is acting as Herrick's "undisclosed agen[t]."

Respondents argue here, as they did below, that Taylor's suit is a collusive attempt to relitigate Herrick's action. We have never defined the showing required to establish that a nonparty to a prior adjudication has become a litigating agent for a party to the earlier case. Because the issue has not been briefed in any detail, we do not discuss the matter elaboratively here. We note, however, that courts should be cautious about finding preclusion on this basis. A mere whiff of "tactical maneuvering" will not suffice; instead, principles of agency law are suggestive. They indicate that preclusion is appropriate only if the putative agent's conduct of the suit is subject to the control of the party who is bound by the prior adjudication.

[V]acated and remanded . . .

NOTES

1. Justice Ginsburg writes of a "federal common law" of preclusion. Do the principles of preclusion law she states apply only in federal question cases or also when federal courts exercise diversity jurisdiction and apply state law to the substance of the case? See also Semtek International Inc. v. Lockheed Martin Corp., presented and discussed at p. 727, infra.

See Smith v. Bayer Corp., 564 U.S. 299, 131 S.Ct. 2368, 2372 (2011): nonparty preclusion only ". . . binds non-named members of 'properly conducted class actions' to judgments entered in such proceedings," citing to *Taylor*. How does a court get jurisdiction to affect the rights of non-residents, who are not in privity with one another, i.e., in so-called class or representative suits? Cf. Hansberry v. Lee, 311 U.S. 32 (1940), involving a suit brought to enjoin the breach of a restrictive covenant against selling land to black persons. The covenant by its terms was not effective unless it had been signed by the owners of 95 percent of the frontage within the area. The defense was that the required 95 percent had not signed. This was answered with a plea of res judicata based on an earlier suit. The defendants were not parties in this suit, but the Supreme Court of Illinois held that the earlier suit was a "class" or "representative" suit, and that all members of the class were bound by the decree. The Supreme Court of the United States reversed, holding that under the facts of the case there was not a "class" since all persons concerned did not have the same interest. It recognized, however, the possibility of binding absent parties in a class suit. It said (pp. 40–42):

> "It is a principle of general application in Anglo-American jurisprudence that one is not bound by a judgment *in personam* in a litigation in which he is not designated as a party or to which he has not been made a party by service of process. . . .

> "To these general rules there is a recognized exception that, to an extent not precisely defined by judicial opinion, the judgment in a 'class' or 'representative' suit, to which some members of the class are parties, may bind members of the class or those represented who were not made parties to it.

> ". . . [T]here is scope within the framework of the Constitution for holding in appropriate cases that a judgment rendered in a class suit is *res judicata* as to members of the class who are not formal parties to the suit. . . . With a proper regard for divergent local institutions and interests, . . . , the Court is justified in saying that there has been a failure of due process only in those cases where it cannot be said that the procedure adopted, fairly insures the protection of the interests of absent parties who are to be bound by it . . ."

A number of decisions have sought to limit, or at least not to extend *Taylor*. See, e.g., Ludwig v. Township of Van Buren, 682 F.3d 457 (6th Cir.2012) (*Taylor* does not extend to state preclusion rules, its footnote 6 makes clear that its list is not exclusive, and, besides, parties were in privity); Lutkauskas v. Ricker, 28 N.E.3d 727, 740 (Ill.2015) (distinguishing *Taylor* where each party had sought to vindicate an individual right, while in this case parties sought to vindicate a right of a third party), explained further in Arellano v. Leach, 2015 WL 5883016, *6 (N.D.Ill. 2015).

2.   Phillips Petroleum Co. v. Shutts, 472 U.S. 797 (1985), involved the question of the jurisdiction of a Kansas court to entertain a class action when the great majority of the plaintiff class were nonresidents of the state. The suit was to recover interest on delayed royalty payments for natural gas extracted from land located in 11 states. The class consisted of some 28,000 members who resided in all 50 states, in the District of Columbia and in several foreign countries. Fewer than 1,000 members of the class were residents of Kansas. Each member had been notified by mail of the pendency of the action and invited to attend in person or by counsel. Otherwise, the absent members would be represented by the class members who initiated the action and would be bound by the judgment unless they "opted out" of the action by returning a "request for exclusion." Held, that the Kansas court had jurisdiction over those members of the class who had not "opted out." The Court declared that the defendant was in error in arguing that Kansas could not exert jurisdiction over absentees' claims unless the absentees have

sufficient minimum contacts with Kansas. The Court said that fewer burdens and fewer risks are placed upon class plaintiffs than upon defendants. Due process requires only that class plaintiffs be given notice of the action, an opportunity to appear in person or by counsel, adequate representation and an opportunity to "opt out." They need not be required affirmatively to "opt into" the class. "The interests of the absent plaintiffs are sufficiently protected by the forum State when those plaintiffs are provided with a request for exclusion that can be returned within a reasonable time to the court." (472 U.S. at 812.) For the part of the Court's opinion dealing with questions of the applicable law, see p. 445, infra.

For an extensive discussion of *Phillips Petroleum* see Miller & Crump, Jurisdiction and Choice of Law in Multistate Class Actions After Phillips Petroleum Co. v. Shutts, 96 Yale L.J. 1 (1986).

3.   State v. Homeside Lending, Inc., 826 A.2d 997 (Vt.2003), held that Vermont members of a national class action in an Alabama state court were not bound by the judgment of that court approving a settlement because the Alabama proceeding violated their due process rights. Notice of the opportunity to opt out of the class action did not adequately inform members of the potential burdens of the litigation. The class representatives did not adequately represent absent class members because the incentive payments to the representatives provided an economic benefit far greater than the value of the settlement. Moreover, when a class action can impose monetary burdens on class members that exceed any benefits, a state court has personal jurisdiction only over those class members who have minimum contacts with the state.

4.   For discussion of limited versus broad collateral review of class action certification, see Hospitality Management Assoc. v. Shell Oil Co., 591 S.E.2d 611 (S.C.2004) (held: the proper scope of collateral review of a rendering court's rulings on the due process requirements for binding absent class members is limited to consideration of whether the procedures in the prior litigation allowed a full and fair opportunity to litigate the due process issues). See also Wolff, Preclusion in Class Action Litigation, 105 Colum.L.Rev. 717 (2005).

5.   For federal law of preclusion drawn from state law, see also Semtek International Inc. v. Lockheed Martin Corp., p. 727, infra.

Kremer v. Chemical Construction Corp.

Supreme Court of the United States, 1982.
456 U.S. 461, 102 S.Ct. 1883, 72 L.Ed.2d 262.

[The plaintiff filed a complaint with the Equal Employment Opportunity Commission (EEOC) under Title VII of the Civil Rights Act of 1964, complaining that his discharge from employment had been caused by illegal discrimination. As required by the Civil Rights Act, the Commission referred the charge to the New York State Division of Human Rights (NYHRD), the agency charged with enforcing the New York law against discrimination. The NYHRD rejected the claim as meritless and, on appeal to the New York Appellate Division, this decision was unanimously affirmed. The plaintiff then brought a Title VII action in a federal district court which dismissed the complaint on res judicata grounds and the Court of Appeals affirmed. This decision was in turn affirmed by the Supreme Court with four Justices dissenting.]

■ JUSTICE WHITE delivered the opinion of the Court.

. . . Section 1738 [quoted on pp. 46, supra] requires federal courts to give the same preclusive effect to state court judgments that those judgments would be given in the courts of the state from which the judgments emerged. Here the Appellate Division of the New York Supreme Court has issued a judgment affirming the decision of the NYHRD Appeals Board that the discharge and failure to rehire Kremer were not the product of the discrimination that he had alleged. There is no question that this judicial determination precludes Kremer from bringing "any other action, civil or criminal, based upon the same grievance" in the New York courts. N.Y.Exec.Law § 300 (McKinney 1972). By its terms, therefore, § 1738 would appear to preclude Kremer from relitigating the same question in federal court.

Kremer . . . suggests that in Title VII cases Congress intended that federal courts be relieved of their usual obligation to grant finality to state court decisions. . . .

. . . The petitioner . . . contends that the judgment should not bar his Title VII action because the New York courts did not resolve the issue that the District Court must hear under Title VII-whether Kremer had suffered discriminatory treatment-and because the procedures provided were inadequate. Neither contention is persuasive. Although the claims presented to the NYHRD and subsequently reviewed by the Appellate Division were necessarily based on New York law, the alleged discriminatory acts are prohibited by both federal and state laws. The elements of a successful employment discrimination claim are virtually identical; petitioner could not succeed on a Title VII claim consistently with the judgment of the NYHRD that there is no reason to believe he was terminated or not rehired because of national origin or religion. The Appellate Division's affirmance of the NYHRD's dismissal necessarily decided that petitioner's claim under New York law was meritless, and thus it also decided that a Title VII claim arising from the same events would be equally meritless. . . .

Our previous decisions have not specified the source or defined the content of the requirement that the first adjudication offer a full and fair opportunity to litigate. But for present purposes, where we are bound by the statutory directive of § 1738, state proceedings need do no more than satisfy the minimum procedural requirements of the Fourteenth Amendment's Due Process Clause in order to qualify for the full-faith-and-credit guaranteed by federal law. It has long been established that § 1738 does not allow federal courts to employ their own rules of res judicata in determining the effect of state judgments. Rather, it . . . commands a federal court to accept the rules chosen by the state from which the judgment is taken. . . .

The State must, however, satisfy the applicable requirements of the Due Process Clause. A state may not grant preclusive effect in its own courts to a constitutionally infirm judgment and other state and federal courts are not required to accord full-faith-and-credit to such a judgment. Section 1738 does not suggest otherwise; other state and federal courts would still be providing a state court judgment with the "same" preclusive effect as the courts of the state from which the judgment emerged. In such a case, there could be no constitutionally recognizable preclusion at all.

We have little doubt that Kremer received all the process that was constitutionally required in rejecting his claim that he had been discriminatorily discharged contrary to the statute. . . .

In our system of jurisprudence the usual rule is that merits of a legal claim once decided in a court of competent jurisdiction are not subject to redetermination in another forum. Such a fundamental departure from traditional rules of preclusion, enacted into federal law, can be justified only if plainly stated by Congress. Because there is no "affirmative showing" of a "clear and manifest" legislative purpose in Title VII to deny res judicata or collateral estoppel effect to a state court judgment affirming that a claim of employment discrimination is unproven, and because the procedures provided in New York for the determination of such claims offer a full and fair opportunity to litigate the merits, the judgment of the Court of Appeals is

Affirmed.

[The dissenters' position was that the New York courts had decided only that the NYHRC's finding of no discrimination was a rational conclusion, not that it was correct in fact. Hence, they said, there was no judicial determination of the issue in the instant proceeding, and Section 1738 did not bar a federal district court from adjudicating the issue.]

NOTES

1.   All of the Justices, including the dissenters, apparently agreed that the obligation of the federal courts to respect state court decisions is based on Section 1738. Does this mean that they thought that the federal courts are not bound by the Full Faith and Credit Clause itself (Article IV, Section 1) and that Congress would be free to limit the conclusive effect of state court judgments in such cases?

2.   In the eyes of the dissenting Justices, would a judicial affirmance of an administrative decision ever be entitled to full faith and credit?

3.   In Davis v. United States Steel Supply, 688 F.2d 166 (3d Cir.1982) (en banc), the facts were much the same as in *Kremer*, except that it was the defendant rather than the plaintiff who appealed from the administrative

decision to a state court. It was held that once the state court had decided the appeal, the plaintiff was barred from seeking relief in a federal court. There were dissents.

See also Storey v. Cello Holdings, L.L.C. et al., 182 F.Supp.2d 355 (S.D.N.Y.2002): dismissal "with prejudice" precludes relitigation of matters that were or could have been litigated, both in subsequent arbitration and in new judicial proceedings; plaintiff's motion, in federal court, for summary judgment barring defendant from seeking state court judgment confirming an arbitration award in its favor: denied (vacated and remanded on appeal to enable plaintiff to claim that events transpired *after* the first action that might constitute a legally sufficient basis for a claim: 347 F.3d 370 (2d Cir.2003)), cited in Bailey v. Interbay Funding, LLC, 2020 WL 3401945, *5 (D.Conn.2020).

4.   Allen v. McCurry, 449 U.S. 90 (1980). At his trial in a state court for possession of heroin and assault with intent to kill, McCurry sought to suppress evidence that he claimed had been obtained by an illegal search and seizure. This motion was denied, and McCurry was convicted. He later brought a damage suit in a federal court against the officers who had entered his home and seized the evidence. The federal court granted summary judgment against McCurry on the ground that collateral estoppel prevented him from re-litigating the search and seizure question that had been decided against him in the criminal trial. On writ of certiorari, this decision was affirmed by the Supreme Court since McCurry had received a "full and fair hearing" on the issue of illegal search and seizure in the state court. The dissent, written by Justice Blackmun and joined by Justices Brennan and Marshall, concluded that "The criminal defendant is an involuntary litigant in the state trial. . . . To force him to a choice between forgoing either a potential defense or a federal forum for hearing his constitutional civil claim is fundamentally unfair."

Marrese v. American Academy of Ortho. Surgeons

Supreme Court of the United States, 1985.
470 U.S. 373, 105 S.Ct. 1327, 84 L.Ed.2d 274.

[Plaintiffs, orthopedic surgeons, applied for membership in the American Academy of Orthopedic Surgeons. Their application was denied, and they then filed suit in the Illinois courts claiming that the Academy had violated their associational rights protected by Illinois law. Upon being denied relief in the state courts, plaintiffs filed a federal antitrust suit in the Illinois federal courts. Here again they were denied relief on the ground that under federal law their claims were precluded by the earlier Illinois judgment. The Supreme Court reversed.]

■ JUSTICE O'CONNOR delivered the opinion of the Court. . . .

The issue presented by this case is whether a state court judgment may have preclusive effect on a federal antitrust claim that could not have been raised in the state proceeding. Although federal antitrust claims are within the exclusive jurisdiction of the federal courts, . . . the

Court of Appeals ruled that the dismissal of petitioners' complaints in state court barred them from bringing a claim based on the same facts under the Sherman Act. The Court of Appeals erred by suggesting that in these circumstances a federal court should determine the preclusive effect of a state court judgment without regard to the law of the State in which judgment was rendered.

The preclusive effect of a state court judgment in a subsequent federal lawsuit generally is determined by the full faith and credit statute. . . .

The fact that petitioners' antitrust claim is within the exclusive jurisdiction of the federal courts does not necessarily make § 1738 inapplicable to this case. Our decisions indicate that a state court judgment may in some circumstances have preclusive effect in a subsequent action within the exclusive jurisdiction of the federal courts. . . .

To be sure, a state court will not have occasion to address the specific question whether a state judgment has issue or claim preclusive effect in a later action that can be brought only in federal court. Nevertheless, a federal court may rely in the first instance on state preclusion principles to determine the extent to which an earlier state judgment bars subsequent litigation. . . .

With respect to matters that were not decided in the state proceedings, we note that claim preclusion generally does not apply where "[t]he plaintiff was unable to rely on a certain theory of the case or to seek a certain remedy because of the limitations on the subject matter jurisdiction of the courts. . . ." Restatement, Second, of Judgments § 26(1)(c) (1982). If state preclusion law includes this requirement of prior jurisdictional competency, which is generally true, a state judgment will not have claim preclusive effect on a cause of action within the exclusive jurisdiction of the federal courts. . . .

Reference to state preclusion law may make it unnecessary to determine if the federal court, as an exception to § 1738, should refuse to give preclusive effect to a state court judgment. The issue whether there is an exception to § 1738 arises only if state law indicates that litigation of a particular claim or issue should be barred in the subsequent federal proceeding. . . . Unless application of Illinois preclusion law suggests, contrary to the usual view, that petitioners' federal antitrust claim is somehow barred, there will be no need to decide in this case if there is an exception to § 1738.

The Court of Appeals did not apply the approach to § 1738 that we have outlined. It expressed the view that § 1738 allows a federal court to give a state court judgment greater preclusive effect than the state courts themselves would give to it. . . .

We are unwilling to create a special exception to § 1738 for federal antitrust claims that would give state court judgments greater preclusive effect than would the courts of the State rendering the judgment. . . .

. . . [W]e have parallel systems of state and federal courts, and the concerns of comity reflected in § 1738 generally allow States to determine the preclusive scope of their own courts' judgments. . . . These concerns certainly are not made less compelling because state courts lack jurisdiction over federal antitrust claims. . . .

In this case the Court of Appeals should have first referred to Illinois law to determine the preclusive effect of the state judgment. Only if state law indicates that a particular claim or issue would be barred, is it necessary to determine if an exception to § 1738 should apply. Although for purposes of this case, we need not decide if such an exception exists for federal antitrust claims, we observe that the more general question is whether the concerns underlying a particular grant of exclusive jurisdiction justify a finding of an implied partial repeal of § 1738. Resolution of this question will depend on the particular federal statute as well as the nature of the claim or issue involved in the subsequent federal action. Our previous decisions indicate that the primary consideration must be the intent of Congress. . . .

The judgment of the Court of Appeals is reversed, and the case is remanded for further proceedings consistent with this opinion.

NOTES

1.   For extensive comment see Shulte, The Claim Preclusive Effect of State Court Judgments on Federal Antitrust Claims: Marrese v. American Academy of Ortho. Surgeons, 71 Iowa L.Rev.609 (1986). See also Migra v. Warren City School District Board of Educ., 465 U.S. 75 (1984); Parsons Steel, Inc. v. First Alabama Bank, 474 U.S. 518 (1986), on remand, 785 F.2d 929 (11th Cir.1986), aff'd, 825 F.2d 1475 (11th Cir.1987), cert. denied, 484 U.S. 1060 (1988).

Matsushita Electric Industrial Co. v. Epstein, 516 U.S. 367 (1996), began as a class action on claims of fraudulent behavior in a securities transaction in Delaware state court and there resulted in a final settlement judgment. A subsequent class action in federal court in California asserted claims under federal securities law and invoked the exclusive federal question jurisdiction of federal courts with respect to such claims. The U.S. Supreme Court recognized the difficulty facing the federal court in determining the reach of state preclusion law concerning cases that state courts could not have entertained: it is most unlikely that there would be state laws on that question. It also rejected the notion, mentioned but left unanswered in *Marrese*, that the grant of exclusive federal jurisdiction created an exception to (partial repeal of) the full faith and credit command of § 1738. The Court concluded that the California federal claim had to be dismissed as a result of the preclusive effect of the Delaware judgment.

Marrese and *Matsushita* thus reject the position of § 26 (1)(c) of the Restatement (Second) of Judgments that the F-1 determination should not have claim preclusive effect when F-2 exercises exclusive federal jurisdiction.

2. An issue similar to that in *Marrese* and *Matsushita* arises in federal bankruptcy cases when a creditor claims that the court cannot discharge a debt because it is for fraud and the claim is based on a state judgment for fraud. The federal court has exclusive jurisdiction to decide what debts are dischargeable in a federal bankruptcy proceeding. In re Calvert, 105 F.3d 315 (6th Cir.1997) held that because California would give collateral estoppel effect to the default judgment for fraud rendered by a California court, a federal bankruptcy court in Tennessee must give preclusive effect to the finding of fraud. The court noted that "[n]umerous bankruptcy courts have faced the issue of whether an exception to § 1738 [the statute implementing the Full Faith and Credit clause] exists in the case of a default judgment and the results have differed." Id. at 320.

In Nestor v. Pratt & Whitney, 466 F.3d 65 (2d Cir.2006), the plaintiff had prevailed on a sex discrimination claim before both the Connecticut Commission on Human Rights and Opportunities and Connecticut state courts. She then sought additional damages in federal court under Title VII of the Civil Rights Act of 1964. While recognizing a circuit split, the court held the federal claim could proceed because the damages claimed were not available in the initial state proceedings. Id. at 69.

3. The difficulties inherent in the application of the *Marrese* holding are illustrated by the comment of the district court judge upon remand of the case. In his view, he was required to decide "a nearly metaphysical question." Marrese v. American Academy of Ortho. Surgeons, 628 F.Supp. 918, 919 (N.D.Ill.1986). The Second Circuit encountered similar problems in Gargiul v. Tompkins, 790 F.2d 265 (2d Cir.1986).

Might *Marrese* encourage gamesmanship in that a party first sues on a non-federal claim in state court and then seeks an additional (or first) recovery on an exclusive federal claim for which state courts lack competence and the particular state therefore would not consider its res judicata law to be applicable? The issue was raised in Valbruna Slater Steel Corp. v. Joslyn Manufacturing Co., 934 F.3d 553 (7th Cir. 2019), but the court discounted it: statutes of limitations (that do not toll when the first claim is pending), issue preclusion (as distinguished from claim preclusion), as well as sanctions for any overt bad faith actions provide sufficient safeguards in its opinion.

Marrese and *Matsushita*, however difficult in application, are consistent with the so-called "*Rooker-Feldman*-Doctrine." See Rooker v. Fidelity Trust Co., 263 U.S. 413 (1923); District of Columbia Court of Appeals v. Feldman, 460 U.S. 462 (1983). Construing 28 U.S.C.A. § 1257 (granting the U.S. Supreme jurisdiction to review state court decisions) and § 1331 (granting original jurisdiction to federal district courts), the doctrine holds that district courts lack original jurisdiction over federal claims that are inextricably bound up with a state law claim decided by a state court. To allow a district court to entertain such a claim would put it in a position "to sit in review of judgments entered by courts of equal—or even greater—authority." Martin

v. Wilks, 490 U.S. 755, 784 n.21 (1989) (Stevens, J., dissenting). Such review may be sought only from the Supreme Court. It is thus important to determine what the state court decided, including what questions are precluded under state law. The *"Rooker-Feldman*-Doctrine" has been criticized as unnecessarily duplicating other doctrines, such as general res judicata (preclusion) law and abstention. For comprehensive review, see Comment, The *Rooker-Feldman*-Doctrine: Toward a Workable Role, 149 U.Pa.L.Rev. 1555 (2001). See also Smith v. Ricci, 2011 WL 1807453, at *7 n.7 (D.N.J.2011).

4.   *Marrese* is discussed in Burbank, Interjurisdictional Preclusion, Full Faith and Credit and Federal Common Law: A General Approach, 71 Cornell L.Rev. 733 (1986); Shreve, Preclusion and Federal Choice of Law, 64 Tex.L.Rev.1209 (1986). See also Weinberg, The Federal-State Conflict of Laws: "Actual" Conflicts, 70 Tex.L.Rev. 1743 (1992).

B. ISSUES AFFECTED

RESTATEMENT, SECOND, CONFLICT OF LAWS:*

§ 95. Issues Affected

What issues are determined by a valid judgment is determined, subject to constitutional limitations, by the local law of the State where the judgment was rendered.

NOTES

1.   Section 95 is in line with opinions of the Supreme Court. See, e.g., Magnolia Petroleum Co. v. Hunt, p. 350, infra; Riley v. New York Trust Co., p. 303, supra. See also, as to splitting a cause of action, Cheatham, Res Judicata and the Full Faith and Credit Clause: Magnolia Petroleum Co. v. Hunt, 44 Colum.L.Rev. 330, 346–48 (1944); Friedman, Under the Law of Federal Jurisdiction: Allocating Cases Between Federal and State Courts, 104 Colum.L.Rev. 1211 (2004). And as to collateral estoppel, United States v. Silliman, 167 F.2d 607 (3d Cir.1948), cert. denied, 335 U.S. 825 (1948). See Erichson, Interjurisdictional Preclusion, 96 Mich.L.Rev. 945 (1998).

2.   When F-1 is a foreign country, what will be the res judicata or collateral estoppel effect in this country of the F-1's determination? See p. 288, Note 1, supra.

3.   Compulsory counterclaims. DeGroot, Kalliel, Traint & Conklin v. Camarota, 404 A.2d 1211 (N.J.Super.Ct.App.Div.1979). Suit by Michigan attorneys to enforce a default judgment obtained in Michigan for professional services rendered. Defendant counterclaimed for legal malpractice in connection with these services. Held that the counterclaim was properly dismissed. Under the Michigan compulsory joinder rule, the claim for malpractice should have been asserted by way of defense or counterclaim. Since the malpractice claim could no longer be asserted in Michigan, it could not, under full faith and credit, be asserted in New Jersey.

---

   *   Quoted with the permission of the copyright owner, The American Law Institute.

Compare Chapman v. Aetna Finance Co., 615 F.2d 361 (5th Cir.1980), where the question was whether plaintiffs' claims under the federal Truth-in-Lending law should be dismissed because of failure to assert them as compulsory counterclaims in prior Georgia state court foreclosure proceedings. Under Georgia law the unasserted claims would have been barred, but the court held that they were not precluded from relitigation by the full faith and credit clause. After noting that the purpose of the Georgia rule was to promote judicial economy and thus was "local in scope," the court said: "We think that Georgia's compulsory counterclaim, for full faith and credit purposes, is more properly analyzed as a legislative act than as an element of that state's judicial proceedings." The Court (now sitting as the 11th Circuit) later disapproved of *Chapman*: ". . . we must apply the doctrine of claim preclusion . . . as faithfully as it would be applied by a court of a state in which the judgment was rendered." McDougald v. Jenson, 286 F.2d 1465, 1485 (11th Cir.1986).

Mutuality of Estoppel

A question of increasing importance is the impact of full faith and credit in situations where F-1 and F-2 have different rules with respect to the collateral estoppel effect of a judgment in a later action between a party to the judgment and a stranger seeking to rely on it as plaintiff (*offensive collateral estoppel*). A case in point is Hart v. American Airlines, Inc., 304 N.Y.S.2d 810 (N.Y.Sup.Ct.1969). That case arose out of a crash in Kentucky of an American Airlines plane in which most of the passengers were killed. Of the various actions involving the crash, the first to go to judgment was an action brought in Texas. The crash was found to have been caused by the negligence of American Airlines and accordingly a judgment was rendered for the plaintiff. Thereafter, in a New York action involving different passengers, the plaintiffs contended that under principles of collateral estoppel American Airlines was precluded by the Texas judgment from denying that its negligence had caused the accident. This was the New York rule of collateral estoppel but not the Texas rule which imposed the requirement of mutuality, namely that one party is not collaterally estopped by a former adjudication if the other party would not have been estopped by a contrary outcome in the earlier suit. The court upheld the plaintiffs' contention, stating that New York's "superior interest in the issue of collateral estoppel" was established by the fact that the plaintiffs and their decedents were New York domiciliaries. The court continued that the defendant's reliance on full faith and credit was "misplaced", since this was not an action to enforce the Texas judgment and that what was here involved was New York's policy determination that "one who has had his day in court should not be permitted to relitigate the question anew." *Hart* was followed in In re Air Crash Disaster Near Dayton, 350 F.Supp. 757, 766 (S.D.Ohio 1972), rev'd on other grounds sub nom.

Humphreys v. Tann, 487 F.2d 666 (6th Cir. 1973), cert. denied, 416 U.S. 956 (1974). Are these cases consistent with *Marrese*, and *Matsushita*,?

Suppose that the New York judgment had been the first to be handed down. Some cases suggest that in this situation Texas would have been required to apply the New York rule of collateral estoppel and hold American Airlines barred from relitigating the question of its negligence although the Airline would have been free to do so under the Texas rule of mutuality. United States v. United Air Lines, Inc., 216 F.Supp. 709 (E.D.Wash., D.Nev.1962), affirmed as to issue of mutuality of collateral estoppel, sub nom. United Air Lines, Inc. v. Wiener, 335 F.2d 379 (9th Cir.1964); Cummings v. Dresher, 218 N.E.2d 688 (N.Y.1966). Non-mutual offensive use of collateral estoppel was approved in Parklane Hosiery Co. v. Shore, 439 U.S. 322 (1979). For an exception, where the federal government was the party against which the estoppel was sought to be raised, see United States v. Mendoza, 464 U.S. 154 (1984).

Can the *Hart* decision be sustained on the reasoning that the New York court gave the Texas judgment greater, rather than less, effect than it would have in Texas and thereby accorded it more full faith and credit, not less? Similar questions can be raised as to the preclusive effect of an F-1 judgment with respect to splitting a cause of action. See Freer, Civil Procedure § 11.3.5 (4th ed. 2017) (discussing various approaches to nonmutual issue preclusion).

See also National Bank of Arizona v. Moore, 122 P.3d 1265 (N.M.App.2005), cert. denied, 122 P.3d 1263 (N.M.2005), enforcing an Arizona judgment against the debtor's separate (non-community property) debt against his New Mexico community property, noted at p. 295, Note 4. While the judgment could not have been enforced against Arizona community property, the court concluded that New Mexico's wider enforcement standard applied, and that the Full Faith and Credit Clause did not prevent the enforcing court from giving a judgment "greater force" than where it was rendered. 122 P.3d at 1269. The problem is the same, but the conflict perhaps more exacerbated, when the local (enforcing) state's policy is the result of an earlier inconsistent judgment. See Colby v. Colby, p 373, Note 4, infra. Does the Supreme Court's decision in *Treinies*, p. 370, infra, speak to either or both of these problems, either as matter of law (*Colby*) or of policy (*Moore* and *Hart*)? In reaching its result in *Moore*, above, the court noted that, after recognition, the other state's judgment becomes a local judgment, to be enforced and subject to the same remedies as any other local judgment. The preclusive effect of the local judgment is therefore a matter of local law. Do you agree? See, in this connection, In re Giron, 610 B.R. 670 (D.N.M. 2019): A California default judgment had been recognized in, domesticated by, New Mexico. Under California law, a default judgment has preclusive effect, under New Mexico law it does not. The domesticated judgment is now a New Mexican judgment and New Mexico preclusion law applies. Logically, the result should be the same

regardless of whether recognition was obtained by suit on the F-1
judgment or on the basis of F-2's version of the uniform recognition act.
In the former, recognition is sought directly on the basis of the mandate
of the Full Faith and Credit Clause and its implementing statute:
does/should the "effect" to be given the F-1 judgment (in the language of
the implementing statute) include that state's law on the preclusive
effect of a judgment?

Besides the question of just what full faith and credit requires of F-
2 when its rules of res judicata (and collateral estoppel) differ from those
of F-1, there are the following issues: (1) If F-1 is a federal diversity court,
is the res judicata effect of its judgment determined pursuant to federal
law or pursuant to the rules of the state that created the underlying
claim? (2) If F-2 is a federal diversity court, is it obliged to give the same
effect to the F-1 judgment that would be given in the state in which it
sits? In Degnan, Federalized Res Judicata, 85 Yale L.J. 741, 773 (1976),
the author asserts that the emerging principle of the res judicata scope
of full faith and credit is that

> "A valid judgment rendered in any judicial system within the
> United States must be recognized by all other judicial systems
> within the United States. . . . [T]he claims and issues precluded
> by that judgment, and the parties bound thereby, are
> determined by the law of the system which rendered the
> judgment."

In accord, see Stovall v. Price Waterhouse Co., 652 F.2d 537 (5th
Cir.1981), holding that federal law should be applied to determine the res
judicata effect of a judgment rendered by a federal court. Restatement,
Second, Judgments § 87 is also in accord.

On the full-faith, *Erie* and choice-of-law aspects of the problem when
different doctrines of mutuality of collateral estoppel prevail in the
concerned jurisdictions, see Gary R. Cunningham, Note, Collateral
Estoppel: The Changing Role of the Mutuality Rule, 41 Mo.L.Rev. 521,
538–42 (1976).

All of the issues discussed above, of course, apply equally to the more
justifiable and more widely recognized *defensive collateral estoppel*.
These are the cases in which a defendant who was not a party to a prior
case is relying on a judgment against the plaintiff in that case. See
Bernhard v. Bank of America, 122 P.2d 892, 894 (1942).

NOTE

See generally Carrington, Collateral Estoppel and Foreign Judgments,
24 Ohio St.L.J. 381 (1963); Lewis, Mutuality in Conflict—Flexibility and Full
Faith and Credit, 23 Drake L.Rev. 364 (1974); Overton, The Restatement of
Judgments, Collateral Estoppel and the Conflict of Laws, 44 Tenn.L.Rev. 927
(1977); Rosenberg, Collateral Estoppel in New York, 44 St. John's L.Rev.165
(1969); Note, Collateral Estoppel in Multistate Litigation, 68 Colum.L.Rev.

1590 (1968); Note, Collateral Estoppel Effects of Administrative Agency Determinations: Where Should Federal Courts Draw the Line?, 73 Cornell L.Rev. 817 (1988).

WARNER V. BUFFALO DRYDOCK CO., 67 F.2d 540 (2d Cir.1933), cert. denied, 291 U.S. 678, 54 S.Ct. 529 (1934): Action in a federal court in New York to recover for damages to plaintiffs' steamer caused by defendant's servants. One of the defendant's pleas in bar was that prior to the commencement of this action plaintiffs had filed a libel action in a federal court in Ohio based upon the same cause of action, and that the libel action had been dismissed "because of laches on the part of libellants in pursuing the alleged claim." Augustus N. Hand, J. "The decisions of the Supreme Court and the English cases all indicate that the judgment of the court of a foreign state which dismisses a cause of action because of the statute of limitations of the forum is not a decision upon the merits and is not a bar to a new action upon the identical claim in the courts of another state. . . . All the court in Ohio decided was that the remedy was barred there because of laches. . . . The Ohio decree does not fail to bar the remedy in the present action because it is not res judicata as to everything which it decided, but because it did not decide that the plaintiffs' claim was extinguished, but only that they could not sue in Ohio on account of the local statute of limitations. . . . In our opinion, the dismissal of the libel by the Ohio court was not a bar to the present action."

NOTES

1.   The *Warner* rule has the support of Restatement of Conflicts, Second, § 110, cmt. *b*. But compare Shoup v. Bell & Howell Co., 872 F.2d 1178 (4th Cir.1989), where a federal court's summary judgment dismissing an action on statute of limitations grounds was held to preclude suit on the same claim in a second federal court. The decision was based entirely on the court's interpretation of the Federal Rules of Civil Procedure. The decision was followed in Payne v. Brake, 439 F.3d 198, 204 (4th Cir.2006).

2.   Would not the Ohio decree in *Warner* have effectively barred the plaintiffs from again suing the defendant in that state on the same cause of action? How then can the result reached in the principal case be reconciled with the statutory command that F-2 must accord F-1 judicial proceedings "such faith and credit . . . as they have by law or usage in the courts" of F-1?

3.   Would an F-1 judgment dismissing plaintiff's suit on the ground of public policy be binding in F-2 whose public policy was different? If not, why should not F-2 also be permitted to apply its own rule as to collateral estoppel and the splitting of a cause of action? Compare Mertz v. Mertz, p. 463, infra.

4.   Does a judgment dismissing plaintiff's suit on the ground that it is barred by the forum's statute of limitations occupy, of necessity, the same status as one basing the dismissal upon the forum's public policy? Is a judgment of the latter type more likely to go to the merits of the cause of action? See Paulsen & Sovern, "Public Policy" in the Conflict of Laws, 56 Colum.L.Rev. 969, 1010–12 (1956); Restatement, Second, Judgments §§ 19–20.

5.   F-1 applies the F-1 statute of limitations to protect a F-1 defendant. The decision states that the court applies the F-1 statute of limitations because F-1 has the most significant relationship to the occurrence and the parties on the limitations issue; the decision is on the merits for the defendant. Is the opinion entitled to full faith and credit in other states barring suit elsewhere? Cf. Sun Oil v. Wortman, p. 449, infra.

C. LIMITATIONS ON FULL FAITH AND CREDIT

Fall v. Eastin

Supreme Court of the United States, 1909.
215 U.S. 1, 30 S.Ct. 3, 54 L.Ed. 65.

■ JUSTICE MCKENNA delivered the opinion of the Court:

The question in this case is whether a deed to land situate in Nebraska, made by a commissioner under the decree of a court of the state of Washington in an action for divorce, must be recognized in Nebraska under the due faith and credit clause of the Constitution of the United States.

[The plaintiff and E.W. Fall were married in Indiana in 1876 and subsequently moved to Nebraska, where E.W. Fall acquired title to the land in controversy. In 1889 they moved to Washington, where in 1895 the plaintiff obtained a divorce on a cross-petition filed by her. The divorce decree, in accordance with a Washington statute concerning the property of divorced parties, was accompanied by a decree awarding plaintiff the Nebraska land and ordering her husband to convey that portion to her. E.W. Fall did not comply with the decree, but a commissioner appointed by the Washington court executed to her a deed to the land. Thereafter, E.W. Fall executed to third parties, W.H. Fall and Elizabeth Eastin, a mortgage on the land and a deed to the land. Plaintiff then brought the present suit in the state court of Nebraska to quiet her title to the land and to cancel the mortgage and the deed executed by E.W. Fall. She set up the Washington decree and the commissioner's deed, and contended that Fall's conveyances were ineffective to impair the rights she claimed under that decree and the deed. E.W. Fall was never served personally in the Nebraska proceedings and did not appear, though his conveyees were duly served. The trial court gave a decree in favor of the plaintiff. The Supreme Court of Nebraska first affirmed (75 Neb. 104, 106 N.W. 412), but on rehearing, it reversed the decree of the trial court (75 Neb. 120, 113 N.W. 175).]

. . . Plaintiff urges the equities which arose between her and her husband, on account of their relation as husband and wife, in the state of Washington, and under the laws of that state. The defendant urges the policy of the state of Nebraska, and the inability of the court of Washington, by its decree alone or the deed executed through the commissioner, to convey the land situate in Nebraska. . . .

. . . The supreme court of the state concedes, as we understand its opinion, the jurisdiction in the Washington court to render the decree. The court said:

"We think there can be no doubt, where a court of chancery has, by its decree, ordered and directed persons properly within its jurisdiction to do or refrain from doing a certain act, it may compel obedience to this decree by appropriate proceedings, and that any action taken by reason of such compulsion is valid and effectual wherever it may be assailed. In the instant case, if Fall had obeyed the order of the Washington court, and made a deed of conveyance to his wife of the Nebraska land, even under the threat of contempt proceedings, or after duress by imprisonment, the title thereby conveyed to Mrs. Fall would have been of equal weight and dignity with that which he himself possessed at the time of the execution of the deed."

But Fall, not having executed a deed, the court's conclusion was, to quote its language, that "neither the decree nor the commissioner's deed conferred any right or title upon her. . . . The decree is inoperative to affect the title to the Nebraska land . . . it remained in E.W. Fall until divested by operation of law or by his voluntary act. He has parted with it to Elizabeth Eastin; and whether any consideration was ever paid for it or not is immaterial so far as the plaintiff is concerned, for she is in no position to question the transaction, whatever a creditor of Fall might be able to do." . . .

The territorial limitation of the jurisdiction of courts of a state over property in another state has a limited exception in the jurisdiction of a court of equity, but it is an exception well defined. A court of equity, having authority to act upon the person, may indirectly act upon real estate in another state, through the instrumentality of this authority over the person. . . .

Whether the doctrine that a decree of a court rendered in consummation of equities, or the deed of a master under it, will not convey title, and that the deed of a party coerced by the decree will have such effect, is illogical or inconsequent, we need not inquire, nor consider whether the other view would not more completely fulfill the Constitution of the United States. . . .

But, however plausibly the contrary view may be sustained, we think that the doctrine that the court, not having jurisdiction of the res, cannot affect it by its decree, nor by a deed made by a master in accordance with the decree, is firmly established. . . .

This doctrine is entirely consistent with the provision of the Constitution of the United States, which requires a judgment in any state to be given full faith and credit in the courts of every other state. This provision does not extend the jurisdiction of the courts of one state to property situated in another, but only makes the judgment rendered conclusive on the merits of the claim or subject-matter of the suit. . . .

Plaintiff seems to contend for a greater efficacy for a decree in equity affecting real property than is given to a judgment at law for the recovery of money simply. The case of Burnley v. Stevenson, 24 Ohio St. 474, in a sense sustains her. . . . [In that case, action was brought in an Ohio court to recover possession of local realty. By way of defense, the defendant relied upon a deed executed by a master commissioner in Kentucky in pursuance of a decree for specific performance rendered by a court of the latter state. The court found for the defendant, holding that, although the commissioner's deed must "be regarded as a nullity," it would recognize the validity of the actual decree "in so far as it determined the equitable rights of the parties in the land in controversy. In our judgment, the parties, and those holding under them with notice are still bound thereby."]

. . . There is . . . much temptation in the facts of this case to follow the ruling of the supreme court of Ohio . . . but, as the ruling of the [Nebraska] court, that the decree in Washington gave no such equities as could be recognized in Nebraska as justifying an action to quiet title, does not offend the Constitution of the United States, we are constrained to affirm its judgment.

So ordered.

■ JUSTICE HARLAN and JUSTICE BREWER dissent.

■ JUSTICE HOLMES, concurring specially:

I am not prepared to dissent from the judgment of the court, but my reasons are different from those that have been stated.

The real question concerns the effect of the Washington decree. As between the parties to it, that decree established in Washington a personal obligation of the husband to convey to his former wife. A personal obligation goes with the person. If the husband had made a contract, valid by the law of Washington, to do the same thing, I think there is no doubt that the contract would have been binding in Nebraska. Ex parte Pollard, 4 Deacon, Bankr. 27, 40; Polson v. Stewart, 167 Mass. 211. So I conceive that a Washington decree for the specific performance of such a contract would be entitled to full faith and credit as between the parties in Nebraska. But it does not matter to its constitutional effect what the ground of the decree may be, whether a contract or something else. Fauntleroy v. Lum, 210 U.S. 230. (In this case it may have been that the wife contributed equally to the accumulation of the property, and so had an equitable claim.) A personal decree is equally within the jurisdiction of a court having the person within its power, whatever its ground and whatever it orders the defendant to do. Therefore I think that this decree was entitled to full faith and credit in Nebraska.

But the Nebraska court carefully avoids saying that the decree would not be binding between the original parties, had the husband been before the court. The ground on which it goes is that to allow the judgment to affect the conscience of purchasers would be giving it an effect in rem. It treats the case as standing on the same footing as that of an innocent purchaser. Now, if the court saw fit to deny the effect of a judgment upon privies in title, or if it considered the defendant an innocent purchaser, I do not see what we have to do with its decision, however wrong. I do not see why it is not within the power of the state to do away with equity or with the equitable doctrine as to purchasers with notice if it sees fit. Still less do I see how a mistake as to notice could give us jurisdiction. If the judgment binds the defendant, it is not by its own operation, even with the Constitution behind it, but by the obligation imposed by equity upon a purchaser with notice. The ground of decision below was that there was no such obligation. The decision, even if wrong, did not deny to the Washington decree its full effect. Bagley v. General Fire Extinguisher Co., 212 U.S. 477, 480.

NOTES

1. Does the majority opinion hold that that part of the Washington decree which ordered Fall to convey the Nebraska land to the plaintiff was entirely without extraterritorial effect? Or can the decision be explained on the ground that the plaintiff had misconceived her remedy? For extensive discussion of the powers of the non-situs court and of the decision in Fall v. Eastin, see Eckard v. Eckard, 636 A.2d 455 (Md.1994). Rejecting the argument that the non-situs court lacked subject matter jurisdiction to compel acts with respect to out-of-state land, the court held that an equity court may "by virtue of its power over a person properly before it . . . compel him to act in relation to property not within the jurisdiction." 636 A.2d at 462. In re Marriage of Kowalewski, 182 P.3d 959 (Wash.2008), held that the Washington court with personal jurisdiction over the parties could determine the spouses' rights to immovables in Poland in exercising its divorce jurisdiction. It acknowledged that Washington lacked power directly to affect title to foreign land but could do so "indirectly . . . by means of an in personam decree operating on the person over whom it has jurisdiction." Id. at 962, followed in OneWest Bank, FSB v. Erickson, 367 P.3d 1063 (Wash.2016, en banc). What effect on title such a decree would have, would still be a matter for the courts of the Polish situs to determine. Id. at 964. See similarly, Guray v. Tacras, 194 P.3d 1174 (Hawaii Ct.App.2008). Id. at 964. What should be the response of the court at the situs? Note that similar problems can arise in reverse, for instance, when a court with jurisdiction over a decedent's estate in the European Union under EU succession law (Decedent's EU domicile at death) exercises jurisdiction over all assets of the estate, regardless where situated. Assume that the estate includes real property in the United States. See p. 1240, infra. See also Note 5, infra. But cf. Kelly Oil Co. v. Svetlik, 975 S.W.2d 762 (Tex.App.1998), review denied, holding that a Texas court with personal jurisdiction over the parties does not have subject-matter jurisdiction to award royalties on oil and gas leases in Mississippi.

The court stated that the royalty rights depended on whether the leases had expired. Whether the leases had expired required determination of title to out-of-state realty and it is "well-settled that Texas courts have no power or jurisdiction to adjudicate title to interests in real property located in another state." In Trutec Oil and Gas, Inc. v. Western Atlas Int'l, Inc., 194 S.W.3d 580 (Tex.App.2006), multiple claims were brought relating to an investment company's interest in a Nigerian oil mining lease. The plaintiff argued that Kelly Oil Co. v. Svetlik, supra, was not applicable because the principal issue was contractual in nature. Held: No jurisdiction because the lawsuit required determining whether the plaintiff had an ownership interest in real property located in Nigeria. See, similarly, Buchanan v. Weber, 567 S.E.2d 413 (N.C.App.), writ of supersedeas denied, 572 S.E.2d 427 (N.C.2002) (portion of Kansas divorce decree purporting to affect title to North Carolina real property not entitled to full faith and credit).

2. Suppose that the defendant Fall had executed a conveyance to the Nebraska land to avoid punishment for contempt at the hands of the Washington court. Such deeds have generally been held effective in passing title to the land. Phillips v. Phillips, 272 S.W.2d 433 (Ark.1954) (defendant signed deed to be released from jail); Deschenes v. Tallman, 161 N.E. 321 (N.Y.1928); Hay, Borchers, Symeonides & Whytock, Conflict of Laws § 24.10 (6th ed.2018). Why should a title deed rendered under duress be valid if the court that exercised the duress could not itself have transferred title?

3. RESTATEMENT, SECOND, CONFLICT OF LAWS § 102, Comment *b* reads:

b. Recognition. A valid foreign judgment that orders the doing of an act other than the payment of money or that enjoins the doing of an act will be given the same degree of recognition as any other judgment (see §§ 93–97). This means that such a judgment will be given the same res judicata effect with respect to the persons, the subject matter of the action and the issues involved that it has in the state of rendition. . . . So, if a court of State X finds that the defendant has broken his contract to convey land in State Y and orders the defendant to make the conveyance, a court of State Y, where the enforcement of the X judgment is sought, must give conclusive effect to the finding of the X court that the defendant has been guilty of breach of contract. Similarly if a court of State X finds that the defendant has procured a judgment in State Y by fraud and enjoins its enforcement, a court of State Y must give conclusive effect to the finding of the X court that the judgment was procured by fraud.

4. *Enforcement.* The great majority of cases dealing with the enforcement of equity decrees that order the doing of an act other than the payment of money have involved an order to convey land in F-2. At one time it was generally believed that such decrees would not be enforced extraterritorially. This conclusion was based on the ground either that (a) since equity decrees are discretionary in nature, F-2 could not be required to accept the relief that F-1 had found appropriate and (b) in any event no action was available for the enforcement of a foreign judgment other than one in the nature of debt. These notions were found baseless in Currie, Full Faith and Credit to

Foreign Land Decrees, 21 U.Chi.L.Rev. 620 (1964). He concluded that an action could be brought in F-2 to establish the F-1 decree as one of F-2 or for a judgment declaring the interests of the parties in the F-2 land in light of the F-1 decree or, if neither of these alternatives was available, an action on the original claim with the F-2 court being required to give res judicata effect to the findings made in F-1. See also Hay, Borchers, Symeonides & Whytock, Conflict of Laws §§ 24.9–24.10 (6th ed.2018); Hay, The Situs Rule in European and American Conflicts Law: Comparative Notes, in Property Law and Legal Education, Essays in Honor of John E. Cribbet 109 (Hay & Hoeflich, eds., 1988).

5. Most of the cases have enforced foreign equity decrees ordering the conveyance of local land. See Andre v. Morrow, 680 P.2d 1355 (Idaho 1984); Ivey v. Ivey, 439 A.2d 425 (Conn.1981); Varone v. Varone, 359 F.2d 769 (7th Cir.1966); Cuevas v. Cuevas, 191 So.2d 843 (Miss.1966). In Weesner v. Weesner, 95 N.W.2d 682 (Neb.1959), the Nebraska court did what it had refused to do in Fall v. Eastin, namely, entertained a cross-petition to quiet title to Nebraska land on the basis of an F-1 decree that ordered conveyance of this land. The F-1 defendant was subjected to the personal jurisdiction of the court in F-2. See also Higinbotham v. Higginbotham, 222 A.2d 120, 126–29 (N.J.Super.Ct.App.Div.1966); Day v. Wiswall, 464 P.2d 626 (Ariz.App.1970), amended and rehearing denied, 467 P.2d 250 (Ariz.App.1970).

6. As to the recognition of decisions with respect to *interests* in land, see Hay, Note 4, supra; Robby Alden, Note, Modernizing the Situs Rule for Real Property Conflicts, 65 Tex.L.Rev. 585 (1987); Weintraub, Commentary on the Conflict of Laws 583–92 (6th ed.2010). In Matter of Estate of Mack, 373 N.W.2d 97 (Iowa 1985), the court recognized a Missouri divorce court's decree setting off, to the former wife, a farm in the Iowa forum. Even though the former husband had not been ordered to convey and the former wife had taken no steps to have the Iowa land put in her name, the court adopted the "preferable" view of Section 43 of the Restatement, Second, Conflict of Laws, that a "judgment in an action determining interests in real or personal property conclusively determines the claims of the parties . . ."

Baker v. General Motors Corp.

Supreme Court of the United States, 1998.
522 U.S. 222, 118 S.Ct. 657, 139 L.Ed.2d 580.

■ JUSTICE GINSBURG delivered the opinion of the Court. JUSTICE SCALIA filed an opinion concurring in the judgment. JUSTICE KENNEDY filed an opinion concurring in the judgment in which JUSTICES O'CONNOR and THOMAS joined.

This case concerns the authority of one State's court to order that a witness' testimony shall not be heard in any court of the United States. In settlement of claims and counterclaims precipitated by the discharge of Ronald Elwell, a former General Motors Corporation (GM) engineering analyst, GM paid Elwell an undisclosed sum of money, and the parties agreed to a permanent injunction. As stipulated by GM and Elwell and entered by a Michigan County Court, the injunction prohibited Elwell from "testifying, without the prior written consent of [GM], . . . as . . . a witness of any kind . . . in any litigation already filed, or to be filed in the future, involving [GM] as an owner, seller, manufacturer and/or designer . . ." GM separately agreed, however, that if Elwell were ordered to testify by a court or other tribunal, such testimony would not be actionable as a violation of the Michigan court's injunction or the GM-Elwell agreement."

After entry of the stipulated injunction in Michigan, Elwell was subpoenaed to testify in a product liability action commenced in Missouri by plaintiffs [the Bakers] who were not involved in the Michigan case. The question presented is whether the national full faith and credit command bars Elwell's testimony in the Missouri case. We hold that Elwell may testify in the Missouri action without offense to the full faith and credit requirement.

[The federal district court in Missouri, in which the plaintiffs were suing GM, allowed the plaintiffs to depose Elwell and call him as a witness at trial. The Eighth Circuit reversed the judgment for the plaintiffs, ruling that Elwell's testimony should not have been admitted.]

II

A

[The Court quoted the Full Faith and Credit Clause and the last paragraph of its implementing statute, 28 U.S.C. § 1738, which are set forth at pp. 45–46, supra.]

Our precedent differentiates the credit owed to laws (legislative measures and common law) and to judgments. "In numerous cases this Court has held that credit must be given to the judgment of another state although the forum would not be required to entertain the suit on which the judgment was founded." Milwaukee County [v. M.E. White Co.], 296 U.S. [268,] 277, 56 S.Ct. 229 [, 234] (1935). The Full Faith and Credit Clause does not compel "a state to substitute the statutes of other states for its own statutes dealing with a subject matter concerning which it is competent to legislate." Pacific Employers Ins. Co. v. Industrial Accident Comm'n, 306 U.S. 493, 501, 59 S.Ct. 629 [, 632], 83 L.Ed.940 (1939). Regarding judgments, however, the full faith and credit obligation is exacting. A final judgment in one State, if rendered by a court with adjudicatory authority over the subject matter and persons governed by the judgment, qualifies for recognition throughout the land. For claim and issue preclusion (res judicata) purposes, in other words, the judgment of the rendering State gains nationwide force. . . .

A court may be guided by the forum State's "public policy" in determining the law applicable to a controversy.[6] But our decisions

---

[6]   See also Paulsen & Sovern, "Public Policy" in the Conflict of Laws, 56 Colum.L.Rev. 969, 980–981 (1956) (noting traditional but dubious use of the term "public policy" to obscure "an assertion of the forum's right to have its [own] law applied to the [controversy] because of the forum's relationship to it").

support no roving "public policy exception" to the full faith and credit due judgments. . . . We are "aware of [no] considerations of local policy or law which could rightly be deemed to impair the force and effect which the full faith and credit clause and the Act of Congress require to be given to [a money] judgment outside the state of its rendition." *Magnolia Petroleum Co. v. Hunt,* 320 U.S. 430, 438, 64 S.Ct. 208, 88 L.Ed. 149 (1943).

The Court has never placed equity decrees outside the full faith and credit domain. Equity decrees for the payment of money have long been considered equivalent to judgments at law entitled to nationwide recognition. . . .

Full faith and credit, however, does not mean that States must adopt the practices of other States regarding the time, manner, and mechanisms for enforcing judgments. Enforcement measures do not travel with the sister state judgment as preclusive effects do; such measures remain subject to the even-handed control of forum law.

Orders commanding action or inaction have been denied enforcement in a sister State when they purported to accomplish an official act within the exclusive province of that other State or interfered with litigation over which the ordering State had no authority. Thus, a sister State's decree concerning land ownership in another State has been held ineffective to transfer title, see *Fall v. Eastin,* 215 U.S. 1, 30 S.Ct. 3, 54 L.Ed. 65 (1909), although such a decree may indeed preclusively adjudicate the rights and obligations running between the parties to the foreign litigation, see, e.g., *Robertson v. Howard,* 229 U.S. 254, 261, 33 S.Ct. 854, 57 L.Ed. 1174 (1913). And antisuit injunctions regarding litigation elsewhere, even if compatible with due process as a direction constraining parties to the decree, in fact have not controlled the second court's actions regarding litigation in that court. See, e.g., *James v. Grand Trunk Western R. Co.,* 14 Ill.2d 356, 372, 152 N.E.2d 858, 867 (1958); see also E. Scoles & P. Hay, Conflict of Laws § 24.21, p. 981 (2d ed. 1992) (observing that antisuit injunction "does not address, and thus has no preclusive effect on, the merits of the litigation [in the second forum]"). Sanctions for violations of an injunction, in any event, are generally administered by the court that issued the injunction.

B

With these background principles in view, we turn to the dimensions of the order GM relies upon to stop Elwell's testimony. Specifically, we take up the question: What matters did the Michigan injunction legitimately conclude?

As earlier recounted, the parties before the Michigan County Court, Elwell and GM, submitted an agreed-upon injunction, which the presiding judge signed. While no issue was joined, expressly litigated, and determined in the Michigan proceeding,[11] that order is claim preclusive between Elwell and GM. Elwell's claim for wrongful discharge and his related contract and tort claims have "merged in the judgment," and he cannot sue again to recover more.

Michigan's judgment, however, cannot reach beyond the Elwell-GM controversy to control proceedings against GM brought in other States, by other parties, asserting claims the merits of which Michigan has not considered. Michigan has no power over those parties, and no basis for commanding them to become intervenors in the Elwell-GM dispute. Most essentially, Michigan lacks authority to control courts elsewhere by precluding them, in actions brought by strangers to the Michigan litigation, from determining for themselves what witnesses are competent to testify and what evidence is relevant and admissible in their search for the truth.

. . . Michigan's decree could operate against Elwell to preclude him from volunteering his testimony. But a Michigan court cannot, by entering the injunction to which Elwell and GM stipulated, dictate to a court in another jurisdiction that evidence relevant in the Bakers' case-a controversy to which Michigan is foreign-shall be inadmissible. This conclusion creates no general exception to the full faith and credit command, and surely does not permit a State to refuse to honor a sister state judgment based on the forum's choice of law or policy preferences. Rather, we simply recognize that, just as the mechanisms for enforcing a judgment do not travel with the judgment itself for purposes of Full Faith and Credit, and just as one State's judgment cannot automatically transfer title to land in another State, similarly the Michigan decree cannot determine evidentiary issues in a lawsuit brought by parties who were not subject to the jurisdiction of the Michigan court.[12]

In line with its recognition of the interference potential of the consent decree, GM provided in the settlement agreement that, if another court ordered Elwell to testify, his testimony would "in no way" render

---

[11] In no event, we have observed, can issue preclusion be invoked against one who did not participate in the prior adjudication. Thus, Justice Kennedy emphasizes the obvious in noting that the Michigan judgment has no preclusive effect on the Bakers, for they were not parties to the Michigan litigation. Such an observation misses the thrust of GM's argument. GM readily acknowledges "the commonplace rule that a person may not be bound by a judgment in personam in a case to which he was not made a party." But, GM adds, the Michigan decree does not bind the Bakers; it binds Elwell only. Most forcibly, GM insists that the Bakers cannot object to the binding effect GM seeks for the Michigan judgment because the Bakers have no constitutionally protected interest in obtaining the testimony of a particular witness. Given this argument, it is clear that issue preclusion principles, standing alone, cannot resolve the controversy GM presents.

[12] Justice Kennedy inexplicably reads into our decision a sweeping exception to full faith and credit based solely on "the integrity of Missouri's judicial processes." The Michigan judgment is not entitled to full faith and credit, we have endeavored to make plain, because it impermissibly interferes with Missouri's control of litigation brought by parties who were not before the Michigan court. Thus, Justice Kennedy's hypothetical, see ibid., misses the mark. If the Bakers had been parties to the Michigan proceedings and had actually litigated the privileged character of Elwell's testimony, the Bakers would of course be precluded from relitigating that issue in Missouri.

him vulnerable to suit in Michigan for violation of the injunction or agreement. The Eighth Circuit regarded this settlement agreement provision as merely a concession by GM that "some courts might fail to extend full faith and credit to the [Michigan] injunction." Ibid. . . . Michigan's power does not reach into a Missouri courtroom to displace the forum's own determination whether to admit or exclude evidence relevant in the Bakers' wrongful death case before it. In that light, we see no altruism in GM's agreement not to institute contempt or breach-of-contract proceedings against Elwell in Michigan for giving subpoenaed testimony elsewhere. Rather, we find it telling that GM ruled out resort to the court that entered the injunction, for injunctions are ordinarily enforced by the enjoining court, not by a surrogate tribunal.

In sum, Michigan has no authority to shield a witness from another jurisdiction's subpoena power in a case involving persons and causes outside Michigan's governance. Recognition, under full faith and credit, is owed to dispositions Michigan has authority to order. But a Michigan decree cannot command obedience elsewhere on a matter the Michigan court lacks authority to resolve. See Thomas v. Washington Gas Light Co., 448 U.S. 261, 282–283, 100 S.Ct. 2647, 65 L.Ed.2d 757 (1980) (plurality opinion) ("Full faith and credit must be given to [a] determination that [a State's tribunal] had the authority to make; but by a parity of reasoning, full faith and credit need not be given to determinations that it had no power to make.").

For the reasons stated, the judgment of the Court of Appeals for the Eighth Circuit is reversed, and the case is remanded for further proceedings consistent with this opinion.

It is so ordered.

■ JUSTICE SCALIA, concurring in the judgment.

I agree with the Court that enforcement measures do not travel with sister-state judgments as preclusive effects do. It has long been established that "the judgment of a state Court cannot be enforced out of the state by an execution issued within it." To recite that principle is to decide this case. . . .

■ JUSTICE KENNEDY, with whom JUSTICES O'CONNOR and THOMAS join, concurring in the judgment.

I concur in the judgment. In my view the case is controlled by well-settled full faith and credit principles which render the majority's extended analysis unnecessary and, with all due respect, problematic in some degree. . . .

I

The majority, of course, is correct to hold that when a judgment is presented to the courts of a second State it may not be denied enforcement based upon some disagreement with the laws of the State of rendition. . . .

My concern is that the majority, having stated the principle, proceeds to disregard it by announcing two broad exceptions. First, the majority would allow courts outside the issuing State to decline to enforce those judgments "purporting to accomplish an official act within the exclusive province of [a sister] State." Second, the basic rule of full faith and credit is said not to cover injunctions "interfering with litigation over which the ordering State had no authority." The exceptions the majority recognizes are neither consistent with its rejection of a public policy exception to full faith and credit nor in accord with established rules implementing the Full Faith and Credit Clause. As employed to resolve this case, furthermore, the exceptions to full faith and credit have a potential for disrupting judgments, and this ought to give us considerable pause.

Our decisions have been careful not to foreclose all effect for the types of injunctions the majority would place outside the ambit of full faith and credit. These authorities seem to be disregarded by today's holding. For example, the majority chooses to discuss the extent to which courts may compel the conveyance of property in other jurisdictions. That subject has proven to be quite difficult. Some of our cases uphold actions by state courts affecting land outside their territorial reach. E.g., Robertson v. Howard, 229 U.S. 254, 261, 33 S.Ct. 854, 57 L.Ed. 1174 (1913) ("It may not be doubted that a court of equity in one State in a proper case could compel a defendant before it to convey property situated in another State"). Nor have we undertaken before today to announce an exception which denies full faith and credit based on the principle that the prior judgment interferes with litigation pending in another jurisdiction. As a general matter, there is disagreement among the state courts as to their duty to recognize decrees enjoining proceedings in other courts.

Subjects which are at once so fundamental and so delicate as these ought to be addressed only in a case necessarily requiring their discussion, and even then with caution lest we announce rules which will not be sound in later application. See Restatement, supra, § 102, Comment C ("The Supreme Court of the United States has not had occasion to determine whether full faith and credit requires a State of the United States to enforce a valid judgment of a sister State that orders the doing of an act other than the payment of money or that enjoins the doing of an act"); E. Scoles & P. Hay, Conflict of Laws § 24.9, p. 964 (2d ed.1992) (noting that interstate recognition of equity decrees other than divorce decrees and decrees ordering payment of money "has been a matter of some uncertainty"). We might be required to hold, if some future case raises the issue, that an otherwise valid judgment cannot intrude upon essential processes of courts outside the issuing State in certain narrow circumstances, but we need not announce or define that principle here. Even if some qualification of full faith and credit were required where the judicial processes of a second State are sought to be controlled in their procedural and institutional aspects, the Court's discussion does not provide sufficient guidance on how this exception should be construed in light of our precedents. The majority's broad review of these matters does not articulate the rationale underlying its conclusions. In the absence of more elaboration, it is unclear what it is about the particular injunction here that renders it undeserving of full faith and credit. The Court's reliance upon unidentified principles to justify omitting certain types of injunctions from the doctrine's application leaves its decision in uneasy tension with its own rejection of a broad public policy exception to full faith and credit.

The following example illustrates the uncertainty surrounding the majority's approach. Suppose the Bakers had anticipated the need for Elwell's testimony in Missouri and had appeared in a Michigan Court to litigate the privileged character of the testimony it sought to elicit. Assume further the law on privilege were the same in both jurisdictions. If Elwell, GM, and the Bakers were before the Michigan court and Michigan law gave its own injunction preclusive effect, the Bakers could not relitigate the point, if general principles of issue preclusion control. Perhaps the argument can be made, as the majority appears to say, that the integrity of Missouri's judicial processes demands a rule allowing relitigation of the issue; but, for the reasons given below, we need not confront this interesting question.

In any event, the rule would be an exception. Full faith and credit requires courts to do more than provide for direct enforcement of the judgments issued by other States. It also "requires federal courts to give the same preclusive effect to state court judgments that those judgments would be given in the courts of the State from which the judgments emerged." Kremer v. Chemical Constr. Corp., 456 U.S. 461, 466, 102 S.Ct. 1883, 1889, 72 L.Ed.2d 262 (1982). Through full faith and credit, "the local doctrines of res judicata, speaking generally, become a part of national jurisprudence. . . ." Riley v. New York Trust Co., 315 U.S. 343, 349, 62 S.Ct. 608, 612, 86 L.Ed. 885 (1942). . . . .

II

In the case before us, of course, the Bakers were neither parties to the earlier litigation nor subject to the jurisdiction of the Michigan courts. The majority pays scant attention to this circumstance, which becomes critical. The beginning point of full faith and credit analysis requires a determination of the effect the judgment has in the courts of the issuing State. . . . A conclusion that the issuing State would not give the prior judgment preclusive effect ends the inquiry, making it unnecessary to determine the existence of any exceptions to full faith and credit. We cannot decline to inquire into these state-law questions when the inquiry will obviate new extensions or exceptions to full faith and credit.

If we honor the undoubted principle that courts need give a prior judgment no more force or effect that the issuing State gives it, the case before us is resolved. Here the Court of Appeals and both parties in their arguments before our Court seemed to embrace the assumption that Michigan would apply the full force of its judgment to the Bakers. Michigan law does not appear to support the assumption.

The simple fact is that the Bakers were not parties to the Michigan proceedings, and nothing indicates Michigan would make the novel assertion that its earlier injunction binds the Bakers or any other party not then before it or subject to its jurisdiction . . . Since the Bakers were not parties to the Michigan proceedings and had no opportunity to litigate any of the issues presented, it appears that Michigan law would not treat them as bound by the judgment. The majority cites no authority to the contrary.

It makes no difference that the judgment in question is an injunction. . . .

GM disavows its desire to issue preclude the Bakers, claiming "the only party being 'bound' to the injunction is Elwell." This is difficult to accept because in assessing the preclusive reach of a judgment we look to its practical effect. Despite its disclaimer, GM seeks to alter the course of the suit between it and the Bakers by preventing the Bakers from litigating the admissibility of Elwell's testimony. Furthermore, even were we to accept GM's argument that the Bakers are essentially irrelevant to this dispute, GM's argument is flawed on its own terms. Elwell, in the present litigation, does not seek to relitigate anything; he is a witness, not a party.

In all events, determining as a threshold matter the extent to which Michigan law gives preclusive effect to the injunction eliminates the need to decide whether full faith and credit applies to equitable decrees as a general matter or the extent to which the general rules of full faith and credit are subject to exceptions. Michigan law would not seek to bind the Bakers to the injunction and that suffices to resolve the case. For these reasons, I concur in the judgment.

NOTES

1.   What does the majority mean when it says that sister-state decrees have been denied faith and credit "when they purported to accomplish an official act within the exclusive province of that other state or interfered with litigation over which the ordering state had no authority?" Note that the majority cites Fall v. Eastin, as support for this assertion, apparently because it considers the transfer of title of land to be "an official act within the exclusive province" of the situs state. Note also that the majority's language is somewhat similar to that used in Section 103 of the Second Restatement, p. 349, infra, which purports to recognize an exception for judgments that "involve an improper interference with important interests of the sister state." Is this consistent with the majority's assertion that it is not recognizing a "roving public policy exception," to judgment recognition? Is this the portion of the majority opinion that Justice Kennedy finds "problematic"?

Taylor v. Sawyer, 284 F.3d 1143 (9th Cir.2002), cert. denied, 537 U.S. 1119 (2003). A federal court sentenced Taylor to a term of imprisonment for distributing crack cocaine. A state court then sentenced Taylor to a term of imprisonment for manslaughter. The state judgment stated that the state sentence would run "concurrently with federal time." After his release from state custody, the Federal Bureau of Prisons refused to credit Taylor with time served in state prison. Held: Federal authorities did not deny Full Faith and Credit to the state judgment "because the state sentence is based on a state prosecution in which the federal government, including its Bureau of Prisons . . . was not and could not have been a party." Id. at 1153.

An Oklahoma statute that categorically rejected adoption decrees when the adopting parents were same-sex couples violated the Full Faith and Credit Clause. Final adoption orders are judgments that must be given full faith and credit under the Constitution. Adar v. Smith, 639 F.3d 146 (5th Cir.2011), cert. denied, 566 U.S. 942 (2011) (mem.).

For a useful discussion of full faith and credit to equity decrees, see Price, Full Faith and Credit and the Equity Conflict, 84 Va.L.Rev. 747 (1998).

2. The majority distinguishes between the faith and credit due judgments—which are stricter and apparently do not allow for a public policy exception—and the faith and credit due laws, which are less strict and allow for a public policy exception. The same distinction is drawn in the next principal case, Magnolia Petroleum Co. v. Hunt. Is the distinction explained by less of a national need to compel deference to sister-state laws than to judgments? If two states had statutes that would produce different results in the same case, could either statute apply if each state had given full faith and credit to the other's statute?

3. Justice Kennedy states: "If we honor the undoubted principle that Courts need give a prior judgment no more force or effect than the issuing state gives it, the case before us is resolved." Then, however, he focuses on what he regards as the false assumption that "Michigan would apply the full force of its judgment to the Bakers." Is it more relevant to the "undoubted principle" whether a Michigan Court would enjoin Elwell from compelled testimony in a Missouri court? Would such an injunction have been likely in light of the stipulation in the Michigan judgment that Elwell's compelled testimony would not violate the injunction?

4. Rash v. Rash, 147 F.3d 1291 (11th Cir.1998) dismissed a husband's action to declare that a Florida divorce decree was valid as opposed to a New Jersey divorce decree. The property settlement in the New Jersey decree was more favorable to the wife than that in the Florida decree. The court held that the Florida court had improperly granted the husband a divorce because this denied full faith and credit to a New Jersey order enjoining the husband from proceeding in Florida.

———

JAMES V. GRAND TRUNK WESTERN RAILROAD CO., 14 Ill.2d 356, 152 N.E.2d 858, cert. denied, 358 U.S. 915, 79 S.Ct. 588 (1958). [The case involved a Michigan injunction and an Illinois counterinjunction. A resident of Michigan was killed in that state by the defendant railroad company. His widow, appointed administratrix in Michigan, brought an action in Illinois under the Michigan wrongful death statute, alleging the death was caused by the negligence of the railroad.

In Michigan, where the administratrix resided, the defendant obtained a temporary injunction restraining her from proceeding with the action in Illinois.

The administratrix then filed a supplemental complaint in the Illinois court, which alleged she believed she could not obtain a fair trial in the county in Michigan where she resided, and the railroad's injunction suit in Michigan was for the purpose of preventing her from obtaining a fair trial in Illinois and of forcing her into an unjust settlement to her irreparable injury. She moved for an injunction restraining the enforcement of the Michigan injunction. The motion was denied by the Illinois trial court and the Appellate Court, and their action is the subject of the present appeal to the Supreme Court of Illinois.]

■ BRISTOW, JUSTICE. . . . The issues are essentially whether the Illinois court, having prior jurisdiction of a wrongful death action instituted by a nonresident plaintiff, must recognize an out-of-State injunction restraining the plaintiff from proceeding with that action; and whether the Illinois court, to protect its jurisdiction of the wrongful death action, may issue a counterinjunction restraining defendant from enforcing its injunction against plaintiff in the State of her residence. . . .

In the instant case it is uncontroverted that the Illinois trial court had proper jurisdiction of the parties. . . . Moreover, it is the undisputed policy of this State to keep its courts open to residents and nonresidents alike.

[W]hile we quite agree with defendant's repeated assertion that a court of equity has power to restrain persons within its jurisdiction from instituting or proceeding with foreign actions (Cole v. Cunningham, 133 U.S. 107, 6 A.L.R.2d 896), we note that the exercise of such power by equity courts has been deemed a matter of great delicacy, invoked with great restraint to avoid distressing conflicts and reciprocal interference with jurisdiction. . . .

Conversely, where other States have enjoined litigants from proceeding with a previously instituted Illinois action, this jurisdiction has followed the overwhelming judicial opinion that neither the full-faith-and-credit clause nor rules of comity require compulsory recognition of such injunctions so as to abate or preclude the disposition of the pending case. . . .

Therefore, [we are not required] to recognize the Michigan injunction, and we may retain jurisdiction and proceed with plaintiff's wrongful death action. Such a course, however, is not practicable in the instant case, unless plaintiff, who is subject to imprisonment and other coercive tactics if she fails to dismiss her Illinois action, is protected by enjoining defendant from enforcing the Michigan injunction by contempt proceedings. A plaintiff cannot be expected or required to risk imprisonment so that the court may retain jurisdiction of a cause.

This brings us to the ultimate issue in this case: whether the court which first acquires jurisdiction of the parties and of the merits of the cause can issue a counterinjunction restraining a party before it from enforcing an out-of-State injunction which requires the dismissal of the local cause and ousts the forum of jurisdiction. . . .

. . . [W]e cannot close our eyes to the fact that the intended effect of the Michigan injunction, though directed at the parties and not at this court, is to prevent the Illinois court from adjudicating a cause of action of which it had proper jurisdiction. For it is patent that if the litigants are coerced to dismiss the Illinois action, it is our rightfully acquired jurisdiction that is thereby destroyed. Therefore, the Michigan injunction was in everything but form an order restraining the Illinois court and determining the cases, it may properly try.

. . . [T]his court need not, and will not, countenance having its right to try cases, of which it has proper jurisdiction, determined by the courts of other States, through their injunctive process. We are not only free to disregard such out-of-State injunctions, and to adjudicate the merits of the pending action, but we can protect our jurisdiction from such usurpation by the issuance of a counterinjunction restraining the enforcement of the out-of-State injunction. . . .

Reversed and remanded, with directions.

■ SCHAEFER, JUSTICE (dissenting). . . .

So far as I have been able to ascertain, no court has as yet held that such an injunction is entitled to full faith and credit in the sense that the action toward which the injunction is directed must be abated. When such injunctions have been recognized, it has been because the State in which the action is pending has chosen to do so as a matter of comity, and not because it was required to do so by constitutional command. . . .

In part this view appears to rest upon the ground that to recognize the injunction is to recognize the claim of the enjoining State to exclusive cognizance of a transitory cause of action, which might abridge constitutional privileges. . . . In part it appears to rest upon the ground that to recognize the injunction would "mean in effect that the courts of one State can control what goes on in another." . . . For these reasons I agree with the majority that the Michigan injunction is not entitled to full faith and credit.

But the question in this case goes a step beyond the issue as to full faith and credit. What is here sought is a counter-injunction to restrain the railroad from enforcing the injunction entered by the Michigan court. . . . Just as the first injunction sired the second, so the second might sire a third. The ultimate end is not foreseeable.

The place to stop this unseemly kind of judicial disorder is where it begins. The peculiar preference of one State for a particular venue in a single class of cases does not, it seems to me, afford a basis for indirect interference with litigation pending in another jurisdiction. The salutary power of a court of equity to restrain the prosecution of inequitable actions in a foreign court originated and developed upon more substantial considerations. But we are not called upon to review the propriety of the Michigan injunction. Plaintiff did not seek to review it in the Michigan courts. . . . Illinois has no connection whatever with the occurrences out of which the administrator's claim arose. The policy of Illinois with respect to the maintenance of foreign wrongful death actions was expressed in section 2 of the Injuries Act (Ill.Rev.Stat.1955, chap. 70, par. 2) which prohibited them. While it is true that this prohibition is no longer effective, the policy that it expressed is also of significance in determining whether or not a counter-injunction should have been issued.

I think that the trial court and the Appellate Court were right, and so I would affirm.

NOTES

1.   Pound, The Progress of the Law—Equity, 33 Harv.L.Rev. 420, 426–27 (1920): "Three types of cases may be distinguished in which courts have enjoined litigation in foreign jurisdictions. In one the foreign court had no jurisdiction, but the threatened foreign judgment would embarrass plaintiff in the assertion of his rights, the legal remedy of collateral attack on the judgment when set up against plaintiff involved danger of impairment of the evidence by which its invalidity could be made to appear, and to compel plaintiff to go to the foreign state to defend or attack the threatened judgment directly involved compelling him to litigate abroad with a wrongdoer whom he could reach at home. In a second type concurrent litigation between the same parties over the same subject matter was in progress or was threatened. In some of the cases of this type there was simply a vexatious multiplicity of actions. Here courts were cautious about interposing. In others, one court was not in as good a position to do complete justice as another. In still others, the defendant was seeking to obtain an inequitable advantage over other creditors by means of concurrent litigation abroad. In a third type there was an attempt of domestic creditors to reach exempt property of a domestic debtor by means of an action outside of the state. To these some courts are adding a fourth: Cases where the foreign court has jurisdiction, in which there is no concurrent litigation or vexatious multiplicity of actions, and in which there is no attempt to reach anything which the policy of the local legislation seeks to secure to the plaintiff, but in which a domestic creditor seeks to sue a domestic debtor, as he has full legal power to do, in another state, where the latter has property, because of more favorable procedure or more favorable views as to what is a defense in the latter jurisdiction. In these cases it cannot be said that plaintiff (in equity) has a legal right only to be sued at home, nor may he claim a legal interest

in the procedure or substantive law of his domicile. Doctrines of Conflict of Laws may sometimes require the court in the other state to judge the cause by the laws of the jurisdiction where the parties are domiciled. But that is a matter for that court to consider and does not give to the latter jurisdiction any claim to exclusive cognizance of the cause nor to its citizens any legal claim to make their defense solely at their domicile. As between a plaintiff and a defendant, each seeking the tribunal more favorable to him, why should not equity leave the matter to the law? ..." For a recent decision following *James* in Illinois federal court, see Love v. Frontier Ins. Co., 526 F.Supp.2d 859 (N.D.Ill.2007).

2. The unwillingness manifested by a court having jurisdiction of the parties to an action to give effect to a foreign decree enjoining the institution or maintenance of that action has its counterpart in the reluctance to treat the pendency of a foreign action on the same cause of action as a defense. A plea in abatement based on the pendency of a prior personal action in another state has often been held to be ineffective. Fitch v. Whaples, 220 A.2d 170 (Me.1966). However, since the granting of a stay does not have the effect of sustaining a plea in abatement in terminating the action, a stay may be allowed when a plea in abatement would be unavailable. See Mahaffey v. Bechtel Associates Professional Corp., 699 F.2d 545 (D.C.Cir.1983); Schering Corp. v. Griffo, 872 F.Supp.2d 1220 (D.N.M.2012). See also Restatement, Second, Conflict of Laws 86. For further discussion of *lis pendens* in the context of forum non conveniens, see p. 248, Note 6 and p. 252, supra.

3. In Amchem Products Inc. v. British Columbia (Workers' Compensation Board), [1993] 1 S.C.R. 897, the Supreme Court of Canada set aside an antisuit injunction against further proceedings in Texas on the ground that Texas was the convenient forum. See also Tetley, Current Developments in Canadian Private International Law, 78 Can. Bar Rev. 152, 162–64, 196–97 (1999).

Yarborough v. Yarborough

Supreme Court of the United States, 1933.
290 U.S. 202, 54 S.Ct. 181, 78 L.Ed.269, 90 A.L.R. 924.

[Facts as taken from the dissent of Justice Stone: The divorce decree of the Georgia court purported to adjudicate finally, both for the present and for the future, the right of a minor child of the marriage to support and maintenance, by directing her father to make a lump sum payment for that purpose. More than two years later, after the minor had become a domiciled resident of South Carolina, and after the sum paid had been exhausted, a court of that State, on the basis of her need as then shown, has rendered a judgment directing further payments for her support out of property of the father in South Carolina, in addition to that already commanded by the Georgia judgment.]

■ JUSTICE BRANDEIS delivered the opinion of the Court.

. . . Fourth. It is contended that the order for permanent alimony is not binding upon Sadie because she was not a resident of Georgia at the time it was entered. Being a minor, Sadie's domicile was Georgia, that of her father; and her domicile continued to be in Georgia until entry of the judgment in question. She was not capable by her own act of changing her domicile. Neither the temporary residence in North Carolina at the time the divorce suit was begun, nor her removal with her mother to South Carolina before entry of the judgment, effected a change of Sadie's domicile. . . .

Fifth. The fact that Sadie has become a resident of South Carolina does not impair the finality of the judgment. South Carolina thereby acquired the jurisdiction to determine her status and the incidents of that status. Upon residents of that State it could impose duties for her benefit. Doubtless, it might have imposed upon her grandfather who was resident there a duty to support Sadie. But the mere fact of Sadie's residence in South Carolina does not give that State the power to impose such a duty upon the father who is not a resident and who long has been domiciled in Georgia. He has fulfilled the duty which he owes her by the law of his domicile and the judgment of its court. Upon that judgment he is entitled to rely. It was settled by Sistare v. Sistare, 218 U.S. 1, that the full faith and credit clause applies to an unalterable decree of alimony for a divorced wife. The clause applies, likewise, to an unalterable decree of alimony for a minor child. We need not consider whether South Carolina would have power to require the father, if he were domiciled there, to make further provision for the support, maintenance, or education of his daughter.

Reversed.

■ JUSTICE STONE, dissenting.

I think the judgment should be affirmed.[W]e may take it that the Georgia decree, as the statutes and decisions of the State declare, is unalterable and, as pronounced, is effective to govern the rights of the parties in Georgia. But there is nothing in the decree itself, or in the history of the proceedings which led to it to suggest that it was rendered with any purpose or intent to regulate or control the relationship of parent and child, or the duties which flow from it, in places outside the State of Georgia where they might later come to reside. . . . But if we are to read the decree as though it contained a clause, in terms, restricting the power of any other state, in which the minor might come to reside, to make provision for her support, then, in the absence of some law of Congress requiring it, I am not persuaded that the full faith and credit clause gives sanction to such control by one state of the internal affairs of another.[1] . . .

Between the prohibition of the due process clause, acting upon the courts of the state from which such proceedings may be taken, and the mandate of the full faith and credit clause, acting upon the state to which

---

[1] It may be assumed for present purposes that the child was sufficiently represented in the Georgia proceedings. But the point is doubtful. . . .

they may be taken, there is an area which federal authority has not occupied. As this Court has often recognized, there are many judgments which need not be given the same force and effect abroad which they have at home, and there are some, though valid in the state where rendered, to which the full faith and credit clause gives no force elsewhere. In the assertion of rights, defined by a judgment of one state, within the territory of another there is often an inescapable conflict of interest of the two states, and there comes a point beyond which the imposition of the will of one state beyond its own borders involves a forbidden infringement of some legitimate domestic interest of the other. That point may vary with the circumstances of the case, and in the absence of provisions more specific than the general terms of the congressional enactment[2] this Court must determine for itself the extent to which one state may qualify or deny rights claimed under proceedings or records of other states. . . .

Just as due process of law will not permit a state by its judgment to inflict parties "with a perpetual contractual paralysis" which will prevent them from altering outside the state their contracts or ordinary business relations entered into within it, New York L. Ins. Co. v. Head, supra (234 U.S. 161), so full faith and credit does not command that the obligations attached to a status, because once appropriately imposed by one state, shall be forever placed beyond the control of every other state, without regard to the interest in it and the power of control which the other may later acquire. . . . Whatever difference there may be between holding that a judgment is invalid under the Fourteenth Amendment because it is "extraterritorial," and in holding that it is not entitled to full faith and credit although it does not infringe the Fourteenth Amendment, is one of degree, or of a difference in circumstances which may prevent the operation of the latter provision of the Constitution. The Georgia judgment with which we are now concerned does not infringe the Fourteenth Amendment, for Georgia had "jurisdiction" of the parties and subject matter at the time its judgment was rendered. The possibility of conflict of the Georgia judgment with the interest of South Carolina first arose when the minor transferred her domicile to South Carolina, long after the Georgia judgment was given.

---

[2] The mandatory force of the full faith and credit clause as defined by this Court may be, in some degree not yet fully defined, expanded or contracted by Congress. Much of the confusion and procedural deficiencies which the constitutional provision alone has not avoided may be remedied by legislation. Cook, "Powers of Congress under the Full Faith and Credit Clause," 28 Yale L.J. 421; Corwin, "The Full Faith and Credit Clause," 81 University of Pa.L.Rev. 371; cf. 33 Columbia L.Rev. 854, 866. The constitutional provision giving Congress power to prescribe the effect to be given to acts, records and proceedings would have been quite unnecessary had it not been intended that Congress should have a latitude broader than that given the courts by the full faith and credit clause alone. It was remarked on the floor of the Constitutional Convention that without the extension of power in the legislature, the provision "would amount to nothing more than what now takes place among all Independent Nations." Hunt and Scott, Madison's Reports of the Debates in the Federal Convention of 1787, p. 503. The play which has been afforded for the recognition of local public policy in cases where there is called in question only a statute of another state, as to the effect of which Congress has not legislated, compared with the more restricted scope for local policy where there is a judicial proceeding, as to which Congress has legislated, suggests the Congressional power.

The question presented here is whether the support and maintenance of a minor child, domiciled in South Carolina, is so peculiarly a subject of domestic concern that Georgia law cannot impair South Carolina's authority.... The maintenance and support of children domiciled within a state, like their education and custody, is a subject in which government itself is deemed to have a peculiar interest and concern.... The states very generally make some provision from their own resources for the maintenance and support of orphans or destitute children, but in order that children may not become public charges the duty of maintenance is one imposed primarily upon the parents, according to the needs of the child and their ability to meet those needs.... Hence, it is no answer in such a suit that at some earlier time provision was made for the child, which is no longer available or suitable because of his greater needs, or because of the increased financial ability of the parent to provide for them, or that the child may be maintained from other sources....

Even though the Constitution does not deny to Georgia the power to indulge in such a policy for itself, it by no means follows that it gives to Georgia the privilege of prescribing that policy for other states in which the child comes to live.[19] South Carolina has adopted a different policy. It imposes on the father or his property located within the state the duty to support his minor child domiciled there. It enforces the duty by criminal prosecution and also permits suit by the minor child maintained by guardian ad litem. The measure of the duty is the present need of the child and the ability of the parent to provide for it....

... The Fourteenth Amendment does not enable a father by the expedient of choosing a domicile other than the state where the child is rightfully domiciled, to avoid the duty which that state may impose for support of his child. The reason seems plain. The locality of the child's residence must see to his welfare.... The conclusion must be the same when the issue is that of the credit to be given the prior Georgia judgment....

... Here the Georgia decree did not end the relationship of parent and child, as a decree of divorce may end the marriage relationship. Had the infant continued to reside in Georgia, and had she sought in the courts of South Carolina to compel the application of property of her father, found there, to her further maintenance and support, full faith and credit to the Georgia decree applied to its own domiciled resident might have required the denial of any relief. [Citing cases.] But when she became a domiciled resident of South Carolina a new interest came into being, the interest of the State of South Carolina as a measure of self-preservation to secure the adequate protection and maintenance of helpless members of its own community and its prospective citizens. That

---

[19] In the custody cases a very similar situation is presented. As conventionally stated the rule has been that the most the full faith and credit clause can require is that the prior ruling shall be deemed conclusive in the absence of an asserted change in circumstances....

interest was distinct from any which Georgia could conclusively regulate or control by its judgment even though rendered while the child was domiciled in Georgia. The present decision extends the operation of the full faith and credit clause beyond its proper function of affording protection to the domestic interests of Georgia and makes it an instrument for encroachment by Georgia upon the domestic concerns of South Carolina.

■ JUSTICE CARDOZO concurs in this opinion.

NOTES

1.   Elkind v. Byck, 439 P.2d 316 (Cal.1968). In that case, the parties had been divorced in Georgia pursuant to a decree under which the husband paid a lump sum for the maintenance and support of his wife and child. Under the Georgia law, his payment was in full satisfaction of the husband's obligation and no further liability could be imposed upon him. Following the divorce, the wife made her home in New York and the husband moved to California. Thereafter, the wife sought additional support from the husband, and it was held that the California court had power to grant her request. Yarborough was said not to stand in the way "[s]ince that decision was based upon the father's continued domicile and residence in Georgia." In this case, the husband's "substantial relationship" with California "justifies the application of its law of support." The court concluded that the facts of the case served to demonstrate "why the divorce state should not be permitted to determine the welfare of the child for all time and in all states. More than ten years following the divorce, none of the parties appears to have any connection at all with Georgia: the mother and child reside in New York and the father resides in California." Similarly: In re Marriage of McCabe, 819 P.2d 1116 (Colo.App.1991) (party had changed domicile). Other courts avoided the result of the main case by finding that the foreign decree at issue did not expressly discharge the support obligation. See, e.g., Dandurand v. Underwood, 332 S.W.3d 907 (Mo.App.2011). For the Supreme Court's own way of dealing with *Yarborough* and *Magnolia* (immediately following), see its focus on what it was that was before the F-1 tribunal and to what the full-faith-and-credit mandate applies in *McCartin* and *Thomas*, pp. 354, 356, infra.

2.   RESTATEMENT, SECOND, CONFLICT OF LAWS.

§ 103. Limitations on Full Faith and Credit

A judgment rendered in one State of the United States need not be recognized or enforced in a sister State if such recognition or enforcement is not required by the national policy of full faith and credit because it would involve an improper interference with important interests of the sister State.

3.   Section 103 was approved in Thompson v. Thompson, 645 S.W.2d 79 (Mo.App.1982). In that case, a divorce decree rendered by a Kansas court had ordered the husband to provide child support. By Kansas statute, a parent's obligation to support a child ceases when the child attains eighteen years. Thereafter, all parties moved to Missouri and there the wife sought to compel

the husband to support a son who was then over eighteen years old. The Missouri court found for the wife, holding that an exception should be made to the normal command of full faith and credit to protect Missouri's "overriding domestic interests." It relied upon Justice Stone's dissent in *Yarborough*, upon Elkind v. Byck, and upon § 103. Was it necessary for the court to rely upon an exception to full faith and credit to reach the desired result?

Section 103 is criticized as inaccurately overbroad in Reynolds, The Iron Law of Full Faith and Credit, 53 Md.L.Rev. 412, 436–49 (1994). Reynolds argues that there is no generalized "improper-interference" exception to full faith and credit and that all of the authorities cited as supporting Section 103 can be more convincingly explained on other grounds.

4.   In the context of footnote 13 in Justice Stone's dissent, above, see the Defense of Marriage Act, P.L. 104–199, 110 Stat. 2419, 28 U.S.C.A. § 1738C, which gave states the authority not to recognize same-sex marriages performed in other states. In Obergefell v. Hodges, the Supreme Court invalidated that provision: it recognized the right to same-sex marriage; the full faith and credit mandate therefore applies to such marriages. For discussion, see p. 918, infra.

5.   See generally Reese & Johnson, The Scope of Full Faith and Credit to Judgments, 49 Colum.L.Rev. 153 (1949).

Magnolia Petroleum Co. v. Hunt

Supreme Court of the United States, 1943.
320 U.S. 430, 64 S.Ct. 208, 88 L.Ed.149, 150 A.L.R. 413.

[Facts, as stated in Justice Black's dissent: The respondent Hunt is a resident of Louisiana, employed in that state by the petitioner and sent by the petitioner to do work in Texas. While in Texas he was seriously injured in the course of his employment. Confined to a hospital he was told that he could not recover compensation unless he signed two forms presented to him. As found by the Louisiana trial judge there was printed on each of the forms "in small type" the designation "Industrial Accident Board, Austin, Texas." To get his compensation Hunt signed the forms and the Texas insurer began to pay. Returning to his home in Louisiana Hunt apparently discovered that his interest would be more fully protected under Louisiana law and notified the insurer of an intention to claim under the statute of that state. The insurer immediately stopped payment to him and notified the Texas Board to that effect. Four days later, without any request from Hunt, the Board notified him at his Louisiana home that a hearing would be held in Texas within two and a half weeks "to determine the liability of the insurance company" under Texas law. Hunt did not participate in that proceeding. The Texas Board thereafter made an award to him which, under the law of Texas, was equivalent to a judgment against the insurer. Before the Texas award became final, Hunt, who had declined to accept any money under it, filed suit against his employer in the courts of Louisiana under the Workmen's

Compensation Law of Louisiana. He recovered a judgment for a substantially larger sum than had been allowed him under the Texas award, from which the Louisiana court deducted the sum he had already received from the Texas insurer. . . .]

■ CHIEF JUSTICE STONE delivered the opinion of the Court.

The question for decision is whether, under the full faith and credit clause, Art. IV, § 1 of the Constitution of the United States, an award of compensation for personal injury under the Texas Workmen's Compensation Law, Title 130 of the Revised Civil Statutes of Texas, bars a further recovery of compensation for the same injury under the Louisiana Workmen's Compensation Law, Title 34, Chapter 15 of the Louisiana General Statutes. . . .

. . .

In Texas a compensation award against the employer's insurer . . . is explicitly made by statute in lieu of any other recovery for injury to the employee, since Art. 8306, § 3 provides that employees subject to the Act "shall have no right of action against their employer or against any agent, servant or employé of said employer for damages for personal injuries . . . but such employés . . . shall look for compensation solely to the association [the insurer]." A compensation award which has become final "is entitled to the same faith and credit as a judgment of a court." . . .

It does not appear, nor is it contended, that Louisiana more than Texas allows in its own courts a second recovery of compensation for a single injury. The contention is that since Louisiana is better satisfied with the measure of recovery allowed by its own laws, it may deny full faith and credit to the Texas award, which respondent has procured by his election to pursue his remedy in that state. In thus refusing, on the basis of state law and policy, to give effect to the Texas award as a final adjudication of respondent's claim for compensation for his injury suffered in Texas, the Louisiana court ignored the distinction, long recognized and applied by this Court . . . between the faith and credit required to be given to judgments and that to which local common and statutory law is entitled under the Constitution and laws of the United States.

In the case of local law, since each of the states of the Union has constitutional authority to make its own law with respect to persons and events within its borders the full faith and credit clause does not ordinarily require it to substitute for its own law the conflicting law of another state, even though that law is of controlling force in the courts of that state with respect to the same persons and events. . . . It was for this reason that we held that the state of the employer and employee is free to apply its own compensation law to the injury of the employee rather than the law of another state where the injury occurred. Alaska Packers Assn. v. Industrial Accident Comm'n, [294 U.S. 532 at] 544–550. And for like reasons we held also that the state of the place of injury is free to apply its own law to the exclusion of the law of the state of the employer and employee. Pacific Employers Ins. Co. v. Industrial Accident Comm'n, [306 U.S. 493 at] 502–505.

But it does not follow that the employee who has sought and recovered an award of compensation in either state may then have recourse to the laws and courts of the other to recover a second or additional award for the same injury. Where a court must make choice of one of two conflicting statutes of different states and apply it to a cause of action which has not been previously litigated, there can be no plea of res judicata. But when the employee who has recovered compensation for his injury in one state seeks a second recovery in another he may be met by the plea that full faith and credit requires that his demand, which has become res judicata in one state, must be recognized as such in every other.

The full faith and credit clause and the Act of Congress implementing it have, for most purposes, placed a judgment on a different footing from a statute of one state, judicial recognition of which is sought in another. . . .

These consequences flow from the clear purpose of the full faith and credit clause to establish throughout the federal system the salutary principle of the common law that a litigation once pursued to judgment shall be as conclusive of the rights of the parties in every other court as in that where the judgment was rendered, so that a cause of action merged in a judgment in one state is likewise merged in every other. The full faith and credit clause like the commerce clause thus became a nationally unifying force. It altered the status of the several states as independent foreign sovereignties, each free to ignore rights and obligations created under the laws or established by the judicial proceedings of the others, by making each an integral part of a single nation, in which rights judicially established in any part are given nation-wide application. . . . Because there is a full faith and credit clause a defendant may not a second time challenge the validity of the plaintiff's right which has ripened into a judgment and a plaintiff may not for his single cause of action secure a second or a greater recovery. . . .

We have no occasion to consider what effect would be required to be given to the Texas award if the Texas courts held that an award of compensation in another state would not bar an award in Texas, for . . . Texas does not allow such a second recovery. And if the award of compensation in Texas were not res judicata there, full faith and credit would, of course, be no bar to the recovery of an award in another state. Chicago, R.I. & P.R. Co. v. Elder, 270 U.S. 611, 622–623.

Whether the proceeding before the State Industrial Accident Board in Texas be regarded as a "judicial proceeding," or its award as a "record" within the meaning of the full faith and credit clause and the Act of Congress, the result is the same. For judicial proceedings and records of the state are both required to have "such faith and credit given to them in every court within the United States as they have by law or usage in the courts of the State from which they are taken." . . .

Respondent was free to pursue his remedy in either state but, having chosen to seek it in Texas, where the award was res judicata, the full faith and credit clause precludes him from again seeking a remedy in Louisiana upon the same grounds. . . .*

■ JUSTICE DOUGLAS, dissenting.

. . . We are dealing here with . . . a clash between the policies of two sovereign States. The question is not which policy we prefer; it is whether the two conflicting policies can somehow be accommodated. The command of the full faith and credit clause frequently makes a reconciliation of the two interests impossible. One must give way in the larger interest of the federal union. The question in each case is whether as a practical matter there is room for adjustment, consistent with the requirements of full faith and credit. . . .

. . . If the Texas award had undertaken to adjudicate the rights and duties of the parties under the Louisiana contract of employment, which we are told carries the right to compensation under the Louisiana Act (10 So.2d 109, 112), the result would be quite different. Then the judgment, . . . would undertake to regulate the relationship of the parties, or their rights and duties which flow from it, as respects their undertakings in another State. . . . But there is nothing in the Texas proceeding or in the Texas award to indicate that that was either intended or done. The most charitable construction is that Texas undertook to adjust the rights and duties of the parties and to regulate their relationship only so long as they remained subject to the jurisdiction of Texas.

JUSTICE MURPHY joins in this dissent.

■ JUSTICE BLACK, dissenting:

. . . As I see it, this case properly involves two separate legal questions: (1) Did Texas intend the award of its Industrial Accident Board against the insurer to bar the right granted the employee by the Louisiana Workmen's Compensation Law to collect from his employer for the same injury the difference between the compensation allowed by Texas and the more generous compensation allowed by Louisiana? (2) Assuming the Texas award was intended to constitute such a bar, does the interest of Louisiana in regulating the employment contracts of its residents nevertheless permit it to grant that larger measure of compensation which as a matter of local policy it believes necessary? The decision of the Court on both of these issues appears to me to be wrong. . . .

It is apparently conceded that Louisiana would not have been required to apply the Texas statute had there not been a judgment in the particular case by the Texas tribunal. This freedom of the state to apply

---

*   A concurring opinion by Justice Jackson is omitted.

its own policy in workmen's compensation cases despite a conflicting statute in the state in which the accident occurs rests on the theory that the state where the workman is hired or is domiciled has a genuine and special interest in the outcome of the litigation. . . . The argument of state interest is hardly less compelling when Louisiana chooses to reject as decisive of the issues of the case a foreign judgment than when it rejects a foreign statute.

The interest of Texas in providing compensation for an injured employee who like respondent was only temporarily employed in the state is not the same as that of Louisiana where the respondent was domiciled and where the contract of employment was made. Someone has to take care of an individual who has received, as has respondent, an injury which permanently disables him from performance of his work. . . . If it chooses to be more generous to injured workmen than Texas, no Constitutional issue is presented. . . .

. . . There should be no Constitutional barrier preventing a state in effect from increasing the workmen's compensation award of another state in a case in which it has jurisdiction over the participants and the social responsibility for the results. Where two states both have a legitimate interest in the outcome of workmen's compensation litigation, the question of whether the second state which considers the case should abide by the decision of the first is a question of policy which should be decided by the state legislatures and courts. . . . State laws vary, and uniformity is not the highest value in the law of workmen's compensation. . . .

■ JUSTICE DOUGLAS, JUSTICE MURPHY, and JUSTICE RUTLEDGE concur in this opinion.

Industrial Commission of Wisconsin v. McCartin

Supreme Court of the United States, 1947.
330 U.S. 622, 67 S.Ct. 886, 91 L.Ed.1140, 169 A.L.R. 1179.

[Kopp and McCartin were both Illinois residents. Pursuant to a contract made in Illinois, Kopp worked for McCartin on a building job in Wisconsin and there suffered an eye injury in the course of his employment. Kopp sought workmen's compensation in both Illinois and Wisconsin. The Illinois award, which was the first to be handed down, provided that it "does not affect any rights" which Kopp might have under the Workmen's Compensation Statute of Wisconsin. Thereafter, the Wisconsin Commission gave Kopp an additional award but on appeal the Wisconsin courts set aside the award on the authority of the Magnolia decision. The Supreme Court granted certiorari.]

■ JUSTICE MURPHY delivered the opinion of the Court. . . .

If it were apparent that the Illinois award was intended to be final and conclusive of all the employee's rights against the employer and the insurer growing out of the injury, the decision in the Magnolia Petroleum Co. case would be controlling here. . . .

But there is nothing in the [Illinois award or in the underlying] statute or in the decisions thereunder to indicate that it was designed to preclude any recovery by proceedings brought in another state for injuries received there in the course of an Illinois employment. . . . And in light of the rule that workmen's compensation laws are to be liberally construed in furtherance of the purpose for which they were enacted . . . we should not readily interpret such a statute so as to cut off an employee's right to sue under other legislation passed for his benefit. Only some unmistakable language by a state legislature or judiciary would warrant our accepting such a construction. . . .

We need not rest our decision, however, solely upon the absence of any provision or construction of the Illinois Workmen's Compensation Act forbidding an employee from seeking alternative or additional relief under the laws of another state. There is even stronger evidence that the employee is free to ask for additional compensation in Wisconsin. . . .

Here the employer and the employee entered into a settlement contract fixing the amount of compensation to which the employee was entitled under the Illinois statute. . . .

One of the provisions in the settlement contract which became the award was the statement that "This settlement does not affect any rights that applicant may have under the Workmen's Compensation Act of the State of Wisconsin." That statement was made a part of the contract at the request of the employee, who had been informed by the Wisconsin Commission that he was entitled to claim an additional amount of compensation in Wisconsin after recovering in Illinois. . . .

This contract provision saving the rights of the employee in Wisconsin thus became part of the Illinois award. . . . [And] when the reservation in this award is read against the background of the Illinois Workmen's Compensation Act, it becomes clear that the reservation spells out what we believe to be implicit in that Act-namely, that an Illinois workmen's compensation award of the type here involved does not foreclose an additional award under the laws of another state. . . .

Since this Illinois award is final and conclusive only as to rights arising in Illinois, Wisconsin is free under the full faith and credit clause to grant an award of compensation in accord with its own laws. Magnolia Petroleum Co. v. Hunt, supra, thus does not control this case.

Reversed.

■ JUSTICE RUTLEDGE concurs in the result.

NOTES

1.   Suppose that a contract made in State X is by its terms to be performed in State Y. Under their respective conflict of laws rules, the courts of State X

look to the law of the place of making to determine the validity of a contract, those of State Y to that of the place of performance; the particular contract in question would be invalid under the local law of State X but valid under that of State Y. Suppose further that the plaintiff, domiciled in State Y, brings suit for breach of the contract in State X and loses. Does the existence of this judgment preclude him from thereafter pressing his claim in State Y even though he would almost certainly have won if he had originally brought suit in that state? If the answer to this question is in the affirmative, does it also follow that the result reached by the majority in the Magnolia case was correct?

2.   Semler v. Psychiatric Institute of Washington, D.C., 575 F.2d 922 (D.C.Cir.1978). The plaintiff's decedent had been murdered in Virginia by a person who had been placed by the defendant Psychiatric Institute in a generally unsupervised outpatient program. The plaintiff initially brought suit in Virginia and recovered $25,000 under that state's wrongful death act. She then sought recovery in the District of Columbia under the District's survival act. Held that full faith and credit required that the second suit be barred by the Virginia judgment. "Under District of Columbia law, negligent conduct resulting in death gives rise to two independent rights of action, one under the Wrongful Death Act and the other under the Survival Act." On the other hand, the Virginia Wrongful Death Act provides the "exclusive right of action in wrongful death cases" and "exists in lieu of an action based on the survival of the deceased's original claim." The court concluded that initially the plaintiff could have brought her action in either Virginia or the District of Columbia and that presumably a greater recovery for the death could have been obtained under District of Columbia law than under that of Virginia. "Either state could have properly applied its law in the first instance. But having elected to seek her remedy in Virginia, where the [effect of the judgment was to bar any further recovery for the wrongful death], the full faith and credit clause precludes her from again seeking a remedy in the District of Columbia upon the same grounds."

Thomas v. Washington Gas Light Co.

Supreme Court of the United States, 1980.
448 U.S. 261, 100 S.Ct. 2647, 65 L.Ed.2d 757.

■ JUSTICE STEVENS announced the judgment of the Court and delivered an opinion in which JUSTICE BRENNAN, JUSTICE STEWART, and JUSTICE BLACKMUN join. . . .

Petitioner is a resident of the District of Columbia and was hired by respondent in the District of Columbia. During the year that he was employed by respondent, he worked primarily in the District but also worked in Virginia and Maryland. He sustained a back injury while at work in Arlington, Va., on January 22, 1971. Two weeks later he entered into an "Industrial Commission of Virginia Memorandum of Agreement as to Payment of Compensation" providing for benefits of $62 per week. . . .

In 1974, petitioner notified the Department of Labor of his intention to seek compensation under the District of Columbia Act. Respondent opposed the claim primarily on the ground that since, as a matter of Virginia law, the Virginia award excluded any other recovery "at common law or otherwise" on account of the injury in Virginia, the District of Columbia's obligation to give that award full faith and credit precluded a second, supplemental award in the District.

I

Respondent contends that the District of Columbia was without power to award petitioner additional compensation because of the Full Faith and Credit Clause of the Constitution or, more precisely, because of the federal statute implementing that Clause. An analysis of this contention must begin with two decisions from the 1940's that are almost directly on point: Magnolia Petroleum Co. v. Hunt and Industrial Commission of Wisconsin v. McCartin.

[Justice Stevens here reviewed the *Magnolia* and *McCartin* decisions]

[In its *McCartin*] opinion, the Court . . . stated that "[o]nly some unmistakable language by a state legislature or judiciary would warrant our accepting . . . a construction" that a workmen's compensation statute "is designed to preclude any recovery by proceedings brought in another state." Id., at 627–628. . . .

The Virginia Workmen's Compensation Act . . . contains no "unmistakable language" directed at precluding a supplemental compensation award in another State. . . . Consequently, *McCartin* by its terms, rather than the earlier *Magnolia* decision, is controlling as between the two precedents. . . .

II

We cannot fail to observe that, in the Court's haste to retreat from *Magnolia,* it fashioned a rule that clashes with normally accepted full faith and credit principles. It has long been the law that "the judgment of a state court should have the same credit, validity, and effect, in every other court in the United States, which it had in the state where it was pronounced." Hampton v. McConnel, 3 Wheat. 234, 235 (Marshall, C.J.). . . .

The *McCartin* rule, however, focusing as it does on the extraterritorial intent of the rendering State, is fundamentally different. It authorizes a State, by drafting or construing its legislation in "unmistakable language," directly to determine the extraterritorial effect of its workmen's compensation awards. . . .

[This] rule represents an unwarranted delegation to the States of this Court's responsibility for the final arbitration of full faith and credit questions.[15] . . . To vest the power of determining the extraterritorial effect of a State's own laws and judgments in the State itself risks the very kind of parochial entrenchment on the interests of other States that it was the purpose of the Full Faith and Credit Clause and other provisions of Art. IV of the Constitution to prevent. . . .

Thus, a re-examination of *McCartin's* unmistakable language test reinforces our tentative conclusion that it does not provide an acceptable basis on which to distinguish *Magnolia*. But if we reject that test, we must decide whether to overrule either *Magnolia* or *McCartin*. . . .

III

. . . It is . . . appropriate to begin the inquiry by considering whether a rule that permits, or a rule that forecloses, successive workmen's compensation awards is more consistent with settled practice. The answer to this question is pellucidly clear.

It should first be noted that *Magnolia,* by only the slimmest majority, . . . effected a dramatic change in the law that had previously prevailed throughout the United States. . . . Of greater importance is the fact that as a practical matter the "unmistakable language" rule of construction announced in *McCartin* left only the narrowest area in which *Magnolia* could have any further precedential value. For the exclusivity language in the Illinois Act construed in *McCartin* was typical of most state workmen's compensation laws. Consequently, it was immediately recognized that *Magnolia* no longer had any significant practical impact. Moreover, since a state legislature seldom focuses on the extraterritorial effect of its enactments,[17] and since a state court has even less occasion to consider whether an award under its State's law is intended to preclude a supplemental award under another State's workmen's compensation act, the probability that any State would thereafter announce a new rule against supplemental awards in other

---

[15] See . . . Reese and Johnson, The Scope of Full Faith and Credit to Judgments, 49 Colum.L.Rev. 153, 161–162 (1949) (hereinafter Reese and Johnson):

"Full faith and credit is a national policy, not a state policy. Its purpose is not merely to demand respect from one state for another, but rather to give us the benefits of a unified nation by altering the status of otherwise 'independent, sovereign states.' Hence it is for federal law, not state law, to prescribe the measure of credit which one state shall give to another's judgment. In this regard, it is interesting to note that in dealing with full faith and credit to statutes the Supreme Court in recent years has accorded no weight to language which purported to give a particular statute extraterritorial effect. There is every reason why a similar attitude should be taken with respect to judgments. [citations omitted]"

[17] Apparently only Nevada's Workmen's Compensation Act contains the unmistakable language required under the McCartin rule. Nevada Rev.Stat. § 616.525 (1979) provides in part:

"[I]f an employee who has been hired or is regularly employed in this state receives personal injury by accident arising out of and in the course of such employment outside this state, and he . . . accepts any compensation or benefits under the provisions of this chapter, the acceptance of such compensation shall constitute a waiver by such employee . . . of all rights and remedies against the employer at common law or given under the laws of any other state, and shall further constitute a full and complete release of such employer from any and all liability arising from such injury. . . ." (Emphasis added.)

States was extremely remote. As a matter of fact, subsequent cases in the state courts have overwhelmingly followed *McCartin* and permitted successive state workmen's compensation awards. . . .

IV

Three different state interests are affected by the potential conflict between Virginia and the District of Columbia. Virginia has a valid interest in placing a limit on the potential liability of companies that transact business within its borders. Both jurisdictions have a valid interest in the welfare of the injured employee—Virginia because the injury occurred within that State, and the District because the injured party was employed and resided there. And finally, Virginia has an interest in having the integrity of its formal determinations of contested issues respected by other sovereigns.

It is . . . perfectly clear that petitioner could have sought a compensation award in the first instance either in Virginia, the State in which the injury occurred . . . or in the District of Columbia, where petitioner resided, his employer was principally located and the employment relation was formed . . . Thus . . . respondent and its insurer would have had to measure their potential liability exposure by the more generous of the two workmen's compensation schemes in any event. It follows that a State's interest in limiting the potential liability of businesses within the State is not of controlling importance.

It is also manifest that the interest in providing adequate compensation to the injured worker would be fully served by the allowance of successive awards. In this respect the two jurisdictions share a common interest and there is no danger of significant conflict.

The ultimate issue, therefore, is whether Virginia's interest in the integrity of its tribunal's determinations forecloses a second proceeding to obtain a supplemental award in the District of Columbia. . . .

We are . . . persuaded that . . . the proposition [set forth in *Magnolia*] that workmen's compensation awards stand on the same footing as court judgments was unwarranted. To be sure . . . the fact findings of state administrative tribunals are entitled to the same res judicata effect in the second State as findings by a court. But the critical differences between a court of general jurisdiction and an administrative agency with limited statutory authority forecloses the conclusion that constitutional rules applicable to court judgments are necessarily applicable to workmen's compensation awards.

A final judgment entered by a court of general jurisdiction normally establishes not only the measure of the plaintiff's rights but also the limits of the defendant's liability. A traditional application of res judicata principles enables either party to claim the benefit of the judgment insofar as it resolved issues the court had jurisdiction to decide. Although a Virginia court is free to recognize the perhaps paramount interests of another State by choosing to apply that State's law in a particular case, the Industrial Commission of Virginia does not have that power. Its jurisdiction is limited to questions arising under the Virginia Workmen's Compensation Act. . . . Typically, a workmen's compensation tribunal may only apply its own State's law. . . . The Virginia Commission could and did establish the full measure of petitioner's rights under Virginia law, but it neither could nor purported to determine his rights under the law of the District of Columbia. Full faith and credit must be given to the determination that the Virginia Commission had the authority to make; but by a parity of reasoning, full faith and credit need not be given to determinations that it had no power to make. Since it was not requested, and had no authority, to pass on petitioner's rights under District of Columbia law, there can be no constitutional objection to a fresh adjudication of those rights. . . .

. . . whether or not the worker has sought an award from the less generous jurisdiction in the first instance, the vindication of that State's interest in placing a ceiling on employers' liability would inevitably impinge upon the substantial interests of the second jurisdiction in the welfare and subsistence of disabled workers-interests that a court of general jurisdiction might consider, but which must be ignored by the Virginia Industrial Commission. . . .

We simply conclude that the substantial interests of the second State in these circumstances should not be overridden by another State through an unnecessarily aggressive application of the Full Faith and Credit Clause, as was implicitly recognized at the time of *McCartin*.

. . . The Full Faith and Credit Clause should not be construed to preclude successive workmen's compensation awards. Accordingly, Magnolia Petroleum Co. v. Hunt should be overruled.

The judgment of the Court of Appeals is reversed.

■ JUSTICE WHITE, with whom THE CHIEF JUSTICE and JUSTICE POWELL join, concurring in the judgment.

. . . Although the plurality argues strenuously that the rule of today's decision is limited to awards by state workmen's compensation boards, it seems to me that the underlying rationale goes much further. . . .

The plurality contends that unlike courts of general jurisdiction, workmen's compensation tribunals generally have no power to apply the law of another State and thus cannot determine the rights of the parties thereunder. . . . Yet I see no reason why a judgment should not be entitled to full res judicata effect under the Full Faith and Credit Clause merely because the rendering tribunal was obligated to apply the law of the forum—provided, of course, as was certainly the case here, that the forum could constitutionally apply its law. The plurality's analysis seems to grant state legislatures the power to delimit the scope of a cause of action for federal full faith and credit purposes merely by enacting choice of law rules binding on the State's workmen's compensation tribunals. . . .

As a matter of logic, the plurality's analysis would seemingly apply to many everyday tort actions. I see no difference for full faith and credit purposes between a statute which lays down a forum-favoring choice of law rule and a common-law doctrine stating the same principle. Hence when a court, having power in the abstract to apply the law of another State, determines by application of the forum's choice of law rules to apply the substantive law of the forum, I would think that under the plurality's analysis the judgment would not determine rights arising under the law of some other State. Suppose, for example, that in a wrongful death action the court enters judgment on liability against the defendant, and determines to apply the law of the forum which sets a limit on the recovery allowed. The plurality's analysis would seem to permit the plaintiff to obtain a subsequent judgment in a second forum for damages exceeding the first forum's liability limit. . . .

Perhaps the major purpose of the Full Faith and Credit Clause is to act as a nationally unifying force. . . . The plurality's rationale would substantially undercut that function. When a former judgment is set up as a defense under the Full Faith and Credit Clause, the court would be obliged to balance the various state interests involved. But the State of the second forum is not a neutral party to this balance. There seems to be a substantial danger-not presented by the firmer rule of res judicata- that the court in evaluating a full faith and credit defense would give controlling weight to its own parochial interests in concluding that the judgment of the first forum is not res judicata in the subsequent suit. . . .

[Justice White concluded that he would not overrule either *Magnolia* or *McCartin,* although, in his opinion, "*Magnolia* states the sounder doctrine" and *McCartin* rests "on questionable foundations." *McCartin,* however, had been on the books for over thirty years and had been widely interpreted as substantially limiting *Magnolia. McCartin* would clearly permit a second award in the instant case, because the Virginia Workmen's Compensation Act lacked the "unmistakable language" which *McCartin* requires if a workers' compensation award is to preclude a further award in a second state.]

■ JUSTICE REHNQUIST, with whom JUSTICE MARSHALL joins, dissenting. . . .

One might suppose that, having destroyed McCartin's ratio decidendi, the plurality would return to the eminently defensible position adopted in Magnolia. But such is not the case. . . .

[Justice Rehnquist concluded that a balancing of state interests as done by Justice Stevens in his plurality opinion could not properly be used in determining the respect owed under full faith and credit to sister-state judgments. Such a balancing would, however, be appropriate in determining questions of constitutional control of choice of law.]

NOTES

1. Pettus v. American Airlines, Inc., 587 F.2d 627 (4th Cir.1978). Pettus, an employee of American Airlines, sustained injury in Virginia while acting in the scope of his employment. He was awarded benefits under the Virginia Workmen's Compensation Act, but these benefits were terminated following a finding that he had unjustifiably refused to undergo surgery to correct his ailment. Pettus then sought and was awarded compensation for the same injury under the District of Columbia Workmen's Compensation Act. On appeal, this latter award was reversed on grounds of full faith and credit and res judicata. The District of Columbia also provides for the termination of benefits if the employee unreasonably refuses to undergo surgery. Should the outcome have been different if the District of Columbia Act had not contained that provision? Would a different result be reached today in the light of the Thomas case? *Pettus* was strongly questioned in Director, Office of Workers' Comp. Pgms. U.S. Dep't of Labor v. National Van Lines, Inc., 613 F.2d 972 (D.C.Cir.1979), cert. denied, 448 U.S. 907 (1980). For a decision questioning *Pettus*, see Exhibit Aids, Inc. v. Kline, 820 F.2d 650, 651 (4th Cir.1987). However, the D.C. Circuit adhered to its earlier decision: Greenfield v. Volpe Constr. Co., 849 F.2d 635, 637 (D.C.Cir.1988).

2. United Airlines, Inc. v. Kozel, 536 S.E.2d 473 (Va.App.2000), relies on *Thomas* in awarding an employee additional workers' compensation despite an Illinois award that expressly barred any subsequent claim for Virginia workers' compensation. For discussion of the U.S. Supreme Court's decisions (from *Magnolia* to *Thomas*), see also Shannon Vrbas v. J R Simplot Co., 2016 WL 3455460 (Neb.Work.Comp.Ct.2016).

3. For a discussion of whether a balancing of state interests is appropriate in the case of full faith and credit to judgments, see Sterk, Full Faith and Credit, More or Less, to Judgments: Doubts About Thomas v. Washington Gas Light Co., 69 Geo.L.J. 1329 (1981).

SECTION 4. DEFENSES

A. NATURE OF THE ORIGINAL PROCEEDINGS

A prerequisite to recognition of a judgment both at common law and under the full faith and credit clause is that it be rendered in the course of proper judicial proceedings. See generally Chapter 3, p. 41, supra. Such proceedings may be said to comprehend all actions taken in the name of a party by a duly authorized representative or representatives in the settlement of an individual controversy. Departing from an earlier decision, the New York Court of Appeals has held that a judgment obtained by warrant of confession (cognovit) is entitled to full faith and credit: Fiore v. Oakwood Plaza Shopping Center, Inc., 585 N.E.2d 364 (N.Y.1991), cert. denied, 506 U.S. 823 (1992). See also Resolution Trust Corp. v. Monga, 1994 WL 517996 (E.D.Pa.1994). Although a state ordinarily exercises judicial jurisdiction through its courts, it may also do so, if it sees fit, through its legislature and its executive and administrative bodies as well. A decision rendered by an administrative tribunal in the course of its judicial functions is entitled to full faith and credit (Magnolia Petroleum Co. v. Hunt, p. 350 supra; City of New York v. Shapiro, p. 395, Note 2, infra), and so too is an arbitration award which is dignified in the state of rendition with the status of a judgment. Wernwag v. Pawling, 5 G. & J. 500 (Md.1833). A divorce granted by the Danish king personally to two of his subjects was also recognized as a judgment in this country. Sorenson v. Sorenson, 202 N.Y.S. 620 (N.Y.Sup.Ct.1924), aff'd, 220 N.Y.S. 242 (N.Y.App.1927).

On the other hand, the mere fact that something is termed a "judgment" by the state of rendition may not entitle it to full faith and credit as such. Thus, for example, the constitutional protection was denied to a commissioner's report appraising the value of property for probate purposes even though the state in which the report was filed denominated it as a judgment and treated it as binding unless appealed from: Taylor v. Barron, 30 N.H. 78 (1855); the decision was overruled by Lomas v. Hilliard, 60 N.H. 148 (1880). In Foote v. Newell, 29 Mo. 400 (1860) effect was denied to a bond given in stay of execution which under the law of F-1 had the effect of a judgment confessed if forfeited. See also, McClure v. Boyle, 141 N.E.2d 229 (Com.Pleas Ohio 1957).

NOTES

1.   In the European Union, the drafters of the Brussels Ia Regulation faced the problem of defining "judgment" broadly enough to ensure wide recognition of judicial or equivalent acts of courts of member states. See p. 275, supra. Art. V(a) of the 1968 Protocol to the predecessor Convention ([1989] Official Journal EC No. L 285, 1) specifically clarified that, for purposes of support decrees, the term "courts" also encompasses Danish administrative agencies. It continues in force. Art. 35 of the Regulation provides that interlocutory measures of relief of national law shall be available to all litigants of EU states. A result of these provisions is, for instance, that Germany is obligated to recognize non-final decrees of other EU states, even though its national law (see §§ 722, 723, 328 Code of Civil Procedure)—still in effect with respect to non-Member States—presupposes that foreign judgments sought to be recognized and enforced are final judgments. However, case law of the European Court has restricted "judgments" entitled to recognition and enforcement to those that issued in an adversary proceeding. Case 125/79, Denilauler v. SNC Couchet Freres, [1980] ECR 1553, [1981] CMLR 62. An English decision goes further: interlocutory decisions obtained ex parte are not entitled to recognition even if the party affected had an opportunity to seek its stay or reversal but failed to avail itself of this opportunity. EMI Records, Ltd. v. Modern Music GmbH, [1992] 1 All E.R. 616 (Q.B.). This means that an English "Anton Piller Order" (permitting the inspection of the other party's premises for evidence) may be sought and obtained ex parte in England by another EU litigant but that the Order is not necessarily entitled to recognition and enforcement in other EU states.

The German Supreme Court followed *Denilauler* in 2006 (Docket No. XI ZB 150/05, 7, [2007] EuLF I-98 and II-55), prompting calls for a reexamination of the decision because of its effect of unduly limiting the efficacy of provisional relief. See Simons and Calabresi-Scholz, id. at 99 and 58, respectively.

2. The fact that the rendering court committed error, either of fact or of law, is not an adequate reason for a failure to recognize the judgment either under full faith and credit or at common law. See in this regard Milliken v. Meyer, 311 U.S. 457 (1940) (pp. 61, 153, 1002, supra), where a Colorado judgment was reversed for failure to give full faith and credit to a Wyoming decree despite the unrebutted contention that there was "an irreconcilable contradiction between the findings [of the Wyoming court] and the decree." Likewise, an English court has enforced a French judgment even though the latter was based upon a misinterpretation of English law. Godard v. Gray, L.R., 6 Q.B. 139 (1870). In effect, these rulings reject, as do legal systems generally today, the notion of *"révision au fond,"* p. 280, Note 3, supra, whereby the second court would judge the correctness of the first court's determinations of law.

3. A judgment, of course, is not entitled to recognition or enforcement either at common law or under full faith and credit if the rendering court lacked jurisdiction or if the defendant was not given reasonable notice and a reasonable opportunity to be heard. Schibsby v. Westenholz, L.R. 6 Q.B. 155 (1870), p. 43, supra; Pennoyer v. Neff, 95 U.S. 714 (1878), pp. 44, 50, supra; cf. Mullane v. Central Hanover Bank & Trust Co., 339 U.S. 306 (1950) p. 192, supra. Where is the line between prohibited review of another court's findings of law and fact (*"révision au fond"*) and a finding that the first court lacked jurisdiction so that its determination is not entitled to recognition for that reason? Under European Union law, even review of the first court's jurisdiction is generally not allowed. Indeed, Art. 45(3) of the Brussels-Ia Regulation ensures that such a review not take place through the "back door:" "The test of public policy . . . may not be applied to the rules relating to jurisdiction." Exceptions are judgments in consumer and insurance transactions or when the Regulation provides for the exclusive jurisdiction of a specified court. In these cases, the second court may review the first court's jurisdiction but is bound by that court's determinations of the underlying facts. Art. 45(2) of the Brussels-Ia Regulation. However, a judgment is not entitled to recognition at all when the defendant, who did not submit to the rendering court's jurisdiction, did not receive the documents commencing suit or did not receive them in sufficient time to prepare a defense. Art. 45(1)(b). Does American law reach a similar result? See Adam v. Saenger, immediately following, *Baldwin*, p. 367, infra, and *Treinies*, p. 370, infra.

Adam v. Saenger

Supreme Court of the United States, 1938.
303 U.S. 59, 58 S.Ct. 454, 82 L.Ed. 649.

■ JUSTICE STONE delivered the opinion of the Court.

The question for decision is whether the action, in this case, of the Texas state courts, in dismissing a suit founded upon a judgment of the Supreme Court of California, denied to the judgment the faith and credit which the Constitution, article 4, § 1, commands.

Petitioner, as assignee of a California judgment against the Beaumont Export & Import Company, a Texas corporation, brought the present suit in the Texas state district court against respondents, directors of the corporation acting as its trustees in dissolution, and against its stockholders as transferees of corporate assets, to collect the judgment. . . .

It appears that the corporation brought suit in the superior court of California, a court of general jurisdiction, against Montes, petitioner's predecessor in interest, to recover a money judgment for goods sold and delivered. Thereupon Montes, following what is alleged to be the California practice, with leave of the court brought a cross-action against the corporation, by service of a cross-complaint upon the corporation's attorney of record in the pending suit, to recover for the conversion of chattels. Judgment in the cross-action, taken by default, was followed by dismissal of the corporation's suit and is the judgment which is the subject of the present suit. . . .

The trial court sustained a general demurrer to the complaint and gave judgment dismissing the cause, which the Texas Court of Civil Appeals affirmed, 101 S.W.2d 1046. Petition to the Texas Supreme Court for a writ of error was denied for want of jurisdiction. . . .

The Texas Court of Civil Appeals rested its decision on a single ground, want of jurisdiction of the California court over the corporation in the cross-action in which the judgment was rendered. Construing the California statutes and decisions which the complaint set out, it concluded that they did not authorize service of the complaint in the cross-action upon the plaintiff's attorney of record. It held further that in any case as the corporation was not present within the state no jurisdiction could be acquired over it by the substituted service, and the California judgment was consequently without due process and a nullity beyond the protection of the full faith and credit clause. To review these rulings we brought the case here. . . .

Congress has not prescribed the manner in which the legal effect of the judgment and the proceedings on which it is founded in the state where rendered are to be ascertained by the courts of another state. It has left that to the applicable procedure of the courts in which they are drawn in question. Where they are in issue this Court, in the exercise of its appellate jurisdiction to review cases coming to it from state courts, takes judicial notice of the law of the several states to the same extent that such notice is taken by the court from which the appeal is taken. . . .

In the present suit petitioner, in conformity to the state procedure, has set out in his complaint the California statutes and the citations of the decisions of California courts which he contends establish the law of that state that a cross-action in a pending suit may be begun by service of a cross-complaint upon the plaintiff's attorney. The question thus raised upon demurrer for decision by the court is the legal effect in California of the service, and hence of the judgment founded upon it.

Whether the question be regarded as one of fact or more precisely and accurately as a question of law to be determined as are other questions of law . . . it is one arising under the Constitution and a statute of the United States which commands that such faith and credit shall be given by every court to the California proceedings "as they have by law or usage" of that state. And since the existence of the federal right turns on the meaning and effect of the California statute, the decision of the Texas court on that point, whether of law or of fact, is reviewable here. . . .

While this Court re-examines such an issue with deference after its determination by a state court, it cannot, if the laws and Constitution of the United States are to be observed, accept as final the decision of the state tribunal as to matters alleged to give rise to the asserted federal right. This is especially the case where the decision is rested, not on local law or matters of fact of the usual type, which are peculiarly within the cognizance of the local courts, but upon the law of another state, as readily determined here as in a state court. . . .

In ruling that the service in the California suit was unauthorized, the Texas Court of Civil Appeals said: "The cross-action was not an ancillary proceeding, but an independent suit in which a final judgment could be rendered without awaiting a decision in the original suit. Farrar v. Steenbergh, 173 Cal. 94, 159 P. 707. It is well settled in this state that a cross-action occupies the attitude of an independent suit and requires service of the cross-action upon the cross-defendant. Harris v. Schlinke, 95 Tex. 88, 65 S.W. 172. This being so, in the absence of a waiver of service, or an appearance by the cross-defendant, personal service on the cross-defendant must be had to confer jurisdiction upon the court to determine the matter and render judgment in the case."

But the question presented by the pleadings is the status of a cross-action under the California statutes, not under those of Texas. We think its status is adequately disclosed by the California statutes and decisions pleaded by petitioner, and is that for which he contends.

[The Court then reviewed the pertinent California statutes.]

There is nothing in the Fourteenth Amendment to prevent a state from adopting a procedure by which a judgment in personam may be rendered in a cross-action against a plaintiff in its courts, upon service of process or of appropriate pleading upon his attorney of record. The plaintiff having, by his voluntary act in demanding justice from the defendant, submitted himself to the jurisdiction of the court, there is nothing arbitrary or unreasonable in treating him as being there for all purposes for which justice to the defendant requires his presence. It is the price which the state may exact as the condition of opening its courts to the plaintiff. . . .

[Reversed.]

NOTE

The full faith and credit clause does not compel F-2 to take judicial notice of F-1 law in determining the effect of a judgment. F-2 may require the party relying on the F-1 judgment to comply with F-2 procedure to bring F-1 law to the F-2 court's attention. Treinies v. Sunshine Mining Co., p. 370, infra.

Thompson v. Whitman

Supreme Court of the United States, 1874.
85 U.S. (18 Wall.) 457, 21 L.Ed. 897.

[The case appears at p. 188, supra]

NOTES

1. Does the opinion in Thompson v. Whitman proceed on the basis that, since the New Jersey court exceeded the power accorded it by local law, the judgment condemning the sloop was legally ineffective? If so, did the Supreme Court ascertain that the judgment did in fact have no binding effect under New Jersey law? See Durfee v. Duke, p. 369, infra. Compare also the problems raised in earlier contexts (pp. 324–326, supra): who determines the (legitimate) reach of preclusion? Or is there some other explanation for the result reached? See Restatement, Second, Judgments § 30, quoted p. 298, supra.

2. Consider the following elements of the F-1 proceedings or judgment to determine whether any of them will preclude F-2 from examining into the jurisdiction of the F-1 court:

    (a)   Recital of jurisdiction.

    (b)   Recital of the jurisdictional facts on which the jurisdiction was based.

    (c)   Recital of a hearing on the jurisdictional facts.

    (d)   Opportunity to litigate the jurisdictional facts in F-1.

    (e)   Actual contest and litigation of the jurisdictional facts.

BALDWIN V. IOWA STATE TRAVELING MEN'S ASSOCIATION, 283 U.S. 522 51 S.Ct. 217 (1931): [Suit in the federal District Court for Southern Iowa to enforce a judgment rendered in the federal District Court for Western Missouri. The defendant had made a special appearance in the Missouri proceedings to claim that the court lacked in personam jurisdiction. This claim was rejected and judgment on the merits rendered in the plaintiff's favor. In defense of the enforcement proceeding in Iowa, the defendant contended that the Missouri judgment had been rendered without jurisdiction. The lower federal courts found for the defendant on this issue, but, on certiorari, the Supreme Court reversed. In the course of his opinion, Justice Roberts said:]

The [plaintiff] suggests that Article IV, Section 1 of the Constitution forbade the retrial of the question determined on respondent's motion in the Missouri District Court; but the full faith and credit required by that clause is not involved since neither of the courts concerned was a state court. . . .

The substantial matter for determination is whether the judgment amounts to res judicata on the question of the jurisdiction of the court which rendered it over the person of the respondent. It is of no moment that the appearance was a special one expressly saving any submission to such jurisdiction. The fact would be important upon appeal from a judgment, and would save the question of the propriety of the court's decision on the matter even though after the motion had been overruled the respondent had proceeded, subject to a reserved objection and exception, to a trial on the merits. . . . The special appearance gives point to the fact that the respondent entered the Missouri court for the very purpose of litigating the question of jurisdiction over its person. It had the election not to appear at all. If, in the absence of appearance, the court had proceeded to judgment and the present suit had been brought thereon, respondent could have raised and tried out the issue in the present action, because it would never have had its day in court with respect to jurisdiction. . . . It had also the right to appeal from the decision of the Missouri District Court. . . . It elected to follow neither of those courses, but, after having been defeated upon full hearing in its contention as to jurisdiction, it took no further steps, and the judgment in question resulted.

Public policy dictates that there be an end of litigation; that those who have contested an issue shall be bound by the result of the contest, and that matters once tried shall be considered forever settled as between the parties. We see no reason why this doctrine should not apply in every case where one voluntarily appears, presents his case and is fully heard, and why he should not, in the absence of fraud, be thereafter concluded by the judgment of the tribunal to which he has submitted his cause. . . .

NOTE

A decision of a state court in a proceeding begun by a motion to set aside a judgment for lack of jurisdiction over the parties is res judicata and is entitled to full faith and credit in a federal court where the defeated movant sought an injunction against enforcement of the judgment of the state court. American Surety Co. v. Baldwin, 287 U.S. 156 (1932); Johnson v. The Pep Boys, 2005 WL 6229590 (E.D.Va.2005), aff'd, 164 Fed.App'x 385 (4th Cir.2006), cert. denied, 549 U.S. 1024 (2006). See also Counsel Financial Services, L.L.C. v. David McQuade Leibowitz, P.C., 311 S.W.3d 45 (Tex.App.2010).

In DURFEE V. DUKE, 375 U.S. 106, 84 S.Ct. 242 (1963), there was first a suit to quiet title in Nebraska with both parties before the court. The land involved lay in the Missouri River, and the question of title turned on the question whether the land was in Nebraska or in Missouri. This depended on whether a shift in the river's course was a result of avulsion or accretion. The Nebraska court decided that the land was in Nebraska, and quieted title in the Nebraska claimant. This was affirmed on appeal by the Nebraska Supreme Court.

Then the Missouri claimant started a suit in Missouri, which was removed to federal court. The United States Court of Appeals for the Eighth Circuit held that the land was in Missouri, and that the Nebraska decree need not be given full faith and credit, since the Nebraska court did not have jurisdiction over the subject matter.

On certiorari to the Supreme Court, this decision was reversed. The Supreme Court held that the issue had been litigated by the parties in Nebraska, both of whom were before the Nebraska court, and that the Nebraska decision was res judicata as between them. Speaking through Justice Stewart, the Court said:

> Full faith and credit thus generally requires every State to give to a judgment at least the res judicata effect which the judgment would be accorded in the State which rendered it. . . .

> It is argued that an exception to this rule of jurisdictional finality should be made with respect to cases involving real property because of this Court's emphatic expressions of the doctrine that courts of one State are completely without jurisdiction directly to affect title to land in other States. This argument is wide of the mark. Courts of one State are equally without jurisdiction to dissolve the marriages of those domiciled in other States. But the location of land, like the domicile of a party to a divorce action, is a matter "to be resolved by judicial determination." Sherrer v. Sherrer, 334 U.S., at 349. The question remains whether, once the matter has been fully litigated and judicially determined, it can be retried in another State in litigation between the same parties. Upon the reason and authority of the cases we have discussed, it is clear that the answer must be in the negative.

> It is to be emphasized that all that was ultimately determined in the Nebraska litigation was title to the land in question as

between the parties to the litigation there. Nothing there decided, and nothing that could be decided in litigation between the same parties or their privies in Missouri, could bind either Missouri or Nebraska with respect to any controversy they might have, now or in the future, as to the location of the boundary between them, or as to their respective sovereignty over the land in question. . . . Either State may at any time protect its interest by initiating independent judicial proceedings here. Cf. Missouri v. Nebraska, 196 U.S. 23.

NOTES

1.   For a discussion of Durfee v. Duke, see B. Currie, Full Faith and Credit, Chiefly to Judgments: A Role for Congress, 1964 Sup.Ct.Rev. 89, 105. Suppose that a court, having jurisdiction over the parties, goes ahead and decides the case. Does this constitute an adjudication that the court had jurisdiction of the subject matter so that the question cannot be reopened in a later case? It was so held in Chicot County Drainage District v. Baxter State Bank, 308 U.S. 371 (1940), and in VI Derivatives LLC v. United States, 671 Fed.App'x 839 (3d Cir.2016), but not in Kalb v. Feuerstein, 308 U.S. 433 (1940), and similarly in York v. State, 373 S.W.3d 32 (Tex.2012), both arising under bankruptcy law. For cases raising the question in a conflict of laws setting, see Sherrer v. Sherrer, p. 948, infra; Coe v. Coe, p. 952, Note 1, infra; cf. Davis v. Davis, p. 948, infra. With respect to foreign in personam decrees affecting forum land, see pp. 332–333, Notes 4–6, supra. See in particular the next principal case (*Treinies*).

2.   In Hodge v. Hodge, 621 F.2d 590 (3d Cir.1980), the Court said in the course of its opinion:

"Reflecting the heightened concern for finality of judgments in post-*Chicot* developments in the law, the Second Restatement of Judgments replaced the First Restatement's simple listing of factors to be considered in weighing finality against validity with a presumption of finality followed by limited, enumerated exceptions. A party is foreclosed from litigating subject matter jurisdiction in a subsequent lawsuit except if the lack of jurisdiction was so clear that its assumption 'was a manifest abuse of authority,' the challenged judgment 'would substantially infringe the authority of another tribunal or [governmental] agency,' or the rendering court was incapable of making an adequately informed assessment of its own jurisdiction."

Treinies v. Sunshine Mining Co.

Supreme Court of the United States, 1939.
308 U.S. 66, 60 S.Ct. 44, 84 L.Ed. 85.

[This case involved a dispute between Mrs. Mason and Evelyn Treinies, and her assignor John Pelkes, with respect to the ownership of a block of Sunshine Mining Company stock which had originally formed part of the estate of Pelkes' wife. The first step in the complicated proceedings was an action brought by Mrs. Mason against Pelkes and

Treinies in an Idaho state court in which she sought to have the stock awarded to her. Before the Idaho court had rendered judgment, Mrs. Mason filed a petition in the probate proceedings in Washington seeking to have Pelkes removed as executor of his wife's estate. Pelkes by cross-petition claimed the stock and despite the protests of Mrs. Mason that it lacked jurisdiction, the Washington court held that Pelkes was the owner. In the meantime, the Idaho litigation continued and, after an appeal to the Supreme Court of Idaho, a final judgment in Mrs. Mason's favor was handed down more than a year after the contrary decision of the Washington court. Pelkes and Treinies thereupon filed suit against Mrs. Mason in the Washington court claiming that the Idaho judgment was void for lack of jurisdiction. At this point, the Sunshine Mining Company took the initiative and brought an interpleader proceeding under the Federal Interpleader Act against all of the contestants in a federal court in Idaho. This court found in favor of Mrs. Mason and its judgment was affirmed by the federal Court of Appeals and by the Supreme Court.]

■ JUSTICE REED delivered the opinion of the Court. . . .

On the merits petitioner's [Treinies] objection to the decree below is that it fails to consider and give effect to the Washington judgment . . . awarding the property in question to Pelkes, petitioner's assignor. It is petitioner's claim that the Washington judgment must be considered as effective in this litigation because the question of the jurisdiction of the Washington court was actually litigated before the Supreme Court of Washington and determined favorably to petitioner by the refusal to grant a writ of prohibition against the exercise of jurisdiction by the Washington Superior Court in probate. This failure to give effect to the judgment is said to infringe the full faith and credit clause of the Constitution. The decree of the Court of Appeals is based upon the doctrine of *res judicata*. The applicability of that doctrine arises from a determination of pertinent matters by the Supreme Court of Idaho. . . .

The [federal] Court of Appeals held that the Idaho suit settled that the stock was distributed in 1923 and that therefore the Idaho court had jurisdiction to determine rights under the alleged oral trust. It was further of the view that the Idaho court's invalidation of the Washington judgment and its decree upholding Mrs. Mason's claim to the disputed property were *res judicata* in this action. Petitioner's only ground for objection to the conclusion that the Idaho decree is *res judicata* rests on the argument that by such ruling below the "judgment of the courts of the State of Washington affecting the same subject matter and parties" is ignored.

In the Idaho proceeding the Washington judgment awarding the stock and dividends to Pelkes was pleaded in bar to Mrs. Mason's suit to recover the stock. The effectiveness of the Washington judgment as a bar depended upon whether the court which rendered it had jurisdiction, after an order of distribution, to deal with settlements of distributees with respect to the assets of an estate. On consideration it was determined in the Idaho proceeding that the Washington court did not have this jurisdiction and that the stock of the Mining Company became the property of Mrs. Mason. In declining to give effect to the Washington decree for lack of jurisdiction over the subject matter, the Idaho court determined also the basic question raised by petitioner in the interpleader action. The contention of petitioner in the interpleader proceedings that the Idaho court did not have jurisdiction of the stock controversy because that controversy was in the exclusive jurisdiction of the Washington probate court must fall, because of the Idaho decision that the Washington probate court did not have exclusive jurisdiction. This is true even though the question of the Washington jurisdiction had been actually litigated and decided in favor of Pelkes in the Washington proceedings. If decided erroneously in the Idaho proceedings, the right to review that error was in those (the Idaho) proceedings. While petitioner sought review from the decree of the Supreme Court of Idaho by petition for certiorari to this Court, which was denied, no review was sought from the final decree of the Idaho District Court of August 18, 1936, on new findings of fact and conclusions of law on remittitur from the Supreme Court of Idaho.[21]

The [federal] Court of Appeals correctly determined that the issue of jurisdiction *vel non* of the Washington court could not be relitigated in this interpleader. As the Idaho District Court was a court of general jurisdiction, its conclusions are unassailable collaterally except for fraud or lack of jurisdiction. The holding by the Idaho court of no jurisdiction in Washington necessarily determined the question raised here as to the Idaho jurisdiction against Miss Treinies' contention. She is bound by that judgment.

The power of the Idaho court to examine into the jurisdiction of the Washington court is beyond question. Even where the decision against

---

[21] It is unnecessary to consider whether the Idaho determination as to the jurisdiction of the Washington court was properly made. As the procedure by which a state court examines into the question of the jurisdiction of the court of a sister state is a matter within the control of the respective states (Adam v. Saenger, 303 U.S. 59, 63), it need only be added that such procedure is subject to question only on direct appeal.

It was stipulated by all parties to the Idaho cause that the Idaho courts might take judicial notice of the statutes and decisions of Washington. Some constitutional and statutory provisions relating to the jurisdiction of the Superior Court were pleaded and admitted. It has long been the rule in Idaho that its courts do not take judicial notice of the laws of another state and that without allegation and evidence it will be assumed the laws are the same as those of Idaho. Maloney v. Winston Bros., 18 Idaho 740, 757, 762, 111 P. 1080, 1086, 47 L.R.A.,N.S., 634; Douglas v. Douglas, 22 Idaho 336, 343, 125 P. 796; Mechanics & Metals Nat. Bk. v. Pingree, 40 Idaho 118, 129, 232 P. 5; State v. Martinez, 43 Idaho 180, 192, 250 P. 239; Kleinschmidt v. Scribner, 54 Idaho 185, 189, 30 P.2d 362. While none of these cases involved a stipulation, the decision of the Supreme Court of Idaho (Mason v. Pelkes, 57 Idaho 10, 59 P.2d 1087) declares the law of that jurisdiction. It follows from the Idaho court's refusal to look into the statutes of Washington that the jurisdiction of the Washington court was presumed to be governed by Idaho law. Under proper proof, the Idaho court would have been compelled to examine the jurisdiction of the Washington court under Washington law.

the validity of the original judgment is erroneous, it is a valid exercise of judicial power by the second court.[23]

One trial of an issue is enough.[24] "The principles of *res judicata* apply to questions of jurisdiction as well as to other issues,"[25] as well to jurisdiction of the subject matter as of the parties.[26]

Decree affirmed.

NOTES

1.   The decisions applying *Treinies* are legion. See, e.g., Morris v. Trust Co. of Virginia, 2015 WL 1475487, at *25 (M.D.Ala.2015).

2.   RESTATEMENT, SECOND, CONFLICT OF LAWS:

§ 114. Inconsistent Judgments

A judgment rendered in a State of the United States will not be recognized or enforced in sister States if an inconsistent, but valid, judgment is subsequently rendered in another action between the parties and if the earlier judgment is superseded by the later judgment under the local law of the State where the later judgment was rendered.

For another application of this principle (relying on *Treinies*), see First Tennessee Nat'l Bank N.A. v. Smith et al., 766 F.2d 255 (6th Cir.1985).

3.   Durfee v. Duke, p. 369, supra, expressly relies on *Treinies*: 375 U.S. at 112. What if Missouri imposes a real property tax on the claimant who lost in that case: can he successfully invoke the Nebraska and U.S. Supreme Court decisions to show that he has no interest in the property? Compare this situation with inconsistent state determinations concerning a person's domicile. See pp. 15–16, Notes 5–6, supra. It has been suggested that the *Treinies* rule should not be applied in situations where it is not possible to obtain review by the Supreme Court of the second inconsistent judgment. Ginsburg, Judgments in Search of Full Faith and Credit: The Last-in-Time Rule for Conflicting Judgments, 82 Harv.L.Rev. 798 (1969). This would be true where the second judgment is that of a foreign country or where the Supreme Court denies certiorari.

4.   Colby v. Colby, 369 P.2d 1019 (Nev.1962), cert. denied, 371 U.S. 888 (1962). W obtained an ex parte divorce in Nevada after H had been served with process in Washington, D.C. but did not appear. Thereafter, H was awarded a separation in Maryland. W appeared in this action and contended that the relief sought could not be granted because of the Nevada divorce. The Maryland court found, however, that W had not been domiciled in Nevada and that therefore the Nevada divorce was not entitled to full faith and credit. H then brought an action in Nevada to have the divorce set aside.

---

[23]   Chicago Life Ins. Co. v. Cherry, 244 U.S. 25, 30; Stoll v. Gottlieb, 305 U.S. 165, 172; Roche v. McDonald, 275 U.S. 449, 454.

[24]   Baldwin v. Traveling Men's Ass'n, 283 U.S. 522, 525.

[25] American Surety Co. v. Baldwin, 287 U.S. 156, 166.

[26]   . . . No decision or statute relative to the reexamination of the decree or judgment of an Idaho court on a contested issue of jurisdiction has been found or called to our attention. It is concluded that the rule here expressed states to the law of Idaho.

Held for W. The divorce decree is still valid in Nevada. A divorce that is not entitled to full faith and credit may nevertheless have satisfied due process requirements and be valid in the state of rendition. Can this result be reconciled with Treinies v. Sunshine Mining Co., p. 370, supra? See Rodgers & Rodgers, The Disparity between Due Process and Full Faith and Credit: The Problem of the Somewhere Wife, 67 Colum.L.Rev. 1363 (1967); Note, Full Faith and Credit Versus State Interest: The Last-in-Time Rule in Texas, 55 Tex.L.Rev. 127 (1976). For an interesting attempt to apply *Colby* outside the area of divorce, see Campion v. State, Department of Community and Regional Affairs, 876 P.2d 1096 (Alaska 1994). On collateral estoppel, see further Sopcak v. Northern Mountain Helicopter Service, 924 P.2d 1006 (Alaska 1996); Wilson v. Golden Valley Electric Assn., 2018 WL 3150342, *2 (D.Alaska 2018).

5.   For a case applying the *Treinies* rule to inconsistent judgments of foreign countries, see Ambatielos v. Foundation Co., 116 N.Y.S.2d 641 (N.Y.Sup.Ct.1952). But see Byblos Bank Europe, S.A. v. Sekerbank Turk Anonym Syrketi, 885 N.E.2d 191, 195 (N.Y.2008), in which the court was faced with three foreign judgments, with the third inconsistent with the first and second. The court noted that the Uniform Foreign-Money Judgments Recognition Act does not specify the order of priority. It considered the last-in-time rule inappropriate for the case before it, where the last court had "departed from normal res judicata principles by permitting a party to relitigate the merits of an earlier judgment" and therefore recognized the first judgment (as also recognized by the second). The Act has since been revised (not yet in force in New York). Sec. 4(c)(4), reproduced at p. 399, infra, repeats the language of § 4(b)(4) of the earlier Act. Which state's "res judicata principles" are applicable? It so happens that Continental systems (here, the first and second courts, Turkish and German respectively) follow a first-in-time rule; *Treinies* does not. Why does the court opt against applying *Treinies* to this international case (assuming that it is free to do so, as the reading of the Uniform Act would suggest)?

In contrast, consider the following: a German court did not accord res judicata effect to an earlier Mississippi determination, but entered its own (consistent) decree. The Fifth Circuit affirmed the lower court's refusal to recognize the German judgment, commingling at least three reasons for its decision: while the German court constituted a fair and impartial tribunal (one of the Uniform Act's requisites for recognition, p. 398, infra), its decree in disregard of the earlier Mississippi decision violated Mississippi's public policy. Perhaps unnecessarily, the Court bolstered its public policy point by distinguishing the problem before it from "race to judgment" cases in which *lis pendens*-notions might argue for deference to the other court: those cases involve ongoing proceedings, the present case presents successive proceedings and decrees. Also, because the German court did not honor the Mississippi decision, the latter would not honor the German court's (i.e., lack of reciprocity as an exception to comity), a ground not mentioned in the Uniform Act. The Court did not invoke sec. 4(c)(4) of the Uniform Act (p. 399, infra) which expressly deals with inconsistent judgments—probably because the decrees in question were not inconsistent. In sum, the Court did not extend the *Treinies* result to foreign-country judgments, as had *Ambatielos* (supra this Note). Its result therefore parallels the rule under European Union law, Note 6, immediately following). Derr v. Swarek, 766 F.3d 430 (5th Cir.2014). A strong dissent disagreed with the majority's resort to public policy to create an exception to the extension of comity. Id. at 449–50.

6. European Union law and the national laws of Continental countries do not follow a last-in-time rule; instead, they give priority to the judgment that was first in time. See Brussels-Ia Regulation Art. 45(1)(d), modified by an exception in favor of inconsistent forum-state judgments (id (c)). Europeans criticize the last-in-time rule on the ground that it legitimizes a judgment that itself failed to give respect to the first court's decision. See Schack, Internationales Zivilverfahrensrecht anno. 945–46, p. 351–52 (7th ed.2017). Is this criticism justified? Does *Treinies* suggest an answer? American law contains no rule providing for a general forum-judgment advantage (whether prior or subsequent in time): why not? Is such a rule any more consistent or acceptable in a system such as that provided by the European Union law?

RESTATEMENT, SECOND, CONFLICT OF LAWS:

§ 112. Vacated Judgment

b.   Proceedings on appeal. Whether proceedings on appeal or error vacate a judgment is determined by the local law of the state of rendition. At common law, a pending writ of error does not vacate a judgment, while an appeal in equity vacates a decree. In the United States, the rule has frequently been changed by statute. If appellate proceedings do not, by the local law of the state of rendition, vacate the judgment, suit to enforce the judgment may be brought in another state. Usually, however, the courts of the state in which enforcement of the judgment is sought will either stay their judgment, or stay execution thereof, pending the determination of the appeal (see § 107, Comment *e*). As between States of the United States, full faith and credit does not prevent in such circumstances either stay of the judgment, or stay of execution, pending determination of the appeal.

NOTES

1. For cases applying this rule, see Maner v. Maner, 412 F.2d 449 (5th Cir.1969); Nowell v. Nowell, 254 A.2d 889 (Conn.1969); Fehr v. McHugh, 413 A.2d 1285 (D.C.App.1980); Fifth Third Bank v. Monet, 2013 WL 1752532 (M.D.Tenn.2013).

2. See generally on the question of the finality of judgments, Restatement, Second, Conflict of Laws § 107.

Barber v. Barber

Supreme Court of the United States, 1944.
323 U.S. 77, 65 S.Ct. 137, 89 L.Ed. 82.

■ CHIEF JUSTICE STONE delivered the opinion of the Court.

The question for decision is whether the Supreme Court of Tennessee, in a suit brought upon a North Carolina judgment for arrears of alimony, rightly denied full faith and credit to the judgment, on the ground that it lacks finality because, by the law of North Carolina, it is subject to modification or recall by the court which entered it.

In 1920 petitioner secured in the Superior Court of North Carolina for Buncombe County, a court of general jurisdiction, a judgment of separation from respondent, her husband. The judgment directed payment to petitioner of $200 per month alimony, later reduced to $160 per month. In 1932 respondent stopped paying the prescribed alimony. In 1940, on petitioner's motion in the separation suit for a judgment for the amount of the alimony accrued and unpaid under the earlier order, the Superior Court of North Carolina gave judgment in her favor. It adjudged that respondent was indebted to petitioner in the sum of $19,707.20, under its former order, that petitioner have and recover of respondent that amount, and "that execution issue therefor".

Petitioner then brought the present suit in the Tennessee Chancery Court to recover on the judgment thus obtained. Respondent, by his answer, put in issue the finality, under North Carolina law, of the judgment sued upon. . . .

The Tennessee Chancery Court held the judgment sued upon to be entitled to full faith and credit, and gave judgment for petitioner accordingly. The Supreme Court of Tennessee reversed on the ground that the judgment was without the finality entitling it to credit under the full faith and credit clause of the Constitution, Art. IV, § 1.180 Tenn. 353, 175 S.W.2d 324. We granted certiorari because of an asserted conflict with Sistare v. Sistare, 218 U.S. 1, . . .

In Sistare v. Sistare, supra, this Court considered whether a decree for future alimony, brought to a sister state, was entitled to full faith and credit as to installments which had accrued, but which had not been reduced to a further judgment. The Court held that a decree for future alimony is, under the Constitution and the statute, entitled to credit as to past due installments, if the right to them is "absolute and vested," even though the decree might be modified prospectively by future orders of the court. See also Barber v. Barber, 21 How. 582. The Sistare case also decided that such a decree was not final, and therefore not entitled to credit, if the past due installments were subject retroactively to modification or recall by the court after their accrual. . . .

Upon full consideration of the law of North Carolina we conclude that respondent has not overcome the prima facie validity and finality of the judgment sued upon. We cannot say that the statutory authority to modify or recall an order providing for future allowances of installments of alimony extends to a judgment for overdue installments or that such a judgment is not entitled to full faith and credit.

Reversed.

■ JUSTICE JACKSON, concurring.

I concur in the result, but I think that the judgment of the North Carolina court was entitled to faith and credit in Tennessee even if it was not a final one. On this assumption I do not find it necessary or relevant to examine North Carolina law as to whether its judgment might under some hypothetical circumstances be modified.

Neither the full faith and credit clause of the Constitution nor the Act of Congress implementing it says anything about final judgments or, for that matter, about any judgments. Both require that full faith and credit be given to "judicial proceedings" without limitation as to finality. Upon recognition of the broad meaning of that term much may some day depend. . . .

NOTE

Is not Justice Jackson correct? How can it be consistent with the mandate of full faith and credit for F-2 to refuse to enforce an F-1 decree merely because it remains subject to modification at the hands of the F-1 court? Such action certainly does not accord the judgment the same effect that it enjoys by "law or usage" in F-1. But, on the other hand, if the F-2 court were to enforce the F-1 decree without question, might it not thereby accord the judgment creditor a greater recovery than he would have obtained in F-1? Would such a result be thought inconsistent with full faith and credit? See also Keeton v. Hustler Magazine, Inc., 815 F.2d 857 (2d Cir.1987) (registration of New Hampshire judgment in New York permitted under New York law despite pendency of an appeal in New Hampshire); Irvin L. Young Foundation, Inc. v. Damrell, 607 F.Supp. 705 (D.Me.1985) (pendency of a motion for relief from a default judgment in the state of rendition does not deprive the judgment of its finality and therefore does not preclude its enforcement in F-2). Note also that European recognition law—including under the Lugano Convention—no longer requires finality of the F-1 judgment.

What recourse does the original judgment debtor have if, after recognition and enforcement of the F-1 judgment against him in F-2, the appeal (or the motion to set aside) is successful in F-1?

Worthley v. Worthley

Supreme Court of California, 1955.
44 Cal.2d 465, 283 P.2d 19.

[Suit by a wife against her husband to recover accrued arrearages under a New Jersey decree for separate maintenance and to have the New Jersey decree "established as a California decree" and the husband ordered to pay her $9 a week (the amount specified in the New Jersey decree) until further order of the court. The trial court entered judgment for the husband and the wife appealed to the Supreme Court of California.]

■ TRAYNOR, JUSTICE. . . . Since the New Jersey decree is both prospectively and retroactively modifiable, N.J.S.A. § 2A:34–23, we are not constitutionally bound to enforce defendant's obligations under it. Sistare v. Sistare, 218 U.S. 1 . . . Nor are we bound *not* to enforce them. People of State of New York ex rel. Halvey v. Halvey, 330 U.S. 610, 615. . . . The United States Supreme Court has held, however, that if such obligations are enforced in this state, at least as to accrued arrearages, due process requires that the defendant be afforded an opportunity to litigate the question of modification. Griffin v. Griffin, 327 U.S. 220, 233–234. . . . It has also clearly indicated that as to either prospective or retroactive enforcement of such obligations, this state "has at least as much leeway to disregard the judgment, to qualify it, or to depart from it as does the State where it was rendered." People of State of New York ex rel. Halvey v. Halvey, supra. . . .

In Biewend v. Biewend, 17 Cal.2d 108, 113–114, 109 P.2d 701, 704 . . . it was held that the California courts will recognize and give prospective enforcement to a foreign alimony decree, even though it is subject to modification under the law of the state where it was originally rendered, by establishing it "as the decree of the California court with the same force and effect as if it had been entered in this state, including punishment for contempt if the defendant fails to comply. . . ." Similar holdings in reference to both alimony and support decrees have repeatedly been made by the District Courts of Appeal . . . and by the courts of other states. . . .

Although the question of retroactive modification has been seldom litigated. . . . there is no valid reason, in a case in which both parties are before the court, why the California courts should refuse to hear a plaintiff's prayer for enforcement of a modifiable sister-state decree and the defendant's plea for modification of his obligations thereunder. If the accrued installments are modified retroactively, the judgment for a liquidated sum entered after such modification will be final and thus will be entitled to full faith and credit in all other states. . . . If the installments are modified prospectively, the issues thus determined will be res judicata so long as the circumstances of the parties remain unchanged. . . . Moreover, the interests of neither party would be served by requiring the plaintiff to return to the state of rendition and reduce her claim for accrued installments to a money judgment. . . . Repeated suits for arrearages would have to be brought in New Jersey as installments accrued, to be followed by repeated actions in California to enforce the New Jersey judgments for accrued installments, with the net result that the costs of litigation and the dilatoriness of the recovery would substantially reduce the value of the support to which plaintiff is entitled.

Furthermore, there is no merit to the contention that as a matter of practical convenience the issue of modification should be tried in the courts of the state where the support decree was originally rendered. [Proof of changed circumstances can be presented to the California court.] Moreover, in most states the problem of modification is dealt with according to general equitable principles, and the law of the state in which the support obligation originated can be judicially noticed, Code Civ.Proc. § 1875, and applied by the California courts.

Accordingly, we hold that foreign-created alimony and support obligations are enforceable in this state. In an action to enforce a modifiable support obligation, either party may tender and litigate any plea for modification that could be presented to the courts of the state where the alimony or support decree was originally rendered.

The judgment is reversed.

LIGHT V. LIGHT, 12 Ill.2d 502, 147 N.E.2d 34 (1957): Proceeding in Illinois to register, under the Uniform Enforcement of Foreign Judgments Act, a divorce decree of Missouri, which ordered the defendant husband to pay alimony in gross and thereafter to pay $100 and $50 a month for alimony and for support of the child. The trial court gave a decree for past due installments only, and "the plaintiff contends [on appeal] ... that the decree is entitled to full faith and credit as to future installments." Held, the decree is entitled to the protection the plaintiff seeks.

■ SCHAEFER, J. . . . Policy considerations argue strongly that such decrees are entitled to full faith and credit. Unless they receive interstate recognition, the insulated judicial systems of the several States may become sanctuaries within which obligations that have been fully and fairly adjudicated in another jurisdiction may be escaped. These policy considerations have found expression in the decisions of many State courts which, on the grounds of comity, have given full effect, . . . Strong as are the considerations of policy, the argument that derives from the language of the constitution itself is at least as strong. . . . We hold, therefore, that the decree is entitled to full faith and credit as to future payments. . . .

NOTES

1. The majority of the recent cases now follow the approach taken in Worthley v. Worthley with respect to interstate alimony decrees that are subject to modification in the state of rendition in application of uniform legislation. The same is generally true with respect to foreign country awards.

2.   The special problems of recognition and enforcement raised by sister-state custody decrees are considered at pp. 979–1001, infra.

Levin v. Gladstein

Supreme Court of North Carolina, 1906.
142 N.C. 482, 55 S.E. 371, 32 L.R.A. N.S. 905, 115 Am.St.Rep. 747.

This was a suit upon a judgment obtained in the Superior Court of Baltimore City, Maryland. . . . At the beginning of the trial . . . counsel for defendant stated he admitted the regularity of the judgment sued upon and withdrew all pleas and defenses to said action, save . . . that the judgment . . . was procured by a fraud practiced by plaintiffs upon the defendant. . . . [Defendant] testified . . . that he knew Philip Levin and Simon Levin, and had bought goods of them. That some time prior to his going to Baltimore he bought a bill of goods of plaintiffs, but had shipped some of them back to Baltimore because they were not up to sample. That plaintiffs had refused to take the goods out of the depot in Baltimore. That upon his visit to Baltimore summons was served upon him in the action brought there by the plaintiffs; but after said summons was served upon him, and before the return day, he saw one of the plaintiffs [who] agreed . . . to withdraw said suit and return the goods to him at Durham, provided he would, upon their receipt pay the plaintiffs a sum of money which they agreed upon, to-wit, $133, and freight and storage not to exceed $3. That relying upon his agreement he returned to Durham and made no defense to the action. Plaintiffs never returned the goods to him at Durham. That the first time he knew of the judgment was when called upon by attorneys for plaintiffs to pay said judgment.

There was testimony contradicting defendant. After hearing testimony from both parties, the Court submitted the following issue to the jury: "Was the alleged judgment . . . obtained by the fraud of plaintiffs?" To which the jury responded "Yes." Judgment was thereupon rendered that the plaintiffs take nothing by their action, and that the defendant go without day, etc. Plaintiffs excepted and appealed.

■ CONNOR, J., . . . The plaintiffs, relying upon the provision of the Constitution of the United States, Article IV, section 1, that "Full faith and credit shall be given in each State to the public acts, records and judicial proceedings of every other State," earnestly contend that the defense is not open to the courts of this State. That the remedy for the fraud in procuring the judgment, if any, must be sought in the courts of Maryland. . . .

In Allison v. Chapman, 19 Fed.Rep. 488, Nixon, J. says: ". . . the allegation, *in a plea,* that a judgment was procured through fraud, is not a good common law defense to a suit brought upon it in the same or a sister State." This conclusion is fully supported by all of the authorities. . . . Notwithstanding the well-settled rule that the judgment when sued upon in another State cannot be impeached or attacked for fraud by any plea known to the common law system of pleading, it is equally clear that upon sufficient allegation and proof defendant is entitled, in a court of equity, to enjoin the plaintiff from suing upon or enforcing his judgment. . . .

The underlying principle is that the judgment of a sister State will be given the *same faith* and credit which is given domestic judgments. It is contended, however, and with force, that the "faith and credit" to be given such judgment is measured by the law of the State in which it is rendered. We find upon examining the decisions made by the Maryland Court that in that State a court of equity will enjoin the enforcement of a judgment obtained by fraud. . . . It is thus apparent that the judgment obtained by the fraud of plaintiffs . . . would be open to attack in the courts of Maryland . . . and in giving the defendant relief we are giving the judgment the same "faith and credit" which it has in that State. . . .

The plaintiff says, however this may be, the defendant can have this relief only in Maryland; that he must go into that State and attack the judgment or enjoin the plaintiff. Mr. Freeman says: "If the judgment was procured under circumstances requiring its enforcement to be enjoined in equity, the question will arise whether these circumstances may be interposed as a defense to an action on the judgment in another State. Notwithstanding expressions to the contrary, we apprehend that in bringing an action in another State, the judgment creditor must submit to the law of the forum, and must meet the charge of fraud in its procurement, when presented in any form in which fraud might be urged in an action on a domestic judgment. If, in the State in which the action is pending, fraud can be pleaded to an action on a domestic judgment, it is equally available and equally efficient in actions on judgments of other States. . . ."

[Affirmed.]

NOTES

1. Accord: Hay, Borchers, Symeonides & Whytock, Conflict of Laws § 24.17 (6th ed.2018); Pryles, The Impeachment of Sister State Judgments for Fraud, 25 Sw.L.J. 697 (1971).

2. The various situations wherein local law affords equitable relief against enforcement of a judgment on the ground of fraud in its procurement are discussed in Restatement, Second, Judgments § 70.

B. NATURE OF ORIGINAL CAUSE OF ACTION

Huntington v. Attrill

Supreme Court of the United States, 1892.
146 U.S. 657, 13 S.Ct. 224, 36 L.Ed. 1123.

■ JUSTICE GRAY delivered the opinion of the court.

This was a bill in equity, filed March 21, 1888, in the Circuit Court of Baltimore City, by Collis P. Huntington, a resident of New York, against the Equitable Gas Light Company of Baltimore, a corporation of Maryland, and against Henry Y. Attrill, his wife and three daughters, all residents of Canada, to set aside a transfer of stock in that company, made by him for their benefit and in fraud of his creditors, and to charge that stock with the payment of a judgment recovered by the plaintiff against him in the State of New York, upon his liability as a director in a New York corporation, under the statute of New York of 1875, c. 611, . . .

The bill alleged that on June 15, 1886, the plaintiff recovered, in the Supreme Court of the State of New York, in an action brought by him against Attrill on March 21, 1883, a judgment for the sum of $100,240, which had not been paid, secured or satisfied; and that the cause of action on which that judgment was recovered was as follows: On February 29, 1880, the Rockaway Beach Improvement Company, Limited, of which Attrill was an incorporator and a director, became a corporation under the law of New York, with a capital stock of $700,000. On June 15, 1880, the plaintiff lent that company the sum of $100,000 to be repaid on demand. On February 26, 1880, Attrill was elected one of the directors of the Company, and accepted the office, and continued to act as a director until after January 29, 1881. On June 30, 1880, Attrill, as a director of the company, signed and made oath to, and caused to be recorded, as required by the law of New York, a certificate, which he knew to be false, stating that the whole of the capital stock of the corporation had been paid in, whereas in truth no part had been paid in; and by making such false certificate became liable, by the law of New York, for all the debts of the company contracted before January 29, 1881, including its debt to the plaintiff. On March 8, 1882, by proceedings in a court of New York, the corporation was declared to be insolvent and to have been so since July, 1880, and was dissolved. A duly exemplified copy of the record of that judgment was annexed to and made part of the bill. . . .

[The bill further alleged that Attrill was insolvent, and that he had transferred the shares of stock to himself as trustee for his wife and daughters in order to hinder, delay, and defraud the plaintiff and other creditors.]

One of the daughters demurred to the bill, because it showed that the plaintiff's claim was for the recovery of a penalty against Attrill arising under a statute of the State of New York. . . .

The Circuit Court of Baltimore City overruled the demurrer. On appeal to the Court of Appeals of the State of Maryland, the order was reversed, and the bill dismissed. 70 Maryland 191. . . .

The question whether due faith and credit were thereby denied to the judgment rendered in another State is a Federal question, of which this court has jurisdiction on this writ of error. . . .

In order to determine this question, it will be necessary, in the first place, to consider the true scope and meaning of the fundamental maxim of international law, stated by Chief Justice Marshall in the fewest possible words: "The courts of no country execute the penal laws of another." The Antelope, 10 Wheat. 66, 123. In interpreting this maxim, there is danger of being misled by the different shades of meaning allowed to the word "penal" in our language.

In the municipal law of England and America, the words "penal" and "penalty" have been used in various senses. Strictly and primarily, they denote punishment, whether corporal or pecuniary, imposed and enforced by the State, for a crime or offence against its laws. . . . But they are also commonly used as including any extraordinary liability to which the law subjects a wrongdoer in favor of the person wronged, not limited to the damages suffered. They are so elastic in meaning as even to be familiarly applied to cases of private contracts, wholly independent of statutes, as when we speak of the "penal sum" or "penalty" of a bond. . . .

The test whether a law is penal, in the strict and primary sense, is whether the wrong sought to be redressed is a wrong to the public, or a wrong to the individual. . . .

The question whether a statute of one State, which in some aspects may be called penal, is a penal law in the international sense, so that it cannot be enforced in the courts of another State, depends upon the question whether its purpose is to punish an offense against the public justice of the State, or to afford a private remedy to a person injured by the wrongful act. . . .

The provision of the statute of New York, now in question, making the officers of a corporation, who sign and record a false certificate of the amount of its capital stock, liable for all its debts, is in no sense a criminal or quasi criminal law. The statute, while it enables persons complying with its provisions to do business as a corporation, without being subject to the liability of general partners, takes pains to secure and maintain a proper corporate fund for the payment of the corporate debts. With this aim, it makes the stockholders individually liable for the debts of the corporation until the capital stock is paid in and a certificate of the payment made by the officers; and makes the officers liable for any false and material representation in that certificate. The individual liability of the stockholders takes the place of a corporate fund, until that fund has been duly created; and the individual liability of the officers takes the place of the fund, in case their statement that it has been duly created is false. If the officers do not truly state and record the facts which exempt them from liability, they are made liable directly to every creditor of the company, who by reason of their wrongful acts has not the security, for the payment of his debt out of the corporate property, on which he had a right to rely. As the statute imposes a burdensome liability on the officers for their wrongful act, it may well be considered penal, in the sense that it should be strictly construed. But as it gives a civil remedy, at the private suit of the creditor only, and measured by the amount of his debt, it is as to him clearly remedial. To maintain such a suit is not to administer a punishment imposed upon an offender against the State, but simply to enforce a private right secured under its laws to an individual. We can see no just ground, on principle, for holding such a statute to be a penal law, in the sense that it cannot be enforced in a foreign state or country.

The decisions of the Court of Appeals of New York, so far as they have been brought to our notice, fall short of holding that the liability imposed upon the officers of the corporation by such statutes is a punishment or penalty which cannot be enforced in another State. . . .

In a later case than any of these, [that] court, in affirming the very judgment now sued on, and adjudging the statute of 1875 to be constitutional and valid, said that "while liability within the provision in question is in some sense penal in its character, it may have been intended for the protection of creditors of corporations created pursuant to that statute." Huntington v. Attrill, 118 N.Y. 365, 378. . . .

[F]or reasons to be stated presently, . . . those decisions [cannot], in any view, be regarded as concluding the courts of Maryland, or this court, upon the question whether this statute is a penal law in the international sense. But they are entitled to great consideration, because made by a court of high authority, construing the terms of a statute with which it was peculiarly familiar; and it is satisfactory to find no adjudication of that court inconsistent with the view which we take of the liability in question. . . .

[T]he question is not one of local, but of international, law. . . . The test is not by what name the statute is called by the legislature or the courts of the State in which it was passed, but whether it appears to the tribunal which is called upon to enforce it to be, in its essential character and effect, a punishment of an offence against the public, or a grant of a civil right to a private person.

. . . [I]f the original liability has passed into judgment in one State, the courts of another State, when asked to enforce it, are bound by the Constitution and laws of the United States to give full faith and credit to that judgment, and if they do not, their decision, as said at the outset of this opinion, may be reviewed and reversed by this court on writ of error. . . .

If a suit to enforce a judgment rendered in one State . . . is brought in the courts of another State, this court, in order to determine, on writ of error, whether the highest court of the latter State has given full faith and credit to the judgment, must determine for itself whether the original cause of action is penal in the international sense. . . .

The Court of Appeals of Maryland, therefore, in deciding this case against the plaintiff, upon the ground that the judgment was not one which it was bound in any manner to enforce, denied to the judgment the full faith, credit and effect to which it was entitled under the Constitution and laws of the United States.

[Judgment reversed.]

NOTES

1. The Supreme Court adhered to *Huntington* in Nelson v. George, 399 U.S. 224, 229 (1970).

In a number of civil law countries, private claims for compensation can be brought as part of (attached to) the criminal action against the wrongdoer. Is an award by the criminal court in favor of the claimant a "penalty?" In keeping with the language of Justice Gray in *Huntington*, a New York court held that it is "the purpose of the judgment, not the court that issued it" that it determines its nature. In the case before the court, the Czech court had awarded a large amount against a corporate officer for "compensation to the victims" of his misconduct. The judgment was not penal, because it was not "vindication of the public justice" but for compensation for "actual damages." Harvardsky Prumyslovy Holding, A.S.-V Lidvidaci v. Kozeny, 983 N.Y.S.2d 240, 243 (App.Div.2014).

2. In City of Philadelphia v. Austin, 429 A.2d 568 (N.J.1981), the New Jersey Supreme Court held that full faith and credit required enforcement of a Pennsylvania judgment for a fine for failure to file tax returns required by the Philadelphia Wage Tax Ordinance. The Court noted that the United States Supreme Court has never decided whether sister state money judgments on penal claims were entitled to full faith and credit. It reserved the question whether full faith and credit was owed to all sister state money judgments for violations other than tax laws. With respect to tax laws, see p. 395, Note 2, infra. For application of *Huntington* in an international case, see L'Institute Nat. de l'Audiovisuel v. Kultur Int'l Films Ltd., 2012 WL 296997, at *3 (D.N.J. 2012).

3. The fact that the plaintiff is a sovereign state does not of itself make the action one for a penalty. The action is not penal where it is brought by the state to vindicate its proprietary interests, and a judgment rendered in such an action is entitled to full faith and credit. Connolly v. Bell, 141 N.Y.S.2d 753 (N.Y.App.Div.1955), aff'd, 132 N.E.2d 852 (N.Y.1956). Accord: United States of America v. Ivey, [1996] 93 D.A.C. 152, leave to appeal dismissed, [1996] S.C.C.A. No. 582 (Ontario Ct.App.).

4. For a discussion of the problems involved when the suit is on the original liability created by a foreign statute alleged to be penal, see p. 459–462, infra.

Fauntleroy v. Lum

Supreme Court of the United States, 1908.
210 U.S. 230, 28 S.Ct. 641, 52 L.Ed. 1039.

By law the State of Mississippi prohibited certain forms of gambling in futures, and inhibited its courts from giving effect to any contract or dealing made in violation of the prohibitive statute. In addition, it was made criminal to do any of the forbidden acts. With the statutes in force two citizens and residents of Mississippi made contracts in that State which were performed therein, and which were in violation of both the civil and criminal statutes referred to. One of the parties asserting that the other was indebted to him because of the contracts, both parties, in the State of Mississippi, submitted their differences to arbitration, and on an award being made in that State the one in whose favor it was made sued in a state court in Mississippi to recover thereon. In that suit, on the attention of the court being called to the prohibited and criminal nature of the transactions, the plaintiff dismissed the case. Subsequently, in a court of the State of Missouri the citizen of Mississippi, in whose favor the award had been made, brought an action on the award, and succeeded in getting personal service upon the other citizen of Mississippi, the latter being temporarily in the State of Missouri. The action was put at issue. Rejecting evidence offered by the defendant to show the nature of the transactions, and that under the laws of Mississippi the same were illegal and criminal, the Missouri court submitted the cause to a jury, with an instruction to find for the plaintiff if they believed that the award had been made as alleged. A verdict and judgment went in favor of the plaintiff. Thereupon the judgment so obtained was assigned by the plaintiff to his attorney, who sued upon the same in a court of Mississippi, where the facts upon which the transaction depended were set up and the prohibitory statutes of the State were pleaded as a defense. Ultimately the case went to the Supreme Court of the State of Mississippi, where it was decided that the Missouri judgment was not required, under the due faith and credit clause, to be enforced in Mississippi, as it concerned transactions which had taken place exclusively in Mississippi, between residents of that State, which were in violation of laws embodying the public policy of that State, and to give effect to which would be enforcing transactions which the courts of Mississippi had no authority to enforce.[8]

■ JUSTICE HOLMES delivered the opinion of the court. . . .

The main argument urged by the defendant to sustain the judgment below is addressed to the jurisdiction of the Mississippi courts.

The laws of Mississippi make dealing in futures a misdemeanor, and provide that contracts of that sort, made without intent to deliver the commodity or to pay the price, "shall not be enforced by any court." Annotated Code of 1892, secs.1120, 1121, 2117. The defendant contends

---

[8]   The statement of the facts is taken from the dissenting opinion. —eds.

that this language deprives the Mississippi courts of jurisdiction, and that the case is like Anglo-American Provision Co. v. Davis Provision Co. No. 1, 191 U.S. 373. There the New York statutes refused to provide a court into which a foreign corporation could come, except upon causes of action arising within the State, etc., and it was held that the State of New York was under no constitutional obligation to give jurisdiction to its Supreme Court against its will. One question is whether that decision is in point.

No doubt it sometimes may be difficult to decide whether certain words in a statute are directed to jurisdiction or to merits, but the distinction between the two is plain. One goes to the power, the other only to the duty of the court. Under the common law it is the duty of a court of general jurisdiction not to enter a judgment upon a parol promise made without consideration; but it has power to do it, and, if it does, the judgment is unimpeachable, unless reversed. Yet a statute could be framed that would make the power, that is, the jurisdiction of the court dependent upon whether there was a consideration or not. Whether a given statute is intended simply to establish a rule of substantive law, and thus to define the duty of the court, or is meant to limit its power, is a question of construction and common sense. When it affects a court of general jurisdiction and deals with a matter upon which that court must pass, we naturally are slow to read ambiguous words, as meaning to leave the judgment open to dispute, or as intended to do more than to fix the rule by which the court should decide.

The case quoted concerned a statute plainly dealing with the authority and jurisdiction of the New York court. The statute now before us seems to us only to lay down a rule of decision. The Mississippi court in which this action was brought is a court of general jurisdiction and would have to decide upon the validity of the bar if the suit upon the award or upon the original cause of action had been brought there. The words "shall not be enforced by any court" are simply another, possibly less emphatic, way of saying that an action shall not be brought to enforce such contracts. . . . We regard this question as open under the decisions below, and we have expressed our opinion upon it independent of the effect of the judgment, although it might be that, even if jurisdiction of the original cause of action was withdrawn, it remained with regard to a suit upon a judgment based upon an award, whether the judgment or award was conclusive or not. But it might be held that the law as to jurisdiction in one case followed the law in the other, and therefore we proceed at once to the further question, whether the illegality of the original cause of action in Mississippi can be relied upon there as a ground for denying a recovery upon a judgment of another State.

The doctrine laid down by Chief Justice Marshall was "that the judgment of a state court should have the same credit, validity, and effect in every other court in the United States, which it had in the State where it was pronounced, and that whatever pleas would be good to a suit thereon in such State, and none others, could be pleaded in any other court of the United States." Hampton v. McConnel, 3 Wheat. 234. . . .

Whether the award would or would not have been conclusive, and whether the ruling of the Missouri court upon that matter was right or wrong, there can be no question that the judgment was conclusive in Missouri on the validity of the cause of action. . . . A judgment is conclusive as to all the media concludendi, United States v. California & Oregon Land Co., 192 U.S. 355; and it needs no authority to show that it cannot be impeached either in or out of the State by showing that it was based upon a mistake of law. Of course a want of jurisdiction over either the person or the subject-matter might be shown. . . . But as the jurisdiction of the Missouri court is not open to dispute the judgment cannot be impeached in Mississippi even if it went upon a misapprehension of the Mississippi law. . . .

We feel no apprehensions that painful or humiliating consequences will follow upon our decision. No court would give judgment for a plaintiff unless it believed that the facts were a cause of action by the law determining their effect. Mistakes will be rare. In this case the Missouri court no doubt supposed that the award was binding by the law of Mississippi. If it was mistaken it made a natural mistake. The validity of its judgment, even in Mississippi, is, as we believe, the result of the Constitution as it always has been understood, and is not a matter to arouse the susceptibilities of the States, all of which are equally concerned in the question and equally on both sides.

Judgment reversed.

■ JUSTICE WHITE, with whom concurred JUSTICE HARLAN, JUSTICE McKENNA, and JUSTICE DAY, dissenting.

. . . Although not wishing in the slightest degree to weaken the operation of the due faith and credit clause as interpreted and applied from the beginning, it to me seems that this ruling so enlarges that clause as to cause it to obliterate all state lines, since the effect will be to endow each State with authority to overthrow the public policy and criminal statutes of the others, thereby depriving all of their lawful authority. . . . The whole theory upon which the Constitution was framed, and by which alone, it seems to me, it can continue, is the recognition of the fact that different conditions may exist in the different States, rendering necessary the enactment of regulations of a particular subject in one State when such subject may not in another be deemed to require regulation; in other words, that in Massachusetts, owing to conditions which may there prevail, the legislature may deem it necessary to make police regulations on a particular subject, although like regulations may not obtain in other States. . . .

. . . Now it cannot be denied that under the rules of comity recognized at the time of the adoption of the Constitution, and which at this time universally prevail, no sovereignty was or is under the slightest moral obligation to give effect to a judgment of a court of another sovereignty, when to do so would compel the State in which the judgment was sought to be executed to enforce an illegal and prohibited contract, when both the contract and all the acts done in connection with its performance had taken place in the latter State. This seems to me conclusive of this case, since both in treatises of authoritative writers (Story, Conflict of Law, sec. 609), and by repeated adjudications of this court it has been settled that the purpose of the due faith and credit clause was not to confer any new power, but simply to make obligatory that duty which, when the Constitution was adopted rested, as has been said, in comity alone. . . .

NOTES

1.   If an appeal to the Supreme Court of the United States had been taken from the decision of the Missouri court (assuming the decision of the Missouri trial court had been affirmed by the Supreme Court of Missouri), would the decision of that court have been reversed on constitutional grounds?

2.   For another decision recognizing an out-of-state judgment on a gambling debt, see MGM Desert Inn, Inc. v. Holz, 411 S.E.2d 399 (N.C.App.1991). See also In re Jafari, 378 B.R. 575, 581 (Bkrptcy.W.D.Wis.2007): out-of-state judgments are being used to "domesticate" gambling claims that would otherwise be illegal under local law, but the recognition command of the Full Faith and Credit Clause applies only to out-of-state judgments, not to the claim itself, even though it might be lawful under the law where contracted. For further discussion of the doctrine that a court will refuse to assume jurisdiction of a suit on an original cause of action because the action is opposed to the public policy of the forum, see ch. 7, infra.

ROCHE V. McDONALD, 275 U.S. 449, 48 S.Ct. 142 (1928): Action in Washington to enforce an Oregon judgment. The Oregon judgment was based on a prior Washington judgment and was rendered after the expiration of the Washington period of limitation. The Washington court, relying on the Washington statute which provided that "No suit, action, or other proceeding shall ever be had on any judgment rendered in this state by which . . . the duration of such judgment . . . shall be extended or continued in force for any greater or longer period than six years from the date of the entry of the original judgment," refused to enforce the Oregon judgment. On appeal, held, reversed. "The Oregon judgment, being valid and conclusive between the parties in that state, was equally conclusive in the courts of Washington, and under the full faith and credit clause should have been enforced by them."

NOTES

1.   Union National Bank of Wichita, Kansas v. Lamb, 337 U.S. 38 (1949). Suit in Missouri to enforce a Colorado judgment obtained in 1927 and revived in 1945, in accordance with the Colorado practice, on personal service upon

the defendant in Missouri. Enforcement was refused by the Missouri courts because of their local statute of limitations which (a) limited the effective life of a judgment to ten years and (b) provided that no judgment could be revived after ten years from its rendition. Held, reversed. "Roche v. McDonald is dispositive of the merits. . . . In this case it is the 1945 Colorado judgment that claims full faith and credit in Missouri. No Missouri statute of limitations is tendered to cut off a cause of action based on judgments of that vintage." The dissenting opinion contended that the judgment should be vacated and the cause remanded to the Missouri court for an initial determination whether the revival proceedings had "created a new Colorado judgment, or whether they merely had the effect of extending the Colorado statute of limitations on the old judgment. Only in the former case would Roche v. McDonald be 'dispositive of the merits'; in the latter case it is equally clear that McElmoyle for Use of Bailey v. Cohen, supra, 13 Pet. 312 . . . would be controlling." See Note, Revival Judgments under the Full Faith and Credit Clause, 17 U.Chi.L.Rev. 520 (1950). A modern application of the point is Johnson Brothers Wholesale Liquor v. Clemmons, 661 P.2d 1242 (Kan.1983). On revival, see also TDK Electronics Corp. v. Draiman, 321 F.3d 677 (7th Cir.2003).

2.   In the European Union, the Brussels-Ia Regulation mandates the recognition of member state judgments, as noted earlier. Does this requirement apply to judgments recognizing a prior judgment of another member state or, for that matter, of a non-member state? What if, in the case of the American judgment sought to be enforced in Germany (and discussed at p. 280, Note 4, supra), the plaintiff had first sought and obtained its recognition in England, including of its punitive damage part: would Germany have had to recognize the English recognition judgment? In traditional European conflicts law, recognition and enforcement of a judgment (the grant of "exequatur") has only territorial effect, and another state will not adopt that effect as its own. If it were otherwise, the argument goes, State A (England, in the example) could undermine the public policy of State B (Germany) by making effective in State B—through the recognition of a State C judgment (the American judgment in our case)—something which State B abhors (punitive damages): "One trusts one's friends [England], but not the friends [U.S.] of one's friends." Kegel, Exequatur sur exequatur ne vaut, Festschrift für Müller-Freienfels 377, 392 (1986); see also Borges, Das Doppelexequatur von Schiedssprüchen 353–77, 424–35 (1997). For disagreement with this view, see Hay, Recognition of a Recognition Judgment Within the European Union—"Double *Exequatur*" and the Public Policy Barrier, in: Hay, Vékás, Elkana, & Dimitrijevic, (eds.), Resolving International Conflicts—Liber Amicorum Tibor Várady 143–164 (2009), reprinted in Eur. Legal F. 2–2009, I-61. Was Mississippi's policy undermined in *Fauntleroy*, p, 386 supra, or Washington's in *Roche*? Is there or should there be a difference in the answer one gives to the basic question ("Is prior recognition in turn entitled to recognition?"), depending on whether States A and B are wholly independent and unrelated jurisdictions or are bound together through a constitutional or treaty-based full-faith-and-credit mandate? The Brussels Ia Regulation has now abolished the exeqatur procedure as among member states. The latter, however, continue to apply

their procedures with respect to non-member state judgments: an American judgment must still obtain an exequatur in Germany in order to be enforced there. The German exequatur may therefor still not be entitled to recognition n another EU state because it will be regarded as having only local effect.

Reading and Bates Construction Co. v. Baker Energy Resources Corp., 976 S.W.2d 702 (Tex.App.1998), held that although a Texas court would enforce a Canadian judgment under the Uniform Foreign Money-Judgments Recognition Act (p. 398, infra), it would not register a Louisiana judgment under the Uniform Enforcement of Foreign Judgments Act (p. 296, supra). The Louisiana judgment had recognized the Canadian judgment. The court held that it need not give full faith and credit to a sister-state judgment enforcing the judgment of a foreign country because this would have the effect of giving full faith and credit to the judgment of a foreign country "through the back door."

In Jaffe v. Accredited Sur. & Cas. Co., 294 F.3d 584, 590–93 (4th Cir. 2002), the lower court was precluded from recognizing a Canadian judgment that a Florida court had previously refused to recognize: the Florida determination was entitled to full faith and credit. Likewise, in Standard Chartered Bank v. Ahmad Hamad Al Gosaibi and Brothers Company, 99 A.3d 936 (Pa.Super.Ct.2014), appeal denied, 108 A.3d 36 (Pa.2015) (mem.), a creditor had domesticated a foreign-country judgment in New York under that state's Uniform Foreign-Money Judgments Recognition Act: the Pennsylvania court recognized the resulting New York judgment under Full Faith and Credit. In contrast, the District of Columbia refused recognition to the same N.Y. recognition judgment. It cited, but did not rely on *Reading and Bates,* supra, but part of the rationale for the decision was the same: "[T]he judgment in issue . . . is a foreign country judgment . . . clothe[d] . . . in the garment of a sister state's judgment." Ahmad Hamad Al Gosaibi and Brothers Company v. Standard Chartered Bank, 98 A.3d 998, 1007 (D.C.2014). The "constitutional demand to give full faith and credit [therefore] does not apply. . . ." Id. at 1008.

The District of Columbia court then looked at the specific judgment involved. In its view, it is not only the jurisdiction of the foreign court (rendering the original judgment) that is subject to review under the Uniform Act, but so is the jurisdiction of the recognizing American forum over the judgment debtor. In this case, New York had lacked personal jurisdiction when it granted recognition: In recognizing the Bahraini judgment in the first place, the New York had held that a judgment creditor may domesticate a foreign judgment that is otherwise entitled to recognition without establishing a basis for personal jurisdiction over the debtor and may do so even when the judgment debtor has no assets in New York: Abu Dhabi Commercial Bank PJSC v. Saad Trading, Contracting, and Financial Services Company, 986 N.Y.S.2d 454 (App.Div.2014). Who is right: the New York court in originally allowing the Bahraini judgment to be established in New York, the Pennsylvania court in accepting the New York action as a New York judgment entitled to full faith and credit, or the District of Columbia court in disagreeing with both of the foregoing? Are *Reading and Bates* as well as *Al Gosabi* inconsistent with the obligation to give a sister-state judgment the same effect as it has where rendered (see *Treinies*, p. 370, supra) and with the limited leeway left states under the public policy defense when a sister-state judgment is for money (see *Fauntleroy*, p. 386, supra)? A Manitoba court also reached the opposite result from *Reading and Bates Constr. Co.*, when it recognized the Ontario recognition of an Illinois judgment: "It must be remembered that the cause of action is the Ontario judgment and not the original Illinois judgment. Thus, [in a suit based on the Ontario judgment], there could be no defence based on the merits of the original Illinois judgment." Girsberger v. Kresz, 135 Man.R.(2d) 34, at [30] (Mant.Q.B.1999). For a decision discussing both the Pennsylvania and D.C. decisions, see Alberta Securities Commission v. Ryckman, 2015 WL 2265473 (Del.Seuper.Ct.2015), aff'd 127 A.3d 399 (Del. 2015), agreeing with the former.

In the European Union, Art. 29 of the Brussels-Ia Regulation requires a European Union court to decline jurisdiction if another European Union court has first acquired jurisdiction of the same case between the same parties. See the *lis pendens* discussion, p. 253, supra. Owens Bank v. Bracco, C-129/92, [1994] ECR I-117 (Eur.Ct. of Justice 1994), held that the identical provision in the predecessor Regulation did not require an English court to stay a suit brought in England to recognize a St. Vincents judgment even though an Italian court was first seized of proceedings to recognize the same St. Vincents judgment. The opinion also contains a statement that a Community judgment recognizing a non-community judgment is not entitled to enforcement in another Community country.

3. Concern has been raised that the strict recognition command of Community law may preclude the kind of review that would assure compliance with Art. 6 of the European Human Rights Convention's guarantee of a fair trial. The EC Court's decision in Denilauler v. SCN Coucher Freres, [1980] ECR 1533, [1981] CMLR 62 addresses this concern in part when it restricts the recognition command to judgments that issue in adversary proceedings. However, violations of Art. 6 might also occur in such a proceeding. It has therefore been suggested that the public policy exception should be used more extensively to assure compliance with Art. 6, "providing that there is some tightening up of when the defence would operate." J. Fawcett, The Impact of Art. 6 of the ECHR on Private International Law, 56 Int'l & Comp.L.Q. 1, 44 (2007).

4. McElmoyle, for Use of Bailey v. Cohen, 38 U.S. (13 Pet.) 312 (1839) held it consistent with full faith and credit for F-2 to refuse to enforce an F-1 judgment on the ground that suit was barred under the F-2 statute of limitations applicable to judgments even though the judgment would still have been enforceable in F-1.

Potomac Leasing Co. v. Dasco Technology Corp., 10 P.3d 972 (Utah 2000) notes a split of authority as to whether a forum's statute of limitations for enforcing sister-state judgments applies to judgments registered under the Uniform Enforcement of Foreign Judgments Act (p. 296, supra). The court sides with those states that have applied the same limitations to suit on and registration of a sister-state judgment. See also Corzo Trucking Corp. v. West, 636 S.E.2d 39 (Ga.App.2006) (holding that Georgia's ten-year statute of limitations for enforcement of judgments began running when the judgment was originally rendered in Florida).

Watkins v. Conway

Supreme Court of the United States, 1966.
385 U.S. 188, 87 S.Ct. 357, 17 L.Ed.2d 286.

■ PER CURIAM. This litigation began when appellant Watkins brought a tort action against Conway in a circuit court of Florida. On October 5, 1955, that court rendered a $25,000 judgment for appellant. Five years and one day later, appellant sued upon this judgment in a superior court of Georgia. Appellee raised § 3–701 of the Georgia Code as a bar to the proceeding:

> "Suits upon foreign judgments. All suits upon judgments obtained out of this State shall be brought within five years after such judgments shall have been obtained."

The Georgia trial court gave summary judgment for appellee. In so doing, it rejected appellant's contention that § 3–701, when read against the longer limitation period on domestic judgments set forth in Ga.Code §§ 110–1001, 1002 (1933), was inconsistent with the Full Faith and Credit and Equal Protection Clauses of the Federal Constitution. The Georgia Supreme Court affirmed, also rejecting appellant's constitutional challenge to § 3–701. 221 Ga. 374, 144 S.E.2d 721 (1965).

Although appellant lays his claim under two constitutional provisions, in reality his complaint is simply that Georgia has drawn an impermissible distinction between foreign and domestic judgments. He argues that the statute is understandable solely as a reflection of Georgia's desire to handicap out-of-state judgment creditors. If appellant's analysis of the purpose and effect of the statute were correct, we might well agree that it violates the Federal Constitution. For the decisions of this Court which appellee relies upon do not justify the discriminatory application of a statute of limitations to foreign actions.[1]

But the interpretation which the Georgia courts have given § 3–701 convinces us that appellant has misconstrued it. The statute bars suits on foreign judgments only if the plaintiff cannot revive his judgment in the State where it was originally obtained. For the relevant date in applying § 3–701 is not the date of the original judgment, but rather it is the date of the latest revival of the judgment. Fagan v. Bently, 32 Ga. 534 (1861); Baty v. Holston, 108 Ga.App.359, 133 S.E.2d 107 (1963). In the case at bar, for example, all appellant need do is return to Florida and

---

[1] The case most directly on point, McElmoyle for Use of Bailey v. Cohen, 13 Pet. 312, upheld the Georgia statute with which we deal today. But the parties in that case did not argue the statute's shorter limitation for foreign judgments as the ground of its invalidity. Instead, the issue presented to this Court concerned the power of the States to impose any statute of limitations upon foreign judgments. See argument for plaintiff, 13 Pet., at 313–320.

revive his judgment.[2] He can then come back to Georgia within five years and file suit free of the limitations of § 3–701.

It can be seen, therefore, that the Georgia statute has not discriminated against the judgment from Florida. Instead, it has focused on the law of that State. If Florida had a statute of limitations of five years or less on its own judgments, the appellant would not be able to recover here. But this disability would flow from the conclusion of the Florida Legislature that suits on Florida judgments should be barred after that period. Georgia's construction of § 3–701 would merely honor and give effect to that conclusion. Thus, full faith and credit is insured, rather than denied, the law of the judgment State. Similarly, there is no denial of equal protection in a scheme that relies upon the judgment State's view of the validity of its own judgments. Such a scheme hardly reflects invidious discrimination.

Affirmed.

––––––––––––

In MILWAUKEE COUNTY V. M.E. WHITE CO., 296 U.S. 268, 56 S.Ct. 229 (1935), the Supreme Court held that a sister state judgment for taxes must be enforced under full faith and credit. In the course of his opinion, Justice Stone said:

. . . Such exception as there may be to [the] all-inclusive command [of full faith and credit] is one which is implied from the nature of our dual system of government, and recognizes that consistently with the full-faith-and-credit clause there may be limits to the extent to which the policy of one state, in many respects sovereign, may be subordinated to the policy of another. That there are exceptions has often been pointed out . . . and in some instances decided. See Haddock v. Haddock, 201 U.S. 562; Maynard v. Hill, 125 U.S. 190; Hood v. McGehee, 237 U.S. 611; Olmsted v. Olmsted, 216 U.S. 386; Fall v. Eastin, 215 U.S. 1. Without attempting to say what their limits may be, we assume for present purposes that the command of the Constitution and of the statute is not all-embracing, and direct our inquiry to the question whether a state to which a judgment for taxes is taken may have a policy against its enforcement meriting recognition as a permissible limitation upon the full-faith and credit clause. Of that question this court is the final arbiter. . . .

Whether one state must enforce the revenue laws of another remains an open question in this court. See Moore v. Mitchell, 281 U.S. 18. . . .

A cause of action on a judgment is different from that upon which the judgment was entered. In a suit upon a money judgment for a civil

––––––––––––––––––––

[2]   The Florida statute of limitations on domestic judgments is 20 years. Fla.Stat.Ann. § 95.11(1) (1960). Thus, it appears that appellant still has ample time to revive his judgment and bring it back to Georgia. . . .

cause of action, the validity of the claim upon which it was founded is not open to inquiry, whatever its genesis. . . .

We can perceive no greater possibility of embarrassment in litigating the validity of a judgment for taxes and enforcing it than any other for the payment of money. The very purpose of the full-faith and credit clause was to alter the status of the several states as independent foreign sovereignties, each free to ignore obligations created under the laws or by the judicial proceedings of the others, and to make them integral parts of a single nation throughout which a remedy upon a just obligation might be demanded as of right, irrespective of the state of its origin. That purpose ought not lightly to be set aside out of deference to a local policy which, if it exists, would seem to be too trivial to merit serious consideration when weighed against the policy of the constitutional provision and the interest of the state whose judgment is challenged. In the circumstances here disclosed, no state can be said to have a legitimate policy against payment of its neighbor's taxes, the obligation of which has been judicially established by courts to whose judgments in practically every other instance it must give full faith and credit. . . .

We conclude that a judgment is not to be denied full faith and credit in state and federal courts merely because it is for taxes.

We intimate no opinion whether a suit upon a judgment for an obligation created by a penal law, in the international sense, see Huntington v. Attrill, supra, 146 U.S. 657, 677, is within the jurisdiction of the federal District Courts, or whether full faith and credit must be given to such a judgment even though a suit for the penalty before reduced to judgment could not be maintained outside of the state where imposed. See Wisconsin v. Pelican Insurance Co., 127 U.S. 265 (1888).

NOTES

1. See also the notes following Huntington v. Attrill, p. 382, supra.

2. City of New York v. Shapiro, 129 F.Supp. 149 (D.Mass.1954). Action by the City of New York to recover a sum assessed by the City Comptroller against the defendants for unpaid use and business taxes, penalties and interest. Held: this administrative determination is entitled to full faith and credit. There is no "reason of policy for distinguishing between a State's duty to give effect to a sister State's binding administrative determination of taxes." To similar effect, see State of Ohio v. Kleitch Brothers, Inc., 98 N.W.2d 636 (Mich.1959).

3. On the question of the enforcement of foreign tax claims, not reduced to judgment, see Attorney General of Canada v. R.J. Reynolds Tobacco Holdings, Inc., 103 F.Supp.2d 134 (N.D.N.Y.2000), aff'd, 268 F.3d 103 (2d Cir.2001), cert. denied, 537 U.S. 1000 (2002). This case involved a RICO action brought by the Canadian government against American tobacco companies alleging a fraudulent scheme to evade Canadian tobacco taxes through a smuggling operation. The court dismissed the complaint relying in part on the Revenue Rule that "courts will normally not enforce foreign tax judgments, the rationale for which is that issues of foreign relations are assigned to, and better handled by, the legislative and executive branches of the government." While expressing some skepticism as to the vitality of the Revenue Rule's rationale—at least insofar as it applies in the judgment-recognition context—the court concluded that it was still established law and precluded a federal court action for recovery of lost foreign tax revenues. The judgment of dismissal was affirmed.

4. In United States v. Harden, [1963] S.C.R. 366, 41 D.L.R.2d 721 (1963), the Supreme Court of Canada refused to enforce a United States judgment for taxes, relying primarily on British authority holding that, "[i]t is perfectly elementary that a foreign government cannot come here" to enforce its tax claims even when reduced to judgment.

Her Majesty the Queen in Right of the Province of British Columbia v. Gilbertson, 433 F.Supp. 410 (D.Or.1977), aff'd, 597 F.2d 1161 (9th Cir.1979). Suit by the Province of British Columbia to enforce a judgment for taxes obtained in its courts against certain citizens of Oregon. Enforcement of the judgment was refused. The court said "Apparently this is the first time in American legal history that a foreign government has sought enforcement of a tax judgment in a court of the United States. The best explanation for this seems to be that the 'well established rule' that it cannot be done has deterred all attempts."

For a thorough discussion of the enforcement of foreign country tax judgments, see Richard E. Smith, Note, The Nonrecognition of Foreign Tax Judgments, International Tax Evasion, 1981 U.Ill.L.Rev. 241. For public policy concerns in international recognition practice see Carter, Rejection of Foreign Law: Some Private International Law Inhibitions, 55 Brit.Ybk.Int'l L. 1984, p. 111 (1985).

5. In Titus v. Wallick, 306 U.S. 282 (1939), suit was brought in Ohio on a judgment obtained in New York by an assignee of a cause of action. The Ohio suit was defended on the ground that the judgment creditor was not the real party in interest, and that in procuring the judgment, he had suppressed and withheld that fact from the defendant and the New York courts. The Ohio court sustained this defense on the ground that the New York judgment was impeachable there for fraud and was to the same extent impeachable in Ohio. The Supreme Court of the United States reversed, holding that the judgment creditor was entitled to maintain the suit under the law of New York. It also held that the Ohio court must recognize the judgment creditor as the real party in interest, since he held the judgment, even though he might not have been the real party in interest if he had sued in Ohio on the original cause of action.

C. Lack of a Competent Court

Kenney v. Supreme Lodge of the World, Loyal Order of Moose

Supreme Court of the United States, 1920.
252 U.S. 411, 40 S.Ct. 371, 64 L.Ed.638, 10 A.L.R. 716.

■ JUSTICE HOLMES delivered the opinion of the court.

This is an action of debt brought in Illinois upon a judgment recovered in Alabama. The defendant pleaded to the jurisdiction that the judgment was for negligently causing the death of the plaintiff's intestate in Alabama. The plaintiff demurred to the plea, setting up Article IV, secs. 1 and 2 of the Constitution of the United States. A statute of Illinois provided that no action should be brought or prosecuted in that State for damages occasioned by death occurring in another State in consequence of wrongful conduct. The Supreme Court of Illinois held that as by the terms of the statute the original action could not have been brought there, the Illinois Courts had no jurisdiction of a suit upon the judgment. The Circuit Court of Kane County having ordered that the demurrer be quashed its judgment was affirmed. 285 Ill. 188.

In the court below and in the argument before us reliance was placed upon Anglo-American Provision Co. v. Davis Provision Co., No. 1, 191 U.S. 373, and language in Wisconsin v. Pelican Insurance Co., 127 U.S. 265, the former as showing that the clause requiring full faith and credit to be given to judgments of other States does not require a State to furnish a court, and the latter as sanctioning an inquiry into the nature of the original cause of action in order to determine the jurisdiction of a court to enforce a foreign judgment founded upon it. But we are of opinion that the conclusion sought to be built upon these premises in the present case cannot be sustained.

Anglo-American Provision Co. v. Davis Provision Co. was a suit by a foreign corporation on a foreign judgment against a foreign corporation. The decision is sufficiently explained without more by the views about foreign corporations that had prevailed unquestioned since Bank of Augusta v. Earle, 13 Pet. 519, 589–591, cited 191 U.S. 373. Moreover, no doubt there is truth in the proposition that the Constitution does not require the State to furnish a court. But it also is true that there are limits to the power of exclusion and to the power to consider the nature of the cause of action before the foreign judgment based upon it is given effect.

In Fauntleroy v. Lum, 210 U.S. 230, it was held that the courts of Mississippi were bound to enforce a judgment rendered in Missouri upon a cause of action arising in Mississippi and illegal and void there. The policy of Mississippi was more actively contravened in that case than the policy of Illinois is in this. Therefore the fact that here the original cause of action could not have been maintained in Illinois is not an answer to a

suit upon the judgment. See Christmas v. Russell, 5 Wall. 290; Converse
v. Hamilton, 224 U.S. 243. But this being true, it is plain that a State
cannot escape its constitutional obligations by the simple device of
denying jurisdiction in such cases to courts otherwise competent. . . .
[T]he Illinois statute . . . read as [the Illinois courts] read it . . . attempted
to achieve a result that the Constitution of the United States forbade. . . .

Judgment reversed.*

D. FOREIGN COUNTRY JUDGMENTS

We have now considered the various defenses that can be raised
under full faith and credit to the recognition and enforcement of a sister
state judgment. How do these defenses differ from those that are
available when the judgment of a foreign country is involved? Consider
in this connection the discussion of defenses to the enforcement of foreign
country judgments in Schibsby v. Westenholz (p. 43, supra); Hilton v.
Guyot (p. 275, supra) and Cowans v. Ticonderoga Pulp & Paper Co. (p.
287, supra). See also Restatement, Second, Conflict of Laws § 98.

Two uniform acts deal with foreign country judgments:

Uniform Foreign Money-Judgments Recognition Act (1962)

Section 4. [*Grounds for Non-Recognition.*]

(a) A foreign judgment is not conclusive if

(1) the judgment was rendered under a system which does not
provide impartial tribunals or procedures compatible with the
requirements of due process of law;

(2) the foreign court did not have personal jurisdiction over the
defendant; or

(3) the foreign court did not have jurisdiction over the subject
matter.

(b) A foreign judgment need not be recognized if

(1) the defendant in the proceedings in the foreign court did not
receive notice of the proceedings in sufficient time to enable him
to defend;

(2) the judgment was obtained by fraud;

(3) the [cause of action] [claim for relief] on which the judgment
is based is repugnant to the public policy of this state;

(4) the judgment conflicts with another final and conclusive
judgment;

---

*   "I also had a case in which Illinois tried to dodge the Constitutional requirement of due
faith and aids to judgments in other states by denying jurisdiction to Courts otherwise
competent. They laid hold of a statement of mine in an earlier case that the Constitution did
not oblige States to furnish a Court, but we said the dodge wouldn't do." Letter from O.W.
Holmes to Sir Frederick Pollock, April 25, 1920, in 2 Holmes-Pollock Letters (1941) 41. —eds.

(5) the proceeding in the foreign court was contrary to an agreement between the parties under which the dispute in question was to be settled otherwise than by proceedings in that court; or

(6) in the case of jurisdiction based only on personal service, the foreign court was a seriously inconvenient forum for the trial of the action.

Which of the defenses listed in Section 4(a), above, would be effective against a sister state judgment?

Uniform Foreign-Country Money Judgments Recognition Act (2005)

Section 4. [*Standards for Recognition of Foreign Country Judgments*]

(a) Except as otherwise provided in subsections (b) and (c), a court of this state shall recognize a foreign-country judgment to which this [act] applies.

(b) A court of this state may not recognize a foreign-country judgment if:

(1) the judgment was rendered under a judicial system that does not provide impartial tribunals or procedures compatible with the requirements of due process of law;

(2) the foreign court did not have personal jurisdiction over the defendant; or

(3) the foreign court did not have jurisdiction over the subject matter.

(c) A court of this state need not recognize a foreign-country judgment if:

(1) the defendant in the proceeding in the foreign court did not receive notice of the proceeding in sufficient time to enable the defendant to defend;

(2) the judgment was obtained by fraud that deprived the losing party of an adequate opportunity to present its case;

(3) the judgment or the [cause of action] [claim for relief] on which the judgment is based is repugnant to the public policy of this state or of the United States;

(4) the judgment conflicts with another final and conclusive judgment;

(5) the proceeding in the foreign court was contrary to an agreement between the parties under which the dispute in question was to be determined otherwise than by proceedings in that foreign court;

(6) in the case of jurisdiction based only on personal service, the foreign court was a seriously inconvenient forum for the trial of the action;

(7) the judgment was rendered in circumstances that raise substantial doubt about the integrity of the rendering court with respect to the judgment; or

(8) the specific proceeding in the foreign court leading to the judgment was not compatible with the requirements of due process of law.

(d) A party resisting recognition of a foreign-country judgment has the burden of establishing that a ground for nonrecognition stated in subsection (b) or (c) exists.

Comment 12 to section 4 reads:

> Subsections 4(c)(7) and (8) both are discretionary grounds for denying recognition, while subsection 4(b)(1) is mandatory. Obviously, if the entire judicial system in the foreign country fails to satisfy the requirements of impartiality and fundamental fairness, a judgment rendered in that foreign country would be so compromised that the forum court should refuse to recognize it as a matter of course. On the other hand, if the problem is evidence of a lack of integrity or fundamental fairness with regard to the particular proceeding leading to the foreign-country judgment, then there may or may not be other factors in the particular case that would cause the forum court to decide to recognize the foreign-country judgment. For example, a forum court might decide not to exercise its discretion to deny recognition despite evidence of corruption or procedural unfairness in a particular case because the party resisting recognition failed to raise the issue on appeal from the foreign-country judgment in the foreign country, and the evidence establishes that, if the party had done so, appeal would have been an adequate mechanism for correcting the transgressions of the lower court.

Is this an adequate reason for not making subsection 4(c)(8) a mandatory basis for non-recognition?

NOTES

The Uniform Act—In General

1.   By 2021, the original 1962 Act was in force in nine states and the Virgin Islands, while the 2005 Revised Act had been enacted by 25 states, the District of Columbia, and Guam. The 1962 Act is discussed in Homburger, Recognition and Enforcement of Foreign Judgments, 18 Am.J.Comp.L. 367 (1970); Kulzer, Recognition of Foreign Country Judgments in New York: The Uniform Foreign Money-Judgments Recognition Act, 18 Buff.L.Rev. 1 (1969). Brand, Enforcement of Judgments in the United States and Europe, 13 J.L. & Com. 193 (1994); Brand, Enforcement of Foreign Money-

Judgments in the United States: In Search of Uniformity and International Acceptance, 67 Notre Dame L.Rev. 253 (1991); Westerheim, The Uniform Foreign-Money Claims Act: No Solution to an Old Problem, 69 Texas L.Rev. 1203 (1991); 100 A.L.R.3d 792. For the 2005 Act, see Graving, The Carefully Crafted 2005 Uniform Foreign-Country Money Judgments Recognition Act Cures Serious Constitutional Defects in Its 1962 Predecessor, 16 Mich.St.J.Int'l L. 289 (2007–2008). The Uniform Act does not apply to judgments for taxes, for penalties, nor for domestic relations matters (in particular, divorce and support and maintenance): Section 3(b)(1)–(3). For a definition of what constitutes a "penalty," see p. 382 supra. With regard to the recognition of foreign-country support decrees, see p. 1014–1015, infra.

For a comprehensive discussion of the recognition and enforcement of foreign country judgments, see Restatement (Fourth) of Foreign Relations Law of the United States §§ 481–90 (2018).

2. Many of the possible defenses to a foreign-country judgment in § 4 of the 1962 and 2005 Uniform Acts parallel those of domestic law, although § 4(b)(3) (1962 Act) which is § 4(c)(3) in the revised 2005 Act, will play a far greater role in the recognition of foreign-country than of sister-state judgments. Note that § 4(c)(3) of the revised 2005 Act pertains to the "judgment or the [cause of action][claim of relief]," while § 4(b)(3) of the 1962 Act pertains only to the latter. For discussion of this defense, see Hay, Comments on Public Policy in Current American Conflicts Law, in Baetge, von Hein & von Hinden (eds.), Die richtige Ordnung—Festschrift für Kropholler, 89, 90–100 (2008).

3. Expanding notions of jurisdiction in this country have led American courts to take a more tolerant view of assertions of jurisdiction by foreign-country courts. Compare in this regard Ross v. Ostrander, 79 N.Y.S.2d 706 (N.Y.Sup.Ct.1948) with Porisini v. Petricca, 456 N.Y.S.2d 888 (N.Y.App.Div.1982). Both cases involved attempts to enforce in New York English judgments obtained by default against defendants who had engaged in transactions in England. Enforcement was refused in *Ross* because the "requirement of jurisdiction according to the laws of this forum" had not been met. On the other hand, enforcement was granted in *Porisini*. By that time, New York law had been amended (CPLR § 302) to permit New York courts to entertain an action in similar circumstances. In Commission Import Export, S.A. v. Republic of Congo, 118 F.Supp.3d 220, 226–27 (D.D.C. 2015), the court, citing *Porisini*, inquired whether the foreign court could have exercised jurisdiction under the standards of forum law (even if it exercised jurisdiction on different grounds provided by its law). Is it correct to make the decision as to the jurisdiction of a foreign court depend upon local rules of competence? Note that the last decision cited might give the foreign judgment the benefit of a rule of forum law when requiring exact equivalence might not have. For a decision denying recognition on public policy grounds when the foreign court had not recognized the res judicata effect of a prior decision of the present recognizing American forum, see Derr v. Swarek, discussed at p. 375, supra.

4. Other provisions (for instance, subsections (4) and (5) of §§ 4(b) and 4(c), respectively), are peculiar to the international setting and the absence of a full faith and credit requirement. The provisions also raise some questions. Consider two of them: First, subsection (1) in §§ 4(b) and 4(c), respectively, states that a judgment "*need not*" be recognized if the defendant had not received notice to present a defense in the foreign court. The implication is that such a judgment *could* be recognized: would such recognition violate the judgment debtor's due-process rights? See *Mullane*, p. 192, supra. Thus, a New York bankruptcy court refused to recognize a German "Mail Interception Order" that had been issued without notice to the debtor. The court based itself on the public policy exception of the Bankruptcy Code (11 U.S.C. § 1506): In re Dr. Jürgen Toft, 453 B.R. 186 (Bkrtcy.S.D.N.Y. 2011).

Second, §§ 4(a)(1) and 4(b)(1), respectively, allow an assessment of the foreign legal system as providing (or not providing) "impartial tribunals and procedures," satisfying American due-process standards. In Society of Lloyd's v. Ashenden, 233 F.3d 473 (7th Cir.2000), the Court affirmed the recognition of an English judgment in application of the Illinois version of the Uniform Act. It assumed that the English system met the standards of § 4(a)(1), but suggested (at p. 477) that there might have to be a closer inquiry if the country of rendition were the Congo, Cuba, North Korea, Iran, or Iraq. In Bridgeway Corp. v. Citibank, 45 F.Supp.2d 276, 288 (S.D.N.Y.1999), aff'd, 201 F.3d 134 (2d Cir.2000), the district court had entered summary judgment in favor of Citibank after concluding that the courts of Liberia were dominated by the political branches and did not afford a "system . . . [for the] impartial administration of justice." The Court of Appeals reviewed the propriety of the procedures followed below and affirmed. It did not address a question that, arguably, could also have been raised: Is it permissible for state courts (or federal courts sitting in diversity) to undertake such a review and arrive at a negative finding or would the latter infringe the federal foreign relations power? See Chapter 9(2)(A), infra, especially Zschernig v. Miller, at p. 773. On public policy, see also Note 6, infra.

5.   Recall the discussion of Latin American statutes designed to block American dismissals on grounds of *forum non conveniens*, p. 249, Note 7, supra. American defendants are eager to obtain dismissals and argue that the particular Latin American country is an acceptable "alternate forum." Texaco, subsequently acquired by Chevron, succeeded in obtaining a dismissal (after agreeing to submit to suit in Ecuador) in Aquina v. Texaco, Inc., 142 F.Supp.2d 534 (S.D.N.Y.2000), affirmed as modified, 303 F.3d 470 (2d Cir.2002). Plaintiffs subsequently obtained a multi-billion dollar judgment against Chevron in a provincial court in Ecuador. Chevron then sought injunctive relief in New York against enforcement of the Ecuadorian judgment in New York or anywhere outside of Ecuador, alleging that the Ecuadorian judiciary is corrupt. See Uniform Act, supra, § 4(b)(1) and § 4(c)(7). The lower court granted the relief requested (Chevron Corp. v. Donziger et al., 768 F.Supp.2d 581 (S.D.N.Y.2011), but the Second Circuit vacated the decree: New York's version of the Uniform Act provides defenses against recognition and enforcement, but does not provide a basis for affirmative relief. 667 F.3d 232 (2d Cir.2012), cert. denied, 568 U.S. 958 (2012). Note that the quality of the foreign judicial system is relevant for the

initial decision whether to dismiss on grounds of *forum non conveniens* (supra p. 248 Note 6. *Texaco/Chevron* thus adopted inconsistent positions with respect to the availability of an adequate alternate forum when it first sought (and obtained) dismissal in the American forum and later sought preemptive relief against the foreign judgment. See notes 6–10, immediately following.

The Public Policy Defense

6.   The problem addressed by *Fauntleroy,* p. 386, supra, and by *Kenney,* p. 397, supra, of course arises also in the international context. With the Full Faith and Credit requirement not applicable, what should be the role and effect of the foreign country judgment? The cases discussed in notes 4 and 5, supra, touch upon the problem of the forum's public policy. For an application of Huntington v. Atrill, p. 382, supra, see L'Institute Nat. de l'Audiovisuel v. Kultur Int'l Films Ltd., 2012 WL 296997, at *3 (D.N.J.2012).

In Ackermann v. Levine, 788 F.2d 830 (2d Cir.1986), a West German judgment for attorneys' fees was recognized and partially enforced despite the fact that it violated New York's public policy because the German attorneys had failed adequately to assure that the defendant understood the fee arrangement. In contrast, in Matusevitch v. Telnikoff, 877 F.Supp. 1 (D.D.C.1995), the court held an English judgment in a libel action not to be entitled to recognition and enforcement on constitutional and on public policy grounds. Citing to the public-policy exception in Maryland's version of the Uniform Foreign-Money Judgments Recognition Act (Md.Code Ann. Cts. & Jud.Proc. § 10–704(b)(2)), the court considered the English standards for libel underlying the judgment to violate Maryland public policy and to deprive the judgment debtor of his First and Fourth Amendment rights. See also Bachchan v. India Abroad Publications Inc., 585 N.Y.S.2d 661 (N.Y.Sup.Ct.1992); World Granite & Marble Corp. v. Wil-Freds Const., 1996 WL 763230 (N.D.Ill.1996); In re Dr. Jürgen Toft, Note 4, supra. For discussion, see Hay, On Comity, Reciprocity, and Public Policy in U.S. and German Judgment Recognition Practice, in: Basedow, et al. (eds.), Private Law in the International Arena—Liber Americorum Kurt Siehr 237 (2000). For critical discussion of Telnikoff and Bachchan, see Rosen, Exporting the Constitution, 53 Emory L.J. 172 (2004). For the "Speech Act of 2010," see Note 8, infra.

7.   In contrast, the Seventh Circuit has suggested that foreign judgments need not comport in a mirror-image fashion with American due process standards. Society of Lloyd's v. Ashenden, 233 F.3d 473, 480 (7th Cir.2000); see also Note 4, supra. "We'll call this the 'international concept of due process' to distinguish it from the complex concept that has emerged from American case law." Id. at 477. For criticism, see Montré D. Carodine, Political Judging: When Due Process Goes International, 48 Wm. & Mary L.Rev. 1159 (2007). For a discussion of the role of public policy as a defense to foreign judgments and as a method of overriding choice-of-law analysis, see Hay, Comments on Public Policy in Current American Conflicts Law, in Baetge & von Hein (eds.), Die richtige Ordnung, Festschrift für Jan Kropholler 89 (2008).

The Fifth Circuit has taken a position similar to that of the Seventh: in DeJoria v. Maghreb Petroleum Exploration S.A., 804 F.3d 373 (5th Cir.2015), Maghreb sought enforcement of a Moroccan judgment in Texas, but the district court refused, holding that Morocco's judicial system was incompatible with due process. Maghreb appealed, and the Fifth Circuit reversed. On appeal, the court's due process inquiry focused on the foreign judicial *system*, rather than on any one of its judgments. It did not matter that political influence could have affected the outcome in *this* case; to defeat recognition, DeJoria had to show that "any judgment rendered by a Moroccan court is to be disregarded as a matter of course," 804 F.3d at 382 (examples that meet this high standard for non-recognition include the courts of a country at war or during a revolution), which DeJoria could not show. Fundamental fairness (not a precise match to the domestic system) is all that recognition requires. 804 F.3d at 383–84. Additional litigation followed. During that time, Texas amended its version of the uniform recognition act by adding two additional grounds for non-recognition: doubts about the integrity of the rendering court with respect to the judgment in question and that the specific judgment is not compatible with due process. Tex.Civ.Prac. & Rem. Code § 36A.001–11. The trial court found the new provisions to be applicable and denied recognition. The Fifth Circuit upheld the retroactive application of the Texas amendment to the recognition statute and held that the trial court had acted within its discretion. Non-recognition was affirmed. 935 F.3d 381 (5th Cir. 2019), cert. denied, 140 S.Ct. 2718 (2020).

The "international concept of due process" was satisfied in Hubei Gezhouba Sanlian Industrial Co., Ltd. v. Robinson Helicopter Company, Inc., 2009 WL 3398931 (C.D.Cal.), involving a helicopter, manufactured by a California corporation, which crashed in China. The California district court recognized and enforced a multi-million dollar Chinese judgment because the defendant did not present any evidence, nor did it contend, that the Chinese court system did not provide impartial tribunals or procedures compatible with the requirements of due process of law. In contrast, in Osorio v. Dole Food Company, 665 F.Supp.2d 1307 (S.D.Fla.2009), aff'd sub nom., Osorio v. Dow Chemical Co., 635 F.3d 1277 (11th Cir.2011), cert. denied, 565 U.S. 1114 (2012), it was held that a 97.4 million dollar Nicaraguan judgment for health effects caused by pesticide use should not be enforced because it did not comport with the international due process norms set forth in *Ashenden*. A Nicaraguan law passed specifically to deal with cases against foreign corporation established strong presumptions in favor of plaintiffs such as an irrefutable presumption of causation.

8.   The "Speech Act of 2010," 28 U.S.C.A. § 4102, essentially adopted *Matusevich* and *Bachchan*, Note 6, supra, as federal law. It followed the earlier adoption by New York of the "Libel Terrorism Protection Act of 2008," N.Y.C.P.L.R. §§ 302, 5304(b), with other states following suit. The federal act requires courts to determine whether the foreign proceedings afforded the judgment debtor essentially the protections guaranteed by the First Amendment of the U.S. Constitution as a prerequisite for the recognition of the ensuing judgment. For criticism, see Hay, Favoring Local Interests, in: Kronke & Thorn (eds.), Grenzen überwinden—Prinzipien bewahren,

Festschrift für von Hoffmann 634, 642 (2011); Rosen, Note 6, supra. The "Speech Act" was a response to what had become known as "libel tourism:" litigation libel claims in England (when England had been the, or one of the places of publication) to take advantage of the then prevailing rule of English procedure (reversal of the burden of proof in defamation action) and English substantive law which provided a much more limited "public figure" defense than American law. For the reform of British libel law in England and Wales, but not yet in Northern Ireland, see p. 284, supra.

When it applies, the "Speech Act" (and similar state statutes) limit the case law as it had developed and is reported in notes 3 and 7, supra. Its underlying rationale—no enforcement of a foreign judgment when it or the proceeding leading to it does not comport with American Constitutional standards—could theoretically lead to rather extensive review of foreign judgments. What about the First Amendment's "Free Exercise Clause" or all of the guarantees a party enjoys in domestic proceedings under the Due Process Clause of the Fifth and Fourteenth Amendments? See Hay, supra this Note, at 644–45. What remains of Judge Posner's idea of an "international concept of due process?" Notes 4 and 7, supra.

9. *An application.* In light of the previous note, consider the following (earlier) case. A French lower court rendered a preliminary decision in actions brought by the French League Against Racism and Discrimination (LICRA) and the French Union of Jewish Students (UEJF) against Yahoo! France and Yahoo! Inc. for providing access to websites offering auction services for Nazi objects and symbols of Nazi ideology. The complaint alleged violations of the French Penal Code and tortious conduct causing injury to plaintiff organizations and their members. The court joined the actions and, with regard to web users in France, ordered Yahoo! Inc. "to take all necessary measures to dissuade and render impossible any access via Yahoo.com to the Nazi artifact auction service and to any other site or service that may be construed as constituting an apology for Nazism or a contesting of Nazi crimes." Yahoo! Inc. took the position that these websites could not be readily filtered out, at least not in geographically defined areas. The court conducted extensive evidentiary hearings and rejected the defense. It ordered Yahoo! Inc. to comply with the order within three months and imposed a fine for each day of non-compliance thereafter. Yahoo! sought declaratory relief in California that the French court's orders are not "recognizable and enforceable" in the United States. After denying the defendants' motion for dismissal for lack of jurisdiction (145 F.Supp.2d 1168 (N.D.Cal.2001)), the court granted Yahoo!'s motion for summary judgment on First Amendment grounds: "Although France has the sovereign right to regulate what speech is permissible in France, this Court may not enforce a foreign order that violates the protections of the United States Constitution by chilling protected speech that occurs simultaneously within our borders." Yahoo! Inc. v. La Ligue Contre Le Racisme et L'Antisémitisme, 169 F.Supp.2d 1181, 1192 (N.D.Cal.2001).

Yahoo! Inc. v. La Ligue Contre Le Racisme et L'Antisemitisme, 379 F.3d 1120 (9th Cir.2004), by a 2–1 panel vote, reversed the district court on the ground that there was no personal jurisdiction over the French defendants.

On rehearing en banc, 433 F.3d 1199 (9th Cir. en banc 2006), a majority of eight judges concluded that the district court had personal jurisdiction over the defendants. Of that majority, 3 judges concluded that the action should be dismissed for lack or ripeness: "[I]t is extremely unlikely that any penalty, if assessed, could ever be enforced against Yahoo! in the United States. Further, First Amendment harm may not exist at all, given the possibility that Yahoo! has now 'in large measure' complied with the French court's orders. . . . There is some possibility that in further restricting access to [Internet users located in France] Yahoo! might have to restrict access by American users. But this possibility is, at this point, highly speculative."

Three judges held that the case is ripe for adjudication but "that the District Court did not properly exercise personal jurisdiction over the defendants and also should have abstained under the Act of State Doctrine (see Banco Nacional de Cuba v. Sabbatino, p. 790, infra) from deciding Yahoo!'s claims." When the 3 votes that the suit is unripe are combined with the 3 votes that there is no personal jurisdiction over the defendants, there is a bare majority (6–5) to dismiss. Therefore the Ninth Circuit en banc reversed the district court and remanded with instructions to dismiss without prejudice.

Five judges held that the case was ripe for adjudication, that there was personal jurisdiction over the defendants, and would remand for further briefing and fact finding on the issue of whether "Yahoo! is not harmed by the very threat of the French orders' possible enforcement."

Assume that the defendant has not complied with the French injunction:

(i) Should the daily monetary amount imposed be characterized as a penalty and refused recognition on that ground or should it be recognized as an instrument for the vindication of private rights?

(ii) Would it make a difference for the purpose of the previous question whether the daily monetary amount imposed was to be paid into court (i.e., to French public authority) or to the plaintiffs?

(iii) If you should favor the recognition and enforcement of the daily amount, would you express your decision in French francs (now euros) or in dollars (see p. 800, Note 2, infra)?

10. In Beals v. Saldanha, [2003] 3 S.C.R. 416, the Supreme Court of Canada required an Ontario court to enforce a Florida default judgment against Ontario residents including both treble and punitive damages. The majority held that the Ontario court must enforce the judgment even if it will bankrupt the defendants. The basis for liability was the sale of Florida land to a developer for $8,000. With interest the judgment is over $1 million Canadian.

Morguard Investments v. De Savoye, [1990] 3 S.C.R. 1077, required full faith and credit to judgments of another Canadian province. *Saldanha* extends *Morguard* to judgments of foreign countries subject to defenses such as those in § 4 of the Uniform Foreign Money-Judgments Recognition Act. See p. 399. Two dissenters agree that Canadian courts should ordinarily enforce foreign judgments but disagree under the circumstances of this case.

One dissenter would impose greater barriers to enforcement of foreign judgments than the majority indicates.

The decision not to defend the Florida action was based on advice by an Ontario solicitor that a Canadian court would not enforce the Florida judgment because the Florida court would not have jurisdiction over the defendants unless they appeared. The defendants were not aware of the risk of a large judgment because, as in many states, Florida courts require pleading only that the amount in controversy is in excess of the stated jurisdictional amount. The solicitor's malpractice insurer paid the judgment.

11. A question that remains relatively unexplored by the courts is the extent to which a foreign-country judgment will be given a lesser res judicata or collateral estoppel effect in this country than that to which a sister state judgment would be entitled under full faith and credit. See GATX Flightlease Aircraft Co. Ltd. v. Airbus S.A.S., 15 Misc.3d 1143(A), at *6 (N.Y.Sup.2007) (slip op.); Alfadda v. Fenn, 966 F.Supp. 1317, 1326 (S.D.N.Y.1997); and R.A. Global Services, Inc. v. Avicenna Overseas Corp., 843 F.Supp.2d 386 (S.D.N.Y.2012). All acknowledge the uncertainty over whether the forum should apply its own or the foreign country's res judicata law. The question has been much discussed in the law reviews. Some writers believe that the difference in treatment should be quite marked. See Smit, International Res Judicata and Collateral Estoppel in the United States, 9 UCLA L.Rev. 44 (1962); von Mehren & Trautman, Recognition of Foreign Adjudications: A Survey and Suggested Approach, 81 Harv.L.Rev. 1601 (1968). See also Kulzer, Some Aspects of Enforceability of Foreign Judgments, 16 Buff.L.Rev. 84 (1966); Reese, The Status in this Country of Judgments Rendered Abroad, 50 Colum.L.Rev. 783 (1950). For a view suggesting essentially similar treatment of international and interstate judgments (same effect as where rendered), see Hay, Merger and Preclusion (Res Judicata) in U.S. Foreign Judgments Recognition—Unresolved Doctrinal Problems, in: R.Schütze et al. (eds.), Festschrift für Reinhold Geimer 325 (2002). For additional case law, on both sides of the issue, but continuing to be inconclusive, see Andes v. Versant Corp., 878 F.2d 147, 149 (4th Cir.1989) (preclusion is governed by the law of the rendering court but also by possibly wider preclusion rules of the enforcing forum), quoted in Seale & Assoc. v. Vector Aero. Corp., 2010 WL 5186410 (E.D.Va.2010), in which the court noted that Virginia generally treats foreign-country judgments the same as sister-state judgments that are entitled to full faith and credit (and to be given the same effect as where rendered), but then observed that the claim would be precluded under both Canadian and Virginia law, i.e., it represented a false conflict.

In interstate practice, the claim merges in the judgment. See Hay, Borchers, Symeonides & Whytock, Conflict of Laws §§ 24.1–24.3, (6th ed.2018). The merger idea also helps to explain the result in *Fauntleroy,* p. 386, supra. A foreign country judgment traditionally does not merge the underlying claim. This explains why the claim and its legal basis remain reviewable in the second court. Does this make sense? See id. at § 24.3.

Decisions in which an American court has given collateral estoppel effect to the judgment of a foreign country include Clarkson Co., Limited v. Shaheen, 544 F.2d 624 (2d Cir.1976); Fairchild, Arabatzis & Smith, Inc. v.

Prometco (Produce & Metals) Co., Limited, 470 F.Supp. 610 (S.D.N.Y.1979); Leo Feist, Inc. v. Debmar Publishing Co., 232 F.Supp. 623 (E.D.Pa.1964); In-Tech Marketing, Inc. v. Hasbro, Inc., 719 F.Supp. 312 (D.N.J.1989); Kim v. Co-op. Centrale Raiffeisen-Boerenleebank B.A., 364 F.Supp.2d 346 (S.D.N.Y. 2005) (Singapore court's dismissal of employee's previous action against bank arising from same facts and asserting same claims was preclusive). The opinions normally are silent on whether they are applying American rules of collateral estoppel or those of the state of rendition. See Peterson, Foreign Country Judgments and the Second Restatement of Conflict of Laws, 72 Colum.L.Rev. 220, 259–64 (1972). See also U.S. v. Kashamu, 656 F.3d 679, 684 (7th Cir.2011).

What reasons can be advanced that would justify an American court in giving a foreign country judgment either greater or less collateral estoppel effect than it would have in the state of rendition?

What is the effect of the grant or denial of recognition of a foreign-country judgment in a second American state: must the second state give full faith and credit to the first state's determination or may it consider the question of recognition anew? See pp. 390–392, Note 2, supra.

12. The Uniform Law Conference of Canada has adopted the Canadian Uniform Enforcement of Foreign Judgments Act, which contains the following provision:

Limit of Damages

(1) Where the enforcing court, on application by a judgment debtor, determines that a foreign judgment includes an amount added to compensatory damages as punitive or multiple damages or for other non-compensatory purposes, it shall limit enforcement of the damages awarded by the foreign judgment to the amount of similar or comparable damages that could have been awarded in [the enacting province or territory.]

Excessive Damages

(2) Where the enforcing court, on application by the judgment debtor, determines that a foreign judgment includes an amount of compensatory damages that is excessive in the circumstances, it may limit enforcement of the award, but the amount awarded may not be less than that which the enforcing court could have awarded in the circumstances.

Costs and Expenses

(3) In this section, a reference to damages includes the costs and expenses of the civil proceeding in the State of origin.

Saskatchewan has enacted the statute: S.S. 2005, c. E–9.121. What burden does this provision impose on the enforcing court? See Janet Walker, Conflict of Laws—Reissue 2016, Halsbury's Laws of Canada 535 et seq. (2016).

Other Issues

13. For currency problems associated with foreign-country claims and judgments, see the Uniform Foreign-Money Claims Act (1989 Act), see infra p. 800, Note 2.

14. For a possible reciprocity requirement, see supra p. 285, Note 8.

E. MATTERS SUBSEQUENT TO F-1 JUDGMENT

A judgment's effectiveness as an enforceable obligation can be affected or destroyed by events which take place thereafter. One obvious example is the running of the forum's statutory period of limitations. McElmoyle for Use of Bailey v. Cohen, p. 392, Note 4, supra. Here we consider the consequences of other supervening occurrences, namely: (1) payment or other discharge, (2) the rendition of a second judgment, which may either be consistent or inconsistent with the first, and (3) the effect on a judgment of the reversal of an earlier one upon which it was based.

1. PAYMENT OR OTHER DISCHARGE

Payment, release, and accord and satisfaction are, of course, valid defenses to the enforcement of a judgment. And where a second judgment has been rendered upon the first, discharge of the obligation created by either of these judgments, in one of the foregoing ways, will also operate to extinguish that created by the other. Restatement, Second, Conflict of Laws § 116. This latter principle has been applied to a situation where payment of the second judgment was made in depreciated currency. Matter of James' Will, 248 N.Y. 1, 161 N.E. 201 (1928). In that case, suit to enforce a New York judgment in the amount of $65,000 was brought in France, and, according to the French procedure, an exequatur was issued, which directed the payment of some 2,300,000 francs, the equivalent of the dollar judgment at the date the French proceeding was begun in 1922. This sum of francs was paid in 1925, and the judgment debtor then moved to have the New York judgment discharged as paid. This was opposed on the ground that, since the value of the franc vis-a-vis the dollar had declined in the intervening years, the francs received in 1925 were not worth $65,000. It was therefore argued that the francs should be valued as of the date of payment and treated only as a payment on account. The court held (4 to 3, with Chief Judge Cardozo dissenting) that the New York judgment was discharged. Is such a result either necessary or desirable? For a discussion of the problem, see Reese, The Status in this Country of Judgments Rendered Abroad, 50 Colum.L.Rev. 783, 798–99 (1950). With respect to currency valuation and conversion, see p. 800, infra.

2. SUCCESSIVE JUDGMENTS

A second judgment, in the sense here used, can be handed down in any one of four situations: (1) in a suit brought to enforce the first judgment; (2) less frequently, in a suit based upon the underlying cause of action;* (3) where the first judgment was for the defendant and

---

*   Such an eventuality might occur in a case where the first judgment was rendered in a foreign country (Eastern Townships Bank v. H.S. Beebe & Co., 53 Vt. 177 (1880)), or where the first judgment was not drawn to the attention of the court in the second action.

constituted a bar to the prosecution of the second action; or (4) where under the principles of collateral estoppel, the first judgment has already determined one or more of the relevant issues involved. Such a judgment may either be consistent or inconsistent with the first. It is consistent so long as it accords the first judgment the same res judicata effect (either by way of merger, bar, or collateral estoppel) that the latter would enjoy at home, or even if it fails to do this, where it reaches the same result with respect to the particular issue involved. It is inconsistent with the first judgment in all other situations. Common examples of the latter sort are where the second court refuses to enforce the first judgment on the ground that it was rendered without jurisdiction or where it permits the issues to be relitigated afresh and then determines them differently.

Where the second judgment is consistent with the first, the legal effectiveness of the latter remains unaffected. The doctrine of merger is inapplicable to judgments, so that the first judgment, even after it has been reduced to a second judgment in another state, continues in full force and effect and can be used, if the judgment creditor so elects, as the basis for a suit in a third state. The first judgment also retains all of its original effect as res judicata. Restatement, Second, Judgments § 18, comment *j*.

The converse is true, however, in situations where the second court hands down an inconsistent judgment. Here the second judgment-assuming always that the court had jurisdiction and that review by the Supreme Court was available-is controlling and destroys the legal effectiveness of the first judgment, so long as it remains unreversed and to the extent that it is inconsistent with the latter. Thus, the plaintiff can no longer maintain an action, or otherwise rely, upon a judgment rendered in his favor once it has been denied enforcement in a second state because of lack of jurisdiction on the part of the original court. And this is true even though the second court violated the mandate of full faith and credit; its finding of no jurisdiction is nevertheless res judicata and binding upon the parties. Plaintiff's remedy in such a case is by way of appeal from the second judgment. Treinies v. Sunshine Mining Co., p. 370, supra; Restatement, Second, Conflict of Laws § 114. For a different approach to inconsistent judgment in Europe, see p. 375, supra.

3.   REVERSAL OF EARLIER JUDGMENT

What is the effect on the second judgment of a subsequent reversal of the earlier one upon which it was based? Assuming that the second court had jurisdiction, its judgment was a valid exercise of judicial power and remains res judicata of the issues involved despite the reversal of the other. Reed v. Allen, 286 U.S. 191 (1932). The judgment debtor, however, is not remediless. Dependent upon the particular law of the second state, he can in that state either have the second judgment vacated or reversed on appeal, or else have its enforcement enjoined by means of an independent action in equity. Restatement, Second, Judgments § 16. As to the debtor's right to restitution on account of any benefits conferred in compliance with a judgment that has subsequently been reversed, see Restatement, Restitution § 74 (1937).

Suppose now that the second judgment is sought to be enforced, or is otherwise placed in issue in the courts of a third state, and that while these proceedings are pending, the first judgment is reversed. What is the status of the second judgment in F-3 upon the happening of this event? Presumably, it cannot under full faith and credit be treated as a nullity so long as it remains valid and effective in F-2. But so long as it is subject to impeachment in F-2 on account of the F-1 reversal, it should likewise be subject to attack on this ground in F-3. And by analogy to the rule prevailing in the case of judgments procured by fraud (Levin v. Gladstein, p. 380, supra), F-3 law would presumably govern the particular method of attack—i.e., whether the issue could be raised by way of defense to the plaintiff's action or only in an independent proceeding in equity for an injunction against the enforcement of the F-2 judgment. Cf. Ellis v. McGovern, 137 N.Y.S. 1029 (N.Y.App.Div.1912).

CHAPTER 6

THE IMPACT OF THE CONSTITUTION

INTRODUCTORY NOTE

The bulk of this course, and particularly the material that follows, is devoted to problems in choice of law. Before plunging into that subject, however, we pause to study constraints that deprive state courts of options they would otherwise have in ruling on conflicts issues. These constraints are rooted, directly or indirectly, in the Constitution of the United States, the most important provisions of which are set out at pp. 45–46, supra. The Supremacy Clause (Art. VI) compels state law to give way to the Constitution and valid federal law, including statutes and treaties. The Interstate Commerce Clause (Article I, § 8) sometimes limits the territorial reach of state economic regulation.

Most importantly for present purposes are constraints imposed by the Full Faith and Credit Clause (Article IV, § 1), the Privileges and Immunities Clause (Article IV, § 2), the Due Process Clauses of the Fifth and Fourteenth Amendments and the Equal Protection Clause of the Fourteenth Amendment.

Sometimes the Constitution compels a state to provide a forum for suit on a claim arising in a sister state. On occasion it prohibits a state from applying its own rule of decision to resolve an issue in a multistate case, for the reason that the state does not have adequate ties, relations, concerns, or interests in the matter to warrant applying its own rule of decision. The same prohibition may prevent application of the rule of decision of some other state which lacks a legitimate interest in the outcome of the dispute. Occasionally, the Constitution may mandate that the law of a particular state be applied to decide the issue presented. Less rarely, a state will be constitutionally prohibited from discriminating unreasonably against citizens of sister states or from dealing unequally with persons in its jurisdiction who are similarly situated.

SECTION 1. THE OBLIGATION TO PROVIDE OR TO REFUSE A FORUM

Hughes v. Fetter

Supreme Court of the United States, 1951.
341 U.S. 609, 71 S.Ct. 980, 95 L.Ed. 1212.

■ JUSTICE BLACK delivered the opinion of the Court.

Basing his complaint on the Illinois wrongful death statute, appellant administrator brought this action in the Wisconsin state court to recover damages for the death of Harold Hughes, who was fatally injured in an automobile accident in Illinois. The allegedly negligent driver and an insurance company were named as defendants. On their motion the trial court entered summary judgment "dismissing the complaint on the merits." It held that a Wisconsin statute, which creates a right of action only for deaths caused in that state, establishes a local public policy against Wisconsin's entertaining suits brought under the wrongful death acts of other states.[2] The Wisconsin Supreme Court affirmed,[1] notwithstanding the contention that the local statute so construed violated the Full Faith and Credit Clause of Art. IV, § 1 of the Constitution. The case is properly here on appeal under 28 U.S.C. § 1257.

We are called upon to decide the narrow question whether Wisconsin, over the objection raised, can close the doors of its courts to the cause of action created by the Illinois wrongful death act. Prior decisions have established that the Illinois statute is a "public act" within the provision of Art. IV, § 1 that "Full Faith and Credit shall be given in each State to the public Acts . . . of every other State." It is also settled that Wisconsin cannot escape this constitutional obligation to enforce the rights and duties validly created under the laws of other states by the simple device of removing jurisdiction from courts otherwise competent. We have recognized, however, that full faith and credit does not automatically compel a forum state to subordinate its own statutory policy to a conflicting public act of another state; rather, it is for this Court to choose in each case between the competing public policies involved. The clash of interests in cases of this type has usually been described as a conflict between the public policies of two or more states. The more basic conflict involved in the present appeal, however, is as follows: On the one hand is the strong unifying principle embodied in the Full Faith and Credit Clause looking toward maximum enforcement in each state of the obligations or rights created or recognized by the statutes of sister states;[9] on the other hand is the policy of Wisconsin, as

---

    [2] Wis.Stat., 1949, § 331.03. This section contains language typically found in wrongful death acts but concludes as follows: "provided, that such action shall be brought for a death caused in this state."

    [1] The Wisconsin court stated in Hughes v. Fetter, 257 Wis. 35, 42 N.W.2d 452 (1950): "It has been repeatedly declared to be the law that it was not intended by the provisions of the Federal Constitution referred to [the full faith and credit clause and the privileges and immunities clause] to give to the laws of one state any operation in other states except by permission, express or implied, by those states. . . . The statute in another state cannot be made the basis of furnishing a remedy for action in Wisconsin whose maintenance would be wholly inconsistent with the public policy of our state as declared by the legislature This clause 'altered the status of the several states as independent foreign sovereignties, each free to ignore rights and obligations created under the laws or established by the judicial proceedings of the others, by making each an integral part of a single nation. . . .' Magnolia Petroleum Co. v. Hunt, 320 U.S. 430, 439. See also Milwaukee County v. White, 296 U.S. 268, 276–277; Order of Travelers v. Wolfe, 331 U.S. 586." —eds.

    [9] This clause "altered the status of the several states as independent foreign sovereignties, each free to ignore rights and obligations created under the laws or established by the judicial proceedings of the others, by making each an integral part of a single nation. . . ."

interpreted by its highest court, against permitting Wisconsin courts to entertain this wrongful death action.[10]

We hold that Wisconsin's policy must give way. That state has no real feeling of antagonism against wrongful death suits in general. To the contrary, a forum is regularly provided for cases of this nature, the exclusionary rule extending only so far as to bar actions for death not caused locally. The Wisconsin policy, moreover, cannot be considered as an application of the forum non conveniens doctrine, whatever effect that doctrine might be given if its use resulted in denying enforcement to public acts of other states. Even if we assume that Wisconsin could refuse, by reason of particular circumstances, to hear foreign controversies to which nonresidents were parties, the present case is not one lacking a close relationship with the state. For not only were appellant, the decedent and the individual defendant all residents of Wisconsin, but also appellant was appointed administrator and the corporate defendant was created under Wisconsin laws. We also think it relevant, although not crucial here, that Wisconsin may well be the only jurisdiction in which service could be had as an original matter on the insurance company defendant. And while in the present case jurisdiction over the individual defendant apparently could be had in Illinois by substituted service, in other cases Wisconsin's exclusionary statute might amount to a deprivation of all opportunity to enforce valid death claims created by another state.

Under these circumstances, we conclude that Wisconsin's statutory policy which excludes this Illinois cause of action is forbidden by the national policy of the Full Faith and Credit Clause.[16] The judgment is reversed and the cause is remanded to the Supreme Court of Wisconsin for proceedings not inconsistent with this opinion.

Reversed and remanded.

■ JUSTICE FRANKFURTER, with whom JUSTICE REED, JUSTICE JACKSON, and JUSTICE MINTON join, dissenting.

Magnolia Petroleum Co. v. Hunt, 320 U.S. 430, 439. See also Milwaukee County v. White, 296 U.S. 268, 276–277; Order of Travelers v. Wolfe, 331 U.S. 586.

[10] The present case is not one where Wisconsin, having entertained appellant's lawsuit, chose to apply its own instead of Illinois' statute to measure the substantive rights involved. This distinguishes the present case from those where we have said that "Prima facie every state is entitled to enforce in its own courts its own statutes, lawfully enacted." Alaska Packers Ass'n v. Industrial Acc. Commission, 294 U.S. 532; see, also, Williams v. State of North Carolina, 317 U.S. 287, 295–296.

[16] In certain previous cases, e.g., Pacific Employers Ins. Co. v. Industrial Accident Commission, 306 U.S. 493, 502; Alaska Packers Ass'n v. Industrial Accident Commission, 294 U.S. 532, 547, this Court suggested that under the Full Faith and Credit Clause a forum state might make a distinction between statutes and judgments of sister states because of Congress' failure to prescribe the extra-state effect to be accorded public acts. Subsequent to these decisions the Judicial Code was revised so as to provide: "Such Acts [of the legislature of any state] . . . and judicial proceedings . . . shall have the same full faith and credit in every court within the United States . . . as they have . . . in the courts of such State . . . from which they are taken." 28 U.S.C. (1946 ed., Supp. III), § 1738. In deciding the present appeal, however, we have found it unnecessary to rely on any changes accomplished by the Judicial Code revision.

. . . In the present case, the decedent, the plaintiff, and the individual defendant were residents of Wisconsin. The corporate defendant was created under Wisconsin law. The suit was brought in Wisconsin. No reason is apparent—and none is vouchsafed in the opinion of the Court— why the interest of Illinois is so great that it can force the courts of Wisconsin to grant relief in defiance of their own law.

Finally, it may be noted that there is no conflict here in the policies underlying the statute of Wisconsin and that of Illinois. The Illinois wrongful death statute has a proviso that "no action shall be brought or prosecuted in this State to recover damages for a death occurring outside of this State where a right of action for such death exists under the laws of the place where such death occurred and service of process in such suit may be had upon the defendant in such place." . . . Thus, in the converse of the case at bar—if Hughes had been killed in Wisconsin and suit had been brought in Illinois—the Illinois courts would apparently have dismissed the suit. There is no need to be "more Roman than the Romans."

NOTES

1.   To what did the Wisconsin court fail to give full faith and credit? Note in this connection Justice Black's intimation in footnote 10 that the Wisconsin court would not have violated full faith and credit if it had decided the "substantive rights" of the parties by application of the Wisconsin wrongful death statute. Professor Brainerd Currie suggested that the proper basis for the decision was the Equal Protection Clause of the Fourteenth Amendment in that the Wisconsin statute discriminated irrationally between Wisconsin citizens killed in Wisconsin and those killed in other states. In Professor Currie's view, Wisconsin could not constitutionally have denied plaintiff a forum if, the facts otherwise being the same, the Wisconsin decedent had met his death in a foreign country rather than in a sister state. Currie, The Constitution and the "Transitory" Cause of Action, 73 Harv.L.Rev. 36, 268 (1959), reprinted in Currie, Selected Essays on the Conflict of Laws, Chap. 6 (1963). See also Weinberg, Against Comity, 80 Geo.L.J. 53 (1991); Weintraub, Who's Afraid of Constitutional Limitations on Choice of Law?, 10 Hofstra L.Rev. 17 (1981). For a full discussion of the principal case, see Reese, Full Faith and Credit to Statutes: The Defense of Public Policy, 19 U.Chi.L.Rev. 339 (1952).

In Wells v. Simonds Abrasive Co., 345 U.S. 514, 73 S.Ct. 856 (1953). the Court held that a Pennsylvania court could apply its own statute of limitations to bar a wrongful death claim arising from an Alabama accident. In meeting the plaintiff's objection that *Hughes* required application of the longer Alabama period, the Court stated: "The crucial factor in [*Hughes*] was that the forum laid an uneven hand on causes of action arising within and without the forum state. . . . Here Pennsylvania applies her one-year limitation to all wrongful death actions wherever they may arise."

Dean Kramer argues that *Hughes* and Broderick v. Rosner, discussed in Note 5 infra, stand for a broader principle of equality in interstate cases:

> "[I]n *Hughes* and *Broderick* we see the Court clearly groping towards a principle that makes considerable sense in its own right. The Full Faith and Credit Clause is one of a bundle of provisions incorporated into the Constitution to bind states more closely together. . . . With respect to full faith and credit in particular, the whole point was that states should not be free to dismiss or ignore the laws of sister states. . . . The central object of the Clause was, in fact, to eliminate a state's prideful unwillingness to recognize other states' laws or judgments on the ground that these are inferior or unacceptable."

Kramer, Same-Sex Marriage, Conflict of Laws, and the Unconstitutional Public Policy Exception, 106 Yale L.J. 1965, 1986 (1997).

Does *Hughes* stand for such a principle? As you read subsequent opinions in this chapter, consider whether the Court has interpreted the Full Faith and Credit Clause in the manner suggested by Dean Kramer. See Borchers, *Baker v. General Motors*: Implications for Inter-jurisdictional Recognition of Non-Traditional Marriages, 32 Creighton L.Rev. 147, 169–70 (1998) (arguing that Kramer's interpretation cannot be reconciled with more modern full-faith-and-credit and due-process cases).

2. First National Bank of Chicago v. United Air Lines, 342 U.S. 396, 72 S.Ct. 421 (1952), was an action in an Illinois federal court for wrongful death in an airplane crash in Utah. An Illinois statute (quoted in Justice Frankfurter's dissent in *Hughes*, at p. 413, supra) was similar to the Wisconsin statute but applied only when the defendant was subject to suit in the place where the death occurred. The Court held that the Illinois statute could not bar the action, and said: "Nor is it crucial here that Illinois only excludes cases that can be tried in other states. We hold again that the Full Faith and Credit Clause forbids such exclusion."

3. If *Hughes* were properly based on full faith and credit, might it lead to the conclusion that there are constitutional limits upon a state's power to refuse to entertain suit on a claim arising in a sister state on the ground of forum non conveniens? Or because the state considers the claim to be penal or contrary to its public policy? Does the Constitution limit the power of a state to refuse to entertain suit on a claim that arose in a sister state because the local courts are congested?

4. In Dick v. Rosner, 294 U.S. 629, 55 S.Ct. 589 (1935), the Court held that New Jersey violated full faith and credit by imposing unreasonable procedural restrictions upon the ability of the New York Superintendent of Banks to recover assessments against New Jersey shareholders of an insolvent New York bank.

5. Under the Supremacy Clause (Article VI), a state cannot decline to hear claims arising under federal law if it hears similar claims under state law. McKnett v. St. Louis & San Francisco Railway Co., 292 U.S. 230, 54 S.Ct. 690 (1934). Likewise, a state cannot refuse to entertain suit on a federal claim on the ground that it is penal (Testa v. Katt, 330 U.S. 386, 67 S.Ct. 810 (1947)), or that it is contrary to the state's public policy, Mondou v. New York, New Haven & Hartford Railroad Co., 223 U.S. 1, 32 S.Ct. 169 (1912).

6. We considered a court's power to refuse to hear cases on the basis of forum non conveniens in Chapter 4, section 3.

SECTION 2. CHOICE OF LAW

A. HISTORICAL APPROACH

Here we study a series of cases, some addressing due process and some addressing full faith and credit. It is helpful to think of these constitutional doctrines as performing two related, but slightly different, tasks. Due process limits the forum state's authority to apply its own law to a dispute, while full faith and credit limits the forum state's authority to ignore the law of another state. Note the sweep of these cases. The Court moves from its early view, in which the Full Faith and Credit Clause imposes a duty on the forum to apply the law of another state (because of that other state's interest), to a consideration of whether the forum state has sufficient contact with the dispute to justify applying its own law. As the Court moved away from balancing interests, it suggested that full faith and credit and due process standards might be merged, a result we will confirm in the next section.

Home Insurance Co. v. Dick

Supreme Court of the United States, 1930.
281 U.S. 397, 50 S.Ct. 338, 74 L.Ed. 926, 74 A.L.R. 701.

Appeal from the Supreme Court of Texas.

■ JUSTICE BRANDEIS delivered the opinion of the Court.

Dick, a citizen of Texas, brought this action in a court of that State against Compania General Anglo-Mexicana de Seguros S.A., a Mexican corporation, to recover on a policy of fire insurance for the total loss of a tug. Jurisdiction was asserted in rem through garnishment, by ancillary writs issued against the Home Insurance Company and Franklin Fire Insurance Company, which reinsured, by contracts with the Mexican corporation, parts of the risk which it had assumed. The garnishees are New York corporations. Upon them, service was effected by serving their local agents in Texas.

Their defense rests upon the following facts: This suit was not commenced till more than one year after the date of the loss. The policy provided: "It is understood and agreed that no judicial suit or demand shall be entered before any tribunal for the collection of any claim under this policy, unless such suits or demands are filed within one year counted as from the date on which such damage occurs." This provision was in accord with the Mexican law to which the policy was expressly made subject. It was issued by the Mexican company in Mexico to one Bonner, of Tampico, Mexico, and was there duly assigned to Dick prior to the loss. It covered the vessel only in certain Mexican waters. The premium was paid in Mexico; and the loss was "payable in the City of

Mexico in current funds of the United States of Mexico, or their equivalent elsewhere." At the time the policy was issued, when it was assigned to him, and until after the loss, Dick actually resided in Mexico, although his permanent residence was in Texas. The contracts of reinsurance were effected by correspondence between the Mexican company in Mexico and the New York companies in New York. Nothing thereunder was to be done, or was in fact done, in Texas.

. . . To this defense Dick demurred, on the ground that article 5545 of the Texas Revised Civil Statutes (1925) provides: "No person, firm, corporation, association or combination of whatsoever kind shall enter into any stipulation, contract, or agreement, by reason whereof the time in which to sue thereon is limited to a shorter period than two years. And no stipulation, contract, or agreement for any such shorter limitation in which to sue shall ever be valid in this State."

The trial court sustained Dick's contention and entered judgment against the garnishees. On appeal, both in the Court of Civil Appeals (8 S.W.2d 354) and in the Supreme Court of the state (15 S.W.2d 1028), the garnishees asserted that, as construed and applied, the Texas statute violated the due process clause of the Fourteenth Amendment and the contract clause. Both courts treated the policy provision as equivalent to a foreign statute of limitation; held that article 5545 related to the remedy available in Texas courts; concluded that it was validly applicable to the case at bar; and affirmed the judgment of the trial court. The garnishees appealed to this Court on the ground that the statute, as construed and applied, violated their rights under the Federal Constitution. Dick moved to dismiss the appeal for want of jurisdiction. Then the garnishees filed, also, a petition for a writ of certiorari. Consideration of the jurisdiction of this Court on the appeal, and of the petition for certiorari, was postponed to the hearing of the case on the merits.

First. Dick contends that this Court lacks jurisdiction of the action, because the errors assigned involve only questions of local law and of conflict of laws. The argument is that, while a provision requiring notice of loss within a fixed period is substantive because it is a condition precedent to the existence of the cause of action, the provision for liability only in case suit is brought within the year is not substantive because it relates only to the remedy after accrual of the cause of action; that, while the validity, interpretation, and performance of the substantive provisions of a contract are determined by the law of the place where it is made and is to be performed, matters which relate only to the remedy are unquestionably governed by the lex fori; and that, even if the Texas court erred in holding the statute applicable to this contract, the error is one of state law or of the interpretation of the contract, and is not reviewable here.

The contention is unsound. There is no dispute as to the meaning of the provision in the policy. It is that the insurer shall not be liable unless suit is brought within one year of the loss. . . . Nor are we concerned with the question whether the provision is properly described as relating to remedy or to substance. However characterized, it is an express term in the contract of the parties by which the right of the insured and the correlative obligation of the insurer are defined. If effect is given to the clause, Dick cannot recover from the Mexican corporation, and the garnishees cannot be compelled to pay. If, on the other hand, the statute is applied to the contract, it admittedly abrogates a contractual right and imposes liability, although the parties have agreed that there should be none.

The statute is not simply one of limitation. It does not merely fix the time in which the aid of the Texas courts may be invoked. Nor does it govern only the remedies available in the Texas courts. It deals with the powers and capacities of persons and corporations. It expressly prohibits the making of certain contracts. As construed, it also directs the disregard in Texas of contractual rights and obligations wherever created and assumed; and it commands the enforcement of obligations in excess of those contracted for. Therefore, the objection that, as applied to contracts made and to be performed outside of Texas, the statute violates the Federal Constitution, raises federal questions of substance; and the existence of the federal claim is not disproved by saying that the statute, or the one-year provision in the policy, relates to the remedy and not to the substance.

. . . The case is properly here on appeal. The motion to dismiss the appeal is overruled; and the petition for certiorari is therefore denied.

Second. The Texas statute as here construed and applied deprives the garnishees of property without due process of law. A state may, of course, prohibit and declare invalid the making of certain contracts within its borders. Ordinarily, it may prohibit performance within its borders, even of contracts validly made elsewhere, if they are required to be performed within the state and their performance would violate its laws. But, in the case at bar, nothing in any way relating to the policy sued on, or to the contracts of reinsurance, was ever done or required to be done in Texas. All acts relating to the making of the policy were done in Mexico. All in relation to the making of the contracts of reinsurance were done there or in New York. And, likewise, all things in regard to performance were to be done outside of Texas. Neither the Texas laws nor the Texas courts were invoked for any purpose, except by Dick in the bringing of this suit. The fact that Dick's permanent residence was in Texas is without significance. At all times here material he was physically present and acting in Mexico. Texas was therefore without power to affect the terms of contracts so made. Its attempt to impose a greater obligation than that agreed upon and to seize property in payment of the imposed obligation violates the guaranty against deprivation of property without due process of law. Compania General de Tabacos v. Collector of Internal Revenue, 275 U.S. 87; Aetna Life Ins. Co.

v. Dunken, 266 U.S. 389; New York Life Ins. Co. v. Dodge, 246 U.S. 357. Compare Modern Woodmen of America v. Mixer, 267 U.S. 544, 551.[5]

The cases relied upon, in which it was held that a state may lengthen its statute of limitations, are not in point. See Atchafalaya Land Co. v. Williams Cypress Co., 258 U.S. 190; National Surety Co. v. Architectural Decorating Co., 226 U.S. 276; Vance v. Vance, 108 U.S. 514. In those cases, the parties had not stipulated a time limit for the enforcement of their obligations. It is true that a state may extend the time within which suit may be brought in its own courts, if, in doing so, it violates no agreement of the parties. And, in the absence of a contractual provision, the local statute of limitation may be applied to a right created in another jurisdiction even where the remedy in the latter is barred.[7] In such cases, the rights and obligations of the parties are not varied. When, however, the parties have expressly agreed upon a time limit on their obligation, a statute which invalidates the agreement and directs enforcement of the contract after the time has expired increases their obligation and imposes a burden not contracted for.

Third. Dick urges that article 5545 of the Texas law is a declaration of its public policy; and that a state may properly refuse to recognize foreign rights which violate its declared policy. Doubtless, a state may prohibit the enjoyment by persons within its borders of rights acquired elsewhere which violate its laws or public policy; and under some circumstances, it may refuse to aid in the enforcement of such rights. Bothwell v. Buckbee-Mears Co., 275 U.S. 274, 277, 279; Union Trust Co. v. Grosman, 245 U.S. 412; compare Fauntleroy v. Lum, 210 U.S. 230. But the Mexican corporation never was in Texas; and neither it nor the garnishees invoked the aid of the Texas courts or the Texas laws. The Mexican corporation was not before the court. The garnishees were brought in by compulsory process. Neither has asked favors. They ask only to be let alone. We need not consider how far the state may go in imposing restrictions on the conduct of its own residents, and of foreign corporations which have received permission to do business within its borders; or how far it may go in refusing to lend the aid of its courts to the enforcement of rights acquired outside its borders. It may not abrogate the rights of parties beyond its borders having no relation to anything done or to be done within them.

---

[5] The division of this court in the Tabacos and Dodge Cases was not on the principle here stated, but on the question of fact whether there were in those cases things done within the state of which the state could properly lay hold as the basis of the regulations there imposed. Compare Bothwell v. Buckbee-Mears Co., 275 U.S. 274; Palmetto Fire Ins. Co. v. Conn, 272 U.S. 295. In the absence of any such things, as in this case, the Court was agreed that a state is without power to impose either public or private obligations on contracts made outside of the state and not to be performed there. Compare Mutual Life Insurance Co. of New York v. Liebing, 259 U.S. 209; E. Merrick Dodd, Jr., The Power of the Supreme Court to Review State Decisions in the Field of Conflict of Laws, 39 Harv.L.Rev. (1926) 533, 548.

[7] Whether a distinction is to be drawn between statutes of limitation which extinguish or limit the right and those which merely bar the remedy, we need not now determine. Compare Davis v. Mills, 194 U.S. 451, and Texas Portland Cement Co. v. McCord, 233 U.S. 157, with Canadian Pac. Ry. Co. v. Johnston, 61 F. 738.

Fourth. Finally, it is urged that the Federal Constitution does not require the states to recognize and protect rights derived from the laws of foreign countries—that as to them the full faith and credit clause has no application. See Aetna Life Ins. Co. v. Tremblay, 223 U.S. 185. The claims here asserted are not based upon the full faith and credit clause. Compare Royal Arcanum v. Green, 237 U.S. 531; Modern Woodmen of America v. Mixer, 267 U.S. 544. They rest upon the Fourteenth Amendment. Its protection extends to aliens. Moreover, the parties in interest here are American companies. The defense asserted is based on the provision of the policy and on their contracts of reinsurance. The courts of the state confused this defense with that based on the Mexican Code. They held that, even if the effect of the foreign statute was to extinguish the right, Dick's removal to Texas prior to the bar of the foreign statute removed the cause of action from Mexico, and subjected it to the Texas statute of limitation. And they applied the same rule to the provision in the policy. Whether or not that is a sufficient answer to the defense based on the foreign law we may not consider; for no issue under the full faith and credit clause was raised. But in Texas, as elsewhere, the contract was subject to its own limitations.

Fifth. . . . Since we hold that the Texas statute, as construed and applied, violates the due process clause, we have no occasion to consider [the contract clause] contention. . . .

Reversed.

_____

NOTES

1. The *Dick* case is a landmark. It establishes that at some point due process prevents a state from making arbitrary choice of law decisions. What is that point? That question requires identifying the critical factors in the *Dick* decision. Which factor or combination of factors was critical?

The nearly total absence of connections to Texas?

The stipulation in the parties' contract limiting the time within which suit had to be brought?

The fact that the Texas statute purported to prohibit the parties from making agreements shortening the time-to-sue period to less than two years?

2. The Court in *Dick* appears to conclude that neither the contract nor a party had any appreciable connection to Texas. In fact, however, though the policy was issued to Bonner of Mexico, the loss was payable to a firm in Texas and to Dick, as their interests might appear. Moreover, several years before the boat burned, the policy was assigned to Dick with the defendant's written consent. See R. Weintraub, Commentary on the Conflict of Laws 632–33 (5th ed.2006). And a comprehensive review of the historical evidence showed that Dick was a bona fide Texan, and that his stay in Mexico (which the Court described as being Dick's "residence" at the time of the underlying events)

was only about six weeks. See Rensberger, Who was Dick? Constitutional Limitations on State Choice of Law, 1998 Utah L.Rev. 37. The Court continued the mythology of the case in a later opinion, Allstate Ins. Co. v. Hague, a principal case at p. 432, infra. There, the Court described Dick as having only a "nominal residence" in Texas, when in fact he had a genuine domicile there.

If the Court had taken account of these "true" facts, could Texas have applied its statute to permit the case to proceed? Professor Rensberger argues that the answer to this question is "yes."

3. Consider Justice Brandeis's statement in *Dick* that in the absence of a contrary agreement by the parties, a state may extend the time within which suit may be brought in its own courts even when the right is created in another jurisdiction. Does this statement imply that:

(a) A state may never extend the time when the parties have made an agreement for a shorter time?

(b) A state may virtually always extend the time to sue in tort cases, where there are seldom agreements as to time-to-sue limits?

(c) A state may always extend the time to sue in contract cases if the only time limits applicable are those supplied by the law of another state rather than the agreement of the parties? Cf. Clay v. Sun Insurance Office, Limited, 377 U.S. 179, 84 S.Ct. 1197 (1964), at p. 430, infra.

JOHN HANCOCK MUTUAL LIFE INSURANCE CO. V. YATES, 299 U.S. 178 (1936). Suit upon a life insurance policy that had been applied for and issued in New York. The insured was a New York domiciliary who was being treated for cancer at the time. In his insurance application, the insured stated that he had not recently been under medical care. Under the law of New York this false statement constituted a material misrepresentation that voided the policy. Following the insured's death, his widow moved to Georgia and there brought suit on the policy. She recovered judgment by application of the Georgia rule that a false statement in an insurance policy is not material if the agent who solicited the policy was aware of the facts. The jury found that the insurance agent knew the insured was suffering from cancer. Thus, the Georgia courts held, forum law was to determine, as a question of procedure, whether the materiality of a misrepresentation was a question of fact for the jury. The Supreme Court reversed. It held that the Georgia courts had denied full faith and credit to the laws of New York. The Court emphasized that "there was no occurrence, nothing done, to which the law of Georgia could apply." Note the similarity to *Dick,* in that the forum could not apply its law because the dispute lacked relevant contacts with Georgia. The Court also said:

. . . Because the statute is a 'public act,' faith and credit must be given to its provisions as fully as if the materiality of this specific misrepresentation in the application, and the consequent non-existence of liability, had been declared by a judgment of a New York court. . . .

———————

ORDER OF UNITED COMMERCIAL TRAVELERS V. WOLFE, 331 U.S. 586 (1947). An Ohio citizen sued a fraternal benefit society in state court in South Dakota to recover benefits owed by the society as a result of the death of an insured member. The member was a citizen of South Dakota at his death. The society was formed in Ohio. The constitution of the society required that suit be brought no later than six months after the society had denied a claim. The six-month limit was valid under Ohio law but not under the law of South Dakota. A five-to-four majority held that South Dakota was required to give full faith and credit to the six-month limit. According to the Court:

> These public acts [of Ohio, permitting the formation of benefits societies] have created and regulated the society and the rights and obligations of its members. They are reflected in its articles of incorporation, constitution and by-laws. They make possible uniformity of rights and obligations among all members throughout the country, provided full faith and credit are given also to the constitution and by-laws of the society insofar as they are valid under the law of the state of incorporation. If full faith and credit are not given to these provisions, the mutual rights and obligations of the members of such societies are left subject to the control of each state. They become unpredictable and almost inevitably unequal.

NOTES

1. *Wolfe* is a rare example of when the Full Faith and Credit Clause forbids application of the forum's rule over that of a sister state's. Compare Clay v. Sun Ins. Office, Ltd., p. 430, infra.

2. The majority in *Wolfe* emphasized the unique relationship between a fraternal benefit society and its members. "The fact of membership . . . is the controlling and central feature of the relationship." This differs from the contractual relationship between a policyholder and an ordinary insurance company; the policyholder is not a member or owner of the ordinary insurance company. A fraternal benefit society and its members form an undivided entity, to be governed by the law of the state in which it is formed.

3. In *Dick*, the Court relied upon due process (not full faith and credit) to forbid the application of Texas law to a contract of insurance. Some have argued that due process should be construed to impose limits only upon personal jurisdiction, while interstate federalism concerns should be addressed under the Full Faith and Credit Clause. Hay, Full Faith and Credit and Federalism in Choice of Law, 34 Mercer L.Rev. 709 (1983) (arguing that the Due Process Clause should be construed to impose limits on judicial jurisdiction only, while interstate (federalism) concerns should be addressed through resort to the Full Faith and Credit Clause). Professor James A. Martin argued that the policies of the Full Faith and Credit Clause should be the sole measures of the constitutional limits on choice of law. See Martin, Constitutional Limitations on Choice of Law, 61 Corn.L.Rev. 185 (1976). If the forum does not violate due process in applying its decisional norm to a multistate case is the full-faith-and-credit requirement automatically satisfied?

ALASKA PACKERS ASSOCIATION V. INDUSTRIAL ACCIDENT COMMISSION OF CALIFORNIA, 294 U.S. 532, 55 S.Ct. 518 (1935). A non-resident alien executed in California a written contract of employment under which he agreed to work for his employer in Alaska during the salmon canning season. The employer agreed to transport him to and from Alaska and to pay him his stipulated wages in California on his return. The contract recited that the employee had elected to be bound by the Alaska Workmen's Compensation Law. The employee was injured in Alaska and, on his return to California, sought an award under that state's compensation act; he won an award. The employer attacked the award, and argued that the application of California law violated due process and full faith and credit. The Court upheld the California award and continued to weigh the relative interests of the states:

> The probability is slight that injured workmen, once returned to California, would be able to retrace their steps to Alaska, and there successfully prosecute their claims for compensation. Without a remedy in California, they would be remediless, and there was the danger that they might become public charges, both matters of grave public concern to the state.

> . . . California, therefore, had a legitimate public interest in controlling and regulating this employer-employee relationship. . . .

> . . . [T]he conflict is to be resolved, not by giving automatic effect to the full faith and credit clause, compelling the courts of each state to subordinate its own statutes to those of the other, but by appraising the governmental interests of each jurisdiction, and turning the scale of decision according to their weight.

> . . . [O]nly if it appears that, in the conflict of interests which have found expression in the conflicting statutes, the interest of Alaska is superior to that of California, is there rational basis for denying to the courts of California the right to apply the laws of their own state.

NOTE

In *Alaska Packers*, the Court picked up on a passage from Bradford Electric v. Clapper, 286 U.S. 145, 52 S. Ct. 571, 76 L.Ed. 1026 (1932). In that case, a Vermont citizen, employed by a Vermont company, was killed while on the job in New Hampshire. The law of Vermont, the place of the employment contract, provided that worker's compensation was the exclusive remedy. New Hampshire, in contrast, permitted an action for wrongful death. The employee's representative sued for wrongful death in New Hampshire. New Hampshire was required to apply Vermont law because that was the state of the employment relationship. In passing, the Court noted that nothing in New Hampshire law indicated that Vermont law governed New Hampshire policy. This comment gave rise to the notion, addressed in *Alaska Packers* and applied in the next case, that a forum need not apply the law of a sister state if that law is "obnoxious" to the policy of the forum-state law.

PACIFIC EMPLOYERS INS. CO. V. INDUSTRIAL ACCIDENT COMMISSION, 306 U.S. 493 (1939). A resident of Massachusetts, while working for a Massachusetts company in California, was injured on the job. He filed a proceeding in the California commission, seeking compensation under the California workmen's compensation scheme. He won an award, despite the fact that the Massachusetts law provided that employees waive the right to seek compensation under the law of another jurisdiction unless they give written notice to their employer. The worker in this case gave no such notice and, under the Massachusetts law, would have been limited to a lesser recovery than that allowed in California. The insurance company that assumed the employer's liability challenged the application of California law as violating the Full Faith and Credit Clause. The Court explained:

> While in the circumstances now presented, either state, if its system for administering workmen's compensation permitted, would be free to adopt and enforce the remedy provided by the statute of the other, here each has provided for itself an exclusive remedy for a liability which it was constitutionally authorized to impose. But neither is bound, apart from the compulsion of the full faith and credit clause, to enforce the laws of the other. . . .

> To the extent that California is required to give full faith and credit to the conflicting Massachusetts statute it must be denied the right to apply in its own courts its own statute, constitutionally enacted in pursuance of its policy to provide compensation for employees injured in their employment within the state. . . . We cannot say that the full faith and credit clause goes so far.

While the purpose of that provision was to preserve rights acquired or confirmed under the public acts and judicial proceedings of one state by requiring recognition of their validity in other states, the very nature of the federal union of states, to which are reserved some of the attributes of sovereignty, precludes resort to the full faith and credit clause as the means for compelling a state to substitute the statutes of other states for its own statutes dealing with a subject matter concerning which it is competent to legislate. . . .

This Court must determine for itself how far the full faith and credit clause compels the qualification or denial of rights asserted under the laws of one state, that of the forum, by the statute of another state. . . . But there would seem to be little room for the exercise of that function when the statute of the forum is the expression of domestic policy, in terms declared to be exclusive in its application to persons and events within the state. Although Massachusetts has an interest in safeguarding the compensation of Massachusetts employees while temporarily abroad in the course of their employment, and may adopt that policy for itself, that could hardly be thought to support an application of the full faith and credit clause which would override the constitutional authority of another state to legislate for the bodily safety and economic protection of employees injured within it. Few matters could be deemed more appropriately the concern of the state in which the injury occurs or more completely within its power. . . .

Here, California legislation . . . expressly provides, . . . that "No contract, rule or regulation shall exempt the employer from liability for the compensation fixed by this Act." The Supreme Court of California has declared in its opinion in this case that . . . "It would be obnoxious to [the policy of the California Act] to deny persons who have been injured in this state the right to apply for compensation when to do so might require physicians and hospitals to go to another state to collect charges for medical care and treatment given to such persons."

Full faith and credit does not here enable one state to legislate for the other or to project its laws across state lines so as to preclude the other from prescribing for itself the legal consequences of acts within it.

NOTE

In *Pacific Employers*, the Court seems to shift away from the interest-appraising and weighing approach to the view, hinted at in passing in *Bradford Electric v. Clapper*, that full faith and credit does not require the forum to apply another state's laws that are "obnoxious" to the forum law's policy. Because the forum court presumably will not often balk at applying sister-state law that is congenial to its own, does this approach in effect read full faith and credit out of the picture? Notice what happens to the interest-weighing and "obnoxious" tests in later Supreme Court decisions, such as the following case.

CARROLL V. LANZA, 349 U.S. 408, 75 S.Ct. 804, 99 L.Ed. 1183 (1955). This is another workers' compensation case. Here, the employer and employee were citizens of Missouri, which is where the contract of employment was entered. The work, however, was done in Arkansas, and the employer was a subcontractor on the project. The employee was injured in Arkansas. Unaware of workers' compensation remedies under Arkansas law, the employee made a successful claim under the Missouri compensation law. The worker then filed a common law claim against the general contractor of the project (not his employer) in Missouri. Arkansas, the site of the injury, permitted such common law claim despite the receipt of workers' compensation benefits. Missouri, the place of employment, did not. The Court upheld the application of Arkansas law, but did so without addressing whether the Missouri law was "obnoxious" to Arkansas policy and without weighing the relative interests of the states. Instead, it appears to permit the forum to apply its law if it has sufficient contacts to the case. The Court explained:

> The Pacific Employers Insurance Co. case teaches that in these personal injury cases the State where the injury occurs need not be a vassal to the home State and allow only that remedy which the home State has marked as the exclusive one. . . . Her interests are large and considerable and are to be weighed not only in the light of the facts of this case but by the kind of situation presented. . . . The State where the tort occurs certainly has a concern in the problems following in the wake of the injury. The problems of medical care and of possible dependents are among these . . . Arkansas therefore has a legitimate interest in opening her courts to suits of this nature, even though in this case Carroll's injury may have cast no burden on her or on her institutions.

> . . . Arkansas, the State of the forum, is not adopting any policy of hostility to the public Acts of Missouri. It is choosing to apply its own rule of law to give affirmative relief for an action arising within its borders.

> . . . Were it otherwise, the State where the injury occurred would be powerless to provide any remedies or safeguards to nonresident employees working within its borders. We do not think the Full Faith and Credit Clause demands that subserviency from the State of the injury.

NOTES

1. Dissenting in *Carroll*, Justice Frankfurter gave a lengthy exegesis of the cases in which the Court had interpreted the Full Faith and Credit Clause in choice of law matters. He concluded that the cases fell into three groups:

- Those in which the forum is required to give effect to a sister-state statute.

- Those in which the forum applied its own statute rather than that of a sister state because the sister-state's law was not exclusive.

- Those in which the forum applied its own law, statutory or judicial, when clearly in conflict with the sister-state law.

He focused on 21 cases in the latter group. In 10 of these, the Court had permitted application of forum law; in the other 11, the Court held that the sister-state law applied.

The 21 cases arose in three fields: (a) commercial law, (b) insurance, and (c) workers' compensation.

In commercial cases, Justice Frankfurter concluded, the Court consistently required forum states to give effect to the law of the state of incorporation in cases involving assessments against out-of-state shareholders.

In cases involving ordinary insurance companies (as opposed to fraternal benefit societies), Frankfurter found that the Court balanced the interests of the competing jurisdictions and considered such factors as the residence of the insured, where premiums were paid or payable, where the policy was applied for and delivered, and where the insured died. He concluded that "the forum has been permitted to protect its residents against insurance companies, but the Court has required the forum to have more than a casual interest. . . ."

Finally, as to workers' compensation cases, Frankfurter argued that the Court had adopted an interests-weighing approach. He found the facts of *Carroll* unique, in that "the interest of the forum here is solely dependent on the occurrence of the injury within its borders. No rights of Arkansas residents are involved, since none of the parties is an Arkansan; the workman was removed immediately to a Missouri hospital and has, so far as appears, remained in Missouri. What might be regarded as the societal interest of Arkansas in the protection of the bodily safety of workers within its borders is an interest equally true of any jurisdiction where a workman is injured." Because *Bradford Electric v. Clapper*, discussed in the Note at p. 1081, required application of the law of the state of the employment relationship—and not the law of the state of injury—Frankfurter wondered whether the Court had not *de facto* overruled that case.

2. Did you find Frankfurter's exegesis of the case law as of 1955 persuasive?

3. In Posnak, Choice of Law: A Very Well-Curried Leflar Approach, 34 Mercer L.Rev. 731 (1983), the author argues that *Carroll v. Lanza may* go over the edge constitutionally because it seems to allow a state with no actual interest in the aftermath of an injury (or any other element of the transaction) to apply its own rule in derogation of the contrary law of a state with strong interests in the case. See also Kramer, Rethinking Choice of Law, 90 Colum.L.Rev. 277 (1990).

In Dillon v. Frazer, 383 S.C. 59, 678 S.E.2d 251 (2009), two residents of Ontario were working in South Carolina for their Ontario employer. One was injured by the other's negligence, and sued other to recover damages. The workers were covered by Ontario workers' compensation law, which (as is common) provides that it is the exclusive remedy for injuries arising in the course of employment. The jury returned a verdict awarding damages to the plaintiff. The defendant asserted that he could not be sued because of the Ontario workers' compensation law.

The South Carolina Supreme Court concluded that the defense based on the law of Ontario was barred by failure to plead that law timely. The court added that even if the defendant had raised the issue properly, South Carolina law governed, as the place of the wrong. Id. at 65, 678 S.E2d at 254. The court remanded the case for a new trial on damages because the jury verdict and the trial judge's additur were too low. The defendant did plead the South Carolina worker's compensation law. The opinion does not discuss why the South Carolina law did not bar tort recovery. (The South Carolina workers' compensation law bars recovery against other employees. Fuller v. Blanchard, 595 S.E.2d 831 (S.C.App.2004).)

CLAY V. SUN INSURANCE OFFICE, LIMITED, 377 U.S. 179, 84 S.Ct. 1197, 12 L.Ed. 2d 229 (1964). Insured, then a citizen of Illinois, purchased an insurance policy to cover his boat. The insurance company was a British firm licensed to do business in several states, including Illinois and Florida. The policy provided "world-wide" coverage for the boat and provided that suit must be brought within twelve months of a loss. Shortly after obtaining the policy, the insured moved to Florida and became a citizen of that state. The loss to the boat was suffered in Florida. Insured brought suit there more than twelve months after the loss. Florida law, however, provided a five-year limitations period on such claims and purported to override a contractual stipulation to the contrary. The Court upheld the application of Florida law:

> While there are Illinois cases indicating that parties may contract—as here—for a shorter period of limitations than is provided by the Illinois statute, we are referred to no Illinois decision extending that rule into other States whenever claims on Illinois contracts are sought to be enforced there. We see no difficulty whatever under either the Full Faith and Credit Clause or the Due Process Clause. We deal with an ambulatory contract on which suit might be brought in any one of several States. Normally, as the Court held in Pacific Employers Ins. Co. v. Industrial Accident Comm'n, [p. 426, supra], a State

having jurisdiction over a claim deriving from an out-of-state employment contract need not substitute the conflicting statute of the other State (workmen's compensation) for its own statute (workmen's compensation)—where the employee was injured in the course of his employment while temporarily in the latter State. . . .

NOTES

1.　Though the policy was purchased in Illinois by a person who at that time had no contacts with Florida, he later moved to Florida, became a citizen of that state, and kept the boat there. The policy provided for "world-wide" coverage. Was it foreseeable that loss of the boat could be suffered in Florida? Is such foreseeability relevant to choice of law? To personal jurisdiction?

2.　Can the *Clay* decision be satisfactorily distinguished from John Hancock Mutual Life Insurance Co. v. Yates, p. 423, supra? Would the decision have been different in *Yates* if, following the issuance of the policy, the insured had moved to Georgia and had died while domiciled there? Can you articulate why some observers feel that *Yates* might no longer be good law, while *Dick,* p. 418, supra, certainly remains vital?

3.　What if the insured risk is immovable? In Burger King Corp. v. Continental Insurance Co., 359 F.Supp. 184 (W.D.Pa.1973), suit was brought in Florida on a casualty policy for property loss and loss of income as a result of damage to a fast-food restaurant because of earth movement. The insured was a Florida corporation, while the defendant was a New York corporation which wrote the insurance policy in New York on property owned by plaintiff in Pennsylvania. The policy provided that no action could be brought on it more than 12 months after the loss. This suit was commenced in Florida approximately 18 months after the loss and transferred to the Pennsylvania federal court. In denying defendant's motion for summary judgment the court applied the Florida statute that declared contractual provisions "illegal and void" as contrary to Florida's public policy if they fixed the period for suit at less than the state's five-year statute of limitations.

　　　The court noted that the constitutionality of the Florida rule had been upheld by the Supreme Court in the *Clay* case. It stressed that in contrast to Quarty v. Insurance Company of North America, 244 So.2d 181 (Fla.App.1971), denying applicability of the Florida rule to a suit for loss by burglary in New York on a policy issued in New York by a New York insurer to a New York resident who became a Florida resident within the 12-month policy claim period but did not sue until later, Burger King was a Florida corporation, with its principal place of business in Florida and at the time of the transaction defendant had a licensed agent in Florida. If the instant decision had been reviewed on appeal, should it have been reversed?

B. MODERN APPROACH

Allstate Insurance Co. v. Hague

Supreme Court of the United States, 1981.
449 U.S. 302, 101 S.Ct. 633, 66 L.Ed.2d 521.

■ JUSTICE BRENNAN announced the judgment of the Court and an opinion in which JUSTICE WHITE, JUSTICE MARSHALL, and JUSTICE BLACKMUN join.

This Court granted certiorari to determine whether the Due Process Clause of the Fourteenth Amendment or the Full Faith and Credit Clause of Art. 4, § 1, of the United States Constitution bars the Minnesota Supreme Court's choice of substantive Minnesota law to govern the effect of a provision in an insurance policy issued to respondent's decedent. . . .

I

Respondent's late husband, Ralph Hague, died of injuries suffered when a motorcycle on which he was a passenger was struck from behind by an automobile. The accident occurred in Pierce County, Wis., which is immediately across the Minnesota border from Red Wing, Minn. The operators of both vehicles were Wisconsin residents, as was the decedent who, at the time of the accident, resided with respondent in Hager City, Wis., which is one and one-half miles from Red Wing. Mr. Hague had been employed in Red Wing for the 15 years immediately preceding his death and had commuted daily from Wisconsin to his place of employment.

Neither the operator of the motorcycle nor the operator of the automobile carried valid insurance. However, the decedent held a policy issued by petitioner Allstate Insurance Company covering three automobiles owned by him and containing an uninsured motorist clause insuring him against loss incurred from accidents with uninsured motorists. The uninsured motorist coverage was limited to $15,000 for each automobile.[3]

After the accident, but prior to the initiation of this lawsuit, respondent moved to Red Wing. Subsequently, she married a Minnesota resident and established residence with her new husband in Savage, Minn. At approximately the same time, a Minnesota Registrar of Probate appointed respondent personal representative of her deceased husband's estate. Following her appointment, she brought this action in Minnesota District Court seeking a declaration under Minnesota law that the $15,000 uninsured motorist coverage on each of her late husband's three automobiles could be "stacked" to provide total coverage of $45,000. Petitioner defended on the ground that whether the three uninsured

---

[3] Ralph Hague paid a separate premium for each automobile including an additional separate premium for each uninsured motorist coverage.

motorist coverages could be stacked should be determined by Wisconsin law, since the insurance policy was delivered in Wisconsin, the accident occurred in Wisconsin, and all persons involved were Wisconsin residents at the time of the accident.

The Minnesota Supreme Court, sitting en banc, affirmed the District Court [and], . . . interpreting Wisconsin law to prohibit stacking,[2] applied Minnesota law after analyzing the relevant Minnesota contacts and interests within the analytical framework developed by Professor Leflar. See Leflar, Choice-Influencing Considerations in Conflicts Law, 41 N.Y.U.L. Rev. 267 (1966). [Professor Leflar's analytical approach, discussed at p. 572, infra, focuses on five considerations as the key factors in choice of law. The Minnesota Supreme Court determined that the fifth consideration—"applying the better rule of law"—called for use of Minnesota's stacking law. The court stressed that most states allow stacking, recent court decisions favor it, and the practice works well by spreading accident costs more broadly. Since insurance companies know that automobiles move freely across state lines, applying the Minnesota rule would not offend due process as too arbitrary or unreasonable.]

II

It is not for this Court to say whether the choice-of-law analysis suggested by Professor Leflar is to be preferred or whether we would make the same choice-of-law decision if sitting as the Minnesota Supreme Court. Our sole function is to determine whether the Minnesota Supreme Court's choice of its own substantive law in this case exceeded federal constitutional limitations. Implicit in this inquiry is the recognition, long accepted by this Court, that a set of facts giving rise to a lawsuit, or a particular issue within a lawsuit, may justify, in constitutional terms, application of the law of more than one jurisdiction. . . . As a result, the forum State may have to select one law from among the laws of several jurisdictions having some contact with the controversy.

In deciding constitutional choice-of-law questions, whether under the Due Process Clause or the Full Faith and Credit Clause,[10] this Court

---

[2] It seems likely that the Minnesota court misunderstood Wisconsin law on this point. While Minnesota and Wisconsin differed on whether they would enforce a clear anti-stacking clause in a policy, even under Wisconsin law the insurance contracts written to the Hagues almost certainly would not have been interpreted to forbid stacking. This point is discussed extensively in Weintraub, Who's Afraid of Constitutional Limitations on Choice of Law?, 10 Hofstra L.Rev. 17 (1981). —eds.

[10] This Court has taken a similar approach in deciding choice-of-law cases under both the Due Process Clause and the Full Faith and Credit Clause. In each instance, the Court has examined the relevant contacts and resulting interests of the State whose law was applied. See, e.g., Nevada v. Hall, 440 U.S. 410, 424 (1979). Although at one time the Court required a more exacting standard under the Full Faith and Credit Clause than under the Due Process Clause for evaluating the constitutionality of choice-of-law decisions, see Alaska Packers Assn. v. Industrial Accident Comm'n, 294 U.S. 532, 549–550 (1935) (interest of State whose law was applied was no less than interest of State whose law was rejected), the Court has since abandoned the weighing of interests requirement. Carroll v. Lanza, 349 U.S. 408 (1955); see

has traditionally examined the contacts of the State, whose law was applied, with the parties and with the occurrence or transaction giving rise to the litigation. . . . In order to ensure that the choice of law is neither arbitrary nor fundamentally unfair, . . . the Court has invalidated the choice of law of a State which has had no significant contact or significant aggregation of contacts, creating state interests, with the parties and the occurrence or transaction.[11]

Two instructive examples of such invalidation are Home Insurance Company v. Dick [p. 418, supra] and John Hancock Mutual Life Insurance Co. v. Yates [p. 423, supra]. In both cases, the selection of forum law rested exclusively on the presence of one nonsignificant forum contact.

. . . [Justice Brennan here reviewed the *Dick* and *Yates* decisions.]

Dick and Yates stand for the proposition that if a State has only an insignificant contact with the parties and the occurrence or transaction, application of its law is unconstitutional. Dick concluded that nominal residence—standing alone—was inadequate; Yates held that a postoccurrence change of residence to the forum State—standing alone—was insufficient to justify application of forum law. Although instructive as extreme examples of selection of forum law, neither Dick nor Yates governs this case. For in contrast to those decisions, here the Minnesota contacts with the parties and the occurrence are obviously significant. Thus, this case is like Alaska Packers, [p. 425, supra] Cardillo v. Liberty Mutual Insurance Co., 330 U.S. 469 (1947), and *Clay II* [p. 430, supra]— cases where this Court sustained choice-of-law decisions based on the contacts of the State, whose law was applied, with the parties and occurrence.

In Alaska Packers, the Court . . . held that the choice of California law was not "so arbitrary or unreasonable as to amount to a denial of due process," 294 U.S., at 542, because "without a remedy in California, [he] would be remediless," ibid., and because of California's interest that the worker not become a public charge, ibid.[15] . . .

Nevada v. Hall, supra; Weintraub, Due Process and Full Faith and Credit Limitations on a State's Choice of Law, 44 Iowa L. Rev. 449 (1959). Different considerations are of course at issue when full faith and credit is to be accorded to acts, records and proceedings outside the choice-of-law area, such as in the case of sister state court judgments.

[11] Prior to the advent of interest analysis in the state courts as the "dominant mode of analysis in modern choice of law theory," Silberman, Shaffer v. Heitner: The End of an Era, 53 N.Y.U.L. Rev. 33, 80, n. 259 (1978) . . . , the prevailing choice of law methodology focused on the jurisdiction where a particular event occurred. See, e.g., Restatement of the Law, Conflict of Laws (1934) (hereinafter cited as "Restatement First"). . . .

[15] The Court found no violation of the Full Faith and Credit Clause, since California's interest was considered to be no less than Alaska's, Alaska Packers Assn. v. Industrial Accident Comm'n, supra, 294 U.S. at 547–548, 549–550, even though the injury occurred in Alaska while the employee was performing his contract obligations there. While Alaska Packers balanced the interests of California and Alaska to determine the full faith and credit issue, such balancing is no longer required.

The lesson from Dick and Yates, which found insufficient forum contacts to apply forum law, and from Alaska Packers, Cardillo, and Clay II, which found adequate contacts to sustain the choice of forum law, is that for a State's substantive law to be selected in a constitutionally permissible manner, that State must have a significant contact or significant aggregation of contacts, creating state interests, such that choice of its law is neither arbitrary nor fundamentally unfair. Application of this principle to the facts of this case persuades us that the Minnesota Supreme Court's choice of its own law did not offend the Federal Constitution.

III

Minnesota has three contacts with the parties and the occurrence giving rise to the litigation. In the aggregate, these contacts permit selection by the Minnesota Supreme Court of Minnesota law allowing the stacking of Mr. Hague's uninsured motorist coverages.

First, and for our purposes a very important contact, Mr. Hague was a member of Minnesota's workforce, having been employed by a Red Wing, Minn., enterprise for the 15 years preceding his death. While employment status may implicate a state interest less substantial than does resident status, that interest is nevertheless important. The State of employment has police power responsibilities towards the nonresident employee that are analogous, if somewhat less profound, than towards residents. Thus, such employees use state services and amenities and may call upon state facilities in appropriate circumstances.

In addition, Mr. Hague commuted to work in Minnesota . . . and was presumably covered by his uninsured motorist coverage during the commute. The State's interest in its commuting nonresident employees reflects a state concern for the safety and well-being of its workforce and the concomitant effect on Minnesota employers.

That Mr. Hague was not killed while commuting to work or while in Minnesota does not dictate a different result. To hold that the Minnesota Supreme Court's choice of Minnesota law violated the Constitution for that reason would require too narrow a view of Minnesota's relationship with the parties and the occurrence giving rise to the litigation. An automobile accident need not occur within a particular jurisdiction for that jurisdiction to be connected to the occurrence. Similarly, the occurrence of a crash fatal to a Minnesota employee in another State is a Minnesota contact. If Mr. Hague had only been injured and missed work for a few weeks the effect on the Minnesota employer would have been palpable and Minnesota's interest in having its employee made whole would be evident. Mr. Hague's death affects Minnesota's interest still more acutely, even though Mr. Hague will not return to the Minnesota workforce. Minnesota's workforce is surely affected by the level of protection the State extends to it, either directly or indirectly. Vindication of the rights of the estate of a Minnesota employee, therefore, is an important state concern.

Mr. Hague's residence in Wisconsin does not—as Allstate seems to argue—constitutionally mandate application of Wisconsin law to the exclusion of forum law. If, in the instant case, the accident had occurred in Minnesota between Mr. Hague and an uninsured Minnesota motorist, if the insurance contract had been executed in Minnesota covering a Minnesota registered company automobile which Mr. Hague was permitted to drive, and if a Wisconsin court sought to apply Wisconsin law, certainly Mr. Hague's residence in Wisconsin, his commute between Wisconsin and Minnesota, and the insurer's presence in Wisconsin should be adequate to apply Wisconsin's law.[22] . . . Employment status is not a sufficiently less important status than residence . . . when combined with Mr. Hague's daily commute across state lines and the other Minnesota contacts present, to prohibit the choice-of-law result in this case on constitutional grounds.

Second, Allstate was at all times present and doing business in Minnesota.[23] By virtue of its presence, Allstate can hardly claim unfamiliarity with the laws of the host jurisdiction and surprise that the state courts might apply forum law to litigation in which the company is involved. "Particularly since the company was licensed to do business in [the forum], it must have known it might be sued there, and that [the forum], courts would feel bound by [forum] law."[24] Clay v. Sun Insurance Office Limited, 363 U.S. 207, 221 (1960) (Black, J., dissenting). Moreover, Allstate's presence in Minnesota gave Minnesota an interest in regulating the company's insurance obligations insofar as they affected both a Minnesota resident and court appointed representative—respondent—and a longstanding member of Minnesota's workforce—Mr. Hague. . . .

Third, respondent became a Minnesota resident prior to institution of this litigation. The stipulated facts reveal that she first settled in Red Wing, Minn., the town in which her late husband had worked. She subsequently moved to Savage, Minn., after marrying a Minnesota

---

[22] Of course, Allstate could not be certain that Wisconsin law would necessarily govern any accident which occurred in Wisconsin, whether brought in the Wisconsin courts or elsewhere. Such an expectation would give controlling significance to the wooden lex loci delicti doctrine. While the place of the accident is a factor to be considered in choice-of-law analysis, to apply blindly the traditional, but now largely abandoned, doctrine, Silberman, supra, 53 N.Y.U.L. Rev., at 80, n. 259; see n.11, supra, would fail to distinguish between the relative importance of various legal issues involved in a lawsuit as well as the relationship of other jurisdictions to the parties and the occurrence or transaction. . . .

[23] The Court has recognized that examination of a State's contacts may result in divergent conclusions for jurisdiction and choice-of-law purposes. See Kulko v. Superior Court, 436 U.S. 84, 98 (1978); Shaffer v. Heitner, supra, 433 U.S., at 215; cf. Hanson v. Denckla, 357 U.S. 235, 254, and n. 27 (no jurisdiction in Florida; the "issue is personal jurisdiction, not choice of law," an issue which the Court found no need to decide). Nevertheless, "both inquiries 'are often closely related and to a substantial degree depend upon similar considerations.'" 433 U.S., at 224–225 (Brennan, J., concurring in part and dissenting in part). . . .

[24] There is no element of unfair surprise or frustration of legitimate expectations as a result of Minnesota's choice of its law. Because Allstate was doing business in Minnesota and was undoubtedly aware that Mr. Hague was a Minnesota employee, it had to have anticipated that Minnesota law might apply to an accident in which Mr. Hague was involved. . . .

resident who operated an automobile service station in Bloomington, Minn. Her move to Savage occurred "almost concurrently," 289 N.W.2d, at 45, with the initiation of the instant case. There is no suggestion that Mrs. Hague moved to Minnesota in anticipation of this litigation or for the purpose of finding a legal climate especially hospitable to her claim. The stipulated facts, sparse as they are, negate any such inference.

While John Hancock Mutual Life Insurance Company v. Yates, supra, held that a postoccurrence change of residence to the forum State was insufficient in and of itself to confer power on the forum State to choose its law, that case did not hold that such a change of residence was irrelevant. Here, of course, respondent's bona fide residence in Minnesota was not the sole contact Minnesota had with this litigation. And in connection with her residence in Minnesota, respondent was appointed personal representative of Mr. Hague's estate by the Registrar of Probate for the County of Goodhue, Minn. Respondent's residence and subsequent appointment in Minnesota as personal representative of her late husband's estate constitute a Minnesota contact which gives Minnesota an interest in respondent's recovery, an interest which the court below identified as full compensation for "resident accident victims" to keep them "off welfare rolls" and able "to meet financial obligations." 289 N.W.2d, at 49.

In sum, Minnesota had a significant aggregation[29] of contacts with the parties and the occurrence, creating state interests, such that application of its law was neither arbitrary nor fundamentally unfair. Accordingly, the choice of Minnesota law by the Minnesota Supreme Court did not violate the Due Process Clause or the Full Faith and Credit Clause.

Affirmed.

■ JUSTICE STEWART took no part in the consideration or decision of this case.

■ JUSTICE STEVENS, concurring in the judgment.

As I view this unusual case—in which neither precedent nor constitutional language provides sure guidance—two separate questions must be answered. First, does the Full Faith and Credit Clause require Minnesota, the forum State, to apply Wisconsin law? Second, does the Due Process Clause of the Fourteenth Amendment prevent Minnesota from applying its own law? The first inquiry implicates the federal interest in ensuring that Minnesota respect the sovereignty of the State of Wisconsin; the second implicates the litigants' interests in a fair adjudication of their rights.

---

[29] We express no view whether the first two contacts, either together or separately, would have sufficed to sustain the choice of Minnesota law made by the Minnesota Supreme Court.

I realize that both this Court's analysis of choice-of-law questions[4] and scholarly criticism of those decisions have treated these two inquiries as though they were indistinguishable. Nevertheless, I am persuaded that the two constitutional provisions protect different interests and that proper analysis requires separate consideration of each.

I

The Full Faith and Credit Clause is one of several provisions in the Federal Constitution designed to transform the several States from independent sovereignties into a single, unified Nation.... The Full Faith and Credit Clause implements this design by directing that a State, when acting as the forum for litigation having multistate aspects or implications, respect the legitimate interests of other States and avoid infringement upon their sovereignty. The Clause does not, however, rigidly require the forum State to apply foreign law whenever another State has a valid interest in the litigation.... On the contrary, in view of the fact that the forum State is also a sovereign in its own right, in appropriate cases it may attach paramount importance to its own legitimate interests. Accordingly, the fact that a choice-of-law decision may be unsound as a matter of conflicts law does not necessarily implicate the federal concerns embodied in the Full Faith and Credit Clause. Rather in my opinion, the Clause should not invalidate a state court's choice of forum law unless that choice threatens the federal interest in national unity by unjustifiably infringing upon the legitimate interests of another State.

In this case, I think the Minnesota courts' decision to apply Minnesota law was plainly unsound as a matter of normal conflicts law. Both the execution of the insurance contract and the accident giving rise to the litigation took place in Wisconsin. Moreover, when both of those events occurred the plaintiff, the decedent, and the operators of both vehicles were all residents of Wisconsin. Nevertheless, I do not believe that any threat to national unity or Wisconsin's sovereignty ensues from allowing the substantive question presented by this case to be determined by the law of another State.

... Since the policy provided coverage for accidents that might occur in other States, it was obvious to the parties at the time of contracting that it might give rise to the application of the law of States other than Wisconsin. Therefore, while Wisconsin may have an interest in ensuring that contracts formed in Wisconsin in reliance upon Wisconsin law are interpreted in accordance with that law, that interest is not implicated in this case.

Petitioner has failed to establish that Minnesota's refusal to apply Wisconsin law poses any direct or indirect threat to Wisconsin's

---

[4] Although the Court has struck down a state court's choice of forum law on both due process, see e.g., Home Insurance Co. v. Dick, 281 U.S. 397 (1930), and full faith and credit grounds, see e.g., John Hancock Insurance Co. v. Yates, 299 U.S. 178 (1936), no clear analytical distinction between the two constitutional provisions has emerged. ...

sovereignty. In the absence of any such threat, I find it unnecessary to evaluate the forum State's interest in the litigation in order to reach the conclusion that the Full Faith and Credit Clause does not require the Minnesota courts to apply Wisconsin law to the question of contract interpretation presented in this case.

II

It may be assumed that a choice-of-law decision would violate the Due Process Clause if it were totally arbitrary or if it were fundamentally unfair to either litigant. I question whether a judge's decision to apply the law of his own State could ever be described as wholly irrational. For judges are presumably familiar with their own state law and may find it difficult and time consuming to discover and apply correctly the law of another State. The forum State's interest in the fair and efficient administration of justice is therefore sufficient, in my judgment, to attach a presumption of validity to a forum State's decision to apply its own law to a dispute over which it has jurisdiction.

The forum State's interest in the efficient operation of its judicial system is clearly not sufficient, however, to justify the application of a rule of law that is fundamentally unfair to one of the litigants. Arguably, a litigant could demonstrate such unfairness in a variety of ways. Concern about the fairness of the forum's choice of its own rule might arise if that rule favored residents over nonresidents, if it represented a dramatic departure from the rule that obtains in most American jurisdictions, or if the rule itself was unfair on its face or as applied.

The application of an otherwise acceptable rule of law may result in unfairness to the litigants if, in engaging in the activity which is the subject of the litigation, they could not reasonably have anticipated that their actions would later be judged by this rule of law. A choice-of-law decision that frustrates the justifiable expectations of the parties can be fundamentally unfair. This desire to prevent unfair surprise to a litigant has been the central concern in this Court's review of choice-of-law decisions under the Due Process Clause.

Neither the "stacking" rule itself, nor Minnesota's application of that rule to these litigants, raises any serious question of fairness. As the plurality observes, "[s]tacking was the rule in most States at the time the policy was issued." ... Moreover, the rule is consistent with the economics of a contractual relationship in which the policyholder paid three separate premiums for insurance coverage for three automobiles, including a separate premium for each uninsured motorist coverage.... Nor am I persuaded that the decision of the Minnesota courts to apply the "stacking" rule in this case can be said to violate due process because that decision frustrates the reasonable expectations of the contracting parties. ...

... [T]he decision of the Minnesota courts to apply the law of the forum in this case does not frustrate the reasonable expectations of the contracting parties, and I can find no fundamental unfairness in that decision requiring the attention of this Court.

In terms of fundamental fairness, it seems to me that two factors relied upon by the plurality—the plaintiff's post-accident move to Minnesota and the decedent's Minnesota employment—are either irrelevant to or possibly even tend to undermine the plurality's conclusion. When the expectations of the parties at the time of contracting are the central due process concern, as they are in this case, an unanticipated post-accident occurrence is clearly irrelevant for due process purposes. . . .

III

Although I regard the Minnesota courts' decision to apply forum law as unsound as a matter of conflicts law, and there is little in this record other than the presumption in favor of the forum's own law to support that decision, I concur in the plurality's judgment. It is not this Court's function to establish and impose upon state courts a federal choice-of-law rule, nor is it our function to ensure that state courts correctly apply whatever choice-of-law rules they have themselves adopted. Our authority may be exercised in the choice-of-law area only to prevent a violation of the Full Faith and Credit or the Due Process Clause. For the reasons stated above, I find no such violation in this case.

■ JUSTICE POWELL, with whom THE CHIEF JUSTICE and JUSTICE REHNQUIST join, dissenting.

My disagreement with the majority is narrow. I accept with few reservations Part II of the majority opinion, which sets forth the basic principles that guide us in reviewing state choice-of-law decisions under the Constitution. The Court should invalidate a forum State's decision to apply its own law only when there are no significant contacts between the State and the litigation. This modest check on state power is mandated by the Due Process Clause of the Fourteenth Amendment and the Full Faith and Credit Clause of Art. 4, § 1. I do not believe, however, that the Court adequately analyzes the policies such review must serve. In consequence, it has found significant what appear to me to be trivial contacts between the forum State and the litigation.

I

. . . The significance of asserted contacts must be evaluated in light of the constitutional policies that oversight by this Court should serve. Two enduring policies emerge from our cases.

First, the contacts between the forum State and the litigation should not be so "slight and casual" that it would be fundamentally unfair to a litigant for the forum to apply its own State's law. Clay v. Sun Ins. Office, Ltd. [p. 430, supra]. The touchstone here is the reasonable expectation of the parties. See Weintraub, Due Process and Full Faith and Credit Limitations on a State's Choice of Law, 44 Iowa L.Rev. 449, 445–57 (1959).

Second, the forum State must have a legitimate interest in the outcome of the litigation before it. Pacific Employers Ins. Co. v. Industrial Accident Comm'n [p. 426, supra]. The Full Faith and Credit Clause addresses the accommodation of sovereign power among the various States. Under limited circumstances, it requires one State to give effect to the statutory law of another State. Nevada v. Hall, 440 U.S. 410, 423 (1979). To be sure, a forum State need not give effect to another State's law if that law is in "violation of its own legitimate public policy." Id., at 624. Nonetheless, for a forum State to further its legitimate public policy by applying its own law to a controversy, there must be some connection between the facts giving rise to the litigation and the scope of the State's lawmaking jurisdiction.

Both the Due Process and Full Faith and Credit Clauses ensure that the States do not "reach out beyond the limits imposed on them by their status as coequal sovereigns in a federal system." World-Wide Volkswagen Corp. v. Woodson, 444 U.S. 286, 292 (1980) (addressing Fourteenth Amendment limitations on state court jurisdiction). . . .

In summary, the significance of the contacts between a forum State and the litigation must be assessed in light of these two important constitutional policies. A contact, or a pattern of contacts, satisfies the Constitution when it protects the litigants from being unfairly surprised if the forum State applies its own law, and when the application of the forum's law reasonably can be understood to further a legitimate public policy of the forum State.

II

Recognition of the complexity of the constitutional inquiry requires that this Court apply these principles with restraint. Applying these principles to the facts of this case, I do not believe, however, that Minnesota had sufficient contacts with the "persons and events" in this litigation to apply its rule permitting stacking. I would agree that no reasonable expectations of the parties were frustrated. The risk insured by petitioner was not geographically limited. . . .

The more doubtful question in this case is whether application of Minnesota's substantive law reasonably furthers a legitimate state interest. The Court attempts to give substance to the tenuous contacts between Minnesota and this litigation. Upon examination, however, these contacts are either trivial or irrelevant to the furthering of any public policy in Minnesota.

First, the post-accident residence of the plaintiff-beneficiary is constitutionally irrelevant to the choice-of-law question. John Hancock Mut. Life Ins. Co. v. Yates, supra. . . . Any possible ambiguity in the Court's view of the significance of a post-occurrence change of residence is dispelled by Home Ins. Co. v. Dick, supra, cited by the Yates Court, where it was held squarely that Dick's post-accident move to the forum State was "without significance." . . .

This rule is sound. If a plaintiff could choose the substantive rules to be applied to an action by moving to a hospitable forum, the invitation to forum shopping would be irresistible. Moreover, it would permit the defendant's reasonable expectations at the time the cause of action accrues to be frustrated, because it would permit the choice-of-law question to turn on a post-accrual circumstance. Finally, post-accrual residence has nothing to do with facts to which the forum State proposes to apply its rule; it is unrelated to the substantive legal issues presented by the litigation.

Second, the Court finds it significant that the insurer does business in the forum State. . . . The State does have a legitimate interest in regulating the practices of such an insurer. But this argument proves too much. The insurer here does business in all 50 States. The forum State has no interest in regulating that conduct of the insurer unrelated to property, persons or contracts executed within the forum State. . . . The Court recognizes this flaw and attempts to bolster the significance of the local presence of the insurer by combining it with the other factors deemed significant: the presence of the plaintiff and the fact that the deceased worked in the forum State. This merely restates the basic question in the case.

Third, the Court emphasizes particularly that the insured worked in the forum State. . . . The insured's place of employment is not, however, significant in this case. Neither the nature of the insurance policy, the events related to the accident, nor the immediate question of stacking coverage are in any way affected or implicated by the insured's employment status. The Court's opinion is understandably vague in explaining how trebling the benefits to be paid to the estate of a nonresident employee furthers any substantial state interest relating to employment. Minnesota does not wish its workers to die in automobile accidents, but permitting stacking will not further this interest. The substantive issue here is solely one of compensation, and whether the compensation provided by this policy is increased or not will have no relation to the State's employment policies or police power. . . .

Neither taken separately nor in the aggregate do the contacts asserted by the Court today indicate that Minnesota's application of its substantive rule in this case will further any legitimate state interest.[6] The Court focuses only on physical contacts vel non, and in doing so pays scant attention to the more fundamental reasons why our precedents

---

[6] The concurring opinion of Justice Stevens supports my view that the forum State's application of its own law to this case cannot be justified by the existence of relevant minimum contacts. As Justice Stevens observes, the principal factors relied on by the Court are "either irrelevant or possibly even tend to undermine the [Court's] conclusion." . . . The interesting analysis he proposes to uphold the State's judgment is, however, difficult to reconcile with our prior decisions and may create more problems than it solves. For example, it seems questionable to measure the interest of a State in a controversy by the degree of conscious reliance on that State's law by private parties to a contract. . . . Moreover, scrutinizing the strength of the interests of a nonforum State may draw this Court back into the discredited practice of weighing the relative interests of various States in a particular controversy. . . .

require reasonable policy-related contacts in choice-of-law cases. Therefore, I dissent.

After Allstate v. Hague, what is the impact of due process and full faith and credit on choice of law? Perhaps it is not realistic to view full faith and credit as retaining any significant function in this context considering that the Supreme Court, despite frequent reference to the full-faith-and-credit command has not since 1947 struck down a choice of law for violating that constitutional stricture. This suggests that the only serious test is due process. Once due process is satisfied the full-faith-and-credit requirement fades away. But there is a possibility, is there not, that the forum's choice might be the equivalent of a "forbidden infringement" on a sister state's interests of the kind that Justice Stone referred to in the judgments area. If so, what are the indicia of such an infringement? Is using part of a sister state statute while rejecting an unmistakably interrelated part an example of a forbidden infringement? Can any state where shareholders reside apply its law to the internal affairs of a corporation (for example, the method of electing directors), even if that law is contrary to the law of the state where the company is incorporated? See Note 3, p. 444, infra.

The law reviews have published floods of commentary on Allstate v. Hague. A major collection is Symposium: Choice of Law Theory After *Allstate Insurance Co. v. Hague*, 10 Hofstra L.Rev. 1 (1981), containing comments by Professors Cavers, Davies, Leflar, Martin, Reese, Sedler, Silberman, Trautman, Twerski, von Mehren, and Weintraub.

Among other useful commentaries are Hay, Full Faith and Credit and Federalism in Choice of Law, 34 Mercer L.Rev. 709 (1983); Hill, Choice of Law and Jurisdiction in the Supreme Court, 81 Colum.L.Rev. 960 (1981); Kozyris, Reflections on Allstate—The Lessening of Due Process in Choice of Law, 14 U.C.Davis L. Rev. 889 (1981); Weinberg, Choice of Law and Minimal Scrutiny, 49 U.Chi.L.Rev. 440 (1982); Note, Legislative Jurisdiction, State Policies and Post-Occurrence Contacts in *Allstate Insurance Co. v. Hague*, 81 Colum.L.Rev. 1134 (1981).

The Restatement, Second, Conflict of Laws, Section 9, reads:

§ 9. Limitations on Choice of Law

A court may not apply the local law of its own state to determine a particular issue unless such application of this law would be reasonable in light of the relationship of the state and of other states to the person, thing or occurrence involved.

Is that as accurate and precise a statement of the law as we can make after Allstate v. Hague?

NOTES

1. See Reese, Legislative Jurisdiction, 78 Colum.L.Rev. 1587 (1978); Müller-Freienfels, Conflicts of Law and Constitutional Law, 45 U.Chi.L.Rev. 598 (1978). As to federal control of choice of law, Justice Jackson, in The Supreme Court in the American System of Government 41–44 (1955), said: "It seems to me that disagreement as to which of conflicting or competing state laws applies raises a federal question under the Full Faith and Credit Clause and that our hope for a better general legal system would be well served by wider application of that clause." Is that the best path in light of Allstate v. Hague? For a rare case in which a plaintiff admitted that a post-accident move (this one also to Minnesota) was part of an effort (this time unsuccessful) to obtain application of a move favorable law, see Nesladek v. Ford Motor Co., 46 F.3d 734 (8th Cir.1995).

2. In re Adoption of Baby Boy S., 12 P.2d 761 (Kan.App.1996), cert. denied, 519 U.S. 870, 117 S.Ct. 185, 136 L.Ed.2d 123 (1996). A child conceived in Ohio where his unmarried parents cohabited, was born in Kansas when his mother moved there after terminating her relationship with the father. In a Kansas adoption proceeding, the court applied Kansas law to terminate the father's parental rights. The court rejected the father's contention that the court's application of Kansas law violated due process and permitted "unwed mothers to 'forum shop' for jurisdictions with stricter statutes to prevent unwed fathers from opposing an adoption." The court stated: "in our current mobile society, the place of conception of a child carries little weight. However, requiring an unwed father to make substantial efforts to remain in contact with an unwed mother and participate in the pregnancy and birth of the child, wherever it occurs, is not an unreasonable expectation." Id. at 766–67.

3. VantagePoint Venture Partners v. Examen, Inc., 871 A.2d 1108 (Del.2005). The merger of two Delaware corporations was imminent. A preferred shareholder of one of the corporations claimed that the corporation was a "quasi-California corporation" under the California Corporation Code because more than 50% of its property, payroll payments, sales, and stockholders were in California. As a quasi-California corporation the shareholder claimed that that the corporation was governed by California law under which, unlike Delaware law, preferred shareholders were entitled to vote as a separate class on the merger. The Delaware Supreme Court held that Delaware law controlled and that the Due Process and Commerce Clauses of the U.S. Constitution mandated this result. Contrary to Justice Brennan's statement in footnote 10 of the principal case, is the result compelled by the Full Faith and Credit Clause because this is a rare instance in which there is a compelling national need for a uniform answer under the law of the state of incorporation?

Phillips Petroleum Co. v. Shutts

Supreme Court of the United States, 1985.
472 U.S. 797, 105 S.Ct. 2965, 86 L.Ed.2d 628.

■ JUSTICE REHNQUIST delivered the opinion of the Court.

Petitioner is a Delaware corporation which has its principal place of business in Oklahoma. During the 1970's it produced or purchased natural gas from leased land located in 11 different States, and sold most of the gas in interstate commerce. Respondents are some 28,000 of the royalty owners possessing rights to the leases from which petitioner produced the gas; they reside in all 50 States, the District of Columbia, and several foreign countries. Respondents brought a class action against petitioner in the Kansas state court, seeking to recover interest on royalty payments which had been delayed by petitioner. They recovered judgment in the trial court, and the Supreme Court of Kansas affirmed the judgment over petitioner's contentions that the Due Process Clause of the Fourteenth Amendment prevented Kansas from adjudicating the claims of all the respondents, and that the Due Process Clause and the Full Faith and Credit Clause of Article IV of the Constitution prohibited the application of Kansas law to all of the transactions between petitioner and respondents. 235 Kan. 195, 679 P.2d 1159 (1984). We granted certiorari to consider these claims. 469 U.S. 879 (1984). We reject petitioner's jurisdictional claim, but sustain its claim regarding the choice of law.

[The part of the Court's decision held that the Kansas court had personal jurisdiction the non-resident class members is omitted.]

III

The Kansas courts applied Kansas contract and Kansas equity law to every claim in this case, notwithstanding that over 99% of the gas leases and some 97% of the plaintiffs in the case had no apparent connection to the State of Kansas except for this lawsuit. Petitioner protested that the Kansas courts should apply the laws of the States where the leases were located, or at least apply Texas and Oklahoma law because so many of the leases came from those States. The Kansas courts disregarded this contention and found petitioner liable for interest on the suspended royalties as a matter of Kansas law, and set the interest rates under Kansas equity principles.

. . . We must first determine whether Kansas law conflicts in any material way with any other law which could apply. There can be no injury in applying Kansas law if it is not in conflict with that of any other jurisdiction connected to this suit.

[At this point, the court determined that Kansas law might differ in material aspects from the law of the other states.]

Four Terms ago we addressed a similar situation in Allstate Ins. Co. v. Hague, 449 U.S. 302 (1981). . . .

The plurality in Allstate noted that a particular set of facts giving rise to litigation could justify, constitutionally, the application of more than one jurisdiction's laws. The plurality recognized, however, that the Due Process Clause and the Full Faith and Credit Clause provided modest restrictions on the application of forum law. These restrictions required "that for a State's substantive law to be selected in a constitutionally permissible manner, that State must have a significant contact or significant aggregation of contacts, creating state interests, such that choice of its law is neither arbitrary nor fundamentally unfair." Id., at 312–313, 101 S.Ct., at 639–640. The dissenting Justices were in substantial agreement with this principle. Id., at 332, 101 S.Ct., at 650 (opinion of Powell, J.). . . . Kansas' contacts to this litigation, as explained by the Kansas Supreme Court, can be gleaned from the opinion below.

Petitioner owns property and conducts substantial business in the State, so Kansas certainly has an interest in regulating petitioner's conduct in Kansas. 235 Kan., at 210, 679 P.2d, at 1174. Moreover, oil and gas extraction is an important business to Kansas, and although only a few leases in issue are located in Kansas, hundreds of Kansas plaintiffs were affected by petitioner's suspension of royalties; thus the court held that the State has a real interest in protecting "the rights of these royalty owners both as individual residents of [Kansas] and as members of this particular class of plaintiffs." Id., at 211–212, 679 P.2d, at 1174. The Kansas Supreme Court pointed out that Kansas courts are quite familiar with this type of lawsuit, and "[t]he plaintiff class members have indicated their desire to have this action determined under the laws of Kansas." Id., at 211, 222, 679 P.2d, at 1174, 1181. Finally, the Kansas court buttressed its use of Kansas law by stating that this lawsuit was analogous to a suit against a "common fund" located in Kansas. Id., at 201, 211–212, 679 P.2d, at 1168, 1174.

We do not lightly discount this description of Kansas' contacts with this litigation and its interest in applying its law. There is, however, no "common fund" located in Kansas that would require or support the application of only Kansas law to all these claims. See, e.g., Hartford Life Ins. Co. v. Ibs, 237 U.S. 662 (1915). As the Kansas court noted, petitioner commingled the suspended royalties with its general corporate accounts. 235 Kan. at 201, 679 P.2d, at 1168. There is no specific identifiable res in Kansas, nor is there any limited amount which may be depleted before every plaintiff is compensated. Only by somehow aggregating all the separate claims in this case could a "common fund" in any sense be created, and the term becomes all but meaningless when used in such an expansive sense.

We also give little credence to the idea that Kansas law should apply to all claims because the plaintiffs, by failing to opt out, evinced their desire to be bound by Kansas law. Even if one could say that the plaintiffs "consented" to the application of Kansas law by not opting out, plaintiff's desire for forum law is rarely, if ever controlling. In most cases the plaintiff shows his obvious wish for forum law by filing there. . . . Even if a plaintiff evidences his desire for forum law by moving to the forum, we have generally accorded such a move little or no significance. John Hancock Mut. Life Ins. Co. v. Yates, 299 U.S. 178, 182 (1936); Home Ins. Co. v. Dick, 281 U.S. 397, 408 (1930). In Allstate the plaintiff's move to the forum was only relevant because it was unrelated and prior to the litigation. 449 U.S., at 318–319, 101 S.Ct., at 643. Thus the plaintiffs' desire for Kansas law, manifested by their participation in this Kansas lawsuit, bears little relevance.

The Supreme Court of Kansas in its opinion in this case expressed the view that by reason of the fact that it was adjudicating a nationwide class action, it had much greater latitude in applying its own law to the transactions in question than might otherwise be the case:

> "The general rule is that the law of the forum applies unless it is expressly shown that a different law governs, and in case of doubt, the law of the forum is preferred. . . . Where a state court determines it has jurisdiction over a nationwide class action and procedural due process guarantees of notice and adequate representation are present, we believe the law of the forum should be applied unless compelling reasons exist for applying a different law. . . ." 235 Kan., at 221–222, 679 P.2d, at 1181.

We think that this is something of a "bootstrap" argument. . . . While a state may, for the reasons we have previously stated, assume jurisdiction over the claims of plaintiffs whose principal contacts are with other States, it may not use this assumption of jurisdiction as an added weight in the scale when considering the permissible constitutional limits on choice of substantive law. . . .

The issue of personal jurisdiction over plaintiffs in a class action is entirely distinct from the question of the constitutional limitations on choice of law; the latter calculus is not altered by the fact that it may be more difficult or more burdensome to comply with the constitutional limitations because of the large number of transactions which the State proposes to adjudicate and which have little connection with the forum.

Kansas must have a "significant contact or aggregation of contacts" to the claims asserted by each member of the plaintiff class, contacts "creating state interests" in order to ensure that the choice of Kansas law is not arbitrary or unfair. Allstate, supra, 449 U.S., at 312–313, 101 S.Ct., at 639–640. Given Kansas' lack of "interest" in claims unrelated to that State, and the substantive conflict with jurisdictions such as Texas, we conclude that application of Kansas law to every claim in this case is sufficiently arbitrary and unfair as to exceed constitutional limits.

When considering fairness in this context, an important element is the expectation of the parties. See Allstate, supra, 449 U.S., at 333, 101 S.Ct., at 650 (opinion of Powell, J.). There is no indication that when the leases involving land and royalty owners outside of Kansas were executed, the parties had any idea that Kansas law would control. Neither the Due Process Clause nor the Full Faith and Credit Clause requires Kansas "to substitute for its own [laws], applicable to persons and events within it, the conflicting statute of another state," Pacific Employers Insurance Co. v. Industrial Accident Comm'n, 306 U.S. 493, 502, 59 S.Ct. 629, 633, 83 L.Ed. 940 (1939), but Kansas "may not abrogate the rights of parties beyond its borders having no relation to anything done or to be done within them." Home Insurance Co. v. Dick, supra, 281 U.S., at 410, 50 S.Ct., at 342.

. . . We make no effort to determine for ourselves which law must apply to the various transactions involved in this lawsuit, and we reaffirm our observation in Allstate that in many situations a state court may be free to apply one of several choices of law. But the constitutional limitations laid down in cases such as Allstate and Home Insurance Co. v. Dick, supra, must be respected even in a nationwide class action. . . .

■ JUSTICE STEVENS, concurring in part and dissenting in part.

. . . I agree that the Kansas courts properly exercised jurisdiction over this class action. . . .

. . . [I]t has long been settled that "a mere misconstruction by the forum of the laws of a sister State is not a violation of the Full Faith and Credit Clause." Carroll v. Lanza, 349 U.S. 408, 414, n. 1, 75 S.Ct. 804, 807, n. 1, 99 L.Ed. 1183 (1955) (Frankfurter, J., dissenting). That clause requires only that States accord "full faith and credit" to other States' laws—that is, acknowledge the validity and finality of such laws and attempt in good faith to apply them when necessary as they would be applied by home state courts. . . .

. . . As the opinion in Shutts I [an earlier case involving a smaller number of royalty owners] indicates, the Kansas court made a careful survey of the relevant laws of Oklahoma and Texas, the only other states whose law is proffered as relevant to this litigation. But, as the Court acknowledges, . . . no other State's laws or judicial decisions were precisely on point, and, in the Kansas court's judgment, roughly analogous Texas and Oklahoma cases supported the results the Kansas court reached. The Kansas court expressly declared that, in a multistate action, a "court should also give careful consideration, as we have attempted to do, to any possible conflict of law problems". . . . While a common law judge might disagree with the substantive legal determinations made by the Kansas court (although nothing in its opinion seems erroneous to me), that court's approach to the possible choices of law evinces precisely the "full faith and credit" that the Constitution requires.

It is imaginable that even a good faith review of another State's law might still "unjustifiably infring[e] upon the legitimate interests of another State" so as to violate the Full Faith and Credit Clause. . . . If, for example, a Texas oil company or a Texas royalty owner with an interest in a Texas lease were treated directly contrary to a stated policy of the State of Texas by a Kansas court through some honest blunder, the Constitution might bar such "parochial entrenchment" on Texas' interests. . . . But this case is so distant from such a situation that I need not pursue this theoretical possibility. Even Phillips does not contend that any stated policies of other States have been plainly contravened, and the Court's discussion is founded merely on an absence of reported decisions and the Court's speculation of what Oklahoma or Texas courts might "most likely" do in a case like this. . . . There is simply no demonstration here that the Kansas Supreme Court's decision has impaired the legitimate interests of any other States or infringed on their sovereignty in the slightest.

III

It is nevertheless possible for a State's choice of law to violate the Constitution because it is so "totally arbitrary or . . . fundamentally unfair" to a litigant that it violates the Due Process Clause. *Allstate*, 449 U.S., at 326 (Stevens, J., concurring in judgment). If the forum court has no connection to the lawsuit other than its jurisdiction over the parties, a decision to apply the forum State's law might so "frustrat[e] the justifiable expectations of the parties" as to be unconstitutional. Id., at 327.

Again, however, a constitutional claim of "unfair surprise" cannot be based merely upon an unexpected choice of a particular State's law—it must rest on a persuasive showing of an unexpected result arrived at by application of that law. Thus, absent any *conflict* of laws, in terms of the results they produce, the Due Process Clause simply has not been violated. This is because the underlying theory of a choice-of-law due process claim must be that parties plan their conduct and contractual relations based upon their legitimate expectations concerning the subsequent legal consequences of their actions. . . .

The crux of my disagreement with the Court is over the standard applied to evaluate the sufficiency of allegations of choice-of-law conflicts necessary to support a constitutional claim. Rather than potential, "putative," or even "likely" conflicts, I would require demonstration of an unambiguous conflict with the *established* law of another State as an essential element of a constitutional choice-of-law claim. Arguments that a State court has merely applied general common law principles in a novel manner, or reconciled arguably conflicting laws erroneously in the face of unprecedented factual circumstances should not suffice to make out a constitutional issue. . . .

NOTE

Sun Oil Co. v. Wortman, 486 U.S. 717, 108 S.Ct. 2117 (1988), p. 449, infra, presented a reprise of *Wortman* (which is treated fully in the next chapter). In *Sun Oil*, the Court held that Kansas may constitutionally apply its own statute of limitations to all claims. The majority opinion, written by Justice Scalia, held that the preference for applying forum law to statute of limitations questions was sufficiently well embedded as a matter of state conflicts law that Kansas's decision to apply its own limitation period was constitutional, even though application of Kansas substantive law to certain claims was found unconstitutional in *Shutts*.

Wortman also raised the question of whether a party has a due-process or full-faith-and-credit right to an accurate reading of the other state's law in cases in which the forum is under a constitutional duty to apply that other state's law. On remand after the *Shutts* decision, the Kansas Supreme Court decided that the Texas, Oklahoma and Louisiana courts would have enforced the parties' "implicit" agreement to a rate of interest different from that specified by statute that the Federal Power Commission required Phillips to pay to customers if the Commission disapproved of Phillip's price increase. In *Wortman*, when the Kansas Supreme Court repeated this assessment of the laws of the other states, the majority concluded that this ruling had not "unconstitutionally distorted" the other states' laws. In order for a state court to violate its constitutional obligation in this regard, the law in the other state must be "clearly established" and "brought to the court's attention. . . ." The majority concluded that the Kansas Supreme Court acted within constitutional bounds because it had "anticipated" possible developments in Texas, Oklahoma and Louisiana law. Justice O'Connor's dissent argued that the laws of Texas, Oklahoma and Louisiana law were clearly established, and that the Kansas Supreme Court's decision had flouted those clearly established principles. See also Pennsylvania Fire Ins. Co. v. Gold Issue Mining and Milling Co., 243 U.S. 93, 96, 37 S.Ct. 344 (1917) (state court fulfilled its duty by engaging in a "candid" appraisal of the other state's law).

Nationwide class actions can run afoul of the *Hague* and *Shutts* requirement that the claims of all parties have some connection to the forum state if forum state law is to be applied to all class claims. See, e.g., Hale v. Emerson Elec. Co., 942 F.3d 401 (8th Cir.2019)(Missouri law could not be applied to class claims involving no significant connection to Missouri). However, choice-of-law issues do not prevent certification of nationwide class actions if a choice-of-law analysis is performed. See, e.g., Senne v. Kan. City Royals Baseball Corp., 934 F.3d 918 (9th Cir.2019)(wage-and-hour law class action certified where District Court decided that the applicable law was where work duties were principally performed).

In a derivative suit involving a Delaware corporation, a New York court held that the plaintiff's right to discovery was a substantive question, to be governed by Delaware law. Lerner v. Prince, 987 N.Y.S.2d 19, 24 (App.Div.2014): Although New York courts have applied the law of the forum when deciding matters, such as discovery, affecting the conduct of the litigation, that this case is a purported derivative action places it into a different context. The demand requirement is based on the 'bedrock principle' of Delaware law that a corporation's directors, and not its shareholders, manage the corporation's business. Thus, the Delaware law on discovery is an integral part of the legal framework governing derivative proceedings; indeed, it is inextricably intertwined with the decision to act or decline to act on a shareholder demand." (citations omitted).

For a discussion of the case and its effect on choice of law, see Miller & Crump, Jurisdiction and Choice of Law in Multistate Class Actions After Phillips Petroleum Co. v. Shutts, 96 Yale L.J. 1 (1986).

_____

NEVADA V. HALL, 440 U.S. 410, 99 S.Ct. 1182 (1979): Suit brought by California residents in the courts of that state to recover for injuries sustained in California in a collision with an automobile owned by the state of Nevada and being driven on state business. Nevada interposed two defenses: sovereign immunity and that full faith and credit was owed to a Nevada statute limiting recovery against the state to $25,000. The California courts rejected both defenses and plaintiffs were awarded judgment of $1,150,000. The Supreme Court granted certiorari and, in an opinion by Justice Stevens, affirmed. On the subject of full faith and credit, Justice Stevens said:

> "[T]his Court's decision in Pacific Employers Insurance Company v. Industrial Accident Commission [p. 426, supra] clearly establishes that the Full Faith and Credit Clause does not require a State to apply another State's law in violation of its own legitimate public policy.

> ". . . In this case, California's interest is the closely related and . . . substantial one of providing 'full protection to those who are injured on its highways through the negligence of both residents and nonresidents.' Hall v. University of Nevada (appendix to petition at 7). To effectuate this interest, California has provided by statute for jurisdiction in its courts over residents and nonresidents alike to allow those injured on its highways through the negligence of others to secure full compensation for their injuries in the California courts.

> "In further implementation of that policy, California has unequivocally waived its own immunity from liability for the torts committed by its own agents and authorized full recovery even against the sovereign. As the California courts have found, to require California either to surrender jurisdiction or to limit respondents' recovery to the $25,000 maximum of the Nevada statute would be obnoxious to its statutorily based policies of jurisdiction over nonresident motorists and full recovery. The Full Faith and Credit Clause does not require this result.[24]"

_____

[24] California's exercise of jurisdiction in this case poses no substantial threat to our constitutional system of cooperative federalism. Suits involving traffic accidents occurring outside of Nevada could hardly interfere with Nevada's capacity to fulfill its own sovereign responsibilities. We have no occasion, in this case, to consider whether different state policies, either of California or of Nevada, might require a different analysis or a different result.

Three Justices dissented with respect to the denial of Nevada's claim to sovereign immunity.

The view of the *Hall* dissenters ultimately prevailed. Gilbert Hyatt had a decades-long dispute with California taxing authorities over whether he owed California state income tax on profits earned on a computer chip patent. The taxation issue turned on where Hyatt was domiciled. He claimed Nevada; California disagreed. Hyatt then sued the California state taxing authority claiming that its aggressive tactics toward him (including searching his mailbox and interviewing people at his church) were tortious. The Supreme Court initially followed *Nevada v. Hall* and held that the suit could proceed under Nevada law. See Franchise Tax Bd. v. Hyatt (Hyatt I), 538 U.S. 488 (2003). Hyatt won a $388 million verdict in Nevada state courts. On a return trip to the U.S. Supreme Court, the California taxing authority asked that *Hall* be overruled. An eight-Justice Court divided 4–4 on whether *Hall* should be overruled, but held that Full Faith and Credit principles allowed Hyatt to recover against California no more than he could have against Nevada, which was $50,000. Franchise Tax Bd. v. Hyatt (Hyatt II), 136 S. Ct. 1277 (2016). After remand to the Nevada Supreme Court, the California taxing authority again sought review by the U.S. Supreme Court, which overruled *Nevada v. Hall* and held that sovereign immunity protected California completely from suit in another state court, unless California expressly consented to suit, which it had not. Franchise Tax Bd. v. Hyatt (Hyatt III), 139 S.Ct. 1485 (2019). After a quarter century of litigation and winning a nine-figure jury verdict, Mr. Hyatt recovered nothing.

STATE FARM MUTUAL AUTOMOBILE INSURANCE CO. V. CAMPBELL, 538 U.S. 408, 123 S.Ct. 1514, 155 L.Ed.2d 585 (2003). After a deadly traffic wreck in which one of its insureds was at fault, the insurance company at first assured the insureds that they had nothing to fear and that "their assets were safe." The company and then refused to settle within policy limits and refused to cover the judgment against its insureds, which was far in excess of policy limits. It told the insureds they had been put their house on the market to cover the liability. Though the company ultimately paid the judgment, the insured sued for fraud and bad faith failure to settle the underlying case. The Utah Supreme Court affirmed a judgment against the insurer of $1,000,000 in compensatory damages and $145,000,000 in punitive damages. The plaintiffs' theory for punitive damages was the insurer's alleged fraudulent practices *nationwide*. The Supreme Court reversed on two principal grounds: (1) Utah lacked authority to apply its punitive damages law to activity occurring in other states and (2) the punitive damages award was unconstitutionally excessive. The majority opinion explained:

> A State cannot punish a defendant for conduct that may have been lawful where it occurred. . . . Bigelow v. Virginia, 421 U.S. 809, 824, 95 S.Ct. 2222, 44 L.Ed.2d 600 (1975) ("A State

does not acquire power or supervision over the internal affairs of another State merely because the welfare and health of its own citizens may be affected when they travel to that State"); New York Life Ins. Co. v. Head, 234 U.S. 149, 161, 34 S.Ct. 879, 58 L.Ed. 1259 (1914) ("[I]t would be impossible to permit the statutes of Missouri to operate beyond the jurisdiction of that State . . . without throwing down the constitutional barriers by which all the States are restricted within the orbits of their lawful authority and upon the preservation of which the Government under the Constitution depends. This is so obviously the necessary result of the Constitution that it has rarely been called in question and hence authorities directly dealing with it do not abound"); Huntington v. Attrill, 146 U.S. 657, 669, 13 S.Ct. 224, 36 L.Ed. 1123 (1892) ("Laws have no force of themselves beyond the jurisdiction of the State which enacts them, and can have extra-territorial effect only by the comity of other States"). Nor, as a general rule, does a State have a legitimate concern in imposing punitive damages to punish a defendant for unlawful acts committed outside of the State's jurisdiction. Any proper adjudication of conduct that occurred outside Utah to other persons would require their inclusion, and, to those parties, the Utah courts, in the usual case, would need to apply the laws of their relevant jurisdiction. Phillips Petroleum Co. v. Shutts, 472 U.S. 797, 821–822, 105 S.Ct. 2965, 86 L.Ed.2d 628 (1985).

Here, the Campbells do not dispute that much of the out-of-state conduct was lawful where it occurred. They argue, however, that such evidence was not the primary basis for the punitive damages award and was relevant to the extent it demonstrated, in a general sense, State Farm's motive against its insured. This argument misses the mark. Lawful out-of-state conduct may be probative when it demonstrates the deliberateness and culpability of the defendant's action in the State where it is tortious, but that conduct must have a nexus to the specific harm suffered by the plaintiff. A jury must be instructed, furthermore, that it may not use evidence of out-of-state conduct to punish a defendant for action that was lawful in the jurisdiction where it occurred. A basic principle of federalism is that each State may make its own reasoned judgment about what conduct is permitted or proscribed within its borders, and each State alone can determine what measure of punishment, if any, to impose on a defendant who acts within its jurisdiction. . . .

Turning to the second . . . guidepost [from BMW of North America, Inc. v. Gore 517 U.S. 559, 116 S.Ct 1589, 134 L.Ed.2d 809 (1996)(excessive punitive damages awards violate substantive due process)], we have been reluctant to identify concrete constitutional limits on the ratio between harm, or potential harm, to the plaintiff and the punitive damages award. . . . Our jurisprudence and the principles it has now established demonstrate, however, that, in practice, few awards exceeding a single-digit ratio between punitive and compensatory damages, to a significant degree, will satisfy due process. . . . Single-digit multipliers are more likely to comport with due process, while still achieving the State's goals of deterrence and retribution, than awards with ratios in range of 500 to 1, or, in this case, of 145 to 1. . . .

The third guidepost in *Gore* is the disparity between the punitive damages award and the "civil penalties authorized or imposed in comparable cases." . . .

Here, we need not dwell long on this guidepost. The most relevant civil sanction under Utah state law for the wrong done to the Campbells appears to be a $10,000 fine for an act of fraud, an amount dwarfed by the $145 million punitive damages award. . . .

An application of the *Gore* guideposts to the facts of this case, especially in light of the substantial compensatory damages awarded (a portion of which contained a punitive element), likely would justify a punitive damages award at or near the amount of compensatory damages. The punitive award of $145 million, therefore, was neither reasonable nor proportionate to the wrong committed, and it was an irrational and arbitrary deprivation of the property of the defendant. The proper calculation of punitive damages under the principles we have discussed should be resolved, in the first instance, by the Utah courts.

NOTES

1.   Observe that the Court cites *Huntington v. Attrill*, p. 382, supra, for the proposition that state laws can have "extra-territorial" effect only by comity from other states. Can this be reconciled, however, with *Hyatt*, in which the court approved of a Nevada court's directly imposing liability on the State of California? Or with *Allstate Insurance Co. v. Hague*, p. 432, supra, in which the Minnesota courts were allowed to impose a Minnesota insurance rule on an insurance policy written to a Wisconsin resident?

2.   What is the practical effect of the Court's admonition that punitive damages must be based upon in-state conduct? Is light of the Court's statement that punitive damages will ordinarily be limited to "single digit" multipliers of the actual damages, will there be any need to rely upon out-of-state conduct? Consider the case of Boyd v. Goffoli, 608 S.E.2d 169 (W.Va.2004). Plaintiffs applied to defendant trucking company in West Virginia for training as truck drivers and for employment. Defendant falsely

told plaintiffs that they could obtain commercial driver's licenses in a course in Pennsylvania and transfer these licenses back to West Virginia. When plaintiffs were denied licenses they sued defendant and were each awarded $75,000 compensatory damages and $250,000 punitive damages. Defendant appealed claiming "that it was improperly punished for a scheme to violate Pennsylvania law in contravention of *State Farm Mut. Auto. Ins. Co. v. Campbell*."

Held: affirmed:

> Reading the Supreme Court's pronouncements in *Campbell* and *Shutts* together, this Court now holds that a State has a legitimate interest in imposing damages to punish a defendant for unlawful acts committed outside of the State's jurisdiction where the State has a significant contact or significant aggregation of contacts to the plaintiffs' claims which arise from the unlawful out-of-state conduct. We now apply this rule to the instant facts.

> First, we note that the facts in *Shutts* are quite different from those below. In *Shutts*, Kansas law was applied to all of the claims despite the fact that the vast majority of those claims had no connection to Kansas. In contrast, Appellees were all West Virginia residents who were initially informed of the Pennsylvania scheme, and wrongly assured that it was legal by Appellant's agent who was a resident of West Virginia. Further, Appellees' economic losses occurred in West Virginia. Therefore, West Virginia has a significant contact with the claims asserted by Appellees. As a result, the fact that a portion of Appellant's misconduct occurred in Pennsylvania is legally insignificant. Certainly, a West Virginia court has an interest in protecting its citizens from tortious conduct and is not precluded from doing so simply because some of the tortious conduct occurred in another state. Id. at 179.

The Control of Choice of Law by Federal Statutes

The Constitution of the United States gives to the Congress wide powers over conflict of laws. This is done in the clearest form by the words of the full faith and credit clause: "And the Congress may by General Laws prescribe the Manner in which such Acts, Records and Proceedings shall be proved, and the Effect thereof." Perhaps, similar power is also conferred by other parts of the Constitution, as, the interstate and foreign commerce clause and the due process clauses.

This power has been sweepingly exercised by the Congress in the field of state judgments, as shown in Chapter 5, supra.

Until 1948 there seems to have been no similar federal statute on choice of law. The statute enacted in 1790 under the full faith and credit clause had dealt with the protection of "records" and "judicial proceedings", but not with "acts". In 1948 the provision was amended, as shown to include "acts" within the scope of its protection.

The Supreme Court has not yet determined the effect, if any, of the amendment. Note, in this connection, that the Court adverted to the question, but did not decide it, in Hughes v. Fetter, p. 413, supra. Note also Justice Frankfurter's statement in his dissent in Carroll v. Lanza, p. 428, supra, that the amendment "cannot be disregarded."

In State ex rel. Swanson v. Integrity Advance, LLC, 846 N.W.2d 435, 441–42 (Minn. App. 2014), a Minnesota state official sued a Delaware online payday lender. The lender was not licensed to do business in Minnesota and the suit alleged that the lender violated Minnesota law on payday lending—*inter alia*, by charging interest over 1300 percent. The Minnesota Court of Appeals held that application of Minnesota law did not violate the Dormant Commerce Clause because it did not regulate conduct occurring outside that state's borders. Minnesota residents submitted applications from computers in Minnesota, the lender contacted the borrower in Minnesota, and also contacted Minnesota financial institutions. The court affirmed summary judgment of over $7,000,000 in favor of the state.

State Efforts to Limit Full Faith and Credit

Since 2010, several states have enacted statutes purporting to ban their courts from applying or enforcing foreign (including sharia) law. Some also forbid forum selection clauses and law selection clauses that would have the same effect. The statutes vary, but tend to prohibit enforcing judgments or laws based upon foreign law that would not grant rights recognized by federal or state law.

The constitutional and other implications of such statutes have sparked considerable academic discussion. See, e.g., An-Na'im, Banning Sharia Is A "Red Herring": The Way Forward For All Americans, 57 St. Louis U.L.J. 287 (2013); Ballou, Sooners vs. Shari'a: The Constitutional and Societal Problems Raised by the Oklahoma State Ban on Islamic Shari'a Law, 30 Law & Ineq. 309 (2012); Chaudhry-Kravitz, The New Facially Neutral "Anti-Shariah" Bills: A Constitutional Analysis, 20 Wash. & Lee J. Civil Rts. & Soc.Just. 25 (2013); Davis, Shadow and Substance: The Impacts of the Anti-International Law Debate on State Court Judges, 47 N.Engl.L.Rev. 631 (2013); Elsayed, Contracting into Religious Law: Anti-Sharia Enactments and the Establishment and Free Exercise Clauses, 20 Geo. Mason L.Rev. 937 (2013); Fallon, Justice for All: American Muslims, Sharia Law, and Maintaining Comity Within American Jurisprudence, 36 B.C. Int'l & Comp.L.Rev. 153 (2013); Hay, The Use and Determination of Foreign Law in Civil Litigation in the United States, 62 Am J.Comp.L. 213 (2014).

Other Constitutional Limits on Unreasonable Discrimination in Choice of Law

The Privileges and Immunities Clause (Art. IV, § 2) and the equal protection clause of the Fourteenth Amendment forbid a state from discriminating unreasonably against citizens of sister states or against persons within its jurisdiction. A leading example is Supreme Court of New Hampshire v. Piper, 470 U.S. 274, 105 S.Ct. 1272 (1985). In that case a Vermont resident, living only about 400 yards from the New Hampshire border, applied for membership in the New Hampshire bar. She passed the bar examination and the character and fitness inquiry, but was not allowed to become a member until she established a domicile in New Hampshire. Doing so would have presented a significant obstacle for her, including forcing her to sell her current residence, which was then secured by a mortgage with a favorable interest rate. She sued and the Supreme Court held that restriction of the privilege of becoming a member of the bar to state residents was a violation of the Privileges and Immunities Clause.

Not all differential treatment of out-of-state residents violates this Clause, however. In Douglas v. New York, New Haven & Hartford Railroad Co., 279 U.S. 377, 49 S.Ct. 355 (1929), the Court held that a state does not violate the privileges and immunities clause by dismissing on a forum non conveniens grounds a suit between residents of sister states that is based on a foreign occurrence. Recall, however, that *Hughes v. Fetter*, p. 413, supra, notes that a dismissal on the merits is much more severe in its impact because it presumably precludes future litigation, while a non-merits dismissal such as a forum non conveniens dismissal allows for re-filing in another state.

It has also come to be recognized that some of the more recent approaches to choice of law reveal a tendency to extend the protection of forum law to forum residents and not to do so for nonresidents, thereby giving rise to privileges and immunities and equal protection problems. For example, suppose that the owner and driver of an automobile, who is domiciled in state X, is involved in an accident in state Y and thereafter is sued in X by two injured guest passengers, one of whom is domiciled in X and the other in Y. Would it be appropriate in these circumstances for the X court to apply X law to determine the rights of the X passenger in a favorable way, but refuse to apply X law to determine the Y passenger's rights on the ground that a state has no interest in favorable treatment of a nonresident but, on the ground that it has no interest in him, Y law to determine the rights of the Y passenger? Problems of this kind are considered in the chapters which follow. The field is intensively discussed in two articles by Professors Currie and Schreter, Unconstitutional Discrimination in the Conflict of Laws: Privileges and Immunities, 69 Yale L.J. 1323 (1960), and Unconstitutional Discrimination in the Conflict of Laws: Equal Protection, 28 U.Chi.L.Rev. 1 (1960). These articles are reprinted in Currie, Selected Essays on the Conflict of Laws,

Chs. 11, 12 (1963). See also Note, Unconstitutional Discrimination in Choice of Law, 77 Colum. L. Rev. 272 (1977).

Another principle of non-discrimination with implications for choice of law is sometimes established by the dormant Commerce Clause. In Healy v. The Beer Institute, 491 U.S. 324, 109 S.Ct. 2491 (1989), the Supreme Court struck down a Connecticut law that required brewers and beer importers to affirm that the prices of beer sold to Connecticut wholesalers were no higher than those in three bordering states. The Court held that because the "practical effect" of the statute was "of controlling commercial activity occurring wholly outside the boundary of the State" that it violated the Commerce Clause. See also Edgar v. MITE Corp., 457 U.S. 624, 102 S.Ct. 2629 (1982) (state anti-takeover legislation).

The Commerce Clause does not, however, prohibit all state economic regulation that has some extraterritorial effect. In Pharmaceutical Research and Manufacturers of America v. Walsh, 538 U.S. 644, 123 S.Ct. 1855 (2003), the Supreme Court upheld against a variety of challenges, including one based upon the Commerce Clause, a Maine statute designed to try to provide lower prescription drug prices to uninsured state citizens. The statute authorized state authorities to enter into negotiations with drug manufacturers for rebates to fund reduced drug prices and if no rebate agreement could be reached to require subject the manufacturer's Medicaid drug sales to a "prior authorization" requirement. The Supreme Court distinguished *Healy* on the grounds that the Maine statute, while undoubtedly affecting out-of-state manufacturers, did not attempt to regulate any out-of-state transactions nor did it impermissibly discriminate against out-of-staters. As states begin to be more aggressive in applying their commercial regulations to transactions substantially connected with other states, the chances of running afoul of the dormant commerce clause increase.

In Midwest Title Loans, Inc. v. Mills, 593 F.3d 660 (7th Cir.), cert denied, 131 S.Ct. 83 (2010), the court invalidated an Indiana law that purported to apply Indiana's credit regulations to out-of-state lending transactions as long as the borrower was a forum-state resident and the lender advertised or solicited the loan in Indiana. The court saw the application of Indiana law based solely on these connecting factors as discriminating against out-of-state lenders wishing to serve the Indiana market

Taxation of out-of-state businesses also presents Commerce Clause issues. In Quill Corp. v. North Dakota, 504 U.S. 298, 112 S.Ct. 1904 (1992), the constitutional due process requisites for personal jurisdiction and jurisdiction to tax were equated, but the Commerce Clause was held to require more than "minimum contacts." The result was to invalidate the state use tax on sales of goods by a non-resident business that had no sales force in the state and little tangible property.

CHAPTER 7

THRESHOLD PROBLEMS OF THE FORUM IN CHOICE OF LAW

INTRODUCTORY NOTE

This chapter focuses on four problems that any system for choosing law must resolve. (1) When choice-of-law analysis selects foreign law, under what circumstances should the court or other adjudicating agency (the "forum") reject that law? If the forum rejects the otherwise applicable law, should it dismiss the case without affecting the merits? (2) When and how should the forum take notice of foreign law? (3) When is choice-of-law analysis unnecessary because the issue is "procedural" and therefore properly decided under forum rules without regard to foreign contacts or policies? (4) When should the forum refer to the choice-of-law rules of another jurisdiction?

The materials raise two questions. First, how does a territorial choice-of-law system, which chooses law based on the location of some event in a transaction, deal with these problems? Second, should the treatment of these issues change if the forum abandons a territorial system for one that takes account of the content and purposes of conflicting laws?

SECTION 1. ADMITTING OR REJECTING THE ACTION OR DEFENSE

Loucks v. Standard Oil Co. of New York

Court of Appeals of New York, 1918.
224 N.Y. 99, 120 N.E. 198.

■ CARDOZO, J. The action is brought to recover damages for injuries resulting in death. The plaintiffs are the administrators of the estate of Everett A. Loucks. Their intestate, while traveling on a highway in the state of Massachusetts, was run down and killed through the negligence of the defendant's servants then engaged in its business. He left a wife and two children, residents of New York. A statute of Massachusetts provides that "if a person or corporation by his or its negligence, or by the negligence of his or its agents and servants while engaged in his or its business, causes the death of a person who is in the exercise of due care, and not in his or its employment or service, he or it shall be liable in damages in the sum of not less than $500, nor more than $10,000, to be assessed with reference to the degree of his or its culpability, or that of his or its servants, to be recovered in an action of tort commenced within two years after the injury which caused the death by the executor or administrator of the deceased; one-half thereof to the use of the widow and one-half to the use of the children of the deceased, or if there are no children, the whole to the use of the widow, or if there is no widow, the whole to the use of the next of kin." The question is whether a right of action under that statute may be enforced in our courts.

"The courts of no country execute the penal laws of another" (The Antelope, 10 Wheat. 66, 123, 6 L.Ed. 268). The defendant invokes that principle as applicable here. Penal in one sense, the statute indisputably is. The damages are not limited to compensation; they are proportioned to the offender's guilt. A minimum recovery of $500 is allowed in every case. But the question is not whether the statute is penal in some sense. The question is whether it is penal within the rules of private international law. A statute penal in that sense is one that awards a penalty to the state, or to a public officer in its behalf, or to a member of the public, suing in the interest of the whole community to redress a public wrong. The purpose must be, not reparation to one aggrieved, but vindication of the public justice (Huntington v. Attrill [supra]; Brady v. Daly, [175 U.S. 148, 20 S.Ct. 62, 44 L.Ed. 109]). The Massachusetts statute has been classified in some jurisdictions as penal, and in others as remedial. * * * The courts of Massachusetts have said that the question is still an open one (Boott Mills v. B. & M. R. R., 218 Mass. 582, 592, 106 N.E. 680). No matter how they may have characterized the act as penal, they have not meant to hold that it is penal for every purpose. * * *

We think the better reason is with those cases which hold that the statute is not penal in the international sense. On that branch of the controversy, indeed, there is no division of opinion among us. It is true that the offender is punished, but the purpose of the punishment is reparation to those aggrieved by his offense (Comm. v. B. & A. R. R. Co., 121 Mass. 36, 37; Comm. v. Eastern R. R. Co., 5 Gray, 473, 474). The common law did not give a cause of action to surviving relatives. In the light of modern legislation, its rule is an anachronism. Nearly everywhere, the principle is now embodied in statute that the next of kin are wronged by the killing of their kinsman. * * * They sue to redress an outrage peculiar to themselves.

We cannot fail to see in the history of the Massachusetts statutes a developing expression of this policy and purpose. The statutes have their distant beginnings in the criminal law. To some extent the vestiges of criminal forms survive. But the old forms have been filled with a new content. The purpose which informs and vitalizes them is the protection of the survivors. * * *

Through all this legislation there runs a common purpose. It is penal in one element and one only; the damages are punitive. * * * But the punishment of the wrongdoer is not designed as atonement for a crime; it is solace to the individual who has suffered a private wrong. This is seen in many tokens. The employer may be innocent himself. * * * The executor or administrator who sues under this statute is not the champion of the peace and order and public justice of the commonwealth of Massachusetts.

He is the representative of the outraged family. He vindicates a private right.

Another question remains. Even though the statute is not penal, it differs from our own. We must determine whether the difference is a sufficient reason for declining jurisdiction. A tort committed in one state creates a right of action that may be sued upon in another unless public policy forbids. That is the generally accepted rule in the United States. * * * The question is whether the enforcement of a right of action for tort under the statutes of another state is to be conditioned upon the existence of a kindred statute here. * * *

A foreign statute is not law in this state, but it gives rise to an obligation, which, if transitory, "follows the person and may be enforced wherever the person may be found." "No law can exist as such except the law of the land; but . . . it is a principle of every civilized law that vested rights shall be protected" (Beale, Conflict of Laws, sec. 51). The plaintiff owns something, and we help him to get it. We do this unless some sound reason of public policy makes it unwise for us to lend our aid. "The law of the forum is material only as setting a limit of policy beyond which such obligations will not be enforced there" (Cuba R. R. Co. v. Crosby, [222 U.S. 473–78]). If aid is to be withheld here, it must be because the cause of action in its nature offends our sense of justice or menaces the public welfare.

Our own scheme of legislation may be different. We may even have no legislation on the subject. That is not enough to show that public policy forbids us to enforce the foreign right. A right of action is property. If a foreign statute gives the right, the mere fact that we do not give a like right is no reason for refusing to help the plaintiff in getting what belongs to him. We are not so provincial as to say that every solution of a problem is wrong because we deal with it otherwise at home. Similarity of legislation has indeed this importance: its presence shows beyond question that the foreign statute does not offend the local policy. But its absence does not prove the contrary. It is not to be exalted into an indispensable condition. The misleading word "comity" has been responsible for much of the trouble. It has been fertile in suggesting a discretion unregulated by general principles (Beale, Conflict of Laws, sec. 71). * * * The courts are not free to refuse to enforce a foreign right at the pleasure of the judges, to suit the individual notion of expediency or fairness. They do not close their doors unless help would violate some fundamental principle of justice, some prevalent conception of good morals, some deep-rooted tradition of the common weal.

This test applied, there is nothing in the Massachusetts statute that outrages the public policy of New York. We have a statute which gives a civil remedy where death is caused in our own state. We have thought it so important that we have now embedded it in the Constitution (Const. art. 1, sec. 18). The fundamental policy is that there shall be some atonement for the wrong. Through the defendant's negligence, a resident of New York has been killed in Massachusetts. He has left a widow and children who are also residents. The law of Massachusetts gives them a recompense for his death. It cannot be that public policy forbids our courts to help in collecting what belongs to them. We cannot give them the same judgment that our law would give if the wrong had been done here. Very likely we cannot give them as much. But that is no reason for refusing to give them what we can. We shall not make things better by sending them to another state, where the defendant may not be found, and where suit may be impossible. Nor is there anything to shock our sense of justice in the possibility of a punitive recovery. The penalty is not extravagant. * * * We shall not feel the pricks of conscience if the offender pays the survivors in proportion to the measure of his offense.

We have no public policy that prohibits exemplary damages or civil penalties. We give them for many wrongs. To exclude all penal actions would be to wipe out the distinction between the penalties of public justice and the remedies of private law. * * *

We hold, then, that public policy does not prohibit the assumption of jurisdiction by our courts, and that this being so, mere differences of remedy do not count. * * * We must apply the same rules that are applicable to other torts; and the tendency of those rules today is toward a larger comity, if we must cling to the traditional term. The fundamental public policy is perceived to be that rights lawfully vested shall be everywhere maintained. At least, that is so among the states of the Union (Beach, Uniform Interstate Enforcement of Vested Rights, 27 Yale Law Journal, 656). There is a growing conviction that only exceptional circumstances should lead one of the states to refuse to enforce a right acquired in another. * * * The test of similarity has been abandoned [in Massachusetts]. If it has ever been accepted here, we think it should be abandoned now.

The judgment of the Appellate Division should be reversed, and the order of the Special Term affirmed, with costs in the Appellate Division and in this court.

NOTES

1.   If Judge Cardozo had found that Massachusetts law violated New York public policy, what would he have done? What is the forum to do under Article 21 of the Regulation of the European Parliament and Council on the Law Applicable to Contractual Obligations or Article 26 of the Regulation of the European Parliament and Council on the Law Applicable to Non-Contractual Obligations (Documentary Appendix, infra) if the law specified by the Convention or Regulation is "manifestly incompatible with the public policy of the forum"?

2.   Judge Cardozo's opinion is a classic statement of the "vested rights" theory of choice of law. Under this theory, did the court even consider the possibility that it could apply New York law? After Babcock v. Jackson, p. 577, infra, would a New York court consider that possibility?

In his jurisprudential writings, Judge Cardozo revealed discomfort with the vested rights theory and the rigid territorial choice-of-law rules that it produced: "When I view the conflict of laws as a whole, I find logic to have been more remorseless here, more blind to final causes, than it has been in other fields. Very likely it has been too remorseless." B. Cardozo, The Paradoxes of Legal Science 68 (1928).

Mertz v. Mertz

Court of Appeals of New York, 1936.
271 N.Y. 466, 3 N.E.2d 597, 108 A.L.R. 1120.

■ LEHMAN, JUDGE. The plaintiff has brought an action in this state against her husband to recover damages for personal injuries which, she alleges, she sustained in the state of Connecticut through her husband's negligent operation of an automobile, owned and controlled by him. Under the law of New York the rule is well established that a husband is not liable to his wife for personal injuries caused by his negligence. . . . The complaint alleges that under the law of the state of Connecticut a husband is liable for such injuries. The parties are residents of the state of New York. The problem presented upon this appeal is whether a wife residing here may resort to the courts of this state to enforce liability for a wrong committed outside of the state, though under the laws of this state a husband is immune from such liability. . . .

The Legislature of Connecticut has chosen to remove the common-law disability. There a wife may maintain an action against her husband for damages caused by his wrong, and no exception has been engrafted there upon the general rule that "illegality established, liability ensues." A cause of action for personal injuries is transitory. Liability follows the person and may be enforced wherever the person may be found. Nonetheless, a cause of action arising in one state may be enforced in another state only by the use of remedies afforded by the law of the forum where enforcement is sought. The courts of the state of New York are not concerned with the wisdom of the law of Connecticut or of the internal policy back of that law. They must enforce a transitory cause of action arising elsewhere, unless enforcement is contrary to the law of this state. . . .

"The term 'public policy' is frequently used in a very vague, loose or inaccurate sense. The courts have often found it necessary to define its juridical meaning, and have held that a state can have no public policy except what is to be found in its Constitution and laws. . . . Therefore, when we speak of the public policy of the state, we mean the law of the state whether found in the Constitution, the statutes or judicial records." (People v. Hawkins, 157 N.Y. 1, 12, 51 N.E. 257.)[1] . . . There is nothing in

---

[1] In People v. Hawkins there was an indictment for offering for sale a scrub brush that was convict-made but not so labeled, in violation of a New York statute that required the label. The brush had been made in an Ohio prison and shipped to New York. The Court of Appeals struck down the statute as an unconstitutional interference with freedom of contract. In the passage quoted from Hawkins, the court was referring to an argument that the New York

the opinion in Loucks v. Standard Oil Co. of New York supra, which could indicate that in the field of conflict of laws the "juridical meaning" of the vague concept of public policy is different.

In that case the administrator of a resident of this state who was killed in Massachusetts sued here to recover the damages caused by his death. . . . This court then held only that in such case the courts may not read into the law a limitation created by a supposed public policy, founded on its own notion of expediency and justice. It did not hold that the courts might disregard a limitation, contained in the law of the state, established by authority and tradition, because the court could not discern a sound public policy back of the law.

The law of the forum determines the jurisdiction of the courts, the capacity of parties to sue or to be sued, the remedies which are available to suitors and the procedure of the courts. Where a party seeks in this state enforcement of a cause of action created by foreign law, he can avail himself only of the remedies provided by our law, and is subject to the general limitations which are part of our law. . . . The law of this state attaches to the marriage status a reciprocal disability which precludes a suit by one spouse against the other for personal injuries. It recognizes the wrong, but denies remedy for such wrong by attaching to the person of the spouse a disability to sue. No other state can, outside of its own territorial limits, remove that disability or provide by its law a remedy available in our courts which our law denies to other suitors. * * * A disability to sue which arises solely from the marital status and which has no relation to a definition of wrong or the quality of an act from which liability would otherwise spring may perhaps be an anachronistic survival of a common-law rule. Even then the courts should not transform an anachrony into an anomaly, and a disability to sue attached by our law to the person of a wife becomes an anomaly if another state can confer upon a wife, even though residing here, capacity to sue in our courts upon a cause of action arising there.

The judgment should be affirmed with costs.

■ CROUCH, JUDGE (dissenting) * * * Without pausing to inquire whether the word "jurisdiction" was accurately used, we accept it as a convenient symbol applying to a refusal to enforce a claim created by a foreign law. In approaching the question whether the refusal was justified, certain general principles may be dogmatically stated. The cause of action rests primarily upon the law of Connecticut. If we entertain it, whether we say we are enforcing the original foreign law or a copy of it incorporated in our own rule of conflicts, is immaterial as a practical matter. It is not penal; it is transitory; and our courts will enforce it according to the substantive law of Connecticut unless it "is contrary to the strong public policy" of our own state. Restatement of Law of Conflict of Laws, section 612. We are left,

Constitution forbade sale of convict-made merchandise to the public. Does the quotation on "public policy" given in this context, guide or control its meaning for conflict of laws purposes? —eds.

then, to determine whether the law of Connecticut, which permits a wife to sue a husband for personal injuries, is contrary to some strong public policy of New York.

The public policy concept is a vague and variable phenomenon. When we find it necessary, in a general way, to embody it in words, we are apt to resort to the language used in People v. Hawkins (157 N. Y. 1, 12) and say that "we mean the law of the state, whether found in the Constitution, the statutes or judicial records." We go further, sometimes, and in explanation say that the law so found evidences "the will of the Legislature," Straus & Co. v. Canadian Pacific Ry. Co., 254 N.Y. 407, 413, 173 N.E. 564, 566, and so, perhaps, represents an inarticulate public opinion on the specific matter involved. In that broad sense it may be true to say that back of every law there is something which is conventionally referred to as public policy. Obviously, however, the bulk of public policy, so defined, relates to "minor morals of expediency and debatable questions of internal policy." Hence the difference between our own public policy and that of our sister states is for the most part disregarded by our own law of conflict of laws. * * *

It may be freely conceded that back of the New York rule which withholds from the wife the right to sue the husband for personal injuries is a public policy of the kind which is back of every other rule of law. But neither in the history of the rule nor in its operation is there anything to indicate that that policy is founded upon a definite view—or even upon some vague feeling—that justice or the public welfare would be affected by a contrary rule. * * * It is enough to say that the rule exists merely as a product of judicial interpretation, is vestigial in character, and embodies no tenable policy of morals or of social welfare. To urge that it survives because it is an aid to conjugal peace disregards reality. Conjugal peace would be as seriously jarred by an action for breach of contract, or on a promissory note, or for an injury to property, real or personal, all of which the law permits, as by one for personal injury. In short, even though we assume that there is some shadowy element of policy back of the rule, it should give way to "the controlling public policy . . . that the courts of each State shall give effect to all valid causes of action created by the laws of another State except possibly in extreme cases." Hubbs, J., in Herzog v. Stern, 264 N.Y. 379, 387, 191 N.E. 23, 26. * * *

■ CRANE, C.J., and O'BRIEN, HUBBS, and LOUGHRAN, JJ. concur with LEHMAN, J.

■ CROUCH, J., dissents in opinion, in which FINCH, J., concurs.

Judgment affirmed.

NOTES

1.   What effect on choice of law would result from literal application of Judge Lehman's definition of public policy?

2. Does affirming the trial court's dismissal of the complaint result in a judgment on the merits for the defendant? What difference does it make if the dismissal is not on the merits but simply bars the wife from suing her husband in New York?

3. Does Judge Lehman satisfactorily distinguish Loucks v. Standard Oil of New York?

Intercontinental Hotels Corp.
(Puerto Rico) v. Golden

Court of Appeals of New York, 1964.
15 N.Y.2d 9, 254 N.Y.S.2d 527, 203 N.E.2d 210.

■ BURKE, JUDGE. On this appeal by the plaintiff from a judgment dismissing the complaint, the only issue is whether the courts of this State must deny access to a party seeking to enforce obligations validly entered into in the Commonwealth of Puerto Rico and enforceable under Puerto Rican law.

Plaintiff, the owner and operator of a government-licensed gambling casino in Puerto Rico, seeks to recover the sum of $12,000 evidenced by defendant's check and I.O.U.'s given in payment of gambling debts incurred in Puerto Rico.

Once again we are faced with the question of when our courts may refuse to enforce a foreign right, though valid where acquired, on the ground that its "enforcement is contrary to [the public] policy of the forum" (Straus & Co. v. Canadian Pacific Ry. Co., 254 N.Y. 407, 414, 173 N.E. 564, 567).* * *

Substantially all of the commentators agree that foreign-based rights should be enforced unless the judicial enforcement of such a contract would be the approval of a transaction which is inherently vicious, wicked or immoral, and shocking to the prevailing moral sense. (Beach, Uniform Interstate Enforcement of Vested Rights, 27 Yale L.J. 656, 662; Goodrich, Conflict of Laws [3d ed., 1949], 305; 2 Rabel, Conflict of Laws: A Comparative Study [1947], 555–575; Paulsen and Sovern, "Public Policy" in the Conflict of Laws, 56 Col.L. Rev. 969; 3 Beale, Conflict of Laws [1935], 1649.)

Applying this test we find decisions in this State involving gambling transactions which put this reasoning into practice. Over 100 years ago this court held in Thatcher v. Morris, 11 N.Y. 437 [1854] that a contract involving lottery tickets if legal and valid without the State would be upheld though illegal in New York. In Harris v. White, 81 N.Y. 532 [1880] suit was permitted for wages earned in out-of-state horse races at a time when horse racing was illegal in the State of New York. In Ormes v. Dauchy, 82 N.Y. 443 [1880] suit was upheld for commissions earned by placing extrastate lottery advertisements in out-of-state newspapers. Thus, aware of the common-law rule which barred the enforcement of gambling contracts and conscious that they were illegal and void in almost all the States of this country, the courts of this State took the position, even in Victorian times, that there was no strong public policy to prevent the enforcement of such contracts according to the law of the place of performance. There is nothing suggested by the respondent which should persuade us that Judge Cardozo was wrong when he said in Loucks v. Standard Oil Co. [p. 459, supra]: "The courts are not free to refuse to enforce a foreign right at the pleasure of the judges, to suit the individual notion of expediency or fairness. They do not close their doors, unless help would violate some . . . prevalent conception of good morals".

It has, however, been urged that suits on gambling debts contracted validly elsewhere are contrary to two public policies of this State, i.e., in this jurisdiction gamblers are outlaws, and all gambling contracts made with them are void. Worthy though such considerations be, they apply only to transactions governed by our domestic law. * * *

Public policy is not determinable by mere reference to the laws of the forum alone. Strong public policy is found in prevailing social and moral attitudes of the community. In this sophisticated season the enforcement of the rights of the plaintiff in view of the weight of authority would not be considered repugnant to the "public policy of this State". It seems to us that, if we are to apply the strong public policy test to the enforcement of the plaintiff's rights under the gambling laws of the Commonwealth of Puerto Rico, we should measure them by the prevailing social and moral attitudes of the community which is reflected not only in the decisions of our courts in the Victorian era, but sharply illustrated in the changing attitudes of the People of the State of New York. The legalization of pari-mutuel betting and the operation of bingo games, as well as a strong movement for legalized off-track betting, indicate that the New York public does not consider authorized gambling a violation of "some prevalent conception of good morals [or] some deep-rooted tradition of the common weal." (Loucks v. Standard Oil Co. [p. 459, supra]).

The trend in New York State demonstrates an acceptance of licensed gambling transactions as a morally acceptable activity, not objectionable under the prevailing standards of lawful and approved social conduct in a community. Our newspapers quote the odds on horse races, football games, basketball games and print the names of the winners of the Irish Sweepstakes and the New Hampshire lottery. Informed public sentiment in New York is only against unlicensed gambling, which is unsupervised, unregulated by law and which affords no protection to customers and no assurance of fairness or honesty in the operation of the gambling devices.

In the present case there is no indication that the evils of gambling, which New York prohibits and Puerto Rico has licensed, will spill over into our community if these debts are enforced in New York courts. The New York constitutional provisions were adopted with a view toward protecting the family man of meager resources from his own imprudence at the gaming tables. (See Carter and Stone, Proceedings and Debates of the Convention, 567 [Hosford, 1821].)

Puerto Rico has made provision for this kind of imprudence by allowing the court to reduce gambling obligations or even decline to enforce them altogether, if the court in its discretion finds that the losses are "[in an] amount [which] may exceed the customs of a good father of a family." (Laws of Puerto Rico Ann., tit. 31, § 4774.) This regulation is consistent with New York policy and would be properly considered in any case before a New York court which may be asked to enforce a Puerto Rican gambling debt.

There is nothing immoral per se in the contract before us, but injustice would result if citizens of this State were allowed to retain the benefits of the winnings in a State where such gambling is legal, but to renege if they were losers.

The cases relied on by the respondent miss the mark.

In the case of Mertz v. Mertz [p. 463, supra], Judge Lehman, writing for the court, said that "a disability to sue attached by our law to the person of a wife becomes an anomaly if another state can confer upon a wife, even though residing here, capacity to sue in our courts upon a cause of action arising there". . . . As distinguished from the present case, in Mertz the court was faced with this State's interest in the marital status situated here. As a practical matter, all the significant contacts of the case were with New York and the language of the opinion indicates that the court was in reality there making a choice of law decision of the kind that this court today follows under the nominal heading of the "contacts" doctrine. * * *

We think, therefore, that this case falls within the consistent practice of enforcing rights validly created by the laws of a sister State which do not tend to disturb our local laws or corrupt the public.

Accordingly, the judgment [dismissing the complaint] should be reversed * * *.

■ DESMOND, CHIEF JUDGE (dissenting). * * * The issue: are our courts open to suits by gambling house proprietors who let their customers run up debts; or do such transactions so offend our concept of good morals that our settled public policy prompts us to reject the suit? Closing our doors to such a lawsuit is in principle and under our decisions and statutes the only possible course. It is not a matter of choice of law as between the Puerto Rican and domestic brands. We refuse the suit not because Puerto Rico's law differs from ours but because we cannot in good conscience use our judicial processes to recognize the gamester's claim by giving him a judgment.

We are here asked to enforce a gambling contract, unenforceable at common law and made void and illegal in our State (and almost every other State) under specific statutes (Penal Law, Consol.Laws, c. 40, §§ 991–996). In truth, not one but two public policies of ours are offended when we give judgment for plaintiff. First, operating a gambling business (as distinguished from casual betting between individuals) was an indictable public nuisance at common law, has always been held criminal conduct in New York State, and professional gamblers are "outlaws" in New York. . . . Second, from earliest times in this State all gambling contracts and loans for gambling have been void and denied enforcement by the professional gambler even to the extent that the bettor-customer may sue for the amount he lost (Penal Law, § 994). * * *

The conclusion that settled New York policy bars suit on a claim like this one is not disproved by pointing to our legalization of bingo games and pari-mutuel betting on horse races. The people of the State in amending their Constitution and the legislators in adopting and revising the statutes have found and acted on important differences between those two forms of gambling and the operation of gambling houses. That these differences are widely recognized elsewhere is evident from the fact that while pari-mutuel betting is lawful in 24 States and bingo is legalized in 11 States (lottery in one) nevertheless only one State (Nevada) licenses gambling rooms and even in Nevada gambling-house debts are not suable in court. * * *

NOTES

1.　The court decided the principal case a year and a half after it decided Babcock v. Jackson, p. 577, infra. In *Babcock*, the court referred to the content and purposes of the conflicting laws and decided to apply New York law even though the defendant injured the plaintiff in Ontario. Is the choice-of-law analysis in *Intercontinental Hotels* consistent with *Babcock*? How would the *Babcock* approach require both the majority and the dissent to rewrite their opinions? For an example of such mock opinions, see Weintraub, Choosing Law with an Eye on the Prize, 15 Mich.J.Int'l L. 705, 716–17 (1994).

Phillips v. General Motors Corp., 995 P.2d 1002, 1011 (Mont.2000) adopted the Second Restatement's approach to choice of law in tort cases and stated: "Considerations of public policy are expressly subsumed within the most significant relationship approach. . . . A 'public policy' exception to the most significant relationship test would be redundant." Is it "redundant"? When should a court use public policy to refuse to apply law selected by a process that has already taken account of the content of that law?

In *Loucks*, p. 459, supra, Judge Cardozo assumes that if he refuses on the ground of public policy to apply Massachusetts law, he must dismiss the case. More recently some courts that use public policy to reject foreign law that the forum's choice-of-law rule has chosen have not dismissed, but instead they have applied forum law. See p. 568, Note 2, infra. Is this a proper use of public policy?

In Kuwait Airways Corp. v. Iraqi Airways Co., [2002] 2 AC 883 (2002, appeal from Eng.), the House of Lords rejected Iraqi law that would justify the seizure of aircraft belonging to the Kuwati State. In his opinion, Lord Hope of Craighead noted that the public policy under which the Lords refused to apply Iraqi law was "based on the Charter of the United Nations and the resolutions which were made under it." He stated that "a principle of English public policy which was purely domestic or parochial in character would not provide clear and satisfying grounds for disapplying the primary rule which favours the lex loci delicti."

2.   Professor Lorenzen wrote: "The doctrine of public policy in the Conflict of Laws ought to have been a warning that there was something the matter with the reasoning upon which the rules to which it is the exception were supposed to be based." Lorenzen, Territoriality, Public Policy and the Conflict of Laws, 33 Yale L.J. 736, 747 (1924). For of the argument that a court should use the "public policy" underlying legal rules to choose law rather than to reject law chosen without knowledge of its contents, see Katzenbach, Conflicts on an Unruly Horse: Reciprocal Claims and Tolerances in Interstate and International Law, 65 Yale L.J. 1087 (1956). The reference, in the title, to an "unruly horse," is taken from Judge Burrough's opinion in Richardson v. Mellish, 2 Bing. 229, 252, 130 Eng.Rep. 294, 303 (C.P.1824), in which he rejected the argument that a contract was unenforceable because against public policy and stated: "I for one, protest . . . against arguing too strongly upon public policy;—it is a very unruly horse, and when once you get astride of it, you never know where it will carry you."

3.   The statement at the end of the dissent, that Nevada does not permit suit on gambling debts, is no longer true. Nevada and New Jersey license gambling casinos and allow such actions. Moreover, both states have long-arm statutes creating jurisdiction over tourist gamblers who have left the state. Judgments against gamblers are entitled to full faith and credit. See, e.g., Marina Associates v. Barton, 563 N.E.2d 1110 (Ill.App.1990) (New Jersey judgment for gambling debt); MGM Desert Inn, Inc. v. Holz, 411 S.E.2d 399 (N.C.App. 1991), rev. denied, 417 S.E.2d 790 (N.C.1992) (Nevada judgment). International Recovery Systems Inc. v. Gabler, 527 N.W.2d 20 (Mich.App.1994), refused to enforce a Nevada gambling judgment, erroneously invoking the "public policy" exception of the Uniform Foreign Money-Judgments Act, which applies to foreign countries, not sister states. On rehearing, the court reversed itself. 210 Mich.App. 422 (1995). Puerto Rico, even after it became a commonwealth in 1952, remained a "territory" within the meaning of 28 U.S.C.A. § 1738 and its judgments are entitled to full faith and credit: see Americana of Puerto Rico, Inc. v. Kaplus, 368 F.2d 431 (3d Cir.1966), cert. denied, 386 U.S. 943, 87 S.Ct. 977(1967).

    The Tokyo District Court ordered Japan to reimburse a Nevada gambling casino for money collected in Japan from Japanese who had incurred debts at the casino. The casino's Japanese agents collected the money and were arrested on charges of issuing threats and violating exchange controls. The casino's agents waived any claim to the money, which was deposited in the state treasury. The court stated, "we hold that there is no ground [on the basis of public policy] to exclude the application of the law of Nevada to the contract between the plaintiff and the Japanese tourists." The court limited the holding to the facts of the case—recovery on the basis of unjust enrichment from money having reverted to the state treasury. Desert Palace Inc. v. State of Japan, [1993] H.J. (1444) 41, [1993] H.T. (818) 56; summarized 37 Japanese Annual of Int'l L. 163 (1994).

Even with the advent of modern choice-of-law approaches, the public policy doctrine still plays a prominent role. See, e.g., Saveraid v. State Farm Ins. Co., 597 Fed. Appx. 492 (9th Cir.2015) holding that the insurer's express anti-stacking clause in its policy did not violate a fundamental public policy of the forum.

4.   Is Judge Burke correct in his conclusion that in Mertz v. Mertz the court made a "choice of law" decision—that is, rejected Connecticut's permissive rule and applied New York's rule that one spouse was without capacity to sue the other—rather than that it refused access to the New York courts for Mrs. Mertz' Connecticut-based cause of action? A refusal to entertain an action may leave the plaintiff with the possibility of suit in a different forum, thus serving as a dismissal without prejudice. On the other hand, a choice-of-law decision may preclude further action anywhere.

5.   In a much-cited article, Paulsen & Sovern, "Public Policy" in the Conflict of Laws, 56 Colum.L.Rev. 969 (1956), the authors warned that the use of the concept is especially insidious and dangerous if it is invoked by a forum court that has only slight contacts with the occurrence or the parties. Often, its use in those circumstances has been for parochial reasons—to give protection to interests of residents. They cautioned that the "principal vice of the public policy concepts is that they provide a substitute for analysis."

Holzer v. Deutsche Reichbahn-Gesellschaft

Court of Appeals of New York, 1938.
277 N.Y. 474, 14 N.E.2d 798.

■ PER CURIAM. The complaint alleges two causes of action arising out of a contract between plaintiff, a German national, and Schenker & Co. G. m. b. H., a German corporation, for services to be performed by plaintiff for three years from January 1, 1932, in Germany and in other locations outside this State. Defendants, German corporations, controlled either through stock ownership or otherwise, the transportation system known as Schenker & Co.

Both causes of action allege that the contract provides that "in the event the plaintiff should die or become unable, without fault on his part, to serve during the period of the contract the defendants would pay to him or his heirs the sum of 120,000 marks, in discharge of their obligations, under the hiring aforesaid."

The first cause of action alleges that on June 21, 1933, defendants discharged plaintiff as of October 31, 1933, upon the sole ground that he is a Jew and that as the result of such discharge he was damaged in a sum upwards of $50,000.

The second cause of action alleges that in April, 1933, the German government incarcerated plaintiff in prison and in a concentration camp for about six months, that his imprisonment was not brought about by any act or fault of plaintiff but solely by reason of the policy of the government which required the elimination of all persons of Jewish blood from leading commercial, industrial and transportation enterprises, that as a result "plaintiff became unable, without any fault on his part, to continue his services from the month of April 1933," and has been damaged in the sum of $50,000.

The second separate defense of defendant Deutsche Reichsbahn-Gesellschaft alleges that the contract of hiring was made and was to be performed in Germany, was terminated in Germany and is governed by the laws of Germany, that subsequent to April 7, 1933, the government of Germany adopted and promulgated certain laws, decrees and orders which required persons of non-Aryan descent, of whom plaintiff is one, to be retired.

The Special Term granted plaintiff's motion to strike out this defense, the Appellate Division affirmed and certified these questions: "(1) Is the second separate defense contained in the answer of the defendant, Deutsche Reichsbahn-Gesellschaft, sufficient in law upon the face thereof? (2) Does the complaint herein state facts sufficient to constitute a cause of action?"

The courts of this State are empowered to entertain jurisdiction of actions between citizens of foreign countries or other States of this Union based upon contracts between non-residents to be performed outside this State. . . . Within its own territory every government is supreme (United States v. Belmont, 301 U.S. 324) and our courts are not competent to review its actions. . . . We have so held, "however objectionable" we may consider the conduct of a foreign government. (Dougherty v. Equitable Life Assur. Soc., 266 N. Y. 71, 83.) "Every sovereign state is bound to respect the independence of every other sovereign state, and the courts of one country will not sit in judgment on the acts of the government of another done within its own territory." (Oetjen v. Central Leather Co., 246 U.S. 297, 303.) In the Dougherty case (supra, at p. 90) we have held: "It cannot be against the public policy of this State to hold nationals to the contracts which they have made in their own country to be performed there according to the laws of that country."

Therefore, in respect to the first cause of action, we are bound to decide, as a matter of pleading, that the complaint does not state facts sufficient to constitute a cause of action and that the second separate defense of the answer is sufficient in law upon its face. Defendants did not breach their contract with plaintiff. They were forced by operation of law to discharge him.

In respect to the second cause of action, the result is necessarily different. We are dealing merely with pleadings. Assuming, as alleged, that plaintiff became unable without any fault on his part to continue his services subsequent to April, 1933, that part of the agreement which is alleged to provide "that in the event the plaintiff should die or become unable, without fault on his part, to serve during the period of the contract the defendants would pay to him or his heirs the sum of 120,000 marks, in discharge of their obligations, under the hiring aforesaid," must be interpreted according to German law and the meaning of German words. What that law is depends upon the solution of questions of fact which must be determined on the trial. If the English words "become unable" are a correct translation of the German words employed in the contract, then they would not appear to be limited to inability caused by physical illness but might be intended to apply to any factor which might prevent his service.

The order should be modified by reversing so much thereof as grants plaintiff's motion to strike out the second separate defense in the answer as applied to the first cause of action. It should be affirmed as to the second cause of action and the certified questions answered as follows: (1) As to the first cause of action, "Yes." As to the second cause of action, "No." (2) As to the first cause of action, "No." As to the second cause of action, "Yes."

NOTES

1.   An understandable emotional reaction to the principal case is outrage. The despicable laws openly discriminating against Jews in Hitler's Germany (to say nothing of the Holocaust) were surely worse on any rational moral scale than, for instance, the gambling laws of Puerto Rico that formed the contract enforced in *Golden*. But before you let your emotions cloud your assessment, think about the posture of the principal case vis-à-vis *Golden, Loucks*, and *Mertz*. In those three cases, the defendants were attempting to keep out a cause of action that was alleged to be so alien to New York law that the forum courts would not assist in enforcing it. Who is invoking the public policy doctrine in *Holzer*? Once you notice that it's the plaintiff, you're on your way to understanding the case. Under the territorial, vested rights theory, any cause of action had to be created under German law. As to the first cause of action, did the plaintiff have a cause of action *under German law*?

2.   Suppose instead that the plaintiff were an "Aryan" and German law provided that Aryans were to be paid double what other workers were. The plaintiff alleges that he is an Aryan, but was only paid at the regular rate. He brings this suit in a New York court for the other half of his wages. What result then? If you see the difference between this hypothetical case and the principal case, then you understand the limited role the public policy doctrine played in the territorial, vested rights era.

Tax Claims

In Holman v. Johnson, 1 Cowp. 341, 343 (K.B.1775), Lord Mansfield said: "No country ever takes notice of the revenue laws of another." In 1935, Milwaukee County v. M. E. White Co., p. 394, supra, held that the Full Faith and Credit Clause compelled states to enforce sister-state tax judgments. The opinion stated that it was an "open question" whether an unadjudicated tax claim was subject to similar constitutional compulsion. After a period of chipping away at the old doctrine, state courts have tended to enforce sister states' revenue claims. See, e.g., City of Detroit v.

Gould, 146 N.E.2d 61 (Ill.1957) (personal property tax); State ex rel. Oklahoma Tax Commission v. Rodgers, 193 S.W.2d 919 (Mo.App.1946) (income tax). See also Scoles, Interstate and International Distinctions in Conflict of Laws in the United States, 54 Calif.L.Rev. 1599, 1607–08 (1966).

At least 44 states had enacted reciprocal statutes for enforcement of tax claims. See Greenberg, Extrastate Enforcement of Tax Claims and Administrative Tax Determinations Under the Full Faith and Credit Clause, 43 Bklyn.L.Rev. 630, 642 (1977). Judicial decisions in Nevada and Wyoming have enforced extrastate tax claims without statutory authority while several other states with reciprocal statutes have gone beyond their provisions in enforcing claims. Id. at 643. Is there any likelihood that the doctrine of Hughes v. Fetter, p. 413, supra, compels enforcement of sister-state tax claims in a non-discriminatory way when the forum state itself levies identical taxes?

The "revenue rule" continues to prevent recognition of the tax claims or judgments of foreign countries. An extreme example is Attorney General of Canada v. R.J. Reynolds Tobacco Holdings, Inc., 268 F.3d 103 (2d Cir.2001), which refused to permit Canada to bring an action under the U.S. Racketeer Influenced and Corrupt Organizations Act (RICO) against a cigarette manufacturer and others to recover tax revenue lost and law enforcement costs incurred as the result of an alleged conspiracy to smuggle cigarettes into Canada. Did this refusal undermine any United States policies?

Pasquantino v. United States, 544 U.S. 349, 125 S.Ct 1766 (2005), held that defendants could be prosecuted under the federal wire fraud statute for actions in the U.S. that were part of a scheme to defraud Canada and the Province of Ontario of excise duties and tax revenues applicable to the importation and sale of liquor. The Court stated: "The present prosecution is unlike these classic examples of actions traditionally barred by the revenue rule. It is not a suit that recovers a foreign tax liability, like a suit to enforce a judgment. This is a criminal prosecution brought by the United States in its sovereign capacity to punish domestic criminal conduct." Id. at 362. "[T]his prosecution poses little risk of causing the principal evil against which the revenue rule was traditionally thought to guard: judicial evaluation of the policy-laden enactments of other sovereigns. . . . True, a prosecution like this one requires a court to recognize foreign law to determine whether the defendant violated U.S. law. But we may assume that by electing to bring this prosecution, the Executive has assessed this prosecution's impact on this Nation's relationship with Canada, and concluded that it poses little danger of causing international friction. We know of no common-law court that has applied the revenue rule to bar an action accompanied by such a safeguard. . . ." Id. at 369.

With regard to cases like Attorney General of Canada v. R.J. Reynolds Holdings, supra, the Court stated: "We express no view on the related question whether a foreign government, based on wire or mail fraud predicate offenses, may bring a civil action under the Racketeer Influenced and Corrupt Organizations Act for a scheme to defraud it of taxes." Id. at 354 n.1. A case that the Court remanded for reconsideration in the light of *Pasquantino*, European Community v. RJR Nabisco, Inc., 424 F.3d 175 (2d Cir.2005), cert. denied, 546 U.S. 1092, 126 S.Ct. 1045 (2006), reaffirmed its earlier ruling that various foreign sovereigns could not recover under RICO against cigarette companies that allegedly directed and facilitated the smuggling of contraband cigarettes depriving the plaintiffs of duties and taxes not paid on the cigarettes. The Second Circuit stated: "The present civil lawsuit [unlike *Pasquantino*] is brought by foreign governments, not by the United States. Moreover, the executive branch has given us no signal that it consents to this litigation. * * * In short, the factors that led the *Pasquantino* Court to hold the revenue rule inapplicable to [wire fraud] smuggling prosecutions are missing here." Id. at 181. The Supreme Court later ruled that RICO's private right of action for damages applied only to damages felt in the United States thus denying the member states of the European Community any redress. See RJR Nabisco v. European Community, 136 S.Ct. 2090 (2016).

The United States has ratified the Council of Europe-Organization for Economic Co-Operation and Development Convention on mutual administrative assistance in tax matters, with a reservation that rejects enforcement of another signatory's tax claims. See Andersen, OECD Mutual Assistance Convention to Amplify Members' Tax Treaties, 1 J.Int'l Tax'n 252 (1990).

SECTION 2. NOTICE AND PROOF OF FOREIGN LAW

Notice and proof of foreign law raises two issues. (1) Must one of the parties inform the court that another jurisdiction has law different from that of the forum and persuade the court that it should apply foreign law rather than forum law? (2) Does the forum have an efficient procedure for determining the content of foreign law?

The answer to the first question may depend on the forum's tradition concerning the role of a judge. The common law view, that it is the parties' responsibility to raise and brief issues, contrasts with the civil law maxim "jura novit curia"—"the court knows the law." Nevertheless, as indicated by James v. Powell, p. 482, infra, sometimes a common law court takes an active role in compelling application of foreign law. In France, Germany, the Netherlands, and Belgium courts must apply foreign law on their own motion if the facts indicate that under the forum's choice-of-law rules foreign law controls. See Sofie Geeroms, Foreign Law In Civil Litigation 43–49, 213–16 (2004); Tetley, Mixed Jurisdictions: Common Law v. Civil Law (Codified and Uncodified), 60 La.L.Rev. 677, 713 (2000).

The answer to the second question, as indicated by Note 1, page 482, infra is "yes" in most states. A desirable procedure for determining foreign law has two elements. First and most important, the determination of foreign law should be a task for the judge, not jury, and should be reviewable de novo as a question of law. Second, the method for determining foreign law should minimize expenditures of time and money. The statutory provisions and rules of court for determining foreign law that most states have enacted meet these requirements

Walton v. Arabian American Oil Co.

United States Court of Appeals, Second Circuit, 1956.
233 F.2d 541, cert. denied 352 U.S. 872 (1956).

■ FRANK, CIRCUIT JUDGE. Plaintiff is a citizen and resident of Arkansas, who, while temporarily in Saudi Arabia, was seriously injured when an automobile he was driving collided with a truck owned by defendant, driven by one of defendant's employees. Defendant is a corporation incorporated in Delaware, licensed to do business in New York, and engaged in extensive business activities in Saudi Arabia. Plaintiff's complaint did not allege pertinent Saudi Arabian "law," nor at the trial did he prove or offer to prove it. Defendant did not, in its answer, allege such "law," and defendant did not prove or offer to prove it. There was evidence from which it might have been inferred, reasonably, that, under well-established New York decisions, defendant was negligent and therefore liable to plaintiff. The trial judge, saying he would not take judicial notice of Saudi Arabian "law," directed a verdict in favor of the defendant and gave judgment against the plaintiff.

1.   As jurisdiction here rests on diversity of citizenship, we must apply the New York rules of conflict of laws. It is well settled by the New York decisions that the "substantive law" applicable to an alleged tort is the "law" of the place where the alleged tort occurred.* * *

It has been suggested that, where suit is brought in an American court by an American plaintiff against an American defendant, complaining of alleged tortious conduct by the defendant in a foreign country, and that conduct is tortious according to the rules of the forum, the court, in some circumstances, should apply the forum's tort rules. See Morris, The Proper Law of a Tort, 64 Harv.L.Rev. (1951) 881, criticizing, inter alia, Slater v. Mexican National Railroad, 194 U.S. 120. [p. 264, supra]. There, and in 12 Modern L. Rev. (1949) 248, Morris decries, as "mechanical jurisprudence," the invariable reference to the "law" of the place where the alleged tort happened. There may be much to Morris' suggestion; and a court—particularly with reference to torts where conduct in reliance on precedents is ordinarily absent—should not perpetuate a doctrine which, upon re-examination, shows up as unwise and unjust.* * * But we see no signs that the New York decisions pertinent here are obsolescent.[5]

2.   The general federal rule is that the "law" of a foreign country is a fact which must be proved. However, under [Fed.Rule Civ.Proc.] 43(a), a federal court must receive evidence if it is admissible according to the rules of evidence of the state in which the court sits. At first glance, then, it may seem that the judge erred in refusing to take judicial notice of Saudi Arabian "law" in the light of New York Civil Practice Act, § 344–a.[7] In Siegelman v. Cunard White Star, 2 Cir., 221 F.2d 189, 196–97, applying that statute, we took judicial notice of English "law" which had been neither pleaded nor proved. Our decision, in that respect, has been criticized; but it may be justified on the ground that an American court can easily comprehend, and therefore, under the statute, take judicial notice of, English decisions, like those of any state in the United States.[9] However, where, as here, comprehension of foreign "law" is, to say the least, not easy, then, according to the somewhat narrow interpretation of the New York statute by the New York courts, a court "abuses" its discretion under that statute perhaps if it takes judicial notice of foreign "law" when it is not pleaded, and surely does so unless the party, who would otherwise have had the burden of proving that "law," has in some way adequately assisted the court in judicially learning it. * * *

4.   In argument, plaintiff's counsel asserted that Saudi Arabia has "no law or legal system," and no courts open to plaintiff, but only a dictatorial monarch who decides according to his whim whether a claim like plaintiff's shall be redressed, i.e., that Saudi Arabia is, in effect, "uncivilized." According to Holmes, J.—in Slater v. Mexican National R. Co., 194 U.S. 120, 129, in American Banana Co. v. United Fruit Co., 213 U.S. 347, 355–356, and in Cuba R. Co. v. Crosby, 222 U.S. 473, 478—the lex loci does not apply "where a tort is committed in an uncivilized country" or in one "having no law that civilized countries would recognize as adequate." If such were the case here, we think the New York courts would apply (and therefore we should) the substantive "law" of the country which is most closely connected with the parties and their conduct—in this case, American "law." But plaintiff has offered no data showing that Saudi Arabia is thus "uncivilized." We are loath to and will not believe it, absent such a showing. * * *

---

[5] Were this not a diversity case, it might perhaps be appropriate to suggest that the Supreme Court should reconsider the accepted doctrine (as to the complete dominance of the "law" of the place where the alleged tort occurred) which seems to have been unduly influenced by notions of sovereignty a la Hobbes.

[7] It reads, in part:

"A. Except as otherwise expressly required by law, any trial or appellate court, in its discretion, may take judicial notice of the following matters of law:

"1. A law, statute, proclamation, edict, decree, ordinance, or the unwritten or common law of a sister state, a territory or other jurisdiction of the United States, or of a foreign country or political subdivision thereof. . . ."

[9] * * * An American court may go astray even in taking judicial notice of English "law." The similarity in language may be deceptive by concealing significant differences. * * *

Since the plaintiff deliberately refrained from establishing an essential element of his case, the complaint was properly dismissed. The majority of the court thinks that, for the following reasons, it is inappropriate to remand the case so that the plaintiff may have another chance: He had abundant opportunity to supply the missing element and chose not to avail himself of it. * * * The judgment of dismissal must therefore be affirmed.

The writer of the opinion thinks we should remand for this reason: Apparently neither the trial judge nor the parties were aware of New York Civil Practice Act, § 344–a; consequently, in the interests of justice, we should remand with directions to permit the parties, if they so desire, to present material which may assist the trial judge to ascertain the applicable "law" of Saudi Arabia.

Affirmed.

NOTES

1.   In *Walton*, Judge Frank indicates that if he were free to fashion a choice-of-law rule, he might apply the "American" rule of respondeat superior as the "proper law" of the tort. Instead he decides that under Klaxon Co. v. Stentor Electric Manufacturing Co., 313 U.S. 487, 61 S.Ct. 1020 (1941), p. 746, infra, he must apply New York conflicts rules and he sees "no signs that the New York decisions [applying the law of the place of injury] are obsolescent." This is only five years before Kilberg v. Northeast Airlines, Inc., 9 N.Y.2d 34, 211 N.Y.S.2d 133, 172 N.E.2d 526 (1961), p. 566, infra, avoided the place-of-injury rule and seven years before Babcock v. Jackson, 191 N.E.2d 279 (N.Y.1963), p. 577, infra, supplied a rationale for displacing that rule.

If you were an attorney arguing a case in a state that, like New York at the time of *Walton*, still adhered to a territorial choice-of-law rule, but you wished to argue that the court should adopt a new rule, where would you prefer to make that argument—in a state court or in a federal court sitting in the state? If you would prefer to be in state court, how would you prevent removal to federal court?

Lee Kreindler, the great plaintiffs' air crash attorney, who died in 2003, argued the landmark case of Griffith v. United Air Lines, 203 A.2d 796 (Pa.1964). A Pennsylvania resident boarded the plane in Pennsylvania. The plane crashed on landing in Colorado resulting in the instant death of the passenger. Kreindler brought a suit in a Pennsylvania state court for survival recovery. Under Colorado law there would be no recovery because that law limited survival recovery to lost earnings between injury and death. Under Pennsylvania law survival recovery was the present value of the decedent's future earnings minus support for himself and his dependents— in this case a very large sum.

The Pennsylvania Supreme Court had recently applied the law of the place of injury in a tort case. Kreindler knew that a federal district court would be bound by this recent decision and apply Colorado law. If he could keep the case in state court, when he reached the Pennsylvania Supreme

Court, Kreindler thought that he could persuade the court to depart from the place-of-injury rule and apply Pennsylvania law. But how could he keep United, which was incorporated in Delaware and had a Chicago headquarters, from removing to federal court? He joined as defendants the Pennsylvania-domiciled mechanics who serviced the plane.[2] He then convinced the Pennsylvania Supreme Court to abandon the place-of-injury rule and apply Pennsylvania law. Kreindler, Luncheon Address, American Association of Law Schools Workshop on Conflict of Laws, Program 8032R Tape 10, July 9, 1988.

Many states have statutes or rules of court permitting a federal court to certify to a state supreme court questions of state law on which there are no controlling precedents. Is this certification procedure useful for assisting a federal court in determining whether state precedent is ripe for overruling?

2. Under a choice-of-law system in which a court chooses law taking account of the law's contents and purposes, will the problem of noticing foreign law change? If there are contacts with the forum that are relevant to a policy underlying forum law, should the court apply forum law unless a party who wishes to displace that law establishes that a foreign jurisdiction has different law and that foreign law should displace forum law? If there are no contacts with the forum that are relevant to any policy underlying forum law, does the answer to the preceding question change? For a discussion approving of the result in *Walton* and disagreeing with the argument that forum law should be applied in default of proof of foreign law, see Kramer, Interest Analysis and the Presumption of Forum Law, 56 U.Chi.L.Rev. 1301 (1989).

Leary v. Gledhill
Supreme Court of New Jersey, 1951.
8 N.J. 260, 84 A.2d 725.

[This is an action between two Americans based on an alleged loan of money, which was made in France and which, so it was assumed, was governed by the law of France. At the trial the defendant moved that the action be dismissed because the law of France was neither pleaded nor proved. The action of the trial court in denying the motion was affirmed on appeal.]

■ VANDERBILT, C. J. * * * Under the common law of England as adopted in this country, * * *. the law of other countries, including sister states, would not be . * * * noticed and applied by a court, but it was deemed an issue of fact to be pleaded and proved as other material facts had to be. * * *

The courts, however, were reluctant to dismiss an action for a failure to plead and prove the applicable foreign law as they would have dismissed it for a failure to prove other material facts necessary to establish a cause of action or a defense. Accordingly the courts frequently indulged in one or another of several presumptions: that the common law prevails in the

---

[2]   28 U.S.C. § 1441(b) provides that a case cannot be removed from state court under federal diversity jurisdiction if any defendant is a citizen of the state in which suit is brought.

foreign jurisdiction; that the law of the foreign jurisdiction is the same as the law of the forum, be it common law or statute; or that certain fundamental principles of the law exist in all civilized countries. As a fourth alternative, instead of indulging in any presumption as to the law of the foreign jurisdiction, the courts would merely apply the law of the forum as the only law before the court on the assumption that by failing to prove the foreign law the parties acquiesce in having their controversy determined by reference to the law of the forum, be it statutory or common law. By the application of these various presumptions the courts have in effect treated the common law rule that foreign law could not be noticed but must be pleaded and proved as if it were a matter of fact merely as a permissive rule whereby either party could, if it were to his advantage, plead and prove the foreign law. Thus the failure to plead and prove the foreign law has not generally been considered as fatal. * * *

In the instant case the transaction occurred in France. Our courts may properly take judicial knowledge that France is not a common law, but rather a civil jurisdiction. It would, therefore, be inappropriate and indeed contrary to elementary knowledge to presume that the principles of the common law prevail there. This does not mean, however, that the plaintiff must fail in his cause of action because of the absence of any proof at the trial as to the applicable law of France. In these circumstances any one of the other three presumptions may be indulged in, i.e., that the law of France is the same as the law of the forum; that the law of France, like all civilized countries, recognizes certain fundamental principles, as, e.g., that the taking of a loan creates an obligation upon the borrower to make repayment; that the parties by failing to prove the law of France have acquiesced in having their dispute determined by the law of the forum.

The court below based its decision upon the presumption that the law of France in common with that of other civilized countries recognizes a liability to make repayment under the facts here present, and its decision is not without substantial merit in reason and support in the authorities. The utilization of this presumption has decided limitations, however, for in many cases it would be difficult to determine whether or not the question presented was of such a fundamental nature as reasonably to warrant the assumption that it would be similarly treated by the laws of all civilized countries. The presumption that in the absence of proof the parties acquiesce in the application of the law of the forum, be it statutory law or common law, does not present any such difficulties for it may be universally applied regardless of the nature of the controversy. * * * We are of the opinion, therefore, that in the instant case the rights of the parties are to be determined by the law of New Jersey which unquestionably permits recovery on the facts proven.

NOTES

1. Would any legal obstacle have stood in the way of the *Walton* court's adopting an approach and reaching a conclusion like that in Leary v. Gledhill?

In Cavic v. Grand Bahama Development Co., Limited, 701 F.2d 879 (11th Cir.1983), plaintiffs claimed they had been defrauded in a land sale deal in the Bahamas. Although the land was situated there and the misrepresentations were made there, Bahamian law was not relied on by any of the parties, each of whom "seems to have assumed that Florida [forum] law governs." The court ruled that the law of Florida would be applied.

See also Belanger v. Keydril Co., 596 F.Supp. 823 (E.D.La.1984), aff'd, 772 F.2d 902 (5th Cir.1985) (age discrimination claim arising from alleged wrongful discharge in Zaire was governed by Louisiana law in the absence of a showing that Zaire law differed); Alameda Films S A De C V. Authors Rights Restoration Corp., 331 F.3d 472, 481 (5th Cir.2003): "When there are gaps in foreign law . . . a U.S. court may use forum law to fill them."

2. In an action arising out of an intersection collision in Nuremberg, Germany, both sides agreed that New York law would be applied. The plaintiff asked the district court to charge the jury that the New York Vehicle and Traffic Law required the defendant to slow down when approaching an intersection. The court refused and the Second Circuit affirmed, stating: "It is unlikely . . . in a case arising out of an accident in Germany, that the courts would add the statutory refinements to the standard of care to include the apparent slight extra duty of care in approaching intersections. Although New York law may be applicable in the absence of proof of German law, strict statutory refinements in New York should not be held binding as the standard of care for operation of a vehicle in Germany." Loebig v. Larucci, 572 F.2d 81, 86 (2d Cir.1978).

Curley v. AMR Corp., 153 F.3d 5 (2d Cir.1998). Plaintiff was a passenger on a flight from the United States to Mexico. On landing, airline employees informed Mexican police that they suspected plaintiff had smoked marijuana during the flight. Plaintiff was strip searched and released. Plaintiff then sued the airline in federal district court in New York. The Second Circuit reversed the district court's determination that New York law applied, held that Mexican law applied, and, applying Mexican law, affirmed the district court's summary judgment for defendant. One of the reasons the district court gave for not applying Mexican law was that "defendant has not presented us with a sufficiently comprehensive statement of Mexican law to permit us to act upon it with confidence." The Second Circuit agreed that the parties' presentations of Mexican law were insufficient, requested further briefings by both sides after oral argument, and conducted its own research into Mexican law, stating that "appellate courts, as well as trial courts, may find and apply foreign law." The Second Circuit also stated that the district court "need not have avoided a full analysis of Mexican law simply on the basis of an inadequate submission by one party" and called attention to the provision in Fed. Rule Civ. Proc. 44.1, p. 482, Note 1, infra, that allows district courts to determine foreign law by considering "any relevant material or source, including testimony, whether or not submitted by a party or admissible under the Federal Rules of Evidence."

3. In a contest in the New York courts over succession to funds in a New York joint bank account opened by a husband and wife domiciled in France, the issue turned on the res judicata effects of a prior French judgment involving the same underlying controversy. Neither side pleaded or offered to rely on the French rules of res judicata, either assuming or agreeing that the preclusive effect of the judgment in France would be the same as a similar New York judgment would enjoy at home. In ascribing "New York" effect to the judgment, the court explained its acceptance of the litigants' submission on the basis that "under modern principles, in the absence of a manifest injustice, a failure to raise or prove foreign law, without objection, should not inevitably prevent the application of forum law. In theory and effect the parties have consented that the forum law be applied to the controversy." Watts v. Swiss Bank Corp., 27 N.Y.2d 270, 276, 265 N.E.2d 739, 743 (1970).

RESTATEMENT, SECOND, CONFLICT OF LAWS:

§ 136. Notice and Proof of Foreign Law

(1) The local law of the forum determines the need to give notice of reliance on foreign law, the form of notice and the effect of a failure to give such notice.

(2) The local law of the forum determines how the content of foreign law is to be shown and the effect of a failure to show such content.

NOTES

1. Most states have statutes or rules of court that provide a procedure for a court to determine the law of other states and foreign countries. The Michigan statute is typical:

> Mich.Comp.L.Ann.ch. 600 § 2114a: "A party who intends to raise an issue concerning the law of any jurisdiction or governmental unit thereof outside this state shall give notice in his pleadings or other reasonable written notice. In determining the law of any jurisdiction or governmental unit thereof outside this state, the court may consider any relevant material or source, including testimony, whether or not submitted by a party or admissible under the rules of evidence. The court, not jury, shall determine the law of any governmental unit outside this state. Its determination is subject to review on appeal as a ruling on a question of law."

The Federal Rules of Civil Procedure contain a similar provision:

> Fed.Rule Civ.Proc. 44.1: "A party who intends to raise an issue about a foreign country's law must give notice by a pleading or other writing. In determining foreign law, the court may consider any relevant material or source, including testimony, whether or not submitted by a party or admissible under the Federal Rules of Evidence. The court's determination must be treated as a ruling on a question of law"

The Advisory Committee Notes on 44.1 state: "There is no requirement that the court give formal notice of its intention to engage in its own research on an issue of foreign law which has been raised by them, or of its intention to raise and determine independently an issue not raised by them. Ordinarily the court should inform the parties of material it has found diverging substantially from the material which they have presented; and in general the court should give the parties an opportunity to analyze and counter new points upon which it proposes to rely."

2. Amiot v. Ames, 693 A.2d 675 (Vt.1997), holds that when the determination of a fact issue controls choice of law, the trial judge and not the jury should determine the fact. A Canadian motorist sued a Vermont motorist for injuries sustained in an automobile collision in Canada just across the Québec-Vermont border. A Québec statute limited the plaintiff to an administrative remedy, but he could sue for damages under Vermont law. The court adopted the "most significant relationship" approach to choice of law for torts. Under the court's view of this approach, a crucial fact was the place where defendant's negligent conduct occurred. The parties disputed whether the cause of the accident was defendant's failure to take insulin in Vermont. The court stated: "Reserving choice-of-law issues for determination by a jury at trial not only raises the problems [of how to instruct the jury], it also precludes the efficient disposal of cases through motions to dismiss or for summary judgment...." Contra Marra v. Bushee, 447 F.2d 1282 (2d Cir.1971), holding that the defendant was entitled to a jury's finding of facts that would control choice of law. The court reversed and remanded for a new trial after the trial judge had made the factual determination.

3. Foreign governments frequently submit statements regarding their law in cases that involve application of their law. Animal Sci. Prods. v. Hebei Welcome Pharm. Co., 138 S.Ct. 1865 (2018), involved an antitrust case against four Chinese manufacturers of Vitamin C, accusing them of price-fixing. The Chinese manufacturers defended on the ground that Chinese law required them to set their prices at the same amount. The Chinese government filed a statement of interest to the effect that Chinese law did require the defendants to set their prices equally. The Second Circuit held that China's statement regarding its own law was conclusive, but a unanimous Supreme Court reversed. It said that while the foreign government's statement was entitled to "respectful consideration," it was inconsistent with F.R.C.P. 44.1 to give it conclusive effect, and that other sources must be weighed in determining foreign law.

SECTION 3. USE OF THE FORUM'S "PROCEDURAL" RULES

When a court labels a rule "procedural" for choice-of-law purposes, the court applies local law without further analysis and without reference to the content or purposes of the rule of another jurisdiction on the same issue. What justifies such insistence on local law? Two variables affect the answer—the difficulty of finding and applying the foreign rule and the likelihood that the forum's rule will change the outcome in a manner that induces forum shopping. The more inconvenient it would be to find and apply a foreign rule and the less likely it is that the rule will affect the result, the greater the justification for a "procedural" label. Examples of procedural rules under this analysis are the proper methods of pleading the action and of preserving objections during trial. Of course even these rules may "affect the result" if a party does not obey them. Neither party, however, is likely to obtain any tactical advantage by application of forum rather than foreign rules on these issues, and local judges and lawyers will avoid the effort of learning and applying the foreign law. On the other hand, the easier it is to find and apply the foreign rule and the greater the likelihood that the rule will affect the result, the greater the justification for a complete choice-of-law analysis before deciding whether to apply that rule.

As the materials in this section indicate, under traditional conflict-of-laws analysis, many rules that were easy to find and apply, and that had high potential for affecting the result, were nevertheless labeled as "procedural." The increased emphasis on the content and purposes of local and foreign rules, which has changed many traditional choice-of-law rules, is also affecting what rules courts regard as "procedural."

A. QUANTIFICATION OF DAMAGES

Harding v. Wealands

House of Lords, 2006.
[2006] UKHL 32.

[Mr. Harding, an Englishman, and Ms. Wealands, an Australian, formed a relationship in Australia. She came to England to live with him. Ms. Wealands returned to Australia to attend a family wedding. He later joined her for a holiday and to visit her parents. While she was driving in New South Wales (NSW) with Mr. Harding as a passenger, she lost control and the car turned over. He was badly injured and is tetraplegic. Ms. Wealands owned the vehicle and carried liability insurance issued by an Australian company. Both Mr. Harding and Ms. Wealands returned to England.

A NSW statute places limits on compensation for various damages including lost earnings and non-economic damages, and in other ways restricts recovery. Under NSW law the plaintiff would recover about 30% less than under English law. Part III of the United Kingdom Private International Law Act abolishes the double actionability choice-of-law rule for torts[3] and creates a presumption that that the law of the place of injury governs unless it is "substantially more appropriate" to apply some other law. Section 14(3)(b) states that the statute does not authorize "questions of procedure in any proceedings to be determined otherwise than in accordance with the law of the forum."

Mr. Harding sued Ms. Wealands in the High Court of Justice in London. That court ruled that English law determined the damages. The judge gave two reasons: (1) damages were "procedural"; (2) even if

---

[3]   The double actionability rule stated that in order for a tort to be actionable in an English court it had to be actionable under both the law of the English forum and the law of the place of wrong. —eds.

damages were substantive it was "substantially more appropriate" to apply English law. The Court of Appeal allowed the appeal and applied Australian law. The three justices were agreed that it was not more appropriate to apply English law, but one justice considered the NSW statutory limits on recovery as "procedural" and therefore not applicable in England. The House of Lords, five Law Lords participating, unanimously allowed the appeal and restored the judgment of the trial court on the ground that damages were procedural.]

LORD HOFFMAN

My Lords, the issue is whether damages for personal injury caused by negligent driving in New South Wales should be calculated according to the applicable law selected in accordance with Part III of the Private International Law (Miscellaneous Provisions) Act 1995 ("Part III") or whether it is a question of procedure which falls to be determined in accordance with English law. * * *

Mr Haddon-Cave, who appeared for the claimant, said that if the House thought that the language of section 14 ["procedure"] was ambiguous or obscure, it should resolve the ambiguity by reference to a statement made in Parliament by the Lord Chancellor during the passage of the Bill. For my part, I do not think that there is any ambiguity or obscurity. Of course, taken out of context, the word "procedure" is ambiguous. In its narrow and perhaps most usual sense it means, as La Forest J expressed it in *Tolofson v Jensen* [1994] 3 SCR 1022, 1072 [Supreme Court of Canada] those rules which "make the machinery of the forum court run smoothly as distinguished from those determinative of the rights of both parties." Or it can have a wider meaning which embraces what Mason CJ in *Stevens v Head* (1993) 176 CLR 433, 445 [High Court of Australia] called "the traditional equation drawn between matters relating to a remedy and matters of procedure." This is the sense it which the term has always been used in English private international law. If section 14 is read in its context, against the background of the existing rules of common law and the report of the Law Commission [which preceded the enactment of the Private International Law Act], there can be no doubt that the latter meaning was intended. For my part, therefore, I see no need for Mr Haddon-Cave to resort to Hansard [report of proceedings in Parliament].

If, however, there had been any ambiguity which needed to be resolved, I am bound to say that this is as clear a case . . . as anyone could hope to find. At the Report stage in the House of Lords, Lord Howie of Troon put down an amendment to add a further paragraph to what is now section 14(3), so that it would read: "[nothing in this Part] (d) authorises any court of the forum to award damages other than in accordance with the law of the forum." Lord Howie declared an interest on behalf of Cape Industries plc, which had a few years earlier been sued in Texas for asbestos-related injuries and was anxious that Part III should not import American scales of compensation into English courts.

In the debate on 27 March 1995 Lord Mackay of Clashfern LC [Lord Chancellor] made what was obviously a carefully prepared statement:

> With regard to damages, issues relating to the quantum or measure of damages are at present and will continue under Part III to be governed by the law of the forum; in other words, by the law of one of the three jurisdictions in the United Kingdom. Issues of this kind are regarded as procedural and, as such, are covered by clause 14(3)(b). It follows from this that the kind of awards to which the noble Lord referred of damages made in certain states, in particular in parts of the United States, will not become a feature of our legal system by virtue of Part III. Our courts will continue to apply our own rules on quantum of damages even in the context of a tort case where the court decides that the "applicable law" should be some foreign system of law so far as concerns the merits of the claim. Some aspects of the law of damages are not regarded as procedural and, in accordance with the views of the Law Commissions in their report on the subject, Part III does not alter this. These aspects concern so-called "heads of damages"—the basic matter which is being compensated for—such as special damage relating to direct financial loss. Whether a particular legal system permits such a head of damage is not regarded as procedural but substantive and therefore not automatically subject to the law of the forum. This seems right given the intimate connection between such a concept and the particular nature of the case in issue. But again, I foresee no significant increase in awards of damages because a particular head of damage permitted by some foreign system of law would continue, so far as the quantum allocated to it in any finding is concerned, to be regulated by our own domestic law of damages. I hope the noble Lord will feel reassured.

* * * My Lords, the next question is whether the provisions of [the NSW statute that imposes limits on damages] should be characterised as relating to the actionability of the economic and non-economic damage suffered by Mr. Harding or to the remedies which the courts of New South Wales provide for such damage. On this point we could not have better authority than that of the High Court of Australia in *Stevens v Head* 176 CLR 433. The majority (Brennan, Dawson, Toohey and McHugh JJ) analysed the equivalent damages-limitation provisions of the Motor Accidents Act 1988 and concluded that they were concerned with quantification rather than heads of damage. Although [the current NSW legislation] is more restrictive of the court's power to award damages than the 1988 Act, the character of the relevant provisions is in my opinion the same. * * *

[Three judges dissented in *Stevens v. Head*.] But there is nothing in the dissenting judgments by Mason CJ and Deane and Gaudron JJ to suggest that, if they had accepted that the court should apply the traditional distinction between actionability and remedy, including quantification of damages, they would have disagreed with the way the majority characterised the provisions of the 1988 Act. It was the traditional distinction itself which the minority rejected. Thus Mason CJ proposed that the court should adopt "a new criterion for the substance-procedure distinction which . . . characterise[s] as procedural 'those rules which are directed to governing or regulating the mode or conduct of court proceedings.' All other provisions or rules are to be classified as substantive." * * *

But Mr Palmer, who appeared for the defendant [in this case] submitted that in English private international law a limit or "cap" on the damages recoverable is regarded as substantive. There is, it is true, some authority for this proposition. The 7th edition (1958) of Dicey's Conflict of Laws edited by Dr. JHC Morris, contained the statement, at p 1092, "statutory provisions limiting a defendant's liability are prima facie substantive; but the true construction of the statute may negative this view." * * *

In my opinion the proposition in Dicey was too widely stated. *Cope v Doherty* [(1858) 4 K & J 367, which Dicey cites] is authority for the proposition that a contractual term which limits the obligation to pay damages for a breach of contract or a tort, or a statutory provision which is deemed to operate as such a term, qualifies the substantive obligation. It is not part of the rules of the lex fori for the assessment of damages. * * *

There is accordingly in my opinion no English authority to cast any doubt upon the conclusion of the Australian High Court in *Stevens v Head* that, for the purposes of the traditional distinction between substance and procedure which treats remedy as a matter of procedure, all the provisions of [the Australian legislation], including limitations on quantum, should be characterised as procedural. * * * In *John Pfeiffer Pty Ltd v Rogerson* (2000) 203 CLR 503, however, the High Court reversed itself, abandoned the traditional rule (at least for torts committed in Australia) and confined the role of the leges fori of the Australian states to procedure in the narrow sense of rules "governing or regulating the mode or conduct of court proceedings." This change was said to be required by constitutional imperatives of Australian federalism. In a later decision (*Regie Nationale des Usines Renault SA v Zhang* (2002) 210 CLR 491, 520, para 76) the court left open the question of whether it would apply to foreign torts. But the decision in the *Pfeiffer* case clearly influenced the judgments of the majority in the Court of Appeal in this case. * * *

There can however be no doubt about the general rule, stated by Lord Mackay in the House of Lords debate, that "issues relating to the quantum or measure of damages" are governed by the lex fori. And this was the rule which Parliament intended to preserve.

Even if there appeared to be more logic in the principle in *Pfeiffer's* case . . . the question is not what the law should be but what Parliament thought it was in 1995. * * *

In my opinion, therefore, Elias J [the High Court trial judge] was right to treat the [NSW statutory] restrictions as entirely inapplicable. In the circumstances it is unnecessary to decide whether, if they had been properly characterised as substantive, it was open to the Court of Appeal to reverse his judgment that it was substantially more appropriate to apply English law. The hypothesis necessary to raise this question is in my view somewhat artificial, because most of the reasons why it may be more appropriate to apply English law are the reasons why the assessment of damages is traditionally characterised as a matter for the lex fori. I would therefore prefer not to express a view on this question. In my opinion the appeal should be allowed and the judgment of Elias J restored.

LORD ROGER OF EARLSFERRY

* * * The passage which Lord Hoffmann has quoted from the Hansard report of the speech of Lord Mackay of Clashfern LC in reply to the probing amendment in the name of Lord Howie of Troon, confirms the construction which I would, in any event, have placed on the words in section 14(3)(b). But more importantly, perhaps, it shows that Parliament was assured that the provision would prevent damages being awarded by reference to the law and standards of other countries. The particular problem raised by Lord Howie related to the high level of damages in the United States which he was anxious should not be replicated here. But it would be equally unacceptable if, say, United Kingdom courts had to award damages according to a statutory scale which, while adequate in another country because of the relatively low cost of services etc. there, would be wholly inadequate in this country, having regard to the cost of the corresponding items here. As Parliament was assured by the Lord Chancellor, section 14(3)(b) guards against such eventualities. The interpretation advocated by the defendant would undermine the basis on which Parliament legislated. * * *

LORD WOOLF

* * * The limits on the amount of damages on which the defendant seeks to rely are contained in the Motor Accidents Compensation Act 1999 of New South Wales. That Act contains in Chapters 3, 4, 5 and 6 a detailed statutory procedural code containing the machinery for recovering compensation for motor accident injuries, including the way damages are to be assessed. The code is clearly one that has provisions which it would be very difficult, if not impossible, to apply in proceedings brought in this country, even though they may be capable of being applied in other parts of Australia. To have different parts of that code dealt with by different systems of law would not be an attractive result and in some cases this would produce an impractical result. (See for example section 132 which requires, in the case of a dispute over non

economic loss, for the degree of impairment to be assessed by a medical assessor in New South Wales.) The greater part of the code is clearly procedural and those parts which could be arguably regarded as substantive should be treated as being procedural as well. * * *

NOTES

1.   The excerpt from the Parliamentary proceedings quoted by Lord Hoffman focuses on avoiding introducing "American scales of compensation into English Courts." Does this policy also apply to rejecting statutory limits on damages that would reduce recovery below the English standard? Lord Roger of Earlsferry addresses this distinction. Does his opinion support treating the NSW limits on recovery as procedural? Does his opinion support applying English law as the substantive law that is "substantially more appropriate" in the light of England's contacts with the parties? Does the fact that Ms. Wealands carried liability insurance issued by an Australian company detract from the appropriateness of applying English law?

2.   Lord Hoffman cites the opinion of the High Court of Australia in Stevens v. Head as precedent for his procedural characterization of the NSW statutory limitations on damages. Lord Hoffman notes that the High Court of Australia overruled Stevens v. Head in John Pfeiffer Pty Ltd. v. Rogerson, but he dismisses this overruling as "required by constitutional imperatives of Australian federalism." *Pfeiffer* states:

> Within a federal nation such as Australia, the capacity of a party to legal proceedings to choose the forum within which to bring such proceedings can be one of the advantages of the interconnected polity. However, such a facility ought not to involve the capacity of one party seriously to prejudice the legal rights of an opponent. * * *
>
> It may be reasonable to recognise the right of a litigant to choose different courts in the one nation by reason of their advantageous procedures, better facilities or greater expedition. However, it is not reasonable that such a choice, made unilaterally by the initiating party, should materially alter that party's substantive legal entitlements to the disadvantage of its opponents. If this could be done, the law would no longer provide a certain and predictable norm, neutrally applied as between the parties. Instead, it would afford a variable rule which particular parties could manipulate to their own advantage. Such a possibility would be obstructive to the integrity of a federal nation, the reasonable expectations of those living within it and the free mobility of people, goods and services within its borders upon the assumption that such movement would not give rise to a significant alteration of accrued legal rights.

203 C.L.R. 552–53.

Does this statement from *Pfeiffer* express a peculiar requirement of the Australian Constitution or does it reflect sound general choice-of-law principles?

3.   United States courts have treated statutory limits on recovery as substantive. See, e.g., Marmon v. Mustang Aviation, 430 S.W.2d 182, 194 (Tex.1968) (applying Colorado statutory limit on wrongful death recovery). Some cases have treated as substantive a court's statement of a limit on recovery. See Cunningham v. Quaker Oats Co., 107 F.R.D. 66, 73 (W.D.N.Y.1985), which treats as substantive a statement by the Supreme Court of Canada that $100,000 should be the upper limit of non-pecuniary damages. Subsequent cases have adjusted this amount for inflation.

4.   On 10 July 2007 the European Parliament voted to adopt a Regulation on the Law Applicable to Non-Contractual Obligations (Rome II), Regulation (EC) No. 864/2007 of 11 July 2007, OJ 2007 L199/40. The Regulation contains the following provisions:

> Article 1(3):
>
> This Regulation shall not apply to evidence and procedure, without prejudice to Articles 21 [choice of law for the formal validity of a unilateral act relating to a non-contractual obligation] and 22 [Regulation's choice-of-law provisions apply to "rules which raise presumption of law or determine the burden of proof"].
>
> Article 15: Scope of the Law Applicable:
>
> The law applicable to non-contractual obligations under this Regulation shall govern in particular ... (c) the existence, the nature and the assessment of damage or the remedy claimed.

Do these provisions abrogate the rule that quantification of damages is procedural? The United Kingdom has agreed to be bound by Rome II, although now that the U.K. has left the European Union presumably it will revert to the rule in the principal case.

In 2008 the European Parliament adopted a Regulation on the Law Applicable to Contractual Obligations (Rome I), to replace the "Rome" Convention. Rome I, art. 15(c), unlike Rome II, retains the language of art. 10(c) of the Rome Convention and includes in the scope of Rome I "the assessment of damages in so far as it is governed by rules of law." Do the words "in so far as it is governed by rules of law" refer to a statute or a court decision placing a specific limit on a head of damages but treat other aspects of quantification of damages as "procedural" to be determined by forum standards? In their report of October 31, 1980 to the European Council on the Rome Convention, Mario Giuliano and Paul Lagarde explain the use of "in so far as it is governed by rules of law." OJ C 282/1 at 33. They state:

> The assessment of damages has given rise to some difficulties. According to some delegations the assessment of the amount of damages is a question of fact and should not be covered by the Convention. To determine the amount of damages the court is obliged to take account of economic and social conditions in its country; there are some cases in which the amount of damages is fixed by a jury; some countries use methods of calculation which might not be accepted in others.

Other delegations countered these arguments, however, by pointing out that in several legal systems there are rules for determining the amount of damages; some international conventions fix limits as to the amount of compensation (for example, conventions relating to carriage); the amount of damages in case of non-performance is often prescribed in the contract and grave difficulties would be created for the parties if these amounts had to be determined later by the court hearing the action.

By way of compromise the Group finally decided to refer in subparagraph (c) solely to rules of law in matters of assessment of damages, given that questions of fact will always be a matter for the court hearing the action.

Does this commentary indicate that the words "in so far as it is governed by rules of law" refer to the procedural/substantive distinction or to the fact/law distinction? Are of the objections referred to in the commentary to extending Rome I's scope to all aspects of quantification of damages cogent?

5. In the absence of a statutory or judicially-declared limit, quantification of damages is typically regarded as procedural and governed by forum law. See Restatement (Second) § 171, cmt. f (stating that "[t]he forum will follow its own local practices in determining whether the damages awarded by a jury are excessive").

A few cases have rejected this procedural characterization. Archuleta v. Valencia, 871 P.2d 198 (Wyo.1994) applied Colorado law "in determining whether the jury's verdict was inadequate as a matter of law." The dissent argued that the issue was procedural and should be governed by Wyoming law. Without discussing the contrary standard rule, Karim v. Finch Shipping Co., 265 F.3d 258 (5th Cir.2001), held that the law of Bangladesh determined the quantification of damages for pain and suffering. Bhatnagar v. Surrendra Overseas Ltd., 52 F.3d 1220 (3d Cir.1995), also without discussing the standard rule, vacated an award of non-pecuniary damages and ordered that they be reassessed in accordance with Indian law. Cf. John Pfeiffer Pty. Ltd. v. Rogerson, 172 A.R. 625, 651 (Austl.2000) ("*all* questions about the kinds of damage, or amount of damages that may be recovered, would likewise be treated as substantive issues governed by the lex loci delicti") (emphasis in original).

6. Louisiana, Wisconsin, and Puerto Rico have statutes that permit a person injured by the fault of another to bring a direct action against the tortfeasor's liability insurance company. Most courts have dismissed suits under the direct action statute of another jurisdiction on the ground that this remedy is "procedural" and therefore is available only if the forum has such a statute. See Noe v. United States Fidelity & Guaranty Co., 406 S.W.2d 666 (Mo.1966), which refuses suit under the Louisiana statute and discusses rulings on the issue in other jurisdictions. Instead of treating the issue as one of substance or procedure, New York and Illinois courts have ruled on whether permitting suit under another jurisdiction's direct action statute would be contrary to the forum's public policy. Oltarsh v. Aetna Ins. Co., 204 N.E.2d 622 (N.Y.1965), permitted suit under the Puerto Rico statute.

Marchlik v. Coronet Ins. Co., 239 N.E.2d 799 (Ill.1968), rejected suit under the Wisconsin statute. Which approach, substance/procedure or public policy, is preferable for ruling on the issue?

7.   Does forum law determine recovery of attorneys' fees? In Mitzel v. Westinghouse Electric Corp., 72 F.3d 414 (3d Cir.1995), a Pennsylvania law firm was admitted pro haec vice to federal district court in New Jersey to represent a Pennsylvania worker injured in New Jersey. The firm's contingent fee agreement was proper under Pennsylvania law, but excessive under New Jersey law. The court held that New Jersey law applied either as a procedural rule adopted by the federal court or as substantive law to protect New Jersey's "paramount concern with its courts." Arno v. Club Med Boutique, Inc., 134 F.3d 1424 (9th Cir.1998), held that although French law applied to liability for sexual assault abroad, California law prevented holding the defendant liable for the plaintiff's attorney's fees. The plaintiff would have recovered the fees under French law. The court distinguished Cutler v. Bank of America National Trust & Savings Ass'n, 441 F.Supp. 863 (N.D.Cal.1977), which applied English law to permit plaintiff to recovery attorney's fees. The opinion in that case characterized the fee-shifting rule as integrally related to England's law of tort compensation. Under English law punitive damages were not available and the level of compensatory damages was low compared with California recoveries.

B. PRESUMPTIONS AND BURDEN OF PROOF

Shaps v. Provident Life & Accident Insurance Co.
Supreme Court of Florida, 2002.
826 So.2d 250.

[In 1987, while residing and working in New York, Ms. Shaps successfully applied to Provident Life & Accident for a disability insurance policy. In July, 1989, Ms. Shaps requested disability benefits asserting that she was unable to work because of pain in her jaw. The insurer paid benefits until September 1990. In October, 1990 the insurer sent a letter to Ms. Shaps stating that it had discontinued payment because "there is no evidence of continuous total disability as defined by your policy." In 1990 Ms. Shaps moved to Florida. In 1995, Ms. Shaps sued the insurer in a Florida State court. The insurer removed the case to federal district court. In early 1996 Ms. Shaps moved to California.

One issue at trial was whether Ms. Shaps or the insurer had the burden of proof on the issue of whether Ms. Shaps was no longer disabled when the insurer stopped paying benefits. Under New York law Ms. Shaps had the burden; under Florida law, the burden was on the insurance company. All parties agreed that New York law applied to determine substantive issues, but disagreed as to whether the burden of proof was "procedural." The trial court charged the jury under New York law. The jury found that Ms. Shaps was not disabled and she appealed.[4]]

■ QUINCE, J.

We have for review two questions of Florida law certified by the United States Court of Appeals for the Eleventh Circuit as determinative of a cause pending before that court and for which there appears to be no controlling precedent. * * * :

(1) Is the burden of proof rule recognized in [Florida cases] part of the substantive law of Florida, such that it would not be applied in a case where under Florida's law of lex loci contractus the substantive law of another state (New York) governs the parties' contract dispute?

(2) Would requiring the insured to prove disability violate the public policy of Florida, such that the burden of proof must be placed on the insurer?

As explained below, we answer the first certified question in the negative and decline to reach the second certified question.* * *

[T]he issue as it relates to the certified question is whether in Florida the burden of proof is procedural or substantive for conflict-of-laws purposes.

Although no Florida case has squarely addressed this issue, generally in Florida the burden of proof is a procedural issue. See Walker & LaBerge, Inc. v. Halligan, 344 So.2d 239, 243 (Fla.1977) ("Burden of proof requirements are procedural in nature"); Ziccardi v. Strother, 570 So.2d 1319, 1321 (Fla. 2d DCA 1990) (modification of the burden of proof in a statute did not amount to substantive change in the law). This Court has explained, "[S]ubstantive law prescribes duties and rights and procedural law concerns the means and methods to apply and enforce those duties and rights." Alamo Rent-A-Car, Inc. v. Mancusi, 632 So.2d 1352, 1358 (Fla.1994). The burden of proof clearly concerns the means and methods to apply and enforce duties and rights under a contract and we find no reason to depart from this general rule for conflict-of-laws purposes.

Accordingly, we find that in Florida the burden of proof is a procedural issue for conflict-of-laws purposes and answer the first certified question in the negative. * * *

NOTES

1. Under the standards proposed in the Note introducing this section, p. 483, supra, should burden of proof be "procedural" for choice-of-law purposes? The two cases cited by the court for its procedural classification, *Walker & LaBerge* and *Ziccardi* characterized burden of proof as "procedural" in the context of

---

[4] Some of the facts are taken from Shaps v. Provident Life & Accident Ins. Co., 244 F.3d 876 (11th Cir.2001) and from defendant's Answer Brief in that case. —eds.

whether a court could constitutionally apply retroactively a statute that changed the burden. Should these cases control the issue in *Shaps*?. The court takes a definition of "procedural" from the decision in *Alamo Rent-A-Car*, which held that a statute limiting punitive damages was "substantive" and therefore did not apply retroactively. Should the same definition of "procedural" apply when that term is used in a different context? See Justice Frankfurter's statement in Guaranty Trust Co. v. York, 326 U.S. 99, 107, 65 S.Ct. 1464, 1469 (1945), p. 700, infra: "Matters of 'substance' and matters of 'procedure' are much talked about in the books as though they defined a great divide cutting across the whole domain of law. But, of course, 'substance' and 'procedure' are the same key-words to very different problems. Neither 'substance' nor 'procedure' represents the same invariants. Each implies different variables depending upon the particular problem for which it is used."

The European Union Regulation on the Law Applicable to Contractual Obligations article 18 and the Regulation on the Law Applicable to Non-Contractual Obligations article 22(1) (Documentary Appendix, infra) apply the Regulations' choice-of-law rules to "rules which raise presumptions of law or determine the burden of proof."

2. Guaranty Trust Co. v. York, held that in diversity cases a statute of limitations is "substantive" so that under Erie R.R. v. Tompkins, p. 695, infra, a federal district court must apply the statute as it would be applied in state court. Is there any relationship between the standards applicable in characterizing issues as procedural for choice of law and for *Erie* cases? See Sedler, The *Erie* Outcome Test as a Guide to Substance and Procedure in the Conflict of Laws, 37 N.Y.U.L.Rev. 813 (1962).

C. RULES OF EVIDENCE: PRIVILEGE

Rules on the admissibility of evidence are among the most diverse of any of the rules that differentiate the way litigation is conducted from forum to forum. The variations from one country to another in the rules for gathering and presenting proof are understandably great. Even among States of the Union the variations are substantial.

In the interests of efficiency and convenience, the local law of the forum is usually applied to determine admissibility of evidence. Familiarity of lawyers and judges with their local rules permits them to deal with evidentiary issues with some measure of assurance a necessary capability, if trials are to proceed swiftly and smoothly. Evidence issues such as hearsay, best evidence, establishing authenticity of documents, and limitations on leading or cross-examining a witness on the stand are thus treated as "procedural" and governed by the forum's rules. Rules determining what communications are privileged and not subject to disclosure under compulsion, however, are more likely to reflect strongly held policies and persons are more likely to act in reliance on them.

RULES OF EVIDENCE FOR UNITED STATES COURTS AND MAGISTRATES*

ARTICLE V. PRIVILEGES

Rule 501

General Rule

Except as otherwise required by the Constitution of the United States or provided by the Act of Congress or in rules prescribed by the Supreme Court pursuant to statutory authority, the privilege of a witness, person, government, State, or political subdivision thereof shall be governed by the principles of the common law as they may be interpreted by the courts of the United States in the light of reason and experience. However, in civil actions and proceedings, with respect to an element of a claim or defense as to which State law supplies the rule of decision, the privilege of a witness, person, government, State, or political subdivision thereof shall be determined in accordance with State law.

Samuelson v. Susen

United States Court of Appeals, Third Circuit, 1978.
576 F.2d 546.

■ SEITZ, CHIEF JUDGE.

Plaintiff, Dr. Gene H. Samuelson, a resident of Steubenville, Ohio, and a neurosurgeon, asserted a claim based upon defamation and tortious interference with business and professional relationships. He alleged that defendants, Drs. Anthony F. Susen and Peter J. Jannetta, [who resided in Pennsylvania] published defamatory statements, either by mail, orally or both, to certain physicians at Ohio Valley Hospital, and other persons, including physicians at St. John Medical Center and Harrison Community Hospital (all in the Steubenville area) and at Weirton General Hospital, Weirton, West Virginia. He seeks damages based on his claim that defendants' conduct has resulted in his being refused privileges at two Ohio hospitals and his staff privileges severely limited at the remaining hospitals.

During the course of discovery, plaintiff sought to depose six physicians and administrators of two Steubenville, Ohio hospitals. All of the proposed deponents (appellees) filed motions for protective orders, which were granted by the district court in Pennsylvania on the basis of Ohio Revised Code § 2305.251, which provides:

> Proceedings and records of all review committees described in section 2305.25 of the Revised Code[1] shall be held in confidence and shall not be subject to discovery or introduction in evidence

---

*   Effective July 1, 1975.

[1]   Section 2305.25 provides in pertinent part: "No member or employee of a utilization review committee . . . shall be deemed liable in damages to any person for any action taken or recommendation made within the scope of the functions of such committee. . . ."

in any civil action against a health care professional or institution arising out of matters which are the subject of evaluation and review by such committee. No person within attendance at a meeting of such committee shall be permitted or required to testify in any civil action as to any evidence or other matters produced or presented during the proceedings of such committee or as to any finding, recommendation, evaluation, opinion or other action of such committee or member thereof. Information, documents, or records otherwise available from original sources are not to be construed as being unavailable for discovery or for use in any civil action merely because they were presented during proceedings of such committee nor should any person testifying before such committee or who is any member of such committee be prevented from testifying as to matters within his knowledge, but the witness cannot be asked about his testimony before such committee or opinion formed by him as a result of such committee hearing.

     This section shall also apply to any member or employee of a ... hospital board or committee reviewing professional qualifications or activities of its medical staff or applicants for admission thereto.

The district court, on April 18, 1977 entered an order designating the following as controlling questions of law pursuant to 28 U.S.C. § 1292(b):

     (1) Do conflicts of law principles require the application of Ohio law to the instant matter?

     (2) Are §§ 2305.25 and 2305.251 of the Ohio Revised Code retrospective in application?

     (3) Do those Ohio statutory provisions prohibit discovery of the publication of allegedly defamatory statements made within the context of committee review of an application for hospital staff privileges?

     (4) If the Ohio statutory provisions do prohibit discovery with regard to alleged defamation occurring in the context of committee review of an application for staff privileges, are those provisions unconstitutional?

I.

     * * * Rule 501 provides that with respect to state issues in "civil actions and proceedings" any privilege "shall be determined in accordance with State law." However, that Rule provides no explicit guidance as to which state's law regarding privilege is to be applied in a diversity case.

     Plaintiff argues that under Rule 501 a federal court must apply the privilege law of the forum, whether or not state courts of the forum would apply their own privilege law. We cannot agree. We believe [that under Erie R.R. v. Tompkins, p. 695, infra and Klaxon v. Stentor Electric Mfg.

Co., p. 746, infra] Rule 501 requires a district court exercising diversity jurisdiction to apply the law of privilege which would be applied by the courts of the state in which it sits.

We thus look to Pennsylvania's conflict-of-laws rules to determine whether Ohio's or Pennsylvania's privilege law applies. We do so even though, it might be argued that the law, of the two jurisdictions, controlling the resolution of the privilege question is essentially the same.

There are no precise Pennsylvania precedents to guide us as to how Pennsylvania courts would rule with respect to the questions before us: consequently, we must predict how Pennsylvania courts would rule. We do know that Pennsylvania has, generally speaking, adopted the "interest analysis" approach to conflict-of-law questions. Griffith v. United Air Lines, 416 Pa. 1, 203 A.2d 796 (1964); Cipolla v. Shaposka, 439 Pa. 563, 267 A.2d 854 (1970). Under that approach "we should apply the law of the predominantly concerned jurisdiction, measuring the depth and breadth of that concern by the relevant contacts each affected jurisdiction had with . . . 'the policies and interests underlying the particular issue before the court.'" Suchomajcz v. Hummel Chemical Company, 524 F.2d 19, 23 (3d Cir.1975).

Here the review committee proceedings were held in Ohio. The participants were Ohio residents. The proceedings were those of an Ohio body seeking to effectuate policies respecting an Ohio physician's use of Ohio medical facilities. Presumably, the proceedings were for the protection of Ohio residents. Under all these circumstances, it seems clear that the district court was justified in concluding that Ohio had the more "significant relationship" to the dispute. It was therefore warranted in prophesying that the Pennsylvania courts would apply Ohio law to the resolution of the conflicts question, particularly since both states have adopted a non-disclosure policy with respect to medical review committee proceedings.

The approach of applying the law of the jurisdiction with the more significant relationship to the dispute is also consistent with that of the Restatement 2d, Conflict of Laws § 139(2).

II

The district court, concluding that Ohio law should apply, granted deponents' motions for protective orders under O.R.C. § 2305.251. Plaintiff contends that it was erroneous to apply O.R.C. § 2305.251 in this litigation because it did not take effect until July 28, 1975, subsequent to plaintiff's February 21, 1975 filing of his complaint in this action.

Article II, Section 28 of the Ohio Constitution denies to the General Assembly the power to enact retroactive legislation. Ohio courts, however, have held that this inhibition applies only to statutes affecting substantive rights, and has no reference to laws of a remedial or procedural nature. * * *

In the context of these proceedings, § 2305.251 works to keep possibly relevant and otherwise admissible evidence from the trier of facts, and is thus clearly procedural. It does not impair the substantive law of defamation, or the substantive right of the plaintiff to bring a cause of action thereon. Therefore, it may be invoked by these deponents even though this action was commenced prior to the effective date of the statute.

[The court considered and rejected plaintiff's contentions that the statute was intended to apply only in malpractice actions and that its application here would abridge federal due process.]

The protective order of the district court dated November 3, 1976, interpreted in its memorandum order denying a motion for reconsideration will be affirmed.

NOTES

1.   How many issues does the court characterize as substantive and for what purposes? What issue is treated as procedural and why? What argument is there that the court did not have to conduct any choice-of-law analysis?

2.   Cases in federal court often have some claims to which federal law applies and others to which state law applies. If evidence relevant to both state and federal claims is privileged under state but not federal law, which standard applies? The Advisory Committee Notes on Rule 501 state:

> Another problem not entirely avoidable is the complexity or difficulty the rule introduces into the trial of a Federal case containing a combination of Federal and State claims and defenses, e.g. an action involving Federal antitrust and State unfair competition claims. Two different bodies of privilege law would need to be consulted. It may even develop that the same witness-testimony might be relevant on both counts and privileged as to one but not the other.

Sprague v. Thorn Americas, Inc., 129 F.3d 1355 (10th Cir.1997) was able to avoid deciding this question because both federal and state privilege law supported application of the attorney-client privilege. The opinion stated: "If such a conflict on the privilege exists, then an analytical solution must be worked out to accommodate the conflicting policies embodied in the state and federal privilege law." In all the cases cited by the court in which the conflict had to be resolved, the courts applied the federal rule favoring admissibility. Id. at 1369.

———————

RESTATEMENT, SECOND, CONFLICT OF LAWS:

§ 139. Privileged Communications

(1) Evidence that is not privileged under the local law of the state which has the most significant relationship with the communication will be admitted, even though it would be privileged under the local law of the

forum, unless the admission of such evidence would be contrary to the strong public policy of the forum.

(2)   Evidence that is privileged under the local law of the state which has the most significant relationship with the communication but which is not privileged under the local law of the forum will be admitted unless there is some special reason why the forum policy favoring admission should not be given effect.

NOTES

1.   If a court does not admit evidence under Restatement (Second) § 139(1), should the court dismiss the case without affecting the merits? Does § 139(2) adequately take account of the policy underlying the foreign privilege?

Ford Motor Co. v. Leggat, 904 S.W.2d 643 (Tex.1995), applied the Michigan attorney-client privilege to bar admission of a report made in Michigan by Ford's general counsel to Ford's Policy and Strategy Committee. Commenting on § 139(2), the court said: "The Restatement . . . goes on to explain that 'the forum will be more inclined to give effect to a foreign privilege that is well established and recognized in many states,' and if the privilege 'was probably relied upon by the parties.' [Section 139 cmt. d.] The purpose of the attorney-client privilege and the reliance placed by the client on the confidential nature of the communications create special reasons why Texas should defer to the broader attorney-client privilege of Michigan in this case. . . . Although we may reach a different result when confronted with other privileges, in view of the nature and purpose of the attorney-client privilege, we hold that it will be governed by the law of the state with the most significant relationship to the communication."

State v. Heaney, 689 N.W.2d 168 (Minn.2004). Heaney was the driver of a vehicle that rolled over in Minnesota killing one of the passengers. Heaney was taken to a nearby hospital in Wisconsin where, against his objections, a sample of his blood was taken, which indicated intoxication. Under Wisconsin law there was no doctor-patient privilege that would prevent admission of the evidence in a criminal trial, but Minnesota law barred the evidence. At Heaney's criminal trial in Minnesota, the judge suppressed the blood-alcohol evidence. Held: reversed:

> Applying the Restatement approach to this case, the state with the most significant relationship to the communication is the state where the communication occurred unless there is a prior relationship between the parties to the communication. Id. § 139 cmt. e. Here, the communication occurred in Wisconsin, the state with the most significant relationship to the communication, and there was no prior relationship between the hospital and Heaney. Furthermore, there is no strong public policy reason in Minnesota for excluding the evidence. On the contrary, the state's interest in prosecuting those who violate the state's criminal vehicular operation laws counsels admission of the evidence.

Id. at 176–77.

In Wellin v. Wellin, 211 F. Supp. 3d 793 (D.S.C.2016), the court held that South Carolina has the most significant relationship to communications between a New York client and South Carolina attorneys, and therefore applied South Carolina's attorney-client privilege law under § 139.

2. On August 1, 2008 The Hague Convention on the Taking of Evidence Abroad in Civil or Commercial Matters was in force in forty-five countries and territories, including the United States (23 U.S.T. 2555, 827 UNTS 231, reprinted in Note following 28 U.S.C.A. § 1781.) Article 11 provides: "In the execution of a Letter of Request the person concerned may refuse to give evidence insofar as he has a privilege or duty to refuse to give evidence (a) under the law of the State of execution; or (b) under the law of the State of origin, and the privilege or duty has been specified in the Letter, or, at the instance of the requested authority, has been otherwise confirmed to that authority by the requesting authority. A Contracting State may declare that, in addition, it will respect privileges and duties existing under the law of States other than the State or origin and the State of execution, to the extent specified in that declaration."

———————

BURGE V. STATE, 443 S.W.2d 720 (Tex.App.1969): Prosecution in Texas for burglary of a home with intent to rape. The victim testified to a struggle with the defendant, during which she managed to "bite him and spit out a piece of the sweater he was wearing." The piece of material was recovered at the scene. Defendant's wife agreed to allow police officers to search their Oklahoma residence without a search warrant. The search uncovered a sweater belonging to Burge, from which a piece of material was missing. It matched the scrap found in the victim's home and was admitted at the Texas trial, which resulted in conviction.

Burge complained that the Oklahoma rule giving each spouse a separate and independent right to insist that a warrant be obtained before search of the home should have been applied to bar the incriminating evidence. The Texas court overruled the objection: "in such instances the law of the forum (Texas in this case) governs as to procedure and rules of evidence. Any other view would lead to endless perplexity."

NOTES

1. In Commonwealth v. Sanchez, 716 A.2d 1221 (Pa.1998), a police dog sniffed a package in California and detected the presence of narcotics. This "canine sniff" provided probable cause for a search warrant in Pennsylvania that produced evidence leading to conviction in Pennsylvania. A canine sniff is not regarded as a search in California and need not be justified by probable cause. Pennsylvania law requires probable cause for a canine sniff. The court affirmed a conviction based on the evidence produced by the Pennsylvania search warrant on the ground that the legality of the canine sniff was substantive and that California law applied because that state "possessed greater interest" in the sniff's validity. A dissenting opinion argued that the legality of the sniff was procedural, but even if substantive, Pennsylvania had a strong interest in protecting the individual rights of persons prosecuted in Pennsylvania courts.

2.　　In People v. Saiken, 275 N.E.2d 381 (Ill.1971), the police in Indiana learned that a body was buried on defendant's farm, obtained a search warrant from an Indiana judge, searched the farm and found the body. The warrant was based on hearsay information and conclusions that were insufficient under Indiana law although adequate in Illinois, the forum state. The Illinois Supreme Court upheld the defendant's conviction for conspiracy to obstruct justice by concealing the body. *Burge* was cited by the court for the proposition that the issue was procedural and governed by forum law. Even if the issue was substantive, Illinois had the significant relationship for choice-of-law purposes.

D.　TIME LIMITATION

Common law conflicts analysis characterized statutes of limitations as procedural. This opened the way for plaintiffs to hunt for a forum in which they could obtain jurisdiction over the defendant and which had an unexpired limitations period. An example is Ferens v. John Deere Co., p. 751, infra. There were two exceptions to this procedural treatment of limitations, one statutory, the so-called "borrowing statute," and one judge-made. These exceptions existed in most, but not all states. Many courts that have adopted modern choice-of-law methods areas have applied these methods to statutes of limitations. Ironically, the borrowing statute, intended to avoid undesirable consequences of the procedural classification of limitations, may prevent modern conflicts analysis of the issue.

Bournias v. Atlantic Maritime Co., Limited

United States Court of Appeals, Second Circuit, 1955.
220 F.2d 152.

■ HARLAN, CIRCUIT JUDGE. Libelant, a seaman, was employed on respondents' vessel at the time she was changed from Panamanian to Honduran registry. As originally filed the libel contained two causes of action. The first was based on several Articles of the Panama Labor Code, under which the libelant claimed an extra three-months' wages payable to seaman upon change of registry, and other amounts for vacation, overtime and holiday pay. The second was for penalties under 46 U.S.C.A. § 596 for failure to pay these amounts promptly. [The district court ruled that the one-year Panama statute of limitations barred all the claims under the Labor Code.]

Article 623 of the Labor Code of Panama, applicable to Articles 127, 154, 166 and 170 of the Code, upon which the libelant based his first cause of action, reads:

Actions and rights arising from labor contracts not enumerated in Article 621 shall prescribe (i.e., shall be barred by the Statute of Limitations) in a year from the happening of the events from which arise or are derived the said actions and rights.

The libelant's employment terminated on December 27, 1950, and since his libel was not filed until December 29, 1952, his first cause of action would be barred by Article 623 if it is controlling in this action.

In actions where the rights of the parties are grounded upon the law of jurisdictions other than the forum, it is a well-settled conflict-of-laws rule that the forum will apply the foreign substantive law, but will follow its own rules of procedure While it might be desirable, in order to eliminate "forum-shopping," for the forum to apply the entire foreign law, substantive and procedural—or at least, as much of the procedural law as might significantly affect the choice of forum, it has been recognized that to do so involves an unreasonable burden on the judicial machinery of the forum and perhaps more significantly, on the local lawyers involved. * * *

The general rule appears established that for the purpose of deciding whether to apply local law or foreign law, statutes of limitations are classified as "procedural." Hence the law of the forum controls. This rule has been criticized as inconsistent with the rationale expressed above, since the foreign statute, unlike evidentiary and procedural details, is generally readily discovered and applied, and a difference in periods of limitation would often be expected to influence the choice of forum. * * *

But as might be expected, some legislatures and courts, perhaps recognizing that in light of the rationale of the underlying conflict-of-laws doctrine it is anomalous to classify across-the-board statutes of limitation as "procedural," have created exceptions to the rule so categorizing such statutes. A legislative example are the so-called "borrowing statutes" which require the courts of the forum to apply the statute of limitations of another jurisdiction, often that where the cause of action arose, when the forum's statute has been tolled. A court-made exception, and the one with which we are concerned here, is that where the foreign statute of limitations is regarded as barring the foreign right sued upon, and not merely the remedy, it will be treated as conditioning that right and will be enforced by our courts as part of the foreign "substantive" law. * * *

It is not always easy to determine whether a foreign statute of limitations should be regarded as "substantive" or "procedural," for the tests applied by the courts are far from precise. In The Harrisburg, 1886, 119 U.S. 199, the Supreme Court held "substantive" a limitation period contained in a wrongful death statute, emphasizing that "the liability and the remedy are created by the same statutes, and the limitations of the remedy are therefore to be treated as limitations of the right." 119 U.S. at page 214. . . . The rule was also carried a step further in Davis v. Mills, 1904, 194 U.S. 451. Suggesting that in the instances where courts have found some statutes of limitation to be "substantive" they were seeking a "reasonable distinction" for escaping from the anomaly of the rule that limitations are generally to be regarded as "procedural," Mr. Justice Holmes continued, "The common case [where limitations are treated as 'substantive'] is where a statute creates a new liability, and in the same section or in the same act limits the time within which it can be enforced, whether using words of condition or not. The Harrisburg, 119 U.S. 199. But the fact that the limitation is contained in the same section or the same statute is material only as bearing on construction. It is merely a ground for saying that the limitation goes to the right created, and accompanies the obligation everywhere. The same conclusion would be reached if the limitation was in a different statute, provided it was directed to the newly created liability so specifically as to warrant saying that it qualified the right." * * *

Two other approaches to the problem were suggested in our opinion in Wood & Selick, Inc. v. Compagnie Generale Transatlantique, 2 Cir., 1930, 43 F.2d 941. First, that the foreign law might be examined to see if the defense possessed the attributes which the forum would classify as "procedural" or "substantive"; that is, for example, whether the defense need be pleaded, as a "substantive" period of limitations need not be in this country. Second, the foreign law might be examined to see if the operation of limitation completely extinguished the right, in which case limitation would be regarded as "substantive." Still other tests are suggested by Goodwin v. Townsend, 3 Cir., 1952, 197 F.2d 970—namely, whether the foreign limitation is regarded as "procedural" or "substantive" by the courts of the foreign state concerned, and possibly whether the limitation is cast in language commonly regarded as "procedural."

Which, then, of these various tests should be applied here? It appears to us that it should be the one which Davis v. Mills, 1904, 194 U.S. 451, suggests for use where the right and its limitation period are contained in separate statutes, viz.: Was the limitation "directed to the newly created liability so *specifically* as to warrant saying that it qualified the right"? 194 U.S., at page 454, 24 S.Ct. at page 694, italics supplied. * * *

Even though the limitation period here is contained in the same statute as enacts the right sought to be enforced, The Harrisburg, supra, still, as noted later, because of the breadth of the Panama Labor Code, as contrasted with the limited scope of the statute involved in The Harrisburg, the limitation period should not automatically be regarded as "substantive." Nor would it be appropriate to make this case turn on the fact that the right sued upon was unknown at common law ... when we are dealing with the statutes of a country where the common law does not exist. And we do not think that it should matter whether the foreign court has interpreted its statute as being "procedural" or "substantive" for some other purpose, which may have happened in Goodwin, supra, or whether the foreign practice requires that limitation be pleaded, Wood & Selick, supra. "The tendency to assume that a word which appears in two or more legal rules, and so in connection with more than one purpose, has and should have precisely the same scope in all of them, runs all through legal discussions. It has all the tenacity of original sin and must constantly be guarded against." Cook, Substance and Procedure in the Conflict of Laws,

42 Yale L.J. 333, 337 (1933). No more should it matter whether the foreign right is extinguished altogether by the mere passage of time, or is instead only repressed into a dormant state, subject to "revival" if the defense of limitation is waived or renounced, Wood & Selick, supra. Such a distinction would generally be difficult to apply, and might also lead to results out of the pattern of the precedents; that is, if the defense could be waived under foreign law, a limitation period might be considered "procedural" even though it was contained in a specific statute giving a remedy for wrongful death. And whether the wording of the limitation period seems more like "procedural" or "substantive" language, Goodwin, supra, does not appear to have been generally considered important.

It is true that the test we prefer leaves much to be desired. It permits the existence of a substantial gray area between the black and the white. But it at least furnishes a practical means of mitigating what is at best an artificial rule in the conflict of laws, without exposing us to the pitfalls inherent in prolonged excursions into foreign law; and it permits us to avoid the short-comings discussed above. We conclude, therefore, that the "specificity" test is the proper one to be applied in a case of this type, without deciding, of course, whether the same test would also be controlling in cases involving domestic or other kinds of foreign statutes of limitations.

Applying that test here it appears to us that the libelant is entitled to succeed, for the respondents have failed to satisfy us that the Panamanian period of limitation in question was specifically aimed against the particular rights which the libelant seeks to enforce. The Panama Labor Code is a statute having broad objectives, viz.: "The present Code regulates the relations between capital and labor, placing them on a basis of social justice, so that, without injuring any of the parties, there may be guaranteed for labor the necessary conditions for a normal life and to capital an equitable return for its investment." In pursuance of these objectives the Code gives laborers various rights against their employers. Article 623 establishes the period of limitation for all such rights, except certain ones which are enumerated in Article 621. And there is nothing in the record to indicate that the Panamanian legislature gave special consideration to the impact of Article 623 upon the particular rights sought to be enforced here, as distinguished from the other rights to which that Article is also applicable. Were we confronted with the question of whether the limitation period of Article 621 (which carves out particular rights to be governed by a shorter limitation period) is to be regarded as "substantive" or "procedural" under the rule of "specificity" we might have a different case; but here on the surface of things we appear to be dealing with a "broad," and not a "specific," statute of limitations. * * *

We therefore conclude that under the proper test the respondents have not made out their defense. In so holding we reach the same result as we did in the similar situation involved in Wood & Selick, 1930, 43 F.2d 941. * * *

Reversed.

NOTE

The distinction between procedural and substantive statutes of limitations, adopted by Judge Harlan in *Bournias* sometimes produced interesting results. In Nelson v. Eckert, 329 S.W.2d 426 (Ark.1959), Arkansas residents were in an automobile returning to Arkansas from Texas. The car crashed in Texas, killing driver and passengers. The administrator of the deceased passengers brought a wrongful death action in Arkansas against the administrator of the deceased driver. This suit was commenced more than two years but less than three years after the fatal crash. Both Texas and Arkansas had two-year statutes of limitations for wrongful death. Nevertheless, the court held the action timely. The Arkansas two-year statute did not apply because it was part of the Arkansas wrongful death act and therefore substantive, applying only to wrongful death occurring in Arkansas. The Texas limitation was not part of the Texas death act. Therefore it was procedural and inapplicable outside of a Texas forum. This left the general Arkansas five-year statute of limitations for personal injury, which the court held to be procedural and applicable.

At the time of the accident, under Arkansas law, the cause of action for wrongful death did not survive the death of the defendant, but the action did survive under Texas law. The court characterized survival as "substantive" and permitted suit.

In Gomez v. ITT Educational Services, Inc., 71 S.W.3d 542 (Ark.2002). the Supreme Court of Arkansas again resolved a clash between Arkansas and Texas statutes of limitations. Defendant's employee murdered a Texas woman in Texas. Her husband brought a wrongful death suit in Arkansas more than two years, but less than three years, after the death. The Texas statute of limitations is two years; the Arkansas period is three years. The court held that Texas limitations barred the action, but gave two different reasons for this result. First, the court applied Restatement (Second) of Conflict of Laws § 143, which states that a limitation on a statutory cause of action is substantive and bars the right, not just the remedy. The court did not note that the 1988 revision of the Restatement superseded § 143 with § 142, p. 507, infra. The court then stated that "Texas has a more significant relationship with the parties and with the issues." Id. at 548. Arkansas had adopted the Uniform Conflict of Laws-Limitations Act, discussed in Cropp v. Interstate Distributor Co., p. 514, infra, but had repealed that act before plaintiff filed this case.

KEETON V. HUSTLER MAGAZINE, INC., 549 A.2d 1187 (N.H.1988). Following reversal by the Supreme Court and remand to the lower federal courts (Keeton v. Hustler Magazine, Inc., p. 100, supra), the United States Court of Appeals certified two questions to the New Hampshire Supreme Court: (1) would the New Hampshire courts apply the interstate single publication rule in the case at hand and (2) would the New Hampshire courts apply their longer (6 year) statute of limitations? The Supreme Court of New Hampshire answered both questions in the affirmative.

The Supreme Court of New Hampshire justified its application of the New Hampshire statute of limitations. It found that application of the statute (1) would be constitutional under the Supreme Court decision in Sun Oil Co. v. Wortman, p. 449, supra; (2) would further New Hampshire's interest because a substantial number of the defendant's magazines had been sold there; (3) would be in line with precedent and hence would simplify the judicial task. There were two dissents.

NOTE

The interstate single publication rule, referred to in Keeton v. Hustler Magazine, would permit the plaintiff to recover for harm suffered from publication of the libel in all jurisdictions. Shevill v. Presse Alliance S.A., [1995] ECR I-415 (Court of Justice of the European Communities, Case C-68/93) interpreted art. 5(3) of the European Union Convention on Jurisdiction and Enforcement of Judgments (the Brussels Convention), in the context of multistate libel. Article 5(3)[5] permitted suit "in matters relating to tort, delict or quasi-delict, in the courts of the place where the harmful event occurred." The Court stated that "the victim of a libel by a newspaper article distributed in several contracting states may bring an action for damages against the publisher either before the courts . . . of the place where the publisher . . . is established, which have jurisdiction to award damages for all the harm caused by the defamation, or before the courts of each contracting state in which the publication was distributed and where the victim claims to have suffered injury to his reputation, which have jurisdiction to rule solely in respect of the harm caused in the state of the court seised."

Waterfield v. Meredith Corp., 20 A.3d 865, 871 (N.H.2011):

On remand, should the trial court determine that the plaintiff was a New will Hampshire resident at the time of the alleged defamation, our limitations period apply and no choice-of-law analysis need be made. Should the trial court determine that the plaintiff was not a New Hampshire resident at the time of the alleged defamation, the issue we left open in Keeton [v. Hustler Magazine, Inc.,131 N.H. 6, 549 A.2d 1187 (1988)] emerges, and we now hold that under such circumstances, our customary balancing test applies. Thus, the court should determine which state's statute of limitations applies by weighing the five choice-influencing considerations: (1) the predictability of results; (2) the maintenance of reasonable orderliness and good relationships among the states in the federal system; (3) simplification of the judicial task; (4) advancement of the governmental interest of the forum; and (5) the court's preference for what it regards as the sounder rule of law.

---

[5]   This is now Article 7(2) of the Council Regulation, which adds "or may occur." See Documentary Appendix, infra.

When the American Law Institute approved the final draft of the Restatement (Second) of Conflict of Laws, the Restatement dealt with statutes of limitations in two sections.

§ 142. Statute of Limitations

(1) An action will not be maintained if it is barred by the statute of limitations of the forum, including a provision borrowing the statute of limitations of another state.

(2) An action will be maintained if it is not barred by the statute of limitations of the forum, even though it would be barred by the statute of limitations of another state, except as stated in § 143.

§ 143. Foreign Statute of Limitations Barring The Right

An action will not be entertained in another state if it is barred in the state of the otherwise applicable law by a statute of limitations which bars the right and not merely the remedy.

Comment c to § 143 stated that "the usual test" of whether a statute of limitations bars the right and not merely the remedy is the "specificity" test as stated by Judge Harlan in Bournias v. Atlantic Maritime Co., p. 501, supra.

After the Restatement (Second) was published, however, courts in jurisdictions that had abandoned territorial choice-of-law rules in favor of rules that took account of the content and purposes of conflicting laws, rejected the procedural characterization of statutes of limitations. Instead they applied to choice of the appropriate statute of limitations the same policy-oriented approach that they applied to other issues. See, e.g., Tomlin v. Boeing Co., 650 F.2d 1065 (9th Cir.1981) (Washington conflicts law); Gianni v. Fort Wayne Air Serv., Inc., 342 F.2d 621 (7th Cir.1965) (Indiana conflicts law); Johnson v. Pischke, 700 P.2d 19 (Id.1985); Cameron v. Hardisty, 407 N.W.2d 595 (Iowa 1987); Heavner v. Uniroyal, Inc., 305 A.2d 412 (N.J.1973); Air Prod. & Chem., Inc. v. Fairbanks Morse, Inc., 206 N.W.2d 414 (Wis.1973). In 1988, responding to these cases, the American Law Institute, under the leadership of the Reporter for the previously published Restatement (Second), Professor Willis Reese, replaced former §§ 142 and 143 with a new § 142:

§ 142. Statute of Limitations

Whether a claim will be maintained against the defense of the statute of limitations is determined under the principles stated in § 6 [p. 574, infra]. In general, unless the exceptional circumstances of the case make such a result unreasonable:

(1) The forum will apply its own statute of limitations barring the claim.

(2) The forum will apply its own statute of limitations permitting the claim unless:

(a) maintenance of the claim would serve no substantial interest of the forum; and

(b) the claim would be barred under the statute of limitations of a state having a more significant relationship to the parties and the occurrence.

Does this revision reflect both the procedural and substantive aspects of statutes of limitations as described by Justice Brennan in Sun Oil v. Wortman, p. 505, supra? With regard to § 142(1), should the forum always apply its own shorter statute of limitations to dismiss an action when the parties and the transaction have significant contacts with a jurisdiction with a longer limitation period? Ledesma v. Jack Stewart Produce, Inc., 816 F.2d 482 (9th Cir.1987), held that the Arizona two-year statute of limitation rather than the California one-year statute applied to a suit in federal district court in California. The plaintiff was a California resident suing Arizona and Oklahoma residents who injured the plaintiff in Arizona. Both Arizona and Oklahoma had two-year limitation periods.

On January 1, 1992, a comprehensive conflict-of-laws code took effect in Louisiana. La.C.C. arts. 3515–49. Article 3549 provides for application of Louisiana time limitations unless (1) the action would be barred under Louisiana law but not "in the state whose law would be applicable to the merits and maintenance of the action in this state is warranted by compelling considerations of remedial justice"; or (2) the action "would be barred in the state whose law is applicable to the merits and maintenance of the action in this state is not warranted by the policies of this state and its relationship to the parties or the dispute nor by any compelling considerations of remedial justice."

In Smith v. ODECO (UK), Inc., 615 So.2d 407 (La.App.1993), writ denied, 618 So.2d 412 (La.1993), the court found that "compelling considerations of remedial justice" permitted a resident and domiciliary of the United Kingdom to sue in Louisiana when the Louisiana period of limitations had expired but the United Kingdom period had not. Louisiana was the only forum in which the plaintiff could obtain jurisdiction over all defendants.

Does § 142(2) require every conflict over limitation policy to be resolved in favor of the forum's longer period if the plaintiff is a forum resident? The following case deals with this issue.

Nierman v. Hyatt Corp.

Supreme Judicial Court of Massachusetts, 2004.
441 Mass. 693, 808 N.E.2d 290.

[The Niermans, a husband and wife, domiciled in Massachusetts, made reservations through a Massachusetts travel agent to stay at a Hyatt

Regency hotel in Texas. Hyatt is incorporated in Delaware, has it principal place of business in Illinois, manages a hotel in Massachusetts, and regularly solicits business in Massachusetts through its reservation system.

Three years after Mrs. Nierman was injured at the Texas hotel, Mr. and Mrs. Nierman sued Hyatt to recover damages resulting from the negligence of Hyatt's employee. The suit was timely under the Massachusetts three-year statute of limitations, but would be barred under the Texas two-year limitation period. The trial court granted summary judgment to Hyatt ruling that the Texas statute applied, The Appeals court reversed on the ground that the Massachusetts statute applied. The Supreme Judicial Court granted Hyatt's application for further appellate review.]

■ GREANEY, J. * * * The parties agree that the substantive laws of Texas on negligence will apply should the Niermans' claims be allowed to proceed. The sole issue before us is whether the Massachusetts or the Texas limitations statute controls the claims.[4]

In New England Tel. & Tel. Co. v. Gourdeau Constr. Co., 419 Mass. 658, 664, 647 N.E.2d 42 (1995), this court departed from the traditional rule of law that characterized limitations statutes as procedural and automatically applied the statute of limitations of the forum State. We adopted instead a functional approach that treats the issue as a choice of law question, as stated in the Restatement (Second) of Conflict of Laws § 142 (Supp.1989). Section 142, as amended, states that, under choice of law principles set forth in § 6, the forum State generally will apply its own statute of limitations to permit a claim unless: "(a) maintenance of the claim would serve no substantial interest of the forum; and (b) the claim would be barred under the statute of limitations of a state having a more significant relationship to the parties and the occurrence." * * *

The Appeals Court reasoned, essentially, that, because the Niermans are residents of this State, Massachusetts has a substantial interest in the maintenance of their claims. Moreover, because Hyatt is not based in Texas, the Appeals Court assumed that Texas has no countervailing interest at stake. The court's resolution of the issue is appealing for its simplicity but fails to engage in the proper choice of law analysis under principles stated in § 142. Specifically, we must consider (1) whether Massachusetts has a substantial interest in permitting the claims to go forward and (2) whether Texas has a more significant relationship to the parties and the negligence claim. The two criteria are necessarily related and should be evaluated "with some sensitivity" to one another, Stanley v. CF-VH Assocs., Inc., 956 F.Supp. 55, 59 * * *

---

[4] No one in this case asserts that the limitations statutes of either Delaware or Illinois apply to the Niermans' claims. Both statutes provide a two-year period within which a personal injury action must be commenced and, thus, would bar the Niermans' claim.

We begin by noting that the more significant relationship test points clearly toward use of the Texas limitations statute. All of the events constituting the alleged negligence took place in Texas, and Texas is where the alleged injuries were suffered. Hyatt, although not a Texas corporation, operates a business there and employs Texans. The operator of the transport cart [whose negligence allegedly injured Mrs. Nierman], presumably, lives in Texas. Although the Niermans are Massachusetts residents, they had traveled to Texas when the alleged accident occurred. The fact that their travel reservations were booked through Massachusetts travel agents carries no weight in our analysis, because that contact has no apparent bearing on any issue in the case, let alone the limitations issue. See Restatement (Second) of Conflict of Laws, supra at § 142 comment e (emerging trend is bar claim if barred by "the state which, *with respect to the issue of limitations*, is the state of most significant relationship to the occurrence and to the parties stated in § 6." [emphasis supplied]).

We next consider whether, regardless that Texas is the State with the closer connections to the issue, Massachusetts has any substantial interest that would be advanced by entertaining the Niermans' claims. We conclude that it does not. Massachusetts has a general interest in having its residents compensated for personal injuries suffered in another State. It cannot be said, however, that its interest in the timeliness of such an action is more compelling than that of Texas. See Restatement (Second) of Conflict of Laws, supra at § 142 comment g (claim generally should not be maintained when some forum interest would be served, but at the expense of the State with closer connection with the case).[6] The Texas Legislature has prescribed a two-year period within which the Niermans could have commenced this action. This time frame reflects its judgment as to the proper balance between the need of its citizens to redress injuries and their right to be protected from protracted exposure to liability. Hyatt has a place of business in Texas, and all of the acts and events that gave rise to this litigation occurred there. Texas has the dominant interest in having its own limitations statute enforced. We conclude that the Texas statute of limitations is the appropriate one to apply in this case.

---

[6]   Comment g states:

Decision becomes difficult in situations where, although the forum is not the state of most significant relationship to important issues in the case, some forum interest would be served by entertainment of the claim, but this would be at the expense of the interests of another state which has a closer connection with the case and under whose statute of limitations the claim would be barred. One such situation is where the domicil of the plaintiff is in the state of the forum and that of the defendant is in the other state with the most significant relationship to important issues in the case. In such a situation, the forum should entertain the claim only in extreme and unusual circumstances.

—eds.

NOTES

1. In the light of this decision and the comments to § 142 noted by the court, is the wording of § 142(2) misleading? The court considers "whether, regardless that Texas is the State with the closer connections to the issue, Massachusetts has any substantial interest that would be advanced by entertaining the Niermans' claims." Despite this has the court effectively rewritten § 142(2) to read: "The forum will apply its own statute of limitations permitting the claim when it has the most significant relationship to the occurrence and the parties under the principles stated in § 6"? Would that revised wording reflect sound choice-of-law policies?

2. DeLoach v. Alfred, 960 P.2d 628 (Ariz.1998), applied revised § 142 and chose the Arizona two-year statute of limitations rather than the Tennessee one-year statute. The suit was by a Californian who was injured in Tennessee while a passenger in a car driven by the Arizona defendant. The court applied § 142(2) and decided that the facts did not rebut the presumption in favor of applying the forum's longer statute. Arizona had an interest in "requiring its citizens to answer for the harm they cause." The court noted that it did not have jurisdiction over the Tennessee driver of the car that had collided with defendant's car and thus Tennessee had no interest in the application of its shorter limitations.

3. The Supreme Court of Canada has held that statutes of limitations are substantive, overruling cases to the contrary. Tolofson v. Jensen, [1994] 3 S.C.R. 1022, 1071–72 (Can.1994).

Civil law countries characterize limitations as substantive for choice-of-law purposes. See Rabel, 3 The Conflict of Laws: A Comparative Study 511–12 (2d ed.1964 by Bernstein). See also European Community Regulations on the Law Applicable to Contractual Obligations Art. 12(1)(d); and on the Law Applicable to Non-Contractual Obligations Art. 15(h) (Documentary Appendix, infra).

PNC Bank v. Sterba (In re Sterba)

United States Court of Appeals for the Ninth Circuit, 2017.
852 F.3d 1175.

■ Before TASHIMA, SMITH, JR., AND KORMAN, JJ.

■ KORMAN, JUDGE.

When it comes to conflicts of law, bankruptcy is a bit of an odd duck. The substantive focus is often on state law, as it always is in diversity cases. But where a federal court sitting in diversity applies the forum state's choice-of-law rules—a straightforward policy that prevents the forum's federal character from determining the outcome of disputes that are really about state law—we have held that in bankruptcy, federal choice-of-law rules control which state's law applies. Lindsay v. Beneficial Reinsurance Co. (In re Lindsay), 59 F.3d 942, 948 (9th Cir. 1995).

This case adds another wrinkle: The dispute here arises out of a clause in a promissory note providing that it should be construed according to Ohio law. So we face two issues—one sounding in contract, the other in conflict of laws. The first is whether such a general choice of law clause encompasses issues relating to the statute of limitations, or whether the parties to an agreement must select a limitations period expressly if they want to do so at all? The second is, if the parties must select a statute of limitations expressly and fail to do so, how should a bankruptcy court determine which state's limitations period applies.

BACKGROUND

In 2007, the Sterbas bought a condo in California. They took out two loans secured by liens against the property, of which National City Bank held the junior one. The Sterbas' promissory note to National City provided in relevant part that: "[T]he Bank is a national bank located in Ohio and Bank's decision to make this Loan . . . was made in Ohio. Therefore, this Note shall be governed by and construed in accordance with . . . the laws of Ohio . . . without regard to conflict of law principles." Less than a year after the loans were made, the Sterbas defaulted, the senior lender foreclosed, and National City was left holding the bag for $42,000.

When the Sterbas filed for bankruptcy in the Northern District of California in 2013, PNC Bank (National City's successor in interest) filed a claim based on the 2007 note. The Sterbas objected, contending that the claim was barred by California's applicable four-year statute of limitations. . . . PNC, in turn, argued that the claim was timely because the promissory note's choice of Ohio law incorporated Ohio's six-year limitations period. . . .

The bankruptcy judge agreed that the promissory note selected Ohio's six-year limitations period, and overruled the Sterbas' objection. The Bankruptcy Appellate Panel reversed. PNC appeals from the BAP's decision.

DISCUSSION

Ordinarily, when parties to an agreement select the law they want to govern an issue, federal courts will enforce that choice. [The majority concluded that the choice-of-law clause in the note did not encompass the applicable statute of limitations, and thus turned to deciding which statute of limitations was applicable in the absence of an applicable choice.]

Federal choice-of-law rules in the Ninth Circuit follow the Restatement (Second) of Conflict of Laws. . . . We have directly adopted § 142, the particular provision of the Second Restatement applicable here.

The 1971 version of § 142 provides that "An action will not be maintained if it is barred by the statute of limitations of the forum, including a provision borrowing the statute of limitations of another state." The 1988 version of § 142 is similarly worded, except that it provides a limited carve-out for "exceptional circumstances." Specifically and in relevant part, it reads as follows: "[I]n general, unless the exceptional circumstances of the case make such a result unreasonable . . . The forum will apply its own statute of limitations barring the claim." (emphasis added).

The Second Restatement's preference for the forum state's statute of limitations, in cases where it has the shorter limitations period, is based on the policy that "[a] state has a substantial interest in preventing the prosecution in its courts of claims which it deems to be 'stale.' " § 142, cmt. f (1988). In the ordinary case, that interest is treated as controlling because vindicating it imposes no real prejudice on the time-barred party—dismissal of a claim as barred by the statute of limitations generally "does not constitute a judgment on the merits," and following such a dismissal "the plaintiff will usually remain free to sue" in a state with a more generous limitations period. Id. But where a countervailing interest exists such that "under the special circumstances of the case dismissal . . . would be unjust," the forum (here, California) will apply another state's longer statute of limitations. Id.

The application of § 142 compels the conclusion that California's shorter statute of limitations does not apply here, because this case presents the sort of "exceptional circumstances" under which the 1988 version of the Second Restatement looks past the law of the forum, and applies a longer foreign limitations period. The Restatement, to be sure, does not provide an exhaustive or technical definition of an exceptional circumstance. Nevertheless, the comment to the 1988 version of § 142 makes clear that the present case comes within that category. Indeed, this case is on all fours with the Restatement's only example of what would constitute such a "special," "unjust" circumstance: "[W]hen through no fault of the plaintiff an alternative forum is not available as, for example, where jurisdiction could not be obtained over the defendant in any [other] state. . . ." Id.

Here—exactly as the comment describes—the unique strictures of the bankruptcy code mean that, through no fault of PNC's, there is no forum for its claim other than the Northern District of California. This is not a case filed voluntarily in California, in which a dismissal on statute of limitations grounds would be without prejudice to bringing the same claim in Ohio. . . . Rather, once the Sterbas declared bankruptcy, PNC was obligated to bring all its claims in the district where the Sterbas filed. Under these circumstances, to reject PNC's claim as time-barred would be the functional equivalent of a dismissal on the merits. Where another jurisdiction—National City's home state of Ohio—would hear the claim, and has a substantial interest in its resolution, disallowing it by mechanical adoption of California's statute of limitations would be wholly unreasonable. We hold that under these exceptional circumstances, the bankruptcy court was correct to apply Ohio's six-year statute of limitations and overrule the Sterbas' objection to PNC's claim. . . .

CONCLUSION

The judgment of the Bankruptcy Appellate Panel is Reversed, and the case is Remanded to the bankruptcy court for further proceedings consistent with this opinion.

[Judge Tashima concurred in the result on the grounds that the choice-of-law clause encompassed the applicable statute of limitations and thus the Ohio six-year period applied under the contract between the parties.]

NOTE

Note that as in Niermann, the court applies a foreign statute of limitations, but unlike Nierman it applies a longer statute of limitations to save the plaintiff's claim. Does section 142 provide sufficient certainty to allow lawyers to predict which limitation period will apply? Would you recommend adopting section 142 in the draft Third Restatement of Conflicts?

Cropp v. Interstate Distributor Co.

Court of Appeals of Oregon, 1994.
129 Or.App. 510, 880 P.2d 464, review denied, 887 P.2d 791 (Or.1994).

■ Before ROSSMAN, P.J., and DE MUNIZ and LEESON, JJ.

■ DE MUNIZ, JUDGE.

Plaintiffs brought this action against defendants seeking money damages for personal injuries and property damage that they sustained when a truck, owned by defendant Interstate Distributor Company (Interstate) and operated by defendant Rust, collided with their parked truck in California. Plaintiffs appeal from a summary judgment that their action was barred by California's one-year statute of limitations. We affirm * * *

Plaintiffs are self-employed truck drivers. They live in Gervais, Oregon, which is also their principal place of business. In 1990, they worked in Oregon, Washington, California, Nevada and Arizona. Rust is a resident of Nevada and an employee of Interstate. He works mainly in California, but also works in Colorado, Wyoming, Montana, Washington and Oregon. He works in Oregon about twice a month and uses Interstate's maintenance and fueling facility in Wilsonville, Oregon. Occasionally, he uses another company's facility in White City, Oregon. Interstate is a Washington corporation with its principal office in Tacoma. It transacts most of its business in California.

On December 18, 1990, plaintiffs were returning to Oregon with a load of lime from Napa Valley, California. Near Doyle, California, they pulled to the side of Highway 395 to change drivers. Rust was also traveling on Highway 395, transporting merchandise north in an Interstate truck. His truck struck plaintiffs' parked truck.

Plaintiffs retained counsel within one month of the accident. They began, but did not complete, the process of filing a lawsuit in Washington. Instead, in April, 1992, they filed this action, and the trial court granted summary judgment for defendants.

In their two assignments of error, which challenge the granting of defendants' motion for summary judgment and the denial of their motion for partial summary judgment, plaintiffs assert that the trial court erred in concluding that, because the "greater contacts are outside of Oregon," California's one-year statute of limitations, applied and barred plaintiffs' claims. Plaintiffs assert that Oregon's two-year statute of limitations, ORS 12.110(1), applies to their personal injury claims, because only Oregon has a substantial interest in having its law applied, and, thus, there is no conflict of laws issue. Alternatively, they assert that ORS 12.110(1) applies according to Oregon tort conflict of laws rules.

We begin with the requirements of ORS 12.430 in the Uniform Conflict of Laws-Limitations Act: "(1) Except as provided by ORS 12.450, if a claim is substantively based: (a) Upon the law of one other state, the limitation period of that state applies; or (b) Upon the law of more than one state, the limitation period of one of those states, chosen by the law of conflict of laws of this state, applies. (2) The limitation period of this state applies to all other claims." * * * In short, the statute requires us to apply the statute of limitations that corresponds to the substantive law forming the basis of plaintiffs' claims. * * *

Plaintiffs allege that Rust was negligent in failing to keep a proper lookout, failing to keep his vehicle under control, driving his truck at a speed that was greater than reasonable and prudent under the circumstances and operating his truck "in violation of PUC regulations." Those allegations concern the parties' rights and responsibilities in operating motor vehicles on highways in California. California law, including its Vehicle Code, defines and regulates those rights. Oregon motor vehicle laws do not define or regulate the operation of motor vehicles in California and thus have no bearing on plaintiffs' claims. Therefore, we conclude that those claims are substantively based on California law only. Accordingly, California's one-year statute of limitations applies and bars plaintiffs' claims. * * *

Affirmed.

■ ROSSMAN, PRESIDING JUDGE, dissenting. * * *

I agree with the majority that the answer to this case depends on which state's substantive law governs the claims. Determining, in turn, whether the claims are based on the substantive law of Oregon or California requires a choice of laws analysis, which the majority does not make. I disagree with the majority's view that the claims here are based on the substantive law of the State of California because the accident took place there. Under a choice of law analysis, I would conclude that plaintiff's tort claims are substantively based only on the law of Oregon. Accordingly,

I would conclude that, pursuant to ORS 12.430(2), Oregon's statute of limitations applies. * * *

For there to be a choice of law issue, there must be a choice to make. Oregon law and another state's law must be different on the disputed issue. Here, there are two different laws on the disputed issue of whether plaintiffs' personal injury claims were timely filed. In Oregon, plaintiffs had to file their action within two years of December 18, 1990. ORS 12.110(1). In California, plaintiffs had to file their action within one year. Thus, the answer to whether there is an actual conflict between Oregon and California law, is yes.

Even if there is a difference between Oregon law and the law of the other state on the disputed issue, there is no choice of law issue unless both states have a substantial interest in having their law apply. Whether a state has a substantial interest in having its law applied to a disputed issue involves identifying that state's interests in the case, and an examination of the policy behind the state's law on the disputed issue and how that policy would be affected by application or non-application of its law in the case.

Perhaps one of the strongest interests that a state can have in a case arises when the parties to the dispute are residents of the state or are to be regarded as such. Here, plaintiffs are Oregonians. Additionally, defendants are considered to be Oregon domiciliaries. According to the Restatement (Second) Conflicts of Law § 145, comment i (1971), when certain contacts involving a tort are located in two or more states with identical local law rules on the issue in question, then the case will be treated, for choice-of-law purposes, as if those contacts were grouped in a single state. Nevada, where Rust lived, and Washington, where Interstate was incorporated and had its principal place of business, each have personal injury statutes of limitations equal to or longer than ORS 12.110(1). Accordingly, for purposes of resolving the conflict, defendants are considered to be Oregon domiciliaries. Additionally, part of the conduct related to the accident—the freight contracts and dispatch instructions—occurred in Oregon, Nevada and Washington, each of which have statutes of limitations similar to ORS 12.110(1). Therefore, at least in part, the conduct causing plaintiffs' personal injuries is considered to have occurred in Oregon. The economic consequences of plaintiff's recovery or lack of recovery would be felt in Oregon, not California. Finally, defendants do business in Oregon. All of those factors require the conclusion that Oregon has a substantial interest in the outcome of the disputed issue.

In contrast, the relevant factors show that any interest that California has in the outcome of the dispute is, at best, minor. Neither plaintiffs nor defendants are, or are considered to be, California domiciliaries for the purpose of resolving the conflict. The majority's holding seems to be based primarily on its view that, because the allegations of the complaint concern the parties' rights and responsibilities in operating motor vehicles on the highways, only California substantive law is implicated. Although

California has an interest in maintaining traffic safety in its state, that interest is met by enforcement of its traffic laws. As between California and Oregon, the only relationship that California has to this action is the entirely fortuitous event that it happened to be the site of the crash. That in itself is not a substantial interest. Additionally, the economic impact of denying plaintiffs the right to recover on their personal injury claims would not be felt in California. Finally, the purpose underlying California's one-year statute of limitations, to make sure that tort claims are brought before they become stale, would not be frustrated by application of Oregon's two-year limitation period. California simply has no substantial interest that would be offended by applying Oregon's statute of limitations to a California automobile accident that does not involve California residents.

In short, the important contacts—where the parties live or are deemed to live and the economic impact of the litigation—are Oregon contacts. The less consequential contact—where the accident occurred—is a California contact. I would conclude that that contact does not create a substantial interest in California. Accordingly, I would conclude that ... Oregon substantive law therefore applies. * * *

NOTES

1.   The principal case reveals the problems encountered when the limitations issue is linked to other issues and not given an independent conflict-of-laws analysis. ORS § 12.450, the exception referred to in the opinion, is § 4 of the Uniform Act. It provides for application of Oregon law if "the limitation period of another state [otherwise applicable under the Act] is substantially different from the limitation of this State and has not afforded a fair opportunity to sue upon, or imposes an unfair burden in defending against, the claim."

Colorado, one of the states that has enacted the Uniform Act, subsequently enacted a borrowing statute that applies the shorter period of limitations where the cause of action arose. Jenkins v. Panama Canal R.R. Co., 208 P.3d 238 (Colo. en banc 2009), declared the two statutes irreconcilable and held the more recent statute "by implication" repealed the Uniform Act. Two dissenters stated the Uniform Act was more specific than later statute and should apply to the case.

2.   The Foreign Limitation Periods Act 1984, applicable to England and Wales, provides that if the law of a foreign country applies, then the time limitations of that country for bringing of proceedings shall also apply. Legislation in Australia and New Zealand contains the same provision.

3.   In Flowers v. Carville, 310 F.3d 1118 (9th Cir.2002), the plaintiff moved to Nevada one year before filing suit there for defamation and other torts. The most recent incident of alleged defamation occurred more than one year but less than two years before suit. The Nevada statute of limitations is two years, but the limitations in all other states that have contacts with the parties or the incidents are one year. The Nevada borrowing statute bars an action that is barred by the laws of the state where the action "has arisen" but has an exception "in favor of a citizen [of Nevada] who has held the cause of action from the time it accrued." The Nevada exception, unlike the exception in some other states, does not expressly state that the plaintiff must have been a citizen of the state at the time that the action accrued. The court construed the Nevada exception as permitting the plaintiff to sue. The opinion stated that this avoids a constitutional issue, citing Saenz v. Roe, 526 U.S. 489, 119 S.Ct. 1518 (1999). *Saenz* held that California legislation limiting benefits to needy families during the recipients' first year of residency violated the Fourteenth Amendment right to travel.

Bendix Autolite Corp. v. Midwesco Enterprises, 486 U.S. 888, 108 S.Ct. 2218 (1988), invalidated, as an unreasonable burden on interstate commerce, the Ohio rule that suspended the running of the statute of limitations against a foreign corporation. The suspension operated even when the corporation was subject to long-arm jurisdiction. To avoid tolling of limitations, the foreign corporation would have to obtain a license to do business in Ohio and appoint a resident agent for service of process. Reynoldsville Casket Co. v. Hyde, 514 U.S. 749, 115 S.Ct. 1745 (1995), holds that *Bendix* applies retroactively to actions accruing before *Bendix* was decided.

Statutes are common that suspend limitations while an action is pending, if suit is terminated without deciding the merits. There is a split of authority whether such statutes apply to actions brought in another state. See Muzingo v. Vaught, 887 S.W.2d 693 (Mo.App.1994), collecting authority and holding that the Missouri statute applies only if the dismissed action was brought in Missouri. For an opposing view see Malone v. Bankhead Enterprises, Inc., 125 F.3d 535 (7th Cir.1997), holding that the Illinois statute applies to an action brought in Missouri.

When limitations have been suspended under a statute referred to in the previous paragraph, the time permitted for refiling the action varies from state to state. Goldsmith v. Learjet, Inc., 917 P.2d 810 (Kan.1996), held that the Kansas borrowing statute, which borrows the statute of limitations of the state where the cause of action arose, did not borrow that state's period for refiling terminated actions when that period is shorter than the Kansas period.

28 U.S.C. § 1367(d) provides: "The period of limitations for any claim asserted [under state law but over which the district court declines to exercise supplemental jurisdiction] shall be tolled while the claim is pending and for a period of 30 days after it is dismissed unless State law provides for a longer tolling period." Raygor v. Regents of the Univ. of Minnesota, 534 U.S. 533, 122 S.Ct. 999 (2002), however, held that § 1367(d) did not apply to "state law claims asserted against nonconsenting state defendants" when those claims "are dismissed on Eleventh Amendment grounds." The Court construed the section not to apply because otherwise there would be "serious doubts about the constitutionality of the provision given principles of state sovereign immunity."

The Eleventh Amendment bars suit in federal court against states by citizens of other states. Hans v. Louisiana, 134 U.S. 1, 10 S.Ct. 504 (1890), extended a state's immunity to suits brought by its own citizens.

Jinks v. Richland County, 538 U.S. 456, 123 S.Ct. 1667 (2003), held that § 1367(d) is constitutional when applied to toll limitations in suits against a political subdivision of a State. The Eleventh Amendment does not apply when the suit is against a political subdivision and not against the state. The Supreme Court granted review in 2017 as to whether § 1367(d) tolls state statutes of limitation or only federal.

In McKinney v. Fairchild Int'l, Inc., 487 S.E.2d 913 (W.Va.1997). A miner who resided in West Virginia was injured in a Kentucky mine by an allegedly defective machine manufactured by a West Virginia company. The Kentucky statute of limitations is one year. A West Virginia statute borrows the limitation of the place where the action accrued if shorter than the West Virginia limitation. The miner and his wife sued the manufacturer in federal court in West Virginia less than one year after the injury. The federal court dismissed this suit for lack of subject-matter jurisdiction. Plaintiffs then sued in a West Virginia state court. This action would be timely if the Kentucky one-year limitation was suspended during the pending of the federal suit. West Virginia law would suspend (toll) the limitation but Kentucky law would not. The court applied West Virginia law and held that the action was timely. The court stated: "where a choice of law question arises about whether the tolling provisions of West Virginia or of the place where the claim accrued should be applied, the [trial] court should ordinarily apply West Virginia law, unless the place where the claim accrued has a more significant relationship to the transaction and the parties. . . . [Here] West Virginia has the more significant relationship because the plaintiffs are West Virginia residents and the defendant is a West Virginia corporation." Id. at 923.

4.   Malone v. Jackson, 652 S.W.2d 170 (Mo.App.1993), held that the Missouri borrowing statute does not apply to the special statute of limitations contained in the Missouri wrongful death act and, under a most significant relationship test, the forum's wrongful death act applied. The holding was based on a provision in the chapter of the Missouri code that contained the borrowing statute. The provision states that the chapter does not apply "to any action which is or shall be otherwise limited by statute." Even without this provision, should the borrowing statute, which was enacted to prevent the undesirable consequences of characterizing limitations as "procedural," apply if the Missouri statute of limitations is "substantive." Most states agree with Bournias v. Atlantic Maritime Co., Ltd., p. 501, supra, that limitations are substantive if part of the same statute creating the cause of action.

5.   Some borrowing statutes that refer to the law of the state where the action "arose" or "originated," state that they do not apply if the plaintiff has been a resident of the forum and has held the cause of action since its inception. Some statutes do not apply if either the plaintiff or defendant is a resident. Are these exceptions for forum residents sufficient to prevent the application of the law of a state that does not have the most significant relationship to the issue? Assume that Plaintiff and Defendant reside in X. X has a borrowing statute that refers to the law of the state where the action "arose," but does not apply if either party was an X resident at that time. Defendant injures Plaintiff while driving in Y with Plaintiff as passenger. Defendant then moves to F, which has the same borrowing statute as X. F and X have two-year limitations, but Y has a one-year period. Plaintiff sues Defendant in F more than one year but less than two years after the accident.

What result? See also Global Financial Corp. v. Triarc Corp., 715 N.E.2d 482 (N.Y.1999) (holding that when the exception for New York plaintiffs does not apply, the borrowing statute's reference to "accruing" means the state where plaintiff suffered harm, not the state indicated by a "grouping of contacts" approach that New York uses for contract choice-of-law analysis).

6.   As contrasted with statutes of limitations, most courts have held that statutes of repose are substantive for choice-of-law purposes. A statute of repose bars suit after a stated time from the sale of a product or other conduct of the defendant even though the plaintiff's injury occurs after that time.

Consolidated Grain & Barge Co. v. Structural Systems, Inc., 212 P.3d 1168 (Okla.2009). The defendant built a grain conveyer system for the plaintiff in Arkansas. A fire at the site of the construction subsequently caused property damage. The plaintiff sued the builder six years and three months after the construction was completed to recover damages for negligent performance of the building contract. Arkansas had a five year statute of repose for construction claims. Oklahoma's statute of repose was ten years. Oklahoma's "backwards" borrowing statute provides: "The period of limitations applicable to a claim accruing out of this state shall that prescribed either by the law of the place where the claim accrued or by the law of this state, *whichever last bars the claim*" [Emphasis added.] The court, responding to a question certified by the Tenth Circuit, held that "period of limitations" does not include statutes of repose. The Tenth Circuit affirmed the district's judgment that the Arkansas statute of repose barred the suit. 318 Fed. Appx. 721 (2009).

Tanges v. Heidelberg North America, Inc., 710 N.E.2d 250 (N.Y.1999) held that the Connecticut statute of repose is substantive and bars a New York resident's claim for injury in Connecticut. The court further held that the New York borrowing statute, which provides that when a cause of action accrues in favor of a New York State resident the time limited by the laws of New York shall apply, does not permit suit because the Connecticut statute prevented an action from ever accruing. Would focusing on the purposes of the borrowing statute provide a more satisfactory explanation of why it did not apply?

Marchesani v. Pellerin-Milnor Corp., 269 F.3d 481 (5th Cir.2001), held that La. C.C. Article 3549 does not distinguish between statutes of limitation and statutes of repose. The court ruled that although Tennessee substantive law applied, Tennessee's 10-year statute of repose for product liability claims does not apply to bar suit by a Tennessee domiciliary injured in Tennessee against a Louisiana manufacturer.

Wenke v. Gehl Co., 682 N.W.2d 405 (Wis.2004). Plaintiff was injured in Iowa while using a baler manufactured by the defendant, a Wisconsin corporation. An Iowa statute bars commencing a product liability action more than 15 years after a product "was first purchased." Plaintiff's injury occurred more than 15 years after defendant had sold the baler to an Iowa buyer. Unable to maintain the action in Iowa, plaintiff sued in Wisconsin. The Wisconsin borrowing statute provides: "If an action is brought in this state on a foreign cause of action and the foreign period of limitation which applies has expired, no action may be maintained in this state." Held: The action is barred in Wisconsin because "the phrase 'period of limitation' . . . pertains equally to foreign statutes of limitation and foreign statutes of repose." Id. at 409.

SECTION 4. REFERENCE TO THE CHOICE-OF-LAW RULES OF ANOTHER JURISDICTION

In re Annesley
Chancery Division, 1926.
[1926] Ch. 692.

[Summons to determine distribution of personal property in England. This turned on the validity of a will. The court applied a choice-of-law rule that determined the validity of a will of personal property by the law of the decedent's domicile at death.

The decedent was a widow over 80 years old at her death in 1924. She was married in England in 1860 to an Army officer, with whom she lived in England until 1866, and then in France until his death in 1884. She then purchased a chateau in Orthez, France, and resided there until her death, making only a few short visits back to England. After 1866 she had no place of residence in England. Two daughters survived her, but she left a will giving most of her estate to others. Under the French law she could dispose by will of only one third of her personal property. Under the English law she could dispose of all of it.]

■ RUSSELL, J. stated the facts and continued: The first question to be decided is whether the domicil of the testatrix was English or French. But for the fact that Mrs. Annesley took no steps to obtain a formal French domicil according to French law, and both in her will and in a codicil to it declared that it was not her intention to abandon her domicil of origin—namely, England, there could not, I conceive, be any room for doubt as to the position according to English law. She died having acquired a French domicil of choice. To use the language of Lord Westbury in Udny v. Udny, L.R. 1 H.L.Sc. 441, 458, Mrs. Annesley fixed voluntarily her sole residence in France, with an intention of continuing to reside there for an unlimited time. The domicil flows from the combination of fact and intention, the fact of residence and the intention of remaining for an unlimited time. The intention required is not an intention specifically directed to a change of domicil, but an intention of residing in a country for an unlimited time. The above recited facts in my opinion clearly establish both the necessary fact and the necessary intention.

Those who seek to establish an English domicil naturally place much reliance on the declarations in her will and codicil. They contend that we have here two statements made at different times by the lady herself, that she had never intended and did not intend to abandon her English domicil, and that in the face of these statements it is impossible for the Court to hold that a French domicil of choice had in fact or in law arisen. The contention is a tempting one to accede to in view of the fact that the finding of an English domicil would solve sundry other knotty points of difficulty which lurk in the background. But I feel unable to accede to it.

It must I think be conceded that domicil cannot depend upon mere declaration, though the fact of the declaration having been made must be one of the elements to be weighed in arriving at a conclusion on the question of domicil. But if a particular domicil clearly emerges from a consideration of the other relevant facts, a declaration of intention to retain some other domicil will not suffice to destroy the result of those facts. If (as I think she had) Mrs. Annesley had by the factum of long residence and by her animus manendi acquired before the date of her codicil a French domicil of choice, her statement that she never intended to abandon her English domicil will not prevent the acquisition of a French domicil of choice, unless weighing the statement with the other relevant facts the Court comes to the conclusion that the animus manendi had not been established. * * *

It was however contended that assuming that all the relevant facts do establish a French domicil, yet in the particular case it was according to English law impossible for Mrs. Annesley to have acquired a French domicil—because not having taken the steps prescribed by art. 13 of the Civil Code she was not and could not be a domiciled Frenchwoman in the eyes of the law of France. In other words the proposition is that no one can, according to English law, acquire a domicil of choice in a foreign country unless that person has also acquired a domicil there according to the law of the foreign country. The contention is founded upon one branch of the judgment of Farwell J. in the well known case In re Johnson, [1903] 1 Ch. 821.

Such a contention appears to me inconsistent with many decisions in the Courts of this country. In In re Martin, [1900] P. 211, 227, Lindley M. R. clearly lays it down that domicil is to be determined by English law. His judgment is no doubt a dissenting judgment, but the effect of his views upon this particular point is not weakened or affected by that fact. "The domicil . . . must be determined by the English Court . . . according to those legal principles applicable to domicil which are recognized in this country and are part of its law." If it were otherwise the question whether an individual were domiciled in France (or in any other country which requires the fulfillment of certain legal requirements before a person can be considered by the Court of that country as domiciled in that country) would be solved quite easily in every case by ascertaining whether those legal requirements had or had not been fulfilled. Yet there have been numerous cases (some of which appear in the books) in which the question has always been considered and answered by an elaborate consideration of the various facts and circumstances in each case. * * *

I hold that the question whether Mrs. Annesley died domiciled in France must be answered by ascertaining whether she had abandoned her English domicil and had acquired a French domicil of choice in accordance with the requirements of English law—namely, by the factum of residence coupled with the animus manendi, and that regardless of the question whether she had or had not complied with the formalities required by French law to be carried out by her before she could rank in its eyes as a domiciled Frenchwoman.

I accordingly decide that the domicil of the testatrix at the time of her death was French. French law accordingly applies, but the question remains: what French law? According to French municipal law, the law applicable in the case of a foreigner not legally domiciled in France is the law of that person's nationality, in this case British. But the law of that nationality refers the question back to French law, the law of the domicil; and the question arises, will the French law accept this reference back, or renvoi, and apply French municipal law?

Upon this question arises acute conflict of expert opinion. Two experts took the view that the renvoi would not be accepted, but that a French Court would distribute the movables of the testatrix in accordance with English municipal law. One expert equally strongly took the view that a French Court would accept the renvoi and distribute in accordance with French municipal law. I must come to a conclusion as best I can upon this question of fact upon the evidence after considering and weighing the reasons given by each side in support of their respective views. It is a case rather of views expressed by the experts as to what the French law ought to be, than what it is. Although there is in France no system of case law such as we understand it here—the decisions of higher Courts not being binding upon inferior tribunals—yet I think I must pay some attention to the fact that this question of renvoi has at different times come for consideration before the Cour de Cassation, the highest Court in France, and each time with the same result—namely, the acceptance of the renvoi and the application of the French municipal law. It is true that the Cour de Cassation is quite free to take the opposite view on a future occasion, but it has never done so. I refer to the cases which were discussed and expounded before me—namely, the Forgo case [Clunet (1883), 64] in 1882, and the Soulié case [Clunet (1910), 888] in 1910. In the former case a decision of the Cour de Cassation, the renvoi was accepted, and French municipal law was applied to the disposition of the estate of a Bavarian national domiciled de facto in France (but not domiciled there according to French law), because according to Bavarian law the law of the domicil or usual residence was applicable. The Forgo case gave rise to grave differences of opinion among French jurists and was followed by many conflicting decisions in lower Courts, some favouring the "Théorie du Renvoi," others against it. The matter again came under the consideration of the branch of the Cour de Cassation entitled Chambre de Requêtes, one of whose functions is to decide whether or not an appeal to the Cour de Cassation should be allowed to proceed. That was the Soulié case, in which the Court below had held that French municipal law governed the succession to the movable property of an American subject who had died in France with a de facto domicil in that country. The Chamber declined to allow an appeal to the Cour de Cassation to proceed. This decision, coming as it did after the grave differences of opinion which resulted from the Forgo case, strikes me as of great importance. As is pointed out in a note to the report in Clunet [Clunet (1910), 888, 892] it shows that the Supreme Court persists with energy in its former view, notwithstanding the views of text writers to the contrary.

In these circumstances, and after careful consideration of the evidence of the experts called before me, I have come to the conclusion that I ought to accept the view that according to French law the French Court, in administering the movable property of a deceased foreigner who, according to the law of his country, is domiciled in France, and whose property must, according to that law, be applied in accordance with the law of the country in which he was domiciled, will apply French municipal law, and that even though the deceased had not complied with art. 13 of the Code.

The result is that as regards her English personal estate and her French movable property the testatrix in this case had power only to dispose of one-third thereof by her will.

Speaking for myself, I should like to reach the same conclusion by a much more direct route along which no question of renvoi need be encountered at all. When the law of England requires that the personal estate of a British subject who dies domiciled, according to the requirements of English law, in a foreign country shall be administered in accordance with the law of that country, why should this not mean in accordance with the law which that country would apply, not to the propositus, but to its own nationals legally domiciled there? In other words, when we say that French law applies to the administration of the personal estate of an Englishman who dies domiciled in France, we mean that French municipal law which France applies in the case of Frenchmen. This appears to me a simple and rational solution which avoids altogether that endless oscillation which otherwise would result from the law of the country of nationality invoking the law of the country of domicil, while the law of the country in turn invokes the law of the country of nationality, and I am glad to find that this simple solution has in fact been adopted by the Surrogates' Court of New York [citing Matter of Tallmadge, Note 1 following]. * * *

NOTES

1.   Matter of Tallmadge, 109 Misc. 696, 181 N.Y.S. 336 (1919), cited at the end of the principal case, is the opinion of a referee in a surrogate's court. It involved the will of a United States citizen, formerly of New York, who died domiciled in France. His will, written in English in New York, left ten dollars to his brother who was his only heir. It left all of the residue of his estate to an aunt and to a cousin, share and share alike. It appeared that the cousin predeceased the testator, and the question was whether the brother took the cousin's share as intestate property according to New York law, or whether

the aunt took the whole of the residue under Article 1044 of the French Civil Code. It was held that the French internal law should be applied.

2.   In re Annesley raises the question of why, when the conflicts law of the forum points to another jurisdiction, a forum court should refer to the choice-of-law rules of that jurisdiction. This problem is called "renvoi," which means "sending back" or "sending away," and occurs when the other state's conflicts rule points back to the forum or to a third state. The first Restatement of Conflict of Laws (1934), which contained territorial rules that selected law according to the location of one element in a transaction, rejected reference to another jurisdiction's conflicts rules, except on questions of title to land and validity of a divorce. Id. §§ 7, 8.

The Restatement (Second) of Conflict of Laws, which chooses law by taking account, among other things, of the policies underlying the laws of "interested states" (Id. § 6(2)(b), (c)), suggests three reasons for the forum to refer to the conflicts rules of other jurisdictions.

(i)   The forum wishes to reach the same result as the other jurisdiction. Id. § 8(2). An example of this would be a court adjudicating interests in realty in another country. Suppose that the courts in the other country would insist on determining those rights under the law of the situs and would not recognize a different determination by a non-situs court. There is no point in the non-situs court attempting to reach a different result, unless there are other assets in the forum that can be distributed to take account of the disposition in the foreign situs. In re Schneider's Estate, 198 Misc. 1017, 96 N.Y.S.2d 652 (Sur.Ct.1950), referred to the Swiss choice-of-law rule to validate the testamentary disposition of realty in Switzerland. The testator was an American citizen who died domiciled in New York. Under Swiss internal law, the testator's heirs were entitled to portions of the estate beyond the portion devised to them. The Swiss conflicts rule, however, applied the law of the domicile at death of a foreign national. A similar result was reached in Matter of Estate of Wright, 637 A.2d 106 (Me.1994). The testator was an American who died domiciled in Switzerland. A Swiss statute permitted a foreigner domiciled in Switzerland to elect the law of his nationality to determine the validity of his will. The testator's will chose Maine law to govern the administration of his estate. The court held that the decedent's children were not entitled to take a forced share of the estate—a power they had under internal Swiss law.

(ii)   "[T]he state of the forum has no substantial relationship to the particular issue or the parties and the courts of all interested states would concur in selecting the local law rule applicable to this issue. . . ." Restatement, Second, Conflict of Laws § 8(3). Matter of Zietz' Estate, 198 Misc. 77, 96 N.Y.S.2d 442 (Sur.Ct.1950), is an illustration. A national of Liechtenstein died in Austria. If he was domiciled in Austria, New York conflicts law would refer to that law to determine which foreign administrator should control ancillary administration in New York, but under a treaty between Austria and Liechtenstein, the law of the nationality controlled. The court stated that under these circumstances it would "accept that reference to the law of the nationality."

(iii) The forum wishes to determine whether the other jurisdiction asserts an "interest" in the application of the other jurisdiction's law. Restatement, Second, Conflict of Laws § 8, comment k. In *Annesley*, is the French rule referring to the law of the nationality, an indication that France disclaims any interest in applying its forced-share rule to a domiciliary who was a national of another country? If so, did it make any sense to insist on applying the French forced-share rule because English conflicts rules pointed to France? Does the extent to which another jurisdiction's choice-of-law rule indicates that state's "interest" in the application of law depend upon whether that rule itself takes account of policies underlying the law chosen? In Pfau v. Trent Aluminum Co., 263 A.2d 129 (N.J.1970), a New Jersey driver, with a Connecticut passenger, crashed in Iowa. The passenger sued the driver. Although the laws of both states have since changed, Iowa had a guest statute, which prevented the passenger from recovering for the driver's ordinary negligence, and Connecticut's choice-of-law rule applied the law of the place of injury. The Supreme Court of New Jersey held that the Iowa guest statute did not apply: "[W]e see no reason for applying Connecticut's choice-of-law rule. . . . Connecticut's choice-of-law rule does not identify that state's interest in the matter. Lex loci delicti was born in an effort to achieve simplicity and uniformity, and does not relate to a state's interest in having its law applied to given issues in a tort case." But see Sutherland v. Kennington Truck Service, Ltd., 562 N.W.2d 466 (Mich.1997), in which an Ontario driver and an Ohio driver collided in Michigan. Michigan had a three-year statute of limitations. Ontario and Ohio had two-year statutes. More than The Ohio driver and his wife sued the Ontario driver and his Ontario employer two years but less than three years after the collision. The court noted that Ontario would apply Michigan's longer statute of limitations as the lex loci delicti. The court state that therefore "we do not see how Ontario can have an interest in having Michigan courts apply Ontario law" to protect the Ontario defendants. Id. at 473. The court applied the Michigan limitation to permit suit between Ontario and Ohio parties although the action would have been barred under both Ontario and Ohio limitations.

For a discussion of reference to foreign choice-of-law rules as an aid in determining the purposes underlying foreign internal law, see Kramer, Return of the Renvoi, 66 N.Y.U.L.Rev. 979 (1991).

3. Another reason to refer to the choice-of-law rule of another jurisdiction is to avoid a statutory choice-of-law rule of the forum. See p. 519 Note 5, supra, suggesting use of this technique in construing borrowing statutes. Richards v. United States, 369 U.S. 1, 82 S.Ct. 585 (1962), construed the Federal Tort Claims Act's reference to "law of the place where the act or omission occurred," to mean the whole law of that place, including its choice-of-law rules. The Court stated: "[T]his interpretation of the Act provides a degree of flexibility to the law to be applied in federal courts. . . . Recently there has been a tendency on the part of some States to depart from the general conflicts rule [which chose the law of the place of injury] in order to take into account the interests of the State having significant contact with the parties to the litigation. We can see no compelling reason to saddle the Act with an interpretation that would prevent the federal courts from implementing this policy in choice-of-law rules where the State in which the negligence occurred has adopted it."

Gould Electronics Inc. v. United States, 220 F.3d 169 (3d Cir.2000), notes that courts have taken five different approaches to choosing law under the Federal Tort Claims Act when the defendant has committed acts and omissions in more than one state: 1) for each injury caused by a different act, apply the whole law of the site of that act; 2) apply the whole law of the site of the last act or omission having causal effect; 3) apply the whole law of the site of the act that had the most significant causal effect; 4) apply the whole law of the site where physical acts could have prevented the injury; 5) apply the whole law of the site of the relevant act or omission. The court holds that the first approach is not applicable on the facts and that under any of the other approaches New York choice-of-law rules determine the liability of the United States for contribution to a settlement of toxic tort claims resulting from pollution in New York. The court also held that New York choice-of-law rules (the *"Neumeier"* rules, p. 592, infra) chose the contribution law of Ohio where the settling companies were headquartered.

The Federal Tort Claims Act provides that it does not apply to "any claim arising in a foreign country." 28 U.S.C. § 2680(k). Federal district courts and courts of appeals developed the "headquarters doctrine," which allowed recovery although the injury was suffered in a foreign country if the decision causing the injury was made in the U.S. Sosa v. Alvarez-Machain, 542 U.S. 692, 124 S.Ct. 2739 (2004), held that the FTCA does not apply to injury abroad even though U.S. government agents in the U.S. ordered the injurious conduct, rejecting the "headquarters doctrine." The court pointed out that at the time the exemption was drafted, the choice-of-law rule applied to torts by all U.S. jurisdictions was the law of the place of injury:

> The object being to avoid application of substantive foreign law, Congress evidently used the modifier "arising in a foreign country" to refer to claims based on foreign harm or injury, the fact that would trigger application of foreign law to determine liability. That object, addressed by the quoted phrase, would obviously have been thwarted, however, by applying the headquarters doctrine, for that doctrine would have displaced the exception by recasting claims of foreign injury as claims not arising in a foreign country because some planning or negligence at domestic headquarters was their cause. And that, in turn, would have resulted in applying foreign law of the place of injury, in accordance with the choice-of-law rule of the headquarters jurisdiction.

Id. at 797–98. Is the choice-of-law reasoning in *osa* compatible with the reasoning in Richards v. United States, supra?

4.   Louisiana Civil Code art. 3517: "Renvoi. Except as otherwise indicated, when the law of another state is applicable under this Book, that law shall not include the law of conflict of laws of that state. Nevertheless, in determining the state whose law is applicable to an issue under Articles 3515 [General Provisions], 3519 [Status], 3537 [Conventional Obligations], and 3542 [Delictual and Quasi-Delictual Obligations], the law of conflict of laws of the

involved foreign states may be taken into consideration." Each of the articles cited in article 3517 refers to "the law of the state whose policies would be most seriously impaired if its law were not applied" to a particular issue.

An Australian court, except with regard to succession, will interpret a reference to the law of another jurisdiction as referring to the law that the courts of that place apply to purely local cases. See Jianfu Chen, Australian Private International Law at the End of the 20th Century: Progress or Regress?, in Private International Law at the End of the 20th Century: Progress or Regress? (Symeonides ed., 1998), 83, 101.

The classic European position is to consider the foreign conflicts rule and to follow its reference forward to the law of a third state, or back to the law of the forum. The principal exceptions, for signatories of the European Union's Regulations on the Law Applicable to Contractual Obligations, and the Law Applicable to Non-Contractual Obligations are Article 20 of the Contractual Obligations Regulation and Article 24 of the Non-Contractual Obligations Regulation, which exclude renvoi. But cf. Article 9(2) of the Contractual Obligations Regulation:

> Effect may be given to the overriding mandatory provisions of the law of the country where the obligations arising out of the contract have to be or have been performed, in so far as those overriding mandatory provisions render the performance of the contract unlawful. In considering whether to give effect to those provisions, regard shall be had to their nature and purpose and to the consequences of their application or non-application.

Documentary Appendix, infra.

In the rest of the world, most modern codifications contain specific provisions on renvoi. About as many accept renvoi as reject it. Both provisions that accept and reject renvoi are likely to state exceptions. See J. Kropholler et al. (eds), Außereuropäische IPR-Gesetze (1999); A.I. Muranov & A.N. Zhilsov (eds), Private International Law—A Collection of Foreign Statutes (2001) (in Russian).

CHAPTER 8

CHOOSING THE RULE OF DECISION

SECTION 1. THE RECEIVED SYSTEM AND TRADITION

A. TERRITORIALITY AND THE JURISDICTION-SELECTING PROCESS

RESTATEMENT, SECOND, CONFLICT OF LAWS, CHAPTER 7, WRONGS, INTRODUCTORY NOTE:

The Position Taken by the Original Restatement

The original Restatement stated that, with minor exceptions, all substantive questions relating to the existence of a tort claim are governed by the local law of the "place of wrong." This was described (in Section 377) as "the state where the last event necessary to make an actor liable for an alleged tort takes place." Since a tort is the product of wrongful conduct and of resulting injury and since the injury follows the conduct, the state of the "last event" is the state where the injury occurred. This rule of the original Restatement was derived from the vested rights doctrine which called for the enforcement everywhere of rights that had been lawfully created under the local law of a state.

"The theory . . . is that, although the act complained of was subject to no law having force in the forum, it gave rise to an obligation, an *obligatio*, which, like other obligations, follows the person, and may be enforced wherever the person may be found. . . . But as the only source of this obligation is the law of the place of the act, it follows that that law determines not merely the existence of the obligation, . . . but equally determines its extent." Justice Holmes in Slater v. Mexican National Railroad Co., 194 U.S. 120, 126, 24 S.Ct. 581, 582–83 (1904), p. 264, supra.

CAVERS, THE CHOICE-OF-LAW PROCESS (1965), PP. 5–9:

In Anglo-American jurisdictions, the development of choice-of-law doctrine has been greatly influenced by the works of the English scholar and jurist, A.V. Dicey, and the American law professor, Joseph H. Beale. Dicey adopted the theory that the task of the court in a choice-of-law case was the enforcement of vested rights. Professor Beale coupled this with the territorial concepts that Story had drawn from Huber and thereby organized a system of choice-of-law rules, simple in structure, which could be applied without regard to the content of the particular laws between which choice had to be made. This theory dominated the American Law Institute's *Restatement of Conflict of Laws* for which Professor Beale served as Reporter.

Professor Beale confronted the welter of conflicting conflicts decisions with bland determination. "Most of the statements in this work will be dogmatic," he wrote at the start of his treatise and then asked— rhetorically: "Does not the Bar desire dogmatic statements?" I need quote only two propositions from the treatise to convey the character of his doctrine and his thought. Thus, at the outset of his discussion of the choice of law as to contracts, he declared: "The question whether a contract is valid . . . can on general principles be determined by no other law than that which applies to the acts [of the parties], that is, by the law of the place of contracting. . . . If . . . the law of the place where the agreement is made annexes no legal obligation to it, *there is no other law which has power to do so.*"

And in expounding choice of law as to torts, Professor Beale explained, "It is impossible for a plaintiff to recover in tort unless he has been given by some law a cause of action in tort; and this cause of action can be given only by the law of the place where the tort was committed. That is the place where the injurious event occurs, and its law is the law *therefore* which applies to it."

While the *Conflicts Restatement* was still in gestation, Beale's basic conceptions came under attack by what he termed "an ephemeral school" of "self-styled realists." Among these Professor Ernest Lorenzen and Professor Walter Wheeler Cook were the foremost. Professor Charles Wesley Hohfeld, famed for his analysis of jural relations, had also been a dissenter from conflicts orthodoxy of his day, and Professor Lorenzen has credited him with the origin of the "local law" theory that, particularly as championed by Professor Cook, became the principal rival of Professor Beale's "vested rights" theory. These critics challenged the logic of the vested rights theory which they found question-begging, but they also challenged its practicality. They complained of its failure to reflect social and economic needs and policies, though they were seldom specific in identifying these. . . .

. . . Though I joined them in asking, in Professor Lorenzen's words: "What are the demands of justice in the particular situation; what is the controlling policy?" I insisted, nevertheless, that these questions could not be answered as long as the questioners continued to seek what I termed "a jurisdiction-selecting" rule,[24] that is, a rule indicating the source of the law to be applied without regard to the law's content. Without taking the

---

[24] Cavers, A Critique of the Choice-of-Law Problem, 47 Harv.L.Rev. 173, 194 (1933): This concept, launched in the article cited, is gradually becoming current. The jurisdiction-selecting rule makes a *state* the object of choice; in theory it is only after the rule has selected the governing state by reference to the "contact" prescribed in the rule that the court ascertains the content of the state's law.

content of the conflicting laws into account, how could one know what would satisfy the demands of justice or the requirements of policy?

---

3 BEALE, A TREATISE ON THE CONFLICT OF LAWS 1929 (1935):

[E]very law has both a territorial and a personal application; and where a conflict arises, it is because one sovereign wishes to apply his own law to a juridical relation arising on his territory, while another wishes to throw around his own subject, who is one of the parties to the relation, the protection of his personal law. Which of the two independent sovereigns should yield is a question not susceptible of a solution upon which all parties would agree.

NOTE

This excerpt from Professor Beale's treatise, published the year after the first Restatement of Conflict of Laws, may be taken as a response to the critics referred to by Professor Cavers. In order to rebut Professor Beale, it is necessary to establish two propositions. First, there are occasions on which a sovereign should not seek "to apply his own law to a juridical relation arising on his territory." Second, when two or more sovereigns do wish their own laws applied, there is a method of resolving this conflict that is more satisfactory than selecting some one event in a multi-state transaction and applying the law of the geographical location of that event. The first proposition may be easier to establish than the second.

As the materials in this chapter indicate, methods that take into account the content and purposes of domestic rules before choosing between them have largely superseded Professor Beale's territorial conflicts system. Which cases created the greatest dissatisfaction with the territorial rules? If Professor Beale's rule for unintentional torts had been, "if both parties have the same domicile, apply that law, otherwise apply the law of the place of injury," would there have been a "conflicts revolution"? Article 4(2) of the European Union Regulation on the Law Applicable to Non-Contractual Obligations (the Rome II Regulation) expresses a same "habitual residence" exception to the general rule applying the law of the place of injury. See Documentary Appendix, infra, p. 1213 .

One would suppose that choice-of-law analysis is not necessary if there is no difference between the relevant rules of forum and all other states that have contacts with the parties or the transaction. As stated in Phillips v. The Marist Society of Washington Province, 80 F.3d 274, 276 (8th Cir.1996): "Having reviewed the relevant laws of Arkansas and the District of Columbia, we conclude that the legal principles involved in this case, rooted as they are in the common law of contracts are the same in both jurisdictions. We thus do not need to engage in a choice-of-law analysis. See Forsyth v. Cessna Aircraft Co., 520 F.2d 608, 613 (9th Cir.1975) ('In the absence of a[n actual] conflict, *lex fori* controls.')."

Nevertheless, because, as Professor Cavers states, traditional choice-of-law rules select law without regard to its content, sometimes these rules created conflict where none existed. See Nelson v. Eckert, 329 S.W.2d 426 (Ark.1959), in which the court held that although both Arkansas and Texas had two-year statutes of limitations for wrongful death, neither applied, and that the Arkansas five-year limit for personal injury made the action timely.

B. EXAMPLES OF THE SYSTEM IN OPERATION

1. UNILATERAL AND MULTILATERAL APPROACHES

Most often a court resolves choice-of-law problems with a multilateral analysis. Under this approach, the court selects the law it views as appropriate in the light of the contacts of the parties and the transaction with the state whose law the court chooses. The law chosen may be that of the state in which the court sits or that of some other state. On some issues, however, the court either applies the law of its own state or dismisses the case. On these matters the court conducts a unilateral analysis of its own law. Typically, this unilateral analysis asks whether applying forum law is fair to the parties and consistent with the policies underlying that law.

United States courts conduct a unilateral choice-of-law analysis in divorce cases. A court has subject matter jurisdiction to grant a divorce if at least one spouse is domiciled there. See Williams v. North Carolina, 317 U.S. 287, 63 S.Ct. 207 (1942), p. 936, infra. In Torlonia v. Torlonia, 142 A. 843 (Conn.1928), the court enunciated the accepted doctrine:

"... [T]he rule is well established that the courts of the State of the domicil may grant a divorce for any cause allowed by its laws, without regard to the place of the commission of the offense for which it is granted or to whether such offense constitutes a ground for divorce in the state in which it was committed. . . ."

Under other legal systems, the forum does not invariably apply its own divorce law. In the European Union Regulation 1259/2010 (commonly known as the "Rome III" regulation) governs divorce law. The regulation gives the spouses the ability to agree on the law applicable to their divorce by choosing among the state of their last common habitual residence if one spouse still resides there, the nationality of either spouse, where the spouses have resided for at least five years, or in which the divorce suit is filed. In the absence of agreement by the spouses the law applicable to a divorce is that of the state: where the spouses have their common habitual residence; if they do not have a common habitual residence, where they last had a common habitual residence if one spouse still resides there; if one spouse does not still reside there; where both spouses are nationals; if the spouses do not have the same nationality, where the divorce suit is filed.

Under Japanese law divorce is governed by the national law that the spouses have in common; in the absence of such law by the law of their common habitual residence, or, if no common habitual residence, by the law of the place with which the spouses are most closely connected. However, a divorce is governed by Japanese law if either of the spouses is a Japanese national, having his or her habitual residence in Japan. Act on the General Rules for Application of Laws, Act No. 78 of 2006, entry into force on January 1, 2007, articles 25, 27.

Workers' Compensation is another subject on which in most states the forum determines whether its own state's law applies because of the contacts of the parties and the employment relationship with that state. If forum law does not apply, the claim is dismissed. For an exception in which a court applies the workers' compensation law of a sister state, see White v. Malone Properties, Inc., 494 So.2d 576 (Miss.1986). The court affirmed a dismissal of the action because time limitations in the Louisiana workers' compensation code had expired.

Criminal law is the classic area in which the state either applies its own law or declines jurisdiction. Many criminal codes have provisions describing the contacts with the state necessary for the code to apply. See, e.g., Model Penal Code § 1.03(1), 10A U.L.A. 1,25 (2001): "[A] person may be convicted under the law of this State of an offense . . . if: (a) either the conduct which is an element of the offense or the result which is such an element occurs within this State. . . ."

Sometimes a state's criminal law refers to the law of another state. For example, the Model Penal Code section quoted above goes on to state: "(3) Subsection (1)(a) does not apply when causing a particular result is an element of an offense and the result is caused by conduct occurring outside the State which would not constitute an offense if the result had occurred there, unless the actor purposely or knowingly caused the result within the State." Laws that increase punishment if there have been previous convictions often include convictions in other states. People v. Laino, 87 P.3d 27 (Cal.2004), cert. denied, 543 U.S. 886, 125 S.Ct. 104 (2004), held that for the purposes of California's "three strikes law," which provides for enhanced punishment of a convicted person who has had prior felony convictions, defendant's guilty plea in Arizona to aggravated assault against his wife counted as a prior felony conviction. Moreover, the Full Faith and Credit Clause of the U.S. Constitution did not preclude a California court from so treating the Arizona plea even though, after defendant successfully completed a domestic violence prevention program, an Arizona court entered a judgment dismissing the aggravated assault charge.

In these circumstances a court is not applying another state's criminal law but is referring to that law as a fact that determines the application of forum law. Some crimes are of such universal concern that international law permits any state that apprehends the perpetrator to try and punish him or her for acts that occurred outside the state and did not affect citizens of the state. See Restatement (Fourth) of the Foreign Relations Law of the United States § 217 (2018) ("International law recognizes a state's jurisdiction to prescribe law with respect to certain offenses of universal concern, such as genocide, crimes against humanity, war crimes, certain acts of terrorism, piracy, slave trade and torture, even if no specific connection exists between the state and the persons or conduct being regulated.").

2.   TRADITIONAL RULES

a)   Tort

Alabama Great Southern Railroad Co. v. Carroll
Supreme Court of Alabama, 1892.
97 Ala. 126, 11 So. 803, 18 L.R.A. 433, 38 Am.St.Rep. 163.

[Plaintiff was a brakeman on defendant's railroad. Both parties were residents of Alabama and plaintiff was hired there. Plaintiff was injured in Mississippi due to a break in a defective car link. The evidence showed negligence on the part of railroad employees who had a duty to inspect the links at various places in Alabama.]

■ MCCLELLAN, J. . . . This was the negligence not of the master, the defendant, but of fellow-servants of the plaintiff, for which at common-law the defendant is not liable. . . . We feel entirely safe in declaring that plaintiff has shown no cause of action under the common-law as it is understood and applied both here and in Mississippi.

It is, however, further contended that the plaintiff . . . has made out a case for the recovery sought under the Employer's Liability Act of Alabama, it being clearly shown that there is no such . . . law . . . in the State of Mississippi. Considering this position in the abstract, that is dissociated from the facts of this particular case which are supposed to exert an important influence upon it, there cannot be two opinions as to its being unsound and untenable. So looked at, we do not understand appellee's counsel even to deny either the proposition or its application to this case, that there can be no recovery in one State for injuries to the person sustained in another unless the infliction of the injuries is actionable under the law of the State in which they were received. Certainly this is the well-established rule of law subject in some jurisdictions to the qualification that the infliction of the injuries would also support an action in the State where the suit is brought, had they been received within that State. . . .

But it is claimed that the facts of this case take it out of the general rule . . . and authorize the courts of Alabama to subject the defendant to the payment of damages under section 2590 of the Code, although the injuries counted on were sustained in Mississippi under circumstances which involved no liability on the defendant by the laws of that State.

This insistence is in the first instance based on that aspect of the evidence which goes to show that the negligence which produced the casualty transpired in Alabama, and the theory that wherever the consequence of that negligence manifested itself, a recovery can be had in Alabama. We are referred to no authority in support of this proposition, and exhaustive investigation on our part has failed to disclose any. . . .

It is admitted, or at least cannot be denied, that negligence of duty unproductive of damnifying results will not authorize or support a recovery. Up to the time this train passed out of Alabama no injury had resulted. For all that occurred in Alabama, therefore, no cause of action whatever arose. The fact which created the right to sue, the injury without which confessedly no action would lie anywhere, transpired in the State of Mississippi. It was in that State, therefore, necessarily that the cause of action, if any, arose; and whether a cause of action arose and existed at all or not must in all reason be determined by the law which obtained at the time and place when and where the fact which is relied on to justify a recovery transpired. Section 2590 of the Code of Alabama had no efficiency beyond the lines of Alabama. . . . Section 2590 of the Code, in other words, is to be interpreted in the light of universally recognized principles of private international or interstate law, as if its operation had been expressly limited to this State and as if its first line read as follows: "When a personal injury is *received in Alabama* by a servant or employee," &c., &c. . . . We have not been inattentive to the suggestions of counsel in this connection, which are based upon that rule of the statutory and common criminal law under which a murderer is punishable where the fatal blow is delivered, regardless of the place where death ensues. This principle is patently without application here. There would be some analogy if the plaintiff had been stricken in Alabama and suffered in Mississippi, which is not the fact. There is, however, an analogy which is afforded by the criminal law, but which points away from the conclusion appellee's counsel desire us to reach. This is found in that well established doctrine of criminal law, that where the unlawful act is committed in one jurisdiction or State and takes effect—produces the result which it is the purpose of the law to prevent, or, it having ensued, punish for—in another jurisdiction or State, the crime is deemed to have been committed and is punished in that jurisdiction or State in which the result is manifested, and not where the act was committed. . . .

[Plaintiff argued that because the contract of employment was entered into in Alabama between Alabama citizens the Alabama Employer's Liability Act became a part of the contract and the defendant was under a contractual duty to the plaintiff. The court rejected this argument.]

[T]he duties and liabilities incident to the relation between the plaintiff and the defendant which are involved in this case, are not imposed by and do not rest in or spring from the contract between the parties. The only office of the contract, under section 2590 of the Code, is the establishment of a relation between them, that of master and servant; and it is upon that relation, that incident or consequence of the contract, and not upon the rights of the parties under the contract, that our statute operates. The law is not concerned with the contractual stipulations, except in so far as to determine from them that the relation upon which it is to operate exists. Finding this relation the statute imposes certain duties and liabilities on the parties to it wholly regardless of the stipulations of the contract as to the rights of the parties under it, and, it may be, in the teeth of such stipulations.

For the error in refusing to instruct the jury to find for the defendant if they believed the evidence, the judgment is reversed and the cause will be remanded.

NOTES

1. The words "in Alabama" did not appear in § 2590 of the Alabama Code. The Alabama Employers' Liability Act was subsequently amended to cover out-of-state injury if the contract of employment was made in Alabama. Ala.Code Ann. § 7540 (1928).

2. The "universally recognized principles of private international or interstate law" that the court refers to in construing § 2590 state that prima facie legislation applies only in the territory of the sovereign that has enacted it. See, e.g. Foley Bros. Inc. v. Filardo, 336 U.S. 281, 284, 69 S.Ct. 575, 577 (1949): "[A]ll legislation of Congress, unless a contrary intent appears, is meant to apply only within the territorial jurisdiction of the United States." In the principal case does this canon of construction assist or impede reaching a result that is consistent with the policies underlying the Alabama statute?

3. The "doctrine of criminal law" that the court refers to is no longer "well established." See Model Penal Code § 1.03(1).

4. Rationis Enterprises Inc. of Panama v. Hyundai Mipo Dockyard Co., 426 F.3d 580 (2d Cir.2005): Defendant shipyard modified plaintiff's ship in Korea. Because of defective welding during the modification, the ship sank on the high seas. Choice of law was governed by the factors set out in Lauritzen v. Larsen [page 687, infra]. The court held that Korean law applied under which a statute of repose barred the claim. Korean law applied because the first *Lauritzen* factor is "place of the wrongful act." "[T]he place of the wrongful act is not where the vessel sinks, but where negligence occurs. The reason for this rule is not difficult to discern because it is the state where the negligence occurs that has the greatest interest in regulating the behavior of the parties." Id. at 587.

Victor v. Sperry

District Court of Appeal, Fourth District, California, 1958.
163 Cal.App.2d 518, 329 P.2d 728.

■ MUSSELL, JUSTICE. This is an action for personal injuries sustained by plaintiff in an automobile accident which occurred on the San Quintin highway, approximately 44 kilometers south of Tiajuana, Baja California, Republic of Mexico.

At the time of the collision on July 3, 1955, defendant John C. Sperry, with the permission and consent of defendant John M. Sperry, was driving a Mercury automobile northerly on said highway when the Mercury collided with a Chevrolet automobile being driven in a southerly direction on said highway by defendant Edward Thornton. Plaintiff Rudolph Victor was an occupant of the Thornton vehicle and was severely injured in the collision. Plaintiff and the drivers of both cars were and now are residents and citizens of the State of California. The accident was the result of the negligence (and of the equivalent of negligence under Mexican law) of the drivers of both cars involved in the accident.

Article 1910 of the Civil Code of 1928 for the Federal District and Territories of Mexico, as amended, which had been adopted by the State of Baja California del Norte and which was in effect at the time of the accident, provided as follows: "A person who, acting illicitly or contrary to good customs, causes damages to another, is obligated to repair it, unless it is shown that the damage was produced as a consequence of the guilt or inexcusable negligence of the victim." Neither said code nor the general law of said state or of said Republic distinguished between guests and passengers in motor vehicles nor did they impose any restrictions upon the right of a guest to recover damages from the negligent operator of a motor vehicle in which he was riding.

Prior to the accident plaintiff had been employed as a house mover and his weekly wage was $99. He had not returned to work at the time of the trial and will not be able to engage in the same occupation or any occupation requiring a substantial amount of physical activity.

The trial court found (and it is not disputed) that as a result of the accident plaintiff's spinal cord was damaged. He suffered a paralysis of the left upper and lower extremities and the disability in his left upper extremity is permanent and total. The disability in his lower extremity is permanent and partial. He is and will continue to be unable to walk without a limp or for protracted periods. The court further found that plaintiff suffered the following actual damages as a result of the accident:

Medical and hospital expenses	$2,962.05
Loss of earnings	7,500.00
Impairment of earning capacity	15,000.00
Pain, suffering and mental anguish	15,000.00
Total	$40,462.05

At the time of the accident the Mexican law in effect imposed restrictions on the recovery of damages for personal injuries regardless of their nature or extent. Under the Mexican law in effect at the time a victim of the negligent conduct of another could recover his medical and hospital expenses. For a temporary total disability he could recover only 75 per cent of his lost wages for a period not to exceed one year. Wages in excess of 25 pesos, or $2 per day, could not be taken into account in computing the amount allowed. If he suffered a permanent and total disability, he could recover lost earnings for only 818 days and, even though he earned more than 25 pesos per day, only that amount could be taken into account in computing the amount of the recovery. Where the disability was permanent but not total, the recovery was scaled down. For a permanent disability of an upper extremity the victim could recover only from 50 to 70 per cent of $2 per day for 918 days, the exact percentage depending upon age, the importance of the disability, and the extent to which the disability prevented the victim from engaging in his occupation. If the injured extremity was the "least useful", the indemnity was reduced by 15 per cent. In addition, "moral damages" up to a maximum of one-third of the other recoverable damages might, in the discretion of the court, be awarded. "Moral damages" are defined as "damages suffered by a person in his honor, reputation, personal tranquility or spiritual integrity of his life, and as damages which are not of a physical nature and not capable of exact monetary evaluation." The trial court concluded that enforcement of these restrictions on the recovery of damages is not contrary to the public policy of this State or to abstract justice or injurious to the welfare of the people of this State and that plaintiff was not entitled to recover his actual damages in the amount of $40,462.05. Judgment was thereupon rendered against defendants John C. Sperry and Edward Thornton in the amount of $6,135.96. The recovery was computed as follows:

Medical and hospital expenses	$2,962.05
Temporary total disability	
(75% of $2.00 for 365 days)	547.50
(75% of $2.00 for 365 days)	
Permanent partial disability	
(70% of $2.00 for 918 days less 15%)	1,092.42
Sub-Total	4,601.97
Moral damages	1,533.99
Total	$6,135.96

Under Article 1913 of the Civil Code of 1928 for the Mexican Federal District and Territories, if a person has the use of mechanisms or instruments which are dangerous per se, by the speed they develop, or otherwise, he is obligated to answer for the damages he causes, even though he does not act illicitly, unless the damage is caused by the guilt or inexcusable negligence of the victim. The Mexican courts hold that an automobile is a dangerous mechanism or instrument within the meaning of this section and that a person injured by a motor vehicle is entitled to recover damages without regard to fault or negligence from both the owner and driver of the automobile. However, if liability exists only under Article 1913 "moral damages" are not recoverable. Since liability under Article 1910 was found to exist on the part of the drivers of both automobiles, it became immaterial whether liability under Article 1913 was found to exist as to them. Plaintiff, however, sought a judgment against John M. Sperry, owner of the Chevrolet automobile, for $4,601.97, under Article 1913. The trial court concluded that this article is contrary to the public policy of this State, is in substantial conflict with the law of this State, and should not be enforced. Judgment was entered in favor of defendant John M. Sperry.

Rudolph Victor appeals from the judgment (a) Insofar as it fails to award damages in excess of $6,135.96 as against defendants John C. Sperry and Edward Thornton; and (b) Insofar as it fails to award any damages against defendant John M. Sperry. . . .

In the instant case, since the accident occurred in Mexico, plaintiff's cause of action arose there and the character and measure of his damages are governed by the laws of Mexico. The measure of damages is inseparably connected to the cause of action and cannot be severed therefrom. The limitation upon the amount of damages imposed by the laws of Mexico is not contrary to the public policy of the State of California or injurious to the welfare of the people thereof.

The trial court herein held that the application of Article 1913 of the Civil Code of 1928 for the Federal District and Territories of Mexico, which provides for liability without fault, was in opposition to the public policy of the State of California and refused to enforce that article against John M. Sperry, owner of one of the automobiles involved in the collision. We find no reversible error in this refusal. . . .

Since no right of action exists in California for damages for liability without fault under the circumstances set forth herein and in Article 1913 of the Civil Code of 1928 for the Mexican Federal District and Territories, the trial court herein properly concluded that this article should not be enforced as against John M. Sperry as owner of one of the automobiles involved.

Judgment affirmed.

NOTES

1. At the end of its opinion, the court states that "no right of action exists in California for damages for liability without fault under the circumstances

set forth herein." Under California Code of 1935 § 402(a), in force at the time of the accident, the owner of a motor vehicle was liable for death or injury resulting from the negligence of "any person using or operating the same with the permission express or implied, of the owner." The court found that "[t]he accident was the result of the negligence . . . of the drivers of both cars." If the owner of the automobile in which the plaintiff was a passenger would have been liable under the law of either California or Mexico, is there a rational basis on which the court could reach a different result in the principal case?

2.   If the plaintiff becomes a public charge as a result of his injuries and inadequate compensation, on which society will the burden fall, Mexico or California?

3.   Without special arrangements with his insurer, the automobile owner's California liability insurance did not cover him "44 kilometers south of Tiajuana," which was more than 25 miles from the United States border. If the court had indicated that it was considering applying the California measure of damages in order to enforce California's "interests," did the owner have a cogent argument that he was unfairly surprised? Would this argument be cogent after the California Supreme Court had adopted interest analysis in Reich v. Purcell, 432 P.2d 727 (Cal.1967), p. 583, infra?

4.   The court did not mention the California "guest statute" in force at the time of the accident. This statute, since repealed, required a showing of "intoxication or willful misconduct" of the driver in order for a guest passenger to recover against the driver or "any person legally liable for the conduct of the driver." California Code of 1935, § 403. Should the court have applied this statute?

5.   Other classic applications of the place-of-wrong rule occurred in marital immunity and guest statute cases. If spouses or host and guest are domiciled in a state that permits them to sue one another for negligence, does it make sense to apply the immunity rule of the place of injury to bar suit in their home state? This was the result reached in many of the cases decided before widespread abandonment of the place-of-wrong rule. For marital immunity cases, see, e.g., Dawson v. Dawson, 138 So. 414 (Ala.1931); Landers v. Landers, 216 A.2d 183 (Conn.1966), abrogated by statute, Conn.Gen.Stat.Ann. § 52–527d; Gray v. Gray, 174 A. 508 (N.H.1934), overruled, Thompson v. Thompson, 193 A.2d 439 (N.H.1963) (abandoning place-of-wrong rule). For guest statute cases: see, e.g., Sharp v. Johnson, 80 N.W.2d 650 (Minn.1957), overruled, Kopp v. Rechtzigel, 141 N.W.2d 526 (Minn.1966) (abandoning place-of-wrong rule); Naphtali v. Lafazan, 8 A.D.2d 22, 186 N.Y.S.2d 1010 (1959); overruled, Babcock v. Jackson, 191 N.E.2d 279 (N.Y.1963), p. 577, infra (abandoning place-of-wrong rule).

b)   Contracts

Unlike the monolithic place-of-wrong rule for torts, the traditional choice-of-law rules applicable to contracts were more diverse. Even the first Restatement had different rules for determining the validity and effect of a contract (§ 332 "the law of the place of contracting") and "matters concerning performance of a contract" (id. cmt. c) "the law of the place of performance." Some classic cases, especially when the issue was usury, expressly chose the law that validated the contract. Moreover, judges applying the contract rules were more likely than in tort cases to address practical effects of choosing law.

Contract choice-of-law issues arise in two contexts—validity and construction. If the issue is one of validity, then no matter how clearly the parties have expressed their intention, one state whose law might be applicable would refuse to give effect to that intention. If the issue is solely one of construction, then any state that has a contact with the parties or the transaction would give effect to the parties' intention if clearly expressed. The problem is that the parties have left a hole in their agreement and the laws of the contact states fill in that hole in different ways. An example of a construction problem is excuse for impossibility or frustration of purpose. Suppose Seller from X promises to manufacture goods and sell them to Buyer in Y. Seller's factory burns down and Buyer obtains the goods from another source but at a higher price. If the contract had specifically addressed this circumstance and stated which party would bear the risk, the courts of X and Y would have enforced the agreement. The contract is silent on the issue, however, and X law excuses Seller, but Y law does not.

Should it make a difference for choice-of-law purposes whether the issue is one of validity or construction? Restatement, Second, Conflict of Laws § 187, p. 627, infra, allows the parties to choose any law to govern construction, but limits their freedom to choose law for validity.

Milliken v. Pratt

Supreme Judicial Court of Massachusetts, 1878.
125 Mass. 374, 28 Am.Rep. 241.

Contract to recover $500 and interest from January 6, 1872. Writ dated June 30, 1875. The case was submitted to the Superior Court on agreed facts, in substance as follows:

The plaintiffs are partners doing business in Portland, Maine, under the firm name of Deering, Milliken & Co. The defendant is and has been since 1850, the wife of Daniel Pratt, and both have always resided in Massachusetts. In 1870, Daniel, who was then doing business in Massachusetts, applied to the plaintiffs at Portland for credit, and they required of him, as a condition of granting the same a guaranty from the defendant to the amount of five hundred dollars, and accordingly he procured from his wife the following instrument:

"Portland, January 29, 1870. In consideration of one dollar paid by Deering, Milliken & Co., receipt of which is hereby acknowledged, I guarantee the payment to them by Daniel Pratt of the sum of five hundred dollars, from time to time as he may want—this to be a continuing guaranty. Sarah A. Pratt."

This instrument was executed by the defendant two or three days after its date, at her home in Massachusetts, and there delivered by her to her husband, who sent it by mail from Massachusetts to the plaintiffs in Portland; and the plaintiffs received it from the post-office in Portland early in February, 1870.

The plaintiffs subsequently sold and delivered goods to Daniel from time to time until October 7, 1871, and charged the same to him, and, if competent, it may be taken to be true, that in so doing they relied upon the guaranty. . . . This action is brought for goods sold from September 1, 1871, to October 7, 1871, inclusive, amounting to $860.12, upon which he paid $300, leaving a balance due of $560.12. The one dollar mentioned in the guaranty was not paid, and the only consideration moving to the defendant therefor was the giving of credit by the plaintiffs to her husband. Some of the goods were selected personally by Daniel at the plaintiffs' store in Portland, others were ordered by letters mailed by Daniel from Massachusetts to the plaintiffs at Portland, and all were sent by the plaintiffs by express from Portland to Daniel in Massachusetts, who paid all express charges. . . .

Payment was duly demanded of the defendant before the date of the writ, and was refused by her.

The Superior Court ordered judgment for the defendant; and the plaintiffs appealed to this court.

■ GRAY, C.J. The general rule is that the validity of a contract is to be determined by the law of the state in which it is made; if it is valid there, it is deemed valid everywhere, and will sustain an action in the courts of a state whose laws do not permit such a contract. Scudder v. Union National Bank, 91 U.S. 406. Even a contract expressly prohibited by the statutes of the state in which the suit is brought, if not in itself immoral, is not necessarily nor usually deemed so invalid that the comity of the state, as administered by its courts, will refuse to entertain an action on such a contract made by one of its own citizens abroad in a state the laws of which permit it. Greenwood v. Curtis, 6 Mass. 358. M'Intyre v. Parks, 3 Metc. 207.

If the contract is completed in another state, it makes no difference in principle whether the citizen of this state goes in person, or sends an agent, or writes a letter across the boundary line between the two states. . . . So if a person residing in this state signs and transmits, either by a messenger or through the post-office, to a person in another state, a written contract, which requires no special forms or solemnities in its execution, and no signature of the person to whom it is addressed, and is assented to and acted on by him there, the contract is made there, just as if the writer personally took the executed contract into the other state, or wrote and signed it there. . . .

. . . The sales of the goods ordered by him from the plaintiffs at Portland, and there delivered by them to him in person or to a carrier for him, were made in the State of Maine.... The contract between the defendant and the plaintiffs was complete when the guaranty had been received and acted on by them at Portland, and not before. Jordan v. Dobbins, 122 Mass. 168. It must therefore be treated as made and to be performed in the State of Maine.

The law of Maine authorized a married woman to bind herself by any contract as if she were unmarried. St. of Maine of 1866, c. 52. Mayo v. Hutchinson, 57 Maine 546. The law of Massachusetts, as then existing, did not allow her to enter into a contract as surety or for the accommodation of her husband or of any third person. Gen.Sts. c. 108, sec. 3. Nourse v. Henshaw, 123 Mass. 96....

The question therefore is, whether a contract made in another state by a married woman domiciled here, which a married woman was not at the time capable of making under the law of this Commonwealth, but was then allowed by the law of that state to make, and which she could now lawfully make in this Commonwealth, will sustain an action against her in our courts.

It has been often stated by commentators that the law of the domicil, regulating the capacity of a person, accompanies and governs the person everywhere. But this statement, in modern times at least, is subject to many qualifications; and the opinions of foreign jurists upon the subject ... are too varying and contradictory to control the general current of the English and American authorities in favor of holding that a contract, which by the law of the place is recognized as lawfully made by a capable person, is valid everywhere, although the person would not, under the law of his domicil, be deemed capable of making it....

In Pearl v. Hansborough, 9 Humph. 426, the rule was carried so far as to hold that where a married woman domiciled with her husband in the State of Mississippi, by the law of which a purchase by a married woman was valid and the property purchased went to her separate use, bought personal property in Tennessee, by the law of which married women were incapable of contracting, the contract of purchase was void and could not be enforced in Tennessee. Some authorities, on the other hand, would uphold a contract made by a party capable by the law of his domicil, though incapable by the law of the place of the contract. In re Hellmann's Will [L.R. 2 Eq. 363], and Saul v. His Creditors [17 Martin (La.) 569], above cited. But that alternative is not here presented.

The principal reasons on which continental jurists have maintained that personal laws of the domicil, affecting the status and capacity of all inhabitants of a particular class, bind them wherever they may go, appear to have been that each state has the rightful power of regulating the status and condition of its subjects ... that laws limiting the capacity of infants or of married women are intended for their protection, and cannot therefore be dispensed with by their agreement; that all civilized states recognize the incapacity of infants and married women; and that a person, dealing with either, ordinarily has notice, by the apparent age or sex, that the person is likely to be of a class whom the laws protect, and is thus put upon inquiry how far, by the law of the domicil of the person, the protection extends.

In the great majority of cases, especially in this country, where it is so common to travel, or to transact business through agents, or to correspond by letter, from one state to another, it is more just, as well as more convenient, to have regard to the law of the place of the contract, as a uniform rule operating on all contracts of the same kind, and which the contracting parties may be presumed to have in contemplation when making their contracts, than to require them at their peril to know the domicil of those with whom they deal, and to ascertain the law of that domicil, however remote, which in many cases could not be done without such delay as would greatly cripple the power of contracting abroad at all. . . .

It is possible also that in a state where the common law prevailed in full force, by which a married woman was deemed incapable of binding herself by any contract whatever, it might be inferred that such an utter incapacity, lasting throughout the joint lives of husband and wife, must be considered as so fixed by the settled policy of the state, for the protection of its own citizens, that it could not be held by the courts of that state to yield to the law of another state in which she might undertake to contract.

But it is not true at the present day that all civilized states recognize the absolute incapacity of married women to make contracts. The tendency of modern legislation is to enlarge their capacity in this respect, and in many states they have nearly or quite the same powers as if unmarried. In Massachusetts, even at the time of the making of the contract in question, a married woman was vested by statute with a very extensive power to carry on business by herself, and to bind herself by contracts with regard to her own property, business and earnings; and, before the bringing of the present action, the power had been extended so as to include the making of all kinds of contracts, with any person but her husband, as if she were unmarried. There is therefore no reason of public policy which should prevent the maintenance of this action.

Judgment for the plaintiffs.

NOTES

1.   Restatement of Conflict of Laws § 324 (1934): "In the case of an informal unilateral contract to guarantee future credits to be given by the promisee, made by giving such credits, the place of contracting is where the credit is given in reliance upon the guaranty."

Under the reasoning of the court in the principal case, would the result have been different if the contract required the seller to deliver the goods by the seller's own wagon or truck to the buyer in Massachusetts? See Uniform Commercial Code § 2–401(2): (a) "if the contract requires or authorizes the seller to send the goods to the buyer but does not require the seller to deliver them at destination, title passes to the buyer at the time and place of shipment; but (b) if the contract requires delivery at destination, title passes on tender there."

2. Did the change in Massachusetts law affect the outcome? Should it?

3. A place-of-making choice-of-law rule may result in the validity of the contract depending on fortuitous circumstances. Restatement of Conflict of Laws § 325, illustration 1 (1934): "A and B being in state X, A offers to buy B's horse for one hundred dollars, the offer to remain open for ten days. Five days later A meets B in state Y and B there accepts A's offer. The contract for the sale of the horse is made in Y."

RESTATEMENT, SECOND, CONFLICT OF LAWS:

§ 203. Usury

The validity of a contract will be sustained against the charge of usury if it provides for a rate of interest that is permissible in a state to which the contract has a substantial relationship and is not greatly in excess of the rate permitted by the general usury law of the state of the otherwise applicable law under the rule of § 188 [p. 675, infra].

KINNEY LOAN & FINANCE CO. V. SUMNER, 65 N.W.2d 240 (Neb.1954). A Nebraska resident borrowed $2,712 from a Colorado corporation. The interest charged conformed with Colorado law, but exceeded the amount permitted in Nebraska. A Nebraska statute that invalidated a small loan contract requiring payment of interest in excess of that permitted in Nebraska contained an exception: "Provided, that the foregoing shall not apply to loans legally made in any state under and in accordance with a regulatory small loan law similar in principle to this act." The court applied Colorado law to validate the contract. "By use of the phrase 'a regulatory small loan law similar in principle to this act', our Legislature clearly did not mean 'identical' or 'precisely like,' or the statute would be of little use. It meant a regulatory small loan law resembling our own installment loan act in origin, purpose, and result, which licenses, controls, and regulates those engaged in lending money at conventional higher rates of interest in order to combat the reservation of extortionate and oppressive rates."

NOTES

1. Should courts distinguish between commercial loans and consumer loans in choosing the law to apply to a usury defense? Restatement § 203 states in comment f that is "uncertain" whether the rule of that section applies to consumer loans.

2. 12 U.S.C. § 85 permits a national bank to charge "interest at the rate allowed by the laws of the State, Territory, or district where the bank is

located." Smiley v. Citibank (South Dakota), N.A., 517 U.S. 735, 116 S.Ct. 1730 (1996), held that this section permitted a national bank located in South Dakota to charge a California resident late-payment fees on credit cards the bank had issued when the fees were legal under South Dakota law but violated California law.

SIEGELMAN V. CUNARD WHITE STAR, LIMITED, 221 F.2d 189 (2d Cir.1955). In New York a husband and wife purchased a ticket for a voyage from New York to Cherbourg on defendant's ship. The "Contract Ticket" was "about 13 inches long and 11 inches wide" and contained 22 "terms and conditions." Condition 10 stated that any suit for personal injury or death had to be brought "within one year from the day when the death or injury occurred." Condition 20 stated: "All questions arising on this contract ticket shall be decided according to English Law with reference to which this contract is made."

On the high seas the wife was injured when her chair, which was not bolted to the floor, toppled over because of the ship's motion. During negotiations to settle the wife's claim, her lawyer asked the defendant's claim agent whether, because of the contractual one-year limitation, it was necessary to file suit to protect his client's rights. The agent replied that it was not necessary because the chance of settlement was excellent. The wife then died of causes not related to her injuries. The defendant withdrew its settlement offer stating that it could only be made to the injured party. The husband then brought suit to recovery for his wife's injuries and for his loss of consortium.

A central issue was whether the claim agent's conduct resulted in a waiver of the one-year contractual limitation. The court held that because the case was in admiralty, federal rather than state choice-of-law rules applied. The court then ruled that under the contractual choice-of-law clause English law applied to the waiver issue and that under English law the defendant could assert as a defense the one-year limitation. The Second Circuit affirmed the trial court's dismissal of the complaint. In his dissent, Judge Jerome Frank stated that he would not construe the choice-of-law clause to cover the waiver issue and that in any event he would not apply that clause because it is in a "contract of adhesion."

NOTE

Siegelman introduces the "party autonomy" rule, which permits contracting parties to choose the law that determines the construction and validity of the contract. This rule has now achieved universal acceptance. The issues on which there is a difference of opinion are: (1) Must the law chosen have a reasonable relation to the parties or the transaction? (2) Should there be special protection for consumers and other parties in an inferior bargaining position who sign form contracts? (3) What rules of validity are the parties unable to avoid by selecting the law of another jurisdiction? See Restatement (Second) of Conflict of Laws § 187, p. 675, infra, Uniform Commercial Code § 1–301, p. 675, infra, European Union Regulation on the Law Applicable to Contractual Obligations arts. 3, 5, 6, 7, Documentary Appendix, infra. Under the Regulation, will a court apply a choice-of-law clause included in a steamship ticket? The Council Directive referred to in art. 6(b) defines "package" as including in the price transportation and accommodation when trip covers a period of more than twenty-four hours or includes overnight accommodation.

c)　*Real Property*

For issues involving interests in real property, once again a monolithic choice-of-law rule emerges—apply the law of the situs. In his typically colorful fashion, Judge Henry Lamm expressed the almost mystical acceptance of this rule: "It follows that the right to redemption as of course under a foreclosure sale is a rule of property in the State of Iowa. It has no extra-territorial force, but dies at the State boundary, as the trees about Troy, under the mandate of the gods, grew no higher than the walls." Hughes v. Winkleman, 147 S.W. 994, 996 (Mo.1912). Moreover, the situs rule for real estate is the territorial rule that has proven most resistant to change.

Sinclair v. Sinclair
Supreme Court of New Hampshire, 1954.
99 N.H. 316, 109 A.2d 851.

Probate Appeal in the estate of Epps E. Sinclair brought by the appellant, brother of the decedent against the appellee, widow of the decedent. The following reserved case was transferred by Griffith, J.:

"The appeal is from a decree of the Judge of Probate for the County of Merrimack dated January 7, 1954, setting off and assigning to the widow $10,000 in value of the real estate of the deceased located in Concord, New Hampshire and one-half in value of the remainder thereof and appointing a committee of three persons pursuant to Chapter 361, Revised Laws, to make a division thereof.

"Epps E. Sinclair died domiciled in Rutland, Vermont on September 6, 1951, leaving no surviving issue. He was survived by his widow, the appellee and by his brother the appellant, who are the sole persons who appear to be interested in his estate. His widow, Edith M. Sinclair, was duly appointed administratrix of his estate by decree of the Probate Court for the District of Rutland, Vermont, dated September 17, 1951. His brother, Quincy V. Sinclair was duly appointed Administrator of his estate in New Hampshire by decree of the Probate Court for Merrimack County, dated October 19, 1951.

"At the time of his death, the deceased owned certain real estate in Concord, New Hampshire, consisting of two tenement properties in

Concord proper and an undivided one-half interest in a summer cottage on the Contoocook River.

"The appellee, Edith M. Sinclair, duly filed in the Registry of Probate for Merrimack County, her waiver of dower and homestead and claim of her distributive share in the decedent's real estate in the value of $10,000 outright and one half in value in excess of said sum, remaining after the payment of debts and expenses of administration. This waiver was filed and recorded seasonably within one year after the decease of the decedent.

"By his probate appeal, the appellant has placed in issue the question whether the amount of real estate to be awarded to the appellee as widow is governed by the law of the State of Vermont or the law of the State of New Hampshire.

"It appearing that justice requires the determination of a certain question of law in advance of further proceedings, the following question of law is reserved and transferred without ruling:

"Should the law of New Hampshire or the law of Vermont be applied in determining what share of the real estate of the decedent situated in Concord, New Hampshire is to be awarded to the widow, Edith M. Sinclair?"

■ KENISON, CHIEF JUSTICE. It is a rule of general application that the descent of real property is governed by the law of the state where the property is located. Since the law of the situs controls, the domicile of the intestate is unimportant. This rule finds specific application in determining the rights of a widow in the real estate of her intestate husband. "The existence and extent of a common law or statutory interest of a surviving spouse in the land of a deceased spouse are determined by the law of the state where the land is." Restatement, Conflict of Laws, § 248(1). While it has been said that there are logical reasons and policy arguments for a different rule, the great weight of authority supports the views of the Restatement.

The widow by proceeding to assert her rights in the ancillary administration in New Hampshire, obtains a larger share of the value of the real estate than she would in the domiciliary administration in Vermont. This fact is immaterial in deciding whether the governing law is in New Hampshire or Vermont. The law of the situs of the real estate has been applied in determining the procedure and time limitations that a widow must conform with in order to claim dower or its statutory equivalent in the real estate of her deceased husband. Although there is limited authority on the point, the cases generally hold that in computing the value or interest due the surviving spouse the value of the real property of the decedent in other states is not to be taken into consideration. This is based on the proposition that only the state where the land is determines the method, extent and amount of succession thereto.

While an estate is a single thing for practical purposes and its unitary character should be emphasized for the convenient administration of estates at the domicile, there are persuasive reasons why the law of the domicile has not been applied to determine rights in real estate. "Any supposed desirability or convenience in the administration of estates arising from this would certainly be counterbalanced by the inconvenience of searching title and the impossibility of determining the validity of title if such foreign judgments are considered as directly affecting the title to land * * *. The domicil theory would make difficult, even impossible, the tracing of title to land." Stimson, Conflict of Laws and the Administration of Decedents' Real Estate, 6 Vanderbilt L.Rev. 545, 548 (1953).

Accordingly we conclude that the appellee's share in the real estate of the decedent is determined by the law of New Hampshire.

Remanded. All concurred.

NOTES

1. What are the "logical reasons and policy arguments for a different rule," referred to by the court?

2. Is it true, as stated in the quotation at the end of the opinion, that applying the law of the decedent's domicile to determine intestate succession to land in another state "would make difficult, even impossible, the tracing of title to land"? What if innocent third parties would be unfairly surprised if this were done in the principal case? If there are none and a court applies the law of Vermont to determine interests in the New Hampshire land, can the New Hampshire land records reflect this result?

3. Craig v. Carrigo, 12 S.W.3d 229 (Ark.2000). A testator died domiciled in Alberta, Canada leaving real and personal property in Arkansas. His will left all his property to a woman with whom he was living. The will did not mention his two children from previous marriages. Under Alberta law, these children would have no claim to the estate. Under Arkansas law, as "pretermitted" children they were entitled to the share in the estate that they would take if the testator had died intestate. The court held that Arkansas law applied to the real estate although Alberta law applied to the personal property. Thus the court construed the same will differently with regard to personal and real property in Arkansas.

For testate and intestate succession of both personalty and realty, the Convention on the Law Applicable to Succession to the Estates of Deceased Persons, promulgated under the auspices of the Hague Conference on Private International Law on August 1, 1989, (not in force) refers to the country in which the decedent was "habitually resident" at death, with alternative references under some circumstances to the law of the decedent's nationality. A survey of countries that are members of the Conference revealed that most civil law jurisdictions applied the same law to both personal and real property (unity principle) for testate and intestate succession. Most applied the law of the decedent's nationality, but some applied the law of the decedent's domicile at death. Droz, Commentary on the Questionnaire on Succession in Private International Law, and Van Loon, Update of the Commentary, in Proceedings of the Sixteenth Session of the Hague Conference on Private International Law.

Toledo Society for Crippled Children v. Hickok
Supreme Court of Texas, 1953.
152 Tex. 578, 261 S.W.2d 692.

[Mr. Hickok died domiciled in Ohio survived by a wife and two children, also Ohio domiciliaries. In a will that he executed within one year of his death, he established a trust, the income to be paid to his widow and two adult children for twenty years and then the corpus to be divided among twenty charities. The charities asserted their rights under the will to certain land and mineral interests in Texas. Some of the land and mineral interests were owned by Mr. Hickok individually at his death, but the most valuable interests were owned by a partnership of which he was a member. Before his death, Mr. Hickok had contracted with his partner to form a corporation and to convey the partnership assets to the corporation in exchange for stock. His will incorporated this contract by reference and directed compliance with it. By the time of trial in the Texas probate proceedings, his executors had carried out Mr. Hickok's instructions and all of his interest in the partnership assets had been conveyed to the corporation in exchange for stock. As to the land and mineral interest that Mr. Hickok owned individually at his death, the trustees of the testamentary trust were given the power, but not directed, to sell any assets and reinvest the proceeds.]

■ GARWOOD, JUSTICE. Our petitioners—sundry charitable, religious and similar enterprises, including the Toledo Society for Crippled Children— seek in this suit against the respondents, who are the two children, widow, executors and trustees of the late Arthur S. Hickok, an Ohio resident, to establish their rights specified in Mr. Hickok's will, but only to the extent of certain lands, and mineral estates in land, located in Texas. All of the parties to the suit appear to reside in Ohio or have their corporate offices there. The facts are without substantial dispute. The sole obstacle to the enjoyment by the petitioners of the benefits conferred by the will is that the latter was executed less than a year before the testator died leaving issue surviving. Under such circumstances, an Ohio statute (which has no counterpart in our law) declares testamentary gifts to enterprises such as the petitioners to be invalid. In previous litigation between the same parties, the Ohio courts have in general terms adjudged the statute to be applicable. In the instant suit, the District Court of Eastland County, on motion for summary judgment, held the gifts valid in respect of part of the Texas property in question and invalid as to the rest. The Eastland Court of Civil Appeals reformed that judgment so as to deny the petitioners any relief whatever—stating that their interest was contingent rather than vested. We granted writ of error upon rehearing of the petition therefor. . . .

It is perhaps appropriate to observe at this point that, minerals in land or "in place" being, by our local law, land, we are admittedly well within our rights in characterizing the mineral estates here in question as Texas land for purposes of the Conflict of Laws as well as for purely domestic purposes. . . .

Assuming, for purposes of discussion, that we are dealing with the simple case of an Ohioan, who dies seized of Texas lands free of any obligation to sell, and whose will makes an ordinary devise of a remainder in such lands to beneficiaries such as the Toledo Society for Crippled Children, it is not disputed or disputable that under proper principles of the Conflict of Laws the validity of the devise is to be determined by reference to Texas law (which permits it) and not by the domiciliary statute (which forbids it). Nor would the above conclusion be varied by the bare fact that the devise runs to a trustee rather than to the beneficiary direct. . . .

In the [Ohio] probate court, the executors and trustees did apparently make the point that there was an equitable conversion—and no doubt with the object of securing a declaration that the Ohio statute governed even as to foreign lands of the testator, but the judge, while apparently of the opinion that we would or should hold that the Ohio statute governs as the result of an equitable conversion, rather clearly indicated that the final answer lay with the Texas law and Texas courts. . . .

The . . . thesis of the respondents is that these circumstances, by the law of Texas as well as that of Ohio, present a case of equitable conversion of all the testator's estate into personalty, with the result that we must regard the will as involving only personalty. Similarly, they appear to say that the will left the petitioners no interest in the Texas property (or other specific property of any kind). Either approach, they argue, forecloses application of any law except that of the testator's domicile to the matter of validity of the trust remainder.

We will consider first the partnership property. The fact since the testator's death, it has been put into the form of corporate stock does not of itself affect the problem, because we are dealing with the validity of what the testator himself did, as judged by the applicable law which depends on what kind of property he had at his death, rather than what kind exists at the time of litigation. As to what happened before his death, it may doubtless be conceded that the will alone, without aid of the subsequent conduct of the testator himself in the organization of the corporation, shows a clear intent that his interest in the partnership should be put into the form of corporate stock at the earliest practical date after his death. The situation is thus comparable to one wherein the testator instructs his executor to trade his land for corporate stock and give the stock to the beneficiary. Or, looking at the contract between the testator and his partner, it is not unnaturally argued that this alone, and aside from the will, was enough to change into a movable or personalty that which had previously been an interest in immovables or land, as would obviously have been the case had the testator sold his interest and received, before his death, stock, cash or an unsecured promissory note in return. That, but for the contract, the testator had, through his partnership interest, an interest in land, does not seem to be contested.

Assuming the theory of equitable conversion to be relevant to the process of determining the applicable law, then, looking at the case from the standpoint of either the will itself or the contract or both, there are presented situations of the type in which our courts, for at least certain domestic law purposes, declare a conversion to have been effected. In Hardcastle v. Sibley, Tex.Civ.App., 107 S.W.2d 432 (writ of error refused) a direction in the will of Mrs. Crosby to sell land and distribute the proceeds to the beneficiary (Mrs. Wood) was held to convert the land in question into personalty so as thereafter to pass as such by the will of the beneficiary herself. (The fact that Mrs. Crosby's executors had actually sold the land after her death was said to be immaterial). The case is also authority for the point that where the testator's contract of sale of his land is virtually carried out during his lifetime, the land is treated as personalty for the purposes of the will. . . .

There appear to be no Texas decisions on the point of whether rules of equitable conversion are to be used in determining whether the nature of the property in question is such as to invoke the law of the situs or that of the domicile. And those very few cases from other jurisdictions, which seem to consider such rules as relevant, apparently follow the same principles exemplified in our Texas decisions in deciding whether a given set of facts is one of conversion or otherwise. The Wisconsin and Michigan decisions in connection with the same will, Ford v. Ford, 70 Wis. 19, 33 N.W. 188; Id., 80 Mich. 42, 44 N.W. 1057, held that the direction to the executors to sell land situated in those states and invest the proceeds in Missouri land to be held in trust, effected a double conversion from land to money to Missouri land, with the result that the Wisconsin and Michigan rules against perpetuities, which would otherwise have invalidated the trusts as to the Wisconsin and Michigan lands of the testator, had no application. But, as to the property which the will gave no positive direction to sell, it was held that no conversion occurred. Penfield v. Tower, 1 N.D. 216, 46 N.W. 413 actually held that no conversion was effected by the terms of a testamentary trust of North Dakota land and personalty for several beneficiaries, not greatly different from that of the Hickok will, and accordingly applied the North Dakota rule against perpetuities, as against that of Pennsylvania, the testator's domicile, thus defeating the trust to the extent of the North Dakota land. But the implication is rather clear that, had the will necessarily disclosed an 'intent' for the land to be sold, the court would have applied the domiciliary law, on the conversion theory. . . .

Contrary to the decisions, or implications thereof, last mentioned are the English and Canadian cases of Re Berchtold (1923), 1 Ch. 192, and Re Burke (1928), 1 D.L.R. 318, each of which, both in result and words, and with considerable citation of English authority, clearly refuses to base the choice between conflicting laws of the situs and domicile upon the principle of equitable conversion. In the first, English land was devised by a Hungarian in trust for the very purpose of being converted to money and thus distributed to two Hungarian beneficiaries, both of whom died intestate before the sale was made. It was held that: (a) the nature of the interests of these beneficiaries as movables or immovables should be determined by English law; (b) by that law the interests were immovables; (c) their distribution was accordingly to be made without regard to the law of the domicile of the two deceased owners and according to English law; (d) the latter requiring that such interests be distributed as personalty (although immovables) they should go to the persons who by English law would take the personalty of a deceased English intestate. Thus, although by English law, the interests in question were personalty for distribution purposes, they were yet immovables for purposes of determining whether the laws of England or those of Hungary applied. In discussing the latter question, the court said that the point of whether the interests were regarded as realty or personalty under principles of conversion or otherwise had nothing to do with the choice of which of the conflicting laws of England and Hungary should govern. . . .

Re Burke, supra, held that where an American contracted to sell his Canadian land and then died intestate, the distribution of his estate was governed by the law of Canada, rather than the domiciliary law, to the extent of this land or its proceeds, including the money which had been actually paid after his death for one particular tract. The court not only declared the fiction of equitable conversion to be irrelevant to the choice between conflicting laws, but also rejected the suggestion that, as a result of actual conversion, the intestate died possessed of merely a chose in action for money, while the purchaser was the owner of the land, thus holding the interest of the intestate at death to be an interest in land, subject to the contract. . . .

We are disposed to agree with the majority of the text writers, whose view appears to be also the view of the Restatement, that the fiction of equitable conversion from realty to personalty or vice versa, "can have no place in the Conflict of Laws". The generally stated reason seems a sound one, to wit, that this body of law is really private international law and not merely a system for operation between the common or English law states of the United States or between these and common or English law nations. Thus to use as a basis for selection of a particular law between conflicting laws a doctrine which may not even exist in some jurisdictions is obviously less desirable than a more realistic basis such as the movable or immovable character of the object in question. As argued by the petitioners, it would in some cases result in state or nation A deferring to the law of state or nation B, when the latter in a converse situation would not reciprocate. It would thus also be more likely to produce unnecessary confusion in particular instances. . . . If the instant case were varied so that Mr. Hickok had no land, but directed by his will that all his stocks and bonds should be forthwith converted into Texas land and the land conveyed to the petitioners, one is inclined to doubt if the Ohio courts would uphold the gift on the theory that an equitable conversion made the Texas law applicable. Or were our case one of a Texas testator, who by will directed conversion of his Texas cattle into Ohio land for the use of these Ohio petitioners, we are disposed to question that the Ohio courts would consider the gift invalid on the theory that equitable conversion made the Ohio statute applicable. . . .

We need not, therefore, decide whether in a proper case for the domestic application of equitable conversion, the partnership mineral interests here in question would be regarded as personal property for the purposes of the will. It is enough to say that at Mr. Hickok's death he was the owner of a half interest in these minerals, subject to a contract that they should be converted into corporate stock. . . . And the circumstances that the will, in effect, directs the contract to be carried out, does not change the fact that, on Mr. Hickok's death, what passed for the benefit of the petitioners and others was his interest in the minerals . . . If this view should impress some as legalistic in the sense of excluding the intent of the testator that his mineral interest should become corporate stock, it is hardly more of a "technical" approach than that of regarding "as done" that which was not done, in order to deprive the petitioners of the last remnant of benefits the testator obviously intended them to have, and, in effect, to enforce here a legislative policy of Ohio, which is contrary to the policy of our own Legislature. . . .

A fortiori we conclude also that our law governs the validity of the trust remainder with respect to the Texas interests owned by Mr. Hickok individually at his death. Indeed, as to these interests, there is insufficient ground on which to claim equitable conversion. . . .

The effect of the foregoing being to hold that as to all the above mentioned lands, and mineral interests in lands, situated in this state, the will of Arthur S. Hickok is valid and passed to the petitioners the interests in trust which it purports to pass, it follows that the judgment of the Court of Civil Appeals should be reversed and the judgment of the trial court modified so as to conform to our holding.

NOTES

1.   The court states that applying the Ohio statute to invalidate the bequest to charities would be "contrary to the policy of our own Legislature." Would it? In the Ohio proceedings, the Supreme Court of Ohio stated that the purpose of the Ohio statute is "to prevent undue influence enhanced by the apprehension of approaching death." Kirkbride v. Hickok, 98 N.E.2d 815, 820 (Ohio 1951). Was this policy applicable to the bequest of the Texas realty?

2.   Lowe v. Plainfield Trust Co., 215 N.Y.S. 50 (App.Div.1926), applied the law of the situs to invalidate half of a bequest to charity that would have been valid under the law of the testator's domicile at death. The situs statute prohibited any person having a spouse or child from devising more than one-half of their estate to a charity.

3.   If a court applied the doctrine of "equitable conversion," discussed in the principal case, in the conflicts context, would the result give greater effect to the policy of the state that had to live with the long-range consequences of validating or invalidating a will? If so, should the principal case have accepted the doctrine? Hancock, Conceptual Devices for Avoiding the Land Taboo in Conflict of Laws: The Disadvantages of Disingenuousness, 20 Stan.L.Rev. 1 (1967) opposes application of the law of the situs in cases like the principal case, but states that use of the equitable conversion fiction may obscure the "real ground" for decision and mislead judges in subsequent cases. What should be the "real ground" for decision?

4.   If only courts at the situs of real estate had the power to adjudicate interests in the realty, the traditional choice-of-law rule could be defended as efficient. The only possible forum would apply its own law.

Section 55 of the Restatement (Second) provides that a court may exercise its personal jurisdiction to order a person to do or refrain from doing an act "although the carrying out of the decree may affect a thing in another state." Comment b states that a court may issue such a decree "whenever the defendant is under a personal obligation, subject to enforcement by a court of equity, to do the act in question." The two illustrations that follow the comment deal with specific performance of a contract to convey land in another state and ordering reconveyance of land in another state that the defendant has obtained title to by fraud.

SECTION 2. ESCAPE DEVICES

A.   CHARACTERIZATION

1.   SUBSTANCE VS. PROCEDURE

Grant v. McAuliffe

Supreme Court of California, 1953.
41 Cal.2d 859, 264 P.2d 944, 42 A.L.R.2d 1162.

[Pullen died shortly after and as a result of the collision of two automobiles in Arizona. After his death, plaintiffs sued the California administrator of Pullen's estate for injuries sustained as a result of Pullen's alleged negligence which caused the accident. All parties were residents of California.

Under Arizona law tort actions did not survive the tortfeasor's death; under California law they did. The court below granted a motion to abate the suits on the ground that Arizona law applied and the causes of action did not survive.]

■ TRAYNOR, JUSTICE. . . . The answer to the question whether the causes of action against Pullen survived and are maintainable against his estate depends on whether Arizona or California law applies. In actions on torts occurring abroad, the courts of this state determine the substantive matters inherent in the cause of action by adopting as their own the law of the place where the tortious acts occurred, unless it is contrary to the public policy of this state.... "[N]o court can enforce any law but that of its own sovereign, and, when a suitor comes to a jurisdiction foreign to the place of the tort, he can only invoke an obligation recognized by that sovereign. A foreign sovereign under civilized law imposes an obligation of its own as nearly homologous as possible to that arising in the place where the tort occurs." Learned Hand, J., in Guinness v. Miller, D.C., 291 F. 769, 770. But the forum does not adopt as its own the procedural law of the place where the tortious acts occur. It must, therefore, be determined whether survival of causes of action is procedural or substantive for conflict of laws purposes.

This question is one of first impression in this state. The precedents in other jurisdictions are conflicting.... Before his death, the injured person himself has a separate and distinct cause of action and, if it survives, the same cause of action can be enforced by the personal representative of the deceased against the tortfeasor. The survival statutes do not create a new cause of action, as do the wrongful death statutes.... They merely prevent the abatement of the cause of action of the injured person, and provide for its enforcement by or against the personal representative of the deceased. They are analogous to statutes of limitation, which are procedural for conflict of laws purposes and are governed by the domestic law of the forum....

Defendant contends, however, that the characterization of survival of causes of action as substantive or procedural is foreclosed by Cort v. Steen, 36 Cal.2d 437, 442, 224 P.2d 723, where it was held that the California survival statutes were substantive and therefore did not apply retroactively. The problem in the present proceeding, however, is not whether the survival statutes apply retroactively, but whether they are substantive or procedural for purposes of conflict of laws. " 'Substance' and 'procedure,' . . . are not legal concepts of invariant content." Black Diamond Steamship Corp. v. Robert Stewart & Sons, 336 U.S. 386, 397, 69 S.Ct. 622, 628, 93 L.Ed. 754. See also Guaranty Trust Co. v. York, 326 U.S. 99, 109, 65 S.Ct. 1464, 89 L.Ed. 2079 [p. 700, infra];... and a statute or other rule of law will be characterized as substantive or procedural according to the nature of the problem for which a characterization must be made....

Defendant also contends that a distinction must be drawn between survival of causes of action and revival of actions, and that the former are substantive but the latter procedural.... The distinction urged by defendant is not a valid one.... In most "revival" statutes, substitution of a personal representative in place of a deceased party is expressly conditioned on the survival of the cause of action itself....

Since we find no compelling weight of authority for either alternative, we are free to make a choice on the merits. We have concluded that survival of causes of action should be governed by the law of the forum. Survival is not an essential part of the cause of action itself but relates to the procedures available for the enforcement of the legal claim for damages. Basically the question is one of the administration of decedents' estate, which is a purely local proceeding. The problem here is whether the causes of action that these plaintiffs had against Pullen before his death survive as liabilities of his estate. . . . Decedent's estate is located in this state, and letters of administration were issued to defendant by the courts of this state. The responsibilities of defendant, as administrator of Pullen's estate, for injuries inflicted by Pullen before his death are governed by the laws of this state. . . . Today, tort liabilities of the sort involved in these actions are regarded as compensatory. When, as in the present case, all of the parties were residents of this state, and the estate of the deceased tortfeasor is being administered in this state, plaintiffs' right to prosecute their causes of action is governed by the laws of this state relating to administration of estates. . . .

■ SCHAUER, JUSTICE. I dissent. . . . [E]ven more regrettable than the failure to either follow or unequivocally overrule the cited cases . . . is the character of the "rule" which is now promulgated: the majority assert that henceforth "a statute or other rule of law will be characterized as substantive or procedural according to the nature of the problem for which a characterization must be made," thus suggesting that the court will no longer be bound to consistent enforcement or uniform application of "a statute or other rule of law" but will instead apply one "rule" or another as the untrammeled whimsy of the majority may from time to time dictate, "according to the nature of the problem" as they view it in a given case. This concept of the majority strikes deeply at what has been our proud boast that ours was a government of laws rather than of men.

Although any administration of an estate in the courts of this State is local in a procedural sense, the rights and claims both in favor of and against such an estate are substantive in nature, and vest irrevocably at the date of death. . . .

NOTES

1. Justice Traynor said the dispositive question in the case was "whether survival of causes of action is procedural or substantive for conflict of laws purposes." Under the standards suggested in the Introduction to Chapter 7, section 3, would survival be characterized as "procedural"?

2. "It may not be amiss to add a postscript that although the opinion [Grant v. McAuliffe] is my own, I do not regard it as ideally articulated, developed as it had to be against the brooding background of a petrified forest. Yet I would make no more apology for it than that in reaching a rational result it was less deft than it might have been to quit itself of the familiar speech of choice of law." Traynor, Is This Conflict Really Necessary?, 37 Tex.L.Rev. 657, 670 (1959). How could the opinion have been made more "deft"? Consider the opinion by the same judge in Reich v. Purcell, p. 583, infra.

MCKINNEY V. FAIRCHILD INTERNATIONAL, INC., 487 S.E.2d 913 (W.V.1997). A machine manufactured by a West Virginia company injured a West Virginia citizen who was using the machine in Kentucky. The injured worker sued the manufacturer in a federal court in West Virginia. The federal court dismissed the action for lack of subject-matter jurisdiction. The worker then sued in a West Virginia state court. The West Virginia "borrowing" statute directed application of the Kentucky one-year statute of limitations rather than the West Virginia two-year statute. Under West Virginia Law, the dismissed federal suit would have suspended ("tolled") the running of the one-year statute of limitations so that the subsequent suit in state court would be timely. Under Kentucky law, the dismissed suit did not toll limitations. The court held that West Virginia law applied to tolling and that the action was timely: "We find that the traditional approach to conflict of laws creates a presumption that the forum state's tolling provisions, as a matter of procedure, apply; however, if another state has a more significant relationship to the transaction and the parties, the modern approach indicates that the tolling provisions of the state with the significant relationship should apply. Based on both our traditional and modern approaches to conflict of laws questions, we hold that where a choice of law question arises about whether the tolling provisions of West Virginia or of the place where the claim accrued should be applied, the circuit court should ordinarily apply West Virginia law, unless the place where the claim accrued has a more significant relationship to the transaction and the parties."

2.   NATURE OF THE ACTION

Haumschild v. Continental Casualty Co.

Supreme Court of Wisconsin, 1959.
7 Wis.2d 130, 95 N.W.2d 814.

[A woman brought this action against her husband for personal injuries sustained through his negligence in a California motor accident. The couple were domiciled in Wisconsin. The trial court dismissed the action because under the local law of California the plaintiff could not recover. The plaintiff appealed.]

■ CURRIE, JUSTICE. This appeal presents a conflict of laws problem with respect to interspousal liability for tort growing out of an automobile accident. Which law controls, that of the state of the forum, the state of the place of wrong, or the state of domicile? Wisconsin is both the state of the forum and of the domicile while California is the state where the alleged wrong was committed. Under Wisconsin law a wife may sue her husband in tort. Under California law she cannot. . . .

This court was first faced with this question in Buckeye v. Buckeye, 1931, 203 Wis. 248, 234 N.W. 342. . . .

The principle enunciated in the Buckeye case and followed in subsequent Wisconsin cases, that the law of the place of wrong controls as to whether one spouse is immune from suit in tort by the other, is the prevailing view in the majority of jurisdictions in this country. . . .

[The court referred to the writings of Messrs. Cook, Rheinstein, Rabel and Ford, and outlined and quoted from Emery v. Emery, 45 Cal.2d 421, 289 P.2d 218 [1955], "the first case to break the ice", and Koplik v. C.P. Trucking Corp., 27 N.J. 1, 141 A.2d 34, all of which advocated or applied the law of the marital domicile to determine spousal and parental immunity.]

. . . [I]t is our considered judgment that this court should adopt the rule that, whenever the courts of this state are confronted with a conflict of laws problem as to which law governs the capacity of one spouse to sue the other in tort, the law to be applied is that of the state of domicile. We, therefore, expressly overrule . . . Buckeye v. Buckeye, supra; . . . the instant decision should not be interpreted as a rejection by this court of the general rule that ordinarily the substantive rights of parties to an action in tort are to be determined in the light of the law of the place of wrong. This decision merely holds that incapacity to sue because of marital status presents a question of family law rather than tort law. . . .

. . . While the appellant's counsel did not request that we overrule Buckeye v. Buckeye, supra, and the subsequent Wisconsin cases dealing with this particular conflict of laws problem, he did specifically seek to have this court apply California's conflict of laws principle, that the law of the domicile is determinative of interspousal capacity to sue, to this particular case. . . .

Wisconsin certainly should not adopt the much criticized renvoi principle in order not to overrule the Buckeye v. Buckeye line of cases, and still permit the plaintiff to recover. Such a result we believe would contribute far more to produce chaos in the field of conflict of laws than to overrule the Buckeye v. Buckeye line of cases and adopt a principle the soundness of which has been commended by so many reputable authorities.

Judgment reversed and cause remanded for further proceedings not inconsistent with this opinion.

■ FAIRCHILD, JUSTICE (concurring). I concur in the reversal of the judgment, but do not find it necessary to re-examine settled Wisconsin law in order to do so. . . .

1. *Solution of this case without overruling previous decisions.* . . . It has been the rule in Wisconsin that the existence or nonexistence of immunity because of family relationship is substantive and not merely procedural, and is to be determined by the law of the locus state. The law of California is that the existence or nonexistence of immunity is a substantive matter, but that it is an element of the law of status, not of tort. . . . Thus it makes no difference under the facts of this case whether

we look directly to the law of Wisconsin to determine that immunity is not available as a defense or look to the law of Wisconsin only because California, having no general tort principle as to immunity, classifies immunity as a matter of status. . . .

I would dispose of the present case upon the theory that California law governs the existence of the alleged cause of action and that in California the immunity question cannot be decided by resort to the law of torts but rather the law of status. I would leave to a later case the consideration of whether the Wisconsin rule of choice of law as to the defense of family immunity should remain as heretofore or, if it is to be changed, which rule will be best.

NOTES

1. *Haumschild* would invariably call for application of the law of the state of the couple's domicile to determine issues of interspousal immunity. Is that rule overly broad? In Haynie v. Hanson, 114 N.W.2d 443 (Wis.1962), the wife was injured in Wisconsin as a result of a collision between automobiles driven by her husband and by Hanson, a Wisconsin resident. The wife brought suit against Hanson and, under Wisconsin's direct action statute, his liability insurer. Hanson sought contribution from the husband's liability insurer. The court dismissed Hanson's cross-complaint on the ground that under the law of Illinois, where the spouses were domiciled, one spouse has no capacity to sue the other spouse in tort.

In Zelinger v. State Sand and Gravel Co., 156 N.W.2d 466 (Wis.1968), an Illinois wife with her daughter as a passenger collided in Wisconsin with a vehicle driven by an employee of a Wisconsin company. The wife, husband, and daughter sued the employer and its insurer for injuries to the wife and daughter. The employer brought a counterclaim against the wife and her insurer for contribution. Under Illinois law the wife was immune from suit by the daughter and, as a host driver, was immune from injury to a guest passenger except for "willful and wanton misconduct." The trial judge applied Illinois law to determine the wife's liability and dismissed the employer's counterclaim. The Supreme Court of Wisconsin reversed. In discussing *Haumschild* the court stated: "The mechanical application of the lex loci delicti was rejected in cases involving interspousal immunity issues, but in its place for such issues another universal mechanical rule was substituted which required the application of the law of the domicile." Instead the court applied "interest analysis." It found that Wisconsin had an interest in permitting the counterclaim "to promote the spreading of the risk and fasten liability in torts on a moral basis of fault." On the other hand in the context of "contribution from an Illinois wife when her husband sues in Wisconsin, we think the Illinois interest of the preservation of family integrity seems hardly to be in jeopardy and also the interest served by the host-guest statute and parental immunity is scarcely impinged upon."

2.   Under California law at the time of the principal case, a spouse's cause of action for personal injury was community property. This was the reason for spousal immunity. Under California choice-of-law rules, the law of the marital domicile determined whether the cause of action was community property. A spouse's cause of action for injury in California was not community property if the marital domicile was not in a community property state. Bruton v. Villoria, 292 P.2d 638 (Cal.App.1956). Do the California choice-of-law rules reveal that in *Haumshild* application of Wisconsin law would not interfere with any policy underlying the California rule of spousal immunity?

LEVY V. DANIELS' U-DRIVE AUTO RENTING CO., 143 A. 163 (Conn.1928): Defendant, a Connecticut automobile rental agency, rented a car in that state. The Connecticut lessee's negligent driving in Massachusetts caused injury to plaintiff, his guest, who was also a Connecticut resident. Plaintiff sued under a Connecticut statute which made the lessor of a motor vehicle "liable for any damage to any person or property caused by the operation of such motor vehicle while so rented or leased." Judgment for the plaintiff was affirmed:

■ WHEELER, C.J. . . . . It is the defendant's contention . . . that the action set forth in the complaint is one of tort and since Massachusetts has no statute like, or substantially like, the Connecticut Act it must be determined by the common law of that State, under which the plaintiff must prove, to prevail, the negligence of the defendant in renting a defective motor vehicle and in failing to disclose the defect. If this were the true theory of the complaint, the conclusion thus reached must have followed. . . . The plaintiff concedes the correctness of this. His counsel, however, construe the complaint as one in its nature contractual. . . .

. . . The statute gives, in terms, the injured person a right of action against the defendant which rented the automobile to Sack, though the injury occurred in Massachusetts. It was a right which the statute gave directly, not derivatively, to the injured person as a consequence of the contract of hiring. The purpose of the statute was not primarily to give the injured person a right of recovery against the tortious operator of the car, but to protect the safety of traffic upon highways by providing an incentive to him who rented motor vehicles to rent them to competent and careful operators by making him liable for damage resulting from the tortious operation of the rented vehicles. . . . The rental of motor vehicles to any but competent and careful operators, or to persons of unknown responsibility, would be liable to result in injury to the public upon or near highways, and this imminent danger justified, as a reasonable exercise of the police power, this statute, which requires all who engage in this business to become responsible for any injury inflicted upon the public by the tortious operation of the rented motor vehicle. . . . The statute made the liability of the person renting motor vehicles a part of every contract of hiring of a motor vehicle in Connecticut. . . .

If the liability of this defendant under this statute is contractual, no question can arise as to the plaintiff's right to enforce this contract, provided the obligation imposed upon this defendant was for the "direct, sole and exclusive benefit" of the plaintiff. The contract was made in Connecticut; at the instant of its making the statute made a part of the contract of hiring the liability of the defendant which the plaintiff seeks to enforce. The law inserted in the contract this provision. The statute did not create the liability; it imposed it in case the defendant voluntarily rented the automobile.... The right of the plaintiff as a beneficiary of this contract to maintain this action is no longer an open question in this State.... The contract was made for him and every other member of the public.

NOTES

1. Cortes v. Ryder Truck Rental, Inc., 581 N.E.2d 1 (Ill.App.1991), appeal dism'd, 587 N.E.2d 1013 (Ill.1992). The court applied the lessor liability statute of Wisconsin, where the rental agreement was executed, to hold the rental company liable for injuries suffered in Indiana: "Although choice-of-law principles might indicate that . . . Indiana law applied to the tort of negligence . . ., Ryder's liability was not based on negligence, directly or vicariously. Ryder's liability . . . arose . . . through its contractual relationship as lessor." The court identified the policy underlying the statute as assuring compensation to a person injured by the rented vehicle.

2. Jack v. Enterprise Rent-A-Car Co. of Los Angeles, 899 P.2d 891 (Wyo.1996), refused to apply a California statute creating vicarious liability for a rental car company. The company rented an automobile in California that injured Wyoming residents in Wyoming. Under Wyoming law, the rental car company was not liable. The court applied Wyoming law as the "lex loci delicti." The court did not cite *Levy, Cortes,* or any other of the numerous cases from other states that would have applied the vicarious liability statute under similar circumstances. Nor did the court discuss the purposes of the California statute.

3. There will be much less occasion to determine the extraterritorial application of a statute like those in notes 1 and 2. As part of its continuing program of "tort reform", Congress has enacted legislation nullifying any state law that imposes vicarious liability on motor vehicle rental companies. 49 U.S.C. § 30106.

3.   SELECTIVE USE OF RENVOI

American Motorists Insurance Co. v. ARTRA Group, Inc.

Court of Appeals of Maryland, 1995.
338 Md. 560, 659 A.2d 1295.

[ARTRA sold a paint manufacturing factory in Maryland to Sherwin-Williams. The Maryland Department of the Environment ordered Sherwin-Williams to investigate and remedy hazardous waste contamination at the site. Sherwin-Williams sued ARTRA to recover the costs of investigation and remediation. ARTRA was insured by American Motorists under a general liability policy. The policy excluded coverage for pollution unless the release of the pollutants "is sudden and accidental". ARTRA requested that American Motorists defend and indemnify ARTRA in the Sherwin-Williams suit. American Motorists refused and sued in the Circuit Court for Baltimore City for a determination that the policy did not cover ARTRA's liability to Sherwin-Williams. ARTRA and American Motorists were both headquartered in Illinois and the policy was countersigned on behalf of American Motorists in Illinois.

Under Maryland law, the pollution exclusion was not ambiguous and did not cover ARTRA's liability to Sherwin-Williams. Under Illinois law, the exclusion was ambiguous and the ambiguity would be construed in favor of ARTRA.

The Circuit Court applied Maryland law and granted American Motorists' motion for summary judgment. The Court of Special Appeals reversed on the grounds that under Maryland choice-of-law rules, the law of Illinois as the *lex loci contractus* governed and that it was irrelevant, as the trial court had found, that an Illinois court would apply Maryland law. The trial court's finding that an Illinois court would apply Maryland law was based on the adoption in Illinois of the "most significant relationship" approach of the Restatement (Second) of Conflict of Laws and on § 193 of the Restatement, under which the rights created by a liability insurance policy are determined by "the local law of the state which the parties understood was to be the principal location of the insured risk during the term of the policy, unless with respect to the particular issue, some other state has a more significant relationship . . . to the transaction and the parties. . . ." The Maryland Court of Appeals reversed, holding that Maryland law applied and that the trial court had properly granted summary judgment for American Motorists.]

■ CHASNOW, J. * * * [F]or the purpose of this opinion we must assume that Illinois choice-of-law rules would dictate the application of Maryland law to the substantive issues in the present case [because the trial judge had so found and ARTRA did not contest this finding].

American Motorists' first suggestion is that we recognize that the rule of *lex loci contractus* is antiquated and should be abandoned in favor of some form of the more modern approaches to choice of law such as the one advocated by Restatement, Second, Conflict of Laws. . . . Based on our holding on the *renvoi* issue, we need not give any consideration to the intriguing question of whether Maryland's traditional *lex loci contractus* test should be abandoned in favor of one of the "modern" most significant relationship tests. American Motorists' second suggestion is that we engraft the doctrine of *renvoi* to our body of conflict of law rules. We need not determine today how far we should go in incorporating the doctrine of *renvoi*, but we do adopt a limited form of *renvoi* which will direct the application of Maryland law to resolve the substantive issues in the instant case. . . .

It has been suggested that the doctrine of *renvoi* was formulated to avoid the harshness of the traditional common law choice-of-law principles. Rhoda S. Barish, Comment, Renvoi and the Modern Approaches to Choice-of-Law, 30 Am.U.L.Rev. 1049, 1061–62 (1981). . . .

A persuasive case for adopting *renvoi* is made by two law school professors in their text on conflict of laws. . . . "[A] mechanical use of renvoi by all concerned jurisdictions could theoretically produce the problem of circularity. In this case, however, it is suggested that the forum accept the reference to its own law, refer no further, and apply its own law. This is the practice of most jurisdictions that do employ renvoi. This is good policy: the foreign conflict rule itself discloses a disinterest to have its own substantive law applied, indeed it recognizes the significance of the forum's law for the particular case; the case therefore probably presents a 'false conflict.' Furthermore, since uniformity in result would not otherwise be achieved in these circumstances, ease in the administration of justice is furthered by the application of forum law rather than by the use of foreign law." Scoles & Hay, Conflict of Laws § 3.13, at 67–70 (2d ed. 1992). . . .

In the absence of some reason to apply foreign law, Maryland courts would ordinarily apply Maryland substantive law, and there is no reason to apply the substantive law of a foreign state if that foreign state recognizes that Maryland has the most significant interest in the issues and that Maryland substantive law ought to be applied to the contract issues. . . .

The limited *renvoi* exception which we adopt today will allow Maryland courts to avoid the irony of applying the law of a foreign jurisdiction when that jurisdiction's conflict of law rules would apply Maryland law. Under this exception, Maryland courts should apply Maryland substantive law to contracts entered into in foreign states' jurisdictions in spite of the doctrine of *lex loci contractus* when:

1)   Maryland has the most significant relationship, or, at least, a substantial relationship with respect to the contract issue presented; and

2)   The state where the contract was entered into would not apply its own substantive law, but instead would apply Maryland substantive law to the issue before the court.

Our holding . . . is not a total jettisoning of *lex loci contractus*. . . . *Lex loci contractus* is still the law in the majority of jurisdictions, although there is a significant modern erosion of the rule. If that erosion continues, however, this Court may, in the proper case, have to reevaluate what the best choice-of-law rules ought to be to achieve simplicity, predictability, and uniformity. . . .

NOTES

1.   Note 2(iii), p. 526, supra, states that a forum court should refer to the choice-of-law rules of another jurisdiction when "[t]he forum wishes to determine whether the other jurisdiction asserts an 'interest' in the application of the other jurisdiction's law." Is the principal case an example of this use of renvoi?

2.   For an extreme example of application Restatement (Second) § 193, see Pfizer, Inc. v. Employers Ins. of Wausau, 712 A.2d 634 (N.J.1998), involving six waste sites in five states and applying the law of each site to determine the construction of "sudden and accidental" pollution coverage. Is this a better result than giving the policy the same interpretation, perhaps under the law of the insured's state, no matter where the pollution occurred? See Maryland Casualty Co. v. Continental Casualty Co., 332 F.3d 145 (2d Cir.2003). The liability policy covered twenty-six sites in twelve states. The policy was issued to W.R. Grace & Co. in New York, which was Grace's principal place of business. Nine of the sites were in New York—more than in any other state. The court held that New York law, which construed the policies to preclude coverage, applied to all the sites. The court rejected Grace's argument that Restatement (Second) of Conflict of Laws § 193 required application of the law of each site:

> The language of § 193 applying the "law of the state" (not the "laws of the states") which the parties understood to be "the *principal location* of the insured risk" (not "all the locations of the insured risks") suggests that the drafters of the Restatement did not intend for courts to apply the laws of more than one state to a single insurance policy. The use of the phrase "principal location" must mean that, where the insured risk is located in more than one state, courts should apply the law of the one state in which the parties understood the risk to be principally located.

> Making this point even more clearly, a comment to § 193 provides, under the heading "Principal location of risk": "The location of the insured risk will be given greater weight than any other single contact in determining the state of the applicable law provided that the risk can be located, at least principally, in a single state. Situations where this cannot be done, and where the location of the risk has less significance, include: . . . where the policy covers a group of risks that are scattered throughout two or more states." Restatement (Second) of Conflict of Laws § 193 cmt. b. This comment lends unambiguous support to the District Court's decision to apply the law of only one state to each insurance policy.

See Borchers, Choice of Law in American Courts in 1992: Observations and Reflections, 42 Am.J.Comp.L. 125 (1994) (most U.S. courts apply §§ 192 and 193 or render decisions consistent with those sections).

The problem of what law applies to the construction of an insurance contract arises frequently with regard to underinsured motorist coverage. Courts differ as to whether the governing law is that of the state where the insured vehicle is principally garaged and where the policy was issued or is that of the state where the insured suffered injury. See, e.g. Mikelson v. United Services Auto. Assoc., 111 P.3d 601, 609 (Haw.2005) (law of Hawaii, where insured injured, applies to permit recovery not available under law of California where policy issued—"Hawai'i has a strong interest in protecting those injured within its borders"); Champagne v. Ward, 893 So.2d 773, 789 (La.2005) (law of Mississippi, where policy issued, applies to reduce coverage of insured injured in Louisiana—"Mississippi has a more substantial interest in the uniform application of its laws governing insurance contracts than Louisiana has in providing an insurance remedy to an out-of-state resident who was injured while transitorily within the borders of Louisiana"); Johnson v. United States Fidelity & Guaranty Co., 696 N.W.2d 431, 443 (Neb.2005) (insured recovers under law of Nebraska where policy issued when recovery would be barred under law of Colorado where insured injured—"the application of Nebraska's laws to resolve the enforceability of contract coverage provisions between Nebraska insurers and insureds enhances the predictability of the parties' contractual rights and obligations by removing the constant variable of different states in which insureds travel").

4.   PUBLIC POLICY

Kilberg v. Northeast Airlines, Inc.

Court of Appeals of New York, 1961.
9 N.Y.2d 34, 172 N.E.2d 526.

[Kilberg, a New York domiciliary, purchased in New York a ticket from the defendant airline, which was incorporated in Massachusetts, for transportation from New York to Nantucket, Massachusetts. The airplane crashed in Nantucket and Kilberg was killed. Both Massachusetts and New York had wrongful death statutes. The Massachusetts statute limited recovery against a common carrier to not less than $2,000 or more than $15,000 assessed with reference to the defendant's culpability. The New York statute had no limit on recovery, which it measured by financial losses to dependents whom the decedent supported. Kilberg's administrator brought suit in New York for the death. On appeal the court considered two of the three causes of action pleaded in the complaint. The first was a cause of action under the Massachusetts wrongful death statute; the second was a cause of action for breach of an alleged contract of safe carriage asking for $150,000 in damages. The trial court denied a motion to dismiss the second cause of action on the ground that, as it was in contract, the law of New York, the place of contracting, governed. The Appellate Division reversed and dismissed the second cause of action because, however labeled, it was in tort for negligently causing death and was subject to the Massachusetts limitation. The Court of Appeals unanimously affirmed the dismissal of the second cause of action, but a majority of the court stated that the first cause of action for wrongful death was not subject to the Massachusetts limitation of damages.]

■ DESMOND, C.J. . . . If the alleged contract breach had caused injuries not resulting in death, a New York-governed contract suit would, we will assume, be available. . . . But it is law long settled that wrongful death actions, being unknown to the common law, derive from statutes only and that the statute which governs such an action is that of the place of wrong. . . .

This does not mean, however, that for the alleged wrong plaintiff cannot possibly recover more than the $15,000 maximum specified in the Massachusetts act. Modern conditions make it unjust and anomalous to subject the traveling citizen of this State to the varying laws of other States through and over which they move. The number of States limiting death case damages has become smaller over the years but there are still 14 of them. . . . An air traveler from New York may in a flight of a few hours' duration pass through several of those commonwealths. His plane may meet with disaster in a State he never intended to cross but into which the plane has flown because of bad weather or other unexpected developments, or an airplane's catastrophic descent may begin in one State and end in another. The place of injury becomes entirely fortuitous. Our courts should if possible provide protection for our own State's people against unfair and anachronistic treatment of the lawsuits which result from these disasters. . . .

Since both Massachusetts . . . and New York . . . authorize wrongful death suits against common carriers, the only controversy is as to amount of damages recoverable. New York's public policy prohibiting the imposition of limits on such damages is strong, clear and old. Since the Constitution of 1894, our basic law has been (N.Y.Const., art. I, § 16; N.Y.Const. [1894], art. I, § 18) that "The right of action now existing to recover damages for injuries resulting in death, shall never be abrogated; and the amount recoverable shall not be subject to any statutory limitation." Each later revision of the State Constitution has included this same prohibition against limitations of death action damages. . . . We will still require plaintiff to sue on the Massachusetts statute but we refuse on public policy grounds to enforce one of its provisions as to damages. . . .

As to conflict of law rules it is of course settled that the law of the forum is usually in control as to procedures including remedies . . . As to whether the measure of damages should be treated as a procedural or a substantive matter in wrongful death cases, there is . . . no controlling New York decision . . . It is open to us, therefore, particularly in view of our own strong public policy as to death action damages, to treat the measure of damages in this case as being a procedural or remedial question controlled by our own State policies. . . .

From all of this it follows that while plaintiff's second or contract cause of action is demurrable, his first count declaring under the Massachusetts wrongful death action is not only sustainable but can be enforced, if the proof so justifies, without regard to the $15,000 limit. Plaintiff, therefore, may apply if he be so advised for leave to amend his first cause of action accordingly. . . .[1]

■ FULD, J., concurred in the decision on the second count. He felt foreclosed by earlier decisions, though if the matter were of first impression New York might be deemed the jurisdiction having "the most significant contact or contacts".

■ FROESSEL, JUDGE (concurring). We concur for affirmance of the judgment appealed from, dismissing plaintiff's second cause of action. We should reach no other question. . . .

Plaintiff's right to maintain this action must . . . stem from the provisions of the Massachusetts statute (Mass.Gen.Stat., ch. 229, § 2). That statute, however, expressly limits the extent of the right given, and declares that the damages assessed thereunder shall not be more than $15,000. . . . The majority, by giving extraterritorial effect to our prohibition against the limitation of recovery in such actions, would permit plaintiff to recover on the basis of the foreign law, and yet not be bound by its express limitation. . . .

No sound reason appears why our courts, in enforcing such a right at all, should not enforce it in its entirety. . . .

The position adopted by the majority may result in the situation where, in a single airplane crash in which numerous passengers from various States are killed, a different law will be applied in each action resulting therefrom. . . .

NOTES

1.   In Davenport v. Webb, 183 N.E.2d 902 (N.Y.1962), the court retracted the "procedural" basis of the *Kilberg* decision. That case involved an action for the wrongful death of persons domiciled in New York in an automobile collision in Maryland. A New York statute provided that a judgment for the plaintiff in a wrongful death action should include interest from the date of death. Maryland law did not authorize prejudgment interest. The Court of Appeals held that the New York statute could not properly be applied to provide for the inclusion of interest and that the *Kilberg* decision "must be held merely to express this State's strong public policy with respect to limitations in wrongful death actions."

2.   *Kilberg* uses "public policy" not only to refuse to apply Massachusetts law, but also to apply New York law. In one of the classic discussions of public policy, Loucks v. Standard Oil of New York, 120 N.E. 198 (N.Y.1918), p. 459, supra, Judge Cardozo assumes that if he refuses on the ground of public policy to apply Massachusetts law, he must dismiss the case: "We cannot give them the same judgment that our law would give if the wrong had been done here. Very likely we cannot give them as much. But that is no reason for refusing to

---

[1]   Kilberg's administrator ultimately settled for less than $15,000 and did not seek leave to amend his first cause of action. Presumably, this was because he did not believe he could prove greater damages. —eds.

give them what we can." Does the use of public policy to apply forum law rather than the law indicated by the forum's choice-of-law rule indicate that the court is in transition to a different method of choosing law? Babcock v. Jackson, 191 N.E.2d 279 (N.Y.1963), p. 577, infra, which adopted as a tort choice-of-law rule "the law of the jurisdiction which has the strongest interest in the resolution of the particular issue presented," followed *Kilberg* by only two years.

Alexander v. General Motors Corp., 478 S.E.2d 123 (Ga.1996), is another case that uses public policy to apply forum law instead of the law indicated by the forum's lex loci delicti conflicts rule. Mr. Alexander, a Georgia citizen, purchased an automobile in Georgia. He was injured when the automobile was involved in a collision in Virginia. Alexander sued the manufacturer alleging that a defective driver's seat increased his injuries. Georgia but not Virginia had a rule of strict liability for defective products. The court stated: "Because Virginia law would place Alexander in exactly the position from which [the Georgia statute enacting strict liability] was intended to protect those who are injured by defective products placed in the stream of commerce in this state, we conclude that it is contrary to the public policy of this state as expressed in that statute. Accordingly, Alexander is entitled to have Georgia law applied to his claims against General Motors."

Dowis v. Mud Slingers, Inc., 621 S.E.2d 413, 419 (Ga.2005), expressly rejects "governmental interest" analysis, Leflar, and the Second Restatement: "The relative certainty, predictability, and ease of the application of lex loci delicti, even though sometimes leading to results which may appear harsh, are preferable to the inconsistency and capriciousness that the replacement choice-of-law approaches have wrought." Is the occasional use of "public policy," as in *Alexander*, consistent with "certainty, predictability, and ease of the application"?

5. EQUITABLE CONVERSION

The materials in section 1(B)(2)(c), supra this chapter, indicate that the traditional rule for issues affecting real property is to apply the law of the situs. Toledo Society for Crippled Children v. Hickok, 261 S.W.2d 692 (Tex.1953), p. 550, supra, discusses and rejects one possible device for escaping from this rule—equitable conversion. This doctrine, which is rooted in the notion that the law will regard as done what ought to have been done, may be applicable if an inter vivos or testamentary document directs the sale of realty and its conversion into personalty. If the realty is regarded as "equitably converted" into personalty, then the relevant choice-of-law rule for personalty would apply. For many issues concerning decedents' estates, the reference would then be to the domicile at death, rather than the situs.

There are several other devices for avoiding the law of the situs. Courts have distinguished between the contract to convey and the conveyance itself (Polson v. Stewart, 45 N.E. 737 (Mass.1897) (Holmes, J.)), between a promissory note and the mortgage securing the note (Thompson v. Kyle, 23 So. 12 (Fla.1897)), and between covenants personal to the parties and those running with the land (Beauchamp v. Bertig, 119

S.W. 75 (Ark.1909)). The effect of these distinctions has often been to treat the second item in each set as a "land" problem to which the law of the situs applies, and the first item as a "contract" problem to be resolved by the contract choice-of-law rule—traditionally the law of the place of making of the contract.

SECTION 3. THE NEW ERA

A. THE CHOICE-OF LAW "REVOLUTION"

One of the most thorough changes in the judge-made rules applied in any area has occurred since the early 1960s with respect to choice-of-law rules. The writings of conflicts scholars heavily influenced this change. The first tentative draft of the Second Restatement of Conflict of Laws was distributed in 1953, when there was little indication from the courts of the changes that were to come. The Reporter was Willis Reese, one of the scholars whose work is represented below. Under his guidance, the Restatement responded to the early indications of a shift from territorial rules and the drafts of the Restatement, in turn, influenced the courts. In many respects the Restatement became a Pre-Statement. Although, as in any field, more persons were doing useful work than can be represented in any short selection, this section presents the theories of some conflicts scholars who had a major role in influencing the conflicts revolution.

CURRIE: THE GOVERNMENTAL INTEREST METHODOLOGY

One of the most influential conflicts scholars of the mid-20th century was Professor Brainerd Currie. He developed the governmental interests analysis, postulating that a choice-of-law case confronts a court with the problem of analyzing the policies that are in competition in the local law rules vying for application. His work fired the imagination and interest of many of the oncoming generation of conflicts scholars and attracted the support of a number of courts. For the 1964 edition of this book,[2] he prepared a succinct statement of his theory, the substance of which follows:

Currie begins by observing that a court may refer to foreign law for quite different purposes. One purpose is to find the "rule of decision"—the answer to such questions as: Is this a valid contract? Does this injury constitute an actionable wrong? On what principle is the estate of this decedent to be distributed? Another purpose is to find some "datum" made relevant by a known rule of decision. Thus, a case otherwise wholly domestic may involve mistake of foreign law. The rule of decision is unquestionably supplied by the law of the forum, but it is necessary to refer to foreign law to establish the fact of mistake. Putting aside for further study all such references to foreign law for other purposes, Currie concentrates on the problem of reference to the foreign law as the source

---

[2] Currie originally set out his theories in an article, Currie, Notes on Methods and Objectives in the Conflict of Laws, 1959 Duke L.J. 171, 178. These he modified quite quickly in a series of articles and statements, culminating in the present statement. See also B. Currie, Selected Essays on the Conflict of Laws (1963).

of the rule of decision. In this context he finds choice-of-law rules of the traditional type unacceptable, and suggests as a substitute for all such rules the following guides:

1.   When a court is asked to apply the law of a foreign state different from the law of the forum, it should inquire into the policies expressed in the respective laws, and into the circumstances in which it is reasonable for the respective states to assert an interest in the application of those policies. In making these determinations the court should employ the ordinary processes of construction and interpretation.

2.   If the court finds that one state has an interest in the application of its policy in the circumstances of the case and the other has none, it should apply the law of the only interested state.

3.   If the court finds an apparent conflict between the interests of the two states it should reconsider. A more moderate and restrained interpretation of the policy or interest of one state or the other may avoid conflict.

4.   If, upon reconsideration, the court finds that a conflict between the legitimate interests of the two states is unavoidable, it should apply the law of the forum.

5.   If the forum is disinterested, but an unavoidable conflict exists between the interests of two other states, and the court cannot with justice decline to adjudicate the case, it should apply the law of the forum, at least if that law corresponds with the law of one of the other states. Alternatively, the court might decide the case by a candid exercise of legislative discretion, resolving the conflict as it believes it would be resolved by a supreme legislative body having power to determine which interest should be required to yield.

6.   The conflict of interest between states will result in different dispositions of the same problem, depending on where the action is brought. If with respect to a particular problem this appears seriously to infringe a strong national interest in uniformity of decision, the court should not attempt to improvise a solution sacrificing the legitimate interest of its own state, but should leave to Congress, exercising its powers under the full faith and credit clause, the determination of which interest shall be required to yield.

————————

Professor Currie's work triggered many responses. Three criticisms are (1) the method slights trans-jurisdictional policies, such as facilitating and encouraging interstate and international transactions; (2) preferring forum law when there is a clash of state policies will be another incentive for forum shopping and reflects interstate chauvinism rather than cooperation; (3) the work represents an approach to resolving choice-of-law problems, but does not provide substitute rules. Professor Currie wrote that "[w]e would be better off without choice-of-law rules." B. Currie, Notes on Methods and Objectives in the Conflict of Laws, 1959 Duke L.J. 171, 177. If a court uses Professor Currie's method to decide a series of cases in the same substantive area, will the court or conflicts scholars inevitably attempt to summarize the results of those cases? Will this summary be a choice-of-law rule?

NOTES

1. For an article by a distinguished judge that espouses the Currie approach, subject to rather substantial limitations, see R. Traynor, War and Peace in the Conflict of Laws, 25 Int'l & Comp.L.Q. 121 (1976).

2. Among commentaries discussing Professor Currie's approach are Brilmayer, Interest Analysis and the Myth of Legislative Intent, 78 Mich.L.Rev. 392 (1980); Hill, Governmental Interest and the Conflict of Laws—a Reply to Professor Currie, 27 U.Chi.L.Rev. 463 (1960); Juenger, Conflict of Law: A Critique of Interest Analysis, 32 Am.J.Comp.L. 1 (1984); Rosenberg, The Comeback of Choice-of-Law Rules, 81 Colum.L.Rev. 946 (1981); M. Traynor, Professor Currie's Restrained and Enlightened Forum, 49 Calif.L.Rev. 845 (1961).

LEFLAR: CHOICE-INFLUENCING CONSIDERATIONS

Professor Robert A. Leflar's American Conflicts Law (4th ed.1986, with L. McDougal III & R. Felix)[3] provides a summary and refinement of the work that he produced in the conflicts field for many years. He reviews the work of other conflicts scholars "to systematize and correlate the choice-influencing considerations" that are useful in resolving choice-of-law problems. Id. § 95. Professor Leflar finds that this produces "a list of five, which seem to incorporate all that are in the longer lists: (A) Predictability of results; (B) Maintenance of interstate and international order; (C) Simplification of the judicial task; (D) Advancement of the forum's governmental interests; (E) Application of the better rule of law." A major ingredient of this last "better rule" is whether one of the competing domestic rules, when compared with the other, "is anachronistic, behind the times." Id. § 107.

Several courts have been attracted to the Leflar formula, with the opinion in Clark v. Clark, 107 N.H. 351, 222 A.2d 205 (1966), showing the way. See, e.g., Satchwill v. Vollrath Co., 293 F.Supp. 533 (E.D.Wis.1968); Schneider v. Nichols, 280 Minn. 139, 158 N.W.2d 254 (1968); Mitchell v. Craft, 211 So.2d 509 (Miss.1968); Tiernan v. Westext Transport, Inc., 295 F.Supp. 1256 (D.R.I.1969); Conklin v. Horner, 38 Wis.2d 468, 157 N.W.2d 579 (1968). See also Allstate Ins. Co. v. Hague, p. 432, supra.

---

[3]   This was the last edition published during Professor Leflar's life. The book in now in a new edition. R. Felix & R. Whitten, American Conflicts Law (6th ed.2011).

NOTES

1. Courts that engage in a search for the "better rule of law" usually end by applying their own local rule in the decision of the case. An exception is Offshore Rental Co. v. Continental Oil Co., 148 Cal.Rptr. 867, 583 P.2d 721 (Cal.1978). Courts that apply Professor Leflar's analysis have grown reluctant to apply a "better law" analysis. See, e.g., Nodak Mut. Ins. Co. v. American Family Mut. Ins. Co., 604 N.W.2d 91, 96 (Minn.2000) ("this court has not placed any emphasis on [the better law] factor in nearly 20 years").

2. Suppose that two states have policies that will be affected if their different domestic laws are not applied. A court determines that the forum's rule is not the "better rule." If forum law is judge-made and can be changed by judicial decision, is the forum's highest court likely to eliminate the conflicts problem by changing forum law to accord with the rule of the other state? If forum law is statutory, should a court have more latitude to reject the rule in a multistate case than in a local case?

CAVERS: PRINCIPLES OF PREFERENCE

On the eve of publication of the first Restatement of Conflict of Laws, Professor David F. Cavers wrote a penetrating critique of the whole conceptual apparatus of the choice-of-law system the American Law Institute was to embrace. See Cavers, A Critique of the Choice-of-Law Problem, 47 Harv.L.Rev. 173 (1933).

He argued that choice-of-law rules should not be oblivious to the contents of the rules of decision whose application they dictated and urged a revised body of choice-of-law rules. In 1965, he presented a limited set of "principles of preference" that he had worked out on the basis of diverse fact-law multistate combinations and that he proposed as guidelines for courts concerned with reaching principled decisions that were neither completely result-selectively ad hoc nor yet blind to consequences.

Using tort cases as his chief subjects, he offered the following as an example of principles of preference (p. 138):

"Where the liability laws of the state of injury set a *higher* standard of conduct or of financial protection against injury than do the laws of the state where the person causing the injury has acted or had his home, the laws of the state of injury should determine the standard and the protection applicable to the case, at least where the person injured was not so related to the person causing the injury that the question should be relegated to the law governing their relationship."

Professor Cavers admitted to greater confidence in the idea that principles of preference are necessary than in the particular formulations he has advanced. He was satisfied that as courts consciously strive for principled decisions and as precedents accumulate, better principles and a more just choice-of-law process will evolve.

JUENGER: MULTISTATE JUSTICE

In Choice of Law and Multistate Justice (1993), Professor Friedrich K. Juenger summarizes his work of many years. He suggests that law be chosen from the best the world has to offer and that the choice not be limited to states that have contacts with the parties and the transaction. Id. 192–94. As a fall-back approach, he suggests the use of alternative references to select, from among states connected to the parties and the transaction, the law that best reflects modern trends and doctrine. Id. 195. He provides an example of such an alternative reference rule for conflicts cases involving products liability:

> In selecting the rules of decision applicable to any issue a multistate liability case presents the court will take into account the laws of the following jurisdictions:
>
>   (a) the place where the injury occurred,
>
>   (b) the place where the conduct causing the injury occurred, and
>
>   (c) the home state (habitual residence, place of incorporation or principal place of business) of the parties.
>
> As to each issue, the court shall select from the laws of these jurisdictions the rule of decision that most closely accords with modern products liability standards.

Professor Juenger's book is reviewed in Weintraub, Choosing Law with an Eye on the Prize, 15 Mich.J.Int'l L. 705 (1994).

RESTATEMENT, SECOND, CONFLICT OF LAWS (1971):

The basic section on choice of law principles in general (§ 6) and the introductory section on torts (§ 145) of the Restatement Second are set forth below:

§ 6. Choice-of-Law Principles

(1) A court, subject to constitutional restrictions, will follow a statutory directive of its own state on choice of law.

(2) When there is no such directive, the factors relevant to the choice of the applicable rule of law include

    (a) the needs of the interstate and international systems,

    (b) the relevant policies of the forum,

    (c) the relevant policies of other interested states and the relative interests of those states in the determination of the particular issue,

    (d) the protection of justified expectations,

    (e) the basic policies underlying the particular field of law,

    (f) certainty, predictability and uniformity of result, and

(g) ease in the determination and application of the law to be applied.

---

§ 145. The General Principle

(1)   The rights and liabilities of the parties with respect to an issue in tort are determined by the local law of the state which, with respect to that issue, has the most significant relationship to the occurrence and the parties under the principles stated in § 6.

(2)   Contacts to be taken into account in applying the principles of § 6 to determine the law applicable to an issue include:

(a)   the place where the injury occurred,

(b)   the place where the conduct causing the injury occurred,

(c)   the domicil, residence, nationality, place of incorporation and place of business of the parties, and

(d)   the place where the relationship, if any, between the parties is centered.

These contacts are to be evaluated according to their relative importance with respect to the particular issue.

RESTATEMENT, THIRD, CONFLICT OF LAWS (COUNCIL DRAFT 3, 2019)

§ 6.09. Residual Rule

For choice-of-law questions not explicitly provided for in this Restatement, a tort issue is governed by the law of the state with the dominant interest in that issue. The state with the dominant interest is identified by an assessment of the relevant policies of the forum and other interested states, the relative interests of those states in the particular issue, and the reasonable expectations of the parties.

"Although it is printed in black letters, section 145 is not much of a rule since it fails to offer a definition of the central word 'significant.' Thus, the Restatement provisions on tort choice of law appear to be programmatic rather than normative." Juenger, Choice of Law in Interstate Torts, 118 U.Pa.L.Rev. 202, 212 (1969). Professor Juenger quotes from the Reporter for the Second Restatement this observation: "This rule of most significant relationship, at the very least, will not stand in the way of progress." Reese, Conflict of Laws and the Restatement Second, 28 Law & Contemp.Prob. 679, 697 (1963). The draft Third Restatement differs in important respects from the Second. The Second Restatement set forth an overarching test in Section 6—"the most significant relationship"—while the draft Third Restatement sets forth relatively clear rules and then uses the "dominant interest" test as a fallback. Which approach is preferable? Would you expect the "dominant interest" and "most significant relationship" tests to differ substantially in application?

1.   THE REVOLUTION BEGINS

With the academic ferment against the traditional rules, and courts becoming more brazen in manipulating the traditional rules to reach results more consistent with the above-noted methodologies, the time was ripe for American courts to break openly from the traditional rules.

Elements of all of the newer methodologies can be found in the more recent cases, but the principal competitors became Currie's interest analysis, Leflar's choice-influencing considerations, and the Second Restatement, the latter of which attempted to bring the modern methodologies under one roof. Numerically, the large majority of states applying one of the newer methodologies purport to follow the Second Restatement, though the open-ended nature of its general sections gives them considerable latitude. As we shall see, however, not all states broke from the First Restatement. Approximately ten states have stayed with the territorial rules.

Moreover, the battleground on which the revolution was fought was principally tort and contract law. Even states firmly in the modern camp have generally continued to adhere to the situs rule for real property disputes, forum law for indisputably procedural matters (such as pleading requirements, the standard for granting a new trial, and so on), as well as in other areas of the law.

While the newer methodologies work reasonably well in cases such as auto accidents, as we shall see later their application in complex and international litigation is more problematic. Also, many of the cases we read involve so-called "guest statutes," which are statutes that either forbid or make difficult recovery of a guest-passenger for injuries suffered as a result of the host-driver's allegedly tortious driving. Guest statutes have all but disappeared from American tort law. Apparently the only enforceable one left in the United States is Alabama Code § 32–1–2, which requires a showing of "willful or wanton misconduct" by host in order for guest to recover.

Of course, none of this renders the guest statute cases irrelevant. Indeed, they remain among the most important U.S. conflicts decisions ever rendered and their methodologies have been adapted to fit more contemporary conflicts problems.

While the matter is not entirely free from debate, the New York Court of Appeals usually gets the credit for firing the first shot in its famous *Babcock* decision immediately below. We will sample cases from many states though we pay outsized attention to the New York decisions as they influenced so many other states.

Babcock v. Jackson

Court of Appeals of New York, 1963.
12 N.Y.2d 473, 240 N.Y.S.2d 743, 191 N.E.2d 279.

■ FULD, JUDGE. On Friday, September 16, 1960, Miss Georgia Babcock and her friends, Mr. and Mrs. William Jackson, all residents of Rochester, left that city in Mr. Jackson's automobile, Miss Babcock as guest, for a week-end trip to Canada. Some hours later, as Mr. Jackson was driving in the Province of Ontario, he apparently lost control of the car; it went off the highway into an adjacent stone wall, and Miss Babcock was seriously injured. Upon her return to this State, she brought the present action against William Jackson, alleging negligence on his part in operating his automobile.

At the time of the accident, there was in force in Ontario a statute providing that "the owner or driver of a motor vehicle, other than a vehicle operated in the business of carrying passengers for compensation, is not liable for any loss or damage resulting from bodily injury to, or the death of any person being carried in . . . the motor vehicle" (Highway Traffic Act of Province of Ontario [Ontario Rev.Stat. (1960), ch. 172], § 105, subd. [2]). Even though no such bar is recognized under this State's substantive law of torts . . . the defendant moved to dismiss the complaint on the ground that the law of the place where the accident occurred governs and that Ontario's guest statute bars recovery. The court at Special Term, agreeing with the defendant, granted the motion and the Appellate Division . . . affirmed the judgment of dismissal without opinion.

The question presented is simply drawn. Shall the law of the place of the tort[2] *invariably* govern the availability of relief for the tort or shall the applicable choice of law rule also reflect a consideration of other factors which are relevant to the purposes served by the enforcement or denial of the remedy?

The traditional choice of law rule, embodied in the original Restatement of Conflict of Laws (§ 384), and until recently unquestioningly followed in this court . . . has been that the substantive rights and liabilities arising out of a tortious occurrence are determinable by the law of the place of the tort. . . . It had its conceptual foundation in the vested rights doctrine, namely, that a right to recover for a foreign tort owes its creation to the law of the jurisdiction where the injury occurred and depends for its existence and extent solely on such law. . . . [T]he vested rights doctrine has long since been discredited. . . . More particularly, as applied to torts, the theory ignores the interest which jurisdictions other than that where the tort occurred may have in the resolution of particular issues. It is for this very reason that, despite the advantages of certainty, ease of application and predictability which it

---

[2] In this case, as in nearly all such cases, the conduct causing injury and the injury itself occurred in the same jurisdiction. The phrase "place of the tort," as distinguished from "place of wrong" and "place of injury," is used herein to designate the place where both the wrong and the injury took place.

affords ... there has in recent years been increasing criticism of the traditional rule by commentators and a judicial trend towards its abandonment or modification.

In Auten v. Auten, 308 N.Y. 155, 124 N.E.2d 99, this court . . . applied what has been termed the "center of gravity" or "grouping of contacts" theory of the conflict of laws. "Under this theory," we declared in the Auten case, "the courts, instead of regarding as conclusive the parties' intention or the place of making or performance, lay emphasis rather upon the law of the place 'which has the most significant contacts with the matter in dispute'" (308 N.Y., at p. 160, 124 N.E.2d, at pp. 101–102). . . .

The "center of gravity" or "grouping of contacts" doctrine adopted by this court in conflicts cases involving contracts impresses us as likewise affording the appropriate approach for accommodating the competing interests in tort cases with multi-State contacts. Justice, fairness and "the best practical result" (Swift & Co. v. Bankers Trust Co., 280 N.Y. 135, 141, 19 N.E.2d 992, 995 . . .) may best be achieved by giving controlling effect to the law of the jurisdiction which, because of its relationship or contact with the occurrence or the parties, has the greatest concern with the specific issue raised in the litigation. . . .

Comparison of the relative "contacts" and "interests" of New York and Ontario in this litigation, vis-a-vis the issue here presented, makes it clear that the concern of New York is unquestionably the greater and more direct and that the interest of Ontario is at best minimal. The present action involves injuries sustained by a New York guest as the result of the negligence of a New York host in the operation of an automobile, garaged, licensed and undoubtedly insured in New York, in the course of a week-end journey which began and was to end there. In sharp contrast, Ontario's sole relationship with the occurrence is the purely adventitious circumstance that the accident occurred there.

New York's policy of requiring a tortfeasor to compensate his guest for injuries caused by his negligence cannot be doubted—as attested by the fact that the Legislature of this State has repeatedly refused to enact a statute denying or limiting recovery in such cases (see, e.g., 1930 Sen.Int.No. 339, Pr.No. 349; 1935 Sen.Int.No. 168, Pr.No. 170; 1960 Sen.Int.No. 3662, Pr.No. 3967)—and our courts have neither reason nor warrant for departing from that policy simply because the accident, solely affecting New York residents and arising out of the operation of a New York based automobile, happened beyond its borders. Per contra, Ontario has no conceivable interest in denying a remedy to a New York guest against his New York host for injuries suffered in Ontario by reason of conduct which was tortious under Ontario law. The object of Ontario's guest statute, it has been said, is "to prevent the fraudulent assertion of claims by passengers, in collusion with the drivers, against insurance companies" (Survey of Canadian Legislation, 1 U.Toronto L.J. 358, 366) and, quite obviously, the fraudulent claims intended to be prevented by the statute are those asserted against Ontario defendants and their insurance carriers, not New York defendants and their insurance carriers. Whether New York defendants are imposed upon or their insurers defrauded by a New York plaintiff is scarcely a valid legislative concern of Ontario simply because the accident occurred there, any more so than if the accident had happened in some other jurisdiction.

It is hardly necessary to say that Ontario's interest is quite different from what it would have been had the issue related to the manner in which the defendant had been driving his car at the time of the accident. Where the defendant's exercise of due care in the operation of his automobile is in issue, the jurisdiction in which the allegedly wrongful conduct occurred will usually have a predominant, if not exclusive, concern. In such a case, it is appropriate to look to the law of the place of the tort so as to give effect to that jurisdiction's interest in regulating conduct within its borders, and it would be almost unthinkable to seek the applicable rule in the law of some other place.

The issue here, however, is not whether the defendant offended against a rule of the road prescribed by Ontario for motorists generally or whether he violated some standard of conduct imposed by that jurisdiction, but rather whether the plaintiff, because she was a guest in the defendant's automobile, is barred from recovering damages for a wrong concededly committed. As to that issue, it is New York, the place where the parties resided, where their guest-host relationship arose and where the trip began and was to end, rather than Ontario, the place of the fortuitous occurrence of the accident, which has the dominant contacts and the superior claim for application of its law. Although the rightness or wrongness of defendant's conduct may depend upon the law of the particular jurisdiction through which the automobile passes, the rights and liabilities of the parties which stem from their guest-host relationship should remain constant and not vary and shift as the automobile proceeds from place to place. Indeed, such a result, we note, accords with "the interests of the host in procuring liability insurance adequate under the applicable law, and the interests of his insurer in reasonable calculability of the premium." (Ehrenzweig, Guest Statutes in the Conflict of Laws, 69 Yale L.J. 595, 603.)

Although the traditional rule has in the past been applied by this court in giving controlling effect to the guest statute of the foreign jurisdiction in which the accident occurred . . . it is not amiss to point out that the question here posed was neither raised nor considered in those cases and that the question has never been presented in so stark a manner as in the case before us with a statute so unique as Ontario's. Be that as it may, however, reconsideration of the inflexible traditional rule persuades us, as already indicated, that, in failing to take into account essential policy considerations and objectives, its application may lead to unjust and anomalous results. This being so, the rule, formulated as it was by the courts, should be discarded. . . .

In conclusion, then, there is no reason why all issues arising out of a tort claim must be resolved by reference to the law of the same jurisdiction. Where the issue involves standards of conduct, it is more than likely that it is the law of the place of the tort which will be controlling but the disposition of other issues must turn, as does the issue of the standard of conduct itself, on the law of the jurisdiction which has the strongest interest in the resolution of the particular issue presented.

The judgment appealed from should be reversed, with costs, and the motion to dismiss the complaint denied.

■ VAN VOORHIS, JUDGE (dissenting). The decision about to be made of this appeal changes the established law of this State. . . . The decision in Auten v. Auten rationalized and rendered more workable the existing law of contracts. . . . The difference between the present case and Auten v. Auten is that Auten did not materially change the law, but sought to formulate what had previously been decided. The present case makes substantial changes in the law of torts. . . .

In my view there is no overriding consideration of public policy which justifies or directs this change in the established rule or renders necessary or advisable the confusion which such a change will introduce. . . .

NOTES

1.   Is Judge Fuld's opinion internally consistent? Can a court consistently call for application of the law of the state that has the greatest interest in the issue to be decided and also declare that "the rights and liabilities of the parties which stem from the guest-host relationship should . . . not vary and shift as the automobile proceeds from place to place"?

2.   The principal case produced a torrent of commentary, mostly approving, starting with a symposium, Comments on Babcock v. Jackson, 63 Colum.L.Rev. 1212 (1963). Professors Cavers, Cheatham, Currie, Leflar and Reese all found the result pleasing, but they gave different reasons for doing so. Each tended to find in the opinion support for his own theories.

3.   The principal case compares rules regulating conduct with rules affecting compensation. The draft Third Restatement adopts this distinction in Sections 6.01 through 6.04. In subsequent New York cases, this concept developed into a distinction between "conduct regulating" rules and "loss allocating" rules. If a rule was conduct regulating, the law of the place where the defendant acted was applicable. If a rule was loss allocating, choice of law followed the approach in the principal case later guided by the "*Neumeier* Rules." See Neumeier v. Kuehner, p. 592, infra.

A case that epitomizes this distinction is Padula v. Lilarn Properties Corp., 644 N.E.2d 1001 (N.Y.1994). A worker, domiciled in New York, was injured by a fall from a scaffold at a construction site in Massachusetts. The site was owned by a New York corporation. The scaffold did not conform with specifications promulgated under New York law for worker safety. The New York Labor Law provided "strict and vicarious liability of the owner of the property" if a worker was injured because of a non-conforming scaffold. The court affirmed a summary judgment for the property owner, holding that because the scaffold requirements were "conduct regulating" rather than "loss allocating," Massachusetts law applied. For comment on this case, see Borchers, The Return of Territorialism to New York's Conflict Law: Padula v. Lilarn Properties Corp., 58 Albany L.Rev. 775 (1995).

Is the distinction between "conduct regulating" and "loss allocating" rules sound? There are some rules so directly conduct regulating, such as speed limits and rules of the road, that the applicable rules must be those where the regulated conduct occurs. Brainerd Currie distinguished between "a rule of decision," which he would select by interest analysis, and a "rule of conduct," which provides the factual "datum" on which the rule of decision will operate. Currie, Selected Essays on the Conflict of Laws 69 (1963). The conflicts code provides separately for "issues of conduct and safety" (La.Civ.C. art. 3543) and "issues of loss distribution and financial protection" (art. 3544). If conduct and injury occur in the same state, issues of conduct and safety are governed by the law of that state. Issues of loss distribution and financial protection are governed by the law of the domicile of the injured person and the person who caused the injury if both are domiciled in the same state or in different states that have "substantially identical" laws on the relevant issue. Whether violation of a rule of conduct constitutes negligence per se is treated as a rule of conduct. Art. 3543, Revision cmt. (e). Should it be? For comments on these and other aspects of the Louisiana conflicts code, see Symeonides, Louisiana's New Law of Choice of Law for Tort Conflicts: An Exegesis, 66 Tul.L.Rev. 677 (1992); Weintraub, The Contributions of Symeonides and Kozyris in Making Choice of Law Predictable and Just: An Appreciation and Critique, 38 Am.J.Comp.L. 511 (1990).

The European Union Regulation on the Law Applicable to Non-Contractual Obligations (Documentary Appendix, infra) contains the following provision:

Article 17: Rules of Safety and Conduct

In assessing the conduct of the person claimed to be liable, account shall be taken, as a matter of fact and insofar as is appropriate, of the rules of safety and conduct which were in force at the place and time of the event giving rise to the liability.

Paragraph 34 of the recitals preceding the text of the Regulation states:

The term "rules of safety and conduct" should be interpreted as referring to all regulations having any relation to safety and conduct, including, for example, road safety rules in the case of an accident.

The Louisiana Civil Code makes a similar distinction referring to issues of "loss distribution."

4. The principal case is typical of the cases in other states that followed its lead to avoid a rule of the place of injury that excluded or limited liability and was perceived to be an anachronistic rule that most states had abandoned. Classic examples were provided by guest statutes, marital immunity rules, and wrongful death statutes that contained a low cap on damages. See, e.g., Griffith v. United Air Lines, Inc., 203 A.2d 796 (Pa.1964) (limit on wrongful death recovery); Mellk v. Sarahson, 229 A.2d 625 (N.J.1967) (guest statute); White v. White, 618 P.2d 921 (Okla.1980) (spousal immunity). Some of the opinions abandoning the place-of-wrong rule, however, do not fit this pattern.

Chambers v. Dakota Charter, Inc., 488 N.W.2d 63 (S.D.1992) applies the law of the forum, rather than Missouri law to deprive a South Dakota resident of a cause of action against a South Dakota corporation. Under South Dakota law, recovery is barred "if the plaintiff's negligence is more than slight in comparison with the negligence of the defendant." (Id. 64). "Under Missouri law, if a plaintiff is determined to be contributorily negligent in any degree, the plaintiff may still recover, but the plaintiff's damages are reduced by the percentage of fault that is attributed to plaintiff's conduct." Id.

Hataway v. McKinley, 830 S.W.2d 53 (Tenn.1992). A Tennessee resident was killed during a scuba dive at a diving class taught in Arkansas by another Tennessee resident. Tennessee barred recovery if the decedent was contributorily negligent, but Arkansas had a doctrine of comparative fault. Held: Tennessee law applied because "Arkansas has no interest in applying its laws to this dispute between Tennessee residents." Id. at 60.

5. Although *Babcock* is usually cited as the case that accelerated the "conflicts revolution," two years previously, in Bernkrant v. Fowler, p. 682, infra, the Supreme Court of California, in an opinion by Justice Traynor, applied "interest analysis" to a choice-of-law problem involving statutes of frauds. Moreover, in the case of Auten v. Auten, 124 N.E.2d 99 (N.Y. 1954), the high court of New York employed a "grouping of contacts" approach that foreshadowed *Babcock*.

6. Rule 8.5(b) of the Model Rules of Professional Conduct of the American Bar Association provides:

In any exercise of the disciplinary authority of this jurisdiction, the rules of professional conduct to be applied shall be as follows:

(1) for conduct in connection with a matter pending before a tribunal, the rules of the jurisdiction in which the tribunal sits, unless the rules of the tribunal provide otherwise; and

(2) for any other conduct, the rules of the jurisdiction in which the lawyer's conduct occurred, or, if the predominant effect of the conduct is in a different jurisdiction, the rules of that jurisdiction shall be applied to the conduct. A lawyer shall not be subject to discipline if the lawyer's conduct conforms to the rules of a jurisdiction in which the lawyer reasonably believes the predominant effect of the lawyer's conduct will occur.

For a conclusion that ABA Model Rule 8.5 fails to bring clarity and certainty to the choice of law problem in ethics proceedings, see J. Mark Little, The Choice of Rules Clause: A Solution to the Choice of Law Problem in Ethics Proceedings, 88 Tex.L.Rev. 855, 865 (2010).

Reich v. Purcell

Supreme Court of California, 1967.
67 Cal.2d 551, 63 Cal.Rptr. 31, 432 P.2d 727.

■ TRAYNOR, CHIEF JUSTICE. This wrongful death action arose out of a head-on collision of two automobiles in Missouri. One of the automobiles was owned and operated by defendant Joseph Purcell, a resident and domiciliary of California who was on his way to a vacation in Illinois. The other automobile was owned and operated by Mrs. Reich, the wife of plaintiff Lee Reich. The Reichs then resided in Ohio and Mrs. Reich and the Reichs' two children, Jay and Jeffry, were on their way to California, where the Reichs were contemplating settling. Mrs. Reich and Jay were killed in the collision, and Jeffry was injured.

Plaintiffs, Lee Reich and Jeffry Reich, are the heirs of Mrs. Reich and Lee Reich is the heir of Jay Reich. Plaintiffs moved to California and became permanent residents here after the accident. The estates of Mrs. Reich and Jay Reich are being administered in Ohio.

The parties stipulated that judgment be entered in specified amounts for the wrongful death of Jay, for the personal injuries suffered by Jeffry, and for the damages to Mrs. Reich's automobile. For the death of Mrs. Reich they stipulated that judgment be entered for $55,000 or $25,000 depending on the court's ruling on the applicability of the Missouri limitation of damages to a maximum of $25,000. Neither Ohio nor California limit recovery in wrongful death actions. The trial court held that the Missouri limitation applied because the accident occurred there and entered judgment accordingly. Plaintiffs appeal.

For many years courts applied the law of the place of the wrong in tort actions regardless of the issues before the court, e.g., whether they involved conduct, survival of actions, applicability of a wrongful death statute, immunity from liability, or other rules determining whether a legal injury has been sustained. . . . It was assumed that the law of the place of the wrong created the cause of action and necessarily determined the extent of the liability. (Slater v. Mexican National R.R. Co., 194 U.S. 120, 126, 24 S. Ct. 581, 48 L. Ed. 900, p. 264, supra.) Aside from procedural difficulties (see Currie, Selected Essays on Conflict of Laws (1963) pp. 10–18), this theory worked well enough when all the relevant events took place in one jurisdiction, but the action was brought in another. In a complex situation involving multistate contacts, however, no single state alone can be deemed to create exclusively governing rights. . . . The forum must search to find the proper law to apply based upon the interests of the litigants and the involved states. Such complex cases elucidate what the simpler cases obscured, namely, that the forum can only apply its own law. . . . When it purports to do otherwise, it is not enforcing foreign rights but choosing a foreign rule of decision as the appropriate one to apply to the case before it. Moreover, it has now been demonstrated that a choice of law resulting from a hopeless search for a governing foreign law to create a foreign vested right may defeat the legitimate interests of the litigants and the states involved. (See generally, Cavers, The Choice of Law Process (1965); Currie, Selected Essays on Conflict of Laws, supra; Ehrenzweig, Conflict of Laws (1962).)

Accordingly, when application of the law of the place of the wrong would defeat the interests of the litigant and of the states concerned, we have not applied that law. (Grant v. McAuliffe [p. 555, supra]; Emery v. Emery, 45 Cal. 2d 421, 428, 289 P.2d 218.) *Grant* was an action for personal injuries arising out of an automobile accident in Arizona between California residents. The driver whose negligence caused the accident died, and the court had to choose between the California rule that allowed an action against the personal representative and the Arizona rule that did not. We held that since "all of the parties were residents of this state, and the estate of the deceased tortfeasor is being administered in this state, plaintiffs' right to prosecute their causes of action is governed by the laws of this state relating to administration of estates." Under these circumstances application of the law of the place of the wrong would not only have defeated California's interest and that of its residents but would have advanced no interest of Arizona or its residents. (Grant v. McAuliffe, supra). In *Emery* members of a California family were injured in Idaho when another member of the family who was driving lost control of the car and it went off the road. The question was whether Idaho or California law determined when one member of a family was immune from tort liability to another. We applied the law of the family domicile rather than the law of the place of the wrong. "That state has the primary responsibility for establishing and regulating the incidents of the family relationship and it is the only state in which the parties can, by participation in the legislative processes, effect a change in those incidents. Moreover, it is undesirable that the rights, duties, disabilities, and immunities conferred or imposed by the family relationship should constantly change as members of the family cross state boundaries during temporary absences from their home." (45 Cal. 2d at p. 428, 289 P.2d at p. 223.)

Defendant contends, however, that there were compelling reasons in the *Grant* and *Emery* cases for departing from the law of the place of the wrong and that such reasons are not present in this case. He urges that application of that law promotes uniformity of decisions, prevents forum shopping, and avoids the uncertainties that may result from ad hoc searches for a more appropriate law in this and similar cases.

Ease of determining applicable law and uniformity of rules of decision, however, must be subordinated to the objective of proper choice of law in conflict cases, i.e., to determine the law that most appropriately applies to the issue involved (see Leflar, Choice-Influencing Considerations in Conflicts Law 41 N.Y.U. L. Rev. 267, 279–282 (1966)). Moreover, as jurisdiction after jurisdiction has departed from the law of the place of the wrong as the controlling law in tort cases, regardless of the issue involved . . . , that law no longer affords even a semblance of the general application that was once thought to be its great virtue. We conclude that the law of the place of the wrong is not necessarily the applicable law for all tort actions brought in the courts of this state . . . [and] cases to the contrary are overruled.

As the forum we must consider all of the foreign and domestic elements and interests involved in this case to determine the rule applicable. Three states are involved. Ohio is where plaintiffs and their decedents resided before the accident and where the decedents' estates are being administered. Missouri is the place of the wrong. California is the place where defendant resides and is the forum. Although plaintiffs now reside in California, their residence and domicile at the time of the accident are the relevant residence and domicile. At the time of the accident the plans to change the family domicile were not definite and fixed, and if the choice of law were made to turn on events happening after the accident, forum shopping would be encouraged. (See Cavers, op. cit., supra, p. 151, fn. 16.) Accordingly, plaintiffs' present domicile in California does not give this state any interest in applying its law, and since California has no limitation of damages, it also has no interest in applying its law on behalf of defendant. As a forum that is therefore disinterested in the only issue in dispute, we must decide whether to adopt the Ohio or the Missouri rule as the rule of decision for this case.

Missouri is concerned with conduct within her borders and as to such conduct she has the predominant interest of the states involved. Limitations of damages for wrongful death, however, have little or nothing to do with conduct. They are concerned not with how people should behave but with how survivors should be compensated. The state of the place of the wrong has little or no interest in such compensation when none of the parties reside there. Wrongful death statutes create causes of action in specified beneficiaries and distribute the proceeds to those beneficiaries. The proceeds in the hands of the beneficiaries are not distributed through the decedent's estate and, therefore, are not subject to the claims of the decedent's creditors and consequently do not provide a fund for local creditors. Accordingly, the interest of a state in a wrongful death action insofar as plaintiffs are concerned is in determining the distribution of proceeds to the beneficiaries and that interest extends only to local decedents and beneficiaries. (Currie, op. cit., supra, pp. 690, 702). Missouri's limitation on damages expresses an additional concern for defendants, however, in that it operates to avoid the imposition of excessive financial burdens on them. That concern is also primarily local and we fail to perceive any substantial interest Missouri might have in extending the benefits of its limitation of damages to travelers from states having no similar limitation. Defendant's liability should not be limited when no party to the action is from a state limiting liability and when defendant, therefore, would have secured insurance, if any, without any such limit in mind. A defendant cannot reasonably complain when compensatory damages are assessed in accordance with the law of his domicile and plaintiffs receive no more than they would have had they been injured at home. (See Cavers, op. cit., supra, pp. 153–157.) Under these circumstances giving effect to Ohio's interests in affording full recovery to injured parties does not conflict with any substantial interest of Missouri. (Cf. Bernkrant v. Fowler, 55 Cal. 2d 588, 595, 12 Cal. Rptr. 266, 360 P.2d 906.) Accordingly, the Missouri limitation does not apply. . . .

The part of the judgment appealed from is reversed with directions to the trial court to enter judgment for the plaintiffs in the amount of $55,000 in accordance with the stipulations of the parties.

NOTES

1. Is the court correct in stating that "if the choice of law were made to turn on events happening after the accident, forum shopping would be encouraged"? (Is perhaps "law shopping" a better term?). Is this likely on the facts of the principal case? If California law permitted greater recovery than the laws of either Ohio or Missouri, could the court have decided that California law applied without confronting the question of the effect of changed residence?

In Nesladek v. Ford Motor Co., 46 F.3d 734 (8th Cir.), cert. denied, 516 U.S. 814, 116 S.Ct. 67 (1995), a products liability action, the majority refused to take into account the plaintiffs' move to Minnesota because they "admitted that they moved to Minnesota in part because they consulted an attorney and were aware that their case was a non-starter [under the law of Nebraska, where they then lived, because of a ten-year statute of repose], whereas Minnesota's law [a "useful life" statute of repose] was more favorable." Id. at 738.

To avoid "forum shopping," HM Holdings, Inc. v. Aetna Casualty & Surety Co., 712 A.2d 645 (N.J.1998), refused to take account of the insured's move to New Jersey in determining which state's law applied to determine the extent of pollution coverage. The court did, however, consider the move to New Jersey in deciding to apply the New Jersey rule that late notice to the insurance company does not eliminate coverage unless the late notice has prejudiced the insurer. The court noted that the late notice occurred after the insured had moved to New Jersey.

2. Because California and Ohio law would produce the same result, was it necessary for Chief Justice Traynor to choose between those two laws? See Restatement (Second) of Conflict of Laws, § 145, cmt. i: "When certain contacts involving a tort are located in two or more states with identical local law rules on the issue in question, the case will be treated for choice-of-law purposes as if these contacts were grouped in a single state."

Milkovich v. Saari

Supreme Court of Minnesota, 1973.
295 Minn. 155, 203 N.W.2d 408.

■ TODD, JUSTICE Defendants appeal from an order of the trial court denying their motion to dismiss plaintiff's complaint for failure to state a cause of action because the law of Ontario, where plaintiff and defendants reside, has a guest statute requiring proof of gross negligence, which was not alleged. Defendants further appeal from the granting of plaintiff's motion to strike their affirmative defense that the law of Ontario should apply. The trial court certified the question as important and doubtful. We affirm.

Plaintiff and both defendants are residents of . . . Ontario, Canada. On November 8, 1968, they left [Ontario] for Duluth, Minnesota, to shop and attend a play. The car belonged to defendant Erma Saari, who drove the first part of the trip. At the United States Customs House at Pigeon River, Minnesota, defendant Judith Rudd took over the driving, and about 40 miles south of the border the car left the road and crashed into rock formations adjacent to the road, causing the injuries to plaintiff. Plaintiff was hospitalized at Duluth for approximately 1 1/2 months and thereafter returned to her home in [Ontario].

Defendant Saari's automobile was garaged, registered, and insured in the Province of Ontario, Canada. Ontario has a guest statute, and if the law of Ontario is to be applied to this case, plaintiff would have to establish gross negligence in order to recover. Minnesota does not have a guest statute, and the rulings of the court would be correct if Minnesota law is to apply.

The field of "conflict of laws" in tort matters has undergone dramatic change in the last decade. Prior to that time, most courts were willing to accept the doctrine of "lex loci," which proved to be easy to administer since the happening of an accident in any particular forum established that the law of the place of the accident would apply. Criticism of this entrenched doctrine mounted from all sides. The issue was met head on in Babcock v. Jackson, 12 N.Y. 2d 473, 240 N.Y.S. 2d 743, 191 N.E. 2d 279, 95 A.L.R. 2d 1 (1963). There the New York Court of Appeals, in an opinion by [Judge] (now Chief [Judge]) Fuld, held that where plaintiff was a New York resident and commenced a trip in the State of New York with the defendant, a New York resident, and was involved in an accident in Ontario, Canada, plaintiff was entitled to have her claim decided under the law of the State of New York. The legislature of New York had rejected the guest statute, which was the law of Ontario and the law of the place of the accident. The decision was premised on the doctrine that New York had the most significant contacts with the litigants and that consequently New York law should apply. The court further held that the law of Ontario, the place of the accident, should not apply, since Ontario had no significant contact with the litigants.

Application of *Babcock* to different fact situations has been confusing. The *Babcock* decision left open the question of the manner of determining each state's interest in a particular situation, and it did not discuss the issues of whether the relationship of the parties is established at the commencement of the trip and whether the relationship continues to be governed by the law of the state in which it was established or changes as state or international lines are crossed.

* * *

Finally, [a] New York court was confronted with the exact factual situation we have in this case. In Kell v. Henderson, 47 Misc. 2d 992, 263 N.Y.S. 2d 647 (1965), affirmed, 26 App. Div. 2d 595, 270 N.Y.S. 2d 552 (1966), the New York Supreme Court [the New York trial court—eds.] allowed the plaintiff to proceed under New York law, and the Appellate Division affirmed. In that case, the plaintiff, a minor child, in the company of the two defendants, a mother and son, set out from Ontario, Canada, to tour nearby New York. The plaintiff and the defendants were all residents of Ontario. The car was garaged in Ontario and insured in Ontario. While being driven in New York by the defendant son, the car went out of control and careened off the highway, striking a bridge and injuring Miss Kell. The defendants in that case argued that under the *Babcock* decision the most significant interests were in Ontario and not New York and therefore the plaintiff could not recover by reason of the Ontario guest statute. The New York Supreme Court, after pointing out that the state had significant interests by reason of its traffic vehicle regulations, its public policy regarding guest statutes, and the fact that its laws applied to residents and nonresidents equally:

"The conflict-of-laws doctrine enunciated in *Babcock* (supra) recognizes that we no longer mechanically turn to the common-law rule of lex loci delicti in tort cases. The courts now have adopted a rule of choice of law in a conflict situation which looks to reason and justice in its selection of which law is to apply and which fits the needs of today's changing world where frequent travel is the rule, rather than the exception."

While New York was experiencing its difficulties in the changing field of conflict of laws, a fact situation arose in a case appealed to the Supreme Court of New Hampshire, which allowed its learned Mr. Chief Justice Kenison to enunciate a doctrine which has been followed by many courts throughout the country, including our own Minnesota court. In Clark v. Clark, 107 N.H. 351, 222 A. 2d 205 (1966), a husband and wife had left their home in New Hampshire to proceed to another part of New Hampshire for a visit and were to return that evening. Part of their trip took them through Vermont, where the accident occurred. The plaintiff wife brought action in New Hampshire against her husband and sought an order of the court that the substantive law of New Hampshire governed the rights of the parties. New Hampshire had no guest statute and Vermont did. In a carefully reasoned opinion, Mr. Chief Justice Kenison traced the history and difficulty of the lex loci rule. He then proceeded to adopt five basic "choice-influencing considerations" to be applied to these cases. The basic premises for the considerations adopted by the court were first proposed by Professor Robert Leflar in his article, Choice-Influencing Considerations in Conflicts Law, 41 N.Y.U. L. Rev. 267, 279, and briefly stated, the tests selected by the New Hampshire court are: (a) Predictability of results; (b) maintenance of interstate and international order; (c) simplification of the judicial task; (d) advancement of the forum's governmental interests; and (e) application of the better rule of law.

The court pointed out that the first three tests caused very few problems. Predictability of results can be overlooked since basically this test relates to consensual transactions where people should know in advance what law will govern their act. Obviously, no one plans to have an accident, and, except for the remote possibility of forum shopping, this test is of little import in an automobile accident case. As to the second consideration, the court found little trouble since under this heading no more is called for than that the court apply the law of no state which does not have substantial connection with the total facts and the particular issue being litigated. The third point, simplification of the judicial task, poses no problem since the courts are fully capable of administering the law of another forum if called upon to do so.

The court observed that in selecting the law of a particular case the last two considerations carry most weight. In the case before it, the court found adequate governmental interest in applying its state's law and concluded that the New Hampshire law was unquestionably the better law and should be applied.

During this same period, the law of the State of Minnesota has undergone a change. Minnesota had followed the doctrine of lex loci as recently as our decision in Phelps v. Benson, 252 Minn. 457, 90 N.W. 2d 533 (1958), where we reiterated our adherence to that doctrine. . . .

Time found the rule [of lex loci delicti] increasingly criticized as a mechanical methodology, predicated on the outmoded "vested right" theory, and emphasizing certainty and predictability at the expense of other, frequently more relevant considerations. . . .

No American state has . . . adopted a guest statute for many years. Courts of states which did adopt them are today construing them much more narrowly, evidencing their dissatisfaction with them. * * * Though still on the books, they contradict the spirit of the times. Unless other considerations demand it, we should not go out of our way to enforce such a law of another state as against the better law of our own state.

The facts of this case now complete the cycle. The choice-influencing considerations proposed by Professor Leflar and set forth by Mr. Chief Justice Kenison in Clark v. Clark, supra, were adopted by our court in Schneider v. Nichols, supra, indicating our preference for the better-law approach and our rejection of the guest statute concept of various jurisdictions. We have come to the conclusion in this case that plaintiff should be allowed to proceed with her action under our common-law rules of negligence and should not be bound by the guest statute requirements of the Province of Ontario.

As we indicated earlier this opinion, the New York case of Kell v. Henderson, supra, is on "all fours" with the facts of this case. . . .

On the consideration of governmental interest, Professor Leflar found adequate support for the decision rendered by the New York court. In so doing, he rejected the concept of the practical interest of the state in the supervision and safety of its state highways since the rule in question, unlike rules of the road and definitions of negligence, does not bear upon vehicle operation as such. Instead, he pointed out that the factor to be considered is the relevant effect the New York rule has on the duty of host to guest and the danger of collusion between them to defraud the host's insurer. New York's interest in applying its own law rather than Ontario law on these issues, he found to be based primarily on its status as a justice-administering state. In that status, it is strongly concerned with seeing that persons who come into the New York courts to litigate controversies with substantial New York connections have these cases determined according to rules consistent with New York concepts of justice, or at least not inconsistent with them. That will be as true for non-domiciliary litigants as for domiciliaries. This interest will not manifest itself clearly if the out-of-state rule does not run contrary to some strong socio-legal policy of the forum, but it will become a major consideration if there is such a strong opposing local policy.

Professor Leflar then pointed out that this consideration leads to preference for what is regarded as the better rule of law, that New York has such a preference, and that it is a vigorous one. He concluded that the combination of the last two items, governmental interest and better rule of law, called for the application of New York law. His statements and reasoning apply equally to the facts of this case and lead to the conclusion that Minnesota should apply its better rule of law and should allow plaintiff to proceed with her action.

* * *

We have already noted the relative unimportance of predictability of results to tort actions. Similarly, the simplification of the judicial task need not concern us to any great extent since we have no doubt our judicial system could in the appropriate case apply the guest statute rule of gross negligence as readily as our common-law rule. Interstate and international relations are maintained without harm where, as here, the forum state has a substantial connection with the facts and issues involved. This requirement is amply met by the fact that the accident occurred in Minnesota, as well as by the fact that plaintiff was hospitalized for well over a month in the state.

The compelling factors in this case are the advancement of the forum's governmental interests and the application of the better law. While there may be more deterrent effect in our common-law rule of liability as opposed to the guest statute requirement of gross negligence, the main governmental interest involved is that of any "justice-administering state." Leflar, Conflicts Law: More on Choice-Influencing Considerations, 54 Calif. L. Rev. 1584, 1594. In that posture, we are concerned that our courts not be called upon to determine issues under rules which, however accepted they may be in other states, are inconsistent with our own concept of fairness and equity. We might also note that persons injured in automobile accidents occurring within our borders can reasonably be expected to require treatment in our medical facilities, both public and private. In the instant case, plaintiff incurred medical bills in a Duluth hospital which have already been paid, but we are loath to place weight on the individual case for fear it might offer even minor incentives to "hospital shop" or to create litigation-directed pressures on the payment of debts to medical facilities. Suffice it to say that we recognize that medical costs are likely to be incurred with a consequent governmental interest that injured persons not be denied recovery on the basis of doctrines foreign to Minnesota.

In our search for the better rule, we are firmly convinced of the superiority of the common-law rule of liability to that of the Ontario guest statute. We can find little reason for the strict limitation of a host's liability to his guest beyond the fear of collusive suits and the vague disapproval of a guest "biting the hand that feeds him." Neither rationale is persuasive. We are convinced the judicial system can uncover collusive suits without such over-inclusive rules, and we do not find any discomfort in the prospect of a guest suing his host for injuries suffered through the host's simple negligence.

Accordingly, we hold that Minnesota law should be applied to this lawsuit.

Affirmed.

■ PETERSON, JUSTICE (dissenting). The "center-of-gravity-of-the contacts" theory of conflict of laws has been adopted in this state, and we have applied it in situations where an automobile trip started and was intended to terminate in this state, where the host-guest relationship was formed in this state, or where the place of registration or garaging of the automobile was in this state. . . .

The "choice-influencing factor" in the majority opinion is simply that Minnesota law is "better law" because, unlike Ontario law, this state has no guest statute. Notwithstanding our undoubted preference for this forum's standard of liability, I am not persuaded that decision should turn on that factor alone. . . .

NOTES

1.   Is the court correct to say that predictability is "relatively unimportant" in tort cases? If the parties are unable to predict what law will apply, wouldn't this lead to more appeals and make it more difficult to settle cases because each side will have a rational hope that the law favoring it will apply?

2.   Can the result in the principal case, or in the New York lower court case of Kell v. Henderson, be explained on any grounds other than a preference for the application of forum law? Under the logic of *Babcock*, does not the defendant and her insurer have an interest in having Ontario's more

demanding standard of culpability be applied? How convincing is the majority opinion's insistence that Minnesota has an interest insuring the payment of medical creditors without any showing that there was such a risk in this case? How well suited are courts to determine whether the forum rule or another one is the better rule of law?

2. THE COURTS AT WORK IN TORT CONFLICTS

Following the decision in Babcock v. Jackson, p. 577, supra, New York's highest court did not live happily ever after with its new approach to choice of law for torts. In the next nine years, the court would decide four more cases in which the issue was whether a guest passenger could recover against a New York host driver under New York's ordinary negligence rule or was required to meet stricter liability standards under the law of the place of injury. Dym v. Gordon, 209 N.E.2d 792 (N.Y.1965), denied recovery to a New York guest suing a New York host for injuries resulting from a collision in Colorado. The court distinguished *Babcock* on the ground that *Dym* involved a two-car accident and one purpose of the Colorado guest statute was to preserve the host's assets for the injured parties in the other car. Moreover, the relationship between host and guest was formed in Colorado, where they met at summer school. Macey v. Rozbicki, 221 N.E.2d 380 (N.Y.1966), applied New York law to a suit between sisters who lived in Buffalo but were vacationing at the host's summer home in Ontario, where the collision occurred during a local trip. The court stated that the relationship between host and guest had been established in New York. Tooker v. Lopez, 249 N.E.2d 394 (N.Y.1969), overruled Dym v. Gordon and applied New York law to a death caused in Michigan, where the New York host and passenger were students at Michigan State University. The court declined to rest its decision on the fact that, unlike Dym v. Gordon, the death was caused by the car overturning, not by a collision with another car.

At this point New York conflicts rules for loss-allocating torts appeared to be in chaos. Understandably, in the next principal case, the court sought to clarify matters.

Neumeier v. Kuehner

Court of Appeals of New York, 1972.
31 N.Y.2d 121, 335 N.Y.S.2d 64, 286 N.E.2d 454.

■ FULD, CHIEF JUDGE. A domiciliary of Ontario, Canada, was killed when the automobile in which he was riding, owned and driven by a New York resident, collided with a train in Ontario. That jurisdiction has a guest statute, and the primary question posed by this appeal is whether in this action brought by the Ontario passenger's estate, Ontario law should be applied and the New York defendant permitted to rely on its guest statute as a defense.

The facts are quickly told. On May 7, 1969, Arthur Kuehner, the defendant's intestate, a resident of Buffalo, drove his automobile from that city to Fort Erie in the Province of Ontario, Canada, where he picked up Amie Neumeier, who lived in that town with his wife and their children. Their trip was to take them to Long Beach, also in Ontario, and back again to Neumeier's home in Fort Erie. However, at a railroad crossing in the Town of Sherkston—on the way to Long Beach—the auto was struck by a train of the defendant Canadian National Railway Company. Both Kuehner and his guest-passenger were instantly killed.

Neumeier's wife and administratrix, a citizen of Canada and a domiciliary of Ontario, thereupon commenced this wrongful death action in New York against both Kuehner's estate and the Canadian National Railway Company. The defendant estate pleaded, as an affirmative defense, the Ontario guest statute and the defendant railway also interposed defenses in reliance upon it. In substance, the statute provides that the owner or driver of a motor vehicle is not liable for damages resulting from injury to, or the death of, a guest-passenger unless he was guilty of gross negligence (Highway Traffic Act of Province of Ontario [Ont.Rev.Stat. (1960), ch. 172], § 105, subd. [2], as amd. by Stat. of 1966, ch. 64, § 20, subd. [2]). It is worth noting, at this point, that, although our court originally considered that the sole purpose of the Ontario statute was to protect Ontario defendants and their insurers against collusive claims (see Babcock v. Jackson, 12 N.Y.2d 473, 482–483, 240 N.Y.S.2d 743, 749–750, 191 N.E.2d 279, 283–284) "Further research . . . has revealed the distinct possibility that one purpose, and perhaps the only purpose, of the statute was to protect owners and drivers against ungrateful guests." (Reese, Chief Judge Fuld and Choice of Law, 71 Col. L. Rev. 548, 558; see Trautman, Two Views on Kell v. Henderson: A Comment, 67 Col. L. Rev. 465, 469.)[4]

The plaintiff, asserting that the Ontario statute "is not available . . . in the present action", moved, pursuant to CPLR 3211 (subd. [b]), to dismiss the affirmative defenses pleaded. The court at Special Term holding the guest statute applicable, denied the motions (63 Misc.2d 766, 313 N.Y.S.2d 468) but, on appeal, a closely divided Appellate Division reversed and directed dismissal of the defenses (37 A.D.2d 70, 322 N.Y.S.2d 867). It was the court's belief that such a result was dictated by Tooker v. Lopez, 24 N.Y.2d 569, 301 N.Y.S.2d 519, 249 N.E.2d 394.

In reaching that conclusion, the Appellate Division misread our decision in the *Tooker* case—a not unnatural result in light of the variant views expressed in the three separate opinions written on behalf of the majority. It is important to bear in mind that in *Tooker*, the guest-passenger and the host-driver were both domiciled in New York, and

---

[4] Another scholar's research into the legislative history of the Ontario statute has led him to the conclusion that the statute was only intended to protect insurance companies. Baade, The Case of The Disinterested Two States: Neumeier v. Kuehner, 1 Hofstra L. Rev. 150, 152–54 (1973). —eds.

our decision—that New York law was controlling—was based upon, and limited to, that fact situation. Indeed [both] . . . Judge Keating (24 N.Y.2d at p. 580, 301 N.Y.S.2d at p. 528, 249 N.E.2d at p. 400) and Judge Burke (at p. 591, 301 N.Y.S.2d at p. 537, 249 N.E.2d at p. 407) expressly noted that the determination then being made left open the question whether New York law would be applicable if the plaintiff passenger happened to be a domiciliary of the very jurisdiction which had a guest statute.[5] Thus, Tooker v. Lopez did no more than hold that, when the passenger and driver are residents of the same jurisdiction and the car is there registered and insured, its law, and not the law of the place of accident, controls and determines the standard of care which the host owes to his guest.

What significantly and effectively differentiates the present case is the fact that, although the host was a domiciliary of New York, the guest, for whose death recovery is sought, was domiciled in Ontario, the place of accident and the very jurisdiction which had enacted the statute designed to protect the host from liability for ordinary negligence. It is clear that although New York has a deep interest in protecting its own residents, injured in a foreign state, against unfair or anachronistic statutes of that state, it has no legitimate interest in ignoring the public policy of a foreign jurisdiction—such as Ontario—and in protecting the plaintiff guest domiciled and injured there from legislation obviously addressed, at the very least, to a resident riding in a vehicle traveling within its borders.

To distinguish *Tooker* on such a basis is not improperly discriminatory. It is quite true that, in applying the Ontario guest statute to the Ontario-domiciled passenger, we, in a sense, extend a right less generous than New York extends to a New York passenger in a New York vehicle with New York insurance. That, though, is not a consequence of invidious discrimination; it is, rather, the result of the existence of disparate rules of law in jurisdictions that have diverse and important connections with the litigants and the litigated issue.

The fact that insurance policies issued in this State on New York-based vehicles cover liability, regardless of the place of the accident (Vehicle and Traffic Law, Consol.Laws, c. 71 § 311, subd. 4), certainly does not call for the application of internal New York law in this case. The compulsory insurance requirement is designed to cover a car-owner's liability, not create it; in other words, the applicable statute was not intended to impose liability where none would otherwise exist. This being so, we may not properly look to the New York insurance requirement to dictate a choice-of-law rule which would invariably impose liability. . . .

When, in Babcock v. Jackson we rejected the inexorable choice-of-law rule in personal injury cases because it failed to take account of underlying policy considerations, we were willing to sacrifice the certainty provided

---

[5]   In the other concurring opinion (24 N.Y.2d at p. 585, 301 N.Y.S.2d at p. 533, 249 N.E.2d at p. 404), I wrote that in such a case—where the passenger is a resident of the state having a guest statute—"the applicable rule of decision will [normally] be that of the state where the accident occurred".

by the old rule for the more just, fair and practical result that may best be achieved by giving controlling effect to the law of the jurisdiction which has the greatest concern with, or interest in, the specific issue raised in the litigation.... In consequence of the change effected—and this was to be anticipated—our decisions in multi-state highway accident cases, particularly in those involving guest-host controversies, have, it must be acknowledged, lacked consistency. This stemmed, in part, from the circumstance that it is frequently difficult to discover the purposes or policies underlying the relevant local law rules of the respective jurisdictions involved. It is even more difficult, assuming that these purposes or policies are found to conflict, to determine on some principled basis which should be given effect at the expense of the others.

The single all-encompassing rule which called, invariably, for selection of the law of the place of injury was discarded, and wisely, because it was too broad to prove satisfactory in application. There, is, however, no reason why choice-of-law rules, more narrow than those previously devised, should not be successfully developed, in order to assure a greater degree of predictability and uniformity, on the basis of our present knowledge and experience.... "The time has come," I wrote in *Tooker* (24 N.Y.2d, at p. 584, 301 N.Y.S.2d, at p. 532, 249 N.E.2d, at p. 403), "to endeavor to minimize what some have characterized as an *ad hoc* case-by-case approach by laying down guidelines, as well as we can, for the solution of guest-host conflicts problems." *Babcock* and its progeny enable us to formulate a set of basic principles that may be profitably utilized, for they have helped us uncover the underlying values and policies which are operative in this area of the law.... "Now that these values and policies have been revealed, we may proceed to the next stage in the evolution of the law—the formulation of a few rules of general applicability, promising a fair level of predictability." Although it was recognized that no rule may be formulated to guarantee a satisfactory result in every case, the following principles were proposed as sound for situations involving guest statutes in conflicts settings (24 N.Y.2d, at p. 585, 301 N.Y.S.2d, at p. 532, 249 N.E.2d, at p. 404):

"1. When the guest-passenger and the host-driver are domiciled in the same state, and the car is there registered, the law of that state should control and determine the standard of care which the host owes to his guest.

"2. When the driver's conduct occurred in the state of his domicile and that state does not cast him in liability for that conduct, he should not be held liable by reason of the fact that liability would be imposed upon him under the tort law of the state of the victim's domicile. Conversely, when the guest was injured in the state of his own domicile and its law permits recovery, the driver who has come into that state should not— in the absence of special circumstances—be permitted to interpose the law of his state as a defense.

"3. In other situations, when the passenger and the driver are domiciled in different states, the rule is necessarily less categorical. Normally, the applicable rule of decision will be that of the state where the accident occurred but not if it can be shown that displacing that normally applicable rule will advance the relevant substantive law purposes without impairing the smooth working of the multi-state system or producing great uncertainty for litigants. (Cf. Restatement, 2d, Conflict of Laws, P.O.D., pt. II, §§ 146, 159 [later adopted and promulgated May 23, 1969].)"

The variant views expressed not only in *Tooker* but by Special Term and the divided Appellate Division in this litigation underscore and confirm the need for these rules. Since the passenger was domiciled in Ontario and the driver in New York, the present case is covered by the third stated principle. The law to be applied is that of the jurisdiction where the accident happened unless it appears that "displacing [that] normally applicable rule will advance the relevant substantive law purposes" of the jurisdictions involved. Certainly, ignoring Ontario's policy requiring proof of gross negligence in a case which involves an Ontario-domiciled guest at the expense of a New Yorker does not further the substantive law purposes of New York. In point of fact, application of New York law would result in the exposure of this State's domiciliaries to a greater liability than that imposed upon resident users of Ontario's highways. Conversely, the failure to apply Ontario's law would "impair"— to cull from the rule set out above—"the smooth working of the multi-state system [and] produce great uncertainty for litigants" by sanctioning forum shopping and thereby allowing a party to select a forum which could give him a larger recovery than the court of his own domicile. In short, the plaintiff has failed to show that this State's connection with the controversy was sufficient to justify displacing the rule of *lex loci* [*delicti*]. . . .

In each action, the Appellate Division's order should be reversed, that of Special Term reinstated, without costs, and the questions certified answered in the negative.

■ BREITEL, JUDGE (concurring).

I agree that there should be a reversal, but would place the reversal on quite narrow grounds. It is undesirable to lay down prematurely major premises based on shifting ideologies in the choice of law. True, Chief Judge Fuld in his concurring opinion in the *Tooker* case . . . took the view that there had already occurred sufficient experience to lay down some rules of law which would reduce the instability and uncertainty created by the recent departures from traditional *lex loci [delicti]*. This case, arising so soon after, shows that the permutations in accident cases, especially automobile accident cases, is disproof that the time has come.

Problems engendered by the new departures have not gone unnoticed and they are not confined to the courts of this State (Juenger, Choice of

Law in Interstate Torts, 118 U. Pa. L. Rev. 202, 214–220). They arise not merely because any new departure of necessity creates problems, but much more because the departures have been accompanied by an unprecedented competition of ideologies, largely of academic origin, to explain and reconstruct a whole field of law, each purporting or aspiring to achieve a single universal principle.

Babcock v. Jackson, an eminently correctly and justly decided case, applied the then current new doctrine of grouping of contacts. Troubles arose only when the universality of a single doctrine was assumed. . . . By the time of Miller v. Miller and the *Tooker* case, the new doctrine had been displaced by a still newer one, that of governmental interests developed most extensively by the late Brainerd Currie, and the court was deeply engaged in probing the psychological motivation of legislatures of other States in enacting statutes restricting recoveries in tort cases. Now, evidently, it is suggested that this State and other States may have less parochial concerns in enacting legislation restricting tort recoveries than had been believed only a short time ago. The trouble this case has given the courts below and now this court stems, it is suggested, more from a concern in sorting out ideologies than in applying narrow rules of law in the traditional common-law process (Juenger, op. cit., supra, at p. 233).

What the *Babcock* case ... taught and what modern day commentators largely agree is that *lex loci [delicti]* is unsoundly applied if it is done indiscriminately and without exception. It is still true, however, that the *lex loci [delicti]* is the normal rule, as indeed Chief Judge Fuld noted in the *Tooker* case, . . . to be rejected only when it is evident that the situs of the accident is the least of the several factors or influences to which the accident may be attributed. . . . Certain it is that States are not concerned only with their own citizens or residents. They are concerned with events that occur within their territory, and are also concerned with the "stranger within the gates" (Juenger, op. cit., supra, at pp. 209–210).

In this case, none would have ever assumed that New York law should be applied just because one of the two defendants was a New York resident and his automobile was New York insured, except for the overbroad statements of Currie doctrine in the *Tooker* case. . . .

Consequently, I agree that there should be a reversal and the defenses allowed to stand. The conclusion, however, rests simply on the proposition that plaintiff has failed by her allegations to establish that the relationship to this State was sufficient to displace the normal rule that the *lex loci [delicti]* should be applied, the accident being associated with Ontario, from inception to tragic termination, except for adventitious facts and where the lawsuit was brought.

■ BERGAN, JUDGE (dissenting). . . .

There is a difference of fundamental character between justifying a departure from *lex loci [delicti]* because the court will not, as a matter of policy, permit a New York owner of a car licensed and insured in New York to escape a liability that would be imposed on him here; and a departure based on the fact a New York resident makes the claim for injury. The first ground of departure is justifiable as sound policy; the second is justifiable only if one is willing to treat the rights of a stranger permitted to sue in New York differently from the way a resident is treated. Neither because of "interest" nor "contact" nor any other defensible ground is it proper to say in a court of law that the rights of one man whose suit is accepted shall be adjudged differently on the merits on the basis of where he happens to live. . . .

. . . What the court is deciding today is that although it will prevent a New York car owner from asserting the defense of a protective foreign statute when a New York resident in whose rights it has an "interest" sues; it has no such "interest" when it accepts the suit in New York of a nonresident. This is an inadmissible distinction.

NOTES

1.   Will Rule 2 produce desirable results when host and guest are on a trip that is intended to enter both of their states?

Foster v. Leggett, 484 S.W.2d 827 (Ky.1972). The defendant driver was domiciled in Ohio, which has a guest statute, but he was employed in Kentucky and spent much of his time there. He and his guest set out from Kentucky for Columbus, Ohio, intending to "have dinner, go to a show or the races" and then return to Kentucky "the night of the same day." In Ohio the defendant's car collided with another car and the passenger was killed. The Kentucky court refused to apply the Ohio guest statute and found for the plaintiff by applying Kentucky's common law standard of negligence. Judge Fuld's second principle would apparently call for application of the law of Ohio.Foster v. Leggett is the subject of a symposium in 61 Ky.L.J. 368–428 (1973).

On the other hand, see Cipolla v. Shaposka, 267 A.2d 854 (Pa.1970). A Delaware host was driving his Pennsylvania guest back to Pennsylvania when the car crashed in Delaware. The court applied the Delaware guest statute declaring that "it seems only fair to permit a defendant to rely on his home state's law when he is acting within that state." Would there be anything unfair about applying the Pennsylvania rule of ordinary negligence when the trip was intended to reach there?

Should *Neumeier* Rule 2 have provided an exception for cases like *Foster* and *Cipolla?* If rules are desirable to provide reasonable predictability, are the *Neumeier* rules good rules for this purpose? Do they sufficiently provide for the most likely variations in host-guest cases? What purpose is served by including the state where the car is "registered" in Rule 1?

The *Neumeier* rules provide for possible exceptions in the second sentence of Rule 2 and in Rule 3. Are these exceptions carefully drafted? Why should there be an exception in the second sentence of Rule 2, but not in the first sentence? For a discussion of the art of drafting exceptions when codifying choice-of-law rules, see Symeonides, Exception Clauses in American Conflicts Law, 42 Am.J.Comp.L. 813 (1994).

2. Subsequent cases in the New York courts have applied Chief Judge Fuld's third principle. Pursuant to this principle, the law of the place of injury was applied and judgment rendered in the defendant's favor in Croft v. National Car Rental, 439 N.E.2d 346 (N.Y.1982) (vicarious liability of owner for negligence of driver); Towley v. King Arthur Rings, Inc., 351 N.E.2d 728 (N.Y.1976) (guest-passenger statute); Blais v. Deyo, 461 N.Y.S.2d 471 (App.Div.1983) (limit on amount of recovery); Rogers v. U-Haul Co., 342 N.Y.S.2d 158 (App.Div.1973) (vicarious liability of owner for negligence of driver).

3. The New York Court of Appeals cited *Neumeier* in an opinion in which it said by way of dictum that "*lex loci delicti* remains the general rule in tort cases to be displaced only in extraordinary circumstances." Cousins v. Instrument Flyers, Inc., 376 N.E.2d 914, 915 (N.Y.1978).

4. Action by a guest-passenger to recover for injuries resulting from an automobile accident in Ohio. The plaintiff was domiciled in New Jersey and the defendant driver in New York. The automobile was registered, principally garaged and "presumably insured" in New York. *Held*: The Ohio guest-passenger statute was not available to the defendant as a defense. Chief Judge Fuld's third principle would not require application of Ohio law in this instance, since "none of the litigants reside in a state having a guest statute, nor presumably did the insurer calculate the defendants' insurance premiums with a guest statute in mind." Chila v. Owens, 348 F.Supp. 1207, 1211 (S.D.N.Y.1972).

See also Diehl v. Ogorewac, 836 F.Supp. 88 (E.D.N.Y.1993). A driver from New Jersey crashed in North Carolina killing one New York passenger and injuring another. Neither passenger was wearing a seat belt. Under North Carolina law, this fact was not admissible in evidence as proof of contributory negligence, but it was admissible under both New Jersey and New York law. The court held the evidence admissible as comporting "with the policies served by the first *Neumeier* rule" and, in any event, within the exception in Rule 3. Article 3544 of the Louisiana codification treats parties domiciled in states that have "substantially" the same rule as if they were domiciled in the same state. See also Borchers, Nebraska Choice of Law: An Updated Synthesis, 53 Creighton L Rev. 339 (2020) (Nebraska courts treat parties domiciled in states with identical laws on the contested issue as domiciled in the same state). Should Rule 1 have expressly included cases in which host and guest live in different states but there is no difference in the laws of the two states?

5. Other states have given Chief Judge Fuld's *Neumeier* principles a mixed reception. First National Bank in Fort Collins v. Rostek, 514 P.2d 314, 319 (Colo.1973), adopted the first two principles; but in Labree v. Major, 306 A.2d 808 (R.I.1973), the court applied the Rhode Island ordinary negligence rule rather than the Massachusetts gross negligence standard, to permit recovery by a Massachusetts guest passenger, injured in Massachusetts by a Rhode Island host driver. The court rejects *Neumeir*'s third rule as "a retreat to the doctrine of lex loci delicti" instead of applying, as the court prefers, "interest analysis." Id. at 817.

6. For a lengthy and scholarly critique of *Neumeier* see Korn, The Choice-of-Law Revolution: A Critique, 83 Colum.L.Rev. 772 (1983). See generally Reese, Chief Judge Fuld and Choice of Law, 71 Colum.L.Rev. 548 (1971); Reese, Choice of Law: Rules or Approach, 57 Corn.L.Q. 315 (1972); Powers, Formalism and Nonformalism in Choice of Law Methodology, 52 Wash. L.Rev. 27 (1976); Haworth, The Mirror Image Conflicts Case, 1974 Wash.U.L.Q. 1.

Bernhard v. Harrah's Club
Supreme Court of California, 1976.
16 Cal.3d 313, 128 Cal.Rptr. 215, 546 P.2d 719, cert. denied
429 U.S. 859, 97 S.Ct. 159, 50 L.Ed.2d 136.

[Action against defendant Harrah's Club, a Nevada corporation, to recover for personal injuries suffered in California. The plaintiff alleged that defendant owned and operated gambling and drinking establishments in Nevada and solicited business for such establishments in California "knowing and expecting that many California residents would use the public highways in going to and from defendant's . . . establishments." In response to defendant's advertisements, in July 1971, two Californians patronized one of defendant's clubs in Nevada where they were served numerous alcoholic beverages "progressively reaching a point of obvious intoxication rendering them incapable of safely driving a car." After they had entered California on their way home, the car, while being driven by one of these Californians in an intoxicated state, crossed the center line and collided head-on with a motorcycle operated by plaintiff Bernhard, also a California domiciliary, who suffered severe injuries. Defendant demurred to the complaint on the ground that Nevada law gave no right to recover against a tavern keeper for injuries caused by the selling of alcoholic beverages to an intoxicated person and that Nevada law governed because defendant's alleged tort had been committed in Nevada. The trial court sustained the demurrer and plaintiff appealed.]

■ SULLIVAN, JUSTICE:

We face a problem in the choice of law governing a tort action. As we have made clear on other occasions, we no longer adhere to the rule that the law of the place of the wrong is applicable in a California forum regardless of the issues before the court. . . . Rather we have adopted in its place a rule requiring an analysis of the respective interests of the states involved—the objective of which is "to determine the law that most appropriately applies to the issue involved." . . .

We observe at the start that the laws of the two states—California and Nevada—applicable to the issue involved are not identical. California imposes liability on tavern keepers in this state for conduct such as here alleged. In Vesely v. Sager, . . . 5 Cal. 3d 153, 166, 95 Cal.Rptr. 623, 486 P.2d 151 (1971), this court [held that such liability should be imposed since not to do so would be] patently unsound and totally inconsistent with the principles of proximate cause established in other areas of negligence law. [Also] the Legislature has expressed its intention in this area with the adoption of Business and Professions Code § 25602 [making it a misdemeanor to sell to an obviously intoxicated person], a statute to which this presumption [of negligence, Evidence Code § 669] applies. . . . Nevada on the other hand refuses to impose such liability. In Hamm v. Carson City Nuggett, Inc., 85 Nev. 99, 450 P.2d 358, 359 (1969), the court held it would create neither common law liability nor liability based on the criminal statute banning sale of alcoholic beverages to a person who is drunk, because "if civil liability is to be imposed, it should be accomplished by legislative act after appropriate surveys, hearings, and investigations to ascertain the need for it and the expected consequences to follow. . . ."

Although California and Nevada, the two "involved states" . . . have different laws governing the issue presented in the case at bench, we encounter a problem in selecting the applicable rule of law only if *both* states have an interest in having their respective laws applied. . . .

Defendant contends that Nevada has a definite interest in having its rule of decision applied in this case in order to protect its resident tavern keepers like defendant from being subjected to a civil liability which Nevada has not imposed either by legislative enactment or decisional law. . . .

Plaintiff on the other hand points out that California also has an interest in applying its own rule of decision to the case at bench. California imposes on tavern keepers civil liability to third parties injured by persons to whom the tavern keeper has sold alcoholic beverages when they are obviously intoxicated "for the purpose of protecting members of the general public from injuries to person and damage to property resulting from the excessive use of intoxicating liquor." (Vesely v. Sager, supra, 5 Cal. 3d 153, 165, 95 Cal.Rptr. 623, 486 P.2d 151 (1971).) California, it is urged, has a special interest in affording this protection to all California residents injured in California.

Thus, since the case at bench involves a California resident (plaintiff) injured in this state by intoxicated drivers and a Nevada resident tavern keeper (defendant) which served alcoholic beverages to them in Nevada, it is clear that each state has an interest in the application of its respective law of liability and nonliability. It goes without saying that these interests conflict. Therefore, unlike Reich v. Purcell, supra, 67 Cal. 2d 551, 63 Cal. Rptr. 31, 432 P.2d 727 (1967), and Hurtado v. Superior Court, supra, 11 Cal. 3d 574, 114 Cal. Rptr. 106, 522 P.2d 666 (1974), where we were faced with "false conflicts," in the instant case for the first time since applying a governmental interest analysis as a choice of law doctrine in *Reich*, we are confronted with a "true" conflicts case. We must therefore determine the appropriate rule of decision in a controversy where each of the states involved has a legitimate but conflicting interest in applying its own law in respect to the civil liability of tavern keepers.

The search for the proper resolution of a true conflicts case, while proceeding within orthodox parameters of governmental interest analysis, has generated much scholarly examination and discussion. The father of the governmental interest approach, Professor Brainerd Currie, originally took the position that in a true conflicts situation the law of the forum should always be applied. (Currie, Selected Essays on Conflicts of Laws p. 184 (1963).) However, upon further reflection, Currie suggested that when under the governmental interest approach a preliminary analysis reveals an apparent conflict of interest upon the forum's assertion of its own rule of decision, the forum should reexamine its policy to determine if a more restrained interpretation of it is more appropriate.... This process of reexamination ... can be approached under principles of "comparative impairment." (Baxter, Choice of Law and the Federal System, supra, 16 Stan. L. Rev. 1–22; Horowitz, The Law of Choice of Law in California—A Restatement, supra, 21 UCLA L. Rev. 719, 748–758.)

... [T]he "comparative impairment" approach to the resolution of such conflict seeks to determine which state's interest would be more impaired if its policy were subordinated to the policy of the other state. This analysis proceeds on the principle that true conflicts should be resolved by applying the law of the state whose interest would be the more impaired if its law were not applied. Exponents of this process of analysis emphasize that it is very different from a weighing process. The court does not " 'weigh' the conflicting governmental interests in the sense of determining which conflicting law manifested the 'better' or the 'worthier' social policy on the specific issue...." Horowitz, The Law of Choice of Law in California—A Restatement, supra, 21 UCLA L.Rev. 719, 753.

Mindful of the above principles governing our choice of law, we proceed to reexamine the California policy underlying the imposition of civil liability upon tavern keepers. At its broadest limits this policy would afford protection to all persons injured in California by intoxicated persons who have been sold or furnished alcoholic beverages while intoxicated regardless of where such beverages were sold or furnished. Such a broad policy would naturally embrace situations where the intoxicated actor had been provided with liquor by out-of-state tavern keepers. Although the State of Nevada does not impose such *civil* liability on its tavern keepers, nevertheless they are subject to *criminal* penalties under a statute making it unlawful to sell or give intoxicating liquor to any person who is drunk or known to be an habitual drunkard. (See Nev. Rev. Stats. 202.100*; see Hamm v. Carson City Nugget, Inc., supra, 85 Nev. 99, 450 P.2d 358 (1969).)

We need not, and accordingly do not here determine the outer limits to which California's policy should be extended, for it appears clear to us that it must encompass defendant, who as alleged in the complaint, "advertis[es] for and otherwise solicit[s] in California the business of

---

* This statute was repealed effective July 1, 1973. 1973 Nev. Stats. 1062, c. 604, § 8, S.B. 359. Eds.

California residents at defendant Harrah's Club Nevada drinking and gambling establishments, knowing and expecting said California residents, in response to said advertising and solicitation, to use the public highways of the State of California in going and coming from defendant Harrah's Club Nevada drinking and gambling establishments." Defendant by the course of its chosen commercial practice has put itself at the heart of California's regulatory interest, namely to prevent tavern keepers from selling alcoholic beverages to obviously intoxicated persons who are likely to act in California in the intoxicated state. It seems clear that California cannot reasonably effectuate its policy if it does not extend its regulation to include out-of-state tavern keepers such as defendant who regularly and purposely sell intoxicating beverages to California residents in places and under conditions in which it is reasonably certain these residents will return to California and act therein while still in an intoxicated state. California's interest would be very significantly impaired if its policy were not applied to defendant.

Since the act of selling alcoholic beverages to obviously intoxicated persons is already proscribed in Nevada, the application of California's rule of civil liability would not impose an entirely new duty requiring the ability to distinguish between California residents and other patrons. Rather the imposition of such liability involves an increased economic exposure, which, at least for businesses which actively solicit extensive California patronage, is a foreseeable and coverable business expense. Moreover, Nevada's interest in protecting its tavern keepers from civil liability of a boundless and unrestricted nature will not be significantly impaired when as in the instant case liability is imposed only on those tavern keepers who actively solicit California business.

. . . [W]e conclude that California has an important and abiding interest in applying its rule of decision to the case at bench, that the policy of this state would be more significantly impaired if such rule were not applied and that the trial court erred in not applying California law.

Defendant argues, however, that even if California law is applied, the demurrer was nonetheless properly sustained because the tavern keeper's duty stated in Vesely v. Sager, supra, 5 Cal. 3d 153, 95 Cal. Rptr. 623, 486 P.2d 151 (1971), is based on Business and Professions Code section 25602, which is a criminal statute and thus without extraterritorial effect. . . .

However, our decision in *Vesely* was much broader than defendant would have it.

. . . [O]ur opinion in *Vesely* struck down the old common law rule of nonliability constructed on the basis that the consumption, not the sale, of alcoholic beverages was the proximate cause of the injuries inflicted by the intoxicated person. Although we chose to impose liability on the *Vesely* defendant on the basis of his violating the applicable statute, the clear import of our decision was that there was no bar to civil liability under modern negligence law. . . .

The judgment is reversed and the cause is remanded to the trial court with directions to overrule the demurrer and to allow defendant a reasonable time within which to answer.

NOTES

1. Was the court right to conclude that Nevada's policies were not impaired substantially by the imposition of civil liability on Harrah's Club? "If Nevada protects its taverns from liability to its own residents, it has an even greater interest in preventing their liability to out-of-state residents." Note, Conflict of Laws, 65 Calif.L.Rev. 290 296 (1977). In an article focusing on the principal case Professor Kanowitz criticized the comparative-impairment method for imprecision, manipulability, and a tendency toward interest counting. Kanowitz, Comparative Impairment and Better Law: Grand Illusions in the Conflict of Laws, 30 Hastings L.J. 255, 293 (1979).

An Ontario husband and wife sued, respectively, for personal injury and consortium damages when he hurt his arm in a meat grinder while at work. Under the Ontario Workmen's Compensation Act the only benefits allowed were those provided in the Act; under the law of California, which was the forum and place of manufacture of the meat grinder, a common law recovery could be had. Held: Although California had some interest in deterring manufacture of defective machines, its interests would be less impaired than Ontario's if the plaintiffs failed to recover. Paulo v. Bepex Corp., 792 F.2d 894 (9th Cir.1986).

2. In 1978 the California legislature amended Cal.Bus.& Prof.Code § 25602 to absolve anyone who "sells, furnishes, [or] gives . . . any alcoholic beverage" from civil liability for acts of drunken patrons or guests. It remained a misdemeanor to serve a person who is obviously intoxicated. The statute overruled by name the *Vesely* and *Bernhard* decisions.

3. Cable v. Sahara Tahoe Corp., 155 Cal.Rptr. 770 (Cal.App.1979). The plaintiff was an employee of the defendant bar located in Nevada. She had been commuting from her residence in California but, at the time of her injury, may have been residing in Nevada. She contended, however, and the court presumed, that she was domiciled in California. A friend was driving her from the bar to a destination in Nevada when the driver lost control because he had become intoxicated at defendant's bar. Following the single-vehicle accident the plaintiff returned to California and, by reason of her injuries, has become and presumably will remain a public charge. Held for the defendant. Nevada's interests would be more impaired by application of California law than would California's interests be impaired by the application of the law of Nevada. "The state with the 'predominant' interest in controlling conduct normally is the state in which such conduct occurs and is most likely to cause injury." The policy that was given effect in the *Bernhard* case is applicable only to injuries that occur in California. Also, by statute enacted after the occurrence of the accident in question, California has repudiated the rule that a bartender is liable for injuries caused by intoxicated patrons. "Though an existing cause of action would not be nullified by the [statute], it is obvious that the impairment of such a repudiated policy [by application of Nevada law] has a minimal effect upon California's governmental interest."

Ruiz v. Blentech Corporation

United States Court of Appeals, Seventh Circuit, 1996.
89 F.3d 320, cert. denied, 519 U.S. 1077, 117 S.Ct. 737, 136 L.Ed.2d 677.

■ CUDAHY, CIRCUIT JUDGE.

Felipe Ruiz's case turns on a rather mystifying choice-of-law problem. Ruiz, a citizen of Illinois, suffered an injury in his home state from an allegedly defective product manufactured in California by a California corporation. The manufacturer has dissolved, but another California corporation has followed in its footsteps by purchasing its principal assets and continuing its business. Ruiz seeks to make the successor corporation answer for his tort claims against the manufacturer. Illinois and California have different rules for determining when one corporation is responsible, as a successor, for the tort liabilities of its predecessors. The district court concluded that Illinois' rules, which are less favorable to Ruiz, should apply. As a consequence of this conclusion, it entered summary judgment against him. Ruiz appeals this judgment, arguing that the district court incorrectly resolved the conflict between the rules adopted, respectively, by Illinois and California. We affirm.

I.

Felipe Ruiz operated a screw conveyor in a food processing plant in Schiller Park, Illinois. On June 16, 1992, he somehow became entangled in the conveyor's machinery and sustained several grievous injuries, the most severe of which left him paralyzed. He soon filed a lawsuit in an Illinois state court, bringing claims of strict products liability and negligence, among others. The case was removed to the district court on the basis of diversity jurisdiction. . . .

[One] defendant was Custom Stainless Equipment, the California corporation that had manufactured the conveyor in 1983 and had dissolved in 1986. [Another] defendant was an entity that Ruiz identified as the successor to Custom Stainless' liabilities in tort. When Custom Stainless dissolved, it sold all of its assets for cash to Blentech, another California corporation. Blentech continued to manufacture Custom Stainless' product lines under its own name, using the same product designs, the same factory, the same management and the same employees. Ruiz contended in the district court that California law defined the relationship between Custom Stainless and Blentech and, therefore, between Blentech and himself. According to Ruiz's interpretation of that law, Blentech's assimilation of Custom Stainless included an assumption of strict liability for any defective products that Custom Stainless had manufactured. . . .

II.

* * *

B.

Ruiz's challenge to the summary judgment for Blentech relies on his argument that the choice of state law governing the crucial issues in the case was in error. In a diversity case, of course, state law governs, and the district court determines what state law to apply in accordance with the choice-of-law principles of the state in which it sits. The district court here was bound by the choice-of-law method defined by the Restatement (Second) of Conflicts of Law, which Illinois has adopted.

The Second Restatement method is constructed around the principle that the state with the most significant contacts to an issue provides the law governing that issue. A court therefore conducts a separate choice-of-law analysis for each issue in a case, attempting to determine which state has the most significant contacts with that issue. The Second Restatement enumerates specific factors that identify the state with the most significant contacts to an issue, and the relevant factors differ according to the area of substantive law governing the issue and according to the nature of the issue itself. To properly apply the Second Restatement method, a court must begin its choice-of-law analysis with a characterization of the issue at hand in terms of substantive law. By prescribing this analytical approach, the Second Restatement follows the principle of dépeçage,[1] which has been long applied in connection with various methods for choice of law.

With respect to Ruiz's claim against Blentech, the choice-of-law analysis had crucial importance. Only two states have significant contacts with the issues raised. California was the place of the legal relationship between Custom Stainless and Blentech; and Illinois was the place of Ruiz's residence and his injury. The decisive issue in the case was whether Blentech had succeeded to Custom Stainless' liabilities by virtue of its purchase of Custom Stainless' assets and its business. Illinois and California shared a basic rule about corporate successor liability, but California provided an exception to that rule that was not available in Illinois.

Illinois mandates that, as a general rule of corporate law, a corporation that purchases the principal assets of another corporation does not assume the seller's liabilities arising from tort claims or from any other kind of claims. Illinois does recognize four exceptions to this rule. The purchasing corporation assumes the seller's liabilities when: (1) it expressly agrees to assume them; (2) the asset sale amounts to a de

---

[1] When roughly translated, dépeçage refers to the process of cutting something into pieces. Here it refers to the process of cutting up a case into individual issues, each subject to a separate choice-of-law analysis.

facto merger; (3) the purchaser is a mere continuation of the seller; (4) the sale is for the fraudulent purpose of escaping liability for the seller's obligations. . . .

California departs from the Illinois rules, however, by adopting a fifth exception. That exception provides that a corporation that purchases a manufacturing business and continues to produce the seller's line of products assumes strict liability in tort for defects in units of the same product line previously manufactured and distributed by the seller. This "products line" exception applies in cases involving tort claims where: (1) the plaintiff lacks an adequate remedy against the seller/manufacturer; (2) the purchaser knows about product risks associated with the line of products that it continues; and (3) the seller transfers good will associated with the product line.

The difference between Illinois' and California's rules is decisive here because Ruiz's case against Blentech depends entirely upon whether the "products line" exception applies. Although Ruiz does argue that he can maintain a cause of action against Blentech even without this exception, it is clear that he cannot do so under the basic rule of successor liability, which both Illinois and California share. . . .

As it must, Ruiz's challenge to the district court's decision depends upon the contention that an Illinois court would choose California's "products line" exception as part of the law governing his claim against Blentech. In deciding whether to apply Illinois or California law, the district court considered whether Illinois or California had the most significant contacts with the tort that Ruiz alleged. It found that the two states had essentially equal contacts with Ruiz's action, but it concluded that the balance tipped towards Illinois because there is a presumption in favor of applying the laws of the state where the alleged tort occurred. On the basis of this conclusion, the district court applied Illinois law to all of the issues in the case, including both of the issues relevant to Ruiz's claim against Blentech.

Ruiz argues that the district court's choice-of-law analysis was fundamentally flawed because it failed to follow the principles of dépeçage. As we have noted, these principles prescribe that the rules of different states can determine different issues in a single case. In Ruiz's view, the issue of Blentech's assumption of Custom Stainless' tort liabilities is separate and distinct from other issues in the case; and he believes it requires an analysis of significant contacts different from the one that the district court performed. When he applies the principles of dépeçage to this issue, Ruiz concludes that the district court should have determined the legal relationship between Custom Stainless and Blentech according to California law with its "products line" exception.

Ruiz correctly invokes the principle of dépeçage and persuasively criticizes the district court's choice-of-law analysis. The district court threw a single analytical blanket over all of the issues in the case, and this is, of course, a departure from the prescriptions of the Second

Restatement. The district court should have conducted one analysis for issues of successor liability and a separate analysis for issues of tort liability. As a matter of corporate law, the issue of successor liability pertains to different significant contacts than does the tort law issue of liability for Ruiz's injury. California clearly has the most significant contacts with a sale of corporate assets by one California corporation to another. Here both corporations have their principal places of business in California. Consequently, California corporate law should determine what liabilities, if any, were conveyed when Custom Stainless sold its business to Blentech. It is equally clear that Illinois has the most significant relationship to an alleged tort befalling one of its citizens within its borders. The district court erred when, ignoring dépeçage, it applied Illinois law to all the issues in the case.

The question we now encounter is whether that error makes any difference here. Ruiz certainly believes that it does. He characterizes California's "product line" exception as a rule of corporate law—a relative of the other four exceptions to the rule determining corporate successor liability. Unlike his argument about the flaws in the district court's choice-of-law analysis, this contention is not so clearly correct. The area of substantive law to which the "product line" exception belongs is a difficult question, and the courts of several states have struggled to decide whether it is a part of corporate law or of tort law. . . .

For our purposes, California's understanding of the nature of the "products line" exception is what matters. See Restatement (Second) at § 7(3).[5] . . . Because the only California rules that we can apply here are the rules of corporate law, we must see whether California characterizes the "products line" exception as a matter of corporate law.

California courts have quite clearly established that the exception is a matter of products liability law, not corporate law. The California Supreme Court derived the exception from its line of cases prescribing strict liability in tort for injuries resulting from defective products. Moreover, California has limited the application of the exception to cases in which it preserves a plaintiff's ability to collect on a valid strict liability claim. In this way, California has established the "products line" exception as a means of advancing the cost-shifting purposes behind its regime of strict liability for injuries caused by defective products. Unlike Michigan, California has not employed the exception generally as a means to limit efforts by corporations to erase corporate identity in the course of asset sales. Instead, California uses the exception to insure that manufacturers generally will bear the costs of defective products.

As we have noted, Ruiz could maintain his case against Blentech only if the "products line" exception applied. Because the exception is a

---

[5]   Restatement (Second) of Conflict of Laws § 7(3): "The classification and interpretation of local law concepts and terms are determined in accordance with the law that governs the issue involved." —eds.

matter of California tort law, not California corporate law, it does not apply to this case. The judgment of the district court is, therefore,

AFFIRMED

NOTES

1. Is the court correct in refusing to apply the California rule of successor liability because California regards this rule as part of tort rather than corporate law? Does Restatement (Second) § 7(3), which the court cites, support the court's ruling? Comment c to § 7(3) states:

> *Differing meanings of same word.* When the same legal term or concept appears in the local law of two states which are involved in a problem, and different meanings are given in these states to the term or concept, the meaning to be applied is that which prevails in the state whose local law governs the issue under the applicable choice-of-law rule.

2. Simon v. United States, 805 N.E.2d 798 (Ind.2004):

> *Dépeçage* is the process of analyzing different issues within the same case separately under the laws of different states. Although Indiana allows different claims to be analyzed separately, it does not allow issues within those counts to be analyzed separately. For example, an Indiana court might analyze a contract claim and a tort claim independently but would not separately analyze and apply the law of different jurisdictions to issues within each claim. *Dépeçage* has not been part of Indiana's lexicon. * * *
>
> On the simple merits of *dépeçage* as a judicial technique, we find ourselves unimpressed. By making separate determinations for each issue within a claim, the process amalgamates the laws of different states, producing a hybrid that may not exist in any state. This is a problem for several reasons. First, legislatures "may enact a given law only because of its expected interaction with a complementary law." Erin A. O'Hara & Larry E. Ribstein, From Politics to Efficiency in Choice of Law, 67 U.Chi.L.Rev. 1151, 1193 (2000) . For example, a legislature may allow recovery for certain injuries or impose a low standard of proof for liability but place a cap on the damages that might be recovered or adopt immunities for certain potential defendants. Consequently, applying the law outside the context of the other laws in the jurisdiction may contravene legislative intent. In addition, applying a law in isolation increases the likelihood that its purpose and importance will be misconstrued, thereby thwarting state policy. Ultimately, by applying *dépeçage* a court may hinder the policy of one or more states without furthering the considered policy of any state.
>
> *Dépeçage* may also produce unfair results because the hybrid law may be more favorable to one party than another, allowing a result that could not be reached if the laws of any one state were applied. * * * Moreover, *dépeçage* compounds the advantage of

parties with greater access to legal resources because it requires a separate analysis of each issue for each state involved.

Id. at 801–03.

Borrower, who is 20 years old, resides in X. Borrower obtains a large business loan at 12 percent interest from Lender. Lender is incorporated and has its only office in Y. Under X law: the maximum legal interest is 10 percent; the penalty for usury is to invalidate the obligation to repay either principal or interest; persons 18 years of age or older have full legal capacity. Under Y law:: the maximum legal interest is 20 percent; contracts made by persons under the age of 21 are void. Should X law apply to determine whether Borrower has capacity to contract and Y law apply to determine the permissible interest rate? See Weintraub, Commentary on the Conflicts of Laws 98–99 (5th ed.2006).

3. Lillegraven v. Tengs, 375 P.2d 139 (Alaska 1962). Plaintiff was injured by an automobile accident in British Columbia. British Columbia law holds the automobile's owner vicariously liable for the driver's negligence. Alaska does not. British Columbia's statute of limitations is one year; Alaska's is two years. Plaintiff brought an action against the automobile's owner more than one year but less than two years after the accident. The trial court granted a summary judgment for defendant based on the British Columbia one-year statute. Held: Reversed. "The trial court erred in applying the British Columbia one-year period of limitation to plaintiff's claim." Do you agree?

4. The Rome Regulation on the Law Applicable to Contractual Obligations, article 3(1): "By their choice the parties can select the law applicable to the whole or to part only of the contract." Id. article 4(1): "To the extent that the law applicable to the contract has not been chosen in accordance with Article 3, the contract shall be governed by the law of the country with which it is most closely connected. Nevertheless, a separable part of the contract which has a closer connection with another country may by way of exception be governed by the law of that other country."

Rowe v. Hoffman-La Roche, Inc.

Supreme Court of New Jersey, 2007
189 N.J. 615, 917 A.2d 767.

[Rowe, a Michigan resident sued two New Jersey manufacturers. of Accutane, a drug used to treat acne. Rowe alleged that the defendants had not adequately warned users that drug might cause depression. After taking the drug, Rowe became depressed and attempted suicide. The federal Food and Drug Administration had approved the warning that accompanied the drug. Under Michigan law, FDA approval bars an action based on the inadequacy of the warning. Under New Jersey law, FDA approval creates a rebuttable presumption that the warning was adequate.]

■ JUDGE LEFELT (temporarily assigned) delivered the opinion of the Court.

* * *

Because an actual conflict exists between New Jersey and Michigan on the very issue in dispute—Rowe's failure-to-warn claim against Hoffmann—we must advance to the next step of the governmental interest analysis. That requires that we identify the policies underlying the New Jersey and Michigan statutes and determine whether those policies are affected by the "state[s'] contacts to the litigation and the parties." Veazey [v. Doremus], 103 N.J. at 248, 510 A.2d 1187 [1986].

* * *

The legislative history ... does not specifically address why the Legislature created only a rebuttable presumption of adequacy for FDA approval of prescription drug warnings. Rowe argues, however, that New Jersey has an interest in applying its rebuttable presumption of adequacy here because Hoffmann is a New Jersey company that has manufactured Accutane in New Jersey. Rowe contends his argument is supported by this Court's decision in Gantes [v. Kason Corp.], 145 N.J. 478, 679 A.2d 106 [1996], a contention we now address.

In Gantes, the representative of a deceased Georgia resident filed a products liability action against a New Jersey manufacturer in New Jersey. The plaintiff alleged that the decedent was killed when a shaker machine, manufactured by the defendant, struck the decedent in the head at the decedent's place of employment in Georgia. The defendant had manufactured the shaker machine in New Jersey thirteen years before the accident. Under Georgia law, the plaintiff's lawsuit was barred because Georgia had a statute of repose that prohibited products liability actions being brought more than ten years after the original sale of the product. New Jersey law, however, contained no statute of repose. Under New Jersey law, the plaintiff was permitted to proceed with the lawsuit because the plaintiff filed suit within New Jersey's two-year statute of limitation. Ibid. The issue before the Court was whether the Georgia statute of repose or the New Jersey statute of limitation applied to the products liability action.

This Court held that New Jersey's statute of limitation, not Georgia's statute of repose applied, reasoning that New Jersey "has a strong interest in encouraging the manufacture and distribution of safe products . . . [and] deterring the manufacture and distribution of unsafe products." In Gantes, although plaintiff was not a New Jersey resident and the injury did not occur in New Jersey, our strong interest in deterring the manufacture of unsafe products in this State was directly furthered because plaintiff's suit was timely and not otherwise barred. Georgia's interest was not frustrated by the application of our statute of limitations because its statute-of-repose was designed to stabilize Georgia's insurance industry and to keep stale claims out of its courts.

New Jersey's interest in allowing Rowe's suit to proceed is not as strong as our interest was in Gantes.

* * *

The [New Jersey statute] impliedly accepts that the presumption of adequacy will not be rebutted in all cases. It accepts FDA regulation as sufficient, at least in part, to deter New Jersey pharmaceutical companies from manufacturing unsafe prescription drugs. The FDA requires that the labeling accompanying a prescription drug "describe serious adverse reactions and potential safety hazards" and that the labeling "be revised to include a warning as soon as there is reasonable evidence of an association of a serious hazard with a drug." 21 C.F.R. § 201.00(e). If any labeling "is false or misleading in any particular and was not corrected within a reasonable time," among other enforcement options, the FDA may withdraw approval for the drug. 21 U.S.C.A. § 355(e). As this Court has stated, "absent deliberate concealment or nondisclosure of after-acquired knowledge of harmful effects, compliance with FDA standards should be virtually dispositive" of a failure-to-warn claim. Perez v. Wyeth Labs., Inc., 161 N.J. 1, 25, 734 A.2d 1245 (1999).[6]

The Legislature also provides in the NJPLA that FDA approval of prescription drugs conclusively prohibits an award of punitive damages in products liability actions. This provision, along with the rebuttable-presumption cede to FDA regulation some of this State's interest in policing local pharmaceutical manufacturers, thereby reducing New Jersey's interest in applying its law to this case.

The predominant object of the law is not to encourage tort recoveries by plaintiffs, whether New Jersey citizens or not, in order to deter this State's drug manufacturers. On the contrary, the law limits the liability of manufacturers of FDA-approved products by reducing the burden placed on them by product liability litigation. The Legislature carefully balanced the need to protect individuals against the need to protect an industry with a significant relationship to our economy and public health. New Jersey's interest in applying its law to Rowe's failure-to-warn issue, when properly discerned, is not antithetical to Michigan's interest but substantially congruent.

* * *

Michigan's interest in making prescription drugs more available to its residents is supported by the legislative history of the law. Commenting on section 600.2946(5), [which exempts from suit a manufacturer of a FDA approved drug] its proponents stated that "[d]rug companies spend large sums of money and expend enormous energy

---

[6]   The Michigan statute stating that FDA approval exempts drug manufacturers from suit contains an exception if a drug manufacturer "intentionally withholds from or misrepresents to the United States food and drug administration information concerning the drug that is required to be submitted under the federal food, drug, and cosmetic act and the drug would not have been approved, or the United States food and drug administration would have withdrawn approval for the drug if the information were accurately submitted." —eds.

getting approval for their products. Many valuable products never reach the market or are withdrawn because of successful lawsuits (or the threat of future lawsuits) even though there is no medical evidence that they are harmful." House Legislative Analysis Section to S.B. 344, at 9 (June 8, 1995). Supporters in the Michigan State Senate recognized that "[c]onsumers . . . suffer when they are denied new products that would increase public safety or improve their quality of life. . . . [P]roduct liability litigation . . . has added substantially to the cost and unavailability of many goods and services." Senate Fiscal Agency Bill Analysis to S.B. 344 & H.B. 4508, at 10 (Jan. 1, 1996).

* * *

This case presents a true conflict of laws because both New Jersey and Michigan have interests that would be furthered by applying their respective statutes to Rowe's failure-to-warn claim against Hoffmann.

* * *

To allow a life-long Michigan resident who received an FDA-approved drug in Michigan and alleges injuries sustained in Michigan to by-pass his own state's law and obtain compensation for his injuries in this State's courts completely undercuts Michigan's interests, while overvaluing our true interest in this litigation.

In this instance, where the challenged drug was approved by the FDA and suit was brought by an out-of-state plaintiff who has no cause of action in his home state, this State's interest in ensuring that our corporations are deterred from producing unsafe products-which was determinative in Gantes and however weighty in other contexts-is not paramount. Our interest in deterring local manufacturing corporations from providing inadequate product warnings, within the context of an FDA approved drug, must yield to Michigan's interest.[1]

The judgment of the Appellate Division [choosing New Jersey law] is reversed and the case is remanded to the Law Division for reinstatement of the trial court's order dismissing the lawsuit.

■ JUDGE STERN (temporarily assigned), dissenting.

* * *

I believe the *Gantes* approach is warranted and controls the disposition of this case. In fact, it seems to me that our Legislature permits recovery, notwithstanding FDA approvals, in the exceptional circumstances in which the presumption can be overcome, because those situations involve matters in which deterrence is needed the most.

---

[1] We note that our dissenting colleagues suggest that we withhold issuing this decision for an unspecified period to determine whether a bill, which has passed the Michigan House, becomes law. The Bill, H.B. 4044–4045, 94th Leg., Reg. Sess. (Mich. 2007), if adopted by Michigan would repeal Mich. Comp. Laws § 600.2946(5), and enact a rebuttable presumption that products are safe if they are subject to, and comply with, pertinent government safety standards. Because of the uncertain duration and predictability of legislative activity, however, we decline to accede to the dissenters' suggestion. We are confident that should the Bill become law, the parties in this case will take whatever actions they believe are warranted.

Michigan's legitimate interests cannot be said to outweigh the need to deter conduct in this State that our Legislature, as a matter of sound public policy, seeks to prevent.

Certainly, as the majority develops, Michigan has significant interests in furthering its legislative design. However, those interests in protecting consumers with respect to prescription costs and availability (and even more broadly with respect to tort reform) are remote and outweighed in a New Jersey forum when the Michigan resident brings his or her suit in New Jersey against a New Jersey manufacturer,[4] particularly because he or she is subject to the "rebuttable" presumption of the warning or label's adequacy.

■ JUSTICE LONG joins in this opinion.

For reversal and remandment-Justices LaVecchia, Wallace, Rivera-Soto and Hoens and Judge Lefelt.

Concurring in part/dissenting in part-Justice Long and Judge Stern.

NOTES

1. Is the majority opinion's distinction of *Gantes* on the ground of Michigan's interest in making affordable prescription drugs available cogent? Could the same argument be made for any product or service? Does the argument have added weight with regard to prescription drugs?

2. Hughes v. Wal-Mart Stores, Inc., 250 F.3d 618 (8th Cir.2001). Parents brought suit for injuries to their child that occurred when a gasoline container exploded. The child's father had purchased the container at defendant's store in Louisiana where parents and child resided and where the injury occurred. The parents sued in Arkansas where defendant has its principal place of business. Under Arkansas law, defendant is subject to strict liability in tort but under Louisiana law is liable only if it should have known that the container was defective. The court affirmed summary judgment for defendant under Louisiana law: "Absent some relevant connection between a state and the facts underlying the litigation, we fail to see how any important Arkansas governmental interest is significantly furthered by ensuring that nonresidents are compensated for injuries that occur in *another state*. The governmental interest factor does not support an application of Arkansas law." Id. at 621.

3. In international product liability cases, some courts have expressed concern that applying United States law more favorable to a foreign user than the law of the user's own country would place United States manufacturers at a competitive disadvantage. See Harrison v. Wyeth Laboratories, 510 F.Supp. 1, 5 (E.D.Pa.1980), aff'd w.o. opn., 676 F.2d 685 (3d Cir.1982). Moreover,

---

[4] Finally, I note there is now pending in the Michigan Senate two bills passed by the Michigan House of Representatives which would enact a rebuttable presumption similar to our own with retroactive applicability. See H.B. 4044–4045, 94th Leg., Reg. Sess. (Mich.2007). It would seem jurisprudentially sound to wait a reasonable period of time in which to see what happens in the Michigan Senate with respect to the proposed legislation in order to evaluate if the actual conflict is resolved and to avoid a split decision on an issue of such significance as the one now being decided.

Harrison found that applying United States law might sometimes interfere with policies of the foreign country: "Faced with different needs, problems and resources . . . India may, in balancing the pros and cons of a drug's use, give different weight to various factors than would our society, and more easily conclude that any risks associated with use of a particular oral contraceptive are far outweighed by its overall benefits to India and its people." Id. at 4–5. Does the cogency of these arguments depend upon whether the manufacturer's liability is based on strict liability, negligence, gross negligence, or intentional misconduct?

The result in *Harrison*, after deciding that United Kingdom rather than Pennsylvania law applied (the reference to India in the quotation above is a hypothetical illustration), was to order a forum non conveniens dismissal. This is frequently the result in such cases once the court decides that foreign law applies.

4.   One effect of permitting suit here, even if foreign law is applied, is that the damages under the foreign damages categories will be determined by a United States jury and will probably be in an amount greater than could be recovered in the foreign country. General levels of damages awarded in the foreign country are not relevant even though the United States court is applying foreign damages law, unless the foreign law places a statutory cap on recovery or there is a judge-made equivalent of a statutory cap. Some commentators have urged courts to stop treating quantification of damages as "procedural" for choice-of-law purposes. See Weintraub, Choice of Law for Products Liability: Demagnetizing the United States Forum, 52 Ark.L.Rev. 157, 171–72 (1999) (suggesting that this practice be changed by informing the trial judge of typical recoveries in the foreign country and giving the judge power to "reduce the verdict to the top of the permissible range abroad"). Gasperini v. Center for Humanities, Inc., 518 U.S. 415, 116 S.Ct. 2211 (1996), p. 720, infra, provides some support for change. *Gasperini* held that in diversity cases, whether damages are excessive is governed by the state law "that gives rise to the claim for relief." Id. at 437 n.22. A few cases have treated quantification of damages as substantive and have applied the standards of the jurisdiction chosen by the forum's choice-of-law rules. Rome II art. 15(c) brings "assessment of damage" within the scope of its rules.

5.   Sutherland v. Kennington Truck Service, Ltd., 562 N.W.2d 466 (Mich.1997), applied the Michigan statute of limitations to permit a suit by an Ohio resident against an Ontario corporation and an Ontario resident although the action would be barred under either Ohio or Ontario limitations. The plaintiff was injured in a collision on a Michigan highway. The court noted that "Professor Borchers' research shows that each of the modern approaches tend to favor significantly the application of forum law" and stated: "Thus on surveying current conflicts of law jurisprudence, one can reasonably conclude that only two distinct conflicts of laws theories actually exist. One, followed by a distinct minority of states, mandates adherence to the lex loci delicti rule. The other, which bears different labels in different states, calls for courts to apply the law of the forum unless important policy considerations dictate otherwise." The court then decided that Ohio had no interest in having Ohio law applied because it would be unconstitutional to impose Ohio law on an Ontario resident if the sole basis for applying Ohio law was plaintiff's residence. Nor, the court reasoned, did Ontario have an interest in applying its statute of limitations to protect the Ontario defendants because Ontario's choice-of-law rule would choose Michigan law, including Michigan time limitations, as the lex loci delicti. The court concluded: "Therefore, no foreign state has an interest in having its law applied to this case. The lex fori presumption is not overcome, and we need not evaluate Michigan's interests."

Would it be unconstitutional to apply Ohio law when this is the same as Ontario law? See Reich v. Purcell, 432 P.2d 727 (Cal.1967), p. 583, supra, applying Ohio law to a crash in Missouri between Ohio and California drivers and stating: "A defendant cannot reasonably complain when compensatory damages are assessed in accordance with the law of his domicile and plaintiffs receive no more than they would have had they been injured at home." Does the Ontario choice-of-law rule indicate that Ontario has no "interest" in having its law applied to protect Ontario defendants? See Pfau v. Trent Aluminum Co., 263 A.2d 129, 137 (N.J.1970): "Connecticut's choice-of-law rule does not identify that state's interest in the matter. Lex Loci delicti was born in an effort to achieve simplicity and uniformity, and does not relate to a state's interest in having its law applied to given issues in a tort case."

6. Piamba Cortes v. American Airlines, Inc., 177 F.3d 1272 (11th Cir.1999), focused on the difficulty of finding and applying Colombian law as the primary reason for applying Florida law to recovery for the death of a Colombian domiciliary. The court assumed Florida law permits higher recovery than Colombian law. The airplane on which the decedent was a passenger took off from Miami and crashed because of pilot error when landing in Colombia. Miami was the center for the airline's Latin American operations. In its choice-of-law analysis the court quoted the Second Restatement's comment that "there is good reason for the court to apply the local law of that state which best achieves the basic policy, or policies, underlying the particular field of law involved." Restatement (Second) § 6 cmt. h. The court then states that if, as the airline contended, Colombian law placed an $8,000 cap on non-pecuniary damages and disallowed some pecuniary damages available under Florida law, "application of Colombian law arguably would frustrate [the goals of tort law to compensate victims and deter wrongful conduct]. Consequently this factor weighs slightly in favor of applying Florida law." The court then noted that expert witnesses on Colombian law disagreed on whether that law limited damages. Furthermore, the trial judge's "review of the available legal authorities failed to reconcile this debate." The court concluded that "[b]ecause the measure of compensatory damages available under Florida law is straightforward and easy to apply . . . this factor weighs heavily in favor of applying Florida law."

As the next principal case shows, the New York Court of Appeals extended the *Neumeier* rules from the guest statute context, for which they were drafted, to include all of "loss allocating" or "loss distribution" rules.

In Schultz v. Boy Scouts of America, 480 N.E.2d 679 (N.Y.1985), the New York Court of Appeals applied New Jersey's rule of charitable immunity to immunize a New Jersey-based charity (the Boy Scouts) and an Ohio-based charity (the Franciscan Brothers) in a suit brought by a New Jersey family against both charities for negligent supervision of an employee alleged to have sexually abused their minor children. [*Schultz* is discussed expensively the *Edwards* case below.] The abuse was alleged to have taken place at a New York campground. As to the Boy Scouts, the Court of Appeals held that the charitable immunity rule was loss-allocating and thus that action fell under the first rule, counseling application of New Jersey law because the parties were all located in New Jersey. The suit against the Francisan Brothers fell under the third rule, because the parties and the conduct covered three different states. Normally the third rule points to the state of the injury, but is more loosely written than the second rule. The Court of Appeals held that this was an unusual case and that application of New Jersey's immunity to only one of the charities would disrupt the smooth interworkings of the multi-state system, and thus also immunized the Francisan Brothers. *Schultz* has been the subject of heavy criticism—much of it surely due to the highly sympathetic nature of the plaintiffs—but remains the law in New York.

Cooney v. Osgood Machinery, Inc.

Court of Appeals of New York, 1993.
81 N.Y.2d 66, 595 N.Y.S.2d 919, 612 N.E.2d 277.

■ KAYE, CHIEF JUDGE.

The issue on this appeal is whether a Missouri statute barring contribution claims against an employer—which conflicts with New York law permitting such claims—should be given effect in a third-party action pending here. Applying relevant choice of law principles, we conclude that the Missouri workers' compensation statute should be given effect, and therefore affirm the dismissal of the third-party complaint seeking contribution against a Missouri employer.

I

The facts relevant to this appeal are essentially undisputed. In 1957 or 1958, Kling Brothers, Inc. (succeeded in interest by third-party defendant Hill Acme Co.) manufactured a 16-foot wide "Pyramid Form Bending Roll," a machine to shape large pieces of metal. The device was sold in 1958 to a Buffalo company, American Standard Inc., through a New York sales agent, defendant Osgood Machinery, Inc., which assisted American in the setup and initial operation of the machine. American closed its Buffalo plant around 1961, and the history of the bending roll is obscured until 1969, when Crouse Company—which obtained the equipment in some unknown manner—sold the machine to Paul Mueller Co., a Missouri domiciliary.

Mueller installed the bending roll in its Springfield, Missouri, plant and subsequently modified it by adding a foot switch. In October 1978, plaintiff Dennis J. Cooney, a Missouri resident working at the Missouri plant, was injured while cleaning the machine. The machine was running at the time—a piece of wood having been wedged in the foot switch—and Cooney was unable to reach the switch to stop the machine and avoid injury.

In Missouri, Cooney filed for and received workers' compensation benefits. Because under Missouri law an employer providing such benefits "shall be released from all other liability whatsoever, whether to the employee or any other person" (Mo. Rev. Stat. § 287.120[1]), he could not additionally sue his employer, Mueller, in tort. Cooney did, however, bring a products liability action against Osgood—the machine's initial sales agent—in Supreme Court, Erie County. (Missouri apparently would not have had personal jurisdiction over Osgood.)

Seeking contribution from parties it deems more culpable in the event it is found liable to Cooney, Osgood brought a third-party action against Mueller, American Standard, and Hill Acme. Mueller invoked the Missouri statute shielding employers from both direct claims by employees and contribution claims by others, and moved for summary judgment dismissing Osgood's third-party complaint. In light of the conflict between the Missouri statute and New York law permitting contribution claims against employers, Supreme Court undertook a choice of law analysis and concluded that New York law should apply. The Appellate Division unanimously reversed and dismissed the third-party complaint as well as all cross claims against Mueller. 179 A.D.2d 240, 582 N.Y.S.2d 873. We now affirm.

II

We conclude . . . that this State has sufficient interest in the litigation so that if we chose to apply New York law on the contribution issue, that decision would not run afoul of the Federal Constitution. Accordingly, we turn to a choice of law analysis.

III

In Neumeier v. Kuehner, 31 N.Y.2d 121, 335 N.Y.S.2d 64, 286 N.E.2d 454, . . . the Court in seeking to return greater predictability and uniformity to the law, adopted a series of three rules that had been proposed by Chief Judge Fuld (see, Tooker v. Lopez, 24 N.Y.2d, at 585, 301 N.Y.S.2d 519, 249 N.E.2d 394 [Fuld, Ch. J., concurring]). Although drafted in terms of guest statutes—drivers and passengers—these rules could, in appropriate cases, apply as well to other loss allocation conflicts (see, Schultz, 65 N.Y.2d, at 200–201, 491 N.Y.S.2d 90, 480 N.E.2d 679 [applying first and third Neumeier rules to conflicting charitable immunity laws]).

The *Neumeier* Rules

[Chief Judge Kaye reviewed the *Neumeier* Rules and concluded:]

Assuming that the interest of each State in enforcement of its law is roughly equal—a judgment that, insofar as guest statutes are concerned, is implicit in the second and third Neumeier rules—the situs of the tort is appropriate as a "tie breaker" because that is the only State with which both parties have purposefully associated themselves in a significant way. . . .

. . . Contribution rules—as involved in the present case—are loss allocating, not conduct regulating. Had conduct regulating been at issue here, our analysis would be greatly simplified, for the traditional rule of lex loci delicti almost invariably obtains. Similarly, if the parties shared the same domicile, we would generally apply that jurisdiction's loss distribution law. Instead, our analysis is necessarily more complicated, calling upon us to evaluate the relative interests of jurisdictions with conflicting laws and, if neither can be accommodated without substantially impairing the other, finding some other sound basis for resolving the impasse.

Interest Analysis

The general scheme of workers' compensation acts is that an employer regardless of culpability is required to make specified payments to an injured employee and in exchange, the law immunizes the employer from further liability. Immunity "is part of the quid pro quo in which the sacrifices and gains of employees and employers are to some extent put in balance, for, while the employer assumes a new liability without fault, [it] is relieved of the prospect of large damage verdicts" (2A Larsen, Workmen's Compensation Law § 65.11 [1993]).

Some States immunize employers only from direct actions by injured workers; others extend protection from third-party contribution actions as well. The Missouri Supreme Court, in rejecting State and Federal constitutional challenges to the Missouri statute at issue here, noted that immunity " 'is the heart and soul of this legislation which has, over the years been of highly significant social and economic benefit to the working [person], the employer and the State.' " (State ex rel. Maryland Hgts. Concrete Contrs. v. Ferriss, 588 S.W.2d 489, 491 [Mo.], quoting Seaboard Coast Line R.R. Co. v. Smith, 359 So.2d 427, 429 [Fla.].) The court, quoting further from the Florida case, also observed that "the right to contribution is not a vested right on which legislation may not impinge" (588 S.W.2d, at 491).

Missouri's decision to shield employers from contribution claims is thus a policy choice implicating significant State interests: "to deny a person the immunity granted by a work[er]'s compensation statute of a given state would frustrate the efforts of that state to restrict the cost of industrial accidents and to afford a fair basis for predicting what these costs will be." (Restatement [Second] of Conflict of Laws § 184, comment b, at 547.) Indeed, as the Restatement concluded in a related context, for another State "to subject a person who has been held liable in work[er]'s compensation to further unlimited liability in tort or wrongful death would frustrate the work[er]'s compensation policy of the State in which the award was rendered." (Restatement [Second] of Conflict of Laws § 183, comment c, at 544.)

Arrayed against Missouri's interest in maintaining the integrity of its workers' compensation scheme is New York's interest in basic fairness to litigants. Under traditional joint and several liability rules, when more than one tortfeasor was responsible for plaintiff's injury, each was potentially liable for the entire judgment, irrespective of relative culpability. Indeed, plaintiff was not even required to sue all the wrongdoers, but could recover the entire judgment from the "deep pocket," who then had no recourse (Sommer v. Federal Signal Corp., 79 N.Y.2d 540, 556, 583 N.Y.S.2d 957, 593 N.E.2d 1365).

In Dole v. Dow Chem. Co., 30 N.Y.2d 143, 148–149, 331 N.Y.S.2d 382, 282 N.E.2d 288 [1972], this Court mitigated the inequity by allowing a defendant that pays more than its fair share of a judgment, as apportioned by the fact finder in terms of relative fault, to recover the difference from a codefendant. The Legislature, also recognizing the desirability of contribution, subsequently codified the Dole principles in CPLR article 14 (L.1974, ch. 742). Stated simply, the "goal of contribution, as announced in Dole and applied since, is fairness to tortfeasors who are jointly liable." (Sommer v. Federal Signal Corp., 79 N.Y.2d, at 556–557, 583 N.Y.S.2d 957, 593 N.E.2d 1365).

Manifestly, the interests of Missouri and New York are irreconcilable in this case. To the extent we allow contribution against Mueller, the policy underlying the Missouri workers' compensation scheme will be offended. Conversely, to the extent Osgood is required to pay more than its equitable share of a judgment, the policy underlying New York's contribution law is affronted. It is evident that one State's interest cannot be accommodated without sacrificing the other's, and thus an appropriate method for choosing between the two must be found.

This is a true conflict in the mold of Neumeier's second rule, where the local law of each litigant's domicile favors that party, and the action is pending in one of those jurisdictions. Under that rule, the place of injury governs, which in this case means that contribution is barred. This holding is consistent with the result reached historically, and reflects application of a neutral factor that favors neither the forum's law nor its domiciliaries. Moreover, forum shopping by defendants—who might attempt to invoke CPLR 1403 and bring a separate action for contribution in New York if sued elsewhere (compare, Grant Co. v. Uneeda Doll Co., 19 A.D.2d 361,

243 N.Y.S.2d 428, affd. 15 N.Y.2d 571, 254 N.Y.S.2d 834, 203 N.E.2d 299)—is eliminated.[2]

A primary reason that locus tips the balance, of course, is that ordinarily it is the place with which both parties have voluntarily associated themselves. In this case, there is some validity to Osgood's argument that it did nothing to affiliate itself with Missouri. Indeed, a decade after Osgood's last contact with the bending roll, the machine wound up in Missouri through no effort, or even knowledge, of Osgood. Moreover, the record establishes that Osgood was not in the business of distributing goods nationwide, but limited its activities to New York and parts of Pennsylvania, and thus Osgood may not have reasonably anticipated becoming embroiled in litigation with a Missouri employer.

For this reason, our decision to apply Missouri law rests as well on another factor that should, at times, play a role in choice of law: the protection of reasonable expectations (see, Restatement [Second] of Conflict of Laws § 6[2][d]; Allstate Ins. Co. v. Hague, 449 U.S. 302, 327 [Stevens, J., concurring]; Schultz, 65 N.Y.2d, at 198, 491 N.Y.S.2d 90, 480 N.E.2d 679 ["protecting the reasonable expectations of the parties" is one reason locus law is generally preferred when there are conflicting conduct-regulating rules]).[3] In view of the unambiguous statutory language barring third-party liability and the Missouri Supreme Court's holding in Ferriss, Mueller could hardly have expected to be haled before a New York court to respond in damages for an accident to a Missouri employee at the Missouri plant. By contrast, in ordering its business affairs Osgood could have had no reasonable expectation that contribution would be available in a products liability action arising out of the sale of industrial equipment. Indeed, Osgood's activity in connection with the bending roll occurred in 1958, some 14 years before Dole was decided and the principles of full contribution were introduced into our law. Moreover, even under present law, contribution is not foolproof. A defendant, for example, may be unable to obtain jurisdiction over a joint tortfeasor; the joint tortfeasor may be insolvent or defunct (like Kling Bros. here); or defendant's own assets may be insufficient to pay its share of the judgment (see, Klinger v. Dudley, 41 N.Y.2d 362, 369, 393 N.Y.S.2d 323, 361 N.E.2d 974).

In sum, we conclude that Missouri law should apply because, although the interests of the respective jurisdictions are irreconcilable, the accident occurred in Missouri, and unavailability of contribution would more closely

---

[2] New York law permitting contribution against an employer is clearly a minority view (see generally, Annotation, Modern Status of Effect of State Workmen's Compensation Act on Right of Third-Person Tortfeasor to Contribution or Indemnity From Employer of Injured or Killed Workman, 100 A.L.R.3d 350). A result that might impose New York law on the carefully structured workers' compensation schemes of other States—especially when the accident occurred there—is undesirable.

[3] We have eschewed reliance on the fictional expectation of the parties based on mere contact with the locus of an accident (Miller v. Miller, 22 N.Y.2d, at 20, 290 N.Y.S.2d 734, 237 N.E.2d 877), but reasonable, justifiable expectations are another matter.

comport with the reasonable expectations of both parties in conducting their business affairs.

IV

[Chief Judge Kaye then considered and rejected the argument that New York's public policy should defeat application of the Missouri rule.]

■ SIMONS, TITONE, HANCOCK, BELLACOSA and SMITH, JJ., concur.

Order affirmed, with costs.

NOTES

1. *Cooney* has stimulated much comment. There is a symposium on the case in 59 Brooklyn L.Rev. 1323 (1994), with articles by professors Sedler, Silberman, and Twerski. Another symposium, Conference on Jurisdiction, Justice, and Choice of Law for the Twenty-First Century, Case Four: Choice of Law Theory, 29 New England L.Rev. 669 (1995), presents a hypothetical variation of *Cooney* decided in mock judicial opinions by professors Borchers, Cox, Kramer, Maier, Silberman, Singer, and Weintraub.

2. In 1996 New York amended its Workers' Compensation Law to exempt an employer from liability for contribution or indemnity to a third person for injury suffered by a worker in the scope of employment unless the injury is "grave" as defined in the statute. N.Y. Work. Comp. L. § 11. In Carnley v. Aid to Hospitals, Inc., 975 F.Supp. 252 (W.D.N.Y.1997) a Texas employee was injured in New York. The worker sued the New York owner of the premises where the injury occurred and the New York defendant impleaded the Texas employer for contribution and indemnity. Texas law did not permit suit against the employer. The court held that even if the amendment to New York's Workers' Compensation law did not apply retroactively, the amendment indicated New York's lack of interest in subjecting the employer to liability. The court applied Texas law and granted a summary judgment for the Texas employer. Quintana v. Ciba-Geigy Corp., 1997 WL 160308 (S.D.N.Y.1997) reached the opposite result. The court refused to apply the amendment to New York Worker's Compensation law retroactively and held a New Jersey employer liable for contribution and indemnity when its New Jersey employee was injured in New York.

3. The principal case chooses law by a method that it refers to as "interest analysis." A little over a month later, in an opinion also by Chief Judge Kaye, the court rejected interest analysis in contract cases in favor of a "grouping of contacts" approach. In the Matter of the Arbitration Between Allstate Ins. Co. and Stolarz, 613 N.E.2d 936 (N.Y.1993). A New York resident driving an automobile leased by her New Jersey employer, was injured by a collision in New York. The driver of the other vehicle had only $20,000 in liability insurance, which was paid to the injured New Yorker. The employer's automobile was insured by a policy that provided $35,000 compensation in the event that a party liable to the insured was uninsured or underinsured. The policy also provided that the $35,000 "shall be reduced by all sums paid by of for anyone who is legally responsible." The injured New Yorker claimed that this provision reducing payment was invalid under New York law and, though valid under New Jersey law, New York law applied. Chief Judge Kaye decided that the provision was valid under New York law, but that even if there were a difference between New York and New Jersey law, as the dissent contended, New Jersey law applied:

> Indeed, in a typical tort case, a car accident, for example—strong governmental interests may underlie the choice of law issue. . . .

> By contrast, contract cases often involve only the private economic interests of the parties, and analysis of the public policy underlying the conflicting contract laws may be inappropriate to resolution of the dispute. It may even be difficult to identify the competing "policies" at stake, because the laws may differ only slightly, and evolve through the incremental process of common-law adjudication as a response to the facts presented.

> The "center of gravity" or "grouping of contacts" choice of law theory applied in contract cases . . . enables the court to identify which law to apply without entering into the difficult, and sometimes inappropriate, policy thicket. Under this approach, the spectrum of significant contacts rather than a single possibly fortuitous event—may be considered (see, Restatement [Second] of Conflict of Laws § 188[2]). Critical to a sound analysis, however, is selecting the contacts that obtain significance in the particular contract dispute. . . .

> There are of course instances where the policies underlying conflicting laws in a contract dispute are readily identifiable and reflect strong governmental interests, and therefore should be considered. For example, in Zeevi & Sons v. Grindlays Bank, 37 N.Y.2d 220, 227, 371 N.Y.S.2d 892, 333 N.E.2d 168, involving an international letter of credit, we held that New York law should control so that our State would maintain its position as a financial capital of the world. Similarly, in a finder's fee dispute, we applied the New York Statute of Frauds instead of New Jersey law which did not require a written agreement. We took into account the policy of the statute as expressed in its legislative history and observed that application of the statute would contribute to New York's economic development, a strong State interest. (See, Intercontinental Planning v. Daystrom, Inc., 24 N.Y.2d 372, 382–385, 300 N.Y.S.2d 817, 248 N.E.2d 576).

> Automobile insurance, highly regulated as it is, may implicate both the private economic interests of the parties and governmental interests in the enforcement of its regulatory scheme. Thus, we may properly consider State interests to determine whether to apply New York law and void the contract's express terms or apply New Jersey law and enforce the contract as written.

> The State interest underlying [Matter of United Community Ins. Co. v. Mucatel, 505 N.E.2d 624 (N.Y.1987), which invalidated a differently-worded policy provision reducing payment] is that consumers purchasing insurance in this State should not be

deceived by misleading policy limits. That interest, however, is irrelevant where, as here, the policy is sold in New Jersey by a New Jersey insurance company to a New Jersey insured, and the clause was written to conform to a New Jersey statute. Indeed, while Stolarz (by virtue of her use of the car) is an additional insured under the policy, she is not a party to the contract, nor did she pay the premiums—her New Jersey employer did. Thus, New York has no governmental interest in applying its law to this dispute and New Jersey law must be applied.

The same result obtains under a "grouping of contacts" analysis that does not consider State interests. When the significant contacts are considered in light of the reality that this is a contract case, not a tort, it is plain that this dispute overwhelmingly centers on New Jersey. The Restatement, for example, enumerates five generally significant contacts in a contract case: the place of contracting, negotiation and performance; the location of the subject matter of the contract; and the domicile of the contracting parties (see, Restatement [Second] of Conflict of Laws § 188[2]).

Indisputably, New Jersey is the place where the contract was negotiated and made. The parties to the contract are both New Jersey entities. The subject matter of the contract, a vehicle, does not have a fixed location but is registered in New Jersey. Thus, four of the five factors identified in the Restatement plainly point to New Jersey law. (The fifth factor, place of performance, is immaterial here because there is no issue as to performance.).

Do you agree with the distinction that Chief Judge Kaye draws between interest analysis and "grouping of contacts"? The last two paragraph of the excerpt above from *Stolarz* count physical contacts without reference to the content of the law in those places or to that law's policies. If these two paragraphs constituted Chief Judge Kaye's entire choice-of-law analysis, would the conclusion be cogent?

Kearney v. Salomon Smith Barney, Inc.

Supreme Court of California, 2006.
39 Cal.4th 95, 137 P.3d 914, 45 Cal.Rptr.3d 730.

[Plaintiffs brought a class action on behalf of California clients of the defendant, Salomon Smith Barney (SSB), a financial institution that had its principal place of business in Georgia. Without the clients' knowledge, the defendant recorded telephone calls between the defendant's Georgia office and California clients. This was permitted under Georgia law but not under California law. The trial court sustained the defendant's demurrer and dismissed the action. The Court of Appeal affirmed the judgment rendered by the trial court, concluding that application of Georgia law is appropriate and supports the denial of all relief sought by plaintiffs. The Supreme Court of California "granted review to consider the novel choice-of-law issue presented by this case."]

■ GEORGE, C.J.

* * *

Past decisions establish that in analyzing a choice-of-law issue, California courts apply the so-called governmental interest analysis, under which a court carefully examines the governmental interests or purposes served by the applicable statute or rule of law of each of the affected jurisdictions to determine whether there is a "true conflict." If such a conflict is found to exist, the court analyzes the jurisdictions' respective interests to determine which jurisdiction's interests would be more severely impaired if that jurisdiction's law were not applied in the particular context presented by the case.

For the reasons discussed at length below, we conclude that this case presents a true conflict between California and Georgia law, and that, as a general matter, the failure to apply California law in this context would impair California's interest in protecting the degree of privacy afforded to California residents by California law more severely than the application of California law would impair any interests of the State of Georgia.

[I]n light of the substantial number of businesses operating in California that maintain out-of-state offices or telephone operators, a resolution of this conflict permitting all such businesses to regularly and routinely record telephone conversations made to or from California clients or consumers without the clients' or consumers' knowledge or consent would significantly impair the privacy policy guaranteed by California law, and potentially would place local California businesses (that would continue to be subject to California's protective privacy law) at an unfair competitive disadvantage vis-à-vis their out-of-state counterparts. At the same time, application of California law will not have a significant detrimental effect on Georgia's interests as embodied in the applicable Georgia law, because applying California law (1) will not adversely affect any privacy interest protected by Georgia law, (2) will affect only those business telephone calls in Georgia that are made to or are received from California clients, and (3) with respect to such calls, will not prevent a business located in Georgia from implementing or maintaining a practice of recording all such calls, but will require only that the business inform its clients or customers, at the outset of the call, of the company's policy of recording such calls. (* * * [I]f a business informs a client or customer at the outset of a telephone call that the call is being recorded, the recording would not violate the applicable California statute.).

Although we conclude that the comparative impairment analysis supports the application of California law in this context, we further conclude that because one of the goals of that analysis is "the 'maximum attainment of underlying purpose by *all* governmental entities'" (Offshore Rental, supra, page 573, italics added), it is appropriate in this instance to apply California law in a restrained manner that accommodates Georgia's reasonable interest in protecting persons who in the past might have undertaken actions in Georgia in reasonable reliance on Georgia law from being subjected to monetary liability for such actions. Prior to our resolution of this case it would have been reasonable for a business entity such as SSB to be uncertain as to which state's law—Georgia's or California's—would be applicable in this context, and the denial of monetary recovery for past conduct that might have been undertaken in reliance upon another state's law is unlikely to undermine significantly the California interest embodied in the applicable invasion-of-privacy statutes. We therefore conclude that it is Georgia's, rather than California's, interest that would be more severely impaired were monetary liability to be imposed on SSB for such past conduct. Under these circumstances, we conclude it is appropriate to decline to impose damages upon SSB (or to require it to provide restitution) on the basis of such past conduct.

Accordingly, we conclude that plaintiffs' action should be permitted to go forward with respect to the request for injunctive relief, but that the judgment rendered by the Court of Appeal should be affirmed insofar as it upholds the dismissal of plaintiffs' claim for damages or restitution based on SSB's past conduct. . . .

II

* * *

On its face, application of the California law here at issue would affect only a business's undisclosed recording of telephone conversations with clients or consumers in California and would not compel any action or conduct of the business with regard to conversations with non-California clients or consumers. * * * Although SSB may attempt to demonstrate, at a later stage in the litigation, that application of the California statute would pose an undue and excessive burden on interstate commerce by establishing that it would be impossible or infeasible for SSB to comply with the California statute without altering its conduct with regard to its non-California clients and that the burden that would be imposed upon it "is clearly excessive in relation to the putative local benefits" (Pike v. Bruce Church, Inc. (1970) 397 U.S. 137, 142, 90 S.Ct. 844, 25 L.Ed.2d 174), SSB clearly cannot prevail on such a theory at the demurrer stage of the proceeding.

Accordingly, we believe that the only substantial issue presented by the case is the choice-of-law issue. We turn to that issue. . . .

IV

* * *

The language of section 632 [of the California statute] does not explicitly address the issue whether the statute was intended to apply when one party to a telephone call is in California and another party is outside California. The legislatively prescribed purpose of the 1967 invasion of privacy statute, however, is "to protect the privacy of the people of this state" (§ 630), and that purpose certainly supports application of the statute in a setting in which a person outside California records, without the Californian's knowledge or consent, a telephone conversation of a California resident who is within California. Furthermore, the companion wiretapping provision of the 1967 act—set forth in section 631, subdivision (a)—specifically applies to any person who attempts to learn the content of any communication "while the same is in transit . . . or is being sent from, or received at any place within this state." Nothing in the language or purpose of the 1967 legislation suggests that the related provisions of section 632 should not similarly apply to protect against the secret recording of any confidential communication that is sent from or received at any place within California.

SSB contends that section 632 should not be interpreted to apply in such a situation, because application of the statute in this setting would constitute a disfavored "extraterritorial" application of the statute. Interpreting that statute to apply to a person who, while outside California, secretly records what a California resident is saying in a confidential communication while he or she is within California, however, cannot accurately be characterized as an unauthorized extraterritorial application of the statute, but more reasonably is viewed as an instance of applying the statute to a multistate event in which a crucial element—the confidential communication by the California resident—occurred in California. The privacy interest protected by the statute is no less directly and immediately invaded when a communication within California is secretly and contemporaneously recorded from outside the state than when this action occurs within the state. A person who secretly and intentionally records such a conversation from outside the state effectively acts within California in the same way a person effectively acts within the state by, for example, intentionally shooting a person in California from across the California-Nevada border. Because there can be no question but that the principal purpose of section 632 is to protect the privacy of confidential communications of California residents while they are in California, we believe it is clear that section 632 was intended, and reasonably must be interpreted, to apply in this setting. . . .

VI

* * *

To be sure, one legitimately might maintain that SSB reasonably should have anticipated that its recording of a telephone conversation with a California client when the client is in California would be governed by California law, regardless of where the SSB employee with whom the client is speaking happens to be located. Although SSB would have reached that conclusion had it undertaken the extended choice-of-law analysis set forth above, we recognize that at the time of SSB's past actions the few lower court decisions that had considered a legal challenge to the recording of an interstate telephone conversation had reached differing conclusions as to which state's law should apply-the law of the state where the person who recorded the conversation was situated, or instead the law of the state where the person whose words were being recorded was located. Although none of the prior cases involved the type of repeated recording of customer telephone calls by a business entity that is involved here, we nonetheless believe that prior to our resolution of the issue in this case a business entity reasonably might have been uncertain as to which state's law was applicable and reasonably might have relied upon the law of the state in which its employee was located. Under these circumstances, we believe Georgia has a legitimate interest in not having SSB subjected to liability on the basis of its employees' past actions in Georgia.

* * *

Accordingly, although we conclude that in general California law is applicable in this setting and that plaintiffs may seek injunctive relief to require SSB to comply with California law in the future, we shall apply Georgia law with respect to SSB's potential monetary liability for its past conduct, thus relieving SSB of any liability for damages for its past recording of conversations. In light of our decision, of course, out-of-state companies that do business in California now are on notice that, with regard to future conduct, they are subject to California law with regard to the recording of telephone conversations made to or received from California, and that the full range of civil sanctions afforded by California law may be imposed for future violations. . . .

NOTE

Professor Arthur von Mehren has suggested that when two or more concerned states have domestic decisional rules that point to opposed results in the case, the proper resolution is to fashion a "special substantive rule" for the problem. The special rule would be different from the domestic rule of any concerned state. See von Mehren, Special Substantive Rules for Multi-State Problems: Their Role and Significance in Contemporary Choice of Law Methodology, 88 Harv.L.Rev. 347 (1974). For the *Neumeier* case, p. 592, supra, the author suggests that a compromise between New York's full-recovery and Ontario's no-recovery rules should be effected in "the form of allowing partial recovery by permitting the guest to recover one-half of the damage suffered." (Id., at p. 369.)

For a further elaboration of the suggestion that special substantive rules should be fashioned for cases involving conflicting substantive policies in multistate situations, see von Mehren, Choice of Law and the Problem of Justice, 41 Law & Contemp.Prob. 27 (1977); Twerski & Mayer, Toward a Pragmatic Solution of Choice-of-Law Problems—at the Interface of Substance and Procedure, 74 Nw.U.L.Rev. 781 (1979); Weintraub, Commentary on the Conflict of Laws §§ 3.5 (in *Haynie* and *Zelinger*, p. 560, supra, apply the guest statute between host and guest but permit the other driver to obtain contribution from the host when the other driver has paid more than his or her share of the judgment), § 7.6 (in interstate small loan case enforce payment of interest in lower amount permitted in borrower's state rather than invalidating the obligation as to either interest or principal under the law of borrower's state) (5th ed.2006).

3. THE COURTS (AND LEGISLATURES) AT WORK IN CONTRACT CONFLICTS

Contract conflicts law in the U.S. was also significantly affected by the conflicts revolution. However, the practical impact has been less than in the field of torts. Section 187 of the Second Restatement (quoted below) gave broad authority to parties to choose the law applicable to govern their contracts and disputes closely related to the contractual relationship. Even states that do not generally follow the Second Restatement often cite and follow Section 187. That, combined with the U.S. Supreme Court's willingness to allow a party with vastly superior bargaining power to dictate the forum by placing a forum selection clause in a contract (see Carnival Cruise Lines v. Shute, 495 U.S. 585 (1991)) or an arbitration clause in a consumer contract (see AT&T Mobility LLC v. Concepcion, 563 U.S. 333 (2011)) have taken many contract conflict questions out of the hands of courts. Yet the field retains enough vitality to merit our attention.

RESTATEMENT, SECOND, CONFLICT OF LAWS (1971):

§ 187. Law of the State Chosen by the Parties

(1) The law of the state chosen by the parties to govern their contractual rights and duties will be applied if the particular issue is one which the parties could have resolved by an explicit provision in their agreement directed to that issue.

(2) The law of the state chosen by the parties to govern their contractual rights and duties will be applied, even if the particular issue is one which the parties could not have resolved by an explicit provision in their agreement directed to that issue, unless either

(a) the chosen state has no substantial relationship to the parties or the transaction and there is no other reasonable basis for the parties' choice, or

(b) application of the law of the chosen state would be contrary to a fundamental policy of a state which has a materially greater interest than the chosen state in the determination of the particular issue and which, under the rule of § 188, would be the state of the applicable law in the absence of an effective choice of law by the parties.

(3) In the absence of a contrary indication of intention, the reference is to the local law of the state of the chosen law.

_____

§ 188. Law Governing in Absence of Effective Choice by the Parties

(1) The rights and duties of the parties with respect to an issue in contract are determined by the local law of the state which, with respect to that issue, has the most significant relationship to the transaction and the parties under the principles stated in § 6.(2) In the absence of an effective choice of law by the parties (see § 187), the contacts to be taken into account in applying the principles of § 6 to determine the law applicable to an issue include:

(a)   the place of contracting,

(b)   the place of negotiation of the contract,

(c)   the place of performance,

(d)   the location of the subject matter of the contract, and

(e)   the domicil, residence, nationality, place of incorporation and place of business of the parties.

These contacts are to be evaluated according to their relative importance with respect to the particular issue.

(3) If the place of negotiating the contract and the place of performance are in the same state, the local law of this state will usually be applied, except as otherwise provided in §§ 189–199 and 203.

NOTES

1.   The Second Restatement expresses "uncertainty" as to whether the parties should be permitted to select the local law of two or more states to govern different aspects of the contract's validity. Restatement, Second, Conflict of Laws § 187, Comment i. Do the reasons supporting party autonomy for choice of law also support freedom to select more than one law? The Rome I Regulation, p. 1198, infra art. 3(1) provides: "By their choice the parties can select the law applicable to the whole or to part only of the contract."

2.   What should be the result when a choice-of-law clause calls for application of a law that would invalidate a contract?

Lilienthal v. Kaufman

Supreme Court of Oregon, 1964.
239 Or. 1, 395 P.2d 543.

■ DENECKE, JUSTICE. This is an action to collect two promissory notes. The defense is that the defendant maker has previously been declared a spendthrift by an Oregon court and placed under a guardianship and that the guardian has declared the obligations void. The plaintiff's counter is that the notes were executed and delivered in California, that the law of California does not recognize the disability of a spendthrift, and that the Oregon court is bound to apply the law of the place of the making of the contract. The trial court rejected plaintiff's argument and held for the defendant.

This same defendant spendthrift was the prevailing party in our recent decision in Olshen v. Kaufman, 235 Or. 423, 385 P.2d 161 (1963). In that case the spendthrift and the plaintiff, an Oregon resident, had gone into a joint venture to purchase binoculars for resale. For this purpose plaintiff had advanced moneys to the spendthrift. The spendthrift had repaid plaintiff by his personal check for the amount advanced and for plaintiff's share of the profits of such venture. The check had not been paid because the spendthrift had had insufficient funds in his account. The action was for the unpaid balance of the check.

The evidence in that case showed that the plaintiff had been unaware that Kaufman was under a spendthrift guardianship. The guardian testified that he knew Kaufman was engaging in some business and had bank accounts and that he had admonished him to cease these practices; but he could not control the spendthrift.

The statute applicable in that case and in this one is ORS 126.335:

"After the appointment of a guardian for the spendthrift, all contracts, except for necessaries, and all gifts, sales and transfers of real or personal estate made by such spendthrift thereafter and before the termination of the guardianship are voidable." (Repealed 1961, ch. 344, § 109, now ORS 126.280).

We held in that case that the voiding of the contract by the guardian precluded recovery by the plaintiff and that the spendthrift and the guardian were not estopped to deny the validity of plaintiff's claim. Plaintiff does not seek to overturn the principle of that decision but contends it has no application because the law of California governs, and under California law the plaintiff's claim is valid.

The facts here are identical to those in Olshen v. Kaufman, supra, except for the California locale for portions of the transaction. The notes were for the repayment of advances to finance another joint venture to sell binoculars. The plaintiff was unaware that defendant had been declared a spendthrift and placed under guardianship. The guardian, upon demand for payment by the plaintiff, declared the notes void. The issue is solely one involving the principles of conflict of laws.

Plaintiff contends that the substantive issue of whether or not an obligation is valid and binding is governed by the law of the place of making, California. This court has repeatedly stated that the law of the place of contract "must govern as to the validity, interpretation, and construction of the contract." . . .

This principle, that *lex loci contractus* must govern, however, has been under heavy attack for years. . . .

There is no need to decide that our previous statements that the law of the place of contract governs were in error. Our purpose is to state that this portion of our decision is not founded upon that principle because of our doubt that it is correct if the *only* connection of the state whose law would govern is that it was the place of making.

In this case California had more connection with the transaction than being merely the place where the contract was executed. The defendant went to San Francisco to ask the plaintiff, a California resident, for money for the defendant's venture. The money was loaned to defendant in San Francisco, and by the terms of the note, it was to be repaid to plaintiff in San Francisco.

On these facts, apart from *lex loci contractus,* other accepted principles of conflict of laws lead to the conclusion that the law of California should be applied. Sterrett v. Stoddard Lumber Co., 150 Or. 491, 504, 46 P.2d 1023 (1935), rests, at least in part, on the proposition that the validity of a note is determined by the law of the place of payment. . . .

There is another conflict principle calling for the application of California law. Stumberg terms it the application of the law which upholds the contract. Stumberg, [Principles of Conflict of Laws (3d ed.)], at 237. Ehrenzweig calls it the "Rule of Validation." Ehrenzweig, Conflict of Laws, 353 (1962). . . .

Thus far all signs have pointed to applying the law of California and holding the contract enforceable. There is, however, an obstacle to cross before this end can be logically reached. In Olshen v. Kaufman, supra, we decided that the law of Oregon, at least as applied to persons domiciled in Oregon contracting in Oregon for performance in Oregon, is that spendthrifts' contracts are voidable. Are the choice-of-law principles of conflict of laws so superior that they overcome this principle of Oregon law?

To answer this question we must determine, upon some basis, whether the interests of Oregon are so basic and important that we should not apply California law despite its several intimate connections with the transaction. The traditional method used by this court and most others is framed in the terminology of "public policy." The court decides whether or not the public policy of the forum is so strong that the law of the forum must prevail although another jurisdiction, with different laws, has more and closer contacts with the transaction. Included in "public policy" we must consider the economic and social interests of Oregon. When these factors are included in a consideration of whether the law of the forum should be applied this traditional approach is very similar to that advocated by many legal scholars. This latter theory is "that choice-of-law rules should rationally advance the policies or interests of the several states (or of the nations in the world community)." Hill, Governmental Interest and the Conflict of Laws—A Reply to Professor Currie, 27 Chi. L. Rev. 463, 474 (1960); Currie, Selected Essays on the Conflict of Laws, 64–72 (1963), reprint from 58 Col. L. Rev. 964 (1958). . . .

Some of the interests of Oregon in this litigation are set forth in Olshen v. Kaufman, supra. The spendthrift's family which is to be protected by the establishment of the guardianship is presumably an Oregon family. The public authority which may be charged with the expense of supporting the spendthrift or his family, if he is permitted to go unrestrained upon his wasteful way, will probably be an Oregon public authority. These, obviously, are interests of some substance.

Oregon has other interests and policies regarding this matter which were not necessary to discuss in Olshen. As previously stated, Oregon, as well as all other states, has a strong policy favoring the validity and enforceability of contracts. This policy applies whether the contract is made and to be performed in Oregon or elsewhere.

The defendant's conduct—borrowing money with the belief that the repayment of such loan could be avoided—is a species of fraud. Oregon and all other states have a strong policy of protecting innocent persons from fraud. . . .

It is in Oregon's commercial interest to encourage citizens of other states to conduct business with Oregonians. If Oregonians acquire a reputation for not honoring their agreements, commercial intercourse with Oregonians will be discouraged. If there are Oregon laws, somewhat unique to Oregon, which permit an Oregonian to escape his otherwise binding obligations, persons may well avoid commercial dealings with Oregonians.

The substance of these commercial considerations, however, is deflated by the recollection that the Oregon Legislature has determined, despite the weight of these considerations, that a spendthrift's contracts are voidable.

California's most direct interest in this transaction is having its citizen creditor paid. . . . California probably has another, although more intangible, interest involved. It is presumably to every state's benefit to have the reputation of being a jurisdiction in which contracts can be made and performance be promised with the certain knowledge that such contracts will be enforced. Both of these interests, particularly the former, are also of substance.

We have, then, two jurisdictions, each with several close connections with the transaction, and each with a substantial interest, which will be served or thwarted, depending upon which law is applied. The interests of neither jurisdiction are clearly more important than those of the other. We are of the opinion that in such a case the public policy of Oregon should prevail and the law of Oregon should be applied; we should apply that choice-of-law rule which will "advance the policies or interests of" Oregon. Hill, supra, 27 Chi. L. Rev. at 474.

Courts are instruments of state policy. The Oregon Legislature has adopted a policy to avoid possible hardship to an Oregon family of a spendthrift and to avoid possible expenditure of Oregon public funds which might occur if the spendthrift is required to pay his obligations. In litigation Oregon courts are the appropriate instrument to enforce this policy. The mechanical application of choice-of-law rules would be the only apparent reason for an Oregon court advancing the interests of California over the equally valid interests of Oregon. The present principles of conflict of laws are not favorable to such mechanical application.

We hold that the spendthrift law of Oregon is applicable and the plaintiff cannot recover.

Judgment affirmed.

■ O'CONNELL, JUSTICE (specially concurring). . . .

In the Olshen case we had to choose between two competing policies; on one hand the policy of protecting the interest of persons dealing with spendthrifts, which, broadly, may be described as the interest in the security of transactions, and on the other hand the policy of protecting the interests of the spendthrift, his family and the county. It was decided that the Oregon Legislature adopted the latter policy in preference to the former.

. . . To distinguish the Olshen case it would be necessary to assume that although the legislature intended to protect the interest of the spendthrift, his family and the county when local creditors were harmed, the same protection was not intended where the transaction adversely affected foreign creditors. I see no basis for making that assumption. There is no reason to believe that our legislature intended to protect California creditors to a greater extent than our own.

■ GOODWIN, JUSTICE (dissenting). . . .

In the case before us, I believe that the policy of both states, Oregon and California, in favor of enforcing contracts, has been lost sight of in favor of a questionable policy in Oregon which gives special privileges to the rare spendthrift for whom a guardian has been appointed.

The majority view in the case at bar strikes me as a step backward toward the balkanization of the law of contracts. Olshen v. Kaufman, 235 Or. 423, 385 P.2d 161 (1963), held that there was a policy in this state to help keep spendthrifts out of the almshouse. I can see nothing, however, in Oregon's policy toward spendthrifts that warrants its extension to permit the taking of captives from other states down the road to insolvency.

I would enforce the contract.

NOTES

1.   How would the result in the principal case have been different if the court had chosen California law under the traditional territorial rule, place of making of the contract, but had refused to apply California law because it violated Oregon public policy?

2.   The Oregon legislature has enacted a comprehensive choice-of-law code for contracts, which contains the following provision: "A party that lacks capacity to enter into a contract under the law of the state in which the party

resides may assert that incapacity against a party that knew or should have known of the incapacity at the time the parties entered into the contract." Or. Stat. § 81.112(2). Would this statute have prevented the result in *Lilienthal?*

DeSantis v. Wackenhut Corporation

Supreme Court of Texas, 1990.
793 S.W.2d 670, cert. denied, 498 U.S. 1048 (1991).

■ HECHT, JUSTICE. . . . This case involving a noncompetition agreement between an employer and employee presents three principal issues: first, whether the law of the state chosen by the parties to govern their agreement should be applied; second, whether the noncompetition agreement is enforceable; third, if the agreement is not enforceable, whether damages for its attempted enforcement are recoverable under the Texas Free Enterprise and Antitrust Act of 1983 or for wrongful injunction, fraud, or tortious interference with contract.

The trial court applied the law of the state of Florida, chosen by the parties to govern the noncompetition agreement, to hold the agreement valid but overly broad as to the geographical territory in which competition was restricted. Based upon a jury finding that the employee breached the agreement, the trial court enjoined any further violation of the agreement within a smaller territory, and denied the employee's claims for damages. The court of appeals affirmed. 732 S.W.2d 29. We hold that Texas law, not Florida law, applies in this case, and that under Texas law, the noncompetition agreement is unenforceable. We further hold that the employee is not entitled to recover damages for his employer's wrongfully obtaining an injunction against him, and that the employee has failed to show fraud, tortious interference, or a violation of the Texas Free Enterprise and Antitrust Act entitling him to damages. We accordingly reverse the judgment of the court of appeals and render judgment in accordance with this opinion.

I

A

Edward DeSantis has been providing international and corporate security services, both in the CIA and the private sector for his entire career. In June 1981, while employed by R.J. Reynolds Industries in North Carolina, DeSantis interviewed for a position with Wackenhut Corporation. At that time, Wackenhut, which was chartered and headquartered in Florida, was the third largest company in the nation specializing in furnishing security guards for businesses throughout the country. DeSantis met with Wackenhut's president, founder, and majority stockholder, George Wackenhut, at the company's offices in Florida, and the two agreed that DeSantis would immediately assume the position of Wackenhut's Houston area manager. According to DeSantis, George Wackenhut promised him that the area manager's position was only temporary, and that he would soon be moved into a top executive position.

George Wackenhut denies that he made any such promises to DeSantis, admitting only that he mentioned advancement to an executive position as a possible opportunity.

At Wackenhut's request, DeSantis signed a noncompetition agreement at the inception of his employment. The agreement recites that it was "made and entered into" on August 13, 1981, in Florida, although DeSantis signed it in Texas. It also recites consideration "including but not limited to the Employee's employment by the Employer". In the agreement DeSantis covenanted that as long as he was employed by Wackenhut and for two years thereafter, he would not compete in any way with Wackenhut in a forty-county area in south Texas. DeSantis expressly acknowledged that Wackenhut's client list "is a valuable, special and unique asset of [Wackenhut's] business" and agreed never to disclose it to anyone. DeSantis also agreed never to divulge any confidential or proprietary information acquired through his employment with Wackenhut. Finally, DeSantis and Wackenhut agreed "that any questions concerning interpretation or enforcement of this contract shall be governed by Florida law."

DeSantis remained manager of Wackenhut's Houston office for nearly three years, until March 1984, when he resigned under threat of termination. DeSantis contends that he was forced to quit because of disagreements with Wackenhut's senior management over the profitability of the Houston office. Wackenhut contends that DeSantis was asked to resign because of his unethical solicitation of business.

Following his resignation, DeSantis invested in a company which marketed security electronics. He also formed a new company, Risk Deterrence, Inc. ("RDI"), to provide security consulting services and security guards to a limited clientele. The month following termination of his employment with Wackenhut, DeSantis sent out letters announcing his new ventures to twenty or thirty businesses, about half of which were Wackenhut clients. He added a postscript to letters to Wackenhut clients in which he disclaimed any intent to interfere with their existing contracts with Wackenhut. Within six months, however, one of Wackenhut's clients, Marathon Oil Company, had terminated its contract with Wackenhut and signed a five-year contract with RDI, and a second Wackenhut client, TRW-Mission Drilling Products, was considering doing the same. Wackenhut claims that DeSantis was acquiring its clients in violation of the noncompetition agreement. DeSantis claims that these clients began considering other security service providers only after the quality of Wackenhut's services declined, following DeSantis' departure.

B

Wackenhut sued DeSantis and RDI in October 1984 to enjoin them from violating the noncompetition agreement, and to recover damages for breach of the agreement and for tortious interference with business relations. Wackenhut alleged that DeSantis and RDI were soliciting its clients' business using confidential client and pricing information which

DeSantis obtained through his employment with Wackenhut. The trial court issued an ex parte temporary restraining order against DeSantis and RDI, and fixed the amount of the requisite bond which Wackenhut filed at $5,000. Following a hearing, the trial court issued a temporary injunction upon a $75,000 bond, which Wackenhut also filed. DeSantis and RDI counterclaimed against Wackenhut, alleging that Wackenhut had fraudulently induced DeSantis to sign the noncompetition agreement, that the agreement violated state antitrust laws, and that enforcement of the agreement by temporary injunction was wrongful and tortiously interfered with DeSantis and RDI's contract and business relationships. RDI claimed damages for loss of the Marathon contract, which Marathon terminated after the injunction issued, for loss of the TRW business, and for injury to its reputation. DeSantis claimed damages for lost salary, impaired reputation, and mental anguish. DeSantis and RDI both sought statutory damages under the Texas Free Enterprise and Antitrust Act, Texas Business and Commerce Code Annotated sections 15.01–15.51 (Vernon 1987 and Supp. 1990), and exemplary damages.

The trial court granted Wackenhut's motion for summary judgment on DeSantis' and RDI's claim for tortious interference, and directed a verdict against them on their fraud claim. At trial, Wackenhut withdrew its tortious interference claim. A jury found that DeSantis breached the noncompetition agreement by competing with Wackenhut.... The jury also failed to find that Wackenhut had ever been unfair, unjust, misleading or deceptive to DeSantis so as to cause him any injury....

The trial court concluded that irreparable harm to Wackenhut was either presumed from DeSantis' breach of the agreement under Florida law, or established as a matter of law because of the absence of an adequate legal remedy for breach of the agreement under Texas law. Accordingly, the trial court permanently enjoined DeSantis from competing with Wackenhut, and RDI from employing DeSantis to compete with Wackenhut, for two years from the date DeSantis left Wackenhut in an area reduced by the trial court from the forty counties stated in the agreement to the thirteen counties found by the trial court to be reasonably necessary to protect Wackenhut's interest. The trial court also permanently enjoined DeSantis from divulging Wackenhut's client list or proprietary information, and RDI from using any proprietary information of Wackenhut's acquired through DeSantis. The trial court denied all relief requested by DeSantis and RDI, based upon the jury's finding that DeSantis had breached his agreement with Wackenhut. The trial court awarded Wackenhut attorney's fees and costs.

The court of appeals affirmed the judgment of the trial court in all respects.

II

We first consider what law is to be applied in determining whether the noncompetition agreement in this case is enforceable. Wackenhut contends that Florida law applies, as expressly agreed by the parties. DeSantis argues that Texas law applies, despite the parties' agreement.

A

... When parties to a contract reside or expect to perform their respective obligations in multiple jurisdictions, they may be uncertain as to what jurisdiction's law will govern construction and enforcement of the contract. To avoid this uncertainty, they may express in their agreement their own choice that the law of a specified jurisdiction apply to their agreement. Judicial respect for their choice advances the policy of protecting their expectations. This conflict of laws concept has come to be referred to as party autonomy. See R. Weintraub, Commentary on the Conflict of Laws 269–271 (1971) ["Weintraub"]. However, the parties' freedom to choose what jurisdiction's law will apply to their agreement cannot be unlimited. They cannot require that their contract be governed by the law of a jurisdiction which has no relation whatever to them or their agreement. And they cannot by agreement thwart or offend the public policy of the state the law of which ought otherwise to apply. So limited, party autonomy furthers the basic policy of contract law. With roots deep in two centuries of American jurisprudence, limited party autonomy has grown to be the modern rule in contracts conflict of laws. See Scoles & Hay, Conflict of Laws § 18.1, p. 657 et seq. (2d ed. 1992); Weintraub, supra at 269–275; Restatement (Second) of Conflict of Laws ["Restatement"] § 187 (1971). . . .

B

[The court quotes Restatement § 187, p. 674, supra, and concludes that this case falls under § 187(2) rather than under § 187(1).]

The parties in this case chose the law of Florida to govern their contract. Florida has a substantial relationship to the parties and the transaction because Wackenhut's corporate offices are there, and some of the negotiations between DeSantis and George Wackenhut occurred there. Thus, under section 187(2) Florida law should apply in this case unless it falls within the exception stated in section 187(2)(b). Whether that exception applies depends upon three determinations: first, whether there is a state the law of which would apply under section 188 of the Restatement absent an effective choice of law by the parties, or in other words, whether a state has a more significant relationship with the parties and their transaction than the state they chose; second, whether that state has a materially greater interest than the chosen state in deciding whether this noncompetition agreement should be enforced; and third, whether that state's fundamental policy would be contravened by the application of the law of the chosen state in this case. More particularly, we must determine: first, whether Texas has a more significant relationship to these parties and their transaction than Florida; second, whether Texas has a materially greater interest than Florida in deciding the enforceability of the noncompetition agreement in this case; and third, whether the application of Florida law in this case would be contrary to fundamental policy of Texas.

1

Section 188 of the Restatement [p. 675, supra] provides that a contract is to be governed by the law of the state that "has the most significant relationship to the transaction and the parties", taking into account various contacts in light of the basic conflict of laws principles of section 6 of the Restatement [p. 574, supra].

In this case, that state is Texas. Wackenhut hired DeSantis to manage its business in the Houston area. Although some of the negotiations between DeSantis and Wackenhut occurred in Florida, the noncompetition agreement was finally executed by DeSantis in Houston. The place of performance for both parties was Texas, where the subject matter of the contract was located. Wackenhut may also be considered to have performed its obligations in part in Florida, from where it supervised its various operations, including its Houston office. Still, the gist of the agreement in this case was the performance of personal services in Texas. As a rule, that factor alone is conclusive in determining what state's law is to apply. See Restatement § 196 (1971).[24] In this case, the relationship of the transaction and parties to Texas was clearly more significant than their relationship to Florida.

2

Texas has a materially greater interest than does Florida in determining whether the noncompetition agreement in this case is enforceable. At stake here is whether a Texas resident can leave one Texas job to start a competing Texas business. Thus, Texas is directly interested in DeSantis as an employee in this state, in Wackenhut as a national employer doing business in this state, in RDI as a new competitive business being formed in the state, and in consumers of the services furnished in Texas by Wackenhut and RDI and performed by DeSantis. Texas also shares with Florida a general interest in protecting the justifiable expectations of entities doing business in several states. Florida's direct interest in the enforcement of the noncompetition agreement in this case is limited to protecting a national business headquartered in that state. Although it is always problematic for one state to balance its own interests fairly against those of another state, the circumstances of this case leave little doubt, if any, that Texas has a materially greater interest than Florida in deciding whether the noncompetition agreement in this case should be enforced.

---

[24] Section 196 states: "Contracts for the Rendition of Services. The validity of a contract for the rendition of services and the rights created thereby are determined, in the absence of an effective choice of law by the parties, by the local law of the state where the contract requires that the services, or a major portion of the services, be rendered, unless, with respect to the particular issue, some other state has a more significant relationship under the principles stated in § 6 to the transaction and the parties, in which event the local law of the other state will be applied."

3

Having concluded that Texas law would control the issue of enforceability of the noncompetition agreement in this case but for the parties' choice of Florida law, and that Texas' interest in deciding this issue in this case is materially greater than Florida's, we must finally determine under section 187(2)(b) of the Restatement whether application of Florida law to decide this issue would be contrary to fundamental policy of Texas. The Restatement offers little guidance in making this determination. Comment g states only that a "fundamental" policy is a "substantial" one, and that "[t]he forum will apply its own legal principles in determining whether a given policy is a fundamental one within the meaning of the present rule. . . ."

Comment g to section 187 does suggest that application of the law of another state is not contrary to the fundamental policy of the forum merely because it leads to a different result than would obtain under the forum's law. We agree that the result in one case cannot determine whether the issue is a matter of fundamental state policy for purposes of resolving a conflict of laws. Moreover, the fact that the law of another state is materially different from the law of this state does not itself establish that application of the other state's law would offend the fundamental policy of Texas. In analyzing whether fundamental policy is offended under section 187(2)(b), the focus is on whether the law in question is a part of state policy so fundamental that the courts of the state will refuse to enforce an agreement contrary to that law, despite the parties' original intentions, and even though the agreement would be enforceable in another state connected with the transaction.

Neither the Restatement nor the cases which have followed section 187 have undertaken a general definition of "fundamental policy", and we need not make the attempt in this case; for whatever its parameters, enforcement of noncompetition agreements falls well within them. This Court has held that "[a]n agreement not to compete is in restraint of trade and will not be enforced unless it is reasonable." Frankiewicz v. National Comp. Assoc., 633 S.W.2d 505, 507 (Tex. 1982). Moreover, that policy is fundamental in that it ensures a uniform rule for enforcement of noncompetition agreements in this state. See Restatement § 187 comment g (1971) ("a fundamental policy may be embodied in a statute which makes one or more kinds of contracts illegal or which is designed to protect a person against the oppressive use of superior bargaining power"). Absent such a policy, agreements involving residents of other states would be controlled by the law and policy of those states. An employee of one out-of-state employer might take a competing job and escape enforcement of a covenant not to compete because of the law of another state, while a neighbor suffered enforcement of an identical covenant because of the law of a third state. The resulting disruption of orderly employer-employee relations, as well as competition in the marketplace, would be unacceptable. Employers would be encouraged to attempt to invoke the most favorable state law available to govern their relationship with their employees in Texas or other states.

These same considerations and others have led virtually every court that has addressed the question of whether enforcement of noncompetition agreements is a matter of fundamental or important state policy to answer affirmatively. Not many of these courts have considered the matter specifically in the context of section 187 of the Restatement, and yet, rather remarkably, many have nevertheless expressed similar conclusions.

We likewise conclude that the law governing enforcement of noncompetition agreements is fundamental policy in Texas, and that to apply the law of another state to determine the enforceability of such an agreement in the circumstances of a case like this would be contrary to that policy. We therefore hold that the enforceability of the agreement in this case must be judged by Texas law, not Florida law.

III

We now consider whether the noncompetition agreement between DeSantis and Wackenhut is enforceable under Texas law. [The court finds the agreement unenforceable because there is insufficient evidence that DeSantis was able to appropriate good will he had developed with customers while working for Wackenhut. Only one customer left Wackenhut for RDI and another was contemplating leaving. Moreover, there was evidence that these customers were dissatisfied with Wackenhut's services. Nor was there a showing that there is a need to protect confidential information relating to Wackenhut's business. DeSantis could have learned of Wackenhut's customers and their needs without working for Wackenhut and there is no showing that Wackenhut's pricing and bidding strategies are unique. DeSantis and RDI cannot recover on the injunction bond because the temporary restraining order and temporary injunction were never dissolved. There was no evidence to support the claim of malicious prosecution.]

NOTES

1.   Would a Florida Court have agreed "that Texas has a materially greater interest than Florida in deciding whether the noncompetition agreement in this case should be enforced"? If not, what planning and litigation strategy does this suggest for an employer like Wackenhut? See In re Autonation, 228 S.W.3d 663 (Tex.2007). A Texas resident worked in Texas at an automobile dealership owned by a corporation that had its principal place of business in Florida (Autonation). The employee signed an agreement that contained (1) a promise not to compete with Autonation for one year after the employment is terminated; (2) a stipulation that any litigation arising from the agreement would be instituted only in Florida state or federal courts; (3) a stipulation that the agreement would be governed by and construed in accordance with Florida law. The employee resigned and accepted employment with a competing automobile dealership. Autonation sued its former employee in a Florida state court to enforce the agreement not to compete. The employee and his new

employer sued Autonation in a Texas state court for (1) a declaratory judgment that the non-compete agreement was governed by Texas law and was unenforceable; (2) an injunction barring Autonation from taking any further action in its Florida lawsuit. The trial court granted the injunction. The Supreme Court of Texas issued a writ of mandamus directing "the trial court to dismiss this suit in favor of the first-filed Florida action in the parties' contracted-for forum." The court stated: "[E]ven if *DeSantis* requires Texas courts to apply Texas law to certain employment disputes, it does not require suit to be brought in Texas when a forum-selection clause mandates venue elsewhere. No Texas precedent compels us to enjoin a party from asking a Florida court to honor the parties' express agreement to litigate a non-compete agreement in Florida, the employer's headquarters and principal place of business."

Beilfuss v. Huffy Corp., 685 N.W.2d 373 (Wis.App.2004). A former employee, residing in Wisconsin, sued his former employer, an Ohio corporation, in a Wisconsin state court seeking a declaration that provisions in the employment contract were unenforceable. The provisions limited the employee's ability to work for a competitor of the employer. The employer moved to dismiss based on provisions in the contract limiting litigation of disputes concerning the employment contract to Ohio courts and selecting Ohio law as governing the contract. The trial judge granted the motion to dismiss. Held: reversed. "[T]he choice of law provision is unenforceable because it violates Wisconsin's long-standing public policy controlling covenants not to compete, in that [the noncompetition agreements are invalid under Wisconsin and valid under Ohio law]. Moreover, we hold that because important public policy considerations are involved, it is unreasonable to enforce the forum selection provision." Id. at 379.

2.   Restatement, Second, Conflict of Laws § 187, cmt. g: "To be 'fundamental' within the meaning of the present rule, a policy need not be as strong as would be required to justify the forum in refusing to entertain suit upon a foreign cause of action under the rule of § 90 [Action Contrary to Public Policy]."

3.   After the decision in the principal case, Texas law firms had difficulty writing "opinion letters" passing on the validity of choice-of-law clauses in interstate and international transactions involving Texas parties. An Ad Hoc Committee on Choice of Law of the Business Law Section of the State Bar of Texas drafted legislation, which provided that in a commercial transaction having "an aggregate value of at least $1,000,000 . . . if the parties . . . agree in writing that the law of a particular jurisdiction governs an issue relating to the transaction, including the validity or enforceability of an agreement relating to the transaction or a provision of the agreement, and the transaction bears a reasonable relation to that jurisdiction, the law, other than conflict of laws rules, of that jurisdiction governs the issue regardless of whether the application of that law is contrary to a fundamental or public policy of this state or of any other jurisdiction." The draft was enacted as Texas Business & Commerce Code § 35.51. If you were a member of the legislature, would you have voted for this bill?

4.   Application Group, Inc. v. Hunter Group, Inc., 61 Cal.App.4th 881 (1998) refused to apply the law chosen in an employment contract. A computer consultant contracted not to compete for one year with her former employer. The employee worked for sixteen months for Hunter in Maryland and at various customer sites in other states, but not in California. Her employment contract contained a clause choosing Maryland law under which the promise not to compete was valid. She resigned from Hunter and took a job with Application Group, a California company, but did not move to California. When Hunter sued in Maryland to enforce the employee's promise not to compete, Application Group obtained a declaratory judgment in California that the covenant not to compete was governed by California law under which it was invalid. The California court found "that California has a materially greater interest than does Maryland in the application of its law to the parties' dispute, and that California's interests would be more seriously impaired if its policy were subordinated to the policy of Maryland."

Govett American Endeavor Fund Ltd. v. Trueger, 112 F.3d 1017 (9th Cir.1997). A company incorporated under the laws of the Channel Island of Jersey asserted claims under the federal Racketeer Influenced and Corrupt Organizations Act (RICO) against a California citizen, several other Jersey companies, and a California subsidiary of a Jersey company. The court, with one dissent, held that plaintiff could assert its RICO claims notwithstanding a contractual agreement choosing Jersey law to govern the parties' relationships. The majority construed the choice-of-law agreements as not covering tort claims and then stated that in any event "[t]o permit [RICO's] fundamental choice of public policy to be frustrated by private choice would be to exalt autonomy in contract over the laws of the United States." Id. at 1022.

The American Law Institute and the National Conference of Commissioners on Uniform State Laws (NCCUSL) promulgated a revision of Uniform Commercial Code section 1–105 (renumbered 1–301) that gave the parties to a contract greater freedom to choose law:

SECTION 1–301. TERRITORIAL APPLICABILITY; PARTIES' POWER TO CHOOSE APPLICABLE LAW.

(a) In this section:

(1) "Domestic transaction" means a transaction other than an international transaction; and

(2) "International transaction" means a transaction that bears a reasonable relation to a country other than the United States.

(b) This section applies to a transaction to the extent that it is governed by another article of the [Uniform Commercial Code]. Except as otherwise provided in this section:

(1) an agreement by parties to a domestic transaction that any or all of their rights and obligations are to be determined by the law of this State or of another State is effective, whether or not the transaction bears a relation to the State designated; and

(2) an agreement by parties to an international transaction that any or all of their rights and obligations are to be determined by the law of this State or of another State or country is effective, whether or not the transaction bears a relation to the State or country designated.

(c) In the absence of an agreement effective under subsection (b), and except as provided in subsections (d) and (f), the rights and obligations of the parties are determined by the law that would be selected by application of this State's conflict of laws principles.

(d) If one of the parties to a transaction is a consumer, the following rules apply:

(1) An agreement referred to in subsection (b) is not effective unless the transaction bears a reasonable relation to the State or country designated.

(2) Application of the law of the State or country determined pursuant to subsection (b) or (c) may not deprive the consumer of the protection of any rule of law governing a matter within the scope of this section, which both is protective of consumers and may not be varied by agreement, of the State or country:

(A) in which the consumer principally resides, unless subparagraph (B) applies; or

(B) if the transaction is a sale of goods, in which the consumer makes the contract and takes delivery of those goods, if such State or country is not the State or country in which the consumer principally resides.

(e) An agreement otherwise effective under subsection (b) is not effective to the extent that application of the law of the State or country designated would be contrary to a fundamental policy of the State or country whose law would govern in the absence of agreement under subsection (c).

(f) To the extent that [the Uniform Commercial Code] governs a transaction, where one of the following provisions of [the Uniform Commercial Code] specifies the applicable law, that provision governs and a contrary agreement is effective only to the extent permitted by the law so specified: [sections 2–402, 2A–105, 2A–106, 4–102, 4A–507, 5–116, 6–103, 8–110, and 9–301 through 9–307].

NOTE

In 2007 the NCCUSL approved of withdrawing the text of § 1–301 and reverting to the wording of former § 1–105. At its annual meeting in May 2008, the American Law Institute (ALI) concurred in the amendment of the wording completing the formal reversion to the wording of § 1–105. At the time of the ALI action, the revised article I of the Uniform Commercial Code had been adopted in 29 states and the Virgin Islands. Only the Virgin Islands adopted the wording of § 1–301. The 29 states retained the wording of § 1–105.

What were the fatal flaws in § 1–301? Under § 1–301 could parties to a domestic transaction from the same state avoid invalidating rules of their own state by selecting the law of another state? Was there any reason to restrict parties to a domestic transaction to choice of U.S. law if the issue is one of construction and not validity? Was it wise to revert to the wording of § 1–105, which was drafted in the 1950s? Do §§ 187 and 188 of the Restatement and the European Union Regulation on the Law Applicable to Contractual Obligations afford models that could have been used to improve the terms of § 1–105?

4. RULES AGAIN?

With the freeform analysis ushered in by the American Conflicts Revolution, it is perhaps not surprising that the pragmatic American judiciary began to crave rules that, while not as hard and fast as those that predated the Revolution (and even those were not as hard and fast as advertised given the escape devices employed), at least gave courts a starting point a rule from which to deviate, if deviation were called for. The *Neumeier* rules were the first serious effort at consolidating the gains of the conflicts revolution (most notably the application of the law of the common geographical basis of two parties involved in a dispute regarding a loss allocating tort rule), but the New York courts expanded them well beyond their humble guest statute origins. Meanwhile, American courts began to pay more attention to the presumptive rules buried beneath the Second Restatement's open-ended pronouncements. And some courts unapologetically hung to the territorial rules enshrined in the First Restatement.

Townsend v. Sears, Roebuck & Co.

Supreme Court of Illinois, 2007.
227 Ill.2d 147, 879 N.E.2d 893.

■ FREEMAN, JUSTICE.

Plaintiffs, Michelle Townsend, individually and on behalf of her minor son, Jacob, brought a personal injury action in the circuit court of Cook County against defendant, Sears, Roebuck and Company. A question arose as to whether Illinois or Michigan law would govern the liability and damages issues presented in the case. . . .

We . . . hold that Michigan law governs the liability and damages issues presented in this case.

I. BACKGROUND

Michelle and James Townsend, and their son, Jacob, reside on North Begole Road in Alma, Michigan. Sears is a New York corporation with its principal place of business and corporate headquarters in Cook County, Illinois. In the spring of 2000, James purchased a Sears Craftsman brand riding lawn tractor from a Sears store in Michigan. The lawn tractor was manufactured by Electrolux Home Products, Inc. (EHP), in South

Carolina. James bought the 20-horsepower, 42-inch-wide lawn tractor for use around his home. This particular lawn tractor developed a faulty engine. In early 2001, James received an identical riding lawn tractor as a warranty replacement. Through early May 2001, James had operated the tractor three or four times to mow the Townsends' 1.8-acre property.

On the afternoon of May 11, 2001, James returned home from work and began to mow his lawn. At this time, his four children, including 3 1/2-year-old Jacob, were inside their home. As James was mowing, he encountered the 16- by 14-foot rectangular railroad-tie-edged planting plot in his front yard. He attempted to mow around the plot by positioning the left edge of the mower deck as close to the ties as possible. However, the tractor became stuck against one of the ties. James shifted the tractor into reverse, looked over his right shoulder, and released the brake. The tractor struggled to move rearward, taking approximately 20 seconds to move approximately six feet. While backing up, he heard a noise, looked to his right, and saw Jacob's sandal on the lawn. He stopped the tractor, turned around, and saw Jacob behind and under the tractor's rear wheels. James overturned the tractor, picked up Jacob, and rushed him to Gratiot Community Hospital in [Michigan]. Jacob was subsequently treated at Sparrow Hospital in Lansing, Michigan. Jacob's right foot was amputated and his lower right leg was severely injured.

Michelle, individually and on behalf of Jacob, filed a complaint against Sears pleading strict product liability and negligence, premised on defective design and failure to warn. . . .

Plaintiffs filed a motion to apply Illinois law to the issues of liability and damages. . . .

II. ANALYSIS

* * *

B. Identifying the Conflict

Subject to constitutional limitations, the forum court applies the choice-of-law rules of its own state. . . . In 1970, this court adopted, for tort cases, the choice-of-law methodology of what would become the Second Restatement of Conflict of Laws. . . .

In the present case, the parties agree that three conflicts exist between Illinois and Michigan law. The first conflict involves liability. Illinois has adopted a rule of strict liability in tort for product design defects. . . . In contrast, Michigan has refused to adopt the doctrine of strict liability, instead imposing a pure negligence standard for product liability actions based on defective design. . . .

The second conflict concerns compensatory damages. Illinois currently does not have a statutory cap on compensatory damages for noneconomic injuries. . . . In contrast, Michigan currently imposes caps on noneconomic damages in product liability actions. . . . The third conflict concerns punitive damages. Illinois does not prohibit the recovery of punitive damages in product liability cases when appropriate.... Subject to specific statutory exceptions, [Michigan does not allow punitive damages].

C. Overview: The Second Restatement of Conflict of Laws

A full understanding of current choice-of-law methodology, including its development, is necessary to properly apply it to the above-identified conflicts. . . .

One scholar has described the Second Restatement as "a document that could not—and cannot—be fairly called a 'restatement' of anything. Instead, it is an amalgamation of different conflict approaches, producing a document of a distinctly normative character." P. Borchers, Courts and the Second Conflicts Restatement: Some Observations and an Empirical Note, 56 Md. L. Rev. 1232, 1237 (1997). Indeed, "the Second Restatement is by far the most popular among the modern methodologies, being followed [as of 2004] in 22 states in tort conflicts." E. Scoles, P. Hay, P. Borchers & S. Symeonides, Conflict of Laws § 2.23, at 98 (4th ed. 2004). Except with respect to the relatively few areas for which it provides clear rules, the Second Restatement's methodology has three principal features: (1) the policies of section 6; (2) the concept of the "most significant relationship"; and (3) the lists of particularized connecting factors.

[The court then quoted Section 6.]

These multiple and diverse principles are not listed in any order of priority, and some of them point in different directions. Thus, in tort cases, for example, these principles, by themselves, do not enable courts to formulate precise choice-of-law rules. Restatement (Second) of Conflict of Laws § 6, Comment c, at 12–13 (1971); accord Scoles, Conflict of Laws § 2.14, at 60. "In some ways, § 6 was a logical response to the perceived flaws of the traditional rules. Critics had identified a variety of concerns that these rules failed to take into account, and § 6 offers a kind of 'laundry list' response that enables the court to consider all of them when appropriate." Crampton, Conflict of Laws: Cases—Comments—Questions, at 117.

Another fundamental concept of the Second Restatement's methodology is the concept of the "most significant relationship." "While section 6 enunciates the guiding principles of the choice-of-law process, the most-significant-relationship formula describes the objective of that process: to apply the law of the state that, with regard to the particular issue, has the most significant relationship with the parties and the dispute." Scoles, Conflict of Laws § 2.14, at 61. For example, in a tort case, the general principle that a court applies is: "The rights and liabilities of the parties with respect to an issue in tort are determined by the local law of the state which, with respect to that issue, has the most significant relationship to the occurrence and the parties under the principles stated in § 6." Restatement (Second) of Conflict of Laws

§ 145(1), at 414 (1971). One scholar has described section 145 as "nearly as amorphous as section 6." [Borchers,] 56 Md. L. Rev. at 1238–39.

Lastly, the Second Restatement provides a list of the factual contacts or connecting factors that the forum court should consider in choosing the applicable law. In a tort case, for example, section 145(2) provides as follows:

"(2) Contacts to be taken into account in applying the principles of § 6 to determine the law applicable to an issue include:

(a) the place where the injury occurred,

(b) the place where the conduct causing the injury occurred,

(c) the domicil, residence, nationality, place of incorporation and place of business of the parties, and

(d) the place where the relationship, if any, between the parties is centered.

These contacts are to be evaluated according to their relative importance with respect to the particular issue." Restatement (Second) of Conflict of Laws § 145(2), at 414 (1971).

In applying the principles of section 6 to these contacts to determine the state with the most significant relationship, the forum court should consider the relevant policies of all potentially interested states and the relevant interests of those states in the decision of the particular issue. Restatement (Second) of Conflict of Laws § 145, Comment e, at 419 (1971). "Thus, section 145 is no more definite than section 6, and perhaps even less so. On top of the 'factors' listed in section 6, section 145 adds a generous dollop of territorial and personal contacts." [Borchers,] 56 Md. L. Rev. at 1239. . . .

D.   Presumption: The Law of the State Where the Injury Occurred

The parties disagree as to the nature and effect of a choice-of-law presumptive rule applicable in this case. The Second Restatement of Conflict of Laws does not abandon rules entirely. "Separate rules are stated for different torts and for different issues in tort. In other words, the identity of the state of the most significant relationship is said to depend upon the nature of the tort and upon the particular issue." Restatement (Second) of Conflict of Laws, ch. 7, Topic 1, Introductory Note 2, at 413 (1971); see Scoles, Conflict of Laws § 2.14, at 62–63 (discussing presumptive rules). The Second Restatement's introduction is an understatement.

"Once one ventures past section 145, however, the chapter dramatically changes character. Instead of infinitely open-ended sections, the Second Restatement, for the most part, articulates reasonably definite rules. To be sure, these succeeding sections contain escape valves that refer to section 6. Many of the rules echo the First Restatement's preference for choosing the law of the injury state. Others do not refer to the injury state directly, but choose connecting factors very likely, if not certain, to lead to the application of the law of the injury state. . . . Only a relatively few sections refer solely to the general formula of section 145 without providing some presumptive choice." [Borchers,] 56 Md. L. Rev. at 1239–40.

Thus, the Second Restatement of Conflict of Laws has been described as "schizophrenic," in that one portion of its split personality consists of general sections such as sections 6 and 145, while the other portion is a set of reasonably definite rules and a preference for territorial solutions, including the injury-state rule for tort cases, endorsed by its predecessor. The general sections embody a free-form approach to choice of law, while the specific sections are quite close to the territorial system embodied by the First Restatement. [Borchers,] 56 Md. L. Rev. at 1240.

We agree with the concern that the bench and bar have overemphasized the general sections of the Second Restatement of Conflict of Laws and have undervalued the specific presumptive rules.

> "The opponents of mechanical rules of conflict of laws may have given too little weight to the virtues of simplicity. The new, flexible standards, such as 'interest analysis,' have caused pervasive uncertainty, higher cost of litigation, more forum shopping (a court has a natural inclination to apply the law it is most familiar with—the forum's law—and will find it easier to go with this inclination if the conflict of law rules are uncertain), and an uncritical drift in favor of plaintiffs" *Kaczmarek*, 836 F.2d at 1057 (dictum). . . .

For example, plaintiffs, in support of the appellate court's judgment, actually contend that this court has never expressly authorized use of legal presumptions in choice-of-law determinations in personal injury actions, observing "that the word 'presumed' is not found in *Ingersoll*." Alternatively, according to plaintiffs: "Even if this court meant to utilize a legal presumption in favor of the state of injury, presumptions in Illinois are governed by the 'bursting bubble hypothesis.'" Therefore, according to plaintiffs, if the presumption exists, it is "evanescent" and "easily overcome" by any contact with another state.

We emphatically reject this contention. . . . [A] presumption exists, which may be overcome only by showing a more or greater significant relationship to another state. . . . As we have explained, this analysis includes the application of presumptive rules.

> "Generally speaking, then, the Second Restatement contemplates a two-step process in which the court (1) chooses a presumptively applicable law under the appropriate jurisdiction-selecting rule, and (2) tests this choice against the principles of § 6 in light of relevant contacts identified by general provisions like § 145 (torts) and § 188 (contracts)." Crampton, Conflict of Laws: Cases—Comments—Questions, at 120. "[M]aking a serious effort to consider the entire Second Restatement would improve the quality of judicial decisionmaking. Courts that are

willing to follow the narrow rules of the Second Restatement would derive vastly more guidance than that which can be gleaned from sections 6, 145 [torts], and 188 [contracts]." [Borchers,] 56 Md. L. Rev. at 1247.

In this personal injury action, the appellate court was correct to cite section 146 of the Second Restatement of Conflict of Laws in holding that, "under Illinois choice-of-law rules, the law of the place of injury controls unless another state has a more significant relationship with the occurrence and with the parties with respect to the particular issue." 368 Ill. App. 3d at 907. "Section 146 is the starting point for any choice-of-law analysis in personal injury claims." *Malena*, 264 Neb. at 766, 651 N.W.2d at 856. . . . Section 146 received insufficient consideration in the appellate court.

Section 146 provides: "In an action for a personal injury, the local law of the state where the injury occurred determines the rights and liabilities of the parties, unless, with respect to the particular issue, some other state has a more significant relationship under the principles stated in section 6 to the occurrence and the parties, in which event the local law of the other state will be applied." Restatement (Second) of Conflict of Laws § 146, at 430 (1971).

One court has explained this presumption as follows: "Often, however, the simple old rules can be glimpsed through modernity's fog, though spectrally thinned to presumptions—in the latest lingo, 'default rules.' For in the absence of unusual circumstances, the highest scorer on the "most significant relationship" test is—the place where the tort occurred. [Citations.] For that is the place that has the greatest interest in striking a reasonable balance among safety, cost, and other factors pertinent to the design and administration of a system of tort law. Most people affected whether as victims or as injurers by accidents and other injury-causing events are residents of the jurisdiction in which the event takes place. So if law can be assumed to be generally responsive to the values and preferences of the people who live in the community that formulated the law, the law of the place of the accident can be expected to reflect the values and preferences of the people most likely to be involved in accidents—can be expected, in other words, to be responsive and responsible law, law that internalizes the costs and benefits of the people affected by it." *Spinozzi*, 174 F.3d at 844–45.

We now apply section 146 to the record before us.

Plaintiffs are domiciled and reside in Michigan, and James works in Michigan. Plaintiffs allege that Sears' tortious conduct occurred in Illinois. Comment e of section 146, entitled "When conduct and injury occur in different states," addresses this specific situation. "The local law of the state where the personal injury occurred is most likely to be applied when the injured person has a settled relationship to that state, either because he is domiciled or resides there or because he does business there." Restatement (Second) of Conflict of Laws § 146, Comment e, at

432 (1971). In contrast: "The state where the conduct occurred is even more likely to be the state of most significant relationship . . . when, in addition to the injured person's being domiciled or residing or doing business in the state, the injury occurred in the course of an activity or of a relationship which was centered there." Restatement (Second) of Conflict of Laws § 146, Comment e, at 432 (1971).

If this guidance were not enough, the comments to section 146 further advise: "The likelihood that some state other than that where the injury occurred is the state of most significant relationship is greater in those relatively rare situations where, with respect to the particular issue, the state of injury bears little relation to the occurrence and the parties." Restatement (Second) of Conflict of Laws § 146, Comment c, at 430–31 (1971).

In this case, Jacob was injured while James was operating the tractor mower in the front yard of their home in Michigan. This activity was centered in plaintiffs' Michigan community. Based on the record before us, a strong presumption exists that the law of the place of injury, Michigan, governs the substantive issues herein, unless plaintiffs can demonstrate that Michigan bears little relation to the occurrence and the parties, or put another way, that Illinois has a more significant relationship to the occurrence and the parties with respect to a particular issue.

E.   Another State With a More Significant Relationship

We now test this presumptive choice against the principles of section 6 in light of the contacts identified in section 145(2). At the outset, we observe that courts describe this analysis differently. This court has essentially first identified the four contacts listed in section 145(2) and then applied the general principles of section 6 to those contacts. . . .

We now consider the section 145 contacts presented in this case. First, the injury occurred in Michigan. As previously discussed, in a personal injury action, this raises a presumption in favor of Michigan law. Restatement (Second) of Conflict of Laws § 146 (1971). In the context of a most-significant-relationship analysis, section 145 cautions that situations exist where the place of the injury will not be an important contact, for example, where the place of the injury is fortuitous. Restatement (Second) of Conflict of Laws § 145, Comment e, at 419 (1971). In this case, however, Michigan has a strong relationship to the occurrence and the parties. Michigan is the place where James purchased the lawn tractor, the place where he used the lawn tractor, and the place where he and the named plaintiffs, his wife Michelle and his son Jacob, are domiciled and reside. . . .

The second contact in section 145 is the place where the conduct causing the injury occurred. According to plaintiffs' theories of the case, Sears committed the allegedly culpable acts in Illinois. . . . However,

Sears pled affirmative defenses alleging contributory negligence on the part of James and Michelle. . . . We view this contact as a wash.

The third contact is the domicile, residence, place of incorporation, and place of business of the parties. Here, plaintiffs reside in Michigan and Sears is headquartered in Illinois. We view this contact as a wash. The fourth contact is the place where the relationship, if any, between the parties is centered. In this case, the relationship between plaintiffs and Sears arose from James' purchase of the lawn tractor at a local Sears store doing business in Michigan. . . .

In sum, the first contact favors Michigan; we consider the second and third contacts each a wash; and the fourth contact favors Michigan. Considered alone, these contacts certainly do not override our presumption that Michigan law governs the substantive issues presented in this case. However, we must not merely "count contacts" but, rather, consider them in light of the general principles embodied in section 6.

A detailed analysis of all seven of the section 6 general principles is unnecessary. The commentary to section 145 explains that in a personal injury action, section 6(2)(d), the protection of justified expectations, and section 6(2)(f), certainty, predictability, and uniformity of result, are implicated only minimally in a personal injury action arising from an accident. Restatement (Second) of Conflict of Laws § 145, Comment b, at 415–16 (1971). Similarly, section 6(2)(a), the needs of the interstate system, is only minimally implicated in personal injury actions. It cannot be said that harmonious relations between states will be advanced by applying either Michigan or Illinois law. . . . Further, section 6(2)(g), the ease in the determination and application of the law to be applied, yields no discernible advantage to Illinois law over Michigan law in this case. . . .

Considering the policies and interests of Michigan and Illinois, and of the field of tort law, we are unable to conclude that Illinois' relationship to this case is so pivotal as to overcome the presumption that Michigan, as the state where the injury occurred, is the state with the most significant relationship.

1. Liability

The first conflict is between Illinois' strict liability standard and Michigan's negligence standard for product liability actions based on defective design. The appellate court characterized the underlying policy of Illinois' law as essentially pro-consumer and pro-corporate regulation, and characterized the underlying policy of Michigan's law as essentially producer protective. . . . The appellate court concluded: "Illinois has a strong interest in applying its products liability law to regulate culpable conduct occurring within its borders, induce the design of safer products, and deter future misconduct.". . . Reasonable minds may disagree as to the accuracy of the appellate court's characterization of the underlying policy of Michigan's negligence standard—the Supreme Court of

Michigan might. In adopting a negligence standard for product liability actions based on defective design, that court viewed a negligence standard as being pro-consumer. First, a negligence standard would reward the careful manufacturer and punish the careless manufacturer. A fault system would produce a greater incentive to design safer products, where the careful and safe design will be rewarded with fewer claims and lower insurance premiums. Second, a verdict for a plaintiff in a design defect case is the equivalent of a determination that an entire product line is defective. . . . But tort rules which limit liability are entitled to the same consideration when determining choice-of-law issues as rules that impose liability." *Malena*, 264 Neb. at 769, 651 N.W.2d at 858. We trust that characterizations such as "pro-consumer" or "pro-business" will not often appear in future choice-of-law cases.

> 2.   Compensatory Damages for Noneconomic Injuries

The next conflict is between the absence of a statutory cap on compensatory damages for noneconomic injuries in Illinois, and the existence of such a cap in Michigan. . . .

We agree with Sears that enforcement by an Illinois court of the Michigan cap on noneconomic damages does not constitute an encroachment of separation of powers in Illinois. Rather, such enforcement simply applies a Michigan statute against a Michigan resident that has been upheld as constitutional in Michigan.

> 3.   Punitive Damages

The last conflict is between the availability of punitive damages in product liability cases when appropriate, in Illinois, and the general unavailability of punitive damages in Michigan. . . .

Again, the purpose of the section 145 analysis is to test our strong presumption that the law of Michigan, where plaintiffs reside and the place of injury, should govern the substantive issues in this case. Restatement (Second) of Conflict of Laws § 146, Comment e, at 432 (1971). The appellate court characterization that Michigan "has an interest" in this conflict is an understatement that fails to recognize the strong presumption in favor of applying Michigan law. . . .

Illinois certainly has a legitimate interest in the liability to be imposed on Illinois-based defendants under strict liability or negligence principles. However, Michigan has an equally legitimate interest in the remedies to be afforded its residents who suffer such tort injuries. And if the substantive law of these two states looks in different directions, each state would seem to have an equal interest in having its tort rule applied in the determination of the conflicting issues presented in this case. . . . We conclude that a section 145 analysis does not override our strong presumption that the law of Michigan, as the state where plaintiffs reside and where the injury occurred, governs the conflicting issues presented in this case. . . .

III. CONCLUSION

For the foregoing reasons, the judgment of the appellate court and the order of the circuit court of Cook County are vacated, and this cause is remanded to the circuit court for further proceedings consistent with this opinion.

P.V. ex rel. T.V. v. Camp Jayee

Supreme Court of New Jersey, 2007.
197 N.J. 132, 462 A.D.2d 463.

■ LONG, JUSTICE.

This choice-of-law case involves the question of whether New Jersey's charitable immunity statute . . . applies to a tort committed in Pennsylvania.

Over thirty years ago, New Jersey Camp Jaycee, Inc. (Camp Jaycee) was organized as a not-for-profit corporation to operate a summer program for mentally challenged individuals. Although Camp Jaycee was incorporated in New Jersey and maintains an administrative office here, it has chosen to carry out its primary charitable mission in the Commonwealth of Pennsylvania at a campsite in the town of Effort.

In 2003, one of Camp Jaycee's campers was P.V., a twenty-one-year-old female from New Jersey with Down syndrome and mental and emotional handicaps. P.V. had attended the camp for at least three consecutive summers. According to the complaint, in August 2003, P.V. was sexually assaulted by another camper, as a result of which she sustained injuries requiring medical treatment.

P.V.'s parents, T.V. and L.V., as guardians ad litem and individually, instituted a personal injury action in New Jersey against Camp Jaycee and several fictitious defendants. . . .

The trial judge granted Camp Jaycee's motion for summary judgment on the ground that, under the CIA, the camp is immune from suit by a beneficiary. . . .

Although the Court recognizes the vitality of New Jersey's own policy of immunizing charities, in this case, it must yield to the presumption favoring application of Pennsylvania law, which has not been overcome.

Traditionally, New Jersey courts, like those of most jurisdictions, followed the bright-line rules embodied in the Restatement (First) of Conflict of Laws (1934). . . . In 1967, New Jersey joined other jurisdictions in abandoning the First Restatement approach to tort cases, embracing the modern governmental interest analysis, traditionally described as an approach by which courts seek to assess countervailing state laws through statutory construction and other interpretative mechanisms to determine whether the states' policies are aligned with either party in the litigation. Four years after our adoption of the governmental interest analysis, and seventeen years after the reform effort had been undertaken, the Second Restatement was finalized. In place of black letter law, the Second Restatement contains presumptions and detailed considerations that bear on conflicts analysis, in particular a "general presumption" (section 146) and factors and principles to be considered in determining which state has the most significant relationship to the occurrence and the parties (sections 6 and 145). Although continuing to denominate our standard as a kind of governmental interest test, we now apply the Second Restatement's most significant relationship standard in tort cases. . . .

The Second Restatement also provides specific guidance for resolving particular types of cases. See, e.g., Restatement, supra, ch. 8 ("Contracts"). In connection with tort, section 145 of chapter 7 is entitled "The General Principle" and prescribes that: "The rights and liabilities of the parties with respect to an issue in tort are determined by the local law of the state which, with respect to that issue, has the most significant relationship to the occurrence and the parties under the principles stated in § 6." Restatement, supra, § 145(1). The contacts that are weighed in making that assessment include:

(a) the place where the injury occurred,

(b) the place where the conduct causing the injury occurred,

(c) the domicil, residence, nationality, place of incorporation and place of business of the parties, and

(d) the place where the relationship, if any, between the parties is centered.

Although the Second Restatement eschews the bright lines established by its predecessor, it does not abandon all rules:

"Once one ventures past section 145, however, the chapter dramatically changes character. Instead of infinitely open-ended sections, the Second Restatement, for the most part, articulates reasonably definite rules. To be sure, these succeeding sections contain escape valves that refer to section 6. Many of the rules echo the First Restatement's preference for choosing the law of the injury state. Others do not refer to the injury state directly, but choose connecting factors very likely, if not certain, to lead to the application of the law of the injury state. . . . Only a relatively few sections refer solely to the general formula of section 145 without providing some presumptive choice." [Patrick J. Borchers, Courts and the Second Conflicts Restatement: Some Observations and an Empirical Note, 56 Md. L. Rev. 1232, 1239–40 (1997) (footnotes omitted).]

The Court must first determine whether an actual conflict exists. Here, it is clear, as the parties have conceded, that an actual conflict exists between the laws of Pennsylvania and New Jersey. . . .

Section 146 of the Second Restatement recognizes the intuitively correct principle that the state in which the injury occurs is likely to have the predominant, if not exclusive, relationship to the parties and issues in the litigation. It is from that vantage point that we turn to the remaining contacts set forth in section 145 and the cornerstone principles of section 6. On one side of the contacts ledger, P.V. and Camp Jaycee are co-domiciliaries of New Jersey. On the other side of the ledger, Camp Jaycee chose to perform the sole charitable function for which it was organized in Pennsylvania; P.V. chose to attend a camp in Pennsylvania; the relationship between P.V. and Camp Jaycee was centered on the camp experience in Pennsylvania; the tortious conduct (negligent supervision) took place solely in Pennsylvania; and P.V. was injured in Pennsylvania. Standing alone, New Jersey's contacts are certainly no greater than those of Pennsylvania. However, because our analysis is not merely quantitative, we also look to the principles of section 6 to measure the significance of those contacts. In other words, do the section 6 considerations gin up or diminish the values to be ascribed to the contacts relative to the issue presented?

* * *

Although both New Jersey and Pennsylvania have strong countervailing policies regarding immunity, Pennsylvania's policy of conduct-regulation and recompense is deeply intertwined with the various Pennsylvania contacts in the case. On the contrary, New Jersey's loss-allocation policy does not warrant the assignment of priority to the parties' domicile in New Jersey in connection with activities outside the state's borders. In short, neither the contacts themselves nor the section 6 considerations support the conclusion that New Jersey has a more significant relationship to the case than Pennsylvania. In fact, the converse is true. Although we recognize the vitality of our own policy of immunizing charities, in this case, it must yield to the presumption favoring application of Pennsylvania law, which has not been overcome.

The judgment of the Appellate Division is affirmed. The case is remanded to the trial court for further proceedings consistent with the principles to which we have adverted.

■ HONES, JUSTICE, dissenting.

Today, a majority of this Court has chosen to adopt a new framework for deciding conflict of law disputes. Although stating that there is nothing novel in its approach, and although supporting that assertion with citations to parts of this Court's prior opinions (both majorities and dissents) as proof that this Court has long used the analytical model embodied in the Restatement (Second) of Conflict of Laws (1971), in reality, the majority has substituted that test for our traditional one. At the same time, the majority has tossed aside our far more nuanced "governmental interest" approach, in which the factors identified by the Restatement (Second) were but an occasionally useful guide, and embraced in its place the Restatement (Second)'s "most-significant-relationship" test. . . .

NOTE

Now consider whether the New York Court of Appeals, the court with the firmest claim to having started the judicial Conflicts Revolution would have reached the same results. Would the expanded *Neumeier* rules have reached the same result as did the Illinois Supreme Court in *Townsend*? In P.V. v. Camp Jaycee, do you think the New Jersey Supreme Court was motivated by dissatisfaction with interest analysis or by a desire to avoid a similar result to the New York *Schultz* decision?

Edwards v. Erie Coach Lines Co.

Court of Appeals of New York, 2011.
17 N.Y.3d 306, 952 N.E.2d 1033, 929 N.Y.S.2d 41.

■ READ, JUDGE.

Near Geneseo, New York on January 19, 2005 a charter bus carrying members of an Ontario women's hockey team plowed into the rear end of a tractor-trailer parked on the shoulder of the highway. Three bus passengers and the tractor driver died; several bus passengers were seriously hurt. We are called upon to decide the choice-of-law issue presented by these six lawsuits, which were brought to recover damages for wrongful death and/or personal injuries. . . .

We have routinely applied the Neumeier [v. Kuehner, p. 592 supra] framework to conflicts in loss-allocation situations not involving guest statutes. For example, the issue in Schultz v. Boy Scouts of Am., 65 N.Y.2d 189, 491 N.Y.S.2d, 90, 480 N.E.2d 679 (1985) was whether the doctrine of charitable immunity would apply in a lawsuit brought by plaintiffs domiciled in New Jersey. The plaintiffs were the parents of two boys, one of whom committed suicide. They sued the Boy Scouts of America and the Brothers of the Poor of St. Francis, Inc. for negligent hiring and supervision of a sexually abusive brother (also a defendant), who was supplied by the Franciscan Brothers, pursuant to an agreement with the Roman Catholic Archdiocese of Newark, as a teacher at a school owned and operated by the Archdiocese, and who was a scoutmaster of a Boy Scout troop sponsored by the school and chartered by the Boy Scouts. The plaintiffs' sons attended the class taught by the brother at the school, and were members of his scout troop.

Acts of sexual abuse were alleged to have taken place mostly during Boy Scout camping outings in New York, but also at the school in New Jersey. The Boy Scouts were domiciled in New Jersey; the Franciscan Brothers in Ohio. At the time the plaintiffs' causes of action arose, New Jersey and Ohio both recognized charitable immunity while New York did not. The Ohio rule, however, denied immunity in actions based on negligent hiring and supervision. And the plaintiffs' claims had already been determined to have been barred by the New Jersey doctrine of charitable immunity in an earlier action brought by the plaintiffs in New Jersey against the Archdiocese. We held that New Jersey law governed, and that the plaintiffs were precluded from relitigating its effect in light of the final determination in their action against the Archdiocese.

Under the first *Neumeier* rule, New Jersey law clearly controlled the plaintiffs' claim against the Boy Scouts because the plaintiffs and this defendant had "chosen to identify themselves in the most concrete form possible, domicile, with a jurisdiction that [had] weighed the interests of charitable tort-feasors and their victims and decided to retain the defense of charitable immunity" But because this was "the first case for our review [where] New York [was] the forum-locus rather than the parties' common domicile," we examined "the reasons most often advanced for applying the law of the forum-locus and those supporting application of the law of the common domicile"

> We identified those reasons "most often urged" to favor the forum-locus as "(1) to protect medical creditors who provided services to injured parties in the locus State, (2) to prevent injured tort victims from becoming public wards in the locus State and (3) the deterrent effect application of locus law [would have] on future tortfeasors in the locus State" We opined that the first two reasons shared "common weaknesses," since neither "necessarily require[d] application of the locus jurisdiction's law, but rather invariably mandate[d] application of the law of the jurisdiction that would either allow recovery or allow . . . greater recovery." As a result, they were "subject to criticism . . . as being biased in favor of recovery." Further, we observed, neither consideration was relevant in Schultz since there was no evidence of unpaid medical creditors or that the plaintiffs were about to become wards of the state. As for the third reason, we acknowledged that although it was "conceivable that application of New York's law in this case would have some deterrent effect on future tortious conduct" in New York, our "deterrent interest [was] considerably less because none of the parties [was] a resident and the rule in conflict [was] loss-allocating rather than conduct-regulating"

On the other side of the ledger, we toted up "persuasive reasons for consistently applying the law of the parties' common domicile." These included (1) reduced opportunities for forum shopping; (2) rebuttal of "charges that the forum-locus is biased in favor of its own laws and in favor of rules permitting recovery"; (3) "the concepts of mutuality and reciprocity support consistent application of the common-domicile rule" since "[i]n any given case, one person could be either plaintiff or defendant and one State could be either the parties' common domicile or the locus, and yet the applicable law would not change depending on their status"; and (4) such a rule was "easy to apply and [brought] a modicum of predictability and certainty to an area of the law needing both."

We then turned our attention to the plaintiffs' claim against the Franciscan Brothers. We evaluated choice of law with respect to this defendant under the third Neumeier rule "because the parties [were] domiciled in different jurisdictions with conflicting loss-distribution rules and the locus of the tort [was] New York, a separate jurisdiction"; and the law of the place of the tort would "normally apply." We decided, however, that this situation fit the proviso to the third rule "[f]or the same reasons stated in our analysis of the action against" the Boy Scouts; namely, this result "would further [New Jersey's] interest in enforcing the decision of its domiciliaries to accept the burdens as well as the benefits of that State's loss-distribution tort rules and its interest in promoting the continuation and expansion of [the Franciscan Brothers'] charitable activities in that State." In addition, "although application of New Jersey's law may not affirmatively advance the substantive law purposes of New York, it will not frustrate those interests because New York has no significant interest in applying its own law to this dispute. Finally, application of New Jersey law will enhance the smooth working of the multi-state system by actually reducing the incentive for forum shopping and it will provide certainty for the litigants whose only reasonable expectation surely would have been that the law of the jurisdiction where plaintiffs are domiciled and defendant sends its teachers would apply, not the law of New York where the parties had only isolated and infrequent contacts as a result of [the brother's] position as Boy Scout leader."

Finally, we rejected the plaintiffs' argument that New York public policy foreclosed application of the New Jersey charitable immunity statute. We emphasized the difficulty of upsetting the choice of law in a conflicts situation on this basis; specifically, the proponent of a public policy bar would have to "establish that to enforce the foreign law 'would violate some fundamental principle of justice, some prevalent conception of good morals, some deep-rooted tradition of the common weal' expressed in them" Further, "the proponent must establish that there [were] enough important contacts between the parties, the occurrence and the New York forum to implicate our public policy and thus preclude enforcement of the foreign law" We concluded that we did not need to decide whether enforcement of New Jersey's charitable immunity statute offended New York public policy "because there [were] not sufficient contacts between New York, the parties and the transactions involved to implicate our public policy and call for its enforcement."

II.

The charter bus's driver (Ryan A. Comfort), his employer (Erie Coach Lines Company), and the company that leased the bus (Trentway-Wagar, Inc.) are Ontario domiciliaries, as are (or were) all the injured and deceased passengers. The tractor-trailer driver (Ernest Zeiset) was a

Pennsylvania domiciliary, as are his employer (Joseph French, doing business as J & J Trucking) and the companies that hired the trailer (Verdelli Farms, Inc. and VF. Transportation, Inc.). The injured passengers and the representatives of those who died (collectively, plaintiffs) filed multiple wrongful death and personal injury lawsuits in Supreme Court.

These split-domicile lawsuits presented an obvious choice-of-law issue because Ontario caps noneconomic damages where negligence causes catastrophic personal injury while New York does not cap such damages in a no-fault case involving serious injury. Following extensive discovery, Erie Coach, Trentway and Comfort (collectively, the bus defendants) and J & J Trucking, the administratrix of Zeiset's estate, Verdelli Farms and V.F. Transportation (collectively, the trailer defendants) moved for orders from Supreme Court determining that, under New York's choice-of-law principles, Ontario law applied to "all loss allocation issues" in these cases.

On March 23, 2009, Supreme Court granted both motions, noting that the Supreme Court of Canada had capped noneconomic damages at CDN $100,000 in 1978 dollars, which was then equivalent to U.S. $310,000. In reaching its decisions, the court concluded that "[p]roper analysis" began with Neumeier. Citing the third Neumeier rule, the judge stated, without elaboration, that "[a]pplying Ontario loss allocation laws [would] not impair the smooth working of the multi-state system, and [would] advance the relevant substantive law purposes of the jurisdiction having the most significant connections to the allocation of loss"; and that Ontario "clearly [had] the predominant interest[ ] in applying its loss allocation laws to its citizens, whereas New York [had] no such interest." Further, Supreme Court discussed Schultz which it regarded as analogous; it saw no reason to consider Pennsylvania law since none of the parties requested this.

The trial of these cases was bifurcated, and, during the course of the jury trial on liability, the parties reached a settlement of that issue. In the stipulation of settlement, placed on the record on June 17, 2009, the bus defendants agreed to 90% and the trailer defendants to 10% liability. Meanwhile, plaintiffs had appealed Supreme Court's orders determining that Ontario law would govern any award of noneconomic damages to be made at a damages trial. The Appellate Division affirmed.

The Appellate Division agreed with Supreme Court's bottom-line conclusion that the Ontario cap applied to damages covered from the bus and trailer defendants, but conducted separate choice-of-law analyses. With respect to the bus defendants, the court looked to the first Neumeier rule, which directs that the law of the parties' common domicile—here, Ontario—governs. The court observed that applying the law of a shared domicile reduced the risk of forum shopping; rebutted the charge of local bias; and served " 'the concepts of mutuality and reciprocity,' " which are "support[ed by the] consistent application of the common domicile law"

As between plaintiffs and the trailer defendants, the Appellate Division applied the third *Neumeier* rule, which prefers the law of the place of the tort. Invoking the proviso to the third rule, the court decided, however, that Ontario law should govern, reasoning that "while applying Ontario law '[might] not affirmatively advance the substantive law purposes of New York, it [would] not frustrate those interests because New York has no significant interest in applying its own law to this dispute'" quoting Schultz The court also commented that New York law created great uncertainty for the litigants because the trailer defendants were only 10% liable for the accident pursuant to the parties' settlement. If the trailer defendants' exposure to noneconomic damages was unlimited while the bus defendants' liability for this item of damages was capped, the trailer defendants might end up paying far more than their stipulated share.

Finally, the Appellate Division concluded that plaintiffs failed to meet the "'heavy burden' of establishing that the application of Ontario law violate[d] the public policy of New York" (quoting *Schultz*). The court pointed out that "resort to the public policy exception should be reserved for those foreign laws that are truly obnoxious" which was not the case here. In any event, the Appellate Division decided that the parties' contacts were too few and limited in scope to implicate New York's public policy.

The Appellate Division granted plaintiffs permission to appeal, and asked us whether its orders were properly made. For the reasons that follow, we answer "No" with respect to the trailer defendants. * * *

Next, plaintiffs press for what they call a "single, joint *Neumeier* analysis" in cases, such as this one, with multiple tortfeasors. As a result, the Edwards plaintiffs argue, the trial judge "properly analyzed both sets of Defendants—those related to the bus and those related to the tractor trailer—together," although he reached the wrong conclusion. In our view, however, the correct way to conduct a choice-of-law analysis is to consider each plaintiff vis-à-vis each defendant, which is essentially the approach taken by the Appellate Division. More to the point, this is the path we ourselves have already traveled: in *Schultz* the plaintiffs likewise demanded judgment, jointly and severally, against multiple defendants, and we applied the Neumeier rules separately in relation to the New Jersey-domiciled Boy Scouts and the Ohio-domiciled Franciscan Brothers. The rules in the Neumeier framework, in fact, by their very nature call for a plaintiff-by-defendant inquiry.

Here, the Ontario cap controls any award of noneconomic damages against the bus defendants because they share an Ontario domicile with plaintiffs. . . .

In sum, Ontario has weighed the interests of tortfeasors and their victims in cases of catastrophic personal injury, and has elected to safeguard its domiciliaries from large awards for nonpecuniary damages. In lawsuits brought in New York by Ontario-domiciled plaintiffs against

Ontario-domiciled defendants, New York courts should respect Ontario's decision, which differs from but certainly does not offend New York's public policy.

Finally, we look to the third *Neumier* rule to decide whether the Ontario cap controls with respect to the trailer defendants. Critically, the third rule establishes the place of the tort—here, New York—as the "normally applicable" choice in a conflicts situation such as this one, where the domicile of plaintiffs, the domicile of the trailer defendants and the place of the tort are different. Initially, the fact that the trailer defendants declined to advocate for Pennsylvania law does not permit them to take advantage of the Ontario cap. To rule otherwise would only encourage a kind of forum shopping. Moreover, the stipulation of settlement on liability is not relevant to "interest analysis," which seeks to recognize and respect the policy interests of a jurisdiction in the resolution of the particular issue where a conflict of law exists.

The trailer defendants contend that *Schultz* controls, meaning that their situation is comparable to that of the Franciscan Brothers, and so the law of New York should not govern, even though the accident occurred there. We do not agree. While New York employs "interest analysis" rather than "grouping of contacts," the number and intensity of contacts is relevant when considering whether to deviate from lex loci delicti under the third Neumeier rule i.e., whether even to analyze if displacing this "normally applicable" choice would "advance the relevant substantive law purposes without impairing the smooth working of the multi-state system or producing great uncertainty for litigants" (*Neumeier*, 31 N.Y.2d at 128, 335 N.Y.S.2d 64, 286 N.E.2d 454).

In *Schultz*, New Jersey was the state where the Franciscan Brothers supplied teachers for a New Jersey school, where some of the acts of sexual abuse allegedly took place, where one of the boys committed suicide, where the two boys allegedly suffered from and were treated for psychological injuries, where the Franciscan Brothers were said to have hired and failed to fire the brother. Under these circumstances, there was every reason to evaluate, under the proviso to the rule, whether New Jersey law should displace New York law with respect to the negligent hiring and supervision claim asserted against the Franciscan Brothers in the plaintiffs' lawsuit. Here, by contrast, there was no cause to contemplate a jurisdiction other than New York, the place where the conduct causing injuries and the injuries themselves occurred. The trailer defendants did not ask Supreme Court to consider the law of their domicile, Pennsylvania, and they had no contacts whatsoever with Ontario other than the happenstance that plaintiffs and the bus defendants were domiciled there.

Accordingly, the orders in these cases should be modified, without costs, in accordance with this opinion and as so modified, affirmed, and the certified questions answered in the negative.

■ CIPARICK, JUDGE (dissenting in part).

Because I believe that a single analysis pursuant to Neumeier v. Kuehner should be applied where nondomiciliary defendants are jointly and severally liable to nondomiciliary plaintiffs in a tort action arising out of a single incident within the State of New York, and that under such an analysis New York law should apply to all defendants for purposes of uniformity and predictability, I respectfully dissent. . . .

While the facts in *Schutlz* lent themselves to a separate analysis for each defendant, the facts in this case do not justify such an analysis. The plaintiffs in Schultz alleged that the two defendants, the Boy Scouts of America and the Brothers of the Poor of St. Francis, had each negligently hired and supervised the same sexually abusive employee. The alleged sexual abuse occurred while the plaintiffs' sons were at a Boy Scout camp in New York and continued at a school in New Jersey. The tortious activities in Schultz took place over varied periods of time and in different locations. Moreover, there was no relationship between the defendants' actions other than the fact that they employed the same alleged bad actor. Because the torts were distinct acts occurring at different times, it was appropriate for us to perform a separate choice-of-law analysis.

In contrast, in the instant case, the causes of action arise from a single incident in New York—the collision of the bus into the parked tractor-trailer—and the liability of the defendants is interrelated.

Furthermore, a separate *Neumeier* analysis for differently domiciled defendants creates additional unpredictability and lack of uniformity in litigation that arises from a single incident. . . . [A]nalyzing this matter under a single *Neumeier* analysis, it is clear that, because plaintiffs and defendants are differently domiciled, the law of the site of the tort—here New York—should apply as set forth in the third *Neumeir* rule. Moreover, the exception to the third Neumeier rule does not apply to these facts.

Indeed, applying New York law here will not "impair . . . the smooth working of the multi-state system and produce great uncertainty for litigants by sanctioning forum shopping." New York was the site of the accident and the only state in which jurisdiction over all defendants could be acquired. New York is a proper location for this action and there is no indication that the cases were brought bore on account of its favorable loss-allocation rules.

In addition, the exception to the third *Neumeier* rule should only apply when a state other than the forum-locus state has a "greate[r] interest in the litigation" Here, it is uncontroverted that both defendants are commercial enterprises that perform significant business in the State of New York and more significantly are frequent users of New York's highways in pursuit of their business. New York has a strong interest in the conduct of business enterprises on its highways and in properly compensating the victims of torts, whether New York or foreign domiciliaries, committed by business enterprises on its highways (see Sullivan v. McNicholas Transfer Co., 224 A.D.2d 966, 967, 638 N.Y.S.2d 260 [4th Dept.1996] [applying Ohio law to an accident in Ohio because "Ohio has a substantial interest in regulating conduct on its highways and in ensuring that those who use its highway(s) will compensate those whom they have injured"]).

Thus, in determining which forum has the greatest interest in this litigation, it is clear that it is New York. Not only does New York have a strong interest in regulating the conduct of commercial vehicles on its highways, it also has an even stronger interest in having commercial vehicles that use its highways maintain insurance to compensate victims of torts committed by said vehicles. In contrast, Ontario's primary interest in having its law applied and capping nonpecuniary losses is to keep motor vehicle insurance costs low (see Arnold v. Teno, [1978] 2 SCR 287 ¶ 109). That interest, however, need not extend to commercial vehicles operating outside of Ontario and subject to the loss-allocation laws of those states.

Finally, because New York is "the only State with which [all] parties have purposefully associated themselves" (*Cooney*, 81 N.Y.2d at 74, 595 N.Y.S.2d 919, 612 N.E.2d 277) and availed themselves of New York highways for profit and tourism, applying New York law is entirely appropriate in this matter.

Accordingly, I would reverse the order of the Appellate Division.

NOTE

Did New York have a greater interest in holding the relevant defendants liable under New York law in *Schultz* or *Edwards*?

Jaffe v. Pallottta Teamworks, 374 F.3d 1223 (D.C.Cir.2004). A D.C. resident, while on a bicycle ride in Virginia to raise funds for charity, died after receiving treatment from the University of Maryland Medical System Corporation (UMMS), which provided medical services for the ride. The decedent had signed a release that exempted UMMS from liability for negligence. Under Virginia law the release was void but its status under D.C. law was unclear. Held: Virginia law applies and the release is void. "Virginia obviously has an interest in preventing non-residents from being negligently injured or killed within its borders." Id. at 1228.

Most states that have abandoned the First Restatement do not articulate rules à la *Neumeier*. Over time, the case law in these states is likely to produce similar responses to similar law-fact patterns. A statement summarizing these responses is a "rule," but one that reflects the results in a series of related cases that the courts regard as reaching desirable choice-of-law results. For a survey of the practice of a number of states against the background of the New York *Neumeier* Rules, see Hay & Ellis, Bridging the Gap Between Rules and Approaches in Tort Choice of Law in the United States: A Survey of Current Case Law, 27 Int'l Law. 369 (1993).

Sterne, Agee & Leach, Inc. v. U.S. Bank Nat'l Ass'n

Supreme Court of Alabama, 2014.
148 So. 3d 1060.

■ BOLIN, JUSTICE.

U.S. Bank National Association and U.S. Bancorp (hereinafter collectively referred to as "U.S. Bank") seek a writ of mandamus ordering the Jefferson Circuit Court to dismiss the malicious-prosecution case filed against them by Sterne, Agee & Leach, Inc. ("Sterne Agee"), that arose out of a lawsuit prosecuted by U.S. Bank entirely in the State of Washington.

Facts and Procedural History

In 2002, Sterne Agee, a Delaware corporation with headquarters in Alabama and offices in Seattle, Washington, acted as the underwriter in Washington for securities offered by a Washington business entity. Under the Washington State Securities Act, Sterne Agee was a "seller" of the securities. In 2004, in federal district court in Washington, U.S. Bank sued Sterne Agee, among others, alleging that the defendants had violated the Washington State Securities Act through a series of material omissions in the securities offering. U.S. Bank obtained default judgments or entered into settlement agreements with all the defendants except Sterne Agee. . . .

On July 1, 2011, Sterne Agee sued U.S. Bank in the Jefferson Circuit Court, alleging malicious prosecution arising out of the lawsuit prosecuted by U.S. Bank in Washington. The case was removed to the United States District Court for the Northern District of Alabama, which subsequently remanded the case to Jefferson Circuit Court. . . . U.S. Bank petitioned . . . for a writ of mandamus. . . .

U.S. Bank sought to have the circuit court certify the conflict-of-laws issue for a permissive appeal. . . .

In light of the foregoing, we now turn to the legal issue before us.

The principle that governs which state's substantive law applies to tort claims in a conflict-of-laws analysis is well settled: "Lex loci delicti has been the rule in Alabama for almost 100 years. Under this principle, an Alabama court will determine the substantive rights of an injured party according to the law of the state where the injury occurred." * * * Accordingly, our review of the denial of the motion to dismiss this malicious-prosecution action is based upon the principle of lex loci delicti.

The parties agree that under the principle of lex loci delicti the governing law is the law of the jurisdiction where the injury occurred. The parties disagree, however, as to where an injury occurs for purposes of a malicious-prosecution claim. U.S. Bank argues that the injury in a malicious-prosecution action occurs in the state where the defense of the allegedly malicious prosecution occurred. It reasons that because "injury" is the last element of a cause of action for any tort, including malicious prosecution, the injury resulting from malicious prosecution occurs where the last event necessary to make the actor liable for the alleged tort takes place. In this case, it argues, the last event necessary occurred in Washington when the securities action was terminated in favor of Sterne Agee. Sterne Agee argues that because the injury suffered in a malicious-prosecution action is financial, the injury occurs where the financial harm was felt. In this case, it argues, the financial harm was felt, and thus the injury occurred, at its corporate headquarters in Alabama.

Unlike Alabama, Washington follows the "English rule" for malicious-prosecution claims, which requires a plaintiff to plead arrest or seizure of property. See Clark v. Baines, 150 Wash. 2d 905, 84 P.3d 245 (2004). Because no arrest or seizure has occurred in this situation, U.S. Bank argues that, under Washington law, Sterne Agee cannot state a malicious-prosecution claim.

For the reasons below, we find that injury in a malicious-prosecution action occurs in the state where the allegedly malicious lawsuit was terminated in favor of the complaining party. Therefore, the principle of lex loci delicti requires that the law of the state in which the antecedent lawsuit was litigated governs a claim of malicious prosecution.

Alabama continues to follow the traditional view of the Restatement (First) of Conflicts of Law, as discussed in Fitts v. Minnesota Min. & Mfg. Co., supra, which looks to the lex loci delicti in tort claims, "in the state where the last event necessary to make an actor liable for an alleged tort takes place." Restatement (First) of Conflict of Laws § 377 (1934). This interpretation adheres to the holding of the seminal lex loci delicti case in Alabama, Alabama Great S. R.R. v. Carroll, 97 Ala. 126, 11 So. 803 (1892). In *Carroll*, the plaintiff resided in Alabama and was employed by an Alabama corporation as a brakeman on the corporation's railroad. The plaintiff was injured when a link between two freight cars broke in Mississippi. However, two employees in Alabama had failed to inspect the link before the train left for Mississippi. Although Alabama law recognized a cause of action for injuries caused by the negligence of fellow employees, Mississippi law did not. Following the traditional rule, the Alabama Supreme Court applied the law of the place of the injury (Mississippi), despite the facts that the acts giving rise to the plaintiff's injuries occurred in Alabama and that the plaintiff was employed in Alabama. The Court stated that negligence without injury will not support recovery.

* * *

In the present case, the "fact which created the right to sue" was the termination of the allegedly malicious lawsuit in favor of Sterne Agee, which occurred in Washington. Thus, the principle of lex loci delicti requires that Washington law govern Sterne Agee's malicious-prosecution claim. . . .

For a malicious-prosecution claim, the event creating the right to sue is not the expenditure of financial resources in order to defend a lawsuit. Such expenses would be made even if the antecedent lawsuit was ultimately terminated in favor of the defendant. It is the determination that such expenses were required to defend an allegedly malicious prosecution (by termination in favor of the complaining party) that creates the right to sue. . . .

Alabama courts' application of the principle of lex loci delicti to cases involving the tort of bad-faith failure to defend a lawsuit are more on point with the present case. Like malicious prosecution, bad-faith failure to defend is based on injury resulting from an antecedent lawsuit, and the injury often involves more than mere financial harm. . . .

Conclusion

The principle of lex loci delicti requires that the law of the state in which the antecedent lawsuit was terminated in favor of the complaining party governs a malicious-prosecution claim. Thus, Washington law governs Sterne Agee's claim of malicious prosecution. Accordingly, U.S. Bank's petition for writ for mandamus is granted, and the circuit court is ordered to dismiss Sterne Agee's malicious-prosecution case.

NOTE

Is the rule that a malicious prosecution tort be judged by where the suit is filed a good rule? If not, what would be a better rule? If the Alabama Supreme Court had applied interest analysis, what result would you expect it to reach?

5.   INTERNATIONAL CONSIDERATIONS

The U.S. conflicts revolution played to mixed reviews abroad. As shown in the summaries of some of the international codifications noted below, its greatest influence was in applying the common geographical link of parties in a conflict involving a loss allocating tort rule and in the fundamental division between loss allocation and conduct regulating rules.

In some respects, the American conflicts revolution merely played "catch up" to international trends. The most notable was in party autonomy in which the U.S. courts were well behind many of their international counterparts in giving effect to effect to party choice as to forum and applicable law. In their enthusiasm, U.S. courts overtook many of their foreign counterparts by enforcing agreements—most notably those involving consumers—what would not be enforced in many other nations.

To be sure, the chapter thus far has not ignored choice-of-law questions involving foreign nations. We have presented cases involving the Canadian province of Ontario as well as Great Britain and Mexican states. Though those have not presented especially difficult questions, and those that a U.S. practicing lawyer is mostly likely to confront, there are many other issues that a lawyer with a truly international practice will confront. Thus, in this section we present a case involving a more involved international conflict and a survey of some of those choice-of-law codes of other nations.

Changes in the Conflicts Rules of Other Countries

As of 2020, forty states plus the District of Columbia and Puerto Rico have adopted a method of choosing law for torts that does not depend entirely on the locus of the liability-creating events. What follows is a summary of international developments.

United Kingdom

Red Sea Insurance Co. v. Bouygues SA, [1994] 3 W.L.R. 926, [1994] 3 All. E.R. 749 (P.C.1994) (appeal taken from Hong Kong). A number of companies were engaged in a joint venture to construct buildings in Saudi Arabia. The joint venturers discovered structural damage to the buildings and, when their insurers rejected a claim for compensation, the joint venturers sued the insurer at its place of incorporation, Hong Kong. The insurer counterclaimed against one member of the joint venture contending the member had supplied faulty materials that caused the damage. The counterclaim was based on the insurer's subrogation to the rights of the other insured members of the venture. Under the law of Saudi Arabia, the insurer could bring its subrogation action before paying the claim, but under Hong Kong law, the insurer first had to pay, which it had not done. The Hong Kong courts, at trial and on appeal, held that the insurer could not bring the subrogation claim in Hong Kong, because under the English rule, the wrong had to be actionable under both the lex loci delicti and the lex fori. The Privy Council reversed on the ground that on the issue of the right to subrogation, the most significant relationship with the occurrence and the parties was with Saudi Arabia and therefore Saudi law applied. Although double actionability remained the usual rule, in order to avoid injustice in particular cases, the law of the place of most significant relationship could be applied either to a single issue and to replace the lex loci delicti (as in Chaplin v. Boys, discussed below), or to all issues and to replace the lex fori (as in this case).

In Chaplin v. Boys, [1971] A.C. 356, a motor vehicle collision in Malta involved two English servicemen who were stationed there. Under Maltese law, the injured serviceman could not recover for his pain and suffering, but under English law he could. The five-member panel of the House of Lords decided unanimously that English law should apply, but each Lord wrote a separate opinion. Lords Hodson and Wilberforce based their analysis on the respective interests of Malta and England in the issue. Lords Guest and Donovan characterized damages as "procedural." Lord Pearson rejected the procedural characterization of damages but stated that if the act was not justifiable where committed, when the plaintiff sued in England, English law should play the predominant role in determining the extent of compensation. Lords Donovan and Pearson stated they would not permit English damages law to apply if, unlike this case, the plaintiff was forum shopping. Could a judge determine whether a plaintiff was forum shopping without inquiring into whether the plaintiff's contacts with England gave England a reasonable interest in applying its law?

On November 8, 1995, Parliament passed The Private International Law (Miscellaneous Provisions) Act. Part III of the Act abolishes the double actionability rule for tort or delict (§ 10) and replaces it with a presumption that the applicable law is that of the place of injury (§ 11). This presumption is rebutted as to one or more issues arising in a case, if it is "substantially more appropriate" to apply the law of another country (§ 12). The Act applies to "acts or omissions giving rise to a claim which occur" after the Act takes effect (§ 14(1)). There is a "public policy" exception (§ 14(3)(a)(i)). The Act does not affect choice of law for defamation (§ 13).

Roerig v. Valiant Trawlers Ltd., [2002] 1 All E.R. 961 (Ct.App.2002), diminished the likelihood that the 1995 Act and its § 12 would lead to decisions more focused on the consequences of choosing law. A Dutch seaman employed by a Dutch company was killed on a trawler registered in England and owned by an English company that was a subsidiary of a Dutch company. His widow sued to recover loss of dependency for herself and the couple's children. Under Dutch law, death benefits that the widow and children would receive, including two pensions, would be deducted from the recovery. The policy underlying the Dutch deduction is "that society provides for its victims and their dependents to an acceptable and reasonably high minimum, which is usually elevated by provisions arranged by the industry they are/were working in." Id. at 964. Under English law there would be no deduction. The court held that English law applied stating that "[t]he general rule [of the law of the place of injury under § 11] is not to be dislodged easily." Id. at 968. As an alternative ground, the court stated that whether there were to be deductions from damages related to quantification of damages and therefore was "procedural." Id. Procedural issues were governed by the law of the forum. In the course of its procedural discussion, the court quoted with approval from Stevens v. Head, 176 C.L.R. 433 (Austl. 1993), (id. at 971–72), which characterized the lex loci's statutory cap on non-economic damages as procedural, apparently unaware that the High Court of Australia had two years previously overruled Stevens. See John Pfeiffer Pty. Ltd. v. Rogerson, 172 A.R. 625 (Austl.2000).

Germany

On June 1, 1999, the long awaited further codification of German conflicts law entered into force. The new code contains rules for torts, unjust enrichment, property, and negotiorum gestio (agent by necessity). The tort rules are as follows (translation by editors):

Article 40

Tort

(1) Claims arising from tort are governed by the law of the state in which the person liable to provide compensation acted. The injured

person may demand, however, that the law of the state where the result took effect be applied instead. The right to make this election may be exercised only in the court of first instance and then only until the end of the first oral proceeding or the end of written pretrial proceeding.

(2) If the person liable to provide compensation and the injured person had their habitual residence in the same state at the time the act took place, the law of that state shall be applied. In the case of enterprises, associations, or legal persons the place of their principal administration, or, in the case of a branch, its location, shall be the equivalent of habitual residence.

(3) Claims that are governed by the law of another state may not be entertained to the extent that they

1.   go substantially beyond that which is required for appropriate compensation for the injured

person,

2.   obviously serve purposes other than provision of appropriate compensation for the injured

person, or

3.   conflict with provisions concerning liability contained in a treaty that is in force with respect to the Federal Republic of Germany.

(4) The injured person may bring his or her claim directly against the insurer of the person liable to provide compensation if the law applicable to the tort or the law applicable to the insurance contract so provides.

Article 41

Substantially Closer Connection

(1) If there is a substantially closer connection to the law of a state other than the law that would be applicable under [Article 40 paragraphs 1 and 2] the law of that state shall be applied.

(2) In particular, a substantially closer connection may be the result of

1.   a special legal or factual relationship between the parties in connection with an obligation . . .

Article 42

Party Autonomy

After the event giving rise to a non-contractual obligation has occurred, the parties may choose the law that shall apply to the obligation; rights of third parties remain unaffected.

Austria

Federal Statute of 15 June 1978 on Private International Law

§ 1(1).   Factual situations with foreign contacts shall be judged, in regard to private law, according to the legal order to which the strongest connection exists.

§ 48(1). Noncontractual damage claims shall be judged according to the law of the state in which the damage-causing conduct occurred. However, if the persons involved have a stronger connection to the law of one and the same other state, that law shall be determinative.

Switzerland

Statute on Private International Law, Entered Into for January 1, 1989, 29 I.L.M. 1254, article 133

1. When the tortfeasor and the injured party have their habitual residence in the same State, claims based on tort are governed by the law of that State.

2. When the tortfeasor and the injured party have no habitual residence in the same state, these claims are governed by the law of the State where the tort was committed. However, if the result occurred in another State, the law of this State shall be applied if the tortfeasor could have foreseen that the damage would be suffered in that State.

3. Notwithstanding the preceding paragraphs, if and when a tort violates a judicial relationship between the tortfeasor and the injured party, claims based on this act are governed by the law applying to this judicial relationship.

———

For product liability, art. 135 allows the injured party to choose either the law of the tortfeasor's place of business or, if the product was sold there with the tortfeasor's permission, the law where the product was acquired. If foreign law applies, "no compensation can be awarded in Switzerland other than the compensation that would be granted for such damage pursuant to Swiss law."

Hungary

Decree 13 of the Presidential Council of the Hungarian People's Republic: The International Private Law, effective July 1, 1979

Section 32

(3) If the domicile of the tortfeasor and the injured party is in the same State, the law of that State shall be applied.

(4) If, according to the law governing the tortious act or omission, liability is conditioned on a finding of culpability, the existence of culpability can be determined by either the personal law of the tortfeasor or the law of the place of injury.

Québec

Civil Code of Québec Book 10 Title 2 Ch. III Sect. II § 10.3126:

The obligation to make reparation for injury caused to another is governed by the law of the country where the injurious act occurred. However, if the injury appeared in another country, the law of the latter country is applicable if the person who committed the injurious act should have foreseen that the damage would occur.

In any case where the person who committed the injurious act and the victim have their domiciles or residences in the same country, the law of that country applies.

———

Hague Convention on the Law Applicable to Traffic Accidents, 4 May 1971 (As of January 1, 2009 in force in Austria, Belarus, Belgium, Bosnia and Herzegovina, Croatia, Czech Republic, France, Latvia, Lithuania, Luxembourg, Macedonia, Netherlands, Poland, Serbia, Slovakia, Slovenia, Spain, and Switzerland; signed but not ratified in Portugal.)

Article 4

Subject to Article 5 [liability for damage to goods] the following exceptions are made to the provisions of Article 3 [applying the "internal law of the State where the accident occurred."]

(a) Where only one vehicle is involved . . . and it is registered in a State other than that where the accident occurred, the internal law of the State of registration is applicable to determine liability—towards the driver, owner or any other person having control of or an interest in the vehicle irrespective of their habitual residence—towards a victim who is a passenger and whose habitual residence is in a State other than that where the accident occurred—towards a victim who is outside the vehicle at the place of the accident and whose habitual residence is in the State of registration. . . .

(b) Where two or more vehicles are involved . . . the provisions of (a) are applicable only if all the vehicles are registered in the same State. . . .

Hague Convention on the Law Applicable to Products Liability, 2 October 1973 (As of January 1, 2009, in force in Croatia, Finland, France, Luxembourg, Macedonia, Netherlands, Norway, Serbia, Slovenia, and Spain; signed but not ratified in Belgium, Italy and Portugal.)

Article 4

The applicable law shall be the internal law of the State of the place of injury, if that state is also—(a) the place of the habitual residence of the person directly suffering damage, or (b) the principal place of business of the person claimed to be liable, or (c) the place where the product was acquired by the person directly suffering damage.

Article 5

Notwithstanding the provisions of Article 4, the applicable law shall be the internal law of the State of the habitual residence of the person directly suffering damage, if that State is also—(a) the principal place of business of the person claimed to be liable, or (b) the place where the product was acquired by the person directly suffering damage.

Article 6

Where neither of the laws designated in Articles 4 and 5 applies, the applicable law shall be the internal law of the State of the principal place of business of the person claimed to be liable, unless the claimant bases his claim upon the internal law of the State of the place of injury.

Article 7 gives the parties to "a juristic act" complete freedom to choose the law governing "formation and effect." In the absence of choice, article 8 applies "the law of the place with which the act is most closely connected," and provides that "where only one party is to effect the characteristic performance of the juristic act, it shall be presumed that the juristic act is most closely connected with the law of his or her habitual residence." Except where the subject of the act is immovables, the presumption is that the law of the situs applies. Under article 11, choice-of-law agreements cannot deprive a consumer of the protection of the mandatory rules of the consumer's habitual residence. In the absence of choice, the law of the consumer's habitual residence applies. The consumer loses this protection if the consumer concludes the contract in a place that has the same law as the place of business, unless the consumer has been invited there by the business operator.

Article 13 applies the law of the situs to rights in rem "to movables and immovables" and to "any other rights requiring registration." In the case of movables, the reference is to the situs "at the time when the events causing the acquisition or loss were completed."

Neither the law of the State of the place of injury nor the law of the State of the habitual residence of the person directly suffering damages shall be applicable by virtue of Articles 4, 5 and 6 if the person claimed to be liable establishes that he could not reasonably have foreseen that the product or his own product of the same type would be made available in that State through commercial channels.

European Community Regulation on the Law Applicable to Non-Contractual Obligations

[For the entire document, see Documentary Appendix, infra]

Article 4 General Rule

1. Unless otherwise provided for in this Regulation, the law applicable to a non-contractual obligation arising out of a tort/delict shall be the law of the country in which the damage occurs irrespective of the country in which the event giving rise to the damage occurred and irrespective of the country or countries in which the indirect consequences of that event occur.

2. However, where the person claimed to be liable and the person sustaining damage both have their habitual residence in the same country at the time when the damage occurs, the law of that country shall apply.

3. Where it is clear from all the circumstances of the case that the tort/delict is manifestly more closely connected with a country other than

that indicated in paragraphs 1 or 2, the law of that other country shall apply. A manifestly closer connection with another country might be based in particular on a pre-existing relationship between the parties, such as a contract, that is closely connected with the tort/delict in question.

———————

Article 28 of the Regulation provides that it "shall not prejudice application of international conventions to which one or more Member States are parties at the time when this Regulation is adopted and which lay down conflict-of-law rules relating to non-contractual obligations." Thus the Regulation does not affect the Traffic Accidents and Products Liability conventions, supra.

What is the meaning of "manifestly more closely connected" in 4(3)? Would it prevent 4(2) from producing the result in Haynie v. Hanson, Note 1 p. 560, supra?

Japan

On 21 June 2006, effective January 1, 2007, Japan adopted a new "Act on General Rules for Application of Laws." An English translation by six Japanese law professors is in 50 Japanese Annual of Int'l L. 87–98 (2007). The 2006 act comprehensively revised and re-titled a law originally enacted in 1898 and formerly known as the Horei.

Article 17 applies to torts the law of the place of the harm, but the law of the acts causing the harm applies if the place of harm is unforeseeable. Article 20 overrides these choices if the tort is "manifestly more closely connected" with another place, "considering that the parties had their habitual residence habitual residence in the same jurisdiction at the time when the tort occurs, the tort constitutes a breach of obligations under a contact between the parties, or other circumstances of the case" Under article 22, the injured person "may not claim any greater recovery of damages or any other remedies than those available under Japanese law." There is no recovery if the event is not unlawful under Japanese law.

There are special rules for other non-contractual obligations including agency by necessity, unjust enrichment, product liability, and defamation.

Russia

A new Russian conflicts law entered into force on March 1, 2002. Civil Code, part 3, chapter VI. Special provisions cover products liability, unfair competition, and unjust enrichment. Article 1219 covers torts.

Article 1219

1.   Rights and duties of the parties under obligations arising as the result of causing harm shall be determined according to the law of the country where the act or other circumstance took place that serves as the basis for the claim for compensation for harm. In case where, as the result of such act or other circumstance, the harm appeared in another country,

the law of this country may be applied if the one that caused harm foresaw or should have foreseen the appearance of harm in this country.

2.   Rights and duties under obligations arising as the result of causing harm abroad, if the parties are citizens or legal persons of one and the same country, shall be determined according to the law of that country. If the parties to such an obligation are not citizens of one and the same country, but are resident in one and the same country, the law of this country shall apply.

3.   The parties may agree on the application to the obligation as a result of causing harm of the law of the country of the court after an act was made or other circumstance happened that resulted in the causing of harm.

NOTE

Do these codes and conventions achieve results that accord with the policies underlying conflicting laws? Under the Products Liability Convention, if the product is foreseeably sold through commercial channels at the victim's habitual residence, should it matter whether the victim acquired it there? Under the Traffic Accidents Convention, should it make a difference that a victim or another car is not from the same state as that where the other car is registered, if they are from a state that has the same law as the state of registration?

Canada has resisted the trend away from the traditional lex loci rules. Tolofson v. Jensen, 120 D.L.R.4th 289 (Can.S.Ct.1994) disapproves of the double actionability rule for choosing law in tort cases [See Red Sea Ins. Co. v. Bouygues SA, p. 668, supra] and adopts the lex loci delicti rule. The court states, incorrectly, that although in the United States there is a trend toward applying the law of the state most concerned with the issue, "the vast majority still apply the law of the place of injury." At the time the of the Canadian decision, only about a dozen American states applied the traditional rule.

The High Court of Australia has also declared that "the lex loci delicti is the governing law with respect to torts committed in Australia but which have an interstate element." John Pfeiffer Pty. Ltd. v. Rogerson, 172 A.R. 625, 648 (Austl.2000). In Regie Nationale des Usines Renault SA v. Zhang [2002] HCA 10, the Court extended the lex loci rule to international cases.

Comparative Perspective: "Closest Connection" and "Characteristic Performance"

The Restatement, Second, § 188 calls for the application of the law of the place of the "most significant relationship" and lists a number of contacts to be taken into account in making this determination. For some contracts, such as insurance, it provides rules, which may be displaced upon a showing that another law is more significantly related to the transaction and the parties.

European Community Regulation on the Law Applicable to
Contractual Obligations (Rome I)

Article 4. Applicable Law in the Absence of Choice

1.   To the extent that the law applicable to the contract has not
been chosen in accordance with Article 3 and without prejudice to
Articles 5 to 8, the law governing the contract shall be determined as
follows:

(a) a contract for the sale of goods shall be governed by the law
of the country where the seller has his habitual residence;

(b) a contract for the provision of services shall be governed by
the law of the country where the service provider has his
habitual residence;

(c) a contract relating to a right *in rem* in immovable property
or to a tenancy of immovable property shall be governed by the
law of the country where the property is situated;

(d) notwithstanding point (c), a tenancy of immovable property
concluded for temporary private use for a period of no more than
six consecutive months shall be governed by the law of the
country where the landlord has his habitual residence, provided
that the tenant is a natural person and has his habitual
residence in the same country;

(e) a franchise contract shall be governed by the law of the
country where the franchisee has his habitual residence;

(f) a distribution contract shall be governed by the law of the
country where the distributor has his habitual residence;

(g) a contract for the sale of goods by auction shall be governed
by the law of the country where the auction takes place, if such
a place can be determined;

(h) a contract concluded within a multilateral system which
brings together or facilitates the bringing together of multiple
third-party buying and selling interests in financial
instruments, as defined by Article 4(1), point (17) of Directive
2004/39/EC, in accordance with non-discretionary rules and
governed by a single law, shall be governed by that law.

2.   Where the contract is not covered by paragraph 1 or where the
elements of the contract would be covered by more than one of points (a)
to (h) of paragraph 1, the contract shall be governed by the law of the
country where the party required to effect the characteristic performance
of the contract has his habitual residence.

3.   Where it is clear from all the circumstances of the case that the
contract is manifestly more closely connected with a country other than

that indicated in paragraphs 1 or 2, the law of that other country shall apply.

4.   Where the law applicable cannot be determined pursuant to paragraphs 1 or 2, the contract shall be governed by the law of the country with which it is most closely connected.

––––––

Under the Japanese Act on General Rules for Application of Laws, in the absence of choice by the parties, article 8 provides "the formation and effect of a juristic act shall be governed by the law of the place with which the act was most closely connected at the time the act was made." Where only one party is to effect the characteristic performance of the juristic act, the presumption is that the juristic act is most closely connected with the law of his or her habitual residence. Except where the subject of the act is immovables, the presumption is that the law of the situs applies.

Article 13 applies the law of the situs to rights in rem "to movables or immovables" and to "other rights requiring registration." In the case of movables, the reference is to the situs "at the time when the events causing the acquisition or loss are completed."

––––––

On March 15, 1999, at the Second Session of the Ninth People's Congress, China adopted a comprehensive Contract Law. Chapter 8, Miscellaneous Provisions, article 126, covers choice of law:

Article 126.

If the parties to a contract involving foreign interests have not made a choice, the law of the country to which the contract is most closely connected shall be applied.

On July 23, 2007, China's Supreme People's Court issued a Regulation on Choice of Law for Foreign Related Civil and Commercial Disputes. The Regulation lists seventeen categories of contracts. For each category it provides a presumption as to which jurisdiction is most closely related. The presumptions are rebutted by clear evidence that another jurisdiction has a closer relationship with the contract.

––––––

The Inter-American Convention on the Law Applicable to International Contracts, opened for signature in 1994, 33 I.L.M. 732, provides: "If the parties have not selected the applicable law, or if their selection proves ineffective, the contract shall be governed by the law of the State with which it has the closest ties." Art. 9. article 10 reflects provisions often found in international commercial agreements: "In addition to the provisions in the foregoing articles, the guidelines, customs, and principles of international commercial law as well as commercial usage and practices generally accepted shall apply in order to discharge the requirements of justice and equity in the particular case."

———

The United Nations Convention on Contracts for the International Sale of Goods (CISG), also known as the "Vienna Convention," entered into force for the United States on January 1, 1988. 53 Fed.Reg. 6262 (1987); 1489 U.N.T.S. 3 (1980).

Instead of choice-of-law rules, the UN Convention replaces the law of signatory countries with the rules of the Convention. The Convention applies when the parties to the contract have their places of business in different Convention countries or if the forum's choice-of-law rules or the parties' own stipulation refer to a contracting state. The Convention provides rules of substantive law on formation of contracts (offer and acceptance) and the rights and obligations of sellers and buyers. The parties can opt out of the Convention or any of its provisions by choosing the law of a non-signatory country or stating that the Convention does not apply. See J. Honnold, Uniform Law for International Sales under the 1980 United Nations Convention (1982).

CONTRACT AUTONOMY ABROAD

Foreign legal systems also permit the parties to stipulate the applicable law, with various limitations.

The European Union Regulation on the Law Applicable to Contractual Obligations. (Rome I) article 3(1) provides: "A contracts shall be governed by the law chosen by the parties." There are two major limitations on this freedom to choose law. Article 3(3) prevents the parties to a wholly domestic transaction from avoiding domestic rules of invalidity. Article 9 provides:

1.   Overriding mandatory provisions are provisions the respect for which is regarded as crucial by a country for safeguarding its public interests, such as its political, social or economic organisation, to such an extent that they are applicable to any situation falling within their scope, irrespective of the law otherwise applicable to the contract under this Regulation.

2.   Nothing in this Regulation shall restrict the application of the overriding mandatory provisions of the law of the forum.

3.   Effect may be given to the overriding mandatory provisions of the law of the country where the obligations arising out of the contract have to be or have been performed, in so far as those overriding mandatory provisions render the performance of the contract unlawful. In considering whether to give effect to those provisions, regard shall be had to their nature and purpose and to the consequences of their application or non-application.

The Regulation limits the parties' freedom to choose the applicable law in consumer (art. 6), insurance (art. 7), and employment (art. 8) contracts. See Documentary Appendix.

Article 6 prevents choice of law that would deprive a consumer of the mandatory provisions of the law of the consumer's habitual residence, provided that provided that the professional conducts activities in that country. Article 8 prevents choice of law that would deprive an employee of the mandatory provisions of the law of the country where the employee habitually works. European Community law protecting consumers or employees is likely to qualify as mandatory. In Case C-381/98, Ingmar GB, Ltd. v. Eaton Leonard Technologies Inc., [2000] ECR I-9305, the Court of Justice of the European Community held that the EC Directive on self-employed commercial agents (Council Directive 86/653/EC, Official Journal 1986 L 382/17), giving commercial agents certain continuing commission claims upon termination, applied despite the parties' express choice of California law. The principal had its headquarters in California. The agent performed its services in the EC. For criticism of this limitation on party autonomy, see Verhagen, The Tension between Party Autonomy and European Union Law: Some Observations on *Ingmar GB Ltd v. Eaton Leonard Technologies Inc.*, 51 Int'l & Comp. L.Q. 135 (2002).

Compare § 187 of the Restatement, Second, p. 674, supra, with Rome I. In what respect does Rome I confer greater freedom to choose law? In what respect does it place greater restrictions on party autonomy?

———

Article 7 of the Japanese Act on General Rules for Application of Laws gives the parties to "a juristic act" complete freedom to choose the law governing "formation and effect." Under article 11, choice-of-law agreements cannot deprive a consumer of the protection of the mandatory rules of the consumer's habitual residence. In the absence of choice, the law of the consumer's habitual residence applies. The consumer loses this protection if the consumer concludes the contract in a place that has the same law as the place of business, unless the consumer has been invited there by the business operator.

———

On March 15, 1999, at the Second Session of the Ninth People's Congress, China adopted a comprehensive Contract Law. Chapter 8, Miscellaneous Provisions, art. 126, covers choice of law:

Article 126 The parties to a contract involving foreign interests may choose the law applicable to the settlement of their contract disputes, except as otherwise stipulated by law. If the parties to a contract involving foreign interests have not made a choice, the law of the country to which the contract is most closely connected shall be applied.

The contracts for Chinese-foreign equity joint ventures, for Chinese-foreign contractual joint ventures and for Chinese-foreign cooperative exploration and development of natural resources to be performed within the territory of the People's Republic of China shall apply the laws of the People's Republic of China.

On July 23, 2007, China's Supreme People's Court issued a Regulation on Choice of Law for Foreign Related Civil and Commercial Disputes. The Regulation provides that the choice of law agreement does not have to be written, but it must be explicit. The choice is not enforceable if it conflicts with China's mandatory rules or is inconsistent with public interests.

———

The Inter-American Convention on the Law Applicable to International Contracts, opened for signature in 1994, 33 I.L.M. 732, except for "mandatory requirements" of forum law and "mandatory provisions of the law of another State with which the contract has close ties" (Art. 11), provides for complete party autonomy: "The contract shall be governed by the law chosen by the parties." Art. 7. For discussion of the Convention, see Juenger, The Inter-American Convention on the Law Applicable to International Contracts: Some Highlights and Comparisons, 42 Am.J.Comp.L. 381 (1994).

NOTES

1.   Can the parties stipulate the law applicable to a tort claim? Such a stipulation will probably be effective for a claim that sounds in tort but arises out of the parties' contractual relationship and could have been brought as a contract claim. Hoes of America, Inc. v. Hoes, 493 F.Supp. 1205 (C.D.Ill.1979) (tortious interference with business claimed after termination of distributorship agreement). In general, however, this is still an open question in most jurisdictions. Compare Twohy v. First Nat. Bank of Chicago, 758 F.2d 1185 (7th Cir.1985) (stipulation upheld) with Ezell v. Hayes Oilfield Const. Co., Inc., 693 F.2d 489 (5th Cir.1982), cert. denied, 464 U.S. 818, 104 S.Ct. 79 (1983) (stipulation ineffective). Watkins & Son Pet Supplies v. The Iams Co., 254 F.3d 607 (6th Cir.2001), held that a choice-of-law clause that does not mention torts does include "promissory fraud"—making promises with an intention not to keep them.

In Kuehn v. Childrens Hospital, Los Angeles, 119 F.3d 1296 (7th Cir.1997), Chief Judge Posner stated that the California tort defendant could have avoided application of Wisconsin law if the defendant had placed a clause in its contract choosing California law. Posner gave his view of the cases dealing with choice-of-law clauses covering torts: "One can, it is true, find cases that say that contractual choice of law provisions govern only contractual disputes and not torts. But what the cases actually hold is that such a provision will not be construed to govern tort as well as contract disputes unless it is clear that this is what the parties intended." Id. at 1302. See also Nedlloyd Lines B.V. v. Superior Court, 3 Cal.4th 459, 11 Cal.Rptr.2d 330, 834

P.2d 1148 (1992), construing a provision that the "agreement shall be governed by and construed in accordance with Hong Kong Law," as including a tort claim for breach of fiduciary duty, and enforcing it as so construed. Two dissenters found that the clause did not cover torts, but indicated that if it did, they would enforce it.

Rayle Tech, Inc. v. Dekalb Swine Breeders, 133 F.3d 1405 (11th Cir.1998), refused to allow a Georgia hog buyer to recover against the seller under Illinois Diseased Animal or Deceptive Business Practices statutes despite the fact that the contract of sale provided that "[t]his contract shall be governed by the laws of the State of Illinois." The court held that under applicable Georgia choice-of-law rules "a choice of law provision simply allows the contracting parties to choose the law of the state to govern their contractual rights and duties." An action under the Illinois statutes "is classified as one arising in tort."

The Regulation of the European Union on the Law Applicable to Non-Contractual Obligations (Documentary Appendix, infra) contains the following provision:

Article 14 Freedom of choice

1.   The parties may agree to submit non-contractual obligations to the law of their choice:

(a) by an agreement entered into after the event giving rise to the damage occurred; or

(b) where all the parties are pursuing a commercial activity, also by an agreement freely negotiated before the event giving rise to the damage occurred.

The choice shall be expressed or demonstrated with reasonable certainty by the circumstances of the case and shall not prejudice the rights of third parties.

2.   Where all the elements relevant to the situation at the time when the event giving rise to the damage occurs, are located in a country other than the country whose law has been chosen, the choice of the parties shall not prejudice the application of provisions of the law of that country which cannot be derogated from by agreement.

3.   Where all the elements relevant to the situation at the time when the event giving rise to the damage occurs, are located in one or more of the Member States, the parties' choice of the law applicable other than that of a Member State shall not prejudice the application of provisions of Community law, where appropriate as implemented in the Member State of the forum, which cannot be derogated from by agreement.

2.   Financial Bancorp Inc. v. Pingree & Dahle, Inc., 880 P.2d 14 (Utah App.1994), holds that a choice-of-law clause will not cover statutes of limitations unless the clause expressly includes this issue. Contra, Hambrecht & Quist Venture Partners v. American Medical International, Inc., 46 Cal.Rptr.2d 33 (Cal.App.1995), holding that "a standard choice of law provision (which states that a contract shall be governed by the 'laws' of a particular jurisdiction) incorporates the statute of limitations of the chosen state." The court that decided *Hambrecht* noted that California no longer adhered to the traditional characterization of statutes of limitation as procedural.

3.   Many cases litigate the scope of choice-of-law provisions such as the issues discussed in Notes 1 and 2 supra. Can the parties draft a provision that eliminates the ambiguities that the courts resolve in these cases? See Weintraub, Commentary on the Conflict of Laws 525–26 (6th ed.2010).

4.   "Floating" forum-selection clauses give one or both parties a choice of fora in which to sue and frequently provide that the applicable law is that of the chosen forum. English law was long hostile to such "floating" clauses, principally on the ground that there had to be some law that applied to the question of validity of the contract (including its forum-selection clause) in the first place. For a review, see North, Reform, Not Revolution, Hague Academy of International Law, 220 Collected Courses 9, 157–60 (1990-I). Art. 3(2) of the Rome Regulation permits the parties to make a choice of law after initially contracting, including changing an earlier choice. The English should now have less objection to an (initially) floating clause. Since the parties are permitted to make an alternative choice later on, there should be no objection to their providing for alternative choices *ab initio*.

A company rented telecommunications equipment to businesses in different states. The rental agreement provided that it was governed by the law of the state where the rental company's principal offices are located and that any suit relating to the rental contract would be brought in that state. The rental company reserved the rights to assign the right to receive rental payments, in which event the rental contract would be governed by the law of the state in which the assignee's principal offices are located and any suit relating to the rental contract would be brought in that state. Actions in different states litigated the right of various assignees to enforce the combined choice-of-law and choice-of-forum agreement. The results varied. See IFC Credit Corp. v. Rieker Shoe Corp., 881 N.E.2d 382 (Ill.App.2007), which enforced the agreement but collects contra authority.

6.   COMPLEX LITIGATION

The most difficult choice-of-law problem for modern methods to resolve occurs when plaintiffs from many different jurisdictions sue defendants from many different jurisdictions. This problem occurs in two contexts. The first is the mass disaster at a single location, such the crash of a commercial airplane. Hundreds of claimants from dozens of states and countries then sue the airline and various other defendants, such as the airplane manufacturer, the manufacturers of component parts, and air traffic controllers. At least the traditional place-of-wrong rule simplified the choice of law in tort, but complications could arise if claims were based on contract theories. Moreover, Philip Morris Inc. v. Angeletti, 358 Md. 689, 752 A.2d 200 (2000) indicated that application of the place-of-wrong rule will not always facilitate class actions by simplifying choice of law for tort claims. Maryland residents brought a class action against tobacco manufacturers for injuries resulting from smoking and for addiction to nicotine. The court decertified the class action holding that the applicable law would be that of the states in which the plaintiffs first suffered injury or addiction.

The second form of the problem is difficult for either traditional or modern methods—many plaintiffs injured at different locations by a defective product produced by the defendant. Can courts adapt modern methods of choosing law to these situations so as to encourage rather than prevent consolidation of the cases for timely disposition? Should they?

Some courts have found that the need to apply different law to different claims is inconsistent with the class-action requirement that common questions of law predominate. See Zandman v. Joseph, 102 F.R.D. 924, 929 (N.D.Ind.1984); In re United States Fin. Sec. Litig., 64 F.R.D. 443, 455 (S.D.Cal.1974). Other courts have found that the need for differential choice-of-law treatment of plaintiffs' claims did not prevent class certification if the parties and applicable laws could be grouped into a manageable number of subclasses. Miner v. Gillette Co., 87 Ill.2d 7, 428 N.E.2d 478, 484 (1981), cert. dism'd, 459 U.S. 86, 103 S.Ct. 484 (1982).

Certification may depend on whether plaintiffs or defendants have the burden of demonstrating that the laws of the states where defendants or plaintiffs reside would produce different results. Castano v. American Tobacco Co., 84 F.3d 734 (5th Cir.1996), held that the trial court abused its discretion in certifying a nationwide class action of all smokers and nicotine dependent persons and their families against tobacco companies. With regard to choice of law, the court stated: "In a multi-state class action, variations in state law may swamp any common issues and defeat predominance. A district court's duty to determine whether the plaintiff has borne its burden on class certification requires that a court consider variations in state law when a class action involves multiple jurisdictions. A requirement that a court know which law will apply before making a predominance determination is especially important when there may be differences in state law. Given the plaintiffs' burden, a court cannot rely on assurances of counsel that any problems with predominance and superiority can be overcome."

Washington Mutual Bank v. Superior Court, 15 P.3d 1071 (Cal.2001), presents a contrasting view. The court compared a case in which there was an enforceable choice-of-law clause with a case in which the parties had not agreed on choice of law. If the choice-of-law clause would require application of the law of many states: "the burden rests upon the party seeking nationwide class certification to identify any variations of applicable state law and to meaningfully demonstrate how a trial on the class causes of action can be conducted fairly and efficiently in light of those variations." Id. at 1086. If, however, there is no controlling choice-of-law clause, a California court will apply California law "unless a party litigant timely invokes the law of a foreign state." If so, "the foreign law proponent must identify the applicable rule of law in each potentially concerned state and must show it materially differs from the law of California. . . . [T]he trial court may properly find California law applicable without [conducting a choice-of-law analysis] if the foreign law proponent fails to identify any actual conflict or to establish the other state's interest in having its own law applied. . . . [S]o long as the requisite significant contacts to California exist, a showing that is properly borne by the class action proponent, California may constitutionally require the other side to shoulder the burden of demonstrating that foreign law, rather than California law, should apply to class claims." Id. at 919–21, 15 P.3d at 1080–81, 103 Cal.Rptr. 2d at 330–31.

Washington Mutual Bank, supra, states that "significant contacts to California" must exist before a California court may constitutionally place the burden on a party who wishes the law of another state to apply. Is this correct if the party has not demonstrated that the law of the other state differs from California law? See Justice Stevens's dissent in Phillips Petroleum Co. v. Shutts, p. 445, supra and the Note following that case, p. 449, supra.

On February 18, 2005, President Bush signed into law the Class Action Fairness Act of 2005. Pub.L.No. 109–002, 119 Stat.4 (2005). The Act applies to "any civil action commenced on or after the date of enactment." § 9. It permits removal from state court and gives federal district courts original jurisdiction on the basis of minimal diversity (28 U.S.C. § 1332(d)(2)(A): "any member of a class of plaintiffs is a citizen of a State different from any defendant") of any class action in which the amount in controversy exceeds $5,000,000. Thus the plaintiffs' attorney can no longer prevent removal from state to federal court by joining a defendant of the same citizenship as any plaintiff (Strawbridge v. Curtiss, 7 U.S. (3 Cranch) 267, 2 L.Ed. 435 (1806), overruled on other grounds, Louisville R.R. v. Letson, 43 U.S. 497 (1844) (holding that for federal diversity jurisdiction to attach, complete diversity is required, each defendant being of diverse citizenship from each plaintiff)) or by suing in a state court in a state where any defendant is a citizen. (28 U.S.C. § 1441(b) provides that a case cannot be removed from state court under federal diversity jurisdiction if any defendant is a citizen of the state in which suit is brought.) The only exception to federal jurisdiction is if "greater than two-thirds of the members of all proposed plaintiff classes in the aggregate are citizens of the State in which the action was originally filed."

Although state courts will no longer be viable forums for multi-state or national class actions, the Act does not contain a choice-of-law provision. Will a federal district court have to apply the choice-of-law rules of the state in which the court is sitting or will the court be free to adopt a federal rule? See Klaxon Co. v. Stentor Elec. Mfg. Co., p. 746; infra; Woolley, Erie and Choice of Law after the Class Action Fairness Act, 80 Tul.L.Rev. 1723 (2006) (*Klaxon* applies and a federal court must apply the choice-of-law rule of the forum state); Issacharoff, Settled Expectations in a World of Unsettled Law: Choice of Law after the Class Action Fairness Act, 106 Colum.L.Rev. 1839 (2006) (urging federal courts to adopt a rule applying the law of the state that was the center of defendant's wrongful acts). If a federal court must apply the conflicts rules of the forum state, where the action is filed will matter and may be the difference between certification and dismissal. See Ysbrand v. DaimlerChrysler Corp. 81 P.3d, 618 (Okla.2003) (applying Michigan law to the warranty claims of all national class members).

Under the Class Action Fairness Act, will an attorney representing a national class improve the chances of certification by suing in a state like California (see Washington Mutual Bank v. Superior Court, p. 683, supra) that in such actions presumes that the law of other states is the same as that of California unless the defendant shows otherwise? After removal to federal court under the Act, the federal judge will have to resolve the problem of whether on this issue the judge must follow California law or is free to apply federal procedural law, which places on the plaintiff the burden of demonstrating that in the light of variations in state law and choice-of-law analysis, "any problems with predominance or superiority can be overcome." Castano v. American Tobacco Co., 84 F.3d 734, 741 (5th Cir.1996).

The answer is likely to be in favor of following the federal placement of burden on the plaintiff to explore variations in state laws. There is a somewhat analogous problem under Federal Rule of Civil Procedure 44.1, which states that when determining the law of a foreign country, the court "may consider any relevant material or source . . . whether or not submitted by a party . . . ." The Advisory Committee Notes on 44.1 state: "There is no requirement that the court give formal notice of its intention to engage in its own research on an issue of foreign law which has been raised by them, or of its intention to raise and determine independently an issue not raised by them."

Moreover, under Federal Rule of Civil Procedure 23, which requires that a class action be "efficient," that common questions of law or fact predominate, and that the class action will present no great difficulties of management, there are, pursuant to Byrd v. Blue Ridge Rural Electric Cooperative, Inc. (p. 706, infra), "affirmative countervailing considerations" militating against the use of state presumptions. Concerns with the quality of justice administered in a federal court may justify putting the burden on the plaintiff to deal with choice of law before certification. Further, under Hanna v. Plumer (p. 711, infra), Congress in enacting FRCP 23 and federal courts in interpreting the rule have the "power to regulate matters which, though falling within the uncertain area between substance and procedure, are rationally capable of classification as either."

In rebuttal it might be argued that the state-law presumption that other laws are the same as the forum's eliminates choice-of-law problems and assures that the requirements of Rule 23 are met insofar as they are affected by variations in state law. Nevertheless, a federal court might wish to preclude such problems from arising when addressed by the defendant and to accomplish this by placing the burden on the plaintiff at the outset. See Woolley, *Erie* and Choice of Law after the Class Action Fairness Act, 80 Tul.L.Rev. 1723, 1724 (2006): "But the claim that Rule 23 permits federal courts to ignore state law presumptions in favor of forum law is paper-thin and may not survive review by the United States Supreme Court."

Because many consumer suits are only feasible if brought as class actions, Shady Grove Orthopedic Associates, P. A. v. Allstate Insurance Co., 559 U.S. 393, 130 S.Ct. 1431 [p. 734, infra], apparently favors consumers, but it only part of the story. In two other opinions the Supreme Court has effectively barred consumer suits.

Stolt-Nielsen SA. v. Animalfeeds Int'l Corp., 559 U.S. 662, 130 S.Ct. 1758 (2010), held that the arbitrators exceeded their powers in imposing class arbitration on parties whose arbitration clauses are silent on that issue:

> Rather than inquiring whether the FAA, maritime law, or New York law contains a "default rule" under which an arbitration clause is construed as allowing class arbitration in the absence of express consent, the panel proceeded as if it had the authority of a common-law court to develop what it viewed as the best rule to be applied in such a situation. Id. at 1768–69.

AT&T Mobility LLC v. Concepcion, 563 U.S. 333 (2011), delivered a further blow to consumer suits. California had a rule that a waiver of a class action in a consumer arbitration agreement is unconscionable and void. See Discover Bank v. Superior Court, 113 P.3d 1100 (Cal.2005). The Supreme Court held (5–4) that the California rule conflicts with the Federal Arbitration Act and is preempted. Although the class argued California rule complied with FAA § 2 because it applied to "any contract"—not just to arbitration agreements—the majority held it incompatible with the FAA. Id. at 1746–47.

A merchant can rid himself of pesky consumer suits by inserting in the contract with the consumer an arbitration agreement that bars class actions. Only Congress can revive consumer suits.

7. DÉPEÇAGE

In its issue-by-issue approach to analysis of a choice-of-law problem, interest analysis has greatly increased the likelihood that the law of one state will be applied to one aspect of the problem while the law of another state is applied to another aspect of the problem. There was some likelihood under the territorial choice-of-law rules that this splitting up of the applicable law would occur. In the first Restatement of Conflict of Laws, for example, the law of the place of contracting determined the validity of a contract (§ 332), but the law of the place of performance determined the sufficiency of performance (§ 358). The first Restatement's tort rule, place of wrong (§ 378), was more monolithic, but with the right chisel even that monolith could be cracked. A particular issue in a "tort" case could be characterized, for example, as "procedural," and would therefore be resolved by the application of forum law, or as a "contract" claim and require use of a different set of guidelines to determine where to place the pin in the map. It is true, however, that the likelihood of applying different laws to different issues in the same case, "dépeçage," is much increased under modern methodology.

The question arises to what extent this issue-by-issue, onion-peeling approach to choice-of-law problems is desirable and to what extent it is fraught with the danger of producing foolish and unjust results. A good example is Edwards v. Erie Coach Lines, p. 657, supra in which the New York Court of Appeals applied different rules depending on the residence of the parties.

8.   ADMIRALTY

Lauritzen v. Larsen

Supreme Court of the United States, 1953.
345 U.S. 571, 73 S.Ct. 921, 97 L.Ed. 1254.

■ MR. JUSTICE JACKSON delivered the opinion of the Court.

The key issue in this case is whether statutes of the United States should be applied to this claim of maritime tort. Larsen, a Danish seaman, while temporarily in New York joined the crew of the *Randa*, a ship of Danish flag and registry, owned by petitioner, a Danish citizen. Larsen signed ship's articles, written in Danish, providing that the rights of crew members would be governed by Danish law and by the employer's contract with the Danish Seamen's Union, of which Larsen was a member. He was negligently injured aboard the *Randa* in the course of employment, while in Havana harbor.

Respondent brought suit under the Jones Act on the law side of the District Court for the Southern District of New York and demanded a jury. Petitioner contended that Danish law was applicable and that, under it, respondent had received all of the compensation to which he was entitled. [The district court ruled that American rather than Danish law applied and gave judgment for the plaintiff.] The Court of Appeals, Second Circuit, affirmed.

[The Supreme Court first conceded that taken literally the Jones Act applied, but]

. . . [I]t has long been accepted in maritime jurisprudence that " . . . if any construction otherwise be possible, an Act will not be construed as applying to foreigners in respect to acts done by them outside the dominions of the sovereign power enacting. That is a rule based on international law, by which one sovereign power is bound to respect the subjects and the rights of all other sovereign powers outside its own territory." Lord Russell of Killowen in The Queen v. Jameson [1896], 2 Q.B. 425, 430. . . .

Congress could not have been unaware of the necessity of construction imposed upon courts by such generality of language and . . . that in the absence of more definite directions than are contained in the Jones Act it would be applied by the courts to foreign events, foreign ships and foreign seamen only in accordance with the usual doctrine and practices of maritime law.

Respondent places great stress upon the assertion that petitioner's commerce and contacts with the ports of the United States are frequent and regular . . . But the virtue and utility of sea-borne commerce lies in its frequent and important contacts with more than one country. If, to serve some immediate interest, the courts of each were to exploit every such contact to the limit of its power, it is not difficult to see that a multiplicity of conflicting and overlapping burdens would blight international carriage by sea. . . .

Maritime law, like our municipal law, has attempted to avoid or resolve conflicts between competing laws by ascertaining and valuing points of contact between the transaction and the states or governments whose competing laws are involved. The criteria, in general, appear to be arrived at from weighing of the significance of one or more connecting factors between the shipping transaction regulated and the national interest served by the assertion of authority. . . .

. . . [I]n dealing with international commerce we cannot be unmindful of the necessity for mutual forbearance if retaliations are to be avoided; nor should we forget that any contact which we hold sufficient to warrant application of our law to a foreign transaction will logically be as strong a warrant for a foreign country to apply its law to an American transaction.

In the case before us, two foreign nations can claim some connecting factor with this tort—Denmark, because, among other reasons, the ship and the seaman were Danish nationals; Cuba, because the tortious conduct occurred and caused injury in Cuban waters. The United States may also claim contacts because the seaman had been hired in and was returned to the United States, which also is the state of the forum. We therefore review the several factors which, alone or in combination, are generally conceded to influence choice of law to govern a tort claim, particularly a maritime tort claim, and the weight and significance accorded them.

1. *Place of the Wrongful Act.*—The solution most commonly accepted as to torts in our municipal and in international law is to supply the law of the place where the acts giving rise to the liability occurred, the *lex loci delicti commissi*. This rule . . . would indicate application of the law of Cuba, in whose domain the actionable wrong took place. The test of location of the wrongful act or omission, however sufficient for torts ashore,

is of limited application to shipboard torts, because of the varieties of legal authority over waters she may navigate. . . .

2. *Law of the Flag.*—Perhaps the most venerable and universal rule of maritime law relevant to our problem is that which gives cardinal importance to the law of the flag. . . .

3. *Allegiance or Domicile of the Injured.*— . . . [T]he longstanding rule . . . was that the nationality of the vessel for jurisdictional purposes was attributed to all her crew. . . . Surely during service under a foreign flag some duty of allegiance is due. But, also, each nation has a legitimate interest that its nationals and permanent inhabitants be not maimed or disabled from self-support. . . . We need not, however, weigh the seaman's nationality against that of the ship, for here the two coincide without resort to fiction. . . .

4. *Allegiance of the Defendant Shipowner.*— . . . [I]n recent years a practice has grown, particularly among American shipowners, to avoid stringent shipping laws by seeking foreign registration . . . Confronted with such operations, our courts on occasion have pressed beyond the formalities of more or less nominal foreign registration to enforce against American shipowners the obligations which our law places upon them. But here . . . it appears beyond doubt that this owner is a Dane by nationality and domicile.

5. *Place of Contract.*—Place of contract, which was New York, is the factor on which respondent chiefly relies to invoke American law. . . .

The place of contracting in this instance . . . was fortuitous. . . . The practical effect of making the *lex loci contractus* govern all tort claims during the service would be to subject a ship to a multitude of systems of law, to put some of the crew in a more advantageous position than others, and not unlikely in the long run to diminish hirings in ports of countries that take best care of their seamen.

But if contract law is nonetheless to be considered, we face the fact that this contract was explicit that the Danish law and the contract with the Danish union were to control. . . .

6. *Inaccessibility of Foreign Forum.*—It is argued . . . that justice requires adjudication under American law to save seamen expense and loss of time in returning to a foreign forum. This might be a persuasive argument for exercising a discretionary jurisdiction to adjudge a controversy; but it is not persuasive as to the law by which it shall be judged. . . .

7. *The Law of the Forum.*—It is urged that, since an American forum has perfected its jurisdiction over the parties and defendant does more or less frequent and regular business within the forum state, it should apply its own law to the controversy between them. . . . The purpose of a conflict-of-laws doctrine is to assure that a case will be treated in the same way under the appropriate law regardless of the fortuitous circumstances which often determine the forum. Jurisdiction of maritime

cases in all countries is so wide and the nature of its subject matter so far-flung that there would be no justification for altering the law of a controversy just because local jurisdiction of the parties is obtainable. . . .

This review of the connecting factors which either maritime law or our municipal law of conflicts regards as significant in determining the law applicable to a claim of actionable wrong shows an overwhelming preponderance in favor of Danish law. . . . [The decision below was reversed on the theory that Danish, not American, law applied. Justice Black dissented.]

NOTE

Romero v. International Terminal Operating Co., 358 U.S. 354, 79 S.Ct. 468 (1959) applied the seven *Lauritzen* factors to deny coverage under the Jones Act or general maritime law of the United States to a Spanish seaman injured in United States territorial waters off Hoboken, New Jersey. Hellenic Lines Ltd. v. Rhoditis, 398 U.S. 306, 90 S.Ct. 1731 (1970), added "base of operations" to the seven *Lauritzen* factors to permit Jones Act recovery for a Greek seaman injured in American territorial waters on a Greek ship based in the United States and operated by a Greek corporation, which had its main office in New York.

Does *Lauritzen* analyze the seven factors it enumerated in the manner a modern court would under a "most significant relationship" approach? When the Court's analysis is complete, the seven factors are reduced to only three that are relevant when suit is by a seaman against the shipowner: the law of the flag which "must prevail unless some heavy counterweight appears"; the allegiance or domicile of the seaman; and the allegiance of the shipowner. Are these the only contacts that are likely to be related to some policy of compensating injured seamen? *Rhoditis* seems even closer to a most-significant-relationship approach: "The significance of one or more factors must be considered in light of the national interest served by the assertion of Jones Act jurisdiction. Moreover, the list of seven factors in *Lauritzen* was not intended as exhaustive." 398 U.S. at 309.

Neely v. Club Med Management Services, Inc., 63 F.3d 166 (3d Cir.1995) permitted a United States citizen injured in a diving accident in St. Lucia to recover under the Jones Act and United States general maritime law. The court characterized *Lauritzen* as having "adopted a form of interest analysis to cabin the sweep of the Jones Act." Then, breaking new ground, a majority of the Third Circuit, sitting en banc, declared that choice of law in Jones Act cases should follow the Restatement (Third) of the Foreign Relations Law of the United States, not the Restatement (Second) of Conflict of Laws.

The difference between the approaches of the Conflicts and Foreign Relations Restatements is between a multilateral and unilateral analysis. Under the multilateral analysis of the Conflicts Restatement, the court attempts to apply the law that will best accommodate the conflicting rules of different states or countries. It is not sufficient for application of forum law that this is reasonable or that forum policies will be advanced if its law applies. It is also necessary that the forum have the most significant relationship to the parties and the transaction. Under a unilateral approach, such as that of the Restatement of Foreign Relations (see Hartford Fire Ins. Co. v. California, 509 U.S. 764, 113 S.Ct. 2891 (1993)), the court looks primarily at the purposes underlying forum law and applies that law if those policies will be advanced, providing this application is reasonable. It does not matter that another country, utilizing the same analysis, would apply its law and not United States law. The only exception is when two countries' laws conflict so completely that a person cannot comply with the laws of both because one country orders the same person at the same time to do what the other forbids. Then "a state should defer to the other state if that state's interest is clearly greater." Restatement (Third) of the Foreign Relations Law of the United States § 403(3).

It would be feasible to apply the Foreign Relations Restatement's unilateral approach to Jones Act cases. Workers' compensation acts are typically applied unilaterally. Would a unilateral approach be feasible in other admiralty cases, such as those involving the construction of a maritime insurance policy when national laws conflict on key issues?

State law applies in admiralty cases if there is no established admiralty rule and if there is no need for a uniform federal rule governing the particular issue. Wilburn Boat Co. v. Fireman's Fund Ins. Co., 348 U.S. 310, 314, 75 S.Ct. 368, 370 (1955). When federal courts use admiralty choice-of-law rules to select state law, they utilize a most significant relationship approach. Albany Ins. Co. v. Anh Thi Kieu, 927 F.2d 882 (5th Cir.), cert. denied, 502 U.S. 901, 112 S.Ct. 278 (1991), held that state law on the effect of misrepresentations by the insured is not pre-empted by federal admiralty law and stated: "Modern choice of law analysis, whether maritime or not, generally requires the application of the law of the state with the 'most significant relationship' to the substantive issue in question." Id. at 891. See also Lien Ho Hsing Steel Enterprise Co. v. Weihtag, 738 F.2d 1455, 1458 (9th Cir.1984) (whether a maritime insurance broker is the insurer's agent is determined by "the law of the state with the greatest interest in the issue"); Edinburgh Assur. Co. v. R.L. Burns Corp., 479 F.Supp. 138, 152–53 (C.D.Cal.1979), aff'd in part and rev'd in part on other grounds, 669 F.2d 1259 (9th Cir.1982) (applying "the points of contact analysis of *Lauritzen* and *Romero* " and holding that English law determines the meaning of "actual total loss," because England has "the most significant relationship to the transaction," citing Restatement (Second) of Conflict of Laws §§ 188 and 193).

CHAPTER 9

CONFLICTS PROBLEMS IN FEDERAL AND INTERNATIONAL SETTINGS

SECTION 1. SPECIAL PROBLEMS IN FEDERAL COURTS

A. THE CONSTRAINTS AND TOLERANCES OF THE ERIE PRINCIPLE

This section addresses issues that have appeared episodically in earlier chapters. Their theme is a broad question: how completely are federal courts bound to follow state conflict-of-law principles in diversity cases? As examples: May the federal diversity court entertain a suit based on state-created rights that would not be entertained in a state court of the forum? Does the *Erie* doctrine compel a diversity court to follow the choice-of-law rules or methods of the forum's state courts and to apply at the end the same decisional rule the state judges would? As the *Erie* doctrine has changed shape over the years, has comparable change occurred in its influence on conflicts methodology?

This chapter also focuses on the issue of federal common law. When the Constitution of the United States, a treaty, or federal statute supplies the rule of decision, state law is superseded. When interstices appear in those sources of law, two issues arise. First, should a uniform federal judge-made rule fill the gap? Second, if state law governs, should state or federal choice-of-law rules select that law?

We take up the problem of state law in the federal courts in a broad context, tracing the movements and counter-movements in state law/federal law relations that bear on the conflicts problems that are the focus of our interest. Two of the important movements concern only the federal courts. The third applies also to the state courts.

(1) *Erie Railroad Co. v. Tompkins*, p. 695, infra, sharply curtailed the growth of a general and independent body of common law rules in the federal courts. For in overruling the doctrine frequently associated with the case of Swift v. Tyson, 41 U.S. (16 Pet.) 1 (1842), it obliterated the more-than-a-century-old doctrine of a separate substantive common law as to commercial matters in the federal courts. It thereby sharpened the question: from what source can the federal courts get separate rules of conflict of laws?

(2) In the same year *Erie* was decided, the area of federal courts law was much expanded by occupying the entire field of federal "procedure". For many years the Conformity Act had directed the federal district

courts hearing actions at law to follow the procedure of the states in which the federal courts were sitting. But in 1938 the Federal Rules of Civil Procedure, went into effect as a uniform set of rules for litigation in all federal district courts. By coincidence the Rules created a special law of procedure for the federal district courts at almost the same time *Erie* was ending the special body of general federal common law on substantive matters lying outside the ordinary sphere of national law.

(3) A third movement, affecting state and federal courts alike but more conspicuous in the federal courts, is concerned with federal law. The increasing regulation of interstate and foreign commerce and the growing activities of the federal government have brought the realization that there are areas of substantive law which are not explicitly dealt with by the federal statutes but which are nevertheless covered by a single national law. This corpus is a part of the law of the land to be applied by all courts, state or federal. Its importance for lawyers with private interstate or international cases is manifest, for in so far as the national law comes into play there is no conflict of laws.

TWO FEDERAL STATUTES

Rules of Decision Act, § 34 of the Judiciary Act of 1789, 1 Stat. 92: "[T]he laws of the several states, except where the constitution, treaties or statutes of the United States shall otherwise require or provide, shall be regarded as rules of decision in trials at common law in the courts of the United States in cases where they apply."

In the 1948 recodification, after the merger in federal courts of law and equity proceedings, the words "civil actions" were substituted for "trials at common law." As so amended, and with the words "Acts of Congress" substituted for "statutes," this Act is now codified as 28 U.S.C. § 1652.

Rules Enabling Act of June 19, 1934, 48 Stat. 1064: "Sec. 1. [T]he Supreme Court of the United States shall have the power to prescribe by general rules, for the district courts of the United States . . . the forms of process, writs, pleadings, and motions, and the practice and procedure in civil actions at law. Said rules shall neither abridge, enlarge, nor modify the substantive rights of any litigant. They shall take effect six months after their promulgation, and thereafter all laws in conflict therewith shall be of no force or effect.

"Sec. 2. The court may at any time unite the general rules prescribed by it for cases in equity with those at law so as to secure one form of civil action and procedure for both: Provided, however, That in such union of rules the right of trial by jury as at common law and declared by the seventh amendment to the Constitution shall be preserved to the parties inviolate. Such unified rules shall not take effect until they shall have been reported to Congress by the Attorney General at the beginning of a regular session thereof and until after the close of such session."

In the 1948 recodification, the provision for uniting of rules for suits in equity and actions at law was deleted because unification had been accomplished. The Act is codified in the following provisions:

28 U.S.C. § 2072: "(a) The Supreme Court shall have the power to prescribe the general rules of practice and procedure and rules of evidence for cases in the United States district courts . . . and courts of appeals.

"(b) Such rules shall not abridge, enlarge or modify any substantive right. All laws in conflict with such rules shall be of no further force or effect after such rules have taken effect. . . ."

The procedure for prescribing rules of evidence and procedure is codified in 28 U.S.C. §§ 2073–74. Section 2074(b) provides: "Any such rule creating, abolishing, or modifying an evidentiary privilege shall have no force or effect unless approved by Act of Congress."

Erie Railroad Co. v. Tompkins

Supreme Court of the United States, 1938.
304 U.S. 64, 58 S.Ct. 817, 82 L.Ed.1188, 114 A.L.R. 1487.

Certiorari to the United States Circuit Court of Appeals for the Second Circuit.

■ JUSTICE BRANDEIS delivered the opinion of the Court.

The question for decision is whether the oft-challenged doctrine of Swift v. Tyson[, 16 Pet. 1 (1842),] shall now be disapproved.

Tompkins, a citizen of Pennsylvania, was injured on a dark night by a passing freight train of the Erie Railroad Company while walking along its right of way at Hughestown in that state. He claimed that the accident occurred through negligence in the operation, or maintenance, of the train; that he was rightfully on the premises as licensee because on a commonly used beaten footpath which ran for a short distance alongside the tracks; and that he was struck by something which looked like a door projecting from one of the moving cars. To enforce that claim he brought an action in the federal court for Southern New York, which had jurisdiction because the company is a corporation of that state. It denied liability; and the case was tried by a jury.

The Erie insisted that its duty to Tompkins was no greater than that owed to a trespasser. It contended, among other things, that its duty to Tompkins, and hence its liability, should be determined in accordance with the Pennsylvania law; that under the law of Pennsylvania, as declared by its highest court, persons who use pathways along the railroad right of way—that is, a longitudinal pathway as distinguished from a crossing—are to be deemed trespassers; and that the railroad is not liable for injuries to undiscovered trespassers resulting from its negligence, unless it be wanton or willful. Tompkins denied that any such rule had been established by the decisions of the Pennsylvania courts;

and contended that, since there was no statute of the state on the subject, the railroad's duty and liability is to be determined in federal courts as a matter of general law.

The trial judge refused to rule that the applicable law precluded recovery. The jury brought in a verdict of $30,000; and the judgment entered thereon was affirmed by the Circuit Court of Appeals, which held (2 Cir., 90 F.2d 603, 604), that it was unnecessary to consider whether the law of Pennsylvania was as contended, because the question was one not of local, but of general, law, and that "upon questions of general law the federal courts are free, in absence of a local statute, to exercise their independent judgment as to what the law is. . . ."

Because of the importance of the question whether the federal court was free to disregard the alleged rule of the Pennsylvania common law, we granted certiorari. 302 U.S. 671.

First. Swift v. Tyson, 16 Pet. 1, 18, held that federal courts exercising jurisdiction on the ground of diversity of citizenship need not, in matters of general jurisprudence, apply the unwritten law of the state as declared by its highest court; that they are free to exercise an independent judgment as to what the common law of the state is—or should be; and that, as there stated by Mr. Justice Story: "the true interpretation of the 34th section [of the Judiciary Act of 1789] limited its application to state laws, strictly local, that is to say, to the positive statutes of the state, and the construction thereof adopted by the local tribunals, and to rights and titles to things having a permanent locality, such as the rights and titles to real estate, and other matters immovable and intraterritorial in their nature and character. It never has been supposed by us, that the section did apply, or was designed to apply, to questions of a more general nature, not at all dependent upon local statutes or local usages of a fixed and permanent operation, as, for example, to the construction of ordinary contracts or other written instruments, and especially to questions of general commercial law, where the state tribunals are called upon to perform the like functions as ourselves, that is, to ascertain, upon general reasoning and legal analogies, what is the true exposition of the contract or instrument, or what is the just rule furnished by the principles of commercial law to govern the case."

. . . The federal courts assumed, in the broad field of "general law," the power to declare rules of decision which Congress was confessedly without power to enact as statutes. Doubt was repeatedly expressed as to the correctness of the construction given section 34, and as to the soundness of the rule which it introduced. But it was the more recent research of a competent scholar, who examined the original document, which established that the construction given to it by the Court was erroneous; and that the purpose of the section was merely to make certain that, in all matters except those in which some federal law is controlling, the federal courts exercising jurisdiction in diversity of citizenship cases would apply as their rules of decision the law of the state, unwritten as well as written.[5]

Criticism of the doctrine became widespread after the decision of Black & White Taxicab & Transfer Co. v. Brown & Yellow Taxicab & Transfer Co., 276 U.S. 518 [(1928). In this case, a Kentucky corporation, by the device of dissolving and re-incorporating in Tennessee, was permitted to manufacture diversity of citizenship jurisdiction and to enforce in a federal court, sitting in Kentucky, a contract that no Kentucky court would have enforced.]

Second. Experience in applying the doctrine of Swift v. Tyson, had revealed its defects, political and social; and the benefits expected to flow from the rule did not accrue. Persistence of state courts in their own opinions on questions of common law prevented uniformity; and the impossibility of discovering a satisfactory line of demarcation between the province of general law and that of local law developed a new well of uncertainties.

On the other hand, the mischievous results of the doctrine had become apparent. Diversity of citizenship jurisdiction was conferred in order to prevent apprehended discrimination in state courts against those not citizens of the state. Swift v. Tyson introduced grave discrimination by noncitizens against citizens. It made rights enjoyed under the unwritten "general law" vary according to whether enforcement was sought in the state or in the federal court; and the privilege of selecting the court in which the right should be determined was conferred upon the noncitizen. Thus, the doctrine rendered impossible equal protection of the law. In attempting to promote uniformity of law throughout the United States, the doctrine had prevented uniformity in the administration of the law of the state.

The discrimination resulting became in practice far-reaching. This resulted in part from the broad province accorded to the so-called "general law" as to which federal courts exercised an independent judgment. . . .

The injustice and confusion incident to the doctrine of Swift v. Tyson have been repeatedly urged as reasons for abolishing or limiting diversity of citizenship jurisdiction. Other legislative relief has been proposed. If only a question of statutory construction were involved, we should not be prepared to abandon a doctrine so widely applied throughout nearly a century. But the unconstitutionality of the course pursued has now been made clear, and compels us to do so.

Third. Except in matters governed by the Federal Constitution or by acts of Congress, the law to be applied in any case is the law of the state. And whether the law of the state shall be declared by its Legislature in a statute or by its highest court in a decision is not a matter of federal

---

[5]   Charles Warren, New Light on the History of the Federal Judiciary Act of 1789 (1923) 37 Harv.L.Rev. 49, 51–52, 81–88, 108.

concern. There is no federal general common law. Congress has no power to declare substantive rules of common law applicable in a state whether they be local in their nature or "general," be they commercial law or a part of the law of torts. And no clause in the Constitution purports to confer such a power upon the federal courts. . . .

The fallacy underlying the rule declared in Swift v. Tyson is made clear by Mr. Justice Holmes.[23] The doctrine rests upon the assumption that there is "a transcendental body of law outside of any particular State but obligatory within it unless and until changed by statute," that federal courts have the power to use their judgment as to what the rules of common law are; and that in the federal courts "the parties are entitled to an independent judgment on matters of general law":

> "but law in the sense in which courts speak of it today does not exist without some definite authority behind it. The common law so far as it is enforced in a State, whether called common law or not, is not the common law generally but the law of that State existing by the authority of that State without regard to what it may have been in England or anywhere else. . . .

> "the authority and only authority is the State, and if that be so, the voice adopted by the State as its own [whether it be of its Legislature or of its Supreme Court] should utter the last word."

Thus, the doctrine of Swift v. Tyson is, as Mr. Justice Holmes said, "an unconstitutional assumption of powers by the Courts of the United States which no lapse of time or respectable array of opinion should make us hesitate to correct." In disapproving that doctrine we do not hold unconstitutional section 34 of the Federal Judiciary Act of 1789 or any other act of Congress. We merely declare that in applying the doctrine this Court and the lower courts have invaded rights which in our opinion are reserved by the Constitution to the several states.

. . . The Circuit Court of Appeals ruled that the question of liability is one of general law; and on that ground declined to decide the issue of state law. As we hold this was error, the judgment is reversed and the case remanded to it for further proceedings in conformity with our opinion.

Reversed.

■ JUSTICE CARDOZO took no part in the consideration or decision of this case.

[JUSTICE BUTLER dissented in an opinion in which JUSTICE MCREYNOLDS concurred. The dissent urged (a) that the doctrine of Swift v. Tyson be adhered to and applied; and (b) that otherwise the case be set down for reargument, for counsel on both sides had assumed in their briefs the

---

[23] Kuhn v. Fairmont Coal Co., 215 U.S. 349, 370–372; Black & White Taxicab, etc., Co. v. Brown & Yellow Taxicab, etc., Co., 276 U.S. 518, 532–536.

validity of Swift v. Tyson; so important a question as the constitutional overruling of that case should not be decided without argument.]

■ JUSTICE REED (concurring in part).

To decide the case now before us and to "disapprove" the doctrine of Swift v. Tyson requires only that we say that the words "the laws" include in their meaning the decisions of the local tribunals. . . . It is unnecessary to go further and declare that the "course pursued" was "unconstitutional," instead of merely erroneous.

The "unconstitutional" course referred to in the majority opinion is apparently the ruling in Swift v. Tyson that the supposed omission of Congress to legislate as to the effect of decisions leaves federal courts free to interpret general law for themselves. I am not at all sure whether, in the absence of federal statutory direction, federal courts would be compelled to follow state decisions. There was sufficient doubt about the matter in 1789 to induce the first Congress to legislate. No former opinions of this Court have passed upon it. . . . If the opinion commits this Court to the position that the Congress is without power to declare what rules of substantive law shall govern the federal courts, that conclusion also seems questionable. . . .

. . . It seems preferable to overturn an established construction of an act of Congress, rather than, in the circumstances of this case, to interpret the Constitution.

NOTES

1. An interesting debate emerged over whether the *Erie* doctrine is constitutionally compelled. In the affirmative, Judge Henry J. Friendly wrote In Praise of *Erie*—and of the New Federal Common Law, 39 N.Y.U.L.Rev. 383, 385–86 (1964). On the other side Judge Charles E. Clark wrote State Law in the Federal Courts: The Brooding Omnipresence of Erie v. Tompkins, 55 Yale L.J. 267–78 (1946). See Wright & Kane, Law of Federal Courts 380–85 (7th ed.2011). Based upon your study of the case, which side is correct?

2. On remand in *Erie*, the district court was required by the majority's opinion to "decide the issue of state law." Did the Supreme Court's decision intend that the federal district court in New York would apply Pennsylvania law? If so, why? Is it because there is a federal choice-of-law rule that applies the law of the place of the tort? Or because the New York courts do so? Or because the Court assumed that "place-of-the-tort" was the uniform conflicts rule in tort? See also Klaxon Co. v. Stentor Electric Manufacturing Co., 313 U.S. 487, 61 S.Ct 1020 (1941), p. 746, infra.

3. For examples of the "new federal common law" or "national common law," see the *D'Oench, Duhme* and *Atherton* cases, pp. 761, 764, infra. Under the interstate commerce power, could not Congress enact rules determining the measure of an interstate railroad's duty to persons walking along the railroad's right of way? See Louise Weinberg, Federal Common Law, 83

Nw.U.L.Rev. 805 (1989), urging expanded use of federal common law for matters of national concern, such as aviation and environmental disasters.

4. The majority opinion in *Erie* relied in part, see n.5 of the opinion, on the historical work of Professor Warren. Warren argued that the earlier versions of the First Judiciary Act of 1789 showed that § 34 (known today commonly as the Rules of Decision Act) was intended to require federal courts to adhere to state substantive law. Warren's conclusion was that, therefore, the *Swift* doctrine had been developed in contravention of the original congressional intent of the Rules of Decision Act. Subsequent research has arguably undermined some of Warren's assertions, however. First, the so-called *Swift* doctrine of federal court application of an independent common law in "general" areas of the law—such as commercial law—began immediately with the passage of the First Judiciary Act in 1789. *Swift*, a decision handed down more than 50 years later, became associated with the doctrine largely because of Justice Story's detailed discussion of it. See, e.g., Gill v. Jacobs, 10 F.Cas. 373, 375 (C.C.D.S.C.1816) (No. 5,426) (applying the general rule and ignoring state law in a commercial case). The fact that *Swift* was consistent with many years of decisional law leading up to it makes it less likely that the doctrine was an historical aberration. Second, some of Warren's specific claims about drafting history of the Judiciary Act, including the history of the Rules of Decision Act, appear to rest on mistaken assumptions about the First Congress's process for debating bills. The most thorough discussion appears in Ritz, Rewriting the History of the Judiciary Act of 1789 (Holt & LaRue eds.1990). See also Borchers, The Origins of Diversity Jurisdiction, the Rise of Legal Positivism, and a Brave New World for Erie and Klaxon, 72 Tex.L.Rev. 79 (1993); Holt, "To Establish Justice": Politics, the Judiciary Act of 1789, and the Invention of the Federal Courts, 1989 Duke L.J. 1421.

As you read the cases following *Erie*, however, consider whether the historical questions were really important to the Court, or whether its other concerns about federal courts applying a general common law were more central to its decision.

———————

For nearly two decades the sway of the Erie doctrine expanded, requiring federal courts to apply one state rule after another as "substantive." The following case, which set out a deceptively simple test, made it rather easy to characterize matters as "substantive," and therefore governed by state law.

Guaranty Trust Co. v. York

Supreme Court of the United States, 1945.
326 U.S. 99, 65 S.Ct. 1464, 89 L.Ed.2079.

[In 1942 York filed a class suit in a Federal district court in New York, charging defendant with breach of trust in connection with transactions in 1931. Defendant obtained a summary judgment on the ground the suit was time-barred under the New York rule, but this was

CHAPTER 9 CONFLICTS PROBLEMS IN FEDERAL AND INTERNATIONAL SETTINGS 701

reversed, the Court of Appeals ruling that in a diversity action brought on its equity side the district court was not bound to apply the statute of limitations as it would have been applied by a New York court. The Supreme Court granted certiorari.]

■ JUSTICE FRANKFURTER delivered the opinion of the Court. . . .

Our starting point must be the policy of federal jurisdiction which Erie R. Co. v. Tompkins, 304 U.S. 64, embodies. . . .

In relation to the problem now here, the real significance of Swift v. Tyson lies in the fact that it did not enunciate novel doctrine. Nor was it restricted to its particular situation. It summed up prior attitudes and expressions in cases that had come before this Court and lower federal courts for at least thirty years, at law as well as in equity. . . .

And so this case reduces itself to the narrow question whether, when no recovery could be had in a State court because the action is barred by the statute of limitations, a federal court in equity can take cognizance of the suit because there is diversity of citizenship between the parties. Is the outlawry, according to State law, of a claim created by the States a matter of "substantive rights" to be respected by a federal court of equity when that court's jurisdiction is dependent on the fact that there is a State-created right, or is such statute of "a mere remedial character" . . . which a federal court may disregard?

Matters of "substance" and matters of "procedure" are much talked about in the books as though they defined a great divide cutting across the whole domain of law. But, of course, "substance" and "procedure" are the same key-words to very different problems. Neither "substance" nor "procedure" represents the same invariants. Each implies different variables depending upon the particular problem for which it is used. See Home Ins. Co. v. Dick, 281 U.S. 397, 409. And the different problems are only distantly related at best, for the terms are in common use in connection with situations turning on such different considerations as those that are relevant to questions pertaining to ex post facto legislation, the impairment of the obligations of contract, the enforcement of federal rights in the State courts and the multitudinous phases of the conflict of laws.

Here we are dealing with a right to recover derived not from the United States but from one of the States. When, because the plaintiff happens to be a non-resident, such a right is enforceable in a federal as well as in a State court, the forms and mode of enforcing the right may at times, naturally enough, vary because the two judicial systems are not identic. But since a federal court adjudicating a state-created right solely because of the diversity of citizenship of the parties is for that purpose, in effect, only another court of the State, it cannot afford recovery if the right to recover is made unavailable by the State nor can it substantially affect the enforcement of the right as given by the State.

And so the question is not whether a statute of limitations is deemed a matter of "procedure" in some sense. The question is whether such a statute concerns merely the manner and the means by which a right to recover, as recognized by the State, is enforced, or whether such statutory limitation is a matter of substance in the aspect that alone is relevant to our problem, namely does it significantly affect the result of a litigation for a federal court to disregard a law of a State that would be controlling in an action upon the same claim by the same parties in a State court?

It is therefore immaterial whether statutes of limitation are characterized either as "substantive" or "procedural" in State court opinions in any use of those terms unrelated to the specific issue before us. Erie R. Co. v. Tompkins was not an endeavor to formulate scientific legal terminology. It expressed a policy that touches vitally the proper distribution of judicial power between State and federal courts. In essence, the intent of that decision was to insure that, in all cases where a federal court is exercising jurisdiction solely because of the diversity of citizenship of the parties, the outcome of the litigation in the federal court should be substantially the same, so far as legal rules determine the outcome of a litigation, as it would be if tried in a State court. The nub of the policy that underlies Erie R. Co. v. Tompkins is that for the same transaction the accident of a suit by a nonresident litigant in a federal court instead of in a State court a block away, should not lead to a substantially different result. And so, putting to one side abstractions regarding "substance" and "procedure," we have held that in diversity cases the federal courts must follow the law of the State as to burden of proof, Cities Service Oil Co. v. Dunlap, 308 U.S. 208, as to conflict of laws, Klaxon Co. v. Stentor Co., 313 U.S. 487, as to contributory negligence, Palmer v. Hoffman, 318 U.S. 109, 117. And see Sampson v. Channell, 1 Cir., 110 F.2d 754. Erie R. Co. v. Tompkins has been applied with an eye alert to essentials in avoiding disregard of State law in diversity cases in the federal courts. A policy so important to our federalism must be kept free from entanglements with analytical or terminological niceties.

Plainly enough, a statute that would completely bar recovery in a suit if brought in a State court bears on a State-created right vitally and not merely formally or negligibly. As to consequences that so intimately affect recovery or nonrecovery a federal court in a diversity case should follow State law. See Morgan, Choice of Law Governing Proof (1944) 58 Harv.L.Rev. 153, 155–158. . . .

Diversity jurisdiction is founded on assurance to non-resident litigants of courts free from susceptibility to potential local bias. The Framers of the Constitution, according to Marshall, entertained "apprehensions" lest distant suitors be subjected to local bias in State courts, or, at least, viewed with "indulgence the possible fears and apprehensions" of such suitors. Bank of the United States v. Deveaux, 5 Cranch 61, 87. And so Congress afforded out-of-State litigants another tribunal, not another body of law. The operation of a double system of conflicting laws in the same State is plainly hostile to the reign of law. Certainly, the fortuitous circumstance of residence out of a State of one of the parties to a litigation ought not to give rise to a discrimination against others equally concerned but locally resident. The source of substantive rights enforced by a federal court under diversity jurisdiction, it cannot be said too often, is the law of the States. Whenever that law is authoritatively declared by a State, whether its voice be the legislature or its highest court, such law ought to govern in litigation founded on that law, whether the forum of application is a State or a federal court and whether the remedies be sought at law or may be had in equity.

The judgment is reversed and the case is remanded for proceedings not inconsistent with this opinion. . . .

■ JUSTICE ROBERTS and JUSTICE DOUGLAS took no part in the consideration or decision of this case.

[JUSTICE RUTLEDGE dissented in an opinion, in which JUSTICE MURPHY joined, which argued that "this case arises from what are in fact if not in law interstate transactions," involving "the rights of security holders in relation to securities which were distributed not in New York or Ohio alone but widely throughout the country."]

NOTES

1. Since the limitations issue in *Guaranty Trust* was statutory, why was *Erie* apposite at all? Does the outcome-determinative test mean that even state rules undoubtedly regulating the conduct of the litigation are subject to the *Erie* command if they can affect the result of the action?

2. In Sun Oil Co. v. Wortman, 486 U.S. 717, 108 S.Ct. 2117 (1988), the Supreme Court held that statutes of limitation are traditionally procedural and that the forum did not violate the Due Process and Full Faith and Credit Clauses by applying its own longer statute to a claim governed by the substantive law of another jurisdiction. A statute of limitations may therefore be "substantive" for *Erie* purposes (since it "substantially affect[s] the enforcement" of a state-law based claim) and, at the same time, "procedural" for due process purposes. Justice O'Connor, in her partial concurrence, left open the question whether *Wortman* should be decided differently if the state whose substantive law applies to the claim also considers its statute of limitations to be "substantive." Why should this make a difference? While *Guaranty Trust* and *Phillips Petroleum*, pp. 700, 445, supra, address different concerns (the *Erie* problem and Due Process, respectively), does either decision turn on the characterization of the issue as "procedural" or as "substantive?"

3. In Chapter 7, we saw that characterization of an issue as substantive or procedural is a pervasive issue in cases presenting state/state conflicts. Under *Erie*, it is also a recurring issue in diversity of citizenship cases in federal court, particularly when a federal rule that is arguably procedural differs significantly from a forum-state rule addressed to the same problem.

To what extent are similar considerations and criteria at work in the federal diversity area? See Meador, State Law and the Federal Judicial Power, 49 Va.L.Rev. 1082 (1963). Servicios Comerciales Andinos, S.A. v. General Electric Del Caribe, Inc., 145 F.3d 463 (1st Cir.1998), affirmed an order of the U.S. District Court for the District of Puerto Rico that defendant pay a portion of plaintiff's attorney's fees under a Puerto Rican Rule of Civil Procedure that permitted this as a sanction for obstinate conduct. The court stated that "the fact that [the Puerto Rican Rule of Civil Procedure] is considered 'substantive' for Erie purposes does not bar a finding that it is 'procedural' for conflict of laws purposes." The court found that a Puerto Rican court would regard its sanction rule as "procedural" and apply it although the parties had stipulated that Peruvian law applied.

Compare Gil de Rebollo v. Miami Heat Associations, Inc., 137 F.3d 56 (1st Cir.1998), which involved the interaction between Federal Rule of Civil Procedure 68 and Puerto Rican Rule of Civil Procedure 35.1. The federal rule provides: "[i]f [the defendant's settlement offer is rejected and] the judgment finally obtained by the offeree is not more favorable than the offer, the offeree must pay the costs incurred after the making of the offer." The Puerto Rican rule provides that under these circumstances, "the offeree must pay the costs, expenses and attorney's fees incurred after the making of the offer." The plaintiff recovered less than the amount offered by defendant, but the First Circuit held that the defendant was not entitled to its attorney's fees incurred after the offer. The court noted that the federal rule did not define "costs" but "incorporates the definition of 'costs' in the relevant substantive statute of the jurisdiction whose substantive law applies to the case." Puerto Rican law applied and the Puerto Rican rule did not regard attorney's fees as "costs" because the rule listed the fees separately from costs. In the clash between the federal and Puerto Rican rules on recovery of attorney's fees, the federal rule controlled because it was "sufficiently broad to cover the point in dispute" and was both constitutional and "within the scope of the Rules Enabling Act."

4. In 1949 a trio of cases accepted the broad view of *Erie* and made major inroads on the independence of federal courts in their handling of state-law-based litigation. In Ragan v. Merchants Transfer and Warehouse Co., 337 U.S. 530, 69 S.Ct. 1233 (1949), a state rule was held to be dispositive of whether a suit had been started in time to avoid being barred by limitations. In Cohen v. Beneficial Industrial Loan Corp., 337 U.S. 541, 69 S.Ct. 1221 (1949), the state security-for-costs rule was held applicable in the diversity suit. Both cases are discussed in the concurring opinion of Harlan, J., in Hanna v. Plumer, p. 711, infra. *Ragan* was confirmed by Walker v. Armco Steel Co., p. 716, infra. Woods v. Interstate Realty Co., 337 U.S. 535, 69 S.Ct. 1235 (1949), held that a corporation barred from state courts because not certified to do business in the state, could not bring a diversity suit in a federal court in that state. But cf. S.J. v. Issaquah School Dist. No. 411, 470 F.3d 1288 (9th Cir.2006) (in an action under federal law when there is no federal statute of limitations and a federal court borrows the state's statute of limitations, the federal rule applies, which, unlike the state rule, tolls the statute when suit is filed rather than when process is served). The three cases have been called a "triple play" on the Federal Rules. Can you articulate why?

5. Though not one of the "triple play" cases, Palmer v. Hoffman, 318 U.S. 109, 117, 63 S.Ct. 477 (1943), has a similar effect: "The question of the burden of [proof in] establishing contributory negligence is a question of local law which federal courts in diversity of citizenship cases . . . must apply."

BERNHARDT V. POLYGRAPHIC CO., 350 U.S. 198, 76 S.Ct. 273 (1956): Plaintiff sued in a Vermont court for damages for breach of a contract of employment. Defendant removed the action to the federal district court and moved for a stay pending arbitration, invoking a provision of the contract. The district judge refused the stay because Vermont law permitted revocation of an arbitration agreement at any time before entry of the arbitration award. Applying that law, the district court refused to enforce the arbitration clause. The Supreme Court agreed, and declared:

> ". . . [The] right to recover . . . owes its existence to one of the States, not to the United States. The federal court enforces the state-created right by rules of procedure which it has acquired from the Federal Government and which therefore are not identical with those of the state courts. Yet, in spite of that difference in procedure, the federal court . . . may not 'substantially affect the enforcement of the right as given by the State.' [Guaranty Trust Co. v. York, 326 U.S. 99, 109, 65 S.Ct. 1464.] If the federal court allows arbitration where the state court would disallow it, the outcome of litigation might depend on the courthouse where suit is brought. For the remedy by arbitration, whatever its merits or shortcomings, substantially affects the cause of action created by the State. The nature of the tribunal where suits are tried is an important part of the parcel of rights behind a cause of action. The change from a court of law to an arbitration panel may make a radical difference in ultimate result. Arbitration carries no right to trial by jury that is guaranteed both by the Seventh Amendment and by Ch. 1, Art. 12th, of the Vermont Constitution. Arbitrators do not have the benefit of judicial instruction on the law; they need not give their reasons for their results; the record of their proceedings is not as complete as it is in a court trial; and judicial review of an award is more limited than judicial review of a trial—all as discussed in Wilko v. Swan, 346 U.S. 427, 435–438. . . . There would in our judgment be a resultant discrimination if the parties suing on a Vermont cause of action in the federal court were remitted to arbitration, while those suing in the Vermont court could not be."

The Federal Arbitration Act is found in Title 9 of the United States Code. 9 U.S.C. § 2 (1988) provides that arbitration agreements in "a contract evidencing a transaction involving commerce . . . shall be valid, irrevocable, and enforceable." 9 U.S.C. § 3 (1988) provides that United States courts shall stay suits brought in violation of such an arbitration agreement. These provisions did not apply in *Bernhardt* because there was no showing that the contract involved interstate commerce. 350 U.S. at 200–01. Wilko v. Swan, cited in the quotation from *Bernhardt*, held that an agreement to arbitrate could not preclude a buyer of a security from seeking a judicial remedy under the Securities Act of 1933, in view of the language of that Act barring a "provision . . . to waive compliance" with the Act. The Court overruled Wilko v. Swan in Rodriguez de Quijas v. Shearson/American Exp., Inc., 490 U.S. 477, 109 S.Ct. 1917 (1989). Moreover, the specific result in *Bernhardt* seems doubtful in light of Allied-Bruce Terminix Cos., Inc. v. Dobson, 513 U.S. 265, 115 S.Ct. 834 (1995), in which the Court held that a consumer contract with a termite protection company had enough of a nexus with interstate commerce so that the Federal Arbitration Act applied, thereby pre-empting an Alabama state law purporting to make arbitration clauses in such contracts unenforceable.

Byrd v. Blue Ridge Rural Electric Cooperative, Inc.

Supreme Court of the United States, 1958.
356 U.S. 525, 78 S.Ct. 893, 2 L.Ed.2d 953.

[Petitioner was injured in South Carolina while working as a lineman for a firm which had a contract to erect electrical power lines for respondent. As a defense to his diversity action for damages resulting from its negligence, respondent asserted that petitioner was a statutory employee and could recover only the statutory compensation benefits. Respondent claimed further that the defense was to be decided by the court and not the jury because of a controlling South Carolina decision. The Court of Appeals reversed a judgment for petitioner entered on a jury verdict.]

■ JUSTICE BRENNAN delivered the opinion of the Court. . . .

. . . The respondent argues on the basis of the decision of the Supreme Court of South Carolina in Adams v. Davison-Paxon Co., 230 S.C. 532, 96 S.E.2d 566, that the issue of immunity should be decided by the judge and not by the jury. That was a negligence action brought in the state trial court against a store owner by an employee of an independent contractor who operated the store's millinery department. The trial judge denied the store owner's motion for a directed verdict made upon the ground that § 72–111 [of the South Carolina Workmen's Compensation Act] barred the plaintiff's action. The jury returned a verdict for the plaintiff. The South Carolina Supreme Court reversed, holding that it was for the judge and not the jury to decide on the evidence whether the owner was a statutory employer, and that the store owner had sustained his defense. . . .

The respondent argues that this state-court decision governs the present diversity case and "divests the jury of its normal function" to decide the disputed fact question of the respondent's immunity under § 72–111. This is to contend that the federal court is bound under Erie R. Co. v. Tompkins, 304 U.S. 64, to follow the state court's holding to secure uniform enforcement of the immunity created by the State.

First. It was decided in Erie R. Co. v. Tompkins that the federal courts in diversity cases must respect the definition of state-created rights and obligations by the state courts. We must, therefore, first examine the rule in Adams v. Davison-Paxon Co. to determine whether it is bound up with these rights and obligations in such a way that its application in the federal court is required. Cities Service Oil Co. v. Dunlap, 308 U.S. 208.

The Workmen's Compensation Act is administered in South Carolina by its Industrial Commission. The South Carolina courts hold that, on judicial review of actions of the Commission under § 72–111, the question whether the claim of an injured workman is within the Commission's jurisdiction is a matter of law for decision by the court, which makes its own findings of fact relating to that jurisdiction. The South Carolina Supreme Court states no reasons in Adams v. Davison-Paxon Co. why, although the jury decides all other factual issues raised by the cause of action and defenses, the jury is displaced as to the factual issue raised by the affirmative defense under § 72–111. The decisions cited to support the holding . . . are concerned solely with defining the scope and method of judicial review of the Industrial Commission. A State may, of course, distribute the functions of its judicial machinery as it sees fit. The decisions relied upon, however, furnish no reason for selecting the judge rather than the jury to decide this single affirmative defense in the negligence action. They simply reflect a policy, cf. Crowell v. Benson, 285 U.S. 22, that administrative determination of "jurisdictional facts" should not be final but subject to judicial review. The conclusion is inescapable that the Adams holding is grounded in the practical consideration that the question had theretofore come before the South Carolina courts from the Industrial Commission and the courts had become accustomed to deciding the factual issue of immunity without the aid of juries. We find nothing to suggest that this rule was announced as an integral part of the special relationship created by the statute. Thus the requirement appears to be merely a form and mode of enforcing the immunity, Guaranty Trust Co. v. York, 326 U.S. 99, 108, and not a rule intended to be bound up with the definition of the rights and obligations of the parties. The situation is therefore not analogous to that in Dice v. Akron, C. & Y. R. Co., 342 U.S. 359, where this Court held that the right to trial by jury is so substantial a part of the cause of action created by the Federal Employers' Liability Act that the Ohio courts could not apply, in an action under that statute, the Ohio rule that the question of fraudulent release was for determination by a judge rather than by a jury.

Second. But cases following Erie have evinced a broader policy to the effect that the federal courts should conform as near as may be—in the absence of other considerations—to state rules even of form and mode where the state rules may bear substantially on the question whether the litigation would come out one way in the federal court and another way in the state court if the federal court failed to apply a particular local rule. E.g., Guaranty Trust Co. v. York, supra; Bernhardt v. Polygraphic Co., 350 U.S. 198. Concededly the nature of the tribunal which tries issues may be important in the enforcement of the parcel of rights making up a cause of action or defense, and bear significantly upon achievement of uniform enforcement of the right. It may well be that in the instant personal-injury case the outcome would be substantially affected by whether the issue of immunity is decided by a judge or a jury. Therefore, were "outcome" the only consideration, a strong case might appear for saying that the federal court should follow the state practice.

But there are affirmative countervailing considerations at work here. The federal system is an independent system for administering justice to litigants who properly invoke its jurisdiction. An essential characteristic of that system is the manner in which, in civil common-law actions, it distributes trial functions between judge and jury and, under the influence—if not the command—of the Seventh Amendment, assigns the decisions of disputed questions of fact to the jury. Jacob v. New York, 315 U.S. 752. The policy of uniform enforcement of state-created rights and obligations, see, e.g., Guaranty Trust Co. v. York, supra, cannot in every case exact compliance with a state rule—not bound up with rights and obligations—which disrupts the federal system of allocating functions between judge and jury. Herron v. Southern Pacific Co., 283 U.S. 91. Thus the inquiry here is whether the federal policy favoring jury decisions of disputed fact questions should yield to the state rule in the interest of furthering the objective that the litigation should not come out one way in the federal court and another way in the state court.

We think that in the circumstances of this case the federal court should not follow the state rule. It cannot be gainsaid that there is a strong federal policy against allowing state rules to disrupt the judge-jury relationship in the federal courts. In Herron v. Southern Pacific Co., supra, the trial judge in a personal-injury negligence action brought in the District Court for Arizona on diversity grounds directed a verdict for the defendant when it appeared as a matter of law that the plaintiff was guilty of contributory negligence. The federal judge refused to be bound by a provision of the Arizona Constitution which made the jury the sole arbiter of the question of contributory negligence. This Court sustained the action of the trial judge, holding that "state laws cannot alter the essential character or function of a federal court" because that function "is not in any sense a local matter, and state statutes which would interfere with the appropriate performance of that function are not binding upon the federal court under either the Conformity Act or the 'rules of decision' Act." Id., at 94. Perhaps even more clearly in light of the influence of the Seventh Amendment, the function assigned to the jury "is an essential factor in the process for which the Federal Constitution provides." Id., at 95. Concededly the Herron case was decided before Erie R. Co. v. Tompkins, but even when Swift v. Tyson, 16 Pet. 1, was governing law and allowed federal courts sitting in diversity cases to disregard state decisional law, it was never thought that state statutes or constitutions were similarly to be disregarded. Green v. Neal's Lessee, 6 Pet. 291. Yet Herron held that state statutes and constitutional provisions could not disrupt or alter the essential character or function of a federal court.

Third. We have discussed the problem upon the assumption that the outcome of the litigation may be substantially affected by whether the issue of immunity is decided by a judge or a jury. But clearly there is not present here the certainty that a different result would follow, cf. Guaranty Trust Co. v. York, supra, or even the strong possibility that this would be the case, cf. Bernhardt v. Polygraphic Co., supra. There are factors present here which might reduce that possibility. The trial judge in the federal system has powers denied the judges of many States to comment on the weight of evidence and credibility of witnesses, and discretion to grant a new trial if the verdict appears to him to be against the weight of the evidence. We do not think the likelihood of a different result is so strong as to require the federal practice of jury determination of disputed factual issues to yield to the state rule in the interest of uniformity of outcome.

The Court of Appeals did not consider other grounds of appeal raised by the respondent because the ground taken disposed of the case. We accordingly remand the case to the Court of Appeals for the decision of the other questions, with instructions that, if not made unnecessary by the decision of such questions, the Court of Appeals shall remand the case to the District Court for a new trial of such issues as the Court of Appeals may direct.

Reversed and remanded.[1]

NOTES

1.   Did *Byrd* change the approach to the *Erie* doctrine? Does *Byrd* mean that a state law need not be applied if doing so would alter the "essential character or function of a Federal court?" See Smith, *Blue Ridge* and Beyond:

---

[1]   Mr. Justice Whittaker dissented on the issue of how integral it was to the South Carolina rule that the question of statutory immunity be decided by the judge. Justices Harlan and Frankfurter also dissented. —eds.

A *Byrd*'s-Eye View of Federalism in Diversity Litigation, 36 Tul.L.Rev. 443 (1962).

2.   Since *Byrd*, to what extent must the forum state's rules be followed as to: availability of a jury; power to remove cases from the jury's determination; review of sufficiency of evidence for directed verdict or new trial purposes, and similar issues?

(a)   As to the grant of trial by jury, the diversity court is not bound to follow the state view, because of the heavy involvement of the Seventh Amendment. See Simler v. Conner, 372 U.S. 221, 83 S.Ct. 609 (1963), rejecting the state view that trial by jury was not available on the ground the suit was in "equity."

(b)   As to tests for a directed verdict and sufficiency of evidence, in pre-*Byrd* days, Stoner v. New York Life Insurance Co., 311 U.S. 464, 61 S.Ct. 336 (1940) was read by some courts to mean that a diversity court is bound by state rules as to the sufficiency of the evidence to go to the jury. The question was explicitly left open in Dick v. New York Life Insurance Co., 359 U.S. 437, 444–445, 79 S.Ct. 921 (1959). Wratchford v. S. J. Groves & Sons Co., 405 F.2d 1061 (4th Cir.1969) and Planters Manufacturing Co. v. Protection Mutual Insurance Co., 380 F.2d 869 (5th Cir.1967) held that federal, not state, law determines when the judge takes an issue from the jury for insufficiency of opposing evidence. Federal law also governs the admissibility of evidence, including admissibility of evidence of insurance. Reed v. General Motors Corp., 773 F.2d 660 (5th Cir.1985). Sometimes it is difficult to distinguish a state rule of evidence from state substantive law. Consider also Snead v. Metropolitan Property & Cas. Ins. Co., 237 F.3d 1080, 1092 (9th Cir.2001), cert. denied, 534 U.S. 888, 122 S.Ct. 201 (2001). That case held that in a suit under the Oregon disability discrimination law, the court applied the federal rather than the state standard for summary judgment. The opinion explained that applying the state standard, which required only that the plaintiff present prima facie evidence of discrimination, would only postpone the inevitable loss for the plaintiff and provide "an increased burden on the district courts' already crowded trial dockets."

(c)   As to size of the jury in civil cases, Wilson v. Nooter Corp., 475 F.2d 497 (1st Cir.1973) ruled that having 12 jurors is not an "integral" part of the state-created right in a diversity action, so that a six-member jury suffices even when the state forum requires 12. See also Palmer v. Ford Motor Co., 498 F.2d 952 (10th Cir.1974). See Moore & Bendix, Congress, Evidence and Rulemaking, 84 Yale L.J. 9 (1974); Note, The Law Applied in Diversity Cases: The Rules of Decision and the Erie Doctrine, 85 Yale L.J. 678 (1976).

(d)   Kamen v. Kemper Financial Services, Inc., 500 U.S. 90, 111 S.Ct. 1711 (1991) held that state law determines whether the plaintiff in a stockholder's derivative suit is excused from making a futile demand that the company's board of directors take action. The Court held that Federal Rule of Civil Procedure 23.1, which requires the complaint in such an action to "allege with particularity the efforts, if any, made by the plaintiff to obtain the action the plaintiff desires from the directors," did not require displacement of state law on the "futility" exception.

Hanna v. Plumer

Supreme Court of the United States, 1965.
380 U.S. 460, 85 S.Ct. 1136, 14 L.Ed.2d 8.

■ CHIEF JUSTICE WARREN delivered the opinion of the Court.

The question to be decided is whether, in a civil action where the jurisdiction of the United States district court is based upon diversity of citizenship between the parties, service of process shall be made in the manner prescribed by state law or that set forth in Rule 4(d)(1) [now Rule 4(e)(2)—eds.] of the Federal Rules of Civil Procedure.

On February 6, 1963, petitioner, a citizen of Ohio, filed her complaint in the District Court for the District of Massachusetts, claiming damages in excess of $10,000 for personal injuries resulting from an automobile accident in South Carolina, allegedly caused by the negligence of one Louise Plumer Osgood, a Massachusetts citizen deceased at the time of the filing of the complaint. Respondent, Mrs. Osgood's executor and also a Massachusetts citizen, was named as defendant. On February 8, service was made by leaving copies of the summons and the complaint with respondent's wife at his residence, concededly in compliance with Rule 4(d)(1), which provides: "The summons and complaint shall be served together. . . . as follows: (1) Upon an individual . . . by delivering a copy . . . to him personally or by leaving copies thereof at his . . . usual place of abode with some person of suitable age and discretion then residing therein. . . ." Respondent filed his answer . . . alleging, inter alia, that the action could not be maintained because [service had not been made in accordance with the "delivery in hand"] provisions of Massachusetts General Laws (Ter.Ed.) Chapter 197, Section 9. . . . On October 17, 1963, the District Court granted respondent's motion for summary judgment, citing Ragan v. Merchants Transfer & Warehouse Co., 337 U.S. 530, and Guaranty Trust Co. of New York v. York, 326 U.S. 99, . . . The Court of Appeals for the First Circuit, . . . unanimously affirmed. . . .

We conclude that the adoption of Rule 4(d)(1), designed to control service of process in diversity actions, neither exceeded the congressional mandate embodied in the Rules Enabling Act nor transgressed constitutional bounds, and that the Rule is therefore the standard against which the District Court should have measured the adequacy of the service. Accordingly, we reverse the decision of the Court of Appeals. . . .

Respondent suggests that the Erie doctrine acts as a check on the Federal Rules of Civil Procedure . . . Reduced to essentials, the argument is: (1) Erie, as refined in York, demands that federal courts apply state law whenever application of federal law in its stead will alter the outcome of the case. (2) In this case a determination that the Massachusetts service requirements obtained will result in immediate victory for respondent. If, on the other hand, it should be held that Rule 4(d)(1) is applicable, the litigation will continue, with possible victory for petitioner. (3) Therefore, Erie demands application of the Massachusetts rule. The syllogism possesses an appealing simplicity, but is for several reasons invalid.

In the first place, it is doubtful that, even if there were no Federal Rule making it clear that in-hand service is not required in diversity actions, the Erie rule would have obligated the District Court to follow the Massachusetts procedure. "Outcome-determination" analysis was never intended to serve as a talisman. . . . Indeed, the message of York itself is that choices between state and federal law are to be made not by the application of any automatic, "litmus paper" criterion, but rather by reference to the policies underlying the Erie rule. Guaranty Trust Co. v. York, supra, at 108–112.

The Erie rule is rooted in part in a realization that it would be unfair for the character or result of a litigation materially to differ because the suit had been brought in a federal court. . . . The decision was also in part a reaction to the practice of "forum-shopping" which had grown up in response to the rule of Swift v. Tyson. . . . Not only are nonsubstantial, or trivial, variations not likely to raise the sort of equal protection problems which troubled the Court in Erie; they are also unlikely to influence the choice of a forum. The "outcome-determination" test therefore cannot be read without reference to the twin aims of the Erie rule: discouragement of forum-shopping and avoidance of inequitable administration of the laws.

The difference between the conclusion that the Massachusetts rule is applicable, and the conclusion that it is not, is of course at this point "outcome-determinative" in the sense that if we hold the state rule to apply, respondent prevails, whereas if we hold that Rule 4(d)(1) governs, the litigation will continue. But in this sense every procedural variation is "outcome-determinative." For example, having brought suit in a federal court, a plaintiff cannot then insist on the right to file subsequent pleadings in accord with the time limits applicable in state courts, even though enforcement of the federal timetable will, if he continues to insist that he must meet only the state time limit, result in determination of the controversy against him. So it is here. Though choice of the federal or state rule will at this point have a marked effect upon the outcome of the litigation, the difference between the two rules would be of scant, if any, relevance to the choice of a forum. Petitioner, in choosing her forum, was not presented with a situation where application of the state rule would wholly bar recovery; rather, adherence to the state rule would have resulted only in altering the way in which process was served. . . .

There is, however, a more fundamental flaw in respondent's syllogism: the incorrect assumption that the rule of Erie R. Co. v. Tompkins constitutes the appropriate test of the validity and therefore the applicability of a Federal Rule of Civil Procedure. The Erie rule has never been invoked to void a Federal Rule. . . .

. . . It is true that both the Enabling Act and the Erie rule say, roughly, that federal courts are to apply state "substantive" law and federal "procedural" law, but from that it need not follow that the tests are identical. For they were designed to control very different sorts of decisions. When a situation is covered by one of the Federal Rules, the question facing the court is a far cry from the typical, relatively unguided Erie choice: the court has been instructed to apply the Federal Rule, and can refuse to do so only if the Advisory Committee, this Court, and Congress erred in their prima facie judgment that the Rule in question transgresses neither the terms of the Enabling Act nor constitutional restrictions.

. . . [T]he opinion in Erie, which involved no Federal Rule and dealt with a question which was "substantive" in every traditional sense (whether the railroad owed a duty of care to Tompkins as a trespasser or a licensee), surely neither said nor implied that measures like Rule 4(d)(1) are unconstitutional. For the constitutional provision for a federal court system (augmented by the Necessary and Proper Clause) carries with it congressional power to make rules governing the practice and pleading in those courts, which in turn includes a power to regulate matters which, though falling within the uncertain area between substance and procedure, are rationally capable of classification as either. . . .

Erie and its offspring cast no doubt on the long-recognized power of Congress to prescribe housekeeping rules for federal courts even though some of those rules will inevitably differ from comparable state rules. . . . To hold that a Federal Rule of Civil Procedure must cease to function whenever it alters the mode of enforcing state-created rights would be to disembowel either the Constitution's grant of power over federal procedure or Congress' attempt to exercise that power in the Enabling Act. Rule 4(d)(1) is valid and controls the instant case.

Reversed.

■ JUSTICE HARLAN, concurring.

It is unquestionably true that up to now Erie and the cases following it have not succeeded in articulating a workable doctrine governing choice of law in diversity actions. I respect the Court's effort to clarify the situation in today's opinion. However, in doing so I think it has misconceived the constitutional premises of Erie and has failed to deal adequately with those past decisions upon which the courts below relied.

Erie was something more than an opinion which worried about "forum-shopping and avoidance of inequitable administration of the laws," . . . although to be sure these were important elements of the decision. I have always regarded that decision as one of the modern cornerstones of our federalism, expressing policies that profoundly touch the allocation of judicial power between the state and federal systems. Erie recognized that there should not be two conflicting systems of law controlling the primary activity of citizens, for such alternative governing authority must necessarily give rise to a debilitating uncertainty in the planning of everyday affairs. And it recognized that the scheme of our Constitution envisions an allocation of law-making functions between state and federal legislative processes which is undercut if the federal judiciary can make substantive law affecting state affairs beyond the bounds of congressional legislative powers in this regard. Thus, in diversity cases Erie commands that it be the state law governing primary private activity which prevails.

The shorthand formulations which have appeared in some past decisions are prone to carry untoward results that frequently arise from oversimplification. The Court is quite right in stating that the "outcome-determinative" test of Guaranty Trust Co. of New York v. York, 326 U.S. 99, if taken literally, proves too much, for any rule, no matter how clearly "procedural," can affect the outcome of litigation if it is not obeyed. In turning from the "outcome" test of York back to the unadorned forum-shopping rationale of Erie, however, the Court falls prey to like oversimplification, for a simple forum-shopping rule also proves too much; litigants often choose a federal forum merely to obtain what they consider the advantages of the Federal Rules of Civil Procedure or to try their cases before a supposedly more favorable judge. To my mind the proper line of approach in determining whether to apply a state or a federal rule, whether "substantive" or "procedural," is to stay close to basic principles by inquiring if the choice of rule would substantially affect those primary decisions respecting human conduct which our constitutional system leaves to state regulation. If so, Erie and the Constitution require that the state rule prevail, even in the face of a conflicting federal rule.

The Court weakens, if indeed it does not submerge, this basic principle by finding, in effect, a grant of substantive legislative power in the constitutional provision for a federal court system . . . , and through it, setting up the Federal Rules as a body of law inviolate. So long as a reasonable man could characterize any duly adopted federal rule as "procedural," the Court, unless I misapprehend what is said, would have it apply no matter how seriously it frustrated a State's substantive regulation of the primary conduct and affairs of its citizens. Since the members of the Advisory Committee, the Judicial Conference, and this Court who formulated the Federal Rules are presumably reasonable men, it follows that the integrity of the Federal Rules is absolute. Whereas the unadulterated outcome and forum-shopping tests may err too far toward honoring state rules, I submit that the Court's "arguably procedural, ergo constitutional" test moves too fast and far in the other direction.

The courts below relied upon this Court's decisions in Ragan v. Merchants Transfer & Warehouse Co., 337 U.S. 530, and Cohen v. Beneficial Indus. Loan Corp., 337 U.S. 541. Those cases deserve more attention than this Court has given them, particularly Ragan which, if still good law, would in my opinion call for affirmance of the result reached by the Court of Appeals. Further, a discussion of these two cases will serve to illuminate the "diversity" thesis I am advocating.

In Ragan a Kansas statute of limitations provided that an action was deemed commenced when service was made on the defendant. Despite Federal Rule 3 which provides that an action commences with the filing of the complaint, the Court held that for purposes of the Kansas statute of limitations a diversity tort action commenced only when service was made upon the defendant. The effect of this holding was that although the plaintiff had filed his federal complaint within the state period of limitations, his action was barred because the federal marshal did not serve a summons on the defendant until after the limitations period had run. I think that the decision was wrong. At most, application of the Federal Rule would have meant that potential Kansas tort defendants would have to defer for a few days the satisfaction of knowing that they had not been sued within the limitations period. The choice of the Federal Rule would have had no effect on the primary stages of private activity from which torts arise, and only the most minimal effect on behavior following the commission of the tort. In such circumstances the interest of the federal system in proceeding under its own rules should have prevailed.

Cohen v. Beneficial Indus. Loan Corp. held that a federal diversity court must apply a state statute requiring a small stockholder in a stockholder derivative suit to post a bond securing payment of defense costs as a condition to prosecuting an action. Such a statute is not "outcome determinative"; the plaintiff can win with or without it. . . . The proper view of Cohen is, in my opinion, that the statute was meant to inhibit small stockholders from instituting "strike suits," and thus it was designed and could be expected to have a substantial impact on private primary activity. Anyone who was at the trial bar during the period when Cohen arose can appreciate the strong state policy reflected in the statute. I think it wholly legitimate to view Federal Rule 23 as not purporting to deal with the problem. But even had the Federal Rules purported to do so, and in so doing provided a substantially less effective deterrent to strike suits, I think the state rule should still have prevailed. That is where I believe the Court's view differs from mine; for the Court attributes such overriding force to the Federal Rules that it is hard to think of a case where a conflicting state rule would be allowed to operate, even though the state rule reflected policy considerations which, under Erie, would lie within the realm of state legislative authority.

It remains to apply what has been said to the present case. The Massachusetts rule provides that an executor need not answer suits unless in-hand service was made upon him or notice of the action was filed in the proper registry of probate within one year of his giving bond. The evident intent of this statute is to permit an executor to distribute the estate which he is administering without fear that further liabilities may be outstanding for which he could be held personally liable. If the Federal District Court in Massachusetts applies Rule 4(d)(1) of the Federal Rules of Civil Procedure instead of the Massachusetts service rule, what effect would that have on the speed and assurance with which estates are distributed? As I see it, the effect would not be substantial. It would mean simply that an executor would have to check at his own house or the federal courthouse as well as the registry of probate before he could distribute the estate with impunity. As this does not seem enough to give rise to any real impingement on the vitality of the state policy which the Massachusetts rule is intended to serve, I concur in the judgment of the Court.

WALKER V. ARMCO STEEL CORP., 446 U.S. 740, 100 S.Ct. 1978 (1980): In a diversity action the complaint was filed within the two year statute of limitations of the forum state, but defendant was not served with process until after the statutory period had run. The Court found these facts "indistinguishable" from those in Ragan v. Merchants Transfer & Warehouse Co., 337 U.S. 530, 69 S.Ct. 1233 (1949), Note 4, p. 704, supra. Contrary to petitioner's claim, *Ragan* was not weakened by Hanna v. Plumer because Rule 3 did not come into "direct collision" with state law by affecting the running of state statutes of limitation. The Court said, 446 U.S., at pp. 751–52:

> "In contrast to Rule 3, the Oklahoma statute is a statement of a substantive decision by that State that actual service on, and accordingly actual notice by, the defendant is an integral part of the several policies served by the statute of limitations. See C & C Tile Co. v. Independent School District No. 7 of Tulsa County, 503 P.2d 554, 559 (Okla.1972). The statute of limitations establishes a deadline after which the defendant may legitimately have peace of mind; it also recognizes that after a certain period of time it is unfair to require the defendant to attempt to piece together his defense to an old claim. A requirement of actual service promotes both of those functions of the statute. See generally ibid.; Seitz v. Jones, 370 P.2d 300, 302 (Okla.1961). See also Ely, The Irrepressible Myth of Erie, 87 Harv.L.Rev. 693, 730–31 (1974).[1] It is these policy aspects

---

[1] The importance of actual service, with corresponding actual notice, to the statute of limitations scheme in Oklahoma is further demonstrated by the fact that under Okla.Stat., Tit. 12, § 97 (1971) the statute of limitations must be tolled as to each defendant through individual service, unless a codefendant who is served is "united in interest" with the unserved defendant. That requirement, like the service requirement itself, does nothing to promote the general policy behind all statutes of limitations of keeping stale claims out of court. Instead, the service requirement furthers a different but related policy decision: that each defendant has a legitimate right not to be surprised by notice of a lawsuit after the period of liability has run. If the defendant is "united in interest" with a codefendant who has been served, then presumably the defendant will receive actual notice of the lawsuit through the codefendant and will not have

which make the service requirement an 'integral' part of the statute of limitations both in this case and in Ragan. As such, the service rule must be considered part and parcel of the statute of limitations."

NOTES

1. After *Hanna* and *Walker* if the Federal Rules of Civil Procedure adopt provisions fixing time limitations for diversity actions in the federal courts, will they be constitutional? If so, would *Guaranty Trust* be overruled?

2. The question addressed in *Walker*, of whether a federal rule or statute is in "direct collision" with the state rule, is very important. If a valid federal provision collides with state law, the Supremacy Clause requires state law to give way; the federal directive must be applied, unless the federal rule violates the Rules Enabling Act. See Semtek Int'l Inc. v. Lockheed Martin Corp., p. 727, infra, in which the Court suggested that if F.R.C.P. 41 were read to bar relitigation in another state contrary to California state law that the rule would then overstep the boundaries of a permissible federal rule. If, however, the federal rule is found not to be in direct collision (as in *Walker*) the state rule is very likely applied under the "twin aims" test articulated in *Hanna*. On some occasions (notably *Ragan* and *Walker*) the Court has read the federal rule narrowly, thus leaving room for application of state law.

But contrast the *Ragan-Walker* approach with some of the Court's later *Erie* decisions. For instance, in Burlington Northern R. Co. v. Woods, 480 U.S. 1, 107 S.Ct. 967 (1987), the Court held that Federal Rule of Appellate Procedure 38, giving the Court of Appeals discretion to assess "just damages" in order to penalize an appellant for filing a frivolous appeal, collided with and displaced a state rule providing a fixed penalty on defendants who took an appeal if the result of the appeal were affirmance of the judgment. Could the Court have accommodated both rules by applying the mandatory penalty provided for under state law and allowing an extra penalty for frivolous appeals under the federal rule with an offset for the amount paid under the state rule?

In Stewart Organization, Inc. v. Ricoh, 487 U.S. 22, 108 S.Ct. 2239 (1988), the Court held that the federal venue transfer statute, 28 U.S.C. § 1404, collided with and thus displaced a state rule forbidding enforcement of exclusive forum selection agreements. The Court held that the statute's policy was broad enough to encompass the parties' consensual expression of a venue preference and thus must control over the state law rule. Again, could the Court have accommodated both rules by requiring district courts to evaluate venue transfer requests under the standards set forth in § 1404 without giving weight to the parties' forum selection agreement?

3. Consider the puzzle created by the application in diversity cases of statutes like Tennessee Code § 29–26–115. That statute requires that for an expert witness to testify as to the standard of care in a malpractice action

---

his peace of mind disturbed when he receives official service of process. Similarly, the defendant will know that he must begin gathering his evidence while that task is still deemed by the State to be feasible.

that the expert either be licensed in Tennessee or a state contiguous to Tennessee. In Legg v. Chopra, 286 F.3d 286 (6th Cir.2002), the court held that statute must be applied in a diversity case. The court first turned to Federal Rule of Evidence 601 which provides that in actions in which "State law supplies the rule of decision, the competency of a witness shall be determined in accordance with State law." As the court noted, the principal application of this sentence of Rule 601 has been with regard to state rules governing the competency of lay witnesses, including so-called Dead Man statutes. The fact that the Tennessee statute governs whether experts can testify, however, required the court to confront a possible conflict between the statute and Federal Rule of Evidence 702, which governs the qualification of expert witnesses in federal court, and makes no express provision for the application of state law. The court concluded, however, that the Tennessee statute did not conflict with Rule 702, because the former governed the competence of a witness, while the latter governed qualification.

Is this approach consistent with the Supreme Court cases discussed at Note 2, supra?

4.   When a federal court finds no controlling precedent from the state supreme court or intermediate appeals court, it may in most states "certify" the question to the highest state court. Some states do not permit certification. Some permit federal appeals courts, but not district courts, to use the procedure. See Hogue, Law in a Parallel Universe: Erie's Betrayal, Diversity Jurisdiction, Georgia Conflict of Laws Questions in Contracts Cases in the Eleventh Circuit, and Certification Reform, 11 Ga.St.U.L.Rev. 531, 536 (1995) (citing statutes). For discussion of the precedential value of intermediate appellate decisions and of plurality decisions of a state supreme court see Klippel v. U-Haul Co. of Northeastern Michigan, 759 F.2d 1176, 1181 (4th Cir.1985) (stating that "we are free to disregard [a decision of a state intermediate appellate court] when it appears to be an aberration and we are reasonably convinced that the [state's highest court] would not embrace it"). In Reiser v. Residential Funding Corp., 380 F.3d 1027 (7th Cir.2004), cert. denied, 543 U.S. 1147, 125 S.Ct. 1301 (2005), the court adhered to its own 16-year old *Erie*-prediction as to how the state supreme court would answer a question of state law, despite intervening state appellate court opinions expressly rejecting that prediction, and reversed the district court which had followed the state appellate courts' view.

Salve Regina College v. Russell, 499 U.S. 225, 111 S.Ct. 1217 (1991) holds that federal courts of appeal must review de novo district courts' determinations of state law, overruling cases from a majority of the circuits that had deferred to district court determinations.

5.   Piper Aircraft Co. v. Reyno, 454 U.S. 235, 102 S.Ct. 252 (1981), p. 233, supra left open the question of whether in diversity cases a federal court must apply the forum non conveniens doctrine of the state in which it sits or whether it should apply a federal standard. Id. at 248 n.13. Forum non conveniens has not been displaced in federal courts by 28 U.S.C. § 1404(a) transfers when the alternative forum is not another federal district court. The *Erie* question is of great tactical importance in states that do not grant

forum non conveniens dismissals or do so in much more limited circumstances than permitted by the federal doctrine. If federal courts are free to dismiss when a state court would not, plaintiffs will sue in states with no or limited conveniens doctrines and will take steps to prevent removal to federal court, such as joining a local defendant. See 28 U.S.C. § 1441(b), providing that a case cannot be removed if any defendant is a citizen of the state in which suit is brought. The defendant may counter such tactics by claiming that the joinder of the local defendant was fraudulent. See Cabalceta v. Standard Fruit Co., 883 F.2d 1553 (11th Cir.1989) (reversing the district court's forum non conveniens dismissal, which was based on a finding of fraudulent joinder under Florida law, and remanding for determination of the fraudulent joinder claim under the applicable Costa Rican law).

American Dredging Co. v. Miller, 510 U.S. 443, 114 S.Ct. 981, 127 L.Ed.2d 285 (1994), held that a Louisiana statute preventing forum non conveniens dismissals in federal maritime actions in state court, including actions under the Jones Act for injuries to seamen, is not pre-empted by federal maritime law. The opinion stated that the doctrine of forum non conveniens is not "either a 'characteristic feature' of admiralty or a doctrine whose uniform application is necessary to maintain the 'proper harmony' of maritime law." 510 U.S. at 447.

6.   *Reverse*-Erie: This doctrine considers the extent to which federal procedural and quasi-procedural rules displace state rules in *state* courts. The phenomenon, which can arise only when the state court adjudicates matters of federal law, is quite rare. See Kevin M. Clermont, Reverse-*Erie*, 82 Notre Dame L.Rev. 1 (2006). An example is Felder v. Casey, 487 U.S. 131, 108 S.Ct. 2302 (1988). In that case, a Wisconsin state court applied a state "notice of claim" statute to a claim against police officers for a violation of federal constitutional rights under 28 U.S.C. § 1983. Analogizing to the *Erie* "outcome" test that was refined in *Hanna*, the Court refused to allow Wisconsin state courts to apply its state statute: "Because the notice-of-claim statute at issue here conflicts in both its purpose and effects with the remedial objectives of § 1983, and because its enforcement in such actions will frequently and predictably produce different outcomes in § 1983 litigation based solely on whether the claim is asserted in state or federal court, we conclude that the state law is pre-empted when the § 1983 action is brought in a state court." *Felder*, 487 U.S. at 138.

Is the "outcome" or "twin aims" test an appropriate guide in reverse-Erie cases? Consider this question again as you read the material on federal questions in relation to state law.

7.   The classic discussion of *Hanna* is Ely, The Irrepressible Myth of Erie, 87 Harv.L.Rev. 693 (1974). A well-known response to that treatment is Chayes, The Bead Game, 87 Harv.L.Rev. 741 (1974). The author of the first article served as law clerk to Chief Justice Warren when *Hanna* was decided.

Gasperini v. Center for Humanities, Inc.

Supreme Court of the United States, 1996.
518 U.S. 415, 116 S.Ct. 2211, 135 L.Ed.2d 659.

■ JUSTICE GINSBURG delivered the opinion of the Court, in which O'CONNOR, KENNEDY, SOUTER, and BREYER, joined. JUSTICE STEVENS filed a dissenting opinion. JUSTICE SCALIA filed a dissenting opinion, in which REHNQUIST and THOMAS joined.

Under the law of New York, appellate courts are empowered to review the size of jury verdicts and to order new trials when the jury's award "deviates materially from what would be reasonable compensation." N.Y. Civ. Prac. Law and Rules [CPLR] § 5501(c) (McKinney 1995). Under the Seventh Amendment, which governs proceedings in federal court, but not in state court, "the right of trial by jury shall be preserved, and no fact tried by a jury, shall be otherwise re-examined in any Court of the United States, than according to the rules of the common law." U.S. Const., Amdt. 7. The compatibility of these provisions, in an action based on New York law but tried in federal court by reason of the parties' diverse citizenship, is the issue we confront in this case. We hold that New York's law controlling compensation awards for excessiveness or inadequacy can be given effect, without detriment to the Seventh Amendment, if the review standard set out in CPLR § 5501(c) is applied by the federal trial court judge, with appellate control of the trial court's ruling limited to review for "abuse of discretion."

I

Petitioner William Gasperini, a journalist for CBS News and the Christian Science Monitor, began reporting on events in Central America in 1984. He earned his living primarily in radio and print media and only occasionally sold his photographic work. During the course of his seven-year stint in Central America, Gasperini took over 5,000 slide transparencies, depicting active war zones, political leaders, and scenes from daily life. In 1990, Gasperini agreed to supply his original color transparencies to The Center for Humanities, Inc. [Center] for use in an educational videotape, Conflict in Central America. Gasperini selected 300 of his slides for the Center; its videotape included 110 of them. The Center agreed to return the original transparencies, but upon the completion of the project, it could not find them.

Gasperini commenced suit in the United States District Court for the Southern District of New York, invoking the court's diversity jurisdiction pursuant to 28 U.S.C. § 1332. He alleged several state-law claims for relief, including breach of contract, conversion, and negligence. The Center conceded liability for the lost transparencies and the issue of damages was tried before a jury.

At trial, Gasperini's expert witness testified that the "industry standard" within the photographic publishing community valued a lost transparency at $1,500. . . . Gasperini estimated that his earnings from photography totaled just over $10,000 for the period from 1984 through 1993. He also testified that he intended to produce a book containing his best photographs from Central America.

After a three-day trial, the jury awarded Gasperini $450,000 in compensatory damages. This sum, the jury foreperson announced, "is [$]1500 each, for 300 slides." Moving for a new trial under Federal Rule of Civil Procedure 59, the Center attacked the verdict on various grounds, including excessiveness. Without comment, the District Court denied the motion.

The Court of Appeals for the Second Circuit vacated the judgment entered on the jury's verdict. Mindful that New York law governed the controversy, the Court of Appeals endeavored to apply CPLR § 5501(c), which instructs that, when a jury returns an itemized verdict, as the jury did in this case, the New York Appellate Division "shall determine that an award is excessive or inadequate if it deviates materially from what would be reasonable compensation. . . ."

Guided by Appellate Division rulings, the Second Circuit held that the $450,000 verdict "materially deviates from what is reasonable compensation." Some of Gasperini's transparencies, the Second Circuit recognized, were unique, notably those capturing combat situations in which Gasperini was the only photographer present. But others "depicted either generic scenes or events at which other professional photojournalists were present." No more than 50 slides merited a $1,500 award, the court concluded, after "giving Gasperini every benefit of the doubt." Absent evidence showing significant earnings from photographic endeavors or concrete plans to publish a book, the court further determined, any damage award above $100 each for the remaining slides would be excessive. . . . [T]he Second Circuit set aside the $450,000 verdict and ordered a new trial, unless Gasperini agreed to an award of $100,000.

II

Before [the adoption of CPLR § 5501(c)], state and federal courts in New York generally invoked the same judge-made formulation in responding to excessiveness attacks on jury verdicts: courts would not disturb an award unless the amount was so exorbitant that it "shocked the conscience of the court."

In both state and federal courts, trial judges made the excessiveness assessment in the first instance, and appellate judges ordinarily deferred to the trial court's judgment.

In 1986, as part of a series of tort reform measures, New York codified a standard for judicial review of the size of jury awards. Placed in CPLR § 5501(c), the prescription reads:

> "In reviewing a money judgment . . . in which it is contended that the award is excessive or inadequate and that a new trial should have been granted unless a stipulation is entered to a

different award, the appellate division shall determine that an award is excessive or inadequate if it deviates materially from what would be reasonable compensation."

As stated in Legislative Findings and Declarations accompanying New York's adoption of the "deviates materially" formulation, the lawmakers found the "shock the conscience" test an insufficient check on damage awards; the legislature therefore installed a standard "inviting more careful appellate scrutiny."

Although phrased as a direction to New York's intermediate appellate courts, § 5501(c)'s "deviates materially" standard, as construed by New York's courts, instructs state trial judges as well. . . .

III

In cases like Gasperini's, in which New York law governs the claims for relief, does New York law also supply the test for federal court review of the size of the verdict? The Center answers yes. The "deviates materially" standard, it argues, is a substantive standard that must be applied by federal appellate courts in diversity cases. . . . Gasperini, emphasizing that § 5501(c) trains on the New York Appellate Division, characterizes the provision as procedural, an allocation of decisionmaking authority regarding damages, not a hard cap on the amount recoverable. Correctly comprehended, Gasperini urges, § 5501(c)'s direction to the Appellate Division cannot be given effect by federal appellate courts without violating the Seventh Amendment's re-examination clause.

As the parties' arguments suggest, CPLR § 5501(c), appraised under Erie R. Co. v. Tompkins, 304 U.S. 64, 58 S.Ct. 817, 82 L.Ed.1188 (1938), and decisions in Erie's path, is both "substantive" and "procedural": "substantive" in that § 5501(c)'s "deviates materially" standard controls how much a plaintiff can be awarded; "procedural" in that § 5501(c) assigns decisionmaking authority to New York's Appellate Division. Parallel application of § 5501(c) at the federal appellate level would be out of sync with the federal system's division of trial and appellate court functions, an allocation weighted by the Seventh Amendment. The dispositive question, therefore, is whether federal courts can give effect to the substantive thrust of § 5501(c) without untoward alteration of the federal scheme for the trial and decision of civil cases.

A

Federal diversity jurisdiction provides an alternative forum for the adjudication of state-created rights, but it does not carry with it generation of rules of substantive law. . . .

Classification of a law as "substantive" or "procedural" for Erie purposes is sometimes a challenging endeavor. Guaranty Trust Co. v. York, 326 U.S. 99, 65 S.Ct. 1464, 89 L.Ed.2079 (1945), an early interpretation of Erie, propounded an "outcome-determination" test: "Does it significantly affect the result of a litigation for a federal court to disregard a law of a State that would be controlling in an action upon the same claim by the same parties in a State court?"_. . . . A later pathmarking case, qualifying Guaranty Trust, explained that the "outcome-determination" test must not be applied mechanically to sweep in all manner of variations; instead, its application must be guided by "the twin aims of the Erie rule: discouragement of forum-shopping and avoidance of inequitable administration of the laws." Hanna v. Plumer, 380 U.S. 460, 468, 85 S.Ct. 1136, 14 L.Ed.2d 8 (1965).

Informed by these decisions, we address the question whether New York's "deviates materially" standard, codified in CPLR § 5501(c), is outcome-affective in this sense: Would "application of the [standard] . . . have so important an effect upon the fortunes of one or both of the litigants that failure to [apply] it would [unfairly discriminate against citizens of the forum State, or] be likely to cause a plaintiff to choose the federal court"? See Hanna, [p. 711, supra].

We start from a point the parties do not debate. Gasperini acknowledges that a statutory cap on damages would supply substantive law for Erie purposes. . . . Although CPLR § 5501(c) is less readily classified, it was designed to provide an analogous control.

New York's Legislature codified in § 5501(c) a new standard, one that requires closer court review than the common law "shock the conscience" test. More rigorous comparative evaluations attend application of § 5501(c)'s "deviates materially" standard. To foster predictability, the legislature required the reviewing court, when overturning a verdict under § 5501(c), to state its reasons, including the factors it considered relevant. We think it a fair conclusion that CPLR § 5501(c) differs from a statutory cap principally "in that the maximum amount recoverable is not set by statute, but rather is determined by case law." In sum, § 5501(c) contains a procedural instruction but the State's objective is manifestly substantive.

It thus appears that if federal courts ignore the change in the New York standard and persist in applying the "shock the conscience" test to damage awards on claims governed by New York law, " 'substantial' variations between state and federal [money judgments]" may be expected. See Hanna.

B

CPLR § 5501(c), as earlier noted is phrased as a direction to the New York Appellate Division. Acting essentially as a surrogate for a New York appellate forum, the [Second Circuit] reviewed Gasperini's award to determine if it "deviated materially" from damage awards the Appellate Division permitted in similar circumstances. The [Second Circuit] performed this task without benefit of an opinion from the District Court, which had denied "without comment" the Center's Rule 59 motion. Concentrating on the authority § 5501(c) gives to the Appellate Division, Gasperini urges that the provision shifts fact-finding responsibility from the jury and the trial judge to the appellate court. Assigning such responsibility to an appellate court, he maintains, is incompatible with the Seventh Amendment's re-examination clause, and therefore, Gasperini concludes, § 5501(c) cannot be given effect in federal court. Although we reach a different conclusion than Gasperini, we agree that the Second Circuit did not attend to "an essential characteristic of [the federal-court] system," Byrd v. Blue Ridge Rural Elec. Cooperative, Inc., 356 U.S. 525, 537, 78 S.Ct. 893, 2 L.Ed.2d 953 (1958), when it used § 5501(c) as "the standard for [federal] appellate review."

That "essential characteristic" was described in Byrd, a diversity suit for negligence in which a pivotal issue of fact would have been tried by a judge were the case in state court. The Byrd Court held that, despite the state practice, the plaintiff was entitled to a jury trial in federal court. In so ruling, the Court said that the Guaranty Trust "outcome-determination" test was an insufficient guide in cases presenting countervailing federal interests. See Byrd, 356 U.S. at 537. The Court described the countervailing federal interests present in Byrd this way:

> "The federal system is an independent system for administering justice to litigants who properly invoke its jurisdiction. An essential characteristic of that system is the manner in which, in civil common-law actions, it distributes trial functions between judge and jury and, under the influence—if not the command—of the Seventh Amendment, assigns the decisions of disputed questions of fact to the jury."

The Seventh Amendment, which governs proceedings in federal court, but not in state court, bears not only on the allocation of trial functions between judge and jury, the issue in Byrd; it also controls the allocation of authority to review verdicts, the issue of concern here. The Amendment reads:

> "In Suits at common law, where the value in controversy shall exceed twenty dollars, the right of trial by jury shall be preserved, and no fact tried by a jury, shall be otherwise re-examined in any Court of the United States, than according to the rules of the common law." U.S. Const., Amdt. 7.

Byrd involved the first clause of the Amendment, the "trial by jury" clause. This case involves the second, the "re-examination" clause. In keeping with the historic understanding, the re-examination clause does not inhibit the authority of trial judges to grant new trials "for any of the reasons for which new trials have heretofore been granted in actions at law in the courts of the United States." Fed. Rule Civ. Proc. 59(a). That authority is large. . . .

In contrast, appellate review of a federal trial court's denial of a motion to set aside a jury's verdict as excessive is a relatively late, and less secure, development. Such review was once deemed inconsonant with the Seventh Amendment's re-examination clause.

[A]ppellate review for abuse of discretion is reconcilable with the Seventh Amendment as a control necessary and proper to the fair administration of justice: "We must give the benefit of every doubt to the judgment of the trial judge; but surely there must be an upper limit, and whether that has been surpassed is not a question of fact with respect to which reasonable men may differ, but a question of law."

C

In Byrd, the Court faced a one-or-the-other choice: trial by judge as in state court, or trial by jury according to the federal practice. In the case before us, a choice of that order is not required, for the principal state and federal interests can be accommodated. The Second Circuit correctly recognized that when New York substantive law governs a claim for relief, New York law and decisions guide the allowable damages.

New York's dominant interest can be respected, without disrupting the federal system, once it is recognized that the federal district court is capable of performing the checking function, i.e., that court can apply the State's "deviates materially" standard in line with New York case law evolving under CPLR § 5501(c).[2] We recall, in this regard, that the "deviates materially" standard serves as the guide to be applied in trial as well as appellate courts in New York.

Within the federal system, practical reasons combine with Seventh Amendment constraints to lodge in the district court, not the court of appeals, primary responsibility for application of § 5501(c)'s "deviates materially" check. Trial judges have the "unique opportunity to consider the evidence in the living courtroom context. . . ."

District court application of the "deviates materially" standard would be subject to appellate review under the standard the Circuits now employ when inadequacy or excessiveness is asserted on appeal: abuse of discretion.

IV

It does not appear that the District Court checked the jury's verdict against the relevant New York decisions demanding more than "industry standard" testimony to support an award of the size the jury returned in this case. . . . Accordingly, we vacate the judgment of the Court of Appeals and instruct that court to remand the case to the District Court so that the trial judge, revisiting his ruling on the new trial motion, may test the jury's verdict against CPLR § 5501(c)'s "deviates materially" standard.

It is so ordered.

■ JUSTICE STEVENS, dissenting.

---

[2]   Whether the damages are excessive for the claim-in-suit must be governed by some law. And there is no candidate other than the law that gives rise to the claim for relief—here the law of New York.

While I agree with most of the reasoning in the Court's opinion, I disagree with its disposition of the case. I would affirm the judgment of the Court of Appeals. I would also reject the suggestion that the Seventh Amendment limits the power of a federal appellate court sitting in diversity to decide whether a jury's award of damages exceeds a limit established by state law.

I agree with the majority that the Reexamination Clause does not bar federal appellate courts from reviewing jury awards for excessiveness. I confess to some surprise, however, at its conclusion that ... [Byrd] requires federal courts of appeals to review district court applications of state law excessiveness standards for an "abuse of discretion."

The majority's persuasive demonstration that New York law sets forth a substantive limitation on the size of jury awards seems to refute the contention that New York has merely asked appellate courts to reexamine facts. The majority's analysis would thus seem to undermine the conclusion that the Reexamination Clause is relevant to this case.

■ JUSTICE SCALIA, with whom the CHIEF JUSTICE and JUSTICE THOMAS join, dissenting.

[JUSTICE SCALIA took the position that the Seventh Amendment prohibits federal appellate re-examination of facts found by a jury, although he agreed "that state law must determine '[w]hether the damages are excessive.' " (Quoting from footnote 22 of the majority opinion.) Justice Scalia also maintained that a federal, not state, review standard would guide the trial judge's comparison of the jury verdict with state awards. He found this standard in Federal Rule of Civil Procedure 59, which provides that "[a] new trial may be granted ... in an action in which there has been a trial by jury for any of the reasons for which new trials have heretofore been granted in actions at law in the courts of the United States. ..." Justice Scalia noted that district judges in the Second Circuit had interpreted Rule 59 to authorize a new trial when " 'it is quite clear that the jury has reach a seriously erroneous result' and letting the verdict stand would result in a 'miscarriage of justice.' " He stated that he had "no reason to question that this is a correct interpretation of what Rule 59 requires."]

NOTES

1.   *Gasperini* applies *Byrd* to the question of allocation of function between the District and Circuit Courts, but the *Hanna* "twin aims" test to the standard to be applied by the District Court in reviewing the jury's verdict. Is this a sensible arrangement? Is it possible that the limited review function given to the Circuit Courts might itself invite forum shopping to avoid the more searching appellate review that might be available in state court? For discussion of *Hanna*, *Walker*, and *Gasperini* in the light of *Byrd*, see Richard D. Freer & Thomas C. Arthur, The Irrepressible Influence of *Byrd*, 44 Creighton L.Rev. 61 (2010).

2.   Gasperini has some implications for the settled rule that quantification of damages is a procedural matter for choice-of-law purposes, and thus governed by forum law. See Dicey, Morris & Collins, The Conflict of Laws 221 et seq. (15th ed.2012): "A distinction must be drawn between remoteness and heads of damages, which are questions of substance governed by the lex causae, and the measure or quantification of damages, which is a question of procedure governed by the lex fori." Cf. Restatement (Second) of Conflict of Laws § 171, cmt. f: "the forum will follow its own local practices in determining whether the damages awarded by a jury are excessive."

3.   Suppose the state in which the federal court is sitting would apply the law of another state to determine what kinds of damages—for example, pain and suffering—are available, but would follow the usual rule that the question of whether the verdict is excessive is determined by forum law. Could the federal court reject this rule as unconstitutional? See Sun Oil v. Wortman, p. 703, supra. If not, would the federal court be compelled to follow the forum state's rule regarding the quantification of damages? See Klaxon Co. v. Stentor Elec. Mfg. Co., p. 746, infra.

Semtek International Inc. v. Lockheed Martin Corp.

Supreme Court of the United States, 2001.
531 U.S. 497, 121 S.Ct. 1021, 149 L.Ed.2d 32.

■ JUSTICE SCALIA delivered the opinion of the Court.

This case presents the question whether the claim-preclusive effect of a federal judgment dismissing a diversity action on statute-of-limitations grounds is determined by the law of the State in which the federal court sits.

I

Petitioner filed a complaint against respondent in California state court, alleging breach of contract and various business torts. Respondent removed the case to the United States District Court for the Central District of California on the basis of diversity of citizenship, and successfully moved to dismiss petitioner's claims as barred by California's 2-year statute of limitations. In its order of dismissal, the District Court, adopting language suggested by respondent, dismissed petitioner's claims "in [their] entirety on the merits and with prejudice." Without contesting the District Court's designation of its dismissal as "on the merits," petitioner appealed to the Court of Appeals for the Ninth Circuit, which affirmed the District Court's order. Petitioner also brought suit against respondent in the State Circuit Court for Baltimore City, Maryland, alleging the same causes of action, which were not time barred under Maryland's 3-year statute of limitations. . . . Following a hearing, the Maryland state court granted respondent's motion to dismiss on the ground of res judicata. Petitioner then returned to the California federal court and the Ninth Circuit, unsuccessfully moving both courts to amend the former's earlier order so as to indicate that the dismissal was not "on the merits." Petitioner also appealed the Maryland trial court's order of dismissal to the Maryland Court of Special Appeals. The Court of Special Appeals affirmed, holding that, regardless of whether California would have accorded claim-preclusive effect to a statute-of-limitations dismissal by one of its own courts, the dismissal by the California federal court barred the complaint filed in Maryland, since the res judicata effect of federal diversity judgments is prescribed by federal law, under which the earlier dismissal was on the merits and claim preclusive. After the Maryland Court of Appeals declined to review the case, we granted certiorari.

II

Petitioner contends that the outcome of this case is controlled by Dupasseur v. Rochereau, 21 Wall. 130, 135 (1875), which held that the res judicata effect of a federal diversity judgment "is such as would belong to judgments of the State courts rendered under similar circumstances," and may not be accorded any "higher sanctity or effect." Since, petitioner argues, the dismissal of an action on statute-of-limitations grounds by a California state court would not be claim preclusive, it follows that the similar dismissal of this diversity action by the California federal court cannot be claim preclusive. While we agree that this would be the result demanded by *Dupasseur*, the case is not dispositive because it was decided under the Conformity Act of 1872, 17 Stat. 196, which required federal courts to apply the procedural law of the forum State in nonequity cases. That arguably affected the outcome of the case. *See Dupasseur*, supra, at 135. See also Restatement (Second) of Judgments § 87, Comment a, p. 315 (1980) (hereinafter Restatement) ("Since procedural law largely determines the matters that may be adjudicated in an action, state law had to be considered in ascertaining the effect of a federal judgment").

Respondent, for its part, contends that the outcome of this case is controlled by Federal Rule of Civil Procedure 41(b), which provides as follows:

> "Involuntary Dismissal: Effect Thereof. For failure of the plaintiff to prosecute or to comply with these rules or any order of court, a defendant may move for dismissal of an action or of any claim against the defendant. Unless the court in its order for dismissal otherwise specifies, a dismissal under this subdivision and any dismissal not provided for in this rule, other than a dismissal for lack of jurisdiction, for improper venue, or for failure to join a party under Rule 19, operates as an adjudication upon the merits."

Since the dismissal here did not "otherwise specify" (indeed, it specifically stated that it was "on the merits"), and did not pertain to the excepted subjects of jurisdiction, venue, or joinder, it follows, respondent contends, that the dismissal "is entitled to claim preclusive effect."

Implicit in this reasoning is the unstated minor premise that all judgments denominated "on the merits" are entitled to claim-preclusive effect. That premise is not necessarily valid. The original connotation of an "on the merits" adjudication is one that actually "passes directly on the substance of [a particular] claim" before the court. Restatement § 19, Comment a, at 161. That connotation remains common to every jurisdiction of which we are aware. See ibid. ("The prototypical [judgment on the merits is] one in which the merits of [a party's] claim are in fact adjudicated [for or] against the [party] after trial of the substantive issues"). And it is, we think, the meaning intended in those many statements to the effect that a judgment "on the merits" triggers the doctrine of res judicata or claim preclusion. *See, e.g.,* Parklane Hosiery Co. v. Shore, 439 U.S. 322, 326, n. 5 (1979) ("Under the doctrine of res judicata, a judgment on the merits in a prior suit bars a second suit involving the same parties or their privies based on the same cause of action"); Goddard v. Security Title Ins. & Guarantee Co., 14 Cal.2d 47, 51, 92 P.2d 804, 806 (1939) ("[A] final judgment, rendered upon the merits by a court having jurisdiction of the cause . . . is a complete bar to a new suit between [the parties or their privies] on the same cause of action" (internal quotation marks and citations omitted)).

But over the years the meaning of the term "judgment on the merits" "has gradually undergone change," and it has come to be applied to some judgments (such as the one involved here) that do not pass upon the substantive merits of a claim and hence do not (in many jurisdictions) entail claim-preclusive effect. *Compare, e.g.,* . . . Plaut v. Spendthrift Farm, Inc., 514 U.S. 211, 228 (1995) (statute of limitations); *with* Federated Department Stores, Inc. v. Moitie, 452 U.S. 394, 399, n. 3 (1981) (demurrer [f]or failure to state a claim). See also Restatement § 19, Comment a and Reporter's Note. That is why the Restatement of Judgments has abandoned the use of the term—"because of its possibly misleading connotations," Restatement § 19, Comment a, at 161.

In short, it is no longer true that a judgment "on the merits" is necessarily a judgment entitled to claim-preclusive effect; and there are a number of reasons for believing that the phrase adjudication "upon the merits" does not bear that meaning in Rule 41(b). To begin with, Rule 41(b) sets forth nothing more than a default rule for determining the import of a dismissal (a dismissal is "upon the merits," with the three stated exceptions, unless the court "otherwise specifies"). This would be a highly peculiar context in which to announce a federally prescribed rule on the complex question of claim preclusion, saying in effect, "All federal dismissals (with three specified exceptions) preclude suit elsewhere, unless the court otherwise specifies."

And even apart from the purely default character of Rule 41(b), it would be peculiar to find a rule governing the effect that must be accorded federal judgments by other courts ensconced in rules governing the internal procedures of the rendering court itself. Indeed, such a rule

CONFLICTS PROBLEMS IN FEDERAL AND INTERNATIONAL SETTINGS

would arguably violate the jurisdictional limitation of the Rules Enabling Act: that the Rules "shall not abridge, enlarge or modify any substantive right," 28 U.S.C. § 2072(b). Cf. Ortiz v. Fibreboard Corp., 527 U.S. 815, 842 (1999) (adopting a "limiting construction" of Federal Rule of Civil Procedure 23(b)(1)(B) in order to "minimize potential conflict with the Rules Enabling Act, and [to] avoid serious constitutional concerns"). In the present case, for example, if California law left petitioner free to sue on this claim in Maryland even after the California statute of limitations had expired, the federal court's extinguishment of that right (through Rule 41(b)'s mandated claim-preclusive effect of its judgment) would seem to violate this limitation.

Moreover, as so interpreted, the Rule would in many cases violate the federalism principle of Erie R. Co. v. Tompkins [p. 695, supra] by engendering " 'substantial' variations [in outcomes] between state and federal litigation" which would "likely . . . influence the choice of a forum," Hanna v. Plumer [p. 711, supra]. See also Guaranty Trust Co. v. York [p. 700, supra]. Cf. Walker v. Armco Steel Corp. [p. 716, supra]. With regard to the claim-preclusion issue involved in the present case, for example, the traditional rule is that expiration of the applicable statute of limitations merely bars the remedy and does not extinguish the substantive right, so that dismissal on that ground does not have claim-preclusive effect in other jurisdictions with longer, unexpired limitation periods. See Restatement (Second) of Conflict of Laws §§ 142(2), 143 (1969); Restatement of Judgments § 49, Comment a (1942). Out-of-state defendants sued on stale claims in California and in other States adhering to this traditional rule would systematically remove state-law suits brought against them to federal court—where, unless otherwise specified, a statute-of-limitations dismissal would bar suit everywhere.[3]

Finally, if Rule 41(b) did mean what respondent suggests, we would surely have relied upon it in our cases recognizing the claim-preclusive effect of federal judgments in federal-question cases. Yet for over half a century since the promulgation of Rule 41(b), we have not once done so. See, e.g., Heck v. Humphrey, 512 U.S. 477, 488–489, n. 9 (1994); Federated Department Stores, Inc. v. Moitie, supra, at 398; Blonder-Tongue Laboratories, Inc. v. University of Ill. Foundation, 402 U.S. 313, 324, n. 12 (1971).

We think the key to a more reasonable interpretation of the meaning of "operates as an adjudication upon the merits" in Rule 41(b) is to be found in Rule 41(a), which, in discussing the effect of voluntary dismissal

---

[3] Rule 41(b), interpreted as a preclusion-establishing rule, would not have the two effects described in the preceding paragraphs—arguable violation of the Rules Enabling Act and incompatibility with Erie R. Co. v. Tompkins [p. 693, supra]—if the court's failure to specify an other-than-on-the-merits dismissal were subject to reversal on appeal whenever it would alter the rule of claim preclusion applied by the State in which the federal court sits. No one suggests that this is the rule, and we are aware of no case that applies it.

by the plaintiff, makes clear that an "adjudication upon the merits" is the opposite of a "dismissal without prejudice":

"Unless otherwise stated in the notice of dismissal or stipulation, the dismissal is without prejudice, except that a notice of dismissal operates as an adjudication upon the merits when filed by a plaintiff who has once dismissed in any court of the United States or of any state an action based on or including the same claim." *See also* 18 Wright & Miller, § 4435, at 329, n. 4 ("Both parts of Rule 41 . . . use the phrase 'without prejudice' as a contrast to adjudication on the merits"); 9 id., § 2373, at 396, n. 4 (" 'With prejudice' is an acceptable form of shorthand for 'an adjudication upon the merits' "). The primary meaning of "dismissal without prejudice," we think, is dismissal without barring the defendant from returning later, to the same court, with the same underlying claim. That will also ordinarily (though not always) have the consequence of not barring the claim from other courts, but its primary meaning relates to the dismissing court itself. Thus, Black's Law Dictionary (7th ed. 1999) defines "dismissed without prejudice" as "removed from the court's docket in such a way that the plaintiff may refile the same suit on the same claim," id., at 482, and defines "dismissal without prejudice" as "[a] dismissal that does not bar the plaintiff from refiling the lawsuit within the applicable limitations period," ibid.

We think, then, that the effect of the "adjudication upon the merits" default provision of Rule 41(b)—and, presumably, of the explicit order in the present case that used the language of that default provision—is simply that, unlike a dismissal "without prejudice," the dismissal in the present case barred refiling of the same claim in the United States District Court for the Central District of California. That is undoubtedly a necessary condition, but it is not a sufficient one, for claim-preclusive effect in other courts.[4]

III

Having concluded that the claim-preclusive effect, in Maryland, of this California federal diversity judgment is dictated neither by Dupasseur v. Rochereau, as petitioner contends, nor by Rule 41(b), as respondent contends, we turn to consideration of what determines the issue. Neither the Full Faith and Credit Clause, U.S. Const., Art. IV, § 1, nor the full faith and credit statute, 28 U.S.C. § 1738, addresses the question. By their terms they govern the effects to be given only to state-court judgments (and, in the case of the statute, to judgments by courts of territories and possessions). And no other federal textual provision,

---

[4] We do not decide whether, in a diversity case, a federal court's "dismissal upon the merits" (in the sense we have described), under circumstances where a state court would decree only a "dismissal without prejudice," abridges a "substantive right" and thus exceeds the authorization of the Rules Enabling Act. We think the situation will present itself more rarely than would the arguable violation of the Act that would ensue from interpreting Rule 41(b) as a rule of claim preclusion; and if it is a violation, can be more easily dealt with on direct appeal.

neither of the Constitution nor of any statute, addresses the claim-preclusive effect of a judgment in a federal diversity action.

It is also true, however, that no federal textual provision addresses the claim-preclusive effect of a federal-court judgment in a federal-question case, yet we have long held that States cannot give those judgments merely whatever effect they would give their own judgments, but must accord them the effect that this Court prescribes. *See* Stoll v. Gottlieb, 305 U.S. 165, 171–172 (1938); Gunter v. Atlantic Coast Line R. Co., 200 U.S. 273, 290–291 (1906); Deposit Bank v. Frankfort, 191 U.S. 499, 514–515 (1903). The reasoning of that line of cases suggests, moreover, that even when States are allowed to give federal judgments (notably, judgments in diversity cases) no more than the effect accorded to state judgments, that disposition is by direction of this Court, which has the last word on the claim-preclusive effect of all federal judgments:

> "It is true that for some purposes and within certain limits it is only required that the judgments of the courts of the United States shall be given the same force and effect as are given the judgments of the courts of the States wherein they are rendered; but it is equally true that whether a Federal judgment has been given due force and effect in the state court is a Federal question reviewable by this court, which will determine for itself whether such judgment has been given due weight or otherwise. . . .

> "When is the state court obliged to give to Federal judgments only the force and effect it gives to state court judgments within its own jurisdiction? Such cases are distinctly pointed out in the opinion of Mr. Justice Bradley in Dupasseur v. Rochereau [which stated that the case was a diversity case, applying state law under state procedure]." Deposit Bank, 191 U.S., at 514–515.

In other words, in Dupasseur the State was allowed (indeed, required) to give a federal diversity judgment no more effect than it would accord one of its own judgments only because reference to state law was the federal rule that this Court deemed appropriate. In short, federal common law governs the claim-preclusive effect of a dismissal by a federal court sitting in diversity. See generally R. Fallon, D. Meltzer, & D. Shapiro, Hart and Wechsler's The Federal Courts and the Federal System 1473 (4th ed. 1996); Degnan, Federalized Res Judicata, 85 Yale L. J. 741 (1976).

It is left to us, then, to determine the appropriate federal rule. And despite the sea change that has occurred in the background law since *Dupasseur* was decided—not only repeal of the Conformity Act but also the watershed decision of this Court in *Erie*—we think the result decreed by *Dupasseur* continues to be correct for diversity cases. Since state, rather than federal, substantive law is at issue there is no need for a uniform federal rule. And indeed, nationwide uniformity in the substance of the matter is better served by having the same claim-preclusive rule (the state rule) apply whether the dismissal has been ordered by a state or a federal court. This is, it seems to us, a classic case for adopting, as the federally prescribed rule of decision, the law that would be applied by state courts in the State in which the federal diversity court sits. See Gasperini v. Center for Humanities, Inc. [p. 720, supra]; Walker v. Armco Steel Corp. [p. 716, supra]; . . . Klaxon Co. v. Stentor Elec. Mfg. Co. [p. 746, infra]. As we have alluded to above, any other rule would produce the sort of "forum-shopping . . . and . . . inequitable administration of the laws" that Erie seeks to avoid, Hanna [p. 711, supra], since filing in, or removing to, federal court would be encouraged by the divergent effects that the litigants would anticipate from likely grounds of dismissal. See Guaranty Trust Co. v. York [p. 700, supra].

This federal reference to state law will not obtain, of course, in situations in which the state law is incompatible with federal interests. If, for example, state law did not accord claim-preclusive effect to dismissals for willful violation of discovery orders, federal courts' interest in the integrity of their own processes might justify a contrary federal rule. No such conflict with potential federal interests exists in the present case. Dismissal of this state cause of action was decreed by the California federal court only because the California statute of limitations so required; and there is no conceivable federal interest in giving that time bar more effect in other courts than the California courts themselves would impose.

* * *

Because the claim-preclusive effect of the California federal court's dismissal "upon the merits" of petitioner's action on statute-of-limitations grounds is governed by a federal rule that in turn incorporates California's law of claim preclusion (the content of which we do not pass upon today), the Maryland Court of Special Appeals erred in holding that the dismissal necessarily precluded the bringing of this action in the Maryland courts. The judgment is reversed, and the case remanded for further proceedings not inconsistent with this opinion.

It is so ordered.

NOTES

1.   Is *Semtek* consistent with *Hanna*, p. 711, supra? Note that in *Hanna* the Court states: "There is, however, a more fundamental flaw in [the argument for applying the state rule instead of the relevant Federal Rule of Civil Procedure]: the incorrect assumption that the rule of Erie R. Co. v. Tompkins constitutes the appropriate test of the validity and therefore the applicability of a Federal Rule of Civil Procedure." In *Semtek*, however, the Court rejects the defendant's proposed reading of Rule 41 in part because so interpreted "the Rule would in many cases violate the federalism principle of Erie R. Co. v. Tompkins." by generating "substantial variations" in the outcomes between state and federal courts. Does *Semtek* therefore call into question the validity of many Federal Rules? For instance, might not the more liberal

"notice pleading" standards of the Federal Rules, see F.R.C.P. 8, generate different outcomes in some cases in states that follow a stricter "fact pleading" standard? Or is the Court merely saying that the broader *Erie* principles should be a guide in resolving ambiguities in the rules?

2. In *Semtek*, the Court does not say that state law applies by its own force, but rather that the preclusive effect of a dismissal in a diversity case is governed by a federal common law rule that normally chooses state law. However this choice of state law appears not to be inflexible: "This federal reference to state law will not obtain, of course, in situations in which the state law is incompatible with federal interests. If, for example, state law did not accord claim-preclusive effect to dismissals for willful violation of discovery orders, federal courts' interest in the integrity of their own processes might justify a contrary federal rule." Suppose, however, that the dismissal involves less clear interests than the Court's hypothetical. As the Court notes in its opinion, federal courts have normally given dismissals on the pleadings without leave to amend preclusive effect. Suppose, however, the federal court hearing a diversity case sits in a state that does not give pleadings dismissals preclusive effect. Is the federal interest in finality sufficient to trump the state interest, or would the plaintiff be able to take advantage of the state rule and refile in another court?

3. What are the implications of *Semtek* for *Klaxon*? In *Klaxon* the Court held that federal courts sitting in diversity must apply the forum state's choice-of-law rules. Yet *Semtek* adopts essentially a federal common law choice-of-law rule that usually, but not invariably, applies the forum state's internal law as to the preclusive effect of dismissals.

4. *Semtek* involves a problem known generally as that of interjurisdictional preclusion. If a judgment is taken from F-1 and the preclusive effect of it becomes an issue in litigation in F-2, then the question of whose preclusion law governs can arise. The general rule is that F-1's law governs. For example, in Angel v. Bullington, 330 U.S. 183, 67 S.Ct. 657, 91 L.Ed. 832 (1947), the Court faced a case that was in some respects the reverse of *Semtek*. In that a case a North Carolina citizen was liable under Virginia law for the balance of the purchase of Virginia real estate remaining after the North Carolina purchaser defaulted and the land was resold. The seller brought suit in a North Carolina state court for the deficiency. The North Carolina Supreme Court held that a North Carolina court did not have jurisdiction because liability for the deficiency was contrary to North Carolina law. The seller then brought suit in a North Carolina federal court. The Supreme Court held that under *Erie*, a federal court in North Carolina must follow the North Carolina law barring suit.

Shady Grove Orthopedic Associates, P. A. v. Allstate Insurance Co.

Supreme Court of the United States, 2010.
559 U.S. 393, 130 S. Ct. 1431, 176 L. Ed.2d 311.

■ JUSTICE SCALIA announced the judgment of the Court and delivered the opinion of the Court with respect to Parts I and II-A, an opinion with respect to Parts II-B and II-D, in which THE CHIEF JUSTICE, JUSTICE THOMAS, and JUSTICE SOTOYMAYOR join, and an opinion with respect to Part II-C, in which THE CHIEF JUSTICE and JUSTICE THOMAS join.

New York law prohibits class actions in suits seeking penalties or statutory minimum damages. We consider whether this precludes a federal district court sitting in diversity from entertaining a class action under Federal Rule of Civil Procedure 23.

I

The petitioner's complaint alleged the following: Shady Grove Orthopedic Associates, P. A., provided medical care to Sonia E. Galvez for injuries she suffered in an automobile accident. As partial payment for that care, Galvez assigned to Shady Grove her rights to insurance benefits under a policy issued in New York by Allstate Insurance Co. Shady Grove tendered a claim for the assigned benefits to Allstate, which under New York law had 30 days to pay the claim or deny it. . . . Allstate apparently paid, but not on time, and it refused to pay the statutory interest that accrued on the overdue benefits (at two percent per month).

Shady Grove filed this diversity suit in the Eastern District of New York to recover the unpaid statutory interest. Alleging that Allstate routinely refuses to pay interest on overdue benefits, Shady Grove sought relief on behalf of itself and a class of all others to whom Allstate owes interest. The District Court dismissed the suit for lack of jurisdiction. . . . The Second Circuit affirmed. The court did not dispute that a federal rule adopted in compliance with the Rules Enabling Act, 28 U.S.C. § 2072, would control if it conflicted with § 901(b) [the New York statute barring class actions in actions seeking penalties]. But there was no conflict because (as we will describe in more detail below) the Second Circuit concluded that Rule 23 and § 901(b) address different issues. Finding no federal rule on point, the Court of Appeals held that § 901(b) is "substantive" within the meaning of Erie R. Co. v. Tompkins, 304 U.S. 64, 58 S. Ct. 817, 82 L. Ed.1188 (1938), and thus must be applied by federal courts sitting in diversity. . . .

II

The framework for our decision is familiar. We must first determine whether Rule 23 answers the question in dispute. Burlington Northern R. Co. v. Woods, 480 U.S. 1, 4–5, 107 S. Ct. 967, 94 L. Ed.2d 1 (1987). If it does, it governs—New York's law notwithstanding—unless it exceeds statutory authorization or Congress's rulemaking power. Id., at 5, 129 S. Ct. 2160; 173 L. Ed.2d 1155; see Hanna v. Plumer, 380 U.S. 460, 463–464, 85 S. Ct. 1136, 14 L. Ed.2d 8 (1965). We do not wade into Erie's murky waters unless the federal rule is inapplicable or invalid. See 380 U.S., at 469–471, 85 S. Ct. 1136, 14 L. Ed.2d 8.

A

The question in dispute is whether Shady Grove's suit may proceed as a class action. Rule 23 provides an answer. It states that "[a] class action may be maintained" if two conditions are met: The suit must satisfy the criteria set forth in subdivision (a) (i.e., numerosity, commonality, typicality, and adequacy of representation), and it also must fit into one of the three categories described in subdivision (b). Fed. Rule Civ. Proc. 23(b).... Thus, Rule 23 provides a one-size-fits-all formula for deciding the class-action question. Because § 901(b) attempts to answer the same question—i.e., it states that Shady Grove's suit "may not be maintained as a class action" (emphasis added) because of the relief it seeks—it cannot apply in diversity suits unless Rule 23 is ultra vires.

The Second Circuit believed that § 901(b) and Rule 23 do not conflict because they address different issues. Rule 23, it said, concerns only the criteria for determining whether a given class can and should be certified; section 901(b), on the other hand, addresses an antecedent question: whether the particular type of claim is eligible for class treatment in the first place—a question on which Rule 23 is silent....

We disagree. To begin with, the line between eligibility and certifiability is entirely artificial. Both are preconditions for maintaining a class action....

There is no reason, in any event, to read Rule 23 as addressing only whether claims made eligible for class treatment by some other law should be certified as class actions.

The dissent argues that § 901(b) has nothing to do with whether Shady Grove may maintain its suit as a class action, but affects only the remedy it may obtain if it wins.... Accordingly, the dissent says, Rule 23 and New York's law may coexist in peace.

We need not decide whether a state law that limits the remedies available in an existing class action would conflict with Rule 23; that is not what § 901(b) does. By its terms, the provision precludes a plaintiff from "maintain[ing]" a class action seeking statutory penalties. Unlike a law that sets a ceiling on damages (or puts other remedies out of reach) in properly filed class actions, § 901(b) says nothing about what remedies a court may award; it prevents the class actions it covers from coming into existence at all....

The dissent all but admits that the literal terms of § 901(b) address the same subject as Rule 23—i.e., whether a class action may be maintained—but insists the provision's purpose is to restrict only remedies..... Unlike Rule 23, designed to further procedural fairness and efficiency, § 901(b) (we are told) "responds to an entirely different concern": the fear that allowing statutory damages to be awarded on a class-wide basis would "produce overkill."...

This evidence of the New York Legislature's purpose is pretty sparse. But even accepting the dissent's account of the Legislature's objective at face value, it cannot override the statute's clear text. Even if its aim is to restrict the remedy a plaintiff can obtain, § 901(b) achieves that end by limiting a plaintiff's power to maintain a class action. We cannot rewrite that to reflect our perception of legislative purpose, see Oncale v. Sundowner Offshore Services, Inc., 523 U.S. 75, 79–80, 118 S. Ct. 998, 140 L. Ed.2d 201 (1998).[6]

The dissent's approach of determining whether state and federal rules conflict based on the subjective intentions of the state legislature is an enterprise destined to produce "confusion worse confounded," Sibbach v. Wilson & Co., 312 U.S. 1, 14, 61 S. Ct. 422, 85 L. Ed. 479 (1941). It would mean, to begin with, that one State's statute could survive pre-emption (and accordingly affect the procedures in federal court) while another State's identical law would not, merely because its authors had different aspirations. It would also mean that district courts would have to discern, in every diversity case, the purpose behind any putatively pre-empted state procedural rule, even if its text squarely conflicts with federal law. That task will often prove arduous. Many laws further more than one aim, and the aim of others may be impossible to discern. Moreover, to the extent the dissent's purpose-driven approach depends on its characterization of § 901(b)'s aims as substantive, it would apply to many state rules ostensibly addressed to procedure. . . .

But while the dissent does indeed artificially narrow the scope of § 901(b) by finding that it pursues only substantive policies, that is not the central difficulty of the dissent's position. The central difficulty is that even artificial narrowing cannot render [it] compatible with Rule 23. If [Rule 23] were susceptible of two meanings—one that would violate § 2072(b) and another that would not—we would agree. See Ortiz v. Fibreboard Corp., 527 U.S. 815, 842, 845, 119 S. Ct. 2295, 144 L. Ed.2d 715 (1999); cf. Semtek Int'l Inc. v. Lockheed Martin Corp., 531 U.S. 497, 503–504, 121 S. Ct. 1021, 149 L. Ed.2d 32 (2001). But it is not. Rule 23 unambiguously authorizes any plaintiff, in any federal civil proceeding, to maintain a class action if the Rule's prerequisites are met. We cannot contort its text, even to avert a collision with state law that might render it invalid. See Walker v. Armco Steel Corp., 446 U.S. 740, 750, n. 9, 100 S. Ct. 1978, 64 L. Ed.2d 659 (1980). What the dissent's approach achieves is not the avoiding of a "conflict between Rule 23 and § 901(b)," but rather the invalidation of Rule 23 (pursuant to § 2072(b) of the Rules Enabling

---

⁶ Our decision in Walker v. Armco Steel Corp., 446 U.S. 740, 100 S. Ct. 1978, 64 L. Ed.2d 659 (1980), discussed by the dissent, is not to the contrary. There we held that Rule 3 (which provides that a federal civil action is " 'commenced' " by filing a complaint in federal court) did not displace a state law providing that " '[a]n action shall be deemed commenced, within the meaning of this article [the statute of limitations], as to each defendant, at the date of the summons which is served on him. . . .' " 446 U.S., at 743, n. 4, 100 S. Ct. 1978, 64 L. Ed.2d 659 (quoting Okla. Stat., Tit. 12, § 97 (1971); alteration in original, emphasis added). Rule 3, we explained, "governs the date from which various timing requirements of the Federal Rules begin to run, but does not affect state statutes of limitations" or tolling rules, which it did not "purpor[t] to displace." 446 U.S., at 751, 750, 100 S. Ct. 1978, 64 L. Ed.2d 659. The texts were therefore not in conflict. While our opinion observed that the State's actual-service rule was (in the State's judgment) an "integral part of the several policies served by the statute of limitations," id., at 751, 100 S. Ct. 1978, 64 L. Ed.2d 659, nothing in our decision suggested that a federal court may resolve an obvious conflict between the texts of state and federal rules by resorting to the state law's ostensible objectives.

Act) to the extent that it conflicts with the substantive policies of § 901. There is no other way to reach the dissent's destination. We must therefore confront head-on whether Rule 23 falls within the statutory authorization.

If all the dissent means is that we should read an ambiguous Federal Rule to avoid "substantial variations [in outcomes] between state and federal litigation," Semtek Int'l Inc. v. Lockheed Martin Corp., 531 U.S. 497, 504, 121 S. Ct. 1021, 149 L. Ed.2d 32 (2001) (internal quotation marks omitted), we entirely agree. We should do so not to avoid doubt as to the Rule's validity—since a Federal Rule that fails Erie's forum-shopping test is not ipso facto invalid, see Hanna v. Plumer, 380 U.S. 460, 469–472, 85 S. Ct. 1136, 14 L. Ed.2d 8 (1965)—but because it is reasonable to assume that "Congress is just as concerned as we have been to avoid significant differences between state and federal courts in adjudicating claims," Stewart Organization, Inc. v. Ricoh Corp., 487 U.S. 22, 37–38, 108 S. Ct. 2239, 101 L. Ed.2d 22 (1988) (Scalia, J., dissenting). The assumption is irrelevant here, however, because there is only one reasonable reading of Rule 23.

B

Erie involved the constitutional power of federal courts to supplant state law with judge-made rules. In that context, it made no difference whether the rule was technically one of substance or procedure; the touchstone was whether it "significantly affect[s] the result of a litigation." Guaranty Trust Co. v. York, 326 U.S. 99, 109, 65 S. Ct. 1464, 89 L. Ed.2079 (1945). That is not the test for either the constitutionality or the statutory validity of a Federal Rule of Procedure. Congress has undoubted power to supplant state law, and undoubted power to prescribe rules for the courts it has created, so long as those rules regulate matters "rationally capable of classification" as procedure. Hanna, 380 U.S., at 472, 85 S. Ct. 1136, 14 L. Ed.2d 8. In the Rules Enabling Act, Congress authorized this Court to promulgate rules of procedure subject to its review, 28 U.S.C. § 2072(a), but with the limitation that those rules "shall not abridge, enlarge or modify any substantive right," § 2072(b).

We have long held that this limitation means that the Rule must "really regulat[e] procedure,—the judicial process for enforcing rights and duties recognized by substantive law and for justly administering remedy and redress for disregard or infraction of them," Sibbach, 312 U.S., at 14, 61 S. Ct. 422, 85 L. Ed. 479; see Hanna, supra, at 464, 85 S. Ct. 1136, 14 L. Ed.2d 8; Burlington, 480 U.S., at 8, 107 S. Ct. 967, 94 L. Ed.2d 1. The test is not whether the rule affects a litigant's substantive rights; most procedural rules do. Mississippi Publishing Corp. v. Murphree, 326 U.S. 438, 445, 66 S. Ct. 242, 90 L. Ed.185 (1946). What matters is what the rule itself regulates: If it governs only "the manner and the means" by which the litigants' rights are "enforced," it is valid; if it alters "the rules of decision by which [the] court will adjudicate [those] rights," it is not. Id., at 446, 66 S. Ct. 242, 90 L. Ed.185 (internal quotation marks omitted).

Applying that test, we have rejected every statutory challenge to a Federal Rule that has come before us. . . .

Applying that criterion, we think it obvious that rules allowing multiple claims (and claims by or against multiple parties) to be litigated together are also valid. See, e.g., Fed. Rules Civ. Proc. 18 (joinder of claims), 20 (joinder of parties), 42(a) (consolidation of actions). Such rules neither change plaintiffs' separate entitlements to relief nor abridge defendants' rights; they alter only how the claims are processed. For the same reason, Rule 23—at least insofar as it allows willing plaintiffs to join their separate claims against the same defendants in a class action—falls within § 2072(b)'s authorization. A class action, no less than traditional joinder (of which it is a species), merely enables a federal court to adjudicate claims of multiple parties at once, instead of in separate suits. And like traditional joinder, it leaves the parties' legal rights and duties intact and the rules of decision unchanged. . . .

In sum, it is not the substantive or procedural nature or purpose of the affected state law that matters, but the substantive or procedural nature of the Federal Rule. We have held since Sibbach, and reaffirmed repeatedly, that the validity of a Federal Rule depends entirely upon whether it regulates procedure. See Sibbach, supra, at 14, 61 S. Ct. 422, 85 L. Ed. 479; Hanna, supra, at 464, 85 S. Ct. 1136, 14 L. Ed.2d 8; Burlington, 480 U.S., at 8, 107 S. Ct. 967, 94 L. Ed.2d 1. If it does, it is authorized by § 2072 and is valid in all jurisdictions, with respect to all claims, regardless of its incidental effect upon state-created rights.

C

A few words in response to the concurrence. We understand it to accept the framework we apply—which requires first, determining whether the federal and state rules can be reconciled (because they answer different questions), and second, if they cannot, determining whether the Federal Rule runs afoul of § 2072(b). The concurrence agrees with us that Rule 23 and § 901(b) conflict, and departs from us only with respect to the second part of the test, i.e., whether application of the Federal Rule violates § 2072(b). Like us, it answers no, but for a reason different from ours.

The concurrence would decide this case on the basis, not that Rule 23 is procedural, but that the state law it displaces is procedural. . . . A state procedural rule is not preempted, according to the concurrence, so long as it is "so bound up with," or "sufficiently intertwined with," a substantive state-law right or remedy "that it defines the scope of that substantive right or remedy."

This analysis squarely conflicts with Sibbach, which established the rule we apply. The concurrence contends that Sibbach did not rule out its approach, but that is not so. Recognizing the impracticability of a test that turns on the idiosyncrasies of state law, Sibbach adopted and applied a rule with a single criterion: whether the Federal Rule "really regulates procedure." 312 U.S., at 14, 61 S. Ct. 422, 85 L. Ed. 479. . . .

Sibbach has been settled law, however, for nearly seven decades. . . .

We must acknowledge the reality that keeping the federal-court door open to class actions that cannot proceed in state court will produce forum shopping. That is unacceptable when it comes as the consequence of judge-made rules created to fill supposed "gaps" in positive federal law. See Hanna, 380 U.S., at 471–472, 85 S. Ct. 1136, 14 L. Ed.2d 8. For where neither the Constitution, a treaty, nor a statute provides the rule of decision or authorizes a federal court to supply one, "state law must govern because there can be no other law." Ibid.; see Clark, Erie's Constitutional Source, 95 Cal. L.Rev. 1289, 1302, 1311 (2007). But divergence from state law, with the attendant consequence of forum shopping, is the inevitable (indeed, one might say the intended) result of a uniform system of federal procedure. Congress itself has created the possibility that the same case may follow a different course if filed in federal instead of state court. Cf. Hanna, 380 U.S., at 472–473, 85 S. Ct. 1136, 14 L. Ed.2d 8. The short of the matter is that a Federal Rule governing procedure is valid whether or not it alters the outcome of the case in a way that induces forum shopping. To hold otherwise would be to "disembowel either the Constitution's grant of power over federal procedure" or Congress's exercise of it. Id., at 473–474, 85 S. Ct. 1136, 14 L. Ed.2d 8.

The judgment of the Court of Appeals is reversed, and the case is remanded for further proceedings.

■ JUSTICE STEVENS, concurring in part and concurring in the judgment.

The New York law at issue . . . is a procedural rule that is not part of New York's substantive law. Accordingly, I agree with Justice Scalia that Federal Rule of Civil Procedure 23 must apply in this case and join Parts I and II-A of the Court's opinion. But I also agree with Justice Ginsburg that there are some state procedural rules that federal courts must apply in diversity cases because they function as a part of the State's definition of substantive rights and remedies. . . .

II

When both a federal rule and a state law appear to govern a question before a federal court sitting in diversity, our precedents have set out a two-step framework for federal courts to negotiate this thorny area. At both steps of the inquiry, there is a critical question about what the state law and the federal rule mean.

The court must first determine whether the scope of the federal rule is " 'sufficiently broad' " to " 'control the issue' " before the court, "thereby leaving no room for the operation" of seemingly conflicting state law. See Burlington Northern R. Co. v. Woods, 480 U.S. 1, 4–5, 107 S. Ct. 967, 94 L. Ed.2d 1 (1987); Walker v. Armco Steel Corp., 446 U.S. 740, 749–750, and n. 9, 100 S. Ct. 1978, 64 L. Ed.2d 659 (1980). If the federal rule does not apply or can operate alongside the state rule, then there is no "Ac[t] of Congress" governing that particular question, 28 U.S.C. § 1652, and the court must engage in the traditional Rules of Decision Act inquiry under Erie and its progeny. In some instances, the "plain meaning" of a federal rule will not come into " 'direct collision' " with the state law, and both can operate. Walker, 446 U.S., at 750, n. 9, 749, 100 S. Ct. 1978, 64 L. Ed.2d 659. In other instances, the rule "when fairly construed," Burlington Northern R. Co., 480 U.S., at 4, 107 S. Ct. 967, 94 L. Ed.2d 1, with "sensitivity to important state interests and regulatory policies," Gasperini, 518 U.S., at 427, n. 7, 116 S. Ct. 2211, 135 L. Ed.2d 659, will not collide with the state law.[5]

If, on the other hand, the federal rule is "sufficiently broad to control the issue before the Court," such that there is a "direct collision," Walker, 446 U.S., at 749–750, 100 S. Ct. 1978, 64 L. Ed.2d 659, the court must decide whether application of the federal rule "represents a valid exercise" of the "rulemaking authority . . . bestowed on this Court by the Rules Enabling Act." Burlington Northern R. Co., 480 U.S., at 5, 107 S. Ct. 967, 94 L. Ed.2d 1; see also Gasperini, 518 U.S., at 427, n. 7, 116 S. Ct. 2211, 135 L. Ed.2d 659; Hanna, 380 U.S., at 471–474, 85 S. Ct. 1136, 14 L. Ed.2d 8. That Act requires, inter alia, that federal rules "not abridge, enlarge or modify any substantive right." 28 U.S.C. § 2072(b) (emphasis added). Unlike Justice Scalia, I believe that an application of a federal rule that effectively abridges, enlarges, or modifies a state-created right or remedy violates this command. . . .

Thus, the second step of the inquiry may well bleed back into the first. When a federal rule appears to abridge, enlarge, or modify a substantive right, federal courts must consider whether the rule can reasonably be interpreted to avoid that impermissible result. See, e.g., Semtek Int'l Inc. v. Lockheed Martin Corp., 531 U.S. 497, 503, 121 S. Ct. 1021, 149 L. Ed.2d 32 (2001) (avoiding an interpretation of Federal Rule of Civil Procedure 41(b) that "would arguably violate the jurisdictional limitation of the Rules Enabling Act" contained in § 2072(b)). And when such a "saving" construction is not possible and the rule would violate the Enabling Act, federal courts cannot apply the rule . . . . A federal rule, therefore, cannot govern a particular case in which the rule would displace a state law that is procedural in the ordinary use of the term but is so intertwined with a state right or remedy that it functions to define

---

[5]   I thus agree with Justice Ginsburg . . . that a federal rule, like any federal law, must be interpreted in light of many different considerations, including "sensitivity to important state interests," and "regulatory policies.". See Stewart Organization, Inc. v. Ricoh Corp., 487 U.S. 22, 37–38, 108 S. Ct. 2239, 101 L. Ed.2d 22 (1988) (Scalia, J., dissenting) ("We should assume. . . when it is fair to do so, that Congress is just as concerned as we have been to avoid significant differences between state and federal courts in adjudicating claims . . . . Thus, in deciding whether a federal . . . Rule of Procedure encompasses a particular issue, a broad reading that would create significant disuniformity between state and federal courts should be avoided if the text permits"). I disagree with Justice Ginsburg, however, about the degree to which the meaning of federal rules may be contorted, absent congressional authorization to do so, to accommodate state policy goals.

the scope of the state-created right. And absent a governing federal rule, a federal court must engage in the traditional Rules of Decision Act inquiry, under the Erie line of cases. This application of the Enabling Act shows "sensitivity to important state interests," and "regulatory policies," but it does so as Congress authorized, by ensuring that federal rules that ordinarily "prescribe general rules of practice and procedure," § 2072(a), do "not abridge, enlarge or modify any substantive right," § 2072(b). . . .

Although the plurality appears to agree with much of my interpretation of § 2072, it nonetheless rejects that approach for two reasons, both of which are mistaken. First, Justice Scalia worries that if federal courts inquire into the effect of federal rules on state law, it will enmesh federal courts in difficult determinations about whether application of a given rule would displace a state determination about substantive rights. I do not see why an Enabling Act inquiry that looks to state law necessarily is more taxing than Justice Scalia's. But in any event, that inquiry is what the Enabling Act requires. . . . The question, therefore, is not what rule we think would be easiest on federal courts. The question is what rule Congress established. Although, Justice Scalia may generally prefer easily administrable, bright-line rules, his preference does not give us license to adopt a second-best interpretation of the Rules Enabling Act. Courts cannot ignore text and context in the service of simplicity. . . .

III

Justice Ginsburg views the basic issue in this case as whether and how to apply a federal rule that dictates an answer to a traditionally procedural question (whether to join plaintiffs together as a class), when a state law that "defines the dimensions" of a state-created claim dictates the opposite answer. As explained above, I readily acknowledge that if a federal rule displaces a state rule that is " 'procedural' in the ordinary sense of the term," S. A. Healy Co., 60 F.3d at 310, but sufficiently interwoven with the scope of a substantive right or remedy, there would be an Enabling Act problem, and the federal rule would have to give way. In my view, however, this is not such a case. . . .

As I have explained, in considering whether to certify a class action such as this one, a federal court must inquire whether doing so would abridge, enlarge, or modify New York's rights or remedies, and thereby violate the Enabling Act. . . . .

In my view, however, the bar for finding an Enabling Act problem is a high one. The mere fact that a state law is designed as a procedural rule suggests it reflects a judgment about how state courts ought to operate and not a judgment about the scope of state-created rights and remedies. And for the purposes of operating a federal court system, there are costs involved in attempting to discover the true nature of a state procedural rule and allowing such a rule to operate alongside a federal rule that appears to govern the same question. The mere possibility that a federal rule would alter a state-created right is not sufficient. There must be little doubt. . . .

■ JUSTICE GINSBURG with whom JUSTICE KENNEDY, JUSTICE BREYER, and JUSTICE ALITO join, dissenting.

The Court today approves Shady Grove's attempt to transform a $500 case into a $ 5,000,000 award, although the State creating the right to recover has proscribed this alchemy. If Shady Grove had filed suit in New York state court, the 2% interest payment authorized by New York Ins. Law Ann. § 5106(a) (West 2009) as a penalty for overdue benefits would, by Shady Grove's own measure, amount to no more than $ 500. By instead filing in federal court based on the parties' diverse citizenship and requesting class certification, Shady Grove hopes to recover, for the class, statutory damages of more than $ 5,000,000. The New York Legislature has barred this remedy. . . . I would continue to interpret Federal Rules with awareness of, and sensitivity to, important state regulatory policies. Because today's judgment radically departs from that course, I dissent. . . . .

I

The Court, I am convinced, finds conflict where none is necessary. Mindful of the history behind § 901(b)'s enactment, the thrust of our precedent, and the substantive-rights limitation in the Rules Enabling Act, I conclude, as did the Second Circuit and every District Court to have considered the question in any detail, that Rule 23 does not collide with § 901(b). As the Second Circuit well understood, Rule 23 prescribes the considerations relevant to class certification and postcertification proceedings—but it does not command that a particular remedy be available when a party sues in a representative capacity. See 549 F.3d 137, 143 (2008). Section 901(b), in contrast, trains on that latter issue. Sensibly read, Rule 23 governs procedural aspects of class litigation, but allows state law to control the size of a monetary award a class plaintiff may pursue. . . .

The absence of an inevitable collision between Rule 23 and § 901(b) becomes evident once it is comprehended that a federal court sitting in diversity can accord due respect to both state and federal prescriptions. Plaintiffs seeking to vindicate claims for which the State has provided a statutory penalty may pursue relief through a class action if they forgo statutory damages and instead seek actual damages or injunctive or declaratory relief; any putative class member who objects can opt out and pursue actual damages, if available, and the statutory penalty in an individual action. . . . On that remedial issue, Rule 23 is silent.

II

Because I perceive no unavoidable conflict between Rule 23 and § 901(b), I would decide this case by inquiring "whether application of the [state] rule would have so important an effect upon the fortunes of one or both of the litigants that failure to [apply] it would be likely to cause a plaintiff to choose the federal court." Hanna, 380 U.S., at 468, n. 9, 85 S. Ct. 1136, 14 L. Ed.2d 8. See Gasperini, 518 U.S., at 428, 116 S. Ct. 2211, 135 L. Ed.2d 659.

Seeking to pretermit that inquiry, Shady Grove urges that the class-action bar in § 901(b) must be regarded as "procedural" because it is contained in [New York's Civil Practice Law and Rules or "CPLR"]. . . . Placement in the CPLR is hardly dispositive. . . .

Shady Grove also ranks § 901(b) as "procedural" because "nothing in [the statute] suggests that it is limited to rights of action based on New York state law, as opposed to federal law or the law of other states"; instead it "applies to actions seeking penalties under any statute." . . . .

It is true that § 901(b) is not specifically limited to claims arising under New York law. But neither is it expressly extended to claims arising under foreign law. The rule prescribes, without elaboration either way, that "an action to recover a penalty . . . may not be maintained as a class action." We have often recognized that "general words" appearing in a statute may, in fact, have limited application; "[t]he words 'any person or persons,' " for example, "are broad enough to comprehend every human being. But general words must not only be limited to cases within the jurisdiction of the state, but also to those objects to which the legislature intended to apply them." . . .

Moreover, Shady Grove overlooks the most likely explanation for the absence of limiting language: New York legislators make law with New York plaintiffs and defendants in mind, i.e., as if New York were the universe. See Baxter, Choice of Law and the Federal System, 16 Stan. L.Rev. 1, 11 (1963) ("[L]awmakers often speak in universal terms but must be understood to speak with reference to their constituents."); cf. Smith v. United States, 507 U.S. 197, 204, n. 5, 113 S. Ct. 1178, 122 L. Ed.2d 548 (1993) (presumption against extraterritoriality rooted in part in "the commonsense notion that Congress generally legislates with domestic concerns in mind").

The point was well put by Brainerd Currie in his seminal article on governmental interest analysis in conflict-of-laws cases. The article centers on a now-archaic Massachusetts law that prevented married women from binding themselves by contract as sureties for their husbands. Discussing whether the Massachusetts prescription applied to transactions involving foreign factors (a foreign forum, foreign place of contracting, or foreign parties), Currie observed:

"When the Massachusetts legislature addresses itself to the problem of married women as sureties, the undeveloped image in its mind is that of *Massachusetts* married women, husbands, creditors, transactions, courts, and judgments. In the history of Anglo-American law the domestic case has been normal, the conflict-of-laws case marginal." Married Women's Contracts: A Study in Conflict-of-Laws Method, 25 U.Chi.L.Rev. 227, 231 (1958) (emphasis added).

Shady Grove's suggestion that States must specifically limit their laws to domestic rights of action if they wish their enactments to apply in federal diversity litigation misses the obvious point: State legislators generally do not focus on an interstate setting when drafting statutes. . . .

In short, Shady Grove's effort to characterize § 901(b) as simply "procedural" cannot successfully elide this fundamental norm: When no federal law or rule is dispositive of an issue, and a state statute is outcome affective in the sense our cases on Erie (pre- and post-Hanna) develop, the Rules of Decision Act commands application of the State's law in diversity suits. Gasperini, 518 U.S., at 428, 116 S. Ct. 2211, 135 L. Ed.2d 659; Hanna, 380 U.S., at 468, n. 9, 85 S. Ct. 1136, 14 L. Ed.2d 8; York, 326 U.S., at 109, 65 S. Ct. 1464, 89 L. Ed.2079. As this case starkly demonstrates, if federal courts exercising diversity jurisdiction are compelled by Rule 23 to award statutory penalties in class actions while New York courts are bound by § 901(b)'s proscription, "substantial variations between state and federal [money judgments] may be expected." Gasperini, 518 U.S., at 430, 116 S. Ct. 2211, 135 L. Ed.2d 659 (quoting Hanna, 380 U.S., at 467–468, 85 S. Ct. 1136, 14 L. Ed.2d 8 (internal quotation marks omitted)). The "variation" here is indeed "substantial." Shady Grove seeks class relief that is ten thousand times greater than the individual remedy available to it in state court. . . .

I would continue to approach Erie questions in a manner mindful of the purposes underlying the Rules of Decision Act and the Rules Enabling Act, faithful to precedent, and respectful of important state interests. I would therefore hold that the New York Legislature's limitation on the recovery of statutory damages applies in this case, and would affirm the Second Circuit's judgment.

NOTES

1. Can Justice Scalia's opinion in *Shady Grove* be reconciled with his majority opinion in *Semtek*? In *Semtek* the Court stated that one reason for reading Rule 41 so narrowly was that a broader reading would mean that it " 'would in many cases violate the federalism principle of Erie R. Co. v. Tompkins by engendering 'substantial' variations [in outcomes] between state and federal litigation' which would 'likely . . . influence the choice of a forum.' " Yet in *Shady Grove*, the Court clearly rejects this test as a guide to applying Federal Rules of Civil Procedure in favor of the *Sibbach* test giving a nearly conclusive presumption of validity to the Rules.

2. Would Justice Stevens's approach require a literal case-by-case analysis of the likely effect of the application of a Federal Rule on a competing state rule? If so, would it be possible that courts could reach conflicting results depending on small factual variations in the case?

3. Is there any practical difference between Justice Ginsburg's proposed resolution of the case and simply finding that Federal Rule 23 overstepped, in this case, the boundaries of the Rules Enabling Act? What is the risk that applying the New York statute forbidding class actions in diversity cases will lead to interstate forum shopping? For instance, suppose that the plaintiff in this case were able to obtain personal jurisdiction over the defendant in a neighboring state that did not have a bar on class actions of this sort. Might not she be able to bring the action in a federal court in a neighboring state and argue that New York's "substantive" law providing for the statutory penalty should apply but that its anti-class-action statute ought not apply as being "procedural" for conflict-of-laws purposes?

4. Several states have adopted provisions aimed at "SLAPP" suits, which are "strategic lawsuits against public participation." When a defendant is sued (typically for defamation) for exercising her right of free speech or to petition the government (e.g., testifying about environmental violations), the defendant may make an "anti-SLAPP" motion to dismiss or strike the case. If the defendant shows that she was sued for the exercise of protected activity, the burden shifts to the plaintiff to show (typically) that she is likely to prevail on the merits.

In a diversity of citizenship case, must a federal court apply such a provision? The most influential decision is Abbas v. Foreign Policy Group, LLC, 783 F.3d 1328, 1334 (D.C. Cir. 2015), written by Judge (now Justice) Kavanaugh. In *Abbas*, the court held that Federal Rules 12 and 56—governing defensive responses and motions for summary judgment—are part of an integrated system for pretrial adjudication. Because the anti-SLAPP provision conflicted directly with this system, *Hanna* and *Shady Grove* required that the Federal Rules govern. Several courts of appeals have adopted this approach and agree that Federal Rules apply, to the exclusion of state anti-SLAPP provisions. See, e.g., La Liberte v. Reid, 966 F.3d 79, 85–86 (2d Cir. 2020); Klocke v. Watson, 936 F.3d 240, 247–48 (5th Cir. 2019); Carbone v. CNN, Inc., 910 F.3d 1345, 1350 (11th Cir. 2018); Los Lobos Renewable Power, LLC v. AmeriCulture, Inc., 885 F.3d 659, 673 (10th Cir. 2018). The Ninth Circuit reached the contrary conclusion in Newsham v. Lockheed Missiles & Space Ctr., 190 F.3d 963, 973 (9th Cir. 1999). After the *Abbas* decision, however, the Ninth Circuit amended its holding to provide that only some parts of the California statute, such as a fee-shifting provision, were to apply in federal court. Planned Parenthood Fed'n of Am. v. Center for Med. Progress, 890 F.3d 828, 833–35 (9th Cir. 2018).

B. THE ERIE DOCTRINE AND CONFLICT OF LAWS IN DIVERSITY CASES

Klaxon Co. v. Stentor Electric Manufacturing Co.

Supreme Court of the United States, 1941.
313 U.S. 487, 61 S.Ct. 1020, 85 L.Ed.1477.

■ JUSTICE REED delivered the opinion of the Court.

The principal question in this case is whether in diversity cases the federal courts must follow conflict of laws rules prevailing in the states in which they sit. We left this open in Ruhlin v. New York Life Insurance Company, 304 U.S. 202, 208, Note 2. The frequent recurrence of the problem, as well as the conflict of approach to the problem between the Third Circuit's opinion here and that of the First Circuit in Sampson v. Channell, 110 F.2d 754, 759–762, 128 A.L.R. 394, led us to grant certiorari.

In 1918 respondent, a New York corporation, transferred its entire business to petitioner, a Delaware corporation. Petitioner contracted to use its best efforts to further the manufacture and sale of certain patented devices covered by the agreement, and respondent was to have a share of petitioner's profits. The agreement was executed in New York, the assets were transferred there, and petitioner began performance there although later it moved its operations to other states. Respondent was voluntarily dissolved under New York law in 1919. Ten years later it instituted this action in the United States District Court for the District of Delaware, alleging that petitioner had failed to perform its agreement to use its best efforts. Jurisdiction rested on diversity of citizenship. In 1939 respondent recovered a jury verdict of $100,000, upon which judgment was entered. Respondent then moved to correct the judgment by adding interest at the rate of six percent from June 1, 1929, the date the action had been brought. The basis of the motion was the provision in section 480 of the New York Civil Practice Act directing that in contract actions interest be added to the principal sum "whether theretofore liquidated or unliquidated." The District Court granted the motion, taking the view that the rights of the parties were governed by New York law and that under New York law the addition of such interest was mandatory. 30 F.Supp. 425, 431. The Circuit Court of Appeals affirmed, 3 Cir., 115 F.2d 268, 275, and we granted certiorari, limited to the question whether section 480 of the New York Civil Practice Act is applicable to an action in the federal court in Delaware, 312 U.S. 674.

The Circuit Court of Appeals was of the view that under New York law the right to interest before verdict under section 480 went to the substance of the obligation, and that proper construction of the contract in suit fixed New York as the place of performance. It then concluded that section 480 was applicable to the case because "it is clear by what we think is undoubtedly the better view of the law that the rules for ascertaining the measure of damages are not a matter of procedure at all, but are matters of substance which should be settled by reference to the law of the appropriate state according to the type of case being tried in the forum. The measure of damages for breach of a contract is determined by the law of the place of performance; Restatement, Conflict of Laws, sec. 413." The court referred also to section 418 of the Restatement, which makes interest part of the damages to be determined by the law of the place of performance. Application of the New York statute apparently followed from the court's independent determination of the "better view" without regard to Delaware law, for no Delaware decision or statute was cited or discussed.

We are of opinion that the prohibition declared in Erie Railroad v. Tompkins, 304 U.S. 64, against such independent determinations by the federal courts extends to the field of conflict of laws. The conflict of laws rules to be applied by the federal court in Delaware must conform to those prevailing in Delaware's state courts. Otherwise the accident of diversity of citizenship would constantly disturb equal administration of justice in coordinate state and federal courts sitting side by side.... Any other ruling would do violence to the principle of uniformity within a state upon which the Tompkins decision is based. Whatever lack of uniformity this may produce between federal courts in different states is attributable to our federal system, which leaves to a state, within the limits permitted by the Constitution, the right to pursue local policies diverging from those of its neighbors. It is not for the federal courts to thwart such local policies by enforcing an independent "general law" of conflict of laws. Subject only to review by this Court on any federal question that may arise, Delaware is free to determine whether a given matter is to be governed by the law of the forum or some other law. Cf. Milwaukee County v. White Co., 296 U.S. 268, 272. This Court's views are not the decisive factor in determining the applicable conflicts rule. Cf. Funkhouser v. J.B. Preston Co., 290 U.S. 163. And the proper function of the Delaware federal court is to ascertain what the state law is, not what it ought to be.... [The opinion states it would be constitutional for Delaware to apply its local law in this case.]

Accordingly, the judgment is reversed and the case remanded to the Circuit Court of Appeals for decision in conformity with the law of Delaware.

NOTES

1.   On remand in *Klaxon* the court of appeals found there was no Delaware statute or decision directly on the conflict of laws point. It thus adhered to its earlier conclusion that the Delaware conflict-of-laws rules was that the New York local law would govern. 125 F.2d 820 (3d Cir.1942). The Supreme Court denied certiorari. 316 U.S. 685, 62 S.Ct. 1284 (1942).

Yohannon v. Keene Corp., 924 F.2d 1255 (3d Cir.1991) held that because a Pennsylvania state court would regard pre-judgment interest as procedural, a federal court sitting in Pennsylvania should apply the Pennsylvania rule even though New Jersey law was applicable to all other aspects of the case.

2.   Is *Klaxon* an inevitable deduction from the logic of *Erie*? Should a federal court in a diversity action be any less able to prescribe its own choice of law rules than a court of State Z in a transaction solely connected with states X and Y? For a penetrating and comprehensive discussion of the subject, see Cavers, Change in Choice-of-Law Thinking and Its Bearing on the *Klaxon* Problem, in the American Law Institute's Study of the Division of Jurisdiction Between State and Federal Courts (Official Draft 1969). See also Borchers, The Origins of Diversity Jurisdiction, the Rise of Legal

Positivism, and a Brave New World for *Erie* and *Klaxon*, 72 Tex.L.Rev. 79 (1993).

3. The Supreme Court went out of its way in Day and Zimmermann v. Challoner, 423 U.S. 3, 96 S.Ct. 167 (1975), to reaffirm *Klaxon*. In a tort action, the Fifth Circuit had held that Cambodia, the country where an artillery round had prematurely exploded and had caused injury to American service personnel, had no interest in having its law applied in an action by American claimants against the American manufacturer. In the absence of a conflict among interested states, the court had applied the law of the forum (Texas). The Supreme Court reversed:

> "... A federal court in a diversity case is not free to engraft onto ... state rules [of choice of law] exceptions or modifications which may commend themselves to the federal court, but which have not commended themselves to the State in which the federal court sits."

4. Should *Klaxon* extend even to cases that state courts would not be able to adjudicate? Seemingly, the answer should be "no" because the primary rationale of *Klaxon* and *Erie* is that litigants should not be able to change the result in a case simply by shifting between state and federal courts located in the same state. However, in Griffin v. McCoach, 313 U.S. 498, 61 S.Ct. 1023 (1941), the Supreme Court held that *Klaxon* forced a Texas federal court hearing an interpleader action to determine rights in an insurance policy to adhere to Texas state conflict-of-laws rules as to whether some of the claimants had an insurable interest in the policy. The action could not have been brought in a Texas (or any) state court because jurisdiction over all the parties could only be obtained through the federal interpleader statute, the modern version of which is 28 U.S.C. § 2361, authorizing nationwide personal jurisdiction.

5. *Evidentiary Privileges:* Federal Rule of Evidence 501 provides that where state law supplies the rule of decision that privileges "shall be determined in accordance with State law." In multistate cases, however, the question of which state's law to apply arises. Following the lead of *Klaxon*, federal courts sitting in diversity have generally followed the forum state's choice-of-law rules with regard to evidentiary privileges. See, e.g., Abbott Laboratories v. Alpha Therapeutic Corp., 200 F.R.D. 401 (N.D.Ill.2001).

6. As we have seen, in some areas of federal competence, such as admiralty, see Note, p. 690, supra, federal courts are free to fashion independent choice-of-law rules. The question of how far *Klaxon's* influence extends beyond diversity cases remains at least partially unsettled, however. Some lower federal courts have, for example, taken the position that *Klaxon* applies to state law claims being litigated in bankruptcy courts. See, e.g., In re Gaston & Snow, 243 F.3d 599 (2d Cir.2001). See also Hay, Borchers, Symeonides & Whytock, Conflict of Laws § 23.15 (6th ed.2018)(noting division in the authorities). In many cases, however, the question is academic, because the approach taken by federal courts in creating federal choice-of-law principles results in a flexible approach substantially similar to one of the modern choice-of-law theories followed in most states. See, e.g., Woods-Tucker Leasing Corp. v. Hutcheson-Ingram Development Co., 642

F.2d 744 (5th Cir.1981) (en banc) (not deciding whether to follow *Klaxon* in a bankruptcy matter because either state or federal choice-of-law principles would lead to the same result).

The Impact of Interest Analysis upon Klaxon

Was *Klaxon* correct to fear that freeing a federal diversity court from the choice-of-law rules of the state forum "would do violence" to *Erie*'s principle? Many commentators believe not. Professor Alfred Hill argued that local bias—the very evil federal diversity jurisdiction was to combat—can make itself felt "particularly through arbitrary choice of law rules" which bear unevenly on out-of-state litigants. Hill, The *Erie* Doctrine and The Constitution, 53 Nw.U.L.Rev. 427, 544 (1958). This was true even in the days when the vested rights approach to choice of law was the norm. It may be even more true in modern times, with the rise of the interest analysis, which several commentators claim has strong forum-favoring tendencies. See also Borchers, The Origins of Diversity Jurisdiction, the Rise of Legal Positivism, and a Brave New World for *Erie* and *Klaxon*, 72 Tex.L.Rev. 79 (1993), which argues that the structural independence of the federal courts places them in a good position to make a non-parochial choice between competing state laws, and that the *Klaxon* doctrine is thus unwise and unnecessary.

The authors of Hart & Wechsler, The Federal Courts and The Federal System 634–35 (1953), argued that the *Klaxon* doctrine is directly opposed to *Erie*'s purpose of avoiding uncertainty for persons conducting primary activities, because when the doctrine is applied results will shift with the happenstance of the forum's choice-of-law rules; and the unpredictability will apply in federal courts as much as in state courts.

Is the *Erie* doctrine misapplied here for yet another reason? When multistate "interests" collide, why should the United States courts not function as federal system umpires, rather than as "ventriloquists' dummies" for the state courts of the forum? See Hart, The Relations Between State and Federal Law, 54 Colum.L.Rev. 489 (1954); Baxter, Choice of Law and The Federal System, 16 Stan.L.Rev. 1 (1963); Horowitz, Toward a Federal Common Law of Choice of Law, 14 UCLA L.Rev. 1191 (1967).

Taking the other side of the argument, Professor Cavers favors the *Klaxon* doctrine for several reasons already noted and also on the pragmatic ground that forum-shopping as between state and federal courts in a given state is a more serious risk than the possibility of shopping across state lines. This is so because the person in control of the choice of forum is the plaintiff's lawyer, who may not want to send the case to an attorney in another state, thus losing or reducing the fee.

Ferens v. John Deere Company

Supreme Court of the United States, 1990.
494 U.S. 516, 110 S.Ct. 1274, 108 L.Ed.2d 443.

■ JUSTICE KENNEDY delivered the opinion of the Court

I

Albert Ferens lost his right hand when, the allegation is, it became caught in his combine harvester, manufactured by Deere & Company. The accident occurred while Ferens was working with the combine on his farm in Pennsylvania. For reasons not explained in the record, Ferens delayed filing a tort suit and Pennsylvania's 2-year limitations period expired. In the third year, he and his wife sued Deere in the United States District Court for the Western District of Pennsylvania, raising contract and warranty claims as to which the Pennsylvania limitations period had not yet run. The District Court had diversity jurisdiction, as Ferens and his wife are Pennsylvania residents, and Deere is incorporated in Delaware with its principal place of business in Illinois.

Not to be deprived of a tort action, the Ferenses in the same year filed a second diversity suit against Deere in the United States District Court for the Southern District of Mississippi, alleging negligence and products liability. Diversity jurisdiction and venue were proper. The Ferenses sued Deere in the District Court in Mississippi because they knew that, under Klaxon Co. v. Stentor Electric Mfg. Co. [p. 746, supra], the federal court in the exercise of diversity jurisdiction must apply the same choice of law rules that Mississippi state courts would apply if they were deciding the case.

The Mississippi courts . . . would apply Mississippi's 6-year statute of limitations to the tort claim arising under Pennsylvania law and the tort action would not be time-barred under the Mississippi statute.

The issue now before us arose when the Ferenses took their forum shopping a step further: having chosen the federal court in Mississippi to take advantage of the State's limitations period, they next moved, under § 1404(a), to transfer the action to the federal court in Pennsylvania on the ground that Pennsylvania was a more convenient forum. The Ferenses acted on the assumption that, after the transfer, the choice of law rules in the Mississippi forum, including a rule requiring application of the Mississippi statute of limitations, would continue to govern the suit.

Deere put up no opposition, the District Court in Mississippi granted the § 1404(a) motion. . . .

[The case was transferred to Pennsylvania. The federal district court applied the Pennsylvania limitation on the ground that Van Dusen, supra, does not apply when plaintiff seeks the transfer. The Third Circuit affirmed, but on the ground that the application of the Mississippi limitation would violate due process because Mississippi had no legitimate interest in the case. The U.S. Supreme Court remanded for further consideration in light of Sun Oil. On remand, the Third Circuit again applied the Pennsylvania limitation, this time for the reason given by the trial court.]

II

Section 1404(a) states only that a district court may transfer venue for the convenience of the parties and witnesses when in the interest of justice. It says nothing about choice of law, and nothing about affording plaintiffs different treatment from defendants. We touched upon these issues in Van Dusen, but left open the question presented in this case. . . . We said:

> "This legislative background supports the view that § 1404(a) was not designed to narrow the plaintiff's venue privilege or to defeat the state-law advantages that might accrue from the exercise of this venue privilege but rather the provision was simply to counteract the inconveniences that flowed from the venue statutes by permitting transfer to a convenient federal court. The legislative history of § 1404(a) certainly does not justify the rather startling conclusion that one might 'get a change of a law as a bonus for a change of venue.' Indeed, an interpretation accepting such a rule would go far to frustrate the remedial purposes of § 1404(a). If a change in the law were in the offing, the parties might well regard the section primarily as a forum-shopping instrument. And, more importantly, courts would at least be reluctant to grant transfers, despite considerations of convenience, if to do so might conceivably prejudice the claim of a plaintiff who initially selected a permissible forum. We believe, therefore, that both the history and purposes of § 1404(a) indicate that it should be regarded as a federal judicial housekeeping measure, dealing with the placement of litigation in the federal courts and generally intended, on the basis of convenience and fairness, simply to authorize a change of courtrooms." . . .

We thus held that the law applicable to a diversity case does not change upon a transfer initiated by a defendant.

III

The quoted part of Van Dusen reveals three independent reasons for our decision. First, § 1404(a) should not deprive parties of state law advantages that exist absent diversity jurisdiction. Second, § 1404(a) should not create or multiply opportunities for forum shopping. Third, the decision to transfer venue under § 1404(a) should turn on considerations of convenience and the interest of justice rather than on the possible prejudice resulting from a change of law.

A

The policy that § 1404(a) should not deprive parties of state law advantages, although perhaps discernible in the legislative history, has its real foundation in Erie R. Co. v. Tompkins. See Van Dusen, 376 U.S. at 637. The Erie rule remains a vital expression of the federal system and the concomitant integrity of the separate States.

The Erie policy had a clear implication for Van Dusen. The existence of diversity jurisdiction gave the defendants the opportunity to make a motion to transfer venue under § 1404(a), and if the applicable law were to change after transfer, the plaintiff's venue privilege and resulting state-law advantages could be defeated at the defendant's option. To allow the transfer and at the same time preserve the plaintiff's state-law advantages, we held that the choice of law rules should not change following a transfer initiated by a defendant.

Transfers initiated by a plaintiff involve some different considerations, but lead to the same result. Applying the transferor law, of course, will not deprive the plaintiff of any state law advantages. A defendant, in one sense, also will lose no legal advantage if the transferor law controls after a transfer initiated by the plaintiff; the same law, after all, would have applied if the plaintiff had not made the motion.

Applying the transferee law, by contrast, would undermine the Erie rule in a serious way. It would mean that initiating a transfer under § 1404(a) changes the state law applicable to a diversity case. We have held, in an isolated circumstance, that § 1404(a) may pre-empt state law. See Stewart Organization, Inc. v. Ricoh Corp., Note 2, p. 717, supra (holding that federal law determines the validity of a forum selection clause). In general, however, we have seen § 1404(a) as a housekeeping measure that should not alter the state law governing a case under Erie.

B

Van Dusen also sought to fashion a rule that would not create opportunities for forum shopping. . . . No interpretation of § 1404(a), however, will create comparable opportunities for forum shopping by a plaintiff because, even without § 1404(a), a plaintiff already has the option of shopping for a forum with the most favorable law. . . . Diversity jurisdiction did not eliminate these forum shopping opportunities; instead, under Erie, the federal courts had to replicate them. . . .

Applying the transferee law, by contrast, might create opportunities for forum shopping in an indirect way. The advantage to Mississippi's personal injury lawyers that resulted from the State's then applicable 6-year statute of limitations has not escaped us; Mississippi's long limitation period no doubt drew plaintiffs to the State. Although *Sun Oil* held that the federal courts have little interest in a State's decision to create a long statute of limitations or to apply its statute of limitations to claims governed by foreign law, we should recognize the consequences of our interpretation of § 1404(a). Applying the transferee law, to the extent that it discourages plaintiff-initiated transfers, might give States incentives to enact similar laws to bring in out-of-state business that would not be moved at the instance of the plaintiff.

C

Van Dusen also made clear that the decision to transfer venue under § 1404(a) should turn on considerations of convenience rather than on the possibility of prejudice resulting from a change in the applicable law. . . .

Some might think that a plaintiff should pay the price for choosing an inconvenient forum by being put to a choice of law versus forum. But this assumes that § 1404(a) is for the benefit only of the moving party. By the statute's own terms, it is not. Section 1404(a) also exists for the benefit of the witnesses and the interest of justice, which must include the convenience of the court. Litigation in an inconvenient forum does not harm the plaintiff alone. . . . The desire to take a punitive view of the plaintiff's actions should not obscure the systemic costs of litigating in an inconvenient place.

D

. . . If we were to hold that the transferee law applies following a § 1404(a) motion by a plaintiff, cases such as this would not arise in the future. . . . The rule would leave unclear which law should apply when both a defendant and a plaintiff move for a transfer of venue or when the court transfers venue on its own motion. The rule also might require variation in certain situations, such as when the plaintiff moves for a transfer following a removal from state court by the defendant, or when only one of several plaintiffs requests the transfer, or when circumstances change through no fault of the plaintiff making a once convenient forum inconvenient. True, we could reserve any consideration of these questions for a later day. But we have a duty, in deciding this case, to consider whether our decision will create litigation and uncertainty. On the basis of these considerations, we again conclude that the transferor law should apply regardless who makes the § 1404(a) motion.

IV

[O]ne might contend that, because no per se rule requiring a court to apply either the transferor law or the transferee law will seem appropriate in all circumstances, we should develop more sophisticated federal choice of law rules for diversity actions involving transfers. To a large extent, however, state conflicts of law rules already ensure that appropriate laws will apply to diversity cases. Federal law, as a general matter, does not interfere with these rules. See Sun Oil Co. v. Wortman, p. 449, supra. Even if more elaborate federal choice of law rules would not run afoul of Klaxon and Erie, we believe that applying the law of the transferor forum effects the appropriate balance between fairness and simplicity.

For the foregoing reasons, we conclude that Mississippi's statute of limitations should govern the Ferenses' action. We reverse and remand for proceedings consistent with this opinion.

■ JUSTICE SCALIA, with whom JUSTICE BRENNAN, JUSTICE MARSHALL, and JUSTICE BLACKMUN join, dissenting.

[J]ust as it is unlikely that Congress, in enacting § 1404(a), meant to provide the defendant with a vehicle by which to manipulate in his favor the substantive law to be applied in a diversity case, so too is it unlikely that Congress meant to provide the plaintiff with a vehicle by which to appropriate the law of a distant and inconvenient forum in which he does not intend to litigate, and to carry that prize back to the State in which he wishes to try the case. [Further], application of the transferor court's law in this context would encourage forum-shopping between federal and state courts in the same jurisdiction on the basis of differential substantive law. It is true, of course, that the plaintiffs here did not select the Mississippi federal court in preference to the Mississippi state courts because of any differential substantive law; the former, like the latter, would have applied Mississippi choice-of-law rules, and thus the Mississippi statute of limitations. But one must be blind to reality to say that it is the Mississippi federal court in which these plaintiffs have chosen to sue. That was merely a way station en route to suit in the Pennsylvania federal court. The plaintiffs were seeking to achieve exactly what Klaxon was designed to prevent: the use of a Pennsylvania federal court instead of a Pennsylvania state court in order to obtain application of a different substantive law. Our decision in Van Dusen compromised "the principle of uniformity within a state," [citing to Klaxon], only in the abstract, but today's decision compromises it precisely in the respect that matters—i.e., insofar as it bears upon the plaintiff's choice between a state and a federal forum. The significant federal judicial policy expressed in Erie and Klaxon is reduced to a laughingstock if it can so readily be evaded through filing-and-transfer.

The Court is undoubtedly correct that applying the Klaxon rule after a plaintiff-initiated transfer would deter a plaintiff in a situation such as exists here from seeking a transfer, since that would deprive him of the favorable substantive law. But that proves only that this disposition achieves what Erie and Klaxon are designed to achieve: preventing the plaintiff from using "the accident of diversity of citizenship," Klaxon, . . . to obtain the application of a different law within the State where he wishes to litigate. In the context of the present case, he must either litigate in the State of Mississippi under Mississippi law, or in the Commonwealth of Pennsylvania under Pennsylvania law.

The Court suggests that applying the choice-of-law rules of the forum court to a transferred case ignores the interest of the federal courts themselves in avoiding the "systemic costs of litigating in an inconvenient place," quoting Justice Jackson's eloquent remarks on that subject in Gulf Oil Corp. v. Gilbert, p. 232, supra. . . . The point, apparently, is that these systemic costs will increase because the change in law attendant to transfer will not only deter the plaintiff from moving to transfer but will also deter the court from ordering sua sponte a transfer that will harm the plaintiff's case. Justice Jackson's remarks were addressed, however, not to the operation of § 1404(a), but to "those rather rare cases where the doctrine [of forum non conveniens] should be applied." Where the systemic costs are that severe, transfer ordinarily will occur whether the plaintiff moves for it or not; the district judge can be expected to order it sua sponte. I do not think that the prospect of depriving the plaintiff of favorable law will any more deter a district judge from transferring than it would have deterred a district judge, under the prior regime, from ordering a dismissal sua sponte pursuant to the doctrine of forum non conveniens.

The Court and I reach different results largely because we approach the question from different directions. For the Court, this case involves an "interpretation of § 1404(a)," and the central issue is whether Klaxon stands in the way of the policies of that statute. For me, the case involves an interpretation of the Rules of Decision Act, and the central issue is whether § 1404(a) alters the "principle of uniformity within a state" which Klaxon says that Act embodies. I think my approach preferable, not only because the Rules of Decision Act does, and § 1404(a) does not, address the specific subject of which law to apply, but also because, as the Court acknowledges, our jurisprudence under that statute is "a vital expression of the federal system and the concomitant integrity of the separate States." To ask, as in effect the Court does, whether Erie gets in the way of § 1404(a), rather than whether § 1404(a) requires adjustment of Erie, seems to me the expression of a mistaken sense of priorities.

NOTES

1.   What are the systemic costs and savings of the decision in *Ferens*? Will fewer cases be tried in really inconvenient forums, will more be filed in forums where no trial is intended, and will a transferee court face an additional burden as a result of the decision (by having to determine the law of the transferor)? For arguments against *Ferens*, see Maltz, Choice of Forum and Choice of Law in the Federal Courts: A Reconsideration of Erie Principles, 79 Ky.L.J. 231 (1991). Spar Inc. v. Information Resources Inc., 956 F.2d 392 (2d Cir.1992), affirmed a district court that dismissed the case on the ground that the forum's statute of limitations had run and refused to transfer the case to a forum whose period had not expired. The court stated "that allowing a transfer in this case would reward plaintiffs for their lack of diligence in choosing a proper forum and this would not be in the interests of justice," disagreeing with Porter v. Groat, 840 F.2d 255 (4th Cir.1988).

Since its law was applied in *Ferens*, Mississippi has shortened its tort limitations to three years (Miss.Code.Ann. § 15–1–49 (Supp.1994)) and has enacted a statute that applies the shorter limitations period of the place where the cause of action "accrued" if the plaintiff is not a Mississippi resident (Miss.Code Ann. § 15–1–65 (Supp.1994)).

In re TMI, 89 F.3d 1106 (3d Cir.1996), cert. denied, 519 U.S. 1077, 117 S.Ct. 739 (1997) avoided the result in *Ferens*. After the Pennsylvania limitations had run, residents of Pennsylvania, site of the Three Mile Island nuclear accident, sued in Mississippi state and federal courts. Congress then enacted legislation providing for consolidation of such actions in the federal district court in the district where the accident occurred and further providing that "the substantive rules of decision in [such actions] shall be derived from the law of the State in which the nuclear incident involved occurs." 42 U.S.C. § 2014(hh). The Mississippi actions were consolidated in federal district court in Pennsylvania. The court holds that the Pennsylvania statute of limitations is "substantive" within the meaning of the federal choice-of-law statute and that the statute applies retroactively to bar the claims.

2.   LaVay Corp. v. Dominion Federal Savings & Loan Ass'n, 830 F.2d 522, 526 (4th Cir.1987), cert. denied, 484 U.S. 1065. 108 S.Ct. 1027 (1988) holds that "a district court receiving a case under the mandatory transfer provisions of § 1406(a) must apply the law of the state in which it is held rather than the law of the transferor district court." Section 1406(a) provides that "[t]he district court of a district in which is filed a case laying venue in the wrong ... district shall dismiss, or if it be in the interest of justice, transfer such case to any district ... in which it could have been brought." See also Tel-Phonic Services, Inc. v. TBS Int'l, Inc., 975 F.2d 1134 (5th Cir.1992) (after transfer under 1406(a), the law of the transferee state applies to state-law claims and the law of the transferee circuit applies on matters of federal law).

If transfer is ordered by a district court without personal jurisdiction over the defendant, the law of the transferee forum applies. See Ross v. Colorado Outward Bound School, Inc., 822 F.2d 1524 (10th Cir.1987) (transfer for lack of personal jurisdiction is under 28 U.S.C. § 1631, which makes *Van Dusen* inapplicable); Levy v. Pyramid Co. of Ithaca, 687 F.Supp. 48, 51 (N.D.N.Y.1988), affirmed, adopting district court opinion, 871 F.2d 9 (2d Cir.1989) (Section1631 applies to lack of subject matter, not personal, jurisdiction, but though transfer for lack of personal jurisdiction is under § 1404 or § 1406, the law of the transferee state applies).

3.   Intrastate forum-shopping, i.e., between the state and federal court in the same state, may also result when a federal court exercises pendent jurisdiction or when it exercises personal jurisdiction pursuant to the 100-mile bulge rule or exercises personal jurisdiction pursuant to a special federal statute authorizing "nationwide" service of process. See, e.g., ESAB Group, Inc. v. Centricut, Inc., 126 F.3d 617 (4th Cir.1997). Supplemental jurisdiction may permit the federal court in a federal-question case to adjudicate a related state-law claim even when the federal claim fails. The Federal Rules of Civil Procedure permit nationwide jurisdiction (consistent with due process) to federal courts when the claim arises under federal law; as a result, federal courts may exercise more far-reaching jurisdiction on pendent state claims than the state courts of the forum could have done. Fed.R.Civ.Proc. 4(k)(2). If *Klaxon* then requires applying the law of the

forum, the result will run counter to the *Erie* policy of intrastate decisional harmony and may encourage forum-shopping.

Similarly, Federal Rule of Civil Procedure 4(k)(1)(B) permits service on third-party defendants and specified additional third parties to a pending claim or counterclaim within a 100-mile radius of the place of suit. Thus, it is quite possible that "the federal court will be able to reach vast population centers outside the state." Vestal, Expanding the Jurisdictional Reach of the Federal Courts: The 1973 Change in Federal Rule 4, 38 N.Y.U.L.Rev. 1053, 1065 (1963). Here too, under *Klaxon*, the plaintiff may gain the benefit of forum law even though the state courts of the forum could not have applied it for lack of personal jurisdiction over the defendant.

Do the Supreme Court's decisions in Allstate Ins. Co. v. Hague, p. 432, supra, and Phillips Petroleum Co. v. Shutts, p. 445, supra, have any relevance to the foregoing?

4. In inter-circuit transfers involving questions of federal law, the transferee court applies the interpretation adopted by its own circuit, not the view of the transferor circuit. See Marcus, Conflicts Among Circuits and Transfers Within the Federal Judicial System, 93 Yale L.J. 677 (1984). This allows the defendant to forum-shop. But see Ragazzo, Transfer and Choice of Federal Law: The Appellate Model, 93 Mich.L.Rev. 703 (1995), contending that federal precedent of the transferee circuit should apply after permanent but not multi-district consolidation transfers. See also Norwood, Double Forum Shopping and the Extension of Ferens to Federal Claims that Borrow State Limitations Periods, 44 Emory L.J. 501, 508–09 (1995) (when a claim under federal law borrows the limitations period from state law, the law of transferor forum should apply to all defendant-initiated transfers, but the law of the transferee forum should apply to all other transfers).

However, the rule is important and desirable when circuits are split on a question of federal law and the case involves a multidistrict consolidation. Adherence to *Van Dusen* in these circumstances would have the court apply not only different state laws but also possibly different interpretations of federal law to different parties in the same case.

5. The parties in *Ferens* assumed that the defendant corporation was subject to personal jurisdiction in Mississippi even for a claim that arose in Pennsylvania. In other words, they assumed that Mississippi had general personal jurisdiction over the defendant. This was true because at the time, courts exercised general jurisdiction over defendants who had continuous and systematic ties with the forum. After *Daimler*, however, p. 126, supra, general jurisdiction is restricted substantially, and it is unlikely that Mississippi would have had general jurisdiction over the *Ferens* defendant today. *Daimler* limits the mischief that can be done under *Ferens*.

C.   FEDERAL QUESTIONS IN RELATION TO STATE LAW

Even when federal power applies and the *Erie* doctrine does not, there can be problems of the interplay between federal and state law. First, in national spheres Congress may choose to specify the rules of decision, which will supplant contrary state rules and thus obviate interstate choice of law problems. For example, the Federal Employers Liability Act did this with reference to the fellow-servant issue, as illustrated in *Alabama Great Southern Railway Co. v. Carroll*, p. 534, supra. Second, Congress may legislate expressly on the conflict of laws problem, as it did in the Federal Tort Claims Act provision making the government liable in certain circumstances "in accordance with the law of the place where the act or omission occurred" (28 U.S.C. § 1346(b)). See Richards v. United States, 369 U.S. 1 (1962), (interpreting "law" in the FTCA to mean that "whole" law of the place, including its choice-of-law rules). Third, Congress may incorporate state definitions of legal rights. For instance, in a copyright case the question of whether the deceased author's illegitimate son came within the federal copyright statute's term "children" for the purpose of sharing in renewal rights. While the "scope of a federal right is, of course, a federal question," the Court declared, "that does not mean that its content is not to be determined by state, rather than federal law." De Sylva v. Ballentine, 351 U.S. 570, 580, 76 S.Ct. 974 (1956). See *United States v. Kimbell Foods, Inc.*, p. 769, infra.

In cases not clearly governed entirely by federal law, a federal court must decide whether it is bound to apply state rules, or, on the other hand, whether it may apply rules from whichever source (federal or state) is rendered appropriate by federal choice of law rules. Then, having decided for the federal source, the court may still look to state law to give content to some terms of the federal law.

CLEARFIELD TRUST CO. V. UNITED STATES, 318 U.S. 363, 63 S.Ct. 573 (1943): Action by the United States to recover the amount of a check on which the payee's name had been forged. The check was drawn on the Treasurer of the United States for services rendered to the Works Progress Administration. It was cashed under the forged endorsement and then endorsed over to the defendant bank, which as agent for collection guaranteed all prior endorsements. Fifteen months after notification of the United States agents of payee's non-receipt of her check, notice of the forgery was communicated to the defendant bank in a demand for reimbursement of the Treasurer who had paid for payee's services a second time. Suit followed upon the express guaranty. The District Court held the rights of the parties to be governed by Pennsylvania law and that since the United States had delayed unreasonably in giving notice of the forgery to defendant, it was barred from recovery. On appeal from a reversal by the Circuit Court of Appeals, affirmed.

■ DOUGLAS, J. . . . We agree with the Circuit Court of Appeals that the rule of Erie Railroad Co. v. Tompkins, 304 U.S. 64, does not apply to this action. The rights and duties of the United States on commercial paper which it issues are governed by federal rather than local law. When the United States disburses its funds or pays its debts, it is exercising a constitutional function or power. . . . The authority to issue the check had its origin in the Constitution and the statutes of the United States and was in no way dependent on the laws of Pennsylvania or of any other state. Cf. Board of Commissioners v. United States, 308 U.S. 343; Royal Indemnity Co. v. United States, 313 U.S. 289. The duties imposed upon the United States and the rights acquired by it as a result of the issuance find their roots in the same federal sources. . . . In absence of an applicable Act of Congress it is for the federal courts to fashion the governing rule of law according to their own standards. United States v. Guaranty Trust Co., 293 U.S. 340, is not opposed to this result. That case was concerned with a conflict of laws rule as to the title acquired by a transferee in Yugoslavia under a forged endorsement. Since the payee's address was Yugoslavia, the check had "something of the quality of a foreign bill" and the law of Yugoslavia was applied to determine what title the transferee acquired.

In our choice of the applicable federal rule we have occasionally selected state law. . . . But reasons which may make state law at times the appropriate federal rule are singularly inappropriate here. The issuance of commercial paper by the United States is on a vast scale and transactions in that paper from issuance to payment will commonly occur in several states. The application of state law, even without the conflict of laws rules of the forum, would subject the rights and duties of the United States to exceptional uncertainty. It would lead to great diversity in results by making identical transactions subject to the vagaries of the laws of the several states. The desirability of a uniform rule is plain. And while the federal law merchant, developed for about a century under the regime of Swift v. Tyson, 16 Pet. 1, represented general commercial law rather than a choice of a federal rule designed to protect a federal right, it nevertheless stands as a convenient source of reference for fashioning federal rules applicable to these federal questions. . . .

NOTE

Clearfield Trust does not apply in all cases involving liability for federal instruments. In Bank of America National Trust & Savings Association v. Parnell, 352 U.S. 29, 77 S.Ct. 119 (1956), the plaintiff sued in federal court in Pennsylvania regarding conversion of his bonds. They were bearer bonds issued by the Home Owners' Loan Corporation, with payment guaranteed by the United States. The bonds were originally due to mature in 1952, but had been called for payment on or about May 1, 1944. On May 2, 1944, someone apparently stole them from the plaintiff. In 1948 they were cashed by the defendant bank in Pennsylvania when presented to it by the individual defendant. At trial the principal issue was who had the burden of establishing that the defendants took the bonds in good faith (without knowledge or notice of the defect in title). The jury held for the plaintiff against both defendants and the court entered judgment against them. The Supreme Court distinguished *Clearfield Trust* in the following paragraph:

"Securities issued by the Government generate immediate interests of the Government. These were dealt with in Clearfield

Trust and in National Metropolitan Bank v. United States, 323 U.S. 454. But they also radiate interests in transactions between private parties. The present litigation is purely between private parties and does not touch the rights and duties of the United States. The only possible interest of the United States in a situation like the one here, exclusively involving the transfer of Government paper between private persons, is that the floating of securities of the United States might somehow or other be adversely affected by the local rule of a particular State regarding the liability of a converter. This is far too speculative, far too remote a possibility to justify the application of federal law to transactions essentially of local concern."

D'Oench, Duhme & Co. v. Federal Deposit Insurance Corp.

Supreme Court of the United States, 1942.
315 U.S. 447, 62 S.Ct. 676, 86 L.Ed. 956.

■ JUSTICE DOUGLAS delivered the opinion of the Court.

Respondent instituted this suit in the United States District Court for the Eastern Division of the Eastern District of Missouri on a demand note for $5,000 executed by petitioner in 1933 and payable to the Belleville Bank & Trust Co., Belleville, Illinois. Respondent insured that bank January 1, 1934; and it acquired the note in 1938 as part of the collateral securing a loan of over $1,000,000 to the bank, made in connection with the assumption of the latter's deposit liabilities by another bank. Since 1935 the note had been among the charged off assets of the bank. The note was executed by petitioner in renewal of notes which it had executed in 1926. Petitioner who was engaged in the securities business at St. Louis, Missouri, had sold the bank certain bonds which later defaulted. The original notes were executed to enable the bank to carry the notes and not show any past due bonds. Proceeds of the bonds were to be credited on the notes. The receipts for the notes contained the statement, "This note is given with the understanding it will not be called for payment. All interest payments to be repaid." Respondent had no knowledge of the existence of the receipts until after demand for payment on the renewal note was made in 1938. Certain interest payments on the notes were made prior to renewal for the purpose of keeping them "as live paper." Petitioner's president who signed the original notes knew that they were executed so that the past due bonds would not appear among the assets of the bank, and that the purpose of the interest payments was "to keep the notes alive." The original notes were signed in St. Louis, Missouri, were payable at petitioner's office there, and were delivered to the payee in Illinois. The evidence does not disclose where the note sued upon was signed, though it was dated at Belleville, Illinois, and payable to the bank there.

The main point of controversy here revolves around the question as to what law is applicable. The District Court held that Illinois law was applicable and that petitioner was liable. The Circuit Court of Appeals applied "general law" to determine that the note was an Illinois rather than a Missouri contract; and it decided that under Illinois law respondent was the equivalent of a holder in due course and entitled to recover. 117 F.2d 491. Petitioner contends that under the rule of Klaxon Company v. Stentor Electric Mfg. Co., 313 U.S. 487, a federal court sitting in Missouri must apply Missouri's conflict of law rules; that if, as was the case here, Illinois law was not pleaded or proved, a Missouri court would have ascertained Illinois law from Missouri decisions since in such a case Illinois law would be presumed to be the same as the Missouri law; and that the District Court was bound to follow that same course. We granted the petition for certiorari, because of the asserted conflict between the decision below and Klaxon Company v. Stentor Electric Mfg. Co., supra.

The jurisdiction of the District Court in this case, however, is not based on diversity of citizenship. Respondent, a federal corporation, brings this suit under an Act of Congress authorizing it to sue or be sued "in any court of law or equity, State or Federal." Section 12B, Federal Reserve Act, 12 U.S.C. § 264(j), 48 Stat. 162, 168, 172, 49 Stat. 684, 692. And see 28 U.S.C. § 42, 43 Stat. 941. Whether the rule of the Klaxon case applies where federal jurisdiction is not based on diversity of citizenship, we need not decide. For we are of the view that the liability of petitioner on the note involves decision of a federal not a state question under the rule of Deitrick v. Greaney, 309 U.S. 190. . . .

Section 12B(s) of the Federal Reserve Act, 12 U.S.C. § 264(s), provides that "Whoever, for the purpose of obtaining any loan from the Corporation . . . or for the purpose of influencing in any way the action of the Corporation under this section, makes any statement, knowing it to be false, or willfully overvalues any security, shall be punished by a fine of not more than $5,000, or by imprisonment for not more than two years or both." Subdivision (y) of the same section provided, at the time respondent insured the Belleville bank, that such a state bank "with the approval of the authority having supervision" of the bank and on "certification" to respondent "by such authority" that the bank "is in solvent condition" shall "after examination by, and with the approval of" the respondent be entitled to insurance.

These provisions reveal a federal policy to protect respondent and the public funds which it administers against misrepresentations as to the securities or other assets in the portfolios of the banks which respondent insures or to which it makes loans. If petitioner and the bank had arranged to use the note for the express purpose of deceiving respondent on insurance of the bank or on the making of the loan, the case would be on all fours with Deitrick v. Greaney, supra. . . . But the reach of the rule which prevents an accommodation maker of a note from setting up the defense of no consideration against a bank or its receiver or creditors is not delimited to those instances where he has committed a statutory offense. . . .

Those principles are applicable here because of the federal policy evidenced in this Act to protect respondent, a federal corporation, from misrepresentations made to induce or influence the action of respondent, including misstatements as to the genuineness or integrity of securities in the portfolios of banks which it insures or to which it makes loans. . . .

Affirmed.

[JUSTICE FRANKFURTER and THE CHIEF JUSTICE concurred on the ground that the result reached by the majority would also follow under Missouri or Illinois law and that it was unnecessary to stretch the federal statute to fit the case.]

■ JUSTICE JACKSON, concurring:

I think we should attempt a more explicit answer to the question whether federal or state law governs our decision in this sort of case than is found either in the opinion of the Court or in the concurring opinion of Mr. Justice Frankfurter. That question, as old as the federal judiciary, is met inescapably at the threshold of this case. . . .

Although by Congressional command this case is to be deemed one arising under the laws of the United States, no federal statute purports to define the Corporation's rights as a holder of the note in suit or the liability of the maker thereof. There arises, therefore, the question whether in deciding the case we are bound to apply the law of some particular state or whether, to put it bluntly, we may make our own law from materials found in common law sources.

This issue has a long historical background of legal and political controversy as to the place of the common law in federal jurisprudence. . . .

I do not understand Justice Brandeis's statement in Erie R. Co. v. Tompkins, 304 U.S. 64, at 78, that "There is no federal general common law," to deny that the common law may in proper cases be an aid to or the basis of decision of federal questions. In its context it means to me only that federal courts may not apply their own notions of the common law at variance with applicable state decisions except "where the Constitution, treaties, or statutes of the United States [so] require or provide." Indeed, in a case decided on the same day as Erie R. Co. v. Tompkins, Justice Brandeis said that "whether the water of an interstate stream must be apportioned between the two States is a question of 'federal common law' upon which neither the statutes nor the decisions of either State can be conclusive." Hinderlider v. La Plata Co., 304 U.S. 92, 110.

Were we bereft of the common law, our federal system would be impotent. This follows from the recognized futility of attempting all-complete statutory codes, and is apparent from the terms of the Constitution itself.

. . . Federal law is no juridical chameleon, changing complexion to match that of each state wherein lawsuits happen to be commenced because of the accidents of service of process and of the application of the venue statutes. It is found in the federal Constitution, statutes, or common law. Federal common law implements the federal Constitution and statutes, and is conditioned by them.[10] Within these limits, federal courts are free to apply the additional common law technique of decision and to draw upon all the sources of the common law in cases such as the present. Board of Commissioners v. United States, 308 U.S. 343, 350.

The law which we apply to this case consists of principles of established credit in jurisprudence selected by us because they are appropriate to effectuate the policy of the governing Act. . . . That a particular state happened to have the greatest connection in the conflict of laws sense with the making of the note involved or that the subsequent conduct happened to be chiefly centered there is not enough to make us subservient to the legislative policy or the judicial views of that state.

I concur in the Court's holding because I think that the defense asserted is nowhere admissible against the Corporation and that we need not go to the law of any particular state as our authority for so holding.

Atherton v. Federal Deposit Insurance Corp.

Supreme Court of the United States, 1997.
519 U.S. 213, 117 S.Ct. 666, 136 L.Ed.2d 656.

■ JUSTICE BREYER delivered the opinion of the Court.

The [FDIC, now the Resolution Trust Corp. ("RTC")] sued several officers and directors of City Federal Savings Bank, claiming that they had violated the legal standard of care they owed that federally chartered, federally insured institution. The case here focuses upon the legal standard for determining whether or not their behavior was improper. It asks where courts should look to find the standard of care to measure the legal propriety of the defendants' conduct—to state law, to federal common law, or to a special federal statute that speaks of "gross negligence"?

We conclude that state law sets the standard of conduct as long as the state standard (such as simple negligence) is stricter than that of the federal statute. The federal statute nonetheless sets a "gross negligence" floor, which applies as a substitute for state standards that are more relaxed.

---

[10] For example, the common-law doctrines of conflict of laws worked out in a unitary system to deal with conflicts between domestic and truly foreign law may not apply unmodified in conflicts between the laws of states within our federal system which are affected by the full faith and credit or other relevant clause of the Constitution.

I

In 1989, City Federal Savings Bank (City Federal), a federal savings association, went into receivership. The RTC, as receiver, brought this action in the bank's name against officers and directors. (Throughout this opinion, we use the more colloquial term "bank" to refer to a variety of institutions such as "federal savings associations.") The complaint said that the defendants had acted (or failed to act) in ways that led City Federal to make various bad development, construction, and business acquisition loans. It claimed that these actions (or omissions) were unlawful because they amounted to gross negligence, simple negligence, and breaches of fiduciary duty.

The defendants moved to dismiss. They pointed to a federal statute, 12 U.S.C. § 1821(k), that says in part that a "director or officer" of a federally insured bank "may be held personally liable for monetary damages" in an RTC-initiated "civil action . . . for gross negligence" or "similar conduct . . . that demonstrates a greater disregard of a duty of care (than gross negligence). . . ." (Emphasis added.) They argued that, by authorizing actions for gross negligence or more seriously culpable conduct, the statute intended to forbid actions based upon less seriously culpable conduct, such as conduct that rose only to the level of simple negligence. The District Court agreed and dismissed all but the gross negligence claims.

The Third Circuit . . . reversed. . . .

II

We begin by temporarily setting the federal "gross negligence" statute to the side, and by asking whether, were there no such statute, federal common law would provide the applicable legal standard. We recognize, as did the Third Circuit, that this Court did once articulate federal common law corporate governance standards, applicable to federally chartered banks. Briggs v. Spaulding, 141 U.S. 132, 35 L.Ed. 662, 11 S.Ct. 924 (1891). . . .

This Court has recently discussed what one might call "federal common law" in the strictest sense, i. e., a rule of decision that amounts, not simply to an interpretation of a federal statute or a properly promulgated administrative rule, but, rather, to the judicial "creation" of a special federal rule of decision. The Court has said that "cases in which judicial creation of a special federal rule would be justified . . . are . . . 'few and restricted.'" "Whether latent federal power should be exercised to displace state law is primarily a decision for Congress," not the federal courts. Nor does the existence of related federal statutes automatically show that Congress intended courts to create federal common-law rules, for "'Congress acts . . . against the background of the total corpus juris of the states. . . .'" Thus, normally, when courts decide to fashion rules of federal common law, "the guiding principle is that a significant conflict between some federal policy or interest and the use of state law . . . must first be specifically shown." . . .

No one doubts the power of Congress to legislate rules for deciding cases like the one before us. Indeed, Congress has enacted related legislation. . . . Consequently, we must decide whether the application of state-law standards of care to such banks would conflict with, and thereby significantly threaten, a federal policy or interest.

We have examined each of the basic arguments that the respondent implicitly or explicitly raises. In our view, they do not point to a conflict or threat that is significant, and we shall explain why. . . .

First, the FDIC invokes the need for "uniformity." Federal common law, it says, will provide uniformity, but "superimposing state standards of fiduciary responsibility over standards developed by a federal chartering authority would 'upset the balance' that the federal chartering authority 'may strike. . . .'" Cf. [United States v.] Kimbell Foods, [440 U.S. 715, 99 S.Ct. 1448] (rejecting "generalized pleas for uniformity").

For one thing, the number of federally insured banks is about equally divided between federally chartered and state-chartered banks, and a federal standard that increases uniformity among the former would increase disparity with the latter.

For another, our Nation's banking system has thrived despite disparities in matters of corporate governance. . . .

Second, the FDIC at times suggests that courts must apply a federal common-law standard of care simply because the banks in question are federally chartered. This argument, with little more, might have seemed a strong one during most of the first century of our Nation's history, for then state-chartered banks were the norm and federally chartered banks an exception—and federal banks often encountered hostility and deleterious state laws.

After President Madison helped to create the second Bank of the United States, for example, many States enacted laws that taxed the federal bank in an effort to weaken it. This Court held those taxes unconstitutional. McCulloch v. Maryland, 17 U.S. 316, 4 Wheat. 316, 431, 4 L.Ed. 579 (1819) ("The power to tax involves the power to destroy"). Still, 10 years later President Andrew Jackson effectively killed the bank. His Secretary of the Treasury Roger Taney (later Chief Justice), believing state banks fully able to serve the Nation, took steps to "usher in the era of expansive state banking."

During and after the Civil War a federal banking system reemerged. Moved in part by war-related financing needs, Treasury Secretary (later Chief Justice) Salmon P. Chase proposed, and Congress enacted, laws providing for federally chartered banks, and encouraging state banks to obtain federal charters. Just before World War I, Congress created the federal reserve system. After that war, it created several federal banking agencies with regulatory authority over both federal and state banks. . . .

This latter history is relevant because in 1870 and thereafter this Court held that federally chartered banks are subject to state law. . . .

The Court subsequently found numerous state laws applicable to federally chartered banks. . . .

For present purposes, the consequence is the following: To point to a federal charter by itself shows no conflict, threat, or need for "federal common law." It does not answer the critical question.

Third, the FDIC refers to a conflict of laws principle called the "internal affairs doctrine"—a doctrine that this Court has described as

"a conflict of laws principle which recognizes that only one State should have the authority to regulate a corporation's internal affairs—matters peculiar to the relationships among or between the corporation and its current officers, directors, and shareholders—because otherwise a corporation could be faced with conflicting demands." Edgar v. MITE Corp., 457 U.S. 624, 645, 73 L.Ed.2d 269, 102 S.Ct. 2629 (1982), p. 1122, infra.

States normally look to the State of a business' incorporation for the law that provides the relevant corporate governance general standard of care. Restatement, Second, Conflict of Laws § 309 (1971). And by analogy, it has been argued, courts should look to federal law to find the standard of care governing officers and directors of federally chartered banks.

To find a justification for federal common law in this argument, however, is to substitute analogy or formal symmetry for the controlling legal requirement, namely, the existence of a need to create federal common law arising out of a significant conflict or threat to a federal interest. The internal affairs doctrine shows no such need, for it seeks only to avoid conflict by requiring that there be a single point of legal reference. Nothing in that doctrine suggests that the single source of law must be federal. In the absence of a governing federal common law, courts applying the internal affairs doctrine could find (we do not say that they will find) that the State closest analogically to the State of incorporation of an ordinary business is the State in which the federally chartered bank has its main office or maintains its principal place of business. So to apply state law, as we have said, would tend to avoid disparity between federally chartered and state-chartered banks (that might be next door to each other). And, of course, if this approach proved problematic, Congress and federal agencies acting pursuant to congressionally delegated authority remain free to provide to the contrary.

Fourth, the FDIC points to statutes that provide the OTS, a federal regulatory agency, with authority to fine, or to remove from office, savings bank officers and directors for certain breaches of fiduciary duty. The FDIC adds that in "the course of such proceedings, the OTS, applying the ordinary-care standard [of Briggs,] . . . has spoken authoritatively respecting the duty of care owed by directors and officers to federal savings associations." The FDIC does not claim, however, that these OTS statements, interpreting a pre-existing judge-made federal common-law standard (i.e., that of Briggs) themselves amounted to an agency effort to promulgate a binding regulation pursuant to delegated congressional authority. Nor have we found, in our examination of the relevant OTS opinions, any convincing evidence of a relevant, significant conflict or threat to a federal interest. . . .

In sum, we can find no significant conflict with, or threat to, a federal interest. . . .

We conclude that the federal common-law standards enunciated in cases such as Briggs did not survive this Court's later decision in Erie v. Tompkins. There is no federal common law that would create a general standard of care applicable to this case.

III

We now turn to a further question: Does federal statutory law (namely, the federal "gross negligence" statute) supplant any state-law standard of care? [The Court concluded that the relevant federal statute did not preempt application of state laws setting a standard stricter than that of gross negligence. The opinion of Justices Scalia and O'Connor concurring in part and concurring in the judgment is omitted.]

NOTES

1.   In *Atherton*, the Court does not cite *D'Oench*. Are the holdings in the two cases consistent?

Another decision of the Supreme Court, also involving a failed thrift institution, likewise rejected application of federal common law. In O'Melveny & Myers v. Federal Deposit Insurance Corp., 512 U.S. 79, 114 S.Ct. 2048, 129 L.Ed.2d 67 (1994) the FDIC became receiver for an insolvent California savings and loan (S & L) and ordered the S & L to make refunds to investors in fraudulent real estate ventures in which the S & L had been represented by O'Melveny & Myers, a law firm. The FDIC filed suit against the law firm in federal court and alleged state causes of action for professional negligence and breach of fiduciary duty. The law firm moved for summary judgment on the ground that the knowledge of the fraudulent conduct of the S & L's officers must be imputed to the S & L and to the FDIC, which, as receiver, stood in the shoes of the S & L. The district court granted the motion, but the Ninth Circuit reversed, holding that a federal common-law rule applied. The Supreme Court reversed the Ninth Circuit, holding that California law rather than federal law governed the issue of whether a corporate officer's knowledge of fraud would be imputed to a corporation asserting a cause of action created by state law, and whether this knowledge would be imputed to the FDIC as receiver. The Court remanded for determination of California law on this issue. The Supreme Court, as in *Atherton*, did not cite *D'Oench*. The Court held that state law applied regardless of whether the Financial Institutions Reform, Recovery, and Enforcement Act of 1989 (FIRREA) applied retroactively to this case, in which the FDIC had taken over as receiver of the S & L in 1986. 12 U.S.C. § 1821(d)(2)(A)(i), part of this Act, provides that the FDIC shall "succeed to all rights, titles, powers and privileges of the insured depository institution." The Court states that this provision "places the FDIC in the shoes of the insolvent S & L, to work out its claims under state law, except where some provision in the extensive framework of the FIRREA provides otherwise." Id. at 2054.

On remand, the Ninth Circuit held that under California law, the FDIC was not barred by equitable defenses that could have been raised against the S & L, and declared that *D'Oench* has "now been overruled by the Supreme Court." F.D.I.C. v. O'Melveny & Myers, 61 F.3d 17, 19 (9th Cir.1995). Was that conclusion correct? Was perhaps the risk of impairment of federal interests greater in *D'Oench* than it was in either *O'Melvny* or *Atherton*? The Eleventh Circuit, disagreeing with the Ninth Circuit opinion cited above, held that *D'Oench* survives. Motorcity of Jacksonville, Ltd. v. Southeast Bank, N.A., 83 F.3d 1317 (11th Cir.1996) (en banc), cert. granted, judgment vacated, 519 U.S. 1087, 117 S.Ct. 760, 136 L.Ed.2d 708 (1997) held that the doctrine bars plaintiff's reliance on oral agreements of officials of a bank, subsequently under FDIC receivership, that the bank would conduct regular audits of plaintiff's business and advise plaintiff of any irregularities. In Murphy v. F.D.I.C., 208 F.3d 959 (11th Cir.2000), the Eleventh Circuit again held that the *D'Oench* doctrine barred investors' claims against the FDIC, thus disagreeing with the Third, Eighth, Ninth and D.C. Circuits on the effect of *O'Melveny* and *Atherton* on the *D'Oench* doctrine. The Supreme Court granted certiorari but later dismissed the writ. Murphy v. Beck, 531 U.S. 1107, 121 S.Ct. 849 (2001).

The FDIC has now issued a "Statement of Policy" regarding when it will assert the federal common law doctrine enunciated in *D'Oench* and when it will assert statutory protections set forth in 12 U.S.C. § 1821(d)(9)(A) and § 1823(e). See 62 Fed.Reg. 5984.

2. In United States v. Kimbell Foods, Inc., 440 U.S. 715, 99 S.Ct. 1448 (1979) the Court held that while federal common law governs the priority of contractual liens arising from certain federal programs, the federal rule need not be uniform, and the Court thus incorporated state law by reference. Is there any practical difference between cases like *Kimbell* which purport to apply state law as a matter of federal common law and cases like *Atherton* in which the Court simply decides to apply state law? Note that *Atherton* cites *Kimbell* with approval. Consider also whether cases like *Atherton* and *Kimbell* are consistent with *Clearfield Trust*, p. 759, supra. See Note, Formulating a Federal Rule of Decision in Commercial Transactions after Kimbell, 66 Iowa L.Rev. 391 (1981).

3. Federal common law generally supplants state law with regard to the application of the "government contractor defense," which immunizes products manufacturers from products liability if their products are built to governmental specifications. See Boyle v. United Tech. Corp., 487 U.S. 500, 108 S.Ct. 2510 (1988)(no liability for alleged design defect in a military aircraft that was built to federal governmental design requirements).

4. Vanston Bondholders Protective Committee v. Green, 329 U.S. 156, 67 S.Ct. 237 (1946) concerned a Delaware corporation with its principal place of business in Kentucky which mortgaged Kentucky property under an indenture. The indenture, executed in New York with a New York bank as trustee, provided that bonds secured by it would be paid in New York or Illinois at the option of the holder. The corporation went into an equity receivership and then into reorganization under the Bankruptcy Act, in a federal court in Kentucky. The indenture and the bonds provided for payment of interest on unpaid interest, and the validity of this provision was in issue. The district court and the circuit court of appeals treated the matter as one of conflict of laws to be governed by the law of New York. The Supreme Court stated: "In determining what claims are allowable and how a debtor's assets shall be distributed, a bankruptcy court does not apply the law of the state where it sits. Erie R.R. v. Tompkins, 304 U.S. 64, has no such implication. . . . [B]ankruptcy courts must administer and enforce the Bankruptcy Act as interpreted by this Court in accordance with authority granted by Congress to determine how and what claims shall be allowed under equitable principles. And we think an allowance of interest on interest under the circumstances shown by this case would not be in accord with the equitable principles governing bankruptcy distributions."

Some issues that must be resolved in bankruptcy are, however, not covered by the bankruptcy code and are thus governed by state law, such as whether a security interest is "perfected" (i.e., effective against third parties, including the bankruptcy trustee) under the U.C.C. Federal courts are split as to whether *Klaxon* applies to state law issues in bankruptcy. Courts in bankruptcy that do not follow state conflicts law generally look to the Second Restatement for guidance as to federal common law conflicts principles. See Borchers, Choice of Law Relative to Security Interests and Other Liens in International Bankruptcies, 46 Am.J.Comp.L. 165, 181–82 (Supp.1998).

5. Federal law may also determine some common law tort issues. In United States v. Standard Oil Co., 332 U.S. 301, 67 S.Ct. 1604 (1947), it was held that federal law determined whether the United States could obtain reimbursement from one who had negligently injured a soldier, for hospital care and pay during his disablement. In Boyle v. United Technologies Corp., 487 U.S. 500, 108 S.Ct. 2510 (1988), the Supreme Court created—as a matter of federal common law—a tort defense against private plaintiffs for military contractors who build military equipment in accord with the government's design specifications. The majority found the defense necessary to avoid conflicts between state tort law and federal military policy.

Some have long argued that federal common law should play a large role in tort liability in aircrash cases. See Note, The Case for a Federal Common Law of Aircraft Disaster Litigation, 51 N.Y.U.L.Rev. 232 (1976), which suggests that federal courts should exercise their power to imply a federal cause of action for victims of air crashes, borrowing from the Supreme Court's decision in Cort v. Ash, 422 U.S. 66, 95 S.Ct. 2080 (1975). There, the Court listed four factors as determinative of when a federal right of action should be implied from a statute not expressly creating one. The Supreme Court, however, rejected an expansive role for federal common law in air crash cases in Miree v. DeKalb County, 433 U.S. 25, 97 S.Ct. 2490 (1977). In that case petitioners sought to recover for the death of passengers asserting a right of recovery as third-party beneficiaries under a government grant contract requiring the county to maintain the airport in a manner permitting normal operations. The Court concluded that, unlike the situation in *Clearfield Trust*: "petitioners' breach-of-contract claim will have no direct effect upon the United States or its Treasury.... The parallel between Parnell and [this case] is obvious ... [N]o substantial rights or duties of the United States hinge on its outcome ... [and any federal interest, e.g., promoting compliance with air safety regulations is] far too speculative ... to justify the application of federal law to transactions essentially of local concern." 433 U.S. at 29–32 passim.

One notable effort to invoke federal common law tort principles arose in In re "Agent Orange" Product Liab. Litigation, 635 F.2d 987 (2d Cir.1980). This was an enormous class action by military veterans asserting a right under federal common law to recover against corporations that supplied the United States government with chemicals that were alleged to have injured the veterans. The court held that the veterans had no claim under federal common law. The court found that there was "no federal interest in uniformity for its own sake" since the litigation was between private parties and "no substantial rights or duties of the government hinged on its outcome." Also, the interests of the federal government were conflicting since it had an interest both in the welfare of its veterans and in that of the suppliers of its material. "The extent to which either group should be favored ... is preeminently a policy determination of the sort reserved in the first instance for Congress." Congress has not yet determined how these two competing interests should be reconciled. "... before common law rules should be fashioned, the use of state law must pose a threat to an 'identifiable' federal policy.... In the present litigation the federal policy is not yet identifiable." The dissent emphasized that it would be unfortunate if veterans' recoveries for Agent Orange injuries were to vary from state to state "despite the fact that these soldiers fought shoulder to shoulder, without regard to state citizenship, in a national endeavor abroad." Is the rejection of a federal common law claim for military personnel in *Agent Orange* consistent with the creation of a federal defense for contractors in *Boyle*?

The *Agent Orange* case was then continued on the basis of the federal court's diversity jurisdiction. Now required to apply state law, the trial court concluded that all of the states involved would apply "a form of national consensus law or of federal law itself" because of the need for a uniform result. In re Agent Orange Product Liability Litigation, 580 F.Supp. 690, 698 (E.D.N.Y.1984). A settlement was reached and ordered. 597 F.Supp. 740, 755 (E.D.N.Y.1984), aff'd, 818 F.2d 145 (2d Cir.1987).

6.   More product liability litigation was filed over asbestos-related injuries than any other product. One prospect in multiple litigation of this magnitude is that the financial resources of defendant manufacturers will be exhausted before the claims of all victims have progressed to judgment or settlement. In Jackson v. Johns-Manville Sales Corp., 750 F.2d 1314 (5th Cir.1985), the

defendants sought a nationwide solution through the development of federal common law. However, the Fifth Circuit held, over strong dissent, "that this case is not an appropriate one for the creation of federal common law because of the absence of a uniquely federal interest and the practical problems that would attend the displacement of state law." 750 F.2d at 1327.

For discussion of the jurisdictional and choice-of-law aspects of mass torts see Symposium: Conflict of Laws and Complex Litigation Issues in Mass Tort Litigation, 1989 U.Ill.L.Rev. 35. For Professor Weintraub's proposed choice-of-law rules to govern products liability, see Weintraub, Commentary on the Conflict of Laws 453 (5th ed.2006).

SECTION 2. CONFLICTS PROBLEMS IN INTERNATIONAL SETTINGS

With international travel, commerce and private transactions increasing by quantum leaps, the subject of "private international law" has become more important for American lawyers. All through the book we have encountered conflicts cases that cut across international boundaries. They were sprinkled, almost interchangeably, among the cases involving states of the Union. See, e.g., In re Annesley, Matter of Schneider, Gilbert v. Burstine, Hilton v. Guyot, Slater v. Mexican Nat'l Ry. Co., Walton v. Arabian American Oil Co., Babcock v. Jackson, Home Insurance Co. v. Dick. In the international sphere, as opposed to cases involving sister-state judgments, enforceability of judgments looks to amorphous principles of comity rather than pointed commands of full faith and credit.

In Hilton v. Guyot, a different question was raised: May the several states impose diverse, individual tests for recognition of foreign judgments, or is the problem one committed to the national government? In somewhat more dilute form, the same sort of issue lurked in the *Holzer* case, where the New York Court of Appeals was asked to refuse to countenance a defense based upon the Nazi government's anti-Jewish laws. In the materials that follow in the first subsection, questions of the effective scope of state law in the international arena are considered against the backdrop of the accepted principle that the United States, in its relations with foreign nations, should speak with a single voice, not with more than fifty voices. Traditionally, for the most part, the spokesperson has been the chief executive and her delegates.

A second subsection explores the growing participation by the United States in international conventions that provide uniform procedural, conflicts and even substantive rules of law. As federal law, these conventions displace inconsistent state law under the Supremacy Clause as well as inconsistent prior federal law. Their application often raises important questions of interpretation—for instance, whether a particular state rule is indeed incompatible with the convention.

Even when the federal control over foreign affairs does not set limits on the states in international conflicts cases and even when no federal law expressly displaces state law, the question remains: Should international conflicts cases be treated differently from interstate cases and, if so, in what circumstances? The third subsection touches upon these issues.

A. INTERNATIONAL CONFLICTS CASES AND THE FEDERAL CONTROL OF FOREIGN AFFAIRS

Zschernig v. Miller

Supreme Court of the United States, 1968.
389 U.S. 429, 88 S.Ct. 664, 19 L.Ed.2d 683.

[An American citizen died in Oregon, leaving property to relatives in the Soviet Zone of Germany. An Oregon statute conditioned a nonresident alien's right to inherit property in Oregon upon the existence of a reciprocal right of American citizens to inherit in the alien's country upon the same terms as citizens of that country; upon the right of American citizens to receive payment within the United States from the estates of decedents dying in that country; and upon proof that the alien heirs of the American decedent would receive the benefit, use, and control of their inheritance without confiscation. The Oregon Supreme Court affirmed the finding of the trial court that the evidence did not establish that American citizens were accorded reciprocal rights to take property from or to receive the proceeds of East German estates. However, it found that a 1923 treaty was still effective with respect to East Germany, and consequently held that under Clark v. Allen, 331 U.S. 503, the East German heirs must be permitted to take the real property despite the Oregon statute. They were not permitted to take the personal property.[2]]

■ JUSTICE DOUGLAS delivered the opinion of the Court.

This case concerns the disposition of the estate of a resident of Oregon who died there intestate in 1962. Appellants are decedent's sole heirs and they are residents of East Germany. Appellees include members of the State Land Board that petitioned the Oregon probate court for the escheat of the net proceeds of the estate under the provisions of Ore.Rev.Stat. § 111.070 (1957), which provides for escheat in cases where a nonresident alien claims real or personal property unless three requirements are satisfied:

(1)   the existence of a reciprocal right of a United States citizen to take property on the same terms as a citizen or inhabitant of the foreign country;

(2)   the right of United States citizens to receive payment here of funds from estates in the foreign country; and

---

[2]   The statement of facts is taken from the concurring opinion of Justice Harlan. —eds.

(3) the right of the foreign heirs to receive the proceeds of Oregon estates "without confiscation."

The Oregon Supreme Court held that the appellants could take the Oregon realty involved in the present case by reason of Article IV of the 1923 Treaty of Friendship, Commerce and Consular Rights with Germany (44 Stat. 2135) but that by reason of the same Article, as construed in Clark v. Allen, 331 U.S. 503, 67 S.Ct. 1431, 91 L.Ed.1633, they could not take the personalty. . . .

We do not accept the invitation to re-examine our ruling in Clark v. Allen. For we conclude that the history and operation of this Oregon statute make clear that § 111.070 is an intrusion by the State into the field of foreign affairs which the Constitution entrusts to the President and the Congress. See Hines v. Davidowitz, 312 U.S. 52, 63. . . .

. . . . It has never been seriously suggested that state courts are precluded from performing [the probate] function, although there is a possibility, albeit remote, that any holding may disturb a foreign nation—whether the matter involves commercial cases, tort cases, or some other type of controversy. At the time Clark v. Allen was decided, the case seemed to involve no more than a routine reading of foreign laws. It now appears that in this reciprocity area under inheritance statutes, the probate courts of various States have launched inquiries into the type of governments that obtain in a particular foreign nation—whether aliens under their law have enforceable rights, whether the so-called "rights" are merely dispensations turning upon the whim or caprice of government officials, whether the representation of consuls, ambassadors, and other representatives of foreign nations are credible or made in good faith, whether there is in the actual administration in the particular foreign system of law any element of confiscation.

As we read the decisions that followed in the wake of Clark v. Allen, we find that they radiate some of the attitudes of the "cold war," where the search is for the "democracy quotient" of a foreign regime as opposed to the Marxist theory. The Oregon statute introduces the concept of "confiscation," which is of course opposed to the Just Compensation Clause of the Fifth Amendment. And this has led into minute inquiries concerning the actual administration of foreign law, into the credibility of foreign diplomatic statements, and into speculation whether the fact that some received delivery of funds should "not preclude wonderment as to how many may have been denied 'the right to receive'. . . ." See State Land Board v. Kolovrat, 220 Or. 448, 461–462, 349 P.2d 255, 262, rev'd sub nom. Kolovrat v. Oregon, 366 U.S. 187 on other grounds.

That kind of state involvement in foreign affairs and international developments—matters which the Constitution entrusts solely to the Federal Government—is not sanctioned by Clark v. Allen. Yet such forbidden state activity has infected each of the three provisions of § 111.070, as applied by Oregon.

It seems inescapable that the type of probate law that Oregon enforces affects international relations in a persistent and subtle way. . . . Reversed.

[The concurring opinion of Justice Stewart is omitted.]

■ JUSTICE HARLAN concurring in the result.

Although I agree with the result reached in this case, I am unable to subscribe to the Court's opinion, for three reasons. *First*, by resting its decision on the constitutional ground that this Oregon inheritance statute infringes the federal foreign relations power, without pausing to consider whether the 1923 Treaty of Friendship, Commerce and Consular Rights with Germany itself vitiates this application of the state statute, the Court has deliberately turned its back on a cardinal principle of judicial review. *Second*, correctly construed the 1923 treaty, in my opinion, renders Oregon's application of its statute in this instance impermissible, thus requiring reversal of the state judgment. *Third*, the constitutional holding, which I reach only because the majority has done so, is in my view untenable. The impact of today's holding on state power in this field, and perhaps in other areas of the law as well, justifies a full statement of my views upon the case. . . .

Upon my view of this case, it would be unnecessary to reach the issue whether Oregon's statute governing inheritance by aliens amounts to an unconstitutional infringement upon the foreign relations power of the Federal Government. However, since this is the basis upon which the Court has chosen to rest its decision, I feel that I should indicate briefly why I believe the decision to be wrong on that score, too.

As noted earlier, the Oregon statute conditions an alien's right to inherit Oregon property upon the satisfaction of three conditions: (1) a reciprocal right of Americans to inherit property in the alien's country; (2) the right of Americans to receive payment in the United States from the estates of decedents dying in the alien's country; and (3) proof that the alien heirs of the Oregon decedent would receive the benefit, use, and control of their inheritance without confiscation. In Clark v. Allen, supra, the Court upheld the constitutionality of a California statute which similarly conditioned the right of aliens to inherit upon reciprocity but did not contain the other two restrictions. The Court in *Clark* dismissed as "farfetched" the contention that the statute unconstitutionally infringed upon the federal foreign relations power. . . .

It seems to me impossible to distinguish the present case from Clark v. Allen in this respect in any convincing way. . . .

The foregoing would seem to establish that the Oregon statute is not unconstitutional on its face. And in fact the Court seems to have found the statute unconstitutional only as applied. Its notion appears to be that application of the parts of the statute which require that reciprocity actually exist and that the alien heir actually be able to enjoy his inheritance will inevitably involve the state courts in evaluations of foreign laws and governmental policies, and that this is likely to result in offense to foreign governments. There are several defects in this rationale. The most glaring is that it is based almost entirely on speculation. . . .

"The Department of State has advised us . . . that State reciprocity laws, including that of Oregon, have had little effect on the foreign relations and policy of this country. . . . Appellants' apprehension of a deterioration in international relations, unsubstantiated by experience, does not constitute the kind of 'changed conditions' which might call for re-examination of Clark v. Allen."

Essentially, the Court's basis for decision appears to be that alien inheritance laws afford state court judges an opportunity to criticize in dictum the policies of foreign governments, and that these dicta may adversely affect our foreign relations. . . .

If the flaw in the statute is said to be that it requires state courts to inquire into the administration of foreign law, I would suggest that that characteristic is shared by other legal rules which I cannot believe the Court wishes to invalidate. For example, the Uniform Foreign Money-Judgments Recognition Act provides that a foreign-country money judgment shall not be recognized if it "was rendered under a system which does not provide impartial tribunals or procedures compatible with the requirements of due process of law." When there is a dispute as to the content of foreign law, the court is required under the common law to treat the question as one of fact and to consider any evidence presented as to the actual administration of the foreign legal system. And in the field of choice of law there is a nonstatutory rule that the tort law of a foreign country will not be applied if that country is shown to be "uncivilized." [See Slater v. Mexican National R. Co., p. 264, supra.] Surely, all of these rules possess the same "defect" as the statute now before us. Yet I assume that the Court would not find them unconstitutional.

I therefore concur in the judgment of the Court upon the sole ground that the application of the Oregon statute in this case conflicts with the 1923 Treaty of Friendship, Commerce and Consular Rights with Germany.

[The dissenting opinion of Justice White is omitted.]

NOTE

In Clark v. Allen, 331 U.S. 503, 67 S.Ct. 1431 (1947), discussed extensively in Justice Harlan's concurrence, Justice Douglas wrote for the Court that a California reciprocal inheritance statute was constitutional and permitted German nationals to take as legatees of a California resident decedent's personal property in that state. (The United States Alien Property Custodian had vested in himself all interest of the German nationals in the decedent's estate, but the question of the validity of the attempted testamentary disposition remained because a California statute provided that nonresident aliens could not inherit real or personal property in the state unless United States citizens had reciprocal rights in property in the aliens' country, but unlike the Oregon statute in *Zschernig*, the California act did not refer to the right of foreign heirs to receive the proceeds of California property "without confiscation.") The opinion said in part:

> ... Rights of succession to property are determined by local law. ... Those rights may be affected by an overriding federal policy, as where a treaty makes different or conflicting arrangements. ... Then the state policy must give way. ... But here there is no treaty governing the rights of succession to the personal property. Nor has California entered the forbidden domain of negotiating with a foreign country, United States v. Curtiss-Wright Export Corp., 299 U.S. 304, 316, 317, or making a compact with it contrary to the prohibition of Article I, Section 10 of the Constitution. What California has done will have some incidental or indirect effect in foreign countries. But that is true of many state laws which none would claim cross the forbidden line.

Was Justice Douglas consistent in the two cases or, as Justice Harlan suggests, are the results inconsistent?

Article 36 of the Vienna Convention on Consular Relations, Apr. 24, 1963, 21 UST 77, 596 UNTS 261, requires signatory nations to inform an arrested alien that the prisoner has a right to notify and communicate with a consular official of the alien's country. Angel Beard, a Paraguayan citizen, was arrested, tried for murder, and sentenced to death in Virginia without having been informed of his rights under the Convention. Beard's petition for habeas corpus, which asserted a violation of the Convention, was denied by a Virginia federal district court and the denial was affirmed by the Fourth Circuit. Breard v. Pruett, 134 F.3d 615 (4th Cir.1998). Paraguay then sued the United States in the International Court of Justice, and asked the Court to declare that the United States had violated the Convention and that Breard was entitled to a new trial. The court found that it had jurisdiction and declared that "[t]he United States should take all measures at its disposal to ensure that Angel Francisco Breard is not executed pending the final decision in these proceedings. ..." Case Concerning the Vienna Convention on Consular Relations, (Paraguay v. United States), Provisional Measures, & 41 (Order of Apr. 9, 1998), 37 ILM 810, 819. The U.S. Secretary of State then sent a letter to the Governor of Virginia requesting that the Governor suspend the execution. The next day the Supreme Court, by a vote of six to three, denied Breard's petitions for habeas corpus and certiorari. Breard v. Greene, 523 U.S. 371, 118 S.Ct. 1352 (1998). The majority held that Breard had "procedurally defaulted his claim" by not raising it in state court and stated that even if the Convention claim were properly raised "it is extremely doubtful that the violation should result in the overturning of a final judgment of conviction without some showing that the violation had an effect on the trial." The majority noted that "[i]n this case, no such showing could even arguably be made." The three dissenters would have granted the application for a stay of execution pending normal consideration of the petitions. The same day the Governor of Virginia refused to stay the execution and Breard was executed. Is *Breard* consistent with *Zschernig*?

Paraguay continued to press its claim in the International Court of Justice for a decision recognizing the Paraguayan claim and granting economic compensation. Paraguay ultimately withdrew its complaint, however, after the U.S. Embassy in Asuncion issued a communique stating that the U.S. government recognized that the Vienna Convention had been violated and extended it apologies to the government and people of Paraguay.

See the International Court of Justice opinion in the *LaGrand* Case (Germany v. United States) 2001 I.C.J. 104 (2001) No. 104, reprinted 40 I.L.M. 1069. The LaGrands were German brothers arrested and convicted of murder without informing them of their rights to consular access. They were executed after Germany had brought an action in the I.C.J. and the I.C.J. had issued an order containing a provisional measure barring execution until final decision of the I.C.J. The I.C.J. found that the U.S. had breached its treaty obligations to Germany and to the LaGrand brothers; that "by failing to take all measures at its disposal to ensure" that execution would not take place pending final decision of the I.C.J. The U.S. had breached "the obligation incumbent upon it under the Order." The Court found that the commitment by the U.S. to ensure implementation of its obligations under the Convention meets Germany's request for a general assurance of no-repetition. The Court then ordered that if nonetheless German national are sentenced to severe penalties without their convention rights having been respected, the U.S. "by means of its own choosing, shall allow the review and reconsideration of the conviction and sentence by taking account of the violation of the rights set forth in that Convention."

In Case Concerning Avena and other Mexican Nationals (Mexico v. U.S.) 2004 I.C.J. No. 128 (2004), the International Court of Justice held that the U.S. had violated article 36 when Mexican nationals were arrested and convicted without being informed of their right to communicate with Mexican consular officials. The I.C.J. further ruled that the U.S. "shall allow the review and reconsideration of the conviction and sentence by taking account of the violation." President George W. Bush then issued a Memorandum to the U.S. Attorney General stating that state courts would give effect to the Avena decision. Sanchez-Llamas v. Oregon, 548 U.S. 331, 126 S.Ct. 2669 (2006), held that (1) violation of the Convention does not require excluding evidence obtained after the violation (id. at 2682); (2) claims for violation of the Convention were subject to the same procedural default rules that apply to other federal law claims.

Jose Ernesto Medellin, a Mexican national, was arrested by Texas police, tried, convicted, and sentenced to death without being informed of his right to contact Mexican consular officials. After his conviction and sentence were affirmed and his applications for habeas corpus denied, Medellin again filed an application for the writ in a Texas court. A Texas rule permits granting such an application only if the factual or legal basis for the review was previously unavailable. Ex Parte Medellin, 223 S.W.3d 315 (Tex.Ct.Crim.App.2006), held that (1) *Avena* is not binding federal law and does not preempt the Texas rule that precludes review in this case; (2) "the

President has exceeded his constitutional power by intruding into the independent power of the judiciary." Id. at 335. The Supreme Court affirmed on the grounds that neither the *Avena* decision of the I.C.J nor the President's memorandum were enforceable to pre-empt state limitations on the filing of habeas petitions. Medellin v. Texas, 552 U.S. 1491, 128 S.Ct. 1346 (2008).

In 2008, the I.C.J. ordered the U.S. to "take all measures necessary to ensure that [Medellin and 4 other Mexican nationals on death row in Texas] are not executed pending judgment on the Request for interpretation [of the Avena decision] submitted by the United Mexican States, unless and until these five Mexican nationals receive review and reconsideration consistent with [the Avena decision]." Request for Interpretation of the Judgment of 31 March 2004 in the Case Concerning Avena and other Mexican Nations, 16 July 2008 (available at the web site of the International Court of Justice www.icj.cij.org). President George W. Bush stated that the I.C.J. did not have jurisdiction. He had previously announced that the United States withdrew from the Optional Protocol to the Vienna Convention on Consular Relations, in which the U.S. had agreed to the compulsory jurisdiction of the I.C.J. to resolve disputes arising out of the interpretation or application of the Vienna Convention. On August 5, 2008, Texas executed Medellin.

In contrast to U.S. courts, the Federal Constitutional Court of Germany held that failure to give the notice required by the Vienna Convention on Consular Relations violates the right to a fair trial guaranteed by the German Constitution. The court ordered the Federal Court of Justice to treat the Convention violation as relevant to criminal proceedings and to reconsider the legal consequences of the violation. Case No. 2BvR2115/01, 60 Neue Juristische Wochenschrift 499 (2007).

Gandara v. Bennett, 528 F.3d 823 (11th Cir.2008) and Mora v. People of the State of New York, 524 F.3d 183 (2d Cir.2008), held that an alien who is not given the notice required by the Vienna Convention on Consular Relations cannot sue the officials who violated the Convention for violation of the alien's civil rights. Contra, Jogi v. Voges, 480 F.3d 822 (7th Cir.2007), held than an Indian citizen, who was prosecuted and imprisoned in the U.S., may sue Illinois law enforcement officials under 42 U.S.C. § 1983 for failing to inform him of his right under the Vienna Convention on Consular Relations to notify his consulate of his arrest. The plaintiff is suing for compensatory and punitive damages. 42 U.S.C. § 1983 provides: "Every person who, under color of any statute, ordinance, regulation, custom, or usage, of any State or Territory or the District of Columbia, subjects, or causes to be subjected, any citizen of the United States or other person within the jurisdiction thereof to the deprivation of any rights, privileges, or immunities secured by the Constitution and laws, shall be liable to the party injured in an action at law, suit in equity, or other proper proceeding for redress * * *." At least one court has held that counsel's failure to raise a violation of article 36 of the Vienna Convention may give rise to a claim for ineffective assistance of counsel. See Osagiede v. United States, 543 F.3d 399 (7th Cir.2008).

American Insurance Association v. Garamendi

Supreme Court of the United States, 2003.
539 U.S. 396, 123 S.Ct. 2374, 156 L.Ed.2d 376.

■ JUSTICE SOUTER delivered the opinion of the Court

California's Holocaust Victim Insurance Relief Act of 1999 (HVIRA or Act), Cal. Ins.Code Ann. §§ 13800–13807 (West Cum.Supp.2003), requires any insurer doing business in that State to disclose information about all policies sold in Europe between 1920 and 1945 by the company itself or any one "related" to it. The issue here is whether HVIRA interferes with the National Government's conduct of foreign relations. We hold that it does, with the consequence that the state statute is preempted.

I

A

The Nazi Government of Germany engaged not only in genocide and enslavement but theft of Jewish assets, including the value of insurance policies, and in particular policies of life insurance, a form of savings held by many Jews in Europe before the Second World War. Early on in the Nazi era, loss of livelihood forced Jews to cash in life insurance policies prematurely, only to have the government seize the proceeds of the repurchase, and many who tried to emigrate from Germany were forced to liquidate insurance policies to pay the steep "flight taxes" and other levies imposed by the Third Reich to keep Jewish assets from leaving the country. . . . Responsibility as between the government and insurance companies is disputed, but at the end of the day, the fact is that the value or proceeds of many insurance policies issued to Jews before and during the war were paid to the Reich or never paid at all.

A vivid precursor of the kind of direct confiscation that would become widespread by 1941 was the Reich's seizure of property and casualty insurance proceeds in the aftermath of the November 1938 Kristallnacht, in which Nazi looting and vandalism inflicted damage to Jewish businesses, homes, and synagogues worth nearly 50 million deutsch marks. Days afterward, a Reich decree mandated that all proceeds of all insurance claims arising from the damage be paid directly to the state treasury, an obligation ultimately settled by German insurance companies with the Reich at a mere pittance relative to full value. . . .

These confiscations and frustrations of claims fell within the subject of reparations, which became a principal object of Allied diplomacy soon after the war. . . .

In the meantime, the western allies placed the obligation to provide restitution to victims of Nazi persecution on the new West German Government. See Convention on the Settlement of Matters Arising Out of the War and the Occupation, May 26, 1952, 6 U.S.T. 4411, 4452–4484, as amended by Protocol on Termination of the Occupation Regime in the

Federal Republic of Germany, Oct. 23, 1954, [1955] 6 U.S.T. 4117, T.I.A.S. No. 3425. . . . Despite a payout of more than 100 billion deutsch marks as of 2000, these measures left out many claimants and certain types of claims. . . . [After reunification of East and West Germany] class-action lawsuits for restitution poured into United States courts against companies doing business in Germany during the Nazi era. . . . These suits generated much protest by the defendant companies and their governments, to the point that the Government of the United States took action to try to resolve "the last great compensation related negotiation arising out of World War II . . . ." From the beginning, the Government's position, represented principally by Under Secretary of State (later Deputy Treasury Secretary) Stuart Eizenstat, stressed mediated settlement "as an alternative to endless litigation" promising little relief to aging Holocaust survivors. Ensuing negotiations at the national level produced the German Foundation Agreement, signed by President Clinton and German Chancellor Schröder in July 2000, in which Germany agreed to enact legislation establishing a foundation funded with 10 billion deutsch marks contributed equally by the German Government and German companies, to be used to compensate all those "who suffered at the hands of German companies during the National Socialist era." Agreement Concerning the Foundation "Remembrance, Responsibility and the Future," 39 Int'l Legal Materials 1298 (2000).

The willingness of the Germans to create a voluntary compensation fund was conditioned on some expectation of security from lawsuits in United States courts, and after extended dickering President Clinton put his weight behind two specific measures toward that end. First, the Government agreed that whenever a German company was sued on a Holocaust-era claim in an American court, the Government of the United States would submit a statement that "it would be in the foreign policy interests of the United States for the Foundation to be the exclusive forum and remedy for the resolution of all asserted claims against German companies arising from their involvement in the National Socialist era and World War II." Though unwilling to guarantee that its foreign policy interests would "in themselves provide an independent legal basis for dismissal," that being an issue for the courts, the Government agreed to tell courts "that U.S. policy interests favor dismissal on any valid legal ground." On top of that undertaking, the Government promised to use its "best efforts, in a manner it considers appropriate," to get state and local governments to respect the foundation as the exclusive mechanism. . . .

B

While these international efforts were underway, California's Department of Insurance began its own enquiry into the issue of unpaid claims under Nazi-era insurance policies, prompting state legislation designed to force payment by defaulting insurers. In 1998, the state legislature made it an unfair business practice for any insurer operating in the State to "fai[l] to pay any valid claim from Holocaust survivors." Cal. Ins.Code Ann. § 790.15(a) (West Cum.Supp.2003). The legislature placed "an affirmative duty" on the Department of Insurance "to play an independent role in representing the interests of Holocaust survivors," including an obligation to "gather, review, and analyze the archives of insurers ... to provide for research and investigation" into unpaid insurance claims. §§ 12967(a)(1), (2).

State legislative efforts culminated the next year with passage of Assembly Bill No. 600, 1999 Cal. Stats. ch. 827, the first section of which amended the State's Code of Civil Procedure to allow state residents to sue in state court on insurance claims based on acts perpetrated in the Holocaust and extended the governing statute of limitations to December 31, 2010. Cal.Civ.Proc.Code Ann. § 354.5 (West Cum.Supp.2003). The section of the bill codified as HVIRA, at issue here, requires "[a]ny insurer currently doing business in the state" to disclose the details of "life, property, liability, health, annuities, dowry, educational, or casualty insurance policies" issued "to persons in Europe, which were in effect between 1920 and 1945." Cal. Ins.Code Ann. § 13804(a) (West Cum.Supp.2003). The duty is to make disclosure not only about policies the particular insurer sold, but also about those sold by any "related company," ibid., including "any parent, subsidiary, reinsurer, successor in interest, managing general agent, or affiliate company of the insurer," § 13802(b), whether or not the companies were related during the time when the policies subject to disclosure were sold, § 13804(a). Nor is the obligation restricted to policies sold to "Holocaust victims" as defined in the Act, § 13802(a); it covers policies sold to anyone during that time, § 13804(a). The insurer must report the current status of each policy, the city of origin, domicile, or address of each policyholder, and the names of the beneficiaries, § 13804(a), all of which is to be put in a central registry open to the public, § 13803. The mandatory penalty for default is suspension of the company's license to do business in the State, § 13806, and there are misdemeanor criminal sanctions for falsehood in certain required representations about whether and to whom the proceeds of each policy have been distributed, § 13804(b). . . .

After HVIRA was enacted, administrative subpoenas were issued against several subsidiaries of European insurance companies participating in the ICHEIC. Immediately, in November 1999, Deputy Secretary Eizenstat wrote to the insurance commissioner of California that although HVIRA "reflects a genuine commitment to justice for Holocaust victims and their families, it has the unfortunate effect of damaging the one effective means now at hand to process quickly and completely unpaid insurance claims from the Holocaust period, the [ICHEIC]." The Deputy Secretary said that "actions by California, pursuant to this law, have already threatened to damage the cooperative spirit which the [ICHEIC] requires to resolve the important issue for Holocaust survivors," and he also noted that ICHEIC Chairman

Eagleburger had expressed his opposition to "sanctions and other pressures brought by California on companies with whom he is obtaining real cooperation." The same day, Deputy Secretary Eizenstat also wrote to California's Governor making the same points, and stressing that HVIRA would possibly derail the German Foundation Agreement: "Clearly, for this deal to work ... German industry and the German government need to be assured that they will get 'legal peace,' not just from class-action lawsuits, but from the kind of legislation represented by the California Victim Insurance Relief Act." These expressions of the National Government's concern proved to be of no consequence, for the state commissioner announced at an investigatory hearing in December 1999 that he would enforce HVIRA to its fullest, requiring the affected insurers to make the disclosures, leave the State voluntarily, or lose their licenses.

II

After this ultimatum, the petitioners here, several American and European insurance companies and the American Insurance Association (a national trade association), filed suit for injunctive relief against respondent insurance commissioner of California, challenging the constitutionality of HVIRA. . . .

III

The principal argument for preemption made by petitioners and the United States as amicus curiae is that HVIRA interferes with foreign policy of the Executive Branch, as expressed principally in the executive agreements with Germany, Austria, and France. The major premises of the argument, at least, are beyond dispute. There is, of course, no question that at some point an exercise of state power that touches on foreign relations must yield to the National Government's policy, given the "concern for uniformity in this country's dealings with foreign nations" that animated the Constitution's allocation of the foreign relations power to the National Government in the first place. Banco Nacional de Cuba v. Sabbatino, 376 U.S. 398, 427, n. 25, 84 S.Ct. 923, 11 L.Ed.2d 804 (1964); see Crosby v. National Foreign Trade Council, 530 U.S. 363, 381–382, n. 16, 120 S.Ct. 2288, 147 L.Ed.2d 352 (2000) (" '[T]he peace of the WHOLE ought not to be left at the disposal of a PART' " (quoting The Federalist No. 80, pp. 535–536 (J. Cooke ed.1961) (A. Hamilton))); The Federalist No. 44, p. 299 (J. Madison) (emphasizing "the advantage of uniformity in all points which relate to foreign powers"); The Federalist No. 42, p. 279 (J. Madison) ("If we are to be one nation in any respect, it clearly ought to be in respect to other nations"); see also First Nat. City Bank v. Banco Nacional de Cuba, 406 U.S. 759, 769, 92 S.Ct. 1808, 32 L.Ed.2d 466 (1972) (plurality opinion) (act of state doctrine was "fashioned because of fear that adjudication would interfere with the conduct of foreign relations"); Japan Line, Ltd. v. County of Los Angeles, 441 U.S. 434, 449, 99 S.Ct. 1813, 60 L.Ed.2d 336 (1979) (negative Foreign Commerce Clause protects the National Government's ability to speak with "one voice" in regulating commerce with foreign countries (internal quotation marks omitted)).

Nor is there any question generally that there is executive authority to decide what that policy should be. . . .

At a more specific level, our cases have recognized that the President has authority to make "executive agreements" with other countries, requiring no ratification by the Senate or approval by Congress, this power having been exercised since the early years of the Republic. Making executive agreements to settle claims of American nationals against foreign governments is a particularly longstanding practice, the first example being as early as 1799, when the Washington administration settled demands against the Dutch Government by American citizens who lost their cargo when Dutch privateers overtook the schooner Wilmington Packet. . . .

The executive agreements at issue here do differ in one respect from those just mentioned insofar as they address claims associated with formerly belligerent states, but against corporations, not the foreign governments. But the distinction does not matter. Historically, wartime claims against even nominally private entities have become issues in international diplomacy, and three of the postwar settlements dealing with reparations implicating private parties were made by the Executive alone. . . .

Generally, then, valid executive agreements are fit to preempt state law, just as treaties are, and if the agreements here had expressly preempted laws like HVIRA, the issue would be straightforward But petitioners and the United States as amicus curiae both have to acknowledge that the agreements include no preemption clause, and so leave their claim of preemption to rest on asserted interference with the foreign policy those agreements embody. Reliance is placed on our decision in Zschernig v. Miller, 389 U.S. 429, 88 S.Ct. 664, 19 L.Ed.2d 683 (1968). . . .

The Zschernig majority relied on statements in a number of previous cases open to the reading that state action with more than incidental effect on foreign affairs is preempted, even absent any affirmative federal activity in the subject area of the state law, and hence without any showing of conflict. . . .

Justice Harlan, joined substantially by Justice White, disagreed with the Zschernig majority on this point, arguing that its implication of preemption of the entire field of foreign affairs was at odds with some other cases suggesting that in the absence of positive federal action "the States may legislate in areas of their traditional competence even though their statutes may have an incidental effect on foreign relations." Thus, for Justice Harlan it was crucial that the challenge to the Oregon statute presented no evidence of a "specific interest of the Federal Government which might be interfered with" by the law. He would, however, have found preemption in a case of "conflicting federal policy," and on this point the majority and Justices Harlan and White basically agreed: state laws "must give way if they impair the effective exercise of the Nation's foreign policy."

It is a fair question whether respect for the executive foreign relations power requires a categorical choice between the contrasting theories of field and conflict preemption evident in the Zschernig opinions, but the question requires no answer here. For even on Justice Harlan's view, the likelihood that state legislation will produce something more than incidental effect in conflict with express foreign policy of the National Government would require preemption of the state law. And since on his view it is legislation within "areas of . . . traditional competence" that gives a State any claim to prevail, it would be reasonable to consider the strength of the state interest, judged by standards of traditional practice, when deciding how serious a conflict must be shown before declaring the state law preempted. Judged by these standards, we think petitioners and the Government have demonstrated a sufficiently clear conflict to require finding preemption here.

IV

A

To begin with, resolving Holocaust-era insurance claims that may be held by residents of this country is a matter well within the Executive's responsibility for foreign affairs. Since claims remaining in the aftermath of hostilities may be "sources of friction" acting as an "impediment to resumption of friendly relations" between the countries involved, there is a "longstanding practice" of the national Executive to settle them in discharging its responsibility to maintain the Nation's relationships with other countries. The issue of restitution for Nazi crimes has in fact been addressed in Executive Branch diplomacy and formalized in treaties and executive agreements over the last half century, and although resolution of private claims was postponed by the Cold War, securing private interests is an express object of diplomacy today, just as it was addressed in agreements soon after the Second World War. Vindicating victims injured by acts and omissions of enemy corporations in wartime is thus within the traditional subject matter of foreign policy in which national, not state, interests are overriding, and which the National Government has addressed.

The exercise of the federal executive authority means that state law must give way where, as here, there is evidence of clear conflict between the policies adopted by the two. The foregoing account of negotiations toward the three settlement agreements is enough to illustrate that the consistent Presidential foreign policy has been to encourage European governments and companies to volunteer settlement funds in preference to litigation or coercive sanctions. . . .

California has taken a different tack of providing regulatory sanctions to compel disclosure and payment, supplemented by a new cause of action for Holocaust survivors if the other sanctions should fail. . . . Whereas the President's authority to provide for settling claims in winding up international hostilities requires flexibility in wielding "the coercive power of the national economy" as a tool of diplomacy, HVIRA denies this, by making exclusion from a large sector of the American insurance market the automatic sanction for noncompliance with the State's own policies on disclosure. "Quite simply, if the [California] law is enforceable the President has less to offer and less economic and diplomatic leverage as a consequence." The law thus "compromise[s] the very capacity of the President to speak for the Nation with one voice in dealing with other governments" to resolve claims against European companies arising out of World War II.

B

The express federal policy and the clear conflict raised by the state statute are alone enough to require state law to yield. If any doubt about the clarity of the conflict remained, however, it would have to be resolved in the National Government's favor, given the weakness of the State's interest, against the backdrop of traditional state legislative subject matter, in regulating disclosure of European Holocaust-era insurance policies in the manner of HVIRA.

The commissioner would justify HVIRA's ambitious disclosure requirement as protecting "legitimate consumer protection interests" in knowing which insurers have failed to pay insurance claims. But, quite unlike a generally applicable "blue sky" law, HVIRA effectively singles out only policies issued by European companies, in Europe, to European residents, at least 55 years ago. Limiting the public disclosure requirement to these policies raises great doubt that the purpose of the California law is an evaluation of corporate reliability in contemporary insuring in the State.

Indeed, there is no serious doubt that the state interest actually underlying HVIRA is concern for the several thousand Holocaust survivors said to be living in the State. § 13801(d) (legislative finding that roughly 5,600 documented Holocaust survivors reside in California). But this fact does not displace general standards for evaluating a State's claim to apply its forum law to a particular controversy or transaction, under which the State's claim is not a strong one. "Even if a plaintiff evidences his desire for forum law by moving to the forum, we have generally accorded such a move little or no significance." Phillips Petroleum Co. v. Shutts, p. 445, supra; see Allstate Ins. Co. v. Hague, p. 432, supra ("[A] postoccurrence change of residence to the forum State—standing alone—[i]s insufficient to justify application of forum law").

But should the general standard not be displaced, and the State's interest recognized as a powerful one, by virtue of the fact that California seeks to vindicate the claims of Holocaust survivors? The answer lies in recalling that the very same objective dignifies the interest of the National Government in devising its chosen mechanism for voluntary settlements, there being about 100,000 survivors in the country, only a small fraction of them in California. As against the responsibility of the United States of America, the humanity underlying the state statute could not give the State the benefit of any doubt in resolving the conflict with national policy.

C

The basic fact is that California seeks to use an iron fist where the President has consistently chosen kid gloves. We have heard powerful arguments that the iron fist would work better, and it may be that if the matter of compensation were considered in isolation from all other issues involving the European allies, the iron fist would be the preferable policy. But our thoughts on the efficacy of the one approach versus the other are beside the point, since our business is not to judge the wisdom of the National Government's policy; dissatisfaction should be addressed to the President or, perhaps, Congress. . . .

■ JUSTICE GINSBURG, with whom JUSTICES STEVENS, SCALIA and THOMAS Join, dissenting.

Responding to Holocaust victims' and their descendents' long-frustrated efforts to collect unpaid insurance proceeds, California's Holocaust Victim Insurance Relief Act of 1999 (HVIRA), Cal. Ins.Code Ann. § 13800 et seq. (West Cum.Supp.2003), requires insurance companies operating in the State to disclose certain information about insurance policies they or their affiliates wrote in Europe between 1920 and 1945. In recent years, the Executive Branch of the Federal Government has become more visible in this area, undertaking foreign policy initiatives aimed at resolving Holocaust-era insurance claims. Although the federal approach differs from California's, no executive agreement or other formal expression of foreign policy disapproves state disclosure laws like the HVIRA. Absent a clear statement aimed at disclosure requirements by the "one voice" to which courts properly defer in matters of foreign affairs, I would leave intact California's enactment. . . .

II

A

California's disclosure law, the HVIRA, was enacted a year after ICHEIC's formation. Observing that at least 5,600 documented Holocaust survivors reside in California, Cal. Ins.Code Ann. § 13801(d) (West Cum.Supp.2003), the HVIRA declares that "[i]nsurance companies doing business in the State of California have a responsibility to ensure that any involvement they or their related companies may have had with insurance policies of Holocaust victims [is] disclosed to the state," § 13801(e). . . .

B

The Federal Government, after prolonged inaction, has responded to the Holocaust-era insurance issue by diplomatic means. . . .

III

A

The President's primacy in foreign affairs, I agree with the Court, empowers him to conclude executive agreements with other countries. Our cases do not catalog the subject matter meet for executive agreement, but we have repeatedly acknowledged the President's authority to make such agreements to settle international claims. And in settling such claims, we have recognized, an executive agreement may preempt otherwise permissible state laws or litigation. . . .

Despite the absence of express preemption, the Court holds that the HVIRA interferes with foreign policy objectives implicit in the executive agreements. I would not venture down that path.

The Court's analysis draws substantially on Zschernig v. Miller, 389 U.S. 429, 88 S.Ct. 664, 19 L.Ed.2d 683 (1968). . . .

We have not relied on Zschernig since it was decided, and I would not resurrect that decision here. The notion of "dormant foreign affairs preemption" with which Zschernig is associated resonates most audibly when a state action "reflect[s] a state policy critical of foreign governments and involve[s] 'sitting in judgment' on them." L. Henkin, Foreign Affairs and the United States Constitution 164 (2d ed.1996); see Constitutionality of South African Divestment Statutes Enacted by State and Local Governments, 10 Op. Off. Legal Counsel 49, 50 (1986) ("[W]e believe that [Zschernig] represents the Court's reaction to a particular regulatory statute, the operation of which intruded extraordinarily deeply into foreign affairs."). The HVIRA entails no such state action or policy. It takes no position on any contemporary foreign government and requires no assessment of any existing foreign regime. It is directed solely at private insurers doing business in California, and it requires them solely to disclose information in their or their affiliates' possession or control. I would not extend Zschernig into this dissimilar domain. . . .

If it is uncertain whether insurance litigation may continue given the executive agreements on which the Court relies, it should be abundantly clear that those agreements leave disclosure laws like the HVIRA untouched. The contrast with the Litvinov Assignment . . . is marked. That agreement spoke directly to claim assignment in no uncertain terms. . . . Here, the Court invalidates a state disclosure law on grounds of conflict with foreign policy "embod[ied]" in certain executive agreements, although those agreements do not refer to state disclosure laws specifically, or even to information disclosure generally. It therefore is surely an exaggeration to assert that the "HVIRA threatens to frustrate the operation of the particular mechanism the President has chosen" to resolve Holocaust-era claims. If that were so, one might expect to find some reference to laws like the HVIRA in the later-in-time executive agreements. There is none.

To fill the agreements' silences, the Court points to statements by individual members of the Executive Branch. But we have never premised foreign affairs preemption on statements of that order. We should not do so here lest we place the considerable power of foreign affairs preemption in the hands of individual sub-Cabinet members of the Executive Branch. Executive officials of any rank may of course be expected "faithfully [to] represen[t] the President's policy," but no authoritative text accords such officials the power to invalidate state law simply by conveying the Executive's views on matters of federal policy. The displacement of state law by preemption properly requires a considerably more formal and binding federal instrument.

Sustaining the HVIRA would not compromise the President's ability to speak with one voice for the Nation. To the contrary, by declining to invalidate the HVIRA in this case, we would reserve foreign affairs preemption for circumstances where the President, acting under statutory or constitutional authority, has spoken clearly to the issue at hand. "[T]he Framers did not make the judiciary the overseer of our government." Dames & Moore, 453 U.S., at 660, 101 S.Ct. 2972 (quoting Youngstown Sheet & Tube Co. v. Sawyer, 343 U.S. 579, 594, 72 S.Ct. 863, 96 L.Ed.1153 (1952) (Frankfurter, J., concurring)). And judges should not be the expositors of the Nation's foreign policy, which is the role they play by acting when the President himself has not taken a clear stand. As I see it, courts step out of their proper role when they rely on no legislative or even executive text, but only on inference and implication, to preempt state laws on foreign affairs grounds.

In sum, assuming, arguendo, that an executive agreement or similarly formal foreign policy statement targeting disclosure could override the HVIRA, there is no such declaration here. Accordingly, I would leave California's enactment in place. . . .

NOTES

1.   Does *Garamendi* signal a retreat from the broad theory of preemption articulated by *Zschernig*? The majority opinion in *Zschernig* does not rely on any particular expression of the United States foreign policy interests but rather assumes that the federal government occupies the entire field without regard to any particular expression of interest. Justice Ginsburg's dissent rejects this theory and Justice Souter's majority opinion describes it as a "fair question" as to whether that broad theory is viable. Is Justice Harlan's concurrence in the result in *Zschernig* now perhaps more important than the majority opinion?

2.   In Crosby v. National Foreign Trade Council, 530 U.S. 363, 120 S.Ct. 2288 (2000), the Supreme Court invalidated a Massachusetts law that largely prohibited state agencies from purchasing from companies with business relations with Burma. The First Circuit held the law

unconstitutional in part based upon the broad preemption theory of the majority opinion in *Zschernig*. Perhaps reflective of the narrower view articulated by Justice Harlan's concurrence in the result, the Supreme Court affirmed, but on the grounds that the state law was preempted by the Foreign Operations, Export Financing, and Related Programs Appropriations Act, a federal enactment.

Banco Nacional de Cuba v. Sabbatino

Supreme Court of the United States, 1964.
376 U.S. 398, 84 S.Ct. 923, 11 L.Ed.2d 804.

[This was a dispute over who was entitled to the proceeds of the sale of sugar. The sugar had been the property of a Cuban corporation whose stock was owned principally by United States residents. Before the sugar was shipped from a Cuban port, it was expropriated without adequate compensation by the Cuban government. The expropriation was in retaliation for a reduction by the United States of the sugar quota for Cuba. An American commodity broker, contrary to its agreement with an instrumentality of the Cuban government, obtained possession of the sugar without paying for it. The broker received payment for the sugar from its customer and deposited the funds with a court-appointed receiver pending judicial determination as to whether Cuba or the former owners were entitled to the money.

Cuba relied on the "act of state doctrine," contending that the legality of Cuba's actions on its own territory could not be questioned by a United States court. The courts below held for the former owners, deciding that the act of state doctrine did not apply because Cuba's action violated international law. The Supreme Court of the United States granted certiorari and reversed.]

■ JUSTICE HARLAN.... Preliminarily, we discuss the foundations on which we deem the act of state doctrine to rest, and more particularly the question of whether state or federal law governs its application in a federal diversity case.

We do not believe that this doctrine is compelled either by the inherent nature of sovereign authority ... or by some principle of international law.... While historic notions of sovereign authority do bear upon the wisdom of employing the act of state doctrine, they do not dictate its existence....

... The text of the Constitution does not require the act of state doctrine; it does not irrevocably remove from the judiciary the capacity to review the validity of foreign acts of state.

The act of state doctrine does, however, have "constitutional" underpinnings. It arises out of the basic relationship between branches of government in a system of separation of powers. It concerns the competency of dissimilar institutions to make and implement particular kinds of decisions in the area of international relations. The doctrine as formulated in past decisions expresses the strong sense of the Judicial Branch that its engagement in the task of passing on the validity of foreign acts of state may hinder rather than further this country's pursuit of goals both for itself and for the community of nations as a whole in the international sphere. Many commentators disagree with this view. . . . Whatever considerations are thought to predominate, it is plain that the problems involved are uniquely federal in nature. If federal authority, in this instance this Court, orders the field of judicial competence in this area for the federal courts, and the state courts are left free to formulate their own rules, the purposes behind the doctrine would be as effectively undermined as if there had been no federal pronouncement on the subject.

. . . [W]e are constrained to make it clear that an issue concerned with a basic choice regarding the competence and function of the Judiciary and the National Executive in ordering our relationships with other members of the international community must be treated exclusively as an aspect of federal law.[23] It seems fair to assume that the Court did not have rules like the act of state doctrine in mind when it decided Erie R. Co. v. Tompkins. Soon thereafter, Professor Philip C. Jessup, now a judge of the International Court of Justice, recognized the potential dangers were Erie extended to legal problems affecting international relations.[24] He cautioned that rules of international law should not be left to divergent and perhaps parochial state interpretations. His basic rationale is equally applicable to the act of state doctrine.

. . . We conclude that the scope of the act of state doctrine must be determined according to federal law.

If the act of state doctrine is a principle of decision binding on federal and state courts alike but compelled by neither international law nor the Constitution, its continuing vitality depends on its capacity to reflect the proper distribution of functions between the judicial and political branches of the Government on matters bearing upon foreign affairs. It should be apparent that the greater the degree of codification or consensus concerning a particular area of international law, the more appropriate it is for the judiciary to render decisions regarding it, since the courts can then focus on the application of an agreed principle to circumstances of fact rather than on the sensitive task of establishing a principle not inconsistent with the national interest or with international justice. It is also evident that some aspects of international law touch much more sharply on national nerves than do others; the less important the implications of an issue are for our foreign relations, the weaker the

---

[23] At least this is true when the Court limits the scope of judicial inquiry. We need not consider whether a state court might, in certain circumstances, adhere to a more restrictive view concerning the scope of examination of foreign acts than that required by the Court.

[24] The Doctrine of Erie Railroad v. Tompkins Applied to International Law, 33 Am.J.Int'l.L. 740 (1939).

justification for exclusivity in the political branches. The balance of relevant considerations may also be shifted if the government which perpetrated the challenged act of state is no longer in existence as in the Bernstein case [Bernstein v. N.V. Nederlandsche-Amerikaansche Stoomvaart-Maatschappij, 173 F.2d 71 (2d Cir.1949), dealing with Nazi decrees], for the political interest of this country may, as a result, be measurably altered. Therefore, rather than laying down or reaffirming an inflexible and all-encompassing rule in this case, we decide only that the Judicial Branch will not examine the validity of a taking of property within its own territory by a foreign sovereign government, extant and recognized by this country at the time of suit, in the absence of a treaty or other unambiguous agreement regarding controlling legal principles, even if the complaint alleges that the taking violates customary international law. [Justice Harlan also concluded that there was a lack of consensus among nations as to whether expropriation without compensation violated international law.]

. . . [W]hatever way the matter is cut the possibility of conflict between the Judicial and Executive Branches could hardly be avoided.

[JUSTICE WHITE dissented.]

NOTES

1. An important sequel to *Sabbatino* is First National City Bank v. Banco Nacional de Cuba, 406 U.S. 759, 92 S.Ct. 1808 (1972), in which a plurality agreed that Banco, an instrumentality of the Cuban government, could not sue for funds that were due it without submitting to a decision on the merits of a counterclaim. City Bank had made a loan to Banco's predecessor. City Bank sold the collateral when the loan was in default and retained a surplus from this sale. When Banco sued for this surplus, City Bank counterclaimed to offset against Banco's claim, the value of City Bank's Cuban properties that had been expropriated. For an enlightening treatment of the main decision, see Henkin, The Foreign Affairs Power of the Federal Courts: Sabbatino, 64 Colum.L.Rev. 805 (1964).

2. Following the *Sabbatino* decision, Congress enacted the so-called Hickenlooper Amendment, (22 U.S.C. § 2370(e)(2)), which provides that ". . . no court in the United States shall decline on the ground of the federal act of state doctrine to make a determination on the merits giving effect to the principles of international law in a case in which a claim . . . is asserted . . . based upon . . . a confiscation or other taking after January 1, 1959 . . . [unless] the President determines that application of the act of state doctrine is required in that particular case by the foreign policy interests of the United States. . . ."

After remand, the court held that the *Sabbatino* case itself came under the scope of the Hickenlooper Amendment and the complaint was dismissed. Banco Nacional de Cuba v. Farr, 383 F.2d 166 (2d Cir.1967), cert. denied, 390 U.S. 956, 88 S.Ct. 1038 (1968). See Paul, The Act of State Doctrine: Revived but Suspended, 113 U.Pa.L.Rev. 691 (1965).

The Cuban Liberty and Democratic Solidarity (Libertad) Act of 1996 [Helms-Burton Act], P.L. 104–114, 110 Stat. 785, reprinted in Note following 22 U.S.C. § 6021, amended the Cuban Democracy Act of 1992. P.L. 202–484, reprinted in Note following 22 U.S.C. § 6001. The new Act enables any United States National who owns property confiscated by Cuba to sue anyone who "traffics" in the property. "Traffics" includes purchasing. No United States court may decline to entertain such an action on the basis of the act of state doctrine. Id. § 302. If a financial institution such as the International Monetary Fund or the Inter-American Development Bank makes a loan to Cuba over United States opposition, the United States will withhold equal amounts in payments to that institution. Id. § 104. The European Union Foreign Ministers have adopted a regulation that authorizes E.U. companies sued under Helms-Burton to bring "clawback" suits against the European subsidiaries of companies that have used the act. Canada has enacted legislation punishing Canadian companies, including subsidiaries of U.S. companies, that refuse to trade with Cuba in compliance with Helms-Burton. Presidents, acting pursuant to his statutory authority, regularly issued six-month suspensions of civil actions under the law, until President Trump ceased the suspensions on May 2, 2019. Several suits have been filed against foreign defendants profiting from the use of property once owned by U.S. citizens but expropriated by Cuba.

3. A Turkish bank raised the act-of-state doctrine unsuccessfully in trying to avoid a commitment to pay the plaintiff bank in Swiss francs in New York. The payment was due on a note executed in Turkey. The court rejected the defense that a Turkish currency regulation barred payment by the defendant in non-Turkish currency. Weston Banking Corp. v. Turkiye Garanti Bankasi, A.S., 442 N.E.2d 1195 (N.Y.1982).

4. For a helpful discussion of the act-of-state doctrine in the *Sabbatino* context, see Cheatham & Maier, Private International Law and Its Sources, 22 Vand.L.Rev. 27, 88 (1968). Its history in relation to sovereign immunity is summarized:

> "The act-of-state doctrine in American law is closely related to the principle of sovereign immunity. Both stemmed, initially, from conceptions of absolute territorial sovereignty and the relationship between those conceptions and a power-oriented theory of jurisdiction which equated physical power over parties with a right to decide their disputes and lack of such power with a lack of jurisdiction. Thus, the adjudication of disputes concerning either the person or the acts of a foreign sovereign was conceived as the application of physical force against the sovereign personality. But the decision to apply force to a foreign sovereign is essentially political in nature. It is not to be made upon the accident of the presence of the sovereign, or of one claiming legal rights based upon the validity of the sovereign's acts, before a court whose even-handed justice could be enforced only by the exercise of its own sovereign's power. . . ."

See also Williams v. Curtiss-Wright Corp., 694 F.2d 300, 303 (3d Cir.1982): "The Act of State doctrine is a policy of judicial abstention from inquiry into the validity of an act by a foreign state within its own sovereignty. . . ." (Emphasis added). The territorial limitation of the Act-of-State doctrine—"within its own sovereignty"—has been recognized in many decisions. How should the doctrine be applied when the asset cannot be located physically, when it is an intangible? Allied Bank International v. Banco Credito Agricola de Cartago, 757 F.2d 516 (2d Cir.1985), cert. dismissed, 473 U.S. 934 (1985), held the act of state doctrine to be inapplicable with respect to Costa Rican decrees purporting to defer payments on foreign debts because the situs of the debts in issue was determined to be in the United States. The Restatement, Third, Foreign Relations Law of the United States § 443, Reporters' Note 4 (1987), suggests that there should not be a search "for an imaginary situs for property that has no real situs, but [a determination] how the act of the foreign state in the particular circumstances fits within the reasons for the act of state doctrine and for the territorial limitation."

5.   In Sosa v. Alvarez-Machain, 542 U.S. 692, 124 S.Ct. 2739 (2004) the Supreme Court confronted another aspect of the potential applicability of the *Erie* doctrine to theories founded on international law. U.S. law enforcement came to believe that Alvarez-Machain had played a role in the torture and killing of a DEA agent in Mexico. It was arranged that Alvarez-Machain would be kidnapped in Mexico and brought to the U.S. to stand trial. He was eventually acquitted and brought a tort action against the federal government under the Federal Tort Claims Act and against the persons responsible for his kidnapping under the Alien Tort Statute, 28 U.S.C. § 1350. That statute, whose origins date back to the Judiciary Act of 1789, provides: "The district courts shall have original jurisdiction of any civil action by an alien for a tort only, committed in violation of the law of nations or a treaty of the United States." The Court concluded that the statute was not only jurisdictional but also provided "a cause of action for the modest number of international law violations with a potential for personal liability at the time." Id. at 724. These violations in 1789 were "offenses against ambassadors, violations of safe conduct . . . and individual actions arising out of prize captures and piracy." Id. at 720. Nor did Erie prevent federal courts from allowing recovery under the statute for violations of international law that were not recognized when Congress first enacted the statute:

> Erie did not in terms bar any judicial recognition of new substantive rules, no matter what the circumstances, and post-Erie understanding has identified limited enclaves in which federal courts may derive some substantive law in a common law way. For two centuries we have affirmed that the domestic law of the United States recognizes the law of nations.

Id. at 729.

Federal courts must, however, exercise caution in recognizing new violations of international law:

> Whatever the ultimate criteria for accepting a cause of action subject to jurisdiction under § 1350, we are persuaded that federal

courts should not recognize private claims under federal common law for violations of any international law norm with less definite content and acceptance among civilized nations than the historical paradigms familiar when § 1350 was enacted.

Id. at 732.

The Court concluded that Alvarez-Machain's claim did not fall within the parameters of the statute as the wrong he asserts against his kidnappers—"a single illegal detention of less than a day"—did not qualify as a violation of international law under the Court's standard.

B. TREATIES

Foreign countries have long used conventions (treaties) to bring about uniform rules of substantive law or, at least, of choice of law. In addition, a number of treaties deal with procedures for handling international cases. With notable exceptions such as the Montreal Convention, which contains rules and limitations with respect to a carrier's liability in international air traffic, the United States has been slow to participate. It does not belong to the Geneva Convention on bills of exchange and checks, and it does not have any treaties with other countries on the recognition of judgments, except to the extent that Friendship, Commerce and Navigation Treaties are occasionally construed by U.S. courts to require recognition of foreign country judgments. See, e.g., Choi v. Kim, 50 F.3d 244, 248 (3d Cir.1995) (stating that "[t]he Treaty of Friendship, Commerce and Navigation Between the United States of America and The Republic of Korea, 8 U.S.T. 2217, elevates a Korean judgment to the status of a sister state judgment").

In 1964, however, the United States joined the Hague Conference on Private International Law which sponsors conventions on conflicts and procedural issues and the Rome Institute on the Unification of Private Law (i.e., dealing with substantive law). One substantive convention—drafted under United Nations auspices—was adopted by the United States and became law in 1988: the Convention on Contracts for the International Sale of Goods. 15 U.S.C. App.

The United States has ratified a number of Hague Conventions, including the Convention Abolishing the Requirement of Legalization for Foreign Public Documents, the Convention on the Service of Documents Abroad, the Convention on the Taking of Evidence Abroad, and the Convention on the Civil Aspects of International Child Abduction. The last of these, in force since 1988, seeks to counteract parental kidnapping in the international arena in a fashion similar to the domestic Uniform Child Custody Jurisdiction Act and the federal Parental Kidnapping Prevention Act. For a decision involving the Hague Service Convention see Volkswagenwerk Aktiengesellschaft v. Schlunk, p. 200, supra.

Société Nationale Industrielle Aerospatiale v. United States District Court for the Southern District of Iowa, 482 U.S. 522, 104 S.Ct. 2542

(1987), involved the Convention on the Taking of Evidence Abroad. The plaintiffs had brought a personal injury action against a French airplane manufacturer in federal court in Iowa. They served a number of discovery requests under the Federal Rules of Civil Procedure. The defendant sought a protective order on the twin grounds that (1) a French "blocking statute" forbids the production of documents located in France in response to foreign judicial orders or requests and that (2) the Hague Convention represents the exclusive means for obtaining evidence located abroad. The District Court denied the motion and the Court of Appeals denied a petition for mandamus.

Upon review of the drafting history of the Convention, the Supreme Court concluded, contrary to some lower court decisions, that the Convention does apply to litigants and third parties who are subject to the U.S. court's jurisdiction. However, its procedures are not exclusive and do not displace American procedural law. Instead, it provides an optional, parallel means for obtaining evidence located abroad. Nor does comity, the respect for other countries' judicial sovereignty, or even the existence of a blocking statute require a rule of first resort to Convention procedures. "[T]he concept of international comity requires in this context a more particularized analysis than petitioners' proposed general rule would generate.... [There must be] prior scrutiny in each case of the particular facts, sovereign interests, and likelihood that resort to . . . [the Convention] procedures will prove effective." 482 U.S. at 543–44. "The French 'blocking statute' . . . does not alter our conclusion. It is well-settled that such statutes do not deprive an American court of the power to order a party subject to its jurisdiction to produce evidence even though the act of production may violate that statute. . . . Extraterritorial assertions of jurisdiction are not one-sided. While the District Court's discovery orders arguably have some impact in France, the French blocking statute asserts similar authority over acts to take place in this country. The lesson of comity is that neither the discovery order nor the blocking statute can have the same omnipresent effect that it would have in a world of only one sovereign. The blocking statute thus is relevant to the court's particularized comity analysis only to the extent that its terms and its enforcement identify the nature of the sovereign interests in nondisclosure. . . ." 482 U.S. at 544 n. 29. The majority concluded by emphasizing the importance of foreign interests and by admonishing trial courts to "exercise special vigilance to protect foreign litigants from the danger that unnecessary, or unduly burdensome, discovery may place them in a disadvantageous position." 482 U.S. at 546.

Justice Blackmun, joined by Justices Brennan, Marshall, and O'Connor, filed a partial dissent. "When there is a conflict, a court . . . should perform a tripartite analysis that considers the foreign interests, the interests of the United States, and the mutual interests of all nations in a smoothly functioning international legal regime." 482 U.S. at 555. This view of comity, of accommodating conflicting interests for the smooth functioning of the international system, led him to favor the adoption of a rule requiring first resort to Convention procedures unless there are "strong indications that no evidence would be forthcoming." 482 U.S. at 566–67. His view was adopted in Hudson v. Hermann Pfauter GmbH & Co., 117 F.R.D. 33 (N.D.N.Y.1987): service of interrogatories in accordance with the Convention ordered, despite plaintiff's objections on the grounds of cost, delay, and unfamiliar procedures. A long line of subsequent cases, however, places the burden of proof on the proponent of Convention procedures. See, e.g., Doster v. Carl Schenk A.G., 141 F.R.D. 50, 51 (M.D.N.C.1991).

NOTES

1. Increasingly, video and audio conferencing take the place of traditional ways of taking evidence in international litigation. The Evidence Convention of course does not address these developments. It is has therefore been suggested that, "if the . . . Convention is not amended by Protocol to produce . . . internationally uniform result[s], it will slowly but surely become a dead letter, at least as so far as the evidence of witnesses is concerned. There will be an international renaissance of the *Aerospatiale* attitude, and the Convention procedures will simply be ignored in favor of the cheaper, speedier and far more effective alternative provided by the new technology." Martin Davies, Bypassing the Hague Evidence Convention: Private International Law Implications of the Use of Video and Audio Conferencing Technology in Transnational Litigation, 55 Am.J.Comp.L. 205, 237 (2007).

2. The Hague Convention on the Law Applicable to Trusts and on Their Recognition, the "Washington" Convention Providing a Uniform Law on the Form of an International Will, and the Inter-American Convention on International Commercial Arbitration have been submitted for congressional action. In 1989, the Hague Conference proposed a new convention on the law applicable to decedents' estates.

3. The area of American conflicts law controlled by treaties is discussed generally in Hay, Borchers, Symeonides & Whytock, Conflict of Laws § 3.56 (6th ed.2018). See also Gaillard & Trautman, Trusts in Non-Trust Countries: Conflict of Laws and the Hague Convention on Trusts, 35 Am.J.Comp.L. 307 (1987).

4. Treaties can displace ordinary conflicts principles even if the treaty does not itself provide a remedy. In El Al Israel Airlines, Ltd. v. Tseng, 525 U.S. 155, 119 S.Ct. 662, 142 L.Ed.2d 576 (1999) the plaintiff was subjected to an intrusive search before boarding the defendant airline's flight. She claimed psychological but no physical injuries as a result. The Warsaw Convention, to which the United States was a signatory, provides in Article 17 that air carriers "shall be liable for damage sustained in the event of a death or wounding of a passenger or any other bodily injury suffered by a passenger, if the accident which caused the damage so sustained took place on board the aircraft or in the course of any of the operations of embarking or disembarking." 49 Stat. 3018. All the parties agreed that the plaintiff had not suffered an injury as a result of an accident within the meaning of Article

17. The plaintiff, however, argued that the failure of the Warsaw Convention to provide her with a tort remedy allowed her to proceed against the airline on a theory of false imprisonment and assault under New York law. The Supreme Court disagreed, however, concluding that the Convention provides the exclusive remedy for alleged torts between the times of embarking and disembarking. The Court noted that this result would also follow under Montreal Protocol No. 4, which was ratified by the United States Senate on September 28, 1998 (after Ms. Tseng's incident), and which amends Article 24 of the Convention to make clear that it is preemptive in effect. Article 29 of the Montreal Convention, which has superseded the Warsaw Convention, also makes clear that the Convention is preemptive in effect. In 2003 the U.S. ratified the Montreal Convention supplying the 30th ratification necessary to have it enter into effect. The Supreme Court also expressed doubt as to the parties' stipulation that an excessive search was not an "accident" within the meaning of the Convention. The Court noted, however, that this matter was inconsequential in the case before it, as the plaintiff could not recover under the Convention for the purely psychological injuries (i.e., injuries without any physical manifestation) that she claimed. This may change under the Montreal Convention. The travaux preparatories indicate that, in light of the withdrawal of a proposal to specifically include compensation for mental injury, the drafters intend to leave the definition of "bodily injury" to each signatory nation.

C. INTERNATIONAL CONFLICTS CASES IN THE ABSENCE OF FEDERAL LIMITATIONS OR PREEMPTION

In the absence of federal limitations or inconsistent federal law, conflicts law is state law, in international cases as well as in interstate cases. Should state conflicts rules affecting international cases be "segregated" from those applicable to sister-state situations? Professor Cheatham doubted the desirability of making such a distinction. He pointed out that the question of which foreign nation is involved and which underlying policies are in issue may be more significant than the simple issue of whether the case is international rather than interstate. Consider three parallel San Francisco cases on judgments or contracts, one with Seattle, another with Vancouver, and a third with Beijing. Surely, it would be unusual for the California court to treat the Vancouver case differently from the Seattle case. Almost certainly, it would find the Vancouver case closer to the Seattle case than to the other international case, the Beijing case. Cheatham, Book Review, 45 A.B.A.J. 1190 (1959).

There is no ipso facto warrant for treating a case differently merely because it is an international instead of an interstate one, or merely because it involves an alien instead of a citizen. The purpose of conflict of laws is to aid in making the international and the interstate systems work well when they affect multistate legal affairs of private persons. Principles must be developed to advance that fundamental purpose. Whenever there is a difference in the treatment of international and interstate cases, it should be justified by differences in the circumstances that call for differences in treatment.

An example is the Uniform Foreign Money-Judgments Recognition Act, in force the majority of states, the District of Columbia, and the Virgin Islands, which, subject to enumerated exceptions, provides for the recognition and enforcement "in the same manner as the judgment of a sister state which is entitled to full faith and credit" of foreign-country judgments which grant or deny the recovery of a sum of money. One of the exceptions, not available for sister-state judgments, is that "the cause of action on which the judgment is based is repugnant to the public policy of this state." Lack of jurisdiction of the F-1 court is a defense, as it would be in the interstate setting. The circumstance that the judgment was rendered in a foreign country rather than in a sister state is reflected in the condition that the judgment must have been rendered in a legal system providing impartial tribunals "or procedures compatible with the requirements of due process. . . ." The versions of the Uniform Act in force in some states require in addition that the foreign country accord reciprocity to American judgments. What policy considerations support or speak against such a requirement? In 2005 the National Conference of Commissioners on Uniform State Laws approved a revision of the Act: the Uniform Foreign-Country Money Judgments Recognition Act. It has been enacted in California, Idaho, Michigan and Nevada and introduced in other states.

NOTES

1.   With respect to foreign-country judgments, the traditional view was that the successful plaintiff's judgment did not merge the underlying claim, thus leaving the plaintiff free to seek either recognition of the judgment or to relitigate the original claim in the United States. See Restatement, Second, Conflict of Laws § 95 (1988 Revision). This view reflected the fact that common law notions of claim and issue preclusion (res judicata and collateral estoppel) are not part of many foreign legal systems, especially civil law systems. See Schlesinger, Baade, Damaska, & Herzog, Comparative Law 454 (5th ed.1988). German law, for instance, attaches res judicata effect only to the claim between the same parties and defines "claim" to include both the facts giving rise to the claim and the remedy sought. If there are different facts or if the plaintiff seeks another remedy, even an additional recovery upon the same facts, a further action may not be precluded. Accordingly, collateral estoppel is unknown in the German system.

Should the fact that notions of res judicata are not the same—for instance, that the plaintiff may be entitled to additional relief under the foreign law—mean that the judgment should not receive the same recognition as a judgment rendered by a sister state? The modern answer is reflected in the Uniform Foreign Money-Judgments Recognition Act. See Hay, Borchers, Symeonides & Whytock, Conflict of Laws § 24.3 (6th ed.2018) ("non-merger rule . . . makes little sense today"). See also Restatement, Second, Conflict of Laws § 98 (1971), which states that valid foreign-country judgments will be recognized "after a fair trial in a contested proceeding . . . so far as the immediate parties and the underlying cause of action are concerned." Even foreign default judgments "will usually be recognized provided that the foreign court had jurisdiction" and the defendant was given notice and opportunity to be heard. Id. comment d. Assume that an American plaintiff seeks and obtains a recovery upon part of her claim in Germany, as permitted by German law. Should German notions of res judicata govern the question of whether the plaintiff may subsequently seek an additional recovery in the United States?

2. Two issues routinely arise when a United States debtor owes a debt payable in foreign currency: (1) Can a United States court render a judgment in foreign currency? (2) If the court orders the foreign debt paid in United States currency, what is the date for converting the foreign currency to dollars?

When enforcement of the judgment is not sought or granted in the foreign currency, the rule with respect to the time for conversion, as stated in Restatement, Second, Conflict of Laws (1971) § 144, comment g: conversion into dollars is of the date of the award. This rule may disadvantage a judgment creditor if, since the award, the dollar has depreciated relative to the foreign currency. As a result, there are substantial variations in the case law. See Competex v. Labow, 783 F.2d 333 (2d Cir.1986). The Uniform Foreign Money-Claims Act, which applies in about half the states, the District of Columbia, and the Virgin Islands, permits the parties to stipulate the currency which is to be used to satisfy claims arising out of their transaction. In the absence of a stipulation, foreign money claims as well as foreign judgments expressed in foreign money are to be stated in the foreign currency, but the judgment debtor may effect payment in dollars at the conversion rate in effect at the time of payment. "The principle of the Act is to restore the aggrieved party to the economic position it would have been in had the wrong not occurred." Id., Prefatory Note. Will the plaintiff really have been restored by receiving today's equivalent of a currency, which may depreciated severely during the course of litigation? Does not the successful plaintiff in a domestic action face the same problem? Is there a difference between domestic plaintiffs and foreign judgment creditors that justifies greater protection of the foreign creditors? Restatement (Third) Foreign Relations Law of the United States § 823, comment c, provides that a court should convert the foreign currency to United States dollars as of the breach day if, compared with the foreign currency in which the debt is owed, the dollar has since appreciated, and should choose judgment-day conversion if the dollar has depreciated.

For the view that such a rule "introduces into a purely procedural rule an element of substantive justice" and that compensation for delay and ensuing loss due to currency fluctuations should therefore be left to the law applicable to the claim or judgment, see F.A. Mann, The Legal Aspect of Money 351 (5th ed.1992); Hay, Fremdwährungsanprüche und-urteile nach dem US-amerikanischen Uniform Act, [1995] Recht der Internationalen Wirtschaft 113, 115 n.35, 118 n.66.

International conflicts cases once again raise the question of the extent to which one state may infringe upon the interests of another, even if the issue has been litigated by the parties. Recall Justice Stone's dissent in Yarborough v. Yarborough, p. 345, supra: that "There is often an inescapable conflict of interest of the two states, and there comes a point beyond which the imposition of the will of one state beyond its own borders involves a forbidden infringement of some legitimate domestic interest of the other." Justice Stone's dissent focused on state interest, not due process to the parties. His views derived from full faith and credit considerations. They were echoed in the position of the New York Times in opposing the exercise of jurisdiction by Alabama in a defamation action against it: "The need for such restraint is emphasized in our system by the full faith and credit clause. . . . If Alabama stood alone it would be impotent . . . to render any judgment that would be of practical importance [but the Full Faith and Credit Clause will give it force throughout the country]. Thus jurisdictional delineations must be based on grounds that command general assent throughout the Union; otherwise full faith and credit will become a burden that the system cannot bear." Petitioner's Brief, at 86, in New York Times Co. v. Sullivan, 376 U.S. 254, 84 S.Ct. 710 (1964). The Supreme Court held for the petitioner but did not address this issue. To what extent do the full faith and credit cases respond to Justice Stone and the petitioner in *New York Times*?

The Full Faith and Credit clause, does not apply, of course, to international cases. Instead, we use the act of state doctrine, invoke notions of comity, and, as the introductory comments stated, treat international cases like domestic ones unless the facts warrant differently. Is "infringement" upon policies of another state such a distinguishing circumstance?

The question becomes whether a federal statute, silent on the question, should be applied "extraterritorially." But what does "extraterritorial" mean? Does it mean that the liability-creating conduct occurred outside the U.S.? Does it refer to the citizenship of the litigants? Does it refer to where the effects of the defendant's conduct will be felt? The Court has not been clear or consistent on which of these characteristics defines "extraterritorial" application of law. Patrick J. Borchers, Kiobel's "Touch and Concern" Test in the Eleventh Circuit (and Elsewhere) and a New Paradigm for the Extraterritorial Application of U.S. Law, 50 Cumb.L.Rev. 259 (2020).

Whatever the definition of "extraterritorial," the question of whether U.S. law governs is one of statutory interpretation. But the Court has not been consistent in the methodology of interpreting statutes to determine their extraterritorial application: "With almost haphazard nonchalance, the Court has applied several fundamentally different rules of construction in international cases." G. Born & P. Rutledge, International Civil Litigation in United States Courts 658 (4th ed.2006).

Traditional presumption. In American Banana Co. v. U.S., 213 U.S. 347, 29 S.Ct. 511, 53 L.Ed. 826 (1909), the Court, in an opinion by Justice Holmes, embraced a strong presumption that congressional acts do not apply extraterritorially. In refusing to apply federal antitrust law (the Sherman Act) to an American company's conduct in Costa Rica, the Court said: "The general and almost universal rule is that the character of an act as lawful or unlawful must be determined wholly by the law of the country where the act is done." 213 U.S. at 356. Two points are noteworthy: (1) the holding reflected then-prevailing conflicts doctrine, with its focus on *lex loci*, and (2) the Court expressed concern with comity, lest the application of American law to activities in Costa Rica interfere with that country's authority.

Conduct and effects. In the mid-twentieth century, some lower federal courts began to embrace a test that looked to where the liability-producing conduct took place and where the effects of that conduct were felt. Finding that the traditional presumption was not absolute, courts sometimes upheld the application of U.S. law to foreign conduct, based upon that conduct's impact in the U.S. For example, in U.S. v. Aluminum Co. of America (Alcoa), 148 F.2d 416, 284 (2d Cir.1945), the Second Circuit held that foreign conduct was subject to Sherman Act sanction when (a) it was intended to have an impact in the U.S., and (b) did have an impact in the U.S.

Reassertion of the traditional presumption. In 1991, the Court reinvigorated the traditional approach in EEOC v. Arabian American Oil Co. (Aramco), 499 U.S. 244, 111 S.Ct. 1227, 113 L.Ed.2d 274 (1991). There, the Court held that Title VII of the Civil Rights Act of 1964 did not reach allegedly discriminatory employment practices in Saudi Arabia, even though the plaintiff and defendant were citizens of the U.S. The opinion was reminiscent of *American Banana*. The Court held that unless Congress clearly expresses its "affirmative intention" to the contrary, it would presume that American law "is primarily concerned with domestic conditions." 499 U.S. at 248. Again, the presumption was rooted to a degree in avoiding ":unintended clashes between our laws and those of other nations, which could result in international discord." Id.

Conduct and effects redux. In Hartford Fire Insurance Co. v. California, 509 U.S. 764, 113 S.Ct. 2891, 125 L.Ed.2d 612 (1993), the Court, five to four, held that the § 1 of the Sherman Act did govern to foreign conduct by foreign defendants. Surprisingly, the Court did not address the territorial presumption; it based its decision on the fact that the conduct was intended to cause—and did cause—anticompetitive effects in the U.S. This conduct-and-effects approach is reminiscent of that adopted by lower courts in the mid-twentieth century.

In *Hartford Fire*, the Court rejected the defendants' comity argument: though British law permitted the defendants to do what they did, that law did not *command* them to do so; thus, said the majority, there was no "true conflict" between the American and the foreign law.

Recent doctrine.

MORRISON V. NATIONAL AUSTRALIA BANK, 561 U.S. 247, 130 S.Ct. 2869, 177 L.Ed.2d 535 (2010). This was a securities fraud case brought by Australian plaintiffs against an Australian bank and some incidental American defendants. The plaintiffs, who purchased stock in the bank on foreign stock exchanges, alleged that the defendants had violated § 10(b) of the Securities and Exchange Act of 1934 by engaging in fraudulent conduct that resulted in overvaluation of the stock. The Second Circuit held that § 10(b) did not apply because the conduct had had no appreciable effect in the U.S. The Court affirmed, but rejected the Second Circuit approach. Rather than assess conduct and effect, the Court returned to the presumption against extraterritorial application of federal law:

> It is a "longstanding principle of American law 'that legislation of Congress, unless a contrary intent appears, is meant to apply only within the territorial jurisdiction of the United States.'" EEOC v. Arabian American Oil Co., 499 U.S. 244, 248, 111 S. Ct. 1227, 113 L. Ed.2d 274 (1991) (Aramco) . . . This principle represents a canon of construction, or a presumption about a statute's meaning, rather than a limit upon Congress's power to legislate. . . . It rests on the perception that Congress ordinarily legislates with respect to domestic, not foreign matters. . . . Thus, "unless there is the affirmative intention of the Congress clearly expressed" to give a statute extraterritorial effect, "we must presume it is primarily concerned with domestic conditions." Aramco, supra, at 248, 111 S. Ct. 1227, 113 L. Ed.2d 274 (internal quotation marks omitted). The canon or presumption applies regardless of whether there is a risk of conflict between the American statute and a foreign law. . . . When a statute gives no clear indication of an extraterritorial application, it has none.
>
> [The Court rejected the Second Circuit approach as "judicial-speculation-made-law—divining what Congress would have wanted if it had thought of the situation before the court." The majority opinion continued:] This analysis demonstrate[s] the wisdom of the presumption against extraterritoriality. Rather than guess anew in each case, we apply the presumption in all cases, preserving a stable background against which Congress can legislate with predictable effects.
>
> [T]here is no affirmative indication in the Exchange Act that § 10(b) applies extraterritorially, and we therefore conclude that it does not. . . .

The Court then discussed the fact that the plaintiffs' underlying claims involved some American contacts. One reason the bank's stock was overvalued, the plaintiffs alleged, was that the bank acquired a Florida company, which it listed as an asset at inflated value. The complaint alleged that the Florida company's executives engaged in deceptive conduct in that state, and that defendants made misleading statements there. The majority opinion addressed these American contacts:

> ...[I]t is a rare case of prohibited extraterritorial application that lacks all contact with the territory of the United States. But the presumption against extraterritorial application would be a craven watchdog indeed if it retreated to its kennel whenever some domestic activity is involved in the case.... [O]ur cases are to the contrary. In Aramco, for example, the Title VII plaintiff had been hired in Houston, and was an American citizen. The Court concluded, however, that neither that territorial event nor that relationship was the "focus" of congressional concern, but rather domestic employment.
>
> Applying the same mode of analysis here, we think that the focus of the Exchange Act is not upon the place where the deception originated, but upon purchases and sales of securities in the United States. Section 10(b) does not punish deceptive conduct, but only deceptive conduct "in connection with the purchase or sale of any security registered on a national securities exchange or any security not so registered." 15 U.S.C. § 78j(b). Those purchase-and-sale transactions are the objects of the statute's solicitude. It is those transactions that the statute seeks to "regulate" ...; it is parties or prospective parties to those transactions that the statute seeks to "protec[t]," ... and it is in our view only transactions in securities listed on domestic exchanges, and domestic transactions in other securities, to which § 10(b) applies.
>
> ... The primacy of the domestic exchange is suggested by the very prologue of the Exchange Act, which sets forth as its object "[t]o provide for the regulation of securities exchanges ... operating in interstate and foreign commerce and through the mails, to prevent inequitable and unfair practices on such exchanges ...." 48 Stat. 881. We know of no one who thought that the Act was intended to "regulat[e]" foreign securities exchanges—or indeed who even believed that under established principles of international law Congress had the power to do so. The Act's registration requirements apply only to securities listed on national securities exchanges. 15 U.S.C. § 78l(a).

NOTES

1. Consider the Court's discussion of the need for a "watchdog." What is the dog guarding against?

2. The watchdog function, according to the Court, is served by assessing the "focus" of the legislation. At what point in the analysis does a court undertake the "focus" assessment?

3.   The majority found that the "focus" of § 10(b) was fraudulent behavior in connection with trading *on U.S. securities markets*. Because the trades in the case had taken place on foreign stock exchanges, the statute did not apply. Should the physical locus of the exchange matter, since the exchange has no physical trading floor, but is entirely computer based?

4.   Does the "focus" assessment in *Morrison* differ in content from the conduct-and-effects test of *Hartford Fire*, p. 802, supra?

5.   Section 402 of the Third Restatement of Foreign Relations provides that nation has "jurisdiction to prescribe" (i.e., to apply its own law) with respect to:

> (1)(a)   conduct that, wholly or in substantial part, takes place within its territory;
>
> (b)   the status of persons, or interests in things, present within its territory;
>
> (c)   conduct outside its territory that has or is intended to have substantial effect within its territory.

> Section 403, however, provides that "a state may not exercise jurisdiction to prescribe law with respect to a person or activity having connections with another state when the exercise of such jurisdiction is unreasonable."

> How is this approach different from that adopted in *Morrison*? Which approach would result in more predictable outcomes?

6.   Shortly after *Morrison* was decided, Congress restored the conduct and effects test for actions brought under § 10(b) by the SEC or the United States (meaning criminal prosecutions) for violations of the Securities and Exchange Act. *Morrison* still applies, however, to private rights of action under § 10.

KIOBEL V. ROYAL DUTCH PETROLEUM CO., 569 U.S. 108,133 S.Ct. 1659, 185 L.Ed.2d 671 (2013). The Court applied the presumption against extraterritorial application of federal statutes to a claim asserted under the Alien Tort Statute (ATS). The claim, by Nigerian nationals residing in the U.S., asserted that Dutch, British, and Nigerian corporations had aided and abetted the Nigerian government in committing violations of the law of nations in Nigeria. Because "all the relevant conduct took place outside the United States," 133 S.Ct. at 1669, the case did not rebut the presumption against extraterritorial application. The Court recognized, however, that the presumption can be rebutted by claims that "touch and concern the territory of the United States . . . with sufficient force." Id.

NOTES

1.   The Court's "touch and concern" statement appeared without elaboration, almost as an afterthought, in the penultimate sentence of the *Kiobel* majority opinion. Is the statement consistent with a conduct-and-effects analysis? If so, when does it apply?

2. Not surprisingly, lower courts have had difficulty dealing with the "touch and concern" concept. The Fourth Circuit held that the presumption against extraterritoriality was rebutted in Al Shimari v. CACI Premier Technology, Inc., 758 F.3d 516, 525 (4th Cir.2014). In that case, former prisoners of the Abu Ghraib prison in Iraq sued a military contractor, which operated the prison, alleging torture, which is a specific and universal obligatory norm for which suit will lie under the ATS. The Fourth Circuit held that extraterritorial application of the statute was justified because the defendant was a United States corporation, its employees were American citizens, the contract engaging the corporation was entered in the United States by the Department of Interior, and managers of the corporation alleged that the government approved its actions. The court found that Congress intended to provide aliens with access to American courts to hold American citizens accountable for torture committed in foreign countries. 758 F.3d at 526–31. See also Mwani v. Laden, 947 F.Supp.2d 1, 3–6 (D.D.C.2013) (terrorist bombing of American embassy in Kenya "touched and concerned" the United States to such a degree as to displace the presumption against extraterritorial application of the ATS). See generally Hay, Borchers, Symeonides & Whytock, Conflict of Laws § 3.76 (6th ed.2018)(discussing cases applying *Kiobel*).

RJR Nabisco, Inc. v. European Community

Supreme Court of the United States, 2016.
579 U.S. ___, 136 S.Ct. 2090, 195 L.Ed.2d 476.

■ JUSTICE ALITO delivered the opinion of the Court.

The Racketeer Influenced and Corrupt Organizations Act (RICO), 18 U.S.C. §§ 1961–1968, created four new criminal offenses involving the activities of organized criminal groups in relation to an enterprise.§§ 1962(a)–(d). RICO also created a new civil cause of action for "[a]ny person injured in his business or property by reason of a violation" of those prohibitions. § 1964(c). We are asked to decide whether RICO applies extraterritorially—that is, to events occurring and injuries suffered outside the United States.

I

A

RICO is founded on the concept of racketeering activity. The statute defines "racketeering activity" to encompass dozens of state and federal offenses, known in RICO parlance as predicates. These predicates include any act "indictable" under specified federal statutes, §§ 1961(1)(B)–(C), (E)–(G), as well as certain crimes "chargeable" under state law, § 1961(1)(A), and any offense involving bankruptcy or securities fraud or drug-related activity that is "punishable" under federal law, § 1961(1)(D). A predicate offense implicates RICO when it is part of a "pattern of racketeering activity"—a series of related predicates that together demonstrate the existence or threat of continued criminal activity. *H.J. Inc. v. Northwestern Bell Telephone Co.*, 492 U.S. 229, 239

(1989); see § 1961(5) (specifying that a "pattern of racketeering activity" requires at least two predicates committed within 10 years of each other).

RICO's § 1962 sets forth four specific prohibitions aimed at different ways in which a pattern of racketeering activity may be used to infiltrate, control, or operate "a[n] enterprise which is engaged in, or the activities of which affect, interstate or foreign commerce." These prohibitions can be summarized as follows. Section 1962(a) makes it unlawful to invest income derived from a pattern of racketeering activity in an enterprise. Section 1962(b) makes it unlawful to acquire or maintain an interest in an enterprise through a pattern of racketeering activity. Section 1962(c) makes it unlawful for a person employed by or associated with an enterprise to conduct the enterprise's affairs through a pattern of racketeering activity. Finally, § 1962(d) makes it unlawful to conspire to violate any of the other three prohibitions.

Violations of § 1962 are subject to criminal penalties, § 1963(a), and civil proceedings to enforce those prohibitions may be brought by the Attorney General, §§ 1964(a)–(b). Separately, RICO creates a private civil cause of action that allows "[a]ny person injured in his business or property by reason of a violation of section 1962" to sue in federal district court and recover treble damages, costs, and attorney's fees. § 1964(c).

B

This case arises from allegations that petitioners—RJR Nabisco and numerous related entities (collectively RJR)—participated in a global money-laundering scheme in association with various organized crime groups. Respondents—the European Community and 26 of its member states—first sued RJR in the Eastern District of New York in 2000, alleging that RJR had violated RICO. Over the past 16 years, the resulting litigation (spread over at least three separate actions, with this case the lone survivor) has seen multiple complaints and multiple trips up and down the federal court system. . . . In the interest of brevity, we confine our discussion to the operative complaint and its journey to this Court.

Greatly simplified, the complaint alleges a scheme in which Colombian and Russian drug traffickers smuggled narcotics into Europe and sold the drugs for euros that—through a series of transactions involving black-market money brokers, cigarette importers, and wholesalers—were used to pay for large shipments of RJR cigarettes into Europe. In other variations of this scheme, RJR allegedly dealt directly with drug traffickers and money launderers in South America and sold cigarettes to Iraq in violation of international sanctions. RJR is also said to have acquired Brown & Williamson Tobacco Corporation for the purpose of expanding these illegal activities.

The complaint alleges that RJR engaged in a pattern of racketeering activity consisting of numerous acts of money laundering, material support to foreign terrorist organizations, mail fraud, wire fraud, and violations of the Travel Act. RJR, in concert with the other participants in the scheme, allegedly formed an association in fact that was engaged in interstate and foreign commerce, and therefore constituted a RICO enterprise that the complaint dubs the "RJR Money-Laundering Enterprise." See § 1961(4) (defining an enterprise to include "any union or group of individuals associated in fact although not a legal entity").

Putting these pieces together, the complaint alleges that RJR violated each of RICO's prohibitions. RJR allegedly used income derived from the pattern of racketeering to invest in, acquire an interest in, and operate the RJR Money-Laundering Enterprise in violation of § 1962(a); acquired and maintained control of the enterprise through the pattern of racketeering in violation of § 1962(b); operated the enterprise through the pattern of racketeering in violation of § 1962(c); and conspired with other participants in the scheme in violation of § 1962(d). These violations allegedly harmed respondents in various ways, including through competitive harm to their state-owned cigarette businesses, lost tax revenue from black-market cigarette sales, harm to European financial institutions, currency instability, and increased law enforcement costs.

RJR moved to dismiss the complaint, arguing that RICO does not apply to racketeering activity occurring outside U.S. territory or to foreign enterprises. The District Court agreed and dismissed the RICO claims as impermissibly extraterritorial. The Second Circuit reinstated the RICO claims. It concluded that, "with respect to a number of offenses that constitute predicates for RICO liability and are alleged in this case, Congress has clearly manifested an intent that they apply extraterritorially." 764 F.3d 129, 133 (2014). "By incorporating these statutes into RICO as predicate racketeering acts," the court reasoned, "Congress has clearly communicated its intention that RICO apply to extraterritorial conduct to the extent that extraterritorial violations of these statutes serve as the basis for RICO liability." Id., at 137. Turning to the predicates alleged in the complaint, the Second Circuit found that they passed muster. The court concluded that the money laundering and material support of terrorism statutes expressly apply extraterritorially in the circumstances alleged in the complaint. Id., at 139–140. The court held that the mail fraud, wire fraud, and Travel Act statutes do *not* apply extraterritorially. Id., at 141. But it concluded that the complaint states *domestic* violations of those predicates because it "allege[s] conduct in the United States that satisfies every essential element" of those offenses. Id., at 142.

RJR sought rehearing, arguing (among other things) that RICO's civil cause of action requires a plaintiff to allege a domestic *injury,* even if a domestic pattern of racketeering or a domestic enterprise is not necessary to make out a violation of RICO's substantive prohibitions. The panel denied rehearing and issued a supplemental opinion holding that RICO does not require a domestic injury. If a foreign injury was caused by the violation of a predicate statute that applies extraterritorially, the court concluded, then the plaintiff may seek recovery for that injury under RICO. The Second Circuit later denied rehearing en banc, with five judges dissenting.

The lower courts have come to different conclusions regarding RICO's extraterritorial application. . . . Because of this conflict and the importance of the issue, we granted certiorari.

II

The question of RICO's extraterritorial application really involves two questions. First, do RICO's substantive prohibitions, contained in § 1962, apply to conduct that occurs in foreign countries? Second, does RICO's private right of action, contained in § 1964(c), apply to injuries that are suffered in foreign countries? We consider each of these questions in turn. To guide our inquiry, we begin by reviewing the law of extraterritoriality.

It is a basic premise of our legal system that, in general, "United States law governs domestically but does not rule the world." *Microsoft Corp. v. AT&T Corp.*, 550 U.S. 437, 454 (2007). This principle finds expression in a canon of statutory construction known as the presumption against extraterritoriality: Absent clearly expressed congressional intent to the contrary, federal laws will be construed to have only domestic application. *Morrison v. National Australia Bank Ltd.*, 561 U.S. 247, 255 (2010). The question is not whether we think "Congress would have wanted" a statute to apply to foreign conduct "if it had thought of the situation before the court," but whether Congress has affirmatively and unmistakably instructed that the statute will do so. *Id.*, at 261. "When a statute gives no clear indication of an extraterritorial application, it has none." *Id.*, at 255.

There are several reasons for this presumption. Most notably, it serves to avoid the international discord that can result when U.S. law is applied to conduct in foreign countries. . . . But it also reflects the more prosaic "commonsense notion that Congress generally legislates with domestic concerns in mind." *Smith v. United States*, 507 U.S. 197, 204, n. 5 (1993). We therefore apply the presumption across the board, "regardless of whether there is a risk of conflict between the American statute and a foreign law." *Morrison, supra*, at 255.

Twice in the past six years we have considered whether a federal statute applies extraterritorially. In *Morrison,* we addressed the question whether § 10(b) of the Securities Exchange Act of 1934 applies to misrepresentations made in connection with the purchase or sale of securities traded only on foreign exchanges. We first examined whether § 10(b) gives any clear indication of extraterritorial effect, and found that it does not. 561 U.S., at 262–265. We then engaged in a separate inquiry to determine whether the complaint before us involved a permissible *domestic* application of § 10(b) because it alleged that some of the relevant misrepresentations were made in the United States. At this second step, we considered the " 'focus' of congressional concern," asking whether § 10(b)'s focus is "the place where the deception originated" or rather "purchases and sale of securities in the United States." *Id.*, at 266. We concluded that the statute's focus is on domestic securities transactions, and we therefore held that the statute does not apply to frauds in connection with foreign securities transactions, even if those frauds involve domestic misrepresentations.

In *Kiobel,* we considered whether the Alien Tort Statute (ATS) confers federal-court jurisdiction over causes of action alleging international-law violations committed overseas. We acknowledged that the presumption against extraterritoriality is "typically" applied to statutes "regulating conduct," but we concluded that the principles supporting the presumption should "similarly constrain courts considering causes of action that may be brought under the ATS." 133 S.Ct., at 1664. We applied the presumption and held that the ATS lacks any clear indication that it extended to the foreign violations alleged in that case. *Id.*, at 1665–1669. Because "all the relevant conduct" regarding those violations "took place outside the United States," *id.*, 133 S.Ct., at 1670, we did not need to determine, as we did in *Morrison,* the statute's "focus."

Morrison and *Kiobel* reflect a two-step framework for analyzing extraterritoriality issues. At the first step, we ask whether the presumption against extraterritoriality has been rebutted—that is, whether the statute gives a clear, affirmative indication that it applies extraterritorially. We must ask this question regardless of whether the statute in question regulates conduct, affords relief, or merely confers jurisdiction. If the statute is not extraterritorial, then at the second step we determine whether the case involves a domestic application of the statute, and we do this by looking to the statute's "focus." If the conduct relevant to the statute's focus occurred in the United States, then the case involves a permissible domestic application even if other conduct occurred abroad; but if the conduct relevant to the focus occurred in a foreign country, then the case involves an impermissible extraterritorial application regardless of any other conduct that occurred in U.S. territory.

What if we find at step one that a statute clearly *does* have extraterritorial effect? Neither *Morrison* nor *Kiobel* involved such a finding. But we addressed this issue in *Morrison,* explaining that it was necessary to consider § 10(b)'s "focus" only because we found that the statute does not apply extraterritorially: "If § 10(b) did apply abroad, we would not need to determine which transnational frauds it applied to; it would apply to all of them (barring some other limitation)." 561 U.S., at 267, n. 9. The scope of an extraterritorial statute thus turns on the limits Congress has (or has not) imposed on the statute's foreign application, and not on the statute's "focus."

III

With these guiding principles in mind, we first consider whether RICO's substantive prohibitions in § 1962 may apply to foreign conduct. Unlike in *Morrison* and *Kiobel*, we find that the presumption against extraterritoriality has been rebutted—but only with respect to certain applications of the statute.

A

The most obvious textual clue is that RICO defines racketeering activity to include a number of predicates that plainly apply to at least some foreign conduct. These predicates include the prohibition against engaging in monetary transactions in criminally derived property, which expressly applies, when "the defendant is a United States person," to offenses that "tak[e] place outside the United States." 18 U.S.C. § 1957(d)(2). Other examples include the prohibitions against the assassination of Government officials, § 351(i) . . . and the prohibition against hostage taking, which applies to conduct that "occurred outside the United States" if either the hostage or the offender is a U.S. national, if the offender is found in the United States, or if the hostage taking is done to compel action by the U.S. Government. At least one predicate— the prohibition against "kill[ing] a national of the United States, while such national is outside the United States"—applies *only* to conduct occurring outside the United States. § 2332(a).

We agree with the Second Circuit that Congress's incorporation of these (and other) extraterritorial predicates into RICO gives a clear, affirmative indication that § 1962 applies to foreign racketeering activity—but only to the extent that the predicates alleged in a particular case themselves apply extraterritorially. . . . To give a simple (albeit grim) example, a violation of § 1962 could be premised on a pattern of killings of Americans abroad in violation of § 2332(a)—a predicate that all agree applies extraterritorially—whether or not any domestic predicates are also alleged.

We emphasize the important limitation that foreign conduct must violate "a predicate statute that manifests an unmistakable congressional intent to apply extraterritorially." 764 F.3d, at 136. Although a number of RICO predicates have extraterritorial effect, many do not. The inclusion of *some* extraterritorial predicates does not mean that *all* RICO predicates extend to foreign conduct. This is apparent for two reasons. First, "when a statute provides for some extraterritorial application, the presumption against extraterritoriality operates to limit that provision to its terms." *Morrison*, 561 U.S., at 265. Second, RICO defines as racketeering activity only acts that are "indictable" (or, what amounts to the same thing, "chargeable" or "punishable") under one of the statutes identified in § 1961(1). If a particular statute does not apply extraterritorially, then conduct committed abroad is not "indictable" under that statute and so cannot qualify as a predicate under RICO's plain terms. . . .

... While the presumption can be overcome only by a clear indication of extraterritorial effect, an express statement of extraterritoriality is not essential. "Assuredly context can be consulted as well." *Morrison, supra,* at 265. Context is dispositive here. Congress has not expressly said that § 1962(c) applies to patterns of racketeering activity in foreign countries, but it has defined "racketeering activity"—and by extension a "pattern of racketeering activity"—to encompass violations of predicate statutes that *do* expressly apply extraterritorially. Short of an explicit declaration, it is hard to imagine how Congress could have more clearly indicated that it intended RICO to have (some) extraterritorial effect. This unique structure makes RICO the rare statute that clearly evidences extraterritorial effect despite lacking an express statement of extraterritoriality.

We therefore conclude that RICO applies to some foreign racketeering activity. A violation of § 1962 may be based on a pattern of racketeering that includes predicate offenses committed abroad, provided that each of those offenses violates a predicate statute that is itself extraterritorial. This fact is determinative as to § 1962(b) and § 1962(c), both of which prohibit the employment of a pattern of racketeering. Although they differ as to the end for which the pattern is employed—to acquire or maintain control of an enterprise under subsection (b), or to conduct an enterprise's affairs under subsection (c)—this difference is immaterial for extraterritoriality purposes.

Section 1962(a) presents a thornier question. Unlike subsections (b) and (c), subsection (a) targets certain uses of *income* derived from a pattern of racketeering, not the use of the pattern itself. ... While we have no difficulty concluding that this prohibition applies to income derived from foreign patterns of racketeering (within the limits we have discussed), arguably § 1962(a) extends only to domestic uses of the income. The Second Circuit did not decide this question because it found that respondents have alleged "a domestic investment of racketeering proceeds in the form of RJR's merger in the United States with Brown & Williamson and investments in other U.S. operations." 764 F.3d, at 138, n. 5. RJR does not dispute the basic soundness of the Second Circuit's reasoning, but it does contest the court's reading of the complaint. See Brief for Petitioners 57–58. Because the parties have not focused on this issue, and because it makes no difference to our resolution of this case, see *infra,* at 2110, we assume without deciding that respondents have pleaded a domestic investment of racketeering income in violation of § 1962(a).

. . .

C

Applying these principles, we agree with the Second Circuit that the complaint does not allege impermissibly extraterritorial violations of §§ 1962(b) and (c). The alleged pattern of racketeering activity consists of five basic predicates: (1) money laundering, (2) material support of foreign terrorist organizations, (3) mail fraud, (4) wire fraud, and (5) violations of the Travel Act. The Second Circuit observed that the relevant provisions of the money laundering and material support of terrorism statutes expressly provide for extraterritorial application in certain circumstances, and it concluded that those circumstances are alleged to be present here. 764 F.3d, at 139–140. The court found that the fraud statutes and the Travel Act do not contain the clear indication needed to overcome the presumption against extraterritoriality. But it held that the complaint alleges *domestic* violations of those statutes because it "allege[s] conduct in the United States that satisfies every essential element of the mail fraud, wire fraud, and Travel Act claims." *Id.*, at 142.

RJR does not dispute these characterizations of the alleged predicates. We therefore assume without deciding that the alleged pattern of racketeering activity consists entirely of predicate offenses that were either committed in the United States or committed in a foreign country in violation of a predicate statute that applies extraterritorially. The alleged enterprise also has a sufficient tie to U.S. commerce, as its members include U.S. companies, and its activities depend on sales of RJR's cigarettes conducted through "the U.S. mails and wires," among other things. App. to Pet. for Cert. 186a, Complaint ¶ 96. On these premises, respondents' allegations that RJR violated §§ 1962(b) and (c) do not involve an impermissibly extraterritorial application of RICO.

IV

We now turn to RICO's private right of action, on which respondents' lawsuit rests. Section 1964(c) allows "[a]ny person injured in his business or property by reason of a violation of section 1962" to sue for treble damages, costs, and attorney's fees. Irrespective of any extraterritorial application of § 1962, we conclude that § 1964(c) does not overcome the presumption against extraterritoriality. A private RICO plaintiff therefore must allege and prove a *domestic* injury to its business or property.

A

. . . [W]e separately apply the presumption against extraterritoriality to RICO's cause of action despite our conclusion that the presumption has been overcome with respect to RICO's substantive prohibitions. "The creation of a private right of action raises issues beyond the mere consideration whether underlying primary conduct should be allowed or not, entailing, for example, a decision to permit enforcement without the check imposed by prosecutorial discretion." *Sosa v. Alvarez-Machain*, 542 U.S. 692, 727. Thus, as we have observed in other contexts, providing a private civil remedy for foreign conduct creates a potential for international friction beyond that presented by merely applying U.S. substantive law to that foreign conduct. See, *e.g.*, *Kiobel, supra,* 133 S.Ct., at 1665 ("Each of th[e] decisions" involved in defining a cause of action based on "conduct within the territory of another sovereign" "carries with it significant foreign policy implications").

Consider antitrust. In that context, we have observed that "[t]he application ... of American private treble-damages remedies to anticompetitive conduct taking place abroad has generated considerable controversy" in other nations, even when those nations agree with U.S. substantive law on such things as banning price fixing. *F. Hoffmann-La Roche Ltd. v. Empagran S.A.*, 542 U.S. 155, 167. Numerous foreign countries—including some respondents in this case—advised us in *Empagran* that "to apply [U.S.] remedies would unjustifiably permit their citizens to bypass their own less generous remedial schemes, thereby upsetting a balance of competing considerations that their own domestic antitrust laws embody." *Ibid.*

We received similar warnings in *Morrison,* where France, a respondent here, informed us that "most foreign countries proscribe securities fraud" but "have made very different choices with respect to the best way to implement that proscription," such as "prefer[ring] 'state actions, not private ones' for the enforcement of law." Brief for Republic of France as *Amicus Curiae,* O.T. 2009, No. 08–1191, p. 20; see *id.,* at 23 ("Even when foreign countries permit private rights of action for securities fraud, they often have different schemes" for litigating them and "may approve of different measures of damages"). Allowing foreign investors to pursue private suits in the United States, we were told, "would upset that delicate balance and offend the sovereign interests of foreign nations." *Id.,* at 26.

Allowing recovery for foreign injuries in a civil RICO action, including treble damages, presents the same danger of international friction. . . . This is not to say that friction would necessarily result in every case, or that Congress would violate international law by permitting such suits. It is to say only that there is a potential for international controversy that militates against recognizing foreign-injury claims without clear direction from Congress. Although "a risk of conflict between the American statute and a foreign law" is not a prerequisite for applying the presumption against extraterritoriality, *Morrison,* 561 U.S., at 255, where such a risk is evident, the need to enforce the presumption is at its apex.

Respondents urge that concerns about international friction are inapplicable in this case because here the plaintiffs are not foreign citizens seeking to bypass their home countries' less generous remedies but rather the foreign countries themselves. Brief for Respondents 52–53. Respondents assure us that they "are satisfied that the[ir] complaint ... comports with limitations on prescriptive jurisdiction under international law and respects the dignity of foreign sovereigns." *Ibid.* Even assuming that this is true, however, our interpretation of § 1964(c)'s injury requirement will necessarily govern suits by nongovernmental plaintiffs that are not so sensitive to foreign sovereigns' dignity. We reject the notion that we should forgo the presumption against extraterritoriality and instead permit extraterritorial suits based on a case-by-case inquiry that turns on or looks to the consent of the affected sovereign. See *Morrison*, supra, at 261 ("Rather than guess anew in each case, we apply the presumption in all cases"); cf. *Empagran*, 542 U.S., at 168. Respondents suggest that we should be reluctant to permit a foreign corporation to be sued in the courts of this country for events occurring abroad if the nation of incorporation objects, but that we should discard those reservations when a foreign state sues a U.S. entity in this country under U.S. law—instead of in its own courts and under its own laws—for conduct committed on its own soil. We refuse to adopt this double standard. "After all, in the law, what is sauce for the goose is normally sauce for the gander." *Heffernan v. City of Paterson*, 136 S.Ct. 1412, 1418 (2016).

B

Nothing in § 1964(c) provides a clear indication that Congress intended to create a private right of action for injuries suffered outside of the United States. The statute provides a cause of action to "[a]ny person injured in his business or property" by a violation of § 1962. § 1964(c). The word "any" ordinarily connotes breadth, but it is insufficient to displace the presumption against extraterritoriality. See *Kiobel,* 133 S.Ct., at 1665–1666. The statute's reference to injury to "business or property" also does not indicate extraterritorial application. If anything, by cabining RICO's private cause of action to particular kinds of injury— excluding, for example, personal injuries—Congress signaled that the civil remedy is not coextensive with § 1962's substantive prohibitions. The rest of § 1964(c) places a limit on RICO plaintiffs' ability to rely on securities fraud to make out a claim. This too suggests that § 1964(c) is narrower in its application than § 1962, and in any event does not support extraterritoriality.

The Second Circuit did not identify anything in § 1964(c) that shows that the statute reaches foreign injuries. Instead, the court reasoned that § 1964(c)'s extraterritorial effect flows directly from that of § 1962. Citing our holding in *Sedima, S.P.R.L. v. Imrex Co.,* 473 U.S. 479 (1985), that the "compensable injury" addressed by § 1964(c) "necessarily is the harm caused by predicate acts sufficiently related to constitute a pattern," *id.,* at 497, the Court of Appeals held that a RICO plaintiff may sue for foreign injury that was caused by the violation of a predicate statute that applies extraterritorially, just as a substantive RICO violation may be based on extraterritorial predicates. 764 F.3d, at 151. . . . This reasoning has surface appeal, but it fails to appreciate that the presumption against extraterritoriality must be applied separately to both RICO's substantive prohibitions and its private right of action. It is not enough to say that a private right of action must reach abroad because the underlying law governs conduct in foreign countries. Something more is needed, and here it is absent.

Respondents contend that background legal principles allow them to sue for foreign injuries, invoking what they call the " 'traditional rule' that 'a plaintiff injured in a foreign country' could bring suit 'in American courts.' " Brief for Respondents 41 (quoting *Sosa,*542 U.S., at 706–707). But the rule respondents invoke actually provides that a court will ordinarily "apply *foreign* law to determine the tortfeasor's liability" to "a plaintiff injured in a foreign country." *Id.,* at 706 (emphasis added). Respondents' argument might have force if they sought to sue RJR for violations of *their own laws* and to invoke federal diversity jurisdiction as a basis for proceeding in U.S. courts. . . . The question here, however, is not "whether a federal court has jurisdiction to entertain a cause of action provided by foreign or even international law. The question is instead whether the court has authority to recognize a cause of action *under U.S. law*" for injury suffered overseas. *Kiobel,* 133 S.Ct., at 1666 (emphasis added). As to that question, the relevant background principle is the presumption against extraterritoriality, not the "traditional rule" respondents cite.

Respondents . . . point out that RICO's private right of action was modeled after § 4 of the Clayton Act, 15 U.S.C. § 15; see *Holmes v. Securities Investor Protection Corporation,* 503 U.S. 258, 267–268 (1992), which we have held allows recovery for injuries suffered abroad as a result of antitrust violations, see *Pfizer Inc. v. Government of India,* 434 U.S. 308, 314–315 (1978). It follows, respondents . . . contend, that § 1964(c) likewise allows plaintiffs to sue for injuries suffered in foreign countries. We disagree. Although we have often looked to the Clayton Act for guidance in construing § 1964(c), we have not treated the two statutes as interchangeable. . . .

There is good reason not to interpret § 1964(c) to cover foreign injuries just because the Clayton Act does so. When we held in *Pfizer* that the Clayton Act allows recovery for foreign injuries, we relied first and foremost on the fact that the Clayton Act's definition of "person"—which in turn defines who may sue under that Act—"explicitly includes 'corporations and associations existing under or authorized by . . . the laws of any foreign country.' " 434 U.S., at 313; see 15 U.S.C. § 12.11 RICO lacks the language that the *Pfizer* Court found critical. See 18 U.S.C. § 1961(3).12 To the extent that the *Pfizer* Court cited other factors that might apply to § 1964(c), they were not sufficient in themselves to show that the provision has extraterritorial effect. For example, the *Pfizer* Court, writing before we honed our extraterritoriality jurisprudence in *Morrison* and *Kiobel,* reasoned that Congress "[c]learly . . . did not intend to make the [Clayton Act's] treble-damages remedy available only to consumers in our own country" because "the antitrust laws extend to trade 'with foreign nations' as well as among the several States of the Union." 434 U.S., at 313–314. But we have emphatically rejected reliance on such language, holding that " 'even statutes . . . that expressly refer to *foreign* commerce" do not apply abroad.' " *Morrison,* 561 U.S., at 262–263. This reasoning also fails to distinguish between extending *substantive antitrust law* to foreign conduct and extending a *private right of action* to foreign injuries, two separate issues that, as we have explained, raise distinct extraterritoriality problems. See *supra,* at 2105–2108. Finally, the *Pfizer* Court expressed concern that it would "defeat th[e] purposes" of the antitrust laws if a defendant could "escape full liability for his illegal actions." 434 U.S., at 314. But this justification was merely an attempt to "divin[e] what Congress would have wanted" had it considered the question of extraterritoriality—an approach we eschewed in *Morrison,* 561 U.S., at 261. Given all this, and in particular the fact that RICO lacks the language that *Pfizer* found integral to its decision, we decline to extend this aspect of our Clayton Act jurisprudence to RICO's cause of action.

. . .

C

Section 1964(c) requires a civil RICO plaintiff to allege and prove a domestic injury to business or property and does not allow recovery for foreign injuries. The application of this rule in any given case will not always be self-evident, as disputes may arise as to whether a particular alleged injury is "foreign" or "domestic." But we need not concern ourselves with that question in this case. As this case was being briefed before this Court, respondents filed a stipulation in the District Court waiving their damages claims for domestic injuries. The District Court accepted this waiver and dismissed those claims with prejudice. Respondents' remaining RICO damages claims therefore rest entirely on injury suffered abroad and must be dismissed.

The judgment of the United States Court of Appeals for the Second Circuit is reversed, and the case is remanded for further proceedings consistent with this opinion.

So ordered.

NOTES

1. Do you agree that *Morrison* established its "focus" inquiry as part of a "two-step framework for analyzing extraterritoriality issues"? What are the two steps? How does "focus" fit into that framework?

2. The Court concluded that RICO § 1962 applied extraterritorially because it targeted racketeering activities affecting interstate or foreign commerce. How does the Court explain that § 1964(c)—which provides a private right of action for persons *injured by violations of § 1962*—did not apply extraterritorially?

3. What is the practical impact of the Court's conclusion that § 1964(c) does not apply extraterritorially?

4. Is it realistic to assume that Congress considers each individual section of an Act for whether it applies extraterritorially? Some conclude that it is not. See, e.g., Gardnera, RJR Nabisco and the Runaway Canon, 102 Va.L. Rev.Online 134, 139 (2016)("unrealistic understanding of how Congress works").

5. Why, according to the Court, would recognition of a private action in this case risk "international friction"? How can there be international friction when, as in this case, foreign governments are attempting to enforce RICO? See Calangelo, The Frankenstein's Monster of Extraterritoriality Law, 110 Am.J.Int'l L. Unbound 51, 55 (2016)(plaintiffs in *RJR Nabisco* were "precisely those nations into whose territories U.S. law would have extended").

D. EXTRATERRITORIAL APPLICATION OF U.S. CONSTITUTIONAL RIGHTS

Boumediene v. Bush

Supreme Court of the United States, 2008.
553 U.S. 723, 128 S.Ct. 2229, 171 L.Ed.2d 41.

■ JUSTICE KENNEDY delivered the opinion of the Court.

Petitioners are aliens designated as enemy combatants and detained at the United States Naval Station at Guantanamo Bay, Cuba. There are others detained there, also aliens, who are not parties to this suit.

Petitioners present a question not resolved by our earlier cases relating to the detention of aliens at Guantanamo: whether they have the constitutional privilege of habeas corpus, a privilege not to be withdrawn except in conformance with the Suspension Clause, Art. I, § 9, cl. 2. . . .

I

Under the Authorization for Use of Military Force (AUMF), § 2(a), 115 Stat. 224, note following 50 U.S.C. § 1541 (2000 ed., Supp. V), the President is authorized "to use all necessary and appropriate force against those nations, organizations, or persons he determines planned, authorized, committed, or aided the terrorist attacks that occurred on September 11, 2001, or harbored such organizations or persons, in order to prevent any future acts of international terrorism against the United States by such nations, organizations or persons."

In Hamdi v. Rumsfeld, 542 U.S. 507, 124 S. Ct. 2633, 159 L. Ed.2d 578 (2004), five Members of the Court recognized that detention of individuals who fought against the United States in Afghanistan "for the duration of the particular conflict in which they were captured, is so fundamental and accepted an incident to war as to be an exercise of the 'necessary and appropriate force' Congress has authorized the President to use." Id., at 518, 124 S. Ct. 2633, 159 L. Ed.2d 578 (plurality opinion of O'Connor, J.), id., at 588–589, 124 S.Ct. 2633, 159 L. Ed.2d 578 (Thomas, J., dissenting). After Hamdi, the Deputy Secretary of Defense established Combatant Status Review Tribunals (CSRTs) to determine whether individuals detained at Guantanamo were "enemy combatants," as the Department defines that term. . . .

Interpreting the AUMF, the Department of Defense ordered the detention of these petitioners, and they were transferred to Guantanamo. Some of these individuals were apprehended on the battlefield in Afghanistan, others in places as far away from there as Bosnia and Gambia. All are foreign nationals, but none is a citizen of a nation now at war with the United States. Each denies he is a member of the al Qaeda terrorist network that carried out the September 11 attacks or of the Taliban regime that provided sanctuary for al Qaeda. Each petitioner appeared before a separate CSRT; was determined to be an enemy combatant; and has sought a writ of habeas corpus in the United States District Court for the District of Columbia.

While [these cases] were pending . . . , Congress passed the [Detainee Treatment Act hereinafter "DTA"]. The DTA provide[s] that "no court, justice, or judge shall have jurisdiction to hear or consider . . . an application for a writ of habeas corpus filed by or on behalf of an alien detained by the Department of Defense at Guantanamo Bay, Cuba." [The DTA] further provides that the Court of Appeals for the District of Columbia Circuit shall have "exclusive" jurisdiction to review decisions of the CSRTs.

[The court then reviewed its earlier decision in Hamdan v. Rumsfeld, 548 U.S. 557, 576–577, 126 S.Ct. 2749, 165 L. Ed.2d 723 (2006), which held that the original version of the DTA did not apply to cases like the petitioners that were pending when the DTA was passed. The Court concluded that the post-Hamdan amendments to the DTA made clear that the DTA, including the withdrawal of jurisdiction to hear habeas corpus cases, did apply to these petitioners.]

III

In deciding the constitutional questions now presented we must determine whether petitioners are barred from seeking the writ or invoking the protections of the Suspension Clause either because of their status, i.e., petitioners' designation by the Executive Branch as enemy combatants, or their physical location, i.e., their presence at Guantanamo Bay. The Government contends that noncitizens designated as enemy combatants and detained in territory located outside our Nation's borders have no constitutional rights and no privilege of habeas corpus. Petitioners contend they do have cognizable constitutional rights and that Congress, in seeking to eliminate recourse to habeas corpus as a means to assert those rights, acted in violation of the Suspension Clause.

We begin with a brief account of the history and origins of the writ. Our account proceeds from two propositions. First, protection for the privilege of habeas corpus was one of the few safeguards of liberty specified in a Constitution that, at the outset, had no Bill of Rights. In the system conceived by the Framers the writ had a centrality that must inform proper interpretation of the Suspension Clause. Second, to the extent there were settled precedents or legal commentaries in 1789 regarding the extraterritorial scope of the writ or its application to enemy aliens, those authorities can be instructive for the present cases.

A

The Framers viewed freedom from unlawful restraint as a fundamental precept of liberty, and they understood the writ of habeas corpus as a vital instrument to secure that freedom. Experience taught, however, that the common-law writ all too often had been insufficient to guard against the abuse of monarchial power. That history counseled the necessity for specific language in the Constitution to secure the writ and ensure its place in our legal system. . . .

B

The broad historical narrative of the writ and its function is central to our analysis, but we seek guidance as well from founding-era authorities addressing the specific question before us: whether foreign nationals, apprehended and detained in distant countries during a time of serious threats to our Nation's security, may assert the privilege of the writ and seek its protection. The Court has been careful not to foreclose the possibility that the protections of the Suspension Clause have expanded along with post-1789 developments that define the present scope of the writ. See INS v. St. Cyr, 533 U.S. 289, 300–301, 121 S.Ct. 2271, 150 L. Ed.2d 347 (2001). But the analysis may begin with precedents as of 1789, for the Court has said that "at the absolute minimum" the Clause protects the writ as it existed when the Constitution was drafted and ratified. Id., at 301, 121 S.Ct. 2271, 150 L. Ed.2d 347.

To support their arguments, the parties in these cases have examined historical sources to construct a view of the common-law writ as it existed in 1789—as have amici whose expertise in legal history the Court has relied upon in the past. See Brief for Legal Historians as Amici Curiae; see also St. Cyr, supra, at 302, n. 16, 121 S.Ct. 2271, 150 L. Ed.2d 347. The Government argues the common-law writ ran only to those territories over which the Crown was sovereign. . . . Petitioners argue that jurisdiction followed the King's officers. . . . Diligent search by all parties reveals no certain conclusions. In none of the cases cited do we find that a common-law court would or would not have granted, or refused to hear for lack of jurisdiction, a petition for a writ of habeas corpus brought by a prisoner deemed an enemy combatant, under a standard like the one the Department of Defense has used in these cases, and when held in a territory, like Guantanamo, over which the Government has total military and civil control.

We know that at common law a petitioner's status as an alien was not a categorical bar to habeas corpus relief. See, e.g., Sommersett's Case,

20 How. St. Tr. 1, 80–82 (1772) (ordering an African slave freed upon finding the custodian's return insufficient); see generally Khera v. Secretary of State for the Home Dept., [1984] A. C. 74, 111 ("Habeas corpus protection is often expressed as limited to 'British subjects.' Is it really limited to British nationals? Suffice it to say that the case law has given an emphatic 'no' to the question"). We know as well that common-law courts entertained habeas petitions brought by enemy aliens detained in England—"entertained" at least in the sense that the courts held hearings to determine the threshold question of entitlement to the writ. See Case of Three Spanish Sailors, 2 Black. W. 1324, 96 Eng. Rep. 775 (C. P. 1779); King v. Schiever, 2 Burr. 765, 97 Eng. Rep. 551 (K. B. 1759); Du Castro's Case, Fort. 195, 92 Eng. Rep. 816 (K. B. 1697). . . .

We find the evidence as to the geographic scope of the writ at common law informative, but, again, not dispositive. Petitioners argue the site of their detention is analogous to two territories outside of England to which the writ did run: the so-called "exempt jurisdictions," like the Channel Islands; and (in former times) India. There are critical differences between these places and Guantanamo, however. . . .

[C]ommon-law courts granted habeas corpus relief to prisoners detained in the exempt jurisdictions. But these areas, while not in theory part of the realm of England, were nonetheless under the Crown's control. See 2 H. Hallam, Constitutional History of England: From the Accession of Henry VII to the Death of George II, pp. 232–233 (reprint 1989). And there is some indication that these jurisdictions were considered sovereign territory. . . . Because the United States does not maintain formal sovereignty over Guantanamo Bay, see Part IV, infra, the naval station there and the exempt jurisdictions discussed in the English authorities are not similarly situated.

Petitioners and their amici further rely on cases in which British courts in India granted writs of habeas corpus to noncitizens detained in territory over which the Moghul Emperor retained formal sovereignty and control. See supra, at 12–13; Brief for Legal Historians as Amici Curiae 12–13. The analogy to the present cases breaks down, however, because of the geographic location of the courts in the Indian example. The Supreme Court of Judicature (the British Court) sat in Calcutta; but no federal court sits at Guantanamo. The Supreme Court of Judicature was, moreover, a special court set up by Parliament to monitor certain conduct during the British Raj. See Regulating Act of 1773, 13 Geo. 3, §§ 13–14. That it had the power to issue the writ in nonsovereign territory does not prove that common-law courts sitting in England had the same power. If petitioners were to have the better of the argument on this point, we would need some demonstration of a consistent practice of common-law courts sitting in England and entertaining petitions brought by alien prisoners detained abroad. We find little support for this conclusion.

The Government argues, in turn, that Guantanamo is more closely analogous to Scotland and Hanover, territories that were not part of England but nonetheless controlled by the English monarch (in his separate capacities as King of Scotland and Elector of Hanover). See Cowle, 2 Burr., at 856, 97 Eng. Rep., at 600. Lord Mansfield can be cited for the proposition that, at the time of the founding, English courts lacked the "power" to issue the writ to Scotland and Hanover, territories Lord Mansfield referred to as "foreign." Ibid. But what matters for our purposes is why common-law courts lacked this power. Given the English Crown's delicate and complicated relationships with Scotland and Hanover in the 1700's, we cannot disregard the possibility that the common-law courts' refusal to issue the writ to these places was motivated not by formal legal constructs but by what we would think of as prudential concerns. This appears to have been the case with regard to other British territories where the writ did not run. See 2 R. Chambers, A Course of Lectures on English Law 1767–1773, p. 8 (T. Curley ed.1986) (quoting the view of Lord Mansfield in Cowle that "[n]otwithstanding the power which the judges have, yet where they cannot judge of the cause, or give relief upon it, they would not think proper to interpose; and therefore in the case of imprisonments in Guernsey, Jersey, Minorca, or the plantations, the most usual way is to complain to the king in Council" (internal quotation marks omitted)). And after the Act of Union in 1707, through which the kingdoms of England and Scotland were merged politically, Queen Anne and her successors, in their new capacity as sovereign of Great Britain, ruled the entire island as one kingdom. Accordingly, by the time Lord Mansfield penned his opinion in Cowle in 1759, Scotland was no longer a "foreign" country vis-B-vis England—at least not in the sense in which Cuba is a foreign country vis-B-vis the United States.

Scotland remained "foreign" in Lord Mansfield's day in at least one important respect, however. Even after the Act of Union, Scotland (like Hanover) continued to maintain its own laws and court system. See 1 Blackstone *98, *109. Under these circumstances prudential considerations would have weighed heavily when courts sitting in England received habeas petitions from Scotland or the Electorate. Common-law decisions withholding the writ from prisoners detained in these places easily could be explained as efforts to avoid either or both of two embarrassments: conflict with the judgments of another court of competent jurisdiction; or the practical inability, by reason of distance, of the English courts to enforce their judgments outside their territorial jurisdiction. . . .

By the mid-19th century, British courts could issue the writ to Canada, notwithstanding the fact that Canadian courts also had the power to do so. See 9 Holdsworth 124 (citing Ex parte Anderson, 3 El. and El. 487 (1861)). This might be seen as evidence that the existence of a separate court system was no barrier to the running of the common-law writ. The Canada of the 1800's, however, was in many respects more analogous to the exempt jurisdictions or to Ireland, where the writ ran, than to Scotland or Hanover in the 1700's, where it did not. Unlike Scotland and Hanover, Canada followed English law. See B. Laskin, The British Tradition in Canadian Law 50–51 (1969).

In the end a categorical or formal conception of sovereignty does not provide a comprehensive or altogether satisfactory explanation for the general understanding that prevailed when Lord Mansfield considered issuance of the writ outside England. In 1759 the writ did not run to Scotland but did run to Ireland, even though, at that point, Scotland and England had merged under the rule of a single sovereign, whereas the Crowns of Great Britain and Ireland remained separate (at least in theory). See Cowle, supra, at 856–857, 97 Eng. Rep., 600; 1 Blackstone *100–101. But there was at least one major difference between Scotland's and Ireland's relationship with England during this period that might explain why the writ ran to Ireland but not to Scotland. English law did not generally apply in Scotland (even after the Act of Union) but it did apply in Ireland. Blackstone put it as follows: "[A]s Scotland and England are now one and the same kingdom, and yet differ in their municipal laws; so England and Ireland are, on the other hand, distinct kingdoms, and yet in general agree in their laws." Id., at *100. This distinction, and not formal notions of sovereignty, may well explain why the writ did not run to Scotland (and Hanover) but would run to Ireland.

The prudential barriers that may have prevented the English courts from issuing the writ to Scotland and Hanover are not relevant here. We have no reason to believe an order from a federal court would be disobeyed at Guantanamo. No Cuban court has jurisdiction to hear these petitioners' claims, and no law other than the laws of the United States applies at the naval station. The modern-day relations between the United States and Guantanamo thus differ in important respects from the 18th-century relations between England and the kingdoms of Scotland and Hanover. This is reason enough for us to discount the relevance of the Government's analogy.

Each side in the present matter argues that the very lack of a precedent on point supports its position. The Government points out there is no evidence that a court sitting in England granted habeas relief to an enemy alien detained abroad; petitioners respond there is no evidence that a court refused to do so for lack of jurisdiction.

Both arguments are premised, however, upon the assumption that the historical record is complete and that the common law, if properly understood, yields a definite answer to the questions before us. There are reasons to doubt both assumptions. Recent scholarship points to the inherent shortcomings in the historical record. See Halliday & White 14–15 (noting that most reports of 18th-century habeas proceedings were not printed). And given the unique status of Guantanamo Bay and the particular dangers of terrorism in the modern age, the common-law courts simply may not have confronted cases with close parallels to this one. We decline, therefore, to infer too much, one way or the other, from the lack of historical evidence on point. Cf. Brown v. Board of Education, 347 U.S. 483, 489, 74 S.Ct. 686, 98 L. Ed. 873 (1954) (noting evidence concerning the circumstances surrounding the adoption of the Fourteenth Amendment, discussed in the parties' briefs and uncovered through the Court's own investigation, "convince us that, although these sources cast some light, it is not enough to resolve the problem with which we are faced. At best, they are inconclusive"); Reid v. Covert, 354 U.S. 1, 64, 77 S.Ct. 1222, 1 L. Ed.2d 1148 (1957) (Frankfurter, J., concurring in result) (arguing constitutional adjudication should not be based upon evidence that is "too episodic, too meager, to form a solid basis in history, preceding and contemporaneous with the framing of the Constitution").

IV

Drawing from its position that at common law the writ ran only to territories over which the Crown was sovereign, the Government says the Suspension Clause affords petitioners no rights because the United States does not claim sovereignty over the place of detention.

Guantanamo Bay is not formally part of the United States. See DTA § 1005(g), 119 Stat. 2743. And under the terms of the lease between the United States and Cuba, Cuba retains "ultimate sovereignty" over the territory while the United States exercises "complete jurisdiction and control." See Lease of Lands for Coaling and Naval Stations, Feb. 23, 1903, U.S.-Cuba, Art. III, T. S. No. 418 (hereinafter 1903 Lease Agreement); Rasul, 542 U.S., at 471, 124 S.Ct. 2686, 159 L. Ed.2d 548. Under the terms of the 1934 Treaty, however, Cuba effectively has no rights as a sovereign until the parties agree to modification of the 1903 Lease Agreement or the United States abandons the base. See Treaty Defining Relations with Cuba, May 29, 1934, U.S.-Cuba, Art. III, 48 Stat. 1683, T. S. No. 866.

The United States contends, nevertheless, that Guantanamo is not within its sovereign control. . . .

We therefore do not question the Government's position that Cuba, not the United States, maintains sovereignty, in the legal and technical sense of the term, over Guantanamo Bay. But this does not end the analysis. Our cases do not hold it is improper for us to inquire into the objective degree of control the Nation asserts over foreign territory. As commentators have noted, " '[s]overeignty' is a term used in many senses and is much abused." . . . Indeed, it is not altogether uncommon for a territory to be under the de jure sovereignty of one nation, while under the plenary control, or practical sovereignty, of another. This condition can occur when the territory is seized during war, as Guantanamo was during the Spanish-American War. . . .

A

The Court has discussed the issue of the Constitution's extraterritorial application on many occasions. These decisions undermine the Government's argument that, at least as applied to noncitizens, the Constitution necessarily stops where de jure sovereignty ends.

The Framers foresaw that the United States would expand and acquire new territories. . . .

Fundamental questions regarding the Constitution's geographic scope first arose at the dawn of the 20th century when the Nation acquired noncontiguous Territories: Puerto Rico, Guam, and the Philippines—ceded to the United States by Spain at the conclusion of the Spanish-American War—and Hawaii—annexed by the United States in 1898. . . .

In a series of opinions later known as the Insular Cases, the Court addressed whether the Constitution, by its own force, applies in any territory that is not a State. . . . The Court held that the Constitution has independent force in these territories, a force not contingent upon acts of legislative grace. Yet it took note of the difficulties inherent in that position.

Prior to their cession to the United States, the former Spanish colonies operated under a civil-law system, without experience in the various aspects of the Anglo-American legal tradition, for instance the use of grand and petit juries. . . .

These considerations resulted in the doctrine of territorial incorporation, under which the Constitution applies in full in incorporated Territories surely destined for statehood but only in part in unincorporated Territories. . . . Yet noting the inherent practical difficulties of enforcing all constitutional provisions "always and everywhere," Balzac, supra, at 312, 312, 42 S.Ct. 343, 66 L. Ed. 627, the Court devised in the Insular Cases a doctrine that allowed it to use its power sparingly and where it would be most needed. This century-old doctrine informs our analysis in the present matter.

Practical considerations likewise influenced the Court's analysis a half-century later in Reid, 354 U.S. 1, 77 S.Ct. 1222, 1 L. Ed.2d 1148. The petitioners there, spouses of American servicemen, lived on American military bases in England and Japan. They were charged with crimes committed in those countries and tried before military courts, consistent with executive agreements the United States had entered into with the British and Japanese governments. Id., at 15–16, 77 S.Ct. 1222, 1 L. Ed.2d 1148, and nn. 29–30 (plurality opinion). Because the petitioners were not themselves military personnel, they argued they were entitled to trial by jury.

Justice Black, writing for the plurality, contrasted the cases before him with the Insular Cases, which involved territories "with wholly dissimilar traditions and institutions" that Congress intended to govern only "temporarily." Id., at 14, 77 S.Ct. 1222, 1 L. Ed.2d 1148. Justice Frankfurter argued that the "specific circumstances of each particular case" are relevant in determining the geographic scope of the Constitution. Id., at 54, 77 S.Ct. 1222, 1 L. Ed.2d 1148 (opinion concurring in result). And Justice Harlan, who had joined an opinion reaching the opposite result in the case in the previous Term, Reid v. Covert, 351 U.S. 487, 76 S.Ct. 880, 100 L. Ed.1352 (1956), was most explicit in rejecting a "rigid and abstract rule" for determining where constitutional guarantees extend. Reid, 354 U.S., at 74, 77 S.Ct. 1222, 1 L. Ed.2d 1148 (opinion concurring in result). He read the Insular Cases to teach that whether a constitutional provision has extraterritorial effect depends upon the "particular circumstances, the practical necessities, and the possible alternatives which Congress had before it" and, in particular, whether judicial enforcement of the provision would be "impracticable and anomalous." Id., at 74–75, 77 S.Ct. 1222, 1 L. Ed.2d 1148; see also United States v. Verdugo-Urquidez, 494 U.S. 259, 277–278, 110 S.Ct. 1056, 108 L. Ed.2d 222 (1990) (Kennedy, J., concurring) (applying the "impracticable and anomalous" extraterritoriality test in the Fourth Amendment context).

That the petitioners in Reid were American citizens was a key factor in the case and was central to the plurality's conclusion that the Fifth and Sixth Amendments apply to American civilians tried outside the United States. But practical considerations, related not to the petitioners' citizenship but to the place of their confinement and trial, were relevant to each Member of the Reid majority. And to Justices Harlan and Frankfurter (whose votes were necessary to the Court's disposition) these considerations were the decisive factors in the case. . . .

[The Court then discussed at length Johnson v. Eisentrager, 339 U.S. 763, 70 S.Ct. 936 (1950), see Note 1, infra, which refused the writ to 21 Germans who had been convicted, by a Military Commission sitting outside the United States, of war crimes. The war crimes took place in the "China Theatre" of operations in World War II. The prisoners were being held in a prison physically located in Germany but under the command of the U.S. military officer.]

B

The Government's formal sovereignty-based test raises troubling separation-of-powers concerns as well. The political history of Guantanamo illustrates the deficiencies of this approach. The United States has maintained complete and uninterrupted control of the bay for over 100 years. . . .

These concerns have particular bearing upon the Suspension Clause question in the cases now before us, for the writ of habeas corpus is itself an indispensable mechanism for monitoring the separation of powers. The test for determining the scope of this provision must not be subject to manipulation by those whose power it is designed to restrain.

C

[W]e conclude that at least three factors are relevant in determining the reach of the Suspension Clause: (1) the citizenship and status of the detainee and the adequacy of the process through which that status determination was made; (2) the nature of the sites where apprehension and then detention took place; and (3) the practical obstacles inherent in resolving the prisoner's entitlement to the writ.

Applying this framework, we note at the onset that the status of these detainees is a matter of dispute . . . In the instant cases . . . the detainees deny they are enemy combatants. They have been afforded some process in CSRT proceedings to determine their status; but . . . there has been no trial by military commission for violations of the laws of war. . . .

In comparison [to a trial by a military commission] the procedural protections afforded to the detainees in the CSRT hearings are far more limited, and, we conclude, fall well short of the procedures and adversarial mechanisms that would eliminate the need for habeas corpus review. Although the detainee is assigned a "Personal Representative" to assist him during CSRT proceedings, the Secretary of the Navy's memorandum makes clear that person is not the detainee's lawyer or even his "advocate." See App. to Pet. for Cert. in No. 06–1196, at 155, 172. The Government's evidence is accorded a presumption of validity. Id., at 159. The detainee is allowed to present "reasonably available" evidence, id., at 155, but his ability to rebut the Government's evidence against him is limited by the circumstances of his confinement and his lack of counsel at this stage. And although the detainee can seek review of his status determination in the Court of Appeals, that review process cannot cure all defects in the earlier proceedings. See Part V, infra.

As to the second factor relevant to this analysis, the detainees . . . are technically outside the sovereign territory of the United States. . . . Guantanamo Bay, [however], is no transient possession. In every practical sense Guantanamo is not abroad; it is within the constant jurisdiction of the United States. . . .

As to the third factor, we recognize . . . that there are costs to holding the Suspension Clause applicable in a case of military detention abroad. Habeas corpus proceedings may require expenditure of funds by the Government and may divert the attention of military personnel from other pressing tasks. While we are sensitive to these concerns, we do not find them dispositive. Compliance with any judicial process requires some incremental expenditure of resources. Yet civilian courts and the Armed Forces have functioned along side each other at various points in our history. See, e.g., Duncan v. Kahanamoku, 327 U.S. 304, 66 S.Ct. 606, 90 L. Ed. 688 (1946); Ex parte Milligan, 71 U.S. 2, 4 Wall. 2, 18 L. Ed.281 (1866). The Government presents no credible arguments that the military mission at Guantanamo would be compromised if habeas corpus courts had jurisdiction to hear the detainees' claims. And in light of the plenary control the United States asserts over the base, none are apparent to us. . . .

There is no indication, furthermore, that adjudicating a habeas corpus petition would cause friction with the host government. No Cuban court has jurisdiction over American military personnel at Guantanamo or the enemy combatants detained there. . . .

It is true that before today the Court has never held that noncitizens detained by our Government in territory over which another country maintains de jure sovereignty have any rights under our Constitution. But the cases before us lack any precise historical parallel. They involve individuals detained by executive order for the duration of a conflict that, if measured from September 11, 2001, to the present, is already among the longest wars in American history. See Oxford Companion to American Military History 849 (1999). The detainees, moreover, are held in a territory that, while technically not part of the United States, is under the complete and total control of our Government. Under these circumstances the lack of a precedent on point is no barrier to our holding.

We hold that Art. I, § 9, cl. 2, of the Constitution has full effect at Guantanamo Bay. If the privilege of habeas corpus is to be denied to the detainees now before us, Congress must act in accordance with the requirements of the Suspension Clause. Cf. Hamdi, 542 U.S., at 564, 124 S.Ct. 2633, 159 L. Ed.2d 578 (Scalia, J., dissenting) ("[I]ndefinite imprisonment on reasonable suspicion is not an available option of treatment for those accused of aiding the enemy, absent a suspension of the writ"). This Court may not impose a de facto suspension by abstaining from these controversies. . . . Petitioners, therefore, are entitled to the privilege of habeas corpus to challenge the legality of their detention.

V

In light of this holding the question becomes whether the statute stripping jurisdiction to issue the writ avoids the Suspension Clause mandate because Congress has provided adequate substitute procedures for habeas corpus. [The Court concluded that the DTA did not provide an adequate substitute for the writ of habeas corpus.]

[The concurring opinion of Justice Souter and the dissenting opinion of Chief Justice Roberts are omitted.]

■ JUSTICE SCALIA with whom THE CHIEF JUSTICE, JUSTICE THOMAS and JUSTICE ALITO join, dissenting.

Today, for the first time in our Nation's history, the Court confers a constitutional right to habeas corpus on alien enemies detained abroad by our military forces in the course of an ongoing war. My problem with today's opinion is . . . fundamental . . . : The writ of habeas corpus does not, and never has, run in favor of aliens abroad; the Suspension Clause thus has no application, and the Court's intervention in this military matter is entirely ultra vires.

I shall devote most of what will be a lengthy opinion to the legal errors contained in the opinion of the Court. Contrary to my usual practice, however, I think it appropriate to begin with a description of the disastrous consequences of what the Court has done today.

I

America is at war with radical Islamists. . . . [O]ne need only walk about buttressed and barricaded Washington, or board a plane anywhere in the country, to know that the threat is a serious one. . . .

At least 30 of those prisoners hitherto released from Guantanamo Bay have returned to the battlefield. See S. Rep. No. 110–90, pt. 7, p. 13 (2007) (Minority Views of Sens. Kyl, Sessions, Graham, Cornyn, and Coburn) (hereinafter Minority Report). Some have been captured or killed. See ibid.; see also Mintz, Released Detainees Rejoining the Fight, Washington Post, Oct. 22, 2004, pp. A1, A12. But others have succeeded in carrying on their atrocities against innocent civilians. In one case, a detainee released from Guantanamo Bay masterminded the kidnapping of two Chinese dam workers, one of whom was later shot to death when used as a human shield against Pakistani commandoes. . . .

II

A

The Suspension Clause of the Constitution provides: "The Privilege of the Writ of Habeas Corpus shall not be suspended, unless when in Cases of Rebellion or Invasion the public Safety may require it." Art. I, § 9, cl. 2. As a court of law operating under a written Constitution, our role is to determine whether there is a conflict between that Clause and the Military Commissions Act. A conflict arises only if the Suspension Clause preserves the privilege of the writ for aliens held by the United States military as enemy combatants at the base in Guantanamo Bay, located within the sovereign territory of Cuba.

We have frequently stated that we owe great deference to Congress's view that a law it has passed is constitutional. . . .

In light of those principles of deference, the Court's conclusion that "the common law [does not] yiel[d] a definite answer to the questions before us," leaves it no choice but to affirm the Court of Appeals. The writ as preserved in the Constitution could not possibly extend farther than the common law provided when that Clause was written. . . .

How, then, does the Court weave a clear constitutional prohibition out of pure interpretive equipoise? The Court resorts to "fundamental separation-of-powers principles" to interpret the Suspension Clause. According to the Court, because "the writ of habeas corpus is itself an indispensable mechanism for monitoring the separation of powers," the test of its extraterritorial reach "must not be subject to manipulation by those whose power it is designed to restrain."

That approach distorts the nature of the separation of powers and its role in the constitutional structure. . . .

B

The Court purports to derive from our precedents a "functional" test for the extraterritorial reach of the writ, which shows that the [statute] unconstitutionally restricts the scope of habeas. That is remarkable because the most pertinent . . . precedent [Johnson v. Eisentrager, 339 U.S. 763, 70 S.Ct. 936 (1950), see Note 1, infra] . . . conclusively establishes the opposite. . . .

C

What drives today's decision is neither the meaning of the Suspension Clause, nor the principles of our precedents, but rather an inflated notion of judicial supremacy. The Court says that if the extraterritorial applicability of the Suspension Clause turned on formal notions of sovereignty, "it would be possible for the political branches to govern without legal constraint" in areas beyond the sovereign territory of the United States. That cannot be, the Court says, because it is the duty of this Court to say what the law is. It would be difficult to imagine a more question-begging analysis. "The very foundation of the power of the federal courts to declare Acts of Congress unconstitutional lies in the power and duty of those courts to decide cases and controversies properly before them." United States v. Raines, 362 U.S. 17, 20–21, 80 S.Ct. 519, 4 L. Ed.2d 524 (1960) (citing Marbury v. Madison, 5 U.S. 137, 1 Cranch 137, 2 L. Ed. 60 (1803); emphasis added). Our power "to say what the law is" is circumscribed by the limits of our statutorily and constitutionally conferred jurisdiction. See Lujan v. Defenders of Wildlife, 504 U.S. 555, 573–578, 112 S.Ct. 2130, 119 L. Ed.2d 351 (1992). And that is precisely the question in these cases: whether the Constitution confers habeas jurisdiction on federal courts to decide petitioners' claims. It is both irrational and arrogant to say that the answer must be yes, because otherwise we would not be supreme.

But so long as there are some places to which habeas does not run— so long as the Court's new "functional" test will not be satisfied in every case—then there will be circumstances in which "it would be possible for the political branches to govern without legal constraint." Or, to put it more impartially, areas in which the legal determinations of the other branches will be (shudder!) supreme. In other words, judicial supremacy is not really assured by the constitutional rule that the Court creates. The gap between rationale and rule leads me to conclude that the Court's ultimate, unexpressed goal is to preserve the power to review the confinement of enemy prisoners held by the Executive anywhere in the world. . . .

III

[I]t is clear that the original understanding of the Suspension Clause was that habeas corpus was not available to aliens abroad. . . .

It is entirely clear that, at English common law, the writ of habeas corpus did not extend beyond the sovereign territory of the Crown. To be sure, the writ had an "extraordinary territorial ambit," because it was a so-called "prerogative writ," which, unlike other writs, could extend beyond the realm of England to other places where the Crown was sovereign. . . .

But prerogative writs could not issue to foreign countries, even for British subjects; they were confined to the King's dominions—those areas over which the Crown was sovereign. . . .

In sum, all available historical evidence points to the conclusion that the writ would not have been available at common law for aliens captured and held outside the sovereign territory of the Crown. . . .

Today the Court warps our Constitution in a way that goes beyond the narrow issue of the reach of the Suspension Clause, invoking judicially brainstormed separation-of-powers principles to establish a manipulable "functional" test for the extraterritorial reach of habeas corpus (and, no doubt, for the extraterritorial reach of other constitutional protections as well). . . .

The Nation will live to regret what the Court has done today. I dissent.

NOTES

1.   Is it possible to construct a general and coherent theory of the applicability of constitutional liberties outside the United States? Questions of this sort generate passionate divisions among the Court's justices no matter what the era.

Consider two decisions invoked repeatedly by both the *Boumediene* majority and dissent. In Reid v. Covert, 354 U.S. 1, 77 S.Ct. 1222 (1957), the Court held that two spouses of service personnel stationed in Japan and England could not be subjected a court martial for murders committed in those countries. In each case the defendant was a wife accused of killing her uniformed husband. Federal law purported to bring both women within the jurisdiction of the military courts. The Court held, however, to allow them to be convicted by a military tribunal would violate their rights under the Fifth and Sixth Amendments of the Constitution as well as Article III. A four-justice plurality announced a sweeping test that seemed to apply the Constitution with full force to U.S. citizens no matter what the locus or circumstances of the wrongful acts. The concurrence, however, was much more cautious and emphasized the capital nature of the crimes and the relatively light burden on the government in providing a jury trial in such serious and rare cases. The dissent, foreshadowing some of Justice Scalia's concerns, worried that the decision placed the political branches in a "distressing situation." Making *Reid* even more unusual, it had been decided the other way the prior Term, but—with some considerable intervening change in the Court's personnel—the Court granted rehearing and substituted a new opinion ruling in favor of the defendants.

The prior Supreme Court decision most like *Boumediene* was Johnson v. Eisentrager, 339 U.S. 763, 70 S.Ct. 936 (1950). As in *Boumediene* and *Reid*, it produced a divided Court. In *Eisentrager*, 21 Germans petitioned the District Court for the District of Columbia for a writ of habeas corpus. They had been tried and convicted for war crimes for continuing to resist U.S. forces after Germany's unconditional May 8, 1945 surrender in World War II. Their base of operation had been in the China Theatre and they were accused of providing the Japanese forces with intelligence as to U.S. troop movements. They were convicted by a U.S. Military Commission sitting in China with the permission of the Chinese government. After conviction, they were repatriated to Germany to serve their sentences under the custody of an American army officer who was the prison commandant.

In holding that the writ did not run to the German prisoners, Justice Jackson's majority opinion emphasized that the Germans were "tried and convicted by a Military Commission sitting outside the United States . . . for offenses against laws of war committed outside the United States . . . and . . . at all times imprisoned outside the United States." Id. at 777, 70 S.Ct. at 943. Justice Scalia argues in his dissent in *Boumediene* that *Eisentrager* is indistinguishable. However, Justice Kennedy argues that *Eisentrager* is distinguishable because of the de facto control exercised by the United States over Guantanamo Bay.

Which view is more convincing? Under the majority's approach, would the result be different if the United States and Cuba had diplomatic relations and, as had the Chinese government in *Eisentrager*, Cuba had given permission to conduct the proceedings in its territory?

2.   View *Boumediene*, *Eisentrager* and *Reid* through the lens of conflicts analysis. Arguably, the *Boumediene* majority reconciles the cases through an application of interest analysis. Seen this way, *Reid* was a clear example of the U.S. having an interest in extending to U.S. citizens the protective cover of important Bill of Rights protections even off U.S. soil, just as New York Court of Appeals asserted an interest in protecting a New York plaintiff through an application of its tort law beyond its state boundaries in Babcock v. Jackson, p. 577, supra. *Eisentrager*, by way of contrast, was a case in which the United States' primary connection was that American defendants were holding the prisoners but the U.S. had no protective interest because the prisoners were not citizens. Moreover, in *Eisentrager* the U.S. lacked any territorial nexus that might give it an interest. Seen that way, *Eisentrager* is perhaps analogous to Neumeier v. Kuehner, p. 592, supra in which the New York Court of Appeals decided that merely having a New York defendant was not enough to justify application of New York law when the plaintiff was a non-New Yorker and the locus of the events was outside New York's borders. *Boumediene*, seen this way, is an intermediate case with the question turning on whether Guantanamo Bay is sufficiently within U.S. control to create a federal regulatory interest, with the majority giving an affirmative answer and the dissent a negative one.

The dissent seems to prefer a more traditional territorial analysis, which would make *Reid* an aberrational case (limited by the narrow concurrence which emphasized the capital nature of the crimes) but would make *Eisentrager* clear precedent for non-application of U.S. constitutional law. Seen this way, the question would be one of under whose formal sovereignty the liability creating events occurred. In that sense, *Eisentrager* and the result urged by the *Boumediene* dissent might be seen as applications of the vested rights theory favored by Justice Holmes and others. See Slater v. Mexican National RR Co., p. 264, supra and Alabama Great Southern RR Co. v. Carroll, p. 534, supra. Note that in his dissent in BMW of North America v. Gore, 517 U.S. 559, 602, 116 S.Ct. 1589 (1996), Justice Scalia criticized the majority for creating a test in "federal punitive damages law (the new field created by today's decision) [that] will be beset by the sort of 'interest analysis' that has laid waste the formerly comprehensible field of conflict of laws."

For a lively debate on the usefulness of viewing these questions through the lens of conflict of laws, see Roosevelt, Guantanamo and the Conflict of Laws: *Rasul* and Beyond, 153 U.Pa.L.Rev. 2017 (2005)(conflicts methodology helpful); Neuman, Extraterritorial Rights and Constitutional Methodology After Rasul v. Bush, 153 U.Pa.L.Rev. 2073 (2005)(conflicts methodology unhelpful).

3. In United States v. Verdugo-Urquidez, 494 U.S. 259, 110 S.Ct. 1056 (1990), the criminal defendant was a Mexican national suspected of trafficking drugs into the United States. Pursuant to a DEA warrant, he was arrested by Mexican police where he was transported to a border station and arrested by U.S. Marshals. The DEA then obtained the approval of Mexican authorities to search the defendant's residences and he moved to suppress, arguing that the searches violated the Fourth Amendment. A closely divided Supreme Court held that the Fourth Amendment had no application to the search. Four Justices treated the case as being essentially controlled by *Eisentrager* because the foreign locus of the search and the non-citizen status of the defendant. Four Justices would have held the Fourth Amendment applicable, though Justice Stevens concurred in the result because he believed the search to be reasonable. Justice Kennedy concurred with the four Justices who held the Fourth Amendment not applicable but clearly did not endorse their absolutist position. He placed weight instead on the fact that "[t]he conditions and considerations of this case would make adherence to the Fourth Amendment's warrant requirement impracticable and anomalous." Id. at 278, 110 S.Ct. at 1078 (Kennedy, J., concurring). Is his test consistent with the majority opinion in *Boumediene*?

4. In Maqaleh v. Gates, 605 F.3d 84 (D.C.Cir.2010), the court considered the habeas corpus applications of three foreign national detainees being held at Bagram Air Force Base in Afghanistan. All three claimed to have been captured outside Afghanistan and were being held by U.S. forces as unlawful enemy combatants. The detainees sought to bring their petitions within the scope of *Boumediene* by arguing that the U.S. held a leasehold interest in the Air Force base, making their confinement similar to the successful petitioners in *Boumediene*. The District Court agreed and ruled that it had jurisdiction over the petitions, but certified the issue for interlocutory review. The Court of Appeals reversed, making two important distinctions with *Boumediene*. One was that unlike Guantanamo Bay, over which the U.S. has exercised essentially complete de facto control for over a century in the face of a hostile Cuban government, the court noted that in the case of Bagram "there is no indication of any intent to occupy the base with permanence, nor is there hostility on the part of the 'host' country." The court also relied heavily on the practical obstacles of extending the run of the writ to Bagram. The court noted that the place of detention it the case before it involved an "active theatre of war," an obstacle not present either in *Boumediene* or *Eisentrager*. For a discussion of *Boumediene* and a prediction that it was likely to present varying results depending on narrow factual distinctions, see Patrick J. Borchers, The Conflict of Laws and Boumediene v. Bush, 42 Creighton L.Rev. 1 (2009).

CHAPTER 10

PROPERTY

INTRODUCTORY NOTE

Cook, The Jurisdiction of Sovereign States and The Conflict of Laws, 31 Colum.L.Rev. 368, 381 (1931): "Since all legislation, all judicial action, creates (and destroys) the rights of persons, even though these have relation to things, there is no logical basis upon which to classify laws into those which affect persons and those which affect things."

SECTION 1. LAND*

RESTATEMENT, SECOND, CONFLICT OF LAWS:

§ 223. Validity and Effect of Conveyance of Interest in Land

(1) Whether a conveyance transfers an interest in land and the nature of the interest transferred are determined by the law that would be applied by the courts of the situs.

(2) These courts would usually apply their own local law in determining such questions.

Thus, the Second Conflicts Restatement refers almost[1] every question concerning land, whether arising from inter vivos transactions or on testate or intestate succession, to the whole law of the situs of the realty, including the conflicts rules of the situs. This is not a typical choice-of-law rule, for it provides no guidance to a court at the situs, except to state that situs courts "would usually apply their own local law in determining such questions." See § 223(2), supra.

The Second Restatement bases its adherence to the traditional situs rule on "principles looking to further the needs of the interstate and international systems, application of the law of the state of dominant interest, protection of justified expectations, certainty, predictability and uniformity of result and ease in the determination and application of the law to be applied." Id. § 223, cmt a. A fair question is if none of the parties to the transaction is domiciled or headquartered at the situs, what policy of the situs is furthered by application of its law to determine the interest of those parties in the land? Perhaps one of the parties will rely on situs law for some purpose, such as the method of foreclosing a mortgage on the land. Title searchers will rely on records at the situs and interpret

---

* See Restatement, Second, Conflict of Laws §§ 223–43.

1 Construction of an instrument of conveyance is "in accordance with the rules of construction of the state designated for this purpose in the instrument." Restatement, Second § 224(1). "A will insofar as it devises an interest in land is construed in accordance with the rules of construction of the state designated for this purpose in the will." Id. § 240(1).

these records under situs law. Are these reasons sufficient for application of situs law when none of the parties has relied on that law and the interests of innocent third parties are not affected? Can the title search problem be resolved by requiring a party whose interest in the land is determined by the law of a jurisdiction other than the situs, to record that determination in records at the situs or lose protection against innocent parties who rely on situs records and law? In how many of the cases in this section is the application of situs law justified by any of the reasons listed in the Restatement?

See Hay, The Situs Rule in European and American Conflicts Law—Comparative Notes, in Hay & Hoeflich, eds., Property Law & Legal Education 109 (1988). For an extensive criticism of the rule that the law of the situs should be applied to determine questions involving transfers of interests in land, see Weintraub, Commentary on the Conflict of Laws 542–46 (5th ed.2006); see also Note, Modernizing the Situs Rule for Real Property Conflicts, 65 Tex.L.Rev. 585 (1987).

Whatever might be said in favor of modification of the situs rule, however, it retains a powerful hold. Even in those states that have departed from territorial choice-of-law rules in other areas, only a few have rejected the situs rule for realty. For example, Cheever v. Graves, 592 N.E.2d 758 (Mass.App.1992), involved a dispute over a purported beach access easement in a residential subdivision on the Massachusetts-Connecticut border. The situs of the disputed easement was in Massachusetts although some of those claiming a right of way owned Connecticut plots. The court upheld application of Massachusetts law and offered the following rationale: "We have said that '[t]he most important interest of the situs in land transactions is the protection of bona fide purchasers or other persons who must rely on record title. Additionally it is desirable for purposes of convenience that a purchaser and his title searchers need consult only the law of one jurisdiction.'" 592 N.E.2d at 764 (quoting Rudow v. Fogel, 12 Mass.App.Ct. 430, 436 (1981)). Moreover, law-and-economics scholarship has now focused on choice of law and defends the situs rule as preserving certainty of title, which makes land more valuable. See O'Hara & Ribstein, From Politics to Efficiency in Choice of Law, 67 U.Chi.L.Rev. 1151, 1220 (2000). Is this argument cogent in light of the comments in preceding paragraph?

A. SUCCESSION ON DEATH

In re Estate of Barrie

Supreme Court of Iowa, 1949.
240 Iowa 431, 35 N.W.2d 658.

■ HAYS, J.—Appeal from an order overruling a motion to strike objections to petition for probate of the alleged last will and testament of Mary E. Barrie, deceased.

Mary E. Barrie, domiciled in Whiteside County, Illinois, died owning real and personal property in Illinois and real property in Tama County, Iowa. The instrument in question was offered for probate in Whiteside County, Illinois. Although first admitted to probate, it was later denied probate after the Illinois Supreme Court had ruled that said instrument had been revoked by cancellation and that decedent died intestate.

Thereafter the instrument was offered for probate in Tama County, Iowa, by one of the beneficiaries named therein. To the petition for probate, decedent's heirs at law filed objections based upon the judgment of the Illinois Supreme Court, to the effect that the said last will and testament had been revoked. Objectors assert that this judgment is conclusive upon the Iowa courts. Proponent's motion to strike said objections for the reason that they do not constitute a valid basis for denying probate, being overruled by the trial court, this appeal was taken.

The instrument offered for probate was duly signed by decedent and witnessed by two witnesses. . . . When found, after the death of decedent, the instrument had the word "void" written across its face in at least five places, including the attestation clause. Also, upon the cover and upon the envelope containing same appears the word "void" written with the name "M. E. Barrie" and "Mary E. Barrie." The Illinois court found that the writing of the word "void" on the instrument, as above related, constituted a revocation by cancellation within the purview of the Illinois Revised Statutes, 1945, chapter 3, section 197. This statute provides for the revocation of a will ". . . (a) by burning, cancelling, tearing, or obliterating it by the testator."

No question is raised as to the due execution of the instrument either under the Illinois or the Iowa statutes. No question is raised as to the testamentary capacity of decedent, nor is it claimed by the objectors that there has been a revocation under the Iowa statute, section 633.10, Code of 1946. The question before this court for determination may be stated thus, "Is the judgment of the Illinois court, holding that said instrument had been revoked and that decedent died intestate, conclusive and binding upon the Iowa courts?" . . .

Decedent was a nonresident of the state and died owning property in Tama county which was subject to administration. Clearly the district court of Tama county has original jurisdiction to probate this instrument unless the Illinois judgment has the effect of nullifying or modifying said statute. . . . That this is in accordance with the recognized rule, see Restatement of the Law, Conflict of Laws, section 469, which states: "The will of a deceased person can be admitted to probate in a competent court of any state in which an administrator could have been appointed had the decedent died intestate", and under comment c of said provision: "Probate in a state other than at the domicil can be had although the will has not been admitted to probate in the state of the decedent's domicil."

. . .

Section 633.33, Code of 1946, provides: "A will probated in any other state or country shall be admitted to probate in this state, without the notice required in the case of domestic wills, on the production of a copy thereof and of the original record of probate."

Upon the general question as to the validity, operation, effect, etc. of a will by which property is devised, there are certain well-established and generally recognized rules, and which definitely differentiate between movable (personal) and immovable (real) property. We are only concerned with immovables in the instant case.

The general rule as stated in Story on Conflict of Laws, Eighth Ed., page 651, is, "the doctrine is clearly established at the common law, that the law of the place where the property [speaking of real (immovable) property] is locally situate is to govern as to the capacity or the incapacity of the testator . . . the forms and solemnities to give the will or testament its due attestation and effect." . . . Restatement of the Law, Conflict of Laws, section 249, states: "The validity and effect of a will of an interest in land are determined by the law of the state where the land is." Upon the specific question as to revocation of a will, . . . Restatement of the Law, Conflict of Laws, section 250, says: "The effectiveness of an intended revocation of a will of an interest in land is determined by the law of the state where the land is." . . .

Under the above-stated rule Iowa courts are free to place their construction, interpretation and sanction upon the will of a nonresident of the state who dies owning real property within the state whether the will be admitted to probate under section 604.3 or section 633.33, Code of 1946, both supra, although it has been admitted to probate in the state of the domicile of testator. . . .

Does a different rule pertain where instead of being admitted to probate in the domicile state probate is denied? We think not. It is generally held that the full faith and credit provision of the Constitution of the United States, Article IV, section 1, does not render foreign decrees of probate conclusive as to the validity of a will as respects real property situated in a state other than the one in which the decree was rendered, nor does the doctrine of res adjudicata or estoppel by judgment apply. . . .

. . . To hold that an act which constitutes a revocation in one state is a revocation in another state where under the law the act does not constitute a revocation is contrary to the general rule, which is stated in 57 Am.Jur., Wills, section 493, to be, "where a statute prescribes the method and acts by which a will may be revoked, no acts other than those mentioned in the statute are to operate as a revocation, no matter how clearly appears the purpose of the testator to revoke his will and his belief that such purpose has been accomplished." . . . That the acts held to be a revocation in Illinois do not constitute such in Iowa, see section 633.10, Code of 1946. . . .

Section 633.49, Code of 1946 provides:

"A last will and testament executed without this state, in the mode prescribed by the law either of the place where executed or of the testator's domicile, shall be deemed to be legally executed, and shall be of the same force and effect as if executed in the mode prescribed by the laws of this state, provided said last will and testament is in writing and subscribed by the testator."

This statute has not been before this court, so far as the writer of this opinion can find. It is clearly a modification of the common law and should not be extended to include matters not clearly included therein. It specifically deals with the formalities in the execution of the will, and nothing more. No question of execution is here involved. That the legislature might have waived the common-law rule as applicable to revocations as well as to the formal execution, as it has done, cannot be denied. However, the legislature has not seen fit to do so. . . . The statute is not applicable.

We hold that the Illinois judgment denying probate to the will in question is not conclusive and binding upon the courts of this state in so far as the disposition of the Iowa real estate is concerned; that the objections filed to the petition do not constitute a basis for denying probate of the will and the appellant's motion to strike should have been sustained. Reversed and remanded for an order in accordance herewith.—Reversed and remanded.

■ SMITH, J. (dissenting)

It is true of course that Code section 633.49 refers to execution and not directly to revocation; and we have here a document, held in Illinois to be nontestamentary, because of revocation and not because of any defect in original execution. In other words, we have an instrument not merely "executed" but also revoked "without this state, in the mode prescribed by the law . . . of the testator's domicile."

But revocation is merely the converse of execution. The power to execute implies the power to revoke. A will can no longer be said to be executed after it has been revoked. Whether an instrument is a will is determined not only by the manner of its execution but also by the manner of its attempted revocation. Both acts are a part of the testamentary process. It is unthinkable that our legislature intended to require recognition of the laws of another jurisdiction in the matter of one and not of the other.

The purpose of both Code sections 633.33 and 633.49 must have been to abolish or minimize confusion and conflict between states in the matter of handling wills. Foreign ownership of property has become common. Owners of property in different jurisdictions should not be required in making and revoking their wills to do more than comply with the law of their own domiciles, or with the law of the jurisdiction where the instrument is drawn or revoked. . . .

The fundamental error in the majority opinion is in assuming that the validity of an instrument offered as a foreign will is to be determined by the same standard that would determine its status if offered as a domestic will. But the Iowa statutes establish a different standard without any differentiation between real and personal property. The lex loci rei sitae is in that respect changed. Code section 633.49 is just as effective in its field as are our general statutes prescribing the forms and solemnities for the execution and revocation of domestic wills.

NOTES

1.   Does the decision protect the reasonable expectations of the testatrix? Suppose that the Illinois decision had exercised in personam jurisdiction over persons before it in order to determine their interests in the Iowa land. Would the Iowa court have had to give this decision full faith and credit insofar as the interests of these persons were concerned? See p. 331, supra.

2.   Statutes in most states provide for alternative places of reference to determine whether a will has been executed in proper form. In the majority of these states a will executed elsewhere, when in writing and subscribed by the testator, is legally effective if executed in the mode prescribed by the law of the forum, or by the law of the place of execution or by the law of the testator's domicile. There are differences among the states as to whether the reference is to the testator's domicile at the time of execution of the will or at the time of death. See, for example, Uniform Probate Code § 2–506 (domicile at time of execution of the will or at time of death). See also Rees, American Wills Statutes: II, 46 Va.L.Rev. 856, 905 (1960).

A liberal provision, recognizing numerous places of alternative reference to determine issues of testamentary formalities, is The English Wills Act 1963, 11 & 12 Eliz. 2, chapter 44. This provision is based upon the Hague Convention of 1960, reprinted in 9 Am.J.Comp.L. 705 (1960).

3.   In Baker v. General Motors, 522 U.S. 222, 235, 118 S.Ct. 657 (1998), the Supreme Court said: "[A] sister State's decree concerning land ownership in another State has been held ineffective to transfer title [citing Fall v. Eastin, p. 328, supra], although such a decree may indeed preclusively adjudicate the rights and obligations running between the parties to the foreign litigation. . . ." Does this summary support the majority's position or the dissent's position?

4.   In re Estate of Hannan, 523 N.W.2d 672 (Neb.1994): Before his death, James Hannan adopted Glover, his wife's daughter from a previous marriage. First James and then his mother died. His mother's will left her estate to her surviving children and to the "issue" of her deceased children. Her will was probated in a court of her domicile at death, Virginia. The Virginia court held that "issue" did not include adopted children. In ancillary probate proceedings of real estate in Nebraska, the court held that Nebraska law applied to determine the construction of the will as it affected Nebraska

real estate. Under Nebraska law "issue" includes adopted children and Glover was awarded 20 percent of the proceeds of the sale of the Nebraska land. The court rejected the argument that the testatrix had relied on Virginia law in drafting her will and stated: "Although Nebraska does grant reciprocal recognition to the final orders of other states as to the validity or construction of a will..., Virginia has no such reciprocal statutory provision. In fact, Virginia has indicated that its policy is to apply its own law to the devise of teal property located in Virginia."

UNIFORM PROBATE CODE, 8 U.L.A. § 2–703:

The meaning and legal effect of a governing instrument is determined by the local law of the state selected in the instrument unless the application of that law is contrary to ... any ... public policy of this State otherwise applicable to the disposition.

Comment:

... [T]his section ... enables the law of a particular state to be selected in the governing instrument for purposes of interpreting the instrument without regard to the location of property covered thereby. So long as local public policy is accommodated, the section should be accepted as necessary and desirable.

NOTE ON INTERNATIONAL SUCCESSION PROBLEMS

In re Estate of Barrie is an example of the traditional American approach and that of most common law countries to the substantive law applicable to succession as well as to the formalities required for a valid testamentary disposition. For both purposes, as well as for jurisdiction, American law distinguished between the movable and immovable assets of the estate. The former is governed by the law of the decedent's domicile at death, the latter by the law of the situs. *Barrie* shows the difficulties than can result when different kinds of property are in different states. Things may be more complicated still when the succession case involves foreign country law, for instance when an American citizen dies domiciled in a civil law country, leaving personal and immovable property both there and in the United States (and perhaps in a third country) or the same in reverse (a foreign national dies domiciled in the United States, leaving property in several countries).

There are two main problems: many non-common law countries view the decedent's estate as a unit, i.e. they do not distinguish between movable and immovable property. Traditionally, they also provided that the applicable law was that of the decedent's nationality (citizenship). More recent statutes now refer to the law of domicile at death. See., e.g., Israeli Succession Law (1965) § 137; Swiss Federal Statute on International Private Law (1987) §§ 86(1), 90. By viewing the estate as a unit, a country where the decedent was domiciled may therefore apply its law to the succession to immovables in other countries. Would a court

like the Iowa court in *Barrie's Estate* accept the disposition decreed by
the foreign court? Swiss law recognizes this problem and provides that if
a foreign state claims exclusive jurisdiction over local immovables, then
that property is excluded from Swiss administration of the estate. Supra
§ 86(2). It thus introduces a limited common law-type bifurcated
approach.

The most far-reaching new foreign law dealing with international
succession cases is the law of the European Union, Regulation (EU) No.
650/2012, [2012] Official Journal L 201/107, in force since August 2015
in twenty-five of the current twenty-seven EU members (Denmark and
Ireland having opted out). The Regulation (statute) retains the civil law
unitary approach to the decedent's estate. It provides for jurisdiction over
the entire estate and the application of the law of the EU state in which
the decedent was "habitually resident" at death. Arts. 1, 21(1). This
replaced the reference to the decedent's nationality in many EU countries
(e.g., Austria, Germany, Netherlands). If the decedent was not habitually
resident in an EU state, but left property in one, the court of that state
may still exercise jurisdiction over the whole estate if the decedent had
been a citizen or had been habitually resident there within the last five
years. Art. 10(1). If these conditions are not met, the court may exercise
jurisdiction only over the local assets, i.e. follow the common law
approach. The local court shall also abstain from the unitary approach
when it appears that the state or country in which an asset is located
would not recognize its decision: in such a case, the court is to exclude
those assets from its proceeding. Art. 12(1). This provision is of course
highly relevant if a decedent whose estate otherwise falls under the EU
Regulation (and the jurisdiction of an EU member state court) leaves real
property in the United States. Under our situs law approach, the
American situs court might not accept the EU court's decision; the latter
court should therefore not even deal with it.

As to the applicable law, the Regulation adopts one modern
American provision and points to a future development with another: the
applicable law (decedent's habitual residence, supra art. 21(1)) may be
disregarded by the court in favor of another "more closely connected" law,
Art. 21(2). Also, the decedent, in a testamentary disposition, may make
a choice of the applicable law, although the choice is limited to the law of
the decedent's nationality (Art. 22).

Three other provisions of the EU law are also of interest. (1) Art. 27
has detailed provisions as to the law applicable to the scope and validity
of a testamentary disposition. These provisions include several
applicable law possibilities, all designed to effectuate the will of the
decedent. Art. 27(2) provides that the same provisions shall apply to
modifications and revocations. *In re Barrie* would have come out
differently under this Article. (2) While most provisions are framed as
applicable to testamentary dispositions, Art. 24 provides that everything
also applies to intestate succession. (3) Art. 34 provides for a limited use

of *renvoi*, i.e. considering and possibly following another state's conflicts law. The Article provides that the local court should accept a reference back to its own law when the other state's conflicts law so provides and should even follow the other state's reference to a third state, but only if that state would then apply its own law.

One Convention of the Hague Conference has achieved substantial support. Forty-two countries, including most of the states of the European Union as well, as the United Kingdom, but not the United States, have ratified the Convention on the Conflict of Laws Relating to the Form of Testamentary Dispositions of 1961, in force since October 1964. Like the European Union Regulation, the Convention lists several ways in which a testamentary disposition shall be regarded as having been validly executed. Its Art. 2 provides that these alternate references also apply to revocations. For European Union members the Convention thus parallels the Regulation described above.

Another Hague Convention—on the Law Applicable to Decedents' Estates—was proposed in 1989 but has gained only one ratification (The Netherlands) and is therefore not in force. The European Union Regulation, above, achieves for its member states what this Convention sought to attain on a worldwide basis.

Bibliographical references: Marongui Buonaiuti, The European Succession Convention and Third Country Courts, 12 J. Private Int'l L. 545 (2016); Pfeiffer, Legal Certainty and Predictability in International Succession Law, 12 J.Priv.Int'l L. 566 (2016); S.I. Strong, The European Succession Regulation and the Arbitration of Trust Disputes, 103 Iowa L.Rev. 2205, 2010 et seq. (2017–18); Zalucki, Attempts to Harmonize the Inheritance Law in Europe: Past, Present, Future, 103 Iowa L.Rev. 2317 (2017–18).

In re Schneider's Estate

Surrogate's Court of New York, New York County, 1950.
198 Misc. 1017, 96 N.Y.S.2d 652.

■ FRANKENTHALER, SURROGATE. This case presents a novel question in this State in the realm of the conflict of laws. Deceased, a naturalized American citizen of Swiss origin, died domiciled in New York County, leaving as an asset of his estate certain real property located in Switzerland. In his will he attempted to dispose of his property, including the parcel of Swiss realty, in a manner which is said to be contrary to the provisions of Swiss internal law. That law confers upon one's legitimate heirs a so-called legitime, i.e., a right to specified fractions of a decedent's property, which right cannot be divested by testamentary act. The precise issue, therefore, is whether this deceased had the power to dispose of the realty in the manner here attempted.

Ordinarily, the courts of a country not the situs of an immovable are without jurisdiction to adjudicate questions pertaining to the ownership of that property. . . . However, in this case the administratrix appointed prior to the probate of the will has liquidated the foreign realty and transmitted the proceeds to this State. She is now accounting for the assets of the estate including the fund representing that realty. As a consequence this court is called upon to direct the administration and distribution of the substituted fund and to determine the property rights therein. . . . In doing so, however, reference must be made to the law of the situs, as the question of whether the fund shall be distributed to the devisee of the realty under the terms of the will is dependent upon the validity of the original devise thereof. . . .

The court is confronted at the outset with a preliminary question as to the meaning of the term "law of the situs"—whether it means only the internal or municipal law of the country in which the property is situated or whether it also includes the conflict of laws rules to which the courts of that jurisdiction would resort in making the same determination. If the latter is the proper construction to be placed upon that term, then this court must, in effect, place itself in the position of the foreign court and decide the matter as would that court in an identical case.

The meaning of the term "law of the situs" can be ascertained best from a consideration of the reasons underlying the existence of the rule which requires the application thereof. The primary reason for its existence lies in the fact that the law-making and law-enforcing agencies of the country in which land is situated have exclusive control over such land. . . . As only the courts of that country are ultimately capable of rendering enforceable judgments affecting the land, the legislative authorities thereof have the exclusive power to promulgate the law which shall regulate its ownership and transfer. . . .

Hence, the rights which were created in that land are those which existed under the whole law of the situs and as would be enforced by those courts which normally would possess exclusive judicial jurisdiction. Griswold, Renvoi Revisited, 51 Harv. L.R. 1165, 1186. . . . The purely fortuitous transfer of the problem to the courts of another state by virtue of a postmortuary conversion of the land, effected for the purpose of administering the entire estate in the country of domicile, ought not to alter the character of the legal relations which existed with respect to the land at the date of death and which continued to exist until its sale. Consequently, this court in making a determination of ownership, must ascertain the body of local law to which the courts of the situs would refer if the matter were brought before them.

It has been urged, however, that a reference to the conflict of laws rules of the situs may involve an application of the principle of renvoi, and if so it would place the court in a perpetually-enclosed circle from which it could never emerge and that it would never find a suitable body of substantive rules to apply to the particular case. . . . This objection is based upon the assumption that if the forum must look to the whole law of the situs, and that law refers the matter to the law of the domicile, this latter reference must be considered to be the whole law of the latter country also, which would refer the matter back to the law of the situs, which process would continue without end. That reasoning is based upon a false premise, for as has been said by Dean Griswold, Renvoi Revisited, op. cit. supra, p. 1190: "Recognition of the foreign conflict of laws rule will not lead us into an endless chain of references if it is clear for any reason that the particular foreign conflicts rule (or any rule along the line of reference) is one which refers to the internal law alone. . . ." . . .

The precise question here considered, namely whether there shall be a reference to the entire law of the situs to determine the ownership of the proceeds of foreign realty, is one of first impression in this State. Nevertheless, the above stated principles, together with the rule enunciated in the Restatement of the Conflict of Laws, in the English authorities on the subject and in analogous cases in courts of this State and others, require us to accept it as a part of our law and to hold that a reference to the law of the situs necessarily entails a reference to the whole law of that country, including its conflict of laws rule.

The rule as formulated in the Restatement is as follows: "Section 8. Rule in questions of title to land or divorce. (1) All questions of title to land are decided in accordance with the law of the state where the land is, including the Conflict of Laws rules of that State. (2) All questions concerning the validity of a decree of divorce are decided in accordance with the law of the domicile of the parties, including the Conflict of Laws rules of that State." In all other cases the Restatement rejects the renvoi principle and provides that where a reference is made to foreign law that law should be held to mean only the internal law of the foreign country. Section 7. . . .

The decisions in this State also indicate the applicability of the doctrine of renvoi in this field. In the early case of Dupuy v. Wurtz, 53 N.Y. 556, which involved personal property, there appears the first reference to the doctrine. The Court there said by way of dictum, 53 N.Y. at page 573: "[W]hen we speak of the law of domicile as applied to the law of succession, we mean not the general law, but the law which the country of the domicile applies to the particular case under consideration. . . ."

The implications of that dictum were disregarded in the celebrated Matter of [Tallmadge], Surr.Ct., New York County, 109 Misc. 696, 181 N.Y.S. 336 per Winthrop, R., where the Referee, rejecting the *renvoi* principle completely, asserted that it "is no part of New York law."

The broad assertion in Matter of [Tallmadge], supra, that the renvoi principle is not applicable in New York is not in accord with the earlier or later cases. The precise limits of its applicability are as yet undefined. . . .

Thus it is now necessary to ascertain the whole of the applicable Swiss law and apply it to this case. . . .

Concerning the actual content of Swiss law, the expert witnesses summoned by the respective parties are in agreement that the Swiss internal law would apply to the real and personal estate of a Swiss citizen domiciled in Switzerland, and that the laws of the country of domicile would, under the Swiss theory of unity of succession, apply to all of the Swiss property belonging to a foreign national.

The experts disagreed, however, upon the ultimate question in the case, i.e., the Swiss rule applicable to the distribution of the Swiss realty of a person of hybrid nationality domiciled not in Switzerland but in the country of his second citizenship. Under Swiss law the decedent herein was vested with dual nationality. The law of that country provides that a citizen, in order to divest himself of the cloak of citizenship must formally renounce his allegiance in the matter prescribed by statute. Such formal act of renunciation was not performed by decedent. . . .

The court has carefully examined the authorities and materials submitted by the experts and has formed its conclusion upon the basis of those authorities. . . .

The language in the Swiss cases . . . indicated that the place in which "property is situated" . . . means, in the case of foreign domiciliaries, the country of domicile, upon the Swiss legal fiction that a decedent's entire estate follows his person and is located at his domicile. Such a rule amounts to a statement that the place of the actual location of property (Switzerland) refers all questions to the law of the place of presumed location, i.e., the country of domicile. The Swiss courts treat the reference to its own as a reference to its own conflict of law rules and policies concerning the devolution of estates of foreigners.

In the case of one who is of both Swiss and American nationality, but who is not a Swiss domiciliary, it appears that the same rule applies; domicile is controlling and its laws provide the substantive rules of decision. . . . [I]n [Matter of Wohlwend (9 B.E. 507) the [Swiss] court was of the opinion that in the case of a hybrid citizen, the place of domicile is controlling in determining the proper jurisdiction and the applicable law. . . .]

Consequently, the court holds that the testamentary plan envisaged by the testator and set out in his will is valid, even in its application to the Swiss realty. The proceeds of that realty must therefore be distributed pursuant to the directions contained in the will. . . .

Submit, on notice, decree settling the account accordingly.[2]

---

[2]   There is a subsequent opinion, further discussing the Swiss law, in In re Schneider's Estate, 198 Misc. 1017, 100 N.Y.S.2d 371 (1950). The decision has been criticized on the ground the Surrogate misunderstood the Swiss law. See Falconbridge, The Renvoi in New York and Elsewhere, 6 Vand.L.Rev. 708, 725–31 (1953) —eds.

NOTE

If Switzerland would have applied its own law, would the decision of the court have been different? Is deference to the whole law of Switzerland, including its choice-of-law rules, more desirable because Switzerland is a foreign country and not a sister state? Should the New York court have determined whether a Swiss court, as a matter of comity, would recognize the New York court's determination of interests in Swiss land? Is the result, in any event, better than if the court had not referred to the Swiss conflicts rules?

B. SECURITY TRANSACTIONS

Swank v. Hufnagle

Supreme Court of Judicature of Indiana, 1887.
111 Ind. 453, 12 N.E. 303.

■ ELLIOTT, J. The appellant sued the appellee, Melissa Hufnagle, and her husband, upon a note and mortgage executed in Darke county, Ohio, on land situate in this State. The appellee, Melissa Hufnagle, answered that she was a married woman, and that the mortgage was executed by her as the surety of her husband, and assumed to convey land in this State owned by her. The appellant replied that the contract was made in Ohio, and that by a statute of that State a married woman had power to execute such a mortgage, but the statute of Ohio is not set forth.

The trial court did right in adjudging the reply bad. The validity of the mortgage of real property is to be determined by the law of the place where the property is situated. . . .

Under the act of 1881 a mortgage executed by a married woman as surety on land owned by her in this State is void. . . .

Judgment affirmed.

NOTES

1.　In Thomson v. Kyle, 23 So. 12 (Fla.1897), the defendant, a married woman, had executed in Alabama a promissory note together with her husband, and also had given a mortgage on Florida land. The note and mortgage were executed by her to secure a debt of the husband. The court enforced the mortgage against the Florida land, even though the note was void as to the defendant under the law of Alabama. "Notwithstanding Mrs. Thomson's incapacity by the laws of Alabama to execute the mortgage sought to be foreclosed here, she was capable under our laws of executing in Alabama, a mortgage upon her separate statutory real property in this State to secure her husband's debt."

2.　In Burr v. Beckler, 106 N.E. 206 (Ill.1914), a married woman domiciled in Illinois, executed and delivered in Florida a note and as security therefor a trust deed to Illinois land. Although the note would have been good if executed and delivered in Illinois, the court held that the note was void since the woman lacked capacity under Florida law. The court held that since the note was void, "the trust deed, which was incidental and intended to secure a performance of the obligation created by the note, could not be enforced." The *Burr* case is discussed in University of Chicago v. Dater, note 4, p. 566, supra.

PROCTOR V. FROST, 197 A. 813 (N.H.1938): A married woman executed and delivered at her home in Massachusetts a mortgage on New Hampshire land to secure her husband's debt. The mortgage was enforceable under Massachusetts law, but a New Hampshire statute provided, "No contract or conveyance by a married woman, as surety or guarantor for her husband . . . shall be binding on her . . ." The court held that the effect of the mortgage was to be determined by New Hampshire law, but that the statute was not meant to apply to mortgages executed outside of New Hampshire. The court stated that New Hampshire had no power to regulate contracts executed elsewhere and that "The primary purpose of the statute . . . was not to regulate the transfer of New Hampshire real estate, but to protect married women in New Hampshire. . . ."

KEY BANK OF ALASKA V. DONNELS, 787 P.2d 382 (Nev.1990). A Nevada corporation borrowed money from an Alaska bank. The note was secured by a deed of trust on Nevada real estate and guaranteed by defendant, the president of the Nevada corporation. The note and guarantee contained provisions choosing Alaska law, but the deed of trust referred to Nevada foreclosure procedures. When the corporate borrower defaulted, the bank sold the Nevada property pursuant to the terms of the deed of trust, effecting a non-judicial foreclosure. The bank then sued the guarantor in Nevada to recover a deficiency between the proceeds of the sale and the loan. The guarantor defended on the ground that under Alaska law there was no right to a deficiency judgment after a non-judicial foreclosure. Nevada law would permit the deficiency judgment. Held: for the bank. Alaska law applied pursuant to the choice-of-law clauses in the note and mortgage, but the Alaska statute precluding a deficiency judgment only applied to foreclosures in Alaska. The Alaska statute provided: "When a sale is made by a trustee under a deed of trust, as authorized by AS 34.20.070–34.20.130, [a deficiency judgment is precluded]." The court stated: "we read the offsetting commas as indicating a clear intent to limit the effect of the statute to foreclosures under those sections, especially because AS 34.20.070 refers to deed of trust conveyances of property located in Alaska. Furthermore, because anti-deficiency statutes derogate from the common law, they should be narrowly construed."

NOTE

In the light of Proctor v. Frost, the decision in Thomson v. Kyle is easier to justify than the decision in Swank v. Hufnagle. Why? Should it have made a difference in Thomson v. Kyle that all of the parties were domiciled in Alabama? Cf. Resolution Trust Corp. v. Northpark Joint Venture, 958 F.2d 1313 (5th Cir.1992), cert. denied, 506 U.S. 1048, 116 S.Ct. 963 (1993), in which a loan by a Texas lender to a Texas joint venture was guaranteed by Texans and secured by a deed of trust on Mississippi land. The loan was not repaid. The lender foreclosed by selling the Mississippi land, but did not recover the full amount of the loan. Under Texas law, the lender was entitled to summary judgment against the guarantors for the deficiency. Under Mississippi law, the lender had the burden of proving that the foreclosure sale was conducted in such a manner that a deficiency judgment would be equitable. Held: Texas law applied and the lender was entitled to summary judgment. "Texas has a direct interest in ensuring that Texas debts are handled properly and that Texas debtors and creditors are treated fairly. By contrast, Mississippi has little interest in this case. In enacting their guaranty laws, Mississippi legislators and judges intended to protect Mississippi citizens. There is no reason why Mississippi would have an interest in the application of its laws to resolve the claims of foreign creditors against foreign debtors." 958 F.2d at 1319.

C. CONVEYANCES AND CONTRACTS

SMITH V. INGRAM, 40 S.E. 984 (N.C.1902): In 1878, the plaintiff, who was then a married woman, sold land located in North Carolina for the sum of $130. Thereafter, the town of Star was built on the land and its value increased to at least $40,000. In this action, the plaintiff claimed the right to recover the land from its present owners on the ground that her deed to the original purchaser was void under North Carolina law since she had not been given a "privy examination", as required by North Carolina law, to ascertain whether she was selling the land of her own free will. No such privy examination was required by the law of South Carolina where the plaintiff was at all times domiciled. The court held, nevertheless, for the plaintiff because the validity of a conveyance of an interest in land is determined by the law of the situs. In denying a petition for rehearing (44 S.E. 643 (N.C.1903)), the court left open the possibility that the dispossessed bona fide purchasers might have an equitable remedy for the value of the improvements.

NOTE

The law of the situs is commonly said to determine the validity and effect of a conveyance of an interest in land including the question of formalities and of the capacity of the respective parties to convey and to receive title. Restatement, Second, Conflict of Laws § 223.

Polson v. Stewart

Supreme Judicial Court of Massachusetts, 1897.
167 Mass. 211, 45 N.E. 737, 36 L.R.A. 771, 57 Am.St.Rep. 452.

Bill in Equity, filed June 6, 1895, to enforce specific performance of a covenant executed by the defendant to his wife, Kitty T.P. Stewart, who died on December 26, 1893, intestate, and of whose estate the plaintiff, who was her brother, was appointed administrator, he having also acquired the rights of the other heirs in her estate. . . .

The defendant demurred to the bill, assigning several grounds therefor. Hearing before Knowlton, J., who, at the request of the parties, reserved the case upon the bill and demurrer for the consideration of the full court.

■ HOLMES, J. This is a bill to enforce a covenant made by the defendant to his wife, the plaintiff's intestate, in North Carolina, to surrender all his marital rights in certain land of hers. The land is in Massachusetts. The parties to the covenant were domiciled in North Carolina. According to the bill, the wife took steps which under the North Carolina statutes gave her the right to contract as a feme sole with her husband as well as with others, and afterwards released her dower in the defendant's lands. In consideration of this release, and to induce his wife to forbear suing for divorce, for which she had just cause, and for other adequate considerations, the defendant executed the covenant. The defendant demurs. . . .

But it is said that the laws of the parties' domicil could not authorize a contract between them as to lands in Massachusetts. Obviously this is not true. It is true that the laws of other States cannot render valid conveyances of property within our borders which our laws say are void, for the plain reason that we have exclusive power over the res. . . . But the same reason inverted establishes that the lex rei sitae cannot control personal covenants, not purporting to be conveyances, between persons outside the jurisdiction, although concerning a thing within it. Whatever the covenant, the laws of North Carolina could subject the defendant's property to seizure on execution, and his person to imprisonment, for a failure to perform it. Therefore, on principle, the law of North Carolina determines the validity of the contract. Such precedents as there are, are on the same side. . . . Lord Cottenham stated and enforced the rule in the clearest way in Ex parte Pollard, 4 Deac. 27, 40 et seq.; S.C. Mont. & Ch. 239, 250. . . .

If valid by the law of North Carolina there is no reason why the contract should not be enforced here. The general principle is familiar. Without considering the argument addressed to us that such a contract would have been good in equity if made here . . . we see no ground of policy for an exception. The statutory limits which have been found to the power of a wife to release dower . . . do not prevent a husband from making a valid covenant that he will not claim marital rights with any person competent to receive a covenant from him. . . . The competency of the wife to receive the covenant is established by the law of her domicil and of the place of the contract. The laws of Massachusetts do not make it impossible for him specifically to perform his undertaking. He can give a release which will be good by Massachusetts law. If it be said that the rights of the administrator are only derivative from the wife, we agree, and we do not for a moment regard anyone as privy to the contract except as representing the wife. But if then it be asked whether she could have enforced the contract during her life, an answer in the affirmative is made easy by considering exactly what the defendant undertook to do. So far as occurs to us, he undertook three things: first, not to disturb his wife's enjoyment while she kept her property; secondly, to execute whatever instrument was necessary in order to release his rights if she conveyed; and thirdly, to claim no rights on her death, but to do whatever was necessary to clear the title from such rights then. All these things were as capable of performance in Massachusetts as they would have been in North Carolina. Indeed, all the purposes of the covenant could have been secured at once in the lifetime of the wife by a joint conveyance of the property to a trustee upon trusts properly limited. It will be seen that the case does not raise the question as to what the common law and the presumed law of North Carolina would be as to a North Carolina contract calling for acts in Massachusetts, or concerning property in Massachusetts, which could not be done consistently with Massachusetts law. . . .

Demurrer overruled.

■ FIELD, C.J. I cannot assent to the opinion of a majority of the court. . . . By our law husband and wife are under a general disability or incapacity to make contracts with each other. . . . It seems to me illogical to say that we will not permit a conveyance of Massachusetts land directly between husband and wife, wherever they may have their domicil, and yet say that they may make a contract to convey such land from one to the other which our courts will specifically enforce. It is possible to abandon the rule of lex rei sitae, but to keep it for conveyances of land and to abandon it for contracts to convey land seems to me unwarrantable. . . .

It is only on the ground that the contract conveyed an equitable title that the plaintiff as heir has any standing in court. His counsel founds his argument on the distinction between a conveyance of the legal title to land and a contract to convey it. . . . On reason and authority I think it cannot be held that, although a deed between a husband and his wife, domiciled in North Carolina, of the rights of each in the lands of the other in Massachusetts, is void as a conveyance by reason of the incapacity of the parties under the law of Massachusetts to make and receive such a conveyance to and from each other, yet, if there are covenants in the deed to make a good title, the covenants can be specifically enforced by our courts, and a conveyance compelled, which, if voluntarily made between the parties, would be void.

. . . Whatever may be true of contracts between husband and wife made in or when they are domiciled in other jurisdictions, so far as personal property or personal liability is concerned, I think that contracts affecting the title to real property situate within the Commonwealth should be such as are authorized by our laws. I am of opinion that the bill should be dismissed.

NOTES

1.   The principal case is often cited as an example of the contract-conveyance distinction, which was sometimes used to avoid applying the law of the situs to issues affecting real property. Courts have drawn distinctions between the contract to convey and the conveyance itself (*Polson*), and between a promissory note and the mortgage securing the note (Thomson v. Kyle, Note 1, p. 847, supra and Burr v. Beckler, Note 2, p. 847, supra). The conveyance and the mortgage are analyzed as a "land" problem to which the law of the situs is applicable. The contract to convey and the promissory note are treated as a "contract" problem to be resolved by a choice-of-law rule appropriate to contracts—typically, in the old cases, the law of the place of making of the contract. The contract-conveyance distinction may, like the equitable conversion fiction (see p. 569, supra), be more likely than the situs rule to give effect to the policies of the state that will experience the consequences of the decision. In Burr v. Beckler (Note 2, p. 847, supra), however, the application of the law of the place of contracting resulted in invalidating a wife's note and the trust deed securing it, though the instruments were valid at her marital domicile, which was also the situs of the land. She executed the note while on a visit in Florida, which denied married women capacity to make the contract in issue.

2.   In Ex parte Pollard, Mont. & C. 239 (1840), relied on by Justice Holmes in the *Polson* case, a borrower had deposited with an English lender title deeds to land in Scotland and a memorandum assuming to give a lien on the land. Under the law of England, an equitable security interest was thereby created, but under the law of Scotland no such interest arose. After the borrower became insolvent, the lender claimed in the English bankruptcy proceedings that his debt should be paid out of the Scottish land in preference to the claims of general creditors. The English court found for the lender and ordered execution by the borrower in the proper Scottish form of an instrument giving the creditor the requisite security interest in the land. In the course of his opinion, the Lord Chancellor said that in cases involving foreign land the English courts "act upon their own rules" in "administering equities between parties residing here" and then continued: "Bills for specific performance of contracts for the sale of lands, or respecting mortgages of estates, in the colonies and elsewhere out of the jurisdiction of this Court, are of familiar occurrence. Why then, consistently with these principles and these authorities, should the fact, that by the law of Scotland no lien or equitable mortgage was created by the deposit and memorandum in this case, prevent the courts of this country from giving such effect to the transactions between the parties as it would have given if the land had been in England? If the contract had been to sell the lands a specific performance

would have been decreed; and why is all relief to be refused because the contract is to sell, subject to a condition for redemption?"

Is this an early example of a governmental interest analysis approach?

3.   Mallory Associates, Inc. v. Barving Realty Co., 90 N.E.2d 468 (N.Y.1949). Lessor and lessee, both of New York, there executed a lease on Virginia property. The lessee sued to recover a deposit given pursuant to the lease as security for performance. He claimed that the lessor had converted this deposit by mingling it with other funds in violation of a New York statute providing that lessees' deposits should be held in trust. The court held the statute to be applicable although the land was in another state. The court first wrote in terms reminiscent of the contract-conveyance distinction, discussed in Note 1, supra: "The provision in the lease for the deposit of security is a personal covenant between the contracting parties, creating rights in personam. . . . The question presented . . . relates solely to the rights and liabilities of the parties as a matter of contractual obligation. Accordingly, it is to be determined by the law governing the contract, even though the subject matter of the contract may be land in another State." The court then, however, focused on the purpose of the statute: "[T]he Legislature was attempting to prevent the depletion of funds deposited with the lessor. . . . The lessee, resident in this State, was the person to be protected. The need for protection is obviously no less, but rather more, when the land to which the lease relates is situated outside of this State."

4.   Estate of Lampert v. Estate of Lampert, 896 P.2d 214 (Alaska 1995) involved the validity of an attempted conveyance by one spouse of a condominium located in Hawaii. The condominium was owned by Mr. and Mrs. Lampert as tenants by the entirety. As part an overall estate plan, Mr. Lampert, an Alaska domiciliary, executed (in Alaska) a series of grant deeds to the daughter (by a previous marriage) of Mrs. Lampert. The court ruled that the law of Hawaii, as the situs of the realty, should govern the validity of the conveyance. The court stated: "We adhere to the rule that the validity of conveyances of real property are governed by the law of the situs of the property." Id. at 220. Hawaii, like most other states that recognize tenancies by the entirety, does not allow one spouse alone to convey, but the court held that the Hawaiian doctrine of quasi-estoppel ratified the transaction, as it was well known to both spouses and its validity was relied upon by the daughter.

5.   Under New York's choice-of-law approach, New York courts make the law of the situs determinative only "when an action involves real estate but does not challenge the title to, or succession or conveyance of, property, the situs of the property" and in other actions "is viewed as one in 'the spectrum of significant contacts' considered in connection with the conflict-of-law analysis." Fieger v. Pitney Bowes Credit Corp., 251 F.3d 386, 395 (2d Cir.2001).

SELOVER, BATES & CO. V. WALSH, 226 U.S. 112, 33 S.Ct. 69 (1912): Action in a state court in Minnesota for damages for breach of an executory contract for the sale by the defendant to the plaintiff's assignor

of land in Colorado. The contract was made and the installments on the
purchase price were to be paid in Minnesota. The contract provided time
was of the essence of the contract, and upon failure to make payments
punctually or to perform literally any covenant in the contract, at the
option of the vendor, the contract should be terminated, the sums paid
being forfeited. The vendee having defaulted in the payment of taxes, the
defendant elected to exercise his option and resold the land to a third
party. Plaintiff relied on a Minnesota statute which provided that a
vendor could not cancel a contract for the sale of land except upon thirty
days' written notice to the vendee, who would then have thirty days in
which to remedy the default. The Supreme Court of Minnesota, in
affirming a judgment for the plaintiff, held the Minnesota statute
applicable. The defendant, contending that the application of the statute
to this contract involving land in Colorado deprived it of its property
without due process of law, carried the case to the Supreme Court of the
United States. In overruling the defendant's contention, the Supreme
Court said: "The argument to support the contention is somewhat
confused, as it mingles with the right of contract simply a consideration
of the state's jurisdiction over the land which was the subject of the
contract. As to the contract simply, we have no doubt of the state's power
over it, and the law of the state, therefore, constituted part of it. . . .
Whether it had extraterritorial effect is another question . . . Courts, in
many ways, through action upon or constraint of the person, affect
property in other states . . . and in the case at bar the action is strictly
personal. . . . The case at bar is certainly within the principle expressed
in Polson v. Stewart. The Minnesota supreme court followed the prior
decision in Finnes v. Selover, Bates & Co., 113 N.W. 883 (Minn.1907), in
which it said that, upon repudiation of a contract by the seller of land,
two courses were open to the purchaser: 'He might stand by the contract,
and seek to recover the land, or he could declare upon a breach of the
contract, and recover the amount of his damages.' If he elected the
former, it was further said, the courts of Colorado alone could give him
relief; if he sought redress in damages, the courts of Minnesota were open
to him. And this, it was observed, was in accordance with the principle
that the law of the situs governs as to the land, and the law of contract
as to the rights of the parties in the contract."

NOTES

1.   In comparing the instant case with Polson v. Stewart, p. 850, supra,
consider the difference in the relief prayed for—in Polson v. Stewart, there
was a suit for specific performance, while in the instant case the plaintiff was
suing for damages.

2.   Kryger v. Wilson, 242 U.S. 171, 37 S.Ct. 34 (1916). By contract "made
and to be performed in Minnesota," the plaintiff agreed to sell North Dakota
land to the defendant. Upon the latter's default, plaintiff caused notice of
cancellation to be served in accordance with the requirements of North
Dakota law and then brought suit in a North Dakota court to quiet title to

the land. Defendant appeared in the action and requested the court to find that the contract was still valid and subsisting since plaintiff had not taken the action prescribed by Minnesota law to entitle a vendor to cancel a contract for the sale of land. From a decree of the North Dakota courts finding that the contract had been legally cancelled and quieting title in plaintiff, defendant appealed to the Supreme Court on the ground that he had been deprived of his property without due process of law. Held: Affirmed. "The most that the plaintiff in error can say is that the state court made a mistaken application of doctrines of the conflict of laws in deciding that the cancellation of a land contract is governed by the law of the situs instead of the place of making and performance. But that, being purely a question of local common law, is a matter with which this court is not concerned. . . ."

> "If the contract properly interpreted or the law properly applied required that this condition [the notice of cancellation] be performed in Minnesota, steps taken by him [the defendant in error] under the North Dakota statute would be ineffective. Whether or not proper proceedings had been taken to secure cancellation could be determined only by a court having jurisdiction; and the North Dakota court had jurisdiction not only over the land but through the voluntary appearance of plaintiff in error, also over him. . . . If the plaintiff in error had not submitted himself to the jurisdiction of the court, the decree could have determined only the title to the land . . . But having come into court . . . he cannot now complain if he has been concluded altogether in the premises. The plaintiff in error relies upon Selover, Bates & Co. v. Walsh, 226 U.S. 112. That was a personal action for breach of contract and not, like the present case, an action merely to determine the title to land. . . ."

BEAUCHAMP V. BERTIG, 119 S.W. 75 (Ark.1909): Action for Arkansas land. An Oklahoma court had rendered a judgment removing the disabilities of nonage of the two minor owners of the land and had specifically authorized them to sell the land. The minors had then executed in Oklahoma a deed of the land to the defendant in which they covenanted to warrant and defend the title against all lawful claims. The deed was recorded in Arkansas. Immediately after the younger had reached his majority, the two executed a deed to the plaintiff of "all their right, title and interest in and to" the land but gave no covenants of title. Plaintiff then brought the present action to determine his interest in the land. The defendant relied on the Oklahoma judgment and the deed pursuant to it.

Held for the plaintiff: "Since immovable property is fixed forever in the State where it lies, and since no other State can have any jurisdiction over it, it follows necessarily that no right, title or interest can be finally acquired therein, unless assented to by the courts of that State, in accordance with its laws." Minor on Conflict of Laws, sec. II. . . .

It has long been the rule in this State that an infant's deed conveys title to his real estate subject to his right to disaffirm when he becomes of age. . . .

But appellees argue that the covenants for title are separate contracts, creating personal obligations and therefore governed by the lex loci contractus . . . even if these covenants create obligations that would, generally speaking, be governed by the lex loci contractus, still that law would have to give way to the local policy as declared by this court.

The covenants under consideration, however, are not personal in the sense that the obligations incurred under them are governed by the law concerning movables. There are many contracts relating to real estate that are so governed. For example, covenants of seisin, of right to convey and against incumbrances, and executory contracts for deeds or other instruments containing covenants that do not run with the land. All these contracts, in the absence of statutory law or an expressed intention to the contrary, are usually governed by the law of the place where such contracts are made. Such is not the case, however, with contracts containing covenants that run with the land—as, for instance, covenants of warranty and for quiet enjoyment; or covenants that can only be performed where the land lies, as, for instance, to defend title, to pay taxes, to repair, etc. These are governed by the law of the place where the land is situated. . . .

. . . It is unnecessary to determine whether the district court of Oklahoma had jurisdiction to render judgment removing the disabilities of the Sitterdings, for it follows from what we have said that they had the right to disaffirm, even if such judgment be valid. . . .

NOTES

1.   If, because of the Oklahoma judgment, the owners could not have disaffirmed their deed in Oklahoma on reaching majority, was the Arkansas court's decision a denial of full faith and credit?

2.   Suppose that in State X, A executes and delivers to B a deed to land situated in State Y. The deed contains no express covenants and for this reason A would not be liable to B under the law of X for any defects in his title. By the law of State Y, however, the usual covenants of title would be implied by the terms of bargain and sale contained in the deed. What law governs B's right to damages against A in the event of a defective title? Should the answer depend upon whether under the law of State Y the covenants are personal to the parties or run with the land in the sense that they impose duties upon the grantor in favor of a remote grantee? See Scoles, Hay, Borchers, Symeonides & Whytock, Conflict of Laws § 19.5 (6th ed.2018): "That a distinction should be made between those covenants for title that run with the land and those which are called purely personal, such as a covenant of seisin, seems doubtful."

3.   Sun Oil Co. v. Guidry, 99 So.2d 424 (La.App.1957). Proceeding to determine ownership of mineral interests in Louisiana land. The question

was whether the interest of one of the parties was barred on account of non-user. This would be so if the prescriptive period commenced running from the date when he was judicially emancipated in Texas, the state of his domicile. Held claimant's interest is barred by non-user. "The general rule is that the law of the individual's domicile determines his status of majority or minority . . . , but the law of the place where the immovable property is situated determines the effect of such status. . . . [Under] Louisiana law . . . prescription runs against the minor over the age of eighteen fully emancipated by marriage . . . or judicially. . . . Thus, in our opinion, prescription commenced running in Louisiana . . . as soon as [the minor] attained the personal status of an emancipated minor under the law of his domicile. . . ." The court distinguished Beauchamp v. Bertig on the ground that under the law of Arkansas, the situs of the land, "even a local decree removing the disability of minority" would not prevent the minor from disavowing the sale after he had reached the age of twenty-one years.

In re French

United States Court of Appeals for the Fourth Circuit, 2006.
440 F.3d 145, cert. denied, 549 U.S. 815, 127 S.Ct. 72.

■ DIANA GRIBBON MOTZ, CIRCUIT JUDGE:

This appeal presents the question of whether a United States bankruptcy court can avoid a constructively fraudulent transfer of foreign real property between United States residents. The transferees here argue that the presumption against extraterritoriality and the doctrine of international comity preclude application of the Bankruptcy Code. Both the bankruptcy court and the district court rejected these arguments and allowed avoidance. For the reasons that follow, we affirm.

I.

In 1976, Betty Irene French, a resident of Maryland, purchased a house in the Bahamas. At a Christmas party held in Maryland in 1981, she gave a deed of gift to the Bahamian property to her children, Randy Lee French, a resident of Maryland, and Donna Marie Shaka, a resident of Virginia (hereinafter "the transferees"). Assertedly to avoid high Bahamian transfer taxes, the transferees decided not to immediately record the deed in the Bahamas.

In the late 1990s, Mrs. French and her husband began experiencing serious financial problems. Concerned by this downturn, the transferees decided at last to record the deed in the Bahamas, a task they accomplished through a Bahamian attorney in mid-2000. In October 2000, Mrs. French's creditors filed an involuntary Chapter 7 bankruptcy petition against her. The bankruptcy court entered an Order for Relief on January 29, 2001.

On August 22, 2002, the bankruptcy trustee, George W. Liebmann, filed an adversary proceeding against the transferees to avoid the transfer of the Bahamian property and to recover the property or its fair market value for the benefit of the estate. In his complaint, the trustee alleged (in pertinent part) that the debtor and the transferees had engaged in a constructively fraudulent transfer, as defined by the Bankruptcy Code, because the debtor had been insolvent at the time of the transfer and had received less than a reasonably equivalent value in exchange. See 11 U.S.C. § 548(a)(1)(B) (2000).

The transferees conceded that the debtor never received a reasonably equivalent value for her gift of the Bahamian property, and they further conceded that the debtor was insolvent in 2000, when the deed was recorded. These facts would normally be sufficient to establish constructive fraud. Nevertheless, the transferees filed a motion to dismiss before the bankruptcy court based on two grounds. First, they invoked the presumption against extraterritoriality, contending that because of it § 548 should not apply to transfers of foreign property. Second, they maintained that considerations of international comity counseled the application of Bahamian (rather than United States) bankruptcy law, which assertedly would allow the transferees to retain the Bahamian property.

The bankruptcy court rejected the transferees' arguments. . . .

II.

"It is a longstanding principle of American law 'that legislation of Congress, unless a contrary intent appears, is meant to apply only within the territorial jurisdiction of the United States.'" EEOC v. Arabian Am. Oil Co., 499 U.S. 244, 248, 111 S. Ct. 1227, 113 L. Ed. 2d 274 (1991) [hereinafter Aramco] (quoting Foley Bros., Inc. v. Filardo, 336 U.S. 281, 285, 69 S. Ct. 575, 93 L. Ed. 680 (1949)). . . .

We have recognized, however, that a similar inquiry—defining "foreign conduct"—is particularly challenging in cases (like this one) that involve a "mixture of foreign and domestic elements." Dee-K Enters., Inc. v. Heveafil Sdn. Bhd., 299 F.3d 281, 286 (4th Cir.2002). In this case too, we believe that any definition must eschew rigid rules in favor of a more flexible inquiry into the "place" of regulated conduct. Minimal contact with the United States should not automatically render conduct domestic. See Gushi Bros. Co. v. Bank of Guam, 28 F.3d 1535, 1538 (9th Cir.1994); Kollias, 29 F.3d at 72; Maxwell Commc'n Corp. PLC v. Societe Generale PLC (In re Maxwell Commc'n Corp.), 186 B.R. 807, 817 (S.D.N.Y.1995) [hereinafter Maxwell II]. Nor should minor contact with another country suffice to render conduct extraterritorial. See Massey, 986 F.2d at 531–32; Maxwell Commun. Corp. v. Barclays Bank (In re Maxwell Commun. Corp.), 170 B.R. 800, 809 (Bankr. S.D.N.Y. 1994) ("Not every transaction that has a foreign element represents an extraterritorial application of our laws."); Jay Westbrook, The Lessons of Maxwell Communications, 64 Fordham L. Rev. 2531, 2538 (1996). . . .

In this case, the perpetrator and most of the victims of the fraudulent transfer—all except a single Bahamian creditor—have long been located in the United States. Given these facts, the effects of this transfer were (naturally) felt most strongly here, and not in the Bahamas.

We also find it significant that the conduct constituting the constructive fraud occurred in the United States. Section 548 defines a constructively fraudulent transfer, inter alia, as one where (1) the debtor was insolvent, and (2) the debtor received "less than a reasonably equivalent value in exchange." 11 U.S.C. § 548(a)(1)(B); see also In re GWI PCS 1 Inc., 230 F.3d 788, 805 (5th Cir. 2000). Here, domestic facts and conduct establish both elements. The determination of Mrs. French's insolvency relies almost entirely upon a comparison of domestic debts and assets. And the decision not to provide a "reasonably equivalent value" for the transfer was made in the United States as well—whether we consider the relevant decision to be Mrs. French's gift of the deed in 1981, or the transferees' recordation of the deed in 2000.

However, we recognize that two aspects of this transfer indisputably involve foreign facts and conduct. The first is relatively insignificant: the transferees' Bahamian lawyer recorded their deed to the property in the Bahamas. . . .

More importantly, the transferees emphasize that the real property at issue in this case is located in the Bahamas. At first blush, this fact does not seem critical because § 548 focuses not on the property itself, but on the fraud of transferring it. In this case, the facts underlying the fraud occurred here. However, the law has long recognized the powerful interest that states and nations have in the real property within their boundaries; the strength of that interest explains why the law of the situs generally applies to real property. See, e.g., Oakey v. Bennett, 52 U.S. 33, 44–45, 13 L. Ed. 593 (1850); Robinson v. Campbell, 16 U.S. 212, 219, 4 L. Ed. 372 n. a (1818); Restatement (Second) of Conflict of Laws § 223 comm. b (1974); cf. Robby Alden, Note, Modernizing the Situs Rule for Real Property Conflicts, 65 Tex. L. Rev. 585, 591–98 (1986–1987) (summarizing arguments on the importance of the location of real property).

Given this long history, the fact that application of United States law could affect Bahamian real property, however indirectly, perhaps merits special weight in the balancing test. The parties in this case certainly seem to believe so—from the outset both sides have treated § 548's reach as extraterritorial. Here, we need not resolve this slippery question. This is so because even if we assume that the application of the Bankruptcy Code would be extraterritorial, the presumption against extraterritoriality does not prevent its application to the transfer at issue here.

III.

Although the presumption against extraterritoriality is important to "protect against unintended clashes between our laws and those of other nations which could result in international discord," it nevertheless must give way when Congress exercises its undeniable "authority to enforce its laws beyond the territorial boundaries of the United States." Aramco, 499 U.S. at 248. . . .

In furtherance of this purpose, Congress provided that creditors are entitled to the "interests of the debtor in property" under § 541—expressly including all property "wherever located"—and that they may avoid a debtor's fraudulent transfer of the same "interests of the debtor in property" under § 548. Congress thus demonstrated an affirmative intention to allow avoidance of transfers of foreign property that, but for a fraudulent transfer, would have been property of the debtor's estate. Therefore, the presumption against extraterritoriality does not prevent application of § 548 here.

IV.

The transferees argue, however, that even if the presumption against extraterritoriality does not prevent extension of § 548 to the transaction here, we should nevertheless refrain from applying the statute under the doctrine of international comity. In particular, they emphasize that disputes concerning real property should be governed by the law of the situs—here, Bahamian law. We disagree. Even if the elements of this transfer do not conclusively render it domestic rather than extraterritorial, a consideration of all the important components of the transfer certainly compels the conclusion that application of the United States Bankruptcy Code is appropriate here.

International comity is "the recognition which one nation allows within its territory to the legislative, executive or judicial acts of another nation, having due regard both to international duty and convenience, and to the rights of its own citizens or of other persons who are under the protection of its laws." Hilton v. Guyot, 159 U.S. 113, 164, 16 S. Ct. 139, 40 L. Ed. 95 (1895). Although there is some dispute as to the precise contours of this doctrine—compare Hartford Fire Ins. Co. v. California, 509 U.S. 764, 798, 113 S. Ct. 2891, 125 L. Ed. 2d 612 (1993), with id. at 813 (Scalia, J., dissenting)—at base comity involves the recognition that there are circumstances in which the application of foreign law may be more appropriate than the application of our own law. In this case, the transferees maintain that application of Bahamian bankruptcy law, which (according to them) only allows avoidance if there is proof of an actual intent to defraud, is more appropriate than application of § 548, which allows avoidance of constructively fraudulent transfers like the one at issue here.

In deciding whether to forego application of our own law under the doctrine of international comity, the Supreme Court has referred to the factors in Restatement (Third) of Foreign Relations Law § 403 (1987). See Hartford Fire Ins., 509 U.S. at 799 & n. 25; id. at 818 (Scalia, J., dissenting); see also Maxwell Commc'n Corp. PLC v. Societe Generale PLC (In re Maxwell Commc'n Corp.), 93 F.3d 1036, 1047–48 (2d Cir.1996) [hereinafter Maxwell III]. The Restatement looks to, inter alia, "the extent to which the activity takes place within the territory" of the regulating state, "the connections, such as nationality, residence, or economic activity, between the regulating state and the person principally responsible for the activity to be regulated," "the extent to which other states regulate such activities" or "may have an interest in regulating [them]," the "likelihood of conflict with regulation by another state," and "the importance of regulation to the regulating state." Restatement (Third), supra, § 403(2). Applying those factors, we can only conclude that the doctrine of international comity does not require that we forego application of the United States Bankruptcy Code in favor of Bahamian bankruptcy law.

The strongest argument in favor of applying Bahamian law is that this case involves real property, which (the transferees argue) should be governed by the law of the situs. When a case involves the definition of property interests, principles of international comity may, in some cases, counsel courts to employ the property law of the situs to resolve those interests, notwithstanding other comity factors. See Koreag, Controle et Revision S.A. v. Refco F/X Assocs., Inc. (In re Koreag, Controle et Revision S.A.), 961 F.2d 341, 349 (2d Cir. 1992). But analogous modern choice-of-law principles recognize that the law of the situs does not necessarily govern "the allocation of interests in land [between] . . . debtor and creditor" if "regulation of the relationship is of greater concern to a state other than the situs." Restatement (Second) of Conflict of Laws ch. 9, topic 2, introductory note. This is "particularly" true "when the land is part of an aggregate of property which it is desirable to deal with as a unit." Id.

Both of these factors are present in this case. The real property at issue is part of an aggregate—the bankruptcy debtor's estate—that is most desirably dealt with as a whole. Furthermore, the United States has a stronger interest than the Bahamas in regulating this transaction. The purpose of the United States Bankruptcy Code is to protect the rights of both debtors and creditors during insolvency. The Code protects debtors by providing them a fresh start. In exchange, the Code's avoidance provisions protect creditors by preserving the bankruptcy estate against illegitimate depletions. The United States has a strong interest in extending these personal protections to its residents— including the vast majority of the interested parties here. The Bahamas, by contrast, has comparatively little interest in protecting nonresidents. Cf. Hurtado v. Superior Court, 11 Cal. 3d 574, 522 P.2d 666, 670, 114 Cal. Rptr. 106 (Cal. 1974) (holding that Mexico has no interest in applying its statutory limitation on damages when defendants in a tort action were not Mexican residents). Thus, applying Bahamian law here would undercut the purpose of the United States Bankruptcy Code by withdrawing its protections from those it is intended to cover, while simultaneously failing to protect any Bahamian residents.

Several other factors make application of United States law more appropriate. Most of the activity surrounding this transfer took place in the United States. Moreover, almost all of the parties with an interest in this litigation—the debtor, the transferees, and all but one of the creditors—are based in the United States, and have been for years. Compare Maxwell III, 93 F.3d at 1051 (deference to British law is appropriate when all of the parties were British). Certainly, Mrs. French, "the person principally responsible for the activity to be regulated," has a strong connection to this country as a long-time United States resident. Finally, there are no parallel insolvency proceedings taking place in the Bahamas. There is thus no danger that the avoidance law of the regulating state—the United States—will in fact conflict with Bahamian avoidance law. Accordingly, we find that the many contacts between this fraudulent transfer and the United States justify the application of United States rather than Bahamian law.

V.

For the foregoing reasons, the judgment of the district court is affirmed.

■ WILKINSON, CIRCUIT JUDGE, concurring:

The unique properties of bankruptcy law compel an affirmance of the district court. The bankruptcy laws provide an integrated scheme for gathering and disbursing the assets of a debtor's estate. Ease and centrality of administration are thus foundational characteristics of bankruptcy law.

For these reasons, Congress has broadly defined property of the estate as property "wherever located and by whomever held." 11 U.S.C. § 541(a) (2000). This broad definition reflects congressional support for the Code's extraterritorial application in appropriate circumstances.

Quite properly, the panel opinion also does not suggest that every portion of the Bankruptcy Code invariably applies to conduct abroad. Instead, it represents a sensitive recognition of the administrative exigencies that are bound up with the avoidance of this fraudulent transfer. . . .

NOTES

1. Would the result in the principal case have been different had most of the creditors been Bahamian? In re Bankruptcy Estate of Midland Euro Exchange, 347 B.R. 708 (Bankr.C.D.Cal. 2006), disagrees with In re French on the ground that the section of the Bankruptcy Act under which the trustee in bankruptcy can recover fraudulent transfers of the bankrupt's property cannot be applied extraterritorially. If the section permitting the avoidance of fraudulent transfers cannot be applied to transfers in other countries, what strategy is available to anyone who wishes to shield assets from the trustee in bankruptcy?

2. See First Commerce Realty Investors v. K-F Land Co., 617 S.W.2d 806, 809 (Tex.Civ.App.1981) in which the court applied the Louisiana Deficiency Judgment Act in a foreclosure proceeding with respect to Texas land. The

secured party's principal place of business had been in Louisiana, the loan was negotiated and to be performed there, the promissory note and the deed of trust selected Louisiana law, and all documents were executed in Louisiana. "It is difficult to conceive of other steps that could have been taken by the parties to imprint this transaction with Louisiana law ... [T]he parties clearly bargained in the most specific terms for the applicability of Louisiana law. We see no reason to frustrate such intention so clearly expressed."

3. In view of how frequently it is uncertain whether a court will apply the law governing the contract or the law of the situs, what precautions can a lawyer take in planning a transaction to insure so far as possible the application of a particular law?

4. See generally Hancock, "In the Parish of St. Mary le Bow, in the Ward of Cheap," 16 Stan.L.Rev. 561 (1964); Hancock, Equitable Conversion and the Land Taboo in Conflict of Laws, 17 Stan.L.Rev. 1095 (1965); Hancock, Full Faith and Credit to Foreign Laws and Judgments in Real Property Litigation, 18 Stan.L.Rev. 1299 (1966); Hancock, Conceptual Devices for Avoiding the Land Taboo in Conflict of Laws: The Disadvantage of Disingenuousness, 20 Stan.L.Rev. 1 (1967); Weintraub, Commentary on the Conflict of Laws §§ 8.1–8.22 (5th ed.2006).

SECTION 2. MOVABLES, IN GENERAL*

A. SUCCESSION ON DEATH

RESTATEMENT, SECOND, CONFLICT OF LAWS

§ 260. Intestate Succession to Movables

The devolution of interests in movables upon intestacy is determined by the law that would be applied by the courts of the state where the decedent was domiciled at the time of his death.

Comment:

a. *Scope of section.* The rule of this Section applies to a decedent's interests in chattels, in rights embodied in a document and in rights that are not embodied in a document.

b. *Rationale. . . .*

It is desirable that insofar as possible an estate should be treated as a unit and, to this end, that questions of intestate succession to movables should be governed by a single law. This is the law that would be applied by the courts of the state where the decedent was domiciled at the time of his death. This state would usually have the dominant interest in the decedent at the time.

Provided that they apply the common law rules of choice of law, the courts of the state where the decedent was domiciled at the time of his

---

* See Restatement, Second, Conflict of Laws §§ 244–66.

death would look to their own local law to determine what categories of persons are entitled to inherit upon intestacy. . . .

§ 263. Validity and Effect of Will of Movables

(1) Whether a will transfers an interest in movables and the nature of the interest transferred are determined by the law that would be applied by the courts of the state where the testator was domiciled at the time of his death.

(2) These courts would usually apply their own local law in determining such questions.

Comment:

a. *Scope of section.* The . . . law selected by application of the present rule determines the capacity of a person to make a will or to accept a legacy, the validity of a particular provision in the will, such as whether it violates the rule against perpetuities or constitutes a forbidden gift to a charity, and the nature of the estate created. Questions concerning the required form of the will and the manner of its execution also fall within the scope of the present rule. The rule applies to a decedent's interests in chattels, in rights embodied in a document and in rights that are not embodied in a document.

b. *Rationale.* For reasons stated in § 260, comment b, questions relating to the validity of a will of movables and the rights created thereby are determined by the law that would be applied by the courts of the state where the decedent was domiciled at the time of his death. These courts would usually apply their own local law to determine such questions as the testator's capacity to make a will, the nature of the estates that can validly be created and the categories of legatees to whom the testator may leave his movables. These courts would also usually apply their own local law in determining whether a legacy for charitable purposes is invalid, in whole or in part, because of statutory restrictions on the power of a testator to make charitable dispositions by will. . . .

NOTES

1. Restatement Second § 260 cmt. b provides the rationale for applying the law of the decedent's domicile at death to testate and intestate succession: "This state would usually have the dominant interest the decedent at the time." Was this true for intestate succession in Estate of Jones, p. 9, supra or White v. Tennant, p. 13, supra; for testate succession in In re Annesley, p. 521, supra? The decedent's last domicile also generally provides the reference for the passage of property outside probate. See Morris v. Cullipher, 306 Ark. 646, 816 S.W.2d 878 (1991) (law of the state of decedent's last domicile governs as to whether personal property is treated as being held in a tenancy by the entirety). Is a preferable rule that of Article 3(2) of the Hague Convention on the Law Applicable to Succession to the Estates of Deceased Persons, referring to the country in which the decedent was "habitually resident . . . for . . . five years [at] death. . . . [unless] in

exceptional circumstances . . . at the time of his death he was manifestly more closely connected with the State of which he was then a national"? See Note, Succession Under Civil Law Concepts, p. 836, supra.

If as stated in Restatement Second § 260, cmt. b, "[i]t is desirable that insofar as possible an estate should be treated as a unit," should the law of the situs apply if the property is land and not movables? As indicated in the notes referred to in the preceding paragraph, both the Convention and most civil law countries apply the same law to personalty and realty in the estate.

2. Most states provide for alternative places of reference to determine whether a will has been executed in proper form. Ester & Scoles, Estate Planning and Conflict of Laws, 24 Ohio St.L.J. 270 (1963). The English Wills Act 1963 (11 and 12 Eliz. 2, chapter 44) provides numerous places of alternative reference.

3. The law of the testator's domicile at death determines whether certain events, such as divorce or the birth of a child to the testator after execution of a will involving movables, operate to revoke the will. Restatement, Second, Conflict of Laws § 263, Comment i. On the other hand, the law of the situs determines whether similar circumstances operate to revoke a will involving land. In re Estate of Barrie, 240 Iowa 431, 35 N.W.2d 658 (1949), p. 836, supra. See also In re Brown, 521 B.R. 205, aff'd, 2014 U.S.Dist.Lexis 176449 (S.D.Tex.) (decedent's last domicile governs application of homestead exemptions to personalty).

4. Some states provide by statute that their own local law shall be applied to govern the validity and effect of the will of a non-resident testator on local movables if the testator has expressed a desire in his will to have this law applied. See, e.g. Ill.Comp.Stat.Ann. ch. 755 § 5/7–6; N.Y.E.P.T. Law § 3–5.1; Uniform Probate Code § 2–602. Are these provisions sound policy if, as in the case of the Illinois and New York statutes, they permit the testator to disinherit family members in a manner not permitted by the testator's domicile? Uniform Probate Code § 2–602 does not permit the testator or testatrix to choose law to evade the rules of the decedent's domicile concerning a surviving spouse's elective share. See In re Estate of Clark, p. 20, supra; In re Estate of Renard, Note 1, p. 22, supra. See generally Bright, Permitting a Non-Resident to Choose a Place of Probate, 95 Trusts & Estates 865 (1956); Lowenfeld, "Tempora Mutantur"—Wills and Trusts and the Conflicts Restatement, 72 Colum.L.Rev. 382 (1972). A choice-of-law clause in a life insurance contract is effective and stipulates the law governing how policies purporting to make ex-spouses beneficiaries in cases in which the divorce occurred after the insurance policy went into effect. See Lincoln Benefit Life Co. v. Manglona, 2014 U.S.Dist.Lexis 90502 (S.D.Tex.)

B. INTER VIVOS TRANSACTIONS

Although the Uniform Commercial Code, by unifying substantive law, decreases the frequency of conflicts problems in commercial property transactions, there are reasons why there remain a substantial number of cases in which the need to choose law arises. (1) The various state versions of the Code are not uniformly enacted or interpreted. (2) The frequent official revisions of the code, even if eventually adopted by all states, go into effect at different times in each state, and 3) in international transactions there may be questions as to whether any version of the Code applies. For example, in 1986, there were three different "official" versions of § 9–103, the primary choice-of-law provision for secured transactions, in force in different states—the 1962, 1972, and 1977 revisions. Comprehensive revisions to Article 9 (including its choice-of-law provisions) went into effect in every state by the end of 2001. As a result, there was not a significant transitional period in which fewer than all of the states have adopted the new version. (3) The Code leaves in force various nonuniform state enactments, such as those concerning usury, small loans, and retail installment sales. (4) Even if all states eventually enact the same Code and construe it in the same manner, international transactions will continue to present conflicts problems.

RESTATEMENT, SECOND, CONFLICT OF LAWS

Topic 3. Movables

§ 244. Validity and Effect of Conveyance of Interest in Chattel

(1) The validity and effect of a conveyance of an interest in a chattel as between the parties to the conveyance are determined by the local law of the state which, with respect to the particular issue, has the most significant relationship to the parties, the chattel and the conveyance under the principles stated in § 6.

§ 245. Effect of Conveyance on Pre-Existing Interests in Chattel

(1) The effect of a conveyance upon a pre-existing interest in a chattel of a person who was not a party to the conveyance will usually be determined by the law that would be applied by the courts of the state where the chattel was at the time of the conveyance.

(2) These courts would usually apply their own local law in determining such questions.

Youssoupoff v. Widener

Court of Appeals of New York, 1927.
246 N.Y. 174, 158 N.E. 64.

[In 1921, the plaintiff, Prince Youssoupoff, a Russian refugee in dire need of funds, agreed to the sale or transfer of two Rembrandt portraits to the defendant, Mr. Widener of Pennsylvania, for one hundred thousand pounds. The negotiations were in England. The writing evidencing the transaction was executed by the defendant in Pennsylvania and was sent to his agent in London, where it was executed by the plaintiff and duly delivered. Thereupon the portraits were delivered to the defendant's representative in London and were removed to the defendant's residence in Pennsylvania.

The writing evidencing the transaction provided: ". . . Mr. Widener grants to Prince Youssoupoff the right and privilege to be exercised on or before January 1, 1924 and not thereafter, of repurchasing these pictures at the purchase price, one hundred thousand pounds (100,000) plus eight per cent. (8%) interest from this date to the date of repurchase; the repurchase to be made in the City of Philadelphia and the pictures to be redelivered to Prince Youssoupoff upon payment of the full purchase money.

"This privilege is a purely personal one granted to Prince Youssoupoff in recognition of his love and appreciation of these wonderful pictures. It is not assignable nor will it inure to the benefit of his heirs, assigns or representatives and Prince Youssoupoff represents that this privilege of repurchase will be exercised only in case he finds himself in the position again to keep and personally enjoy these wonderful works of art. . . ."

In 1923, the plaintiff tendered to the defendant in Pennsylvania in money of the United States the equivalent of the stipulated one hundred thousand pounds plus interest at eight per cent., and demanded the return of the portraits; but the money so tendered was borrowed by the plaintiff from a lender with whom the portraits if returned by the defendant were to be pledged as security.]

■ LEHMAN, J. . . . The defendant declined the tender and refused to transfer the pictures to the plaintiff. In effect the defendant's reply to the plaintiff's demand is that the defendant is the absolute owner of the pictures under the contract of sale, subject only to the right of the plaintiff to repurchase the pictures in accordance with the terms contained in the contract. That right is, by its terms, to be exercised only in case the plaintiff "finds himself in the position again to keep and personally enjoy these wonderful works of art." It may not be exercised for the purpose of enabling the plaintiff to transfer the pictures to another. . . .

The plaintiff has brought this action in equity to compel the defendant to accept the money tendered to him, and to transfer the pictures.

It is said . . . that under the law of Pennsylvania, where Mr. Widener resided, where he kept his collection of paintings and where any option to repurchase must be exercised, the contract between the parties hereto would be conclusively presumed to be a mortgage, regardless of the actual intention of the parties, and enforced only as a mortgage. The courts below have made no finding to that effect. We have not analyzed the testimony or the Pennsylvania decisions introduced in evidence to determine whether they would support such a finding. We hold that the law of England and not the law of Pennsylvania governs this transaction.

The general rule is well established that the construction and legal effect of a contract for the transfer of, or the creation of a lien upon, property situated in the jurisdiction where the contract is made is governed by the law of that jurisdiction. (Goetschius v. Brightman, 245 N.Y. 186, 156 N.E. 660.) Various grounds, however, are urged upon which it is said that this case presents an exception to the general rule. We dispose of them briefly. . . .

The fact that Mr. Widener obtained the pictures with the intention of removing them to his home, does not change the general rule. It is true that it has been held in some States that where property, transferred by contract in one jurisdiction, must be removed to another jurisdiction in order to carry out the purpose of the contract, the construction and effect of the contract may be governed, in accordance with the intention of the parties, not by the law of the jurisdiction where the contract was made and where the property was then situated, but by the law of the jurisdiction to which the property was removed thereafter and where the parties intended that it should be permanently located. (Beggs v. Bartels, 73 Conn. 132, 46 A. 874.) We need not now consider whether upon a similar state of facts we should reach a similar conclusion. If under such circumstances exception to the general rule may be created, that may be done only for the purpose of carrying out a presumed intention of the parties. Here the parties have given convincing evidence that the parties intended that the law of England should apply. . . .

Finally, it is said that since the provisions for the repurchase of the paintings in Pennsylvania were the only executory provisions of the contract, we should construe the contract according to the law of Pennsylvania where performance was to be made. (International Text-Book Co. v. Connelly, 206 N.Y. 188, 99 N.E. 722.) The contract in effect is primarily a bill of sale of the paintings, and was so intended. The right to repurchase was merely an incident to the transfer. The transfer of title was completed simultaneously with the signing of the contract. The parties certainly did not intend the law of Pennsylvania should apply to the transfer of property completed in England by contract made and dated there and by delivery accepted there. Under the law of England, full ownership was then transferred to the defendant, subject only to a condition that plaintiff should have a limited right to repurchase in Pennsylvania. Since full ownership had then been transferred to the defendant, and the plaintiff no longer held an equity of redemption, he might regain the pictures only by exercising his option of repurchase in accordance with the provisions of the contract. If we assume that the parties intended that the law of Pennsylvania should apply to the provisions giving an option of repurchase, and construe those provisions accordingly (Hamlyn & Co. v. Talisker Distillery, [1894] Appeal Cases 202), we must begin construction upon the basis, fatal to plaintiff's claim, that these provisions apply to property of which the defendant is the full owner and in which the plaintiff has no equity of redemption. . . .

Judgment affirmed, etc.

NOTES

1. When faced with the question of what law governs a consensual transaction involving movables, should a court adopt the approach ordinarily used in contracts cases, i.e., formerly "place of making," "place of performance," or an approach based on property concepts, i.e., "title," "situs"? Which approach was used in the principal case?

2. See Cavers, The Conditional Seller's Remedies and the Choice-of-Law Process, 35 N.Y.U.L.Rev. 1126 (1960).

C. SECURITY TRANSACTIONS

Green v. Van Buskirk

Supreme Court of the United States, 1866, 1868.
72 U.S. (5 Wall.) 307, 18 L.Ed. 599; 74 U.S. (7 Wall.) 139, 19 L.Ed. 109.

[Bates, who lived in New York, executed and delivered to Van Buskirk, who lived in the same State, a chattel mortgage on certain iron safes which were then in the City of Chicago. Two days after this, Green, who was also a citizen of New York, being ignorant of the existence of the mortgage, sued out a writ of attachment in the courts of Illinois, levied on the safes, and subsequently had them sold in satisfaction of the judgment obtained in the attachment suit. There was no appearance or contest in this attachment suit, and Van Buskirk was not a party to it, although he could have made himself such party and contested the right of Green to levy on the safes, being expressly authorized by the laws of Illinois so to do. It was conceded that by the law of Illinois mortgages of personal property, until acknowledged and recorded, were [unenforceable] against third persons. Subsequently Van Buskirk sued Green in New York for the value of the safes mortgaged to him by Bates, of which Green had thus received the proceeds. The courts of New York gave judgment in favor of Van Buskirk, holding that the law of New York was to govern and not the law of Illinois, although the property was situated in the latter state, and that the title passed to Van Buskirk by the execution of the mortgage. The cause was then brought to this court and first considered upon a motion to dismiss for want of jurisdiction.[2]]

■ JUSTICE MILLER delivered the opinion of the Court:

... It is claimed by the plaintiff in error that the faith and credit which these proceedings have by law and usage in the state of Illinois, were denied to them by the decision of the courts of New York, and that in doing so, they decided against a right claimed by him under section 1, article IV of the Constitution and the act of Congress of May 26, 1790, on that subject. ...

---

[2] The statement of facts is taken from the outline of the principal case given in Cole v. Cunningham, 133 U.S. 107, 132. —eds.

The record before us contains the pleadings in the case, the facts found by the court, and the conclusions of law arising thereon.

Among the latter, the court decides "that, by the law of the state of New York, the title to the property passed on the execution and delivery of the instrument under the facts found in the case, and overreached the subsequent attachment of the state of Illinois and actual prior possession under it at the suit of defendant, although he was a creditor having a valid and fair debt against Bates, and had no notice of the previous assignment and sale. And that the law of the state of New York was to govern the transaction and not the law of the state of Illinois, where the property was situated." . . .

It is said that Van Buskirk, being no party to the proceedings in Illinois, was not bound by them, but was at liberty to assert his claim to the property in any forum that might be open to him; and, strictly speaking, this is true. He was not bound by way of estoppel, as he would have been if he had appeared and submitted his claim, and contested the proceedings in attachment. He has a right to set up any title to the property which is superior to that conferred by the attachment proceedings; and he has the further right to show that the property was not liable to the attachment—a right from which he would have been barred if he had been a party to that suit. And this question of the liability of the property in controversy to that attachment is the question which was raised by the suit in New York, and which was there decided. That court said that this question must be decided by the laws of the state of New York, because that was the domicil of the owner at the time the conflicting claims to the property originated.

We are of opinion that the question is to be decided by the effect given by the laws of Illinois, where the property was situated, to the proceedings in the courts of that state, under which it was sold.

There is no little conflict of authority on the general question as to how far the transfer of personal property by assignment or sale, made in the country of the domicil of the owner, will be held to be valid in the courts of the country where the property is situated, when these are in different sovereignties. . . . And it may be conceded that as a question of comity, the weight of . . . authority is in favor of the proposition that such transfers will, generally, be respected by the courts of the country where the property is located, although the mode of transfer may be different from that prescribed by the local law. . . .

But, after all, this is a mere principle of comity between the courts, which must give way when the statutes of the country where property is situated, or the established policy of its laws prescribe to its courts a different rule. . . .

We do not here decide that the proceedings in the state of Illinois have there the effect which plaintiff claims for them; because that must remain to be decided after argument on the merits of the case. But we

CHAPTER 10

hold that the effect which these proceedings have there, by the law and usage of that state was a question necessarily decided by the New York courts, and that it was decided against the claim set up by plaintiff in error under the constitutional provision and statute referred to, and that the case is, therefore, properly here for review.

The motion to dismiss the writ of error is overruled. . . .

■ JUSTICE NELSON, dissenting. . . . The court below decided that the instrument was to be governed by the law of the state of New York, where it was made, and which was the domicil of the parties. . . . The question here is whether, in so deciding, the court denied full faith, credit, and effect to the judgment in Illinois. In other words, did the court, in holding that the prior assignment was not fraudulent and void but valid and effectual to transfer the title, thereby discredit the Illinois judgment? The answer to the question, I think, is obvious. These assignees were not parties to the judgment. It could not bind them. They were free, therefore, to set up and insist upon this prior title to the property; and, if there was nothing else in the case, it is clear the junior attachment could not hold it. . . .

I agree, if the attachment had been levied before the assignment, and the court had given effect to this instrument over the levy, it might be said that full faith and credit had not been given to it; but, being posterior, these proceedings could not have the effect, per se, to displace the assignment as against a stranger. Another element must first be shown, namely; fraud or other defect in the instrument, to render it inoperative.

My conclusion is that the regularity of the attachment proceedings was not called in question in the court below; but, on the contrary, full force and credit were given to them, and the case should be dismissed for want of jurisdiction.

■ JUSTICE SWAYNE concurs in this opinion.

[The case then came up for final adjudication. 7 Wall. 139 (1868).]

■ JUSTICE DAVIS delivered the opinion of the Court:

That the controversy in this case was substantially ended when this court refused, 5 Wall. 312, to dismiss the writ of error for want of jurisdiction, is quite manifest, by the effort which the learned counsel for the defendants in error now made, to escape the force of that decision. . . .

This decision, supported as it was by reason and authority, left for consideration on the hearing of the case, the inquiry, whether the Supreme Court of New York did give to the attachment proceedings in Illinois the same effect they would have received in the courts of that State. . . .

[The court here stated the law of Illinois, and showed that under that law the purchaser at the attachment sale would prevail over the New York mortgagee.]

. . . And as the effect of the levy, judgment and sale is to protect Green if sued in the courts of Illinois, and these proceedings are produced for his own justification, it ought to require no argument to show that when sued in the court of another State for the same transaction, and he justifies in the same manner, that he is also protected. Any other rule would destroy all safety in derivative titles, and deny to a State the power to regulate the transfer of personal property within its limits and to subject such property to legal proceedings. . . .

The judgment of the Supreme Court of the State of New York is reversed, and the cause remitted to that court, with instructions to enter judgment for the plaintiff in error.

NOTES

1.   In the principal case, was full faith and credit denied to a judgment of the courts of Illinois or to that state's law? Would the decision be followed today?

2.   Does the decision in the principal case require, as a compliance with full faith and credit, that in a case involving tangible things the reference to the law of the state of the situs be to that state's conflict-of-laws rules?

Choice-of-law questions involving secured transactions in movables fall into two broad categories: those arising between the secured creditor and his immediate debtor and those involving the rights of the creditor against some third person, such as an attaching creditor or a transferee of the immediate debtor.

Today, such questions are governed in large measure by the Uniform Commercial Code, which has obtained almost universal enactment throughout the United States. Initially, there was some question whether the rights inter se of the secured creditor and his immediate debtor were governed exclusively by Section 1–105 or also by Sections 9–102 and 9–103. This uncertainty was removed by a 1972 revision of the Code, which removes all references to choice of law in Section 9–102 and amends Section 9–103 to deal exclusively with problems of perfection of security interests and the effect of perfection or non-perfection. As a result, it is now clear that choice-of-law questions arising between the secured creditor and his immediate debtor are governed by Section 1–105.

The 2001 revisions to Article 9 (which went into effect in all states except Alabama, Connecticut, Florida and Mississippi as of July 1, 2001, and shortly thereafter in those four) contain a complete overhaul of the choice-of-law provisions. Most of the choice-of-law rules are now found in a separate subpart encompassing U.C.C. §§ 9–301 through 9–307. These new provisions follow the 1972 version in making clear that they exclusively govern all questions of perfection, the effect of non-perfection and now even the priority of security interests. Questions of "attachment" of a security interest (i.e., the relationship between the creditor and the immediate debtor) continue to be governed by the U.C.C.'s more general choice-of-law provisions. See U.C.C. § 9–301, cmt. 2 (2001 version).

The 2001 version, however, makes dramatic changes in the U.C.C.'s approach to choice-of-law questions involving question of perfection. The principal choice-of-law concern involves a situation in which a chattel has first been subjected to a security interest in state X and then is taken to state Y where it becomes involved in a transaction with a third person who is unaware of the existence of the security interest. The question is whether the interests of the secured creditor or of the third person should be preferred. This question is now governed by §§ 9–103 through 9–107 of the 2001 version of the Uniform Commercial Code.

Prior to the nearly universal adoption of the Uniform Commercial Code, the usual position of the courts was that the secured creditor would be preferred over the third person if (a) the security interest had been perfected under the law of the state (X) where the chattel was situated at the time and (b) the chattel was taken to another state (Y) without the creditor's knowledge or consent and was there dealt with by the third person before the secured creditor had become aware of the chattel's presence in the state. On the other hand, the third person would usually be preferred over the secured creditor if the security interest had not been perfected in state Y and either the chattel had been taken to Y with the creditor's knowledge and consent or the creditor had become aware of the chattel's presence in Y prior to the time that it was there dealt with by the third person. Perfection of security interests is usually accomplished by filing them with the appropriate governmental official so that third persons have reasonable access to the information.

Significant portions of the 2001 version of the Uniform Commercial Code are set forth below:

§ 9–301. Law Governing Perfection and Priority of Security Interests

Except as otherwise provided in Sections 9–303 through 9–306, the following rules determine the law governing perfection, the effect of perfection or nonperfection, and the priority of a security interest in collateral.

(1) Except as otherwise provided in this section, while a debtor is located in a jurisdiction, the local law of that jurisdiction governs perfection, the effect of perfection or nonperfection, and the priority of a security interest in collateral.

(2) While collateral is located in a located in a jurisdiction, the local law of that jurisdiction governs perfection, the effect of perfection or nonperfection, and the priority of a *possessory* [emphasis added— eds.] security interest in that collateral.

(3) Except as otherwise provided in paragraph (4), while negotiable documents, goods, instruments, money or tangible chattel paper is located in a jurisdiction, the local law of that jurisdiction governs:

(A) perfection of a security interest in the goods by a fixture filing;

(B) perfection of a security interest in timber to be cut; and

(C) the effect of perfection or nonperfection and the priority of a nonpossessory security interest in the collateral.

(4) The local law of the jurisdiction in which the wellhead or minehead is located governs perfection, the effect of perfection or nonperfection, and the priority of a security interest in as-extracted collateral.

§ 9–307. Location of Debtor

(a) ["Place of business"] In this section, "place of business" means a place where a debtor conducts its affairs.

(b) [Debtor's location: general rules.] Except as otherwise provided in this section the following rules determine a debtor's location:

(1) A debtor who is an individual is located at the individual's principal residence.

(2) A debtor that is an organization and has only one place of business is located at its place of business.

(3) A debtor that is an organization and has more than one place of business is located at its chief executive office.

(c) [Limitation of applicability of subsection (b).] Subsection (b) applies only if a debtor's residence, place of business, or chief executive office, as applicable, is located in a jurisdiction whose law generally requires information concerning the existence of a nonpossessory security interest to be made generally available in a filing, recording, or registration system as a condition or result of the security interest's obtaining priority over the rights of a lien creditor with respect to the collateral. If subsection (b) does not apply, the debtor is located in the District of Columbia.

(d) [Continuation of location: cessation of existence, etc.] A person that ceases to exist, have a residence, or have a place of business continues to be located in the jurisdiction specified by subsections (b) and (c).

(e) [Location of registered organization organized under State law.] A registered organization that is organized under the law of a State is located in that State.

(f) [Location of registered organization organized under federal law; bank branches and agencies.] Except as otherwise provided in subsection (i), a registered organization that is organized under the law of the United States and a branch or agency of a bank that is not organized under the law of the United States or a State are located:

(1) in the State that the law of the United States designates, if the law designates a State of location;

(2) in the State that the registered organization, branch, or agency designates, if the law of the United States authorizes the registered organization, branch, or agency to designate its State of location; or

(3) in the District of Columbia, if neither paragraph (1) nor paragraph (2) applies.

(g) [Continuation of location: change in status of registered organization.] A registered organization continues to be located in the jurisdiction specified by subsection (e) or (f) notwithstanding:

(1) the suspension, revocation, forfeiture, or lapse of the registered organization's status as such in its jurisdiction of organization; or

(2) the dissolution, winding up, or cancellation of the existence of the registered organization.

(h) [Location of United States.] The United States is located in the District of Columbia.

(i) [Location of foreign bank branch or agency if licensed in only one state.] A branch or agency of a bank that is not organized under the law of the United States or a State is located in the State in which the branch or agency is licensed, if all branches and agencies of the bank are licensed in only one State.

(j) [Location of foreign air carrier.] A foreign air carrier under the Federal Aviation Act of 1958, as amended, is located at the designated office of the agent upon which service of process may be made on behalf of the carrier.

(k) [Section applies only to this part.] This section applies only for purposes of this part.

Dayka & Hackett, LLC v. Del Monte Fresh Produce N.A., Inc.

Court of Appeals of Arizona, 2012.
269 P.3d 709.

■ BRAMMER, JUDGE.

Del Monte Fresh Produce, N.A., Inc. (Del Monte) appeals from the trial court's order granting summary judgment to Dayka & Hackett, LLC (D&H) on its claims of lien priority and conversion regarding the proceeds from the sale of Rolando Castelo de la Rosa and Maria Olivia Aguirre Ramos's (growers) 2008 table grape crop. Del Monte argues its security interest in the crop had priority over D&H's security interest in the same collateral, it had a right of recoupment pursuant to A.R.S. § 47–9404(A)(1), it did not engage in conversion because it had acted in accordance with A.R.S. §§ 47–9610 and 47–9615, and D&H had permitted it to sell the collateral without first having made a demand for possession. We affirm.

Factual and Procedural Background

We view the facts in the light most favorable to the party against whom summary judgment was entered, drawing all justifiable inferences in its favor. . . . In January 2007, D&H agreed to finance and sell the growers' 2007 grape crop to be grown in Sonora, Mexico. D&H entered into marketing and security agreements with the growers and, on January 18, 2007, it filed a financing statement pursuant to A.R.S. § 47–9307(C) [identical to U.C.C. § 9–307[c] above] in Washington, D.C. to perfect its interest. The security agreement granted D&H an interest in the 2007 and any future crops the growers produced together with any proceeds generated by the sale of the crops. The 2007 grape crop was not profitable and the growers were unable to repay to D&H what they owed. The growers subsequently defaulted on their obligations to D&H, eventually owing $688,587.71.

Del Monte, unaware of the relationship between the growers and D&H, advanced the growers funds to produce their 2008 crop. After conducting a lien search of the public registry in Sonora, Del Monte entered into a marketing and security agreement with the growers. Under its marketing agreement, Del Monte was obligated to market and sell the crop it was advancing the growers funds to raise, and to pay the growers a portion of the sales proceeds. The growers granted Del Monte a security interest in collateral, which included the 2008 crop and any proceeds from its sale. In May 2008, Del Monte registered its security interest with the public registry in Sonora.

On April 24, 2008, D&H sent Del Monte a letter informing Del Monte of its security interest in the growers' crops. Del Monte responded with a letter on May 14, 2008 asserting a superior interest in the crops. Del Monte marketed the 2008 crop and collected and retained all the sales proceeds.

D&H filed a complaint against the growers and Del Monte seeking to enforce its security interest in the growers' 2008 crop and its proceeds. The trial court granted summary judgment in favor of D&H on its conversion claim and awarded it damages of $688,587.71, the amount the growers owed D&H. The judgment also declared D&H's security interest in the 2008 crop and proceeds to be superior to Del Monte's interest and denied Del Monte's asserted right of recoupment. The court denied Del Monte's motion for reconsideration and entered a final judgment pursuant to Rule 54(b), Ariz. R. Civ. P. This appeal followed. . . .

Priority

Del Monte argues its security interest in the 2008 crop was superior to and had priority over D&H's security interest because D&H did not perfect its interest by taking possession of the collateral or by filing notice of its interest in a proper jurisdiction. D&H recorded its security interest with the Registrar of Deeds in Washington, D.C., on January 18, 2007. Del Monte recorded its security agreement in Mexico's Real Property Registry and Movables Registry on May 7, 2008 in Hermosillo, Sonora, Mexico. To assess which party's filing was effective to perfect its interest and give it priority, we must determine whether United States or Mexican law applies.

The Uniform Commercial Code (UCC) as adopted in Arizona provides that, "while a debtor is located in a jurisdiction, the local law of that jurisdiction governs perfection ... and the priority of a security interest in collateral." A.R.S. § 47–9301(1) [identical to U.C.C. § 9–301(1) above].

An individual generally "is located at the individual's principal residence," A.R.S. § 47–9307(B)(1) [identical to U.C.C. § 9–307(b)(1) above], and it is undisputed that the growers are residents of Sonora, Mexico. However, § 47–9307(B) applies only if:

> [the] debtor's residence ... is located in a jurisdiction whose law generally requires information concerning the existence of a nonpossessory security interest to be made generally available in a filing, recording or registration system as a condition or result of the security interest's obtaining priority over the rights of a lien creditor with respect to the collateral. [U.C.C. § 9–307[c]].

If the requirements of [U.C.C. § 9–307[c]] are not met, the debtor is considered to be "located in the District of Columbia." Id.

Therefore, whether priority is determined by United States or Mexican law depends on whether, during the relevant time period, Mexican law "generally require[d]" such information "to be made generally available in a filing, recording or registration system" in order to obtain priority. See id. HN4To determine whether Mexico's law meets the test in [U.C.C. § 9–307[c]] we "may consider any relevant material or source, including testimony." Ariz. R. Civ. P. 44.1. . . .

Both parties presented expert testimony regarding whether Mexican law during the relevant period satisfied the conditions set forth in [U.C.C. § 9–307[c]]. D&H expert Dale Furnish has authored articles and book chapters on Mexican law, has consulted with the Mexican government regarding the amendment of its laws, and has assisted in drafting Arizona's secured transactions laws and the Organization of American States model on secured transactions. According to Furnish, Mexican law in 2007 and 2008 was a "crazy quilt" of different security devices that did not meet the requirements of [U.C.C. § 9–307[c]]. Checking public records in Mexico provided no assurance of the priority of an interest because it was "possible for several common types of credit guaranties to be unrecorded, and still gain priority over even a recorded security interest." According to Furnish, one of the major flaws in the Mexican registration system preventing the growers from being "located" in Mexico is that it did not include a provision stating it applied to any device acting in practical effect as a security interest.

D&H expert . . . Bringas Acedo has practiced law in Mexico for over twenty-eight years representing borrowers, growers, finance companies, and distributors in crop-financing transactions. He agreed that Mexican law does not "generally require[ ]" filing as described in [U.C.C. § 9–307[c]] noting that a financier like Del Monte, to perfect its interest in a crop, need only "notify any third party who may be in possession of that same fruit . . . such that perfection of the guaranty . . . is not the result of recording in any registry but rather by way of notification."

Amendments to Mexico's laws in 2009 recognized and defined a "security interest," created a single federal registry for recording security interests, and generally required that all security interests be recorded in the federal registry. Furnish offered that the Mexican system before the 2009 amendments "resemble[d] the United States system prior to the 1962 advent of UCC Article 9." Both Furnish and Bringas Acedo opined that once the 2009 amendments are implemented they will, for the first time, create a system that " 'generally requires' recording to establish priority between competing claims or security interests in personal property."

Furnish added that "[e]very authoritative source available agrees that Mexico did not have . . . a law" satisfying [U.C.C. § 9–307[c]] in 2007 and 2008. . . .

Additional authority supports Furnish's and Bringas Acedo's conclusions. A 2006 article . . . reiterates the concern that "Mexican law recognizes various types of nonpossessory security devices in personal property that do not require registration yet may take priority over lien creditors and registered nonpossessory pledges." Arnold S. Rosenberg, Where to File Against Non-U.S. Debtors: Applying UCC § 9–307(c) [Rev] to Foreign Filing, Recording, and Registration Systems, 39 UCC L.J., no. 2, 2006, art. 1. A 2004 article recognized that "current mechanisms [in Mexico] undermine secured transactions . . . [and] create secret liens, making it difficult for a secured party to determine if potential debtor's assets are encumbered." Alejandro Lopez-Velarde & John M. Wilson, A Practical Point-by-Point Comparison of Secured Transactions Law in the United States and Mexico, 36 UCC L.J., no. 4, 2004, art. 1. And a recent article by Furnish noted that, even after reforms in 2003, "the pre-existing secret liens and diverse security mechanisms continued unabated." Dale Beck Furnish, The Impact of the Organization of American States Model Law of Secured Transactions in Latin America: The First Decade, 43 UCC L.J., no. 4, 2011, art. 1. . . .

Del Monte expert Steven Weise specializes in UCC secured transactions. He was the chairperson of the ABA committee on Article 9, and is a member of the editorial board for the UCC. He is not an expert on Mexican law, and based his opinions on the testimony of Bringas Acedo, Furnish, and a Mexican attorney hired by Del Monte. Although he deferred to the interpretation of Mexican law offered by other experts, Weise testified that, pursuant to [U.C.C. § 9–307[c]], a jurisdiction's registration system should be examined with regard to the specific collateral at issue, rather than for nonpossessory secured interests as a whole. Based on his interpretation of the other experts' descriptions of the Mexican system, he contended the Mexican security interest devices discussed by Bringas Acedo were either similar to the UCC or irrelevant to grape crops. He further opined that, based on his conversations with Del Monte's Mexican attorney, a security interest in crops must be filed in Mexico to gain priority over third parties.

Del Monte urges us to accept Weise's interpretation of [U.C.C. § 9–307[c]] as collateral-specific. There is no Arizona case law addressing the issue. One article by Rosenberg on the topic acknowledged it is an "unsettled question" whether U.C.C. § 9–307(c) should be interpreted to require a system for the specific collateral or for nonpossessory security interests as a whole, but noted a comprehensive test is the more likely interpretation. Rosenberg, Where to File, supra. One reason supporting this prediction is that U.C.C. § 9–307 cmt. 3 appears to support a comprehensive interpretation of the phrase "generally requires," stating in relevant part:

The phrase "generally requires" is meant to include legal regimes that generally require notice in a filing or recording system as a condition of perfecting nonpossessory security interests, but which permit perfection by another method . . . in limited circumstances. A jurisdiction that has adopted this Article or an earlier version of this Article is such a jurisdiction.

Policy implications also favor interpreting [U.C.C. § 9–307[c]] as requiring the jurisdiction's system to satisfy the test generally. One risk of a comprehensive test is that, if a jurisdiction's system satisfies [U.C.C. § 9–307[c]] generally but leaves a void for a particular type of collateral, a lender could find it impossible to perfect a security interest in that type of collateral because it would be required to file in that jurisdiction. See Rosenberg, Where to File, supra. However, a comprehensive approach "has the advantage of clarity and might reduce transaction costs," and a collateral-specific approach would require secured parties "to retain foreign counsel in almost all cases to ascertain foreign law on the subject." Id. As noted in Rosenberg's 2008 article, admitted in evidence during Furnish's testimony, under a collateral-specific approach a debtor could be "located" in more than one jurisdiction and, "in a single transaction, a secured party might have to file in the limited-purpose registry to perfect as to some security interests or collateral, while having to file in the District of Columbia to perfect as to others." For these reasons, and based on the comments to the UCC, we interpret § 47–9307(C) to adopt the comprehensive approach, requiring a system for perfecting nonpossessory security interests as a whole.

The expert testimony and secondary authority on the topic establish that Mexico's law in 2007 and 2008 did not meet the requirements of [U.C.C. § 9–307[c]] and, therefore, the growers for the purpose of perfecting security interests in their property were located in the District of Columbia pursuant to the statute. Thus, D&H perfected its security interest by filing in the District of Columbia, and its security interest in the 2008 crop and its proceeds had priority over Del Monte's conflicting, unperfected security interest. See A.R.S. § 47–9322(A)(2) ("A perfected security interest . . . has priority over a conflicting unperfected security interest . . . .").

[Because D & H's security interest was perfected and Del Monte's was not, the court affirmed the trial court's grant of summary judgment to D & H.]

NOTES

1.   The case turns on a close question as to what is meant by U.C.C. § 9–307[c]'s requirement that a foreign jurisdiction's "law generally requires information concerning the existence of a nonpossessory security interest to be made generally available in a filing, recording, or registration system. . . ." Could Del Monte have hedged its bet by filing both where it did and in the District of Columbia?

2.   The 2001 version effects a major change in philosophy from the 1972 version. While the 1972 version generally looked to the law of the state of the situs of the collateral, the 2001 version looks to the debtor's "location" for nonpossessory security interests. For possessory security interests (i.e., those security interests that are perfected by the creditor taking possession of the collateral) the 2001 version retains the situs nexus. A debtor's location is elaborately defined in § 9–307, but generally looks to an individual's "principal residence", a non-corporate business's "chief executive" office, and a "registered organization's" (most obviously a corporation's) state of registration. In the case of foreign debtors, the 2001 version goes to great lengths to assign such debtors a location in a place where the local law requires publicly available filings of security interests. If none of § 9–307's rules would point to such a local law, the 2001 version assigns such debtors a location in the District of Columbia.

What advantages are there to the debtor location nexus? Are those advantages sufficient to warrant the major revisions to the existing choice-of-law regime?

In 2010, the National Conference of Commissioners on Uniform State Laws and the American Law Institute drafted further amendments to Article 9 of the Uniform Commercial Code with a suggested enactment date of July 1, 2013. Most of the amendments are technical in nature and designed to resolve difficulties that arose with respect to the much more extensive amendments that were drafted in 1998 and went into effect in most states as of July 1, 2001. The 2010 amendments add the following clause to the end of Section 9–307(f)(2): "including by designating its main office, home office, or other comparable office . . ." The comments explain that in the case of an organization organized under federal law that designating a main office or making a similar declaration is sufficient to fix that organization's "location" for security perfection purposes in that state.

3. Under the 2001 version, a change in the law applicable to perfection will usually occur because the debtor changes location. If the applicable law changes, and the holder of the security interest does not refile in the state whose law is newly applicable, the security interest can then become unperfected. Once the security interest becomes unperfected, a third party who takes the collateral in good faith does so free of the security interest, leaving the holder of the security interest with only personal rights against the debtor, which will be worthless if the debtor does not have assets.

The holder of the security interest four months to refile in the new state. See U.C.C. § 9–316(a)(2), (f)(2). The holder of the security interest has a full year to refile if the collateral is transferred to another debtor who has a location in a new state. U.C.C. § 9–316(a)(3).

4. In 2010, Mexico created a Unified Registry of Movable Property Collateral (RUG), which creates a public registration system of security interests more in line with the Uniform Commercial Code. Although enacted before the decision in the principal case, but after the security interests in the crops were created, it was not germane to the principal case. It is possible that registration in the RUG might now be sufficient to perfect a security interest under the U.C.C. However, the safest route in doubtful cases is to register the security interest in multiple jurisdictions. For a discussion of the move to a debtor-location nexus and its implications for international transactions, see Borchers, Choice of Law Relative to Security Interests and Other Liens in International Bankruptcies, 46 Am.J.Comp.L. 165 (Supp.1998).

5. The movement of motor vehicles from state to state gives rise to difficult problems involving the conflicting interests of a secured creditor and a bona fide purchaser. At the present time all states have adopted certificate-of-title laws which provide for the perfection of the security interests in vehicles on the certificate. Some have such laws for mobile homes and water craft as well. There are, however, significant differences among these laws. In some states, perfection of the security interest is completed by the notation of the interest on the certificate of title or by the issuance of a new certificate after such notation. Other states provide that perfection is complete as soon as delivery of the appropriate papers has been made by the secured creditor to the proper official, even though the interest is not noted on the certificate of title or indeed even though no certificate is ever issued.

The 2001 version of the U.C.C. devotes a special section to security interests in goods covered by a certificate of title. U.C.C. § 9–303. That section chooses the law of the state that issues the certificate of title, and provides that goods "become covered by a certificate of title when a valid application for the certificate of title and the applicable fee are delivered to the appropriate authority." Other specialized types of collateral, including agricultural liens, deposit accounts, investment property and letter-of-credit rights are subject to special sections in the 2001 version. See U.C.C. §§ 9–302, 9–304, 9–305, 9–306.

Frequently, however, these provisions in the U.C.C. conflict with non-uniform motor vehicle title laws. For example, in In re Sorsby, 559 S.E.2d 45 (W.V.2001), the court confronted a conflict between U.C.C. § 9–103(2)(b) (1972 version) (which provides that security interests remain perfected until re-registration of the vehicle and for not less than four months) and a non-uniform West Virginia statute which provided that such liens become unperfected after three months without regard to whether the vehicle is re-registered in West Virginia. The court held that the U.C.C. had repealed by implication the non-uniform enactment and thus controlled. Hendrickson v. HW Partners, LLC, 2013 Bankr.Lexis 3820 (E.D.Wash.)

6.   Consider in this vein the United Nations Convention on the Assignment of Receivables in International Trade: Annex to General Assembly Resolution 56/81, 12 December 2001:

> The Convention sets out rights and duties of assignors, assignees, and debtors and contains choice-of-law rules to determine law applicable to priority of the assignee over other claimants.
>
> Art. I(1)(a): Applies to assignments of international receivables and to international assignments of receivables if at time of conclusion of contract of assignment, assignor located in a Contracting State. (3) Rights and obligations of debtor not affected by Convention unless at that time debtor located in Contracting State or law governing original contract is law of a Contracting State.
>
> Art. 3: Receivable international if at time of conclusion of original contracts, assignor and debtor are located in different States. Assignment is international if, at time of conclusion of contract of assignment, the assignor and the assignee are located in different States.
>
> Art. 4: Exclusions: Not applicable to assignments made to an individual for individual's personal, family or household purposes; or to receivables arising under or from . . . bank deposits, letter of credit or independent guarantee.
>
> Art. 5(h): Location of a assignor or assignee is in State where central administration. Location of debtor is place of business having closest relationship to original contract. If no place of business, person is located at habitual residence.
>
> Art. 6: Assignor, assignee, and debtor may derogate from provisions of Convention relating to their rights and obligations.
>
> Art. 22: Law where assignor located governs priority of the right of an assignee in the assigned receivable over rights of competing claimants.
>
> Art. 23: (1) Forum may refuse to apply law of assignor's State only if "manifestly contrary to the public policy of the forum State." (3) State other than assignor's location may in an insolvency

proceeding give effect to a preferential right that arises under its law over the rights of the assignee.

Ch. V contains conflict-of-laws rules for other issues.

Art. 27: Formal validity of assignment: law that governs contract or law of State in which one or both parties located.

Art. 28(1): "The mutual rights and obligations of the assignor and the assignee arising from their agreement are governed by law chosen by them; (2) if no choice, by the law of the State with which the contract of assignment is most closely connected."

Art. 29: Law governing original contract governs rights and obligations as between debtor and assignee.

Art. 31: except for law applicable to priority of assignee over other claimants, none of rules restrict application of mandatory rules of forum or of other State having close connection with matters dealt with in the rules.

Art. 30: repeats rules of arts. 23 and 23, without mentioning right to refuse if against forum's public policy, but art. 32 contains general public policy exception for all rules in the chapter.

Opt outs include the following. A signatory State may elect not to be bound by Ch. V (art. 39) or will not apply the Convention to categories of receivables that it specifies in its declaration (art. 41).

Art. 45: Convention enters into force six months after deposit of fifth instrument of ratification.

Section I of an Annex to the Convention sets out priority rules among assignees, and between the assignee and an insolvency administrator or the creditors of the assignor. Priorities depend on date of registration of the assignment under Section II. Section II requires establishment of a registration system that persons may search by the name of the assignor.

Art. 42 provides that signatories may declare that they are bound by the priorities in section I and will participate in the international registration system under section II. Or signatories may establish a registration system that fulfills the purpose of the priorities set out in section I.

D. FUTURE INTERESTS AND TRUSTS[*]

1.   VALIDITY—INTER VIVOS TRUSTS

Hutchison v. Ross

Court of Appeals of New York, 1933.
262 N.Y. 381, 187 N.E. 65, 89 A.L.R. 1007.

[Under an ante-nuptial agreement executed in 1902 in Québec, where the parties to it were both domiciled, John Ross promised to establish by deed or will a trust fund of $125,000 for the benefit of his prospective wife. In 1916, after inheriting $10,000,000 from his father, Ross decided to set up a trust of $1,000,000 for the benefit of his wife and children, and he directed that some securities then in New York City be used for that purpose. The trust instrument was drawn in New York and was signed in Québec by Ross and his wife. It was then sent back to New York City where the trustee, the Equitable Trust Company of New York, signed it and where the securities constituting the corpus of the trust were thereupon delivered to it. The trust instrument contained a clause to the effect that the $1,000,000 trust was in lieu of the $125,000 trust.

Ross had lost almost the entire fortune by 1926 when he discovered that under the law of Québec an antenuptial agreement cannot be modified in any way and under that law the trust of $1,000,000 with respect to the wife was invalid. In consideration for a further loan, Ross promised a creditor to institute proceedings to have the trust set aside and to deliver the trust res to the creditor as collateral. Ross commenced the action and, upon his involuntary bankruptcy, his trustee in bankruptcy was substituted as party plaintiff. The trial court held that the attempted modification of the antenuptial agreement was governed by the law of Québec, the matrimonial domicile, and, therefore, that the $1,000,000 trust was invalid. The Appellate Division reversed the trial court, and the plaintiff appealed.]

■ LEHMAN, J. . . . With possible limitations, not relevant to the question here presented . . . the rule is well established that the essential validity of a testamentary trust must be determined by the law of the decedent's domicile. . . . The plaintiff urges that the same rule should be applied to a conveyance in trust inter vivos, especially where such trust is established for the benefit of the wife and children of the settlor.

It cannot be gainsaid that there are expressions in the opinions of the courts of this State which support the plaintiff's contentions. In considering the effect of these expressions, we must give due weight to the circumstances under which they were made. The paucity of old judicial decisions upon conveyances in trust inter vivos, compared with the number of decisions upon testamentary trusts, shows that conveyances in trust inter vivos were comparatively rare. Thus the

---

[*]   See Restatement, Second, Conflict of Laws §§ 267–282.

possible importance of drawing distinctions between the rules applicable to testamentary trusts and trusts inter vivos, was not apparent or brought to the attention of the courts. . . . Today the courts cannot close their eyes to the fact that trusts of personal property and securities are created by settlors during their lifetime for many purposes, and for the first time our court is called upon to decide directly the question whether conveyances in trust of securities made inter vivos shall be governed by the same rules as testamentary trusts or by the same rules as other conveyances inter vivos. . . .

. . . [N]ow that we are called upon to decide that question, we must weigh other considerations not then apparent to the courts which seem to point logically to the need for differentiation between the rule to be applied to testamentary trusts and the rule to be applied to trusts inter vivos.

In all the affairs of life there has been a vast increase of mobility. Residence is growing less and less the focal point of existence and its practical effect is steadily diminishing. Men living in one jurisdiction often conduct their affairs in other jurisdictions, and keep their securities there. Trusts are created in business and financial centers by settlors residing elsewhere. A settlor, regardless of residence, cannot establish a trust to be administered here which offends our public policy. If we hold that a non-resident settlor may also not establish a trust of personal property here which offends the public policy of his domicile, we shackle both the non-resident settlor and the resident trustee.

Our courts have sought whenever possible to sustain the validity even of testamentary trusts to be administered in a jurisdiction other than the domicile of the testator. . . . In regard to other conveyances or alienations of personal property situated here, they have steadfastly applied the law of the jurisdiction where the personal property is situated. . . . Where a non-resident settlor establishes here a trust of personal property intending that the trust should be governed by the law of this jurisdiction, there is little reason why the courts should defeat his intention by applying the law of another jurisdiction. . . .

. . . We may throw in the balance also expressions of public policy by the Legislature of this State. It has provided that: "Whenever a person being a citizen of the United States, or a citizen or a subject of a foreign country, wherever resident, creates a trust of personal property situated within this State at the time of the creation thereof, and declares in the instrument creating such trust that it shall be construed and regulated by the laws of this State, the validity and effect of such trust shall be determined by such laws." (Pers.Prop.Law; Const. Laws, ch. 41, sec. 12-a). It is true that the statute was enacted long after the creation of the trust now the subject of this litigation and the validity of the trust must, probably, be determined by the law as it then existed. The statute does not change retroactively a well-established rule of law. It merely establishes a definite public policy in a field where the rules of law were still fluid and undefined. When the courts are called upon to define these rules even as of an earlier date, they cannot entirely disregard this public policy. . . .

It is said that the statute establishes a public policy only where there is an express declaration of intention in the instrument that it shall be construed and regulated by the laws of this State. Here there is no express declaration of intention, but the intention is implied in every act and word of the parties. The statute makes express declaration of intention conclusive, but a construction which would deny effect to intention appearing by implication would be unreasonable. . . . It follows that the validity of a trust of personal property must be determined by the law of this State, when the property is situated here and the parties intended that it should be administered here in accordance with the laws of this State. . . .

The judgment in each action should be affirmed, with costs. . . .

[Two judges dissented.]

Shannon v. Irving Trust Co.

Court of Appeals of New York, 1937.
275 N.Y. 95, 9 N.E.2d 792.

■ RIPPEY, JUDGE. . . . a trust indenture was duly executed in the city of New York between Joseph G. Shannon, who was . . . domiciled within the State of New Jersey, and the Irving Trust Company, a corporation organized and existing under the laws of the State of New York . . . as trustee, whereby an irrevocable trust was created for the benefit, among others, of Goewey F. Shannon, wife of the settlor, and plaintiff herein, John Shannon, the son of the settlor, both of which beneficiaries were then . . . domiciled within the State of New Jersey. . . . The trust created for the wife consisted of fixed items of income with the provision that all income in excess of the amount named should accumulate and become part of the principal of the trust. Up to December 26, 1933, when Goewey F. Shannon died, she continued to be . . . domiciled within the State of New Jersey. . . . The trust instrument provided that upon her death the trustee should thereafter pay to the son, John Shannon, monthly, an aggregate annual income of $3,000 until the son should arrive at twenty-five years of age; that thereafter the income to the son, payable in monthly installments, should aggregate $5,000 per year until the son arrived at the age of thirty years; that thereafter the income to the son should be increased to $10,000 per year until he should arrive at the age of thirty-five years, after which time he should receive the full income from the trust estate for the balance of his life. All income in excess of the amounts thus payable to the son was directed to become a part of the trust estate. The trust instrument provided that, at the death of the son, the principal and accumulated income should pass to the issue of the son, or, if the son should die without issue surviving, to the Hill School of

Pottstown, Pa. At the time the trust was created, the plaintiff was a resident of and domiciled within the State of New Jersey and his domicile has continued in that state to the time of the commencement of the action. . . . the trust instrument [provided] "The Trustee shall receive for its services, its necessary expenses and the commissions allowed testamentary trustees by the laws of the State of New York instead of the laws of the State of New Jersey, but otherwise the laws of the State of New Jersey shall govern this trust indenture and any construction to be placed thereupon or interpretation thereof."

. . . [T]he plaintiff contended that the validity of the trust is to be determined by the laws of the State of New York and, inasmuch as the provisions for accumulations of income are void under section 16 of the Personal Property Law (Consol. Laws, c. 41) of the State of New York (Laws 1909, c. 45), the accumulations should be paid over to him as the person presumptively entitled to the next eventual estate . . . while the defendants assert that the validity of the trust provisions is to be determined by the laws of the State of New Jersey, where the accumulations are valid. . . . The Appellate Division found that the trust was valid and certified to this court that a question of law was involved which ought to be here reviewed.

. . . Where the domicile of the owner of the res and the actual and business situs of the trust do not coincide, the law applicable to the interpretation, construction, and validity of the trust and the legal obligations arising out of it . . . depend upon facts involved in and circumstances surrounding the particular case. In such a situation, the express or clearly implied intent of the settlor may control. . . .

In the case at bar the execution of the trust instrument, the location of the res, the domicile of the trustee, and the place of administration of the trust are in the city of New York. The intent of the settlor that in all matters affecting the trust except remuneration of the trustee his domiciliary law shall govern is expressly stated in the body of the trust instrument. . . . The instrument should be construed and a determination of its validity made according to the law chosen by the settlor unless so to do is contrary to the public policy of this state. . . .

Consideration of the New Jersey law and our own relating to perpetuities and accumulations of income will indicate that our policy in that connection is substantially the same as that of New Jersey. . . . The general policy of New Jersey and New York to put some limitation on the absolute suspension of the power of alienation of property and the accumulation of income from trusts is the same. Difference arises only as to the ending of the period during which such power to suspend alienation and to provide for accumulation of income may be permitted.

Under the facts existing in the case at bar, . . . we find nothing in our public policy which forbids extending comity and applying the New Jersey law so as to carry out the wish of the settlor and sustain the trust. The positive direction contained in the trust instrument that the validity of the trust should be determined by the law of the settlor's domicile must prevail. Our decision here does not extend, however, beyond instances where conflict arises between the domiciliary law of the settlor and the law of the situs of the trust where the construction and validity of trusts inter vivos are involved.

Judgment affirmed.

NOTES

1. What common principle reconciles the *Hutchison* and *Shannon* decisions?

2. Would *Shannon* be differently decided if an interests analysis were applied? To what extent is the settlor's expressed choice of one applicable law to determine the trustee's reimbursement for expenses and commissions, and another to determine other aspects of the trust analogous to the problem of autonomy in contract choice of law? Is there anything wrong with the dépeçage employed here?

3. National Shawmut Bank v. Cumming, 91 N.E.2d 337 (Mass.1950). S, a Vermont resident, transferred a fund to a Massachusetts trustee to pay the income to himself for life and after his death to distribute it in equal shares among his widow, mother, brothers and sister; upon the death of the life beneficiaries, the corpus was to go to the settlor's nephews and nieces. After S's death, his widow claimed the principal of the trust contending that the trust was invalid under Vermont law since it was made for the purpose of depriving her of her inheritance rights. Held: Massachusetts law governs and under that law the trust is valid. "The general tendency of authorities . . . is away from the adoption of the law of the settlor's domicil where the property, the domicil and place of business of the trustee and the place of administration intended by the settlor are in another State."

Did not Vermont have a greater interest than Massachusetts in the decision of the particular issue? Did the court place too much weight upon the policy in favor of upholding the validity of a trust? Was the issue one where the respective policies of Massachusetts and Vermont differed markedly?

RESTATEMENT, SECOND, CONFLICT OF LAWS:

§ 270. Validity of Trust of Movables Created Inter Vivos

An inter vivos trust of interests in movables is valid if valid

(a) under the local law of the state designated by the settlor to govern the validity of the trust, provided that this state has a substantial relation to the trust and that the application of its law does not violate a strong public policy of the state with which, as to the matter at issue, the trust has its most significant relationship under the principles stated in § 6, or

(b) if there is no such effective designation, under the local law of the state with which, as to the matter at issue, the trust has its most significant relationship under the principles stated in § 6.

Comment:

a. *The general principle.* It is desirable that a trust should be treated as a unit and, to this end, that the trust as to all of the movables included therein, no matter where they happen to be at the time of the creation of the trust, should be governed by a single law. The creation of a trust is different from an outright conveyance, which is either valid or invalid at the outset. In the case of a trust there is something more. In the first place, the creation of a trust establishes a continuing relationship between the trustee and the beneficiaries, and the state in which the trust is to be administered or which is otherwise connected with the trust may be different from the state in which the trust property is situated when the trust is created. In the second place, the trust property is ordinarily not a single movable but includes a group of movables which may be situated in different states at the time of the creation of the trust. The validity of a trust of movables, therefore, should be governed by a single law and not held valid as to some of the movables included in the trust and invalid as to others. This is true whether the movables consist of chattels, rights embodied in a document or intangibles. The rule of this Section is applicable to all these types of movables, no matter where they are situated at the time of the creation of the trust. It does not follow, however, that all questions of validity are determined by the same law. See Comment e.

Wilmington Trust Co. v. Wilmington Trust Co.

Supreme Court of Delaware, 1942.
26 Del.Ch. 397, 24 A.2d 309, 139 A.L.R. 1117.

[In 1920, William Donner as settlor created a trust through the deposit of personal property with the trustee, Dora Donner. The trust instrument provided that the income was to be paid to members of the settlor's family, and gave to each of his children a power of appointment over a part of the trust property. The settlor and the trustee were domiciled in New York and the trust was created there.

Subsequent to 1920, a successor trustee was named under a power given by the trust instrument. The new trustee was a trust company of Delaware.

In 1929, Joseph W. Donner, one of the settlor's children assumed to exercise the power of appointment given him. In doing so he set up trusts which were invalid under the New York rules against perpetuities but were valid under the law of Delaware.

From a decree of the Court of Chancery upholding the validity of the exercise of the power, an appeal was taken to the Supreme Court of Delaware.[3]]

■ LAYTON, CHIEF JUSTICE. . . . The power of appointment exercised by Joseph W. Donner for the benefit of his two children had its origin in the donor's deed of trust; the provisions of the deed of appointment are viewed in law as though they had been embodied in that instrument. . . . The validity of the deed of appointment and of the rights and interests assigned thereunder depend upon the law of the jurisdiction in which the trust had its seat when the power of appointment was exercised.

The diversity of judicial opinion with respect to the discovery of the jurisdiction under whose law the validity of a trust inter vivos of intangible personal property is to be determined is such that no useful purpose will be served by an attempted analysis of the decisions. Courts have variously looked to the domicile of the donor, the place of execution of the trust instrument, the situs of the trust property, the place of administration of the trust, the domicile of the trustee, the domicile of the beneficiaries, and to the intent or desire of the donor, or to a combination of some of these denominators, in deciding the troublesome question of conflict of law. . . . The place of one's residence no longer is a sure indication of one's place of business; nor is ownership of property closely tied to residence. The domicile of the donor is, of course, a circumstance to be considered in the ascertainment of the seat of the trust; but courts, today, . . . are disposed to take a more realistic and practical view of the problem; and the donor's domicile is no longer regarded as the decisive factor. The place of execution of the trust instrument and the domicile of the beneficiaries are not important indicia. The domicile of the trustee and the place of administration of the trust—quite generally the same place—are important factors; and the intent of the donor, if that can be ascertained, has been increasingly emphasized. . . .

Where the donor in a trust agreement has expressed his desire, or if it pleases, his intent to have his trust controlled by the law of a certain state, there seems to be no good reason why his intent should not be respected by the courts, if the selected jurisdiction has a material connection with the transaction. More frequently, perhaps, the trust instrument contains no expression of choice of jurisdiction; but, again, there is no sufficient reason why the donor's choice should be disregarded if his intention in this respect can be ascertained . . . provided that the same substantial connection between the transaction and the intended jurisdiction shall be found to exist. . . .

The donor was careful to provide for a change of trustee subject to his approval in his lifetime. In the event of such change he declared that

---

[3]   The statement of facts is taken in part from the report of the case on the original hearing in the Court of Chancery, 180 A. 597 (Del.Ch. 1936).

the successor trustee should "hold the said trust estate subject to all the conditions herein *to the same effect as though now named herein*". The italicized language either has a significance of its own or it is to be considered as no more than a superfluous or redundant phrase. . . . We are of opinion that the phrase "to the same effect as though now named herein", as applied to the power to appoint a successor trustee in another state, must be accepted as authorizing a removal of the seat of the trust from its original location, and its re-establishment under the law of another jurisdiction. . . .

There is no substantial reason why a donor, in dealing with that which is his own, may not provide for a change in the location of his trust with a consequent shifting of the controlling law. In an era of economic uncertainty, with vanishing returns from investments and with tax laws approaching confiscation, such a provision would seem to amount to no more than common foresight and prudence. The rights of beneficiaries may, it is true, be disturbed by a shift of jurisdiction, but if such change has been provided for, they have no more cause to complain that other persons who are the recipients of bounty under some condition or limitation.

The adult beneficiaries, with the donor's approval, transferred the seat of the trust from New York to Delaware. On October 9, 1929, when Joseph W. Donner availed himself of the power of appointment conferred on him by the trust agreement, the home of the trust was in this State, and, being subject then to local law, the validity and effect of his deed of appointment and of the rights and interests of the appointees thereunder are to be adjudged and determined by the law of Delaware. . . .

[Affirmed.]

NOTES

1. See Cavers, Trusts Inter Vivos and the Conflict of Laws, 44 Harv.L.Rev. 161 (1930); Ester & Scoles, Estate Planning and Conflict of Laws, 24 Ohio St.L.J. 270 (1963); Scott, What Law Governs Trusts? 99 Trusts and Estates, 186 (1960); Scott, Spendthrift Trusts and the Conflict of Laws, 77 Harv.L.Rev. 845 (1964); Comment, Choice of Law: The Validity of Trusts of Movables—Intention and Validation, 64 Nw.L.Rev. 388 (1969).

2. For the Hague Convention on the Law Applicable to Trusts and Their Recognition, see Note 3, p. 897, infra.

In re Bauer's Trust

New York Court of Appeals, 1964.
14 N.Y.2d 272, 251 N.Y.S.2d 23, 200 N.E.2d 207.

■ DESMOND, CHIEF JUDGE. In 1917 Dagmar Bauer, then a resident of New York, executed in New York City an irrevocable trust indenture which stipulated that she should receive the life income and that the remainder should go to her husband. In the event her husband predeceased her, the principal was to be distributed to such person or persons as she appointed by her will and, failing a valid disposition in her will, to the settlor's next of kin pursuant to the statutes of the State of New York. Settlor's husband predeceased her. She died a resident of London, England, in 1956. A codicil [to her will probated in England] left the trust fund to Midland Bank for the benefit of two nieces for life with the remainder to Dr. Barnardo's Homes, etc., a charitable corporation of the United Kingdom and Northern Ireland. . . .

We . . . summarize our holdings as follows:

(1)   The law to be applied here is the law of New York which was the donor's domicile and where there was executed the trust agreement containing the power of appointment. . . . This rule applies where the same person is donor and donee. . . .

(2)   The trust was irrevocable and created a remainder interest but no reversionary interest in Mrs. Bauer. She retained no more than a testamentary power of appointment and hers was, therefore, one of the "measuring lives". . . .

(3)   The original trust plus the codicil trust thus involved three lives in being, resulting in unenforceability under the applicable former New York law . . . and thus the attempt in the will and codicil to exercise the power of appointment was ineffective. . . .

(5)   Since . . . there has been no valid testamentary disposition of the trust principal it must, as directed by the indenture itself, be distributed to the settlor's next of kin pursuant to the statutes of New York.

The order appealed from should be modified accordingly, with costs to parties filing separate briefs.

[The dissenting opinion of Judge Dye is omitted.]

■ FULD, JUDGE (dissenting). . . .

We deal here with a testatrix (Dagmar Bauer) who died in England, where she had long been domiciled, after there executing a will in which she exercised a general power of appointment, of which she was donor as well as donee, pursuant to a trust indenture executed in New York almost 40 years earlier. The court's decision to apply New York law to test the validity of Mrs. Bauer's exercise in England (in 1954) of the power of appointment which she had reserved to herself (in 1917) strikes me as an unfortunate example of adherence to mechanical and arbitrary formulae. The same considerations which prompted a departure from the inflexible and traditional choice-of-law rules in other cases (see, e.g., Auten v. Auten, 308 N.Y. 155, 124 N.E.2d 99, 50 A.L.R.2d 246; Babcock v. Jackson, 12 N.Y.2d 473, 240 N.Y.S.2d 743, 191 N.E.2d 279), it seems to me, should move the court to re-examine the wisdom and justice of continuing to apply similarly inflexible rules, with regard to significant underlying factors, in disposing of cases such as the present one.

The traditional rule which identifies the instrument exercising the power with the instrument creating it, for the purpose of testing the validity of the exercise of the power . . . assumes that ownership of the appointive property remains at all times in the donor of the power and that the donee of the power serves merely as a conduit or agency through which the donor's intention with respect to the appointive property is realized. . . . Such an assumption is, perhaps, justified where the power created is "special" and confines the donee's exercise of the power within the limits prescribed by the instrument creating the power. However, the assumption is certainly not justified when the power created is "general" or "beneficial", whether exercisable by deed or will or by will alone, and no restrictions of any other kind are imposed on its exercise by the donee. In the latter case—and in the one before us upon the death of Mrs. Bauer's husband—it is evident that the donee is vested with the equivalence of ownership as to the appointive property. . . . And this is particularly true where the donor and donee of the general power are the same person. This being so, it runs counter to reason to assume that the donor in such a case becomes his own agent to preserve an attachment to the place where the original trust agreement was executed, even though he has abandoned that place as his residence and acquired a new domicile in another jurisdiction, to the laws of which he voluntarily subjected himself.

In exercising the general power of appointment in England 37 years after she had conferred such power upon herself, Mrs. Bauer was justified in treating the appointive property as her own, and it is reasonable to suppose that, in disposing of such property under a will executed in England by an English solicitor, designating an English institutional executor and trustee to administer the trust and conferring benefits, at least in part, upon an English charity, Mrs. Bauer (through her English solicitor) had exercised the power in the light of English, rather than New York, law. The inference is inescapable that she intended the disposition of the appointive property to be governed by the same law which would govern the disposition of her personal estate, namely, the law of her last domicile. Since no discernible New York policy or interest dictates the application of its law to invalidate the disposition by the English testatrix valid under her personal law—and, indeed, now valid under present New York law—such intention should be given effect.

I do not, of course, mean to suggest that New York law would not govern the validity and effect of the provisions of the trust indenture. That instrument was executed in 1917 against the background of New York law, which Mrs. Bauer at that time undoubtedly intended would control. . . . However, I reject as insupportable any suggestion . . . that the law governing the trust conclusively governs the exercise of the power of appointment in every case, even to the extent of overriding the manifest intent of the donor-donee to have the law of his last domicile apply so as to effect a valid exercise of the general power. . . .

In sum, then, I would disavow the rule requiring the inexorable application of the law governing the instrument creating the power and I would apply the law of the jurisdiction intended by the donor-donee to control—in the case before us, England which, quite obviously, has the principal, if not the sole, interest and concern with " 'the outcome of . . . [this] litigation' ". . . .

2. VALIDITY—TESTAMENTARY TRUSTS

Farmers and Merchants Bank v. Woolf

Supreme Court of New Mexico, 1974.
86 N.M. 320, 523 P.2d 1346.

■ MONTOYA, JUSTICE.

The plaintiff-trustee (trustee), Farmers and Merchants Bank of Las Cruces, New Mexico, filed this action for declaratory judgment to determine the rights of the parties involved in a trust estate. From a judgment awarding the balance of the trust estate of Mabel Evelyn Jones (testatrix) to the Alcoholics Foundation of San Antonio, Texas (Foundation), Dale Woolf (Woolf), the administrator with will annexed of the estate of Gordon Vance Jones brings this appeal. . . .

[By will the testatrix, who died domiciled in Arizona, left her residuary estate in trust to the Farmers and Merchants Bank with the provision that following the death of her brother, the corpus of the trust should be paid to Alcoholics Anonymous of San Antonio, Texas. The trial court upheld the provision for Alcoholics Anonymous under Texas law although it would have been invalid under the law of Arizona. Woolf, the administrator of the deceased brother's estate appealed on the ground, among others, that the trial court had erred in not applying the law of Arizona, the state of the testatrix' domicil, since her estate consisted entirely of personal property.]

We first consider which law governs the disposition of the trust property. The testatrix was domiciled in Arizona and the main probate proceeding was held there. Ancillary probate proceedings were completed by the Dona Ana County Probate Court, since the funds involved in the trust were in the custody of the trustee in New Mexico. The legatee of the trust property is organized under the laws of the State of Texas, and the administration of the trust will also be in the State of Texas.

Under Restatement, Second, Conflict of Laws, Ch. 10 Trusts, § 269, at 152–153, it is stated:

"269. Validity of Trust of Movables Created by Will

"The validity of a trust of interests in movables created by will is determined "(a) as to matters that affect the validity of the will as a testamentary disposition, by the law that would be applied by the courts of the state of the testator's domicil at death, and

"(b) as to matters that affect only the validity of the trust provisions, except when the provision is invalid under the strong public policy of the state of the testator's domicil at death,

"(i) by the local law of the state designated by the testator to govern the validity of the trust, provided that this state has a substantial relation to the trust, or

"(ii) if there is no such effective designation, by the local law of the state of the testator's domicil at death, except that the local law of the state where the trust is to be administered will be applied if application of this law is necessary to sustain the validity of the trust."

Since the testatrix did not designate what law was to govern the validity of the trust, the provisions of § 269(b)(ii), supra, would apply. In the commentary to the foregoing section in Restatement, supra, the following appears in comment (h) at 157:

"h. Charitable trusts. In the case of charitable trusts, the courts have been even more ready than in the case of private trusts to uphold the trust if valid under the local law of the state of administration, even though the trust would be invalid under the local law of the testator's domicil. . . .

"When a testator bequeaths movables to be administered for charitable purposes in a state other than that of his domicil, the disposition is valid if valid under the local law of the state of administration, even though it would be invalid under the local law of the state of the testator's domicil. . . ."

In Fletcher v. Safe Deposit & Trust Co., 193 Md. 400, 410–411, 67 A.2d 386, 390 (Ct.App.1949), in considering the question of the applicable law to determine the validity of a trust estate, the court stated:

"The general rule is that the validity of a will of movables, or of a trust of movables created by will, is determined by the law of the testator's domicile. . . . 'However, where a trust is to be administered in a state other than that of the domicile, but is by the domiciliary law invalid from the outset under a rule grounded in a feeling that the administration of such a trust would be difficult or against the policy of the domicile, if such objections do not prevail at the place of administration the courts of the domicile will hold the trust valid.' [Citations omitted.]" . . .

Accordingly, we hold that the trial court did not err as claimed by Woolf under his first point. . . .

NOTES

1. Cross v. United States Trust Co., 30 N.E. 125 (N.Y.1892). The will of testatrix who died domiciled in Rhode Island was admitted to probate in that state. The will created a trust of personal property to be administered in New York by a New York trust company. The provisions of the trust violated the New York rule against perpetuities but were valid under the law of Rhode Island. The court applied Rhode Island law and held the trust valid. It stated that application of Rhode Island law would not be contrary to New York public policy. "The only material difference in the law of the two states on this subject [rule against perpetuities] is that in each a different rule is adopted for measuring the period within which absolute ownership may lawfully be suspended. . . . If . . . a person desiring to make a will must not only know the law of his domicile, but also the law of every country in which his personal estate may happen to be at his death . . . our courts would become the resort of dissatisfied heirs, or legatees, seeking to nullify wills, valid by the laws of the state where the persons who made them were domiciled. The question is not changed by the circumstance that the trustee and the trust fund is within our jurisdiction and all the beneficiaries but one are now residents of this state."

Matter of Chappell, 213 P. 684 (Wash.1923). By will, the testator, who died domiciled in California, established a trust covering personal property situated in Washington. The trust provisions were valid under Washington law; they were invalid under the California rule against perpetuities. Held that the validity of the trust should be sustained by application of Washington law. The trust did not contain any choice-of-law provision. But the court reasoned that the testator had obviously intended that the trust should be valid and that his intentions should be given effect "if that be possible and lawful."

In re Estate of Mullin, 155 A.3d 155 (N.H.2017). A choice-of-law clause selecting California law to govern all personal property, and the law of the situs of all realty, in an inter vivos trust, even though the decedent died domiciled in New Hampshire. The settlor of the trust had a substantial connection to California.

2. Hope v. Brewer, 32 N.E. 558 (N.Y.1892). The will of testator, a domiciliary of New York, directed his executors to convert his New York real estate into money and to pay over the proceeds to three named Scottish trustees, in trust, for the purpose of founding and endowing an infirmary "for the care and relief of the sick and infirm of Langholm, in Dunfrieshire, Scotland." This disposition was void under New York law on the ground of indefiniteness of beneficiaries; under the law of Scotland it was valid. On appeal from a judgment, upholding the validity of the trust against attack by a legatee, held, affirmed. "I have not been able to find any well-considered case . . . where a gift to a foreign charity in trust, contained in a valid testamentary instrument, has been held void, where there was a trustee competent to take and hold, and the trust was capable of being executed and enforced, according to the law of the place to which the property was to be transmitted under the will of the donor. . . . Our law with respect to the creation and validity of trusts . . . was designed only to regulate the holding of property under our laws, and in our state, and a trust intended to take effect in another state, or in a foreign country, would not seem to be within either its letter or spirit."

3. Trusts have no exact counterpart in the legal systems of civil law countries. Their recognition and enforcement in those countries has therefore been uncertain. Since trusts increasingly contain assets located abroad, common law countries have pressed for a resolution of these uncertainties. The 1984 Hague Convention on the Law Applicable to Trusts and Their Recognition (not yet in force, but ratification by the United States is pending) provides that a trust shall be governed by the law chosen by the settlor or, in the absence of a choice, by the law of the country with which it is most closely connected. The governing law applies to validity, construction, and effect of the trust. The same law, or another, may apply to administration. See Gaillard & Trautman, Trusts in Non-Trust Countries: Conflict of Laws and The Hague Convention on Trusts, 35 Am.J.Comp.L. 307 (1987).

4. As to the law governing the validity of testamentary trusts of movables, see 5A Scott & Fratcher, Trusts §§ 588–96A (4th ed.1989). As to the law governing powers of appointment of movables, see id. §§ 629–42.

Administration of Trusts

RESTATEMENT, SECOND, CONFLICT OF LAWS:

§ 271. Administration of Trust of Movables Created by Will

The administration of a trust of interests in movables created by will is governed as to matters which can be controlled by the terms of the trust

    (a) by the local law of the state designated by the testator to govern the administration of the trust, or

    (b) if there is no such designation, by the local law of the state of the testator's domicil at death, unless the trust is to be administered in some other state, in which case the local law of the latter state will govern.

Comment:

    a. *What are matters of administration.* The term "administration of a trust," as it is used in the Restatement of this Subject, includes those matters which relate to the management of the trust. Matters of administration include those relating to the duties owed by the trustee to the beneficiaries. . . . They include the powers of a trustee, such as the power to lease, to sell and to pledge, the exercise of discretionary powers, the requirement of unanimity of the trustees in the exercise of powers, and the survival of powers. . . . They include the liabilities which may be incurred by the trustee for breach of trust. . . . They include questions as to what are proper trust investments. . . . They include the trustee's right to compensation. . . . They include the trustee's right to indemnity for expenses incurred by him in the administration of the trust. . . . They include the removal of the trustee and the appointment of successor trustees. . . . They include the terminability of the trust. . . .

On the other hand, where the question is as to who are beneficiaries of the trust and as to the extent of their interests, the question is one of construction rather than of administration. . . .

c. *Law designated by the testator to govern administration of the trust.* The testator may designate in the will a state whose local law is to govern the administration of the trust. As to the effectiveness of such designation, a distinction must be made between those matters of administration which the testator can control by provisions in the will and those which he cannot control.

As to those matters which are subject to his control, he may designate a state which has no relation to the trust. The testator can freely regulate most matters of administration. . . .

The testator may provide that different matters of administration shall be governed by different laws. Thus, he may provide that the local law of one state shall govern the compensation of the trustee, and that the local law of another state shall govern investments. . . .

h. *Matters which cannot be controlled by the terms of the trust.* Certain matters of administration may be such that the testator cannot regulate them by any provision in the terms of the trust. Thus, . . . under the local law of the state of the testator's domicil there may be unusually strict rules as to self-dealing. If a testator fixes the administration of a trust in a state other than that of his domicil, it is not certain whether the courts will apply the rule of the domicil or the rule of the place of administration.

―――――

§ 272. Administration of Trust of Movables Created Inter Vivos

The administration of an inter vivos trust of interests in movables is governed as to matters which can be controlled by the terms of the trust

(a) by the local law of the state designated by the settlor to govern the administration of the trust, or

(b) if there is no such designation, by the local law of the state to which the administration of the trust is most substantially related.

NOTES

1. Appointment of a trust company as trustee provides persuasive evidence that the settlor of either an inter vivos or a testamentary trust intended that the trust should be administered in the state where the trust company is incorporated. Restatement, Second, Conflict of Laws §§ 271–72;

see also Boston Safe Deposit & Trust Co. v. Alfred University, 157 N.E.2d 662 (Mass.1959).

2. Application of New York Trust Co., 187 N.Y.S.2d 787 (Sup.Ct.1949). The case involved the question whether the situs of an inter vivos trust created in New York by a resident of that state with a New York trust company as trustee could be removed to California. The trust deed appointed two trustees, an individual and a corporation, and provided that the individual trustee, who was also the life beneficiary, could "request in writing the resignation of the corporate trustee, and upon receiving such request such corporate trustee shall forthwith resign. . . ." Acting under this provision, the individual trustee, who was a resident of California, requested the resignation of the New York corporate trustee and appointed a California trust company in its stead. Held, in a proceeding brought by the New York trust company, that the situs of the trust could be removed to California and that the California trust company was qualified to act as trustee. ". . . the express provision in the clause under discussion . . . makes it perfectly clear that the grantor contemplated the substitution when she executed the trust agreement. . . . The grantor must have realized that her son might find it more convenient to have the trust administered in a place readily accessible to him and that he might request the resignation of the corporate trustee for the very purpose of bringing about this result." Neither the law nor the public policy of New York were found to be offended by such a transfer.

Would the change in the place of administration in the New York Trust Co. case result in a change in the law governing the administration of the trust?

Does a provision of the type found in this case afford a convenient and effective way of giving a beneficiary power to change the law governing the validity of a trust?

Mullane v. Central Hanover Bank & Trust Co.

Supreme Court of the United States, 1950.
339 U.S. 306, 70 S.Ct. 652, 94 L.Ed. 865.

[The case appears p. 192, supra.]

NOTE

Jurisdiction to supervise the administration of a trust of interests in movables and, if necessary, to remove a trustee and to appoint a successor trustee is usually exercised by the court in which the trustee has qualified as trustee or by the courts of the state in which the trust is to be administered. Restatement, Second, Conflict of Laws § 267.

SECTION 3. INTANGIBLES

Morson v. Second National Bank of Boston

Supreme Court of Massachusetts, 1940.
306 Mass. 588, 29 N.E.2d 19, 131 A.L.R. 189.

■ QUA, JUSTICE. This is a bill in equity by the administrator of the estate of Herbert B. Turner . . . alleging . . . that a certificate for one hundred and fifty shares of the stock of the defendant Massachusetts Mohair Plush Company, a Massachusetts corporation, had been originally issued to Herbert B. Turner, but had been delivered to the defendant bank as "transfer agent" of the Plush company by the defendant Mildred Turner Copperman for transfer to her on the ground that Herbert B. Turner in his lifetime had made her a gift of the stock. The prayers are for injunctions against the transfer of the stock and for recovery of the certificate.

The judge . . . entered a decree for the plaintiff. The issue is whether the facts found show a valid gift of the stock, which should now be recognized by a transfer on the books of the corporation and the issuance of a new certificate to Mildred Turner Copperman. We think that they do.

Among the facts found are these: About September 20, 1937, while Turner and Mildred Turner Copperman were traveling together in Italy, Turner handed to Mildred Turner Copperman a sealed envelope previously marked by him "Property of Mildred Turner Copperman." As he did so he said, "These are yours." The certificate in his name, dated October 6, 1933, was in the envelope. He also said that he would have to sign the back of the certificate. Two days later a notary and two witnesses came to the hotel where the parties were staying. Mildred Turner Copperman produced the certificate, and "Turner signed his name on the back . . . and then he filled in the name of Miss Copperman and her address" and delivered the certificate to Mildred Turner Copperman, who "accepted it." Turner's intention at that time was "to make an absolute gift to Mildred Copperman to take effect at once."

It is provided by G.L.(Ter. Ed.) c. 155, sec. 27 (Uniform Stock Transfer Act sec. 1), that title "to a certificate and to the shares represented thereby shall be transferred only—(a) By delivery of the certificate endorsed either in blank or to a specified person by the person appearing by the certificate to be the owner of the shares represented thereby; or (b) By delivery of the certificate and a separate document containing a written assignment of the certificate or a power of attorney to sell, assign or transfer the same or the shares represented thereby, signed by the person appearing by the certificate to be the owner of the shares represented thereby. . . ." Plainly that which was done in Italy would have been sufficient, if it had been done in Massachusetts, to effect a transfer of legal title to the shares.

But it is argued that the validity of the transfer is to be judged by the law of Italy, and that certain formalities required by that law for the making of gifts in general were not observed. Doubtless it is true that whether or not there is a completed gift of an ordinary tangible chattel is to be determined by the law of the situs of the chattel. . . . Shares of stock, however, are not ordinary tangible chattels. A distinction has been taken between the shares and the certificate, regarded as a piece of paper which can be seen and felt, the former being said to be subject to the jurisdiction of the state of incorporation and the latter subject to the jurisdiction of the state in which it is located. . . . The shares are part of the structure of the corporation, all of which was erected and stands by virtue of the law of the state of incorporation. The law of that state determines the nature and attributes of the shares. If by the law of that state the shares devolve upon one who obtains ownership of the certificate it may be that the law of the state of a purported transfer of the certificate will indirectly determine share ownership. . . . But at the least when the state of incorporation has seen fit in creating the shares to insert in them the intrinsic attribute or quality of being assignable in a particular manner it would seem that that state, and other states as well, should recognize assignments made in the specified manner wherever they are made, even though that manner involves dealing in some way with the certificate. . . .

The final decree is reversed, and a final decree is to be entered dismissing the bill with costs to the defendant Mildred Turner Copperman.

NOTES

1. Does the principal case establish an alternative reference rule to determine the effect of a voluntary transfer of a stock certificate which embodies the underlying share—i. e., such a transfer will be held effective so long as this result would follow by applying either the law of the state of incorporation or that of the situs of the certificate?

2. *Travelers Insurance Co. v. Fields*, 451 F.2d 1292 (6th Cir.1971). While domiciled in Kentucky with his first wife, the decedent obtained employment in Ohio. He designated his first wife as beneficiary of group insurance policies issued by Travelers and which insured the employees of the Ohio employer against accidental death. The policies expressly provided that they should be governed by Ohio law. Thereafter, the decedent was divorced by his first wife in Kentucky. In due course, the decedent remarried but did not amend the provision in the policies which designated his first wife as beneficiary. He later changed his domicile to Ohio and there met an accidental death. Both the first and second wives claimed the proceeds of the policies. Held for the second wife. The divorce took place in Kentucky where the decedent and his first wife were domiciled at the time. Hence Kentucky law, under which the divorce extinguished the first wife's rights under the policy, was applicable. The first wife would have won if Ohio law had been held applicable.

SECTION 4. INTERPRETATION AND CONSTRUCTION OF DOCUMENTS

The meaning and effect of words contained in wills, trusts, deeds and other instruments of transfer may be determined in any one of three ways:

(1) *Interpretation.* This is the process used most frequently. It involves the attempt to determine the meaning which the words in question were actually intended to bear. In ascertaining the intentions of the party or parties, the court will consider the ordinary meaning of the words, the context in which they appear in the instrument, and the circumstances in which the instrument was drafted. It will consider who drafted the instrument (whether the party or parties or some third person) and whether the draftsman was probably using the language of his domicile or of the place of execution or of the situs of the land or chattel. The tribunal will also consider any other properly admissible evidence that casts light on the actual intentions of the party or parties. The question to be determined is one of fact rather than one of law. The forum will apply its own rules in determining the admissibility of evidence, and it will use its own standards in drawing conclusions from the evidence. Accordingly, interpretation does not involve choice-of-law problems.

(2) *Construction.* Sometimes it proves impossible to determine the meaning the words in an instrument were intended to bear, either because the party or parties did not give thought to the question or left no evidence of their thinking. In such cases, a rule of construction must be employed to fill what would otherwise be a gap in the instrument.

A typical problem of this sort arises when the question is whether an adopted child should be included within the scope of the word "heirs," as used in an instrument of conveyance, and there is no satisfactory evidence of what was actually intended. Here a rule of construction must be employed to provide an answer to this question.

(3) *Legal Effect.* Sometimes the law ascribes definite legal consequences, irrespective of the parties' actual intent, to the use of certain words in an instrument of transfer. Here the sole inquiry is as to the legal effect of the language, and so the term "legal effect" is used to describe the process. Instances of this sort are comparatively rare and, generally speaking, are confined to transfers of interests in land. One example is the common law rule that, in order to convey a fee simple interest in land by transfer inter vivos, the words "his heirs" must appear in the deed following the name of the grantee. Another is the rule in Shelley's Case, that when an owner of land made a conveyance to a person for life and limited a remainder to the heirs of the same person, he created an estate in fee simple in that person and not a life estate in him with a remainder to his heirs.

Where the contacts are divided among two or more states, determination of the meaning and effect of the language contained in an instrument of transfer may involve the preliminary inquiry: what law governs questions of construction and legal effect, and, assuming a change in this law during the period involved, at what time did the meaning and effect of the language become fixed?

"Construction" is likewise a fertile field for choice-of-law questions. Canons of construction are actual rules of law, and where the laws of the interested states differ in this regard, the problem of making a selection between them is essentially the same as that arising in any other field of choice of law.

Typical of the conflicts problems which may arise in this field is what law determines (1) the meaning of a term, such as "heirs," "issue" or "next of kin," contained in a will or conveyance inter vivos, (2) whether covenants for title will be implied from ordinary words of grant (e.g., "bargain, sell and convey") in a deed of land, (3) whether, in the absence of any provision on the point in her husband's will, a wife can take under the will and claim dower as well or whether she must make an election between the two and (4) assuming again that the will is silent, whether a devisee of land that is encumbered by a mortgage receives only the remaining equity or whether the mortgage must be paid from the personal property in the estate.

In the absence of a choice-of-law provision, words in a will of movables will be construed in accordance with the rules of construction that would be applied by the courts of the state where the testator was domiciled at the time of his death. These courts, in the absence of controlling circumstances to the contrary, would usually construe the words in accordance with the rules of construction prevailing in the state where the testator was domiciled at the time the will was executed. Restatement, Second, Conflict of Laws § 264; White v. United States, 511 F.Supp. 570 (S.D.Ind.1981), affirmed 680 F.2d 1156 (7th Cir.1982); Hamilton National Bank of Chattanooga v. Hutcheson, 357 F.Supp. 114 (E.D.Tenn.1973); In re Sewart, 342 Mich. 491, 70 N.W.2d 732, 52 A.L.R.2d 482 (1955) (law of testator's domicile at time of death applies to construction of the will for all purposes).

On occasion, the meaning of a term, such as "heirs" or "next of kin," has been determined by applying the law of the testator's domicile as of the time of the death of the person to whose heirs or next of kin the remainder was given. Second Bank-State Street Trust Co. v. Weston, 342 Mass. 630, 174 N.E.2d 763 (1961); Matter of Battell, 286 N.Y. 97, 35 N.E.2d 913 (1941); cf. Carnegie v. First National Bank of Brunswick, 218 Ga. 585, 129 S.E.2d 780 (1963). It may be suspected that in such cases the courts frequently apply that law which they believe will achieve the fairest and most desirable result for all concerned.

Words in a trust of movables, in the absence of a choice-of-law provision, will be construed, as to matters pertaining to administration, in accordance with the rules of construction of the state whose law governs the administration of the trust and, as to other matters, in accordance with the rules of construction of the state which the testator or settlor would probably have wished to be applied. Restatement, Second, Conflict of Laws § 268.

CHAPTER 11

FAMILY LAW

RESTATEMENT (SECOND) OF CONFLICT OF LAWS

INTRODUCTORY NOTE

In law, a [person's] status can be viewed from two standpoints. It can be viewed as a relationship which continues as the parties move from state to state, or it can be viewed from the standpoint of the incidents that arise from it. So marriage can be viewed as a relationship, namely solely from the point of view of whether [two] given [persons are "married."] On the other hand, marriage can be viewed from the standpoint of its incidents, such as . . . [the right to support during or after the termination of the relationship], the interests which the one has in the other's assets and the right of each to inherit, or to take a forced share in, the other's estate. . . .

On occasion, the courts are faced with a question of pure status [whether there exists a marital, or a legitimate, or an adoptive relationship between the parties]. For example, in the case of marriage, a question of pure status may arise in an action for an annulment, in an action for a declaratory judgment that a marriage does or does not exist or in a criminal prosecution for bigamy. It is clear, however, that questions involving the incidents of a status arise more frequently than do questions which purely involve the status as such. One problem is whether a question involving the incidents of a status can properly be decided without having made a preliminary determination of whether the status does, or does not, exist. For example, can a court properly determine that [one person] may inherit from the deceased as a "surviving spouse" within the meaning of its intestacy statute without having first determined that [the parties were] validly married . . .? Or can a court properly determine that a child born before the marriage of his parents may inherit from his father under its intestacy statute without having first determined that the child is legitimate . . .? By and large, the courts have acted on the assumption that a decision of questions involving the incidents of a marriage should be preceded by a determination of the validity of the marriage. On the other hand, the courts have been more inclined to decide questions of incidents involving legitimacy and adoption without having first determined whether legitimacy or adoption existed as a status.

SECTION 1. MARRIAGE*

Introduction

The *Restatement (Second)* statement reproduced above was drafted in 1971 against the background of the traditional marriage between a man and a woman. In the United States, "marriage," at that time,

---

*   See Restatement (Second) of Conflict of Laws §§ 283–84 (1971).

encompassed both a marriage formalized in accordance with state law (before a public official or a member of the clergy) and the informal, so-called "common law" marriage under the law of some (but not all) states. Since that time, and as a reaction to the ease with which modern law facilitates the dissolution of marriage, some states have introduced the "covenant marriage" to strengthen the parties' commitment to their marriage and to discourage its ready dissolution.

Parties to same-sex relationships have long sought formal recognition of their relationships and of their rights and duties ("incidents," see above) analogous to or identical with those of a traditional marriage. The watershed cases of *United States v. Windsor* (2013) and *Obergefell v. Hodges* (2015) made this so in all U.S. states. Before these decisions, a minority of states had "civil union" legislation, according same-sex partners to such a union essentially marriage-like rights. While same-sex partners may now wed, treatment of existing civil unions differs from state to state. For example, Vermont no longer allows new civil unions and Illinois allows partners to a civil union to "upgrade" their pre-*Obergefell* status to that of a marriage by simply completing the appropriate paperwork.

The federal Defense of Marriage Act (DOMA) defined marriage as heterosexual for federal law purposes and allowed states to deny effect to same-sex legal relationships entered into in states permitting them. The decision in *Windsor* overturned the first provisions, and *Obergefell* required countrywide recognition of same-sex marriage. Both decisions are considered at p. 918, infra.

In re May's Estate

Court of Appeals of New York, 1953.
305 N.Y. 486, 114 N.E.2d 4.

■ LEWIS, CHIEF JUDGE. In this proceeding, involving the administration of the estate of Fannie May, deceased, we are to determine whether the marriage in 1913 between the respondent Sam May and the decedent, who was his niece by the half blood—which marriage was celebrated in Rhode Island, where concededly such marriage is valid—is to be given legal effect in New York where statute law declares incestuous and void a marriage between uncle and niece. Domestic Relations Law, § 5, subd.3, McK.Consol.Laws.

The question thus presented arises from proof of the following facts: The petitioner Alice May Greenberg, one of six children born of the Rhode Island marriage of Sam and Fannie May, petitioned in 1951 for letters of administration of the estate of her mother Fannie May, who had died in 1945. Thereupon, the respondent Sam May, who asserts the validity of his marriage to the decedent, filed an objection to the issuance to petitioner of such letters of administration upon the ground that he is the surviving husband of the decedent and accordingly under section 118 of the Surrogate's Court Act, he has the paramount right to administer her estate. . . .

The record shows that for a period of more than five years prior to his marriage to decedent the respondent Sam May had resided in Portage, Wisconsin; that he came to New York in December, 1912, and within a month thereafter he and the decedent—both of whom were adherents of the Jewish faith—went to Providence, Rhode Island, where, on January 21, 1913, they entered into a ceremonial marriage performed by and at the home of a Jewish rabbi. The certificate issued upon that marriage gave the age of each party as twenty-six years and the residence of each as "New York, N.Y." Two weeks after their marriage in Rhode Island the respondent May and the decedent returned to Ulster County, New York, where they lived as man and wife for thirty-two years until the decedent's death in 1945. Meantime the six children were born who are parties to this proceeding. . . .

In Surrogate's Court, where letters of administration were granted to the petitioner, the Surrogate ruled that although the marriage of Sam May and the decedent in Rhode Island in 1913 was valid in that State, such marriage was not only void in New York as opposed to natural law but is contrary to the provisions of subdivision 3 of section 5 of the Domestic Relations Law. . . .

At the Appellate Division the order of the Surrogate was reversed on the law and the proceeding was remitted to Surrogate's Court with direction that letters of administration upon decedent's estate be granted to Sam May who was held to be the surviving spouse of the decedent. . . .

We regard the law as settled that, subject to two exceptions presently to be considered and in the absence of a statute expressly regulating within the domiciliary State marriages solemnized abroad, the legality of a marriage between persons *sui juris* is to be determined by the law of the place where it is celebrated. . . .

The statute of New York upon which the appellants rely is subdivision 3 of section 5 of the Domestic Relations Law which, insofar as relevant to our problem, provides:

"§ 5. *Incestuous and void marriages*

"A marriage is incestuous and void whether the relatives are legitimate or illegitimate between either: . . .

"3. An uncle and niece or an aunt and nephew.

"If a marriage prohibited by the foregoing provisions of this section be solemnized it shall be void, and the parties thereto shall each be fined not less than fifty nor more than one hundred dollars and may, in the discretion of the court in addition to said fine, be imprisoned for a term not exceeding six months. Any person who shall knowingly and wilfully solemnize such marriage, or procure or aid in the solemnization of the same, shall be deemed guilty of a misdemeanor and shall be fined or imprisoned in like manner."

Although the New York statute quoted above declares to be incestuous and void a marriage between an uncle and a niece and imposes penal measures upon the parties thereto, it is important to note that the statute does not by express terms regulate a marriage solemnized in another State where, as in our present case, the marriage was concededly legal. . . .

[T]he statute's scope should not be extended by judicial construction. . . . Accordingly, as to the first exception to the general rule that a marriage valid where performed is valid everywhere, we conclude that, absent any New York statute expressing clearly the Legislature's intent to regulate within this State marriages of its domiciliaries solemnized abroad, there is no "positive law" in this jurisdiction which serves to interdict the 1913 marriage in Rhode Island of the respondent Sam May and the decedent.

As to the application of the second exception to the marriage here involved—between persons of the Jewish faith whose kinship was not in the direct ascending or descending line of consanguinity and who were not brother and sister—we conclude that such marriage, solemnized, as it was, in accord with the ritual of the Jewish faith in a State whose legislative body has declared such a marriage to be "good and valid in law", was not offensive to the public sense of morality to a degree regarded generally with abhorrence and thus was not within the inhibitions of natural law. . . .

■ DESMOND, JUDGE (dissenting). It is fundamental that every State has the right to determine the marital status of its own citizens [citing cases]. Exercising that right, New York has declared in section 5 of the Domestic Relations Law that a marriage between uncle and niece is incestuous, void and criminal. Such marriages, while not within the Levitical forbidden degrees of the Old Testament, have been condemned by public opinion for centuries (see 1 Bishop on Marriage, Divorce and Separation, § 738), and are void, by statute in (it would seem) forty-seven of the States of the Union (all except Georgia, see Martindale-Hubbell, Law Digests, and except, also, that Rhode Island, one of the forty-seven, exempts from its local statute "any marriage which shall be solemnized among the Jews, within the degrees of affinity or consanguinity allowed by their religion", Gen.L. of R.I., ch. 415, § 4). It is undisputed here that this uncle and niece were both domiciled in New York in 1913, when they left New York for the sole purpose of going to Rhode Island to be married there, and that they were married in that State conformably to its laws (see above) and immediately returned to New York and ever afterwards resided in this State. That Rhode Island marriage, between two New York residents, was in New York, absolutely void for any and all purposes, by positive New York law which declares a strong public policy of this State. See Penal Law, § 1110.

The general rule that "a marriage valid where solemnized is valid everywhere" (see Restatement, Conflict of Laws, § 121) does not apply. To that rule there is a proviso or exception, recognized, it would seem, by all the States, as follows: "unless contrary to the prohibitions of natural law or the express prohibitions of a statute". See Thorp v. Thorp, 90 N.Y. 602, 605. Section 132 of the Restatement of Conflict of Laws states the rule apparently followed throughout America: "A marriage which is against the law of the state of domicil of either party, though the requirements of the law of the state of celebration have been complied with, will be invalid everywhere in the following cases: . . . (b) incestuous marriage between persons so closely related that their marriage is contrary to a strong public policy of the domicil". . . .

. . . Section 5 of the Domestic Relations Law, the one we are concerned with here, lists the marriages which are "incestuous and void" in New York, as being those between parent and child, brother and sister, uncle and niece, and aunt and nephew. All such misalliances are incestuous, and all, equally, are void. The policy, language, meaning and validity of the statute are beyond dispute. It should be enforced by the courts.

Decree affirmed.

NOTES

1.   See likewise Ghassemi v. Ghassemi, 998 So.2d 731 (La.App.2008), after remand confirmed, 103 So.3d 401 (La.App.2012) (Iranian marriage of first cousins did not violate Louisiana's public policy). See also Verma v. Verma, 903 N.E.2d 343 (Ohio Ct.App.2008) (recognition of marriage celebrated in India, in Hindu ceremony, and valid there); Tshiani v. Tshiani, 81 A.3d 414 (Md.2013) (foreign marriage by proxy, valid under law of celebration did not violate the public policy of the forum and was recognized). For the converse see Note 2, infra.

As indicated by In re May's Estate, a marriage will usually be held valid everywhere if it is valid under the law of the state of celebration. This state has an obvious interest in the manner in which the marriage is celebrated. On the other hand, this state will not, simply by reason of the fact that it is the state of celebration, be the state of most significant relationship for purposes of questions that do not relate to formalities, e.g., whether the parties have the capacity to marry or are within one of the forbidden degrees of relationship. Application of the law of the state of celebration to uphold the validity of the marriage with respect to such questions must therefore rest on other grounds. See Restatement, Second, Conflict of Laws § 283, Comments f–h; Baade, Marriage and Divorce in American Conflicts Law: Governmental-Interests Analysis and the Restatement (Second), 72 Colum.L.Rev. 329 (1972); Fine, The Application of Issue-Analysis to Choice of Law Involving Family Law Matters in the United States, 26 Loyola L.Rev. 295 (1980); Weintraub, Commentary on the Conflict of Laws § 5.1 (6th ed.2010); Hay, Borchers, Symeonides, Whytock Conflict of Laws §§ 13.1–13.18 (6th ed.2018). See the Introduction, supra, with respect to DOMA.

2.   Does it follow that a marriage that is invalid under the law of the state of celebration must necessarily be invalid everywhere? In this connection, should a distinction be drawn between questions of formalities and questions of substance? See Restatement, Second, Conflict of Laws § 283, Comment *i*. In re Estate of Shippy, 678 P.2d 848 (Wash.App.1984), involved the question of whether the claimant was the deceased putative husband's spouse. In selecting the applicable law, the court held: "There are, however, exceptions to applying the traditional rule that the validity of a marriage is governed by the law of the state where the marriage was contracted. . . . One of the exceptions . . . is that a marriage should not necessarily be invalid in other states if it would be valid under the law of some other state having a substantial relation to the parties and the marriage. . . . [In] light of this state's strong present interests [as the parties' last domicile], and to protect the expectations of James and Inge, we will . . . validate Inge's otherwise void marriage [entitling her to be treated] as the 'surviving spouse' . . . for all purposes in the administration and distribution of [James'] estate." Id. at 850–52. But see Randall v. Randall, 345 N.W.2d 319 (Neb.1984), confirming older decisions that strictly follow the place-of-celebration rule: ". . . [I]f valid there, [the marriage] will be held valid everywhere, and conversely if invalid by the [law of the place of celebration], it will be invalid wherever the question may arise." See also McPeek v. McCardle, 888 N.E.2d 171 (Ind.2008) (Ohio marriage, voidable there because contracted with Indiana, i.e. out-of-state, marriage license, recognized in Indiana).

In re Farrai, 900 N.Y.S.2d 340 (N.Y.App.Div.2010) (Islamic wedding of two New Yorkers in New Jersey: While invalid there for failure to conform with formal requirements, accepted as valid in New York under statutory language recognizing marriages "properly solemnized"). But see Ponorovskaya v. Stecklow, 987 N.Y.S.2d 543, 544 (N.Y.Sup.Ct.2014) ("pseudo-Jewish" marriage performed in Mexico, by a dentist appointed a Universal Life Church minister, and invalid there for non-compliance with formal requirements also not recognized in New York, distinguishing *In re Farrai*, supra, on the ground that the ceremony in the latter had been performed by an Imam in accordance with Islamic law). In Marriage of Medina, the Supreme Court of the North Marina Islands distinguished *In re Farrari* on the basis of Restatement (Second) Conflict of Laws § 283(2), which refers to the law of celebration, the Restatement (Second) having been adopted by statute as the Commonwealth's choice of law rules. 7 CMC § 3401. In the instant case, the marriage did not comply with the law of the Philippines (where it was celebrated), and therefore was not entitled to recognition. 2019 WL 7212282, *3 n. 4 (S.Ct. No. Marina Islands 2019).

3.   The general rule is that the validity of a marriage celebrated on board a vessel on the high seas is governed by the law of the vessel's flag. When the flag is that of the United States, this rule alone is insufficient to determine the applicable law since there is no federal law of marriage. In Fisher v. Fisher, 165 N.E. 460 (N.Y.1929) (an action for separation and support), the law of the shipowner's domicile was applied to validate the marriage in preference to that of the ship's registry, which would have invalidated the marriage.

4. See Starkowski v. Attorney General, [1954] A.C. 155 (H.L.), which upheld a marriage celebrated in Austria by application of an Austrian statute enacted subsequent to the marriage at a time when the spouses were no longer living in Austria. The marriage was originally invalid under Austrian law because it had been celebrated by a priest rather than by the civil authorities. The validating act was held to relate to formalities. See Da Costa, The Formalities of Marriage in the Conflict of Laws, 7 Int'l & Comp.L.Q. 217 (1958).

5. Under the place-of-celebration rule, states that do not permit informal methods of creating the matrimonial status ("common law" marriage) usually will recognize a marriage of that kind when it was contracted in a state permitting such a method. See, e.g., Enis v. State, 408 So.2d 486 (Miss.1981); Mott v. Duncan Petroleum Transp., 414 N.E.2d 657 (N.Y.1980); In re Succession of Hendrix, 990 So.2d 742 (La.App.2008), review denied, 998 So.2d 729 (La.2009). The same is generally true with respect to marriages by proxy. See In re Marriage of Holemar, 557 P.2d 38 (Or.1976); Morris v. Morris, 2010 WL 2342659 (La.App.2010) (marriage by proxy, valid under Texas law, recognized in Louisiana, where marriages "by procuration" are prohibited). However, the courts in the state of the parties' domicile have refused recognition to out-of-state common law marriages when the link with the state of celebration was insubstantial. See, e.g., Matter of Estate of Brack, 329 N.W.2d 432 (Mich.App.1982) (one night in a Georgia motel while en route to Florida insufficient to establish a Georgia common law marriage); Collier v. City of Milford, 537 A.2d 474 (Conn.1988) ("periodic sojourns" to Alabama and South Carolina). See also p. 922, Note 4, infra. State courts may also refuse to recognize a foreign country determination of marital status. See, e.g., Dion v. Rieser, 285 P.3d 678 (N.M.App.2012), cert. denied, 294 P.3d 1243 (N.M.2012) (Australian "de facto spouse" status is not a recognizable marriage; petitioners is therefore not a surviving spouse entitled to appointment as personal representative of decedent's estate); Miezgiel v. Holder, 33 F.Supp.3d 184 (E.D.N.Y.2014) (marriage performed at Polish Consulate in New York not valid for immigration purposes for non-compliance with New York law).

6. Problems arise when the validity of a second marriage depends upon the dissolution or invalidity of the first marriage. It has been said that the "generally accepted American view is that the presumption of the validity of the second marriage is 'stronger' than the presumption of the continuance of the first marriage." Headen v. Pope & Talbot, Inc., 252 F.2d 739, 743 (3d Cir.1958). But cf. Woolery v. Metro. Life Ins. Co., 406 F.Supp. 641 (E.D.Va.1976) (first marriage valid because never dissolved, second marriage license fraudulently obtained); Tostado v. Tostado 151 P.3d 1060 (Wash.App.2007) (California marriage a "nullity" because parties had earlier wed in Mexico).

Wilkins v. Zelichowski

Supreme Court of New Jersey, 1958.
26 N.J. 370, 140 A.2d 65.

■ JACOBS, J. . . . The plaintiff and the defendant were domiciled in New Jersey as were their respective parents. They ran away from New Jersey to marry and they chose Indiana because they believed "it was the quickest place." The Indiana statutes provide that "females of the age of sixteen" are capable of marriage although they also provide that where the female is within the age of 18 the required marriage license shall not be issued without the consent of her parents. See Burns, Indiana Statutes Annotated, §§ 44–101, 44–202. After their marriage in Indiana on April 23, 1954, the plaintiff and defendant returned immediately to New Jersey where they set up their home. On February 22, 1955 the plaintiff bore the defendant's child. . . . On January 4, 1956 the plaintiff filed her annulment complaint under N.J.S. 2A:34–1(e), N.J.S.A., which provides that a judgment of nullity may be rendered on the wife's application upon a showing that she was under the age of 18 years at the time of her marriage and that the marriage has not been "confirmed by her after arriving at such age"; the statute also provides that where a child has been born there shall be no judgment of nullity unless the court is of the opinion that the judgment "will not be against the best interests of the child." . . .

The plaintiff's evidence adequately established that she was 16 years of age when she was married and that she did not confirm her marriage after she had reached 18 years of age and the Chancery Division expressly found that an annulment would be "for the best interests of the child"; nevertheless it declined to grant the relief sought by the plaintiff on the ground that the marriage was valid in Indiana and should therefore, under principles of the conflict of laws, not be nullified by a New Jersey court because of the plaintiff's nonage. In reaching the same result the Appellate Division recognized that the Chancery Division had ample power to nullify the Indiana marriage of the New Jersey domiciliaries . . . but expressed the view that comity dictated that it should not take such action unless there was an imperative New Jersey policy (which it did not find) against marriages of 16-year-old females. . . .

In 1905 the Court of Chancery had occasion to deal with an application by a New Jersey resident for annulment of an English marriage entered into when she was 14 years of age; the court expressed the view that there could be "no doubt" as to its jurisdiction. After reviewing the plaintiff's evidence of fraud and duress and pointing out that while our law is interested in the permanency and inviolability of the marriage contract "it is equally interested in having it entered into by persons of competent age and judgment," it awarded a decree of annulment. See Avakian v. Avakian, 69 N.J.Eq. 89, 100, 60 A. 521, 525 (Ch.1905, per Pitney, V.C.), affirmed, 69 N.J.Eq. 834, 66 A. 1133 (E. & A.1906). In 1907 the Legislature revised the statutory provisions relating to annulments (L.1907, c. 216, p. 474); it directed that a decree of nullity could be rendered not only in the case of a bigamous or incestuous marriage (see L.1902, c. 157, p. 502) but also in any case, among others, where the wife sought the decree and established that she was under 16 at the time of the marriage and had not confirmed it after attaining such age. . . . In 1928 the Legislature strengthened its policy by increasing the wife's age requirement and providing that the wife could obtain a decree of nullification "when she was under the age of eighteen years at the time of the marriage, unless such marriage be confirmed by her after arriving at such age." See L.1928, c. 65, p. 139.

The vigor of New Jersey's policy against marriages by persons under the prescribed age is evidenced not only by the breadth of the statutory language but also by the judicial decisions. [The court discussed at this point a number of New Jersey decisions.]

It is undisputed that if the marriage between the plaintiff and the defendant had taken place here, the public policy of New Jersey would be applicable and the plaintiff would be entitled to the annulment; and it seems clear to us that if New Jersey's public policy is to remain at all meaningful it must be considered equally applicable though their marriage took place in Indiana. While that State was interested in the formal ceremonial requirements of the marriage it had no interest whatever in that marital status of the parties. Indeed, New Jersey was the only State having any interest in that status, for both parties were domiciled in New Jersey before and after the marriage and their matrimonial domicile was established here. The purpose in having the ceremony take place in Indiana was to evade New Jersey's marriage policy and we see no just or compelling reason for permitting it to succeed. . . .

. . . We are not here concerned with a collateral attack on an Indiana marriage or with a direct attack on an Indiana marriage between domiciliaries of Indiana or some state other than New Jersey. We are concerned only with a direct and timely proceeding, authorized by the New Jersey statute (N.J.S. 2A:34–1(e), N.J.S.A.), by an underage wife for annulment of an Indiana marriage between parties who have at all times been domiciled in New Jersey. We are satisfied that at least in this situation the strong public policy of New Jersey (see Restatement, Conflict of Laws § 132(b), comment *b*) requires that the annulment be granted. The annulment will not render the plaintiff's child illegitimate (N.J.S. 2A:34–20, N.J.S.A.) and, as the Chancery Division found, it will be for his best interests. The annulment will also serve the plaintiff's best interests for it will tend to reduce the tragic consequences of her immature conduct and unfortunate marriage. The Legislature has clearly fixed the State's policy in her favor and has granted her the right to apply for a judgment nullifying her marriage; we know of no considerations of equity or justice or overriding principles of the law which would lead us to deprive her of the relief she seeks under the circumstances she presents. . . .

Reversed.

NOTES

1. The *Wilkins* case demonstrates that a marriage which satisfies the place of celebration rule will occasionally be held invalid under the law of another jurisdiction. This typically occurs only when the marriage is celebrated outside the domicile of one of the parties and where they intend to live thereafter. Restatement, Second, Conflict of Laws § 283; Taintor, Marriage to a Paramour after Divorce: The Conflict of Laws, 43 Minn.L.Rev. 889 (1959). For an exception, see Catalano v. Catalano, 170 A.2d 726 (Conn.1961). It has been suggested that the law of the state where the parties intend to make their home should have the ultimate voice in determining the validity of their marriage. See Cook, The Logical and Legal Bases of the Conflict of Laws 452–56 (1942). What objections could be advanced to the adoption of such a rule?

2. Did the marriage in the *Wilkins* case represent a more objectionable union than the one upheld in In re May's Estate, p. 906, supra? In the absence of statutory guidance, what criteria should a court use to invalidate a marriage that satisfies the requirements of the state of celebration? In Leszinske v. Poole, 798 P.2d 1049 (N.M.App.1990), cert. denied, 797 P.2d 983 (N.M.1990), a father appealed a lower court decision to permit the mother to retain primary physical custody of the three minor children only if the mother and her uncle, who wished to marry each other, could enter into a valid marriage. A marriage between uncle and niece was prohibited by the laws of New Mexico and California (where the mother wished to reside). Soon thereafter, niece and uncle were married in Costa Rica, which permits such marriages. The lower court recognized the marriage because it was valid where celebrated and awarded physical custody of the children to the mother. On appeal, the father argued that the lower court had encouraged the mother to violate New Mexico public policy. The court of appeals affirmed. The lower court had properly recognized the strong probability of the mother seeking such a marriage, considered the possible impact of any attack on the validity of such a marriage upon the best interests of the children, and concluded that the children should remain with the mother. See also Note 2, p. 910.

3. Statutes in a number of states expressly declare that a marriage, valid where contracted, is valid within the state. See, e.g., Cal.Fam.Code Ann. § 308; Idaho Code Ann. § 32–209; Kan.Gen.Stat.Ann. § 23–2508; Ky.Rev.Stat. § 402.040; Neb.Rev.Stat. § 42–117; N.M.Stat.Ann. § 40–1–4; N.D.Code 14–03–08 (but note exception as to its residents' contracting a marriage prohibited by North Dakota); S.D.C.L. 25–1–38; Utah Code Ann. § 30–1–4

Section 210 of the Uniform Marriage and Divorce Act (currently in effect in six states) carries the validation preference even further. It provides:

All marriages contracted within this State prior to the effective date of this Act, or outside this State, that were valid at the time of the contract or subsequently validated by the laws of the place in which they were contracted or by the domicile of the parties, are valid in this State.

Are general provisions of this sort desirable? Would § 210 have required the court to reach a different result in the Wilkins case? Would it be possible to frame a general choice-of-law rule on the subject of marriage that would permit the court to give consideration to the particular issue?

4.   Several states have enacted marriage evasion statutes, based on the Uniform Marriage Evasion Act (now withdrawn). These statutes typically provide that marriages contracted outside the forum will be void if the marriage is of a type prohibited under forum law and the parties are residents of the forum. Some states also prohibit solemnization of marriages within the forum by out-of-state residents whose home state would not permit the marriage. See, e.g. Ill.Comp.Stat. 750 § 5/216–219 (2015); N.H. Stat. § 457:3 (2014); W.Va. Code § 48–2–602 (West 2020); Wis.Stat.Ann. § 765.04 (West 2020).

Some states make it unlawful for their residents to cohabit within the state if they have elsewhere contracted a marriage which is prohibited by the law of the state. See, e.g., Del.Code Ann. tit. 13 § 104; Miss.Code Ann. § 97–29–9; Va.Code § 20–40 (1983); W.Va.Code § 48–2–503. But see State v. Austin, 234 S.E.2d 657 (W.Va.1977), involving a charge of contributing to the delinquency of a 15-year old by marrying her out of state. The court said that although the marriage was voidable (by or on behalf of the minor) it was valid until then, hence no crime had been committed.

5.   If a divorce does not become final until the termination of the period within which remarriage is prohibited, a new marriage within this period in a second state will usually be invalid under the law of the second state and, if so, will be held invalid everywhere. Randall v. Randall, 345 N.W.2d 319 (Neb.1984); Marek v. Flemming, 192 F.Supp. 528 (S.D.Tex.1961), judgment vacated, 295 F.2d 691 (5th Cir.1961).

6.   With the redefinition of marriage by *Windsor* and *Obergefell*, 918, infra, the introduction in some states of other forms of legal relationships (civil unions, registered partnerships), and the dissolution of marriage or such other relationships being relatively easy, the "covenant marriage" represents a trend in the opposite direction. This alternative—a stricter form of marriage—has been adopted by Arizona, Arkansas, and Louisiana. Ariz.Rev.Stat.Ann. § 25–901; Ark.C.Ann. § 9–11–801; La.Rev.Stat.Ann. § 9:272. Similar legislation has been introduced in other states. In a "covenant marriage", the parties execute a "declaration of intent" to make all reasonable efforts to preserve the marriage. Dissolution is possible on fault grounds or, after a two-year waiting period, on a no-fault basis. The parties stipulate the applicability of the covenant state's law. Will the stricter preconditions for dissolution be honored in a non-covenant state, if dissolution is later sought there by one or both parties? See p. 940, Note 2, infra. For discussion, see K. Shaw Spaht & S. Symeonides, Covenant

Marriage and the Law of Conflicts [sic] of Laws, 32 Creighton L.Rev. 1085 (1999); P. Hay, The American "Covenant Marriage" in the Conflict of Laws, 64 Louisiana L.Rev. 43 (2003); reprinted in John Witte, Jr. and Eliza Ellison (eds.), Covenant Marriage in Comparative Perspective 294 (2004); Blackburn v. Blackburn, 180 So.3d 16 (Ala.Civ.App.2015) (Alabama courts need not enforce covenant marriage after spouses become Alabama domiciliaries). See comment on *Blackburn* in Melki v. Melki 2020 WL 5797869, *3, n. 5 (Md.Ct.Spec.App. Sept. 29, 2020).

Redefinition of marriage can also go the opposite way, viz. advocating its abolition in any kind of traditional form. One proposal called for the removal of most restrictions relating to gender or number of persons that can be party to a marriage. E. Brake, Minimizing Marriage: Marriage, Morality, and the Law (2012). Assuming that any state were to go this way, would such a "minimal marriage" benefit from the recognition-friendly approaches summarized in Note 3, supra? For polygamous marriages, see In re Dalip Singh Bir's Estate and Notes 2–4 following it, p. 921, infra.

7.   *Validity of sequential marriages.* In Seaton v. Seaton, 133 Cal.Rptr.3d 50 (Cal.App.2011), the issue was whether appellant's third marriage in California should be nullified because her prior Nevada (second) marriage had not been dissolved as bigamous in view of a still prior (first) marriage that was still undissolved at the time of the Nevada marriage. The appellate court reversed the trial court's declaration that the third marriage was a nullity in view of the Nevada marriage. Instead, the Nevada marriage itself was null and void from the beginning because of the undissolved first marriage. Since the latter was dissolved before the third marriage, the appellant did have capacity to contract the third marriage. The court based itself on both California and Nevada law (the latter as the law of the place of celebration of the second "marriage") and found them to be the same: a marriage contracted when one of the parties is still married to another is void from the beginning and "its invalidity may be shown collaterally." Id. at 55. In contrast, a formal decree of dissolution is needed when the marriage is voidable (see *Wilkins*, p. 912, supra), rather than void, as here. The court noted in dictum that "the legal fiction that a void marriage never existed has been abandoned where the rights of children are involved. Thus, children born during a bigamous marriage are considered legitimate even though the marriage was void from inception." Id. at 57.

8.   *Estoppel.* Parties who benefit from a marriage may be estopped from denying its validity, even if that marriage was not valid. In Bedard v. Corliss, 973 N.E.2d 691 (Mass.App.2012), the decedent mother's children challenged the validity of her second marriage as not complying with the laws of the place where contracted (Mexico). The trial court held that the couple had never legally married and ousted the presumptive husband from administering the decedent's estate. On appeal, this court reversed, holding that the challenge itself was improper. Under the Restatement (Second) of Conflict of Laws, a child of a first marriage is estopped from challenging the validity of its dissolution to prevent a second spouse from sharing the decedent's inheritance. § 74 cmt. *b*. This court extended this reasoning to a challenge to the validity of a marriage. The couple had held themselves out as married for more than 20 years, and the decedent spouse had benefitted from that relationship. The children's claim derived from that of their mother, who herself would have been estopped (by virtue of that benefit), so they, too were estopped from challenging the validity of their mother's marriage. See also *Suneson v. Suneson*, 508 N.E.2d 891 (Mass.App.1987) (stranger to marriage in privity with deceased spouse estopped from challenging validity of marriage when decedent would have been estopped).

NOTES: FORMAL SAME-SEX DOMESTIC RELATIONSHIPS

1.   In an early decision, the Hawaii Supreme Court appeared willing to require, on constitutional grounds, the availability of solemnization of same-sex marriages: *Baehr v. Lewin*, 852 P.2d 44 (Haw.1993), abrogated by *Obergefell*, Note 2 infra. In response, Congress passed the Defense of Marriage Act, 28 U.S.C. § 1738C, 1 U.S.C. § 7. The Act was the fourth implementing statute adopted under the Constitution's Full Faith and Credit Clause (p. 45, supra). It provided: "No state, territory, or possession of the United States, or Indian tribe, shall be required to give effect to any public act, record, or judicial proceeding of any other State, territory, possession, or tribe, respecting any relationship between persons of the same sex that is treated as a marriage under the laws of such other State, territory, possession, or a right or claim arising from such relationship." As of November 2012, 39 states had adopted legislation or constitutional amendments expressly prohibiting same-sex marriages.

Civil Union

2.   Vermont was the first state to enact a statute permitting "civil unions" of same-sex couples, assuring them the benefits enjoyed by married couples. As of 2015, civil union was available in Colorado, Hawaii, Illinois, and New Jersey. After the decision in *Obergefell v. Hodges*, 576 U.S. 644 (2015) these statutes are largely irrelevant.

In *United States v. Windsor*, 570 U.S. 744 (2013), the United States Supreme Court struck down Section 3 of DOMA, which defined marriage as the union of man and woman for purposes of federal law, but did not address Section 2, which permits states to refuse to recognize such marriages, i.e., the Act exempted same-sex unions from the Constitution's Full Faith and Credit command. See p. 909, Note 1. While most states had originally adopted legislation or state constitutional amendments rejecting such unions and refusing recognition to out-of-state unions, even if valid where entered, increasing numbers changed their approach, either by legislation or as a result of judicial decision, so that same-sex marriage was permitted by 35 states and the District of Columbia by 2015. The status of the law of the remaining states therefore became increasingly important: would Section 2 of DOMA be upheld or struck down by the Supreme Court?

In 2015, the Supreme Court addressed the issues presented by Section 2 of DOMA. The Court had granted certiorari in four cases, and consolidated them, in January of that year with respect to two questions: (1) does the Fourteenth Amendment require a state to license a marriage between two people of the same sex, and (2) must a state recognize such a marriage if validly entered in a sister state? In *Obergefell v. Hodges*, 576 U.S. 644 (2015), the Court answered both questions in the affirmative. Justice Kennedy, writing for the 5–4 majority, identified four "principles and traditions" as inherent in the Due Process Clause of the Fourteenth Amendment, among them the right to marry (as "a keystone of the Nation's social order") and the right to "individual dignity and autonomy." Together, these principles meant that the safeguarding of individual dignity and the right to autonomy required same-sex partners also to have the right to marry. Justice Kennedy also invoked the Equal Protection Clause in support of the majority's conclusion, but without much elaboration. Four vigorous, individual dissents by Chief Justice Roberts and Justices Scalia, Thomas, and Alito shared one common ground: that concern with a definition of the Nation's social structure should be left to the democratically elected legislature rather than be determined by the judiciary.

While the *Obergefell* decision now permits, and requires recognition of, same-sex marriages throughout the United States, much additional litigation now involves the protection of personal religious beliefs. The federal Religious Freedom Restoration Act of 1993, 42 U.S.C. §§ 2000bb–2000bb–4, was intended as an instrument to balance possible infringements of religious beliefs against compelling state interests. State law versions (passed in response to the decision in City of Boerne v. Flores, 521 U.S. 507 (1997)) go further and have been criticized as possibly permitting homophobic action. See, e.g., Ind.Code § 34–13–9 (signed in April 2015, effected July 15, 2015); Indiana Family Institute, Inc. v. City of Carmel, 155 N.E.3d 1209 (Ind.Ct.App.2020) (affirming dismissal of challenge of statute because plaintiff failed to show exclusion of or discrimination against its same-sex members, so that the constitutional question was not reached). Such potential developments may raise constitutional, but not conflict-of-laws issues, and are not addressed further here.

Foreign Jurisdictions

3. American developments with respect to formal legal relationships between same-sex partners have their counterparts abroad. In the European Union, Austria, Belgium, Denmark, Finland, France, Germany, Greece, Iceland Ireland, Luxembourg, Malta, the Netherlands, Portugal, Spain, Sweden, and the United Kingdom have legislation permitting same-sex marriage. E.U. members that grant spouse-like rights to same-sex domestic partners include Croatia, Cyprus, Czech Republic, Estonia, Hungary, Italy, and Slovenia. In contrast, Bulgaria, Latvia, Poland, and Slovakia prohibit same-sex marriage. Serbia, an E.U.-applicant, also prohibits same-sex marriage. Outside of the E.U., Argentina, Australia, Brazil, Canada, Colombia, Ecuador, Mexico City, New Zealand, South Africa, Taiwan, Uruguay, and parts of Mexico permit same-sex marriage. Israel does not provide for same-sex marriage under its religious law, but does recognize such marriages concluded abroad.

Conflicts Problems

4. In the wake of *Obergefell*, one issue appears settled: a same-sex marriage entered into in F-1 must be recognized by F-2. It also seems settled that F-2 must now entertain claims for incidents to a same-sex F-1 marriage that F-2 would accord a similar opposite-sex marriage. After all, the court held in *Obergefell* that the state laws at issue were invalid to the extent they excluded same-sex couples from civil marriage "on the same terms and conditions as same-sex couples." Examples of incidents that should no longer be an issue are pension rights, inheritance rights, claims for support following an out-of-state dissolution of the relationship, and petitions for custody or changes in custody of children raised in the common household.

Surprisingly, Florida officials have refused to issue new death certificates listing same-sex spouses who died before the decision in *Obergefell*, even though a death certificate was at issue before the court in *Obergefell*. Instead, the surviving same-sex spouse must obtain a court order to make the correction. A case challenged this procedural state of affairs, which imposes an additional burden on same-sex couples not imposed on opposite-sex couples. Birchfield v. Jones, 2017 WL 4399811 (N.D.Fla.Mar.23, 2017) (summary judgment for plaintiffs granted).

The conflict-of-laws problems posed by the previous availability of same-sex marriages or civil unions in some states and unavailability or illegality in others generated considerable commentary, much of which remains relevant to analysis of recognition of incidents of same-sex marriages. See Borchers, Baker v. General Motors: Implications for Inter-Jurisdictional Recognition of Non-Traditional Marriages, 32 Creighton L.Rev. 147 (1998); Cox, Same-Sex Marriage and Choice-of-Law: If We Marry in Hawaii, Are We Still Married When We Return Home?, 1994 Wis.L.Rev. 1033; Hay, Recognition of Same-Sex Legal Relationships in the United States, in: John C. Reitz & David S. Clark, American Law in the Twenty-First Century: U.S. National Reports to the XVIIth International Congress of Comparative Law, 54 Am.J.Comp.L. 257 (Supp.2006); Kramer, Same-Sex Marriage, Conflict of Laws, and the Unconstitutional Public Policy Exception, 106 Yale L.J. 1965 (1997); Reppy, The Framework of Full Faith and Credit and Interstate Recognition of Same-Sex Marriages, 3 Ave Maria L.Rev. 393 (2005); Baude, Beyond DOMA: Choice of State Law in Federal Statutes, 64 Stan.L.Rev. 1371 (2012). Some additional conflicts problems are raised below in Note 8.

Numerous problems related to granting or recognizing incidents of a same-sex marriage remain undecided, even after the decision in *Obergefell*. The opinion itself identified many of them in its rationale for marriage's averred status as a "keystone of [American] social order[:] taxation; inheritance and property rights; rules of intestate succession; spousal privilege in the law of evidence; hospital access; medical decisionmaking authority; adoption rights; the rights and benefits of survivors; birth and death certificates; professional ethics rules; campaign finance restrictions; workers' compensation benefits; health insurance; and child custody, support, and visitation rules." Obergefell v. Hodges, 576 U.S. 644, 669 (2015).

5. To protect the religious freedom of public officials opposed to same-sex marriage, North Carolina passed a law allowing judges to recuse themselves "from performing all lawful marriages . . . based upon any sincerely held religious objection." N.C.Gen.Stat. § 51–5.5 (2015). A challenge was dismissed for lack of standing in Ansley v. Warren, 2016 WL 5213937 (W.D.N.C.2016).

6. For same-sex marriage abroad, see also supra Note 4. For the Netherlands legislation, see J. Wasmuth, in: H. Krüger and H.-P. Mansel (eds.), Liber Amicorum Gerhard Kegel 237 (2002). For Belgium, see Fiorini, New Belgian Law on Same Sex Marriage and the PIL Implications, 52 Int'l & Comp.L.Q. 1039 (2003). In a number of European countries, same-sex partnerships can now be registered and are analogized to marriage for purposes of property and succession rights, support, and dissolution. For overviews, see K. Boele-Woelki, The Legal Recognition of Same-Sex Relationships Within the European Union, 82 Tul.L.Rev. 1949 (2008); J. Basedow, K. Hopt, H. Kötz & P. Dopffel (eds.), Die Rechtsstellung gleichgeschlechtlicher Lebensgemeinschaften (= Vol.70, Beiträge zum Ausländischen und Internationalen Privatrecht, 2000). Many countries recognize same-sex couples for immigration purposes. Although same-sex marriages cannot be performed in Israel, the Israeli Supreme Court recognized same-sex marriages validly entered into abroad in Yosi Ben Ari v. Ministry of the Interior, Case 05–3045 (Consolidated Cases 05–3045, 3046, 10218, 110468, 10597 (Nov. 21, 2006)) (Canadian marriage).

In Belgium, which permits same-sex marriage, an administrative circular directs state registrars to treat registered same-sex partnerships (such as civil unions) concluded in other countries as "marriages" and to register them as such. Belgium, Staatsblad, May 31, 2007, 29469. If parties from, say, Hungary or Switzerland, register their same-sex partnership as a marriage in Belgium or another EU country that has adopted same-sex marriage legislation, will their home states now recognize their relation as a marriage? For Germany, see Art. 17(b)(4) EGBGB (referring to the law of original registration of the partnership. Is there a problem with a "limping marriage" (married in one state, but not another)?

The question has also been raised whether recognition of same-sex unions may even be required as a matter of European Union law, particularly EC Directive 2004/38, which guarantees the free movement of EU citizens and their family members. If an EU citizen is married to a non-EU citizen, the latter is a "spouse" and entitled to the same rights of movement and residence as if s/he were an EU citizen herself/himself. Do these rights extend to a same-sex spouse who is regarded as a spouse in the EU country of celebration? A lower German administrative court said "no" in a decision issued before the Directive was adopted. VG Karlsruhe, Decision of Sept. 9, 2004, [2006] IPRax 284. The EU Court of Justice ruled in 2018 that the right to free movement of EU domiciliaries extends to their spouses, as defined (or recognized) by the law of their EU country of domicile from which they come. Coman, Hamilton and Asociata Accept v. Inspectoratul General pentru Imigrâri and Ministeral Afacerilor Interne (C-673/16), [2018] Official Journal C-268, p. 7 (June 2018).

How would/should these issues be resolved in the United States— interstate or international?

7. What is the status of a married person after a sex-change operation? Before same-sex marriage became legal in Germany, the German Constitutional Court held the restriction of "marriage" to heterosexual unions to be inapplicable in the case of a married person seeking a change in official records to reflect the change in gender. In the Court's view, the law impermissibly required a transgendered person either to disavow his or her marriage or the (new) sexual identity. Bundesverfassungsgericht, Decision of May 27, 2008, 1 BvL 10/05. The result of the decision is a same-sex marriage, at that time not otherwise available under German law. How should another country deal with this transgendered person's civil status?

IN RE DALIP SINGH BIR'S ESTATE, 188 P.2d 499 (Cal.App.1948): While domiciled in the Punjab Province of India, the decedent legally married two wives. Thereafter, he moved to California where he died intestate. The question was whether both women could inherit as "wives" of the decedent. The court held that they could so inherit. The conclusion might be different "if the decedent had attempted to cohabit with his two wives in California." But the "public policy" of California would not be violated by dividing money equally between them. Accord: In re Estate of Diba, 28 Misc.3d 1207(A), 2010 WL 2696611 (N.Y.Surr.Ct.2010). A Minnesota district court cited *In re Dalip Singh Bir's Estate* in support of its decision to allow the surviving partner of a valid California same-sex marriage to inherit as a spouse, even though Minnesota had adopted DOMA-type legislation. The court recognized the marriage as valid only for the purpose of inheritance. In re Estate of Proehl, 2012 WL 3191246 (Minn.Dist.Ct. Aug. 1, 2012).

NOTES

1. A state will usually afford the same incidents—in the sense of resulting legal interests—to a valid foreign marriage that it gives to a marriage contracted within its territory. Restatement, Second, Conflict of Laws § 284. However, it will not do so in situations where recognition would violate public policy. See, e.g., Loucks v. Standard Oil Co., p. 459, supra. People v. Ezeonu, 588 N.Y.S.2d 116 (N.Y.Sup.Ct.1992); In re Takahashi's Estate, 129 P.2d 217 (Mont.1942) (inheritance); State v. Bell, 66 Tenn. 9 (1872) (cohabitation).

2. Section 47 of the English Matrimonial Causes Act of 1973 provides that a court in England or Wales may grant (a) "matrimonial relief" and (b) make "a declaration concerning the validity of a marriage" even though "the marriage in question was entered into under a law which permits polygamy." The first of these provisions addresses the incidents of an actually or potentially polygamous marriage, as in *Dalip Singh Bir's Estate,* supra. The second addresses the validity of a persisting marriage, between actually *monogamous* spouses, contracted in a legal system in which a polygamous marriage would also be valid. Section 5(1) of the Private International Law (Miscellaneous Provisions) Act 1995 (c 42) now specifies more generally that a marriage contracted by parties not already married is "not void under the law of England and Wales" on the ground that it was entered into in a legal system permitting polygamous marriages. Section 7(2), making essentially the same provision with respect to Scots law, specifies further: "so long as neither party marries a second spouse during the subsistence of the marriage." See also Hussain v. Hussain, [1982] 3 All E.R. 369 (C.A.); R. v. Secretary of State for the Home Dep't ex parte Rahman, Court of Appeal, Nov. 20, 1985, UK library, ALLCAS file; Fentiman, The Validity of Marriage and the Proper Law, 44 Cambridge L.J. 256, 273 (1985).

3. Marriage among the American Indians according to their laws and customs, where tribal regulations and government exist, has been almost universally recognized in the United States, even though both polygamy and termination by mutual consent may be permitted. See Kobogum v. Jackson Iron Co., 43 N.W. 602 (Mich.1889) (recognizing U.S.-Indian polygamous marriage). See also Ponina v. Leland, 454 P.2d 16 (Nev.1969); In re Marriage of Red Fox, 542 P.2d 918 (Or.App.1975); Strasser, Tribal Marriages, Same-Sex Unions, and an Interstate Recognition Conundrum, 30 B.C. Third World L.J. 207 (2010); Hay, Borchers, Symeonides & Whytock, Conflict of Laws § 13.17 (6th ed.2018). When states began to amend their constitutions to prohibit same-sex marriage, some Native American tribal governments followed suit and adopted laws prohibiting same-sex marriage. Jacobi, Note, Two Spirits, Two Eras, Same Sex: For a Traditionalist Perspective on Native American Tribal Same-Sex Policy, 39 U.Mich.J.L.Reform 823 (2006).

4. What incidents should be attached to a relationship or status that is unknown to the forum law? In Nevarez v. Bailon, 287 S.W.2d 521 (Tex.Civ.App.1956), appellant and the deceased had lived together in Mexico in a relationship termed "concubinage" by Mexican law but which would have constituted a common-law marriage had they lived in Texas. Her petition for a widow's allowance and to be appointed administratrix of the decedent's Texas estate was denied. Although Mexican law would attach certain inheritance rights to concubine relationships, the Texas court refused to do so. "[B]ecause the relationship between appellant and deceased was entered into and existed wholly within [Mexico], it must be regulated and defined by the Code Law of that state. . . . The courts of Texas must therefore recognize her as do the courts of her residence, viz., as a concubine, and there is no provision in the Texas law for her to inherit as such. . . . [S]he could not claim as a common-law wife in Texas for such a relationship non-existent in the jurisdiction of her residence." How could that result have been avoided by the court? Could it have applied forum law? See chapters 7 and 8, supra. See also Rosales v. Battle, 7 Cal.Rptr.3d 13 (Cal.Ct.App.2003) (Petitioner lacked standing to bring wrongful death action in California despite Mexican status as a heir resulting from "concubinage" relationship); Estate of Duval v. Duval-Couetil, 777 N.W.2d 380, 384 (S.D.2010) ("[A] Mexican concubinage is not the legal equivalent of a common law marriage in the United States"). Foreign legal systems may do exactly what the Texas court rejected: apply a functionally equivalent solution of forum law to the foreign facts and law.

For a German example, see Hay, Internationales Privat-und Zivilverfahrensrecht 196–198 (PdW Series, 4th ed.2010). For same-sex relationships, see pp. 917–921, supra.

SECTION 2. DIVORCE*

A. CONDITIONS FOR DECREEING DIVORCE

Alton v. Alton

United States Court of Appeals, Third Circuit, 1953.
207 F.2d 667.

■ GOODRICH, CIRCUIT JUDGE. This case involves an important and novel question with regard to jurisdiction for divorce. The plaintiff, Sonia Alton, left her home in West Hartford, Connecticut, and went to the Virgin Islands, where she arrived February 10, 1953. After six weeks and one day continuous presence there she filed a suit for divorce on March 25, 1953. Her husband, David Alton, defendant, entered an appearance and waived service of summons. He did not contest the allegations of the complaint. . . . When the case came to the judge of the district court he asked for further proof on the question of domicile. This was not furnished. He thereupon denied the plaintiff the relief sought, and the case comes here on her appeal. The defendant has filed no brief and made no argument.

The core of our question is found in two acts of the Legislative Assembly of the Virgin Islands. The first is the Divorce Law of 1944, section 9 of which requires six weeks' residence in the Islands prior to commencement of a suit for divorce. In Burch v. Burch, 3 Cir., 1952, 195 F.2d 799, this court construed the words "inhabitant" and "residence" in that statute to mean "domiciliary" and "domicile." In 1953 the Legislative Assembly passed another act which must be stated in full in order to understand the specific problem involved in this case. It amends section 9 of the Divorce Law of 1944 by adding to it an additional subsection (a) which reads:

"Notwithstanding the provisions of sections 8 and 9 hereof, if the plaintiff is within the district at the time of the filing of the complaint and has been continuously for six weeks immediately prior thereto, this shall be prima facie evidence of domicile, and where the defendant has been personally served within the district or enters a general appearance in the action, then the Court shall have jurisdiction of the action and of the parties thereto without further reference to domicile or to the place where the marriage was solemnized or the cause of action arose."

---

* See Restatement, Second, Conflict of Laws §§ 70–74.

[W]e think it pretty clear as a matter of construction of the English language that there are here two separable provisions. There are two rules provided and they are connected with a conjunctive "and." We think, therefore, that we must give attention to the two clauses independently.

[The Court struck down the first clause of the statute on the ground that "If domicile is really the basis for divorce jurisdiction . . . six weeks' physical presence without more is not a reasonable way to prove it."]

. . . The second part of the statute goes on to provide that the court shall have jurisdiction, after six weeks' residence by the plaintiff, where the defendant has been personally served or appeared, "without further reference to domicile." . . . The action, in other words, is to become a simple transitory action like a suit for tort or breach of contract. . . . Can divorce be turned into a simple, transitory action at the will of any legislature?

The background of divorce legislation and litigation shows that it has not been considered a simple transitory personal action. The principle said to govern is that marriage is a matter of public concern, as well as a matter of interest to the parties involved. Because it is a matter of public concern, the public, through the state, has an interest both in its formation and in its dissolution, and the state which has that interest is the state of domicile, because that is where the party "dwelleth and hath his home."

* * *

So deeply has it been thought that the responsibility for divorce was that of the domicile, that divorce litigation has been called an action in rem, the res being the marital relationship between the parties. One may question whether the analogy has not caused more confusion than clarity, but at any rate it shows the way in which the matter has been regarded in the law. It is of significance upon the importance of domicile as the foundation for jurisdiction that the Supreme Court has recently held that a divorce action at the domicile of one of the parties is entitled to full faith and credit as a matter of constitutional compulsion even without the presence of the defending spouse.[20] On the other hand, a divorce not at the domicile gives no protection against a prosecution for bigamy in the state of the domicile,[21] although if the defendant is in court he, himself, may be precluded from questioning the decree on the grounds of res judicata.[22]

We now go out beyond the place where legal trails end. The Supreme Court has never had occasion to say what would happen in a case where two parties, being personally before the court, are purportedly divorced by a state which has no domiciliary jurisdiction, and the question of the

---

[20] Williams v. North Carolina (I), 1942, 317 U.S. 287.

[21] Williams v. North Carolina (II), 1945, 325 U.S. 226.

[22] Sherrer v. Sherrer, 1948, 334 U.S. 343; Coe v. Coe, 1948, 334 U.S. 378.

validity of the decree comes up in a second state in a prosecution for bigamy, or in a suit for necessaries by a creditor, or in some other such fashion. Granted that the parties are precluded from attacking the decree, does that immunity extend only to attacks by them or by those in privity with them?[23] Here is an unanswered question. . . .

But assume that the Virgin Islands cannot grant to a nondomiciliary a decree which will be impregnable elsewhere by the shield of full faith and credit. Can it not, if it pleases, provide for the granting of a divorce decree to any plaintiff who has a defendant in court in the Virgin Islands? If the decree is good by the law of the Islands and the parties thereto and those in privity with them cannot attack it, it may well be good enough for practical purposes in a world where divorce decrees as well as everything else may fall short of perfection. But is such a decree, which the parties might regard as good enough, one which a nondomiciliary court may grant?

Before the days of the Fourteenth Amendment, a state could and some states did, pass rules for the exercise of jurisdiction against nonconsenting, nonresident absentee defendants. These rules were not based upon what are now considered the fundamental requisites for such jurisdiction. The judgments were not recognized in other states under the full faith and credit clause, but there was no foundation for testing their validity in the state where they were rendered. After the Fourteenth Amendment provided a way for testing the validity of these judgments in the rendering state under the due process clause, it became well settled that an attempt to give a personal judgment for money against one not subject to the state's jurisdiction was invalid at home under due process, as well as invalid abroad under full faith and credit. With regard to this type of case one can generalize and say that due process at home and full faith and credit in another state are correlative.

We think that adherence to the domiciliary requirement is necessary if our states are really to have control over the domestic relations of their citizens. The instant case would be typical. In the Virgin Islands incompatibility of temperament constitutes grounds for divorce. In Connecticut it does not. We take it that it is all very well for the Virgin Islands to provide for whatever matrimonial regime it pleases for people who live there. But the same privilege should be afforded to those who control affairs in Connecticut.

Our conclusion is that the second part of this statute conflicts with the due process clause of the Fifth Amendment. . . . Domestic relations are a matter of concern to the state where a person is domiciled. An attempt by another jurisdiction to affect the relation of a foreign domiciliary is unconstitutional even though both parties are in court and

---

[23] Following the *Sherrer* and *Coe* cases, supra, note 22, the Supreme Court has held that if a person cannot collaterally attack the decree by the law of the state which rendered it, he cannot do so in the second state. Johnson v. Muelberger, 1951, 340 U.S. 581. See also Cook v. Cook, 1951, 342 U.S. 126.

neither one raises the question. The question may well be asked as to what the lack of due process is. The defendant is not complaining. Nevertheless, if the jurisdiction for divorce continues to be based on domicile, as we think it does, we believe it to be lack of due process for one state to take to itself the readjustment of domestic relations between those domiciled elsewhere. . . .

The judgment of the district court will be affirmed.

■ HASTIE, CIRCUIT JUDGE (dissenting). The majority of the court think that both . . . changes [in the Virgin Islands statute] violate the Constitution of the United States. Dissenting, I think both changes are within legislative competency. . . .

[That part of Judge Hastie's opinion dealing with the first clause of the statute is omitted.]

In striking down the second amendment of the statute . . . this court now says that the Fifth Amendment requires the exercise of legal power to grant divorce be restricted to those cases where one party at least is a local domiciliary. The agreed starting point in this phase of the case is the fact that English and American judges in recent times have refrained, in the absence of statute, from exercising their divorce power except in cases involving local domiciliaries. But what is it that raises this judicial rule of self-restraint to the status of an invariable Constitutional principle? . . .

I can find nothing in the history of the present judge-made rule which entitles it to Constitutional sanction. Certainly it is no ancient landmark of the common law. . . .

[T]he rule . . . is a creation of nineteenth century American judges. It is also clear that the rule did not become settled in England . . . until the 1895 decision of the Privy Council in Le Mesurier v. Le Mesurier, [1895] A.C. 517. . . .

I do not mean to suggest that pre-revolutionary existence is essential to Constitutional protection of a doctrine. . . . I think our real question on this phase of the case is whether it is clearly arbitrary or unfair for a legislature to adopt an alternative for domicil as an appropriate foundation for divorce power.

When I get to this point I am impressed that a number of states in the British Commonwealth have by legislation made domicil unnecessary to divorce jurisdiction in various situations. See Griswold, Divorce Jurisdiction and Recognition of Divorce Decrees—A Comparative Study, 1951, 65 Harv.L.Rev. 193, 197–208. I find it difficult to see in what respect these abandonments of domicil as a fundamental basis of divorce are patently unfair and arbitrary, even though a particular legislature may not have been restrained by a written Constitution. . . .

Actually, the concept of domicil as a basis of jurisdiction is in practice elusive and very unsatisfactory for several reasons. It is a highly technical concept depending upon the proof of the mental attitude of a person toward a place. Whether in taxation or in divorce, the use of domicil as a jurisdictional base gives trouble when it is applied to people who really have no "home feeling" toward any place or, at the other end of the scale, to those who have more than one home. And . . . in the divorce field difficulties are multiplied because the estranged spouses so often establish separate homes. Thus, when a court is asked to grant a divorce it very often finds that not one domicil but at least two—potentially more through refinements of the "marital domicil" concept—may be interested in the parties and their relationship. In these all too familiar situations of divided domicil, the jurisdictional requirement which the majority regards as so essential to fairness that it can not be changed is a troublemaker and a potential source of injustice.

[I]t seems to me that a reasonable person can say that the domiciliary rule does not accomplish what its proponents, including the majority here, claim for it. If it is socially justified in some circumstances, it works unfairly without social justification in others. Perhaps the trouble is that it exaggerates the theoretical interest of the technical domicil of a plaintiff at the time of suit for divorce at the expense of personal and community interests on the defendant's side. . . .

In the Virgin Islands it has seemed to the legislature that an alternative to the domiciliary rule is worth a trial. And in selecting the alternative of personal jurisdiction over both parties, the legislature has obviated that very disregard of interests on the defendant's side which is the great weakness of the domiciliary rule. In this action I can find nothing arbitrary or unfair; hence, nothing inconsistent with the Fifth Amendment.

One other matter should be mentioned. Although the court recognizes that, as concerns authoritative precedents, this case requires us to travel beyond the place "where legal trails end", the majority opinion places some reliance upon the less than pellucid body of case law which is concerned with various aspects of the problem of recognition of divorce granted in one state of the union by a sister state. For present purposes I do not find these cases very helpful. The due process question in divorce jurisdiction which we have to decide is whether it is fair for a state and its courts to adjudicate the merits of a petition for the dissolution of a particular marriage. The problem of the full faith and credit cases is to what extent a second state must subordinate its notions of policy about a marital matter in which it wants to have a voice to what a sister state has already decided. Perhaps full faith should be given to every American divorce decree which satisfies due process. But until the Supreme Court makes it clear that in this area due process and full faith are of the same dimensions, I mistrust any inversion of reasoning which would extract from the not invariant line of decisions on full faith and credit the essentials of due process in the original exercise of divorce power.

[I]t seems proper to point out that if a state proceeds upon this new basis of divorce jurisdiction another conflict of laws difficulty must be faced before the merits of the claim can be decided. That difficulty is the proper choice of the law to govern the controversy.

So long as one of the spouses has had a domiciliary relationship to the forum it has been conventional theory that the forum has sufficient connection with the domestic relation which is the subject matter of suit to justify not only the exercise of its judicial power to decide the controversy but also the application of its own substantive law of divorce as well. Stewart v. Stewart, 1919, 32 Idaho 180, 180 P. 165. It is quite possible that some of the difficulties which have arisen in this field are the result of failure to keep in view that these are distinct problems although the existence of a domiciliary relationship is thought to solve both.

But once the power to decide the case is based merely upon personal jurisdiction a court must decide as a separate question upon what basis, if any, the local substantive law of divorce can properly be applied to determine whether the plaintiff is entitled to the relief sought. In this case, if it should appear that Mr. and Mrs. Alton were both domiciled in Connecticut at the time of suit in the Virgin Islands and that their estrangement had resulted from conduct in the matrimonial home state, it may well be that under correct application of conflict of laws doctrine, and even under the due process clause, it is encumbent upon the Virgin Islands, lacking connection with the subject matter, to apply the divorce law of some state that has such connection, here Connecticut. . . .

Of course such a solution would be a novelty in divorce procedure. But the entire situation presented by this statute is very unusual. And the legislation is an innovation in a very important area. I think, therefore, that we should try to answer no more questions than the exigencies of this litigation require. . . . Accordingly, I do no more than point out that this choice of law question would have to be considered if the court's power to decide this case depended upon personal jurisdiction and that basis of jurisdiction were sustained, as I believe it should be.

I am authorized to state that CHIEF JUDGE BIGGS and CIRCUIT JUDGE KALODNER concur in the views stated in this opinion.

NOTES

1. The Supreme Court granted certiorari in the *Alton* case, but then dismissed the proceeding as moot upon learning that, in the meantime, one of the spouses had procured a second divorce in another jurisdiction, 347 U.S. 610 (1954). In Granville-Smith v. Granville-Smith, 349 U.S. 1 (1955), the Supreme Court invalidated the Virgin Islands statute, however, without passing upon the constitutionality of the statute under the Due Process Clause. The decision was based on the ground that in enacting the statute the Virgin Islands Legislative Assembly had exceeded the power granted it by Congress. This power was to legislate on "all subjects of local application,"

and this language was held not to include the granting of a divorce to non-residents.

2. How can a state violate due process by giving spouses a divorce which both desire? Apart from considerations of fairness to the individual parties, should there be some restriction upon the power of a member state of a federal union to hear and adjudicate issues which are of far greater concern to a sister state? See Rheinstein, The Constitutional Bases of Jurisdiction, 22 U.Chi.L.Rev. 775 (1955).

3. The Supreme Court has never had occasion to determine whether domicile of one of the spouses in the divorce state is an essential jurisdictional basis for the granting of a divorce. The *Williams* cases, pp. 936, 941, infra, have been cited for the proposition that domicile is a required jurisdictional basis for divorce. However, the Nevada statute in *Williams,* as interpreted by the Nevada courts, required the petitioner to be a domiciliary. The issue in *Williams,* therefore, was whether domicile of the petitioning spouse was a sufficient jurisdictional basis, not whether it was the only one.

Statutes in an increasing number of states permit the rendering of a divorce on some basis other than domicile. The most common type of statute is one that authorizes the granting of a divorce to military personnel who have been stationed in the state for a given period, which is frequently a year but is only 90 days under § 302 of the Uniform Marriage and Divorce Act.

An Arkansas statute (Ark.Stats. §§ 34–1208, 34–1208.1 (1947)) empowered the Arkansas courts to grant a divorce to one who alleges and proves "actual presence" within the state for a three-month period. The constitutionality of this statute was upheld in Wheat v. Wheat, 318 S.W.2d 793 (Ark.1958). This provision is now codified at Ark.Code Ann. § 9–12–307(a)(1)(A) (2020). Section 307(b) provides that " 'Residence' . . . is defined to mean actual presence, and upon proof that . . . the party . . . shall be considered domiciled in the state. . . ."

4. Comment *b* of § 72 of Restatement, Second, Conflict of Laws reads as follows:

> *b.   Relationships other than domicil.* If one or both of the spouses are domiciled in the state, the state has a sufficient interest in the marriage status to give it judicial jurisdiction to dissolve the marriage (see §§ 70–71). The domicil of one or of both of the spouses in the state is not, however, the only possible basis of jurisdiction. A state may have a sufficient interest in a spouse by reason of some relationship other than domicil, to give the state judicial jurisdiction to dissolve the marriage. In the present state of the authorities, few definite statements can be made as to what relationships with a state, other than domicil, will suffice. Residence, as distinguished from domicil, by one of the spouses in the state for a substantial period, such as a year, is an adequate jurisdictional basis for the rendition of a divorce. On the other hand, the fact that the spouses were married in the state should not of itself provide an adequate jurisdictional basis. A distinction may ultimately be drawn between situations where both spouses

are subject to the personal jurisdiction of the divorce court and where there is jurisdiction over only one spouse. One or more jurisdictional bases may be found adequate for the granting of a divorce in the first situation and inadequate in the second.*

5. Indyka v. Indyka, [1967] 3 W.L.R. 510. The case involved the status in England of a divorce granted in Czechoslovakia. H and W were Czech nationals who married in Czechoslovakia. After H moved to England, W, who remained in Czechoslovakia, obtained an ex parte divorce. H remarried in England and, when his second wife sought a divorce, defended on the ground that their marriage was void for bigamy, attacking the Czech divorce as invalid. The House of Lords unanimously held that the Czech divorce was valid and that domicile of at least one of the spouses is not the only jurisdictional basis for divorce. Other jurisdictional bases included nationality and residence. Cases citing Indyka have used it for the proposition that a state has jurisdiction to grant a divorce if it has a "real and substantial connection" with a plaintiff spouse. See Dicey, Morris & Collins, The Conflict of Laws 1062 et seq. (15th ed.2012). Indyka's common law standard was abolished by the Family Law Act 1986, which implements the 1968 Hague Convention and provides that a foreign divorce decree will be recognized only if it comports with the standards of the Act or other statutes. Id.

6. As made clear by both opinions in the *Alton* case, one of the most peculiar aspects of American divorce litigation is that the law of the forum is usually applied to determine whether there are adequate grounds for a divorce. So if the action is brought in state X, the law of X will usually be applied even though the complained-of conduct took place in state Y. Restatement, Second, Conflict of Laws § 285.

Would adoption of Judge Hastie's suggestion in *Alton*, with respect to the choice of law for divorce, place as serious a roadblock in the way of a nonresident seeking a divorce as the majority decision? Continental countries traditionally applied the law of the parties' nationality or forum law if one of the parties was a national of the forum. As a result of conflicts law reform in Austria and Germany, those countries now use a series of references (in order of priority) to the law of the parties' common nationality, last common nationality, common habitual residence or, if all else fails, the law of the country with the closest connection to the spouses. Would such an approach adequately address the concerns?

7. In the European Union, except Denmark, there is divorce jurisdiction in the Member State in which (1) the spouses are "habitually resident," (2) the spouses were last "habitually resident" and one of them still is, (3) the respondent is habitually resident (or if petitioner is, in the case of a consensual bilateral divorce), among other grounds, and (4) in the Member State of the spouses' common citizenship (or "domicile" in the case of English or Irish parties, with "domicile" given the common-law meaning of those countries). Art. 5, Council Regulation (EC) No. 2201/2003, [2003] Official

---

* Quoted with the permission of the copyright owner, The American Law Institute.

Journal L 338/1*. As does American law, European law thus requires a relationship of some sort to the forum for divorce jurisdiction—even in the case of consensual bilateral divorce. EU legislation, the "Rome III" Regulation, in force in seventeen of the Member States, now provides rules for the selection of the law applicable to divorce, even permitting the parties to choose the law from among four options. For details see infra at p. 1227 et seq. For discussion, see Corneloup, The Rome III Regulation—A Commentary on the Law Applicable to Divorce and Legal Separation (2020).

8. The Supreme Court has not yet squarely passed upon the question of what sort of notice of the divorce proceedings must be given the defendant spouse. State statutes sometimes authorize the giving of notice to a nonresident spouse by some form of publication. If the respondent spouse's address is known to the petitioner, would such statutes be upheld today by the Supreme Court? See Mullane v. Central Hanover Bank & Trust Co., p. 192, supra.

9. Compare Hartford v. Superior Court, 304 P.2d 1 (Cal.1956). Plaintiff, domiciled in California, brought an action to have it determined that defendant was his father. Defendant was not domiciled in California and was served with process outside the state. Plaintiff contended that the California courts had jurisdiction on the ground that the proceeding to establish paternity was a proceeding in rem by analogy to ex parte divorce proceedings. Held (Traynor, J.), California has no judicial jurisdiction over the defendant. Plaintiff's action against the defendant is in personam. "Basically the difference [between this action and an ex parte divorce action] is between the state's power to insulate its domiciliary from a relationship with one not within its jurisdiction and its lack of power to reach out and fasten a relationship upon a person over whom it has no jurisdiction." See also Conlon by Conlon v. Heckler, 719 F.2d 788 (5th Cir.1983): the court at the plaintiff's domicile had divorce jurisdiction but lacked jurisdiction for a declaration of paternity in the absence of personal jurisdiction over the putative father. The petitioner therefore could not claim social security benefits as the deceased putative father's "child." Is the distinction sound? See also p. 969, infra, with respect to annulment jurisdiction.

SOSNA V. IOWA, 419 U.S. 393 (1975): In recent years, a frequently litigated question has been whether a state may constitutionally impose a durational residence requirement for obtaining a divorce. The cases were divided. In the principal case, the Supreme Court upheld the constitutionality of the Iowa one-year residence requirement. The suit was a class action on behalf of all Iowa residents who had resided in the state for less than one year but wished to institute divorce proceedings there. For the majority, Justice Rehnquist wrote:

---

*   This Regulation entered into force on August 1, 2004, and applied from March 1, 2005. It replaced Council Regulation (EC) 1347/2000, [2000] Official Journal L 160/19. This law will be replaced, effective August 1, 2022, by Council Regulation (EU) 2019/1111, [2019] Official Journal 178. The statements in the text remain unaffected.

"The imposition of a durational residency requirement for divorce is scarcely unique to Iowa, since 48 States impose such a requirement as a condition for maintaining an action for divorce.[15] As might be expected, the periods vary among the States and range from six weeks[16] to two years.[17] The one-year period selected by Iowa is the most common length of time prescribed.[18]

Appellant contends that the Iowa requirement of one year's residence is unconstitutional for two separate reasons: first, because it establishes two classes of persons and discriminates against those who have recently exercised their right to travel to Iowa ... and, second, because it denies a litigant the opportunity to make an individualized showing of bona fide residence and therefore denies such residents access to the only method of legally dissolving their marriage. . . .

Iowa's residency requirement may reasonably be justified on grounds other than purely budgetary considerations or administrative convenience. Cf. Kahn v. Shevin, 416 U.S. 351 (1974). . . . Both spouses are obviously interested in the proceedings, since it will affect their marital status and very likely their property rights. Where a married couple has minor children, a decree of divorce would usually include provisions for their custody and support. With consequences of such moment riding on a divorce decree issued by its courts, Iowa may insist that one seeking to initiate such a proceeding have the modicum of attachment to the State required here.

Such a requirement additionally furthers the State's parallel interests in both avoiding officious intermeddling in matters in which another State has a paramount interest, and in minimizing the susceptibility of its own divorce decrees to collateral attack. A State such as Iowa may quite reasonably decide that it does not wish to become a divorce mill for unhappy spouses who have lived there as short a time as appellant had when she commenced her action in the state court after having long resided elsewhere. . . . Perhaps even more importantly, Iowa's interests extend beyond its borders and include the

---

[15] Louisiana and Washington are the exceptions. La.Civ.Code, Art. 10A(7) (Supp.1974). . . . Wash.Laws 1973, 1st Ex.Sess., c. 157. . . [However, Louisiana requires that couples have been separated for at least six months (or 12, if there are children) as a precondition for a no-fault divorce. La. Civil Code Arts. 102 and 103(1) (2008); Washington law requires that the petitioner be a "resident." Residence is equated with "domicile" and does not require a specific time. Wash. Rev. Code Ann.2 §§ 26.09.020–0.30 (2008); Odegard v. Behla, 134 Wash.App. 1005 (2006).—Eds.]

[16] See, e.g., Idaho Code § 32–701 (1963); Nev.Rev.Stat. § 125.020 (1973).

[17] See, e.g., R.I.Gen.Laws Ann. § 15–2–2 (1970); Mass.Gen.Laws Ann., c. 208, §§ 4–5 (1958 and Supp.1974).

[18] [More than] a majority of the States impose a one-year residency requirement of some kind. . . .

recognition of its divorce decrees by other States under the Full Faith and Credit Clause of the Constitution, Art. IV, § 1. . . . For that reason, the State asked to enter such a decree is entitled to insist that the putative divorce petitioner satisfy something more than the bare minimum of constitutional requirements before a divorce may be granted. The State's decision to exact a one-year residency requirement as a matter of policy is therefore buttressed by a quite permissible inference that this requirement not only effectuates state substantive policy but likewise provides a greater safeguard against successful collateral attack than would a requirement of bona fide residence alone.[21]"

In his dissenting opinion, Justice Marshall wrote:

"The Court omits altogether what should be the first inquiry: whether the right to obtain a divorce is of sufficient importance that its denial to recent immigrants constitutes a penalty on interstate travel. In my view, it clearly meets that standard. . . .

Having determined that the interest in obtaining a divorce is of substantial social importance, I would scrutinize Iowa's durational residency requirement to determine whether it constitutes a reasonable means of furthering important interests asserted by the State. The Court, however, has not only declined to apply the 'compelling interest' test to this case, it has conjured up possible justifications for the State's restriction in a manner much more akin to the lenient standard we have in the past applied in analyzing equal protection challenges to business regulations. . . . I continue to be of the view that the 'rational basis' test has no place in equal protection analysis when important individual interests with constitutional implications are at stake. . . .

Certainly the stakes in a divorce are weighty both for the individuals directly involved in the adjudication and for others immediately affected by it. The critical importance of the divorce process, however, weakens the argument for a long residence requirement rather than strengthens it. The impact of the divorce decree only underscores the necessity that the State's regulation be evenhanded.

It is not enough to recite the State's traditionally exclusive responsibility for regulating family law matters; some tangible

---

[21] Since the majority of States require residence for at least a year, see n. 18, supra, it is reasonable to assume that Iowa's one-year 'floor' makes its decrees less susceptible to successful collateral attack in other States. As the Court of Appeals for the Fifth Circuit observed in upholding a six-month durational residency requirement imposed by Florida, an objective test may impart to a State's divorce decrees "a verity that tends to safeguard them against the suspicious eyes of other states' prosecutorial authorities, the suspicions of private counsel in other states, and the post-decree dissatisfaction of parties to the divorce who wish a second bite. Such a reputation for validity of divorce decrees is not, then, merely cosmetic." . . .

interference with the State's regulatory scheme must be shown. Yet in this case, I fail to see how any legitimate objective of Iowa's divorce regulations would be frustrated by granting equal access to new state residents. . . .

Iowa has a legitimate interest in protecting itself against invasion by those seeking quick divorces in a forum with relatively lax divorce laws, and it may have some interest in avoiding collateral attacks on its decree in other States. These interests, however, would adequately be protected by a simple requirement of domicile—physical presence plus intent to remain—which would remove the rigid one-year barrier while permitting the State to restrict the availability of its divorce process to citizens who are genuinely its own.[6] . . . If, as the majority assumes, Iowa is interested in assuring itself that its divorce petitioners are legitimately Iowa citizens, requiring petitioners to provide convincing evidence of bona fide domicile should be more than adequate to the task.[9]"

NOTES

1. In *Sosna*, the state's durational residence requirement had not been met, and the United States Supreme Court agreed that a state could condition its exercise of jurisdiction in this way. It takes matters a step further to say that a state may dismiss a petition on grounds of *forum non conveniens* in circumstances when jurisdictional prerequisites have been met. An Illinois appellate court did so when the petitioner, formerly an Illinois domiciliary, had lived for six years in Ireland with his spouse but sought a divorce in Illinois because of its shorter waiting period and the availability there of divorce on no-fault grounds. The court found insufficient ties to Illinois and that petitioner's motives were irrelevant to a *forum non conveniens* determination. In re Marriage of Townley and Carraz, 2014 Ill.App. (4th) 130935-U (Ill.App.Ct.2014). The second point is, of course, standard for these determinations. But what if the petitioner had not been

---

[6] The availability of a less restrictive alternative such as a domicile requirement weighs heavily in testing a challenged state regulation against the 'compelling interest' standard. See Shapiro v. Thompson, 394 U.S., at 638. . . ; Dunn v. Blumstein, 405 U.S. 330, 342, 350–352. . . ; Memorial Hospital v. Maricopa County, 415 U.S., at 267. . . ; Shelton v. Tucker, 364 U.S. 479, 488 (1960). . . . Since the Iowa courts have in effect interpreted the residency statute to require proof of domicile as well as one year's residence, see Korsrud v. Korsrud, 242 Iowa 178, 45 N.W.2d 848 (1951); Julson v. Julson, 255 Iowa 301, 122 N.W.2d 329 (1963), a shift to a 'pure' domicile test would impose no new burden on the State's fact-finding process.

[9] The majority argues that since most States require a year's residence for divorce, Iowa gains refuge from the risk of collateral attack in the understanding solicitude of States with similar laws. Of course, absent unusual circumstances, a judgment by this Court striking down the Iowa statute would similarly affect the other states with one-and two-year residency requirements. For the same reason, the risk of subjecting Iowa to an invasion of divorce seekers seems minimal. If long residency requirements are held unconstitutional, Iowa will not stand conspicuously alone without a residency requirement 'defense.' Moreover, its 90-day conciliation period, required of all divorce petitioners in the State, would still serve to discourage peripatetic divorce seekers who are looking for the quickest possible adjudication.

candid about his motives: should the exercise of divorce jurisdiction include a review of whether another court might not be more convenient?

2. Similarly, should parties be able to *exclude* a divorce action in a court with proper jurisdiction by including an exclusive forum selection clause for the eventuality of divorce in an antenuptial agreement? In Ofer v. Sirota, 984 N.Y.S.2d 312 (N.Y.App.Div.2014), the New York Appellate Division affirmed a dismissal of a divorce petition in favor of Israel when the antenuptial agreement had provided for the latter's jurisdiction. It seems, however, that, in contrast to *Townley*, above, the circumstances to permit the action to go forward in New York were more compelling: In Israel, the petitioner wife could not obtain a divorce without the husband's delivering a *Get* (letter of divorcement) to the wife (see infra, p. 971) and compelling him to do so is not easy. The need for and the importance for a *Get* is expressly recognized by New York statutory law (infra, p. 971), but the Appellate Division considered that policy not strong enough to overcome the policy favoring upholding forum selection agreements. None of the cases the court cited in the context of antenuptial agreements concerned divorce, but rather the settlement of matrimonial property issues. By way of comparison, the rules for divorce jurisdiction under the Brussels IIa Regulation of the European Union are exclusive and not subject to variation by the parties: see Arts. 3, 6, 12, infra, pp. 1173, 1174, 1176, respectively. For further explanation of the *Get*, and discussion of Jewish divorce law, see Traum, Note, Involved, Empowered and Inspired: How Mediating Halakhic Prenuptial Agreements Honors Jewish and American Law and Builds Happy Families, 17 Cardozo J.Conflict Resol. 179 (2015) .

B. EXTRATERRITORIAL RECOGNITION

Three principal different situations should be distinguished. In the first, the divorce is handed down in a state where both spouses are domiciled. In the second, the divorce state is the domicile of only one spouse, and in the third, this state is the domicile of neither spouse. Foreign-country divorces and non-judicial (e.g., religious) divorces raise additional problems and are treated briefly at p. 968, infra.

Prior to the Williams decisions, the situation which gave rise to most litigation was the second, in which a divorce had been rendered in State F-1 where one spouse was domiciled, and its effect was questioned in State F-2. Many states recognized such a divorce under their rules of conflict of laws, but some states refused to do so except as compelled by the full faith and credit requirement.

The two leading decisions on full faith and credit were Atherton v. Atherton, 181 U.S. 155 (1901) and Haddock v. Haddock, 201 U.S. 562 (1906). Both involved the second situation. In the Atherton case, a divorce granted to the husband in the state of matrimonial domicile was held entitled to full faith and credit and thus to constitute a bar to an action for separation brought by the wife in a second state. But in the Haddock case, a divorce granted to the husband in a state where he was then domiciled, but which was not the state of matrimonial domicile, was denied constitutional protection in the second state where the wife brought a suit for separation and alimony. In neither case did State F-1 have personal jurisdiction over the respondent. These decisions led to the belief that a divorce at the domicile of one spouse was not entitled to full faith and credit, unless there was some additional strengthening factor, e.g., that F-1 was the matrimonial domicile or had personal jurisdiction over the respondent.

Williams v. North Carolina (I)

Supreme Court of the United States, 1942.
317 U.S. 287, 63 S.Ct. 207, 87 L.Ed.279, 143 A.L.R. 1273.

Certiorari to the Supreme Court of North Carolina.

■ JUSTICE DOUGLAS delivered the opinion of the Court.

Petitioners were tried and convicted of bigamous cohabitation under § 4342 of the North Carolina Code, 1939, and each was sentenced for a term of years to a state prison. The judgment of conviction was affirmed by the Supreme Court of North Carolina. 220 N.C. 445, 17 S.E.2d 769. The case is here on certiorari.

Petitioner Williams was married to Carrie Wyke in 1916 in North Carolina and lived with her there until May, 1940. Petitioner Hendrix was married to Thomas Hendrix in 1920 in North Carolina and lived with him there until May, 1940. At that time petitioners went to Las Vegas, Nevada, and on June 26, 1940, each filed a divorce action in the Nevada court. The defendants in those divorce actions entered no appearance nor were they served with process in Nevada. In the case of defendant Thomas Hendrix, service by publication was had by publication of the summons in a Las Vegas newspaper and by mailing a copy of the summons and complaint to his last post-office address. In the case of defendant Carrie Williams, a North Carolina sheriff delivered to her in North Carolina a copy of the summons and complaint. A decree of divorce was granted petitioner Williams by the Nevada court on August 26, 1940, . . . the court finding that "the plaintiff has been and now is a *bona fide* and continuous resident of the County of Clark, State of Nevada, and had been such resident for more than six weeks immediately preceding the commencement of this action in the manner prescribed by law." The Nevada court granted petitioner Hendrix a divorce on October 4, 1940 . . . and made the same finding as to this petitioner's *bona fide* residence in Nevada as it made in the case of Williams. Petitioners were married to each other in Nevada on October 4, 1940. Thereafter they returned to North Carolina where they lived together until the indictment was returned. . . . The Supreme Court of North Carolina in affirming the judgment held that North Carolina was not required to recognize the Nevada decrees under the full faith and credit clause of the Constitution (Art. IV, § 1) by reason of Haddock v. Haddock, 201 U.S. 562. The intimation in the majority opinion (220 N.C. pp. 460–464) that the

Nevada divorces were collusive suggests that the second theory on which the State tried the case may have been an alternative ground for the decision below, adequate to sustain the judgment under the rule of Bell v. Bell, 181 U.S. 175—a case in which this Court held that a decree of divorce was not entitled to full faith and credit when it had been granted on constructive service by the courts of a state in which neither spouse was domiciled. But . . . North Carolina does not seek to sustain the judgment below on that ground. Moreover it admits that there probably is enough evidence in the record to require that petitioners be considered "to have been actually domiciled in Nevada. . . ." Accordingly, we cannot avoid meeting the Haddock v. Haddock issue in this case . . . on the easy assumption that petitioners' domicil in Nevada was a sham and a fraud. Rather, we must treat the present case for the purpose of the limited issue before us precisely the same as if petitioners had resided in Nevada for a term of years and had long ago acquired a permanent abode there. . . .

The Haddock case involved a suit for separation and alimony, brought in New York by the wife on personal service of the husband. The husband pleaded in defense a divorce decree obtained by him in Connecticut where he had established a separate domicil. This Court held that New York, the matrimonial domicil where the wife still resided, need not give full faith and credit to the Connecticut decree, since it was obtained by the husband who wrongfully left his wife in the matrimonial domicil, service on her having been obtained by publication and she not having entered an appearance in the action. But we do not agree with the theory of the Haddock case that so far as the marital status of the parties is concerned, a decree of divorce granted under such circumstances by one state need not be given full faith and credit in another. . . .

Haddock v. Haddock is not based on the . . . theory . . . that a decree of divorce granted by the courts of one state need not be given full faith and credit in another if the grounds for the divorce would not be recognized by the courts of the forum. It does not purport to challenge or disturb the rule, earlier established by Christmas v. Russell [5 Wall. 290], and subsequently fortified by Fauntleroy v. Lum [210 U.S. 230] that, even though the cause of action could not have been entertained in the state of the forum, a judgment obtained thereon in a sister state is entitled to full faith and credit. . . . [Haddock was based on the theory that] the state granting the divorce had no jurisdiction over the absent spouse, since it was not the state of the matrimonial domicil, but the place where the husband had acquired a separate domicil after having wrongfully left his wife. . . .

The historical view that a proceeding for a divorce was a proceeding *in rem* (2 Bishop, Marriage & Divorce, 4th ed., § 164) was rejected by the Haddock case. We likewise agree that it does not aid in the solution of the problem presented by this case to label these proceedings as proceedings *in rem*. Such a suit, however, is not a mere *in personam* action. Domicil of the plaintiff, immaterial to jurisdiction in a personal action, is recognized in the Haddock case and elsewhere (Beale, Conflict of Laws, § 110.1) as essential in order to give the court jurisdiction which will entitle the divorce decree to extraterritorial effect, at least when the defendant has neither been personally served nor entered an appearance. The findings made in the divorce decrees in the instant case must be treated on the issue before us as meeting those requirements. For it seems clear that the provision of the Nevada statute that a plaintiff in this type of case must "reside" in the State for the required period requires him to have a domicil, as distinguished from a mere residence, in the state. . . . Hence, the decrees in this case, like other divorce decrees, are more than *in personam* judgments. They involve the marital status of the parties. Domicil creates a relationship to the state which is adequate for numerous exercises of state power. . . . Each state as a sovereign has a rightful and legitimate concern in the marital status of persons domiciled within its borders. The marriage relation creates problems of large social importance. Protection of offspring, property interests, and the enforcement of marital responsibilities are but a few of commanding problems in the field of domestic relations with which the state must deal. Thus it is plain that each state, by virtue of its command over its domiciliaries and its large interest in the institution of marriage, can alter within its own borders the marriage status of the spouse domiciled there, even though the other spouse is absent. There is no constitutional barrier if the form and nature of the substituted service . . . meet the requirements of due process. . . .

[I]f one is lawfully divorced and remarried in Nevada and still married to the first spouse in North Carolina, [a] . . . complicated and serious condition would be realized. . . . Under the circumstances of this case, a man would have two wives, a wife two husbands. The reality of a sentence to prison proves that that is no mere play on words. Each would be a bigamist for living in one state with the only one with whom the other state would permit him lawfully to live. Children of the second marriage would be bastards in one state but legitimate in the other. And all that would flow from the legalistic notion that where one spouse is wrongfully deserted he retains power over the matrimonial domicil so that the domicil of the other spouse follows him wherever he may go, while, if he is to blame, he retains no such power. But such considerations are inapposite. As stated by Mr. Justice Holmes in his dissent in the Haddock case (201 U.S. p. 630), they constitute a "pure fiction, and fiction always is a poor ground for changing substantial rights." Furthermore, the fault or wrong of one spouse in leaving the other becomes under that view a jurisdictional fact on which this Court would ultimately have to pass. Whatever may be said as to the practical effect which such a rule would have in clouding divorce decrees, the question as to where the fault lies has no relevancy to the existence of state power in such circumstances. See Bingham, In the Matter of Haddock v. Haddock, 21 Corn.L.Q. 393, 426. The existence of the power of a state to alter the marital status of its domiciliaries, as distinguished from the wisdom of its exercise, is not dependent on the underlying causes of the domestic rift. . . . Moreover, so far as state power is concerned, no distinction between a matrimonial domicil and a domicil later acquired has been suggested or is apparent. . . . It is one thing to say as a matter of state law that jurisdiction to grant a divorce from an absent spouse should depend on whether by consent or by conduct the latter has subjected his interest in the marriage status to the law of the separate domicil acquired by the other spouse. . . . But where a state adopts, as it has the power to do, a less strict rule, it is quite another thing to say that its decrees affecting the marital status of its domiciliaries are not entitled to full faith and credit in sister states. Certainly if decrees of a state altering the marital status of its domiciliaries are not valid throughout the Union even though the requirements of procedural due process are wholly met, a rule would be fostered which could not help but bring "considerable disaster to innocent persons" and "bastardize children hitherto supposed to be the offspring of lawful marriage" (Mr. Justice Holmes dissenting in Haddock v. Haddock, supra, 201 U.S. at page 628), or else encourage collusive divorces. Beale, Constitutional Protection of Decrees for Divorce, 19 Harv.L.Rev. 586, 596. These intensely practical considerations emphasize for us the essential function of the full faith and credit clause in substituting a command for the former principles of comity [Broderick v. Rosner, 294 U.S. 629 at p. 643] and in altering the "status of the several states as independent foreign sovereignties" by making them "integral parts of a single nation." Milwaukee County v. White Co. [296 U.S. 268 at p. 380].

It is objected, however, that if such divorce decrees must be given full faith and credit, a substantial dilution of the sovereignty of other states will be effected. For it is pointed out that under such a rule one state's policy of strict control over the institution of marriage could be thwarted by the decree of a more lax state. But such an objection goes to the application of the full faith and credit clause to many situations. It is an objection in varying degrees of intensity to the enforcement of a judgment of a sister state based on a cause of action which could not be enforced in the state of the forum. Mississippi's policy against gambling transactions was overridden in Fauntleroy v. Lum [210 U.S. 230], when a Missouri judgment based on such a Mississippi contract was enforced by this Court. Such is part of the price of our federal system.

This Court, of course, is the final arbiter when the question is raised as to what is a permissible limitation on the full faith and credit clause. . . . But the question . . . as to what is a permissible limitation on the full faith and credit clause does not involve a decision on our part as to which state policy on divorce is the most desirable one. . . . It is a Constitution which we are expounding—a Constitution which in no small measure brings separate sovereign states into an integrated whole through the medium of the full faith and credit clause. Within the limits of her political power North Carolina may, of course, enforce her own policy regarding the marriage relation—an institution more basic in our civilization than any other. But society also has an interest in the avoidance of polygamous marriages . . . and in the protection of innocent offspring of marriages deemed legitimate in other jurisdictions. And other states have an equally legitimate concern in the status of persons domiciled there as respects the institution of marriage. So, when a court of one state acting in accord with the requirements of procedural due process alters the marital status of one domiciled in that state by granting him a divorce from his absent spouse, we cannot say its decree should be excepted from the full faith and credit clause merely because its enforcement or recognition in another state would conflict with the policy of the latter. . . .

Haddock v. Haddock is overruled. The judgment is reversed and the cause is remanded to the Supreme Court of North Carolina for proceedings not inconsistent with this opinion.

Reversed.

■ JUSTICE FRANKFURTER concurred in a separate opinion and JUSTICE MURPHY and JUSTICE JACKSON dissented in separate opinions.

NOTES

1. Was attention given in the principal case to the value of fairness to the defendant that was stressed so heavily in International Shoe Co. v. State of Washington, p. 65, supra? What about the admonition, in Shaffer v. Heitner, p. 173, supra, that "all" assertions of state court jurisdiction must be evaluated in light of the standards of *International Shoe?* Does *Shaffer* affect the decision in *Williams?* See p. 176 n. 30, supra.

2. Was the application in the principal case of Nevada law to determine the plaintiff spouse's right to a divorce consistent with the rule of Home Ins. Co. v. Dick and Allstate Ins. Co. v. Hague, pp. 418, 432, supra, respectively? Compare the European approach: p. 930, Note 7, supra. What if the law of the place of celebration of the marriage, perhaps reinforced by the parties' express choice of that law (as in covenant-state marriages, p. 915, Note 6, supra), imposes restrictions (grounds, waiting periods) as a precondition to dissolution? May the forum disregard them? Accord, Blackburn v. Blackburn, 180 So.3d 16 (Ala.Civ.App.2015). Assume that a spouse who had entered into a covenant marriage later becomes domiciled in another (non-covenant marriage) state and there obtains an ex parte no-fault divorce. Must the original marital domicile (the covenant state, the state of celebration) accord the divorce full faith and credit? For an affirmative answer to both questions, see Hay, p. 915, Note 6, supra. Would the other spouse (respondent) have any remedy against the spouse who has obtained the no-fault divorce? See Spaht, Louisiana's Covenant Marriage: Social Analysis and Legal Implications, 59 La.L.Rev. 63, 105–106 (1998) (suggesting an action for breach of contract).

3.   In Von Schack v. Von Schack, 893 A.2d 1004 (Me.2006), the court held that it could a grant a divorce to a Maine domiciliary without personal jurisdiction over the other spouse, but may not determine collateral issues of property division, parental rights, or support. The decision was consistent with Shaffer v. Heitner. The court declined to base its holding on the ground that the action was in rem over the marriage status:

> Because Maine has a unique interest in assuring that its citizens are not compelled to remain in such personal relationships against their wills and because no personal or real property interests would be determined in the proceeding, we conclude that Maine courts have jurisdiction to enter a divorce judgment without personal jurisdiction over the defendant. . . . We do not, however, alter or re-evaluate the requirement of personal jurisdiction in any other type of litigation affecting the parties' children, financial responsibilities, or property.

> We also caution that when Maine lacks personal jurisdiction over a defendant in a divorce proceeding, Maine courts must exercise their limited jurisdiction with care. Courts must uphold the due process requirements of notice and an opportunity to be heard . . . and must consider a defendant's assertions of forum non conveniens if the exercise of jurisdiction would further a fraud or create an unwarranted burden or inconvenience for the defendant.

Id. at 1011.

Williams v. North Carolina (II)
Supreme Court of the United States, 1945.
325 U.S. 226, 65 S.Ct. 1092, 89 L.Ed.1577, 157 A.L.R. 1366.

Certiorari to the Supreme Court of North Carolina.

■ JUSTICE FRANKFURTER delivered the opinion of the Court.

This case is here to review judgments of the Supreme Court of North Carolina, affirming convictions for bigamous cohabitation, assailed on the ground that full faith and credit, as required by the Constitution of the United States, was not accorded divorces decreed by one of the courts of Nevada. Williams v. North Carolina, 317 U.S. 287, decided an earlier aspect of the controversy. . . . The record then before us did not present the question whether North Carolina had the power "to refuse full faith and credit to Nevada divorce decrees because, contrary to the findings of the Nevada court, North Carolina finds that no *bona fide* domicil was acquired in Nevada." Williams v. North Carolina, supra, at 302. This is the precise issue which has emerged after retrial of the cause following our reversal. Its obvious importance brought the case here. 322 U.S. 725.

Under our system of law, judicial power to grant a divorce—jurisdiction, strictly speaking—is founded on domicil. Bell v. Bell, 181 U.S. 175; Andrews v. Andrews, 188 U.S. 14. The framers of the Constitution were familiar with this jurisdictional prerequisite, and since 1789, neither this Court nor any other court in the English-speaking world has questioned it. Domicil implies a nexus between person and place of such permanence as to control the creation of legal relations and responsibilities of the utmost significance. The domicil of one spouse within a State gives power to that State, we have held, to dissolve a marriage wheresoever contracted. . . . Williams v. North Carolina, supra . . .

It is one thing to reopen an issue that has been settled after appropriate opportunity to present their contentions has been afforded to all who had an interest in its adjudication. This applies also to jurisdictional questions. After a contest these cannot be relitigated as between the parties. . . . But those not parties to a litigation ought not to be foreclosed by the interested actions of others; especially not a State which is concerned with the vindication of its own social policy and has no means, certainly no effective means, to protect that interest against the selfish action of those outside its borders. The State of domiciliary origin should not be bound by an unfounded, even if not collusive, recital in the record of a court of another State. As to the truth or existence of a fact, like that of domicil, upon which depends the power to exert judicial authority, a State not a party to the exertion of such judicial authority in another State but seriously affected by it has a right, when asserting its own unquestioned authority, to ascertain the truth or existence of that crucial fact.

These considerations of policy are equally applicable whether power was assumed by the court of the first State or claimed after inquiry. This may lead, no doubt, to conflicting determinations of what judicial power is founded upon. Such conflict is inherent in the practical application of the concept of domicil in the context of our federal system. . . .[7] What was said in Worcester County Trust Co. v. Riley . . . is pertinent here. "Neither the Fourteenth Amendment nor the full faith and credit clause requires uniformity in the decisions of the courts of different states as to the place of domicil, where the exertion of state power is dependent upon domicil within its boundaries." 302 U.S. 292, 299. If a finding by the court of one State that domicil in another State has been abandoned were conclusive upon the old domiciliary State, the policy of each State in matters of most intimate concern could be subverted by the policy of every other State. . . .

Although it is now settled that a suit for divorce is not an ordinary adversary proceeding, it does not promote analysis, as was recently pointed out, to label divorce proceedings as actions *in rem*. Williams v. North Carolina, supra, at 297. But insofar as a divorce decree partakes of some of the characteristics of a decree *in rem*, it is misleading to say

---

[7]   Since an appeal to the Full Faith and CredIt Clause raises questions arising under the Constitution of the United States, the proper criteria for ascertaining domicil, should these be in dispute, become matters of federal determination. See Hinderlider v. La Plara Co., 804 U.S. 92, 110.

that all the world is party to a proceeding *in rem*. . . . All the world is not party to a divorce proceeding. What is true is that all the world need not be present before a court granting the decree and yet it must be respected by the other . . . States provided—and it is a big proviso—the conditions for the exercise of power by the divorce-decreeing court are validly established whenever that judgment is elsewhere called into question. In short, the decree of divorce is a conclusive adjudication of everything except the jurisdictional facts upon which it is founded, and domicil is a jurisdictional fact. To permit the necessary finding of domicil by one State to foreclose all States in the protection of their social institutions would be intolerable.

But to endow each State with controlling authority to nullify the power of a sister State to grant a divorce based upon a finding that one spouse had acquired a new domicil within the divorcing State would, in the proper functioning of our federal system, be equally indefensible. . . . The necessary accommodation between the right of one State to safeguard its interest in the family relation of its own people and the power of another State to grant divorces can be left to neither State.

The problem is to reconcile the reciprocal respect to be accorded by the members of the Union to their adjudications with due regard for another most important aspect of our federalism whereby "the domestic relations of husband and wife . . . were matters reserved to the States," Popovici v. Agler, 280 U.S. 379, 383–84 . . . The rights that belong to all the States and the obligations which membership in the Union imposes upon all, are made effective because this Court is open to consider claims . . . that the courts of one State have not given the full faith and credit of a sister State that is required by Art. IV, § 1 of the Constitution.

But the discharge of this duty does not make of this Court a court of probate and divorce. Neither a rational system of law nor hard practicality calls for our independent determination, in reviewing the judgment of a State court, of that rather elusive relation between person and place which establishes domicil. . . . The challenged judgment must, however, satisfy our scrutiny that the reciprocal duty of respect owed by the States to one another's adjudications has been fairly discharged, and has not been evaded under the guise of finding an absence of domicil and therefore a want of power in the court rendering the judgment.

What is immediately before us is the judgment of the Supreme Court of North Carolina. We have authority to upset it only if there is want of foundation for the conclusion that that Court reached. The conclusion it reached turns on its findings that the spouses who obtained the Nevada decrees were not domiciled there. The fact that the Nevada court found that they were domiciled there is entitled to respect, and more. The burden of undermining the verity which the Nevada decrees import rests heavily upon the assailant. But simply because the Nevada court found that it had power to award a divorce decree cannot, we have seen, foreclose reexamination by another State. . . . If this Court finds that proper weight was accorded to the claims of power by the court of one State in rendering a judgment the validity of which is pleaded in defense in another State, that the burden of overcoming such respect by disproof of the substratum of fact—here domicil—on which such power alone can rest was properly charged against the party challenging the legitimacy of the judgment, that such issue of fact was left for fair determination by appropriate procedure, and that a finding adverse to the necessary foundation for any valid sister-State judgment was amply supported in evidence, we cannot upset the judgment before us. And we cannot do so even if we also found in the record of the court of original judgment warrant for its finding that it had jurisdiction. If it is a matter turning on local law, great deference is owed by the courts of one State to what a court of another State has done. . . . But when we are dealing as here with an historic notion common to all English-speaking courts, that of domicil, we should not find a want of deference to a sister State on the part of a court of another State which finds an absence of domicil where such a conclusion is warranted by the record. . . .

. . . The trial judge charged that the State had the burden of proving beyond a reasonable doubt that (1) each petitioner was lawfully married to one person; (2) thereafter each petitioner contracted a second marriage with another person outside North Carolina; (3) the spouses of petitioners were living at the time of this second marriage; (4) petitioners cohabited with one another in North Carolina after the second marriage. The burden, it was charged, then devolved upon petitioners "to satisfy the trial jury, not beyond a reasonable doubt nor by the greater weight of the evidence, but simply to satisfy" the jury from all the evidence, that petitioners were domiciled in Nevada at the time they obtained their divorces. The court further charged that "the recitation" of *bona fide* domicil in the Nevada decree was "prima facie evidence" sufficient to warrant a finding of domicil in Nevada but not compelling "such an inference." If the jury found . . . that petitioners had been domiciled in North Carolina and went to Nevada "simply and solely for the purpose of obtaining divorces, intending to return to North Carolina on obtaining" them, they never lost their North Carolina domicils nor acquired new domicils in Nevada. . . .

The scales of justice must not be unfairly weighted by a State when full faith and credit is claimed for a sister-State judgment. But North Carolina has not so dealt with the Nevada decrees. She has not raised unfair barriers to their recognition. North Carolina did not fail in appreciation or application of federal standards of full faith and credit. Appropriate weight was given to the finding of domicil in the Nevada decrees, and that finding was allowed to be overturned only by relevant standards of proof. There is nothing to suggest that the issue was not fairly submitted to the jury and that it was not fairly assessed on cogent evidence. . . .

We conclude that North Carolina was not required to yield her State policy because a Nevada court found that petitioners were domiciled in Nevada when it granted them decrees of divorce. North Carolina was entitled to find, as she did, that they did not acquire domicils in Nevada and that the Nevada court was therefore without power to liberate the petitioners from amenability to the laws of North Carolina governing domestic relations. And, as was said in connection with another aspect of the Full Faith and Credit Clause, our conclusion "is not a matter to arouse the susceptibilities of the States, all of which are equally concerned in the question and equally on both sides." Fauntleroy v. Lum, 210 U.S. 230, 238.

Affirmed.

■ [JUSTICE MURPHY wrote a concurring opinion, joined in by CHIEF JUSTICE STONE and JUSTICE JACKSON, which reemphasizes the jurisdictional fact rationale of the majority opinion.

■ JUSTICE RUTLEDGE wrote a dissenting opinion questioning the entire domiciliary concept, reasoning that "jurisdictional fact" has been used to cloak "unitary domicil" so that divorce is back to the era of Haddock with respect to effects.

■ JUSTICE BLACK wrote a dissenting opinion, joined in by JUSTICE DOUGLAS, which reasons that civil liberties are endangered when a criminal offense is grounded on refusal to recognize what another state has apparently regarded as sufficient domicil, and on the further reasoning that the Constitution does not "measure the power of state courts to pass upon petitions for divorce."]

NOTES

1. What law should the F-2 court apply in determining whether the plaintiff spouse acquired a bona fide domicile in F-1? See footnote 7 of the opinion in *Williams II*, at p. 941, supra. Did the Court apply a federal standard? If so, what is it? See also Rice v. Rice, 336 U.S. 674 (1949), where the Supreme Court sustained the finding of a Connecticut court that a Nevada divorce was not supported by a bona fide domicile.

2. A helpful article on the problems presented by the *Williams* cases is D. Currie, Suitcase Divorce in the Conflict of Laws: *Simons, Rosenstiel,* and *Borax,* 34 U.Chi.L.Rev. 26 (1967).

3. For a discussion of professional ethics problems that may arise in connection with matrimonial litigation, see Adams & Adams, Ethical Problems in Advising Migratory Divorce, 16 Hastings L.J. 60 (1964); Drinker, Problems of Professional Ethics in Matrimonial Litigation, 66 Harv.L.Rev. 443 (1953); Drinker, Legal Ethics 80, 122–28 (1953); Neuman, Legal Advice Toward Illegal Ends, 28 U.Rich.L.Rev. 287, 304–08 (1994).

Foreign Jurisdictions

4. The effect given U.S. divorces in foreign countries may depend on whether the particular country has adopted the Hague Convention on the

Recognition of Divorces and Legal Separations of 1970. The Convention provides for recognition of divorces decreed in observance of its jurisdictional standards (including either party's domicile). When the Convention applies, the divorce has the same effect in F-2 as where rendered. See, e.g., Lawrence v. Lawrence, [1985] 3 W.L.R. 125, 2 All E.R. 733 (C.A.): a Brazilian woman obtained a Nevada divorce, remarried in Nevada, and subsequently contested the validity of her remarriage in England on the ground that Brazil would not have recognized the Nevada divorce so that she lacked capacity to remarry. The court held that the Nevada divorce met the Convention's jurisdictional requirements and was valid; its effect, including capacity to remarry, was determined by Nevada law. See contributions by Downes and Lipstein in 35 Int'l & Comp.L.Q. 170, 178 respectively (1986). The matter may be different in civil law countries which have not adopted the Hague Convention and which combine jurisdiction and choice-of-law considerations. For instance, if validity of a divorce depends, in addition to jurisdiction of the F-1 court, on a requirement that the divorcing court apply the right substantive law (e.g., the law of nationality), then a U.S. divorce of a foreign national by application of the local law of F-1 may prevent recognition of the decree in F-2. *Lawrence,* supra, illustrates this fact situation: the validity of the Nevada decree was placed in issue in Brazil. Compare for Germany: Decision of the OLG Koblenz, IPRax 1996, 278; Decision of the OLG Bamberg, NJW-RR 1997, 4; summarized in Hay, Internationales Privat-und Zivilverfahrensrecht, 84–86, 204, 205–207 (PdW Series, 4th ed.2010). See also Verschraegen, Internationales Privatrecht no. 140 et seq. (2012), for Austria.

The effect given foreign divorces in the U.S. may depend on the operation of the doctrine of comity. In re Estate of Toland, 329 P.3d 878 (Wash.2014) (recognizing Japanese divorce of U.S. citizens married in Japan).

5.   The Japanese Supreme Court has held that when spouses are domiciled in different countries, Japanese courts have subject-matter jurisdiction for divorce if this is reasonable in the light of the "plaintiff's domicile and other factors." One of these factors is the "obstacles which a plaintiff may face in filing an action for divorce in the country of the defendant's domicile." The Court upheld jurisdiction in the case of a Japanese man domiciled in Japan when his wife was domiciled in Germany and she had already obtained a German divorce. X v. Y, June 24, 1996, 50 Minshu (7) 1451, [1996] H.J. (1578) 56, summary and partial English translation in 40 Japanese Annual of Int'l L. 132 (1997).

6.   In the European Union, except Denmark, EC Regulation 2201/2003, [2003] Official Journal L 338/1 ("Brussels IIa"), now governs "Jurisdiction and Recognition and Enforcement of Judgments in Matrimonial Matters and in Matters of Parental Responsibility." Article 27(d) provides that a judgment in these matters "shall not be recognised . . . if it is irreconcilable with an earlier judgment given in another Member State or in a non-Member State between the same parties, provided that the earlier judgment fulfills the conditions necessary for its recognition in the Member State in which recognition is sought." This law will be replaced, as of August 1, 2022, by

Council Regulation (EU) 2019/1111, [2010] Official Journal 178. The current provision, cited above, is retained in the new Regulation as Art. 38(c) and (d).

The EU Regulation only deals with jurisdiction to grant a divorce to EU nationals or residents. It does not provide a substantive divorce law The "Rome III" Regulation, reproduced in the Appendix, provides choice-of-law rules for the determination of the applicable law. However, it is in force in only seventeen EU states. In the others, the applicable substantive law is still determined on the basis of their respective national conflicts law.

The Rome III Regulation allows the parties, within limits, to stipulate the substantive law applicable to the divorce. In the absence of such a stipulation, it provides, in order of preference, for the application of the law of the parties' common habitual residence, their last common habitual residence, the law of their common nationality (or domicile, in the case of UK or Irish parties), or the lex fori. In all cases, except the last, the applicable law is that of a state with which the parties have or had a close relationship. Do these rules sufficiently address Judge Goodrich's concerns in *Alton*? May F-2 review F-1's findings (e.g., as to the parties' habitual residence), which underlay F-1's choice of the applicable law? Compare Arts. 22, 24–25 of the current Brussels II Regulation (reproduced in the Appendix). Note that *Williams II* did not concern the law applicable to the divorce (e.g., on what grounds it might be granted), but rather the Nevada court's *jurisdiction* to proceed at all. In *Williams*, jurisdiction and applicable law were intertwined: "domicile" answered both questions. Back to the European Union: could F-2, like North Carolina, avoid recognizing the F-1 divorce by finding that the "habitual residence" requirement—relevant for both jurisdiction and applicable law—had not been met in F-1? See Art. 24 of the current EU Regulation. Finally, what about application of the lex fori, the last reference in the EU Regulation's choice-of-law rules? Note that the least link required for jurisdiction (Brussels II and its replacement Regulation Art. 3(1)(a)) is petitioner's six-month residence. Is this sufficient/reasonable in the light of *Alton* and *Sosna*, above?

Even in the EU countries in which the Rome III Regulation is in force, it applies only to divorces granted by courts in those states; it does not address the recognition of divorces granted in non-EU countries. Substantive grounds for divorce differ (e.g., no-fault vs. fault divorce), so it is possible that a non-EU state's divorce granted on no-fault grounds may run afoul of the standards of the recognizing court. See Verschraegen, supra n. 4, at no. 146. In particular, recognition of private (especially religious) divorces—valid where rendered—may present problems when the recognizing court does not provide for such divorces. See infra pp. 968–971. For a discussion of the challenges facing international couples who divorce in the United States, see Geffner-Mihlsten, Note, Lost in Translation: The Failure of the Interstate Divorce System to Adequately Address the Needs of International Divorcing Couples, 21 S.Cal.Interdisc.L.J. 403 (2012).

C. EXTRATERRITORIAL RECOGNITION: LIMITS ON ATTACK FOR JURISDICTIONAL DEFECTS

DAVIS V. DAVIS, 305 U.S. 32 (1938): Husband, alleging he was a Virginia domiciliary, instituted divorce action there. Wife was served personally in the District of Columbia, her domicile, and appeared in the Virginia action to contest husband's allegations as to his domicile. The court found that husband was domiciled in Virginia and granted the divorce. Husband thereafter brought suit in the District of Columbia to have a prior separation decree modified as a result of the Virginia divorce. The District of Columbia court refused to recognize the Virginia divorce on the grounds of lack of jurisdiction. Held, reversed. Both parties having appeared, and the domicile question having been fully argued, the Virginia decision is res judicata.

Sherrer v. Sherrer

Supreme Court of the United States, 1948.
334 U.S. 343, 68 S.Ct. 1087, 92 L.Ed.1429, 1 A.L.R.2d 1355.

Certiorari to the Probate Court for Berkshire County, Massachusetts.

■ CHIEF JUSTICE VINSON delivered the opinion of the Court.

We granted certiorari in this case and in Coe v. Coe . . . to consider the contention of petitioners that Massachusetts has failed to accord full faith and credit to decrees of divorce rendered by courts of sister States.

Petitioner Margaret E. Sherrer and the respondent, Edward C. Sherrer, were married in New Jersey in 1930, and from 1932 until April 3, 1944, lived together in Monterey, Massachusetts. Following a long period of marital discord, petitioner, accompanied by the two children of the marriage, left Massachusetts on the latter date, ostensibly for the purpose of spending a vacation in the State of Florida. Shortly after her arrival in Florida, however, petitioner informed her husband that she did not intend to return to him. . . .

On July 6, 1944, a bill of complaint for divorce was filed at petitioner's direction in the Circuit Court of the Sixth Judicial Circuit of the State of Florida. The bill alleged extreme cruelty as grounds for divorce and also alleged that petitioner was a "bona fide legal resident of the State of Florida." The respondent received notice by mail of the pendency of the divorce proceedings. He retained Florida counsel who entered a general appearance and filed an answer denying the allegations of petitioner's complaint, including the allegation as to petitioner's Florida residence.

On November 14, 1944, hearings were held in the divorce proceedings. Respondent appeared personally to testify with respect to a stipulation entered into by the parties relating to the custody of the children. Throughout the entire proceedings respondent was represented by counsel. Petitioner introduced evidence to establish her Florida residence and testified generally to the allegations of her complaint. Counsel for respondent failed to cross-examine or to introduce evidence in rebuttal.

The Florida court on November 29, 1944, entered a decree of divorce after specifically finding that petitioner "is a bona fide resident of the State of Florida, and that this court has jurisdiction of the parties and the subject matter in said cause . . ." Respondent failed to challenge the decree by appeal to the Florida Supreme Court.

On December 1, 1944, petitioner was married in Florida to one Henry A. Phelps, whom petitioner had known while both were residing in Massachusetts and who had come to Florida shortly after petitioner's arrival in that State. Phelps and petitioner lived together as husband and wife in Florida, where they were both employed, until February 5, 1945, when they returned to Massachusetts.

In June, 1945, respondent instituted an action in the Probate Court of Berkshire County, Massachusetts, which has given rise to the issues of this case. Respondent alleged that he is the lawful husband of petitioner, that the Florida decree of divorce is invalid, and that petitioner's subsequent marriage is void. Respondent prayed that he might be permitted to convey his real estate as if he were sole and that the court declare that he was living apart from his wife for justifiable cause. Petitioner joined issue on respondent's allegations.

In the proceedings which followed, petitioner gave testimony in defense of the validity of the Florida divorce decree. The Probate Court, however, resolved the issues of fact adversely to petitioner's contentions, found that she was never domiciled in Florida, and granted respondent the relief he had requested. The Supreme Judicial Court of Massachusetts affirmed the decree on the grounds that it was supported by the evidence and that the requirements of full faith and credit did not preclude the Massachusetts courts from reexamining the finding of domicile made by the Florida court. . . .

That the jurisdiction of the Florida court to enter a valid decree of divorce was dependent upon petitioner's domicile in that State is not disputed. This requirement was recognized by the Florida court which rendered the divorce decree, and the principle has been given frequent application in decisions of the State Supreme Court. But whether or not petitioner was domiciled in Florida at the time the divorce was granted was a matter to be resolved by judicial determination. Here, unlike the situation presented in Williams v. North Carolina, 325 U.S. 226 (1945), the finding of the requisite jurisdictional facts was made in proceedings in which the defendant appeared and participated. The question with which we are confronted, therefore, is whether such a finding made under the circumstances presented by this case may, consistent with the requirements of full faith and credit, be subjected to collateral attack in the courts of a sister State in a suit brought by the defendant in the original proceedings.

The question of what effect is to be given to an adjudication by a court that it possesses requisite jurisdiction in a case, where the judgment of that court is subsequently subjected to collateral attack on jurisdictional grounds has been given frequent consideration by this Court over a period of many years. Insofar as cases originating in the federal courts are concerned, the rule has evolved that the doctrine of *res judicata* applies to adjudications relating either to jurisdiction of the person or of the subject matter where such adjudications have been made in proceedings in which those questions were in issue and in which the parties were given full opportunity to litigate. . . .

We believe that the decision of this Court in the Davis case [p. 948, supra] and those in related situations are clearly indicative of the result to be reached here. Those cases stand for the proposition that the requirements of full faith and credit bar a defendant from collaterally attacking a divorce decree on jurisdictional grounds in the courts of a sister State where there has been participation by the defendant in the divorce proceedings, where the defendant has been accorded full opportunity to contest the jurisdictional issues, and where the decree is not susceptible to such collateral attack in the courts of the State which rendered the decree.

Applying these principles to this case, we hold that the Massachusetts courts erred in permitting the Florida divorce decree to be subjected to attack on the ground that petitioner was not domiciled in Florida at the time the decree was entered. . . .

It is urged further, however, that because we are dealing with litigation involving the dissolution of the marital relation, a different result is demanded from that which might properly be reached if this case were concerned with other types of litigation. It is pointed out that under the Constitution the regulation and control of marital and family relationships are reserved to the States. It is urged, and properly so, that the regulation of the incidents of the marital relation involves the exercise by the States of powers of the most vital importance. Finally, it is contended that a recognition of the importance to the States of such powers demands that the requirements of full faith and credit be viewed in such a light as to permit an attack upon a divorce decree granted by a court of a sister State under the circumstances of this case even where the attack is initiated in a suit brought by the defendant in the original proceedings.

But the recognition of the importance of a State's power to determine the incidents of basic social relationships into which its domiciliaries enter does not resolve the issues of this case. This is not a situation in which a State has merely sought to exert such power over a domiciliary. This is, rather, a case involving inconsistent assertions of power by courts of two States of the Federal Union and thus presents considerations which go beyond the interests of local policy, however vital. In resolving the issues here presented, we do not conceive it to be a part of our function to weigh the relative merits of the policies of Florida and Massachusetts with respect to divorce and related matters. Nor do we understand the decisions of this Court to support the proposition that the obligation imposed by Article IV, § 1 of the Constitution and the Act of Congress passed thereunder amounts to something less than the duty to accord *full* faith and credit to decrees of divorce entered by courts of sister States. The full faith and credit clause is one of the provisions incorporated into the Constitution by its framers for the purpose of transforming an aggregation of independent, sovereign States into a nation. If in its application local policy must at times be required to give way, such "is part of the price of our federal system." Williams v. North Carolina, 317 U.S. 287, 302 (1942).

This is not to say that in no case may an area be recognized in which reasonable accommodations of interest may properly be made. But as this Court has heretofore made clear, that area is of limited extent. We believe that in permitting an attack on the Florida divorce decree which again put in issue petitioner's Florida domicile and in refusing to recognize the validity of that decree, the Massachusetts courts have asserted a power which cannot be reconciled with the requirements of due faith and credit. We believe that assurances that such a power will be exercised sparingly and wisely render it no less repugnant to the constitutional commands.

It is one thing to recognize as permissible the judicial reexamination of findings of jurisdictional fact where such findings have been made by a court of a sister State which has entered a divorce decree in *ex parte* proceedings. It is quite another thing to hold that the vital rights and interests involved in divorce litigation may be held in suspense pending the scrutiny by courts of sister States of findings of jurisdictional fact made by a competent court in proceedings conducted in a manner consistent with the highest requirements of due process and in which the defendant has participated. We do not conceive it to be in accord with the purposes of the full faith and credit requirement to hold that a judgment rendered under the circumstances of this case may be required to run the gauntlet of such collateral attack in the courts of sister States before its validity outside of the State which rendered it is established or rejected. That vital interests are involved in divorce litigation indicates to us that it is a matter of greater rather than lesser importance that there should be a place to end such litigation. And where a decree of divorce is rendered by a competent court under the circumstances of this case, the obligation of full faith and credit requires that such litigation should end in the courts of the State in which the judgment was rendered.

Reversed.

■ JUSTICE FRANKFURTER, with whom JUSTICE MURPHY concurs, dissented. In the course of the dissenting opinion, he wrote, "A divorce may satisfy due process requirements, and be valid where rendered, and still lack the jurisdictional requisites for full faith and credit to be mandatory." 334 U.S. at 368.

NOTES

1. In Coe v. Coe, 334 U.S. 378 (1948), decided the same day as Sherrer v. Sherrer, H sued for divorce in Nevada after residing there six weeks. W appeared personally, and through her attorney filed an answer admitting H's residence in Nevada and a cross-complaint for divorce. The Nevada court found it had jurisdiction of the parties and of the subject matter, and entered a decree granting W a divorce. H remarried and returned to Massachusetts, where W brought proceedings against him under a decree for support rendered in Massachusetts before the Nevada divorce. The Massachusetts court disregarded the Nevada divorce as void for lack of jurisdiction. The court held that Massachusetts could not, under the requirements of full faith and credit, subject the Nevada decree to collateral attack by readjudicating the existence of jurisdictional facts. The dissent in Sherrer v. Sherrer also encompassed Coe v. Coe. For discussion of the Sherrer and Coe cases, see Carey & MacChesney, Divorces by the Consent of the Parties and Divisible Divorce Decrees, 43 Ill.L.Rev. 608 (1948); Paulsen, Migratory Divorce: Chapters III and IV, 24 Ind.L.J. 25 (1948). For a recent application of *Sherrer* and *Coe*, see Kelley v. Kelley, 147 So.3d 597 (Fla.App.2014) (collateral attack on sister-state divorce decree by a third-party barred by Full Faith and Credit Clause).

2. There are differences among the state courts as to whether the rule of the Sherrer case applies in a situation where the defendant enters an appearance through an attorney in the divorce proceedings but is not physically present and does not contest any issues. In Boxer v. Boxer, 177 N.Y.S.2d 85 (N.Y.Sup.Ct.1958), aff'd, 163 N.E.2d 149 (N.Y.1959) (mem.), H obtained a divorce in Alabama after having been in that state only one day. W appeared through an Alabama attorney whom she had appointed by an instrument mailed from New York. The decree was held entitled to full faith and credit. A similar result was reached in Boudreaux v. Welch, 192 So.2d 356 (La.1966).

On the other hand, a divorce has been held subject to collateral attack when the defendant spouse did not appear personally in the divorce proceedings and either (a) was represented by an attorney employed and controlled by the plaintiff spouse (Pelle v. Pelle, 182 A.2d 37 (Md.1962); Staedler v. Staedler, 78 A.2d 896 (N.J.1951)); or (b) filed in the divorce proceedings an answer admitting that plaintiff spouse was domiciled in the divorce state. Donnell v. Howell, 125 S.E.2d 448 (N.C.1962). Can these decisions be reconciled with Johnson v. Muelberger, which appears immediately below, and Cook v. Cook, p. 955, infra?

Johnson v. Muelberger

Supreme Court of the United States, 1951.
340 U.S. 581, 71 S.Ct. 474, 95 L.Ed. 552.

■ JUSTICE REED delivered the opinion of the Court.

The right of a daughter to attack in New York the validity of her deceased father's Florida divorce is before us. She was his legatee. The divorce was granted in Florida after the father appeared there and contested the merits. The issue turns on the effect in New York under these circumstances of the Full Faith and Credit Clause of the Federal Constitution.

Eleanor Johnson Muelberger, respondent, is the child of decedent E. Bruce Johnson's first marriage. After the death of Johnson's first wife in 1939, he married one Madoline Ham, and they established their residence in New York. In August 1942, Madoline obtained a divorce from him in a Florida proceeding, although the undisputed facts as developed in the New York Surrogate's hearing show that she did not comply with the jurisdictional ninety-day residence requirement. The New York Surrogate found that

> "In the Florida court, the decedent appeared by attorney and interposed an answer denying the wrongful acts but not questioning the allegations as to residence in Florida. The record discloses that testimony was taken by the Florida court and the divorce granted Madoline Johnson. Both parties had full opportunity to contest the jurisdictional issues in that court and the decree is not subject to attack on the ground that petitioner was not domiciled in Florida."

In 1944 Mr. Johnson entered into a marriage, his third, with petitioner, Genevieve Johnson, and in 1945 he died, leaving a will in which he gave his entire estate to his daughter, Eleanor. After probate of the will, the third wife filed notice of her election to take the statutory one-third share of the estate, under § 18 of the New York Decedent's Estate Law. This election was contested by respondent daughter, and a trial was had before the Surrogate, who determined that she could not attack the third wife's status as surviving spouse, on the basis of the alleged invalidity of Madoline's divorce, because the divorce proceeding had been a contested one, and "[s]ince the decree is valid and final in the State of Florida, it is not subject to collateral attack in the courts of this state."

The Appellate Division affirmed the Surrogate's decree *per curiam,* but the New York Court of Appeals reversed. 301 N.Y. 13, 92 N.E.2d 44. . . . The Court . . . held that the Florida judgment finding jurisdiction to decree the divorce bound only the parties themselves. This followed from their previous opportunity to contest the jurisdictional issue. As the court read the Florida cases to allow Eleanor to attack the decree collaterally in Florida, it decided she should be equally free to do so in

New York. The Court of Appeals reached this decision after consideration of the Full Faith and Credit Clause. Because the case involves important issues in the adjustment of the domestic-relations laws of the several states, we granted certiorari, 340 U.S. 874.

... There is substantially no legislative history to explain the purpose and meaning of the [full faith and credit] clause and of the [implementing] statute. From judicial experience with and interpretation of the clause, there has emerged the succinct conclusion that the Framers intended it to help weld the independent states into a nation by giving judgments within the jurisdiction of the rendering state the same faith and credit in sister states as they have in the state of the original forum. The faith and credit given is not to be niggardly but generous, full....

This constitutional purpose promotes unification, not centralization. It leaves each state with power over its own courts but binds litigants, wherever they may be in the Nation, by prior orders of other courts with jurisdiction....

[At this point, the Court discussed the *Davis*, *Williams*, *Sherrer*, and *Coe* cases.]

It is clear from the foregoing that, under our decisions, a state by virtue of the clause must give full faith and credit to an out-of-state divorce by barring either party to that divorce who has been personally served or who has entered a personal appearance from collaterally attacking the decree. Such an attack is barred where the party attacking would not be permitted to make a collateral attack in the courts of the granting state. This rule the Court of Appeals recognized. 301 N.Y. 13, 17, 92 N.E.2d 44. It determined, however, that a "stranger to the divorce action," as the daughter was held to be in New York, may collaterally attack her father's Florida divorce in New York if she could have attacked it in Florida.

No Florida case has come to our attention holding that a child may contest in Florida its parent's divorce where the parent was barred from contesting, as here, by *res judicata*.... If the laws of Florida should be that a surviving child is in privity with its parent as to that parent's estate, surely the Florida doctrine of res judicata would apply to the child's collateral attack as it would to the father's. If, on the other hand, Florida holds ... that the child of a former marriage is a stranger to the divorce proceedings, late opinions of Florida indicate that the child would not be permitted to attack the divorce, since the child had a mere expectancy at the time of the divorce. [At this point, the Court discussed certain Florida cases.]

We conclude that Florida would not permit Mrs. Muelberger to attack the Florida decree of divorce between her father and his second wife as beyond the jurisdiction of the rendering court. In that case New York cannot permit such an attack by reason of the Full Faith and Credit Clause. When a divorce cannot be attacked for lack of jurisdiction by parties actually before the court or strangers in the rendering state, it cannot be attacked by them anywhere in the Union. The Full Faith and Credit Clause forbids.

Reversed.

■ JUSTICE FRANKFURTER dissents, substantially for the reasons given in the opinion of the New York Court of Appeals, 301 N.Y. 13, 92 N.E.2d 44, in light of the views expressed by him in Sherrer v. Sherrer and Coe v. Coe, 334 U.S. 343, 356.

■ JUSTICE MINTON took no part in the consideration or decision of this case.

Cook v. Cook

Supreme Court of the United States, 1951.
342 U.S. 126, 72 S.Ct. 157, 96 L.Ed. 146.

[Shortly after he had gone through a marriage ceremony with W, H discovered that she was still the lawful wife of one Mann. H and W thereupon agreed to remarry after W had procured a Florida divorce from Mann. This course was followed, but after the remarriage, marital difficulties developed and H eventually brought suit in Vermont to have the marriage annulled. This relief was granted by the Vermont courts on the ground that the divorce, and hence the remarriage, were void because W had never acquired a Florida domicile. The case was then taken on certiorari to the Supreme Court.]

■ JUSTICE DOUGLAS delivered the opinion of the Court.

On this record we do not know what happened in the Florida divorce proceedings except that the Florida court entered a divorce decree in favor of petitioner and against Mann. So far as we know, Mann was a party to the proceedings. So far as we know, the issue of domicile was contested, litigated and resolved in petitioner's favor. If the defendant spouse appeared in the Florida proceedings and contested the issue of the wife's domicile, Sherrer v. Sherrer, 334 U.S. 343, or appeared and admitted her Florida domicile, Coe v. Coe, 334 U.S. 378 he would be barred from attacking the decree collaterally; and so would a stranger to the Florida proceedings, such as respondent, unless Florida applies a less strict rule of *res judicata* to the second husband than it does to the first. See Johnson v. Muelberger, supra. On the other hand, if the defendant spouse had neither appeared nor been served in Florida, the Vermont court, under the ruling in Williams v. State of North Carolina, 325 U.S. 226, could reopen the issue of domicile.

... The Vermont Supreme Court recognized that there were no findings on those issues in the present record. The Court in referring to the case of Williams v. State of North Carolina, 325 U.S. 226, said, "It was there held that the question of bona fide domicile was open to attack, notwithstanding the full faith and credit clause when the other spouse neither had appeared nor been served with process in the state. The findings here do not show either of these criteria." 116 Vt. 374, 378, 76 A.2d 593, 595. Yet it is essential that the court know what transpired in Florida before this collateral attack on the Florida decree can be resolved. For until Florida's jurisdiction is shown to be vulnerable, Vermont may not relitigate the issue of domicile on which the Florida decree rests. . . .

Reversed.

■ JUSTICE FRANKFURTER dissented in a separate opinion.

NOTES

1.   A Nevada statute bars all third-party attacks on Nevada divorce decrees that are binding on the parties to the action. Nev.Rev.Stat. § 125.185. Would this statute also have the effect of barring third-party attacks in sister states?

2.   In the *Williams* cases, pp. 936, 941, supra, the absent spouses had not questioned the validity of the Nevada divorces obtained by Mr. Williams and Ms. Hendrix. It was the State of North Carolina that asserted the invalidity of the divorces and prosecuted Williams and Hendrix for bigamy. Does the state of the ex-spouses' last matrimonial domicile have an independent interest in the validity of the out-of-state divorce which it may assert (a) when the divorce was ex parte (as in *Williams*) and (b) even when both parties participated? Does Johnson v. Muelberger answer this question? See Weber v. Weber, 265 N.W.2d 436, 440 (Neb.1978), refusing to recognize a Dominican Republic bilateral divorce: "The state is impliedly a party to the marriage contract, and has an interest in the continuance and dissolution of the marital relation."

Krause v. Krause
Court of Appeals of New York, 1940.
282 N.Y. 355, 26 N.E.2d 290.

■ FINCH, JUDGE. This is an action for separation brought by a wife in which she seeks support. The husband seeks to avoid liability to plaintiff by alleging the invalidity of a Nevada divorce which he obtained from his first wife. May he avail himself of such a defense?

The facts presented by the defense are as follows: Defendant and his first wife domiciled in this State, were married here in 1905. There are two children by that marriage. In 1932 the present defendant, while retaining his residence in this State, made a visit to Reno, Nev., where he invoked the jurisdiction of the courts of that State and obtained a decree of divorce from his first wife, who neither entered an appearance nor was personally served in that action, and who at all times has remained a resident of this State. . . . Consequently this divorce against the first wife is not recognized by the courts of this State. . . . The subsequent marriage between plaintiff and defendant, therefore, was void for the incapacity of the defendant to marry. But nonetheless plaintiff and defendant participated in a complete marriage ceremony and did live together as man and wife for six years pursuant thereto, after which time defendant abandoned plaintiff, who now brings this action. Defendant entered the defense already noted, viz., that he lacked capacity to marry plaintiff because the court, which upon his petition purported to accord him a divorce from his first wife, lacked jurisdiction to act in the premises. Upon motion of plaintiff Special Term struck out the defense as insufficient in law . . . The Appellate Division affirmed by a divided court . . .

The question upon this appeal, therefore, depends upon whether defendant husband may now be heard to assert in this action, brought by his second "wife," that the judgment of divorce which he sought and obtained failed of its purpose and thereby did not give to the defendant that freedom to remarry which he appeared to possess by virtue of said judgment.

In general, a person who invokes the jurisdiction of a court will not be heard to repudiate the judgment which that court entered upon his seeking and in his favor. . . . The rule has been applied in this State in cases where property rights arising out of the marriage have been involved. . . . It is said, however, that in Stevens v. Stevens [273 N.Y. 157, 7 N.E.2d 26] we have answered the question upon which the case at bar turns. But in the Stevens case an action for separation was brought in this State by a wife against her husband who had previously secured a divorce in a Nevada court which was admittedly without jurisdiction. The husband counterclaimed for a divorce. At the trial the wife sought to defeat the counterclaim by introducing in evidence the Nevada divorce obtained by the husband in order to put him in a position where he could not maintain his claim for divorce because he was no longer the husband of the wife. Upon the facts of that case this court held that the husband was not prevented from maintaining the action for divorce despite the prior Nevada decree which he had obtained. . . . In the Stevens case the position which the husband assumed in the proceedings in this State was inconsistent with the decree which he had obtained in Nevada only in the sense that as part of a cause of action for divorce it is necessary to prove the marriage. . . . But the action which he sought to take was parallel with that which he had previously undertaken in the Nevada proceedings in that the object of both was the same, to wit, termination of the marriage with his wife. Such is not the situation in the case at bar where the action which defendant seeks to take is inconsistent with the result purportedly achieved by the invalid Nevada decree. . . .

We come, then, to a consideration of the principle applicable in the case at bar. We cannot lose sight of the fact that the present defendant was himself the party who had obtained the decree of divorce which he now asserts to be invalid and repudiates in order that he may now disown any legal obligation to support the plaintiff, whom he purported to marry. To refuse to permit this defendant to escape his obligation to support plaintiff does not mean that the courts of this State recognize as valid a judgment of divorce which necessarily is assumed to be invalid in the case at bar, but only that it is not open to defendant in these proceedings to avoid the responsibility which he voluntarily incurred. . . .

But it is urged that even though the prior authorities in this State do not compel a contrary result, a different conclusion should be reached as a matter of principle. It is said that public policy requires that the interest of the State in the first marriage be protected even though that may also give to the individual defendant an incidental advantage to which he is not entitled in his private right. Thus defendant seeks to avoid the obligation which he has purported to undertake to support his second wife, upon the pretext that such is inconsistent with his obligations toward his first wife. Objection upon this score is fully met by the fact that the needs of the first wife are to be taken into account in arriving at the ability of defendant to support plaintiff in the case at bar. Defendant would altogether disavow any obligation toward this plaintiff because of his obligation to his first wife. The result which we reach here is the only one which awards justice to this plaintiff, prevents her from becoming a public charge if she should be impecunious and at the same time protects the first wife in adequate degree. Thus there is complete observance of not only the interest of the State in the protection of the first marriage, but also of the other interest of the State that marriage obligations shall not be lightly undertaken and lightly discarded.

Nothing in this decision should be taken to mean that because the defendant may not in these proceedings avail himself of the invalidity of his Nevada decree he is not the husband of his first wife. On the contrary, the very theory that defendant is precluded in these proceedings presupposes that the true situation is the contrary of that which he may show in the case at bar.

It follows, therefore, that the order appealed from should be affirmed, with costs, and the question certified answered in the negative.

Order affirmed, etc.

[The dissenting opinion is omitted.]

NOTES

1.   Suppose that a spouse is estopped from attacking the divorce in F-1. Does the Constitution require in such a case that he likewise be estopped in F-2? Will the *Sherrer, Coe, Johnson,* and *Cook* cases result in a narrower application of the estoppel doctrine?

2.   The estoppel principle is frequently applied to a spouse who did not obtain the divorce but who took advantage of it by remarrying. Carbulon v. Carbulon, 57 N.E.2d 59 (N.Y.1944); Torres v. Colvin, 2014 WL 795961 (N.D.Ala.2014).

D. EXTRATERRITORIAL RECOGNITION: DIVISIBLE DIVORCE

Estin v. Estin

Supreme Court of the United States, 1948.
334 U.S. 541, 68 S.Ct. 1213, 92 L.Ed.1561, 1 A.L.R.2d 1412.

Certiorari to the Court of Appeals of New York.

■ Opinion of the Court by JUSTICE DOUGLAS, announced by JUSTICE REED.

This case, here on certiorari to the Court of Appeals of New York, presents an important question under the Full Faith and Credit Clause of the Constitution. Article IV, § 1. It is whether a New York decree awarding respondent $180 per month for her maintenance and support in a separation proceeding survived a Nevada divorce decree which subsequently was granted petitioner.

The parties were married in 1937 and lived together in New York until 1942 when the husband left the wife. There was no issue of the marriage. In 1943 she brought an action against him for a separation. He entered a general appearance. The court, finding that he had abandoned her, granted her a decree of separation and awarded her $180 per month as permanent alimony. In January 1944 he went to Nevada where in 1945 he instituted an action for divorce. She was notified of the action by constructive service but entered no appearance in it. In May, 1945, the Nevada court, finding that petitioner had been a bona fide resident of Nevada since January 30, 1944, granted him an absolute divorce "on the ground of three years continual separation, without cohabitation." The Nevada decree made no provision for alimony, though the Nevada court had been advised of the New York decree.

Prior to that time petitioner had made payments of alimony under the New York decree. After entry of the Nevada decree he ceased paying. Thereupon respondent sued in New York for a supplementary judgment for the amount of the arrears. Petitioner appeared in the action and moved to eliminate the alimony provisions of the separation decree by reason of the Nevada decree. The Supreme Court denied the motion and granted respondent judgment for the arrears. 63 N.Y.S.2d 476. The judgment was affirmed by the Appellate Division, 271 App.Div. 829, 66 N.Y.S.2d 421, and then by the Court of Appeals, 296 N.Y. 308, 73 N.E.2d 113.

We held in Williams v. North Carolina, 317 U.S. 287; 325 U.S. 226 (1) that a divorce decree granted by a State to one of its domiciliaries is entitled to full faith and credit in a bigamy prosecution brought in another State, even though the other spouse was given notice of the divorce proceeding only through constructive service; and (2) that while the finding of domicile by the court that granted the decree is entitled to *prima facie* weight, it is not conclusive in a sister State but might be relitigated there. And see Esenwein v. Esenwein, 325 U.S. 279. The latter course was followed in this case, as a consequence of which the Supreme Court of New York found, in accord with the Nevada court, that petitioner "is now and since January, 1944, has been a bona fide resident of the State of Nevada."

Petitioner's argument therefore is that the tail must go with the hide—that since by the Nevada decree, recognized in New York, he and respondent are no longer husband and wife, no legal incidence of the marriage remains.

[T]he highest court in New York has held in this case that a support order can survive divorce and that this one has survived petitioner's divorce. That conclusion is binding on us, except as it conflicts with the Full Faith and Credit Clause. . . . The only question for us is whether New York is powerless to make such a ruling in view of the Nevada decree.

We can put to one side the case where the wife was personally served or where she appeared in the divorce proceedings. . . . The only service on her in this case was by publication and she made no appearance in the Nevada proceeding. The requirements of procedural due process were satisfied and the domicile of the husband in Nevada was foundation for a decree effecting a change in the marital capacity of both parties in all the other States of the Union, as well as in Nevada. Williams v. North Carolina, 317 U.S. 287. But the fact that marital capacity was changed does not mean that every other legal incidence of the marriage was necessarily affected.

Although the point was not adjudicated in Barber v. Barber, 21 How. 582, 588, the Court in that case recognized that while a divorce decree obtained in Wisconsin by a husband from his absent wife might dissolve the *vinculum* of the marriage, it did not mean that he was freed from payment of alimony under an earlier separation decree granted by New York. An absolutist might quarrel with the result and demand a rule that once a divorce is granted, the whole of the marriage relation is dissolved, leaving no roots or tendrils of any kind. But there are few areas of the law in black and white. The greys are dominant and even among them the shades are innumerable. For the eternal problem of the law is one of making accommodations between conflicting interests. This is why most legal problems end as questions of degree. That is true of the present problem under the Full Faith and Credit Clause. . . .

Marital status involves the regularity and integrity of the marriage relation. It affects the legitimacy of the offspring of marriage. It is the basis of criminal laws, as the bigamy prosecution in Williams v. North Carolina dramatically illustrates. The State has a considerable interest in preventing bigamous marriages and in protecting the offspring of marriages from being bastardized. The interest of the State extends to its domiciliaries. The State should have the power to guard its interest in them by changing or altering their marital status and by protecting them in that changed status throughout the farthest reaches of the nation. For a person domiciled in one State should not be allowed to suffer the penalties of bigamy for living outside the State with the only one which the State of his domicile recognizes as his lawful wife. And children born of the only marriage which is lawful in the State of his domicile should not carry the stigma of bastardy when they move elsewhere. These are matters of legitimate concern to the State of the domicile. They entitle the State of the domicile to bring in the absent spouse through constructive service. In no other way could the State of the domicile have and maintain effective control of the marital status of its domiciliaries.

Those are the considerations that have long permitted the State of the matrimonial domicile to change the marital status of the parties by an *ex parte* divorce proceeding . . . considerations which in the Williams case we thought were equally applicable to any State in which one spouse had established a bona fide domicile. See 817 U.S. pp. 300–301. But those considerations have little relevancy here. In this case New York evinced a concern with this broken marriage when both parties were domiciled in New York and before Nevada had any concern with it. New York was rightly concerned lest the abandoned spouse be left impoverished and perhaps become a public charge. The problem of her livelihood and support is plainly a matter in which her community had a legitimate interest. The New York court, having jurisdiction over both parties, undertook to protect her by granting her a judgment of permanent alimony. Nevada, however, apparently follows the rule that dissolution of the marriage puts an end to a support order. . . . But the question is whether Nevada could under any circumstances adjudicate rights of respondent under the New York judgment when she was not personally served or did not appear in the proceeding.

Bassett v. Bassett, 141 F.2d 954, held that Nevada could not. We agree with that view.

The New York judgment is a property interest of respondent, created by New York in a proceeding in which both parties were present. . . . The property interest which it created was an intangible, jurisdiction over which cannot be exerted through control over a physical thing. Jurisdiction over an intangible can indeed only arise from control of power over the persons whose relationships are the source of the rights and obligations. . . .

Jurisdiction over a debtor is sufficient to give the State of his domicile some control over the debt which he owes. . . . But we are aware of no power which the State of domicile of the debtor has to determine the personal rights of the creditor in the intangible unless the creditor has been personally served or appears in the proceeding. . . .

We know of no source of power which would take the present case out of that category. The Nevada decree that is said to wipe out respondent's claim for alimony under the New York judgment is nothing less than an attempt by Nevada ... to exercise an *in personam* jurisdiction over a person not before the court. That may not be done. Since Nevada had no power to adjudicate respondent's rights in the New York judgment, New York need not give full faith and credit to that phase of Nevada's judgment. A judgment of a court having no jurisdiction to render it is not entitled to the full faith and credit which the Constitution and statute of the United States demand. . . .

The result in this situation is to make the divorce divisible—to give effect to the Nevada decree insofar as it affects marital status and to make it ineffective on the issue of alimony. It accommodates the interests of both Nevada and New York in this broken marriage by restricting each State to the matters of her dominant concern.

Since Nevada had no jurisdiction to alter respondent's rights in the New York judgment, we do not reach the further question whether in any event that judgment would be entitled to full faith and credit in Nevada. . . . And it will be time enough to consider the effect of any discrimination shown to out-of-state *ex parte* divorces when a State makes that its policy.

Affirmed.

■ JUSTICE FRANKFURTER and JUSTICE JACKSON dissent in separate opinions.

NOTES

1.   Vanderbilt v. Vanderbilt, 354 U.S. 416 (1957) (affirming 135 N.E.2d 553 (N.Y.1956)). H and W's marital domicile was California at the time of their separation. Thereafter, H became domiciled in Nevada and obtained there an ex parte divorce with the purported effect of ending his alimony obligation. W had moved to New York before the Nevada action, and, after the handing down of the Nevada decree, sued H for alimony in New York under a New York statute (now Dom.Rel. § 236), which authorizes such an action. The New York courts found for W, and the Supreme Court affirmed on the ground that "[s]ince the wife was not subject to its jurisdiction, the Nevada divorce court had no power to extinguish any right which [the wife] had under the law of New York to financial support from her husband." 354 U.S., at 418. There were dissents by Justices Frankfurter and Harlan. Justice Frankfurter believed that Nevada had as much power under due process to affect support rights ex parte as it had to dissolve the marriage. Justice Harlan summarized the grounds of his dissent in his concurring opinion in Simons v. Miami Beach First Nat. Bank, p. 963, infra.

2.   Suppose that after a Nevada ex parte divorce, the non-appearing spouse brings an original suit for alimony and support against the other spouse in the Nevada courts. May these courts refuse to entertain the action on the ground that, so far as Nevada is concerned, plaintiff's right to such relief was terminated by the divorce decree? This question was answered in the affirmative, with one judge dissenting, in Cavell v. Cavell, 526 P.2d 330

(Nev.1974). Is this result consistent with—or does it go beyond—the *Simons* case, immediately following?

3. In the United States the doctrine of "divisible divorce" is based on the fact that the sister-state court that granted an ex parte divorce did not have personal jurisdiction over the spouse now seeking a support order. In England, part III of the Marital and Family Proceedings Act 1984, in force in England and Wales, gives a court the power to grant financial relief to a spouse whose marriage has been dissolved in a foreign country even when that spouse had appeared in the foreign proceedings. In Agbaje v. Akinnoye-Agbaje, [2010] UKSC 13 (U.K. Supreme Court 2010), a Nigerian court divorced the spouses and granted the wife a portion of the marital assets. The wife, who had been living in England since 1999, appeared in the Nigerian proceedings. The court held that, although the divorce was valid, the trial judge had the power, which he exercised, to make additional financial provisions for the wife. The court left open the question of whether, if the other country were a member of the European Union, proceedings under the Act would be precluded because an English court must recognize the foreign court's determination of the maintenance issue.

Simons v. Miami Beach First National Bank

Supreme Court of the United States, 1965.
381 U.S. 81, 85 S.Ct. 1315, 14 L.Ed.2d 232.

■ JUSTICE BRENNAN delivered the opinion of the Court.

The question to be decided in this case is whether a husband's valid Florida divorce, obtained in a proceeding wherein his nonresident wife was served by publication only and did not make a personal appearance, unconstitutionally extinguished her dower right in his Florida estate.

The petitioner and Sol Simons were domiciled in New York when, in 1946, she obtained a New York separation decree that included an award of monthly alimony. Sol Simons moved to Florida in 1951 and, a year later, obtained there a divorce in an action of which petitioner had valid constructive notice but in which she did not enter a personal appearance. After Sol Simons' death in Florida in 1960, respondent, the executor of his estate, offered his will for probate in the Probate Court of Dade County, Florida. Petitioner appeared in the proceeding and filed an election to take dower under Florida law, rather than have her rights in the estate governed by the terms of the will, which made no provision for her. The respondent opposed the dower claim, asserting that since Sol Simons had divorced petitioner she had not been his wife at his death, and consequently was not entitled to dower under Florida law. Petitioner thereupon brought the instant action in the Circuit Court for Dade County in order to set aside the divorce decree and to obtain a declaration that the divorce, even if valid to alter her marital status, did not destroy or impair her claim to dower. The action was dismissed after trial, and the Florida District Court of Appeal for the Third District affirmed. 157

So.2d 199. The Supreme Court of Florida declined to review the case, 166 So.2d 151. We granted certiorari, 379 U.S. 877. We affirm.

Petitioner's counsel advised us during oral argument that he no longer challenged the judgment below insofar as it embodied a holding that the 1952 Florida divorce was valid and terminated the marital status of the parties. We therefore proceed to the decision of the question whether the Florida courts unconstitutionally denied petitioner's dower claim.

Petitioner argues that since she had not appeared in the Florida divorce action the Florida divorce court had no power to extinguish any right which she had acquired under the New York decree. She invokes the principle of Estin v. Estin, 334 U.S. 541, where this Court decided that a Nevada divorce court, which had no personal jurisdiction over the wife, had no power to terminate a husband's obligation to provide the wife support as required by a pre-existing New York separation decree. . . .

The short answer to this contention is that the only obligation imposed on Sol Simons by the New York decree, and the only rights granted petitioner under it, concerned monthly alimony for petitioner's support. Unlike the ex-husband in Estin, Sol Simons made the support payments called for by the separate maintenance decree notwithstanding his *ex parte* divorce. . . . when he died there was consequently nothing left of the New York decree for Florida to dishonor. . . .

Insofar as petitioner argues that since she was not subject to the jurisdiction of the Florida divorce court its decree could not extinguish any dower right existing under Florida law, Vanderbilt v. Vanderbilt, 354 U.S. 416, 418, the answer is that under Florida law no dower right survived the decree. The Supreme Court of Florida has said that dower rights in Florida property, being inchoate, are extinguished by a divorce decree predicated upon substituted or constructive service. Pawley v. Pawley, 46 So.2d 464.[6]

---

[6] In Pawley the Supreme Court of Florida distinguished the dower right from the right to support saying at 46 So.2d 464, 472–473, n. 2:

"In this, if not in every jurisdiction, right of dower can never be made the subject of a wholly independent issue in any divorce suit. It stands or falls as a result of the decree which denies or grants divorce. It arises upon marriage, as an institution of the law. The inchoate right of dower has some of the incidents of property. It partakes of the nature of a lien or encumbrance. It is not a right which is originated by or is derived from the husband; nor is it a personal obligation to be met or fulfilled by him, but it is a creature of the law, is born at the marriage altar, cradled in the bosom of the marital status as an integral and component part thereof, survives during the life of the wife as such and finds its sepulcher in divorce. Alimony too is an institution of the law but it is a personal obligation of the husband which is based upon the duty imposed upon him by the common law to support his wife and gives rise to a personal right of the wife to insist upon, if she be entitled to, it. It has none of the incidents of, and is in no sense a lien upon or interest in, property. Consequently, the right of the wife to be heard on the question of alimony should not, indeed lawfully it cannot, be destroyed by a divorce decree sought and secured by the husband in an action wherein only constructive service of process was effected." . . .

It follows that the Florida courts transgressed no constitutional bounds in denying petitioner dower in her ex-husband's Florida estate.

Affirmed.

■ JUSTICE HARLAN, concurring.

I am happy to join the opinion of the Court because it makes a partial retreat from Vanderbilt v. Vanderbilt, 354 U.S. 416, a decision which I believe must eventually be rerationalized, if not entirely overruled.

The Vanderbilt case was this. The Vanderbilt couple was domiciled in California. Mr. Vanderbilt went to Nevada, established a new domicile, and obtained an *ex parte* divorce decree which did not provide for alimony payments to Mrs. Vanderbilt. In the meantime Mrs. Vanderbilt went to New York. After the Nevada decree had become final, she sued in New York for support under New York law, sequestering Mr. Vanderbilt's property located there. New York ordered support payments, rejecting full-faith-and-credit arguments based on the Nevada decree. . . .

Two rules emerged from the case, neither of which, I suggest with deference, commends itself: (1) an *ex parte* divorce can have no effect on property rights; (2) a State in which a wife subsequently establishes domicile can award support to her regardless of her connection with that State at the time of the *ex parte* divorce and regardless of the law in her former State of domicile.[2]

The first rule slips unobtrusively into oblivion in today's decision, for Florida is allowed to turn property rights on its *ex parte* decree. . . .

Because New York was petitioner's State of domicile at all times relevant to this case and did not purport to invest her with any rights to property beyond those she received from her husband, the second rule is not involved here. My hope is that its time will come too. . . .

■ JUSTICE BLACK, with whom JUSTICE DOUGLAS joins, concurring. . . .

I do not think that today's decision marks any "retreat" at all from the opinion or holding in Vanderbilt, . . . Vanderbilt held that a wife's right to support could not be cut off by an *ex parte* divorce. In the case before us, Mrs. Simons' Florida dower was not terminated by the *ex parte* divorce. It simply never came into existence. No one disputes that the *ex parte* divorce was effective to end the marriage, so that after it Mrs.

---

[2] The Vanderbilt result might have been proper on any of three grounds. (1) If New York was Mrs. Vanderbilt's State of domicile at the time of the *ex parte* Nevada divorce, New York law investing a wife with support rights should not be overborne by an *ex parte* decree in another State. (2) If California was Mrs. Vanderbilt's domicile at the time of the Nevada divorce and under California law support could have been awarded, New York should also be free (though not bound) to award support. (3) If Mr. Vanderbilt owned property in New York at the time of the *ex parte* divorce, New York might arguably be free to hold that ownership of New York property carries with it the obligation to support one's wife, at least to the extent of the value of that property.

The Court did not concern itself with the location of Mrs. Vanderbilt's domicile or Mr. Vanderbilt's property at the time of the Nevada divorce.

Simons was no longer Mr. Simons' wife. Florida law, as the Court's opinion shows, grants dower only to a woman who is the legal wife of the husband when he dies. Mrs. Simons therefore had no property rights cut off by the divorce. She simply had her marriage ended by it, and for that reason was not a "widow" within the meaning of the Florida law. Unless this Court were to make the novel declaration that Florida cannot limit dower rights to widows, I see no possible way in which the Vanderbilt case, which dealt with rights which a State did give to divorced wives, could be thought to apply.

[A dissenting opinion by JUSTICE STEWART, joined in by JUSTICE GOLDBERG, is omitted.]

NOTES

1.   The *Simons* case makes clear that an absent spouse can constitutionally lose "inchoate" property interests as a result of an ex parte divorce decree. Can this case be reconciled with Estin v. Estin? See D. Currie, Suitcase Divorce in the Conflict of Laws, 34 U.Chi.L.Rev. 26 (1967).

2.   Domicile in the state by at least one of the parties is not the only jurisdictional basis for divorce under the law of most foreign countries. Indeed, "most countries do not even have a concept equivalent to our notion of domicile." Juenger, Recognition of Foreign Divorces—British and American Perspectives, 20 Am.J.Comp.L. 1, 19 (1972). For the European Union, see p. 946, Note 6, supra. To the extent that ties other than domicile in the state suffice as a jurisdictional basis for divorce in the forum state, some foreign country divorces will be entitled to recognition in the United States. On the other hand, many divorces denied recognition in this country involved situations in which the divorce was sought by an American citizen seeking to escape divorce restrictions in his state of domicile. For example, in some Mexican states, a divorce could be obtained for practically any reason, sometimes without residence, and in some cases without requiring the petitioning spouse to appear in person. In the latter instance, the petitioning spouse could arrange by mail to have an appearance entered on his or her behalf. For these reasons, thousands of Americans sought Mexican divorces. The question of what extraterritorial effect should be given these divorces frequently came before American courts. Mexican "mail-order divorces"—i.e. those where neither spouse personally appears before the divorce court—have almost invariably been denied legal effect. Divorces granted upon the personal appearance of one or both spouses have also been denied recognition in most states on the ground that neither spouse had a bona fide domicile in Mexico. The New York courts, on the other hand, gave effect to Mexican divorces if one spouse was before the divorce court and the other appeared either personally or by attorney.

ROSENSTIEL V. ROSENSTIEL, WOOD V. WOOD, 209 N.E.2d 709, 712 (N.Y.1965): Both of these cases involved divorces obtained in Chihuahua, Mexico by New Yorkers. In both cases the plaintiff spouse was in Mexico for less than twenty-four hours, during which time he appeared personally before the divorce court. The defendant spouse in both cases entered an appearance by an attorney but did not personally go to Mexico. Held, the divorces should be recognized in New York. "The State or county of true domicile has the closest real public interest in a marriage but, when a New York spouse goes elsewhere to establish a synthetic domicile to meet technical acceptance of a matrimonial suit, our public interest is not affected differently by a formality of one day than by a formality of six weeks. Nevada gets no closer to the real public concern with the marriage than Chihuahua."

In 1971, the Federal Government of Mexico issued a decree stating that an alien may not obtain a divorce in any Mexican state without having been present in Mexico for a period of not less than six months. As a result, "quickie" divorces are no longer obtainable in Mexico. Haiti and the Dominican Republic then entered the field by enacting legislation similar to that of the Mexican states referred to above. A whole new industry sprang up, with tour packages complete with weekend divorces. Guam, a U.S. territory, similarly facilitates quick divorces. Haitian and Dominican Republic divorces have been recognized as freely in New York as had been those of Mexico. Greschler v. Greschler, 414 N.E.2d 694 (N.Y.1980); Becker v. Becker, 541 N.Y.S.2d 699 (N.Y.Sup.Ct.1989), later proceeding at 588 N.Y.S.2d 45 (N.Y.App.Div.1992). Note that in *Kulko*, p. 1001, infra, the parties had obtained a Haitian divorce, although the decision did not turn on this fact. For limitations, see Note 1, infra.

NOTES

1.   In addition to New York, it seems that Connecticut, Indiana, Massachusetts, New Jersey, Tennessee, and the Virgin Islands will either recognize Haitian and Dominican Republic divorces, or estop a party who participated in or earlier invoked the benefits of such a divorce, from attacking its validity. Hay, Borchers, Symeonides, Whytock, Conflict of Laws § 15.20 (6th ed.2018). "Mail order" divorces, or those in which the respondent received no or insufficient notice, will not be recognized. An extreme example is Kushnick v. Kushnick, 763 N.Y.S.2d 889 (N.Y.Sup.Ct.2003): the petitioner in a Mexican divorce had merely filled out an Internet form, never resided in Mexico nor appeared in the proceeding there, and the respondent had not received notice. See also Jimenez v. Jimenez, 2006 WL 2949095 (Conn.Super.Ct.2006) (Dominican Republic divorce; no actual notice and notice by publication insufficient); Juma v. Aomo, 68 A.3d 148 (Conn.App.2013) (Kenyan divorce; insufficient notice).

2.   Suppose that parties previously domiciled in a state that does not recognize *Rosenstiel*-type divorces have obtained such a divorce in a foreign country. They subsequently engage in litigation in New York with both parties participating to determine rights to property there. The New York court recognizes the foreign divorce (i.e., it decides the "preliminary question") before then turning to the property determination. Would a

subsequent collateral attack by one of the parties or by a third party on the foreign-country divorce (e.g., in the state of the parties' original domicile) be successful? Does Sherrer v. Sherrer, p. 948, supra, apply?

Suppose the following variation:

In a foreign country, a New Yorker gets a *Rosenstiel*-type divorce that New York would recognize as valid. He then returns to New York and remarries. Should a second state, to which he subsequently moves, recognize the divorce and the remarriage as valid, even though it would have held invalid a similar divorce obtained by one of its own domiciliaries? See Note, New York Approved Mexican Divorces: Are They Valid in Other States?, 114 U.Pa.L.Rev. 771 (1966), and the discussion supra at p. 915, Note 4, with respect to the Uniform Marriage Evasion Act. What if the New Yorker did not remarry in New York but now seeks to do so in the state to which he has moved? In the European Union, Arts. 21 et seq. of EC Regulation 2201/2003, as well as Arts. 30 et seq. the replacement Regulation (effective August 1, 2022), p. 945, Note 4, supra and p. 1179, infra only mandate recognition of divorces granted by EU Member States. What about an EU Member State court's decision recognizing a divorce obtained outside the EU? For the same problem with respect to other civil judgments, see pp.400 et seq., supra.

3. *Estoppel.* In Caldwell v. Caldwell, 81 N.E.2d 60 (N.Y.1948), a spouse who procured a "mail order" Mexican divorce was held not estopped from attacking it because "there is not even the slightest color of jurisdiction." The rule of *Caldwell* was extended somewhat in Alfaro v. Alfaro, 169 N.Y.S.2d 943 (N.Y.App.Div.1958), aff'd, 165 N.E.2d 880 (N.Y.1960) (mem.): a spouse was permitted collaterally to attack an ex parte Mexican divorce that he had procured, even though the decree recited that he had appeared before the court and testified that he had visited the court and "picked up" the decree. See also Estate of Pringle, 43 V.I. 15 (Terr.Ct.V.I., St. Croix 2000): even though an out-of-state divorce may not be entitled to recognition (in the case at bar, a Dominican Republic divorce), for instance, for reasons of fraud in the procurement or lack of notice to the respondent, the party who procured may nevertheless be barred from taking a distributive share (as the surviving spouse) of the decedent's estate. The court relied in part on *Considine* and the consideration that the party procuring the divorce should not be able to invoke its invalidity for his financial gain. In England, the House of Lords refused to recognize a Belgian annulment of a prostitute's sham marriage, which she sought to avoid in order to claim, as the surviving spouse, the substantial English estate of her employer, whom she had subsequently married in Italy and who died at the wedding reception. Vervaeke v. Smith, [1982] 2 All E.R. 144 (H.L.).

Non-Judicial Divorces

Non-judicial divorces, by unilateral act or by contract of the parties, are possible under Islamic and Jewish religious law, as well as under Chinese, Japanese, and Korean law. According to American Indian tribal custom, a divorce may also be effected by agreement on an Indian reservation. The effect of non-judicial divorces has been a question of considerable difficulty, especially in countries of immigration from Muslim countries (e.g., in England with respect to immigrants from Arab and Asian countries)

The Islamic Talaq. Under Islamic law, a husband of Muslim faith may divorce a wife by issuing the *talaq,* the triple repetition of words of divorce before witnesses. In a number of Islamic countries, some public act—notice, registration, or confirmation of the talaq—is now required. Judaic law permits divorce by delivery to the wife of a bill of divorcement, the *get.* In Aleem v. Aleem, 947 A.2d 489 (Md.2008), the court refused to recognize a Pakistani divorce by *talaq,* which the respondent attempted to interpose to the wife's action in Maryland. The unilateral divorce violated the wife's constitutional rights, the court concluded. A contrary result would have been especially detrimental because a valid *talaq* would have cut off her property rights. Cf. Ashfaq v. Ashfaq, 467 S.W.3d 539 (Tex.App.2015) (recognizing a divorce by *talaq* that the husband obtained by more formal procedures, including notice to the wife, a ninety-day waiting period, and an attempt at reconciliation).

The German Supreme Court had to decide whether a Syrian divorce, obtained by the husband by delivery of a talaq before a Syrian Sharia court, was entitled to recognition in Germany. Both parties were dual citizens of Syria and Germany. The European Union Court of Justice had decided earlier in this case that EU law was not applicable ("Sayouni II," Case C 281-15), [2016] FamRZ 1137 no. 16), thus German law applied (though it incorporates EU law principles—Art. 17 II Introductory Law to the German Civil Code, EGBGB). Under German law, a divorce must have been decreed by a court to be valid. Sec. 1564 Civil Code (BGB). Even if non-judicial divorces might be entitled to recognition under certain circumstances, a divorce by *talaq* would violate German public policy (for the same reason as in the American decision *Aleem,* supra). The Court therefore denied recognition to the Syrian divorce. BGH (*Bundesgerichtshof*), Case XII ZB 158/18, Decision of Aug. 26, 2020.

The Jewish Get. In both the United States and in England, religious divorces will be recognized if they were obtained by foreign domiciliaries abroad and are valid where obtained. In contrast, a valid domestic divorce requires compliance with domestic law. Section 253 of N.Y. Dom.Rel. (Consol.1994) now requires the plaintiff in a divorce action to file, prior to final judgment, a verified statement that he or she has taken all steps to remove all barriers to the defendant's remarriage. "Barriers" includes "religious constraints." The purpose of the provision is to require compliance with religious requirements (for instance, the delivery of a *get*) when a *foreign* country (e.g., Israel) would not recognize a New York civil divorce, standing alone, and therefore would not permit remarriage. In the United States, courts differ on whether to assist in obtaining a *get.* See Kaplinsky v. Kaplinsky, 603 N.Y.S.2d 574 (N.Y.App.Div.1993) (affirming contempt sanction against husband for failure to cooperate in obtaining a *get* pursuant to a stipulation of the parties that was incorporated in the divorce judgment). See also infra, Note 3. Non-compliance with a judicial order to obtain a Jewish *get* in compliance with a stipulation to that effect may result in an order holding the husband in contempt, and imprisoning him until he has purged himself of the contempt by compliance, payment of a fine, payment of the wife's attorneys' fees, or upon other condition imposed by the court. Schwartz v. Schwartz, 913 N.Y.S.2d 313 (N.Y.App.Div.2010). *But* see A.W. v. I.N., 117 N.Y.S.3d 527, 530 (N.Y.Sup.Ct.2020): in the absence of a stipulation to comply with religious requirements (as in *Kaplinsky,* supra), it would be a violation of the First Amendment "to order the Wife to participate in a religious ritual" to receive a *get* from her husband. Another complicating factor may be the Jewish religious body's (Beth Din's) reluctance to supervise the delivery of a *get* because not done voluntarily, but under compulsion. Id. at 1008. See also p. 935, supra, Note 2.

Native American Marriages. Similar to the Beth Din, the Navajo nation will not recognize a divorce unless a certificate of divorce has been issued by the Courts of the Navajo Nation. United States v. Jarvison, 409 F.3d 1221, 1230 (10th Cir.2005) (citing Navajo Code, tit. 9, § 407 (1993)). See also Senator v. U.S., 2010 WL 723792 (E.D.Wash.2010).

NOTES

1. See Comment, United States Recognition of Foreign, Nonjudicial Divorces, 53 Minn.L.Rev. 612 (1969). In England, the matter is now largely regulated by the Family Law Act of 1986, which replaced the Recognition of Divorces and Legal Separations Act of 1971. It has been held that a *get* may constitute a "proceeding" within the meaning of § 46(1) of the Act and that the resulting divorce is entitled to recognition in England. However, the "proceeding" must be a single act, effected outside of Britain. Hence, a *get* written in England and delivered to the wife at a rabbinical court in Israel might serve to divorce the parties under Jewish law, but such a divorce would not be entitled to recognition under the Act in England. Berkovits v. Grinberg, [1995] Fam. 142, [1995] 2 All E.R. 681, [1995] 2 W.L.R. 553 (Fam.Div.). For a decision involving a *talaq,* see Z. v. Z., [1992] F.L.R. 291 (Australia). For comprehensive review of English law, see Stone, The Recognition in England of Talaq Divorces, 14 Anglo-American L.Rev. 363 (1985). See also Pilkington, Transnational Divorces Under the Family Law Act 1986, 37 Int'l & Comp.L.Q. 131 (1988); Reed, Transnational Non-Judicial Divorces: A Comparative Analysis of Recognition Under English and U.S. Jurisprudence, 18 Loy.L.A.Int'l & Comp.L.J. 311 (1996); Hay, Borchers, Symeonides. Whytock, Conflict of Laws §§ 15.24–15.25 (6th ed.2018); Dicey, Morris & Collins, Conflict of Laws 994–1057 (15th ed.2012) & 262–71 (15th ed. Supp. 4th 2017). For a comparison of Belgian and U.S. recognition law, see Katayoun Alidadi, The Western Judicial Answer to Islamic *Talaq*: Peeking Through the Gate of Conflict of Laws, 5 UCLA J. Islamic & Near.E.L. 1 (2005–2006). For France, see Moatly v. Zagha, [1982] Revue critique de droit int. privé 298 (Ct.App., Aix-en-Provence); for Germany BGH

(Supreme Court), supra. For Austria, with respect to the *talaq*, see Verschraegen, Internationales Privatrecht no. 144 (2012).

2. In India, a wife received a *talaq* by e-mail from her Pakistani husband and subsequently remarried. Would her divorce and remarriage be recognized in the United States? Revisit the hypotheticals in Note 2 on p., 968, supra. In a number of countries, including India (by Supreme Court decision in 2019), triple talaq is now banned. It is still practiced in other countries, such as Syria (see text supra).

3. In Shapiro v. Shapiro, 442 N.Y.S.2d 928 (N.Y.Sup.Ct.1981), the New York court enforced an order of the Rabbinical Court of Israel by entering its own order that the husband perform the ritual acts of the *get* to enable the wife to remarry. In Avitzur v. Avitzur, 446 N.E.2d 136 (N.Y.1983), cert. denied, 464 U.S. 817 (1983), the court ordered specific performance of a marriage contract requiring submission of marital disputes to a Jewish tribunal (Beth Din). See also Golding v. Golding, 581 N.Y.S.2d 4 (N.Y.App.1992) (separation agreement not enforced because wife signed under duress when husband threatened to withhold the *get*); Tal v. Tal, 601 N.Y.S.2d 530 (N.Y.Sup.Ct.1993) (Israeli rabbinical court divorce not recognized for lack of personal jurisdiction; prior New York rabbinical court divorce not given weight because non-judicial). The change in New York's Domestic Relations Law now also covers cases in which there is no prior decree of another court or tribunal or any marriage contract. For an overview and comment, see Broyde, The 1992 New York Jewish Divorce Law, 29–4 Tradition: A Journal of Jewish Thought 3 (1997); Broyde, Marriage, Divorce and the Abandoned Wife in Jewish Law at 35 (2001). See also Berger and Lipstadt, Women in Judaism from the Perspective of Human Rights, in: Witte and Van der Vyver (eds.), Religious Human Rights in Global Perspective 295, 304 et seq. (1995); Einhorn, Jewish Divorce in the International Arena-Liber Amicorum Kurt Siehr 135 (2000); Ann Laquer Estin, Embracing Tradition: Pluralism in American Family Law, 63 Md.L.Rev. 540, 578 et seq. (2004).

4. With respect to divorce in accordance with Indian tribal customs, see Marris v. Sockey, 170 F.2d 599 (10th Cir.1948); United States v. Jarvison, 409 F.3d 1221 (10th Cir.2005). See also Begay v. Miller, 222 P.2d 624 (Ariz.1950); A. Sedillo Lopez, Evolving Indigenous Law: Navajo Marriage-Cultural Traditions and Modern Challenges, 17 Ariz.J.Int'l & Comp.L. 283, 295 n.76 (2000), with references to tribal court decisions.

SECTION 3. ANNULMENT*

Whealton v. Whealton
Supreme Court of California, 1967.
67 Cal.2d 656, 63 Cal.Rptr. 291, 432 P.2d 979.

■ TRAYNOR, CHIEF JUSTICE. Defendant appeals from a default judgment annulling her marriage to plaintiff on the ground of fraud.

---

* See Restatement, Second, Conflict of Laws §§ 76, 286.

Plaintiff, a petty officer on active duty with the United States Navy, married defendant at Bel Air, Maryland, on June 15, 1964. Thereafter his military duties took him from place to place on the east coast until he was assigned to the U.S.S. *Reposte* at the San Francisco Naval Shipyard. He arrived in California on July 14, 1965. Plaintiff and defendant lived together for only six or seven weeks on the east coast.

On September 3, 1965, plaintiff filed this action for annulment of the marriage. Summons was issued and an order for publication of summons was filed on the same day. Publication of the summons was accomplished as prescribed by law. Defendant received a copy of the summons by mail at her home in Maryland on September 7, 1965. . . . On October 11, 1965, the court entered her default, heard testimony in support of the complaint, and entered a judgment annulling the marriage. On October 19, 1965, defendant made a motion to set aside the default and the judgment by default and to permit the filing of an answer and a cross-complaint. The motion was denied on November 9, 1965.

[The Court first found that the judgment was void because it had been prematurely entered.]

Even if the default judgment were not premature, it would have to be reversed, for neither the pleadings nor the evidence establish that either party was a domiciliary of California. The court therefore lacked jurisdiction to award an ex parte annulment. . . .

Ex parte divorces are a striking exception to the rule that a court must have personal jurisdiction over a party before it may adjudicate his substantial rights. . . . The legal fiction that explains the exception by regarding the marital status as a res present at the permanent home of either of the spouses provides doctrinal consistency with other rules governing jurisdiction over things, but the appellation "in rem" is unnecessary to support the conclusion that jurisdiction is properly assumed. (Williams v. State of North Carolina (1945) 325 U.S. 226.) *Williams* does hold, however, that due process requires something more than mere presence of a party within a jurisdiction before that party can invoke the legal process of the forum to force an absent spouse to defend her marital status in an inconvenient forum and to subvert the policies of other interested jurisdictions in preserving marriages. When the forum state is also the domicile of one of the parties, however, its interest and that of its domiciliary justify subordinating the conflicting interests of the absent spouse and of any other interested jurisdiction.

Jurisdiction to grant annulments has followed an analogous, but somewhat divergent course. An annulment differs conceptually from a divorce in that a divorce terminates a legal status, whereas an annulment establishes that a marital status never existed. The absence of a valid marriage precluded reliance on the divorce cases in formulating a theory of ex parte jurisdiction in annulment, for no res or status could be found within the state. . . . The courts, however, did not let jurisdictional concepts of in personam and in rem dictate results in annulment actions. They recognized a state's interest in providing a forum for some annulment actions even though the court lacked personal jurisdiction over one of the parties. . . . The crucial question, then, is whether there are sufficient factors to justify the court's exercising ex parte annulment jurisdiction. . . .

. . . The primary issue under the facts of this case is whether due process concepts of fairness to defendant permit plaintiff to choose a forum inconvenient to her absent personal jurisdiction over her. . . . We find no factor here that would justify an exception to the general rule requiring personal jurisdiction and thereby shift the burden of inconvenience to defendant. The marriage ceremony took place elsewhere, defendant lives elsewhere, the matrimonial domicile was elsewhere, and witnesses are likely to be located elsewhere. Although domicile of a plaintiff here would afford jurisdiction to award an ex parte annulment, plaintiff in this case did not plead or prove that he was a domiciliary of California when the default judgment was entered. The court was therefore without jurisdiction to enter the default judgment. . . .

[After the original judgment, the defendant appeared in the action.] Since both parties are [now] properly before the court, we confront the questions whether we may treat the action as a transitory cause . . . and whether the interest of another state compels us to refuse to hear this cause. . . .

However valid the rationale for the domicile prerequisite may be in divorce actions, it does not apply to annulment actions. In divorce actions, the applicable substantive law changes as parties change their domicile, but in annulment actions courts uniformly apply the law of the state in which the marriage was contracted. . . . We conclude, therefore, that the interests of the state of celebration of the marriage or the state of domicile of either party do not preclude a court that has personal jurisdiction over both parties from entertaining an annulment action.

It does not follow that because a court may exercise that jurisdiction it must do so in all cases. In the present case plaintiff was under a special disability in terms of access to any forum other than California. Moreover, defendant was not caught inadvertently within California, and personal jurisdiction was not exercised on a territorial power theory but was obtained over defendant through her consent. Hence, we assume that no undue burdens are placed on her by the trial of the action in California. In other annulment actions where personal jurisdiction is the sole jurisdictional basis, however, the doctrine of *forum non conveniens* might well be invoked by one of the parties, or asserted by the court, to cause a discretionary dismissal when fairness and the interests of judicial administration so demand. . . .

The judgment is reversed.

Wilkins v. Zelichowski

Supreme Court of New Jersey, 1958.
26 N.J. 370, 140 A.2d 65.

[The case appears p. 912, supra.]

NOTE

There is uncertainty about the bases of judicial jurisdiction for annulment. It is usually held that, at the least, a court has jurisdiction to decree an annulment if it could render a divorce. Under this view, personal jurisdiction over the defendant spouse is not necessary, but suit must ordinarily be brought in the domicile of the plaintiff spouse. A few courts, on the other hand, believe that personal jurisdiction over the defendant spouse is essential. See, e.g., Owen v. Owen, 257 P.2d 581 (Colo.1953). Rarely, however, has this latter view been carried to the extreme of holding that an annulment action can be brought in any state where personal jurisdiction over both spouses can be obtained. A number of cases hold that the state where the marriage was celebrated has jurisdiction to annul it if both spouses are before the court. See, e.g., Feigenbaum v. Feigenbaum, 194 S.W.2d 1012 (Ark.1946); Sawyer v. Slack, 146 S.E. 864 (N.C.1929).

According to § 76 of the Restatement, Second, a state has jurisdiction to annul a marriage (a) if it would have jurisdiction to dissolve the marriage by divorce, or (b) if the respondent spouse is subject to the judicial jurisdiction of the state, and either the marriage was contracted there or the validity of the marriage is determined under its law. See, e.g., Vanvelzor v. Vanvelzor, 219 P.3d 184, 191 n.24 (Alaska 2009).

SECTION 4. JUDICIAL SEPARATION

RESTATEMENT, SECOND, CONFLICT OF LAWS

§ 75. Judicial Separation.

(1) A state has power to exercise judicial jurisdiction to grant a judicial separation under the circumstances which would give the state jurisdiction to dissolve the marriage by divorce.

(2) A state has power to exercise judicial jurisdiction to grant a judicial separation when both spouses are personally subject to the jurisdiction of the state.

Comment on Subsection (1):

b. ... A state which lacks personal jurisdiction over the respondent spouse, but which nevertheless would have judicial jurisdiction to grant a divorce, either because it is the state of domicil of the plaintiff spouse or because it has some other appropriate relationship to the plaintiff spouse ... may exercise judicial jurisdiction to grant a judicial separation. As between States of the United States, such a decree is entitled to full faith and credit.... Under these circumstances, however, the state lacks judicial jurisdiction to affect the respondent spouse's economic rights and duties . . . except to the extent that it has jurisdiction over the respondent's property . . .

SECTION 5. LEGITIMATION

RESTATEMENT, SECOND, CONFLICT OF LAWS

Topic 2. Legitimacy

§ 287. Law Governing Legitimacy

(2) The child will usually be held legitimate if this would be his status under the local law of the state where either (a) the parent was domiciled when the child's status of legitimacy is claimed to have been created or (b) the child was domiciled when the parent acknowledged the child as his own.

§ 288. Incidents of Legitimacy Created by Foreign Law

A state usually gives the same incidents to a status of legitimacy created by a foreign law under the principles stated in § 287 that it gives to the status when created by its own local law.

NOTE

At common law, illegitimate children inherited from no one; by statute, however, most states granted inheritance rights to such a child with respect to the mother. In Trimble v. Gordon, 430 U.S. 762 (1977), the Supreme Court struck down such a restriction. Equal Protection requires that illegitimate children may also inherit from their father by intestate succession. However, state law may require that the decedent's paternity have been judicially determined during his lifetime. Lalli v. Lalli, 439 U.S. 259 (1978). State statutes and decisions differ widely on how paternity is to be established. The Uniform Parentage Act (1979), revised several times, most recently in 2017 and 2019, provides several means. The 2017 version had been adopted by only four states as of 2021; it had been introduced in one other. The Uniform Probate Code, in force in its entirety in only a minority of states (19 as of 2021), provides that if a state has not adopted the Uniform Parentage Act, a person is a "child" for purposes of interstate succession if paternity was adjudicated before the decedent's death "or is established thereafter by clear and convincing proof. . . ." The 2017 amendments to the Uniform Parentage Act brought about amendments to the intestacy and class gift provisions of the Uniform Probate Code in 2019. See also Seaton v. Seaton, 133 Cal.Rptr.3d 50, 57 (Cal.App.2011), p. 916, Note 7, supra, and Morales v. City of Delano, 2012 WL 1669398, at *6 (E.D.Cal.2012): children born of a bigamous marriage are considered legitimate, even though the marriage is considered void from the beginning as between the parties to it.

If paternity must be established by adjudication, the Supreme Court has held, in the context of support claims, that equal protection requires that the claimant be given an adequate opportunity to do so. In Clark v. Jeter, 486 U.S. 456 (1988), the Court invalidated a six-year statute of limitations as too short. The 1984 federal child support amendments require states wishing to qualify under the federal program to enact 18-year statutes of limitations. 42 U.S.C.A. § 666(a)(5)(ii).

See generally Hay, Borchers, Symeonides, Whytock, Conflict of Law §§ 16.1–16.3 (6th ed.2018).

SECTION 6. ADOPTION*

INTRODUCTORY NOTE

Adoption was unknown to the common law and is purely a creature of statute. In the sense here used, it is the process whereby the adoptive parent is substituted for the natural parents, and whereby in many states the child's legal relationship with the latter is severed entirely. Some statutes, however, employ the term in a sense closely akin to legitimation, such as when provision is made for the so-called adoption by a natural parent of his illegitimate child. On rare occasions, adoption is used in a restricted sense to describe a process whereby the child becomes no more than an heir presumptive of the adopter, and his relations with his natural parents remain undisturbed. Adoption, as here defined, exists by virtue of statutory enactment in the great majority of States in this country.

Unlike legitimation, adoption is usually effected by court proceedings. The two main conflicts problems in the field are the judicial jurisdiction of a state to grant an adoption and the effect which will be accorded an adoption in another state. The statutes differ rather widely in their details, particularly as to the circumstances under which a court can decree an adoption and with respect to the rights of inheritance of the adopted child. There is agreement in common law countries that in determining whether to grant the adoption, the forum will apply the local provisions of its own law and not those of some other state. See, e.g., In re Adoption of M.L.L., 810 N.E.2d 1088 (Ind.App.2004); Stubbs v. Weathersby, 869 P.2d 893 (Or.App.1994).

There is some uncertainty as to what jurisdictional bases must exist to enable a state to grant an adoption through its courts. It is believed that such jurisdiction exists in a state (a) which is the domicile of either the child or the adoptive parent and (b) which has personal jurisdiction over the adoptive parent and over either the adopted child or the person having legal custody of the child. Two principal questions are involved in an adoption proceeding: first, whether the child's situation is such that adoption is in the best interests of the child and, if so, whether the would-be adopter is a desirable person from the child's point of view. Courts sitting in either the domicile of the child or in that of the adoptive parent will normally be equally well-situated to determine such issues. And the interests of the two states in the matter are of approximately equal weight.

An adoption, decreed in a state with judicial jurisdiction, will usually be given the same legal incidents in another state as the latter gives to a decree of adoption by its own courts.

---

* See Restatement, Second, Conflict of Laws §§ 78, 289–90.

Incidents arising from an adoption include such matters as the right of the adoptive parent to the custody and control of the child and the right of either the child or the adoptive parent to share in the other's estate and to recover damages for the other's wrongful death. To date, the bulk of the cases involving the effect of a foreign adoption have concerned the inheritance rights of the adopted child. According to most of the decisions, such rights are determined by the law governing succession; that is to say by the law of the situs in the case of immovables and by the law of the decedent's last domicile in the case of movables. So, if the question concerns the right of a child adopted in state X to inherit the movables of an adoptive or of a natural parent or some other relative who died domiciled in state Y, the case will be decided by Y law rather than by that of X. See, e.g., Pazzi v. Taylor, 342 N.W.2d 481 (Iowa 1984); In re Underhill, 450 So.2d 786 (Miss.1984); Warren v. Foster, 262 So.3d 1111 (Miss.2019). See also Tate v. Whitehead, 2010 WL 11613989, at *3 n.3 (S.D. Iowa 2010).

NOTES

1.   In Anglo-American countries, the forum will look to its own law in determining whether to grant an adoption. 1 Rabel, Conflict of Laws 681 (2d ed.1958). The courts of civil law countries, on the other hand, apply what they deem to be the proper law (frequently the state of the adoptive parent's domicile or nationality) to govern the case. Hay, Borchers, Symeonides, Whytock, Conflict of Laws §§ 16.4–.5 (6th ed.2018). An adoption decree entered by a court with competent jurisdiction will ordinarily be recognized everywhere. See, e.g., Bonwich v. Bonwich, 699 P.2d 760 (Utah 1985), cert. denied, 474 U.S. 848 (1985). See also In re Adoption of Baby E.Z., 266 P.3d 702 (Utah 2011) (federal Parental Kidnapping Prevention Act applies to custody proceedings and biological father waived right to refuse to consent to adoption by failing to raise it); In Adoption of B.B., 417 P.3d 1 (Utah 2017) (Native American birth father was parent under Indian Child Welfare Act and entitled to intervene in an adoption proceeding to which the mother had consented).

The Hague Convention on Protection of Children and Co-operation in Respect of Intercountry Adoption (the Hague Adoption Convention) sets minimum standards for the intercountry adoption of children. As of 2020, 101 states had ratified this Convention, including the United States. The U.S. ratification states that Arts. 1 through 39 are not self-executing. For the text of the convention and an introductory note by Pfund, see 32 Int'l Legal Materials 1134 (1993). For comment, see McKinney, International Adoption and The Hague Convention: Does Implementation of the Convention Protect the Best Interests of Children?, 6 Whittier J.Child & Fam.Adv. 361 (2007); Wardle, The Hague Convention on Intercountry Adoption and American Implementing Law: Implications for International Adoptions by Gay and Lesbian Couples or Partners, 18 Ind.Int'l & Comp.L.Rev. 113 (2008); Milbrandt, Adopting the Stateless, 39 Brook.J.Int'l L. 695 (2014); Mabry-King, Outgoing Adoptions: What Should Happen When Things Go Wrong?, 44 Cap.U.L.Rev. 1 (2016).

In early 2010, controversy arose when a Tennessee woman sent the young Russian boy she had recently adopted back to Russia—unaccompanied. The Russian foreign ministry subsequently renewed demands for a bilateral adoption treaty between the U.S. and Russia and indicated that U.S. adoptions might be suspended if a treaty were not concluded. The U.S. had previously urged Russia to ratify the Hague Convention, which it had not done. Russia, however, sought protections not provided by the Hague Convention, such as legal guarantees regarding the specific screening process for potential adoptive parents, guarantees that Russian children sent to the U.S. will maintain their Russian cultural awareness (including their Russian language if they were old enough to speak it), and the ability to prosecute individuals who harm children adopted from Russia. After additional problems had arisen, Russia adopted a law in 2012 prohibiting all adoptions of Russian children by Americans. DeBose & DeAngelo, *The New Cold War: Russia's Ban on Adoptions by U.S. Citizens*, 28 J.Am.Acad.Matrim.Law. 51 (2015).

2.   In Armstrong v. Manzo, 380 U.S. 545 (1965), no notice of the Texas adoption proceedings was given to the natural father, although those seeking the adoption (the mother and her new husband) "well knew his precise whereabouts in . . . Texas." It was held that, as a result of this failure to give notice, the adoption decree was constitutionally invalid. In Quilloin v. Walcott, 434 U.S. 246 (1978), and Lehr v. Robertson, 463 U.S. 248 (1983), the Supreme Court held that an unwed father who had not lived in a home situation with the child nor legitimated his child was not allowed to object to the child's adoption by the man whom the mother subsequently married. By statute, Oklahoma now requires notice of adoption proceedings to the unwed father. Okla.St.Ann. tit.10, § 7505–4.1C. See also *Adoption of Baby E.Z.*, Note 1, supra.

3.   May same-sex couples adopt a child and, if so, will the adoption be recognized elsewhere? In V.L. v. E.L., 136 S.Ct. 1017 (2016), the Court reversed an Alabama order that failed to recognize a Georgia decree by which a same-sex spouse had adopted her estranged spouse's biological children. Citing Fauntleroy v. Lum, p. 386, supra the Court held that the Alabama Supreme Court had impermissibly construed Georgia law as pertaining to jurisdiction instead of the merits of the case, and thereby violated the federal Full Faith and Credit mandate. See also In re Jacob, 660 N.E.2d 397 (N.Y.1995) (held, unmarried partners have standing to become adoptive parents without terminating the biological mother's parental rights). Florida was the only state that denied adoption by gay and lesbian couples. Its denial of adoption by a "homosexual" person was upheld against federal constitutional challenge in Lofton v. Sec'y of Dep't of Children and Family Servs., 358 F.3d 804 (11th Cir.2004), cert. denied, 543 U.S. 1081 (2005), but held to be unconstitutional under the Florida Constitution: In re Adoption of Doe, 2008 WL 5070056 (Fl.Cir.Ct.2008). When Virginia children were adopted in another state, the same-sex adoptive parents sought to compel, by mandamus, the issuance of a new birth certificate listing the names of both adoptive parents. In holding that such certificates must be issued, the Virginia Supreme Court explained that the relevant statute refers to

"adoptive parents" and "intended parents," not to mother and father. The case before the court "[was] not about homosexual marriage, nor ... about same-sex relationships, nor adoption policy in Virginia." It was about the issuance of birth certificates only. Davenport v. Little-Bowser, 611 S.E.2d 366, 369 (Va.2005). See also Newman, Same-Sex Parenting Among a Patchwork of Laws: An Analysis of New York Same-Sex Parents' Options for Gaining Legal Parental Status, 2016 Cardozo L.Rev. de novo 77 (2016).

The United States has become a party to the Hague Convention on Intercountry Adoptions. See p. 977, supra. For analysis in the present context, see Lynn D. Wardle, The Hague Convention on Intercountry Adoption and American Implementing Law: Implications for International Adoptions by Gay and Lesbian Couples or Partners, 18 Ind.Int'l & Comp.L.Rev. 113 (2008).

SECTION 7. CUSTODY OF CHILDREN

May v. Anderson

Supreme Court of the United States, 1953.
345 U.S. 528, 73 S.Ct. 840, 97 L.Ed. 1221.

■ JUSTICE BURTON delivered the opinion of the Court.

The parties were married in Wisconsin and, until 1947, both were domiciled there. After marital troubles developed, they agreed in December, 1946, that appellant should take their children to Lisbon, Columbiana County, Ohio, and there think over her future course. By New Year's Day, she had decided not to return to Wisconsin and by telephone, she informed her husband of that decision.

Within a few days he filed suit in Wisconsin, seeking both an absolute divorce and custody of the children. The only service of process upon appellant consisted of the delivery to her personally, in Ohio, of a copy of the Wisconsin summons and petition. . . . Appellant entered no appearance and took no part in this Wisconsin proceeding which produced not only a decree divorcing the parties from the bonds of matrimony but a decree purporting to award the custody of the children to their father, subject to a right of their mother to visit them at reasonable times. Appellant contests only the validity of the decree as to custody. . . .

Armed with a copy of the decree and accompanied by a local police officer, appellee, in Lisbon, Ohio, demanded and obtained the children from their mother. The record does not disclose what took place between 1947 and 1951, except that the children remained with their father in Wisconsin until July 1, 1951. He then brought them back to Lisbon and permitted them to visit their mother. This time, when he demanded their return, she refused to surrender them.

Relying upon the Wisconsin decree, he promptly filed in the Probate Court of Columbiana County, Ohio, the petition for a writ of habeas corpus now before us. Under Ohio procedure that writ tests only the immediate right to possession of the children. It does not open the door for the modification of any prior award of custody on a showing of changed circumstances. Nor is it available as a procedure for settling the future custody of children in the first instance.

Separated as our issue is from that of the future interests of the children, we have before us the elemental question whether a court of a state, where a mother is neither domiciled, resident nor present, may cut off her immediate right to the care, custody, management and companionship of her minor children without having jurisdiction over her *in personam*. Rights far more precious to appellant than property rights will be cut off if she is to be bound by the Wisconsin award of custody. . . .

In Estin v. Estin, [p. 959, supra,] . . . this Court upheld the validity of a Nevada divorce obtained *ex parte* by a husband, resident in Nevada, insofar as it dissolved the bonds of matrimony. At the same time, we held Nevada powerless to cut off, in that proceeding, a spouse's right to financial support under the prior decree of another state. In the instant case, we recognize that a mother's right to custody of her children is a personal right entitled to at least as much protection as her right to alimony.

In the instant case, the Ohio courts gave weight to appellee's contention that the Wisconsin award of custody binds appellant because, at the time it was issued, her children had a technical domicile in Wisconsin, although they were neither resident nor present there. We find it unnecessary to determine the children's legal domicile because, even if it be with their father, that does not give Wisconsin, certainly as against Ohio, the personal jurisdiction that it must have in order to deprive their mother of her personal right to their immediate possession. . . .

Reversed and remanded.

■ JUSTICE CLARK, not having heard oral argument, took no part in the consideration or decision of this case.

■ JUSTICE FRANKFURTER, concurring.

The views expressed by my brother Jackson make it important that I state, in joining the Court's opinion, what I understand the Court to be deciding and what it is not deciding in this case.

What is decided—the only thing the Court decides—is that the Full Faith and Credit Clause does not require Ohio, in disposing of the custody of children in Ohio, to accept, in the circumstances before us, the disposition made by Wisconsin. The Ohio Supreme Court felt itself so bound. This Court does not decide that Ohio would be precluded from recognizing, as a matter of local law, the disposition made by the Wisconsin court. For Ohio to give respect to the Wisconsin decree would not offend the Due Process Clause. Ohio is no more precluded from doing so than a court of Ontario or Manitoba would be, were the mother to bring the children into one of these provinces.

Property, personal claims, and even the marriage status ... generally give rise to interests different from those relevant to the discharge of a State's continuing responsibility to children within her borders. Children have a very special place in life which law should reflect. Legal theories and their phrasing in other cases readily lead to fallacious reasoning if uncritically transferred to determination of a State's duty towards children. . . . But the child's welfare in a custody case has such a claim upon the State that its responsibility is obviously not to be foreclosed by a prior adjudication reflecting another State's discharge of its responsibility at another time. Reliance on opinions regarding out-of-State adjudications of property rights, personal claims or the marital status is bound to confuse analysis when a claim to the custody of children before the courts of one State is based on an award previously made by another State. Whatever light may be had from such opinions, they cannot give conclusive answers.

■ JUSTICE JACKSON, whom JUSTICE REED joins, dissenting.

The Court apparently is holding that the Federal Constitution prohibits Ohio from recognizing the validity of this Wisconsin divorce decree insofar as it settles custody of the couple's children. In the light of settled and unchallenged precedents of this Court, such a decision can only rest upon the proposition that Wisconsin's courts had no jurisdiction to make such a decree binding upon appellant. . . .

The Ohio courts reasoned that although personal jurisdiction over the wife was lacking, domicile of the children in Wisconsin was a sufficient jurisdictional basis to enable Wisconsin to bind all parties interested in their custody. This determination that the children were domiciled in Wisconsin has not been contested either at our bar or below. Therefore, under our precedents, it is conclusive. . . .

The Court's decision holds that the state in which a child and one parent are domiciled and which is primarily concerned about his welfare cannot constitutionally adjudicate controversies as to his guardianship. The state's power here is defeated by the absence of the other parent for a period of two months. The convenience of a leave-taking parent is placed above the welfare of the child, but neither party is greatly aided in obtaining a decision. The Wisconsin courts cannot bind the mother, and the Ohio courts cannot bind the father. A state of the law such as this, where possession apparently is not merely nine points of the law but all of them and self-help the ultimate authority, has little to commend it in legal logic or as a principle of order in a federal system. . . .

The difference between a proceeding involving the status, custody and support of children and one involving adjudication of property rights is too apparent to require elaboration. In the former, courts are no longer concerned primarily with the proprietary claims of the contestants for the *"res"* before the court, but with the welfare of the *"res"* itself. Custody is viewed not with the idea of adjudicating rights *in* the children, as if they were chattels, but rather with the idea of making the best disposition possible for the welfare of the children. To speak of a court's "cutting off" a mother's right to custody of her children, as if it raised problems similar to those involved in "cutting off" her rights in a plot of ground, is to obliterate these obvious distinctions. Personal jurisdiction of all parties to be affected by a proceeding is highly desirable, to make certain that they have had valid notice and opportunity to be heard. But the assumption that it overrides all other considerations and in its absence a state is constitutionally impotent to resolve questions of custody flies in the face of our own cases. . . .

I fear this decision will author new confusions. The interpretative concurrence, if it be a true interpretation, seems to reduce the law of custody to a rule of seize-and-run. I would affirm the decision of the Ohio courts that they should respect the judgment of the Wisconsin court, until it or some other court with equal or better claims to jurisdiction shall modify it.

[A dissenting opinion by JUSTICE MINTON is omitted.]

NOTES

1.   Is Justice Burton's notion that personal jurisdiction over the defendant parent is essential to the rendition of a valid custody decree out of line with the realities of the situation? How, under these circumstances, could a custody issue be resolved in a situation where each parent is domiciled in a different state and neither proves willing to appear in the courts of the other's domicile? Does the reference in *Shaffer* to the special case of jurisdiction in "status" matters on p. 176, n.30, supra permit the inference that custody may be awarded in an ex parte proceeding? The general consensus has rejected Justice Burton's position in favor of Justice Frankfurter's. Weintraub, Affecting the Parent-Child Relationship Without Jurisdiction Over Both Parents, 36 Sw.L.J. 1167 (1983).

Personal jurisdiction over the defendant parent, although not essential to the rendition of a valid custody decree, is essential for the rendition against the parent of a valid judgment for support. Kumar v. Santa Clara Cnty. Superior Court, 177 Cal.Rptr. 763 (Cal.App.1981), vacated, 186 Cal.Rptr. 772 (Cal.App.1982); In re Marriage of Hudson, 434 N.E.2d 107 (Ind.App.1982). Is this sensible? See also Kulko v. California Superior Court, 436 U.S. 84 (1978), p. 1001, infra.

A number of courts have expressly held that "the status exception" applies in child custody jurisdiction and that personal jurisdiction over an absent parent is not required: In re JJC, 2001 WL 256161 (Tenn.App. Mar. 15, 2001); State ex rel. W.A., 63 P.3d 607 (Utah 2002); In re R.W., 39 A.3d 682 (Vt.2011)(jurisdiction is based on the uniform act, see following case); Matter of F.S.T.Y., 843 S.E.2d 160, 165, 166–67 (N.C. 2020). The "status exception" comes from footnote 30 in the United States Supreme Court's decision in Shaffer v. Heitner, p. 173.

2. In New York ex rel. Halvey v. Halvey, 330 U.S. 610 (1947), the Supreme Court held that under full faith and credit, a custody decree is as subject to modification in F-2 as it is in F-1. Almost invariably, custody decrees are subject to modification in the state of their rendition on a showing of changed circumstances. Since these can usually be found, the net effect of the Halvey decision was to attenuate markedly the role of full faith and credit in the custody area. This had the disadvantage of making it possible for a parent who was displeased with a custody decision of one state to seek a fresh determination in another state. Moreover, to give the courts of that other state jurisdiction, one parent might in effect kidnap the child and take it there. The other parent might then retaliate in kind, and the custody battle might go on and on unless and until the courts of one state choose, of their own volition, to respect the other state's decree. The child would, of course, be the principal victim in the tug-of-war.

Today, the situation has drastically changed. Questions involving the recognition, enforcement, and modification of sister state and foreign country decrees are now regulated in large part by statute. As of 2020, every state except Massachusetts has adopted the Uniform Child Custody Jurisdiction and Enforcement Act (UCCJEA), replacing the earlier Uniform Child Custody Jurisdiction Act (UCCJA). See, e.g., Gjertsen v. Haar, 347 P.3d 1117, 1124 (Wyo.2015). The federal Parental Kidnapping Prevention Act of 1980 (28 U.S.C.A. § 1738A) entitles some custody decrees to full faith and credit. The interplay of uniform state legislation and § 1738A is illustrated by the next case (on the basis of the old UCCJA).

Section 201 of the UCCJEA gives the child's home state jurisdiction for an initial custody determination, as well as continuing jurisdiction (until there is a new "home state") and, unlike § 3 of the former Act, permits jurisdiction in other states only if no state qualifies for home-state jurisdiction or if the home state has declined to exercise jurisdiction. The new priority given to the home state mirrors the Parental Kidnapping Prevention Act. The case that follows arose under the UCCJA. It remains instructive as an illustration of the interpretative problems with the UCCJA. It is equally instructive to inquire how the case would/should be decided under the UCCJEA.

3. In Debra H. v. Janice R., 930 N.E.2d 184 (N.Y.2010), cert. denied, 562 U.S. 1136 (2011), the former same-sex partner of a Vermont civil union sought visitation rights from the biological mother of a child born after the civil union had been contracted. At that time, a non-biological parent who had not adopted the partner's child lacked standing to seek visitation rights under New York's Domestic Relations Law. However, the Court of Appeals concluded that comity required recognition of the former civil union of the parties, and that Vermont law, which recognizes parentage created by civil union, applied: petitioner thus could seek custody rights. Six years later, (perhaps in the shadow of *Obergefell*), New York's highest court promulgated a more permissive interpretation of the same Domestic Relations Law that was at issue in Debra H. v. Janice R.: if the petitioner can prove by clear and convincing evidence that he or she entered into a pre-conception agreement with the biological parent to conceive and raise a child as co-parents, then such a person "who is not a biological or adoptive parent may obtain standing to petition for custody or visitation" under New York Domestic Relations Law. Brooke S.B. v. Elizabeth A.C.C., 61 N.E.3d 488 (N.Y.2016). See also Tomeka N.H. v. Jesus R., 122 N.Y.S.3d 461 (N.Y.App.Div.2020) (biological mother's same-sex ex partner, who had helped raise the child for a period after birth, lacked standing in action against both biological parents for a "tri-custodial" arrangement, the N.Y. statute referred to "either parent," thus meaning no more than two persons).

Quenzer v. Quenzer

Supreme Court of Wyoming, 1982.
653 P.2d 295, cert. denied, 460 U.S. 1041 (1983).

■ THOMAS, JUSTICE.

The task confronting our court in this case is that of reconciling, in the context of the power to enter a judgment modifying a child-custody decree, the laws of the State of Texas, the State of Wyoming, and the United States of America. . . .

The appellant, Fred August Quenzer, Jr., and the appellee, Nola Kathleen Quenzer (now Sharrard), were divorced in Texas in 1975. Primary custody of the parties' daughter was awarded to the mother pursuant to the Decree of Divorce which followed the provisions of a Property Settlement Agreement previously entered into by the parties. Not long after the divorce the mother removed herself from Texas with the result that the father could not exercise weekend visitation rights as provided for in the Decree of Divorce. . . .

In August of 1977 the father petitioned the circuit court in Oregon [to which the mother had gone] to enforce the visitation provisions of the Texas decree in accordance with Oregon's adoption of the Uniform Child Custody Jurisdiction Act. A cross-petition by the mother sought modification of the Texas decree and also arrearages in child and spousal support payments, and an increase in the amount of monthly child support. . . . The father then filed a motion for a change in custody of the daughter. . . . Essentially the Oregon decree continued custody in the mother; . . . Although appealed, that judgment was affirmed by the Oregon Court of Appeals.

. . . In August of 1979 the mother married her present husband and the mother, daughter and the stepfather moved to . . . Alaska . . . In June of 1980 the daughter was sent to visit in Texas. The father was entitled to custody for a six-week period starting on the second Sunday of June of each year. During the period of this visit the mother and her husband moved from Alaska to Teton County, Wyoming, where they intended to establish a permanent residence. On July 8, 1980, which was less than a week before the scheduled visitation in Texas was to end, the father filed a motion in the Texas district court, seeking a modification in custody of the child. Process was served upon the mother in Eugene, Oregon, where she was visiting prior to returning to Wyoming.

Thereafter the mother instituted a separate habeas corpus proceeding in the Texas court, seeking enforcement of the Oregon decree returning the child to her custody. The return to her custody was ordered by the Texas court, and on August 16, 1980, the mother and daughter left Texas, and since that time they have resided in Wyoming. . . . In the meantime the modification proceeding had been held in abeyance pending a determination of the status of the mother, who had attempted to appear specially. The Texas court, by the same judge who had heard the habeas corpus proceeding, entered an order denying the mother's special appearance and ordering the case to proceed to trial on the merits. Thereafter, in January of 1981, trial was held with respect to the proceeding seeking modification of custody. On January 12, 1981, an Order of Modification in Suit Affecting Parent-Child Relationship was entered in Texas in which the court held that custody should be given to the father with visitation rights to the mother. January 26, 1981, was specified as the date for transferring possession of the child, and the Texas court did enter findings that it had jurisdiction and that the mother had not been a continuous domiciliary or resident of any state for six months preceding the filing of this action. It further found that no other court had or has continuing jurisdiction of the suit or of the daughter and that it had jurisdiction of the child because it was the most convenient forum to determine the best interest of the child.

The proceeding in Wyoming was commenced on February 23, 1981. . . . The Wyoming court found that it had jurisdiction under the Wyoming version of the Uniform Child Custody Jurisdiction Act; that the mother was the proper person to have custody of the child; and that the circumstances before the court showed that any orders of any court in the past should be modified, because of a change in circumstances, to give the mother custody of the child. While critical of the Texas proceeding, the Wyoming district court premised its authority upon the existence of jurisdiction pursuant to Wyoming statute, and it did proceed to modify the Texas modification order by restoring permanent custody to the mother; denying visitation rights in the father "at the present time unless substantial safeguards are erected in that regard" . . . The father has appealed from this order. . . .

The father argues earnestly, that the Parental Kidnapping Prevention Act of 1980, Pub.L. 96–611, 94 Stat. 3569 (1980) . . . forecloses the Wyoming court from modifying the modification decree entered by the Texas court. . . .

This legislation, if applicable, must be afforded primary consideration under the Supremacy Clauses of our federal and state constitutions. Constitution of the United States, Art.VI, Cl. 2; Constitution of the State of Wyoming, Art.1, § 37. By this statute

Congress has provided for the effect to be given to the judicial proceedings in the state originally exercising jurisdiction, and thus has defined what full faith and credit requires in such instances.[1]

Any child-custody determination made consistently with the provisions of the Parental Kidnapping Prevention Act is required to be enforced according to its terms by the courts of every other state (28 U.S.C.A. § 1738A), and the authorities of another state are not permitted to modify except as provided in subsection (f) of 28 U.S.C.A. § 1738A such a child-custody determination. Subsection (f), which is referred to, provides as follows:

"(f) A court of a State may modify a determination of the custody of the same child made by a court of another state, if—

"(1) it has jurisdiction to make a child custody determination; and

"(2) the court of the other State no longer has jurisdiction, or it has declined to exercise such jurisdiction to modify such determination." . . .

There is, however, a threshold test which must be applied. . . . The modification order in Texas must have been made consistently with the provisions of the Parental Kidnapping Prevention Act. Subsection (c) of the Parental Kidnapping Prevention Act provides as follows:

"(c) A child custody determination made by a court of a State is consistent with the provisions of this section only if—

"(1) such court has jurisdiction under the law of such State; and

"(2) one of the following conditions is met:

"(A) such State (i) is the home State of the child on the date of the commencement of the proceeding, or (ii) had been the child's home State within six months before the date of the commencement of the proceeding and the child is absent from such State because of his removal or retention by a contestant or for other reasons, and a contestant continues to live in such State;

"(B)(i)   it appears that no other State would have jurisdiction under subparagraph (A), and (ii) it is in the best interest of the child that a court of such State assume jurisdiction because (I) the child and his parents, or the child and at least one contestant, have

---

[1] It would appear that this legislation was intended to supplement existing state legislation such as the Uniform Child Custody Jurisdiction Act to promote interstate judicial cooperation and communication, facilitate the enforcement of custody and visitation decrees of sister states, discourage interstate controversies over child custody, prevent jurisdictional competition and conflicts between state courts, and to deter parental kidnapping and forum shopping. See § 7(c), Pub.L. 96–611, 94 Stat. 3569 (1980). . . .

a significant connection with such State other than mere physical presence in such State, and (II) there is available in such State substantial evidence concerning the child's present or future care, protection, training, and personal relationships;

"(C) the child is physically present in such State and (i) the child has been abandoned, or (ii) it is necessary in an emergency to protect the child because he has been subjected to or threatened with mistreatment or abuse;

"(D)(i)   it appears that no other State would have jurisdiction under subparagraph (A), (B), (C), or (E), or another State has declined to exercise jurisdiction on the ground that the State whose jurisdiction is in issue is the more appropriate forum to determine the custody of the child, and (ii) it is in the best interest of the child that such court assume jurisdiction; or

"(E) The court has continuing jurisdiction pursuant to subsection (d) of this section." . . .

The Texas determination . . . was not made consistently with the second requirement of the Parental Kidnapping Prevention Act, in that its exercise of jurisdiction did not fit any of the conditions contained in 28 U.S.C.A. § 1738A(c)(2). Obviously Texas was not the home state of the child under subsection (A) of that provision. The father cannot rely upon subsection (B) of that provision because the daughter had been living in Alaska for at least six consecutive months immediately preceding the time she went to visit the father, and [therefore] Alaska would be the home state of the child as defined in 28 U.S.C.A. § 1738A(b)(4). The Texas court therefore could not, and it did not, find that no other state would have jurisdiction under subparagraph (A) of 28 U.S.C.A. § 1738A(c)(2)(A). Subsections (C), (D), and (E) of the title similarly are not applicable, and we must conclude that the jurisdiction of the district court in Wyoming was not foreclosed by the provisions of the Parental Kidnapping Prevention Act because the modification order entered in the State of Texas was not a "custody determination made consistently with the provisions of this section by a court of another State."

Having concluded that neither the Full Faith and Credit Clause nor the provisions of the Parental Kidnapping Prevention Act foreclosed the exercise of jurisdiction by the district court in Wyoming, we still must consider whether the exercise of that jurisdiction was precluded under some provision of Wyoming law. Our conclusion with respect to this proposition will also dispose of the first issue urged by the father in his appeal. Section 20–5–104, W.S.1977 [U.C.C.J.A. § 3] is the provision governing the jurisdiction of Wyoming courts in child-custody proceedings, and it provides as follows:

"(a) A court of this state competent to decide child custody matters has jurisdiction to make a child custody determination by initial decree or modification decree if:

"(i) This state is the home state of the child at the time of commencement of the proceeding, or was the child's home state within six (6) months before commencement of the proceeding and the child is absent from the state because of his removal or retention by a person claiming his custody or for other reasons, and a parent or person acting as parent continues to live in this state;

"(ii) It is in the best interest of the child that a court of this state assume jurisdiction because the child and his parents, or the child and at least one (1) contestant, have a significant connection with the state and there is available in this state substantial evidence concerning the child's present or future care, protection, training and personal relationships;

"(iii)The child is physically present in this state and has been abandoned or if it is necessary in an emergency to protect the child because he has been subjected to or threatened with mistreatment or abuse or is otherwise neglected or dependent; or

"(iv) It appears that no other state would have jurisdiction under prerequisites substantially in accordance with paragraphs [subdivisions] (i), (ii) or (iii) of this subsection, or another state has declined to exercise jurisdiction on the ground that this state is the more appropriate forum to determine the custody of the child and it is in the best interest of the child that this court assume jurisdiction.

"(b) Except under paragraphs [subdivisions] (a)(iii) and (iv) of this section, physical presence in this state of the child or of the child and one (1) of the contestants is not alone sufficient to confer jurisdiction on a court of this state to make a child custody determination.

"(c) Physical presence of the child, while desirable, is not a prerequisite for jurisdiction to determine his custody."

Both subsections (a)(i) and (a)(ii) in this instance justify the exercise of jurisdiction by the courts of the State of Wyoming. In § 20–5–103(a)(v), W.S.1977, [U.C.C.J.A. § 2] "Home state" is defined as follows:

"... 'Home state' means the state in which the child immediately preceding the time involved has lived with his parents, a parent or a person acting as parent, for at least six

(6) consecutive months, and in the case of a child less than six (6) months old the state in which the child has lived since birth with any of the persons mentioned. Periods of temporary absence of any of the names [sic] persons are counted as part of the six (6) month or other period; . . ."

The record is clear that the daughter had resided with her mother in Wyoming from the time of the conclusion of the habeas corpus proceeding in Texas until the commencement of the Wyoming proceeding, which was more than six months. It is equally apparent that there did exist in this instance a significant connection with the State of Wyoming, and that there was available in this state substantial evidence concerning the child's present or future care, protection, training and personal relationships. Friends, neighbors, school personnel, and a professional psychologist were all present to assist the court in making determinations with respect to the best interest of the child. We note by contrast that the testimony in the Texas proceeding duplicated some of this testimony, and that the Texas witnesses appeared primarily as character witnesses for the father and his second wife. Any balanced comparison of these factors results in a clear preference for the State of Wyoming as the appropriate forum. The district court [determined] that it was in the best interest of the child that it exercise its jurisdiction. The evidence present in the record sustains this determination, and in the absence of some other inhibiting factor or prohibition the district court had jurisdiction over this matter under Wyoming law.

The father, however, points to the provisions of § 20–5–107(a), W.S.1977, [U.C.C.J.A. § 6] and urges that this section prohibits the exercise of jurisdiction in Wyoming. Section 20–5–107(a), W.S.1977, provides:

"(a) A court of this state shall not exercise its jurisdiction under this act if at the time of filing the petition a proceeding concerning the custody of the same child was pending in a court of another state exercising jurisdiction substantially in conformity with this act, unless the proceeding is stayed by the court of the other state because this state is a more appropriate forum or for other reasons."

Again the record is clear that when this proceeding was commenced in the Wyoming district court the proceedings in the courts of Texas had been concluded, and become final there according to local law. Since there was no proceeding pending in Texas, § 20–5–107(a) did not interfere with the exercise of jurisdiction by the district court in Wyoming. We note in this regard that the father apparently has abandoned his claim that the district court abused its discretion by failing to decline jurisdiction as an inconvenient forum in favor of Texas under § 20–5–08, W.S.1977 [U.C.C.J.A. § 7].

Relying upon still another contention, the father argues that the district court committed error in asserting and exercising jurisdiction to determine child custody in the light of §§ 20–5–14 [U.C.C.J.A. § 13] and 20–5–15(a) [U.C.C.J.A. § 14] W.S.1977. The provisions of those statutes read as follows:

"§ 20–5–14. Recognition and enforcement of initial or modification decree made by court of another state.

> "The courts of this state shall recognize and enforce an initial or modification decree of a court of another state which had assumed jurisdiction under statutory provisions substantially in accordance with this act, or which was made under factual circumstances meeting the jurisdictional standards of the act, so long as this decree has not been modified in accordance with jurisdictional standards substantially similar to those of this act."

"§ 20–5–15. Modifying custody decree made by court of another state.

> "(a) If a court of another state has made a custody decree a court of this state shall not modify that decree unless it appears that the court which rendered the decree does not now have jurisdiction under jurisdictional prerequisites substantially in accordance with this act or has declined to assume jurisdiction to modify the decree, and the court of this state has jurisdiction."

The mother meets these contentions by asserting that the district court correctly refused to recognize and enforce the Texas order because the statutory provisions in Texas are not substantially in accordance with the Uniform Child Custody Jurisdiction Act, and she asserts that the factual circumstances were such that the jurisdictional standards of the Uniform Act were not met in Texas. . . . She points out that, while tit. 2, § 11.045(1)(2)(A), Tex.Fam.Code Ann. (Vernon 1975), facially is similar to § 20–5–104(a)(ii), W.S.1977, the State of Texas has no provision similar to § 20–5–109(b), W.S.1977. [U.C.C.J.A. § 8] This latter provision provides as follows:

> "(b) Unless required in the interest of the child and subject to W.S. 20–5–115(a), the court shall not exercise its jurisdiction to modify a custody decree of another state if the petitioner without consent of the person entitled to custody has improperly removed the child from the physical custody of the person entitled to custody or has improperly retained the child after a visit or other temporary relinquishment of physical custody. If the petitioner has violated any other provision of a custody decree of another state the court in its discretion and subject to W.S. 20–5–115(a) may decline to exercise jurisdiction."

The record before us discloses that while the father filed his action for modification in Texas during the period that the daughter was visiting him pursuant to the provisions of the Oregon decree, his retention of custody beyond the time provided by the decree was wrongful and in derogation of the mother's rights. We agree with the mother that

. . . a Wyoming court under these circumstances would not be permitted to exercise its jurisdiction to modify a custody decree.

It would appear from the circumstances that the policy of the State of Texas differs. Consequently, if the issue in this case were confined to the enforcement of the Texas order it well might be that the doctrine of res judicata, combined with the provisions of our Wyoming law and the Parental Kidnapping Prevention Act, would require the recognition and enforcement of the Texas decree. . . . Still the availability of the jurisdiction of the district court to modify the provisions of the Texas order is not foreclosed. Unless the prohibition contained in § 20–5–115(a), W.S.1977, is applicable, the district court in Wyoming had the power to act and enter its own order modifying the custody provisions upon a sufficient showing of a change in circumstances to warrant a different decree. . . .

We conclude that it is the duty of the Wyoming court to determine the applicability of § 20–5–115(a), W.S.1977, i.e., to determine whether the Texas court at the time the jurisdiction of the Wyoming court was exercised had jurisdiction under jurisdictional prerequisites substantially in accordance with the Uniform Child Custody Jurisdiction Act or had declined to assume jurisdiction to modify the decree. . . . This determination, which must be made by the Wyoming court, is to be made not at the commencement of the Wyoming action, but rather at the time of the hearing on the matter in light of the evidence presented. . . . Other courts which have construed this Uniform Child Custody Jurisdiction Act generally have applied a two-stage test in determining whether the local court had jurisdiction to modify a foreign custody determination. First the court must consider whether the court whose decree is sought to be modified no longer has jurisdiction under standards such as those set forth in § 20–5–104, W.S.1977 [U.C.C.J.A. § 4], and secondly it may consider whether the court whose decree is sought to be modified has declined jurisdiction to modify its prior judgment. If either of these tests is met, then the forum state must determine whether it has jurisdiction under its own laws. . . .

On the date that the Wyoming court held its hearing the Texas court no longer had jurisdiction under standards which substantially comply with the Uniform Child Custody Jurisdiction Act. This test having been met, the Wyoming court was not foreclosed from exercising jurisdiction by the provisions of § 20–5–115(a), W.S.1977. We justify this holding first by alluding to one of the general purposes of the Uniform Child Custody Jurisdiction Act set forth in § 20–5–102, W.S.1977 [U.C.C.J.A. § 1] as follows:

"(a) The general purposes of this act are:

* * *

"(iii) To assure that litigation concerning the custody of a child take place ordinarily in the state with which the child and his family have the closest connection and where significant evidence concerning his care, protection, training and personal relationships is most readily available, and that courts of this state decline the exercise of jurisdiction when the child and his family have a closer connection with another state;"

We find in this statement of policy an explicit recognition that the paramount consideration of the best interest of the child mandates that custody determinations be made in the forum having the best access to the relevant evidence. . . .

At the time that Wyoming exercised its jurisdiction in this matter it was the "home state" under the Uniform Child Custody Jurisdiction Act and § 20–5–104(a)(i), W.S.1977. . . . At the pertinent date the state which had the most significant connections with the child and her mother was Wyoming. In February of 1982 the daughter had been present in Wyoming nearly eighteen months. She was attending local schools and receiving weekly counseling in Jackson, Wyoming, from a professional psychologist. Evidence of the mother's parental fitness and her relationship with the daughter was most accessible in Wyoming. Most importantly, however, the child's presence in this state gave the district court the best opportunity to gather evidence concerning the daughter's emotional and personal development, as well as furnishing to it the opportunity for the child to testify directly with respect to her early allegations in the Texas habeas corpus proceeding of drug use and mistreatment at the hands of her mother. She had earlier recanted that testimony by a letter to the Texas judge, and the Wyoming court had the opportunity to evaluate personally with the daughter the two versions of her prior testimony. The evidence available in Wyoming was relevant and substantial with respect to the issue of the best interest of the child. Under these criteria the Wyoming court properly exercised jurisdiction in the matter and entered its decree modifying the custody provisions of the Texas decree. . . .

[T]he last argument of the father relates to the sufficiency of the evidence to justify the finding by the district court of a substantial change in circumstances. . . . He also urges the proposition that the brief period between the date of the modification order in Texas and the beginning of the Wyoming proceedings negates the possibility that a change of circumstances occurred in the interim.

Once vested with jurisdiction over the cause, it is the duty of the court to hear evidence to determine whether a substantial material change in circumstances has occurred so that the welfare of the child will be best served by a change in custody. . . . Although the brief period of time between the entry of the order sought to be modified and the institution of new proceedings may indicate that circumstances have not changed, we cannot as a matter of law hold that the movant, who bears the burden of proof, could not present such sufficient evidence. . . .

. . . The district court in this instance made detailed and explicit findings concerning the changes in the daughter's circumstances. In addition, the record contains exhibits . . . including the depositions of the daughter and the psychologist, both of which support the findings made by the district court. The evidence is sufficient to support a conclusion that the mother has established a stable home with her new husband, and this has greatly aided the daughter's own emotional stability and maturity. The deposition of the psychologist details the advances the daughter has made since treatment was obtained. The daughter is happy and manifesting significant improvement in her school work and social development under the mother's care and supervision. She has established a strong parent-child relationship with her stepfather. Other improvements in the daughter and the mother's circumstances are detailed in the record. The record in this case is adequate to support the action of the district court. . . .

The order of the trial court hereby is affirmed on the basis of the conclusions reached in the foregoing opinion.

NOTES

1.   For a subsequent application of *Quenzer*, see Crites v. Alston, 837 P.2d 1061 (Wyo.1992). See also Gjertsen v. Haar, 347 P.3d 1117 (Wyo.2015) (modification of California decree which acknowledged impending change of child's home state from California to Wyoming and that California would then be an inconvenient forum).

As mentioned earlier, § 201 of the Uniform Child Custody Jurisdiction and Enforcement Act (UCCJEA) gives the home state exclusive jurisdiction to make the original custody determination. Art. 3 of the UCCJA, which the UCCJEA replaces, provided the same standard for the identification of "home state" for original determinations and later modifications. Under § 201 UCCJEA, the original court retains exclusive continuing jurisdiction unless the state no longer has "a significant connection" with the child, the parents, or a person acting as parent, or when "substantial evidence . . . concerning . . . the child's protection, training, and personal relationships" is no longer available in the state. Sec. 201(a)(1). However, the court may determine that it is an inconvenient forum and decline to exercise jurisdiction. Sec. 207(a). See also *Gjertsen*, supra. It should obviously do so when the child has moved away and acquired a new home state. See Moore v. Richardson, 964 S.W.2d 377 (Ark.1998) (Texas did not have jurisdiction to modify custody decree from Arkansas when father still lived in Arkansas and when custody arrangement was still in compliance with Arkansas decree, despite mother's claim that Texas was the child's home state; continuing jurisdiction state has priority over home state). In Wilson v. Beckett, 236 S.W.3d 527 (Ark.Ct.App.2006), the court noted that "home state" means the same under both the UCCJA and the UCCJEA. As a consequence, Arkansas' original and exclusive jurisdiction terminated when the child had lawfully lived for more than six months in Missouri, which had become the "home state" and had properly exercised jurisdiction in an adoption proceeding. In

In re Marriage of Kneitz, 793 N.E.2d 988 (Ill.App.2003), decided under the UCCJA, the mother had been unsuccessful in obtaining a modification of the father's visitation rights in Illinois. Rather than appeal, she sought and obtained an ex parte modification in Louisiana. The Illinois court pointed to its continuing jurisdiction (which it had not relinquished), refused to recognize the Louisiana decree, held the mother in contempt for not honoring the original decree, and noted that any difficulty she might now have under the inconsistent Louisiana decree was of her own making. Her remedies, if any, lay with the Illinois courts. What result under the UCCJEA?

The Parental Kidnapping Prevention Act, 28 U.S.C.A. § 1738A, implements the Full Faith and Credit Clause with respect to custody decrees entered by courts with appropriate jurisdiction. It also makes available the facilities of the Federal Parent Locator Service to aid attempts to ascertain the whereabouts of a kidnapped child.

The Parental Kidnapping Prevention Act does not confer custody jurisdiction on the federal courts, nor does it give them jurisdiction to determine which of two or more competing state courts has jurisdiction. Compliance with the Act must therefore be tested by appeal within the state court system and thereafter by petition for certiorari to the Supreme Court. Thompson v. Thompson, 484 U.S. 174 (1988). See also California v. Superior Court of California, 482 U.S. 400 (1987): the Extradition Act required California to extradite a father to Louisiana, where he had been charged with parental kidnapping. California could not refuse to do so on the ground that the father had custody under a prior and valid California decree. The effect to be given to the California decree was to be determined by the Louisiana courts. For comment on *Thompson*, see R. Weintraub, Commentary on the Conflict of Laws § 5.3C (6th ed.2010).

2.   In Greenlaw v. Smith, 869 P.2d 1024 (Wash.1994), cert. denied, 513 U.S. 935 (1994), a father asked the Washington court to modify its custody decree in his favor even though the minor child and his mother, the custodial parent, had not resided in Washington State for six years prior to the request for modification. The Washington Supreme Court held that the lower court's exercise of jurisdiction was proper because the father remained in Washington State and the child continued to have more than slight contact with Washington as a result of visiting his father. See Juliet A. Cox, Note, Judicial Wandering Through a Legislative Maze: Application of the Uniform Child Custody Jurisdiction Act and the Parental Kidnapping Prevention Act to Child Custody Determinations, 58 Mo.L.Rev. 427 (1993); Linda M. DeMelis, Note, Interstate Child Custody and the Parental Kidnapping Prevention Act: The Continuing Search for a National Standard, 45 Hastings L.J. 1329 (1994). See also In re Jorgensen, 627 N.W.2d 550 (Iowa 2001), cert. denied, 535 U.S. 1000 (2002): the court undertook a separate review of whether the joint custody agreement incorporated in a New York divorce decree was entitled to recognition under the PKPA and, if not, whether it should be recognized under Iowa's version of the UCCJA. It answered both questions in the negative because New York was not the home state of the child at the time of the determination, and its court therefore lacked

jurisdiction with respect to custody. See also In re K.A.K., 2006 WL 2058322, 723 N.W.2d 449 (Table) (Iowa App.2006).

For further discussion of the relationship between the Parental Kidnapping Act and the UCCJA, see Coombs, Custody Conflicts in the Courts: Judicial Resolution of the Old and New Questions Raised by Interstate Child Custody Cases, 16 Fam.L.Q. 251 (1982); Coombs, Interstate Child Custody: Jurisdiction, Recognition, and Enforcement, 66 Minn.L.Rev. 711 (1982); Lea Hixson, Note, The Parental Kidnapping Prevention Act—Analysis and Impact on Uniform Child Custody Jurisdiction, 27 N.Y.L.Sch.L.Rev. 553 (1982); Jeanne K. Pettenati, Note, The Effect of the Parental Kidnapping Prevention Act of 1980 on Child Snatching, 17 New Eng.L.Rev. 499 (1982); Baron, Federal Preemption in the Resolution of Child Custody Jurisdiction Disputes, 45 Ark.L.Rev. 885 (1993); Arkin, Jurisdiction and the Interstate Child: How to Avoid the Avoidable Complications, 26 Colo.Law. 75 (March 1997).

Articles on the original Uniform Child Custody Jurisdiction Act by Professor Brigitte Bodenheimer, its principal draftsman, include Bodenheimer, Interstate Custody: Initial Jurisdiction and Continuing Jurisdiction Under the UCCJA, 14 Fam.L.Q. 203 (1981); Bodenheimer, The Rights of Children and The Crisis in Custody Litigation: Modification of Custody In and Out of State, 46 U.Colo.L.Rev. 495 (1975); Bodenheimer, The Uniform Child Custody Jurisdiction Act: A Legislative Remedy for Children Caught in the Conflict of Laws, 22 Vand.L.Rev. 1207 (1969).

For the UCCJEA, see David Carl Minneman, Annotation, Construction and Operation of Uniform Child Custody Jurisdiction and Enforcement Act, 100 A.L.R.5th 1 (2002 & Supp.2004); Wessel, Home Is Where the Court Is: Determining Residence for Child Custody Matters under the UCCJEA, 79 U.Chi.L.Rev. 1141 (2012). For the Uniform Deployed Parents Custody and Visitation Act, see Gromek, Comment, Military Child Custody Disputes: The Need for Federal Encouragement for the States' Adoption of the Uniform Deployed Parents Custody and Visitation Act, 44 Seton Hall L.Rev. 873 (2014).

3. The Parental Kidnapping Prevention Act is applicable only to sister-state custody decrees. The International Parental Kidnapping Crime Act of 1993, 107 Stat. 1988, 18 U.S.C.A. § 1204, makes the removal of a child from the United States with intent to obstruct the exercise of parental rights a federal crime. Parental rights include custody based on a court order or derived from a legally binding agreement between the parties. The Parental Kidnapping Prevention Act is also applicable to adoption proceedings. In re Adoption of Baby E.Z., 266 P.3d 702 (Utah 2011).

4. The UCCJA (§ 23) and the UCCJEA (§ 105) also apply to custody decrees rendered in foreign countries. See, e.g., Custody of a Minor (No. 3), 468 N.E.2d 251, 254 (Mass.1984) (Massachusetts court would not modify an Australian custody decree): "We see no basis ... for concluding that the Australian custody determination was not made in substantial conformity with [the UCCJA] or ... that the Australian court does not now have jurisdiction under the jurisdictional prerequisites of [the Act].... If a

Massachusetts court had the power to disregard a foreign judgment by considering [its] propriety . . . in a substantive, rather than a procedural sense, the very purpose of the law would be undermined. . . ." See, similarly, Vause v. Vause, 409 N.W.2d 412 (Wis.Ct.App.1987) (the mother had received reasonable notice of the German proceeding and had an opportunity to appear, the German proceeding satisfied the standards of the UCCJA, and the resulting decree was entitled to recognition); Khan v. Saminni, 842 N.E.2d 453 (Mass.2006) (Trinidad custody determination was made "in substantial conformity" with forum law, so this court was required to enforce said decree under Massachusetts version of the UCCJA). In contrast to Custody of a Minor (3), supra, the court in El Chaar v. Chehab, 941 N.E.2d 75 (Mass.App.Ct.2010), denied a father's action for recognition and enforcement of a Lebanese decree in his favor because it had not been shown, for purposes of considering the best interests of the child, that the procedures and substantive law applied by the Lebanese court were reasonably comparable to those of Massachusetts. It appeared in the case that the mother's removal of the child from Lebanon had been wrongful under Lebanese law. Lebanon is not a member of the Hague Convention, Note 6, infra. See also Abbott v. Abbott, Note 7, infra.

In the case of In re Stephanie M., 867 P.2d 706 (Cal.1994), cert. denied, 513 U.S. 908 (1994), the Supreme Court of California upheld the jurisdiction of a lower court over a custody action involving the minor child of Mexican nationals despite the assertion of concurrent jurisdiction by Mexico. California asserted jurisdiction over the matter because of the emergency presented by the abuse of the minor. Much of the evidence regarding the abuse and the investigation of the parents' capacity to provide a future home free from abuse was located in California. The state supreme court held that the lower court had not abused its discretion, although it had been informed of the child's Mexican grandmother's interest in having the child live with her in Mexico. For the appropriateness of basing jurisdiction for adoption on the UCCJA and its successor act, see Kay, Adoption in the Conflict of Laws: The UAA, Not the UCCJA, Is the Answer, 84 Cal.L.Rev. 703 (1996).

When the decree of an American court provides for the child to visit a parent abroad, it becomes important that the continuing jurisdiction of the American court be preserved and that no inconsistent decree be entered abroad. See Tischendorf v. Tischendorf, 321 N.W.2d 405 (Minn.1982), cert. denied, 460 U.S. 1037 (1983) (father, residing in Germany, required to post security in the form of an irrevocable letter of credit and to obtain German court order recognizing the exclusive jurisdiction of the American court). See also Annotation, Court-Authorized Permanent or Temporary Removal of Child by Parent to Foreign Country, 30 A.L.R.4th 548 (1984).

5. Under § 109 of the UCCJEA, a nonresident who participates in a child custody proceeding in the state "is not subject to personal jurisdiction in th[e] State for another proceeding . . . solely by reason of having participated . . . in the proceeding." However, in Friedetzky v. Hsia, 117 A.3d 660 (Md.App.2015), a nonresident father's demands for discovery on child support in response to the mother's petition for custody triggered a long-arm statute under the Uniform Interstate Family Support Act (UIFSA) and waived immunity from suit under the UCCJEA. For the same result, see Ihenachor v. Martin, 2019 WL 2913974 (Md.Spec.App.2019).

6. The Hague Convention on the Civil Aspects of International Child Abduction came into force for the United States on July 1, 1988, by the International Child Abduction Remedies Act, 42 U.S.C. §§ 9001–11. The Convention does not provide a mechanism for the determination of custody disputes. Instead, it seeks "to restore the factual situation that existed prior to the child's removal or retention. . . . The international abductor is denied legal advantage from the abduction to or retention in the country where the child is located, as resort to the Convention is to effect the child's swift return to his or her circumstances before the abduction or retention." President Reagan's message to the Senate, 99th Cong., 1st Sess., Sen. Treaty Doc. 99–11 (Nov. 5, 1985). An aggrieved parent may enlist the aid of the "Central Authority" designated by each ratifying country and may resort to the courts. Under the federal implementing Act, state and federal courts have concurrent original jurisdiction. Halabi, Abstention, Parity, and Treaty Rights: How Federal Courts Regulate Jurisdiction under the Hague Convention on the Civil Aspects of International Child Abduction, 32 Berkeley J.Int'l L. 144 (2014). See also the International Parental Kidnapping Act of 1993, 18 U.S.C.A. § 1204, making it a crime to remove a child from the United States with intent to obstruct the exercise of parental rights. See Lynda R. Herring, Comment, Taking Away the Pawns: International Parental Abduction & the Hague Convention, 20 N.C.J.Int'l L. & Com.Reg. 137 (1994); Julia A. Todd, Note, The Hague Convention on the Civil Aspects of International Child Abduction: Are the Convention's Goals Being Achieved?, 2 Ind.J.Global Legal Stud. 553 (1995).

The Convention does not define "habitual residence." In a case of first impression, the Second Circuit adopted the following test: the trial court should first determine the shared intent of those responsible to establish the child's residence at the last time they shared such an intent. The court should then inquire whether the evidence unequivocally points to the conclusion that the child has acclimatized to the new location and thus acquired a habitual residence there, notwithstanding the last shared intent of the parents. Gitter v. Gitter, 396 F.3d 124 (2d Cir.2005). See also Thompson v. Brown, 2007 WL 54100 (N.D.Ill. Jan. 3, 2007). But see Kijowska v. Haines, 463 F.3d 583, 587 (7th Cir.2006): the *Gitter* test is not workable when the parents have lived apart for a considerable length of time, thus making reference to their "last shared intent" not very helpful. In such circumstances, only the second part of the *Gitter* test helps, representing the case-by-case determination of the child's circumstances, which generally already characterizes the case law on this issue. *Kijowska* is explained and applied in Ovalle v. Perez, 2016 WL 6082404 (S.D.Fla. Oct. 18, 2016) (child returned to Guatemala), and in Rodriguez Palomo v. Howard, 426 F.Supp.3d 160 (M.D.N.C.2019), aff'd 812 Fed.App'x (4th Cir. 2020) (mem.). For other decisions applying the Convention, see Diorinou v. Mezitis, 237 F.3d 133 (2d Cir.2001) (removal of child from Greece was wrongful, child ordered returned; the District Court correctly deferred to the Hague Convention ruling made by the Greek courts on the critical issue of whether the mother had wrongfully retained the children in Greece); Rydder v. Rydder, 49 F.3d 369 (8th Cir.1995) (child returned to Poland); Brooke v. Willis, 907 F.Supp. 57 (S.D.N.Y.1995) (United Kingdom found to be the child's habitual residence: even though child spent only one summer there, he had become "settled" in England); Silverman v. Silverman, 338 F.3d 886 (8th Cir.2003) ("habitual residence" of children was Israel when parents had sold their house in Minnesota, moved the family and their belongings to Israel, and enrolled the children in school in Israel, despite having named Minnesota as their permanent address for bankruptcy proceedings and having listed Minnesota as their permanent address on federal income tax forms; nor is Israel a "zone of war" for purpose of "grave risk" inquiry); In Robert v. Tesson, 507 F.3d 981 (6th Cir.2007), the court granted that the children might have acquired habitual residence in France during a 15-month stay there, but noted that they had then lived for a year with their mother in the United States, with little contact with their father. Their habitual residence had thus changed to the United States. This result was not changed by a three-week visit to France. The court's determination was influenced by its evaluation of the children's French surroundings as not constituting a proper "home." Should these considerations enter into a habitual-residence determination?

Art. 12 of the Hague Convention provides that a court shall order the return of a child who has been wrongfully removed from his or her country of habitual residence when an application to this effect is made within one year. The Article also provides for the child's return after a year unless the child has become settled in the new environment in the meantime. In Lozano v. Montoya Alvarez, 572 U.S. 1 (2014), the mother left the United Kingdom with the child and settled in the United States. The father, who had custody rights, was unable to locate the child's whereabouts until 16 months after the child's removal. The New York courts denied his application for the child's return because more than twelve months had elapsed and the child (about four years old at the time of removal) was now settled in the new environment. A unanimous United States Supreme Court affirmed. The doctrine of "equitable tolling" did not apply to modify the one-year period envisioned by Article 12: it is a common law notion that has no place in interpretation and application of a multilateral convention. The latter itself specifies the only exceptions to its provisions. In the case of Art. 12, the Convention extends the one-year only on the condition that the child has not yet become fully integrated in the new environment and commits that determination to the trial court. The trial court did undertake such a determination. See, similarly, MG v. WZ, 998 N.Y.S.2d 563 (N.Y.Fam.Ct.2014), applying Lozano: while the child was not as young as in that case, he had lived in the United States since 2010; "equitable tolling" was not argued. It seems likely that the exception of Art. 12 will rarely lead to the return of the child, especially when the child is very young. Similarly, Art. 13 (providing for the court to hear children who have attained sufficient maturity) may provide an avenue to prevent return of the child: In Custodio v. Samillan, 842 F.3d 1084 (8th Cir.2016), the court held that the trial court had not abused its discretion in denying the request for the return of a 15 year old boy to Peru who had testified that he did not want to see his father again (who had visitation rights and of whom the boy was afraid) and that he did not like living in Peru.

7.   In Abbott v. Abbott, 560 U.S. 1 (2010), a father held a ne exeat right under Chilean law as a consequence of a custody decree granted by a Chilean family court. The father's ne exeat right required the mother to obtain the father's consent before removing the child from Chile. She removed the child to the United States without the father's consent. Resolving a conflict among the Courts of Appeal, the Supreme Court held that the ne exeat right was a "right of custody," rather than a "right of access," under the Hague Convention on the Civil Aspects of International Child Abduction. The father was therefore entitled to seek the remedy of the child's return to Chile, as provided for in the Hague Convention for the violation of a right of custody. Justice Kennedy's majority decision combined textual interpretation with consideration of the overarching purpose of the treaty and of the practice of other signatory countries. The dissent pointed out that the mother had sole custody (while some of the foreign cases had involved joint custody by the parents), so the mother's actions were undoubtedly in violation of Chilean law but not violations of "custody rights."

8.   In the European Union, except Denmark, Council Regulation (EC) No. 2201/2003 on Jurisdiction and the Recognition and Enforcement of Judgments in Matrimonial Matters and in Matters of Parental Responsibility, to be replaced by Council Regulation No. 2019/1111 as of August 1, 2022, and reproduced in the Appendix, contains comprehensive provisions on child custody. The Regulation provides for general jurisdiction in questions relating to "parental responsibility" (defined broadly as relating to the child's person or property and confined to the child and its parents, Art. 2(6 and 7)) in the courts of the Member State of the child's habitual residence (Art. 10). These courts retain jurisdiction ("continuing jurisdiction") when the child is lawfully removed to another Member State and until it has acquired a new habitual residence there (Art. 11). Spouses may also confer jurisdiction by agreement on the divorce court, and other "holders of parental responsibility" may similarly agree on a court ("prorogation of jurisdiction," Art. 12). Transfer to another court, on grounds similar to forum non conveniens, may be made in specified, limited cases (Art. 15). With the emphasis on the child's habitual residence, detailed provisions became necessary with respect to child abduction and its leading to the relitigation of the custody decision in a second state. Art. 21 provides that the courts of the state to which the child has been abducted lacks jurisdiction unless the child has resided there for at least one year after the holder of the custodial right gained knowledge of its whereabouts and made no application for its return, and the child has settled in its new environment. Granting of access rights and the unlawful exercise of them (for instance, failure to return the child) are expressly covered by the jurisdiction and enforcement provisions. Arts. 45–47. Indeed, a certificate from the court of the child's habitual residence "shall be enforced in all other Member States without any special procedure being required" (Art. 47(1)).

The following case was decided by the European Court of Justice, under the Regulation summarized above, upon referral to it from the Lithuanian

Supreme Court. Compare it with *Quenzer* and the provisions of the UCCJEA: The parties, a Lithuanian and a German, had married and lived in Germany, and their child was born there. After they separated and while divorce proceedings had been initiated and were pending, the mother took the child to Lithuania for a vacation, with the father's consent. The German court awarded him provisional custody. When the mother did not return, he sought the child's return and protracted litigation commenced in Lithuania. Meanwhile, the German court issued the divorce, awarded custody to the father, and issued the certificate specified by Art. 42 of the Regulation (reproduced in the Documentary Appendix). The ex-wife filed for a decree of non-recognition of the German decree in Lithuania; in another application there, she had requested modification of the custody award on grounds of changed circumstances. In response to questions posed to it by the Lithuanian Supreme Court, the European Court of Justice wrote:

> "[A] judgment given in a Member State is to be recognised in the other Member States without any special procedure being required. . . . [The] provisions [of the Regulation] seek not only to secure the immediate return of the child to the Member State where he or she was habitually resident immediately before the wrongful removal or retention, but also to enable the court of origin to assess the reasons for and evidence underlying the [current state's position that their child should not be returned]. . . . [W]ere [it] otherwise, there would be a risk that the Regulation would be deprived of its useful effect, since the objective of the immediate return of the child would remain subject to the condition that the redress procedures allowed under the domestic law of the Member State in which the child is wrongfully retained have been exhausted. That risk [should not be incurred] because as far as concerns young children biological time cannot be measured according to general criteria [i.e., according to a time table], given [the speed of their] intellectual and psychological [development] . . . By excluding any appeal against the issuance of a certificate [supra] . . . the Regulation seeks to ensure that the effectiveness of its provisions is not undermined by abuse of the procedure. . . . As is apparent from the . . . previous [discussion], an application for non-recognition of a judicial decision is not permitted if a certificate has been issued pursuant to Article 42 . . . . In such a situation, the decision which has been certified is enforceable and no opposition to its recognition is permitted." Rinau v. Rinau, Case C-195/08 PPU, [2008] ECR 5271, at nn. 61, 78, 81, 85, 109 (European Court of Justice, July 11, 2008). Review (and possible modification) of the custody determination is therefore in the exclusive jurisdiction of the German court and the child must be returned to Germany."

Several other cases concerning child custody have been decided under Regulation No. 2201/2003. Case C-4/14, Bohez v. Wiertz, 2015 Official Journal C 363, 6–7 (penalty payment imposed to ensure enforcement of rights of access not reviewable "as to the substance of the matter" outside the court of origin); Case C-523/07, 2007 E.C.R. I-02805, the Regulation "does not oblige the court which has taken a provisional measure" for the protection of a child under Art. 20(1) "to transfer the case to the court of another Member State with jurisdiction"); Case C-435/06, C, 2007 E.C.R. I-10141 (term "civil matters" in Art. 1(1) includes "a single decision ordering a child to be taken into care and placed outside his original home in a foster family"); Case C-256/09, Purrucker v. Vallés Pérez, 2010 E.C.R. 7353 (Art. 21 et seq. "do not apply to provisional measures, relating to rights of custody, falling within the scope of Article 20").

9. The Hague Conference on Private International Law adopted a "Convention on Jurisdiction, Applicable Law, Recognition, Enforcement and Co-operation in Respect of Parental Responsibility and Measures for the Protection of Children" in 1996. As of 2021, the Convention was in force in 54 contracting states (but not in the United States). The EU Regulation discussed in Note 7, supra, is modeled after this Hague Convention as well as the 1980 Hague Child Abduction Convention, Note 6, supra. The EU Member States that ratified the Convention did so with the declaration that a judgment of an EU Member State court "in respect of matters relating to the Convention shall be recognized and enforced in [the state making the declaration] by application of the relevant internal rules of Community law."

10. Alley v. Parker, 707 A.2d 77 (Me.1998). Husband and wife, two well-known actors, based most of their professional activities in California, owned property in Maine, Kansas and Oregon, and claimed Maine as their domicile for tax and other purposes. They adopted two children during their marriage. Upon separation, the husband filed for divorce and custody in California while the wife filed in Maine. The Maine trial court dismissed the wife's complaint on forum non conveniens grounds. The Maine Supreme Court left undisturbed the trial court's factual finding that California was the home state of the children, as they had resided there for the previous six months, with only brief absences. The Maine and California trial judges had conferred by telephone, and it had been agreed that California would assume jurisdiction for purposes of determining temporary custody.

SECTION 8. SUPPORT

A. ENFORCEMENT OF SUPPORT CLAIMS WITHOUT REGARD TO RECIPROCAL SUPPORT LEGISLATION

Kulko v. California Superior Court

Supreme Court of the United States, 1978.
436 U.S. 84, 98 S.Ct. 1690, 56 L.Ed.2d 132.

[Sharon Kulko Horn commenced a custody and support action in a California state court against her former husband, Ezra Kulko. Prior to their separation, the former spouses resided in New York with their two minor children. After the couple separated, the mother moved to California. A subsequent Haitian divorce obtained by her incorporated a separation agreement that had been negotiated in New York. The agreement provided that the children were to live with the father during the school year and with the mother during vacations. The father made support payments in the amount of $3,000 per year for the time in which the children were in the mother's care. When the daughter asked to live with her mother in California during the school year, the father acquiesced and bought the daughter a one-way ticket to California. The son also joined his mother in California after she sent him a ticket, unbeknownst to the father. The mother then brought an action in a California state court to seek full custody and an increase in child support payments. The father did not object to the court's assertion of jurisdiction with respect to the custody claim, but did object to the court's assertion of personal jurisdiction with respect to the claim for increased child support. The father had visited California only twice during brief military stopovers years earlier. California courts held that California could exercise personal jurisdiction over the father because the father had "purposefully availed himself of the benefits and protections of California." The Supreme Court reversed.]

■ JUSTICE MARSHALL delivered the opinion of the Court.

The issue before us is whether, in this action for child support, the California state courts may exercise in personam jurisdiction over a nonresident, nondomiciliary parent of minor children domiciled in the State. For reasons set forth below, we hold that the exercise of such jurisdiction would violate the Due Process Clause of the Fourteenth Amendment.

II

The Due Process Clause of the Fourteenth Amendment operates as a limitation on the jurisdiction of state courts to enter judgments affecting rights or interests of nonresidents. See Shaffer v. Heitner, 433 U.S. 186, 198–200, 97 S.Ct. 2569, 2577, 53 L.Ed.2d 683 (1977). It has long been the rule that a valid judgment imposing a personal obligation or duty in favor of the plaintiff may be entered only by a court having jurisdiction over the person of the defendant. Pennoyer v. Neff, 95 U.S. 714, 732–733, 24 L.Ed. 565, 572 (1877); International Shoe Co. v. Washington, 326 U.S., at 316, 66 S.Ct., at 158. The existence of personal jurisdiction, in turn, depends upon the presence of reasonable notice to the defendant that an action has been brought. Mullane v. Central Hanover Trust Co., 339 U.S. 306, 313–314, 70 S.Ct. 652, 656–657, 94 L.Ed. 865 (1950), and a sufficient connection between the defendant and the forum State to make it fair to require defense of the action in the forum. Milliken v. Meyer, 311 U.S. 457, 463–464, 61 S.Ct. 339, 342–343, 85 L.Ed. 278 (1940). In this case, appellant does not dispute the adequacy of the notice given, but contends that his connection with the State of California is too attenuated, under the standards implicit in the Due Process Clause of the Constitution, to justify imposing upon him the burden and inconvenience of defense in California.

The parties are in agreement that the constitutional standard for determining whether the State may enter a binding judgment against appellant here is that set forth in this Court's opinion in International Shoe Co. v. Washington, supra: that a defendant "have certain minimum contacts with [the forum State] such that the maintenance of the suit does not offend 'traditional notions of fair play and substantial justice.'" 326 U.S., at 316, 66 S.Ct., at 158, quoting Milliken v. Meyer, supra, 311 U.S., at 463, 61 S.Ct., at 342.

... But we believe that the California Supreme Court's application of the minimum-contacts test in this case represents an unwarranted extension of International Shoe and would, if sustained, sanction a result that is neither fair, just, nor reasonable.

A

[I]n holding that personal jurisdiction existed, the court below carefully disclaimed reliance on the fact that appellant had agreed at the time of separation to allow his children to live with their mother three months a year and that he had sent them to California each year pursuant to the agreement. As was noted below, 19 Cal.3d, at 523–524, 138 Cal.Rptr., at 590, 564 P.2d, at 357, to find personal jurisdiction in a State on this basis, merely because the mother was residing there, would discourage parents from entering into reasonable visitation agreements. Moreover, it could arbitrarily subject one parent to suit in any State of the Union where the other parent chose to spend time while having custody of their offspring pursuant to the separation agreement.[6] As we have emphasized:

> "The unilateral activity of those who claim some relationship with a nonresident defendant cannot satisfy the requirement of contact with the forum State.... [I]t is essential in each case that there be some act by which the defendant purposefully avails [him]self of the privilege of conducting activities within the forum State...." Hanson v. Denckla, supra, 357 U.S., at 253, 78 S.Ct., at 1240.

The "purposeful act" that the California Supreme Court believed did warrant the exercise of personal jurisdiction over appellant in California was his "actively and fully consent[ing] to [the daughter] living in California for the school year ... and ... sen[ding] her to California for that purpose." 19 Cal.3d, at 524, 138 Cal.Rptr., at 591, 564 P.2d, at 358. We cannot accept the proposition that appellant's acquiescence in [the daughter's] desire to live with her mother conferred jurisdiction over appellant in the California courts in this action. A father who agrees, in

---

[6] Although the separation agreement stated that appellee Horn resided in California and provided that child-support payments would be mailed to her California address, it also specifically contemplated that appellee might move to a different State. The agreement directed appellant to mail the support payments to appellee's San Francisco address or "any other address which the Wife may designate from time to time in writing." App. 10.

the interests of family harmony and his children's preferences, to allow them to spend more time in California that was required under a separation agreement can hardly be said to have "purposefully availed himself" of the "benefits and protections" of California's laws. See Shaffer v. Heitner, 433 U.S., at 216, 97 S.Ct., at 2586.[7]

Nor can we agree with the assertion of the court below that the exercise of in personam jurisdiction here was warranted by the financial benefit appellant derived from his daughter's presence in California for nine months of the year. 19 Cal.3d, at 524–525, 138 Cal.Rptr., at 590–591, 564 P.2d, at 358. This argument rests on the premise that, while appellant's liability for support payments remained unchanged, his yearly expenses for supporting the children in New York decreased. But this circumstance, even if true, does not support California's assertion of jurisdiction here. Any diminution in appellant's household costs resulted, not from the child's presence in California, but rather from her absence from appellant's home. Moreover, an action by appellee Horn to increase support payments could now be brought, and could have been brought when [the daughter] first moved to California, in the State of New York; a New York court would clearly have personal jurisdiction over appellant and, if a judgment were entered by a New York court increasing appellant's child support obligations, it could be properly enforced against him in both New York and California. Any ultimate advantage to appellant thus results not from the child's presence in California, but from appellee's failure earlier to seek an increase in payments under the separation agreement. The argument below to the contrary, in our view, confuses the question of appellant's liability with that of the proper forum in which to determine that liability.

B

In light of our conclusion that appellant did not purposefully derive any benefit from any activities relating to the State of California, it is apparent that the California Supreme Court's reliance on appellant's having caused an "effect" in California was misplaced. See supra, at 1695. This "effects" test is derived from the American Law Institute's Restatement, Second, of Conflict of Laws § 37 (1971), which provides:

> "A state has power to exercise judicial jurisdiction over an individual who causes effects in the state by an act done elsewhere with respect to any cause of action arising from these effects unless the nature of the effects and of the individual's relationship to the state makes exercise of such jurisdiction unreasonable."

---

[7] The court below stated that the presence in California of appellant's daughter gave appellant the benefit of California's "police and fire protection, its school system, its hospital services, its recreational facilities, its libraries and museums...." 19 Cal.3d, at 522, 138 Cal.Rptr., at 589, 564 P.2d, at 356. But, in the circumstances presented here, these services provided by the State were essentially benefits to the child, not the father, and in any event were not benefits that appellant purposefully sought for himself.

While this provision is not binding on this Court, it does not in any event support the decision below. As is apparent from the examples accompanying § 37 in the Restatement, this section was intended to reach wrongful activity outside of the State causing injury inside of the State, see, e.g., Comment *a*, p. 157 (shooting bullet from one State into another), or commercial activity affecting state residents, ibid. Even in such situations, moreover, the Restatement recognizes that there might be circumstances that would render "unreasonable" the assertion of jurisdiction over the nonresident defendant.

The circumstances in this case clearly render "unreasonable" California's assertion of personal jurisdiction. There is no claim that appellant has visited physical injury on either property or persons within the State of California. . . . The cause of action herein asserted arises, not from the defendant's commercial transactions in interstate commerce, but rather from his personal, domestic relations. . . . Furthermore, the controversy between the parties arises from a separation that occurred in the State of New York; appellee Horn seeks modification of a contract that was negotiated in New York and that she flew to New York to sign. As in Hanson v. Denckla, 357 U.S., at 252, 78 S.Ct., at 1239, the instant action involves an agreement that was entered into with virtually no connection with the forum state. See also n. 6, supra.

Finally, basic considerations of fairness point decisively in favor of appellant's State of domicile as the proper forum for adjudication of this case, whatever the merits of appellee's underlying claim. It is appellant who has remained in the State of the marital domicile, whereas it is appellee who has moved across the continent. Cf. May v. Anderson, 345 U.S. 528, 534–535, n. 8, 73 S.Ct. 840, 843–844, 97 L.Ed. 1221 (1953). Appellant has at all times resided in New York State, and, until the separation and appellee's move to California, his entire family resided there as well. As noted above, appellant did no more than acquiesce in the stated preference of one of his children to live with her mother in California. This single act is surely not one that a reasonable parent would expect to result in the substantial financial burden and personal strain of litigating a child-support suit in a forum 3,000 miles away, and we therefore see no basis on which it can be said that appellant could reasonably have anticipated being "haled before a [California] court" Shaffer v. Heitner, 433 U.S., at 216, 97 S.Ct., at 2586. To make jurisdiction in a case such as this turn on whether appellant bought his daughter a ticket or instead unsuccessfully sought to prevent her departure would impose an unreasonable burden on family relations, and one wholly unjustified by the "quality and nature" of appellant's activities in or relating to the State of California. International Shoe Co. v. Washington, 326 U.S., at 319, 66 S.Ct., at 159.

III

In seeking to justify the burden that would be imposed on appellant were the exercise of in personam jurisdiction in California sustained, appellee argues that California has substantial interests in protecting the welfare of its minor residents and in promoting to the fullest extent possible a healthy and supportive family environment in which the children of the State are to be raised. These interests are unquestionably important. But while the presence of the children and one parent in California arguably might favor application of California law in a lawsuit in New York, the fact that California may be the " 'center of gravity' " for choice-of-law purposes does not mean that California has personal jurisdiction over the defendant. Hanson v. Denckla, supra, 357 U.S., at 254, 78 S.Ct., at 1240. And California has not attempted to assert any particularized interest in trying such cases in its courts by, e.g., enacting a special jurisdictional statute. Cf. McGee v. International Life Ins. Co., supra, 355 U.S., at 221, 224, 78 S.Ct., at 200–201.

California's interest in ensuring the support of children resident in California without unduly disrupting the children's lives, moreover, is already being served by the State's participation in the Revised Uniform Reciprocal Enforcement of Support Act of 1968. . . .

IV

. . . But the mere act of sending a child to California to live with her mother is not a commercial act and connotes no intent to obtain or expectancy of receiving a corresponding benefit in the State that would make fair the assertion of that State's judicial jurisdiction.

Accordingly, we conclude that the appellant's motion to quash service, on the ground of lack of personal jurisdiction, was erroneously denied by California courts. The judgment of the California Supreme Court is, therefore,

Reversed.

[JUSTICE BRENNAN, JUSTICE WHITE, and JUSTICE POWELL dissenting.]

NOTES

1.   The Montana Supreme Court held that the Kulko decision barred assertion of jurisdiction over a father (resident of California) in an action that sought an increase in child support, even though the father had helped the children move to Montana. Heinle v. Fourth Judicial Dist. Ct. In & For Cnty. of Missoula, 861 P.2d 171 (Mont.1993). See also Jaworowski v. Kube, 648 A.2d 261 (N.J.App.1994) (Arizona had jurisdiction over New Jersey resident in support case who lived in Arizona when the child was born and support obligation arose, was a resident there after the child was born, and received unemployment benefits in Arizona); Cardneaux v. Cardneaux, 967 P.2d 410 (Mont.1998) (father became subject to Montana jurisdiction through consent when he and his ex-wife filed a stipulation modifying a Louisiana support agreement in Montana district court, over his objection that he did not consent to jurisdiction).

2. In the European Union, the Regulation (EC) 44/2001 provides for jurisdiction "in matters relating to maintenance, in the courts for the place where the maintenance creditor is domiciled or habitually resident." As of June 18, 2011, this provision was replaced by the more far-reaching provisions of Council Regulation (EC) No. 4/2009, reproduced in the Documentary Appendix.

Yarborough v. Yarborough
Supreme Court of the United States, 1933.
290 U.S. 202, 54 S.Ct. 181, 78 L.Ed.269, 90 A.L.R. 924.

[The case appears at p. 345, supra.]

Barber v. Barber
Supreme Court of the United States, 1944.
323 U.S. 77, 65 S.Ct. 137, 89 L.Ed. 82.

[The case appears at p. 376, supra.]

Worthley v. Worthley
Supreme Court of California, 1955
44 Cal.2d 465, 283 P.2d 19

[The case appears at p. 377, supra.]

Estin v. Estin
Supreme Court of the United States, 1948.
334 U.S. 541, 68 S.Ct. 1213, 92 L.Ed.1561, 1 A.L.R.2d 1412.

[The case appears at p. 959, supra.]

---

1. THE LAW GOVERNING SUPPORT

"[I]t is little realized how different are the duties [of support] existing in our . . . states. Some enforce a duty toward illegitimate children, others do not. Forty jurisdictions require children to support their parents, the others do not. A dozen states require support between brothers and sisters, the others do not. Seventeen states require a wife to support a husband under certain circumstances, the others do not. And even in the duty of a parent to support his child the several states require this support up to different ages, varying from 14 to 21 years."

Commissioners' Prefatory Note to the Uniform Reciprocal Enforcement of Support Act (1950), 9 U.L.A. 885.

State of California v. Copus

Supreme Court of Texas, 1958.
158 Tex. 196, 309 S.W.2d 227.

[In 1936 Mrs. Copus, the mother of defendant Dale Copus, was adjudged mentally ill in California and admitted to a California state institution where she had been a patient ever since. A California statute imposed a duty on a son to pay for the support of his incompetent mother in a state hospital. On July 16, 1951, the son changed his domicile from California to Texas. On May 21, 1953, the State of California brought the present action in a Texas court against the son for the amounts accrued under the California statute during the four years preceding.

California had a four year statute of limitations for the enforcement of the obligation. Texas had a general statute of limitations setting a period of two years for such an obligation. The trial court gave a judgment for the plaintiff for the full amount sued for, $3,470, stating: "... the liability of the defendant ... is a continuing one; and the removal of the defendant ... does not discharge him from such continuing liability under the laws of the State of California, the defendant having been a resident of California at the time of the commencement of such continuing liability."]

■ CULVER, JUSTICE. . . . The general rule rather universally recognized is that the statutes of a state ex proprio vigore have no extraterritorial effect. It must be concluded, therefore, that the California statute could not create a legal obligation upon a citizen of Texas who was not a citizen of California when the obligation arose, that is, at the time the mother became institutionalized in California or at any time thereafter. We are aware of no rule of law that would make the obligation a continuing one after removal from California even though it attached to him while a resident of that state. Citizens of a state equally share the burdens and privileges of citizenship regardless of when or how that status is attained. To say that the support statute compelled liability for that period of time after the respondent moved to Texas would seem to deny to him equality with other citizens of the state. . . .

This cause of action in so far as it concerns the accruals after respondent's removal to Texas cannot be said to have arisen while respondent was under the legislative jurisdiction of California. . . . We hold, therefore, that respondent is not liable for any sums accrued after his removal to this state.

[W]e prefer to follow those decisions that would treat the [time] limitation in the California statute as substantive and not procedural. . . .

It cannot be said that the maintenance of this suit in Texas and the rendition of a judgment in California's favor for the amount accruing before the respondent became a citizen of Texas is against the public policy of this state. It is true that our Legislature has not seen fit to enact a statute to impose legal liability upon a son for the maintenance of a parent inmate in a state institution, although it does by statute obligate the husband or wife and the father or mother, if financially able, to bear the expense of maintaining a patient in a state hospital where the patient has not sufficient estate of his own. . . . And not only that, but our Probate Code, Sec. 423, requires that an incompetent person, having no estate of his own, shall be maintained by the husband or wife and by the father or mother and even by the children and grandchildren, if able to do so. . . .

This California statutory requirement of support does not run counter to good morals or natural justice or appear prejudicial in any way to the general interest of the citizens of Texas.

We, therefore, hold that the petitioner is entitled to judgment for the sum of money charged by the State of California for the support of his mother while the respondent was a citizen of that state that accrued within four years of the commencement of this suit and will be denied recovery for any sums that accrued after respondent's removal to this state.

■ GREENHILL, JUSTICE. I respectfully dissent. . . .

As I view it, the bare legal point here is: does the fact that Copus moved to Texas, standing alone, relieve him of his legal obligation to contribute thereafter to his mentally-ill mother's support? I think not. Texas should not become a haven for deserting providers who would ignore or repudiate their duty to support.

Viewed the other way, if Copus and his mother had been Texas citizens and he were obligated in Texas to contribute to her support, should he be able to shirk that responsibility by just moving out of the State?

There is no evidence before us that Copus is unable to support his mother, that other relatives should bear or share in the burden, or that she has forfeited any right to support from her son. . . .

The majority opinion correctly states that it is not against the public policy of Texas to enforce such an obligation. Our policy in that regard has been fixed in comparatively recent times by the enactment of our Uniform Support Act and the Texas Probate Code.

Section 423 of the Probate Code provides:

"Where an incompetent has no estate of his own, he shall be maintained: (a) By the husband or wife . . . if able to do so; or, if not, (b) By the father or mother . . . if able to do so; or, if not, (c) *By the children and grandchildren of such person,* respectively if able to do so; or, if not, (d) By the county. . . ."

The Legislature has thus determined that it is the policy of Texas that under the circumstances above set out, an incompetent person (such as the mother here) shall be supported by her children, if able. The mother here was incompetent. . . .

The Texas trial court found that "the liability of . . . Copus is a continuing one; and that the removal of the defendant [Copus] to Texas . . . does not discharge him from such continuing liability."

I would affirm the judgment of the trial court.

NOTE

In *Copus*, the relationship (mother-son) was not in question, but rather whether it gave rise to a continuing support obligation. In State ex rel. Simons v. Simons, 336 P.3d 557 (Or.App.2014), the support obligation was clear if the defendant was the child's father. He was married to the child's mother in Louisiana when the child was born and, under Louisiana law, was presumed to be the father and was so named in the birth certificate. Later, the parents divorced in Louisiana, she remained in Louisiana, and the father moved to Oregon, where she sought support. He defended on the ground that he was not the father and that, in any case, the divorce terminated his Louisiana presumed parentage. The Oregon court applied the Oregon statute, which provided that non-parentage could not be invoked if parentage was "previously determined by or pursuant to law." The statutory language amounted to such a determination in the court's view, although it might have also pointed to the entry on the birth certificate. His status as the child's father, once so determined, was not terminated by the divorce. Compare Elkind v. Byck, 439 P.2d 316 (Cal.1968) (p. 349, Note 2, supra). Following a divorce in Georgia, the wife and children moved to New York and the husband moved to California. In New York, the wife initiated support proceedings against the husband and the case was then transferred to a court in California for proceedings pursuant to the Uniform Reciprocal Enforcement of Support Act, which is discussed below. Held, pursuant to the Act, the husband's duty of support should be determined under California law. See, similarly, Petersen v. Petersen, 100 Cal.Rptr. 822 (Cal.App.1972): California, as the current domicile of the obligor and with jurisdiction over both parties, "can best exercise its discretion by utilizing its familiarity with living costs in California, and applying the California standard. . . ."

B. RECIPROCAL SUPPORT LEGISLATION

Originally, attempts to recover support from one who has left the state where his dependents live faced almost insuperable difficulties. Where a support judgment had been obtained against the deserter prior to his flight, it was frequently not enforced by the state of his refuge on the ground that it was modifiable in the state of rendition. In this situation two suits, as well as delay, became inevitable. First, it was necessary to wait until there had been time for installments under the support decree to accrue. Next, the claimant was forced to recover judgment for the accrued installments in the first state and then sue to enforce this judgment in the second state. In the absence of statute, the entire process would have to be repeated after still further installments had become due, unless, as in Worthley v. Worthley, p. 377, supra, the second court were willing to order the defendant to pay future installments of alimony as they accrued.

If no judgment for support had been obtained before the defendant left the state, the plight of the dependent might have been hopeless. At least in the absence of a modern long-arm statute (see p. 78, supra), presumably, no judgment could be obtained against the defendant in the first state for lack of jurisdiction or competence. An action to recover support, brought against the defendant in the state of his refuge, might involve traveling and legal expenses beyond the means of the dependent. Moreover, the action might be dismissed in the latter state on the ground that no duty of support was there recognized, except with respect to dependents who were residing within the state at the time the claim arose.

Until the Uniform Interstate Family Support Act (UIFSA) was promulgated in 1992, every state in the country, except New York, had some form of the Uniform Reciprocal Enforcement of Support Act (URESA). UIFSA has had unusual success. It is now law in all states and has replaced URESA. In 1996, a new UIFSA was promulgated that all states subsequently adopted, and in 2001 and 2008. The 2008 version is now in force in all fifty states, the District of Columbia, Puerto Rico, and the U.S. Virgin Islands.

Under UIFSA § 205, if a forum court has issued a child support order, that court has continuing, exclusive jurisdiction over the order so long as the obligor, the obligee, or the child resides in the state, or unless each party files a written consent for a court of another state to modify the order and assume jurisdiction. If a forum court has issued a spousal support order, that court has continuing, exclusive jurisdiction over the order throughout the existence of the support obligation. Under § 303, however, when a forum court is responding to a request from another state to establish a support obligation, the law of the forum "shall determine the duty of support and the amount payable in accordance with the law and support guidelines of this State." See In re Marriage of Crosby and Grooms, 10 Cal.Rptr.3d 146 (Cal.App.2004): the parties had entered into a marital settlement as part of their 1996 Idaho divorce, stipulating the application of Idaho law to their agreement. The ex-wife and the couple's minor children then moved to Oregon, and the ex-husband moved to California, where the Idaho support order was registered. Modification of support was sought in 2001 and granted by the trial court, applying the support guidelines of California law. On appeal, held: affirmed. Under California's version of UIFSA, California now had jurisdiction and application of its law was proper. As to the choice-of-law clause in the parties' agreement, the court wrote: ". . . [D]ue to the special nature of child support, parents are bound by public policy extrinsic to their own agreements. . . .[citing cases]. In the present case, since the clause requiring application of Idaho law would serve to limit [the father's] child support obligation and undermine the mandate of UIFSA, it is contrary to public policy and not enforceable. . . . Idaho has passed the UIFSA. . . . Consequently, Idaho law requires that the guidelines of the forum tribunal—here California—be used to modify the child support order. . . ." Id. at 152. What is the basis for the decision—application of California law as the result of renvoi (p. 562, supra) (i.e., because Idaho law refers to California law)? A false conflict (p. 570, supra), between Idaho and California law? Or California's public policy? Asked differently: what if Idaho had not yet enacted UIFSA?

For an application of "continuing and exclusive jurisdiction" and transfer of jurisdiction from one court to another under UIFSA, see Lombardi v. Van Deusen, 938 N.E.2d 219 (Ind.Ct.App.2010), and Hornblower v. Hornblower, 94 A.3d 1218, 1222 n.5 (Conn.App.2014) ("Georgia and Colorado have statutes that prevent . . . [them] from modifying a spousal support order issued by a court of another state that has continuing exclusive jurisdiction.") In application of *Hornblower*, a Connecticut court honored the continuing exclusive jurisdiction of the English court under the United Kingdom's Reciprocal Enforcement of Maintenance Orders (United States of America) Order 2007 and dismissed the local action for modification: Olson v. Olson, 2020 WL 1744665 (Conn.Super.Ct. Feb. 21, 2020).

Once a support obligation has been judicially established, federal law and mechanisms are now increasingly important means for enforcement. See Krause, Child Support in America 281 passim (1981). An example is Title IV-D of the Social Security Act, 42 U.S.C.A. § 651 et seq. See also the 1984 Child Support Amendments, 98 Stat. 1305.[1] 42 U.S.C.A. § 666(a)(5)(ii) (West 1994).

For comment, see Weintraub, Commentary on the Conflict of Laws § 5.2E4 (6th ed.2010); Tina M. Fielding, Note, The Uniform Interstate Family Support Act: The New URESA, 20 U.Dayton L.Rev. 425 (1994). The UIFSA extends to obligations established in foreign countries that have substantially similar procedures. Canada, for instance, is such a country. See Weintraub, Recognition and Enforcement of Judgments and Child Support Obligations in United States and Canadian Courts, 34 Texas Int'l L.J. 361 (1999); Elrod, Child Support Reassessed: Federalization of Enforcement Nears Completion, 1997 U.Ill.L.Rev. 695.

The Full Faith and Credit for Child Support Orders Act of 1994 (PL 103–383, 108 Stat. 4063, 28 U.S.C. § 1738B) is designed to counteract the possibility that the usual recognition mechanism may frustrate full

---

[1] The Uniform Civil Liability for Support Act was approved in 1954 by the National Conference of Commissioners on Uniform State Laws. It is designed to make the substantive law of support uniform among the states and to make readily ascertainable who owes support duties to whom under the law of a particular state and what factors should be considered in determining the level of support owed. The act has been adopted only by three states: Maine, New Hampshire, and Utah.

enforcement of a child support order of a sister state. In this Act, Congress exercised its powers under the "effect" provision of the Full Faith and Credit Clause (p. 45, supra) to require more credit for sister-state child support orders than the Constitutional Clause itself would require. Under § 1738B, a child support order made consistently with the Act must be "enforced according to its terms" by sister states, and sister states may not modify the order unless (1) the court that issued the order no longer is the residence of the child or of any contestants, or (2) each contestant files a written consent to the modification. A support order is made consistently with the Act if the court, under the laws of its state, has subject matter jurisdiction to enter the order and personal jurisdiction over the contestants. The federal Act does not preempt the UIFSA, but provides for enforcement of orders made in conformity with the UIFSA. Jackson v. Holiness, 961 N.E.2d 48 (Ind.App.2012). In interpreting a child support order, a court must apply the law of the state of the court that issued the order. In Hamilton v. Hamilton, 914 N.E.2d 747 (Ind.2009), the trial court had suspended the defendant's obligation under a Florida decree to pay child support of $1,473 per month, so long as he paid $1,000 per month, sought gainful employment, and executed a wage assignment. Held: affirmed. The reduction in monthly payments did not constitute a modification, violating the recognition obligation, but rather related to the manner of enforcement of the obligation established by the Florida decree. Do you agree with the court's distinction between (impermissible) modification and (permissible) enforcement of the obligation in reduced amount? See also Matter of Cleopatra Cameron Gift Trust, Dated May 26, 1998, 931 N.W.2d 244 (S.D.2019) : California order requiring direct payment of child support from beneficiary's trust is an enforcement measure and, as such, is not entitled to full faith and credit. Why not, for instance if the beneficiary (who is the support debtor) has no other means? Because the trustee may not be bound? See Baker v. General Motors Corp., p. 333, supra ("enforcement measures do not travel") and Riley v. New York Trust Co., p. 303, supra.

Time limitations are governed by either the law of the state that issued the order or the law of the forum, whichever provides the longer period of limitation. See, e.g., Martin v. Phillips, 347 P.3d 1033 (Kan.App.2015); In re Marriage of Edelman and Preston, 38 N.E.3d 50 (Ill.App.2015) (shorter period applies under law of issuing state).

NOTES

1. Reciprocal support legislation involves planned and directed cooperation between courts of different states of the Union in hearing and deciding a single controversy and in enforcing the judgment. Are there areas other than support in which such cooperation is needed, and in which it should be established, either through legislation or on the initiative of the courts? What are these areas? How should the cooperation be carried out?

2. Reciprocal support legislation has survived many constitutional attacks. Among the claims of invalidity that have been urged are those asserting that this legislation confers "extraterritorial jurisdiction" on the initiating court, and that it denies defendant the opportunity to confront and cross-examine the petitioner and his or her witnesses. The former objection has been overruled on the ground that jurisdiction over the respondent is acquired by the responding court by operation of its own statute rather than by that of the initiating state. See Duncan v. Smith, 262 S.W.2d 373 (Ky.1953). With respect to the latter objection, cross-examination by deposition has been held sufficient. Reciprocal support legislation also does not violate the Compact Clause of the Constitution, Fraser v. Fraser, 415 A.2d 1304 (R.I.1980).

3. Two international conventions, the United Nations Convention on the Recovery Abroad of Maintenance and the Hague Convention on the Recognition and Enforcement of Decisions Relating to Maintenance Obligations, are in force among a number of countries. However, neither convention has been adopted by the United States. Instead, some states of the Union and a number of foreign countries have worked out bilateral arrangements which are based on the "reciprocal" provision of the 1968 version of the Uniform Reciprocal Enforcement of Support Act. For a list of these arrangements see Hay, Borchers, Symeonides, Whytock, Conflict of Laws, §§ 15.37–15.38 (6th ed.2018). See also Dehart, Comity, Conventions and the Constitution: State and Federal Initiatives in International Support Enforcement. 28 Fam.L.Q. 89 (1994); Cavers, International Enforcement of Family Support, 81 Colum.L.Rev. 994 (1981).

Under the Hague Maintenance Convention, the law of the obligee's habitual residence applies to the support obligation. If that law does not provide for a support obligation, the law of the common nationality of the parties applies. When the claimant is related to the obligor only laterally or by marriage, the obligor may defend on the ground that the law of the parties' common nationality or of the obligor's habitual residence does not impose an obligation. These rules apply regardless of whether the state to which they refer is also a contracting state. Some countries, e.g., Germany, incorporated these rules directly into their national conflicts statute. See Art. 18 German Introductory Law to the Civil Code (EGBGB). Compare these rules with § 7 of URESA (now superseded) (support obligation determined by the law of the state where the obligor resided during the time for which support is claimed), the Uniform Act, and the decision in Copus, p. 1008, supra. What speaks for and against § 7 of URESA? For and against the Hague Convention? Would the Convention be constitutional in the United States? See also Note 2, supra. Note that the German provision has now been replaced by EU law: Note 4, supra.

On November 23, 2007, the Hague Conference on Private International Law adopted a Convention on the International Recovery of Child Support and other Forms of Family Maintenance. The Convention covers "maintenance obligations arising from a parent-child relationship towards a person under the age of 21" (art. 2(1)(a)) and "with the exception of Chapters II and III, to spousal support" (art. 2(1)(c)). Chapter II requires contracting states to designate a Central Authority to discharge Convention duties. Chapter III routes applications for enforcement and establishment of child maintenance obligations through the Central Authority. Chapter V provides that decisions made in one contracting state regarding child and spousal support shall be recognized and enforced in other contracting states. The Convention entered into force for the United States on Jan.1, 2017, subject to a number of reservations concerning the jurisdiction of the court issuing the award.

4. For the new EU Regulation on Maintenance Obligations (Council Regulation (EC) No. 4/2009) and its relation to the Protocol of the 2007 Hague Convention, supra, see the Documentary Appendix.

5. See Sanson v. Sanson, 466 N.E.2d 770 (Ind.App.1984) (judgment for alimony payable in installments, entered in German divorce proceeding, was enforceable in Indiana); Herczog v. Herczog, 9 Cal.Rptr. 5 (Cal.Ct.App.1960) (English decree entitled to recognition in California); Olson v. Olson, p. 1012, supra; Dart v. Dart, 568 N.W.2d 353 (Mich.App.1997), aff'd, 597 N.W.2d 82 (Mich.1999), cert. denied, 529 U.S. 1018 (2000) (English divorce judgment obtained by husband awarding lump sum, child support, and property to wife was enforceable against wife in Michigan).

SECTION 9. MARITAL PROPERTY*

INTRODUCTORY NOTE

"Marital property" may be defined as the interests which one spouse acquires, solely by reason of the marital relation, in the property, whether movable or immovable, of the other spouse, apart from the bare expectancy of inheriting upon the death of the other intestate. Two marital property systems are in effect in the United States. The common law system prevails in more than forty states and the District of Columbia, while community property is to be found in Arizona, California, Idaho, Louisiana, Nevada, New Mexico, Texas, Washington, and Wisconsin. There have been many drastic statutory modifications, and marked divergencies are to be found between states having the same general system.

There is no need to discuss these two systems in detail or to describe the form they originally took. They protect a spouse's economic interests in different ways. In common law states, a spouse is entitled to a fraction of all the property owned by the other spouse at the time of death. This interest is contingent upon surviving the other, but cannot be affected by any testamentary disposition the other spouse makes. Under community property systems, a spouse has a one-half interest in that part of the other's property which falls into the community. This is a present and vested interest which is not dependent upon surviving the other. Upon the dissolution of the marriage by death or divorce, the community property is divided equally among the spouses or their estates. Some property, however, does not fall into the community. A spouse retains full ownership to (and the

---

* Restatement, Second, Conflict of Laws §§ 233–234, 257–259.

other spouse has no marital interest in) property which belonged to him or her at the time of marriage, or which he or she acquires thereafter by gift, will, or descent. All other acquisitions after marriage belong to the community, with the exception (in some states) of income derived from a spouse's separate property.

Marital property is a fertile field for conflict-of-laws problems in this country. This is not only because of the differences between common law and community property systems but because of frequent divergencies in the laws of states belonging to the same general system.

NOTES

1.   Property is usually classified as a spouse's separate property or as the spouses' community property on the basis of the law of domicile at the time of its acquisition. The "domicile" will usually be the spouses' (common) marital domicile, although the rule may be stated in terms of the domicile of the acquiring spouse, as it is in Louisiana. What if the spouses separate, one of them moves into a community property state, while the other remains in a common law state or moves from such a state into another common law state: will property acquired by the first spouse after the move be community property? In Hand v. Hand, 834 So.2d 619 (La.App.2002), the court said "no." Without domicile of both spouses in the state at some time in their marriage, no community was created. The property acquired by the in-state party therefore did not fall into a community. What if the parties had married in Louisiana, had subsequently lived in a common law state, and one of them, as in *Hand*, had later returned to Louisiana and acquired property there; would that property be community property? In Louisiana's view? See Bertrand, What's Mine Is Mine Is Mine: The Inequitable Intersection of Louisiana's Choice-of-Law Provisions and the Movables of Migratory Spouses, 79 Tul.L.Rev. 493 (2004); Tooley-Knoblett, A Step by Step Guide to Louisiana's Choice of Law Provisions on Marital Property, 52 Loy.L.Rev. 759 (2006). In the view of courts of another state? See supra, this Note. What about property earned by either one of them while both, or the acquiring party, lived in a common law state? See Kingma, Property Division at Divorce or Death for Married Couples Migrating Between Common Law and Community Property States, 35 ACTEC J. 74 (2009). In De Nicols v. Curlier, [1900] A.C. 21, the House of Lords treated a marriage in France between French citizens as creating by tacit contract an agreement that French community property law was to govern acquisition of personal property in England after the parties had become domiciled there. In De Nicols v. Curlier, [1900] 2 Ch. 410, the same rule was applied to real property acquired in England. The rule of the Curlier cases is not followed in the United States. Saul v. His Creditors, 5 Mart. (N.S.) 569 (La.1827).

2.   Spouses-to-be may wish to provide by contract for ownership rights in property, for modification or elimination of spousal support rights, for the making of wills, and for the law applicable to their agreement. See Uniform Premarital Agreement Act (1983 Act), 9C U.L.A. 35, 39 (2001), as of 2021, in force in 26 states and the District of Columbia. For discussion, see Brashier, Disinheritance and the Modern Family, 45 Case W.Res.L.Rev. 83 (1995). See

also Henderson, Marital Agreements and the Rights of Creditors, 19 Idaho L.Rev. 177 (1983); Belcher & Pomeroy, A Practitioner's Guide for Negotiating, Drafting and Enforcing Premarital Agreements, 37 Real Prop.Prob. & Tr.J. 1 (2002). In 2012, The Uniform Law Commission completed the Uniform Premarital and Marital Agreements Act. As of 2021, it is in force in only Colorado and North Dakota.

In Holston v. Holston, 128 So.3d 736 (Ala.Civ.App.2013), an Alabama court upheld an antenuptial agreement's choice of Mississippi law. Beyond the validity of a premarital agreement's choice of law, the validity of the agreement itself may be at issue. For decisions upholding prenuptial agreements, valid where contracted, against challenges elsewhere, see Van Kipnis v. Van Kipnis, 900 N.E.2d 977 (N.Y.2008) (upholding French prenuptial agreement). See also Muchmore v. Trask, 666 S.E.2d 667 (N.C.App.2008) (enforcing California prenuptial agreement); Bradshaw v. Bradshaw, 826 S.E.2d 779 (N.C.App.2019) (Virginia prenuptial property settlement barred wife's claim for equitable distribution). In both *Muchemore* and *Bradshaw*, the North Carolina court followed the Restatement First approach: rights and obligations are fixed by the law of the sovereign where the agreement was concluded, except if in violation of the forum's public policy. On the enforceability of a postnuptial agreement, see Hussemann ex rel. Ritter v. Hussemann, 847 N.W.2d 219 (Iowa 2014).

Rozan v. Rozan

Supreme Court of California, 1957.
49 Cal.2d 322, 317 P.2d 11.

■ TRAYNOR, JUSTICE. Plaintiff brought this action against her husband, Maxwell M. Rozan, for divorce, support, custody of their minor child, and division of their community property....

The trial court granted plaintiff an interlocutory judgment of divorce on the ground of extreme cruelty, awarded her the custody of the minor child, ordered defendant to pay $75 per month for child support, $250 per month for plaintiff's support, and $12,500 for attorney's fees. The court adjudged that the parties became domiciled in California ... in any event not later than July 1948 and that the property thereafter acquired was community property....

Although defendant "does not challenge the lower Court for granting the divorce" ... he contends ... that certain oil properties outside of California adjudged to be community property were his separate property....

The first finding essential to the division of the property is that plaintiff and defendant "established their residence and domicile in California ... in any event not later than July, 1948" and "that ever since they have been and still are residents of and domiciled in the State of California." A determination of the domicile is essential, for marital interests in movables acquired during coverture are governed by the law of the domicile at the time of their acquisition.... Moreover, the interests of the spouses in movables do not change even though the movables are taken into another state or are used to purchase land in another state. . . .

. . . The . . . evidence amply supports the trial court's finding of domicile not later than July, 1948. . . .

The last finding on which the division of property depends is that the North Dakota properties "were acquired with community property and community property money." It is undisputed that these properties were acquired after 1949. . . . It . . . appears that the purchase money for the North Dakota properties was acquired by the efforts and skill of defendant as an oil operator subsequent to the establishment of the California domicile and was therefore community property. . . . Moreover there is a presumption that in the absence of evidence of gift, bequest, devise or descent, all property acquired by the husband after marriage is community property. . . . There is no evidence that the purchase money was acquired by gift, bequest, devise, or descent. There is, therefore, substantial evidence to sustain the trial court's finding that the North Dakota properties were purchased with community property funds. . . .

After acquiring the real property in North Dakota, defendant divested himself of title thereto by means of various conveyances, and title was eventually put in the name of Eugene Rosen, defendant's nephew, either individually or as trustee of a purported trust for the minor child. . . . there is abundant evidence to support the trial court's findings that these transactions were fraudulent as to plaintiff.

Defendant contends finally that the judgment directly affects the title to land in another state and therefore exceeded the court's jurisdiction. A court of one state cannot directly affect or determine the title to land in another. Fall v. Eastin, 215 U.S. 1 . . . It is well settled, however, that a court, with the parties before it, can compel the execution of a conveyance in the form required by the law of the situs and that such a conveyance will be recognized there. . . . Currie, Full Faith and Credit to Foreign Land Decrees, 21 U. of Chi.L.Rev. 620, 628–629. If the court has entered a decree of specific performance, but the conveyance has not been executed, the majority of states, including California, will give effect to the decree. . . . Thus in Redwood Investment Co. of Stithton, Ky. v. Exley, 64 Cal.App. 455, 459, 221 P. 973, 975, the court stated with reference to a Kentucky decree of specific performance to land in California: "It may be pleaded as a basis or cause of action or defense in the courts of the state where the land is situated, and is entitled in such a court to the force and effect of record evidence of the equities therein determined, unless it be impeached for fraud." There is no sound reason for denying a decree of a court of equity the same full faith and credit accorded any other kind of judgment. "Without exception, the courts recognize the validity of a deed executed under the compulsion of a foreign decree. But if the decree did not deal rightfully and constitutionally with the title to the land it would be voidable for duress. Recognition of the deed necessarily involves acceptance of the decree.

Whatever intrusion on the state's exclusive control is implied in the recognition of the decree is accomplished through the recognition of the deed. A policy so easily evaded, so dependent on the success of the defendant in eluding the enforcement process of the foreign court, is a formal, lifeless thing, and the truth must be that foreign judicial proceedings of this type pose no real threat to the legitimate interest of the situs state." (Currie, supra, 21 U. of Chi.L.Rev. 620, 628–629.) Thus in the majority of states, such decrees are given effect as a res judicata declaration of the rights and equities of the parties. . . . Fall v. Eastin, 215 U.S. 1, on which defendant relies did not hold otherwise. In that case the Washington decree directly affected title to land in Nebraska. A commissioner of the Washington court had executed a deed to that land and Mrs. Fall attempted to use this deed as a muniment of title in her action to quiet title against a grantee of the husband.

In the light of the foregoing principles the judgment in the present case is res judicata and entitled to full faith and credit in North Dakota to the extent that it determines the rights and equities of the parties with respect to the land in question. An action on that judgment in North Dakota, however, is necessary to effect any change in the title to the land there. Thus, the judgment must be affirmed to the extent that it declares the rights of the parties before the court and modified to the extent that it purports to affect the title to the land.

Neither Eugene Rosen, who holds record title, nor the minor child, who is the beneficiary of the purported trust, were parties to this action and the judgment is therefore not binding on them. . . .

In several respects the judgment purports to affect title to the land and must therefore be modified. Thus, paragraph . . . 21 . . . awards 65 per cent of the North Dakota properties and the past, present, and future rents, issues and profits therefrom to plaintiff as her sole and separate property and awards 35 per cent thereof to Rozan subject to a lien for alimony, child support, and attorney's fees. This paragraph . . . is therefore modified to read as follows: "21. It Is Further Ordered and Adjudged, that each and every one of the aforementioned North Dakota properties . . . were acquired with community property funds of plaintiff and Rozan; . . . that plaintiff is entitled to 65% of the aforementioned properties and of the rents, issues and profits thereof as against Rozan; that Rozan is entitled to 35% of the aforementioned properties and of the rents, issues and profits thereof as against plaintiff' . . .

The judgment is affirmed as modified. Defendant shall bear the costs on appeal.

NOTES

1. Following the decision in the principal case, the wife instituted an action in North Dakota to enforce the California decree. The North Dakota court awarded the wife judgment for the sums accrued under the California decree.

It also gave res judicata effect to the California finding that the North Dakota real property was purchased with community funds and accordingly held that the wife was entitled to a one-half interest in this property. On the other hand, the court held that it would not recognize the California decree insofar as it purported to award the wife a 65% interest in this property. This was because the decree (a) did not order the husband to convey such an interest to his wife, and (b) did not have to be recognized under full faith and credit because it directly affected title to North Dakota real property. Rozan v. Rozan, 129 N.W.2d 694 (N.D.1964). See also Fall v. Eastin, p. 328, supra. For arguments that, in certain circumstances, the law of the marital domicile rather than the law of the situs should apply to disposition of real property at divorce, see Singer, Property Law Conflicts, 54 Washburn L.J. 129 (2014); Symeonides, The Choice-of-Law Revolution Fifty Years After Currie: An End and a Beginning, 2015 U.Ill.L.Rev. 1847, 1915 (2015); Roberts v. Locke, 304 P.3d 116 (Wyo.2013) (domestic court ordered sale of foreign marital property incident to divorce action; wife held in contempt for impeding such sale).

2. Estate of Warner, 140 P. 583 (Cal.1914). H and W made their home in Illinois, a common law state. During the marriage, H sent from Illinois certain funds which were used to purchase land in California. After H's death, W renounced her rights under H's will and claimed a community property interest in the California land. W's claim was, however, rejected by the California courts on the ground that "it is well settled that separate personal property, enjoyed under the law of the domicile by one of the spouses at the time it was acquired is not lost by its investment in real property in another jurisdiction where a different law is in force." In states that have adopted the quasi-community concept (p. 1037, Note 6 infra), the result may be otherwise if the spouses had changed their domicile from the common law to the community property state prior to the death of one spouse or to the dissolution of the marriage. See Addison v. Addison, p. 1032, infra.

3. For a discussion of the converse situation, where persons move from a community property state to a common law property state, see Lay, Community Property in Common Law States: A Comparative Analysis of its Treatment in Foreign Jurisdictions, 41 Temp.L.Q. 1 (1967); Leflar, From Community to Common Law State; Estate Problems of Citizens Moving from One to Other, 99 Trusts & Estates 882 (1960).

4. Depas v. Mayo, 11 Mo. 314 (1848). While domiciled in Louisiana, a community property state, H and W accumulated considerable assets. They then moved to Missouri, where H used part of the assets accumulated in Louisiana to purchase, in his own name, a lot in the city of St. Louis. Thereafter the parties resumed their Louisiana domicile and ultimately were divorced. Action was brought by W for determination that she was entitled to a one-half interest in the St. Louis property. Held for the wife. Missouri law must decide "all questions" concerning title to the land in St. Louis. "[A]ccording to the law in this state, if A purchases land with the money of B, and takes legal title to himself, a court of equity will regard him as a trustee. . . ." H purchased the land with assets in which his wife had a one-half interest. She is therefore entitled to one-half interest in the land. It makes no difference that prior to the purchase the parties had changed their domicile to Missouri.

Compare Savelle v. Savelle, 650 So.2d 476 (Miss.1995). The spouses lived in Louisiana for thirty years. They moved to Mississippi after the husband retired. Two years after the move, they were granted a divorce. Under Louisiana law, the wife would be entitled to fifty percent of the husband's retirement benefits, but under Mississippi law she was entitled only to an equitable distribution. In a 6:3 decision, the court applied Mississippi law and granted the wife a lump sum that was smaller than the amount she would have received under Louisiana law. Similarly, in Zeolla v. Zeolla, 908 A.2d 629, 631 (Me.2006), the court held that the trial court has broad discretion "to equitably divide all the marital and nonmarital property, wherever that property is located." In contrast, in Mbatha v. Cutting, 848 S.E.2d 920 (Ga.App.2020), the court declined to depart from the traditional rule (Note 5, infra) that the classification and distribution of real property upon divorce is determined by the law of its situs and that of personal property by the parties' domicile at the time of acquisition. It rejected the petitioner's argument that the parties' property should be equitably distributed under Georgia law.

5.   Restatement, Second, of Conflict of Laws § 258 cmt. c. "When the spouses have separate domiciles at the time of the acquisition of the movable, the local law of the state where the spouse who acquired the movable was domiciled at the time will usually be applied, in the absence of an effective choice of law by the parties, to determine the extent of the other spouse's marital interest therein." See also Litner, Marital Property Rights and Conflict of Laws When Spouses Reside in Different States, 11 Comm.Prop.J. 283 (1984).

6.   Restatement, Second, of Conflict of Laws § 166 cmt. b. "[At times] one spouse is injured either through the negligence of the other spouse or through the joint negligence of the other spouse and of a third person. Then, if the injured spouse brings suit against the employer or insurer of the other spouse or against the third person, he may be met with the argument that relief should be denied because the negligent spouse would share in any recovery that might be obtained. It might be thought that the law [selected to determine related issues of tort law] should be applied to determine whether the negligence of one person should be imputed to another if the negligent person would share in any recovery that the other might obtain. On the other hand, it might be thought that the local law of the state of the spouses' domicile should be applied to determine whether any recovery would be community property and thus would be shared by the negligent spouse. . . . In the majority of the few cases in point, the plaintiff spouse has been permitted to recover." See also Marsh, Marital Property in Conflict of Laws 193–94 (1952); Oldham, Conflict of Laws and Marital Property Rights, 39 Baylor L.Rev. 1255 (1987).

7.   In recent years, community property interests have been recognized in intangible assets such as pension rights and other contractual interests. To what extent should the value of a professional degree earned by a spouse during marriage be considered? See Boyer, Note, Equitable Interest in

Enhanced Earning Capacity: The Treatment of a Professional Degree at Dissolution, 60 Wash.L.Rev. 431 (1985). See also Shaheen v. Khan, 142 So.3d 257 (La.App.2014) (in divorce proceedings, husband could not recover amounts paid for wife's tuition during marriage because, at his request, she did not work, so he thus had no expectation of a shared benefit from said expenditure).

On pension rights, see also Robinson v. Robinson, 778 So.2d 1105 (La.2001). A wife's waiver of Louisiana pension rights was not recognized by Louisiana because the chosen law (North Carolina) did not have a sufficient "link" to the parties. As has been pointed out (Symeonides, Choice-of-Law in the American Courts in 2001, 50 Am.J.Comp.L. 1, 31–33 (2002)), the court could have reached the same result by treating Louisiana law as "mandatory law" (in European conflicts tradition, as sanctioned by the Louisiana conflicts statute) and therefore applicable regardless of any choice-of-law clause.

8.   Choice-of-law problems also occur in the area of community debts. In one case, a couple lived in New Mexico, a community property state. The husband signed a loan note with an Ohio bank. His wife was not a party to the transaction. He defaulted on the note. The bank sued him in Ohio state court and obtained a default judgment. The bank then domesticated the Ohio judgment in New Mexico and sought to foreclose on the marital residence there. The wife argued that the loan agreement contained a choice-of-law clause in favor of Ohio law, under which her husband's loan was not a community debt, so the bank could not foreclose on her half of the marital residence to satisfy the judgment. Rejecting this argument, the New Mexico court applied New Mexico law, as the choice-of-law clause in the note no longer applied: the note had merged in the judgment, which, once domesticated, ceased to exist as an Ohio judgment. It became a New Mexico judgment, enforceable under the laws of New Mexico. The husband's loan did not comply with New Mexico statutory requirements necessary to overcome the presumption that a debt created during marriage is a community debt, so the Bank was allowed to seek enforcement against property of the community. Huntington Nat'l Bk. v. Sproul, 861 P.2d 935 (N.M.1993). See also Am. Nat'l Bank v. Medved, 801 N.W.2d 230 (Neb.2011) (similar facts, involving Nebraska and Arizona law). See also Nationstar Mortgage LLC v. O'Malley, 415 P.3d 1022, 1028 (N.M.Ct.App.2018). For the opposite outcome under a common law property regime, see In re Estate of Greb, 848 N.W.2d 611, 622 (Neb.2014) (wife not jointly and severally liable for husband's debt because she never signed an obligation or guarantee).

9.   In a number of states that have traditionally adhered to the common law spousal property system, "equitable distribution" of assets now takes the place of alimony obligations to be paid out of "separate" assets. In some respects, the "equitable distribution" concept resembles the community property system. The conflict-of-laws problems identified above—when spouses move from one state to another, or live in one state while acquiring assets in another, or live and acquire assets separately and in different states—also arise when an "equitable division" state is involved.

A court also has subject matter jurisdiction to divide property acquired by the parties whose out-of-state "marriage" was void under forum law, because it was bigamous. Marriage of Thomas v. Smith, 794 N.E.2d 500 (Ind.App.2003).

10. In some instances, federal law preempts state marital property law. One example is protecting annuitants under the amendments to the Employee Retirement Income Security Act (ERISA), 29 U.S.C.A. § 1001 et seq. by the Retirement Equity Act of 1984, Pub.L.No. 98–397 (1984) (spouses to be provided for in qualified retirement plans). In other instances, state law controls. See, e.g., Uniformed Services Former Spouses' Protection Act, 10 U.S.C.A. § 1408(c)(1) (states may treat military pensions either as separate or as community property under state law; the act overturned McCarty v. McCarty, 453 U.S. 210 (1981), holding that federal law preempted state law). See Reppy, Conflict of Laws Problems in the Division of Marital Property, 1 Valuation and Distribution of Marital Property § 10.03 (1985). See also Polacheck, The "Un-Worth-y" Decision: The Characterization of a Copyright as Community Property, 17 Hastings Comm. & Ent.L.J. 601 (1995).

11. Dawson-Austin v. Austin, 968 S.W.2d 319 (Tex.1998), cert. denied, 525 U.S. 1067 (1999). A couple, with assets consisting principally of the lone stock certificate of a corporation founded by the husband, was domiciled in Minnesota and owned another house in California. After separation, the wife left to live in the California house and filed for divorce in that State. The husband left for Texas, taking the stock certificate, opening bank accounts, and acquiring a residence. He filed for divorce in Texas, as well as for a determination of their respective interests in the property. Held, the Texas courts had jurisdiction to divorce, but not to determine the wife's interest in the property, as there was no basis for in personam jurisdiction over her. The holding in Shaffer v. Heitner, p. 173, supra, requires a showing that the wife had minimum contacts with Texas, which were lacking. The court stated:

> "We do not believe that one spouse may leave the other, move to another state in which neither has ever lived, buy a home or open a bank account or store a stock certificate there, and by those unilateral actions, and nothing more, compel the other spouse to litigate their divorce in the new domicile consistent with due process." Id. at 327.

Accord: Mason v. Mason, 321 S.W.3d 178 (Tex.App.2010).

Wyatt v. Fulrath
Court of Appeals of New York, 1965.
16 N.Y.2d 169, 264 N.Y.S.2d 233, 211 N.E.2d 637.

■ BERGAN, JUDGE. The Duke and Duchess of Arion were nationals and domiciliaries of Spain. Neither of them had ever been in New York, but through a long period of political uncertainty in Spain, from 1919 to the end of the [Spanish] Civil War, they sent cash and securities to New York for safekeeping and investment.

Under the law of Spain this was the community property of the spouses. Substantial parts of it were placed with the New York custodians in joint accounts. In establishing or in continuing these accounts, the husband and wife either expressly agreed in writing that the New York law of survivorship would apply or agreed to a written form of survivorship account conformable to New York law.

The husband died in November, 1957; the wife in March, 1959. After the husband's death the wife took control of the property in New York and undertook to dispose of it by a will executed according to New York law and affecting property in New York. . . . Some additional property in joint account in England was transferred by the wife to New York after the husband's death which had not been placed by either spouse in New York during the husband's life.

This action is by plaintiff as an ancillary administrator in New York of the husband against defendant as executor of the wife's will to establish a claim of title to one half of the property which at the time of the husband's death was held in custody accounts under sole or joint names of the spouses by banks in New York and London.

The total value of the property in New York is about $2,275,000, of which about $370,000 was transferred by the wife after the husband's death from the London accounts to New York. . . .

The main issue in the case is whether the law of Spain should be applied to the property placed in New York during the lives of the spouses, in which event only half of the property would have gone to the wife at her husband's death, or the law of New York, in which event all of such jointly held property would have gone to her as survivor. . . .

The controversy here is . . . to be governed by the legal capacity of the husband and wife, as citizens and domiciliaries of Spain, to make an agreement as to their community property inconsistent with Spanish law.

The agreements giving full title to the survivor in the joint accounts were executed either in Spain, or if not there at least not in New York, and were, in any event, executed by persons who were domiciliaries and citizens of Spain. Usually rights flowing from this kind of legal act are governed by the law of the domiciliary jurisdiction. . . .

Dispositions of property in violation of this prohibition are shown to be void according to Spanish law. . . .

But New York has the right to say as a matter of public policy whether it will apply its own rules to property in New York of foreigners who choose to place it here for custody or investment, and to honor or not the formal agreements or suggestions of such owners by which New York law would apply to the property they place here. (Cf. Decedent Estate Law, § 47; Personal Property Law, Consol.Laws, c. 41, § 12–a).

It seems preferable that as to property which foreign owners are able to get here physically, and concerning which they request New York law to apply to their respective rights, when it actually gets here, that we should recognize their physical and legal submission of the property to our laws, even though under the laws of their own country a different method of fixing such rights would be pursued.

Thus we would at once honor their intentional resort to the protection of our laws and their recognition of the general stability of our Government which may well be deemed inter-related things. . . .

The Special Term in the case before us found for the defendant. . . . We agree that this disposition is the correct one as to property placed in New York during the husband's lifetime.

This effect would include, too, those accounts which had formerly been joint accounts but which during the lifetime of the husband were transferred to the wife's sole name. . . .

The assent of the husband to arrangements in respect of joint property transferred to the sole account of the wife with the legal consequence of sole ownership to be anticipated from the effect of New York law would lead us to treat the property as the property of the wife and to be controlled by the same principle applicable to joint accounts. . . .

We would treat the wife's own separate property similarly where, during the lifetime of her husband and apparently with his recognition and assent, she was able to transfer the separate property to New York and keep it here in her own name.

But the property in the value of about $370,000 transferred from London to New York by the wife after the husband's death raises a somewhat different question. Adjudication of its title requires further factual exploration. At the time of the husband's death this property and other property were held in three-name custody accounts by London depositories. The accounts were in the names of the husband, the wife and their daughter Hilda, who had no proprietary interest. . . .

The reasons grounded on New York policy and affected by the physical transfer of the property to New York during the lifetime of the spouses and by their directions relating to it do not necessarily apply to property of Spanish nationals placed in a third country during their lifetime.

If the local law of the third country would deem title to have passed to the wife on the death of the husband, we would treat this property as we now treat that placed in New York during their lives.

But if the third country would have applied the Spanish community property law or, if it is not demonstrated what rule would be applied by the third country and the subject is open or equivocal, we would, under general principles, feel bound to apply the law of Spain to the title of property owned by these Spanish nationals.

The order should be modified to direct the remission to Special Term to determine the rights of parties in respect of the property transferred by the wife from London to New York after the husband's death in accordance with this opinion and, as modified, affirmed, without costs.

■ DESMOND, CHIEF JUDGE (dissenting). Resolution of the dispute as to this property (or any part of it) by any law other than that of Spain, the matrimonial domicile, is utterly incompatible with historic and settled conflict of laws principles and is not justifiable on any ground. No policy ground exists for upsetting the uniform rules and no precedent commands such a result. . . .

The majority of this court is throwing overboard not one but three of the oldest and strongest conflict rules: first, that with exceptions not pertinent here the law of the domicile of the owner governs as to the devolution of personal property . . . ; second, that the law of the matrimonial domicile controls as to the property and contract rights of husband and wife *inter sese* . . . ; and, third, that whether such personalty is separate or community property is determined by the law of the matrimonial domicile. . . .

. . . The Duke and Duchess of Arion were Spanish nationals, were married in Spain and always had their domicile there as had their ancestors for generations or centuries. Neither was ever in New York. New York State's only contact with this property was that for purposes of convenience or safety the husband and wife left valuable property in the custody of New York banks for safekeeping only. The banks were mere bailees without other title or interest. To say that setting up of joint accounts of personalty in New York subjected that personalty to New York law rather than to the law of the matrimonial domicile is to refuse to follow one of the most basic of Conflict of Laws rules. . . .

. . . The signing by the Duke and Duchess in Spain of routine joint-account-for-custody agreements on forms supplied by the New York banks is not substantial proof that these people (who had no apparent reason for so doing) were attempting to abrogate as to these items of property the ancient community laws of their country. There is no other proof of such an intent to substitute New York law and a much more reasonable explanation of the documents exacted by the banks is that they operated and were intended merely to release the banks on payment to one spouse or the other. . . .

———

MATTER OF CRICHTON, 228 N.E.2d 799 (N.Y.1967): [Crichton died domiciled in New York, where he had moved early in life, owning movables in Louisiana. His will made no provision for his wife, from whom he had been separated for twenty-seven years, and the question was whether she had a community property interest in the Louisiana movables or whether her rights were limited to a forced share under New York law. A Louisiana statute provided that all property acquired in the state by a nonresident should be treated as community property. It was held that the wife's rights in the Louisiana movables were limited to a forced share under New York law. Speaking for the court, Judge Keating wrote: . . .]

The choice of law problem here should be resolved by an examination of the contacts which Louisiana and New York have with this controversy for the purpose of determining which of those jurisdictions has the paramount interest in the application of its law. . . .

The issue in this case is whether the community property laws of Louisiana should be applied to govern the property rights of New York domiciliaries in intangible personal property acquired during coverture. . . . [I]t is clear that the community property system is designed to regulate the property rights of married persons and, in particular, to protect the interest of each spouse in the property accumulated during marriage. . . . For reasons which become obvious merely in stating the purpose of the rule, Louisiana has no such interest in protecting and regulating the rights of married persons residing and domiciled in New York.

The State of New York which has such an interest has not adopted a community property system. Instead it has sought to protect a *surviving* spouse by giving her a right to take one third of the entire estate of the deceased as against a testamentary disposition by which the deceased has attempted to exclude her from a share of the estate. (Decedent Estate Law, § 18.) And, depending upon the nature of the property in the estate, a surviving spouse under New York law might well be entitled to receive a greater portion of the over-all estate than under the community property system.

By affording the surviving spouse such a right in the estate of the deceased spouse, the Legislature has sought to preserve the right of the testator to distribute his property as he desires, while at the same time to provide protection for the surviving spouse. New York, as the domicile of Martha and Powell Crichton, has not only the dominant interest in the application of its law and policy but the only interest. . . .

It is urged by the appellant that the Louisiana contacts with this case give it the paramount interest in the application of its law. Among the contacts which are urged as being significant are the facts the deceased was born in Louisiana, that, although he was domiciled in New York, the bulk of his fortune was made in Louisiana, and that the documentary evidences of his intangible property are located in that jurisdiction. Exactly how these contacts are related to the policies sought to be vindicated by Louisiana's community property laws is not made clear. The reason, no doubt, is that they have no relation whatever. [8] . . .

---

[8] Contacts obtain significance only to the extent that they relate to the policies and purposes sought to be vindicated by the conflicting laws. Once these contacts are discovered and

[T]his case is distinguishable from Hutchison v. Ross, 262 N.Y. 381, 187 N.E. 65, 89 A.L.R. 1007, supra, and Wyatt v. Fulrath, 16 N.Y.2d 169, 264 N.Y.S.2d 233, 211 N.E.2d 637, supra, relied upon by the appellant in support of her argument for the application of Louisiana law.

In the latter case . . . [r]elying upon sections 12–a of the Personal Property Law, Consol.Laws, c. 41, and 47 of the Decedent Estate Law, which are designed to encourage investment of funds in this State by permitting a nondomiciliary to designate New York law as applicable to determine questions of law relating to testamentary dispositions of personal property located here as well as *inter vivos* trusts having a situs in this State, we held that New York law and not the Spanish community property laws would govern. In so doing, we cited the earlier case of Hutchison v. Ross (supra) in which the court, speaking through Judge Lehman, relying upon section 12–a of the Personal Property Law, held that it was the policy of this State to permit out-of-State settlors of trusts to designate that rights in that property be determined by New York law.

In both these cases we were giving effect to New York's policy and governmental interest. . . .

NOTES

1. Subsequent to the New York decision in the principal case, the Louisiana court held, in Mrs. Crichton's action against her husband's estate, that the New York courts had misinterpreted Louisiana law and that under that law Mrs. Crichton was entitled to a one-half interest in the movable property left by Mr. Crichton in Louisiana. The court found for the estate, however, for the reason that it felt required by full faith and credit to give res judicata effect to the New York judgment. Crichton v. Succession of Crichton, 232 So.2d 109 (La.App.1970), appeal denied, 236 So.2d 39 (La.1970) (mem.), cert. denied, 400 U.S. 919 (1970).

In Shaheen v. Khan, 142 So.3d 257 (La.App.2014), the parties were married in India in a Muslim wedding and had entered into a marital contract (*mahr*). In Muslim tradition the *mahr* executes or promises a gift in contemplation of marriage from the husband to the wife. The question arises with some frequency in Western courts whether this gift also has the effect of settling (cutting off) any future claims for support or inheritance, i.e., whether it is in lieu of any other claims the wife may have against the husband or his estate. In *Shaheen*, the husband moved to Louisiana, and the wife followed some time later. In a subsequent divorce proceeding, the wife

---

analyzed they will indicate (1) that there exists no true conflict of laws, as in the case at bar and as in most choice of law cases, or (2) that a true conflict exists, i.e., both jurisdictions have an interest in the application of their law. In the former case, of course, the law of the jurisdiction having the only real interest in the litigation will be applied. . . . (Oltarsh v. Aetna Ins. Co., 15 N.Y.2d 111, 256 N.Y.S.2d 577, 204 N.E.2d 622.) In the case of a true conflict, while our decisions have normally resulted in application of forum law (Wyatt v. Fulrath, 16 N.Y.2d 169, 264 N.Y.S.2d 233, 211 N.E.2d 637, supra), we are not as yet prepared to formulate what may be deemed a rule of general application but prefer rather to give further consideration to the question as the cases arise. (See Currie, The Disinterested Third State, 28 Law & Contemp.Prob., 754, 756–764.)

sought division of the property acquired in Louisiana as her interest in the community property. The husband asserted that the execution of the *mahr* had the effect of establishing that the parties had agreed to a separate marital property regime. Without addressing the difficult questions of how to characterize a *mahr* in terms of Western legal concepts, the court pointed to Louisiana's community property law, which indeed permits parties to opt out of it and to adopt a separate property regime for themselves, provided that they make a declaration to that effect within the time period provided by law. The *mahr* (probably) was not such a declaration and, in any event, was not made within the required period after the parties moved to Louisiana and became subject to its law. The situation was clearer in Neivens v. Estrada-Belli, 228 So.3d 238 (La.Ct.App. 2017): The parties had married in Tennessee and there concluded a prenuptial agreement by which they provided for a "separate property marriage" and for the application of Tennessee law. In a divorce proceeding in Louisiana after their move to that state, the court distinguished *Shaheen*: it recognized the prenuptial agreement as valid and enforceable under Tennessee law and as applicable, under Tennessee law to property outside of that state. It therefore refused to apply Louisiana's version of community property law for purposes of division of the assets held by the wife.

2. Is Judge Keating's approach in Crichton a sound one? Is marital property an area where there is real need for actual rules of choice of law?

3. Granted that in Wyatt v. Fulrath, New York had an interest in applying its law, can it convincingly be urged that New York, rather than Spain, was the state of paramount interest? If not, what is the status of the Wyatt holding in light of Matter of Crichton? Can the Wyatt decision be justified on other grounds? Does it bear an analogy to the power of the parties to select the law governing their contract? See pp. 629, 643, 678, supra. For premarital agreements, see p. 1016, Note 2, supra.

4. For a fine article comparing the American, French, and English approaches to marital property in conflict of laws, see Juenger, Marital Property and the Conflict of Laws: A Tale of Two Countries, 81 Colum.L.Rev. 1061 (1981).

5. See generally Clausnitzer, Property Rights of Surviving Spouse and the Conflict of Laws, 18 J.Fam.L. 471 (1980).

Estate of O'Connor

Supreme Court of California, 1933.
218 Cal. 518, 23 P.2d 1031, 88 A.L.R. 856.

[Plaintiff and defendant were married in Indiana, where both were domiciled at the time. Shortly after the marriage, defendant deserted plaintiff and went to California, where he died, leaving a will in which he bequeathed his property to a third person. At the time of the marriage, defendant owned some $200,000 worth of stocks and bonds, and these, or property acquired in exchange therefor, were in his estate at the time of his death. In the California administration proceedings, plaintiff claimed one-third of the estate relying upon the Indiana law which permits a widow to take this amount against the will of her deceased husband. The plaintiff is now appealing from the action of the trial court in sustaining the executor's demurrer to her petition.]

■ THE COURT. We have re-examined the questions involved in this appeal and find ourselves in entire accord with the conclusion and opinion of the District Court of Appeal, Division One of the First Appellate District, and we hereby adopt that opinion as the opinion of this court in this cause. . . .

Appellant contends that she is entitled to the portion of decedent's personal estate which she could have claimed under the laws of Indiana notwithstanding his attempted disposal thereof by his will.

. . . The community system does not prevail in Indiana, and appellant admits that prior to 1891 there was no statute of that state giving to a surviving widow an interest in her deceased husband's personal estate akin to the common-law right of dower and not subject to be defeated by will. . . . She claims, however, that the act of March 9, 1891 (Acts 1891, p. 404) (Burns' Annotated Indiana Statutes 1926, sec. 3343 (3025)), gives such right. [The statute, which gives the widow the right to elect, is omitted.] . . .

[N]o statute or decision from that state has been called to our attention which provides or holds that the wife enjoys any ordinary rights of ownership in her husband's personal property during his lifetime, or has a more complete interest therein than that of an expectancy as heir if she survives him.

Appellant concedes that the property in question if governed by the California law would be the separate property of decedent and subject to his testamentary disposition; also that as a general rule the descent of personal property is governed by the laws of the state where decedent was domiciled at the time of his death, but she insists that the contract of marriage in relation to property rights should be governed, as other contracts, by the laws of the jurisdiction where it was to be carried out-in this instance by the laws of Indiana.

This doctrine has been recognized and applied in instances where rights in the property of one spouse were held to have vested at the time of the marriage. The rule is stated in Wharton on Conflict of Laws, section 193a, as follows: "While . . . it is undoubtedly true that the intestacy laws of the last domicile of the deceased govern the distribution of the personal estate of either husband or wife in case of intestacy, a distinction is to be observed between the mere inchoate rights of either spouse to share in the distribution of the other's estate at his death and a vested right which attaches at the time of marriage though its enjoyment may be postponed until the death of the other spouse." The author says further that the latter right is not divested by a change of domicile, but that a mere statute of distribution of the original matrimonial domicile, or any domicile other than the last, by which either spouse is to share in the other's personal estate upon the latter's death creates no vested right, and therefore offers no obstacle to the application of the statute of distribution of the last domicile. . . .

The mere fact that under the Indiana laws, above cited, the power of the husband to dispose of his personal property by will was subject to the right of his wife at her election to claim a third thereof gave her no more than an expectancy in this portion of his estate. As was held in Spreckels v. Spreckels, 116 Cal. 339 (48 P. 228, 58 Am.St.Rep. 170, 36 L.R.A. 497), such a limitation of the husband's right would give the wife no interest in his property during his lifetime. We are satisfied that appellant had no present fixed right or interest in decedent's personal estate, or more than a mere expectancy, which depended upon survivorship to become a vested right. This being true, and he having established his domicile in California, as he might do (Civ.Code, sec. 129), the property was subject to the law of this state, which governs its disposition and distribution whether he died testate or intestate.

The order appealed from is affirmed.

NOTES

1.   It will be noted that in the principal case the plaintiff wife was denied the economic protection accorded a spouse by either the California or Indiana law. Could the court have properly reached a different result? If so, by what reasoning?

2.   A pervasive problem is whether a given issue should be characterized as one of marital property or of succession. Questions of marital property are governed by the rules set forth in this Section, while those involving succession are determined by the law of the situs in the case of land and by that of the state where the decedent died domiciled in the case of movables. Whether a spouse has a community property interest in the other's property is considered a problem of marital property. On the other hand, whether a spouse has a nonbarrable interest in the property owned by the other spouse at the time of death is considered a question of succession. See, e.g., In re Sylvester, 181 So.3d 250 (La.App.2015) (characterized Florida tenancy by the entirety as issue of succession, rather than marital property; under Florida law, title to a timeshare passed immediately to the surviving spouse, and was not subject to partition with the rest of decedent's estate).

Should application of a given rule of foreign law depend upon the way in which it is characterized by the forum or by the courts of the foreign state? For example, was the court in the principal case correct in refusing to apply the Indiana rule on the ground that it was one of succession rather than of marital property?

3.   The law of a decedent's domicile at death may not govern the interest of a surviving spouse in the decedent's immovable property located in another state. In Whatley v. Smart, the husband owned real property in Louisiana and died intestate while domiciled in Alabama. By operation of Alabama law, his surviving spouse inherited all of his property. She died intestate there a

year later, at which time the administratrix of her estate initiated Louisiana proceedings to recover the value of real property, an interest in which it was alleged the deceased wife had inherited at the time of her husband's death. However, under Louisiana law, such a surviving out-of-state spouse acquires only a claim against the decedent's estate for the *value* of the real property, and not actual title. Having not exercised that claim during her life, it was extinguished by her death and not inherited by her heirs. 174 So.3d 1273 (La.App.2015), appeal denied, 182 So.3d 952 (La.2016).

Addison v. Addison

Supreme Court of California, 1965.
62 Cal.2d 558, 43 Cal.Rptr. 97, 399 P.2d 897.

■ PETERS, JUSTICE. Plaintiff Leona Addison (hereafter referred to as Leona) was granted an interlocutory decree of divorce from defendant Morton Addison (hereafter referred to as Morton) on the ground of his adultery. . . .

At the time of their marriage in Illinois in 1939, Morton, having previously engaged in the used car business, had a net worth which he estimated as being between $15,000 and $20,000. Leona, however, testified that her husband's net worth was almost nothing at the time of their marriage. In 1949 the Addisons moved to California bringing with them cash and other personal property valued at $143,000 which had been accumulated as a result of Morton's various Illinois business enterprises. Since that time Morton has participated in several California businesses.

On February 20, 1961, Leona filed for divorce and requested an equitable division of the marital property. On trial, Leona . . . attempted to apply the recently enacted quasi-community property legislation[3] by

---

[3]   The key sections of the 1961 legislation which are involved in the instant case are as follows:

Civil Code section 140.5: "As used in Sections 140.7, 141, 142, 143, 146, 148, 149 and 176 of this code, 'quasi-community property' means all personal property wherever situated and all real property situated in this State heretofore or hereafter acquired:

"(a)   By either spouse while domiciled elsewhere which would have been community property of the husband and wife had the spouse acquiring the property been domiciled in this State at the time of its acquisition; or

"(b)   In exchange for real or personal property, wherever situated, acquired other than by gift, devise, bequest or descent by either spouse during the marriage while domiciled elsewhere.

"For the purposes of this section, personal property does not include and real property does include leasehold interests in real property."

Civil Code section 146 provides in part: "In case of the dissolution of the marriage by decree of a court of competent jurisdiction or in the case of judgment or decree for separate maintenance of the husband or the wife without dissolution of the marriage, the court shall make an order for disposition of the community property and the quasi-community property and for the assignment of the homestead as follows:

"(a)   If the decree is rendered on the ground of adultery, incurable insanity or extreme cruelty, the community property and quasi-community property shall be

contending that the property presently held in Morton's name was acquired by the use of property brought from Illinois and that the property would have been community property had it been originally acquired while the parties were domiciled in California.

The trial court . . . held the quasi-community property legislation to be unconstitutional.

The trial court . . . did find the household furniture and furnishings to be community property and, pursuant to Civil Code section 146, awarded them to Leona. In addition, the court found that the residence of the parties was held in joint tenancy and thus each owned an undivided one-half separate interest therein. Finally, all other property which had been in Morton's name alone was found to be his sole and separate property.

The sociological problem to which the quasi-community property legislation addresses itself has been an area of considerable legislative and judicial activity in this state. One commentator has expressed this thought as follows: "Among the perennial problems in the field of community property in California, the status of marital personal property acquired while domiciled in another State has been particularly troublesome. Attempts of the Legislature to designate such personalty as community property uniformly have been thwarted by court decisions." (Comment 8 So.Cal.L.Rev. 221, 222 (1935)).

The problem arises as a result of California's attempts to apply community property concepts to the foreign, and radically different (in hypotheses) common-law theory of matrimonial rights. In fitting the common-law system into our community property scheme the process is of two steps. First, property acquired by a spouse while domiciled in a common-law state is characterized as separate property. (Estate of O'Connor, 218 Cal. 518, 23 P.2d 1031, 88 A.L.R. 856.) Second, the rule of tracing is invoked so that all property later acquired in exchange for the common-law separate property is likewise deemed separate property. . . . Thus, the original property, and all property subsequently acquired through use of the original property is classified as the separate property of the acquiring spouse.

One attempt to solve the problem was the 1917 amendment to Civil Code section 164 which had the effect of classifying all personal property wherever situated and all real property located in California into California community property if that property would not have been the separate property of one of the spouses had that property been acquired while the parties were domiciled in California. Insofar as the amendment attempted to affect personal property brought to California which was

---

assigned to the respective parties in such proportions as the court, from all the fact of the case, and the condition of the parties, may deem just.

"(b)   If the decree be rendered on any other ground than that of adultery, incurable insanity or extreme cruelty, the community property and quasi-community property shall be equally divided between the parties."

the separate property of one of the spouses while domiciled outside this state Estate of Thornton, 1 Cal.2d 1, 33 P.2d 1, 92 A.L.R. 1343, held the section was unconstitutional. The amendment's effect upon real property located in California was never tested but generally was considered to be a dead letter as the section was never again invoked on the appellate level.

Another major attempt to alter the rights in property acquired prior to California domicile was the passage of Probate Code section 201.5. This section gave to the surviving spouse one half of all the personal property wherever situated and the real property located in California which would not have been the separate property of the acquiring spouse had it been acquired while domiciled in California. As a succession statute, its constitutionality was upheld on the theory that the state of domicile of the decedent at the time of his death has full power to control rights of succession. (In re Miller, 31 Cal.2d 191, 196, 187 P.2d 722). In other words, no one has a vested right to succeed to another's property rights, and no one has a vested right in the distribution of his estate upon his death. Hence succession rights may be constitutionally altered. This theory was a basis of the dissent in Thornton.

In the present case it is contended that Estate of Thornton, supra, 1 Cal.2d 1, 33 P.2d 1, is controlling and that the current legislation, by authority of Thornton, must be held to be unconstitutional. Thornton involved a situation of a husband and wife moving to California and bringing with them property acquired during their former domicile in Montana. Upon the husband's death, his widow sought to establish her community property rights in his estate as provided by the then recent amendment to Civil Code section 164. The majority held the section unconstitutional on the theory that upon acquisition of the property the husband obtained vested rights which could not be altered without violation of his privileges and immunities as a citizen and also that "to take the property of A and transfer it to B because of his citizenship and domicile, is also to take his property without due process of law. This is true regardless of the place of acquisition or the state of his residence." (Estate of Thornton, supra, 1 Cal.2d 1, 5, 33 P.2d 1, 3, 92 A.L.R. 1343.)

The underlying rationale of the majority was the same in Thornton as it had been since Spreckels v. Spreckels, 116 Cal. 339, 48 P. 228, 36 L.R.A. 497, which established, by a concession of counsel, that changes in the community property system which affected "vested interests" could not constitutionally be applied retroactively but must be limited to prospective application.

Langdon, J., in his dissent in Thornton, conceded the correctness of the vested right theory but argued that the statute was merely definitional, giving no rights to anyone except as provided by other legislation. Therefore, the widow would only be acquiring rights pursuant to a right of succession as granted by statute. As to the constitutionality of this application of amended Civil Code section 164 he declared: "It is a rule of almost universal acceptance that the rights of testamentary disposition and of succession are wholly subject to statutory control, and may be enlarged, limited, or abolished without infringing upon the constitutional guaranty of due process of law." (Estate of Thornton, supra, 1 Cal.2d 1, 7, 33 P.2d 1, 3.) The majority refused to construe amended Civil Code section 164 in this limited fashion.

The constitutional doctrine announced in Estate of Thornton, supra, has been questioned. Justice (now Chief Justice) Traynor in his concurring opinion in Boyd v. Oser, 23 Cal.2d 613, at p. 623, 145 P.2d 312, at page 318, had the following to say: "The decisions that existing statutes changing the rights of husbands and wives in community property can have no retroactive application have become a rule of property in this state and should not now be overruled. It is my opinion, however, that the constitutional theory on which they are based is unsound. [Citations.] That theory has not become a rule of property and should not invalidate future legislation in this field intended by the Legislature to operate retroactively." . . .

Thus, the correctness of the rule of Thornton is open to challenge. But even if the rule of that case be accepted as sound, it is not here controlling. This is so because former section 164 of the Civil Code has an entirely different impact from the legislation presently before us. The legislation under discussion, unlike old section 164, makes no attempt to alter property rights merely upon crossing the boundary into California. It does not purport to disturb vested rights "of a citizen of another state, who chances to transfer his domicile to this state, bringing his property with him. . . ." (Estate of Thornton, supra, 1 Cal.2d 1, at p. 5, 33 P.2d 1, at p. 3.) Instead, the concept of quasi-community property is applicable only if a divorce or separate maintenance action is filed here after the parties have become domiciled in California. Thus, the concept is applicable only if, after acquisition of domicile in this state, certain acts or events occur which give rise to an action for divorce or separate maintenance. These acts or events are not necessarily connected with a change of domicile at all. . . .

Clearly the interest of the state of the current domicile in the matrimonial property of the parties is substantial upon the dissolution of the marriage relationship. . . .

In recognition of much the same interest as that advanced by the quasi-community property legislation, many common-law jurisdictions have provided for the division of the separate property of the respective spouses in a manner which is "just and reasonable" and none of these statutes have been overturned on a constitutional basis.

In the case at bar it was Leona who was granted a divorce from Morton on the ground of the latter's adultery and hence it is the spouse guilty of the marital infidelity from whom the otherwise separate property is sought by the operation of the quasi-community property legislation. We are of the opinion that where the innocent party would otherwise be left unprotected the state has a very substantial interest and one sufficient to provide for a fair and equitable distribution of the marital property without running afoul of the due process clause of the Fourteenth Amendment. . . .

Morton also asserts that there is an abridgment of the privileges and immunities clause of the Fourteenth Amendment citing Estate of Thornton, supra . . . Aside from the due process clause, already held not to be applicable, Thornton may be read as holding that the legislation there in question impinged upon the right of a citizen of the United States to maintain a domicile in any state of his choosing without the loss of valuable property rights. As to this contention, the distinction we have already noted between former Civil Code section 164 and quasi-community property legislation is relevant. Unlike the legislation in Thornton, the quasi-community property legislation does not cause a loss of valuable rights through change of domicile. The concept is applicable only in case of a decree of divorce or separate maintenance. . . .

The judgment is affirmed insofar as it decrees divorce and custody of the minor child. In all other respects the judgment is reversed. . . .

NOTES

1. The facts of In re Thornton's Estate are stated in the principal case. The statute declared unconstitutional in Thornton provided in effect that all movables originally owned by a spouse as separate property, but which would be community property under California rules, would be converted into community property as soon as the spouse acquired a domicile in California. It should be noted that Mrs. Thornton had a nonbarrable interest in her husband's movables under Montana law. The decision in effect held that Mrs. Thornton lost this interest in her husband's movables as soon as she and he acquired a domicile in California. This was the result the California statute sought to avoid.

2. The California Probate Code contains the following sections:

Section 66 (derived from former § 201.5) defines "quasi-community property" as all personal property wherever situated, and all real property situated in California (a) "acquired by a decedent while domiciled elsewhere that would have been the community property of the decedent and the surviving spouse if the decedent been domiciled in this state at the time of its acquisition" and (b) "acquired in exchange for real or personal property, wherever situated, that would have been the community property of the decedent and the surviving spouse if the decedent had been domiciled in this state at the time the property so exchanged was acquired."

Section 101 (also derived from former § 201.5) provides that a surviving spouse is entitled to one-half of the decedent's quasi-community property.

Section 102 (derived from former § 201.8) provides that the surviving spouse may require restoration to the estate of one-half of any property transferred by the deceased spouse without consideration of substantial value if the surviving spouse had an expectancy in this property under § 101, and the deceased spouse had an ownership interest in the property at death.

3.　The California statutes were further amended to provide for "quasi community property" interests in the event of a divorce. These provisions are set forth in footnote 3 to the Addison opinion. See also Miller & Starr, California Real Estate (3d ed.2012) § 12:40.

4.　The California legislation is discussed in Gardner, Note, Marital Property and the Conflict of Laws: The Constitutionality of the "Quasi-Community Property" Legislation, 54 Calif.L.Rev. 252 (1966); Schreter, "Quasi-Community Property" in Conflict of Laws, 50 Calif.L.Rev. 206 (1962). See also Buchschacher, Rights of a Surviving Spouse in Texas in Marital Property Acquired While Domiciled Elsewhere, 45 Tex.L.Rev. 321 (1966) (comparing various approaches to marital property when common law spouses move to a community property state).

5.　In Sample v. Sample, 663 P.2d 591 (Ariz.App.1983), the court upheld the constitutionality of Arizona's legislation, citing to *Addison* and invoking the "strong interest of the state in the marital relationship and in marital property upon dissolution." 663 P.2d, at 594–95. Note that the *Addison* court saw the relevant difference from *Estate of Thornton* in the fact that "after acquisition of domicile in this state, certain acts or events occur which give rise to an action for divorce." The reference is to the fault-based divorce under substantive divorce law at that time. What justifies the application of community-property law to a new resident's property, acquired out of state, in the era of no-fault divorce? Is the reason given by the *Sample* court enough? For discussion, see Mark Patton, Quasi-Community Property in Arizona: Why Just at Divorce and Not Death?, 47 Ariz. L.Rev. 167, 183 et seq. (2005).

6.　Other community-property states have also adopted the quasi-community property concept. Wisconsin, Washington, and New Mexico, like California, have adopted the concept for purposes of distribution upon dissolution of the marriage and on the death of a spouse, while Arizona and Texas have done so for divorce and Idaho for distribution on death. The Texas Supreme Court declined to extend the concept beyond dissolution to distribution on death. Estate of Hanau v. Hanau, 730 S.W.2d 663 (Tex.1987); Bauer v. White, 2016 WL 3136608 (Tex.App. June 2, 2016). For criticism, see Patton, previous note.

The "quasi-community property" concept assures that the surviving spouse does not run the risk of receiving nothing. When migration occurs from a community property state to a common law property state, the surviving spouse may receive too much: his or her half of the community property as well as what the succession laws of the new (common law) state of the domicile at the time of the decedent's death provide. The Uniform Disposition of Community Property Rights at Death Act, 8A U.L.A. 191

(1993), addresses this problem: the survivor takes his or her part of the community property as of the time of the change of domicile. As of 2020, the Act is in force in sixteen states.

7.   Cameron v. Cameron, 641 S.W.2d 210 (Tex.1982): in the case of divorce, common law marital property acquired by one spouse should not be regarded as the "separate" property of that spouse but, if acquired during marriage, should be divided in the same manner as community property, regardless of the spouses' domicile at the time of acquisition. If it were otherwise, the common law property of the particular spouse would be insulated from division even though it would have been subject to claims for alimony or equitable division in the state of acquisition. Compare Note 2, p. 1020, supra. For commentary on *Cameron*, see Brock, Note, Community Property—Division of Property Upon Divorce, 14 St. Mary's L.J. 789 (1983); Levy, Note, Cameron v. Cameron: Divestiture of Separate Personalty on Divorce, 35 Baylor L.Rev. 168 (1983).

8.   A basic book in the area is Marsh, Marital Property in Conflict of Laws (1952). For other discussions of marital property, see R. Felix & R. Whitten, American Conflicts Law § 201 (6th ed.2011); Hay, Borchers, Symeonides, Whytock, Conflict of Laws ch. 14 (6th ed.2018); Weintraub, Commentary on the Conflict of Laws § 8.14 (6th ed.2010). From among the older literature, see McClanahan, Community Property Law in the United States (1982, 1984 Supp.); Oldham, Conflict of Laws and Marital Property Rights, 39 Baylor L.Rev. 1255 (1987); Lay, The Role of the Matrimonial Domicile in Marital Property Rights, 4 Fam.L.Q. 61 (1970); Norsigian, Note, Community Property and the Problem of Migration, 66 Wash.U.L.Q. 773 (1988); Chappell, A Uniform Resolution to the Problem a Migrating Spouse Encounters at Divorce and Death, 28 Idaho L.Rev. 993 (1991–1992). See also Oldham, What if the Bechkams Move to L.A. and Divorce? Marital Property Rights of Mobile Spouses When They Divorce in the United States, 42 Fam.L.Q. 263 (2008).

9.   Similar problems also arise in conflicts cases in other legal systems, either because they have different rules on marital property (e.g., in English-Swedish cases on facts comparable to *O'Connor* and *Addison*) or because different laws apply to the succession and the marital property issues of a case. The following illustrates the second type of case: an Austrian husband and German wife are habitually resident in Germany, where he dies, leaving his widow and two children. The European Union's Succession Regulation (see the Documentary Appendix) refers succession to the entire estate (both personal and real property) to the law of the decedent's state of habitual residence at death, but permits selection of the law of nationality by stipulation in the will. Under Austrian law (if it had been chosen by the Austrian decedent), each survivor takes one-third. However, the law of the common habitual residence (absent common nationality) applies to matrimonial property issues. Under German law, the surviving spouse's inheritance rights (one-third, § 1931(1) BGB) are increased by one-quarter. Arts.15(1), 14(1) No. 2 EGBGB; § 1371(1) BGB. In the example, the surviving spouse would receive a total of seven twelfths, when Austrian law would give one third or German law, if applicable, one half. The German solution: to give the greater of the two, but not to cumulate them. See Hay, Internationales Privat- und Zivilverfahrensrecht 241–42 (PdW Series, 4th ed.2010). See also Decision of Landgericht Moosbach, [1999] JuS 296. For an overview, see Clarkson, Matrimonial Property on Divorce: All Change in Europe, 4 J.Priv.Int'l L. 421 (2008).

CHAPTER 12

ADMINISTRATION OF ESTATES

SECTION 1. DECEDENTS' ESTATES

INTRODUCTORY NOTE

This casebook has dealt in earlier chapters with the substantive law applicable to succession to a decedent's property. This section is concerned with the machinery for the transfer of wealth from generation to generation. In the United States the method of transfer is through the personal representative, who is either an executor (if the decedent had a will) or administrator (if the decedent died intestate) and who has been confirmed or appointed by a competent court.

The first stage is the determination in a judicial proceeding that the alleged decedent is dead and that he died either testate or intestate in a certain domicile. These determinations are followed by the appointment or qualification of the personal representative to administer the estate. At this stage there are problems of jurisdiction of courts, the nature of an administration proceeding, whether in rem or in personam, and the effect of foreign judgments.

The second stage is administration of the estate by the personal representative. The representative's functions are essentially three: to collect and protect the property of the decedent, whether by voluntary payment or delivery or by suit; to pay creditors either voluntarily or after suit; and to distribute the net proceeds.

The last stage is the termination of the administration through a report to the court and its discharge of the personal representative.

The second stage presents the greatest difficulties. The central question is whether a personal representative appointed in one state may act and sue or be sued in another state, or whether the representative is confined to the state of his or her appointment. In support of wider powers are practical considerations: "An estate is for practical purposes a single thing, whether the items of property which compose it are all within the borders of one State or are scattered among several. . . . It is difficult to administer an estate as a unit, if that portion of it in each State is to be treated as a completely separate affair." (Restatement, Second, Conflict of Laws, Chap. 14, Topic 1, Introductory Note (1971).) The principal support of the narrower view is the traditional conception of a personal representative as an artificial legal person who, as such, may only act in the state of appointment. There are further complicating elements: the desire to protect local creditors out of local assets and the nature of the property involved, whether it is immovable or movable, tangible or intangible, or represented by a specialty.

Matters of probate and administration, as well as of the substantive validity of wills, are frequently affected by statutes, some of which are designed to simplify the handling of estates with assets in two or more states. An example is the Uniform Probate Code, some provisions of which will be referred to at various places in this chapter. A number of other uniform acts are in effect in some states.

Milmoe v. Toomey

United States Court of Appeals, District of Columbia Circuit, 1966.
123 U.S.App.D.C. 40, 356 F.2d 793.

■ McGOWAN, CIRCUIT JUDGE. This appeal challenges the jurisdiction of the District Court . . . to appoint an ancillary administrator by reason of an asset in the District of Columbia consisting solely of the protection against liability afforded by an automobile insurance policy. . . .

The decedent was a girl who, for some time prior to June 6, 1964, had been residing in Washington while working for the Peace Corps. On the morning of that day, in company with a fellow employe[e], she rented a Hertz car and set out for her family home in New York State. In Lebanon County, Pennsylvania, during the early afternoon, the rented car was in a collision, and both of its occupants were killed. Also dying in the crash were a married couple from Illinois who were in the other car; and a minor child with them was seriously injured.

The rental agreement executed by the decedent with Hertz recites her "local address" in Washington to be 3336 P Street. An affidavit submitted in the District Court by her father asserts, however, that before leaving Washington the decedent had resigned from the Peace Corps and given up her P Street apartment; and that her purpose was to return to the family home in New York to live. Execution of the rental agreement with Hertz operated to bring the decedent directly within the coverage of a liability policy issued to Hertz by Royal Indemnity Company. Although not District of Columbia corporations, both Hertz and Royal Indemnity are doing business in the District so as to be subject to suit here.

Appellee O'Keefe is the Illinois administrator of the estate of the deceased Illinois couple. He filed a petition in the District Court reciting the rental agreement and the accompanying insurance coverage, and asked that letters of administration issue to a disinterested attorney in order that suit might be brought against such appointee in the District on behalf of the deceased Illinois couple and their surviving minor child. Appellee Toomey is the ancillary administrator appointed in response to this petition.

Appellant, the decedent's father, appeared in the District Court to oppose the appointment. It was urged by him that the decedent was, at the time of her death, domiciled in New York, and that any relationship of significance between her and the District of Columbia had ended before her death. As the administrator of his daughter's estate duly appointed in New York, appellant represented that he could be sued in New York or in Pennsylvania, as could Hertz and the estate of the decedent's companion on the fatal journey. He further asserted that the insurance policy running to Hertz and its customers was nationwide in character, and that its benefits could be claimed in both New York and Pennsylvania.

At the hearing before the District Court it appeared that a suit had in fact been filed in Pennsylvania; and, promptly after the appointment of the ancillary administrator in the District of Columbia, suit was brought against him in the District Court. So far as we are aware, these actions remain pending before trial.

The immediately relevant statute is Title 20 D.C.Code § 201, which provides as follows:

> "On the death of any person leaving real or personal estate in the District, letters of administration on his estate may be granted, on the application of any person interested, on proof satisfactory to the probate court, that the decedent died intestate."

The District Judge conceived that the controversy before him was to be resolved by a scrupulous attention to the terms of this statute; and that, accordingly, the question before him was whether the decedent was an intestate person "leaving ... personal estate in the District" within the contemplation of the statute. He did not find it necessary to choose explicitly and finally between the conflicting contentions as to whether the decedent was a resident of the District at her death. He thought that the decedent's interest in the insurance policy was "personal estate," and that the circumstances surrounding the creation of that interest gave it a *locus* "in the District," within the scope of those phrases as used in the statute. Thus, he considered the conditions of the statute to be met, and that the appointment by him of an ancillary administrator was in order.

We agree with this concept of the issue presented, and see no occasion to disturb the resolution made of it. With respect to the narrow question of whether coverage under an insurance policy constitutes a personal property interest supporting administration, we think the answer is as clear in reason as it is settled in authority.... And, whatever may be the precise outer limits of the relationship of such an interest to the District of Columbia contemplated by Congress as warranting administration here, we agree with the District Judge that they were not exceeded in this case. The decedent was certainly not an ordinary transient in her relationship with the District of Columbia at the time she entered into the Hertz contract which created her insurance rights. Those rights came into being here; and we think that, on this record, they continue to constitute a "personal estate in the District" within the statutory prescription.

Appellant's claim of an absence of jurisdictional power to make the appointment is largely cast ... in terms of the lack of necessity for bringing the tort action here and of the greater appropriateness of other forums for its trial. This argument essentially is that, since the District Court should decline jurisdiction over the tort action from *forum non conveniens* considerations, it must be taken to have lacked jurisdiction to appoint the ancillary administrator. But the logic of this, if such there be, is not to be discovered from the language of the governing statute. Section 201 does not address itself generally to the purposes for which administration is sought, and, in particular, it prescribes nothing with respect to which lawsuits may be appropriately brought in the District of Columbia against the administrator, and which may not. Its concern appears to be mainly, if not exclusively, with the designation of a legal custodian of an asset in the District of an intestate decedent.

The District Judge ... looking only to Section 201, refused to be drawn into the question of whether the tort claim should be tried here or in Pennsylvania. In this he was ... wholly right. He regarded that question as one reserved to the judge before whom the tort suit comes ... There may or may not be persuasive reasons why the issue of liability in negligence should be tried elsewhere than in the District of Columbia ... But that is a matter for exploration and resolution in the tort action itself, and not in [this] proceeding.

The judgment appealed from is Affirmed.

NOTES

1. The circumstances in which a will may be probated, and an executor or administrator appointed, are usually regulated by statute. The District of Columbia statute involved in the principal case is similar to statutes commonly found among the states. The statutes do not usually require that a representative be appointed but authorize the making of such an appointment in the court's discretion—e.g., if the appointment would be in the best interests of the estate and is required for the protection of local creditors. Restatement, Second, Conflict of Laws §§ 314–15 (1971).

2. Local ancillary administrators have frequently been appointed in the circumstances involved in the principal case. See e.g., Gordon v. Shea, 14 N.E.2d 105 (Mass.1938); Estate of Riggle, 181 N.E.2d 436 (N.Y.1962). One reason for the appointment of local ancillary administrators in these circumstances is the perceived difficulty involved in bringing suit against a foreign domiciliary administrator. See p. 1047, infra.

3. On the privileges and functions of a consul in dealing with the estate of a national of his country, see Boyd, Consular Functions in Connection with Decedents' Estates, 47 Iowa L.Rev. 823 (1962); Boyd, Constitutional, Treaty, and Statutory Requirement of Probate Notice to Consuls and Aliens, 47 Iowa L.Rev. 29 (1961).

4. On the administration of estates in which aliens have an interest, see Boyd, The Administration in the United States of Alien Connected Decedents' Estates, 2 Int'l L. 601 (1968).

In re Fischer's Estate

Prerogative Court of New Jersey, 1935.
118 N.J.Eq. 599, 180 A. 633.

■ BUCHANAN, VICE ORDINARY. Mrs. Mae Platto Fischer died at Denville (Indian Lake), Morris county, N.J., on August 21, 1933. She left no descendants, but was survived by her husband, Frederick G. Fischer, and by one brother, George Platto, but by no other brother or sister or representative thereof. No will being found, her husband applied to this court for letters of administration, and letters of general administration were issued to him on September 12, 1933.

These letters were issued on Fischer's allegation that decedent was a resident of ("late of") New Jersey, and without notice to the brother, Platto. It is the law of the state of domicile of an intestate decedent, which governs and determines the rights of intestate succession. Under the law of New Jersey, if the decedent had been domiciled here at her death, the husband would have had the sole right to succeed to all the decedent's personal property, and the sole right to letters of administration, and no notice was required to be given to Platto or anyone else.

If the decedent, however, were domiciled in New York at the time of her death, the New York law would control, and under that law the brother, Platto, would succeed to a substantial share in the estate.

On October 20, 1933, the brother, Platto, filed petition for administration of Mrs. Fischer's estate, in the Surrogate's Court in New York, alleging her to have been a resident of New York at her death; and process was issued and served on the husband, Fischer.

Fischer had become mentally deranged, and on November 8, 1933, the letters of administration which had been issued to him by this court were revoked on that ground and letters issued in their stead to one Milton Mermelstein. . . .

Mermelstein, as substituted administrator of Mrs. Fischer's estate, appointed by this court, entered appearance and answer in the New York proceeding above mentioned. He also himself filed a petition in the New York court for the issuance of ancillary letters to himself, on the basis of the allegation that Mrs. Fischer had been domiciled in New Jersey and that original letters of administration had been issued to him here. Under the New York law it is a requisite to the grant of ancillary letters that it be shown that original letters have been issued in the state of decedent's domicile. To this petition Platto answered, denying that Mrs. Fischer's residence was in New Jersey, and alleging such residence to have been in New York.

Both proceedings in New York therefore involved the issue as to whether Mrs. Fischer had been domiciled in New York or New Jersey. Both proceedings were consolidated and duly tried in New York, and . . . Mr. Fischer also appeared as a party, and contended that the domicile of Mrs. Fischer was not New York but New Jersey. The determination of the issue in and by the New York court was that Mrs. Fischer had been domiciled in New York, and original letters of administration were issued to Platto. In re Fischer's Estate, 151 Misc. 74, 271 N.Y.S. 101. . . .

Following the determination aforesaid in the New York Surrogate's Court, Platto, as general administrator appointed by the New York court, commenced the present proceeding in this court, being a petition for the revocation of the letters issued by this court to Mermelstein and for the issuance of letters to him (Platto), in the place and stead thereof. The basis of this petition is the allegation that Mrs. Fischer was not a resident of New York but of New York; that hence New Jersey had not the right to issue letters of general or original administration on her estate; that although New Jersey had the right to issue letters of administration for the administration of such assets of the estate as were in this state, such letters (on Fischer's becoming incompetent) should have been issued to Platto and not to Mermelstein; that the issuance of the letters to Mermelstein was the result of mistake and misrepresentation, to wit, the mistake of this court in believing that Mrs. Fischer's residence had been in this state, which mistake was caused by the misrepresentation to that effect made to this court by Fischer in his original petition . . . that Platto, not having been brought in to the proceedings in this court nor given notice thereof, had had no opportunity to raise or be heard on the issue as to the domicile of Mrs. Fischer, in this court.

. . . Fisher . . . and the New Jersey substituted administrator, are all bound by the determination in the New York proceeding, because they were all parties to that proceeding, and not only had the opportunity to be heard therein, but therein actively litigated, against Platto, the same issue now sought by them to be relitigated against him herein. . . .

Reopening the action and finding of this court of 1933, and according to Platto, now, the opportunity to be heard on the question of the right to letters of ancillary administration, results in the revocation of Mermelstein's letters and the grant of ancillary letters to Platto. . . .

Riley v. New York Trust Co.

Supreme Court of the United States, 1942.
315 U.S. 343, 62 S.Ct. 608, 86 L.Ed. 885.

[The case appears at p. 303, supra.]

NOTE

An application of the rationale in *In re Fischer's Estate* is In the Matter of the Estate of Jack Franklin Tolson, et al., 947 P.2d 1242 (Wash. App.1997).

RESTATEMENT, SECOND, CONFLICT OF LAWS (1971):

§ 317. Effect Given in Other States to Judgments in Administration Proceedings

(1) A judgment in administration proceedings by a competent court in the state where the decedent was domiciled at the time of his death will usually be followed by the forum with respect to local movables insofar as the judgment deals with questions of succession that under the choice-of-law rules of the forum are governed by the law that would be applied by the courts of the state of the decedent's domicil.

(2) A judgment in administration proceedings by a competent court in the state where the decedent was domiciled at the time of his death will not of itself invalidate a prior inconsistent judgment by a court in another state in administering the estate of the same decedent in that state.

(3) A judgment in administration proceedings by a competent court of any state will be held conclusive in other states as to the issues determined upon all persons who were subject to the jurisdiction of the original court if the judgment is conclusive upon such persons in the state of rendition.

(4) If an issue as to the state in which a decedent was domiciled at the time of his death is raised by a person not precluded from raising this issue under Subsection (3), a court will not regard itself as concluded by a prior finding made in another state as to the place of the decedent's domicil.

NOTE

To facilitate solution of these problems, the Uniform Probate Code (2013) provides in § 3–202 that when probate or appointment proceedings are pending at the same time in the state of the forum and in one or more other states, "[t]he determination of domicile in the proceeding first commenced must be accepted as determinative in the proceeding in this state." The Comment explains that the "section is designed to reduce the possibility that conflicting findings of domicile in two or more states may result in inconsistent administration and distribution of parts of the same estate," and that "the local suitor always will have a chance to contest the question of domicile in the other state." The official commentary to this section also provides: "Even if parties to a present proceeding were not personally before the court in an earlier proceeding in State A involving the same decedent, the prior judgment would be binding as to property subject to the power of the courts in A, on persons to whom due notice of the proceeding was given."

Section 3–203 provides that in the absence of a contrary provision in the decedent's will, the domiciliary administrator "has priority over all other persons" for appointment as ancillary administrator of local assets.

Section 3–408 provides that a previous determination by a court of another state of testacy or of the validity or construction of a will must be accepted as conclusive by the local courts provided the previous determination was rendered after proper notice and opportunity to be heard and included "a finding that the decedent was domiciled at his death in the state where the [previous determination] was made." The Comment makes clear that the section applies to cases where parties before the local court were not subject to the personal jurisdiction of the foreign court. The official commentary also provides: "If conflicting claims of domicile are made in proceedings which are commenced in different jurisdictions, Section 3–202 applies." In other words, parties not before the first court are not bound as to property not subject to the power of the first court *unless* they concede that the first court was at the domicile.

Wilkins v. Ellett, Adm'r

Supreme Court of the United States, 1883.
108 U.S. 256, 2 S.Ct. 641, 27 L.Ed. 718.

■ GRAY, J. This is an action of *assumpsit* on the common counts, brought in the circuit court of the United States for the western district of Tennessee. The plaintiff is a citizen of Virginia, and sues as administrator, appointed in Tennessee, of the estate of Thomas N. Quarles. The defendant is a citizen of Tennessee and surviving partner of the firm of F.H. Clark & Co. The answer sets up that Quarles was a citizen of Alabama at the time of his death; that the sum sued for has been paid to William Goodloe, appointed his administrator in that state, and has been inventoried and accounted for by him upon a final settlement of his administration; and that there are no creditors of Quarles in Tennessee. The undisputed facts, appearing by the bill of exceptions, are as follows:

Quarles was born at Richmond, Virginia, in 1835. In 1839 his mother, a widow, removed with him, her only child, to Courtland, Alabama. They lived there together until 1856, and she made her home there until her death, in 1864. In 1856, he went to Memphis, Tennessee, and there entered the employment of F.H. Clark & Co., and continued in their employment as a clerk, making no investments himself, but leaving the surplus earnings on interest in their hands until January, 1866, when he went to the house of a cousin in Courtland, Alabama, and while there died by an accident, leaving personal estate in Alabama. On the twenty-seventh of January, 1866, Goodloe took out letters of administration in Alabama, and in February, 1866, went to Memphis, and there, upon exhibiting his letters of administration, received from defendant the sum of money due to Quarles, amounting to $3,455.22 (which is the same for which this suit is brought,) and included it in his inventory and in his final account, which was allowed by the probate court in Alabama. There were no other debts due from Quarles in Tennessee. All his next of kin resided in Virginia or in Alabama; and no administration was taken out on his estate in Tennessee until June, 1866, when letters of administration were there issued to the plaintiff.

[W]e are of opinion that the court erred in instructing the jury that if the domicile was in Tennessee they must find for the plaintiff; and in refusing to instruct them, as requested by the defendant, that the payment to the Alabama administrator before the appointment of one in Tennessee, and there being no Tennessee creditors, was a valid discharge of the defendant, without reference to the domicile.

There is no doubt that the succession to the personal estate of a deceased person is governed by the law of his domicile at the time of his death; that the proper place for the principal administration of his estate is that domicile; that administration may also be taken out in any place in which he leaves personal property; and that no suit for the recovery of a debt, due to him at the time of his death, can be brought by an administrator as such in any state in which he has not taken out administration. But the reason for this last rule is the protection of the rights of citizens of the state in which the suit is brought; and the objection does not rest upon any defect of the administrator's title in the property, but upon his personal incapacity to sue as administrator beyond the jurisdiction which appointed him.

If a debtor, residing in another state, comes into the state in which the administrator has been appointed, and there pays him, the payment is a valid discharge everywhere. If the debtor, being in that state, is there sued by the administrator, and judgment recovered against him, the administrator may bring suit in his own name upon that judgment in the state where the debtor resides. Talmage v. Chapel, 16 Mass. 71.

The administrator, by virtue of his appointment and authority as such, obtains the title in promissory notes or other written evidences of debt, held by the intestate at the time of his death, and coming to the possession of the administrator; and may sell, transfer, and indorse the same; and the purchasers or indorsees may maintain actions in their own names against the debtors in another state, if the debts are negotiable promissory notes, or if the law of the state in which the action is brought permits the assignee of a chose in action to sue in his own name. . . .

In accordance with these views, it was held by this court, when this case was before it after a former trial, at which the domicile of the intestate appeared to have been in Alabama, that the payment in Tennessee to the Alabama administrator was good as against the administrator afterwards appointed in Tennessee. Wilkins v. Ellett, 9 Wall. 740.

The fact that the domicile of the intestate has now been found by the jury to be in Tennessee does not appear to us to make any difference.

There are neither creditors nor next of kin in Tennessee. The Alabama administrator has inventoried and accounted for the amount of this debt in Alabama. The distribution among the next of kin, whether made in Alabama or in Tennessee, must be according to the law of the domicile; and it has not been suggested that there is any difference between the laws of the two states in that regard.

The judgment must, therefore, be reversed, and the case remanded with directions to set aside the verdict and to order a new trial.

NOTES

1.   It would seem convenient to permit the decedent's domicile to appoint a universal successor whose title to the decedent's assets in other states would be recognized under full faith and credit. Further, this person should be permitted to sue everywhere as of right to collect these assets. The existence of such a successor would vastly simplify the handling of a multistate estate. So far as is known, only one court has attempted to appoint such a universal successor, and this appointment was vacated on appeal on the ground that no jurisdiction could be exercised over assets in other states. In re De Lano's Estate, 315 P.2d 611 (Kan.1957); cf. Hanson v. Denckla, p. 75, supra. On the other hand, universal succession has been achieved in the area of debtors' estates through the appointment of a statutory successor. See pp. 1064–1082, infra and Cheatham, The Statutory Successor, the Receiver and the Executor in Conflict of Laws, 44 Colum.L.Rev. 549 (1944). Why should what is possible in the area of debtors' estates not likewise be possible in decedents' estates? See D. Currie, The Multiple Personality of the Dead: Executors, Administrators and the Conflict of Laws, 33 U.Chi.L.Rev. 429, 435–38 (1966).

2.   The Uniform Probate Code provides in §§ 4–201 to 4–203 that, unless he has been given notice not to do so by a resident creditor, a debtor may without danger of double liability pay a debt owed a nonresident decedent to a foreign domiciliary representative upon the latter's affidavit stating, among other things that "no local administration, or application or petition therefor, is pending in this state." Also under §§ 4–204 to 4–205, that a foreign domiciliary representative, upon filing copies of his appointment and giving bond, "may exercise as to assets in this state all powers of a local personal representative," including the bringing of suit, if no local representative has been appointed and no petition for such an appointment is pending.

3.   "Most of the difficulty found in the reported decisions has concerned the effect of a voluntary payment made to an administrator outside the state of his appointment. The results are conflicting and reflect the divergent theoretical conceptions, heretofore discussed, of territorial restriction upon the legal personality of an administrator.... [T]he great majority of decisions have upheld such payments, at least where no local representative has been appointed at the time of payment." Hopkins, Conflict of Laws in Administration of Decedents' Intangibles, 28 Iowa L.Rev. 422, 435–37 (1943).

4. Most case authority holds that a domiciliary administrator may assign, and the assignee may enforce, a claim which is not represented by a negotiable instrument and which is owed the decedent by a person who is not subject to suit in a state where an ancillary administrator has been appointed. Restatement, Second, Conflict of Laws § 333 (1971); Hay, Borchers, Symeonides &Whytock, Conflict of Laws § 22.17 (6th ed.2018); McDowell, Foreign Personal Representatives 63–66 (1957).

5. For examples of achieving uniformity in the administration of the estate see Matter of Estate of Jones, 858 P.2d 983 (Utah 1993), which gave full faith and credit to the California determination, in an ancillary administration concerning California realty, of the Utah claimant's status as pretermitted child. See also O'Keefe v. O'Keefe (In re Estate of O'Keefe), 833 So.2d 157 (Fla.App.2002): full faith and credit given in Florida probate proceeding to California determination upholding a settlement with disinherited child against latter's claim that the settlement was the result of forgery and fraud; the California court had jurisdiction and the place to raise these objections was there. See also Cuevas v. Kelly, 873 So.2d 367 (Fla.App.2004): full faith and credit given to Mississippi determination of domicile when testator moved from Florida after being adjudicated incompetent; the Mississippi court had jurisdiction and appellee had notice of the Mississippi proceeding.

Cf. West v. White, 758 P.2d 424 (Or.App.1988), aff'd en banc, 766 P.2d 383 (Or.1988): domiciliary administration in Massachusetts involved a Trust deed to Oregon real property. The Trust deed was "personal property" and had its situs at the decedent's domicile at death. Without property in Oregon, the Oregon probate court lacked jurisdiction.

Administration of Land

Land owned by a decedent is subject to administration as part of his estate only when and to the extent that a statute of the state of the situs so provides. When assets within State X, where the land is located, are insufficient to satisfy claims proved and allowed in X, the land will be ordered sold even though there may be other assets in State Y. The land will also be ordered sold to satisfy claims proved and allowed in State Y when the assets in State Y are insufficient to satisfy creditors. When a will confers upon an executor the power to sell land, he need not receive an appointment from the court of the state where the land is to exercise the power to sell. This is because he is said to be acting in an individual and not in a representative capacity. Bacharach v. Spriggs, 292 S.W. 150 (Ark.1927).

An order from the domiciliary state denying probate of a will precludes heirs from submitting that will for probate in another state where the decedent owned real property. The will may comply with the execution formalities of one state but not the other. "Principles of res judicata and full faith and credit have no application in matters involving probate and title to realty." In re Estate of Latek, 960 N.E.2d 193 (Ind.App.2012).

Unless authorized by a State X statute, an executor or administrator appointed in State Y may not foreclose a mortgage on land in State X. Under certain circumstances, however, his assignee will be permitted to do so. See Restatement, Second, Conflict of Laws §§ 339–40 (1971).

Estate of Hanreddy

Supreme Court of Wisconsin, 1922.
176 Wis. 570, 186 N.W. 744.

One Joseph Hanreddy, a resident citizen of Chicago, Illinois, died there testate April 8, 1918. On June 25, 1918, his widow, Margaret Hanreddy, was duly appointed, qualified, and ever since has acted and is still acting as executrix of his estate in the probate court of Cook county, Illinois. Claims were therein filed aggregating more than $50,000. The available assets subject to that jurisdiction do not exceed $4,000.

In August, 1918, in the county court of Milwaukee county, Wisconsin, the will of said Joseph Hanreddy was duly probated and the said Margaret Hanreddy appointed executrix in ancillary proceedings, there being assets aggregating over $50,000 belonging to said estate as well as resident creditors within the state of Wisconsin. Claims have been filed therein by both resident and nonresident creditors in amounts in excess of the assets. Some creditors have filed their respective claims in both jurisdictions.

In August, 1919, the said executrix filed a petition in the county court of Milwaukee county reciting the probate proceedings in Illinois and in this state; the claims filed in the respective proceedings and their respective assets substantially as above set forth; the fact that the assets of the said estate are insufficient to pay all of the debts of the said estate and that the said estate is insolvent; that if all the claims filed were allowed there would be assets in the Wisconsin jurisdiction sufficient to pay the claims filed in that jurisdiction to approximately ninety per cent. thereof, and that as to the claims in the Illinois jurisdiction the assets there would not be sufficient to pay more than a ten per cent. dividend thereon. . . . She asked that no payment be made upon the claims filed in the Wisconsin jurisdiction until after final adjudication in both states upon all the claims and a determination had of the pro rata percentage that could properly be paid from the entire assets in both jurisdictions upon the respective claims in the several jurisdictions and that after such ascertainment and payment upon such pro rata percentage of the claims filed and allowed in the Wisconsin jurisdiction the surplus should be turned over to her as executrix in the jurisdiction of Illinois, to be there likewise applied.

. . . After a hearing the court made his findings of fact reciting substantially as above stated and his conclusions of law as follows:

"I. That the assets in said ancillary administration constitute a fund out of which the claims of creditors residing in Wisconsin, and who have duly filed their claims, be paid in full. . . .

"III. That this court has no jurisdiction to consider or allow claims of foreign creditors . . .

"IV. That any residue in the possession of the ancillary administrator after the payment of the claims of Wisconsin creditors duly allowed, and after the payment of the costs and expenses of the ancillary administration, are hereby ordered to be paid and delivered by said ancillary administrator to the executrix of the domiciliary estate."

An appeal was taken from the judgment or order entered in conformity with said conclusions of law. . . .

■ ESCHWEILER, J. . . .

Where the assets of a deceased, though found in several jurisdictions, are sufficient to pay the debts allowed against his estate in the several jurisdictions, ordinarily each of the separate jurisdictions proceeds to adjust claims and provide for their payment out of the assets in their control, each independently of the other; but where, as here, the entire assets of the deceased are insufficient to pay all his just obligations, there is such an interdependence between the various jurisdictions as to require the application of the old maxim that "Equality is equity"; and the several courts administering the affairs of the deceased, each being apprised of that situation, must no longer consider the assets within their respective controls as separate and distinct funds for distribution to the creditors within such jurisdictions, but as one entire fund in which all creditors of the deceased having just claims of equal standing shall share pro rata. It makes no material difference by whom or how the situation is brought to the knowledge of the court. In this case the petition of the executrix alone was sufficient. It is the fact of insolvency that raises the equity. It then becomes the duty of the court itself, administering the assets, to subordinate the demands of the local creditors to be paid in full or to the exhaustion of the assets to the broader rights of the creditors as a whole to share on an equal footing in the assets as a whole. . . .

[This] is but the application in another form of the rule that is applied in the distribution of the assets of an insolvent corporation foreign to the distributing jurisdiction, where resident and nonresident creditors must share pro rata. Blake v. McClung, 172 U.S. 239, 19 S.Ct. 165, 43 L.Ed. 432; . . .

It is of course proper that sufficient of the assets belonging to the estate and found in Wisconsin should be held here so that when the proper percentage is ultimately determined in the two jurisdictions the creditors whose claims are filed and allowed in this jurisdiction shall be here paid their proper percentage.

[I]t is clear that, there being assets of the deceased and resident creditors within the state of Wisconsin, the county court of Milwaukee county had ... the duty ... to receive, examine, and adjust the claims and demands of all persons against the deceased ...

Under [the Wisconsin] statute as well as under the general principles governing such matters, no distinction can be made between ancillary administration and domiciliary administration as to the rights of nonresident creditors to file, in accordance with the established practice of this state, their claims against such an estate for adjustment and allowance. ...

■ BY THE COURT. Judgment reversed, and the cause remanded with directions to enter judgment in accordance with this opinion.

NOTES

1. Sister-state creditors of an insolvent decedent's estate are undoubtedly entitled to the same constitutional protection that is given to the creditors of an insolvent corporation. See Blake v. McClung, p. 1064, infra, cited in the principal case.

2. Although the law of the domicile provides that claims not presented against the estate there within the period of limitations shall be forever barred, a claim may be presented in any other state where there is an administration and whose period of limitations has not yet run. Restatement, Second, Conflict of Laws § 345 (1971).

3. For decisions similar to *Hanreddy*, see Sanders v. Boyer, 613 P.2d 1291 (Ariz.App.1980) (residuary estate chargeable with estate taxes and cost related to ancillary administration); In re Hirsch's Estate, 66 N.E.2d 636 (Ohio 1946) (unsecured claims against insolvent estate paid at equal rate to foreign and domestic creditors); In re Eaton, 202 N.W. 309 (Wis.1925) (court without jurisdiction to make allowance for widow in ancillary proceeding of solvent estate with no known local creditors). But see Matter of Estate of Mason, 947 P.2d 886 (Ariz.App.1997) (no estate tax apportionment between probate and non-probate assets).

4. In support of treating the estate as a unit even though it is composed of assets located in different states or nations, see Hay, Borchers, Symeonides & Whytock, Conflict of Laws §§ 22.6–10 (6th ed.2018); Scoles, Conflict of Laws and Creditors' Rights in Decedents' Estates, 42 Iowa L.Rev. 341 (1957).

Lenn v. Riche

Supreme Judicial Court of Massachusetts, 1954.
331 Mass. 104, 117 N.E.2d 129.

[During his life, Paul Bonn made a gift to plaintiff of a valuable painting. The gift was made in Germany. Later in France plaintiff loaned the painting to Bonn so that he could exhibit and preserve it. Bonn died in France and by his will duly "allowed" there named his wife as "universal legatee." After she refused to return the painting to plaintiff,

plaintiff brought this suit against the ancillary administrator of Bonn's Massachusetts estate. Plaintiff recovered in the court below and defendant excepted.]

■ QUA, CHIEF JUSTICE. [T]he defendant insists that this action cannot be maintained against the administrator of Bonn's estate in Massachusetts because Bonn left a will duly established in France, in which he made his wife ... his universal legatee, and because under French law, the universal legatee, who takes all the property of the deceased, becomes personally chargeable with his obligations. The argument is that if suit had been brought in France it must have been brought against [his wife] personally. This may be true. . . . But it is not controlling over the law governing the administration of estates in this Commonwealth. Here the administrator is liable to suit upon obligations of the deceased, and creditors resident here, of whom the plaintiff is one, are entitled to secure payment of their claims out of Massachusetts assets in the manner provided by Massachusetts law. At the moment of Bonn's death he owed to the plaintiff an obligation which had arisen under French law to return her property to her upon request. This obligation was chargeable against his Massachusetts assets. It was like a promissory note owed but not yet due. Even though at Bonn's death there was as yet no breach of his obligation, there was a breach when the plaintiff made her request to the universal legatee for a return of her property. We think the request, if any was necessary, was properly made to the universal legatee in France. She was the general representative of the succession and of the personalty of the deceased at the domicil of the deceased. The defendant had not at that time been appointed administrator here. A request to the defendant after his appointment would have been a barren gesture. There was no reason to suppose that the plaintiff's property was in this Commonwealth or in the control of the administrator appointed here in his capacity as ancillary administrator. The plaintiff can maintain her action here. She was not obliged to see Massachusetts assets swept away and then go to France to assert her rights. . . .

Exceptions overruled.

NOTES

1. The principal case is in line with authority. But was the result a desirable one? The administration of a multistate estate would obviously be facilitated by requiring all creditors to file their claims in the court of domiciliary administration. Would the advantages that such a rule would bring to estate administration be outweighed by the hardship that it would visit upon out-of-state creditors? Compare D. Currie, The Multiple Personality of the Dead: Executors, Administrators and the Conflict of Laws, 33 U.Chi.L.Rev. 429, 453–62 (1966).

2. On the different methods in the civil law and the common law for the determination of death and the administration of the property of a decedent and the coordination of the two methods, see Ehrenzweig, Conflict of Laws

180–82 (1962). In Wren, Problems in Probating Foreign Wills and Using Foreign Personal Representatives, 17 Sw.L.J. 55 (1963), special attention is given to differences in the laws of Mexico and Texas.

The Uniform International Wills Act, which constitutes Art. II, Part 10 of the Uniform Probate Code, provides formalities for the execution and registration of an "international will," to be valid "as regards form, irrespective . . . of the place where it was made, of the location of the assets and of the nationality, domicile, or residence of the testator." Sec. 2 [§ 2–1002 of the Uniform Probate Code]. Such a will must be executed before an "authorized person," defined as "individuals who have been admitted to practice . . . [in] this state" (§ 9) as well as "members of the diplomatic and consular service of the United States, designated by Foreign Service Regulation" (1(2)). For discussion, see Averill & Brantley, A Comparison of Arkansas's Current Law Concerning Succession, Wills, and Other Donative Transfers with Article II of the 1990 Uniform Probate Code, 17 U.Ark.Little Rock L.J. 631 (1995).

Ghilain v. Couture

Supreme Court of New Hampshire, 1929.
84 N.H. 48, 146 A. 395, 65 A.L.R. 553.

■ SNOW, J. This action was brought by the plaintiff as administratrix by appointment in Massachusetts, the domicile of the deceased, against defendants resident in this state, to recover for death from an injury received here.

In claims for death the nature of the right of action, and the party in whom it is vested, are fixed by the lex loci delicti. . . . The plaintiff's right of action, if any, is therefore determined by the law of this state. At the time of the accident the sole basis for such a right was P.S., c. 191, ss. 10–13. Poff v. New England Tel. & Teleg. Company, 72 N.H. 164, 55 A. 891. This statute authorized an action to recover damages for death caused by wrongful physical injury to the person, for the benefit of the widow or widower and the children, if any, otherwise for the benefit of the heirs at law of the deceased; said action to be brought at any time within two years after the death of the injured party and not afterwards. Though not expressed in so many words, the statute clearly contemplated that actions to enforce the right should be brought by the "administrator of the deceased party." P.S. c. 191, s. 12; Cogswell v. Concord & M. Railroad, 68 N.H. 192, 194, 44 A. 293. See Laws 1887, c. 71, s. 1. The interpretation of the quoted words is the principal and the controlling issue presented.

The contentions of the defendants are that the plaintiff, domiciliary administratrix, was not an "administrator of the deceased party" within the meaning of the statute, and that she was, therefore, wholly without authority to bring the suit; that her attempted action was a mere nullity; and that, the limitation having run, the plaintiff's writ is incapable of amendment by substitution of herself as the ancillary administratrix so as to relate back and cure her defective suit.[1]

In support of their contention of the plaintiff's want of authority the defendants cite the general rule that an administrator cannot sue outside of the state of his appointment, . . .

While the rule presupposes that an administrator has no claim to recognition *as a matter of right,* beyond the bounds of the state of his appointment . . . such want of *legal right* is not the reason for the rule. The rule does not arise from any want of inherent authority in the court to accord such recognition. . . . No statute or . . . principle of the common law forbids it. . . .

[I]n a larger sense, the so-called rule that executors and administrators will not ordinarily be granted extra-territorial recognition, and therefore will not generally be permitted to bring actions in the courts of foreign jurisdictions . . . is but an exception to the broader doctrine that the acts of foreign representatives or fiduciaries, as a matter of practice, convenience and expediency, will be given effect through the exercise of a liberal comity. . . . An exception is made whenever such a course would conflict with any principle of public policy. It is in such a conflict with state policy that the denial of the right of action generally to foreign administrators, without first taking out letters here, finds a sufficient, and its only, justification. Upon whatever ground the rule calling for such denial may formerly have been thought to rest it is now generally recognized that it is based solely upon the policy of the courts of each state to protect resident creditors of the decedent against the withdrawal into another state of assets on which they may equitably rely for the payment of the debts that may be due them. . . .

The damages recoverable under the statute by its terms (s. 13) "shall belong and be distributed" to the designated beneficiaries. They are not assets of the estate within the ordinary meaning of the word. . . . As no creditor of the deceased can be either benefited or burdened by any action brought under the statute or have "the slightest . . . interest in the recovery sought" . . . it is clear that the legislature, in designating the person who shall bring the action, could not have been influenced by a rule which had as its sole justification the protection of local creditors. In interpreting the statute the rule relied upon by the defendants may, therefore, be laid out of the case.

Nor is it perceived that the recognition of a domiciliary administrator as the plaintiff in actions under our death statute offends any state policy so as to require his exclusion under the broader principles of comity. . . . To assume otherwise would be in effect saying that it would be impolitic to extend the courtesy of our courts to a

---

[1]   The decedent, a resident of Massachusetts, was killed in New Hampshire on May 13, 1924. The present action was brought on May 12, 1926. The plaintiff was appointed administratrix in New Hampshire in 1928. —eds.

Massachusetts representative for fear that the courts of that commonwealth would not hold its own appointee accountable for his special trust according to its definitive terms. The acceptance of such a postulate would be to impugn the mutual confidence possessed by the courts of the respective states in each other so essential to the very existence of the doctrine of comity. . . .

We therefore come to the interpretation of the statute unhampered by any rules or questions of state policy peculiar to the ordinary administration of intestate property to which it has no relation, except as it utilizes the personal representative of the decedent, ex officio, as the instrument of enforcement of the right of action which it provides. . . .

While it may fairly be assumed that the legislature had in mind the domestic administrator if there be one, there is nothing in the language showing an intention to restrict the court in the exercise of its powers, under the principles of comity, to recognize the domiciliary administrator in the absence of a local representative. It is our conclusion that the legislature used the words "the administrator of the deceased party" as inclusive of any representative who, by comity or otherwise, may be admitted to sue in this forum without infringing any principle of state policy. . . .

. . . The suggestion in argument that the defendant would not be protected by a judgment in the suit as instituted is without merit. It seems to be well settled that a judgment for damages for the wrongful death of a person is a bar to an action in another state to recover damages of the same character and for the same death, where the real parties in interest are the same, even though the nominal parties are different. . . .

. . . There was no error in the ruling that the plaintiff was not precluded by law on the record from maintaining the suit for her beneficiaries under the statute.

Exceptions overruled.

NOTES

1.   See also Morris v. Solow Mgt. Corp., 779 N.Y.S.2d 29 (App.Div.2004); Wiener v. Specific Pharmaceuticals, 83 N.E.2d 673 (N.Y.1949); Briggs v. Pennsylvania R. Co., 153 F.2d 841 (2d Cir.1946).

2.   The common law rule is that a foreign personal representative lacks capacity to maintain an action outside the state of appointment. One way to overcome the ban, where it persists, is for the foreign representative to be appointed ancillary representative in the second state.

3.   Courts have created several exceptions to the rule: (a) The defendant waives the defense of incapacity of the representative by failing to plead it promptly. (b) When the representative has "title" in himself personally, he may sue, as when he makes a contract or recovers a judgment after the death of the decedent, or holds negotiable paper. This result may be wise, though the form of expression can scarcely be justified since the personal representative does not hold these assets for himself but must account for them as representative. (c) An action for the death of a decedent may be maintained, at least if the proceeds will go to the members of the family rather than to the general estate, so creditors are not concerned. See Hatas v. Partin, 175 So.2d 759 (1965). (d) An action may be maintained by a foreign personal representative when this would be for the best interests of the estate and would not prejudice the interests of local creditors. The states vary in their recognition of the exceptions mentioned. See Restatement, Second, Conflict of Laws § 354 (1971).

Eubank Heights Apartments, Limited v. Lebow

United States Court of Appeals, First Circuit, 1980.
615 F.2d 571.

■ ALDRICH, SENIOR CIRCUIT JUDGE.

On September 28, 1972, Saul L. Lebow executed in Massachusetts a limited partnership agreement and, in connection therewith, six promissory notes. . . . The payee was the partnership, Eubank Heights Apartments, Ltd. The partnership was created under Texas law, with its general partners and its principal office in Texas. Lebow, a resident of Massachusetts, died on March 12, 1973. His wife, Estelle, was appointed executrix on May 22, 1973. Apparently not until March, 1974, did the partnership, hereinafter plaintiff, learn of Lebow's death and of the probate proceedings. On April 3, 1974, plaintiff exercised its right to make the notes payable in Texas by notifying defendant. On December 13, 1974, plaintiff brought suit on the notes in the state court of Texas, naming as defendant the Estate of Saul L. Lebow. Service was made on the Secretary of State, and notice was sent to, and received by, the executrix. She made no response, and on May 16, 1975, a default judgment for the amounts of the notes, interest, and attorney's fees was entered, naming the Estate as the judgment debtor. There is, of course, no such entity; at least none such is recognized in Massachusetts. . . . Nor were there any assets, to be denominated an estate, in Texas.

Action was brought on the judgment in the district court for the District of Massachusetts on February 12, 1976, naming as defendant Estelle I. Lebow, Executrix of the Estate of Saul L. Lebow. The above facts having been made to appear by affidavits, plaintiff moved for summary judgment. . . . The court granted the motion . . . and defendant appeals.

The first defense asserted is that decedent did not have sufficient connection with Texas to give that state jurisdiction over him under its longarm statute, Tex.Rev.Civ.Stat.Ann. art. 2031b, §§ 3, 4. This is a conventional statute, whose reach is restricted only by the Constitution. . . . Although the partnership was created to deal with New Mexico land, it was a Texas-run enterprise, by the terms of the agreement governed by Texas law, and had cumulatively such Texas connections that we see no merit in defendant's attack on the Texas court's in personam jurisdiction so far as the decedent was concerned. . . .

This, however, is only one step. However labeled, this was not an action against the decedent—he no longer existed. The suit was, in effect, against his former assets; obviously defendant would not be liable individually. The fact that Texas would have had in personam jurisdiction over him does not mean that it had jurisdiction in rem, or quasi in rem. Indeed, he died before there even was a claim against his assets. What happens to a person's intangible assets after death is determined by the state of domicile. . . . We must look, accordingly, to the law of Massachusetts to determine whether plaintiff took adequate steps to secure an interest chargeable against the assets. . . .

. . . In the district court defendant did not claim that the Estate of Saul L. Lebow was a nonentity, but asserted that it was "a different party . . . than the defendant in this action." We think defendant's present claim, that there was no party at all, hypertechnical. Identification was clear, and statutory service was made on the executrix. We would not hold this judgment a worthless piece of paper simply because defendant's name as estate representative was not included thereon. Rather, we take the issue to be whether plaintiff could obtain a judgment in Texas valid against estate assets in Massachusetts by suing the executrix in Texas. . . .

A long held view is that a court-appointed estate representative cannot represent the estate for purposes of suit, whether as plaintiff or defendant, beyond the state borders. It would have advanced consideration of this case substantially if plaintiff had called our attention to Saporita v. Litner, 1976, 371 Mass. 607, 358 N.E.2d 809. It is not our primary obligation to be acquainted with Massachusetts law; counsel owe a duty to the court.[3]

In *Saporita* a Massachusetts creditor succeeded in obtaining a judgment in Massachusetts against an executor of a Connecticut estate. The court, after extensive discussion of the old cases, held that such procedure was in accord with the times. We cannot think that Massachusetts would decline to take the reciprocal view, and refuse to recognize a Texas judgment against a Massachusetts executor. It is true that plaintiff Saporita obtained service in hand on the foreign executor in Massachusetts, whereas defendant here received only substituted service by mail, but we do not think that a significant difference. If the Texas long arm would have reached the decedent, we do not believe it withered on his death. . . . We hold the judgment valid.

---

[3] We are also critical of defendant, who either shared plaintiff's negligence in not discovering *Saporita,* or else was disingenuous in arguing that defendant "had no standing to be subject to an action in Texas" without mentioning it.

NOTES

1. Most of the modern long-arm statutes provide that in the event of the defendant's death suit may be brought against the defendant's personal representative. For a good discussion of the problem, see D. Currie, The Multiple Personality of the Dead: Executors, Administrators and the Conflict of Laws, 33 U.Chi.L.Rev. 429 (1966).

2. Section 4–302 of the Uniform Probate Code provides that "a foreign personal representative is subject to the jurisdiction of the courts of this state to the same extent that his decedent was subject to jurisdiction immediately prior to death."

3. RESTATEMENT, SECOND, CONFLICT OF LAWS (1971):

§ 358. Suit Against Foreign Executor or Administrator

An action may be maintained against a foreign executor or administrator upon a claim against the decedent when the local law of the forum authorizes suit in the state against the executor or administrator and

(a) suit could have been maintained within the state against the decedent during his lifetime because of the existence of a basis of jurisdiction other than mere physical presence . . . , or

(b) the executor or administrator has done an act in the state in his official capacity.

INGERSOLL V. CORAM, 211 U.S. 335, 29 S.Ct. 92 (1908). [An action was brought in a state court of Montana by the Montana ancillary administrator of a New York lawyer against the lawyer's clients for a large fee alleged to have been earned in Montana. On motion of the defendants the complaint was dismissed for failure to state a cause of action. The present action was then brought in the federal court in Massachusetts by the New York domiciliary administratrix, who had also been appointed ancillary administratrix in Massachusetts, of the lawyer to recover the fee. The defense was that the judgment in the Montana proceeding was a bar. The Supreme Court of the United States held, two justices dissenting without opinion, that it was not a bar.]

■ JUSTICE MCKENNA . . . Respondents assert the identity of the action in Montana with the present suit, and upon that identity they urge that such action constitutes *res judicata*. Petitioner denies the identity of the actions, and urges besides that there is no such privity between the parties as to make the Montana action *res judicata* of the pending case. In support of the latter contention petitioner urges that an ancillary administrator in one jurisdiction is not in privity with an ancillary administrator in another jurisdiction, and that therefore a judgment against one is not a bar to a suit by the other. . . .

We shall assume that there is identity of subject-matter between the Montana action and that at bar, but the question remains, Was there identity of parties? An extended discussion of the question is made unnecessary by the case of Brown v. Fletcher, 210 U.S. 82, 28 S.Ct. 702 . . . The latter case [Stacy v. Thrasher, 6 How. 44] was quoted from as follows: "Where administrations are granted to different persons in different states, they are so far deemed independent of each other that a judgment obtained against one will furnish no right of action against the other, to affect assets received by the latter in virtue of his own administration; for, in contemplation of law, there is no privity between him and the other administrator." . . . That there is a certain amount of artificiality in the doctrine was pointed out in Stacy v. Thrasher, and that it leads to the inconvenience and burdensome result of retrying controversies and repeating litigations. The doctrine, however, was vindicated as a necessary consequence of the different sources from which the different administrators received their powers, and the absence of privity between them, and that the imputations against it were not greater than could be made against other "logical conclusions upon admitted legal principles." It is not necessary, therefore, to review in detail the argument of respondents.

[The Supreme Court reversing the Circuit Court of Appeals, held the Montana judgment was not binding in the later proceeding in the federal court in Massachusetts and allowed recovery of the fee.]

NOTES

1. It seems likely that if the issue were to arise today the Supreme Court would overrule Ingersoll v. Coram and hold that a judgment involving one administrator is binding on administrators appointed in other states. See Hay, Borchers, Symeonides & Whytock, Conflict of Laws § 22.19 (6th. ed.2018). The Supreme Court of the United States has held that, if the same person is executor in two states, an adverse judgment in one state will be recognized as binding in the other state.

2. Nash v. Benari, 105 A. 107 (Me.1918). The decedent died domiciled in Massachusetts and Benari was appointed both domiciliary administrator in Massachusetts and ancillary administrator in Maine. The plaintiff recovered judgment in Massachusetts against Benari, as domiciliary administrator, on an alleged debt owed her by the decedent. This judgment being largely unsatisfied, the plaintiff brought an action on the original claim against Benari, as ancillary administrator, in Maine. Benari claimed by way of defense that this claim had been merged in the Massachusetts judgment. Held for the plaintiff. There is no privity between administrators for the same decedent appointed in different states. ". . . the fact that one and the same person is administrator in both states does not alter the doctrine." Accord: Wisemantle v. Hull Enterprises, Inc., 432 N.E.2d 613 (Ill.App.1981).

3. According to the majority rule, when a claimant brings suit against an administrator to recover on an alleged debt owed by the decedent and loses, the claimant will thereafter be precluded from bringing an action on the same claim against another administrator in a second state. Restatement, Second, Conflict of Laws § 357 (1971).

4. Section 4–401 of the Uniform Probate Code provides that "An adjudication rendered in any jurisdiction in favor of or against any personal representative of the estate is as binding on the local personal representative as if he were a party to the adjudication."

Distribution, Taxes, and Planning

Distribution. The domiciliary representative distributes the net estate in his hands after payment of debts and expenses to those entitled to it. The ancillary representative may, subject to the order of the court, transmit the net estate in his hands to the domiciliary representative, or he may turn the net proceeds over to the distributees directly when this is the fair and economical thing to do. The distribution may be made more complex by the assertion of nonbarrable interests or the necessity of election. See, generally, D. Currie, The Multiple Personality of the Dead: Executors, Administrators and the Conflict of Laws, 33 U.Chi.L.Rev. 429 (1966).

Taxes. Problems of disputed domicile in relation to state succession taxes are discussed at pp. 15–18, supra. There are also problems on the apportionment of the burden of the federal estate tax, as the following decision illustrates:

In Gellerstedt v. United Missouri Bank of Kansas City, 865 S.W.2d 707 (Mo.App.1993), the decedent had died domiciled in Missouri. Her will, executed some seventeen years earlier while domiciled in Kansas, was silent as to the allocation of state and federal tax burdens. The defendant bank paid the federal estate tax, thereafter made distribution to specific distributees but did not deduct a prorata portion of the tax liability. Plaintiff seeks a declaratory judgment to the effect that the tax should be prorated among all of the recipients under the will (the Missouri rule) and not be borne solely by the residue (the Kansas rule). The court selected the law of the testator's domicile at death but noted that "such law should not be blindly and mechanically applied. It may be that in some cases the application of the law of domicile at death would produce an absurd and inequitable result, or one that clearly would have been abhorrent to the testator."

See also 26 U.S.C.A. § 2207 (2003) (Internal Revenue Code), concerning the tax liability of the recipient of property over which the decedent had a power of appointment.

Estate Planning. In Estate of Prestie, 138 P.3d 520 (Nev.2006), the decedent's will provided that the "estate may be administered under the California Independent Administration of Estates Act." In Nevada, the decedent's domicile at death, the district court held, and the Supreme Court affirmed, that Nevada law applied and that decedent's marriage subsequent to the execution of the will revoked the will as to his surviving spouse. The quoted language was not a choice-of-law provision but merely permitted administration of the estate with limited court supervision, as provided by California law. The provision thus addressed the probate process, not applicable substantive law. Moreover, it was discretionary. The opponent had argued that the use of "estate" in the will included the right to take under the will and made that issue subject to California law. In passing, the court offered this advice: "We are cognizant of the fact that modern estate planning regularly utilizes revocable inter vivos trusts with pour-over wills. This approach to estate planning usually results in amendments, if any, being made to the revocable trust and not the pour-over will. Given the clear and unambiguous language of NRS 133.110, we caution that a testator must modify his or her will in order to avoid the consequences resulting from the unintentional omission of a surviving spouse pursuant to NRS 133.110." Id. at 524 n. 13. Estate planning with attention to conflict of laws is considered in Casner & Pennell, Estate Planning (8th ed.2012); Ester and Scoles, Estate Planning and Conflict of Laws, 24 Ohio St.L.J. 270 (1963); Scoles & Rheinstein, Conflict Avoidance in Succession Planning, 21 Law & Contemp.Probs. 427 (1956); J. Schoenblum, Multistate and Multinational Estate Planning (3d ed.2007).

See generally Hay, Borchers, Symeonides & Whytock, Conflict of Laws §§ 22.1–22.13 (6th ed.2018).

SECTION 2. DEBTORS' ESTATES

INTRODUCTORY NOTE

The national reach of the Federal Bankruptcy Act has, for the most part, supplanted the old system of administration of insolvent estates through state court receiverships and so has obliterated interstate conflicts problems. The Act does not apply to municipal, insurance, or banking corporations or to building and loan associations. As to them the old problems of interstate conflicts continue and are similar, in large part, to those arising in decedents' estates. Often the liquidator is elevated from the position of a receiver to that of a "statutory successor" and given the enlarged rights in other states that cases in this section reveal. The section is directed principally to the rights of foreign creditors and of foreign liquidators, especially statutory successors. To the last, the full faith and credit clause gives important protection.

Blake v. McClung

Supreme Court of the United States, 1898.
172 U.S. 239, 19 S.Ct. 165, 43 L.Ed. 432.

[The Embreeville Company, a British corporation, qualified to do business in Tennessee under a statute of the state which contained this provision:

". . . creditors who may be residents of this State shall have a priority in the distribution of assets . . . over all simple contract creditors, being residents of any other country or countries, . . ." The corporation acquired property in Tennessee. In a proceeding in a court of the state it was alleged that the corporation was insolvent and a receiver of its property in the state was appointed. Several classes of creditors filed claims against the corporation in the receivership proceedings. They included British creditors, Ohio individual creditors, a Virginia corporation, and residents of Tennessee. The state court applied the statute quoted above so as to give the Tennessee creditors priority over all the others. The state court judgment was appealed to the Supreme Court of the United States.]

■ JUSTICE HARLAN delivered the opinion of the court. . . .

The plaintiffs in error contend that the judgment of the state court, based upon the statute, denies to them rights secured by the second section of the Fourth Article of the Constitution of the United States providing that "the citizens of each State shall be entitled to all privileges and immunities of citizens in the several States," as well as by the first section of the Fourteenth Amendment, declaring that no State shall "deprive any person of life, liberty or property without due process of law," nor "deny to any person within its jurisdiction the equal protection of the laws." . . .

The suggestion is made that as the statute refers only to "residents," there is no occasion to consider whether it is repugnant to the provision of the National Constitution relating to citizens. We cannot accede to this view. . . . The State did not intend to place creditors, citizens of other States, upon an equality with creditors, citizens of Tennessee, and to give priority only to Tennessee creditors over creditors who resided in, but were not citizens of, other States. The manifest purpose was to give to all Tennessee creditors priority over all creditors residing out of that State, whether the latter were citizens or only residents of some other State or country. . . .

We hold such discrimination against citizens of other States to be repugnant to the second section of the Fourth Article of the Constitution of the United States, although, generally speaking, the State has the power to prescribe the conditions upon which foreign corporations may enter its territory for purposes of business. Such a power cannot be exerted with the effect of defeating or impairing rights secured to citizens of the several States by the supreme law of the land. . . .

It may be appropriate to observe that the objections to the statute of Tennessee do not necessarily embrace enactments that are found in some of the States requiring foreign insurance corporations, as a condition of their coming into the State for purposes of business, to deposit with the state treasurer funds sufficient to secure policy holders in its midst. Legislation of that character does not present any question of discrimination against citizens forbidden by the Constitution. Insurance funds set apart in advance for the benefit of home policy holders of a foreign insurance company doing business in the State are a trust fund of a specific kind to be administered for the exclusive benefit of certain persons. . . .

As to the plaintiff in error, the Hull Coal & Coke Company of Virginia, different considerations must govern our decision. It has long been settled that, for purposes of suit by or against it in the courts of the United States, the members of a corporation are to be conclusively presumed to be citizens of the state creating such corporation . . . ; and therefore it has been said that a corporation is to be deemed, for such purposes, a citizen of the state under whose laws it was organized. But it is equally well settled, and we now hold, that a corporation is not a citizen within the meaning of the constitutional provision that "the citizens of each state shall be entitled to all privileges and immunities of citizens in the several states". . . . The Virginia corporation, therefore, cannot invoke that provision for protection against the decree of the state court denying its right to participate upon terms of equality with Tennessee creditors in the distribution of the assets of the British corporation in the hands of the Tennessee court.

Since, however, a corporation is a "person," within the meaning of the fourteenth amendment . . . may not the Virginia corporation invoke for its protection the clause of the amendment declaring that no state shall deprive any person of property without due process, nor deny to any person within its jurisdiction the equal protection of the laws?

[T]his question must receive a negative answer. . . . this court has adjudged that the prohibitions of the fourteenth amendment refer to all the instrumentalities of the state, to its legislative, executive, and judicial authorities . . . [But the] corporation was not, in any legal sense, deprived of its claim, nor was its right to reach the assets of the British corporation in other states or countries disputed. It was only denied the right to participate upon terms of equality with Tennessee creditors in the distribution of particular assets of another corporation doing business in that state. . . .

It is equally clear that the Virginia corporation cannot rely upon the clause declaring that no state shall "deny to any person within its jurisdiction the equal protection of the laws." That prohibition manifestly relates only to the denial by the state of equal protection to persons "within its jurisdiction." . . . Without attempting to state what is the full import of the words, "within its jurisdiction," it is safe to say that a corporation not created by Tennessee, nor doing business there under conditions that subjected it to process issuing from the courts of Tennessee at the instance of suitors, is not, under the above clause of the fourteenth amendment, within the jurisdiction of that state. . . . Nor do we think it came within the jurisdiction of Tennessee, within the meaning of the amendment, simply by presenting its claim in the state court, and thereby becoming a party to this cause. . . .

What may be the effect of the judgment of this court in the present case upon the rights of creditors not residing in the United States it is not necessary to decide. Those creditors are not before the court on this writ of error. The final judgment of the supreme court of Tennessee must be affirmed as to the Hull Coal & Coke Company . . . Rev.St. § 709. As to the other plaintiffs in error, citizens of Ohio, the judgment must be reversed, and the cause remanded for further proceedings not inconsistent with this opinion. It is so ordered.

■ JUSTICE BREWER, with whom CHIEF JUSTICE FULLER concurred, dissenting. . . .

NOTES

1.   On the rights of a corporate creditor under the equal protection of the laws clause, see Kentucky Finance Corp. v. Paramount Auto Exchange Corp., 262 U.S. 544, 43 S.Ct. 636 (1923), p. 1108, infra.

2.   In 2005, § 508 of the Bankruptcy Code was amended to refer only to a creditor of a partnership who receives payment from a partner. Congress also adopted the United Nations Commission on International Trade Law (UNCITRAL) Model Law on Cross-Border Insolvency as chapter 15 of the Bankruptcy Act. The purpose of chapter 15 is to facilitate cooperation between U.S. and foreign courts and authorities in cross-border insolvency cases. 11 U.S.C. § 1501. The chapter authorizes a representative in a foreign bankruptcy proceeding to petition a U.S. court for recognition of the foreign proceeding. Id. § 1509. 11 U.S.C. § 1521 provides:

> (a)   Upon recognition of a foreign proceeding . . . where necessary to effectuate the purpose of this chapter and to protect the assets of the debtor or the interests of the creditors, the court may, at the request of the foreign representative, grant any appropriate relief, including—
>
>> (1)   staying the commencement or continuation of an individual action or proceeding concerning the debtor's assets, rights, obligations or liabilities. . . .
>>
>> (2)   staying execution against the debtor's assets. . . .
>>
>> (3)   suspending the right to transfer, encumber or otherwise dispose of any assets of the debtor. . . .
>>
>> (5)   entrusting the administration or realization of all or part of the debtor's assets within the territorial jurisdiction of the United States to the foreign representative. . . .
>
> (b)   Upon recognition of a foreign proceeding . . . the court may, at the request of the foreign representative, entrust the distribution of all or part of the debtor's assets located in the United States to the foreign representative . . . provided that the court is satisfied that the interests of creditors in the United States are sufficiently protected.

11 U.S.C. § 1524 provides that if a foreign proceeding is recognized, "the foreign representative may intervene in any proceedings in a State or Federal court in the United States in which the debtor is a party."

3. Similar questions arise in bankruptcy proceedings in the European Union. Since 2002, Council Regulation (EC) 1346/2000, [2000] Official Journal L 160/1, now governs the jurisdiction and recognition of decrees in inter-EU insolvencies in all Member States, except Denmark. For discussion see Lueke, The New European Law on International Insolvencies: A German Perspective, 17 Bank.Dev.J. 369 (2001). For an overview of American and European law, see Westbrook, Multinational Enterprises in General Default: Chapter 15, The ALI Principles, and the EU Insolvency Regulation, 76 Am.Bankr.L.J. 1 (2002).

Morris v. Jones

Supreme Court of the United States, 1947.
329 U.S. 545, 67 S.Ct. 451, 91 L.Ed.488, 168 A.L.R. 656.

Certiorari to the Supreme Court of Illinois.

■ JUSTICE DOUGLAS delivered the opinion of the Court.

This case presents a substantial question under the Full Faith and Credit Clause (Art. IV, § 1) of the Constitution.

Chicago Lloyds, an unincorporated association, was authorized by Illinois to transact an insurance business in Illinois and other States. It qualified to do business in Missouri. In 1934 petitioner sued Chicago Lloyds in a Missouri court for malicious prosecution and false arrest. In 1938, before judgment was obtained in Missouri, respondent's predecessor was appointed by an Illinois court as statutory liquidator for Chicago Lloyds. The Illinois court fixed a time for the filing of claims against Chicago Lloyds and issued an order staying suits against it. Petitioner had notice of the stay order but nevertheless continued to prosecute the Missouri suit. At the instance of the liquidator, however, counsel for Chicago Lloyds withdrew from the suit and did not defend it, stating to the Missouri court that the Illinois liquidation proceedings had vested all the property of Chicago Lloyds in the liquidator. Thereafter petitioner obtained a judgment in the Missouri court and filed an exemplified copy of it as proof of his claim in the Illinois proceedings. An order disallowing the claim was sustained by the Illinois Supreme Court against the contention that its allowance was required by the Full Faith and Credit Clause. People ex rel. Jones v. Chicago Lloyds, 391 Ill. 492, 63 N.E.2d 479. . . .

First. We can put to one side, as irrelevant to the problem at hand, several arguments which have been pressed upon us. We are not dealing here with any question of priority of claims against the property of the debtor. For in this proceeding petitioner is not seeking, nor is respondent denying him, anything other than the right to prove his claim in judgment form. No question of parity of treatment of creditors, or the lack thereof (see Blake v. McClung, 172 U.S. 239, 19 S.Ct. 165), is in issue. Nor is there involved in this case any challenge to the Illinois rule, which follows Relfe v. Rundle, [p. 1076, Note 2, infra], that title to all the property of Chicago Lloyds, wherever located, vested in the liquidator. Nor do we have here a challenge to the possession of the liquidator either through an attempt to obtain a lien on the property or otherwise. As pointed out in Riehle v. Margolies, 279 U.S. 218, 224, 49 S.Ct. 310, 312, the distribution of assets of a debtor among creditors ordinarily has a "two-fold aspect." It deals "directly with the property" when it fixes the time and manner of distribution. No one can obtain part of the assets or enforce a right to specific property in the possession of the liquidation court except upon application to it. But proof and allowance of claims are matters distinct from distribution. They do not "deal directly with any of the property." "The latter function, which is spoken of as the liquidation of a claim is strictly a proceeding in personam." Id., 279 U.S. at 224, 49 S.Ct. at 313. The establishment of the existence and amount of a claim against the debtor in no way disturbs the possession of the liquidation court, in no way affects title to the property, and does not necessarily involve a determination of what priority the claim should have. . . .

Moreover, we do not have here a situation like that involved in Pendleton v. Russell, 144 U.S. 640, 12 S.Ct. 743, where it was sought to prove in a New York receivership of a dissolved corporation a judgment obtained in Tennessee after dissolution. The proof was disallowed, dissolution having operated, like death, as an abatement of the suit. No such infirmity appears to be present in the Missouri judgment; and the Illinois Supreme Court did not hold that the appointment of a liquidator for Chicago Lloyds operated as an abatement of the suit. . . . The Missouri judgment represents a liability for acts committed by Chicago Lloyds, not for those of the liquidator. The claims for which the Illinois assets are being administered are claims against Chicago Lloyds. The Missouri judgment represents one of them. There is no more reason for discharging a liquidator from the responsibility for defending pending actions than there is for relieving a receiver of that task. Riehle v. Margolies, supra.

Second. "A judgment of a court having jurisdiction of the parties and of the subject matter operates as res judicata, in the absence of fraud or collusion, even if obtained upon a default." Riehle v. Margolies, supra, 279 U.S. at page 225, 49 S.Ct. at page 313. . . . The full faith and credit to which a judgment is entitled is the credit which it has in the State from which it is taken, not the credit that under other circumstances and conditions it might have had. Moreover, the question whether a judgment is entitled to full faith and credit does not depend on the presence of reciprocal engagements between the States. . . .

As to respondent's contention that the Illinois decree, of which petitioner had notice, should have been given full faith and credit by the Missouri court, only a word need be said. Roche v. McDonald [p. 389, supra], makes plain that the place to raise that defense was in the Missouri proceedings. And see Treinies v. Sunshine Mining Co., [p. 370, supra]. And whatever might have been the ruling on the question, the rights of the parties could have been preserved by a resort to this Court which is the final arbiter of questions arising under the Full Faith and Credit Clause. Williams v. State of North Carolina, [p. 936, supra]. In any event the Missouri judgment is res judicata as to the nature and amount of petitioner's claim as against all defenses which could have been raised. . . .

It is finally suggested that since the Federal Bankruptcy Act provides for exclusive adjudication of claims by the bankruptcy court and excepts insurance companies from the Act (§ 4, 52 Stat. 840, 845, 11 U.S.C. § 22; . . .), the state liquidators of insolvent insurance companies should have the same control over the determination of claims as the bankruptcy court has. This is to argue that by reason of its police power a State may determine the method and manner of proving claims against property which is in its jurisdiction and which is being administered by its courts or administrative agencies. We have no doubt that it may do so except as such procedure collides with the federal Constitution or an Act of Congress. . . . There is such a collision here. When we look to the general statute which Congress has enacted pursuant to the Full Faith and Credit Clause, we find no exception in case of liquidations of insolvent insurance companies. The command is to give full faith and credit to every judgment of a sister State. And where there is no jurisdictional infirmity, exceptions have rarely, if ever, been read into the constitutional provision or the Act of Congress in cases involving money judgments rendered in civil suits. . . .

The function of the Full Faith and Credit Clause is to resolve controversies where state policies differ. Its need might not be so greatly felt in situations where there was no clash of interests between the States. The argument of convenience in administration is at best only another illustration of how the enforcement of a judgment of one State in another State may run counter to the latter's policies. But the answer given by Fauntleroy v. Lum [p. 386, supra], is conclusive. If full faith and credit is not given in that situation, the Clause and the statute fail where their need is the greatest. The argument of convenience, moreover, proves too much. In the first place, it would often be equally appealing to individuals or corporations engaging in multistate activities which might well prefer to defend law suits at home. In the second place, against the convenience of the administration of assets in Illinois is the hardship on the Missouri creditor if he were forced to drop his Missouri litigation, bring his witnesses to Illinois, and start all over again. But full faith and credit is a more inexorable command; its applicability does not turn on a balance of convenience as between litigants. If this were a situation where Missouri's policy would result in the dismemberment of the Illinois estate so that Illinois creditors would go begging, Illinois would have such a large interest at stake as to prevent it. See Clark v. Williard [p. 1074, infra]. But, as we have said, proof and allowance of claims are matters distinct from distribution of assets.

The single point of our decision is that the nature and amount of petitioner's claim has been conclusively determined by the Missouri judgment and may not be relitigated in the Illinois proceedings, it not appearing that the Missouri court lacked jurisdiction over either the parties or the subject matter. . . .

Reversed.

■ JUSTICE FRANKFURTER, with whom concur JUSTICE BLACK and JUSTICE RUTLEDGE, dissenting.

[T]he real issue is this. May Illinois provide that when an insurance concern to which Illinois has given life can, in the judgment of the State courts, no longer be allowed to conduct the insurance business in Illinois, the State may take over the local assets of such an insurance concern for fair distribution among all who have claims against the defunct concern? May the State, pursuant to such a policy, announce in advance, as a rule of fairness, that all claims not previously reduced to valid judgment, no matter how or where they arose, if they are to be paid out of assets thus administered by the State, must be proven on their merits to the satisfaction of Illinois? And may the State specify that this mode of proof apply also to out-of-State creditors so as to require such creditors to prove the merit of their claims against the Illinois assets in liquidation as though they were Illinois creditors, and preclude them from basing their claims merely on a judgment against the insurance concern, obtained after it had legally ceased to be, and after its Illinois assets had by appropriate proceedings passed into ownership of an Illinois liquidator?

. . . The Full Faith and Credit Clause does not eat up the powers reserved to the States by the Constitution. That clause does not embody an absolutist conception of mechanical applicability. As is so often true of constitutional problems, an accommodation must be struck between different provisions of the Constitution. When rights are asserted in one State on the basis of a judgment procured in another, it frequently becomes necessary, as it does here, to define the duty of the courts of the former State in view of that State's power to regulate its own affairs. . . . Surely, the Full Faith and Credit Clause does not require a State to give an advantage to persons dwelling without, when State policy may justifiably restrict its own citizens to a particular procedure in proving claims against a State fund. . . .

Precedent and policy sustain the right of Illinois to have each claimant prove his fair share to the assets in Illinois by the same procedure. . . . Of course Missouri has a right to provide for its methods of administration, in case of default, as to Missouri assets. But we are not here concerned with an attempt to enforce the Missouri judgment against Missouri assets. . . .

. . . The precise relation of the liquidator's legal position to the Missouri judgment, on the basis of which Morris asserts a claim against the liquidator's assets, reinforces the more general considerations.

Morris had no judgment against the company when by Illinois law title to Lloyds' assets passed to the liquidator. . . . The liquidator, as trustee for the creditors of the extinct Illinois company, represented interests that were not the same as those represented by the extinct company when it conducted its own business. In short, the Illinois liquidator was thus a stranger to the Missouri judgment and it cannot be invoked against him in Illinois. . . . Indeed, to subject the assets of the Illinois liquidator to the claim of a judgment obtained against Lloyds in Missouri subsequent to the passage of those assets to the liquidator may well raise constitutional questions. Riley v. New York Trust Co. [p. 303, supra].

. . . Against the claim of out-of-State creditors must be set not merely the interests of Illinois creditors, but also the importance of a unified liquidation administration, the burden to the liquidator of defending suits anywhere in the United States, and the resulting hazards to a fair distribution of the estate. . . . The resolution of this conflict so that the out-of-State creditor must take his place with the Illinois creditors is another instance of a price to be paid for our federalism . . .

This is not to say that the Missouri judgment is invalid. Whether recovery may be based on this judgment in Missouri, or in any other State except Illinois or even in Illinois should the assets go out of the State's hands and return to a reanimated Chicago Lloyds, are questions that do not now call for consideration.

The judgment should be affirmed.

NOTES

1.   Can Pendleton v. Russell, discussed by Justice Douglas in his opinion, satisfactorily be distinguished from Morris v. Jones?

2.   RESTATEMENT, SECOND, CONFLICT OF LAWS (1971):

§ 299. Termination or Suspension of Corporate Existence

(1) Whether the existence of a corporation has been terminated or suspended is determined by the local law of the state of incorporation.

(2) The termination or suspension of a corporation's existence by the state of incorporation will be recognized for most purposes by other states.

Comment . . .

e.   Statute of state of incorporation extending life of corporation. To facilitate collection by the corporation of its assets, and the assertion of creditors' claims against it, statutes commonly provide that for a period of time after the termination or suspension of the corporate existence, suits may be brought by or against the corporation. Likewise, such statutes usually permit the corporation to settle and discharge claims, to transfer its assets, and to do other acts incidental to the winding-up of its affairs.

A corporation whose existence has been terminated or suspended will usually be permitted to exercise in another state such powers as are accorded it by the state of incorporation even though the other state does not give similar powers to domestic corporations. . . .

f. Statute of other state making corporation subject to suit after termination or suspension of existence. Primarily for the purpose of saving local creditors from the inconvenience of having to present their claims in the state of incorporation, statutes sometimes provide that foreign corporations which own things or do business in the state can sue, and remain subject to suit, in the corporate name for a period after their existence has been terminated or suspended. Even if there is no similar statute in the state of incorporation, such a statute will permit suit to be brought in the state of enactment to wind up the corporation's business in that state or to proceed against corporate property located there. . . .

Reporter's Note: . . .

Whether full faith and credit should require extraterritorial enforcement of a judgment rendered against a dissolved foreign corporation under a statute of a State where the corporation did business depends upon which of two considerations is the weightier. The first is the desirability of having a unified winding-up of the corporation's affairs. This can best be achieved by limiting the effect of such statutes to property located within the particular State so as to permit the state of incorporation to insist that, in general, claims against the corporation must be proved before its courts. The second consideration is the convenience of the corporation's creditors who would usually prefer to prove their claims at home and might find it a serious hardship to be compelled to do so in the state of incorporation. . . .

MARTYNE V. AMERICAN UNION FIRE INSURANCE CO., 110 N.E. 502 (N.Y.1915): [The American Union Fire Insurance Company was a Pennsylvania corporation, authorized to carry on business in New York. In 1913, it was ordered dissolved in a court proceeding in Pennsylvania, and its liquidation was directed to be made by the insurance commissioner of that state. There was in force in Pennsylvania a statute which provided that on the dissolution of such a corporation, the insurance commissioner of the state "shall be vested by operation of law with title to all the property, contracts and rights of action of such corporation as of the date of the order so directing him to liquidate." As a result of the dissolution, the policies of fire insurance issued by the corporation became void. After the dissolution, the present action was instituted in New York for the return of unearned premiums under some of the canceled policies, and an alleged indebtedness to the corporation or to the insurance commissioner was attached. A few days later, the New York superintendent of insurance was appointed liquidator of the corporation under the insurance law of New York.

The Pennsylvania insurance commissioner appeared specially in the New York action and moved to have the garnishment and all other proceedings in the action set aside. The trial court granted the motion, and the order was affirmed by the Appellate Division. Appeal, with certain questions of law certified.]

■ CHASE, J. This action is brought against a corporation that has ceased to exist as such. . . .

The insurance commissioner of Pennsylvania is a statutory liquidator and as such took the title to all of the corporate property of the dissolved corporation. The title of foreign statutory assignees is recognized and enforced where it can be without injustice. (Matter of Waite, 99 N.Y. 433, 2 N.E. 440 (1885); Relfe v. Rundle, [p. 1076, Note 2, infra]. See Supreme Council of the Royal Arcanum v. Green, 237 U.S. 531, 35 S.Ct. 724 (1915)) . . .

. . . The rule in this state seems to be so thoroughly established that the title of an assignee or receiver under involuntary or bankruptcy proceedings in a foreign state will not be upheld as against an attachment obtained and served by a resident of this state, that perhaps it should not be changed except by an act of the legislature.

To hold, however, in this case that the title which vested by the Statutes of Pennsylvania in the insurance superintendent of that state as a statutory liquidator does not extend to property in this state as against an attaching creditor here, would be to extend the rule which permits a local creditor to ignore the laws of a foreign state. We are of the opinion that the plaintiff and those from whom he received assignments of claims against the dissolved corporation have no equity that should prevent enforcing the general rule of comity in this case. . . .

The order should be affirmed, with costs. . . .

CLARK V. WILLIARD, 292 U.S. 112, 54 S.Ct. 615 (1934): [An Iowa insurance company was adjudged insolvent and ordered dissolved in a state court proceeding in Iowa, and pursuant to a statute of Iowa the state commissioner of insurance was adjudged "the successor to said corporation" and as such to hold "title to all property owned by [the corporation] at the time it so ceased to exist." The Iowa insurance company had been authorized to do business in Montana under a statute providing in effect that the dissolution of a domestic or foreign corporation did not impair any remedy against the corporation for a liability previously incurred. Two creditors had brought an action in a Montana state court against the Iowa corporation prior to its dissolution and recovered a judgment by default after the dissolution.

Another creditor then brought a suit in a Montana state court against the corporation and the Iowa liquidator in which he prayed for an ancillary receivership and a receiver was appointed. The judgment creditors mentioned above then filed a petition for leave to satisfy their judgment out of Montana assets, and the Iowa liquidator filed a cross-petition asserting his title as statutory successor to the dissolved corporation and urging that his title should be recognized under the full faith and credit clause. The Montana Supreme Court held that the Iowa liquidator was only an equity receiver, and that as against such a liquidator the Montana creditors were entitled to satisfy their claims out of Montana assets. On certiorari, the Supreme Court of the United States vacated the state court decree and remanded the cause to the Supreme Court of Montana for further proceedings not inconsistent with its opinion.]

■ JUSTICE CARDOZO. . . . The question is whether full faith and credit has been given by the courts of Montana to the statutes and judicial proceedings of the state of Iowa. . . .

We assume in accordance with the decision of the Montana court that the respondents' action against the surety company did not abate on dissolution, but was lawfully pursued to judgment. . . . But this . . . is only a partial statement of the problem. To ascertain the procedure by which the [judgment] is to be enforced, whether by the levy of execution or by a ratable division, other considerations must be weighed. In particular, it must be known whether superior interests or titles have developed between the summons and the judgment, and whether the quality or operation of those interests affects the method of distribution. Something did intervene here, the appointment of a liquidator under the statutes of the domicile. That much is undisputed. Did the Supreme Court of Montana misjudge the quality and operation of this intervening interest, and in so doing did it deny to the statutes and decrees of Iowa the faith and credit owing to them under the Constitution of the United States?

In our judgment, the statutes of Iowa have made the official liquidator the successor to the corporation, and not a mere receiver. . . . His title is not the consequence of a decree of a court whereby a corporation still in being has made a compulsory assignment of its assets with a view to liquidation. . . . His title is the consequence of a succession established for the corporation by the law of its creation. . . . So the lawmakers have plainly said. So the Iowa court adjudged in decreeing dissolution.

We think the Supreme Court of Montana denied full faith and credit to the statutes and judicial proceedings of Iowa in holding, as it did, that the petitioner was a receiver deriving title through a judicial proceeding, and not through the charter of its being and the succession there prescribed. . . .

In thus holding we do not say that there is an invariable rule by which the title of a statutory liquidator must prevail over executions and attachments outside of the state of his appointment. The subject is involved in confusion, with decisions pro and con. . . .

Whether there is in Montana a local policy, expressed in statute or decision, whereby judgments and attachments have a preference over the title of a charter liquidator, is a question as to which the Supreme Court of that state will speak with ultimate authority.

NOTES

1. When the case was remanded to the Supreme Court of Montana, that court by a divided vote again held the judgment creditors had priority over the Iowa statutory liquidator because Montana's law permitted attachments on property in Montana of insolvent corporations, both domestic and foreign, for which a statutory liquidator had been appointed. Mieyr v. Federal Surety Co., 34 P.2d 982 (Mont.1934). The Supreme Court of the United States affirmed this decision. "Iowa may say that one who is a liquidator with title, appointed by her statutes, shall be so recognized in Montana with whatever rights and privileges accompany such recognition according to Montana law . . . Iowa may not say . . . that a liquidator with title who goes into Montana may set at naught Montana law as to the distribution of Montana assets, and carry over into another state the rule of distribution prescribed by the statutes of the domicile." Clark v. Williard, 294 U.S. 211, 55 S.Ct. 356 (1935).

2. In Relfe v. Rundle, 103 U.S. 222 (1880), a Missouri insurance company had been dissolved under the law of Missouri and its property vested in the Missouri State Superintendent of Insurance. The Missouri Superintendent of Insurance had himself made a party defendant to a suit which had been instituted in Louisiana against this insurance company. Held, this is proper, and the Superintendent can remove the suit to the federal court in Louisiana on the ground of diversity of citizenship. "Relfe is not an officer of the Missouri state court. . . . He was the statutory successor of the Corporation for the purpose of winding up its affairs. . . . He is an officer of the State, and as such represents the State in its sovereignty while performing its public duties connected with the winding up of the affairs of one of its insolvent and dissolved corporations."

Converse v. Hamilton

Supreme Court of the United States, 1912.
224 U.S. 243, 32 S.Ct. 415 (1912).

[A creditor of a Minnesota corporation brought a suit in a Minnesota state court against the corporation for the sequestration of its property and the appointment of a receiver. The court found the corporation was insolvent, appointed a receiver, and ascertained it was necessary to resort to the double liability of the stockholders imposed by Minnesota law for the payment of the creditors. The court then levied upon the corporation's stockholders assessments amounting to 100 per cent. of the par value of their shares, and directed the receiver to prosecute such actions within or without the state as were necessary to enforce the assessment.

The present actions were brought by the Minnesota receiver in Wisconsin against Wisconsin stockholders of the corporation to recover the assessments. The Wisconsin stockholders had not been made parties to the Minnesota suit and were not notified, otherwise than by publication or by mail, of the application for the orders levying the assessments. The Wisconsin court refused to enforce the assessments because they were contrary to Wisconsin policy. The receiver sued out writs of error to the Supreme Court of the United States.]

■ JUSTICE VAN DEVANTER delivered the opinion of the court. . . . This liability is not to the corporation but to the creditors collectively, is not penal but contractual, is not joint but several, and the mode and means of its enforcement are subject to legislative regulation. . . .

The proceedings in the sequestration suit, looking to the enforcement of this liability, were had under chapter 272, Laws of 1899, and sections 3814–3490, Revised Laws of 1905, the latter being a continuation of the former with changes not here material. . . . It expressly prescribed the mode of enforcement pursued in the present instance; that is to say, it made provision for bringing all the creditors into the sequestration suit, for the presentation and adjudication of their claims, for ascertaining the relation of the corporate debts and the expenses of the receivership to the available assets, and whether and to what extent it was necessary to resort to the stockholders' double liability for levying such assessments upon the stockholders according to their respective holdings as should be necessary to pay the debts, and for investing the receiver with authority to collect the assessments on behalf of the creditors. . . .

Under this statute, as interpreted by the Supreme Court of the State, as also by this court, the receiver is not an ordinary chancery receiver or arm of the court appointing him, but a quasi-assignee and representative of the creditors, and when the order levying the assessment is made he becomes invested with the creditors' rights of action against the stockholders and with full authority to enforce the same in any court of competent jurisdiction in the State or elsewhere.

The constitutional validity of chapter 272 has been sustained by the Supreme Court of the State, as also by this court; and this because (1) the statute is but a reasonable regulation of the mode and means of enforcing the double liability assumed by those who become stockholders in a Minnesota corporation; (2) while the order levying the assessment is made conclusive, as against all stockholders, of all matters relating to the amount and propriety of the assessment and the necessity therefor, one against whom it is sought to be enforced is not precluded from showing that he is not a stockholder, or is not the holder of as many shares as is alleged, or has a claim against the corporation which in law or equity he is entitled to set off against the assessment, or has any other defense personal to himself, and (3) while the order is made conclusive as against a stockholder, even although he may not have been a party to the suit in which it was made and may not have been notified that an assessment was contemplated, this is not a tenable objection, for the order is not in the nature of a personal judgment against the stockholder and as to him is amply sustained by the presence in that suit of the corporation, considering his relation to it and his contractual obligation in respect of its debts. . . .

This statement of the nature of the liability in question, of the laws of Minnesota bearing upon its enforcement, and of the effect which judicial proceedings under those laws have in that State, discloses, as we think, that in the cases now before us the Supreme Court of Wisconsin failed to give full faith and credit to those laws and to the proceedings thereunder, upon which the receiver's right to sue was grounded. It is true that an ordinary chancery receiver is a mere arm of the court appointing him, is invested with no estate in the property committed to his charge, and is clothed with no power to exercise his official duties in other jurisdictions. . . . But here the receiver was not merely an ordinary chancery receiver, but much more. By the proceedings in the sequestration suit, had conformably to the laws of Minnesota, he became a quasi-assignee and representative of the creditors, was invested with their rights of action against the stockholders, and was charged with the enforcement of those rights in the courts of that State and elsewhere. So when he invoked the aid of the Wisconsin court the case presented was, in substance, that of a trustee, clothed with adequate title for the occasion, seeking to enforce, for the benefit of his cestuisquetrustent, a right of action, transitory, in character, against one who was liable contractually and severally, if at all. . . .

In these circumstances we think the conclusion is unavoidable that the laws of Minnesota and the judicial proceedings in that State, upon which the receiver's title, authority and right to relief were grounded, and by which the stockholders were bound, were not accorded that faith and credit to which they were entitled under the Constitution and laws of the United States.

The judgments are accordingly reversed, and the cases are remanded for further proceedings not inconsistent with this opinion.

Reversed.

Broderick v. Rosner

Supreme Court of the United States, 1935.
294 U.S. 629, 55 S.Ct. 589, 79 L.Ed.1100.

■ JUSTICE BRANDEIS delivered the opinion of the Court.

Pursuant to article 8, section 7, of the Constitution of New York, its Banking Law (Consol.Laws, c. 2) provides, section 120: "The stockholders of every bank will be individually responsible, equally and ratably and not one for another, for all contracts, debts and engagements of the bank, to the extent of the amount of their stock therein, at the par value thereof, in addition to the amount invested in such shares."

The Bank of the United States is a corporation organized under the Banking Law of New York and had its places of business in New York City. Its outstanding capital stock is $25,250,000 represented by 1,010,000 shares of $25 par value. On November 17, 1933, Joseph A. Broderick, as Superintendent of Banks of the State of New York, brought, in the Supreme Court of New Jersey, this action against 557 of its stockholders who are residents of New Jersey, to recover unpaid assessments levied by him upon them pursuant to law.

The defendant moved to strike out the complaint on the ground, among others, that, by reason of section 94b of the Corporation Act of New Jersey (2 Comp.St.1910, p. 1656), it failed to set out a cause of action enforceable in any court of that State. The section, first enacted March 30, 1897, provides: "No action or proceeding shall be maintained in any court of law in this state against any stockholder, officer or director of any domestic or foreign corporation by or on behalf of any creditor of such corporation to enforce any statutory personal liability of such stockholder, officer or director for or upon any debt, default or obligation of such corporation, whether such statutory personal liability be deemed penal or contractual, if such statutory personal liability be created by or arise from the statutes or laws of any other state or foreign country, and no pending or future action or proceeding to enforce such statutory personal liability shall be maintained in any court of this state other than in the nature of an equitable accounting for the proportionate benefit of all parties interested, to which such corporation and its legal representatives, if any, and all of its creditors and all of its stockholders shall be necessary parties."

Broderick seasonably claimed that to sustain the asserted bar of the statute would violate article 4, section 1, of the Federal Constitution, which provides that, "Full Faith and Credit shall be given in each State to the public Acts, Records and judicial Proceedings of every other State," and the legislation of Congress enacted pursuant thereto. The trial court sustained the motion to strike out the complaint, Broderick v. Abrams, 112 N.J.L. 309, 170 A. 214, on the ground that the statute of the State constituted a bar to the action. Judgment against the plaintiff, with costs, was entered in favor of each of the defendants, and the judgment was affirmed by the Court of Errors and Appeals "for the reasons expressed in the opinion" of the trial court. 113 N.J.L. 305, 174 A. 507. An appeal to this Court was allowed. Broderick v. Rosner, 293 U.S. 613.

First. The conditions imposed by section 94b of the New Jersey statute upon the bringing of suits to enforce such assessments, as here applied, deny to the Superintendent the right to resort to the courts of the State to enforce the assessment of liability upon the stockholders there resident. The requirement that the proceeding be by bill in equity, instead of by an action at law, would, if standing alone, be no obstacle. But by withholding jurisdiction unless the proceeding be a suit for an equitable accounting to which the "corporation and its legal representatives, if any, and all of its creditors and all of its stockholders shall be necessary parties," it imposes a condition which, as here applied, is legally impossible of fulfillment. For it is not denied that according to the decisions of the New Jersey courts "necessary parties" means those whose presence in a suit is essential as a jurisdictional prerequisite to the entry of judgment, so that no decree can be made respecting the subject-matter of litigation until they are before the court . . . and that to secure jurisdiction personally over those who are not residents of New Jersey, or engaged in business there, is impossible. . . . The corporation has no place of business in New Jersey; only a few of the many stockholders and creditors have either residence or place of business there.

Moreover, even if it were legally possible to satisfy the statutory condition by making substituted service by publication upon non-resident stockholders and creditors . . . , the cost would be prohibitive. The number of the stockholders is 20,843; the number of depositors and other creditors exceeds 400,000; and the amounts assessed against the individual defendants are relatively small—against some only $50. The aggregate of sheriff's fees alone as to the nonresident defendants, aside from expenses of publication and mailing, would exceed the aggregate amount due from the New Jersey stockholders. The suggestion, in the opinion of the Supreme Court, that leave might be granted to file a bill in equity is, therefore, without legal significance.

Second. But for the statute, the action would have been entertained. . . . The plaintiff is not, as in Booth v. Clark, 17 How. 322, 15 L.Ed. 164, a foreign receiver. He sues as an independent executive in whom has been vested by statute the cause of action sued on. Converse v. Hamilton, 224 U.S. 243, 257. . . .

Third. The power of a State to determine the limits of the jurisdiction of its courts and the character of the controversies which shall be heard therein is subject to the limitations imposed by the Federal Constitution. . . . A "State cannot escape its constitutional obligations [under the full faith and credit clause] by the simple device of denying jurisdiction in such cases to courts otherwise competent." Kenney v. Supreme Lodge, [p. 397, supra][3] . . . it may not, under the guise of merely affecting the remedy, deny the enforcement of claims otherwise within the protection of the full faith and credit clause, when its courts have general jurisdiction of the subject-matter and the parties. . . . For the States of the Union, the constitutional limitation imposed by the full faith and credit clause abolished, in large measure, the general principle of

---

[3]   Chambers v. Baltimore & Ohio R. Co., 207 U.S. 142, is not to the contrary; there no claim was made under the full faith and credit clause.

international law by which local policy is permitted to dominate rules of comity.

Here the nature of the cause of action brings it within the scope of the full faith and credit clause. The statutory liability sought to be enforced is contractual in character. The assessment is an incident of the incorporation. Thus the subject-matter is peculiarly within the regulatory power of New York, as the State of incorporation. . . . In respect to the determination of liability for an assessment, the New Jersey stockholders submitted themselves to the jurisdiction of New York. . . . Obviously recognition could not be accorded to a local policy of New Jersey, if there really were one, of enabling all residents of the State to escape from the performance of a voluntarily assumed statutory obligation, consistent with morality, to contribute to the payment of the depositors of a bank of another State of which they were stockholders.

Fourth. The fact that the assessment here in question was made under statutory direction by an administrative officer does not preclude the application of the full faith and credit clause. If the assessment had been made in a liquidation proceeding conducted by a court, New Jersey would have been obliged to enforce it, although the stockholders sued had not been made parties to the proceedings, and, being nonresidents, could not have been personally served with process. Converse v. Hamilton [p. 1076, supra]. The reason why in that case the full faith and credit clause was held to require Wisconsin courts to enforce the assessment made in Minnesota was not because the determination was embodied in a judgment. Against the nonresident stockholders there had been no judgment in Minnesota. Wisconsin was required to enforce the Minnesota assessment because statutes are "public acts" within the meaning of the clause, Bradford Electric Light Co. v. Clapper, 286 U.S. 145, 155; Alaska Packers Association v. Industrial Accident Commission [294 U.S. 532 (1935)]; and because the residents of Wisconsin had, by becoming stockholders of a Minnesota corporation, submitted themselves to that extent, to the jurisdiction and laws of the latter State. Where a State has had jurisdiction of the subject-matter and the parties, obligations validly imposed upon them by statute must, within the limitations above stated, be given full faith and credit by all the other states. . . .

Fifth. The Superintendent contends that his assessment is a "public act" within the meaning of the full faith and credit clause, and is entitled to receive in every other State of the Union, the same recognition accorded to it by the laws of New York. He insists that, while under the law of New York defenses personal to individual stockholders are open to them whenever and wherever sued, Selig v. Hamilton, 234 U.S. 652, 662, 663, his determinations as to the propriety and amount of the assessment, in so far as they involve merely the exercise of judgment, are conclusive; and are not subject to review by any court, except on grounds for which equity commonly affords relief against administrative orders. . . . Whether this contention is sound, we have no occasion to consider now. . . . It is sufficient to decide that, since the New Jersey courts possess general jurisdiction of the subject-matter and the parties, and the subject-matter is not one as to which the alleged public policy of New Jersey could be controlling, the full faith and credit clause requires that this suit be entertained.

Reversed.

■ JUSTICE CARDOZO is of the opinion that the judgment should be affirmed.

NOTE

In Wilson v. Louisiana-Pacific Resources, Inc., 138 Cal.App.3d 216, 224 187 Cal.Rptr. 852 (1982), the court questioned whether "there [is] vitality left" in *Broderick* after Allstate Ins. Co. v. Hague, p. 432, supra. In any event, the court considered *Broderick* distinguishable on the ground that New Jersey, in *Broderick*, had no conflicting interests to New York's, while in the case at bar, California had an interest in regulating "pseudo-foreign" corporations. A state's freedom to concern itself with the "internal affairs" of a foreign corporation in turn is now in doubt: see pp. 1112–1131, infra for the "internal affairs" rule, "pseudo-foreign corporations," and the U.S. Supreme Court's decision in *CTS*. See also VantagePoint Venture Partners v. Examen, Inc., 871 A.2d 1108 (Del.2005), which held unconstitutional the application of the California Corporation Code to the internal affairs of a Delaware corporation.

See generally Cheatham, The Statutory Successor, The Receiver and the Executor in Conflict of Laws, 44 Colum.L.Rev. 549 (1944).

CHAPTER 13

AGENCY, PARTNERSHIPS AND CORPORATIONS

SECTION 1. AGENCY

INTRODUCTORY NOTE

A relationship of agency or of partnership may give rise to several choice-of-law problems: what law governs the rights and duties (a) of the principal and agent, or of the partners, as between themselves, (b) of the principal, or of the partnership and partners, on the one hand, and of some third person on the other, on account of one or more acts done on behalf of the principal or partnership by an agent, who in the case of a partnership will frequently be a partner, and (c) as between the agent and the third person on account of an act done by the agent. The second of these questions is the one primarily dealt with in this chapter. The third question is not considered, since the law governing a person's individual liability for an act is the same irrespective of whether he was acting for himself or for another.

YOUNG V. MASCI, 289 U.S. 253, 53 S.Ct. 599 (1933): Action brought by a New Yorker in a New Jersey court to recover for injuries suffered in an automobile accident in New York. The defendant, a New Jersey resident, had loaned his automobile in that state "without restriction upon its use" to one Balbino who drove the automobile into New York and there negligently injured the plaintiff. The New Jersey courts gave judgment to the plaintiff by application of a New York statute which made the "owner of a motor vehicle" liable for injuries caused by the negligence of any person operating the same with the "permission, express or implied, of such owner." The defendant appealed to the Supreme Court of the United States, contending that application of the New York statute under the circumstances violated due process. Affirmed. "When Young [the defendant] gave permission to drive his car to New York, he subjected himself to the legal consequences imposed by that state upon Balbino's negligent driving as fully as if he had stood in the relation of master to servant. A person who sets in motion in one state the means by which injury is inflicted in another may, consistently with the due process clause, be made liable for that injury whether the means employed be a responsible agent or an irresponsible instrument. . . . The power of the state to protect itself and its inhabitants is not limited by the scope of the doctrine of principal and agent. . . . No good reason is suggested why, when there is permission to take the automobile into a state for use upon its highways, personal liability should not be imposed upon the owner in case of injury inflicted there by the driver's negligence. . . ."

Agency relationships are usually created by contract but they can arise otherwise. For example, one person may act at another's direction without any express agreement between them but the law may raise the existence of an agency or there may be a ratification by the principal of the alleged agent's acts. The obligations between principal and agent are determined, according to Restatement, Second, Conflict of Laws § 291 (1971) "by the local law of the state which, with respect to the particular issue, has the most significant relationship to the parties and the transaction under the principles stated in § 6." The law is selected by applying the rules set forth in Sections 187–188 with regard to contracts. Comment f to Section 291 states that "the state where performance by the agent is to take place will usually be given the greatest weight, in the absence of an effective choice of law by the parties (see § 187), in determining what law governs the rights and duties owed by the principal and agent to each other."

Consider again Young v. Masci, supra: may the state of injury impose its vicarious liability statute on a nonresident owner who had entrusted the car to the driver but expressly forbidden the driver from leaving the state? Judge Learned Hand said "no" in Scheer v. Rockne Motors Corp., 68 F.2d 942 (2d Cir.1934). Does this make sense? Also, it is not clear whether Judge Hand would require express or only implied authority. See Cavers, The Two "Local Law" Theories, 63 Harv.L.Rev. 822, 827–28 (1950).

The civil law concept of *negotiorum gestio* is an agency raised as a matter of law, in the sense mentioned at the beginning of this note. In German law, for instance, it is descriptively styled "agency without mandate." The legal relationship arises when someone fulfills the obligations of another or performs the task for another without having received a mandate or request to do so. See §§ 677 et seq. German Civil Code; Dawson, Negotiorum Gestio: The Altruistic Intermeddler, 74 Harv.L.Rev. 817 (1961). The European Union's "Rome II" Regulation (reproduced in the Documentary Appendix), in force in all EU countries except Denmark, replaces prior national conflicts law and provides four conflicts rules, in order of priority, for *negotiorum gestio*: the law of the underlying relationship giving rise to the claim (usually a contract or a tort), the law of the parties' common habitual residence, the law of the place where the act was performed, or—instead of the foregoing—the law of the country that is "manifestly more closely related" to the claim. Art. 11.

Mercier v. John Hancock Mutual
Life Insurance Co.

Supreme Court of Maine, 1945.
141 Me. 376, 44 A.2d 372.

■ MANSER, JUSTICE. [Action to recover on a life insurance policy, the application for which had been written in Maine. From a jury verdict in favor of the plaintiff, the insurance company appealed.]

The defendant Company contested payment upon the ground that [the insured] made false representations to the effect that no albumin or sugar had ever been found in his urine, and that he had never been told that he had symptoms of diabetes, when in truth he had been diabetic for ten years and had used the insulin treatment therefor. Also that he stated his brother was in good health, when he was at the time a patient in a tuberculosis sanitarium, and died soon thereafter. . . .

The issues presented to the jury were whether there were, in fact, any material misrepresentations or concealments by or on behalf of the [insured]; whether the agent knew or was informed of the diabetes and took the responsibility of assuring the [insured] that it made no difference and need not be mentioned in the application; and again whether the agent failed to ask the question as to the health of the brother of the [insured], and instead assumed the responsibility of inserting a favorable answer.

The testimony was flatly contradictory. The instructions by the presiding Justice were clear and lucid upon the factual issues. It was for the jury to determine as to the credibility of witnesses and the weight of the evidence. The record would not warrant a ruling by this Court that the verdict was manifestly wrong.

This brings us to a consideration of the exceptions. [The defendant complained of the refusal of the trial judge to charge that the Maine statute, which provided that an insurance company could not rely as a defense on misrepresentations known to the agent, was not applicable because the insurance contract was a "Massachusetts contract".]

The question of whether the policy was, technically, a Maine or a Massachusetts contract was not passed upon by the presiding Justice or the jury. It did not need to be.

The situation presented here is simply whether the defendant Company is responsible for the acts of a duly authorized agent, licensed in the State of Maine, in connection with an application for insurance which he procured in Maine from a citizen thereof, when our statute says that such agent stands in the place of the Company with regard to all insurance effected by him.

In the Restatement of the Law upon the title Conflict of Laws, § 345, the rule is succinctly stated as follows:

"The law of the state in which an agent or a partner is authorized or apparently authorized to act for the principal or other partners determines whether an act done on account of the principal or other partners imposes a contractual duty upon the principal or other partners."

Then under the Comment, after discussing the effect of an agent's acts, we find the definite statement:

"But whether or not a particular act of the agent or partner is authorized, the law of the state where the act is done determines whether the principal is bound by a contract with a third person. . . ."

Exceptions overruled.

RESTATEMENT, SECOND, CONFLICT OF LAWS (1971):

§ 292. Contractual Liability of Principal to Third Person

(1) Whether a principal is bound by action taken on his behalf by an agent in dealing with a third person is determined by the local law of the state which, with respect to the particular issue, has the most significant relationship to the parties and the transaction under the principles stated in § 6.

(2) The principal will be held bound by the agent's action if he would so be bound under the local law of the state where the agent dealt with the third person, provided at least that the principal had authorized the agent to act on his behalf in that state or had led the third person reasonably to believe that the agent had such authority.

NOTES

1. See generally Reese & Flesch, Agency and Vicarious Liability in Conflict of Laws, 60 Colum.L.Rev. 764 (1960).

The 1978 Hague Convention on Agency is in force in Argentina, France, The Netherlands, and Portugal. The United States participated in the drafting, but did not ratify. For comment, see Hay & Müller-Freienfels, Agency in the Conflict of Laws and the 1978 Hague Convention, 27 Am.J.Comp.L. 1 (1979).

2. For cases applying the principles of the Restatement, Second, Conflict of Laws (1971), to determine the law governing the liability of an undisclosed principal to the person with whom the agent dealt, see Guardian Angel Credit Union v. Metabank, 2010 WL 1794713, at *6–7 (D.N.H.2010); Francis v. Starwood Hotels & Resorts Worldwide, Inc., 2011 WL 3351320, at *3–5 (D.Colo.2011).

3. In State X, P authorizes A to manage P's farm in State X and to use the livestock on it as required. A drives the livestock to State Y and sells them to T, remitting the proceeds to P. By what law will it be determined whether A is liable to P for having exceeded the terms of his authority? By what law will it be determined whether T obtained title to the livestock? See Restatement, Second, Conflict of Laws §§ 291–92 (1971).

4. The law governing the agent's contract with the third person will usually be applied to determine whether the principal is bound by the contract and entitled to its benefits.

Maspons y Hermano v. Mildred, Goyeneche & Co., L.R. 9 Q.B.D. 530 (1882), aff'd, 8 App. Cas. 874 (1883). Defendants, a London firm, entered into an agreement with Demestre & Co. whereby defendants were to receive a cargo of tobacco for purposes of resale and were also to insure the cargo for the benefit of all concerned. Defendants realized that Demestre & Co. were acting in the capacity of agents but did not know the names of their principals, who in fact were the present plaintiffs, a Spanish firm carrying on business in Havana. The ship carrying the tobacco sank and plaintiffs brought suit for the proceeds of the insurance which had been paid to the defendants. The defense was that under Spanish law an undisclosed principal was not entitled to sue the person with whom his agent had contracted. Held, for the plaintiffs. Spanish law is material only for the purpose of determining the nature and extent of the authority given by plaintiffs to their agent. "The contract between Demestre & Co. and the defendants is governed by English law, not Spanish, and the persons who can sue and be sued on that contract in England must also be determined by our law, and not by the law of Spain."

5. In the case of land, the law of the situs governs questions relating to the validity and effect of the deed executed by the agent. Clark v. Graham, 19 U.S. (6 Wheat.) 577 (1821); Restatement, Second, Conflict of Laws § 223 (1971), applied in Miller v. Stuckey, 42 N.E.3d 304 (Ohio App.2015). See Combs v. Combs and Fall v. Eastin, at pp. 167, 328, supra, respectively. On the other hand, since a contract whereby a broker is authorized to buy or sell land does not create an interest in the land, the obligations owed by the principal and broker to each other under the contract are determined by the law governing the contract. This law may or may not be that of the state where the land is. Johnson v. Allen, 158 P.2d 134 (Utah 1945); Richland Development Company, Inc. v. Staples, 295 F.2d 122 (5th Cir.1961); Olsen v. Celano, 600 N.E.2d 1257 (Ill.App.1992).

Ratification. A ratification by the principal of the agent's act will usually bind the principal if the ratification would be effective under the law of either (a) the state where the agent dealt with the third person or (b) the state whose law governs the principal-agent relationship. Restatement, Second, Conflict of Laws § 293 (1971). This is an example of an alternative reference rule to accomplish validation of the contract.

SECTION 2. PARTNERSHIPS AND OTHER ASSOCIATIONS

RESTATEMENT, SECOND, CONFLICT OF LAWS (1971):

§ 294. Relationship of Partners Inter Se

The rights and duties owed by partners to each other are determined by the local law of the state which, with respect to the particular issue, has the most significant relationship to the partners and the transaction under the principles stated in § 6. This law is selected by application of the rules of §§ 187–88.

NOTES

1. The paucity of conflict-of-laws cases involving the rights and duties owed by partners to each other is perhaps due in part to the nearly universal adoption of the Uniform Partnership Act.

2. Among the legal issues that arise between partners are questions as to the share of each partner in the control and profits of the business, the extent of their liabilities to one another, and the effect of death or withdrawal of a partner on continuation of the firm. Usually, the partnership will conduct its business in the state where it was organized Treeline OCR, LLC v. Nassau County Indus. Development Agency, 918 N.Y.S.2d 128, 131 (App.Div.) (law of state of organization—Texas—applies). However, the courts will also give effect to the parties' choice of another law, if the choice was entered into in good faith and the state of the chosen law has a sufficient connection to the partnership's business: Engel v. Ernst, 724 P.2d 215 (Nev.1986); Wright v. Armwood, 107 A.2d 702 (D.C.Mun.App. 1954); Rose v. Chase Manhattan Bank USA, 2006 WL 1520238 (D.Nev.2006).

RESTATEMENT, SECOND, CONFLICT OF LAWS (1971):

§ 295. Contractual Liability of Partnership, Partners and Third Person

(1) Whether a partnership is bound by action taken on its behalf by an agent in dealing with a third person is determined by the local law of the state selected by application of the rule of § 292.

(2) Whether a general partner is bound by action taken on behalf of the partnership by an agent in dealing with a third person is determined by the local law of the state selected by application of the rule of § 292.

(3) The liability of a limited partner for action taken on behalf of the partnership by an agent in dealing with a third person is determined by the local law of the state selected by application of the rule of § 294 [the law governing the relationship of partners inter se], unless the limited partner has taken a significant part in the control of the partnership business or has led the third person reasonably to believe that he was a general partner. In either of these latter events, the liability of the limited partner will be determined by application of the local law of the state selected by application of the rule of § 292.

First National Bank of Waverly v. Hall

Supreme Court of Pennsylvania, 1892.
150 Pa. 466, 24 A. 665.

[Action against Hall and others on promissory notes signed by Crandall. The defendants and Crandall made in Pennsylvania a contract, with the following provisions: Crandall agreed to establish and operate under his sole control a toy factory in New York; the defendants agreed to furnish the necessary working capital, not to exceed three thousand dollars; the defendants were to receive 6 per cent per annum on all sums so furnished, and in addition 40 per cent of the net profits of the business; Crandall was to have the privilege to repay in installments the money so advanced and as the money was repaid the share of the net profits going to the defendants would be correspondingly reduced; the defendants should have a mortgage lien on the machinery and fixtures of the business to secure the repayment of the money advanced; and "nothing in this writing shall be construed to create a partnership between the respective parties except with respect to the net profits as herein provided." The notes sued upon were made by Crandall to a New York bank, apparently in New York, in connection with the operation of the business in that state.]

■ Opinion by JUSTICE HEYDRICK. . . .

The plaintiff sues upon notes made by C.M. Crandall, one of the defendants, in his own name, and seeks to charge the other defendants as partners of Crandall in a business in which the proceeds of certain other notes, of which these were renewals, were used. . . .

[The court here outlined the agreement between Crandall and the defendants.] These provisions are all consistent with the relation of borrower and lender, and some of them are inconsistent with any other relation. It is therefore manifest that that relation was intended to be established; and the next question is whether, in spite of the intention of the parties, the community of interest in the profits constituted them a partnership as to creditors.

[The court held that this question should be determined by the law which governed the agreement between Crandall and the defendants and that this law was that of New York, the state where the toy factory was to be established. The court found that under the law of New York the agreement did not create a partnership as to third persons, and the judgment for the defendants was affirmed.]

Barrows v. Downs & Co.

Supreme Court of Rhode Island, 1870.
9 R.I. 446.

These were two actions of assumpsit, one brought by Henry F. Barrows against the defendants, to recover the sum of $8,494.39 alleged to be due on book account for goods sold and delivered, and the other by the Meriden Britannia Company, upon a promissory note for $8,467.82, made by the said J.F. Downs & Co., and also to recover the sum of $1,142.09, alleged to be due on book account for goods sold and delivered.

Service of the writ in each of these cases was made solely upon William C. Downs, described therein as one of the co-partners of the firm of Joseph F. Downs & Co., the said Joseph F. Downs not being found within the state. . . .

■ POTTER, J. . . .

The plaintiffs rely on evidence that said William, while on a visit to this country, held himself out as a partner, and a general partner, in the firm.

The defendant denies these representations, and contends that he was only a special partner in the Havana firm, and under the Spanish law not liable as a general partner.

He testifies to a special partnership existing between him and Joseph for several years previous to 1866, the terms of which were, however, not reduced to writing until April, 1866, a copy of which he produces, and he also offers the evidence of A.F. Bramoso, a Spanish lawyer formerly of Havana, but now of New York, that said verbal special partnership was valid there. . . .

Being satisfied, . . . that the partnership in Havana was a special one and authorized by Spanish law, the next inquiry is, what is the liability of William C. Downs, the special partner in this case.

The orders for these goods were by the general partner, Joseph, by letter or personally. No goods were ever ordered by William except once,—some ear-drops from Mr. Barrows.

Now, if the parties had remained in Havana, and the general partner had made contracts abroad by letter or otherwise, there can be no doubt but that the extent to which he could bind his copartners and make them liable for his acts, would depend upon the law of the place of the partnership; the extent to which they had made him their agent with power to bind them, would be regulated by the law of Cuba. And if the general partner himself went abroad, (the special partners remaining at home,) his authority to bind them would still be regulated by the law of Cuba. . . .

But the plaintiffs offer evidence to show that the defendant, W.C. Downs, was in New York in the summer of 1865, and there represented himself as a partner, and, as they contend, a general partner in the firm. Of course, if he was actually a general partner, he would be liable for the whole amount.

And if he was not a general partner in fact, yet if he made such representations to these parties as to his interest in the concern, his responsibility, and his share in the profits, as to lead them to suppose he was a partner personally liable, and the goods or any portion of them were advanced on the strength of his representations, then he should be liable for all so advanced.

And this is the view we take from all the evidence in the case; that the defendant should be held liable for all the goods advanced after these representations made in the summer of 1865.

Judgment for plaintiffs for $2,054.61 and costs.

NOTES

1. Section 901 of the Uniform Limited Partnership Act (1976) provides that "the laws of the state under which a foreign limited partnership is organized governs its organization and internal affairs and the liability of its limited partners."

2. For discussion of the choice-of-law problems relating to limited partnerships, see Vestal, A Comprehensive Uniform Limited Partnership Act? The Time Has Come, 28 U.C.Davis L.Rev. 1195, 1233–34 (1995); Vestal, Choice of Law and the Fiduciary Duties of Partners under the Revised Uniform Partnership Act, 79 Iowa L.Rev. 219 (1994); Johnson, Risky Business: Choice-of-Law and the Unincorporated Entity, 1 J. Small & Emerging Bus. 249 (1997).

Greenspun v. Lindley

New York Court of Appeals, 1975.
36 N.Y.2d 473, 369 N.Y.S.2d 123, 330 N.E.2d 79.

■ JONES, J. In the circumstances of this case we conclude that holders of beneficial shares of interest in this real estate investment trust who desire to challenge investment decisions of the trustees and the payment by them of what are alleged to be excessive management fees must first make a demand on the trustees before commencing what is the equivalent of a shareholders' derivative action against the trustees individually.

Mony Mortgage Investors was organized as a business trust under the laws of the Commonwealth of Massachusetts to carry on business as a "real estate investment trust" as described in the REIT provisions of the Internal Revenue Code (§§ 856–858; US Code, tit 26, §§ 856–58). . . .

The declaration of trust, initially dated February 25, 1970, provides that there shall be no less than 3 and no more than 15 trustees, to be elected by the shareholders, except that a majority of the trustees shall not be affiliated with the manager to be employed for the transaction of the business of the trust. On April 6, 1970, the trustees approved a management contract with the Mutual Life Insurance Company of New York. At the time of the institution of the present action there were 11 trustees, 5 of whom were officers of the insurance company and 6 of whom were unaffiliated. The 11 trustees, the insurance company and the investment trust were all named as defendants.

The gravamen of the complaint, pleaded in conclusory terms only, is that in consequence of the subservience of the trustees to domination by the insurance company they are paying excessive management fees to the insurance company and make investment decisions only if the interest of the insurance company is thereby served, and that the investments so made are unsuitable for the purposes of the investment trust and inconsistent with its stated investment policy. Plaintiff seeks an accounting by defendants to the investment trust for damages sustained by the trust and for profits realized by defendants, together with counsel fees.

Defendants moved to dismiss the complaint, principally on the ground that plaintiff failed, prior to the commencement of the action, to make a demand on either the trustees or the other shareholders. . . .

We hold, as did the Appellate Division, that the law of the Commonwealth of Massachusetts governs the disposition of the present motions.

The investment trust is a business trust organized and existing under the laws of Massachusetts. The declaration of trust, with which the shareholders became associated only by voluntary choice on the part of each of them, expressly provides that the law of Massachusetts shall be the applicable law as to the rights of all parties. Thus, prima facie Massachusetts law is applicable. . . .

We conclude . . . in the circumstances of this case that reference must be made to the authorities in the Commonwealth of Massachusetts to determine the rights of the parties in this litigation. In so holding we incidentally note the pragmatic as well as the theoretical advantages which would appear to flow from a conclusion that the rights of all shareholders of this real estate investment trust in comparable situations should be determined on a trust-wide basis rather than in consequence of the litigants' choice of forum or the assessment by several courts as to which State it is where the investment trust may be said to be present.

In deciding this case as we do, however, we expressly leave open what law we might apply were there proof from which it could properly be found, in consequence of significant contacts with New York State, that this investment trust, although a Massachusetts business trust, was nonetheless so "present" in our State as perhaps to call for the application of New York law. In that sense we reject any automatic application of the so-called "internal affairs" choice-of-law rule, under which the relationship between shareholders and trustees of a business trust by strict analogy to the relationship between shareholders and directors of a business corporation would be governed by the law of the State in which the business entity was formed.

Similarly we do not reach the question of what significance we would accord the explicit agreement of the parties that their rights are to be governed by Massachusetts law, were we disposed, entirely without reference to that provision of the declaration of trust, to apply the law of New York or the law of some State other than Massachusetts.

Turning then to the law of Massachusetts, we conclude ... that the courts of that Commonwealth would treat the shareholders of a Massachusetts business trust the same as they would the shareholders of a Massachusetts business corporation in enforcing conditions precedent to the institution of a shareholders' derivative action. There is no question that the shareholders of a Massachusetts corporation are required to make a demand on the corporate directors prior to bringing a derivative action. ... We conclude that a parallel rule would be applied by the Massachusetts courts to a business trust. ...

Order affirmed ...

NOTES

1. Similarly: Rotz v. Van Kampen Asset Mgmt., 2014 WL 5431156 (N.Y.Sup.Ct.2014).

2. What law determines the legal power of an unincorporated association to engage in a particular activity? For material dealing with the analogous problem of the powers of a foreign corporation, see pp. 1109–1122, infra.

3. Should the same law be used to govern all of the following problems: (a) the capacity of an association to take legal or equitable title to property; (b) the liabilities of the members of an association to third parties; (c) the liabilities of the members of an association inter se; (d) the liabilities of the members of an association to an agent of the association?

4. On the power of a state to impose upon foreign partnerships that wish to do business in its territory essentially the same qualification requirements that are imposed upon foreign corporations, see Note, 52 Cornell L.Q. 157 (1966); Forst, The U.S. International Tax Treatment of Partnerships: A Policy Based Approach, 14 Berk.J.Int'l L. 239 (1996).

SECTION 3. CORPORATIONS

A. CORPORATE PERSONALITY; BASIC PRINCIPLES

INTRODUCTORY NOTE

With rare exceptions, Anglo-American law holds that the law of the state of incorporation governs such questions as whether the corporation exists at all, what it is authorized to do, and when it ceases to exist. That state's law also determines the rights and liabilities of the corporate officers and of the shareholders with respect to the corporation.

States in which a corporation formed elsewhere (a "foreign corporation") carries on part of its business normally have an interest in regulating or applying their law to its activities. The principles under which a state may subject a foreign corporation to judicial jurisdiction were discussed in

Chapter 3 supra. The related question of the state's power to tax a foreign corporation arose in tandem with the issue of judicial jurisdiction in the fountainhead International Shoe case.

A state will also want to regulate conduct and to supervise the activities of foreign corporations, just as it exercises control over its domestic corporations. Qualification statutes and other legislation are designed to make this possible. As in the area of judicial jurisdiction, federal constitutional law may impose limitations.

The materials that follow first explore in historical perspective the concept of corporate personality as it relates to problems of conflict of laws. They then deal with regulation of corporate activity by the state where it takes place, the "internal affairs rule," and issues related to winding-up the corporation.

American legal theory on the subject of foreign corporations was based largely upon four principles embodied in Chief Justice Taney's opinion in Bank of Augusta v. Earle, 38 U.S. 519, 10 L.Ed. 274 (1839), to wit:

(1)   A corporation, being a creature of law, cannot exist outside the boundaries of the state of incorporation.

(2)   Being a creature of law, a corporation can nowhere exercise powers not granted it either by its charter or by the general laws of the state of incorporation.

(3)   A state is under no obligation to adhere to the doctrine of comity and hence has the power not only to refuse recognition to the foreign corporation but also to prevent the corporation from acting within its territory.

This principle was reaffirmed by the Supreme Court in Paul v. Virginia, 75 U.S. 168, 19 L.Ed. 357 (1868), in which Justice Field stated: ". . . Having no absolute right of recognition in other States, but depending for such recognition and the enforcement of its contracts upon their assent, it follows, as a matter of course, that such assent may be granted upon such terms and conditions as those States may think proper to impose. They may exclude the foreign corporation entirely; they may restrict its business to particular localities, or they may exact such security for the performance of its contracts with their citizens as in their judgment will best promote the public interest. The whole matter rests in their discretion."

(4)   The fourth principle, largely complementary of the third, is that a state is under no obligation to accord a foreign corporation the privileges which are enjoyed by natural persons who are citizens.

In Paul v. Virginia, the Supreme Court held that a corporation is not a "citizen" within the meaning of the privileges and immunities clause (Art. IV, § 2) and refused to look through the corporation to the stockholders, because ". . . the privileges and immunities secured to citizens of each State in the several States, by the provision in question, are those privileges and immunities which are common to the citizens in the latter States under their constitution and laws by virtue of their being citizens. Special privileges enjoyed by citizens in their own States are not secured in other States by this provision. . . . Now a grant of corporate existence is a grant of special privileges to the corporators, enabling them to act for certain designated purposes as a single individual, and exempting them (unless otherwise specially provided) from individual liability. . . ."

Do the conclusions reached by these four principles follow logically from the stated premises and do these principles adequately explain the results reached by the actual decisions? Consider the following:

1. In the course of his opinion in Bank of Augusta v. Earle, p. 1094 supra. Chief Justice Taney stated that ". . . it has been decided in many of the state Courts, we believe in all of them where the question has arisen, that a corporation of one state may sue in the courts of another." Can these decisions be reconciled with the principle that a corporation has "no existence" outside of the state of incorporation? Is consistency attained by the Chief Justice's suggestion that a corporation can act through agents in other states? How can there be an agent in a state which does not recognize the existence of the principal?

Can this principle of "non-existence" be squared with the present rule that a corporation subjects itself to the judicial jurisdiction of a foreign state by "doing business" within the latter's territory or, as stated by the Supreme Court in International Shoe Co. v. State of Washington, p. 65, supra, when the corporation's contacts with the forum "make it reasonable, in the context of our federal system of government, to require the corporation to defend the particular suit which is brought there"?

Does it follow that because a corporation is "a creature of law," it cannot exist outside the state of incorporation? Does the fact that corporations owe their legal existence to the laws of the incorporating state adequately serve to distinguish them from individuals for the purpose at hand? The problem of legal personality extends throughout the field of conflict laws. An individual's "legal personality"—i.e., one's particular bundle of rights, duties, privileges and powers—is the creation of law. As such, would it not follow that if a New York corporation has no existence in other states, neither would a man and woman who were legally married in New York be considered married elsewhere because their marriage status (like the status of incorporation) is a creation of New York law which is without force in other states?

The problem of legal personality has caused the courts least trouble in the case of individuals, presumably because the need was always apparent of recognizing rights and duties acquired by them under the law of other states. With respect to corporations, a similar need became apparent as soon as significant numbers of them began to spread their activities through two or more states. As a result, the courts have tended more and more to bypass questions of corporate personality and to concentrate instead upon practical problems. In other areas, particularly in the case of foreign administrators, executors and receivers, difficulties posed by the concept of legal personality have not yet been overcome.

2.   The validity of the second principle should be considered in the light of the material contained in Section 2(A), infra. If the first principle is incorrect, must not the same also be true of the second principle?

Since an individual's rights and powers are as much "creations of law" as those of a corporation, it could as logically be contended that an individual can exercise no powers in a foreign state that were not granted by the state of his domicile. That obviously is not the law. See, e.g., Milliken v. Pratt, p. 541, supra.

3.   The third principle—that a state has the absolute power to prevent foreign corporations from entering its territory—is frequently repeated in the opinions. See, e.g., Wheeling Steel Corp. v. Glander, 337 U.S. 562, 571, 69 S.Ct. 1291, 1296 (1949); Asbury Hospital v. Cass County, 326 U.S. 207, 211, 66 S.Ct. 61, 63 (1945).

The development of constitutional law, however, has placed limitations upon premise and conclusion alike. The commerce clause provides one source of limitation. A state cannot forbid corporations from carrying on business in foreign or interstate commerce within its borders (Pensacola Telegraph Co. v. Western Union Telegraph Co., 96 U.S. 1 (1877)) and cannot attach conditions upon their entrance which amount to an undue burden on interstate commerce. Thus, for example, the states do not have unfettered power to tax such corporations or to make them amenable to suit in the local courts (Davis v. Farmers' Co-op Equity Co., p. 68, supra; Oregon Waste Systems, Inc. v. Department of Environmental Quality of State of Oregon, 511 U.S. 93, 114 S.Ct. 1345 (1994); South Central Bell Telephone Co. v. Alabama, 526 U.S. 160, 119 S.Ct. 1180 (1999)). For a more recent application, see Harley-Davidson, Inc. v. Franchise Tax Bd., 187 Cal.Rptr.3d 672 (Cal.App.2015). Nor can states place unreasonable conditions upon access by such corporations to the local courts. Eli Lilly & Co. v. Sav-On-Drugs, p. 1101, infra; Sioux Remedy Co. v. Cope, p. 1106, infra. On the other hand, reasonable taxation and reasonable regulation is permissible. International Shoe Co. v. State of Washington, p. 65, supra; Union Brokerage Co. v. Jensen, p. 1106, infra. States can favor their own citizens over others, however, when they are acting as market participants, rather than as regulators. Glacier State Distribution Services, Inc. v. Wisconsin Dept. of Transp., 585 N.W.2d 652 (Wis.App.1998).

Corporations are also "persons" within the due process and equal protection clauses of the Fourteenth Amendment. Thus, a state, once it has permitted a foreign corporation to enter its territory and acquire property therein, cannot subject the corporation to unduly burdensome legislation or discriminate against it unreasonably in favor of domestic corporations. WHYY, Inc. v. Borough of Glassboro, 393 U.S. 117, 89 S.Ct. 286 (1968); Wheeling Steel Corp. v. Glander, 337 U.S. 562, 69 S.Ct. 1291 (1949).

The Supreme Court has also developed the doctrine of "unconstitutional conditions" which, in effect, prohibits the states from demanding the surrender of constitutional rights either as the price of admission or to avoid the penalty of expulsion. A state cannot, for example, require foreign corporations to refrain from invoking the jurisdiction of the federal courts. Terral v. Burke Construction Co., 257 U.S. 529, 42 S.Ct. 188 (1922). *But compare* National Jewish Democratic Council v. Adelson, 417 F.Supp.3d 416, 422 (S.D.N.Y.2019)(imposition by federal court of compensatory and punitive damages in application of state's anti-SLAPP statute is not a denial of free exercise of the right of access to federal court because the latter is bound to apply state law, when sitting in diversity, and the liability provision was substantive in nature).

4. A state, of course, need not accord to foreign corporations privileges which under its law can be enjoyed only by its citizens in their individual capacity. Situations of this sort, however, are unlikely to arise today. General incorporation laws are now common, and these permit the formation of corporations to engage in a great variety of activities. Incorporation, in other words, is no longer a special privilege as it was at the time of Bank of Augusta v. Earle, p. 1094, supra.

Nevertheless, it is still firmly established that a corporation is not a "citizen" within the meaning of the privileges and immunities clauses of Article IV, Sec. 2 of the Constitution and of the Fourteenth Amendment. Asbury Hospital v. Cass County, 326 U.S. 207, 66 S.Ct. 61 (1945). Apart from the doctrine of Blake v. McClung, p. 1064, supra, what is the precise effect of this rule? Is the rule necessary to permit the states to exercise adequate control over foreign corporations within their borders? Note in this regard the control that the states may constitutionally exercise over individuals, partnerships and unincorporated associations which transact business or do certain acts within their borders. Hess v. Pawloski, p. 64, supra; Doherty & Co. v. Goodman, 294 U.S. 623, 55 S.Ct. 553 (1935). Yet individuals and partnerships, at least, are included within the protection of the privileges and immunities clauses. Flexner v. Farson, 248 U.S. 289, 39 S.Ct. 97 (1918); Grimes v. Alteon, 804 A.2d 256 (Del.2002). But see FCNB Spiegel Inc. v. Dimmick, 619 N.Y.S.2d 935 (Civil Ct., City of New York 1994) (jurisdiction based on activities in the state, rather than on whether the party was an individual or corporation).

Now that the privilege of incorporation is considered no more special or peculiar than that of forming a partnership, is there any reason why corporations should receive less constitutional protection than partnerships?

NOTES

1. What law determines whether a given association is a corporation for the purpose at hand? In Liverpool & L. Life & Fire Insurance Co. v.

Massachusetts, 77 U.S. (10 Wall.) 566, 19 L.Ed. 1029 (1870), the Supreme Court affirmed a determination by the Massachusetts courts that a joint-stock association, formed under a British statute which expressly declared an intention not to incorporate, was properly taxed as a corporation under a Massachusetts tax statute. Cf. Greenspun v. Lindley, p. 1091, supra.

2. State v. United Royalty Co., 363 P.2d 397 (Kan.1961), involved a "Massachusetts trust," organized in Oklahoma and doing business in Kansas. As a trust, United Royalty was unincorporated, but its organization and powers were very similar to those of a corporation. In a suit in quo warranto, the Kansas Supreme Court held that the trust was in effect an unlicensed foreign corporation, and was subject to penalties for doing corporate type business without a permit. The court enjoined United Royalty from doing any business in Kansas until it had complied with the Kansas corporation laws. See Shafran, Comment, Limited Liability of Shareholders in Real Estate Investment Trusts and the Conflict of Laws, 50 Calif.L.Rev. 696 (1962).

3. For discussions of the history of the corporation and the development of the theories of corporate personality, see Freer & Moll, Principles of Business Organizations 189–91 (2d.ed.2018); Gevurtz's Corporation Law § 1.1.3 (3d ed. 2021). For a state's power to tax the intrastate activities of a corporation which is also engaged in interstate commerce, see Nowak and Rotunda, Constitutional Law 319 (7th ed.2004). On the subject of unconstitutional conditions, see Hale, Unconstitutional Conditions and Constitutional Rights, 35 Colum.L.Rev. 321 (1935) ; Sullivan, Unconstitutional Conditions, 102 Harv.L.Rev. 1413 (1989); see also Holby, Note, "Doing Business:" Defining State Control over Foreign Corporations, 32 Vand.L.Rev. 1105 (1979); Schauer, Too Hard: Unconstitutional Conditions and the Chimera of Constitutional Consistency, 72 Denv.U.L.Rev. 989 (1995).

4. A corporation is often said to have its domicile in the state of incorporation. Bergner & Engel Brewing Co. v. Dreyfus, 51 N.E. 531 (Mass.1898). Dicey, Morris, & Collins, Conflict of Laws 1528 (15th ed.2012), and Supp. 4th (2017), at 411–12. Can the concept of domicile, developed in the law of individuals and based on the idea of home, appropriately be applied to corporations? Consider what is said in Section 11 of the Restatement, Second, Conflict of Laws (1971):

> 1. ... No useful purpose is served by assigning a domicil to a corporation. Most of the uses ... which the concept of domicil serves for individuals ... are inapplicable to corporations, which do not, for example, vote, marry, become divorced, beget or bear children and bequeath property. Certain problems, such as judicial jurisdiction and the power to tax and to regulate, are common both to individuals and corporations. But unlike an individual, a corporation has a state of incorporation. This state may tax the corporation, exercise judicial jurisdiction over it and regulate its corporate activities. It is both inaccurate and unnecessary to explain the existence of these powers on the ground that the corporation has its domicil in the state of incorporation. ...

But see the decisions of the U.S. Supreme Court in *Goodyear* and *Daimler*, p. 126, supra, restricting the exercise of general jurisdiction over corporations to states in which they are not only doing general "continuous and systematic business," but where their connection to the forum is such that they can be said to be "at home" there.

5. A corporation is generally said to be a national of the state of incorporation regardless of the nationality of its stockholders. See Sumitomo Shoji America, Inc. v. Avagliano, 457 U.S. 176, 102 S.Ct. 2374 (1982): Defendant, incorporated in New York, was a wholly-owned subsidiary of a Japanese corporation. In an employment discrimination suit, defendant sought to invoke a provision of the U.S.-Japanese Treaty of Friendship, Commerce and Navigation which allows companies of each contracting state to do business in the other and to engage employees "of their choice." The Court held that the defendant was a United States company as a result of its New York incorporation and was not entitled to rely on the U.S.-Japanese treaty as if it were Japanese by reason of the nationality of its parent. See also Kirmse v. Hotel Nikko, 59 Cal.Rptr.2d 96 (Cal.App.1996). Practical exigencies, particularly those arising in times of war, may demand a departure from the ordinary rule and on occasion the courts are specifically directed by statute to look through the corporation to the individual stockholder. See Corcoran, The Trading with the Enemy Act and the Controlled Canadian Corporation, 14 McGill L.J. 174 (1968). See also Sealing, Sex, Allies, and BFOQS: The Case for Not Allowing Foreign Corporations to Violate Title VII in the United States, 55 Me.L.Rev. 89 (2003).

6. For legislation providing for the application of local law to corporations incorporated elsewhere but with a high degree of local ownership ("pseudo-foreign corporations") see p. 1119–1122, infra.

7. For purposes of diversity of citizenship, a corporation is deemed a citizen both of the state of incorporation and of the state where it has its principal place of business, 28 U.S.C.A. § 1332(c). A corporation's principal place of business for purposes of diversity jurisdiction is its "nerve center." Hertz Corp. v. Friend, 559 U.S. 77, 130 S.Ct. 1181 (2010). The nerve center is the place where the corporation's high level officers direct, control, and coordinate the corporation's activities, which will typically be found at its corporate headquarters. For application of the "nerve center" test in a choice of law case rather than the more "flexible" state law test under the Restatement Second, see Starr Indemnity & Liability Company v. Rolls-Royce Corporation, 725 Fed.Appx 592 (9th Cir. 2018) ; relied on in Bagwell v. CBS Corporation, No. 2:19-CV-08423-DSF, 2019 WL 6329631, at *4 (C.D.Cal.2019) ("The existence of an "office with thousands of employees does not mean that location is the 'nerve center'.") As a result of a 2012 amendment to 28 U.S.C.A. § 1332(c), corporations with a U.S. place of incorporation and a foreign principal place of business—or vice versa—are deemed to be citizens of both the U.S. state and the foreign country. Thus, for example, a Mexican individual plaintiff could not assert either diversity or alienage jurisdiction in a suit against a corporation incorporated in Delaware with its principal place of business in France.

B. CORPORATE ACTIVITY

1. "DOING BUSINESS" AND QUALIFICATION STATUTES

The term "doing business" is found in three general types of statutes. The first type is directed to the amenability of foreign corporations to service of process in the state, on the basis of their "doing business" in the state. The second type of statute is concerned with the taxing of foreign corporations for the privilege of "doing business" in the state. The third type involves statutes which declare that a foreign corporation which desires to carry on activities constituting "doing business" in the state must "qualify." Qualification traditionally meant that the foreign company had to provide information from its articles, prove good standing in its home state, appoint an agent for service of process, and pay fees and file reports. Increasingly, the process is changed from "qualifying" to "registering." That is, the foreign business need not get permission to do business, but simply files a registration statement with the appropriate state officer. The registering company must still provide information, maintain a registered agent, and pay fees. The usual penalty imposed for failure to comply with a qualification or registration statute is to deny the corporation the right to bring suit in the state courts. In some states, a civil penalty is imposed upon the company. Failure to qualify or register, under modern law, does not affect the validity of contracts entered by the foreign business. See generally Freer & Moll, Principles of Business Organizations 189–91 (2d ed. 2018).

Thus, the term "doing business" is used in three distinct situations. But "doing business" for one purpose may not satisfy the requirements of "doing business" for another purpose.

NOTES

1. The Model Business Corporation Act (2016), § 15.05, provides that the following activities do not constitute "doing business" for purposes of requiring a foreign corporation to register:

(1) maintaining, defending, mediating, arbitrating, or settling any proceeding;

(2) carrying on any activity concerning the internal affairs of the foreign corporation, including holding meetings of its shareholders or board of directors;

(3) maintaining accounts in financial institutions;

(4) maintaining offices or agencies for the transfer, exchange, and registration of securities of the foreign corporation or maintaining trustees or depositories with respect to those securities;

(5) selling through independent contractors;

(6) soliciting or obtaining orders by any means if the orders require acceptance outside this state before they become contracts;

(7) creating or acquiring indebtedness, mortgages, or security interests in real or personal property;

(8) securing or collecting debts or enforcing mortgages or security interests in property securing the debts, and holding, protecting, or maintaining property so acquired;

(9) conducting an isolated transaction that is not in the course of similar transactions;

(10) owning, protecting and maintaining property; and

(11) doing business in interstate commerce.

See also Restatement, Second, Conflict of Laws § 311 (1971).

2. Suppose that on the facts of International Shoe Co. v. State of Washington, p. 65, supra, a Washington retailer had failed to pay for a consignment of shoes. Could the International Shoe Co. have maintained an action in a Washington court to recover the price, assuming that (a) the company had not qualified to do business in that state and (b) the Washington courts were closed by statute to foreign corporations which did business there without having so qualified?

3. See Netherlands Shipmortgage Corp. v. Madias, 717 F.2d 731 (2d Cir.1983), holding "clearly erroneous" the application of New York's qualification statute to a Bermuda company engaged in international and interstate as well as intrastate business.

4. For a detailed discussion of the various statutory penalties for failure to qualify, see Note, Sanctions for Failure to Comply with Corporate Qualification Statutes: An Evaluation, 63 Colum.L.Rev. 117 (1963).

5. See Okilski, Foreign Corporations: What Constitutes "Doing Business" under New York's Qualification Statute?, 44 Ford.L.Rev. 1042 (1976).

Eli Lilly & Co. v. Sav-On-Drugs, Inc.

Supreme Court of the United States, 1961.
366 U.S. 276, 81 S.Ct. 1316, 6 L.Ed.2d 288.

■ JUSTICE BLACK delivered the opinion of the Court.

The appellant Eli Lilly and Company, an Indiana corporation dealing in pharmaceutical products, brought this action in a New Jersey state court to enjoin the appellee Sav-On-Drugs, Inc., a New Jersey corporation, from selling Lilly's products in New Jersey at prices lower than those fixed in minimum retail price contracts into which Lilly had entered with a number of New Jersey drug retailers. . . . Sav-On moved to dismiss this complaint under a New Jersey statute that denies a foreign corporation transacting business in the State the right to bring any action in New Jersey upon any contract made there unless and until it files with the New Jersey Secretary of State a copy of its charter together with a limited amount of information about its operations[2] and obtains from him a certificate authorizing it to do business in the State.

Lilly opposed the motion to dismiss, urging that its business in New Jersey was entirely in interstate commerce and arguing, upon that ground, that the attempt to require it to file the necessary information and obtain a certificate for its New Jersey business was forbidden by the Commerce Clause of the Federal Constitution. . . . the trial court . . . granted Sav-On's motion to dismiss . . . The State Supreme Court . . . affirmed . . .

The record shows that the New Jersey trade in Lilly's pharmaceutical products is carried on through both interstate and intrastate channels. Lilly manufactures these products and sells them in interstate commerce to certain selected New Jersey wholesalers. These wholesalers then sell the products in intrastate commerce to New Jersey hospitals, physicians and retail drug stores, and these retail stores in turn sell them, again in intrastate commerce, to the general public. It is well established that New Jersey cannot require Lilly to get a certificate of authority to do business in the State if its participation in this trade is limited to its wholly interstate sales to New Jersey wholesalers. Under the authority of the so-called "drummer" cases . . . Lilly is free to send salesmen into New Jersey to promote this interstate trade without interference from regulations imposed by the State. On the other hand, it is equally well settled that if Lilly is engaged in intrastate as well as interstate aspects of the New Jersey drug business, the State can require it to get a certificate of authority to do business. In such a situation, Lilly could not escape state regulation merely because it is also engaged in interstate commerce. . . .

We agree with the trial court that "[t]o hold . . . that plaintiff [Lilly] is not doing business in New Jersey is to completely ignore reality." Eighteen "detailmen," working out of a big office in Newark, New Jersey, with Lilly's name on the door and in the lobby of the building, and with Lilly's district manager and secretary in charge, have been regularly engaged in work for Lilly which relates directly to the intrastate aspects of the sale of Lilly's products. These eighteen "detailmen" have been traveling throughout the State of New Jersey promoting the sales of Lilly's products, not to the wholesalers, Lilly's interstate customers, but to the physicians, hospitals and retailers who buy those products in intrastate commerce from the wholesalers. To this end, they have provided these hospitals, physicians and retailers with up-to-date knowledge of Lilly's products and with free advertising and promotional material designed to encourage the general public to make more intrastate purchases of Lilly's products. And they sometimes even

---

[2]   The information required is: (1) the amount of the corporation's authorized capital stock; (2) the amount of stock actually issued by the corporation; (3) the character of the business which the corporation intends to transact in New Jersey; (4) the principal office of the corporation in New Jersey; and (5) the name and place of abode of an agent upon whom process against the corporation may be served. N.J.Rev.Stat. 14:15–3.

directly participate in the intrastate sales themselves by transmitting orders from the hospitals, physicians and drugstores they service to the New Jersey wholesalers. . . .

Lilly also contends that even if it is engaged in intrastate commerce in New Jersey and can by virtue of that fact be required to get a license to do business in that State, New Jersey cannot properly deny it access to the courts in this case because the suit is one arising out of the interstate aspects of its business. . . . We do not think that . . . the present suit is . . . of that kind. Here, Lilly is suing upon a contract entirely separable from any particular interstate sale . . .

Affirmed.

■ JUSTICE HARLAN, concurring. . . .

It is clear that sending "drummers" into New Jersey seeking customers to whom Lilly's goods may be sold and shipped . . . and suing in the state courts to enforce contracts for sales from an out-of-state store of goods . . . are both so intimately connected with Lilly's right to access to the local market, free of local controls, that they cannot be separated off as "local business" even if they are conducted wholly within New Jersey. However, I do not think that the systematic promotion of Lilly's products among local retailers and consumers who, as Lilly conducts its affairs, can only purchase them from a New Jersey wholesaler bears the same close relationship to the necessities of keeping the channels of interstate commerce state-unburdened. I believe that New Jersey can treat as "local business" such promotional activities, which are pointed at and result initially in local sales by Lilly's customers, and not in direct sales from its own out-of-state store of goods. . . .

. . . The only aspect of the present case that resembles the "drummer" cases is the fact that Lilly's promotion of local sales ultimately serves to increase its interstate sales. To treat this factor as bringing the present situation within the drummer cases would, in my view, be substantially to extend the reach of those cases. . . .

■ JUSTICE DOUGLAS, with whom JUSTICE FRANKFURTER, JUSTICE WHITTAKER and JUSTICE STEWART concur, dissenting. . . .

(1) If New Jersey sought to collect from appellant a tax apportioned to some local business activity which it carries on in *that State,* I would see no constitutional objection to it. . . .

(2) If appellant were sued in New Jersey, I think its connections with that State have been sufficient to make it subject to the jurisdiction of the state courts . . . at least as to suits which reveal a "substantial connection" with the State. . . .

(3) The present case falls in neither of those two categories. New Jersey demands that appellant obtain from it a certificate authorizing it to do business in the State, absent which she denies appellant access to

her courts. The case thus presents the strikingly different issue-whether an interstate business can be subjected to a licensing system. . . .

In this case, appellant's employees within the State were engaged solely in the "drumming up" of appellant's interstate trade. They did this, not by direct solicitation of the interstate buyers, but by contacts with the customers of the buyers. . . . The Court finds these activities to be separable from appellant's interstate business; appellant is "inducing" sales, not "soliciting" them. It is not a distinction I can accept. . . .

ALLENBERG COTTON COMPANY, INC. V. PITTMAN, 419 U.S. 20, 95 S.Ct. 260 (1974): [Action for breach of a contract under which the defendant of Mississippi agreed to sell cotton to the plaintiff, a Tennessee corporation. Plaintiff had no office in Mississippi, did not own or operate a warehouse there and had no employees soliciting business in the state on a regular basis. It did employ an independent broker to identify farmers in the state who would be prepared to sell cotton to the plaintiff. The actual contracts were prepared by the plaintiff in Tennessee and signed by it there; they were then forwarded to the individual farmers in Mississippi for their signatures. The contracts provided that the farmer was to be paid for the cotton upon its delivery to a local warehouse in Mississippi. After delivery to the warehouse, the plaintiff would sort and classify the cotton preliminary to its shipment to mills in other states. The defendant failed to deliver the cotton he had contracted to sell the plaintiff and, when suit was brought against him in a Mississippi state court, claimed that the Mississippi courts were not open to the plaintiff since it was doing business in the state without having obtained the requisite certificate. The defendant was successful in having the suit dismissed by the state courts, but the Supreme Court reversed on the ground that the plaintiff was doing business in interstate commerce.]

■ JUSTICE DOUGLAS delivered the opinion of the Court.

Appellant's arrangements with Pittman and the broker, Covington, are representative of a course of dealing with many farmers whose cotton, once sold to appellant, enters a long interstate pipeline. That pipeline ultimately terminates at mills across the country or indeed around the world, after a complex sorting and matching process designed to provide each mill with the particular grade of cotton which the mill is equipped to process.

Due to differences in soil, time of planting, harvesting, weather and the like, each bale of cotton, even though produced on the same farm, may have a different quality. Traders or merchants like appellant, with the assistance of the Department of Agriculture, must sample each bale and classify it according to grade, staple length, and color. Similar bales, whether from different farms or even from different collection points, are then grouped in multiples of 100 into "even-running lots" which are uniform as to all measurable characteristics. This grouping process typically takes place in card files in the merchant's office; when enough bales have been pooled to make an even-running lot, the entire lot can be targeted for a mill equipped to handle cotton of that particular quality, and the individual bales in the lot will then be shipped to the mill from their respective collection points. It is true that title often formally passes to the merchant upon delivery of the cotton at the warehouse, and that the cotton may rest at the warehouse pending completion of the classification and grouping processes; but as the description above indicates, these fleeting events are an integral first step in a vast system of distribution of cotton in interstate commerce. . . .

We deal here with a species of control over an intricate interstate marketing mechanism. . . . Delivery of the cotton to a warehouse, taken in isolation, is an intrastate transaction. But that delivery is also essential for the completion of the interstate transaction, for sorting and classification in the warehouse are essential before the precise interstate destination of the cotton, whether in this country or abroad, is determined. The determination of the precise market cannot indeed be made until the classification is made. The cotton in this Mississippi sale . . . though temporarily in a warehouse, was still in the stream in interstate commerce. . . .

Much reliance is placed on Eli Lilly & Co. v. Sav-On-Drugs, Inc. [p. 1101, supra], for sustaining Mississippi's action. The case is not in point. There the Court found that the foreign corporation had an office and salesmen in New Jersey selling drugs intrastate. Since it was engaged in an intrastate business it could be required to obtain a license even though it also did an interstate business. . . .

In short, appellant's contacts with Mississippi do not exhibit the sort of localization or intrastate character which we have required in situations where a state seeks to require a foreign corporation to qualify to do business. Whether there were local tax incidents of those contacts which could be reached is a different question on which we express no opinion. Whether the course of dealing would subject appellant to suits in Mississippi is likewise a different question on which we express no view. We hold only that Mississippi's refusal to honor and enforce contracts made for interstate or foreign commerce is repugnant to the Commerce Clause. . . .

■ JUSTICE REHNQUIST, dissenting.

But even if I were able to agree with the Court that Allenberg's activities in Mississippi were purely "interstate," I do not believe that our cases, properly understood, prevent Mississippi from exacting qualification from a foreign corporation as a condition for use of the Mississippi courts.

. . . Mississippi's qualifications statute is concededly not discriminatory. Domestic corporations organized under her laws must submit themselves to her taxing jurisdiction, to service of process within the State, and to a number of other incidents of corporate existence which state law may impose.... [Q]ualifications statutes [aid] in the collection of state taxes by identifying foreign corporations operating within the State and in the protection of citizens within the State through insuring ready susceptibility to service of process of the corporation. The qualification statute also serves an important informational function making available to citizens of the State who may deal with the foreign corporation details of its financing and control. Although the result of Allenberg's failure to comply with the qualification statute is a drastic one, our decisions hold that the burden imposed on interstate commerce by such statutes is to be judged with reference to the measures required to comply with such legislation, and not to the sanctions imposed for violation of it.... The steps necessary in order to comply with this statute are not unreasonably burdensome.

For a review of several cases and distinguishing *Allenberg*, see Hurst v. Buczek Enterprises, LLC, 870 F.Supp.2d 810 (N.D.Cal.2012).

———

SIOUX REMEDY CO. V. COPE, 235 U.S. 197, 35 S.Ct. 57 (1914): Action by an Iowa corporation brought in a South Dakota court. It arose out of a contract made in South Dakota for goods to be shipped by the plaintiff from Iowa to South Dakota. The plaintiff had not "qualified" to do business in South Dakota, and a statute of the latter state provided that if a foreign corporation did business in the state without qualifying (which included the appointment of an agent for the service of process on any and all claims), the foreign corporation could not maintain any action in South Dakota courts. The Supreme Court held that this statute, requiring a general consent to the jurisdiction of the South Dakota courts, was unreasonable and an undue burden on interstate commerce. It held that the South Dakota courts must entertain the action.

In First Family Mortg. Corp. of Florida v. Durham, 528 A.2d 1288 (N.J.1987), New Jersey law barred foreign corporations from maintaining any action to pursue claims that accrued during any time in which it had not filed a local Activity Report. In application of *Sioux City Remedy*, the New Jersey Supreme Court considered this to be an impermissible restraint on interstate commerce. But without declaring the statute to be unconstitutional, it interpreted it to require the filing of an Activity Report as a condition for maintaining claims, regardless of when accrued (i.e., including claims accrued before filing).

Union Brokerage Co. v. Jensen

Supreme Court of the United States, 1944.
322 U.S. 202, 64 S.Ct. 967, 88 L.Ed. 1227, 152 A.L.R. 1072.

[Plaintiff, a North Dakota corporation, which was licensed under federal statute to do business in Minnesota as a custom house broker, brought suit in the Minnesota courts against two former employees for breach of fiduciary obligations. Suit was dismissed by the state courts under a Minnesota statute which denied access to the local courts to all foreign corporations doing business in the state unless they had previously obtained a certificate of authority. The requirements for obtaining such a certificate included (1) the payment of a license fee of $50.00, (2) the filing of a statement containing the name of the corporation, the names and addresses of its directors and officers, the aggregate number of its authorized shares and kindred information and (3) the filing of a consent by the corporation to service of process upon it and appointment of an agent upon whom service of process could be made. Plaintiff appealed to the Supreme Court of the United States contending that, as applied to it, the Minnesota statute was unconstitutional since it placed an undue burden upon a federal instrumentality engaged in foreign commerce.]

■ JUSTICE FRANKFURTER delivered the opinion of the Court.

... In a situation like the present, where an enterprise touches different and not common interests between Nation and State, our task is that of harmonizing these interests without sacrificing either. ... The Tariff Act of 1930 ... confers upon licensees certain privileges, and secures to the Federal Government by means of these licensing provisions a measure of control over those engaged in the customhouse brokerage business. But such circumscribed control by the Federal Government does not imply immunity from control by the State within the sphere of its special interests. ... The state and federal regulations here applicable have their separate spheres of operation. ... Minnesota is legitimately concerned with safeguarding the interests of its own people in business dealings with corporations not of its own chartering but who do business within its borders. ... To safeguard responsibility in all such dealings ... Minnesota has made the same exactions of Union as of every other foreign corporation engaged in similar transactions.

[W]e have not here a case of a foreign corporation merely coming into Minnesota to contribute to or to conclude a unitary interstate transaction ... nor of the State's withholding "the right to sue even in a single instance until the corporation renders itself amenable to suit in all the courts of the state by whosoever chooses to sue it there." Sioux Remedy Co. v. Cope, 235 U.S. 197, 205, 35 S.Ct. 57, 59 (1914). The business of Union, we have seen, is localized in Minnesota, and Minnesota, in the requirement before us, merely seeks to regularize its conduct. ... In the absence of applicable federal regulation, a State may impose non-discriminatory regulations on those engaged in foreign commerce. ...

The Commerce Clause ... does not imply relief to those engaged in interstate or foreign commerce from the duty of paying an appropriate share for the maintenance of the various state governments. Nor does it preclude a State from giving needful protection to its citizens in the course of their contacts with businesses conducted by outsiders when the legislation by which this is accomplished is general in its scope, is not aimed at interstate or foreign commerce, and involves merely burdens incident to effective administration. . . .

Judgment affirmed.

NOTES

1.   A corporation that has failed to comply with a state qualification statute and is thereby barred from suing in the state courts on a contract made in the state is also precluded from bringing suit on the same claim in a local federal court. Woods v. Interstate Realty Co., 337 U.S. 535, 69 S.Ct. 1235 (1949). A foreign corporation that has failed to comply with a state qualification statute may also be precluded from defending itself against a state claim of breach of contract filed in federal court. Farris v. Sambo's Restaurants, Inc., 498 F.Supp. 143 (N.D.Tex.1980) (damage action for breach of a lease); Vahlco Corp. v. C.I.R., 97 T.C. 428 (U.S.Tax Ct.1991). It has been held, however, that the federal courts remain open to the corporation when the issue involves a federal question. Lisle Mills, Inc. v. Arkay Infants Wear, Inc., 90 F.Supp. 676 (E.D.N.Y.1950) (validity of a patent). See also *First Family Mortg. Corp. of Florida*, p. 1106, supra.

2.   Fed.R.Civ.P. 17(b) provides in part that ". . . The capacity of a corporation to sue or be sued shall be determined by the law under which it was organized. . . ." See Sable Corporation v. Dual Office Suppliers, Inc., 1987 WL 14607 (N.D.Ill.1987). For cases applying this rule to a dissolved foreign corporation, see Johnson v. Helicopter & Airplane Services Corp., 404 F.Supp. 726 (D.Md.1975); Stone v. Gibson Refrigerator Sales Corp., 366 F.Supp. 733 (E.D.Pa.1973); Domino Media, Inc. v. Kranis, 9 F.Supp.2d 374 (S.D.N.Y.1998).

KENTUCKY FINANCE CORP. V. PARAMOUNT AUTO EXCHANGE, 262 U.S. 544, 43 S.Ct. 636 (1923): [A Kentucky corporation brought an action of replevin in a Wisconsin State court against a Wisconsin corporation to recover an automobile which the plaintiff alleged had been stolen from it in Kentucky and turned over in Wisconsin to the defendant. Except for the present suit, the plaintiff had engaged in no business activities of any kind in Wisconsin. On the defendant's motion under a Wisconsin statute (applicable only to foreign corporations), the court ordered the plaintiff to send its secretary from Louisville, Kentucky, to Milwaukee, Wisconsin, for an examination before trial. Upon the plaintiff's refusal to comply with the order, the court made a further order that the complaint be dismissed. The plaintiff appealed to the state supreme court, contending that the statute under which both orders were made violated the equal protection clause of the Fourteenth Amendment. The Supreme Court of Wisconsin affirmed the lower court and the plaintiff appealed to the Supreme Court of the United States. Held, reversed.]

■ VAM DEVANTER, J. "The State court whose aid it [the plaintiff] invoked was one whose jurisdiction was general and adequate for the purpose. . . . [W]hen the plaintiff went into Wisconsin, as it did, for the obviously lawful purpose of repossessing itself, by a permissible action in her courts, of specific personal property unlawfully taken out of its possession elsewhere and fraudulently carried into that state, it was, in our opinion, within her jurisdiction for all the purposes of that undertaking. . . . And we think there is no tenable ground for regarding it as any less entitled to the equal protection of the laws in that state than an individual would have been in the same circumstances; . . . The discrimination was essentially arbitrary."

■ JUSTICE BRANDEIS, with whom JUSTICE HOLMES concurred, dissented. "To sustain the contention that the statute denies to plaintiff equal protection of the laws would seem to require the court to overrule Blake v. McClung [p. 1064, supra] . . . and many other cases."

C. THE LAW GOVERNING CORPORATE ACTIVITIES

RESTATEMENT, SECOND, CONFLICT OF LAWS (1971):

§ 301. Rights Against and Liabilities to Third Person

The rights and liabilities of a corporation with respect to a third person that arise from a corporate act of a sort that can likewise be done by an individual are determined by the same choice-of-law principles as are applicable to noncorporate parties.

NOTES

1. Stone v. Southern Illinois & Mo. Bridge Co., 206 U.S. 267, 27 S.Ct. 615 (1907). Suit by the plaintiff bridge company, an Illinois corporation, to condemn a strip of Missouri land which was to form one of the approaches to a bridge which the plaintiff was about to construct over the Mississippi river. The Missouri courts found for the plaintiff and the defendant landowners appealed to the Supreme Court of the United States on the ground, among others, that the plaintiff did not have the power of eminent domain under the law of Illinois, the state of its incorporation, and that "a corporation of Illinois can only exercise in Missouri such powers as are conferred upon it by the State of its creation." Held for the plaintiff. The question involved ". . . the powers of corporations under the laws of Missouri . . . no federal right was taken from the [defendants] by the action complained of under the state laws as interpreted by the Supreme Court of the State of Missouri. . . ."

2. See generally Kozyris, Corporate Wars and Choice of Law, 1985 Duke L.J. 1 (1985); Reese & Kaufman, The Law Governing Corporate Affairs: Choice of Law and the Impact of Full Faith and Credit, 58 Colum.L.Rev. 1118 (1958). See also Goldsmith, Interest Analysis Applied to Corporations: The Unprincipled Use of a Choice of Law Method, 98 Yale L.J. 597 (1989); Note, Corporate Chaos: Who Should Govern Internal Affairs?, 24 T.Jefferson L.Rev. 83 (2001).

RESTATEMENT, SECOND, CONFLICT OF LAWS (1971):

§ 302. Other Issues with Respect to Powers and Liabilities of a Corporation

(1) Issues involving the rights and liabilities of a corporation, other than those dealt with in '301, are determined by the local law of the state which, with respect to the particular issue, has the most significant relationship to the occurrence and the parties under the principles stated in § 6.

(2) The local law of the state of incorporation will be applied to determine such issues, except in the unusual case where, with respect to the particular issue, some other state has a more significant relationship to the occurrence and the parties, in which event the local law of the other state will be applied.

Comment:

a.   *Scope of section.* The rule of this Section is to be contrasted with that of § 301. The rule of this Section is concerned with issues involving matters that are peculiar to corporations and other associations, whereas the rule of § 301 is concerned with issues arising from corporate acts of a sort that can also be done by individuals. Many of the matters that fall within the scope of the rule of this Section involve the "internal affairs" of a corporation-that is, the relations inter se of the corporation, its shareholders, directors, officers or agents. . . . Other such matters affect the interests of the corporation's creditors.

Matters falling within the scope of the rule of this Section and which involve primarily a corporation's relationship to its shareholders include steps taken in the course of the original incorporation, the election or appointment of directors and officers, the adoption of bylaws, the issuance of corporate shares, preemptive rights, the holding of directors' and shareholders' meetings, methods of voting including any requirement for cumulative voting, shareholders' rights to examine corporate records, charter and by-law amendments, mergers, consolidations and reorganizations and the reclassification of shares. Matters which may also affect the interests of the corporation's creditors include the issuance of bonds, the declaration and payment of dividends, loans by the corporation to directors, officers and shareholders, and the purchase and redemption by the corporation of outstanding shares of its own stock.

The rule of this Section will be applied in the absence of a local statute that is explicitly applicable to the situation at hand. All States of the United States have statutes which regulate in various ways the affairs of foreign corporations within their territory. Blue sky laws and statutes regulating the activities of public utilities are typical examples. . . .

e.   *Rationale.* Application of the local law of the state of incorporation will usually be supported by those choice-of-law factors favoring the needs of the interstate and international systems, certainty, predictability and uniformity of result, protection of the justified expectations of the parties and ease in the application of the law to be applied. Usually, application of this law will also be supported by the factor looking toward implementation of the relevant policies of the state with the dominant interest in the decision of the particular issue.

Uniform treatment of directors, officers and shareholders is an important objective which can only be attained by having the rights and liabilities of those persons with respect to the corporation governed by a single law. . . .

In addition, many matters involving a corporation cannot practicably be determined differently in different states. Examples of such matters, most of which have already been mentioned in Comment *a,* include steps taken in the course of the original incorporation, the election or appointment of directors and officers, the adoption of bylaws, the issuance of corporate shares ..., the holding of directors' and shareholders' meetings, methods of voting including any requirement for cumulative voting, the declaration and payment of dividends and other distributions, charter amendments, mergers, consolidations, and reorganizations, the reclassification of shares and the purchase and redemption by the corporation of outstanding shares of its own stock.

Matters such as these must be contrasted with the acts dealt with in § 301, which include, for example, the making of contracts, the commission of torts and the transfer of property. There is no reason why corporate acts of the latter sort should not be governed by the local law of different states. There is no reason, for example, why an issue involving one corporate contract should not be governed by the local law of state X while an issue involving another corporation contract is governed by the local law of state Y. On the other hand, it would be impractical to have matters of the sort mentioned in the previous paragraph, which involve a corporation's organic structure or internal administration, governed by different laws. It would be impractical, for example, if an election of directors, an issuance of shares, a payment of dividends, a charter amendment, or a consolidation or reorganization were to be held valid in one state and invalid in another. Possible alternatives would be either to have matters of this sort governed by the local law of a particular state or else to hold applicable the local law of any state having a reasonable relationship to the corporation which imposed the strictest requirement. . . .

It should be added that certain issues which are peculiar to corporations or to other organizations do not affect matters of organic structure or internal administration and need not, as a practical matter, be governed by a single law. An example is the transfer of individual shares of a share issue. There is no practical reason, for example, why a corporation incorporated in state X should not comply with the requirements of state Y when it seeks to sell its shares in the latter state.

Even as to such matters, however, the local law of the state of incorporation has usually been applied in the absence of an explicitly applicable local statute. . . .

The "Internal Affairs" Rule. At one time American courts took the position that they would not entertain actions involving the internal organization, management, capitalization, issuance of dividends, etc., of foreign corporations. This view has given way in more recent times to the thought that this is but one aspect of the forum non conveniens principle. A court will exercise jurisdiction over an action involving the internal affairs of a foreign corporation unless it is an inappropriate or an inconvenient forum for the trial of the action." Restatement, Second, Conflict of Laws § 313 (1971).

NOTES

1.   Hausman v. Buckley, 299 F.2d 696 (2d Cir.1962), cert. denied, 369 U.S. 885, 82 S.Ct. 1157 (1962). This was a derivative action brought by minority stockholders on behalf of the Pantepec Oil Company against its officers and directors to recover damages for what was alleged to be the unlawful sale of the corporation's assets. The Pantepec Company was incorporated in Venezuela, its shareholders' meetings were held there, and it had substantial assets in that country. On the other hand, Pantepec was an American financed and American controlled corporation, and all the parties to the action were American citizens. The defendants moved to dismiss the complaint on the ground that under Venezuelan law actions on behalf of a corporation cannot be brought by minority stockholders but only by persons appointed at a stockholders' meeting. Held for the defendants. The law of the state of incorporation determines the right of a shareholder to object to action taken by the directors and officers on behalf of the corporation. Whether a derivative action can be brought is a substantive, rather than a procedural, question and the Venezuelan law is not contrary to the public policy of New York. Mansfield Hardwood Lumber Co. v. Johnson (Note 2, infra) was distinguished on the ground that Pantepec is not a "paper" corporation of Venezuela. See also *CTS Corp.*, p. 1125, infra.

2.   The internal affairs rule applies to claims by the corporation for breach of a fiduciary duty by one of its corporation's principals: Enzo Life Scis., Inc. v. Adipogen Corp., 82 F.Supp.3d 568 (D.Del.2015). But see Mansfield Hardwood Lumber Co. v. Johnson, 268 F.2d 317 (5th Cir.1959), cert. denied, 361 U.S. 885 (1959). Suit in a federal court in Louisiana by minority shareholders against the officers and majority shareholders of a Delaware corporation complaining that the defendants had breached their fiduciary obligations to the plaintiffs in purchasing the plaintiffs' stock. The corporation did all of its business in Louisiana. Held for the plaintiffs. Under Delaware law there was no breach of fiduciary obligation, but the rule calling for application of the law of the state of incorporation should not be applied to determine the internal affairs of a corporation "where the only contact point with the incorporating state is the naked fact of incorporation and

where all other contact points . . . are found" in the state of the forum. The decision was distinguished and limited in Sommers Drug Stores Co. Employee Sharing Trust v. Corrigan, 883 F.2d 345 (5th Cir.1989).

3. See also McDermott Inc. v. Lewis, 531 A.2d 206 (Del.1987) and Draper v. Paul N. Gardner Defined Plan Trust, 625 A.2d 859 (Del.1993), extending the internal affairs rule to foreign-country corporations.

4. In European and other civil law countries, the basic law governing a corporation's internal affairs and the liability of its officers, directors and shareholders is the law of the corporation's "social seat" which can generally be described as the main office or executive headquarters of the corporation. Latty, Pseudo-Foreign Corporations, 65 Yale L.J. 137, 166–73 (1955); 2 Rabel, Conflict of Laws 33 et seq. (2d ed.1958); Note, Basedow, Pseudo-Foreign Corporations and the Internal Affairs Rule, 1960 Duke L.J. 477. For a European perspective and comparative treatment, see Kegel/Schurig, Internationales Privatrecht 498–512 (8th ed.2000), with numerous references. See also Basedow, Conflicts of Economic Regulation, 42 Am.J.Comp.L. 423 (1994).

In the European Community, some states follow the incorporation rule, while others observe the "seat" rule. The European Court has held that a corporation's status as a legal person must be recognized throughout the Community if it was established in accordance with the law of its state of incorporation and continues to enjoy legal personality there. Case C-212/97, Centros Ltd. v. Erhvervs-og Selskabsstyrelsen, [1999] ECR I-1459, 1999 WL 477587. However, the law of the state of formation still determines whether the corporation must maintain its seat there and what consequences (e.g., possible dissolution) might result from a change of the seat to another state. In this respect, the *Centros* decision does not affect the Court's earlier decision in Case 81/87 (*Daily Mail*), [1988] ECR 5483. For comment, see Behrens, Das Internationale Gesellschaftsrecht nach dem Centros-Urteil des EuGH, 1999 IPRax 323. In Case C-208/00, Überseering BV v. Nordic Construction Company Baumanagement GmbH (NCC), [2002] ECR I-9919, the Court held that a seat-principle state (Germany) must recognize the legal capacity of an entity formed in an incorporation-principle EU Member State, even when its principal place of business is (now) in Germany. The Member State cannot require the branch of such a company to comply with stricter domestic rules on share capital and director's liability. Case C-167/01, Kamer van Koophandel en Fabrieken voor Amsterdam v. Inspire Art Ltd., [2003] ECR I-10155.

However, while the seat-doctrine may not be applied to impede the cross-border movement and establishment of companies within the EU, member states are free to retain the doctrine and to apply it to companies established under their own law. In response to a reference from a Hungarian court, the European Court held that a member state could deny a company organized under its law the right to move its seat to another member state, resulting in a change in the applicable law. Clarifying its earlier decisions, the Court stated that EU law precluded: (a) refusal to recognize a company validly organized in another member state and continued to be governed by its law despite the move of its seat and (b) preventing a domestic company as well as to prohibit a domestic company from reorganizing itself under the law of another member state (thereby effecting not only a move of its seat but also a change in the applicable law). Case C-210/06, In re Cartesio, [2008] ECR I-9641.

The *seat* principle, in those countries adhering to it, applied both to foreign companies moving their seat *into* the country and to local (domestic) companies moving their seat *abroad*. See preceding paragraph, this note. The case law of the EC Court of Justice, supra, makes it clear that the free-movement-of-establishment law of the EU requires recognition of companies validly established where incorporated in the EU. The case law does not affect national law as it deals with its own companies. Might continued application of the seat principle still result in loss of legal personality when such a company moves its seat abroad? A German appellate decision distinguishes strictly between movement into Germany and movement of local companies abroad and suggests that the answer to the question posed is "yes." Bayrisches Oberlandesgericht, Decision of Feb. 11, 2004 (3Z BR 175/03), in: [2004] IPRax No. 4, p. XI. For discussion of European national company conflicts law after *Inspire Art*, see, e.g., Schnelle, Die Regeln des deutschen internationalen Gesellschaftsrechts in der Zusammenschau der Inspire-Art-Rechtsprechung des EuGH und der europäischen und deutschen Gesetzgebung, in: Rasmussen-Bonne, Freer, Lüke, Weitnauer (eds.), Balancing of Interests—Festschrift für Peter Hay 343 (2005); Schurig, Das deutsch-amerikanische Gesellschaftsrecht im Fahrwasser des europäischen?, id. at 369.

5. While mergers within a member state are possible, cross-border mergers (as distinguished from the acquisition of minority or controlling stock interests) had not been possible, the seat problem being one obstacle. Regulation (EC) 21257/2001, [2001] Official Journal L 294/1, on the Statute of a European Company (SE) provides a vehicle to achieve such a goal. The regulation provides for the establishment, by one or more companies, of a *Societas Europea* (SE) which is free to move its center of operations within the Community. It is a *European*, rather than a national company, although regulatory or protective provisions of national law (such as worker codetermination under German law) may carry over into the way such a company may need to be structured. As the first company to avail itself of this new corporate form, the German insurance and banking giant Allianz AG decided in early 2006 to transform itself into Allianz SE and, as part of that process, to acquire the Italian insurer Riunione Adriatica di Sicurtà Spa. The merger documentation can be found at https://www.allianz.com/en/investor_relations/shareholders/annual-general-meeting/agm-archive.html#2006eo (last visited Feb. 28, 2021). By 2014, there were 2,423 SEA registrations. A 2011 Directive provides for the merger of limited liability companies: Directive 2011/35/EU, [2011] Official Journal L. 110/1.

Another Directive concerns the cross-border establishment of limited liability companies, which could be one-man companies. The cross-border requirement prevents adoption of this model for a purely domestic business. Thus, for instance, a German wishing to establish such a business, intending to be primarily active in Germany, would need to establish it in another member state and then operate by way of a branch in Germany, invoking the free-movement principles of the decisions discussed in Note 4. Basedow, Das facultative Unionsprivatrecht und das international Privatrecht, in: Kronke and Thorn (eds.), Grenzen überwinden—Prinzipien bewahren, Festschrift von Hoffmann 50, 52 (2012). The Directive is 2009/102/EC, [2009] Official Journal L 258/20.

The new European corporate form (SE), supra, also raises difficult question with respect to the law applicable in the case of possible insolvency: Bachmann, Das auf die insolvente Societas Europea (SE) anwendbare Recht, in: Kronke and Thorn (eds).

6.   The U.S.-German Treaty of Friendship, Commerce, and Navigation of 1954 (7 U.S.T. 1839, 273 UNTS 3) provides for the mutual recognition of companies established in the respective other contracting state and for national and most-favored-nation treatment in the host state. Art. XXV, para. 2, sentence 2. What about a company incorporated in a U.S. state but with its principal (or only) place of business in Germany (without having complied with German requirements for incorporation there): is it a legal person, does it have capacity to sue? In a first interpretation of the 1954 Treaty, the German Supreme Court (BGH) said "yes" to both questions, both as a matter of interpreting the US-American treaty on the basis of its explicit language and with reference to the ECJ's decisions holding that the "right of establishment" includes recognition of the legal status accorded by the state of origin. Decision of the Bundesgerichtshof (BGH) of January 29, 2003, Docket No. VIII ZR 155/02, [2003] Betriebsberater 810; [2003] IPRax 265 (Company incorporated in Florida with administrative seat in Germany). As a consequence, the "incorporation approach" has supplanted the "seat theory" within the EU and, in the case of Germany, with respect to the United States. See also BGH Docket No. VII ZR 370/98, March 13, 2003, 58 Juristenzeitung 525 (2003) (Dutch Company with "seat" in Germany).

In response to the European Union Court's Inspire Art decision, Note 4, supra, the German Justice Ministry presented a draft law in early 2008 to amend the German conflicts statute (Einführungsgesetz zum Bürgerlichen Gesetzbuch). A new Art. 10(1) would have provided that the law applicable to corporations is that of the state of their registration or, absent a registration, that of their formation. The applicable law would extend to the corporation's internal affairs (Art. 10(2)) and to the prerequisites, procedures, and effects of a transformation by way of merger, transfer of assets, or change of corporate form (Art. 10a). The new provisions would have general application (i.e., extend also to companies from non-EC states), thereby generalizing the results of the German Supreme Court's case law with respect to states with commercial treaties with Germany, supra this note. See Leuring, Neue Entwicklungen im Internationalen Gesellschaftsrecht, [2008–4] NJW-Spezial 111; Rotheimer, Referentenentwurf zum Internationalen Gesellschaftsrecht, [2008–5] id. 181. The draft has not been adopted, the combination of EU law (within the EU) and national law (with respect to non-EU companies), as described above, therefore continues to apply. For compresensive treatment (for

Germany), see Münchner Handbuch des Gesellschaftsrechts, Vol. 6: Internationales Gesellschaftsrecht (4th ed.2013).

German-American Coffee Co. v. Diehl

Court of Appeals of New York, 1915.
216 N.Y. 57, 109 N.E. 875.

[Action brought under a former New York statute by a New Jersey corporation against one of its directors to recover damages for the declaration of a dividend that was illegal under a New York statute. The dividend was also illegal under New Jersey law but under that law an action against the directors could only be brought by the stockholders. The plaintiff corporation has "maintained in New York its main business office; has held in New York the regular and most of the special meetings of its directors; and in New York has 'generally,' to follow the words of the complaint, 'managed, directed and conducted its business.'" Held that the statute was intended to apply to this situation and could constitutionally be so applied.]

■ CARDOZO, J. . . . We come, then, to the question of power. On that question the argument has taken a wide range, yet the decision, when confined to the facts of the case at hand, is brought within a narrow compass. As long as a foreign corporation keeps away from this state, it is not for us to say what it may do or not do. But when it comes into this state, and transacts its business here, it must yield obedience to our laws. . . . This statute makes no attempt to regulate foreign corporations while they keep within their domicile. A prohibition which lasts while business within the state continues, and may be escaped when business within the state is stopped, is, in effect, a condition imposed on the right to do business, and nothing more. . . .

Also cited in: Culligan Soft Water Co., et al. v. Clayton Dubilier & Rice LLC, et al., 988 N.Y.S.2d 134 (App.Div.2014). Is the problem of local regulation of the affairs of a foreign corporation as simple as Judge Cardozo apparently conceived it to be in his opinion in the *Diehl* case? Does the fact that a corporation does some business in a state give that state power to regulate all aspects of the corporation's internal affairs? See Edgar v. MITE Corp., p. 1122, infra, and CTS Corp. v. Dynamics Corp. of America, infra, p. 1125.

As seen from the preceding material in this Section, the courts will not hesitate to apply their local law to a corporate act, such as the making of a contract or the commission of a tort, which is of the sort that can likewise be done by an individual. Restatement, Second, Conflict of Laws § 301 (1971). On the other hand, the courts will rarely, in the absence of an explicit statute, apply their local law to matters that are peculiar to corporations. Restatement, Second, Conflict of Laws § 302 (1971).

Matters that are peculiar to corporations can be grouped into two categories: those that practically can be regulated differently in different states and those where this cannot be done. Examples of matters falling within the first category are individual sales of a corporation's stock and the power of shareholders to inspect the corporate books. Many states have statutes, such as blue sky laws, that regulate matters falling within this category.

Examples of matters falling within the second category are the declaration and payment of dividends, cumulative voting and the issuance of stock. Other matters falling within this category are set forth in Comment *e* of § 302 of the Restatement, Second, Conflict of Laws (1971), which is set forth above. Relatively few statutes are directed to foreign corporations with regard to matters in this second category. Presumably, a state, which is not that of incorporation, can appropriately apply its law to such matters if the foreign corporation involved does all, or nearly all, of its business within the territory of that state and if all, or nearly all, of the corporation's shareholders reside there. On the other hand, there are undoubtedly constitutional limitations upon the power of a state to apply its law in circumstances where its contacts with the foreign corporation are of lesser extent.

Western Air Lines, Inc. v. Sobieski

California District Court of Appeal, 1961.
191 Cal.App.2d 399, 12 Cal.Rptr. 719.

[Western Airlines, a Delaware corporation, had originally been formed for the purpose of acquiring the assets of a California corporation. Western did substantial business in California and in several other states. It did no business in Delaware. Residents of California held 30% of its stock; 55% of its passenger traffic started or ended in that state; 60% of its wages were paid there; and there were other substantial contacts.

The Board of Directors of Western wished to eliminate cumulative voting on its stock, and, in accordance with Delaware law, started to seek shareholders' approval when the California Commissioner of Corporations intervened. He ruled that this would be a "sale" of stock in California within the meaning of Section 25009(a) of the California Corporations Code which defines "sale" to include "any change in the rights, preferences, privileges, or restrictions on outstanding securities."

The Commissioner granted a permit to proceed with the shareholder vote on condition that the amendment of the articles should not be filed with the Secretary of State of Delaware until a hearing had been held in California on the "fairness" of the proposal, pursuant to the California Corporation Code. At that hearing, the Commissioner found that the plan was "unfair" and disallowed it. The Commissioner noted a strong public policy in favor of cumulative voting which is required for all California corporations. He also treated Western as a "pseudo-foreign corporation," saying that "the fiction of Delaware residence should yield to the totality of California contacts so as to require, in addition to compliance with the Delaware law, the approval of the California Corporations Commissioner as a condition to eliminating the right of cumulative voting by the shareholders."

The ruling of the Commissioner was upheld by the California District Court of Appeal. The court relied, among other things, on the fact that Western had originally been a California corporation and that, when it applied to the California Corporations Commissioner for permission to exchange its shares for those of its California predecessor, it represented to the Commissioner that the shareholders of the California corporation would not be hurt in any way by the exchange.

The Court also said:]

> It would appear that the provisions of the Corporate Securities Act here before us are a proper exercise of legislative discretion in requiring that corporate dealings with residents of this state be authorized by the Commissioner of Corporations, particularly where such corporation does a substantial amount of business within the state, and the act is not violative of the constitutional clauses of equal protection, contract, due process and full faith and credit if such legislative enactments operate equally upon such foreign corporations and domestic corporations in this state. . . .

When we consider the complexity of present-day corporate structure and operation, and the far-flung area of corporate activities where transportation or nation-wide distribution of products may be involved, we are persuaded that the commissioner has this discretion. To hold otherwise, and to follow the argument of Western to its conclusion, would be to say that the commissioner might have the power in the first instance to require certain rights to be guaranteed to shareholders before he would permit the sale or issuance of a foreign corporation's stock in this state, but that immediately thereafter, by the device of amending the charter of such corporation in another state, the entire structure of that corporation, even to substantial changes in the rights of shareholders in California, might be legally affected. Such a holding would enable a foreign corporation to destroy the rights which the State of California has deemed worthy of protection by the enactment of the Corporate Securities Act.

This position is not without support in other jurisdictions. The mere fact that the last act here necessary to effectuate the change in the voting rights of the numerous California residents who are shareholders of Western will take place in Delaware does not of itself necessitate a finding that the commissioner for that reason was without jurisdiction in this matter. . . .

NOTES

1. The problem of this case is discussed in Reese & Kaufman, The Law Governing Corporate Affairs: Choice of Law and the Impact of Full Faith and Credit, 58 Colum.L.Rev. 1118 (1958). *Sobieski* was followed in Friese v. Superior Court of San Diego County, 36 Cal.Rptr.3d 558 (Cal.Ct.App.2005), cert. denied, 549 U.S. 821, 127 S.Ct. 138 (2006).

2. Article 8–110 of the Uniform Commercial Code (1994 Revision) deals with choice of law with respect to investment securities, for instance, the questions of what law governs the validity of a security and the rights and duties of an issuer with respect to registration of transfer of a security. It distinguishes between direct and indirect holding of securities. In direct holding, the investor is registered on the corporation's books and the applicable law is determined by the corporation's state of incorporation. That state also determines whether the issuer may choose another law. Art. 8–110(d). In indirect holding, the investor has an entitlement, a claim, against a securities intermediary. The intermediary's "jurisdiction" is defined by Art. 8–110(e). In all cases, the "applicable law" is the "local" law of the particular jurisdiction and thus excludes its conflicts rules. Official Comment (1). For discussion see Heidenreich, Article Eight-Article Eight?, 22 Wm.Mitchell L.Rev. 985 (1996); Strauss, Reviewing Revised Article 8 of the Uniform Commercial Code, 44 Wayne L.Rev. 203 (1998); Facciolo, Father Knows Best: Revised Article 8 and the Individual Investor, 27 Fla.St.U.L.Rev. 615 (2000); Schwarcz & Benjamin: Intermediary Risk in the Indirect Holding System for Securities, 12 Duke J.Comp. & Int'l L. 309 (2002); Hakes, UCC Article 8: Will the Indirect Holding of Securities Survive the Light of Day?, 35 Loy.L.A.L.Rev. 661 (2002).

California (in 1976)[1] and New York (in 1962)[2] enacted statutes which provide for application of their law in certain circumstances to foreign corporations with which they have a substantial relationship. Both statutes are expressly made inapplicable to corporations whose shares are listed on a national securities exchange. Hence, in the nature of things, they will rarely affect corporations that do a substantial multistate business. The California statute only becomes operative if two additional tests are met. "[T]he average of the property factor, the payroll factor and the sales factor" (all factors being a proportion of the corporation's California activity to its total activity) must exceed 50 percent during the corporation's "latest full income year." Also, "more than one-half of [the corporation's] outstanding voting securities [must be] held of record by persons having addresses" in California. Once these conditions are met, California law is made applicable to a variety of issues, including the election of directors, the liability and indemnification of directors and the payment of dividends. It seems apparent that California law would not have been applied if this statute

---

[1]   West's Ann.Cal.Corp.Code § 2115.

[2]   N.Y.Bus.Corp.Law § 1320.

had been in effect at the time that Western Airlines, Inc. v. Sobieski was decided.

The New York statute only becomes applicable if the shares of the foreign corporation are not listed on a national securities exchange and if at least half of the corporation's "business income for the preceding three fiscal years . . . was allocable to this state for franchise tax purposes under the tax law." In contrast to the California statute, the New York statute does not apply to shareholders' voting rights.

To date, only the California statute appears to have given rise to much litigation. Its application to require cumulative voting by the shareholders of a Utah corporation was upheld in Wilson v. Louisiana-Pacific Resources, Inc., 187 Cal.Rptr. 852 (Cal.App.1982). The corporation in question "had initially no business connection with Utah and had maintained" its principal place of business in California since at least 1975. In addition, the meetings of its shareholders and directors were held in California and all of its employees and bank accounts were located in that state. Utah law provides for straight voting in an election of directors, but permits cumulative voting if the articles of incorporation so provide. The court held that application of the California statute was not prohibited by any provision of the Constitution, saying:

> . . . California's present law requiring cumulative voting by shareholders continues in effect a policy which has existed in this state since the Constitution of 1879. . . .

> Utah, on the other hand, has no interests which are offended by cumulative voting; and, whatever interest it might have in maintaining a laissez faire policy on that score would seem to be clearly outweighed by the interests of California, in which a majority of shareholders and the corporation's business activity is located. . . .

> There is no suggestion, or evidence, that section 2115 was adopted for the purpose of deterring foreign corporations from doing business in this state; nor is there any direct evidence that it has had or will have such an effect. On the contrary, what evidence there is in the record on this point consists of testimony by appellant's president that he knew of no adverse effect on appellant's business which would be caused by cumulative voting.

> Appellant argues that adverse consequences are predictable from "potentially conflicting claims of shareholders as to which state [law] governs" the method of voting by shareholders, and from the "transient nature of the applicability of the California statute." . . .

> The potential for conflict and resulting uncertainty from California's statute is substantially minimized by the nature of the criteria specified in section 2115. A corporation can do a majority of its business in only one state at a time; and it can have a majority of its shareholders resident in only one state at a time. If a corporation meets those requirements in

this state, no other state is in a position to regulate the method of voting by shareholders on the basis of the same or similar criteria. It might also be said that no other state could claim as great an interest in doing so. In any event, it does not appear that any other state has attempted to do so. If California's statute were replicated in all states, no conflict would result. We conclude that the potential for conflict is, on this record, speculative and without substance.

What appellant refers to as the "transient nature" of the statute's applicability, i.e., its application from year to year based upon the prior year's activity, could conceivably be a problem for a corporation whose business activity within the state fluctuated widely, but the "worst-case" scenario that such a corporation might find it necessary to adopt cumulative voting as a means of assuring compliance on a continuing basis-does not appear to be so burdensome as to result in a significant restraint upon commerce among the states. . . .

Wilson, supra, was mentioned with approval in Greb v. Diamond Intern. Corp., 295 P.3d 353 (Cal.2013), but the constitutionality of the underlying California statute was questioned in light of the U.S. Supreme Court's *CTS* decision, p. 1125, infra, in VantagePoint Venture Partners 1996 v. Examen, Inc., 871 A.2d 1108 (Del.2005).

New York's statute has been raised as a defense against indemnification of corporate employees: Stewart v. Continental Copper & Steel Industries, Inc., 414 N.Y.S.2d 910 (App.Div.1979); Sierra Rutile Limited v. Katz, 1997 WL 431119 (S.D.N.Y.1997).

NOTES

1. Application of the California statute to require cumulative voting and the annual election of directors of a publicly owned Delaware corporation was held unconstitutional in Louart Corp. v. Arden-Mayfair, Inc., No. c192091 (Sup.Ct.Cal., Aug. 5, 1977) (unreported). The court noted that there was an irreconcilable conflict between California and Delaware law and that the corporation might have the requisite contacts with California in some years but not in others. It concluded that application of the California statute would impose an improper burden on interstate commerce because of the uncertainty that would result from the corporation's being subject in different years to different state laws.

2. The choice-of-law problems dealt with here would be mitigated if Congress were to prescribe minimum standards for corporations doing business in interstate commerce. Such a statute, proposed by Professor William L. Cary, would permit corporations to incorporate in the state of their choosing, but would remove many of the present incentives for incorporating in states, such as Delaware, which have lenient corporation laws. See Cary, Federalism and Corporate Law: Reflections upon Delaware, 83 Yale L.J. 663 (1974); Loewenstein, Delaware as Demon: Twenty-five Years After Professor Cary's Polemic, 71 U.Colo.L.Rev. 497 (2000).

3. Articles on the general subject include Oldham, Regulating the Regulators: Limitations Upon a State's Ability to Regulate Corporations with Multi-State Contacts, 57 Denver L.J. 345 (1980); Ratner & Schwartz, The Impact of Shaffer v. Heitner on the Substantive Law of Corporations, 45 Brooklyn L.Rev. 641 (1979); Halloran & Hammer, Section 2115 of the New California General Corporation Law, 23 UCLA L.Rev. 1282 (1976); Kaplan, Foreign Corporations and Local Corporate Policy, 21 Vand.L.Rev. 433 (1968); Bebchuk, Cohen & Ferrell, Does the Evidence Favor State Competition in Corporate Law?, 90 Cal.L.Rev. 1775 (2002).

Edgar v. MITE Corp.

Supreme Court of the United States, 1982.
457 U.S. 624, 102 S.Ct. 2629, 73 L.Ed.2d 269.

■ JUSTICE WHITE delivered . . . the opinion of the Court. . . .

Appellee MITE Corporation and its wholly-owned subsidiary, MITE Holdings, Inc., are corporations organized under the laws of Delaware with their principal executive offices in Connecticut. Appellant James Edgar is the Secretary of State of Illinois and is charged with the administration and enforcement of the Illinois Act. Under the Illinois Act any takeover offer for the shares of a target company must be registered with the Secretary of State. Ill.Rev.Stat., ch. 121, ¶ 137.54.A (1979). A target company is defined as a corporation or other issuer of securities of which shareholders located in Illinois own 10% of the class of equity securities subject to the offer, or for which any two of the following three conditions are met: the corporation has its principal executive office in Illinois, is organized under the laws of Illinois, or has at least 10% of its stated capital and paid-in surplus represented within the state. Id., at ¶ 137.52–10. An offer becomes registered 20 days after a registration statement is filed with the Secretary unless the Secretary calls a hearing. Id., at ¶ 137.54.E. The Secretary may call a hearing at any time during the 20-day waiting period to adjudicate the substantive fairness of the offer if he believes it is necessary to protect the shareholders of the target company, and a hearing must be held if requested by a majority of a target company's outside directors or by Illinois shareholders who own 10% of the class of securities subject to the offer. Id., at & 137.57.A. If the Secretary does hold a hearing, he is directed by the statute to deny registration to a tender offer if he finds that it "fails to provide full and fair disclosure to the offerees of all material information concerning the take-over offer, or that the take-over offer is inequitable or would work or tend to work a fraud or deceit upon the offerees. . . ." Id., at ¶ 137.57.E.

On January 19, 1979, MITE initiated a cash tender offer for all outstanding shares of Chicago Rivet and Machine Co., a publicly held Illinois corporation, by filing a Schedule 14D–1 with the Securities and

Exchange Commission in order to comply with the Williams Act.[2] . . . MITE did not comply with the Illinois Act, however, and commenced this litigation on the same day by filing an action in the United States District Court for the Northern District of Illinois. The complaint asked for a declaratory judgment that the Illinois Act was preempted by the Williams Act and violated the Commerce Clause. In addition, MITE sought a temporary restraining order and preliminary and permanent injunctions prohibiting the Illinois Secretary of State from enforcing the Illinois Act. . . .

[In the first part of his opinion, Justice White held that the Illinois Act was preempted by the Williams Act. This part of the opinion did not gain the support of a majority of the Court.]

The Illinois Act is . . . unconstitutional under the test of Pike v. Bruce Church, Inc., 397 U.S., at 142, 90 S.Ct., at 847, for even when a state statute regulates interstate commerce indirectly, the burden imposed on that commerce must not be excessive in relation to the local interests served by the statute. The most obvious burden the Illinois Act imposes on interstate commerce arises from the statute's previously-described nationwide reach which purports to give Illinois the power to determine whether a tender offer may proceed anywhere.

The effects of allowing the Illinois Secretary of State to block a nationwide tender offer are substantial. Shareholders are deprived of the opportunity to sell their shares at a premium. The reallocation of economic resources to their highest-valued use, a process which can improve efficiency and competition, is hindered. The incentive the tender offer mechanism provides incumbent management to perform well so that stock prices remain high is reduced. . . .

Appellant claims the Illinois Act furthers two legitimate local interests. He argues that Illinois seeks to protect resident security holders and that the Act merely regulates the internal affairs of companies incorporated under Illinois law. We agree with the Court of Appeals that these asserted interests are insufficient to outweigh the burdens Illinois imposes on interstate commerce.

While protecting local investors is plainly a legitimate state objective, the state has no legitimate interest in protecting non-resident shareholders. Insofar as the Illinois law burdens out-of-state

---

[2] The Williams Act, 82 Stat. 454, et seq., codified at 15 U.S.C. §§ 78m(d)–(e) and 78n(d)B(f), added new sections 13(d), 13(e) and 14(d)–(f) to the Securities Exchange Act of 1934. Section 14(d)(1) of the Securities Exchange Act requires an offeror seeking to acquire more than five percent of any class of equity security by means of a tender offer to first file a Schedule 14D-1 with the Securities and Exchange Commission. The Schedule requires disclosure of the source of funds used to purchase the target shares, past transactions with the target company, and other material financial information about the offeror. In addition, the offeror must disclose any anti-trust or other legal problems which might result from the success of the offer. 17 CFR § 240.14d-100 (1981). Section 14(d)(1) requires the offeror to publish or send a statement of the relevant facts contained in the Schedule 14D-1 to the shareholders of the target company. . . .

transactions, there is nothing to be weighed in the balance to sustain the law. . . .

We are also unconvinced that the Illinois Act substantially enhances the shareholders' position. The Illinois Act seeks to protect shareholders of a company subject to a tender offer by requiring disclosures regarding the offer, assuring that shareholders have adequate time to decide whether to tender their shares, and according shareholders withdrawal, proration and equal consideration rights. However, the Williams Act provides these same substantive protections . . . [T]he Court of Appeals . . . also was of the view that the possible benefits of the potential delays required by the Act may be outweighed by the increased risk that the tender offer will fail due to defensive tactics employed by incumbent management. We are unprepared to disagree with the Court of Appeals in these respects, and conclude that the protections the Illinois Act affords resident security holders are, for the most part, speculative.

Appellant also contends that Illinois has an interest in regulating the internal affairs of a corporation incorporated under its laws. The internal affairs doctrine is a conflict of laws principle which recognizes that only one state should have the authority to regulate a corporation's internal affairs-matters peculiar to the relationships among or between the corporation and its current officers, directors, and shareholders-because otherwise a corporation could be faced with conflicting demands. See Restatement (Second) of Conflict of Laws, § 302, Comment b at 307–08 (1971). That doctrine is of little use to the state in this context. Tender offers contemplate transfers of stock by stockholders to a third party and do not themselves implicate the internal affairs of the target company. . . . Furthermore, the proposed justification is somewhat incredible since the Illinois Act applies to tender offers for any corporation for which 10% of the outstanding shares are held by Illinois residents, . . . The Act thus applies to corporations that are not incorporated in Illinois and have their principal place of business in other states. Illinois has no interest in regulating the internal affairs of foreign corporations.

We conclude with the Court of Appeals that the Illinois Act imposes a substantial burden on interstate commerce which outweighs its putative local benefits. It is accordingly invalid under the Commerce Clause.

The judgment of the Court of Appeals is

Affirmed.

[The concurring opinions of JUSTICES POWELL, O'CONNOR and STEVENS are omitted. JUSTICES MARSHALL and REHNQUIST dissented on the ground that the case was moot.]

NOTE

The decision was interpreted and distinguished in Alliant Energy Corp. v. Bie, 336 F.3d 545 (7th Cir.2003).

CTS Corp. v. Dynamics Corp. of America

Supreme Court of the United States, 1987.
481 U.S. 69, 107 S.Ct. 1637, 95 L.Ed.2d 67.

■ JUSTICE POWELL delivered the opinion of the Court.

[The "Control Share Acquisitions Chapter" of the Indiana Business Corporation Law applies to corporations that are incorporated in Indiana and meet several additional tests. They must have at least 100 shareholders, the principal office or substantial assets must be in Indiana; and either 10,000 shareholders or 10% of the shareholders must be Indiana residents or more than 10% of all shares must be owned by Indiana residents. When the acquisition of shares in a company covered by the Act would bring the acquiror's voting power above specified levels, voting rights will not accompany the acquisition unless a majority of the pre-existing shareholders agrees. Dynamics Corporation made a tender offer which would have raised its ownership in CTS above the level specified in the Act. Dynamics sought declaratory relief, which the District Court granted. The Court of Appeals affirmed, holding, on the basis of the plurality opinion in *MITE*, that the Indiana statute was preempted by the Williams Act. It also held that the statute violates the Commerce Clause.

Addressing the first question in the case, Justice Powell concluded that the Williams Act does not preempt the statute because the latter does not frustrate the purposes of the federal law. The Indiana Act protects shareholders against coercive tender offers by permitting them to vote as a group and does not give an advantage to any party in communicating with shareholders. That some tender offers may suffer some delay also does not call for preemption.]

III

As an alternative basis for its decision, the Court of Appeals held that the Act violates the Commerce Clause. . . .

A

The principal objects of dormant Commerce Clause scrutiny are statutes that discriminate against interstate commerce. . . . The Indiana Act is not such a statute. It has the same effects on tender offers whether or not the offeror is a domiciliary or resident of Indiana. Thus, it "visits its effects equally upon both interstate and local business. . . ."

Dynamics nevertheless contends that the statute is discriminatory because it will apply most often to out-of-state entities. This argument rests on the contention that, as a practical matter, most hostile tender offers are launched by offerors outside Indiana. But this argument avails

Dynamics little. "The fact that the burden of a state regulation falls on some interstate companies does not, by itself, establish a claim of discrimination against interstate commerce." Exxon Corp. v. Governor of Maryland, 437 U.S. 117, 126, 98 S.Ct. 2207, 2214, 57 L.Ed.2d 91 (1978). . . . Because nothing in the Indiana Act imposes a greater burden on out-of-state offerors than it does on similarly situated Indiana offerors, we reject the contention that the Act discriminates against interstate commerce.

B

This Court's recent Commerce Clause cases also have invalidated statutes that adversely may affect interstate commerce by subjecting activities to inconsistent regulations. E.g., Brown-Forman Distillers Corp. v. New York State Liquor Authority, 476 U.S. 573, 584, 106 S.Ct. 2080, 2086–2087, 90 L.Ed.2d 552 (1986); Edgar v. MITE Corp., 457 U.S., at 642, 102 S.Ct., at 2640–2641 (plurality opinion of White, J.). . . . The Indiana Act poses no such problem. So long as each State regulates voting rights only in the corporations it has created, each corporation will be subject to the law of only one State. No principle of corporation law and practice is more firmly established than a State's authority to regulate domestic corporations, including the authority to define the voting rights of shareholders. See Restatement (Second) of Conflict of Laws § 304 (1971) (concluding that the law of the incorporating State generally should "determine the right of a shareholder to participate in the administration of the affairs of the corporation"). Accordingly, we conclude that the Indiana Act does not create an impermissible risk of inconsistent regulation of different States.

C

The Court of Appeals did not find the Act unconstitutional for either of these threshold reasons. Rather, its decision rested on its view of the Act's potential to hinder tender offers. We think the Court of Appeals failed to appreciate the significance for Commerce Clause analysis of the fact that state regulation of corporate governance is regulation of entities whose very existence and attributes are a product of state law. . . .

. . . Every State in this country has enacted laws regulating corporate governance. By prohibiting certain transactions, and regulating others, such laws necessarily affect certain aspects of interstate commerce. This necessarily is true with respect to corporations with shareholders in States other than the State of incorporation. Large corporations that are listed on national exchanges, or even regional exchanges, will have shareholders in many States and shares that are traded frequently. . . .

It thus is an accepted part of the business landscape in this country for States to create corporations, to prescribe their powers, and to define the rights that are acquired by purchasing their shares. A State has an interest in promoting stable relationships among parties involved in the corporations it charters, as well as in ensuring that investors in such corporations have an effective voice in corporate affairs.

There can be no doubt that the Act reflects these concerns. The primary purpose of the Act is to protect the shareholders of Indiana corporations. It does this by affording shareholders, when a takeover offer is made, an opportunity to decide collectively whether the resulting change in voting control of the corporation, as they perceive it, would be desirable. A change of management may have important effects on the shareholders' interests; it is well within the State's role as overseer of corporate governance to offer this opportunity. . . .

Dynamics argues in any event that the State has " 'no legitimate interest in protecting the nonresident shareholders.' " . . . Dynamics relies heavily on the statement by the *MITE* Court that "[i]nsofar as the . . . law burdens out-of-state transactions, there is nothing to be weighed in the balance to sustain the law." 457 U.S., at 644, 102 S.Ct., at 2641. But that comment was made in reference to an Illinois law that applied as well to out-of-state corporations as to in-state corporations. We agree that Indiana has no interest in protecting nonresident shareholders *of nonresident corporations.* But this Act applies only to corporations incorporated in Indiana. We reject the contention that Indiana has no interest in providing for the shareholders of its corporations the voting autonomy granted by the Act. Indiana has a substantial interest in preventing the corporate form from becoming a shield for unfair business dealing. Moreover, unlike the Illinois statute invalidated in *MITE,* the Indiana Act applies only to corporations that have a substantial number of shareholders in Indiana. . . . Thus, every application of the Indiana Act will affect a substantial number of Indiana residents, whom Indiana indisputably has an interest in protecting. . . .

[W]e reverse the judgment of the Court of Appeals.

It is so ordered.

[Justice Scalia concurred in Parts III-A and III-B but would not engage in the interest balancing test, first adopted in *Pike* and invoked in *MITE:* "As long as a State's corporation law governs only its own corporations and does not discriminate against out-of-state interests, it should survive this Court's scrutiny under the Commerce Clause, whether it promotes shareholder welfare or industrial stagnation."

Justice White, joined by Justices Blackmun and Stevens, dissented on the ground that the Indiana statute violates the Williams Act because it will prevent minority shareholders from selling their stock at a premium to a tender offeror. Justice White, by himself, also dissented on the ground that the Indiana statute regulates the purchase and sale of stock in interstate commerce and that the attendant restraint violates the Commerce Clause.]

NOTES

1. The Supreme Court explained that the *CTS* analysis contained two elements: that the Indiana statute furthered the federal policy of investor protection and did not violate federal law. Crosby v. Nat'l Foreign Trade Council, 530 U.S. 363, 380 n. 14, 120 S.Ct. 2288, 2298 n.14 (2000). *CTS* was followed in IMS Health, Inc. v. Mills, 616 F.3d 7, 28 (1st Cir.2010) ("[C]oncerns about hidden protectionism and excessive barriers to interstate trade arise when states enact laws likely to subject entities engaged in interstate commerce to incompatible cross-state regulatory regimes."). Similarly: IMS Health, Inc. v. Sorrell, 630 F.3d 263 (2d Cir.2010). In LaPlant v. Northwestern Mutual Life Ins. Co., 701 F.3d 1137 (7th Cir.2012), the Seventh Circuit sharpened the reach of the internal affairs rule. It held that the method of calculating payments under annuity contracts did not implicate the corporation's internal affairs; the state class action therefore did not fall under the exception to the Class Action Fairness Act (CAFA) for cases involving a corporation's internal affairs and could be removed to federal court: "This is a contract case, not a corporate-governance Case."

2. The *CTS* case involved the application of forum law to a corporation incorporated under forum law. May the forum state apply its regulatory law to a *foreign* corporation which does a stated amount of business in the state or which is owned to a large extent by local residents? For instance, may it require cumulative voting or specify how directors are to be elected? Does the *CTS* decision limit the applicability of "pseudo-foreign corporation" legislation, pp. 1119–1122, supra?

Delaware has passed a statute controlling corporate takeovers: 8 Del.Code.Ann. § 203. For discussion, see Suggs, Business Combination Antitakeover Statutes: The Unintended Repudiation of the Internal Affairs Doctrine and Constitutional Constraints on Choice of Law, 56 Ohio State L.J. 1097 (1995). For an examination of similar California legislation and a review of U.S. Supreme Court cases, see Mahjchrzak, Corporate Chaos: Who Should Govern Internal Affairs? 24 T.Jefferson L.Rev. 83 (2001). See also Jacobs, The Reach of State Corporate Law Beyond State Borders: Reflections on Federalism, 84 N.Y.U.L.Rev. 1149 (2009).

In a case involving parallel litigation in Delaware and California and concerning a Delaware corporation, the Supreme Court of Delaware forcefully restated and confirmed the internal affairs doctrine (applicability of the law of the state of incorporation) and referred to its "constitutional underpinnings." Draper v. Paul N. Gardner Defined Plan Trust, 625 A.2d 859, 867 (Del.1993), followed in Hamilton Partners, L.P. v. England, 11 A.3d 1180, 1211 (Del.Ch. 2010).

Art. 10 of the Uniform Limited Liability Company Act also adopts the internal affairs rule: the law applicable to the internal affairs of a foreign limited liability company is that of the state or country where it was organized. The Uniform Act as such has not yet been adopted by any state, but almost all states now have Limited Liability Company Acts with an essential similar provision. See, e.g., Del.Corp.Laws Ann. 1994–95, Title 6, § 18–901(a) (1995).

Compare VantagePoint Venture Partners v. Examen, Inc., 871 A.2d 1108 (Del.2005) (Delaware adheres to law-of-incorporation rule), with Friese v. Superior Court, 36 Cal.Rptr.3d 558 (Cal.App.2005) (internal-affairs rule does not preclude suit against corporate officers and directors for insider trading under California law because that law does not regulate, but rather protects, the corporation and its shareholders and because California had sufficient contact to apply its law). Does the *Friese* court's distinction between regulation and protection answer the question raised in the first paragraph, supra? Did the decision in *CTS* turn on the sufficiency of Indiana contacts? Is *Friese* consistent with *Crosby*, Note 1, supra? See also *IMS Health*, same note.

3.   The *CTS* decision probably does not affect a state's ability to regulate the intrastate *conduct* of foreign corporations, so long as the balancing test of *Pike* and *MITE* is satisfied. See, for instance, Haberman v. Washington Public Power Supply System, 744 P.2d 1032 (Wash.1987), in which securities fraud claims against out-of-state defendants were adjudicated under Washington law:

> [W]ashington is clearly the state with the most substantial contacts with the subject matter of this case. The bonds . . . were issued . . . to finance two nuclear power plants in Washington. The [respondent] Supply System, respondent members and directors, one respondent bond counsel, as well as the majority of the respondent Participants are Washington residents. . . . [O]ur application of the [Washington statute] does not impinge on federal regulation of commerce as did the Illinois statute under scrutiny in [*MITE*]. . . . Unlike the Illinois Statute . . . , we do not attempt to apply [the Washington statute] to transactions completely unrelated to Washington. Moreover, in contrast to the corporate takeover regulations at issue in [*MITE*], Congress explicitly provided that federal and state securities regulation may co-exist absent conflict. . . . Washington's interests in regulating bond issues by municipal corporations, and in providing a forum for claims arising from those issues outweigh the impact that our application of the [Washington statute] will have on interstate commerce, particularly when considering the substantial relationship between this state and the case in controversy.

744 P.2d at 1053–54. In Alliant Energy Corp. v. Bie, 330 F.3d 904 (7th Cir.2003), cert. denied, 540 U.S. 1105, 124 S.Ct. 1047 (2004), the Court held that there was no constitutional violation when a Wisconsin statute required local incorporation for a company conducting local business in local markets.

In Colaco v. Cavotec SA, 236 Cal.Rptr.3d 542 (Cal.App.2018), the court acknowledged that a company's contractual relationship with its CEO is usually a matter of the company's internal affairs and therefore governed by the law of the state of its incorporation. However, the instant case involved a discharge of the CEO in retaliation to his complaints about illegal acts. California's governmental interest in the integrity of its securities market called for and justified the application of California law.

The potential international implications are discussed in Swaine, Negotiating Federalism: State Bargaining and the Dormant Treaty Power, 49 Duke L.J. 1127, 1146 (2000).

In *CTS*, the U.S. Supreme Court made express reference to Restatement, Second, Conflict of Laws § 304 (1971). Comment *d* to that section expressly excludes access to stockholder lists from the internal affairs rule. While acknowledging that the Supreme Court did not necessarily "endorse" this exception, the Second Circuit found compelling reason to permit resident stockholders to gain access, under New York law, to an out-of-state corporation's list of non-objecting beneficial owners ("NoBo" list). It held that the Commerce Clause did not preclude such access. Sadler v. NCR Corp., 928 F.2d 48 (2d Cir.1991). For an application, see Airtran N.Y., LLC v. Midwest Air Group, Inc., 844 N.Y.S.2d 233 (N.Y.App.Div.2007). In both *Sadler* and *Airtran* the courts found that the defendant was "doing business" in New York and equated that statutory requirement with the "doing business" test for jurisdictional purposes. That test changed with *Goodyear Dunlop* (see next Note (4), infra, at the end). Arguably, the facts in *Airtran* would have satisfied the new "at home" test. 844 N.Y.S.2d 233, at 241.

4. What law governs for jurisdictional or choice-of-law purposes whether the separate corporate entity of parent and subsidiary may be disregarded? Piercing of the corporate veil is an important part of interstate and international enterprise liability. See the *Bhopal* decision, p. 244, Note 2, supra.

The Restatement, Second, Conflict of Laws §§ 303 et seq. (1971) would seem to favor the law of incorporation of the parent. The result may be otherwise when the claim implicates interests of the forum. In such cases, the applicable law may well follow the jurisdictional decision, i.e. result in the application of forum law. Delaware, in particular, asserts adjudicatory jurisdiction and applies forum law when a Delaware parent *or* subsidiary is involved. See Mobil Oil Corp. v. Linear Films, Inc., 718 F.Supp. 260 (D.Del.1989). However, a subsidiary's Delaware contacts (insufficient to amount to "general doing of business") did not warrant drawing in the likewise non-Delaware parent in C.R. Bard, Inc. v. Guidant Corp., 997 F.Supp. 556 (D.Del.1998). Is this result not required today in the light of *Goodyear Dunlop*, p. 126, supra? See also Note (3), supra.

Under Texas law, the law of the state of incorporation of a foreign corporation governs whether the parent shareholders are liable: in Alberto v. Diversified Group, Inc., 55 F.3d 201 (5th Cir.1995), the court applied Delaware law and did not pierce the corporate veil. See also MCR Oil Tools, LLC v. SPEX Offshore, Ltd., 2018 WL 10425906 (N.D.Tex.2018) (Scottish law).

5. Dividends on stock shares often remain unclaimed by shareholders when stock changes hands and the bank or brokerage houses that hold securities do not know the identity of the new owners. In Delaware v. New York, 507 U.S. 490, 113 S.Ct. 1550 (1993), the question was which of the two states had the right to escheat the unclaimed dividends. A special master, appointed by the Court, recommended that the right to escheat was in the state where the dividend-paying corporation had its principal place of business. The Supreme Court, dividing 6 to 3, rejected the special master's recommendation and ruled that the right to escheat belonged to the state of incorporation of the brokerage house or bank holding the dividends. Delaware thus became entitled to hundreds of millions of dollars, with New York losing out. Since many brokerage houses are incorporated in Delaware, that state will enjoy a bonanza.

With respect to the application of the law of the state of incorporation, see *CTS* decision. What is the relevance of the broker's state of incorporation to this escheat problem? Are the funds the broker's? If not, does its state of incorporation have regulatory concerns that justify escheat of these funds by it? Are these regulatory concerns greater than those of the state of incorporation of the debtor (the dividend-paying corporation)? Does either of these states have anything to do with the generation of the profits underlying the dividends? Which state does? What is the role of the broker? Is a single rule (state of incorporation-whether that state be that of the broker or of the dividend-paying company) more easily administered than the one proposed by the special master? Bankers and brokers argued against the special master's recommendation on the ground it would be an enormous burden for them to search out the headquarters of every dividend-paying corporation.

6. Ruiz v. Blentech Corp., 89 F.3d 320 (7th Cir.1996), cert. denied, 519 U.S. 1077, 117 S.Ct. 737 (1997) applied the law of Illinois, the place of injury, rather than the law of California, the place of incorporation of the dissolved and successor corporations, to absolve the successor corporation of liability in a products liability action. The court stated that "California courts have quite clearly established that [the California law under which the successor corporation would have been liable] is a matter of product liability law, not corporate law." The case is discussed at p. 605, supra. The Alaska Supreme Court applied tort principles to find that Alaska law applied as the state with the most significant relationship to the injury, not Texas law, the state of the successor's purchase of the manufacturing business. Savage Arms, Inc. v. Western Auto Supply Co., 18 P.3d 49 (Alaska 2001). Similarly: Van Doren v. Coe Press Equip. Corp., 592 F.Supp.2d 776, 784 (E.D.Pa.2008); JobPro Temporary Services, Inc. v. Giftcorp, Inc., 2014 WL 341895 (Conn.Super.2014) (tort choice of law analysis determines the law applicable to successor corporation liability).

SECTION 4. DISSOLUTION AND WINDING-UP

NOTE

The dissolution of a corporation is also governed by the law of the state of incorporation. Restatement, Second, Conflict of Laws § 299 (1971). However, most state statutes provide for a limited time during which the corporation continues to exist, and is empowered to act, so that it may wind-up its affairs. The time extension provided by the state of incorporation will ordinarily be recognized in other states as well.

Subject to limitations of federal law, especially federal bankruptcy law, a state may also wind-up the local business of a foreign corporation which has not been dissolved in the state of its incorporation. This follows from the state's authority to regulate the intrastate activities of foreign corporations. Restatement, Second, Conflict of Laws § 300 (1971). The rule is the same in England: Dicey, Morris & Collins, Conflict of Laws 1548 (15th ed.2012) and Supp. 4th (2017) at 411–12.

What law determines whether a successor corporation is liable for the wrongs of the business it acquired? In Webb v. Rodgers Machinery Mfg. Co., 750 F.2d 368 (5th Cir.1985), the plaintiff was injured in Texas while operating a "Rodgers" wood shaping machine. The defendant enterprise had a long history. Rodgers began business in 1928 as a proprietorship, sold the production equipment of this proprietorship to Olympic Machinery Co., Inc., a California corporation in 1959–60, which ran an operating division called Rodgers from 1960–64, separately incorporating it in 1964 as Rodgers Machinery Manufacturing Co., Inc. The type of machinery that injured plaintiff was discontinued prior to 1959, hence manufactured by the Rodgers proprietorship. The Fifth Circuit noted that Texas, the forum, has adopted the "most significant relationship" test of the Restatement, Second, Conflict of Laws (1971). "Although Texas law under that test governs many of the substantive issues of this case such as those dealing with the manufacturer's duty, causation, and damages, the Restatement makes clear that choice of law considerations should be viewed 'with respect to the particular issue'. . . . Here, the particular issue to be decided is the liability of a succeeding business entity using the trade name of a previously existing proprietorship. All the contacts with respect to that issue occurred in California. The corporations and proprietorships were all Californian. Thus, California clearly has the most significant relationship with respect to the particular issue of whether the defendant Rodgers corporation can be held liable for the torts of the preceding Rodgers proprietorship." 750 F.2d at 374. See also Young v. Fulton Iron Works Co., 709 S.W.2d 927 (Mo.App.1986) (tort, not contract, choice-of-law rule determines tort liability of successor corporation); Ruiz v. Blentech, *Savage Arms, Inc.,* and *JonPro,* see Note 6, supra. For an extensive overview of different exceptions to the general rule that an acquiring company is not liable for the debts and liabilities of the selling company, see Savage Arms, Inc. v. Western Auto Supply Co., 18 P.3d 49 (Alaska 2001).

DOCUMENTARY APPENDIX: CONFLICT OF LAWS IN THE EUROPEAN UNION

I.   "FEDERALIZING" ASPECTS OF PROCEDURAL LAW IN THE EUROPEAN UNION

INTRODUCTORY NOTE

Law Making in the European Union

The European Union presently consists of 27 countries with a total population in excess of 500 million. The Union started, with only six member countries in 1958, as the European Common Market, later renamed the European Economic Community. Today it is named the European Union. Over the years, the Union grew to 28 member states until the United Kingdom withdrew in 2020 ("Brexit"). The initial principal aim of the then "Common Market" was economic integration through the establishment of a single market for the movement of goods. Realizing that economic integration requires more, provisions on the free movement of workers, companies (establishment and services), and capital were added (the "four freedoms"). Powers were conferred on the central authorities to implement the four freedoms through actions binding not only on the member states but also directly on individuals and business. These competences have increased over the years, through successive revisions of the basic treaties, and today encompass many areas of what traditionally was purely national law, including matters of civil jurisdiction and conflict of laws. The legislative competences of the European Union are exercised by the Council (representing the member states), upon a proposal of the Commission (the Union's executive arm), together with the European Parliament (elected directly by the Union's population), under the supervision of the Court of Justice.[1]

---

[1] The European Union legislates by means of "regulations," "directives," and other instruments. The Treaty on the Functioning of the European Union, TFEU (Consolidated Versions, also including the Treaty on European Union, [2008] Official Journal C 115/01) provides in Art. 288, paras. 2 and 3:

"A regulation shall have general application. It shall be binding in its entirety and directly applicable in all Member States.

A directive shall be binding, as to the result to be achieved, upon each Member State to which it is addressed, but shall leave to the national authorities the choice of form and method."

As the quote shows, "regulations" have the same function as federal statutes in the United States. The nature of Community law as a "kind of federal law" in the U.S. sense is reinforced by the institution of the "Court of Justice," which has jurisdiction to review the legality of Community legislative and administrative action (Art. 263 et seq. TFEU) and, upon referral from national courts (Art. 267 TFEU Treaty), issues binding rulings on the interpretation of the Treaty on the Functioning of the European Union (TFEU) and on the validity and interpretation of acts of Community institutions (such as its executive arm, the "Commission").

When the European Union issues a regulation, it draws that subject matter into its regulatory ambit, without regard to whether it was previously the subject of intergovernmental cooperation between or among member states, or had been the subject of bi- or multilateral treaties (for instance, the Brussels Convention, the forerunner of the "Brussels I and Ia," Regulations, for which see below). It thereby preempts state law (and interpretation through state courts), as the references to Arts. 267 and 288 EC Treaty, respectively, show. We therefore refer to the "federalizing" of certain areas of private law (not public, regulatory law in the Community). In some respects, this process reflects the American experience. Europeans refer to the "communitarization" of various aspects of private law, to express exactly the same

Civil Procedure: Jurisdiction and Judgment Recognition

From 1968–2002, the "Brussels Convention" on Jurisdiction and the Recognition of Judgments applied among the member states of the European Community. A Protocol conferred jurisdiction to issue binding interpretations on the EC Court of Justice. In March 2002, Regulation No. 44/2001 replaced the Convention as to all then-current members, except Denmark (see below). With the accession of ten new member states in 2004[2], Bulgaria and Romania in 2007, and Croatia in 2013, the Regulation extended also to them. The Regulation was popularly known as "Brussels I." It was revised ("recast") in 2012 by Regulation No. 1215/2012, which entered into force on January 10, 2015. It is popularly known as "Brussels Ia" or "Brussels Ibis".

Many provisions of the recast Regulation track the earlier law; the Court's case law to that Regulation therefore remains highly relevant and should be consulted. Annex III of the Brussels Ia Regulation provides a correlation table for its provisions with those of its predecessor Regulation, and we reproduce it below.

Note also that all Regulations begin with a large number of "Whereas" recitals. These are important indications of the legislative intent of the Council and Parliament. The excerpts of the Regulations reproduced below therefore also reproduce the most important ones of the Recitals.

Civil Procedure: Lugano Convention

The "Lugano Convention" (also "Parallel Convention") was in most respects identical with ("parallels") the early Brussels Convention by extending essentially the same jurisdictional regime to the non-EU countries of Iceland, Norway, Liechtenstein, and Switzerland.[3] Thus Lugano applied to jurisdictional matters as between those three states as well as between one of those states and an EU state. Of course, Lugano did not apply as between EU states because jurisdiction as between them is regulated by the Brussels regulations. On 30 October 2007 a new Convention was signed in Lugano ("Lugano II")[4], answering the need to align the 1988 Convention with the new Brussels I Regulation. The new treaty entered into force in 2009. Unlike Lugano I, which was a multilateral treaty of all the states involved, Lugano II is a treaty concluded by the EU and is therefore "EU law." Its application by courts

---

thought, but perhaps less readily understandable to the American reader. See Fauvarque-Cosson, Comparative Law and Conflict of Laws: Allies or Enemies?—New Perspectives on an Old Couple, 49 Am.J.Comp.L. 407, especially at 417 n. 39 (2001). See also Basedow, The Communitarization of the Conflict of Laws under the Treaty of Amsterdam, [2000] Common Market Law Review 687.

[2]   Czech Republic, Cyprus, Estonia, Hungary, Latvia, Lithuania, Malta, Poland, Slovakia, Slovenia.

[3]   The Brussels Convention may be found (in consolidated version) in [1998] Official Journal C 27/1; the Lugano-I Convention may be found in [1988] Official Journal L 319/9.

[4]   Text of the new Lugano Convention: [2007] Official Journal L 339/3; signature on behalf of the Community is not binding upon or applicable in Denmark.

in the EU is therefore reviewable by the European Court of Justice. In April 2020, the United Kingdom applied to accede to the Lugano II Convention upon leaving the European Union ("Brexit"). Its accession requires the unanimous assent of all Convention member states. If given, and in light of the United Kingdom's accession to the Hague Choice of Court Convention, p 208, supra, much of what the Brussels and Lugano Conventions achieved will be preserved. If the United Kingdom does not accede, jurisdiction and judgment law will no longer be shared. Judgments, for instance, would no longer benefit from inter-countries recognition requirements; their recognition would depend on comity (see p. 276, supra).

Civil Procedure: Family Law

Another Regulation (No. 2201/2003)—known as "Brussels IIa", which replaced an earlier regulation—deals with jurisdiction and the recognition and enforcement of judgments in matrimonial matters and in matters of parental responsibility (child custody). This Regulation was revised again in 2019. The new version—"Brussels IIa Recast"—will enter into force and replace its predecessor in August 2022. The materials below reproduce the existing Regulation and also indicate the changes or additions under the Recast Regulation.

Opting Out

The Treaty of Amsterdam (1999) permitted Denmark, Ireland, and the United Kingdom to opt out of certain future EU legislation. Denmark, but not the two other states, exercised that right with respect to both the old and new versions of "Brussels I" and "Brussels II." As a result, the Brussels Convention has not been replaced by "Brussels I" with respect to Denmark. As between that country, on the one hand, and all other member states, on the other hand, the Brussels Convention remained in effect. In October 2005 the European Community and the Kingdom of Denmark reached an agreement that extends the scope of "Brussels I" to Denmark. According to its article 12 (2), the agreement entered into force on 1 July 2007 ([2007] Official Journal L94/70).

"Brexit"

In 2015, voters in the United Kingdom adopted a referendum in favor of leaving the European Union. Art. 50 of the Treaty on European Union ("TEU") required that a country wishing to exit the Union give notice of its intention to the European Union, and that any negotiations for an accommodation or arrangement for future relations be completed within two years thereafter. The required notice was given, and the United Kingdom left the European Union in 2020, with EU law continuing in effect until the end of that year. Negotiated agreements define future relations.

Without an arrangement between the European Union and the United Kingdom with respect to the Brussels I and II Regulations, these Regulations ceased to have effect when "Brexit" entered into force because their provisions deal with litigants who are habitual residents of "Member States." However, with respect to "Brussels Ia," the old "Brussels Convention" (which the United Kingdom had joined) could revive as between the original member states (excluding all new EU members): as an independent treaty without a unilateral cancellation provision, it should be unaffected by EU membership. However, in early 2021, the United Kingdom gave notice that it considered its participation in the Brussels Convention to have ended. An alternative might be mutual cancellation of that treaty and British accession to the Lugano Convention (see above). No such solutions exist with respect to "Brussels IIa," or its Recast (see above), although Hague Conventions provide solutions to some problems, for instance, with respect to enforcement of custody rights and child support.

In contrast, the Rome I, II, and III Regulations, dealing with applicable law (see below), do not focus on Member State litigants. Rather, they replace national conflicts law in the areas covered by them: they are of "universal application." The United Kingdom has decided to keep the Rome I and II Regulations in force as national law: pp. 1194 n. 24 and 1209 n. 31 infra.

A. CIVIL AND COMMERCIAL MATTERS

Council Regulation (EU) No. 1215/2012 on Jurisdiction and the Recognition of Judgments in Civil and Commercial Matters (recast) ["Brussels Ia"]

[2012] Official Journal L 351/1

(excerpts; footnotes omitted)

. . .

Whereas:

. . .

(4) Certain differences between national rules governing jurisdiction and recognition of judgments hamper the sound operation of the internal market. Provisions to unify the rules of conflict of jurisdiction in civil and commercial matters, and to ensure rapid and simple recognition and enforcement of judgments given in a Member State, are essential.

(6) In order to attain the objective of free circulation of judgments in civil and commercial matters, it is necessary and appropriate that the rules governing jurisdiction and the recognition and enforcement of judgments be governed by a legal instrument of the Union which is binding and directly applicable.

. . .

(13) There must be a connection between proceedings to which this Regulation applies and the territory of the Member States. Accordingly, common rules of jurisdiction should, in principle, apply when the defendant is domiciled in a Member State.

(14) A defendant not domiciled in a Member State should in general be subject to the national rules of jurisdiction applicable in the territory of the Member State of the court seised.

However, in order to ensure the protection of consumers and employees, to safeguard the jurisdiction of the courts of the Member States in situations where they have exclusive jurisdiction and to respect the autonomy of the parties, certain rules of jurisdiction in this Regulation should apply regardless of the defendant's domicile.

(15) The rules of jurisdiction should be highly predictable and founded on the principle that jurisdiction is generally based on the defendant's domicile. Jurisdiction should always be available on this ground save in a few well-defined situations in which the subject-matter of the dispute or the autonomy of the parties warrants a different connecting factor. The domicile of a legal person must be defined autonomously so as to make the common rules more transparent and avoid conflicts of jurisdiction.

(16) In addition to the defendant's domicile, there should be alternative grounds of jurisdiction based on a close connection between the court and the action or in order to facilitate the sound administration of justice. The existence of a close connection should ensure legal certainty and avoid the possibility of the defendant being sued in a court of a Member State which he could not reasonably have foreseen. This is important, particularly in disputes concerning non-contractual obligations arising out of violations of privacy and rights relating to personality, including defamation.

. . .

(18) In relation to insurance, consumer and employment contracts, the weaker party should be protected by rules of jurisdiction more favourable to his interests than the general rules.

(19) The autonomy of the parties to a contract, other than an insurance, consumer or employment contract, where only limited autonomy to determine the courts having jurisdiction is allowed, should be respected subject to the exclusive grounds of jurisdiction laid down in this Regulation.

(20) Where a question arises as to whether a choice-of-court agreement in favour of a court or the courts of a Member State is null and void as to its substantive validity, that question should be decided in accordance with the law of the Member State of the court or courts designated in the agreement, including the conflict-of-laws rules of that Member State.

(21) In the interests of the harmonious administration of justice it is necessary to minimise the possibility of concurrent proceedings and to ensure that irreconcilable judgments will not be given in different Member States. There should be a clear and effective mechanism for resolving cases of *lis pendens* and related actions, and for obviating problems flowing from national differences as to the determination of the time when a case is regarded as pending. For the purposes of this Regulation, that time should be defined autonomously.

(22) However, in order to enhance the effectiveness of exclusive choice-of-court agreements and to avoid abusive litigation tactics, it is necessary to provide for an exception to the general *lis pendens* rule in order to deal satisfactorily with a particular situation in which concurrent proceedings may arise. This is the situation where a court not designated in an exclusive choice-of-court agreement has been seised of proceedings and the designated court is seised subsequently of proceedings involving the same cause of action and between the same parties. In such a case, the court first seised should be required to stay its proceedings as soon as the designated court has been seised and until such time as the latter court declares that it has no

jurisdiction under the exclusive choice-of-court agreement. This is to ensure that, in such a situation, the designated court has priority to decide on the validity of the agreement and on the extent to which the agreement applies to the dispute pending before it. The designated court should be able to proceed irrespective of whether the non-designated court has already decided on the stay of proceedings.

(23) This Regulation should provide for a flexible mechanism allowing the courts of the Member States to take into account proceedings pending before the courts of third States, considering in particular whether a judgment of a third State will be capable of recognition and enforcement in the Member State concerned under the law of that Member State and the proper administration of justice.

(24) When taking into account the proper administration of justice, the court of the Member State concerned should assess all the circumstances of the case before it. Such circumstances may include connections between the facts of the case and the parties and the third State concerned, the stage to which the proceedings in the third State have progressed by the time proceedings are initiated in the court of the Member State and whether or not the court of the third State can be expected to give a judgment within a reasonable time.

That assessment may also include consideration of the question whether the court of the third State has exclusive jurisdiction in the particular case in circumstances where a court of a Member State would have exclusive jurisdiction.

(25) The notion of provisional, including protective, measures should include, for example, protective orders aimed at obtaining information or preserving evidence as referred to in Articles 6 and 7 of Directive 2004/48/EC of the European Parliament and of the Council of 29 April 2004 on the enforcement of intellectual property rights. It should not include measures which are not of a protective nature, such as measures ordering the hearing of a witness. . . .

(26) Mutual trust in the administration of justice in the Union justifies the principle that judgments given in a Member State should be recognised in all Member States without the need for any special procedure. In addition, the aim of making cross-border litigation less time-consuming and costly justifies the abolition of the declaration of enforceability prior to enforcement in the Member State addressed. As a result, a judgment given by the courts of a Member State should be treated as if it had been given in the Member State addressed.

(27) For the purposes of the free circulation of judgments, a judgment given in a Member State should be recognised and enforced in another Member State even if it is given against a person not domiciled in a Member State.

(28) Where a judgment contains a measure or order which is not known in the law of the Member State addressed, that measure or order, including any right indicated therein, should, to the extent possible, be adapted to one which, under the law of that Member State, has equivalent effects attached to it and pursues similar aims. How, and by whom, the adaptation is to be carried out should be determined by each Member State.

(29) The direct enforcement in the Member State addressed of a judgment given in another Member State without a declaration of enforceability should not jeopardise respect for the rights of the defence. Therefore, the person against whom enforcement is sought should be able to apply for refusal of the recognition or enforcement of a judgment if he considers one of the grounds for refusal of recognition to be present. This should include the ground that he had not had the opportunity to arrange for his defence where the judgment was given in default of appearance in a civil action linked to criminal proceedings. It should also include the grounds which could be

invoked on the basis of an agreement between the Member State addressed and a third State concluded pursuant to Article 59 of the 1968 Brussels Convention.

(30) A party challenging the enforcement of a judgment given in another Member State should, to the extent possible and in accordance with the legal system of the Member State addressed, be able to invoke, in the same procedure, in addition to the grounds for refusal provided for in this Regulation, the grounds for refusal available under national law and within the time-limits laid down in that law.

The recognition of a judgment should, however, be refused only if one or more of the grounds for refusal provided for in this Regulation are present.

(31) Pending a challenge to the enforcement of a judgment, it should be possible for the courts in the Member State addressed, during the entire proceedings relating to such a challenge, including any appeal, to allow the enforcement to proceed subject to a limitation of the enforcement or to the provision of security.

(32) In order to inform the person against whom enforcement is sought of the enforcement of a judgment given in another Member State, the certificate established under this Regulation, if necessary accompanied by the judgment, should be served on that person in reasonable time before the first enforcement measure. In this context, the first enforcement measure should mean the first enforcement measure after such service.

(33) Where provisional, including protective, measures are ordered by a court having jurisdiction as to the substance of the matter, their free circulation should be ensured under this Regulation. However, provisional, including protective, measures which were ordered by such a court without the defendant being summoned to appear should not be recognised and enforced under this Regulation unless the judgment containing the measure is served on the defendant prior to enforcement. This should not preclude the recognition and enforcement of such measures under national law.

. . .

(38) This Regulation respects fundamental rights and observes the principles recognised in the Charter of Fundamental Rights of the European Union, in particular the right to an effective remedy and to a fair trial guaranteed in Article 47 of the Charter.

CHAPTER I

SCOPE AND DEFINITIONS

Article 1

1.   This Regulation shall apply in civil and commercial matters whatever the nature of the court or tribunal. It shall not extend, in particular, to revenue, customs or administrative matters or to the liability of the State for acts and omissions in the exercise of State authority (*acta iure imperii*).

2.   This Regulation shall not apply to:

(a)   the status or legal capacity of natural persons, rights in property arising out of a matrimonial relationship or out of a relationship deemed by the law applicable to such relationship to have comparable effects to marriage;

(b)   bankruptcy, proceedings relating to the winding-up of insolvent companies or other legal persons, judicial arrangements, compositions and analogous proceedings;

(c)   social security;

(d)   arbitration;

(e) maintenance obligations arising from a family relationship, parentage, marriage or affinity;

(f) wills and succession, including maintenance obligations arising by reason of death.

Article 2

For the purposes of this Regulation:

(a) 'judgment' means any judgment given by a court or tribunal of a Member State, whatever the judgment may be called, including a decree, order, decision or writ of execution, as well as a decision on the determination of costs or expenses by an officer of the court.

For the purposes of Chapter III, 'judgment' includes provisional, including protective, measures ordered by a court or tribunal which by virtue of this Regulation has jurisdiction as to the subject of the matter. It does not include a provisional, including protective, measure which is ordered by such a court or tribunal without the defendant being summoned to appear, unless the judgment containing the measure is served on the defendant prior to enforcement;

(b) 'court settlement' means a settlement which has been approved by a court of a Member State or concluded before a court of a Member State in the course of proceedings; . . .

(e) 'Member State addressed' means the Member State in which the recognition of the judgment is invoked or in which the enforcement of the judgment, the court settlement or the authentic instrument is sought; . . .

(f) 'court of origin' means the court which has given the judgment the recognition of which is invoked or the enforcement of which is sought.

. . .

CHAPTER II
JURISDICTION
SECTION 1
General provisions
Article 4

1. Subject to this Regulation, persons domiciled in a Member State shall, whatever their nationality, be sued in the courts of that Member State.

2. Persons who are not nationals of the Member State in which they are domiciled shall be governed by the rules of jurisdiction applicable to nationals of that Member State.

Article 5

1. Persons domiciled in a Member State may be sued in the courts of another Member State only by virtue of the rules set out in Sections 2 to 7 of this Chapter.

2. In particular, the rules of national jurisdiction of which the Member States are to notify the Commission pursuant to point (a) of Article 76(1) shall not be applicable as against the persons referred to in paragraph 1.

Article 6

1. If the defendant is not domiciled in a Member State, the jurisdiction of the courts of each Member State shall, subject to Article 18(1), Article 21(2) and Articles 24 and 25, be determined by the law of that Member State.

2.   As against such a defendant, any person domiciled in a Member State may, whatever his nationality, avail himself in that Member State of the rules of jurisdiction there in force, and in particular those of which the Member States are to notify the Commission pursuant to point (a) of Article 76(1), in the same way as nationals of that Member State.

SECTION 2

Special jurisdiction

Article 7

A person domiciled in a Member State may be sued in another Member State:

(1)(a)   in matters relating to a contract, in the courts for the place of performance of the obligation in question;

(b)   for the purpose of this provision and unless otherwise agreed, the place of performance of the obligation in question shall be:

— in the case of the sale of goods, the place in a Member State where, under the contract, the goods were delivered or should have been delivered,

— in the case of the provision of services, the place in a Member State where, under the contract, the services were provided or should have been provided;

(c) if point (b) does not apply then point (a) applies;

(2)   in matters relating to tort, delict or quasi-delict, in the courts for the place where the harmful event occurred or may occur;

(3)   as regards a civil claim for damages or restitution which is based on an act giving rise to criminal proceedings, in the court seised of those proceedings, to the extent that that court has jurisdiction under its own law to entertain civil proceedings;

(4)   as regards a civil claim for the recovery, based on ownership, of a cultural object as defined in point 1 of Article 1 of Directive 93/7/EEC initiated by the person claiming the right to recover such an object, in the courts for the place where the cultural object is situated at the time when the court is seised;

(5)   as regards a dispute arising out of the operations of a branch, agency or other establishment, in the courts for the place where the branch, agency or other establishment is situated;

(6)   as regards a dispute brought against a settlor, trustee or beneficiary of a trust created by the operation of a statute, or by a written instrument, or created orally and evidenced in writing, in the courts of the Member State in which the trust is domiciled;

(7)   as regards a dispute concerning the payment of remuneration claimed in respect of the salvage of a cargo or freight, in the court under the authority of which the cargo or freight in question:

(a)   has been arrested to secure such payment; or

(b)   could have been so arrested, but bail or other security has been given;

provided that this provision shall apply only if it is claimed that the defendant has an interest in the cargo or freight or had such an interest at the time of salvage.

Article 8

A person domiciled in a Member State may also be sued:

(1)   where he is one of a number of defendants, in the courts for the place where any one of them is domiciled, provided the claims are so closely connected that it is expedient to hear and determine them together to avoid the risk of irreconcilable judgments resulting from separate proceedings;

(2)   as a third party in an action on a warranty or guarantee or in any other third-party proceedings, in the court seised of the original proceedings, unless these were instituted solely with the object of removing him from the jurisdiction of the court which would be competent in his case;

(3)   on a counter-claim arising from the same contract or facts on which the original claim was based, in the court in which the original claim is pending;

(4)   in matters relating to a contract, if the action may be combined with an action against the same defendant in matters relating to rights *in rem* in immovable property, in the court of the Member State in which the property is situated.

Article 9

Where by virtue of this Regulation a court of a Member State has jurisdiction in actions relating to liability from the use or operation of a ship, that court, or any other court substituted for this purpose by the internal law of that Member State, shall also have jurisdiction over claims for limitation of such liability.

SECTION 3

Jurisdiction in matters relating to insurance

Article 10

In matters relating to insurance, jurisdiction shall be determined by this Section, without prejudice to Article 6 and point 5 of Article 7.

Article 11

1.   An insurer domiciled in a Member State may be sued:

(a)   in the courts of the Member State in which he is domiciled;

(b)   in another Member State, in the case of actions brought by the policyholder, the insured or a beneficiary, in the courts for the place where the claimant is domiciled; or

(c)   if he is a co-insurer, in the courts of a Member State in which proceedings are brought against the leading insurer.

(2)   An insurer who is not domiciled in a Member State but has a branch, agency or other establishment in one of the Member States shall, in disputes arising out of the operations of the branch, agency or establishment, be deemed to be domiciled in that Member State.

Article 12

In respect of liability insurance or insurance of immovable property, the insurer may in addition be sued in the courts for the place where the harmful event occurred. The same applies if movable and immovable property are covered by the same insurance policy and both are adversely affected by the same contingency.

Article 13

1.   In respect of liability insurance, the insurer may also, if the law of the court permits it, be joined in proceedings which the injured party has brought against the insured.

2.   Articles 10, 11 and 12 shall apply to actions brought by the injured party directly against the insurer, where such direct actions are permitted.

3.   If the law governing such direct actions provides that the policyholder or the insured may be joined as a party to the action, the same court shall have jurisdiction over them.

Article 14

1.   Without prejudice to Article 13(3), an insurer may bring proceedings only in the courts of the Member State in which the defendant is domiciled, irrespective of whether he is the policyholder, the insured or a beneficiary.

2.   The provisions of this Section shall not affect the right to bring a counter-claim in the court in which, in accordance with this Section, the original claim is pending.

Article 15

The provisions of this Section may be departed from only by an agreement:

(1)   which is entered into after the dispute has arisen;

(2)   which allows the policyholder, the insured or a beneficiary to bring proceedings in courts other than those indicated in this Section;

(3)   which is concluded between a policyholder and an insurer, both of whom are at the time of conclusion of the contract domiciled or habitually resident in the same Member State, and which has the effect of conferring jurisdiction on the courts of that Member State even if the harmful event were to occur abroad, provided that such an agreement is not contrary to the law of that Member State;

(4)   which is concluded with a policyholder who is not domiciled in a Member State, except in so far as the insurance is compulsory or relates to immovable property in a Member State; or

(5)   which relates to a contract of insurance in so far as it covers one or more of the risks set out in Article 16.

Article 16

The following are the risks referred to in point 5 of Article 15:

(1)   any loss of or damage to:

(a)   seagoing ships, installations situated offshore or on the high seas, or aircraft, arising from perils which relate to their use for commercial purposes;

(b)   goods in transit other than passengers' baggage where the transit consists of or includes carriage by such ships or aircraft;

(2)   any liability, other than for bodily injury to passengers or loss of or damage to their baggage:

(a)   arising out of the use or operation of ships, installations or aircraft as referred to in point 1(a) in so far as, in respect of the latter, the law of the Member State in which such aircraft are registered does not prohibit agreements on jurisdiction regarding insurance of such risks;

(b)   for loss or damage caused by goods in transit as described in point 1(b);

(3)   any financial loss connected with the use or operation of ships, installations or aircraft as referred to in point 1(a), in particular loss of freight or charter-hire;

(4)   any risk or interest connected with any of those referred to in points 1 to 3;

(5)   notwithstanding points 1 to 4, all 'large risks' as defined in Directive 2009/138/EC of the European Parliament and of the Council of 25 November 2009 on

the taking-up and pursuit of the business of Insurance and Reinsurance (Solvency II).

SECTION 4

Jurisdiction over consumer contracts

Article 17

1. In matters relating to a contract concluded by a person, the consumer, for a purpose which can be regarded as being outside his trade or profession, jurisdiction shall be determined by this Section, without prejudice to Article 6 and point 5 of Article 7, if:

(a) it is a contract for the sale of goods on instalment credit terms;

(b) it is a contract for a loan repayable by instalments, or for any other form of credit, made to finance the sale of goods; or

(c) in all other cases, the contract has been concluded with a person who pursues commercial or professional activities in the Member State of the consumer's domicile or, by any means, directs such activities to that Member State or to several States including that Member State, and the contract falls within the scope of such activities.

2. Where a consumer enters into a contract with a party who is not domiciled in a Member State but has a branch, agency or other establishment in one of the Member States, that party shall, in disputes arising out of the operations of the branch, agency or establishment, be deemed to be domiciled in that Member State.

3. This Section shall not apply to a contract of transport other than a contract which, for an inclusive price, provides for a combination of travel and accommodation.

Article 18

1. A consumer may bring proceedings against the other party to a contract either in the courts of the Member State in which that party is domiciled or, regardless of the domicile of the other party, in the courts for the place where the consumer is domiciled.

2. Proceedings may be brought against a consumer by the other party to the contract only in the courts of the Member State in which the consumer is domiciled.

3. This Article shall not affect the right to bring a counter- claim in the court in which, in accordance with this Section, the original claim is pending.

Article 19

The provisions of this Section may be departed from only by an agreement:

(1) which is entered into after the dispute has arisen;

(2) which allows the consumer to bring proceedings in courts other than those indicated in this Section; or

(3) which is entered into by the consumer and the other party to the contract, both of whom are at the time of conclusion of the contract domiciled or habitually resident in the same Member State, and which confers jurisdiction on the courts of that Member State, provided that such an agreement is not contrary to the law of that Member State.

SECTION 5

Jurisdiction over individual contracts of employment

Article 20

1.   In matters relating to individual contracts of employment, jurisdiction shall be determined by this Section, without prejudice to Article 6, point 5 of Article 7 and, in the case of proceedings brought against an employer, point 1 of Article 8.

2.   Where an employee enters into an individual contract of employment with an employer who is not domiciled in a Member State but has a branch, agency or other establishment in one of the Member States, the employer shall, in disputes arising out of the operations of the branch, agency or establishment, be deemed to be domiciled in that Member State.

Article 21

1.   An employer domiciled in a Member State may be sued:

   (a)   in the courts of the Member State in which he is domiciled; or

   (b)   in another Member State:

   (i)   in the courts for the place where or from where the employee habitually carries out his work or in the courts for the last place where he did so; or

   (ii)   if the employee does not or did not habitually carry out his work in any one country, in the courts for the place where the business which engaged the employee is or was situated.

2.   An employer not domiciled in a Member State may be sued in a court of a Member State in accordance with point (b) of paragraph 1.

Article 22

1.   An employer may bring proceedings only in the courts of the Member State in which the employee is domiciled.

2.   The provisions of this Section shall not affect the right to bring a counter-claim in the court in which, in accordance with this Section, the original claim is pending.

Article 23

The provisions of this Section may be departed from only by an agreement:

(1)   which is entered into after the dispute has arisen; or

(2)   which allows the employee to bring proceedings in courts other than those indicated in this Section.

SECTION 6

Exclusive jurisdiction

Article 24

The following courts of a Member State shall have exclusive jurisdiction, regardless of the domicile of the parties:

(1)   in proceedings which have as their object rights in rem in immovable property or tenancies of immovable property, the courts of the Member State in which the property is situated.

However, in proceedings which have as their object tenancies of immovable property concluded for temporary private use for a maximum period of six consecutive months, the courts of the Member State in which the defendant is domiciled shall also have jurisdiction, provided that the tenant is a natural person and that the landlord and the tenant are domiciled in the same Member State;

(2)   in proceedings which have as their object the validity of the constitution, the nullity or the dissolution of companies or other legal persons or associations of natural or legal persons, or the validity of the decisions of their organs, the courts of the Member State in which the company, legal person or association has its seat. In order to determine that seat, the court shall apply its rules of private international law;

(3)   in proceedings which have as their object the validity of entries in public registers, the courts of the Member State in which the register is kept;

(4)   in proceedings concerned with the registration or validity of patents, trade marks, designs, or other similar rights required to be deposited or registered, irrespective of whether the issue is raised by way of an action or as a defence, the courts of the Member State in which the deposit or registration has been applied for, has taken place or is under the terms of an instrument of the Union or an international convention deemed to have taken place.

Without prejudice to the jurisdiction of the European Patent Office under the Convention on the Grant of European Patents, signed at Munich on 5 October 1973, the courts of each Member State shall have exclusive jurisdiction in proceedings concerned with the registration or validity of any European patent granted for that Member State;

(5)   in proceedings concerned with the enforcement of judgments, the courts of the Member State in which the judgment has been or is to be enforced.

SECTION 7

Prorogation of jurisdiction

Article 25

1.   If the parties, regardless of their domicile,[5] have agreed that a court or the courts of a Member State are to have jurisdiction to settle any disputes which have arisen or which may arise in connection with a particular legal relationship, that court or those courts shall have jurisdiction, unless the agreement is null and void as to its substantive validity under the law of that Member State. Such jurisdiction shall be exclusive unless the parties have agreed otherwise. The agreement conferring jurisdiction shall be either:

(a)   in writing or evidenced in writing;

(b)   in a form which accords with practices which the parties have established between themselves; or

(c)   in international trade or commerce, in a form which accords with a usage of which the parties are or ought to have been aware and which in such trade or commerce is widely known to, and regularly observed by, parties to contracts of the type involved in the particular trade or commerce concerned.

2.   Any communication by electronic means which provides a durable record of the agreement shall be equivalent to 'writing'.

3.   The court or courts of a Member State on which a trust instrument has conferred jurisdiction shall have exclusive jurisdiction in any proceedings brought against a

---

[5]   Note: In the Lugano Convention, p. 1133, supra, the parallel provision requires that one of the parties be domiciled in a Convention state.

settlor, trustee or beneficiary, if relations between those persons or their rights or obligations under the trust are involved.

4.   Agreements or provisions of a trust instrument conferring jurisdiction shall have no legal force if they are contrary to Articles 15, 19 or 23, or if the courts whose jurisdiction they purport to exclude have exclusive jurisdiction by virtue of Article 24.

5.   An agreement conferring jurisdiction which forms part of a contract shall be treated as an agreement independent of the other terms of the contract.

The validity of the agreement conferring jurisdiction cannot be contested solely on the ground that the contract is not valid.

Article 26

1.   Apart from jurisdiction derived from other provisions of this Regulation, a court of a Member State before which a defendant enters an appearance shall have jurisdiction. This rule shall not apply where appearance was entered to contest the jurisdiction, or where another court has exclusive jurisdiction by virtue of Article 24.

2.   In matters referred to in Sections 3, 4 or 5 where the policyholder, the insured, a beneficiary of the insurance contract, the injured party, the consumer or the employee is the defendant, the court shall, before assuming jurisdiction under paragraph 1, ensure that the defendant is informed of his right to contest the jurisdiction of the court and of the consequences of entering or not entering an appearance.

SECTION 8

Examination as to jurisdiction and admissibility

Article 27

Where a court of a Member State is seised of a claim which is principally concerned with a matter over which the courts of another Member State have exclusive jurisdiction by virtue of Article 24, it shall declare of its own motion that it has no jurisdiction.

Article 28

1.   Where a defendant domiciled in one Member State is sued in a court of another Member State and does not enter an appearance, the court shall declare of its own motion that it has no jurisdiction unless its jurisdiction is derived from the provisions of this Regulation.

2.   The court shall stay the proceedings so long as it is not shown that the defendant has been able to receive the document instituting the proceedings or an equivalent document in sufficient time to enable him to arrange for his defence, or that all necessary steps have been taken to this end.

3.   Article 19 of Regulation (EC) No 1393/2007 of the European Parliament and of the Council of 13 November 2007 on the service in the Member States of judicial and extrajudicial documents in civil or commercial matters (service of documents) (1) shall apply instead of paragraph 2 of this Article if the document instituting the proceedings or an equivalent document had to be transmitted from one Member State to another pursuant to that Regulation.

4.   Where Regulation (EC) No 1393/2007 is not applicable, Article 15 of the Hague Convention of 15 November 1965 on the Service Abroad of Judicial and Extrajudicial Documents in Civil or Commercial Matters shall apply if the document instituting the proceedings or an equivalent document had to be transmitted abroad pursuant to that Convention.

SECTION 9

Lis pendens—related actions

Article 29

1.   Without prejudice to Article 31(2), where proceedings involving the same cause of action and between the same parties are brought in the courts of different Member States, any court other than the court first seised shall of its own motion stay its proceedings until such time as the jurisdiction of the court first seised is established.

2.   In cases referred to in paragraph 1, upon request by a court seised of the dispute, any other court seised shall without delay inform the former court of the date when it was seised in accordance with Article 32.

3.   Where the jurisdiction of the court first seised is established, any court other than the court first seised shall decline jurisdiction in favour of that court.

Article 30

1.   Where related actions are pending in the courts of different Member States, any court other than the court first seised may stay its proceedings.

2.   Where the action in the court first seised is pending at first instance, any other court may also, on the application of one of the parties, decline jurisdiction if the court first seised has jurisdiction over the actions in question and its law permits the consolidation thereof.

3.   For the purposes of this Article, actions are deemed to be related where they are so closely connected that it is expedient to hear and determine them together to avoid the risk of irreconcilable judgments resulting from separate proceedings.

Article 31

1.   Where actions come within the exclusive jurisdiction of several courts, any court other than the court first seised shall decline jurisdiction in favour of that court.

2.   Without prejudice to Article 26, where a court of a Member State on which an agreement as referred to in Article 25 confers exclusive jurisdiction is seised, any court of another Member State shall stay the proceedings until such time as the court seised on the basis of the agreement declares that it has no jurisdiction under the agreement.

3.   Where the court designated in the agreement has established jurisdiction in accordance with the agreement, any court of another Member State shall decline jurisdiction in favour of that court.

4.   Paragraphs 2 and 3 shall not apply to matters referred to in Sections 3, 4 or 5 where the policyholder, the insured, a beneficiary of the insurance contract, the injured party, the consumer or the employee is the claimant and the agreement is not valid under a provision contained within those Sections.

Article 32

1.   For the purposes of this Section, a court shall be deemed to be seised:

(a)   at the time when the document instituting the proceedings or an equivalent document is lodged with the court, provided that the claimant has not subsequently failed to take the steps he was required to take to have service effected on the defendant; or

(b)   if the document has to be served before being lodged with the court, at the time when it is received by the authority responsible for service, provided that the claimant has not subsequently failed to take the steps he was required to take to have the document lodged with the court.

The authority responsible for service referred to in point (b) shall be the first authority receiving the documents to be served.

2.   The court, or the authority responsible for service, referred to in paragraph 1, shall note, respectively, the date of the lodging of the document instituting the proceedings or the equivalent document, or the date of receipt of the documents to be served.

Article 33

1.   Where jurisdiction is based on Article 4 or on Articles 7, 8 or 9 and proceedings are pending before a court of a third State at the time when a court in a Member State is seised of an action involving the same cause of action and between the same parties as the proceedings in the court of the third State, the court of the Member State may stay the proceedings if:

(a)   it is expected that the court of the third State will give a judgment capable of recognition and, where applicable, of enforcement in that Member State; and

(b)   the court of the Member State is satisfied that a stay is necessary for the proper administration of justice.

2.   The court of the Member State may continue the proceedings at any time if:

(a)   the proceedings in the court of the third State are themselves stayed or discontinued;

(b)   it appears to the court of the Member State that the proceedings in the court of the third State are unlikely to be concluded within a reasonable time; or

(c)   the continuation of the proceedings is required for the proper administration of justice.

3.   The court of the Member State shall dismiss the proceedings if the proceedings in the court of the third State are concluded and have resulted in a judgment capable of recognition and, where applicable, of enforcement in that Member State.

4.   The court of the Member State shall apply this Article on the application of one of the parties or, where possible under national law, of its own motion.

Article 34

1.   Where jurisdiction is based on Article 4 or on Articles 7, 8 or 9 and an action is pending before a court of a third State at the time when a court in a Member State is seised of an action which is related to the action in the court of the third State, the court of the Member State may stay the proceedings if:

(a)   it is expedient to hear and determine the related actions together to avoid the risk of irreconcilable judgments resulting from separate proceedings;

(b)   it is expected that the court of the third State will give a judgment capable of recognition and, where applicable, of enforcement in that Member State; and

(c)   the court of the Member State is satisfied that a stay is necessary for the proper administration of justice.

2.   The court of the Member State may continue the proceedings at any time if:

(a) it appears to the court of the Member State that there is no longer a risk of irreconcilable judgments;

(b) the proceedings in the court of the third State are themselves stayed or discontinued;

(c) it appears to the court of the Member State that the proceedings in the court of the third State are unlikely to be concluded within a reasonable time; or

(d) the continuation of the proceedings is required for the proper administration of justice.

3. The court of the Member State may dismiss the proceedings if the proceedings in the court of the third State are concluded and have resulted in a judgment capable of recognition and, where applicable, of enforcement in that Member State.

4. The court of the Member State shall apply this Article on the application of one of the parties or, where possible under national law, of its own motion.

SECTION 10

Provisional, including protective, measures

Article 35

Application may be made to the courts of a Member State for such provisional, including protective, measures as may be available under the law of that Member State, even if the courts of another Member State have jurisdiction as to the substance of the matter.

CHAPTER III

RECOGNITION AND ENFORCEMENT

SECTION 1

Recognition

Article 36

1. A judgment given in a Member State shall be recognised in the other Member States without any special procedure being required.

2. Any interested party may, in accordance with the procedure provided for in Subsection 2 of Section 3, apply for a decision that there are no grounds for refusal of recognition as referred to in Article 45.

3. If the outcome of proceedings in a court of a Member State depends on the determination of an incidental question of refusal of recognition, that court shall have jurisdiction over that question.

Article 37

1. A party who wishes to invoke in a Member State a judgment given in another Member State shall produce:

(a) a copy of the judgment which satisfies the conditions necessary to establish its authenticity; and

(b) the certificate issued pursuant to Article 53.

2. The court or authority before which a judgment given in another Member State is invoked may, where necessary, require the party invoking it to provide, in accordance with Article 57, a translation or a transliteration of the contents of the certificate referred to in point (b) of paragraph 1. The court or authority may require the party to provide a translation of the judgment instead of a translation of the contents of the certificate if it is unable to proceed without such a translation.

Article 38

The court or authority before which a judgment given in another Member State is invoked may suspend the proceedings, in whole or in part, if:

(a) the judgment is challenged in the Member State of origin; or

(b)   an application has been submitted for a decision that there are no grounds for refusal of recognition as referred to in Article 45 or for a decision that the recognition is to be refused on the basis of one of those grounds.

SECTION 2

Enforcement

Article 39

A judgment given in a Member State which is enforceable in that Member State shall be enforceable in the other Member States without any declaration of enforceability being required.

Article 40

An enforceable judgment shall carry with it by operation of law the power to proceed to any protective measures which exist under the law of the Member State addressed.

Article 41

1.   Subject to the provisions of this Section, the procedure for the enforcement of judgments given in another Member State shall be governed by the law of the Member State addressed. A judgment given in a Member State which is enforceable in the Member State addressed shall be enforced there under the same conditions as a judgment given in the Member State addressed.

2.   Notwithstanding paragraph 1, the grounds for refusal or of suspension of enforcement under the law of the Member State addressed shall apply in so far as they are not incompatible with the grounds referred to in Article 45.

3.   The party seeking the enforcement of a judgment given in another Member State shall not be required to have a postal address in the Member State addressed. Nor shall that party be required to have an authorised representative in the Member State addressed unless such a representative is mandatory irrespective of the nationality or the domicile of the parties.

Article 42

1.   For the purposes of enforcement in a Member State of a judgment given in another Member State, the applicant shall provide the competent enforcement authority with:

(a)   a copy of the judgment which satisfies the conditions necessary to establish its authenticity; and

(b)   the certificate issued pursuant to Article 53, certifying that the judgment is enforceable and containing an extract of the judgment as well as, where appropriate, relevant information on the recoverable costs of the proceedings and the calculation of interest.

2.   For the purposes of enforcement in a Member State of a judgment given in another Member State ordering a provisional, including a protective, measure, the applicant shall provide the competent enforcement authority with:

(a)   a copy of the judgment which satisfies the conditions necessary to establish its authenticity;

(b)   the certificate issued pursuant to Article 53, containing a description of the measure and certifying that:

(i)   the court has jurisdiction as to the substance of the matter;

(ii)   the judgment is enforceable in the Member State of origin; and

(c)   where the measure was ordered without the defendant being summoned to appear, proof of service of the judgment.

3.   The competent enforcement authority may, where necessary, require the applicant to provide, in accordance with Article 57, a translation or a transliteration of the contents of the certificate.

4.   The competent enforcement authority may require the applicant to provide a translation of the judgment only if it is unable to proceed without such a translation.

Article 43

1.   Where enforcement is sought of a judgment given in another Member State, the certificate issued pursuant to Article 53 shall be served on the person against whom the enforcement is sought prior to the first enforcement measure. The certificate shall be accompanied by the judgment, if not already served on that person.

2.   Where the person against whom enforcement is sought is domiciled in a Member State other than the Member State of origin, he may request a translation of the judgment in order to contest the enforcement if the judgment is not written in or accompanied by a translation into either of the following languages:

(a)   a language which he understands; or

(b)   the official language of the Member State in which he is domiciled or, where there are several official languages in that Member State, the official language or one of the official languages of the place where he is domiciled.

Where a translation of the judgment is requested under the first subparagraph, no measures of enforcement may be taken other than protective measures until that translation has been provided to the person against whom enforcement is sought. This paragraph shall not apply if the judgment has already been served on the person against whom enforcement is sought in one of the languages referred to in the first subparagraph or is accompanied by a translation into one of those languages.

. . .

Article 44

1.   In the event of an application for refusal of enforcement of a judgment pursuant to Subsection 2 of Section 3, the court in the Member State addressed may, on the application of the person against whom enforcement is sought:

(a)   limit the enforcement proceedings to protective measures;

(b)   make enforcement conditional on the provision of such security as it shall determine; or

(c)   suspend, either wholly or in part, the enforcement proceedings.

2.   The competent authority in the Member State addressed shall, on the application of the person against whom enforcement is sought, suspend the enforcement proceedings where the enforceability of the judgment is suspended in the Member State of origin.

SECTION 3

Refusal of recognition and enforcement

Subsection 1

Refusal of recognition

Article 45

1.   On the application of any interested party, the recognition of a judgment shall be refused:

(a)   if such recognition is manifestly contrary to public policy (ordre public) in the Member State addressed;

(b)   where the judgment was given in default of appearance, if the defendant was not served with the document which instituted the proceedings or with an equivalent document in sufficient time and in such a way as to enable him to arrange for his defence, unless the defendant failed to commence proceedings to challenge the judgment when it was possible for him to do so;

(c)   if the judgment is irreconcilable with a judgment given between the same parties in the Member State addressed;

(d)   if the judgment is irreconcilable with an earlier judgment given in another Member State or in a third State involving the same cause of action and between the same parties, provided that the earlier judgment fulfils the conditions necessary for its recognition in the Member State addressed; or

(e)   if the judgment conflicts with:

(i)   Sections 3, 4 or 5 of Chapter II where the policyholder, the insured, a beneficiary of the insurance contract, the injured party, the consumer or the employee was the defendant; or

(ii)   Section 6 of Chapter II.

2.   In its examination of the grounds of jurisdiction referred to in point (e) of paragraph 1, the court to which the application was submitted shall be bound by the findings of fact on which the court of origin based its jurisdiction.

3.   Without prejudice to point (e) of paragraph 1, the jurisdiction of the court of origin may not be reviewed. The test of public policy referred to in point (a) of paragraph 1 may not be applied to the rules relating to jurisdiction.

4.   The application for refusal of recognition shall be made in accordance with the procedures provided for in Subsection 2 and, where appropriate, Section 4.

Subsection 2

Refusal of enforcement

Article 46

On the application of the person against whom enforcement is sought, the enforcement of a judgment shall be refused where one of the grounds referred to in Article 45 is found to exist.

Article 47

1.   The application for refusal of enforcement shall be submitted to the court which the Member State concerned has communicated to the Commission pursuant to point (a) of Article 75 as the court to which the application is to be submitted.

2.   The procedure for refusal of enforcement shall, in so far as it is not covered by this Regulation, be governed by the law of the Member State addressed.

3.   The applicant shall provide the court with a copy of the judgment and, where necessary, a translation or transliteration of it.

The court may dispense with the production of the documents referred to in the first subparagraph if it already possesses them or if it considers it unreasonable to require the applicant to provide them. In the latter case, the court may require the other party to provide those documents.

4.   The party seeking the refusal of enforcement of a judgment given in another Member State shall not be required to have a postal address in the Member State addressed. Nor shall that party be required to have an authorised representative in the Member State addressed unless such a representative is mandatory irrespective of the nationality or the domicile of the parties.

Article 48

The court shall decide on the application for refusal of enforcement without delay.

Article 49

1.   The decision on the application for refusal of enforcement may be appealed against by either party.

2.   The appeal is to be lodged with the court which the Member State concerned has communicated to the Commission pursuant to point (b) of Article 75 as the court with which such an appeal is to be lodged.

Article 50

The decision given on the appeal may only be contested by an appeal where the courts with which any further appeal is to be lodged have been communicated by the Member State concerned to the Commission pursuant to point (c) of Article 75.

Article 51

1.   The court to which an application for refusal of enforcement is submitted or the court which hears an appeal lodged under Article 49 or Article 50 may stay the proceedings if an ordinary appeal has been lodged against the judgment in the Member State of origin or if the time for such an appeal has not yet expired. In the latter case, the court may specify the time within which such an appeal is to be lodged.

2.   Where the judgment was given in Ireland, Cyprus or the United Kingdom, any form of appeal available in the Member State of origin shall be treated as an ordinary appeal for the purposes of paragraph 1.

SECTION 4

Common provisions

Article 52

Under no circumstances may a judgment given in a Member State be reviewed as to its substance in the Member State addressed.

. . .

Article 54

1.   If a judgment contains a measure or an order which is not known in the law of the Member State addressed, that measure or order shall, to the extent possible, be adapted to a measure or an order known in the law of that Member State which has equivalent effects attached to it and which pursues similar aims and interests.

Such adaptation shall not result in effects going beyond those provided for in the law of the Member State of origin.

2.   Any party may challenge the adaptation of the measure or order before a court.

3.   If necessary, the party invoking the judgment or seeking its enforcement may be required to provide a translation or a transliteration of the judgment.

Article 55

A judgment given in a Member State which orders a payment by way of a penalty shall be enforceable in the Member State addressed only if the amount of the payment has been finally determined by the court of origin.

Article 56

No security, bond or deposit, however described, shall be required of a party who in one Member State applies for the enforcement of a judgment given in another Member State on the ground that he is a foreign national or that he is not domiciled or resident in the Member State addressed.

. . .

CHAPTER IV
AUTHENTIC INSTRUMENTS AND
COURT SETTLEMENTS

Article 58

1.   An authentic instrument which is enforceable in the Member State of origin shall be enforceable in the other Member States without any declaration of enforceability being required. Enforcement of the authentic instrument may be refused only if such enforcement is manifestly contrary to public policy (ordre public) in the Member State addressed.

The provisions of Section 2, Subsection 2 of Section 3, and Section 4 of Chapter III shall apply as appropriate to authentic instruments.

. . .

Article 59

A court settlement which is enforceable in the Member State of origin shall be enforced in the other Member States under the same conditions as authentic instruments.

. . .

CHAPTER V

GENERAL PROVISIONS

Article 61

No legalisation or other similar formality shall be required for documents issued in a Member State in the context of this Regulation.

Article 62

1.   In order to determine whether a party is domiciled in the Member State whose courts are seised of a matter, the court shall apply its internal law.

2.   If a party is not domiciled in the Member State whose courts are seised of the matter, then, in order to determine whether the party is domiciled in another Member State, the court shall apply the law of that Member State.

Article 63

1.   For the purposes of this Regulation, a company or other legal person or association of natural or legal persons is domiciled at the place where it has its:

    (a)   statutory seat;

    (b)   central administration; or

    (c)   principal place of business.

2.   For the purposes of Ireland, Cyprus and the United Kingdom, 'statutory seat' means the registered office or, where there is no such office anywhere, the place of incorporation or, where there is no such place anywhere, the place under the law of which the formation took place.

3.   In order to determine whether a trust is domiciled in the Member State whose courts are seised of the matter, the court shall apply its rules of private international law.

Article 64

Without prejudice to any more favourable provisions of national laws, persons domiciled in a Member State who are being prosecuted in the criminal courts of another Member State of which they are not nationals for an offence which was not intentionally committed may be defended by persons qualified to do so, even if they do not appear in person. However, the court seised of the matter may order appearance in person; in the case of failure to appear, a judgment given in the civil action without the person concerned having had the opportunity to arrange for his defence need not be recognised or enforced in the other Member States.

CHAPTER V
FINAL PROVISIONS

Article 76

1.   The Member States shall notify the Commission of:

(a)   the rules of jurisdiction referred to in Articles 5(2) and 6(2);

(b)   the rules on third-party notice referred to in Article 65; and

(c)   the conventions referred to in Article 69.

2.   The Commission shall, on the basis of the notifications by the Member States referred to in paragraph 1, establish the corresponding lists.

3.   The Member States shall notify the Commission of any subsequent amendments required to be made to those lists. The Commission shall amend those lists accordingly.

4.   The Commission shall publish the lists and any subsequent amendments made to them in the Official Journal of the European Union.

5.   The Commission shall make all information notified pursuant to paragraphs 1 and 3 publicly available through any other appropriate means, in particular through the European Judicial Network.

Article 77

The Commission shall be empowered to adopt delegated acts in accordance with Article 78 concerning the amendment of Annexes I and II.

. . .

Article 79

By 11 January 2022 the Commission shall present a report to the European Parliament, to the Council and to the European Economic and Social Committee on the application of this Regulation. That report shall include an evaluation of the possible need for a further extension of the rules on jurisdiction to defendants not domiciled in a Member State, taking into account the operation of this Regulation and possible developments at international level. Where appropriate, the report shall be accompanied by a proposal for amendment of this Regulation.

. . .

ANNEX III
CORRELATION TABLE

Regulation (EC) No 44/2001	This Regulation
Article 1(1)	Article 1(1)
Article 1(2), introductory words	Article 1(2), introductory words
Article 1(2) point (a)	Article 1(2), points (a) and (f)
Article 1(2), points (b) to (d)	Article 1(2), points (b) to (d)

Regulation (EC) No 44/2001	This Regulation
—	Article 1(2), point (e)
Article 1(3)	—
—	Article 2
Article 2	Article 4
Article 3	Article 5
Article 4	Article 6
Article 5, introductory words	Article 7, introductory words
Article 5, point (1)	Article 7, point (1)
Article 5, point (2)	—
Article 5, points (3) and (4)	Article 7, points (2) and (3)
—	Article 7, point (4)
Article 5, points (5) to (7)	Article 7, points (5) to (7)
Article 6	Article 8
Article 7	Article 9
Article 8	Article 10
Article 9	Article 11
Article 10	Article 12
Article 11	Article 13
Article 12	Article 14
Article 13	Article 15
Article 14	Article 16
Article 15	Article 17
Article 16	Article 18
Article 17	Article 19
Article 18	Article 20
Article 19, points (1) and (2)	Article 21(1)
—	Article 21(2)
Article 20	Article 22
Article 21	Article 23
Article 22	Article 24
Article 23(1) and (2)	Article 25(1) and (2)
Article 23(3)	—
Article 23(4) and (5)	Article 25(3) and (4)

Regulation (EC) No 44/2001	This Regulation
—	Article 25(5)
Article 24	Article 26(1)
—	Article 26(2)
Article 25	Article 27
Article 26	Article 28
Article 27(1)	Article 29(1)
—	Article 29(2)
Article 27(2)	Article 29(3)
Article 28	Article 30
Article 29	Article 31(1)
—	Article 31(2)
—	Article 31(3)
—	Article 31(4)
Article 30	Article 32(1), points (a) and (b)
—	Article 32(1), second subparagraph
—	Article 32(2)
—	Article 33
—	Article 34
Article 31	Article 35
Article 32	Article 2, point (a)
Article 33	Article 36
—	Article 37
—	Article 39
—	Article 40
—	Article 41
—	Article 42
—	Article 43
—	Article 44
Article 34	Article 45(1), points (a) to (d)
Article 35(1)	Article 45(1), point (e)
Article 35(2)	Article 45(2)
Article 35(3)	Article 45(3)
—	Article 45(4)

Regulation (EC) No 44/2001	This Regulation
Article 36	Article 52
Article 37(1)	Article 38, point (a)
Article 38	—
Article 39	—
Article 40	—
Article 41	—
Article 42	—
Article 43	—
Article 44	—
Article 45	—
Article 46	—
Article 47	—
Article 48	—
—	Article 46
—	Article 47
—	Article 48
—	Article 49
—	Article 50
—	Article 51
—	Article 54
Article 49	Article 55
Article 50	—
Article 51	Article 56
Article 52	—
Article 53	—
Article 54	Article 53
Article 55(1)	—
Article 55(2)	Article 37(2), Article 47(3) and Article 57
Article 56	Article 61
Article 57(1)	Article 58(1)
Article 57(2)	—
Article 57(3)	Article 58(2)
Article 57(4)	Article 60

Regulation (EC) No 44/2001	This Regulation
Article 58	Article 59 and Article 60
Article 59	Article 62
Article 60	Article 63
Article 61	Article 64
Article 62	Article 3
Article 63	—
Article 64	—
Article 65	Article 65(1) and (2)
—	Article 65(3)
Article 66	Article 66
Article 67	Article 67
Article 68	Article 68
Article 69	Article 69
Article 70	Article 70
Article 71	Article 71
Article 72	Article 72
—	Article 73
Article 73	Article 79
Article 74(1)	Article 75, first paragraph, points (a), (b) and (c), and Article 76(1), point (a)
Article 74(2)	Article 77
—	Article 78
—	Article 80
Article 75	—
Article 76	Article 81
Annex I	Article 76(1), point (a)
Annex II	Article 75, point (a)
Annex III	Article 75, point (b)
Annex IV	Article 75, point (c)
Annex V	Annex I and Annex II
Annex VI	Annex II
—	Annex III

NOTES

The Regulation ("Brussels Ia") contains a number of clarifications and changes compared to its predecessor, the Brussels I Regulation. The following are among the most important ones:

1.   The original Brussels Convention and, later, the Brussels I Regulation proscribed the use of exorbitant bases of jurisdiction again EU defendants ("persons domiciled in a Member State"), with Brussels I listing these bases in an Annex. The new Brussels I (recast) Regulation provides for the same: Arts. 4(1) and 5(1) make it clear that, with exceptions, an EU person may be sued only at his or her domicile, while Art. 6 makes it clear that national rules, including those providing for the exercise of exorbitant jurisdiction remain in effect as against non-EU defendants. The Member States inform the Commission of the national rules, and the latter keeps a list. As before, the list includes jurisdiction based on the plaintiff's nationality, the presence of assets unrelated to the claim, and common-law type transient jurisdiction. Art. 6(2) broadens the use of exorbitant rules as against non-EU defendants by making a Member State's exorbitant jurisdictional provisions available to any EU-plaintiffs, not only their own nationals. Example: French law provides for jurisdiction over a defendant with no connection to France (e.g., a non-resident American) when the plaintiff is a French citizen. This provision can now also be utilized by plaintiffs who are citizens of other EU countries.

2.   Art. 7 of the Regulation makes provision for "special [specific] jurisdiction," thereby enlarging upon the basic rules of Arts. 4 and 5 (defendant's domicile). The list is more extensive than in the predecessor Regulation. However, for claims arising from contract, difficulties remain.

(a)   If jurisdiction for a contract claim cannot be determined under Art. 7(1)(b), letter (c) refers back to (a): "the place of performance of the obligation in question." This will require a court to determine first what law applies to the "obligation in question," then to inquire where the place of performance is under that law, only perhaps to find that that place is in a state other than its own, so that it does not have jurisdiction after all.

(b)   As in all cases in which a party has a choice of forum, jurisdiction and applicable law may diverge, for instance when one court would apply the Vienna Sales Convention (because both countries are Contracting States or its conflicts law refers to the Convention), while another would not (because, like the United States, its state does not apply the Convention by way of conflicts law).

3.   Art. 7(2) retains specific jurisdiction at the place where "the harmful event occurred"—presumably, incorporating the interpretation of the Court of Justice, this means either the place of acting or the place of injury (p. 1142, supra)—but extends this to include the place where such harm "may occur." The addition says nothing directly about injunctive relief, but jurisdiction to grant such relief (if available under the particular national law) has now been clarified to exist in the state of potential harm. There is no general provision dealing with injunctive relief. As in tort, it would seem that such jurisdiction lies wherever there is general or specific jurisdiction under provisions of the Regulation. Cases potentially in doubt, or uncovered, are

those involving protective measures, especially when the principal litigation is taking place elsewhere. The Regulation addresses the problem in Art. 35. Recall that orders that issue ex parte, such as British freezing orders (formerly "Mareva injunctions") may not be entitled to recognition in other member states: see p. 184, supra.

4. Specific jurisdiction with respect to consumer contracts is the subject of Arts. 17–19. Art. 15(3) requires that the consumer have concluded a contract with a supplier who "pursues commercial or professional activities in the Member State of the consumer's domicile or, by any means, directs such activities to that Member State or to several countries, including that Member State, and the contract falls within the scope of such activities." Note: (a) solicitation of the particular consumer or advertising in the particular member state is not required—"direct[ing] activities" to that member state is enough; (b) "direct[ing] activities" is clearly less than "targeting" as the "several countries, including . . ." language makes clear; (c) the consumer need not have taken any steps to conclude the contract in his or her home state to be able to sue there, so long as the requirements under (a) of this summary are met; (d) "by any means" today would seem to include the maintenance (passive, interactive? see p. 115, supra) of web sites. Add to this (2nd paragraph of Art. 17) that non-Community suppliers that maintain "a branch, agency or other establishment in one of the Member States" shall be "deemed to be domiciled in that Member State" (and accordingly be subject to suit there (Art. 4, supra)) and the jurisdictional reach over Internet suppliers may be very extensive indeed. Suppliers engaged in e-commerce vociferously objected to the proposal, and the Commission undertook to hold hearings. Some suggested that e-commerce traders might henceforth stipulate that no goods would be supplied to named member states. Would that avoid the assertion of jurisdiction there? What if orders were made contingent upon acceptance by the seller's home office: any different result? The EC's "E-commerce Directive," [2000] Official Journal L 178/1, states in its Art. 1(4) that the Directive neither creates additional rules of private international law nor addresses judicial jurisdiction. The Directive's main thrust is to focus on the country of origin of e-commerce. But that does not necessarily answer the question of what constitutes "activity" sufficient for assertion of jurisdiction by the forum state.

The Court of Justice has given some guidance as to what constitutes "directing activity" to a member state for purposes of Art. 17(1)(c) when a trader, or an intermediary acting on its behalf, maintains a website. It held in a preliminary ruling that "the mere accessibility of the trader's . . . website in the Member State in which the consumer is domiciled is insufficient. The same is true of mention of an email address and of other contact details. . . ." Joined Cases C-585/08 and C-144/09 (Pammer v. Schlüter and Hotel Alpenhof v. Heller), [2010] E.C.R. I-12527 (Dec. 7. 2010), 10 Eur. Legal Forum I-263, 269 (para. 94) (5/6, 2010). However, matters that could be considered "directing activity" (in the context of a tourist contract) were: the mention of directions from another Member State to where the trader pursues its activities; use of language or currency other than or in addition to those used in the trader's country; the possibility of making or confirming a reservation in a language other than the trader's; reimbursement for expenses; mention of international telephone accessibility. Id. at para. 78 et seq.

In 2015, the Court held that a contract that does not itself fall within Art. 17(1)(c) may nevertheless give rise to jurisdiction under Art. 18(1) if it is closely linked to a previous contract that clearly met the conditions of Art. 17(1)(c) (in the case at bar, to effectuate the economic goals of the earlier contract). Case 297/14 (Hobohm v. Benedikt Kampik Ltd. Co. KG, [2016] Official Journal C 68/11. The case arose under the original Brussels I Regulation.

Art. 19 seeks to insure that choice-of-court clauses, for instance in standard form contracts, do not negate the protection Arts. 17–18 are intended to provide. Such clauses are valid only if entered into after the dispute has arisen (this guards against standard form contracts), or afford the consumer additional places of suit, or when the contract is between residents of the same state and selects the courts of that state. The same problem arises also in the choice-of-law context. See p. 1208, infra, and Borchers, Categorical Exceptions to Party Autonomy in Private International Law, 82 Tul.L.Rev. 1645 (2008). Note that Art. 19 does not permit the kind of mandatory private arbitration provisions in consumer contracts (thereby precluding a consumer to seek relief in court, either by private action or as a member of the class) as the U.S. Supreme Court has sanctioned in the United States. See Hay, One-sided (Asymmetrical) Remedy Clauses and Weaker Party Protection in American Law, in Rolf A. Schütze (ed.), Fairness Justice Equity—Festschrift für Reinhold Geimer) 217–230 (Germany, 2017).

5. There is some uncertainty whether jurisdiction over contract claims under Art. 7(1) may draw in related tort claims. In an early decision, the European Court had strictly limited Art. 7(1) claims arising from obligations freely assumed (as distinguished from imposed as a matter of law): Case C-344/00 (Taconi), 2002 ECR I-7357. In another decision, however, the Court countenanced the possibility of invoking the consumer-contract jurisdiction to seek relief for a claim in tort: C-96/00 (Gabriel), 2002 ECR I-6367. In 2011 and 2012, the German Supreme Court—in cases arising under the original Lugano ("Parallel") Convention—held that a consumer could assert a claim for precontractual misconduct (*culpa in contrahendo*) in a consumer contract action. BGH, Judgment of May 31, 2011, Docket No. VI ZR 154/10, 15 GWR 349, 367 (2011). The court did not consider that legal systems differ in the way that they deal with *culpa in contrahendo*—some treat it as "related" to contract (such as the German), others regard it as being closer to tort. National court interpretations and applications therefore may diverge. In consumer judgment recognition cases, a recognizing court may review the jurisdiction of the rendering court (Art. 45(1)(c)), see also Note (9) below). If its view of the scope of Art. 7(1) and 17 differs, it might refuse recognition. Such a result may now be avoided under the revised Lugano Convention because, as EU law, questions arising under it in EU national courts should now be referred to the European Court when they reach the highest national court. The decision in the 2015 *Hobohm* case (supra Note (4)), on reference from the German Supreme Court, is case in point. For further comment, see Hay and Rasmussen-Bonne, Uniform Interpretation of Brussels-I and Lugano—The Example of Jurisdiction "In Matters Relating to Contract" in Consumer Transactions, 2011 Eur. Legal F. 105. See also Bogdan, Contract or Tort under Article 5 of the Brussels I Regulation: Tertium non Datur?, in: Kronke and Thorn (eds.), Grenzen überwinden—Prinzipien bewahren, Festschrift für von Hoffmann 561 (2011).

6.   Art. 25 governs forum selection clauses (p. 1147, supra), except in insurance, consumer, and employment contracts (for these, see Arts. 15, 19, and 23, respectively). The chosen forum has exclusive jurisdiction, unless the parties expressly provided otherwise, i.e., that they only meant to prorogate an additional forum. Art. 25(2) adds to prior law that "any communication by electronic means which can provide a durable record of the agreement shall be deemed to be in writing." Note that the addition softens the general writing requirement and does so in keeping with modern technology. In addition, a form that "accords with a usage" in "international trade or commerce," of which the parties were or should have been aware, will suffice. The Court had much earlier permitted the parties to arrive at a forum selection by means of an informal (oral) stipulation of the place of performance: Art. 7(1) requires no form. See case 56/79, [1980] ECR 89. The Court drew the line when the parties stipulated a place of performance solely for forum selection purposes. Case 106/95, [1997] 1 All. E.R. 385; [1997] ECR–I 911. How realistic is this limitation? How does one prove such an (improper) purpose? As noted in a footnote to Art. 25, supra, the parallel provision of the Lugano Convention requires that one party be domiciled in a signatory country. The Hague Choice of Court Convention, like EU law, lacks such a requirement. That Convention was signed by the EU Council on behalf of the European Union (excluding Denmark) and entered into force in 2015.

Taking a possibly stricter view, the Austrian Supreme Court held that a jurisdiction clause must be properly incorporated in the contract, and that a clause contained in several pages of standard terms, which were attached to an offer sent by e-mail without express reference to the clause, would be effective. OGH, Decision of June 21, 2011, Docket No. 1Ob09/11k, 2011 Eur. Legal F. 137.

Brussels Ia now remedies a problem that the original Brussels I Regulation had overlooked: the *lis pendens* provision (now Art. 29) requires courts to stay a proceeding in favor of another court where the action was brought first. This provision could be used (and was) to undercut the jurisdiction of the court chosen in the parties' agreement (Art. 25), until such time as the court where suit had been brought dismissed the action as improperly brought (because the chosen court has exclusive jurisdiction— Art. 25). This practice was popularly known as the "torpedo." Art. 31 now makes an exception to the first-court-seized rule in favor of the chosen court.

7.   Where is the "domicile" of a company or other legal person for purposes, for instance, of the general jurisdiction provision of Art. 4? The Brussels Convention had left the determination to national conflicts law. Given the differences in the national laws of the member states ("seat" rule or "law of

incorporation," see p. 1113, supra), moving a company from one type of state to one with a different rule presented problems. Even before Regulation No. 44/2001, the Court of Justice had begun to emphasize the need for recognition of companies formed in another member state in the interest of a free and integrated market. See the *Centros* and *Überseering* decisions, p. 1113, supra.

Art. 60 of "Brussels I," now followed by Art. 63 of Brussels Ia, narrows the choices for the determination of a company's domicile to the places where the company (or other legal person) "has its statutory seat, central administration, or principal place of business." This closely resembles the Treaty on the Functioning of the European Union, defining legal persons for the purposes of the right of establishment. Note, however, that the jurisdictional provision of Art. 4, in combination with Art. 63, says nothing about rules of substantive national corporate law, for instance, that a company registered and with original seat in Germany may become subject to dissolution there when it moves its seat to another Community state. Indeed, whenever a proceeding concerns "the validity of the constitution, the nullity or the dissolution of companies or other legal persons," the courts of the state of a company's seat have exclusive jurisdiction. To determine where the seat is, the court shall continue "to apply its rules of private international law" (Art. 24(2)). German law therefore could still result in the dissolution of a German company that moves its seat elsewhere. But can Germany entertain an action for the dissolution of a company, validly incorporated elsewhere, that has moved its seat to Germany without re-incorporating there? The Court's decisions in *Überseering* and *Inspire Art*, p. 1113 supra, suggest that the answer is no.

8.   Note that a company's "location" may be defined differently for different purposes: see, for instance, Art. 23 of the Rome-II Regulation, p. 1221, infra, defining a company's "habitual residence" for purposes of that law.

9.   For recognition of judgments, Art. 36(1) says that such a "judgment shall be recognized without any special procedure being required." Traditionally, the procedural law of civil-law countries requires a "declaration of enforceability" of a foreign judgment ("exequatur") before it can be enforced domestically. In view of the recognition command of Art. 36(1), this requirement became more or less a mere formality and Art. 39 now expressly abolishes it. Nonetheless, there are grounds (listed in Art. 45) on which a party may resist recognition and enforcement (typically when enforcement is sought, Art. 45(4)). The grounds for non-recognition listed in Art. 45 are the same as under prior law, with additional clarification in Art. 45(1)(b). Note, in particular, that the first court's jurisdiction may only be challenged at the recognition stage for the limited types of cases listed in Art. 45(1)(c), and that the recognizing court may not invoke public policy to get around this prohibition (Art. 45(3)). The practical result of these provisions is that a defendant who had notice of a proceeding (Art. 45(1)(b)) must challenge jurisdiction in the court where sued or risk losing that defense; he or she cannot default and then raise the defense collaterally in the second court to resist recognition and enforcement. For cases of inconsistent judgments, the Regulation, like its predecessor, adopts a first-in-time rule,

except that an inconsistent local judgment always takes precedence (Art. 45(1)(c)–(d)).

10. Note that the scope of review in the second state is quite narrow. First, the trial court must immediately declare the judgment enforceable once the requirements of Art. 55 have been fulfilled. Art. 41. Matters in opposition to enforcement may first be considered upon appeal of the trial court's order. Art. 45. Second, even the appellate court's scope of review is very limited. It may not review the first court's jurisdiction, except in the limited group of cases listed in Art. 35(1), for instance, in consumer cases, and it is limited even then by the first court's findings of fact (Art. 35(2)). It also may not review the first court's judgment as to substance. Art. 36. What may it properly examine (apart from the somewhat special case—Art. 34(3)–(4)—of an irreconcilable judgment by another court in the same matter)? Art. 34(2) requires notice to the defendant "in sufficient time and in such a way as to enable him to arrange for his defense." Lack of such notice requires denial of recognition. The provision refers expressly to judgments "given in default of appearance." It follows that, if proper notice was given, a defendant must litigate any jurisdictional objections in the first court or lose them (Art. 35(1)); the defendant does not have the option to default in F-1, and litigate F-1's jurisdiction in F-2. See Krombach v. Bamberski, Case C–7/98, [2000] ECR I–1935 (EC Court of Justice); German Court of Appeal Köln, Jan. 12, 2004, Case 16 W 20/03, unalex DE–470. This is a harsh rule, especially when, after initial notice and commencement of the action, the claim is later amended. See German Court of Appeal Frankfurt, Dec. 16, 2004, Case 20 W 507/04, unalex DE–451; German Supreme Court, December 12, 2007, Case XII ZB 240/05, 8 Eur. Legal F. II-8 (1–2008) (irregularities in the manner of service and notification do not matter so long as the defendant had actual notice and either an opportunity to defend or, after entry of judgment, to seek a remedy against it in the state of rendition). See the earlier ECJ decision in Case 283/05, ASML Netherlands v. SEMIS, [2006] ECR I-12041. What about fairness in the first proceedings after first notice and commencement of the action? Art. 34 is silent, the only other ground for non-recognition being violation of F-2's public policy. Faced with such a case (notice had been given, the court hypothesized, but only in the last minute), a German Court of Appeal used the public-policy provision as a source of a broader right to what might, in American law, be called "procedural due process." Everyone has a right to a fair procedure, and notice of suit in the last moment violates "essential legal principles" of the recognizing state. OLG Zweibrücken, May 10, 2005, Case 3 W 165/04, [2006] IPRax 487, with anno. by Roth, id. at 466. For all of the foregoing, see also Hay, The Development of the Public Policy Barrier to Judgment Recognition Within the European Community, 7 Eur. Legal F. I-289 (6–2007). The revision in Art. 45(1)(b) may serve to clarify this "due process" requirement.

11. The European Court held in Case 125/9, Denilauler v. Coucher [1980] ECR I-1553 (under the Regulation's predecessor Brussels Convention) that "judgments," for purposes of the recognition requirement, means decrees issued as a result of adversary proceedings, thus excluding ex parte decisions (for instance, freezing orders—formerly "Mareva injunctions"). However, a

judgment entered upon the defendant's default of appearance after service (previous paragraph) is not therefore an excluded *ex parte* decision. See Advocate General Kokott in Case C 394/07, Gambazzi v. Daimler Chrysler, 126. But see the decision of the Dutch Supreme Court in Realchemie Nederland BV v. Fa. Feinchermie Schwebda GmbH. Nov. 7, 2008, Case 07/12641, LJN: BD7568 (Hoge Raad 2008): decisions (such as one setting court fees) that issued *ex parte* but were served on the defendant and subject to challenge in the state of rendition are covered by the recognition command.

12. Litigation in transborder cases can be expensive. The potential financial exposure is particularly great in legal systems, such as the German, in which the loser also pays the winner's expenses (costs and attorneys' fees) and therefore, in effect, bars the prosecution of claims. In order to ensure access to justice, the Community obligates member states, by directive,[6] to provide legal aid for (a) "pre-litigation advice with a view to reaching a settlement" and (b) "legal assistance and representation in court,"[7] including the costs of the other side, if national law so provides, and to do so in a non-discriminatory fashion. The right to legal aid applies to suits by a person habitually resident in one member state against a person habitually resident in another. Member states determine the financial threshold for eligibility for aid.

13. For detailed review of the Regulation, see Micklitz & Rott, Vergemeinschaftung des EuGVÜ in der Verordnung (EG) Nr. 44/2001, [2002] Europäische Zeitschrift für Wirtschaftsrecht 16; Mankowski and Magnus, Commentary on the Brussels I Regulation (2007); Hess, Pfeiffer & Schlosser, The Brussels I Regulation (2008). Simons and Hausmann (eds.), unalex Commentary on the Brussels I Regulation (print volumes in English, German, French, Italian 2012).

14. In 2019 the Hague Conference on Private International Law proposed a new worldwide convention for the recognition of judgments. It is much narrower in scope than the Brussels Ia (Recast) Regulation. For brief discussion see p. 285, supra. The Convention is not yet in force. The United States has not signed it and therefore not indicated its intention to ratify it. For discussion, see Coco, The Value of a New Judgments Convention for U.S. Litigants, 94 N.Y.U.L.Rev. 1209 (2019); Cuniberti, Signalling the Enforceability of the Forum's Judgments Abroad, 56 Rivista di diritto internazionale private e processuale 33 (2020).

---

[6]   In contract to a regulation, a directive as no direct (self-executing) effect in the member states, but obligates them to enact domestic law or to adopt domestic administrative measures giving effect to the directives goals and objectives. See n.1, supra.

[7]   The Directive is reproduced at p. 1175, infra. For the definition of a "directive," see n. 1, supra.

B. DIVORCE, CUSTODY, AND MAINTENANCE

INTRODUCTORY NOTE

The Regulation concerning Jurisdiction and the Recognition and Enforcement of Judgments in Matrimonial Matters and the Matters of Parental Responsibility was adopted in 2003[8], replacing the earlier Regulation No. 1347/2000 ("Brussels II").[9] The 2003 Regulation is popularly known as "Brussels IIa or Brussels II*bis*." It was revised in 2019 and becomes "Brussels IIa Recast," effective in August 2022.[10]

The 2003 Regulation contains a comprehensive treatment of child custody jurisdiction and the recognition of awards and in the recognition and provision for enforcement of a right of access.[11] The 2019 recast introduces a number of revisions and, in particular, strengthens the rules designed to protect children in cross-border disputes.[12]

In reviewing the provisions of the 2003 "Brussels IIa," it is important to keep in mind some of the explanatory and policy statements contained in the introductory recitals. The following paragraphs should be noted in particular: 4, 5, 7–9, 11–13, 16, 23, and 33. See also the further comments on it and on the 2019 Recast Regulation in the Note following the text of the Regulation.

The jurisdictional provisions for divorce of the 2003 Brussels IIa Regulation were supplemented by Regulation (EU) No. 1259/2010, which provides for the law applicable to divorce. The 2019 Recast made small changes. The jurisdictional provision for maintenance of the Brussels I Regulation (Art. (2)) has been expanded and supplemented by Regulation (EU) 4/2009. These Regulations are considered at pp. 1137, 1189, infra, respectively.

1. COUNCIL REGULATION (EC) NO. 2201/2003 CONCERNING JURISDICTION AND THE RECOGNITION AND ENFORCEMENT OF JUDGMENTS IN MATRIMONIAL MATTERS AND THE MATTERS OF PARENTAL RESPONSIBILITY (REPEALING REGULATION (EC) NO. 1347/2000)—"BRUSSELS IIA"

[2003] Official Journal L 338/1

(excerpts; footnotes omitted)

. . .

---

[8] Council Regulation (EC) 2201/2003, [2003] Official Journal L 338/1.

[9] Council Regulation (EC) 1347/2000, [2000] L 160/90.

[10] Council Regulation (EU) 2019/1111 on Jurisdiction, the Recognition and Enforcement of Decisions in Matrimonial Matters and the Matters of Parental Responsibility, and on International Child Abduction (recast), [2019] Official Journal 1-115.

[11] For American decisions on whether "custody rights" include rights of access, see p. 997, supra.

[12] See EU Commission Fact Sheet, Adoption of new rules to better protect children in cross-border disputes, https://ec.europa.eu/commission/presscorner/detail/en/Memo_19_3374 (last visited November 12, 2020),

Whereas:

. . .

(5)   In order to ensure equality for all children, this Regulation covers all decisions on parental responsibility, including measures for the protection of the child, independently of any link with a matrimonial proceeding.

(6)   Since the application of the rules on parental responsibility often arises in the context of matrimonial proceedings, it is more appropriate to have a single instrument for matters of divorce and parental responsibility.

(7)   The scope of this Regulation covers civil matters, whatever the nature of the court or tribunal.

(8)   As regards judgments on divorce, legal separation or marriage annulment, this Regulation should apply only to the dissolution of matrimonial ties and should not deal with issues such as the grounds for divorce, property consequences of the marriage or any other ancillary measures.

(9)   As regards the property of the child, this Regulation should apply only to measures for the protection of the child, i.e. (i) the designation and functions of a person or body having charge of the child's property, representing or assisting the child, and (ii) the administration, conservation or disposal of the child's property. In this context, this Regulation should, for instance, apply in cases where the parents are in dispute as regards the administration of the child's property. Measures relating to the child's property which do not concern the protection of the child should continue to be governed by Council Regulation (EC) No 44/2001 of 22 December 2000 on jurisdiction and the recognition and enforcement of judgments in civil and commercial matters.

(10)   This Regulation is not intended to apply to matters relating to social security, public measures of a general nature in matters of education or health or to decisions on the right of asylum and on immigration. In addition it does not apply to the establishment of parenthood, since this is a different matter from the attribution of parental responsibility, nor to other questions linked to the status of persons. Moreover, it does not apply to measures taken as a result of criminal offences committed by children.

(11)   Maintenance obligations are excluded from the scope of this Regulation . . . [13]

(12)   The grounds of jurisdiction in matters of parental responsibility established in the present Regulation are shaped in the light of the best interests of the child, in particular on the criterion of proximity. This means that jurisdiction should lie in the first place with the Member State of the child's habitual residence, except for certain cases of a change in the child's residence or pursuant to an agreement between the holders of parental responsibility.

(13)   In the interest of the child, this Regulation allows, by way of exception and under certain conditions, that the court having jurisdiction may transfer a case to a court of another Member State if this court is better placed to hear the case. However, in this case the second court should not be allowed to transfer the case to a third court.

. . .

(16)   This Regulation should not prevent the courts of a Member State from taking provisional, including protective measures, in urgent cases, with regard to persons or property situated in that State.

---

[13]   See Regulation (EC) No. 4/2009, summarized below at 1187.

(17) In cases of wrongful removal or retention of a child, the return of the child should be obtained without delay, and to this end the Hague Convention of 25 October 1980 would continue to apply as complemented by the provisions of this Regulation, in particular Article 11. The courts of the Member State to or in which the child has been wrongfully removed or retained should be able to oppose his or her return in specific, duly justified cases. However, such a decision could be replaced by a subsequent decision by the court of the Member State of habitual residence of the child prior to the wrongful removal or retention. Should that judgment entail the return of the child, the return should take place without any special procedure being required for recognition and enforcement of that judgment in the Member State to or in which the child has been removed or retained.

(18) Where a court has decided not to return a child on the basis of Article 13 of the 1980 Hague Convention, it should inform the court having jurisdiction or central authority in the Member State where the child was habitually resident prior to the wrongful removal or retention. Unless the court in the latter Member State has been seised, this court or the central authority should notify the parties. This obligation should not prevent the central authority from also notifying the relevant public authorities in accordance with national law.

(19) The hearing of the child plays an important role in the application of this Regulation, although this instrument is not intended to modify national procedures applicable.

. . .

(21) The recognition and enforcement of judgments given in a Member State should be based on the principle of mutual trust and the grounds for non-recognition should be kept to the minimum required.

. . .

(29) For the proper functioning of this Regulation, the Commission should review its application and propose such amendments as may appear necessary.

(30) The United Kingdom and Ireland, in accordance with Article 3 of the Protocol on the position of the United Kingdom and Ireland annexed to the Treaty on European Union and the Treaty establishing the European Community, have given notice of their wish to take part in the adoption and application of this Regulation.

(31) Denmark, in accordance with Articles 1 and 2 of the Protocol on the position of Denmark annexed to the Treaty on European Union and the Treaty establishing the European Community, is not participating in the adoption of this Regulation and is therefore not bound by it nor subject to its application.

. . .

(33) This Regulation recognises the fundamental rights and observes the principles of the Charter of Fundamental Rights of the European Union. In particular, it seeks to ensure respect for the fundamental rights of the child as set out in Article 24 of the Charter of Fundamental Rights of the European Union,

HAS ADOPTED THE PRESENT REGULATION:

CHAPTER I

SCOPE AND DEFINITIONS

Article 1

Scope

1.   This Regulation shall apply, whatever the nature of the court or tribunal, in civil matters relating to:

(a)   divorce, legal separation or marriage annulment;

(b)   the attribution, exercise, delegation, restriction or termination of parental responsibility.

2.   The matters referred to in paragraph 1(b) may, in particular, deal with:

(a)   rights of custody and rights of access;

(b)   guardianship, curatorship and similar institutions;

(c)   the designation and functions of any person or body having charge of the child's person or property, representing or assisting the child;

(d)   the placement of the child in a foster family or in institutional care;

(e)   measures for the protection of the child relating to the administration, conservation or disposal of the child's property.

3.   This Regulation shall not apply to:

(a)   the establishment or contesting of a parent-child relationship;

(b)   decisions on adoption, measures preparatory to adoption, or the annulment or revocation of adoption;

(c)   the name and forenames of the child;

(d)   emancipation;

(e)   maintenance obligations;[14]

(f)   trusts or succession;

(g)   measures taken as a result of criminal offences committed by children.[15]

Article 2

Definitions

For the purposes of this Regulation:

1.   the term "court" shall cover all the authorities in the Member States with jurisdiction in the matters falling within the scope of this Regulation pursuant to Article 1;

2.   the term "judge" shall mean the judge or an official having powers equivalent to those of a judge in the matters falling within the scope of the Regulation;

3.   the term "Member State" shall mean all Member States with the exception of Denmark;

4.   the term "judgment" shall mean a divorce, legal separation or marriage annulment, as well as a judgment relating to parental responsibility, pronounced by a court of a Member State, whatever the judgment may be called, including a decree, order or decision;

5.   the term "Member State of origin" shall mean the Member State where the judgment to be enforced was issued;

---

[14] At the time of the adoption of this Regulation, Art. 5(2) of the then Brussels-I Regulation governed jurisdiction for maintenance obligations, but left the matter of the applicable substantive law to be determined by the national court on the basis of its national conflicts law. Regulation No. 4/2009, p. 1187, *infra*, replaced Art. 5(2) of the Brussels-I Regulation with respect to jurisdiction and now provides EU-wide rules for the determination of the applicable substantive law.

[15] Art. 1(2) of the 2019 Recast Regulation also excludes provisional measures ordered ex parte unless notice was given.

6.   the term "Member State of enforcement" shall mean the Member State where enforcement of the judgment is sought;

7.   the term "parental responsibility" shall mean all rights and duties relating to the person or the property of a child which are given to a natural or legal person by judgment, by operation of law or by an agreement having legal effect. The term shall include rights of custody and rights of access;

8.   the term "holder of parental responsibility" shall mean any person having parental responsibility over a child;

9.   the term "rights of custody" shall include rights and duties relating to the care of the person of a child, and in particular the right to determine the child's place of residence;

10.   the term "rights of access" shall include in particular the right to take a child to a place other than his or her habitual residence for a limited period of time;

11.   the term "wrongful removal or retention" shall mean a child's removal or retention where:

   (a)   it is in breach of rights of custody acquired by judgment or by operation of law or by an agreement having legal effect under the law of the Member State where the child was habitually resident immediately before the removal or retention;

and

   (b)   provided that, at the time of removal or retention, the rights of custody were actually exercised, either jointly or alone, or would have been so exercised but for the removal or retention. Custody shall be considered to be exercised jointly when, pursuant to a judgment or by operation of law, one holder of parental responsibility cannot decide on the child's place of residence without the consent of another holder of parental responsibility.

CHAPTER II

JURISDICTION

SECTION 1

Divorce, legal separation and marriage annulment

Article 3

General jurisdiction

1.   In matters relating to divorce, legal separation or marriage annulment, jurisdiction shall lie with the courts of the Member State

   (a)   in whose territory:

      —   the spouses are habitually resident, or

      —   the spouses were last habitually resident, insofar as one of them still resides there, or

      —   the respondent is habitually resident, or

      —   in the event of a joint application, either of the spouses is habitually resident, or

      —   the applicant is habitually resident if he or she resided there for at least a year immediately before the application as made, or

      —   the applicant is habitually resident if he or she resided there for at least six months immediately before the application was made and is either a national of the Member State in question or, in the case of the United Kingdom and Ireland, has his or her "domicile" there;

(b)   of the nationality of both spouses or, in the case of the United Kingdom and Ireland, of the "domicile" of both spouses.

2.   For the purpose of this Regulation, "domicile" shall have the same meaning as it has under the legal systems of the United Kingdom and Ireland.

. . .

Article 5

Conversion of legal separation into divorce

Without prejudice to Article 3, a court of a Member State that has given a judgment on a legal separation shall also have jurisdiction for converting that judgment into a divorce, if the law of that Member State so provides.

Article 6

Exclusive nature of jurisdiction under Articles 3, 4 and 5

A spouse who:

(a)   is habitually resident in the territory of a Member State; or

(b)   is a national of a Member State, or, in the case of the United Kingdom and Ireland, has his or her "domicile" in the territory of one of the latter Member States,

may be sued in another Member State only in accordance with Articles 3, 4 and 5.

Article 7

Residual jurisdiction

1.   Where no court of a Member State has jurisdiction pursuant to Articles 3, 4 and 5, jurisdiction shall be determined, in each Member State, by the laws of that State.

2.   As against a respondent who is not habitually resident and is not either a national of a Member State or, in the case of the United Kingdom and Ireland, does not have his "domicile" within the territory of one of the latter Member States, any national of a Member State who is habitually resident within the territory of another Member State may, like the nationals of that State, avail himself of the rules of jurisdiction applicable in that State.

SECTION 2

Parental responsibility

Article 8

General jurisdiction

1.   The courts of a Member State shall have jurisdiction in matters of parental responsibility over a child who is habitually resident in that Member State at the time the court is seised.

2.   Paragraph 1 shall be subject to the provisions of Articles 9, 10 and 12.

Article 9

Continuing jurisdiction of the child's former habitual residence

1.   Where a child moves lawfully from one Member State to another and acquires a new habitual residence there, the courts of the Member State of the child's former habitual residence shall, by way of exception to Article 8, retain jurisdiction during a three-month period following the move for the purpose of modifying a judgment on access rights issued in that Member State before the child moved, where the holder

of access rights pursuant to the judgment on access rights continues to have his or her habitual residence in the Member State of the child's former habitual residence.

2.   Paragraph 1 shall not apply if the holder of access rights referred to in paragraph 1 has accepted the jurisdiction of the courts of the Member State of the child's new habitual residence by participating in proceedings before those courts without contesting their jurisdiction.

Article 10

Jurisdiction in cases of child abduction

In case of wrongful removal or retention of the child, the courts of the Member State where the child was habitually resident immediately before the wrongful removal or retention shall retain their jurisdiction until the child has acquired a habitual residence in another Member State and:

(a)   each person, institution or other body having rights of custody has acquiesced in the removal or retention;

or

(b)   the child has resided in that other Member State for a period of at least one year after the person, institution or other body having rights of custody has had or should have had knowledge of the whereabouts of the child and the child is settled in his or her new environment and at least one of the following conditions is met:

(i)   within one year after the holder of rights of custody has had or should have had knowledge of the whereabouts of the child, no request for return has been lodged before the competent authorities of the Member State where the child has been removed or is being retained;

(ii)   a request for return lodged by the holder of rights of custody has been withdrawn and no new request has been lodged within the time limit set in paragraph (i);

(iii)   a case before the court in the Member State where the child was habitually resident immediately before the wrongful removal or retention has been closed pursuant to Article 11(7);

(iv)   a judgment on custody that does not entail the return of the child has been issued by the courts of the Member State where the child was habitually resident immediately before the wrongful removal or retention.

Article 11

Return of the child

1.   Where a person, institution or other body having rights of custody applies to the competent authorities in a Member State to deliver a judgment on the basis of the Hague Convention of 25 October 1980 on the Civil Aspects of International Child Abduction (hereinafter "the 1980 Hague Convention"), in order to obtain the return of a child that has been wrongfully removed or retained in a Member State other than the Member State where the child was habitually resident immediately before the wrongful removal or retention, paragraphs 2 to 8 shall apply.

2.   When applying Articles 12 and 13 of the 1980 Hague Convention, it shall be ensured that the child is given the opportunity to be heard during the proceedings unless this appears inappropriate having regard to his or her age or degree of maturity.

3.   A court to which an application for return of a child is made as mentioned in paragraph 1 shall act expeditiously in proceedings on the application, using the most expeditious procedures available in national law.

Without prejudice to the first subparagraph, the court shall, except where exceptional circumstances make this impossible, issue its judgment no later than six weeks after the application is lodged.

4.   A court cannot refuse to return a child on the basis of Article 13b of the 1980 Hague Convention if it is established that adequate arrangements have been made to secure the protection of the child after his or her return.

5.   A court cannot refuse to return a child unless the person who requested the return of the child has been given an opportunity to be heard.

6.   If a court has issued an order on non-return pursuant to Article 13 of the 1980 Hague Convention, the court must immediately either directly or through its central authority, transmit a copy of the court order on non-return and of the relevant documents, in particular a transcript of the hearings before the court, to the court with jurisdiction or central authority in the Member State where the child was habitually resident immediately before the wrongful removal or retention, as determined by national law. The court shall receive all the mentioned documents within one month of the date of the non-return order.

7.   Unless the courts in the Member State where the child was habitually resident immediately before the wrongful removal or retention have already been seised by one of the parties, the court or central authority that receives the information mentioned in paragraph 6 must notify it to the parties and invite them to make submissions to the court, in accordance with national law, within three months of the date of notification so that the court can examine the question of custody of the child.

Without prejudice to the rules on jurisdiction contained in this Regulation, the court shall close the case if no submissions have been received by the court within the time limit.

8.   Notwithstanding a judgment of non-return pursuant to Article 13 of the 1980 Hague Convention, any subsequent judgment which requires the return of the child issued by a court having jurisdiction under this Regulation shall be enforceable in accordance with Section 4 of Chapter III below in order to secure the return of the child.

Article 12

Prorogation of jurisdiction

1.   The courts of a Member State exercising jurisdiction by virtue of Article 3 on an application for divorce, legal separation or marriage annulment shall have jurisdiction in any matter relating to parental responsibility connected with that application where:

(a)   at least one of the spouses has parental responsibility in relation to the child;

and

(b)   the jurisdiction of the courts has been accepted expressly or otherwise in an unequivocal manner by the spouses and by the holders of parental responsibility, at the time the court is seised, and is in the superior interests of the child.

2.   The jurisdiction conferred in paragraph 1 shall cease soon as:

(a)   the judgment allowing or refusing the application for divorce, legal separation or marriage annulment has become final;

(b)   in those cases where proceedings in relation to parental responsibility are still pending on the date referred to in (a), a judgment in these proceedings has become final;

(c)   the proceedings referred to in (a) and (b) have come to an end for another reason.

3.   The courts of a Member State shall also have jurisdiction in relation to parental responsibility in proceedings other than those referred to in paragraph 1 where:

(a)   the child has a substantial connection with that Member State, in particular by virtue of the fact that one of the holders of parental responsibility is habitually resident in that Member State or that the child is a national of that Member State;

and

(b)   the jurisdiction of the courts has been accepted expressly or otherwise in an unequivocal manner by all the parties to the proceedings at the time the court is seised and is in the best interests of the child.

4.   Where the child has his or her habitual residence in the territory of a third State which is not a contracting party to the Hague Convention of 19 October 1996 on jurisdiction, applicable law, recognition, enforcement and cooperation in respect of parental responsibility and measures for the protection of children, jurisdiction under this Article shall be deemed to be in the child's interest, in particular if it is found impossible to hold proceedings in the third State in question.

Article 13

Jurisdiction based on the child's presence

1.   Where a child's habitual residence cannot be established and jurisdiction cannot be determined on the basis of Article 12, the courts of the Member State where the child is present shall have jurisdiction.

2.   Paragraph 1 shall also apply to refugee children or children internationally displaced because of disturbances occurring in their country.

Article 14

Residual jurisdiction

Where no court of a Member State has jurisdiction pursuant to Articles 8 to 13, jurisdiction shall be determined, in each Member State, by the laws of that State.

Article 15

Transfer to a court better placed to hear the case

1.   By way of exception, the courts of a Member State having jurisdiction as to the substance of the matter may, if they consider that a court of another Member State, with which the child has a particular connection, would be better placed to hear the case, or a specific part thereof, and where this is in the best interests of the child:

(a)   stay the case or the part thereof in question and invite the parties to introduce a request before the court of that other Member State in accordance with paragraph 4; or

(b)   request a court of another Member State to assume jurisdiction in accordance with paragraph 5.

2.   Paragraph 1 shall apply:

(a)   upon application from a party; or

(b)   of the court's own motion; or

(c)   upon application from a court of another Member State with which the child has a particular connection, in accordance with paragraph 3.

A transfer made of the court's own motion or by application of a court of another Member State must be accepted by at least one of the parties.

3.   The child shall be considered to have a particular connection to a Member State as mentioned in paragraph 1, if that Member State:

(a)   has become the habitual residence of the child after the court referred to in paragraph 1 was seised; or

(b)   is the former habitual residence of the child; or

(c)   is the place of the child's nationality; or

(d)   is the habitual residence of a holder of parental responsibility; or

(e)   is the place where property of the child is located and the case concerns measures for the protection of the child relating to the administration, conservation or disposal of this property.

4.   The court of the Member State having jurisdiction as to the substance of the matter shall set a time limit by which the courts of that other Member State shall be seised in accordance with paragraph 1.

If the courts are not seised by that time, the court which has been seised shall continue to exercise jurisdiction in accordance with Articles 8 to 14.

5.   The courts of that other Member State may, where due to the specific circumstances of the case, this is in the best interests of the child, accept jurisdiction within six weeks of their seisure in accordance with paragraph 1(a) or 1(b). In this case, the court first seised shall decline jurisdiction. Otherwise, the court first seised shall continue to exercise jurisdiction in accordance with Articles 8 to 14.

6.   The courts shall cooperate for the purposes of this Article, either directly or through the central authorities designated pursuant to Article 53.

SECTION 3

Common provisions

. . .

Article 17

Examination as to jurisdiction

Where a court of a Member State is seised of a case over which it has no jurisdiction under this Regulation and over which a court of another Member State has jurisdiction by virtue of this Regulation, it shall declare of its own motion that it has no jurisdiction.

Article 18

Examination as to admissibility

1.   Where a respondent habitually resident in a State other than the Member State where the action was brought does not enter an appearance, the court with jurisdiction shall stay the proceedings so long as it is not shown that the respondent has been able to receive the document instituting the proceedings or an equivalent document in sufficient time to enable him to arrange for his defence, or that all necessary steps have been taken to this end.

. . .

Article 19

Lis pendens and dependent actions

1.   Where proceedings relating to divorce, legal separation or marriage annulment between the same parties are brought before courts of different Member States, the court second seised shall of its own motion stay its proceedings until such time as the jurisdiction of the court first seised is established.

2.   Where proceedings relating to parental responsibility relating to the same child and involving the same cause of action are brought before courts of different Member States, the court second seised shall of its own motion stay its proceedings until such time as the jurisdiction of the court first seised is established.

3.   Where the jurisdiction of the court first seised is established, the court second seised shall decline jurisdiction in favour of that court.

In that case, the party who brought the relevant action before the court second seised may bring that action before the court first seised.

Article 20

Provisional, including protective, measures

1.   In urgent cases, the provisions of this Regulation shall not prevent the courts of a Member State from taking such provisional, including protective, measures in respect of persons or assets in that State as may be available under the law of that Member State, even if, under this Regulation, the court of another Member State has jurisdiction as to the substance of the matter.

2.   The measures referred to in paragraph 1 shall cease to apply when the court of the Member State having jurisdiction under this Regulation as to the substance of the matter has taken the measures it considers appropriate.

CHAPTER III

RECOGNITION AND ENFORCEMENT

SECTION 1

Recognition

Article 21

Recognition of a judgment

1.   A judgment given in a Member State shall be recognised in the other Member States without any special procedure being required.

. . .

3.   Without prejudice to Section 4 of this Chapter, any interested party may, in accordance with the procedures provided for in Section 2 of this Chapter, apply for decision that the judgment be or not be recognised.

The local jurisdiction of the court appearing in the list notified by each Member State to the Commission pursuant to Article 68 shall be determined by the internal law of the Member State in which proceedings for recognition or non-recognition are brought.

4.   Where the recognition of a judgment is raised as an incidental question in a court of a Member State, that court may determine that issue.

Article 22

Grounds of non-recognition for judgments relating to divorce, legal separation or marriage annulment

A judgment relating to a divorce, legal separation or marriage annulment shall not be recognised:

(a)   if such recognition is manifestly contrary to the public policy of the Member State in which recognition is sought;

(b)   where it was given in default of appearance, if the respondent was not served with the document which instituted the proceedings or with an equivalent document in sufficient time and in such a way as to enable the respondent to arrange for his or her defence unless it is determined that the respondent has accepted the judgment unequivocally;

(c)   if it is irreconcilable with a judgment given in proceedings between the same parties in the Member State in which recognition is sought; or

(d)   if it is irreconcilable with an earlier judgment given in another Member State or in a non-Member State between the same parties, provided that the earlier judgment fulfils the conditions necessary for its recognition in the Member State in which recognition is sought.

Article 23

Grounds of non-recognition for judgments relating to parental responsibility

A judgment relating to parental responsibility shall not be recognised:

(a)   if such recognition is manifestly contrary to the public policy of the Member State in which recognition is sought taking into account the best interests of the child;

(b)   if it was given, except in case of urgency, without the child having been given an opportunity to be heard, in violation of fundamental principles of procedure of the Member State in which recognition is sought;

(c)   where it was given in default of appearance if the person in default was not served with the document which instituted the proceedings or with an equivalent document in sufficient time and in such a way as to enable that person to arrange for his or her defence unless it is determined that such person has accepted the judgment unequivocally;

(d)   on the request of any person claiming that the judgment infringes his or her parental responsibility, if it was given without such person having been given an opportunity to be heard;

(e)   if it is irreconcilable with a later judgment relating to parental responsibility given in the Member State in which recognition is sought;

(f)   if it is irreconcilable with a later judgment relating to parental responsibility given in another Member State or in the non-Member State of the habitual residence of the child provided that the later judgment fulfills the conditions necessary for its recognition in the Member State in which recognition is sought;

or

(g)   if the procedure laid down in Article 56 has not been complied with.

Article 24

Prohibition of review of jurisdiction of the court of origin

The jurisdiction of the court of the Member State of origin may not be reviewed. The test of public policy referred to in Articles 22(a) and 23(a) may not be applied to the rules relating to jurisdiction set out in Articles 3 to 14.

Article 25

Differences in applicable law

The recognition of a judgment may not be refused because the law of the Member State in which such recognition is sought would not allow divorce, legal separation or marriage annulment on the same facts.

Article 26

Non-review as to substance

Under no circumstances may a judgment be reviewed as to its substance.

. . .

SECTION 2

Application for a declaration of enforceability

Article 28

Enforceable judgments

1. A judgment on the exercise of parental responsibility in respect of a child given in a Member State which is enforceable in that Member State and has been served shall be enforced in another Member State when, on the application of any interested party, it has been declared enforceable there.

2. However, in the United Kingdom, such a judgment shall be enforced in England and Wales, in Scotland or in Northern Ireland only when, on the application of any interested party, it has been registered for enforcement in that part of the United Kingdom.

Article 29

Jurisdiction of local courts

1. An application for a declaration of enforceability shall be submitted to the court appearing in the list notified by each Member State to the Commission pursuant to Article 68.

2. The local jurisdiction shall be determined by reference to the place of habitual residence of the person against whom enforcement is sought or by reference to the habitual residence of any child to whom the application relates.

Where neither of the places referred to in the first subparagraph can be found in the Member State of enforcement, the local jurisdiction shall be determined by reference to the place of enforcement.

Article 30

Procedure

1. The procedure for making the application shall be governed by the law of the Member State of enforcement.

. . .

SECTION 4

Enforceability of certain judgments concerning rights of access and of certain judgments which require the return of the child

Article 40

Scope

1.   This Section shall apply to:

(a)   rights of access;

and

(b)   the return of a child entailed by a judgment given pursuant to Article 11(8).

2.   The provisions of this Section shall not prevent a holder of parental responsibility from seeking recognition and enforcement of a judgment in accordance with the provisions in Sections 1 and 2 of this Chapter.

Article 41

Rights of access

1.   The rights of access referred to in Article 40(1)(a) granted in an enforceable judgment given in a Member State shall be recognised and enforceable in another Member State without the need for a declaration of enforceability and without any possibility of opposing its recognition if the judgment has been certified in the Member State of origin in accordance with paragraph 2.

Even if national law does not provide for enforceability by operation of law of a judgment granting access rights, the court of origin may declare that the judgment shall been enforceable, notwithstanding any appeal.

2.   The judge of origin shall issue the certificate referred to in paragraph 1 using the standard form in Annex III (certificate concerning rights of access) only if:

(a)   where the judgment was given in default, the person defaulting was served with the document which instituted the proceedings or with an equivalent document in sufficient time and in such a way as to enable that person to arrange for his or her defense, or, the person has been served with the document but not in compliance with these conditions, it is nevertheless established that he or she accepted the decision unequivocally;

(b)   all parties concerned were given an opportunity to be heard;

and

(c)   the child was given an opportunity to be heard, unless a hearing was considered inappropriate having regard to his or her age or degree of maturity.

The certificate shall be completed in the language of the judgment.

3.   Where the rights of access involve a cross-border situation at the time of the delivery of the judgment, the certificate shall be issued ex officio when the judgment becomes enforceable, even if only provisionally. If the situation subsequently acquires a cross-border character, the certificate shall be issued at the request of one of the parties.

Article 42

Return of the child

1.   The return of a child referred to in Article 40(1)(b) entailed by an enforceable judgment given in a Member State shall be recognised and enforceable in another Member State without the need for a declaration of enforceability and without any

possibility of opposing its recognition if the judgment has been certified in the Member State of origin in accordance with paragraph 2.

Even if national law does not provide for enforceability by operation of law, notwithstanding any appeal, of a judgment requiring the return of the child mentioned in Article 11(b)(8), the court of origin may declare the judgment enforceable.

2.   The judge of origin who delivered the judgment referred to in Article 40(1)(b) shall issue the certificate referred to in paragraph 1 only if:

(a)   the child was given an opportunity to be heard, unless a hearing was considered inappropriate having regard to his or her age or degree of maturity;

(b)   the parties were given an opportunity to be heard; and

(c)   the court has taken into account in issuing its judgment the reasons for and evidence underlying the order issued pursuant to Article 13 of the 1980 Hague Convention.

In the event that the court or any other authority takes measures to ensure the protection of the child after its return to the State of habitual residence, the certificate shall contain details of such measures.

The judge of origin shall of his or her own motion issue that certificate using the standard form in Annex IV (certificate concerning return of the child(ren)).

The certificate shall be completed in the language of the judgment.

. . .

SECTION 6

Other provisions

Article 47

Enforcement procedure

1.   The enforcement procedure is governed by the law of the Member State of enforcement.

2.   Any judgment delivered by a court of another Member State and declared to be enforceable in accordance with Section 2 or certified in accordance with Article 41(1) or Article 42(1) shall be enforced in the Member State of enforcement in the same conditions as if it had been delivered in that Member State.

In particular, a judgment which has been certified according to Article 41(1) or Article 42(1) cannot be enforced if it is irreconcilable with a subsequent enforceable judgment.

Article 48

Practical arrangements for the exercise of rights of access

1.   The courts of the Member State of enforcement may make practical arrangements for organising the exercise of rights of access, if the necessary arrangements have not or have not sufficiently been made in the judgment delivered by the courts of the Member State having jurisdiction as to the substance of the matter and provided the essential elements of this judgment are respected.

2.   The practical arrangements made pursuant to paragraph 1 shall cease to apply pursuant to a later judgment by the courts of the Member State having jurisdiction as to the substance of the matter.

. . .

Article 50

Legal aid

An applicant who, in the Member State of origin, has benefited from complete or partial legal aid or exemption from costs or expenses shall be entitled, in the procedures provided for in Articles 21, 28, 41, 42 and 48 to benefit from the most favourable legal aid or the most extensive exemption from costs and expenses provided for by the law of the Member State of enforcement.

. . .

CHAPTER V
RELATIONS WITH OTHER
INSTRUMENTS

. . .

Article 61

Relation with the Hague Convention of 19 October 1996[16] on Jurisdiction, Applicable law, Recognition, Enforcement and Cooperation in Respect of Parental Responsibility and Measures for the Protection of Children

As concerns the relation with the Hague Convention of 19 October 1996 on Jurisdiction, Applicable law, Recognition, Enforcement and Cooperation in Respect of Parental Responsibility and Measures for the Protection of Children, this Regulation shall apply:

(a)   where the child concerned has his or her habitual residence on the territory of a Member State;

(b)   as concerns the recognition and enforcement of a judgment given in a court of a Member State on the territory of another Member State, even if the child concerned has his or her habitual residence on the territory of a third State which a contracting Party to the said Convention.

Article 62

Scope of effects

1.   The agreements and conventions referred to in Articles 59(1), 60 and 61 shall continue to have effect in relation to matters not governed by this Regulation.

2.   The conventions mentioned in Article 60, in particular the 1980 Hague Convention, continue to produce effects between the Member States which are party thereto, in compliance with Article 60.

. . .

NOTES

The following Notes comment on the 2003 Brussels IIa Regulation. The 2019 Brussels IIa Recast Regulation (p. 1169, n. 10, supra) contains more detailed provisions dealing with international child abduction, both within

---

[16] As of February 2017, the Convention was in force in Albania, Armenia, Australia, Austria, Belgium, Bulgaria, Croatia, Cyprus, Czech Republic, Denmark, Dominican Republic, Ecuador, Estonia, Finland, France, Georgia, Germany, Greece, Hungary, Ireland, Italy, Latvia, Lithuania, Luxembourg, Malta, Monaco, Montenegro, Morocco, Netherlands, Norway, Poland, Portugal, Romania, Slovakia, Slovenia, Spain, Sweden, Switzerland, Turkey, Ukraine, United Kingdom, and Uruguay. It has also been signed, but not yet ratified, by Argentina and the United States.

the European Union and with respect to non-member states, and implementing the rules and policies of the Hague Convention (p. 997, supra).

1.   *Scope.* The Regulation combines, in a single instrument, provisions for jurisdiction and recognition of decisions for divorce and custody, thereby acknowledging that "the rules on parental responsibility often arise in the context of matrimonial proceedings" (introductory recitals ¶ 6). Of course, this is true everywhere else as well. To make the combination of both subjects work, rules of jurisdiction must be circumscribed narrowly and uniformly. Even so, there may be jurisdiction for divorce in a given case (see, e.g., Art 3(1)(a), sixth situation—unilateral divorce) when it would not be appropriate to allow the court to deal with custody. Separate rules therefore deal with custody (Art. 8 et seq.) and do not necessarily coincide with those for divorce jurisdiction. Similarly, a custody law must address jurisdiction for the modification of an original decree when the parties' territorial affiliations have changed. The Regulation's rules for these questions may therefore well diverge from those for divorce jurisdiction.

In recognition of the fact that different states confer jurisdiction for family law matters to different types of institutions, the 2003 Regulation and the 2019 Recast define "court" broadly. The Introduction to the 2019 Brussels IIa Recast Regulation states that the term also covers administrative agencies and "others" (such as notaries) that "exercise authority." Id at ¶ (14). Note that a notary in European legal systems is usually a member of a limited specialized bar of legal professionals, rather than someone who only authenticates signatures.

The Regulation addresses jurisdiction and recognition of decisions, *not* substantive law. The grounds for divorce (or even the absence of divorce in a particular state) remain matters for national law. However, national law, and underlying national social values, are affected by the requirement that a divorce decreed by a court with jurisdiction by Regulation standards is entitled to recognition in all other member states, even in those with different substantive rules on divorce (see Art. 25, infra). Regulation No. 1259/2010, infra p. 1227, provides the conflicts rules for the determination of the applicable national substantive law.

As to custody, the Regulation is no longer restricted (as was its predecessor) to the parental responsibility "for the children of both spouses," but deals generally with custody and other rights (such as the right to access). The Regulation's distinguishing feature is its overriding concern for the "best interests of the child." It finds expression in the "criterion of proximity" (introductory recital ¶ 12), exemplified by provisions like Art. 15.

The Regulation does not define who has custody rights. This is a matter to be determined by the appropriate national court under national laws. Thus, when an unmarried father sought the return of his child to Ireland whom the mother had taken to England, the European Court held that Ireland was entitled to require a judicial determination of the acquisition of custody rights by an unmarried father before the child's removal could be considered to be a violation of Art. 2(11) of the Regulation. Case C-400/10 (J.McB. v. L.E.), [2010] ECR I-8985, (4-2010) Eur. Legal F. I-195 (Oct. 5,

2010). The Court noted, however, that, for purposes of the application of the Regulation, as well as under the European Convention of Human Rights, the natural father must have the means, under national law, to request, and to obtain custody rights, which go to "the very essence of the right ... to a private and family life," and that denial of such a possibility to obtain custody rights would be a violation of Art. 14, in combination with Art. 8, of the ECHR. Id. at paras. 55 and 56.

Among other things (see Art. 1(3)), the Regulation does not apply to adoption and to maintenance obligations (the latter are dealt with by Regulation (EC) No. 4/2009, summarized infra, p. 1189.

In the first case to reach the Court of Justice under this Regulation, a Swedish public agency had ordered a child to be removed from its home and placed with a foster family. The child was removed to Finland by its mother, where a court ordered its return. Two of the questions presented to the Court concerned the applicability of the Regulation: was the subject matter of the case (placement of the child in foster care) encompassed by Art. 1(2), and did the case involve a "civil matter" (Art. 1(1))? The Court answered both questions in the affirmative: Art. 1(2) contains a non-exclusive list of subjects ("in particular") and is to be construed broadly, in keeping with Introductory Recital (5); placement of a child in foster care for its protection is a "civil matter." Case C-435/06 (Applicant C), [2007] ECR I-10141 (Nov. 27, 2007). See comments by Pirrung, Auslegung der Brüssel IIa-Verordnung in Sorgerechtssachen, in Baetge, von Hein & von Hinden (eds.), Die richtige Ordnung-Festschrift für Kropholler 399 (2008).

Like the Brussels I Regulation, and unlike the Rome I and Rome II Regulations (on applicable law in contract and tort, respectively), the Regulation applies only with respect to cases between parties who are habitually resident in a member state; it does not have "universal application" (see Art. 2 of the other two instruments named), and therefore does not displace national law with respect to third states.

2.   The provisions for jurisdiction for divorce generally reflect the approaches of national law (Art. 3), including jurisdiction based the forum's nationality of both spouses (Art. 3(1)(b)). Divorce decrees, as mentioned, are entitled to recognition elsewhere in the Union, without review as to substance (Art. 26, see also Art. 31(3)). The usual grounds for non-recognition apply, including that the other state's judgment is "manifestly contrary to [the recognizing state's] public policy" (Art. 23(a)). But "public policy" may not serve as a vehicle to reexamine the first court's jurisdiction (Art. 24) or to deny recognition because of differences in the law applied by the first court, which is particularly important in a sensitive area like divorce (Art. 25). For comparative comment and analysis, see Silberman, Rethinking Rules of Conflict of Laws in Marriage and Divorce in the United States: What Can We Learn From Europe?, 82 Tul. L.Rev. 1999 (2008).

The "Rome III" Regulation (p. 1227, infra) permits the parties to enter into a choice-of-court agreement. In its Explanatory Memorandum, the Commission states its view that the ability to select the applicable law would "enhance access to court for spouses who are of different nationalities. The rule . . . applies regardless of whether the couple lives in a Member State or in a third State."

Though uncommon, recognition of a divorce decree may be the subject of an independent enforcement proceeding. More likely, however, is that it will be an incidental question, for instance, as part of a custody or support action. See Art. 21(3) and (4). In cases of support claims, it should be noted, the Brussels II Regulation applies for purposes of divorce recognition, while the Brussels I Regulation applies to maintenance.

3.   The custody provisions, as stated, focus on the best interests of the child. While European law generally does not recognize a doctrine of *forum non conveniens* (since competing interests are supposedly reflected in the stated jurisdictional rules), Article 15 does envision transfer to a more convenient forum, not only upon application by a party, but also upon request of a court seeking to exercise jurisdiction. The focus on the "best interest of the child" finds particular expression in the provision that a judgment relating to parental responsibility (i.e., a custody decree) "shall not be recognized", if given "without the child having been given an opportunity to be heard" (Art. 23(b)). The 2019 "Brussels IIa Recast Regulation" (p. 1169 n. 10, supra) emphasizes the requirement to hear and thereby the child directly in its Arts. 21 and 39(2).

The "best interests of the child" are also an important consideration when the issue involves potential parallel litigation, which Art.19, the Regulation's *lis pendens* provision, addresses. Does an action for provisional relief in the first court involve the "same cause of action" (Art. 19(2)) as an action seeking custody rights in a second court? It might or it might not: the second court should inquire of the first court and, if no answer has been received within a reasonable time, go ahead an exercise jurisdiction. The duration of a "reasonable time" should take account of the best interests of the child in the light of the circumstances of the particular case. Case C-296/10 (Bianca Purrucker v. Guillermo Vallés Pérez), 2010 E.C.R. I-11163, [2011] O.J. C 013).

Rights of access to the child fall under issues of "parental responsibility" and within the purview of the Regulation. Decisions with respect to the right of access are therefore entitled to recognition. In making right-of-access decisions, the child is to be heard (Art. 41(2)(c)).

The enforcement of custody rights requires effective enforcement, including return of a child wrongfully held over after a visit or even abducted with the intent to relitigate custody elsewhere. The Hague Convention on the Civil Aspects of International Child Abduction[17] calls for the return of the child in these circumstances and provides a mechanism. The Regulation's provisions (Arts. 11, 40 et seq.) are modeled after the Hague Convention, but are stricter and, to that extent, take precedence over the Convention within the Union (see Art. 11(4), (6), (8), and Art. 60(e)). The right of access similarly is reinforced by a provision on the "return of the child" (Art. 42). Annexes

---

[17] P. 995, supra.

(not reproduced) specify the content of documentation ("certificates") to be used for transborder enforcement proceedings.

The 2019 revision—the "Brussels IIa Recast" Regulation (p. 1227, n. 10, supra)—devotes three subchapters (III, IV, and VI) to detailed provisions for the return of a child after wrongful removal from one EU member state to another and from a non-member state to a member state, in both cases with particular attention to the Hague Convention (p. 997, supra). In the 2003 Regulation, in effect until August 2022, Arts. 61 et seq. deal in far shorter fashion with the interrelation of EU and Hague Convention law.

4.   The concept of "habitual residence" of a child is central for the determination of jurisdiction to award or to modify custody, including for the determination of whether the child was wrongfully removed to the forum state. What constitutes "habitual residence?" The European Court provided the following guidance: "The concept of 'habitual residence', for the purposes of Articles 8 and 10 . . . must be interpreted as meaning that such residence corresponds to the place which reflects some degree of integration by the child in a social and family environment. To that end, where the situation concerned is that of an infant who has been staying with her mother only a few days in a Member State—other than that of her habitual residence— to which she has been removed, the factors which must be taken into consideration include, first, the duration, regularity, conditions and reasons for the stay in the territory of that Member State and for the mother's move to that State and, second, with particular reference to the child's age, the mother's geographic and family origins and the family and social connections which the mother and child have with that Member State. It is for the national court to establish the habitual residence of the child, taking account of all the circumstances of fact specific to each individual case. If the application of the abovementioned tests were, in the case in the main proceedings, to lead to the conclusion that the child's habitual residence cannot be established, which court has jurisdiction would have to be determined on the basis of the criterion of the child's presence, under Article 13 of the Regulation." Case C-497/10 (Barbara Mercredi v. Richard Chaffe), [2011] O.J. C 055/17.

5.   *Legal Aid.* Article 50 provides that a person who has benefited from legal aid in the country of origin shall benefit from the "most favorable" provisions for legal aid in the state of enforcement (lest he or she hold an empty title for lack of means to enforce it). See also Arts. 49 and 51. How about an indigent person's ability to pursue an initial action (for divorce or custody) in another member state? Council Directive 2002/8/EC on legal aid also applies to proceedings under the Brussels IIa Regulation.

6.   *Relation to Other Instruments.* The member states are parties to a number of multilateral and bilateral conventions, including Concordats with the Holy See (Art. 63). Chapter V (Art. 59 et seq.) defines the Regulation's relationship to these instruments. The provision for its precedence, within the Union, over the Hague Child Abduction Convention (Art. 60(e)) was noted earlier.

7. For comment, see Maire Ni Shuilleabháin, Ten Years of European Family Law: Retrospective Reflections from a Common Law Perspective, 59 Int'l & Comp. L.Q. 1021 (2010).

8. See also the Proposal for a Regulation on Jurisdiction, Applicable Law, and the Recognition and Enforcement of Decisions regarding the Property Consequences of Registered Partnerships, p. 1241, infra.

2. MAINTENANCE OBLIGATIONS COUNCIL REGULATION (EC) NO. 4/2009 ON JURISDICTION, APPLICABLE LAW, RECOGNITION AND ENFORCEMENT OF DECISIONS AND COOPERATION IN MATTERS RELATING TO MAINTENANCE OBLIGATIONS

[2009] Official Journal L 7/1
(Textual Summary)

Introduction

Maintenance obligations are the subject of a number of Hague conventions, both with respect to recognition and enforcement of decisions as well as the applicable law. Two new Hague instruments are designed to consolidate and revise Hague convention law in these matters: the Convention of 23 November 2007 on the International Recovery of Child Support and Other Forms of Family Maintenance and the Protocol of 23 November 2007 on the Law Applicable to Maintenance Obligations. Of these, the former provides a mechanism, through the designation of cooperating "Central Authorities," for the establishment of maintenance obligations in support of children and for the enforcement of maintenance decisions for child or spousal support. As of 2020, the Convention was in force in forty-two countries. The European Union joined in 2014 on behalf of all of its member states. Because it left the European Union, the United Kingdom acceded anew in April 2020.

The European Union had participated in the work of the Hague Conference on these two instruments. Its aim was to adopt the second of these, the Protocol on the Law Applicable to Maintenance Obligations, as part of European law. See Regulation No. 4/2009, Recital (20). This objective is accomplished by the European Union's signing and adopting the Protocol on behalf of participating member states and providing, by Regulation, for the applicability of its provisions in those member states.

Council Regulation No. 4/2009 makes comprehensive provision for the jurisdiction of courts to establish maintenance obligations, for the law applicable to them, and for the recognition and enforcement of decisions. It also provides mechanisms for cooperation between and among national authorities and for legal aid. The Regulation's scope—as well as that of the 2007 Hague Protocol, which it incorporates by means of its Art. 15— is wide and deliberately left undefined: it applies to "maintenance obligations arising from a family relationship, parentage, marriage or affinity." Art. 1(1). The focus is on maintenance, not on the underlying relationship. The latter remains a matter of national law, for instance, whether informal domestic relationships or formalized same-sex relationships give rise to maintenance obligations. Art. 22 emphasizes that recognition of a maintenance decision "shall not in any way imply the recognition of the family relationship, parentage, marriage or affinity underlying the maintenance obligation which gave rise to the decision." See also Recitals (21) and (25).

As of June 18, 2011, the Regulation replaced the maintenance provision (Art. 5 (2)) of the original Brussels I Regulation; the European Enforcement Order Regulation will no longer apply to maintenance obligations. Art. 68 (1)–(2). Of the member states that may opt out of legislation of this type, Denmark and the United Kingdom exercised that right. Recitals (47) and (48). Ireland, on the other hand, participated in the Regulation, Recital (46), and the United Kingdom later declared its acceptance. Since the application of the Brussels I Regulation was extended to Denmark by agreement between it and the Community (p. 1136, supra), Art. 5(2) of the original Brussels I Regulation will continue in force as to Denmark.

Jurisdiction and Recognition and Enforcement of Decisions

Jurisdiction. The jurisdictional provisions of the Regulation are based on those of Arts. 2, 5(2), 23, and 24 of the Brussels I Regulation, but broaden them considerably. While Art. 5(2) of Brussels I provides for specific jurisdiction, in the courts of the maintenance creditor's habitual residence, over a defendant "domiciled in a Member State," Art. 3(b) of the new Regulation drops the requirement that the defendant have such a connection (or any other) to a member state; it focuses on the creditor's habitual residence alone. In addition, a court has jurisdiction of maintenance claims that are ancillary to status (e.g., divorce) or custody cases over which it has jurisdiction "according to its own law" (for instance, in a case involving a non-EU defendant to whom the Brussels II Regulation does not apply). Art. 3(c) and (d). Also new is a provision for "jurisdiction by necessity," i.e., when no court of a member state has jurisdiction otherwise and "proceedings cannot reasonably be brought or conducted or would be impossible in a third State." In these circumstances, however, the dispute must have "a sufficient connection" to the forum state. Art. 7.

Whether a judgment obtained on the basis of some of these jurisdictional provisions—for instance, one based on Art. 3(b), above—will be recognized outside the EU, e.g., in the United States, is questionable. Nonetheless, any assets that the judgment debtor has in any EU member state will be at risk.

Other provisions address jurisdiction by submission (Art. 5) and on the basis of a choice-of-forum agreement (Art. 4). An interesting provision seeks to prevent forum shopping to improve on a court's decision. There is no jurisdiction to entertain a new action or an action for modification by the debtor so long as the creditor remains habitually resident in the state in which the decision was originally rendered. This restriction is bypassed, however, if the parties have a valid choice-of-forum agreement, if the creditor submits to another court's jurisdiction, or in certain cases involving non-EU decisions. Art. 8.

Recognition and Enforcement. The Regulation deals only with the recognition and enforcement of decisions of member states. As under Brussels Ia, the recognition and enforcement of third-country decisions is a matter of national law in each member state. As to member state decisions, the Regulation distinguishes between those rendered in a state *bound* by the 2007 Hague Protocol and those rendered in states not so bound. The expectation is of course that the Protocol will be in effect in the Community when the Regulation enters into effect: see the Introduction, supra.

With respect to decisions entered by member states bound by the 2007 Hague Protocol, Art. 17 abolishes the need for a national declaration of enforceability (the exequatur), just as had the European Enforcement Order regulation which it replaces. The decision is directly enforceable in other member states, the judgment creditor may invoke protective measures available in the state of enforcement (Art. 18), and review is generally limited to the courts of the state of origin (Arts. 19, 21).

The matter is different if the decision originates in a member state not bound by the 2007 Hague Protocol. The procedure parallels, in all material respects, that of the Brussels I Regulation, including continued use of the exequatur (Arts. 26–27), listing of grounds for the refusal of enforcement (Art. 24), but limiting their invocation to the appeal stage (Arts. 30, 34).

Central Authorities. Chapter VII of the Regulation (Arts. 49 et seq.) provides for cooperation between "Central Authorities" to be established by member states. Upon application of a maintenance creditor, a central authority, with the cooperation of its counterpart in the "requested state," assists with the establishment, enforcement, and modification of maintenance obligations, including, where necessary, the establishment of parentage, and similarly assists a maintenance debtor in securing modification or recognition of a suspension or other limitation of a maintenance obligation (Art. 56).

NOTES

1. Will maintenance decrees based on the jurisdictional provisions of the new Regulation be vulnerable when their recognition is sought in the United States? See supra pp. 1014–1015. Would it affect your answer if the EU court that rendered the decree applied a law other than its own?

2. The Regulation's provisions regarding the law applicable to maintenance obligations are considered at p. 1237, infra.

II. CHOICE OF LAW IN CONTRACT, TORT, AND MATRIMONIAL MATTERS

INTRODUCTORY NOTE

Early attempts, dating to 1972, to establish common rules for choice of law for both contract and tort by treaty proved too difficult and failed. A treaty dealing only with contract was concluded in 1980 ("Rome Convention"). When the Treaty of Amsterdam (1999) conferred additional powers on the Community, work first centered on procedural law, resulting in the enactment of the Brussels I (now Ia) Regulation (p. 1137 supra). The Brussels II and IIa Regulations, p. 1169, supra and other procedural laws followed.

At the same time, work resumed with respect to choice-of-law in contract and tort, with the Rome Convention an obvious candidate for enactment in form of a regulation. It became the "Rome I Regulation." Work progressed more quickly with respect to tort and other non-contractual obligations, so that a regulation on these matters (the "Rome II Regulation") was in fact enacted first. The following reproduces both Regulations, followed by Notes with commentary and further references.

In 2006, the Commission proposed a further Regulation, to be known as "Rome III," to provide rules for the determination of the law applicable to divorce and legal separations. While a number of member states favored adoption of such a regulation, others did not. The European Council therefore utilized its authority under the Treaty on the Functioning of the European Union to authorize "enhanced cooperation" among some, but not all member states (Art. 329). The result was the adoption of the "Rome III" Regulation, applicable in participating member states in divorce proceedings filed after June 21, 2012). It is also reproduced below.

1. CHOICE OF LAW IN CONTRACT REGULATION (EC) NO. 593/2008 OF THE EUROPEAN PARLIAMENT AND OF THE COUNCIL OF THE EUROPEAN UNION ON THE LAW APPLICABLE TO CONTRACTUAL OBLIGATIONS ("ROME I")

[2008] Official Journal L 177/6

. . .

Whereas:

. . .

(6)   The proper functioning of the internal market creates a need, in order to improve the predictability of the outcome of litigation, certainty as to the law applicable and the free movement of judgments, for the conflict-of-law rules in the Member States to designate the same national law irrespective of the country of the court in which an action is brought.

(7)   The substantive scope and the provisions of this Regulation should be consistent with Council Regulation (EC) No 44/2001 of 22 December 2000 on jurisdiction and

the recognition and enforcement of judgments in civil and commercial matters[18] ("Brussels I") and Regulation (EC) No 864/2007 of the European Parliament and of the Council of 11 July 2007 on the law applicable to non-contractual obligations (Rome II)[19].

(8) Family relationships should cover parentage, marriage, affinity and collateral relatives. The reference in Article 1(2) to relationships having comparable effects to marriage and other family relationships should be interpreted in accordance with the law of the Member State in which the court is seised.

(9) Obligations under bills of exchange, cheques and promissory notes and other negotiable instruments should also cover bills of lading to the extent that the obligations under the bill of lading arise out of its negotiable character.

. . .

(11) The parties' freedom to choose the applicable law should be one of the cornerstones of the system of conflict-of-law rules in matters of contractual obligations.

(12) An agreement between the parties to confer on one or more courts or tribunals of a Member State exclusive jurisdiction to determine disputes under the contract should be one of the factors to be taken into account in determining whether a choice of law has been clearly demonstrated.

(13) This Regulation does not preclude parties from incorporating by reference into their contract a non-State body of law or an international convention.

(14) Should the Community adopt, in an appropriate legal instrument, rules of substantive contract law, including standard terms and conditions, such instrument may provide that the parties may choose to apply those rules.

(15) Where a choice of law is made and all other elements relevant to the situation are located in a country other than the country whose law has been chosen, the choice of law should not prejudice the application of provisions of the law of that country which cannot be derogated from by agreement. This rule should apply whether or not the choice of law was accompanied by a choice of court or tribunal. Whereas no substantial change is intended as compared with Article 3(3) of the 1980 Convention on the Law Applicable to Contractual Obligations[20] ("the Rome Convention"), the wording of this Regulation is aligned as far as possible with Article 14 of Regulation (EC) No 864/2007.

(16) To contribute to the general objective of this Regulation, legal certainty in the European judicial area, the conflict-of-law rules should be highly foreseeable. The courts should, however, retain a degree of discretion to determine the law that is most closely connected to the situation.

(17) As far as the applicable law in the absence of choice is concerned, the concept of "provision of services" and "sale of goods" should be interpreted in the same way as when applying Article 5 of Regulation (EC) No 44/2001 [now Art. 7 of "Brussels Ia"] in so far as sale of goods and provision of services are covered by that Regulation. Although franchise and distribution contracts are contracts for services, they are the subject of specific rules.

---

[18] OJ L 12, 16.1.2001, p. 1. Regulation as amended by Regulation (EC) No 1791/2006 (OJ L 363, 20.12.2006, p. 1).

[19] OJ L 199, 31.7.2007, p. 40.

[20] OJ C 334, 30.12.2005, p. 1.

(18) As far as the applicable law in the absence of choice is concerned, multilateral systems should be those in which trading is conducted, such as regulated markets and multilateral trading facilities as referred to in Article 4 of Directive 2004/39/EC of the European Parliament and of the Council of 21 April 2004 on markets in financial instruments[21], regardless of whether or not they rely on a central counterparty.

(19) Where there has been no choice of law, the applicable law should be determined in accordance with the rule specified for the particular type of contract. Where the contract cannot be categorised as being one of the specified types or where its elements fall within more than one of the specified types, it should be governed by the law of the country where the party required to effect the characteristic performance of the contract has his habitual residence. In the case of a contract consisting of a bundle of rights and obligations capable of being categorised as falling within more than one of the specified types of contract, the characteristic performance of the contract should be determined having regard to its centre of gravity.

(20) Where the contract is manifestly more closely connected with a country other than that indicated in Article 4(1) or (2), an escape clause should provide that the law of that other country is to apply. In order to determine that country, account should be taken, inter alia, of whether the contract in question has a very close relationship with another contract or contracts.

(21) In the absence of choice, where the applicable law cannot be determined either on the basis of the fact that the contract can be categorised as one of the specified types or as being the law of the country of habitual residence of the party required to effect the characteristic performance of the contract, the contract should be governed by the law of the country with which it is most closely connected. In order to determine that country, account should be taken, inter alia, of whether the contract in question has a very close relationship with another contract or contracts.

(22) As regards the interpretation of contracts for the carriage of goods, no change in substance is intended with respect to Article 4(4), third sentence, of the Rome Convention. Consequently, single-voyage charter parties and other contracts the main purpose of which is the carriage of goods should be treated as contracts for the carriage of goods. For the purposes of this Regulation, the term "consignor" should refer to any person who enters into a contract of carriage with the carrier and the term "the carrier" should refer to the party to the contract who undertakes to carry the goods, whether or not he performs the carriage himself.

(23) As regards contracts concluded with parties regarded as being weaker, those parties should be protected by conflict-of-law rules that are more favourable to their interests than the general rules.

(24) With more specific reference to consumer contracts, the conflict-of-law rule should make it possible to cut the cost of settling disputes concerning what are commonly relatively small claims and to take account of the development of distance-selling techniques. Consistency with Regulation (EC) No 44/2001 requires both that there be a reference to the concept of directed activity as a condition for applying the consumer protection rule and that the concept be interpreted harmoniously in Regulation (EC) No 44/2001 and this Regulation, bearing in mind that a joint declaration by the Council and the Commission on Article 15 of Regulation (EC) No 44/2001 states that "for Article 15(1)(c) to be applicable it is not sufficient for an

---

[21]   OJ L 145, 30.4.2004, p. 1. Directive as last amended by Directive 2007/44/EC (OJ L 247, 21.9.2007, p. 1).

undertaking to target its activities at the Member State of the consumer's residence, or at a number of Member States including that Member State; a contract must also be concluded within the framework of its activities". The declaration also states that "the mere fact that an Internet site is accessible is not sufficient for Article 15 to be applicable, although a factor will be that this Internet site solicits the conclusion of distance contracts and that a contract has actually been concluded at a distance, by whatever means. In this respect, the language or currency which a website uses does not constitute a relevant factor."

(25) Consumers should be protected by such rules of the country of their habitual residence that cannot be derogated from by agreement, provided that the consumer contract has been concluded as a result of the professional pursuing his commercial or professional activities in that particular country. The same protection should be guaranteed if the professional, while not pursuing his commercial or professional activities in the country where the consumer has his habitual residence, directs his activities by any means to that country or to several countries, including that country, and the contract is concluded as a result of such activities.

. . .

(27) Various exceptions should be made to the general conflict-of-law rule for consumer contracts. Under one such exception the general rule should not apply to contracts relating to rights in rem in immovable property or tenancies of such property unless the contract relates to the right to use immovable property on a timeshare basis within the meaning of Directive 94/47/EC of the European Parliament and of the Council of 26 October 1994 on the protection of purchasers in respect of certain aspects of contracts relating to the purchase of the right to use immovable properties on a timeshare basis[22].

(28) It is important to ensure that rights and obligations which constitute a financial instrument are not covered by the general rule applicable to consumer contracts, as that could lead to different laws being applicable to each of the instruments issued, therefore changing their nature and preventing their fungible trading and offering. Likewise, whenever such instruments are issued or offered, the contractual relationship established between the issuer or the offeror and the consumer should not necessarily be subject to the mandatory application of the law of the country of habitual residence of the consumer, as there is a need to ensure uniformity in the terms and conditions of an issuance or an offer. The same rationale should apply with regard to the multilateral systems covered by Article 4(1)(h), in respect of which it should be ensured that the law of the country of habitual residence of the consumer will not interfere with the rules applicable to contracts concluded within those systems or with the operator of such systems.

. . .

(32) Owing to the particular nature of contracts of carriage and insurance contracts, specific provisions should ensure an adequate level of protection of passengers and policy holders. Therefore, Article 6 should not apply in the context of those particular contracts.

(33) Where an insurance contract not covering a large risk covers more than one risk, at least one of which is situated in a Member State and at least one of which is situated in a third country, the special rules on insurance contracts in this Regulation should apply only to the risk or risks situated in the relevant Member State or Member States.

---

[22] OJ L 280, 29.10.1994, p. 83.

(34) The rule on individual employment contracts should not prejudice the application of the overriding mandatory provisions of the country to which a worker is posted in accordance with Directive 96/71/EC of the European Parliament and of the Council of 16 December 1996 concerning the posting of workers in the framework of the provision of services[23].

(35) Employees should not be deprived of the protection afforded to them by provisions which cannot be derogated from by agreement or which can only be derogated from to their benefit.

(36) As regards individual employment contracts, work carried out in another country should be regarded as temporary if the employee is expected to resume working in the country of origin after carrying out his tasks abroad. The conclusion of a new contract of employment with the original employer or an employer belonging to the same group of companies as the original employer should not preclude the employee from being regarded as carrying out his work in another country temporarily.

(37) Considerations of public interest justify giving the courts of the Member States the possibility, in exceptional circumstances, of applying exceptions based on public policy and overriding mandatory provisions. The concept of "overriding mandatory provisions" should be distinguished from the expression "provisions which cannot be derogated from by agreement" and should be construed more restrictively.

. . .

(39) For the sake of legal certainty there should be a clear definition of habitual residence, in particular for companies and other bodies, corporate or unincorporated. Unlike Article 60(1) of Regulation (EC) No 44/2001 [now Art. 63 of "Brussels Ia"], which establishes three criteria, the conflict-of-law rule should proceed on the basis of a single criterion; otherwise, the parties would be unable to foresee the law applicable to their situation.

. . .

(44) In accordance with Article 3 of the Protocol on the position of the United Kingdom and Ireland, annexed to the Treaty on European Union and to the Treaty establishing the European Community, Ireland has notified its wish to take part in the adoption and application of the present Regulation.

(45) In accordance with Articles 1 and 2 of the Protocol on the position of the United Kingdom and Ireland, annexed to the Treaty on European Union and to the Treaty establishing the European Community, and without prejudice to Article 4 of the said Protocol, the United Kingdom is not taking part in the adoption of this Regulation and is not bound by it or subject to its application.[24]

(46) In accordance with Articles 1 and 2 of the Protocol on the position of Denmark, annexed to the Treaty on European Union and to the Treaty establishing the European Community, Denmark is not taking part in the adoption of this Regulation and is not bound by it or subject to its application,

---

[23] OJ L 18, 21.1.1997, p. 1.

[24] The United Kingdom subsequently notified the Commission of its intent to accept and to participate in the Regulation and the Commission then declared the Regulation's application to the United Kingdom by decision of December 22, 2008: [2009] Official Journal L 10/22. The situation changed again when the United Kingdom left the EU in 2020 ("Brexit"). This circumstance makes no difference within the EU in relation to the UK because the Regulation has "universal application" (Art. 2). The UK, on the other hand, has adopted the Regulation as domestic law. *The Law Applicable to Contractual Obligations and Non-Contractual Obligations (Amendment etc.) (UK Exit) Regulations 2019 (SI 2019/834)* (Regulations)

HAVE ADOPTED THIS REGULATION:

CHAPTER I
SCOPE
Article 1
Material Scope

1.   This Regulation shall apply, in situations involving a conflict of laws, to contractual obligations in civil and commercial matters.

It shall not apply, in particular, to revenue, customs or administrative matters.

2.   The following shall be excluded from the scope of this Regulation:

(a)   questions involving the status or legal capacity of natural persons, without prejudice to Article 13;

(b)   obligations arising out of family relationships and relationships deemed by the law applicable to such relationships to have comparable effects, including maintenance obligations;

(c)   obligations arising out of matrimonial property regimes, property regimes of relationships deemed by the law applicable to such relationships to have comparable effects to marriage, and wills and succession;[25]

(d)   obligations arising under bills of exchange, cheques and promissory notes and other negotiable instruments to the extent that the obligations under such other negotiable instruments arise out of their negotiable character;

(e)   arbitration agreements and agreements on the choice of court;

(f)   questions governed by the law of companies and other bodies, corporate or unincorporated, such as the creation, by registration or otherwise, legal capacity, internal organisation or winding-up of companies and other bodies, corporate or unincorporated, and the personal liability of officers and members as such for the obligations of the company or body;

(g)   the question whether an agent is able to bind a principal, or an organ to bind a company or other body corporate or unincorporated, in relation to a third party;

(h)   the constitution of trusts and the relationship between settlors, trustees and beneficiaries;

(i)   obligations arising out of dealings prior to the conclusion of a contract;

(j)   insurance contracts arising out of operations carried out by organisations other than undertakings referred to in Article 2 of Directive 2002/83/EC of the European Parliament and of the Council of 5 November 2002 concerning life assurance the object of which is to provide benefits for employed or self-employed persons belonging to an undertaking or group of undertakings, or to a trade or group of trades, in the event of death or survival or of discontinuance or curtailment of activity, or of sickness related to work or accidents at work.

3.   This Regulation shall not apply to evidence and procedure, without prejudice to Article 18.

4.   In this Regulation, the term "Member State" shall mean Member States to which this Regulation applies. However, in Article 3(4) and Article 7 the term shall mean all the Member States.

---

[25]   With regard to succession, see infra p. 1238 —eds.

Article 2

Universal application

Any law specified by this Regulation shall be applied whether or not it is the law of a Member State.

CHAPTER II
UNIFORM RULES

Article 3

Freedom of choice

1.   A contract shall be governed by the law chosen by the parties. The choice shall be made expressly or clearly demonstrated by the terms of the contract or the circumstances of the case. By their choice the parties can select the law applicable to the whole or to part only of the contract.

2.   The parties may at any time agree to subject the contract to a law other than that which previously governed it, whether as a result of an earlier choice made under this Article or of other provisions of this Regulation. Any change in the law to be applied that is made after the conclusion of the contract shall not prejudice its formal validity under Article 11 or adversely affect the rights of third parties.

3.   Where all other elements relevant to the situation at the time of the choice are located in a country other than the country whose law has been chosen, the choice of the parties shall not prejudice the application of provisions of the law of that other country which cannot be derogated from by agreement.

4.   Where all other elements relevant to the situation at the time of the choice are located in one or more Member States, the parties' choice of applicable law other than that of a Member State shall not prejudice the application of provisions of Community law, where appropriate as implemented in the Member State of the forum, which cannot be derogated from by agreement.

5.   The existence and validity of the consent of the parties as to the choice of the applicable law shall be determined in accordance with the provisions of Articles 10, 11 and 13.

Article 4

Applicable law in the absence of choice

1.   To the extent that the law applicable to the contract has not been chosen in accordance with Article 3 and without prejudice to Articles 5 to 8, the law governing the contract shall be determined as follows:

(a)   a contract for the sale of goods shall be governed by the law of the country where the seller has his habitual residence;

(b)   a contract for the provision of services shall be governed by the law of the country where the service provider has his habitual residence;

(c)   a contract relating to a right in rem in immovable property or to a tenancy of immovable property shall be governed by the law of the country where the property is situated;

(d)   notwithstanding point (c), a tenancy of immovable property concluded for temporary private use for a period of no more than six consecutive months shall be governed by the law of the country where the landlord has his habitual residence, provided that the tenant is a natural person and has his habitual residence in the same country;

(e)   a franchise contract shall be governed by the law of the country where the franchisee has his habitual residence;

(f)   a distribution contract shall be governed by the law of the country where the distributor has his habitual residence;

(g)   a contract for the sale of goods by auction shall be governed by the law of the country where the auction takes place, if such a place can be determined;

(h)   a contract concluded within a multilateral system which brings together or facilitates the bringing together of multiple third-party buying and selling interests in financial instruments, as defined by Article 4(1), point (17) of Directive 2004/39/EC, in accordance with non-discretionary rules and governed by a single law, shall be governed by that law.

2.   Where the contract is not covered by paragraph 1 or where the elements of the contract would be covered by more than one of points (a) to (h) of paragraph 1, the contract shall be governed by the law of the country where the party required to effect the characteristic performance of the contract has his habitual residence.

3.   Where it is clear from all the circumstances of the case that the contract is manifestly more closely connected with a country other than that indicated in paragraphs 1 or 2, the law of that other country shall apply.

4.   Where the law applicable cannot be determined pursuant to paragraphs 1 or 2, the contract shall be governed by the law of the country with which it is most closely connected.

Article 5

Contracts of carriage

1.   To the extent that the law applicable to a contract for the carriage of goods has not been chosen in accordance with Article 3, the law applicable shall be the law of the country of habitual residence of the carrier, provided that the place of receipt or the place of delivery or the habitual residence of the consignor is also situated in that country. If those requirements are not met, the law of the country where the place of delivery as agreed by the parties is situated shall apply.

2.   To the extent that the law applicable to a contract for the carriage of passengers has not been chosen by the parties in accordance with the second subparagraph, the law applicable shall be the law of the country where the passenger has his habitual residence, provided that either the place of departure or the place of destination is situated in that country. If these requirements are not met, the law of the country where the carrier has his habitual residence shall apply.

The parties may choose as the law applicable to a contract for the carriage of passengers in accordance with Article 3 only the law of the country where:

(a)   the passenger has his habitual residence; or

(b)   the carrier has his habitual residence; or

(c)   the carrier has his place of central administration; or

(d)   the place of departure is situated; or

(e)   the place of destination is situated.

3.   Where it is clear from all the circumstances of the case that the contract, in the absence of a choice of law, is manifestly more closely connected with a country other than that indicated in paragraphs 1 or 2, the law of that other country shall apply.

Article 6

Consumer contracts

1.   Without prejudice to Articles 5 and 7, a contract concluded by a natural person for a purpose which can be regarded as being outside his trade or profession ("the consumer") with another person acting in the exercise of his trade or profession ("the professional") shall be governed by the law of the country where the consumer has his habitual residence, provided that the professional:

(a)   pursues his commercial or professional activities in the country where the consumer has his habitual residence, or

(b)   by any means, directs such activities to that country or to several countries including that country,

and the contract falls within the scope of such activities.

2.   Notwithstanding paragraph 1, the parties may choose the law applicable to a contract which fulfills the requirements of paragraph 1, in accordance with Article 3. Such a choice may not, however, have the result of depriving the consumer of the protection afforded to him by provisions that cannot be derogated from by agreement by virtue of the law which, in the absence of choice, would have been applicable on the basis of paragraph 1.

3.   If the requirements in points (a) or (b) of paragraph 1 are not fulfilled, the law applicable to a contract between a consumer and a professional shall be determined pursuant to Articles 3 and 4.

4.   Paragraphs 1 and 2 shall not apply to:

(a)   a contract for the supply of services where the services are to be supplied to the consumer exclusively in a country other than that in which he has his habitual residence;

(b)   a contract of carriage other than a contract relating to package travel within the meaning of Council Directive 90/314/EEC of 13 June 1990 on package travel, package holidays and package tours[26];

(c)   a contract relating to a right in rem in immovable property or a tenancy of immovable property other than a contract relating to the right to use immovable properties on a timeshare basis within the meaning of Directive 94/47/EC;

(d)   rights and obligations which constitute a financial instrument and rights and obligations constituting the terms and conditions governing the issuance or offer to the public and public take-over bids of transferable securities, and the subscription and redemption of units in collective investment undertakings in so far as these activities do not constitute provision of a financial service;

(e)   a contract concluded within the type of system falling within the scope of Article 4(1), point (h).

Article 7

Insurance contracts

1.   This Article shall apply to contracts referred to in paragraph 2, whether or not the risk covered is situated in a Member State, and to all other insurance contracts covering risks situated inside the territory of the Member States. It shall not apply to reinsurance contracts.

2.   An insurance contract covering a large risk as defined in Article 5(d) of the First Council Directive 73/239/EEC of 24 July 1973 on the coordination of laws, regulations

---

[26]   OJ L 158, 23.6.1990, p. 59.

and administrative provisions relating to the taking-up and pursuit of the business of direct insurance other than life assurance[27] shall be governed by the law chosen by the parties in accordance with Article 3 of this Regulation.

To the extent that the applicable law has not been chosen by the parties, the insurance contract shall be governed by the law of the country where the insurer has his habitual residence. Where it is clear from all the circumstances of the case that the contract is manifestly more closely connected with another country, the law of that other country shall apply.

3. In the case of an insurance contract other than a contract falling within paragraph 2, only the following laws may be chosen by the parties in accordance with Article 3:

(a) the law of any Member State where the risk is situated at the time of conclusion of the contract;

(b) the law of the country where the policy holder has his habitual residence;

(c) in the case of life assurance, the law of the Member State of which the policy holder is a national;

(d) for insurance contracts covering risks limited to events occurring in one Member State other than the Member State where the risk is situated, the law of that Member State;

(e) where the policy holder of a contract falling under this paragraph pursues a commercial or industrial activity or a liberal profession and the insurance contract covers two or more risks which relate to those activities and are situated in different Member States, the law of any of the Member States concerned or the law of the country of habitual residence of the policy holder.

Where, in the cases set out in points (a), (b) or (e), the Member States referred to grant greater freedom of choice of the law applicable to the insurance contract, the parties may take advantage of that freedom.

To the extent that the law applicable has not been chosen by the parties in accordance with this paragraph, such a contract shall be governed by the law of the Member State in which the risk is situated at the time of conclusion of the contract.

4. The following additional rules shall apply to insurance contracts covering risks for which a Member State imposes an obligation to take out insurance:

(a) the insurance contract shall not satisfy the obligation to take out insurance unless it complies with the specific provisions relating to that insurance laid down by the Member State that imposes the obligation. Where the law of the Member State in which the risk is situated and the law of the Member State imposing the obligation to take out insurance contradict each other, the latter shall prevail;

(b) by way of derogation from paragraphs 2 and 3, a Member State may lay down that the insurance contract shall be governed by the law of the Member State that imposes the obligation to take out insurance.

5. For the purposes of paragraph 3, third subparagraph, and paragraph 4, where the contract covers risks situated in more than one Member State, the contract shall be considered as constituting several contracts each relating to only one Member State.

---

[27] OJ L 228, 16.8.1973, p. 3. Directive as last amended by Directive 2005/68/EC of the European Parliament and of the Council (OJ L 323, 9.12.2005, p. 1).

6.   For the purposes of this Article, the country in which the risk is situated shall be determined in accordance with Article 2(d) of the Second Council Directive 88/357/EEC of 22 June 1988 on the coordination of laws, regulations and administrative provisions relating to direct insurance other than life assurance and laying down provisions to facilitate the effective exercise of freedom to provide services[28] and, in the case of life assurance, the country in which the risk is situated shall be the country of the commitment within the meaning of Article 1(1)(g) of Directive 2002/83/EC.

Article 8
Individual employment contracts

1.   An individual employment contract shall be governed by the law chosen by the parties in accordance with Article 3. Such a choice of law may not, however, have the result of depriving the employee of the protection afforded to him by provisions that cannot be derogated from by agreement under the law that, in the absence of choice, would have been applicable pursuant to paragraphs 2, 3 and 4 of this Article.

2.   To the extent that the law applicable to the individual employment contract has not been chosen by the parties, the contract shall be governed by the law of the country in which or, failing that, from which the employee habitually carries out his work in performance of the contract. The country where the work is habitually carried out shall not be deemed to have changed if he is temporarily employed in another country.

3.   Where the law applicable cannot be determined pursuant to paragraph 2, the contract shall be governed by the law of the country where the place of business through which the employee was engaged is situated.

4.   Where it appears from the circumstances as a whole that the contract is more closely connected with a country other than that indicated in paragraphs 2 or 3, the law of that other country shall apply.

Article 9
Overriding mandatory provisions

1.   Overriding mandatory provisions are provisions the respect for which is regarded as crucial by a country for safeguarding its public interests, such as its political, social or economic organisation, to such an extent that they are applicable to any situation falling within their scope, irrespective of the law otherwise applicable to the contract under this Regulation.

2.   Nothing in this Regulation shall restrict the application of the overriding mandatory provisions of the law of the forum.

3.   Effect may be given to the overriding mandatory provisions of the law of the country where the obligations arising out of the contract have to be or have been performed, in so far as those overriding mandatory provisions render the performance of the contract unlawful. In considering whether to give effect to those provisions, regard shall be had to their nature and purpose and to the consequences of their application or non-application.

---

[28] OJ L 172, 4.7.1988, p. 1. Directive as last amended by Directive 2005/14/EC of the European Parliament and of the Council (OJ L 149, 11.6.2005, p. 14).

Article 10

Consent and material validity

1. The existence and validity of a contract, or of any term of a contract, shall be determined by the law which would govern it under this Regulation if the contract or term were valid.

2. Nevertheless, a party, in order to establish that he did not consent, may rely upon the law of the country in which he has his habitual residence if it appears from the circumstances that it would not be reasonable to determine the effect of his conduct in accordance with the law specified in paragraph 1.

Article 11

Formal validity

1. A contract concluded between persons who, or whose agents, are in the same country at the time of its conclusion is formally valid if it satisfies the formal requirements of the law which governs it in substance under this Regulation or of the law of the country where it is concluded.

2. A contract concluded between persons who, or whose agents, are in different countries at the time of its conclusion is formally valid if it satisfies the formal requirements of the law which governs it in substance under this Regulation, or of the law of either of the countries where either of the parties or their agent is present at the time of conclusion, or of the law of the country where either of the parties had his habitual residence at that time.

3. A unilateral act intended to have legal effect relating to an existing or contemplated contract is formally valid if it satisfies the formal requirements of the law which governs or would govern the contract in substance under this Regulation, or of the law of the country where the act was done, or of the law of the country where the person by whom it was done had his habitual residence at that time.

4. Paragraphs 1, 2 and 3 of this Article shall not apply to contracts that fall within the scope of Article 6. The form of such contracts shall be governed by the law of the country where the consumer has his habitual residence.

5. Notwithstanding paragraphs 1 to 4, a contract the subject matter of which is a right in rem in immovable property or a tenancy of immovable property shall be subject to the requirements of form of the law of the country where the property is situated if by that law:

(a) those requirements are imposed irrespective of the country where the contract is concluded and irrespective of the law governing the contract, and

(b) those requirements cannot be derogated from by agreement.

Article 12

Scope of the law applicable

1. The law applicable to a contract by virtue of this Regulation shall govern in particular:

(a) interpretation;

(b) performance;

(c) within the limits of the powers conferred on the court by its procedural law, the consequences of a total or partial breach of obligations, including the assessment of damages in so far as it is governed by rules of law;

(d) the various ways of extinguishing obligations, and prescription and limitation of actions;

(e)   the consequences of nullity of the contract.

2.   In relation to the manner of performance and the steps to be taken in the event of defective performance, regard shall be had to the law of the country in which performance takes place.

Article 13

Incapacity

In a contract concluded between persons who are in the same country, a natural person who would have capacity under the law of that country may invoke his incapacity resulting from the law of another country, only if the other party to the contract was aware of that incapacity at the time of the conclusion of the contract or was not aware thereof as a result of negligence.

Article 14

Voluntary assignment and contractual subrogation

1.   The relationship between assignor and assignee under a voluntary assignment or contractual subrogation of a claim against another person ("the debtor") shall be governed by the law that applies to the contract between the assignor and assignee under this Regulation.

2.   The law governing the assigned or subrogated claim shall determine its assignability, the relationship between the assignee and the debtor, the conditions under which the assignment or subrogation can be invoked against the debtor and whether the debtor's obligations have been discharged.

3.   The concept of assignment in this Article includes outright transfers of claims, transfers of claims by way of security and pledges or other security rights over claims.

Article 15

Legal subrogation

Where a person ("the creditor") has a contractual claim against another ("the debtor") and a third person has a duty to satisfy the creditor, or has in fact satisfied the creditor in discharge of that duty, the law which governs the third person's duty to satisfy the creditor shall determine whether and to what extent the third person is entitled to exercise against the debtor the rights which the creditor had against the debtor under the law governing their relationship.

Article 16

Multiple liability

If a creditor has a claim against several debtors who are liable for the same claim, and one of the debtors has already satisfied the claim in whole or in part, the law governing the debtor's obligation towards the creditor also governs the debtor's right to claim recourse from the other debtors. The other debtors may rely on the defences they had against the creditor to the extent allowed by the law governing their obligations towards the creditor.

Article 17

Set-off

Where the right to set-off is not agreed by the parties, set-off shall be governed by the law applicable to the claim against which the right to set-off is asserted.

Article 18

Burden of proof

1.   The law governing a contractual obligation under this Regulation shall apply to the extent that, in matters of contractual obligations, it contains rules which raise presumptions of law or determine the burden of proof.

2.   A contract or an act intended to have legal effect may be proved by any mode of proof recognised by the law of the forum or by any of the laws referred to in Article 11 under which that contract or act is formally valid, provided that such mode of proof can be administered by the forum.

CHAPTER III

OTHER PROVISIONS

Article 19

Habitual residence

1.   For the purposes of this Regulation, the habitual residence of companies and other bodies, corporate or unincorporated, shall be the place of central administration. The habitual residence of a natural person acting in the course of his business activity shall be his principal place of business.

2.   Where the contract is concluded in the course of the operations of a branch, agency or any other establishment, or if, under the contract, performance is the responsibility of such a branch, agency or establishment, the place where the branch, agency or any other establishment is located shall be treated as the place of habitual residence.

3.   For the purposes of determining the habitual residence, the relevant point in time shall be the time of the conclusion of the contract.

Article 20

Exclusion of renvoi

The application of the law of any country specified by this Regulation means the application of the rules of law in force in that country other than its rules of private international law, unless provided otherwise in this Regulation.

Article 21

Public policy of the forum

The application of a provision of the law of any country specified by this Regulation may be refused only if such application is manifestly incompatible with the public policy ("ordre public") of the forum.

Article 22

States with more than one legal system

1.   Where a State comprises several territorial units, each of which has its own rules of law in respect of contractual obligations, each territorial unit shall be considered as a country for the purposes of identifying the law applicable under this Regulation.

2.   A Member State where different territorial units have their own rules of law in respect of contractual obligations shall not be required to apply this Regulation to conflicts solely between the laws of such units.

Article 23

Relationship with other provisions of Community law

With the exception of Article 7, this Regulation shall not prejudice the application of provisions of Community law which, in relation to particular matters, lay down conflict-of-law rules relating to contractual obligations.

Article 24

Relationship with the Rome Convention

1.   This Regulation shall replace the Rome Convention in the Member States, except as regards the territories of the Member States which fall within the territorial scope of that Convention and to which this Regulation does not apply pursuant to Article 299 of the Treaty [Art. 355 TFEU—eds.].

2.   In so far as this Regulation replaces the provisions of the Rome Convention, any reference to that Convention shall be understood as a reference to this Regulation.

Article 25

Relationship with existing international conventions

1.   This Regulation shall not prejudice the application of international conventions to which one or more Member States are parties at the time when this Regulation is adopted and which lay down conflict-of-law rules relating to contractual obligations.

2.   However, this Regulation shall, as between Member States, take precedence over conventions concluded exclusively between two or more of them in so far as such conventions concern matters governed by this Regulation.

. . .

NOTES

The following Notes offer explanations and also compare the provisions of the Rome I Regulation with those of its predecessor Rome Convention.

1.   *Sphere of Application; Scope*

The provisions on the sphere of application of the Regulation essentially parallel those of the earlier Rome Convention of 1980. The rule relating to time limitations is now in Art. 12(d); that on burden of proof is now in Art. 18. In the list of excluded subjects (Art. 1), the Regulation is more specific than the Convention had been concerning excluded insurance matters; for insurance contracts see Art. 7 and Recital (33). Art. 1(2)(j) adds "dealings prior to the conclusion of a contract." In decisions under the predecessor convention to the Brussels I and now Ia Regulations, the Court of Justice had held that contractual obligations include only those consensually undertaken, thus excluding other obligations that might arise in connection with a contract, but are imposed by law. The Rome II Regulation (infra p. 1211) now provides choice-of-law rules for pre-contractual liability in the context of "non-contractual obligations" (Art. 12 of the Rome II Regulation), and Art. 1(2)(i) of the Rome I Regulation takes account of this: see also its Recitals (7) and (10).

2.   *Parties' Freedom of Choice (Party Autonomy)*

Recital (11) declares party autonomy to be "one of the cornerstones" of conflicts law in contracts. Art. 3 continues the liberal tradition of Art. 3 of the Convention. "Demonstrated with reasonable certainty" (in the language of the Convention) now becomes "clearly demonstrated" by the "terms of the contract or the circumstances." Recital (12) adds, as an interpretative aid, that a choice-of-court clause may be such a circumstance. The rules concerning dépeçage and validity of the choice remain the same.

May the parties choose rules that are not part of a particular state's law, such as the lex mercatoria, the Vienna Sales Convention (CISG), or the UNIDROIT Principles? Like the Rome Convention, the Regulation's Art. 3 contains no answer. However, Recital (13) expressly so stipulates. What is its effect? Since it states the intent and understanding ("whereas") of the legislator, the Recital may serve to define the meaning of "law" in Art. 3. The latter's reference to Art. 10 (on material validity) might present a problem: when the non-state rules are silent on the matter (for instance, CISG refers this question to the applicable national law), the reference to Art. 11 (formal validity) might result in the application of the law of the place of contracting (absent a rule in the chosen non-state body of rules), and the condition of Art. 12(1)(c) (a statute making the assessment of damages substantive) would not apply. The same might be true of other provisions that contemplate the existence of positive rules of law. For comprehensive discussion, see R. Wagner, Der Grundsatz der Rechtswahl und das mangels Rechtswahl anwendbare Recht (Rom I-Verordnung), [2008] IPRax 377; Martiny, in Münchner Kommentar, BGB—VO(EG) 593:2008, Art. 3 Freie Rechtswahl nos. 1–7 (5th ed.2010).

3. *The Applicable Law in the Absence of a Choice: The General Default Rule*

The Regulation's default rule for choice of law (i.e., in the absence of a choice by the parties) in Art. 4 is quite different from that of the Convention. The latter established the basic rule that the applicable law is that of the "closest connection" of the contract to the law of a country. For many contracts, the closest connection, in turn, was presumed to be the state of habitual residence of the party rendering the "characteristic performance." For sales or service contracts, this was the place of the seller or the person rendering the service; the other party's payment of money was not regarded as "characteristic" of the contract. Art. 4(2) of the original Convention. Other presumptions applied in other circumstances. Art. 4(3)–(4). In all cases, the result was subject to an adjustment (Art. 4(5)) in favor of another more closely connected law.

The Regulation, in effect, turns the presumptions into rules. See Recitals (6), (19)–(21). The rules specified for the contract types listed in Art. 4(1)(a)–(h) presumably reflect judgments as to the place of the "characteristic performance" of these contracts. The original Convention's "characteristic performance" test reappears in Art. 4(2) of the Regulation when there is no predetermined rule in paragraph (1) or when a contract straddles its categories.

The original Convention addressed two situations in its Art. 4(5): that the place of the characteristic performance cannot be determined or that a different law is more closely connected. For the first case, the provision simply says that the presumption should be disregarded. That makes the general provision applicable again: search for the "most closely connected" law. If, however, another law is "more closely connected" to the contract than the law specified by the presumptions, then it should apply. The Regulation retains these provisions, distributing them now over Art. 4(3) and (4). The Regulation's structure improves on the Convention: the general test now comes at the end, i.e., after it has been determined that there is no otherwise applicable law. Note, with respect to Art. 4(3), that the Regulation now envisions the displacement of a law by another law—determined on the basis of one of the rules or of the characteristic performance test—only if it is "manifestly more closely connected with [another] country" (emphasis added). Can "manifestly more closely" be less than "most closely" in Art. 4(4)? Note also that a determination of a "manifestly more closely connected" relationship should take account of whether this contract has a "very close relationship with another contract. . . :" Recital (20).

The parallel between the "closest connection" test of European law and the "most significant relationship" of § 188, Restatement (Second), p. 629, supra, is obvious. Note, however, the difference in the manner of determining the closest connection or most significant relationship: while the Restatement (§ 188(2)) presents a non-exclusive and non-prioritized list of factors that are to be evaluated according to their relative importance in the light of the general policies of § 6, supra p. 574, Art. 4(2)–(4) of the Convention presents a number of (rebuttable) *presumptions*, which the Regulation now turns into rules. The Convention's principal presumption invokes the law of the place of the rendition of the "characteristic performance" (supra) of *the contract.*

The italicized language at the end of the previous paragraph quotes Art. 4(2) of both the Convention and the Regulation: contrary to § 188(3), Restatement (Second), Art. 4 seeks to determine a law applicable to the *entire* contract, not to a "particular issue." Indeed, while the original Convention still made provision for limited *dépeçage* under some limited and exceptional circumstances, this provision no longer appears in the Regulation.

4. *Special Default Rules: Consumer Contracts*

Under the Rome Convention, there had been a discrepancy between it and the Brussels I Regulation in the way they protected consumers.

The Regulation's Art. 6 now brings the choice-of-law provision in line with Brussels I. See Recitals (7) and (23)–(24). Particularly significant is the inclusion of language from the Council's and Commission's joint statement in Recital (24), addressing the question of what is meant by a seller/provider's "by any means . . . direct[ing] his activities," leading to the contract, to the consumer's country of habitual residence. Assume that a Belgian consumer had accessed a Swedish seller's interactive French-language website in her Paris hotel room, ordered merchandise, and upon its receipt in Belgium is dissatisfied and wants to sue? Where? See p. 1145. What law applies? What if the consumer had accessed the website in Austria by means of a satellite dish?[29]

---

[29]   See also Case 297/14 (Hobohm), [2016] Official Journal C 68/11, supra p. 1162.

Consumer protection may also result in substantive terms from other instruments of Community law that supplement or displace otherwise applicable law. See particularly EC Directive No. 93/13, [1995] O.J. L 95/29, on Unfair Terms in Consumer Contracts. See also, with respect to the "Consumer Sales Directive" EC Directive No. 99/44, [1999] O.J. L 171/12, which is modeled after the CISG. This directive has been amended by Directive No. 2011/83/EU, [2011] O.J. L. 304/64, effective June 13, 2014, specifying a number of "consumer rights," especially in "distance contracts" and "off-premise" transactions (e.g., to receive certain information and to have the right to withdraw from the contract). For a summary of earlier Community legislation protecting "weaker parties," such as consumers and employees, see Michael Bogdan, Concise Introduction to EU Private International Law 155 (2006). See also Hill, Cross-Border Consumer Contracts (2008). Note also that the Brussels Ia Regulation protects consumers by disallowing disadvantageous choice of court stipulations in consumer contracts: see p. 1145, supra.

5. *Employment Contracts*

The Regulation's rules on individual employment contracts (Art. 8) restate, in redrafted form, those of Art. 6 of the Convention. Recital (34) draws particular attention to EC Directive No. 96/71, [1997] O.J. L 18/1, on the Posting of Workers in the Framework of the Provision of Services, which is to prevent "social dumping" in the case of workers from low wage and working standard countries securing employment in higher standard states.

6. *Mandatory Rules*

Art. 7 of the original Convention is now Art. 9 in the Regulation. The new provision is a considerable improvement over its predecessor in several respects. Its title ("overriding mandatory provisions") already signals the special quality of the mandatory provisions addressed by it: not every "mandatory" provision of national law is meant to be an "overriding" provision internationally (see Recital (37)). The definition in Art. 9(1), lacking in the Convention, underlines this. Overriding mandatory rules are an affirmative application of public policy, as distinguished from its defensive use, such as in Art. 21.

Mandatory rules may be rules of national law or of Community law itself. See European Court of Justice Case C-381/98, Ingmar GB v. Eaton Leonard Technologies, [2000] ECR I-9305, in which a commercial agent's contract for services in England stipulated the application of California law; upon termination, he sought compensation. Held, that Art. 17 of EC Council Directive 86/653, [1986] O.J. L 382/17, providing for such compensation, applies regardless of the choice-of-law clause.

Art. 9(3) preserves in much limited form Art. 7(1) of the Convention. Art. 9(3) limits the (*discretionary*) consideration of a third country's law (i.e., a country other than the forum or that of the otherwise applicable law) to provisions that would render performance unlawful. Even in such a case, the last sentence directs an evaluation of the purpose and strength of the third country's rule. In addition to Germany, Luxembourg, and the United Kingdom (which had done so early), Ireland and Portugal had also opted out of the original Convention's Art. 7(1), which had *directed* the consideration of a third country's mandatory rules. There is no provision in the Regulation for an opting out: it will apply to all member states (Art. 29), except Denmark (Recital (46)). But recall that the Regulation's Art. 9(3) is entirely discretionary. See Dickinson, Third-Country Mandatory Rules in the Law Applicable to Contractual Obligations: So Long, Farewell, Auf Wiedersehen, Adieu?, 3 J. Priv. Int'l L. 53 (2007). Note that opting out of Art. 7(1) of the Convention (or exercising discretion under Art. 9(3) of the Regulation) does not affect a forum's obligation to give effect to the mandatory rules of law of another state when the Regulation itself so provides. Examples are Regulation Arts. 3(3) (choice of foreign law in a domestic contract); 6(2) (consumer contracts); 8(1) (employment contracts); and 11(5) (formal requirements of situs law for contracts concerning rights in immovables).

7. *Habitual Residence*

Art. 19 of the new Regulation adopts a narrower definition of "habitual residence" than earlier law for "bodies corporate" in Art. 1 (for the reason stated in Recital (39)).

8. See also Guinchard (ed.), Rome I and II in Practice (2020); Kronke, Transnational Commercial Law: General Doctrines: Thirty Years On, in Baetge, von Hein & von Hinden (eds.), Die richtige Ordnung-Festschrift für Kropholler 39 (2008); Callies & Renner (eds.), Rome Regulations—Commentary on European Rules of Conflict of Laws (3d ed. 2020).

2.   CHOICE OF LAW FOR NON-CONTRACTUAL OBLIGATIONS

INTRODUCTORY NOTE

The reference to "non-contractual obligations" in Continental law encompasses more than tort. As the name indicates, the concept extends to obligations incurred—not in contract and beyond tort—as a result of unjust enrichment (an obligation that also cannot be classified readily in the common law) and to "agency without mandate" (a concept derived from Roman law, for which there is no direct common law counterpart). An early attempt to deal, in one convention, with both contract and tort was unsuccessful. After success with the Rome Convention and its conversion into community law ("Rome I"), the Commission also proposed, and the Council and Parliament adopted Regulation "Rome II" on choice of law for non-contractual obligations. It is presented below, together with explanatory notes.

For contracts, the Rome Convention had provided conflicts rules since 1980, but tort conflicts law had remained the national law of the member states of the European Community. Like tort conflicts law elsewhere, national laws had undergone change in the last quarter century or so.[30] The new regulation serves to provide a uniform approach. Note, in particular,

---

[30] See Hay, Borchers, Symeonides, Whytock, Conflict of Laws § 2.27 (6th ed.2018); Hay, From Rule Orientation to "Approach" in German Conflicts Law—The Effect of the 1986 and 1999 Codifications, 47 Am.J.Comp.L. 501 (1999). With regard to substantive law, see von Bar (ed.), The Common European Law of Torts, 2 vols. (1998, 2000).

that—like Rome I (Art. 2, p. 1198 , supra)—Rome II also provides for its "universal application" (Art. 2): the rules of the Regulation apply "both to 'intra-Community' situations and to situations involving an 'extra-Community' element. . . . [If it were otherwise, the different conflicts rules of the member states might lead to different substantive laws in essentially similar cases involving Community and third-country parties, and thereby] provoke a distortion of competition." Paragraph 6 of the introductory recitals addresses this concern. Moreover, the "highly complex" nature of conflict[s] rules would be compounded if practitioners had to deal with two sets of rules—Community and national.[31]

Regulation (EC) No 864/2007 of the European Parliament and of the Council of 11 July 2007 on the Law Applicable to Non-Contractual Obligations
(Rome II)
[2007] Official Journal L 199/40

. . .

Whereas:

. . .

(6) The proper functioning of the internal market creates a need, in order to improve the predictability of the outcome of litigation, certainty as to the law applicable and the free movement of judgments, for the conflict-of-law rules in the Member States to designate the same national law irrespective of the country of the court in which an action is brought.

. . .

(8) This Regulation should apply irrespective of the nature of the court or tribunal seised.

. . .

(11) The concept of a non-contractual obligation varies from one Member State to another. Therefore for the purposes of this Regulation non-contractual obligation should be understood as an autonomous concept. The conflict-of-law rules set out in this Regulation should also cover non-contractual obligations arising out of strict liability.

(12) The law applicable should also govern the question of the capacity to incur liability in tort/delict.

(13) Uniform rules applied irrespective of the law they designate may avert the risk of distortions of competition between Community litigants.

---

[31] Commission, Explanatory Memorandum for a Regulation on the Law Applicable to Non-Contractual Obligations ("Rome II"), COM/2003/0427 final, Art. 2 (2003). Note that this Regulation is not affected by the UK's "Brexit" from the EU as far as the remaining member states is concerned, since the Regulation provides for "universal application" (Art. 3). In the UK, on the other hand, it no longer applies as EU law. However, the UK retains the Regulation as domestic law: The Law Applicable to Contractual Obligations and Non-Contractual Obligations (Amendment etc.) (UK Exit) Regulations 2019 (SI 2019/834) (Regulations).

(14) The requirement of legal certainty and the need to do justice in individual cases are essential elements of an area of justice. This Regulation provides for the connecting factors which are the most appropriate to achieve these objectives. Therefore, this Regulation provides for a general rule but also for specific rules and, in certain provisions, for an "escape clause" which allows a departure from these rules where it is clear from all the circumstances of the case that the tort/delict is manifestly more closely connected with another country. This set of rules thus creates a flexible framework of conflict-of-law rules. Equally, it enables the court seised to treat individual cases in an appropriate manner.

(15) The principle of the lex loci delicti commissi is the basic solution for non-contractual obligations in virtually all the Member States, but the practical application of the principle where the component factors of the case are spread over several countries varies. This situation engenders uncertainty as to the law applicable.

(16) Uniform rules should enhance the foreseeability of court decisions and ensure a reasonable balance between the interests of the person claimed to be liable and the person who has sustained damage. A connection with the country where the direct damage occurred (lex loci damni) strikes a fair balance between the interests of the person claimed to be liable and the person sustaining the damage, and also reflects the modern approach to civil liability and the development of systems of strict liability.

(17) The law applicable should be determined on the basis of where the damage occurs, regardless of the country or countries in which the indirect consequences could occur. Accordingly, in cases of personal injury or damage to property, the country in which the damage occurs should be the country where the injury was sustained or the property was damaged respectively.

(18) The general rule in this Regulation should be the lex loci damni provided for in Article 4(1). Article 4(2) should be seen as an exception to this general principle, creating a special connection where the parties have their habitual residence in the same country. Article 4(3) should be understood as an 'escape clause' from Article 4(1) and (2), where it is clear from all the circumstances of the case that the tort/delict is manifestly more closely connected with another country.

(19) Specific rules should be laid down for special torts/delicts where the general rule does not allow a reasonable balance to be struck between the interests at stake.

(20) The conflict-of-law rule in matters of product liability should meet the objectives of fairly spreading the risks inherent in a modern high-technology society, protecting consumers' health, stimulating innovation, securing undistorted competition and facilitating trade. Creation of a cascade system of connecting factors, together with a foreseeability clause, is a balanced solution in regard to these objectives. The first element to be taken into account is the law of the country in which the person sustaining the damage had his or her habitual residence when the damage occurred, if the product was marketed in that country. The other elements of the cascade are triggered if the product was not marketed in that country, without prejudice to Article 4(2) and to the possibility of a manifestly closer connection to another country.

(21) The special rule in Article 6 is not an exception to the general rule in Article 4(1) but rather a clarification of it. In matters of unfair competition, the conflict-of-law rule should protect competitors, consumers and the general public and ensure that the market economy functions properly. The connection to the law of the country where competitive relations or the collective interests of consumers are, or are likely to be, affected generally satisfies these objectives.

(22) The non-contractual obligations arising out of restrictions of competition in Article 6(3) should cover infringements of both national and Community competition law. The law applicable to such non-contractual obligations should be the law of the country where the market is, or is likely to be, affected. In cases where the market is, or is likely to be, affected in more than one country, the claimant should be able in certain circumstances to choose to base his or her claim on the law of the court seised.

(23) For the purposes of this Regulation, the concept of restriction of competition should cover prohibitions on agreements between undertakings, decisions by associations of undertakings and concerted practices which have as their object or effect the prevention, restriction or distortion of competition within a Member State or within the internal market, as well as prohibitions on the abuse of a dominant position within a Member State or within the internal market, where such agreements, decisions, concerted practices or abuses are prohibited by Articles 81 and 82 of the Treaty or by the law of a Member State.

(24) "Environmental damage" should be understood as meaning adverse change in a natural resource, such as water, land or air, impairment of a function performed by that resource for the benefit of another natural resource or the public, or impairment of the variability among living organisms.

(25) Regarding environmental damage, Article 174 of the Treaty, which provides that there should be a high level of protection based on the precautionary principle and the principle that preventive action should be taken, the principle of priority for corrective action at source and the principle that the polluter pays, fully justifies the use of the principle of discriminating in favour of the person sustaining the damage. The question of when the person seeking compensation can make the choice of the law applicable should be determined in accordance with the law of the Member State in which the court is seised.

(26) Regarding infringements of intellectual property rights, the universally acknowledged principle of the lex loci protectionis should be preserved. For the purposes of this Regulation, the term 'intellectual property rights' should be interpreted as meaning, for instance, copyright, related rights, the sui generis right for the protection of databases and industrial property rights.

(27) The exact concept of industrial action, such as strike action or lock-out, varies from one Member State to another and is governed by each Member State's internal rules. Therefore, this Regulation assumes as a general principle that the law of the country where the industrial action was taken should apply, with the aim of protecting the rights and obligations of workers and employers.

. . .

(30) Culpa in contrahendo for the purposes of this Regulation is an autonomous concept and should not necessarily be interpreted within the meaning of national law. It should include the violation of the duty of disclosure and the breakdown of contractual negotiations. Article 12 covers only non-contractual obligations presenting a direct link with the dealings prior to the conclusion of a contract. This means that if, while a contract is being negotiated, a person suffers personal injury, Article 4 or other relevant provisions of this Regulation should apply.

(31) To respect the principle of party autonomy and to enhance legal certainty, the parties should be allowed to make a choice as to the law applicable to a non-contractual obligation. This choice should be expressed or demonstrated with reasonable certainty by the circumstances of the case. Where establishing the existence of the agreement, the court has to respect the intentions of the parties. Protection should be given to weaker parties by imposing certain conditions on the choice.

(32) Considerations of public interest justify giving the courts of the Member States the possibility, in exceptional circumstances, of applying exceptions based on public policy and overriding mandatory provisions. In particular, the application of a provision of the law designated by this Regulation which would have the effect of causing non-compensatory exemplary or punitive damages of an excessive nature to be awarded may, depending on the circumstances of the case and the legal order of the Member State of the court seised, be regarded as being contrary to the public policy (ordre public) of the forum.

(33) According to the current national rules on compensation awarded to victims of road traffic accidents, when quantifying damages for personal injury in cases in which the accident takes place in a State other than that of the habitual residence of the victim, the court seised should take into account all the relevant actual circumstances of the specific victim, including in particular the actual losses and costs of after-care and medical attention.

(34) In order to strike a reasonable balance between the parties, account must be taken, in so far as appropriate, of the rules of safety and conduct in operation in the country in which the harmful act was committed, even where the non-contractual obligation is governed by the law of another country. The term "rules of safety and conduct" should be interpreted as referring to all regulations having any relation to safety and conduct, including, for example, road safety rules in the case of an accident.

. . .

(39) In accordance with Article 3 of the Protocol on the position of the United Kingdom and Ireland annexed to the Treaty on European Union and to the Treaty establishing the European Community, the United Kingdom and Ireland are taking part in the adoption and application of this Regulation.

(40) In accordance with Articles 1 and 2 of the Protocol on the position of Denmark, annexed to the Treaty on European Union and to the Treaty establishing the European Community, Denmark does not take part in the adoption of this Regulation, and is not bound by it or subject to its application

HAVE ADOPTED THIS REGULATION:

CHAPTER I

SCOPE

Article 1

Scope

1.   This Regulation shall apply, in situations involving a conflict of laws, to non-contractual obligations in civil and commercial matters. It shall not apply, in particular, to revenue, customs or administrative matters or to the liability of the State for acts and omissions in the exercise of State authority (acta iure imperii).

2.   The following shall be excluded from the scope of this Regulation:

(a)   non-contractual obligations arising out of family relationships and relationships deemed by the law applicable to such relationships to have comparable effects including maintenance obligations;

(b)   non-contractual obligations arising out of matrimonial property regimes, property regimes of relationships deemed by the law applicable to such relationships to have comparable effects to marriage, and wills and succession;

(c)   non-contractual obligations arising under bills of exchange, cheques and promissory notes and other negotiable instruments to the extent that the obligations under such other negotiable instruments arise out of their negotiable character;

(d) non-contractual obligations arising out of the law of companies and other bodies corporate or unincorporated regarding matters such as the creation, by registration or otherwise, legal capacity, internal organisation or winding-up of companies and other bodies corporate or unincorporated, the personal liability of officers and members as such for the obligations of the company or body and the personal liability of auditors to a company or to its members in the statutory audits of accounting documents;

(e) non-contractual obligations arising out of the relations between the settlors, trustees and beneficiaries of a trust created voluntarily;

(f) non-contractual obligations arising out of nuclear damage;

(g) non-contractual obligations arising out of violations of privacy and rights relating to personality, including defamation.

3.   This Regulation shall not apply to evidence and procedure, without prejudice to Articles 21 and 22.

4.   For the purposes of this Regulation, "Member State" shall mean any Member State other than Denmark.

Article 2

Non-contractual obligations

1.   For the purposes of this Regulation, damage shall cover any consequence arising out of tort/delict, unjust enrichment, negotiorum gestio or culpa in contrahendo.

2.   This Regulation shall apply also to non-contractual obligations that are likely to arise.

3.   Any reference in this Regulation to:

(a) an event giving rise to damage shall include events giving rise to damage that are likely to occur; and

(b) damage shall include damage that is likely to occur.

Article 3

Universal application

Any law specified by this Regulation shall be applied whether or not it is the law of a Member State.

CHAPTER II

TORTS/DELICTS

Article 4

General rule

1.   Unless otherwise provided for in this Regulation, the law applicable to a non-contractual obligation arising out of a tort/delict shall be the law of the country in which the damage occurs irrespective of the country in which the event giving rise to the damage occurred and irrespective of the country or countries in which the indirect consequences of that event occur.

2.   However, where the person claimed to be liable and the person sustaining damage both have their habitual residence in the same country at the time when the damage occurs, the law of that country shall apply.

3.   Where it is clear from all the circumstances of the case that the tort/delict is manifestly more closely connected with a country other than that indicated in

paragraphs 1 or 2, the law of that other country shall apply. A manifestly closer connection with another country might be based in particular on a pre-existing relationship between the parties, such as a contract, that is closely connected with the tort/delict in question.

Article 5

Product liability

1.   Without prejudice to Article 4(2), the law applicable to a non-contractual obligation arising out of damage caused by a product shall be:

(a)   the law of the country in which the person sustaining the damage had his or her habitual residence when the damage occurred, if the product was marketed in that country; or, failing that,

(b)   the law of the country in which the product was acquired, if the product was marketed in that country; or, failing that,

(c)   the law of the country in which the damage occurred, if the product was marketed in that country.

However, the law applicable shall be the law of the country in which the person claimed to be liable is habitually resident if he or she could not reasonably foresee the marketing of the product, or a product of the same type, in the country the law of which is applicable under (a), (b) or (c).

2.   Where it is clear from all the circumstances of the case that the tort/delict is manifestly more closely connected with a country other than that indicated in paragraph 1, the law of that other country shall apply. A manifestly closer connection with another country might be based in particular on a pre-existing relationship between the parties, such as a contract, that is closely connected with the tort/delict in question.

Article 6

Unfair competition and acts restricting free competition

1.   The law applicable to a non-contractual obligation arising out of an act of unfair competition shall be the law of the country where competitive relations or the collective interests of consumers are, or are likely to be, affected.

2.   Where an act of unfair competition affects exclusively the interests of a specific competitor, Article 4 shall apply.

3.

(a)   The law applicable to a non-contractual obligation arising out of a restriction of competition shall be the law of the country where the market is, or is likely to be, affected.

(b)   When the market is, or is likely to be, affected in more than one country, the person seeking compensation for damage who sues in the court of the domicile of the defendant, may instead choose to base his or her claim on the law of the court seised, provided that the market in that Member State is amongst those directly and substantially affected by the restriction of competition out of which the non-contractual obligation on which the claim is based arises; where the claimant sues, in accordance with the applicable rules on jurisdiction, more than one defendant in that court, he or she can only choose to base his or her claim on the law of that court if the restriction of competition on which the claim against each of these defendants relies directly and substantially affects also the market in the Member State of that court.

4. The law applicable under this Article may not be derogated from by an agreement pursuant to Article 14.

Article 7

Environmental damage

The law applicable to a non-contractual obligation arising out of environmental damage or damage sustained by persons or property as a result of such damage shall be the law determined pursuant to Article 4(1), unless the person seeking compensation for damage chooses to base his or her claim on the law of the country in which the event giving rise to the damage occurred.

Article 8

Infringement of intellectual property rights

1. The law applicable to a non-contractual obligation arising from an infringement of an intellectual property right shall be the law of the country for which protection is claimed.

2. In the case of a non-contractual obligation arising from an infringement of a unitary Community intellectual property right, the law applicable shall, for any question that is not governed by the relevant Community instrument, be the law of the country in which the act of infringement was committed.

3. The law applicable under this Article may not be derogated from by an agreement pursuant to Article 14.

Article 9

Industrial action

Without prejudice to Article 4(2), the law applicable to a non-contractual obligation in respect of the liability of a person in the capacity of a worker or an employer or the organisations representing their professional interests for damages caused by an industrial action, pending or carried out, shall be the law of the country where the action is to be, or has been, taken.

CHAPTER III

UNJUST ENRICHMENT, NEGOTIORUM GESTIO AND CULPA IN CONTRAHENDO

Article 10

Unjust enrichment

1. If a non-contractual obligation arising out of unjust enrichment, including payment of amounts wrongly received, concerns a relationship existing between the parties, such as one arising out of a contract or a tort/delict, that is closely connected with that unjust enrichment, it shall be governed by the law that governs that relationship.

2. Where the law applicable cannot be determined on the basis of paragraph 1 and the parties have their habitual residence in the same country when the event giving rise to unjust enrichment occurs, the law of that country shall apply.

3. Where the law applicable cannot be determined on the basis of paragraphs 1 or 2, it shall be the law of the country in which the unjust enrichment took place.

4. Where it is clear from all the circumstances of the case that the non-contractual obligation arising out of unjust enrichment is manifestly more closely connected with a country other than that indicated in paragraphs 1, 2 and 3, the law of that other country shall apply.

Article 11

Negotiorum gestio

1.   If a non-contractual obligation arising out of an act performed without due authority in connection with the affairs of another person concerns a relationship existing between the parties, such as one arising out of a contract or a tort/delict, that is closely connected with that non-contractual obligation, it shall be governed by the law that governs that relationship.

2.   Where the law applicable cannot be determined on the basis of paragraph 1, and the parties have their habitual residence in the same country when the event giving rise to the damage occurs, the law of that country shall apply.

3.   Where the law applicable cannot be determined on the basis of paragraphs 1 or 2, it shall be the law of the country in which the act was performed.

4.   Where it is clear from all the circumstances of the case that the non-contractual obligation arising out of an act performed without due authority in connection with the affairs of another person is manifestly more closely connected with a country other than that indicated in paragraphs 1, 2 and 3, the law of that other country shall apply.

Article 12

Culpa in contrahendo

1.   The law applicable to a non-contractual obligation arising out of dealings prior to the conclusion of a contract, regardless of whether the contract was actually concluded or not, shall be the law that applies to the contract or that would have been applicable to it had it been entered into.

2.   Where the law applicable cannot be determined on the basis of paragraph 1, it shall be:

(a)   the law of the country in which the damage occurs, irrespective of the country in which the event giving rise to the damage occurred and irrespective of the country or countries in which the indirect consequences of that event occurred; or

(b)   where the parties have their habitual residence in the same country at the time when the event giving rise to the damage occurs, the law of that country; or

(c)   where it is clear from all the circumstances of the case that the non-contractual obligation arising out of dealings prior to the conclusion of a contract is manifestly more closely connected with a country other than that indicated in points (a) and (b), the law of that other country.

Article 13

Applicability of

Article 8

For the purposes of this Chapter, Article 8 shall apply to non-contractual obligations arising from an infringement of an intellectual property right.

CHAPTER IV
FREEDOM OF CHOICE

Article 14

Freedom of choice

1.   The parties may agree to submit non-contractual obligations to the law of their choice:

>   (a)   by an agreement entered into after the event giving rise to the damage occurred;

>   or

>   (b)   where all the parties are pursuing a commercial activity, also by an agreement freely negotiated before the event giving rise to the damage occurred.

The choice shall be expressed or demonstrated with reasonable certainty by the circumstances of the case and shall not prejudice the rights of third parties.

2.   Where all the elements relevant to the situation at the time when the event giving rise to the damage occurs are located in a country other than the country whose law has been chosen, the choice of the parties shall not prejudice the application of provisions of the law of that other country which cannot be derogated from by agreement.

3.   Where all the elements relevant to the situation at the time when the event giving rise to the damage occurs are located in one or more of the Member States, the parties' choice of the law applicable other than that of a Member State shall not prejudice the application of provisions of Community law, where appropriate as implemented in the Member State of the forum, which cannot be derogated from by agreement.

CHAPTER V
COMMON RULES

Article 15

Scope of the law applicable

The law applicable to non-contractual obligations under this Regulation shall govern in particular:

(a)   the basis and extent of liability, including the determination of persons who may be held liable for acts performed by them;

(b)   the grounds for exemption from liability, any limitation of liability and any division of liability;

(c)   the existence, the nature and the assessment of damage or the remedy claimed;

(d)   within the limits of powers conferred on the court by its procedural law, the measures which a court may take to prevent or terminate injury or damage or to ensure the provision of compensation;

(e)   the question whether a right to claim damages or a remedy may be transferred, including by inheritance;

(f)   persons entitled to compensation for damage sustained personally;

(g)   liability for the acts of another person;

(h)   the manner in which an obligation may be extinguished and rules of prescription and limitation, including rules relating to the commencement, interruption and suspension of a period of prescription or limitation.

Article 16

Overriding mandatory provisions

Nothing in this Regulation shall restrict the application of the provisions of the law of the forum in a situation where they are mandatory irrespective of the law otherwise applicable to the non-contractual obligation.

Article 17

Rules of safety and conduct

In assessing the conduct of the person claimed to be liable, account shall be taken, as a matter of fact and in so far as is appropriate, of the rules of safety and conduct which were in force at the place and time of the event giving rise to the liability.

Article 18

Direct action against the insurer of the person liable

The person having suffered damage may bring his or her claim directly against the insurer of the person liable to provide compensation if the law applicable to the non-contractual obligation or the law applicable to the insurance contract so provides.

Article 19

Subrogation

Where a person (the creditor) has a non-contractual claim upon another (the debtor), and a third person has a duty to satisfy the creditor, or has in fact satisfied the creditor in discharge of that duty, the law which governs the third person's duty to satisfy the creditor shall determine whether, and the extent to which, the third person is entitled to exercise against the debtor the rights which the creditor had against the debtor under the law governing their relationship.

Article 20

Multiple liability

If a creditor has a claim against several debtors who are liable for the same claim, and one of the debtors has already satisfied the claim in whole or in part, the question of that debtor's right to demand compensation from the other debtors shall be governed by the law applicable to that debtor's non-contractual obligation towards the creditor.

Article 21

Formal validity

A unilateral act intended to have legal effect and relating to a non-contractual obligation shall be formally valid if it satisfies the formal requirements of the law governing the non-contractual obligation in question or the law of the country in which the act is performed.

Article 22

Burden of proof

1.   The law governing a non-contractual obligation under this Regulation shall apply to the extent that, in matters of non-contractual obligations, it contains rules which raise presumptions of law or determine the burden of proof.

2.   Acts intended to have legal effect may be proved by any mode of proof recognised by the law of the forum or by any of the laws referred to in Article 21 under which that act is formally valid, provided that such mode of proof can be administered by the forum.

CHAPTER VI
OTHER PROVISIONS

Article 23

Habitual residence

1.   For the purposes of this Regulation, the habitual residence of companies and other bodies, corporate or unincorporated, shall be the place of central administration.

Where the event giving rise to the damage occurs, or the damage arises, in the course of operation of a branch, agency or any other establishment, the place where the branch, agency or any other establishment is located shall be treated as the place of habitual residence.

2.   For the purposes of this Regulation, the habitual residence of a natural person acting in the course of his or her business activity shall be his or her principal place of business.

Article 24

Exclusion of renvoi

The application of the law of any country specified by this Regulation means the application of the rules of law in force in that country other than its rules of private international law.

Article 25

States with more than one legal system

1.   Where a State comprises several territorial units, each of which has its own rules of law in respect of non-contractual obligations, each territorial unit shall be considered as a country for the purposes of identifying the law applicable under this Regulation.

2.   A Member State within which different territorial units have their own rules of law in respect of non-contractual obligations shall not be required to apply this Regulation to conflicts solely between the laws of such units.

Article 26

Public policy of the forum

The application of a provision of the law of any country specified by this Regulation may be refused only if such application is manifestly incompatible with the public policy (ordre public) of the forum.

. . .

Commission Statement on the treatment of foreign law

The Commission, being aware of the different practices followed in the Member States as regards the treatment of foreign law, will publish at the latest four years after the entry into force of the "Rome II" Regulation and in any event as soon as it is available a horizontal study on the application of foreign law in civil and commercial matters by the courts of the Member States, having regard to the aims of the Hague Programme. It is also prepared to take appropriate measures if necessary.

NOTES

Further Reading: For comment on the Rome II Regulation, see E. Guinchard (ed.), Rome I and Rome II in Practice (2020); A. Dickinson, The

Rome II Regulation—The Law Applicable to Non-Contractual Obligations (2008); Weintraub, The Choice-of-Law Rules of the European Community Regulation on the Law Applicable to Non-Contractual Obligations: Simple and Predictable, or Consequence-Based, or Neither?, 43 Tex.Int'l L.J. 401 (2008); Hay, Contemporary Approaches to Non-Contractual Obligations in Private International Law and the European Community's "Rome II" Regulation, 7 European Law Forum I-137 (4–2007); von Hein, Something Old and Something Borrowed, but Nothing New?, 82 Tul.L.Rev. 1663 (2008); Symeonides, Rome II and Tort Conflicts: A Missed Opportunity, 56 Am.J.Comp.L. 173 (2008) and the Reply by Kozyris, 56 Am.J.Comp.L. 471 (2008). See also Junker, Die Rome II-Verordnung: Neues Internationales Deliktsrecht auf europäischer Grundlage, [2007] Neue Juristische Wochenschrift 3675; Leible & Matthias, Die neue EC-Verordnung über das auf ausservertragliche Schuldverhältnisse anzuwendende Recht ("Rome II"), [2007] Recht der Internationalen Wirtschaft 721; Wagner, Die neue Rome II-Verordnung, [2008] IPRax 1. See generally, Callies & Renner, Rome Regulations (3d ed. 2020).

1.   The Regulation retains the law of the place of injury as its default rule (Art. 4(1)). The reference to damage that "is likely to" occur is part of a definitional section: Art. 2(3)(b). See Recitals (15) through (18). Reference to the place of conduct remains an option in cases of environmental damage (Art. 7 and Note 7, infra); see also Art. 17.[32] Art. 4(1) makes clear that the place where "indirect consequences" are felt is not the relevant place of injury (see Recital (17)). For another instance, in which the plaintiff may choose among alternatively applicable laws, see Art. 6(3)(b).

Subsection (2) of Art. 4 adopts the exception to the default rule in favor of the law of the parties' common habitual residence (see Recital (18)) that was previously part of German and English law and is known in American law since Babcock v. Jackson, p. 577, supra. May a court (for instance, at the defendant's domicile) apply a rule of forum law (for instance, as to damages) that differs from the law applicable under Art. 4(1) but is the same as the law in the plaintiff's state of habitual residence? More generally: does Art. 4(2) permit the application of the common law of the parties' different states of habitual residence? From an American perspective, it would seem that the court might take a functional (policy) view of the matter and apply the (identical) domiciliary laws in circumstances when there are no forum interests to be advanced. Subsection (3) of Art. 4, an "escape" clause (Recital (14)), may permit recourse to the common law of the parties' different domiciles, as suggested in the previous paragraph (see Weintraub, in

---

[32] The Hague Conventions on Traffic Accidents and Products Liability (Arts. 7 and 9, respectively) contain similar provisions as do the conflicts laws of most member states. But note: "Taking account of foreign law is not the same thing as applying it: the court will apply only the law that is applicable under the conflict rule, but it must take account of another law as a point of fact, for example when assessing the seriousness of the fault or the author's good or bad faith. . . ." EC Commission, Memorandum at 25. The question has been raised whether this provision may unduly favor the tortfeasor by not actually requiring application of law of the state of acting when these impose higher standards than the state of injury. The actor's expectations would hardly be disappointed and the interests of the state of conduct would be addressed. Symeonides, Tort Conflicts and Rome II: A View from Across, in: Festschrift für Erik Jayme 935, ¶ 4.1–6 (H–P. Mansel, et al., eds. 2004).

"Further Readings," supra). Such a reading is supported by Recital (18), which states the intent that the subsection provide an escape, when appropriate, from both subsections (1) and (2). See also Hay, Borchers & Symeonides, Conflict of Laws § 17.40 (5th ed.2010); Hay, supra, at I-142; Symeonides, supra at 196; Dornis, "When in Rome, do as the Romans do?"— A Defense of the Lex Domicilii Communis in the Rome-II—Regulation, 7 European Law Forum I-152 (4-2007).

However, it seems unlikely that a court would take such a wide view of the exception in favor of the parties' law of domicile. Article 4 has a territorial orientation; it seeks to identify one state that, on the basis of territorially affiliating facts, has the closest connection to the case. Neither of the two hypothetical states of habitual residence fulfills the tests of Art. 4(2) or (3), nor do these states do so together (Art. 4(2): ". . . the same country . . .").

2. The escape clause of Art. 4(3) is a recurring theme in the Regulation: see, e.g., Arts. 5(2), 10(4), 11(4), 12(2)(c).

3. The Regulation does not contemplate or provide for dépeçage. It refers to "the" law applicable to "the" non-contractual obligation. However, there are situations in which the rules of the Regulation itself may lead to the application of more than one law to the case: see Arts. 8(2), 17,[33] 18–20. See also Recital (33) and consider subjects that may be considered "procedural," resulting in the application of forum law. See below Note 8. In addition, mandatory rules (Art. 16) and the public policy exception (Art. 26) of course displace the otherwise applicable law, although—arguably—this is not a choice of an applicable law in the sense that *dépeçage* is usually understood. In one commentator's opinion, the lack of an express issue-by-issue orientation as represented by the American Restatement (Second), the lack of a differentiation between loss-allocating and conduct-regulating rules as developed by case law in New York (*Schultz*, p. 657, supra), and there being only indirect consideration of state interests and policies are all serious shortcomings of Rome II, making its provisions too inflexible. Symeonides, Introductory Note, supra, at p. 1222. Calling for greater attention to the consequences of a choice of law (which country bears the consequence of having its law applied or not applied?) and making a number of concrete suggestions (e.g., with respect to Art. 4): Weintraub. Substantially less critical, particularly with regard to the limited dépeçage: Hay, supra at I–144, I–148, I–151. Does the last sentence of Recital (14) provide a way for achieving greater flexibility, for instance, by guiding the interpretation and application of the escape clause or does the use of "manifestly"—for instance in Art. 4(3)—preclude this?

4. Does Art. 5, on the law applicable to products liability, adequately address the concerns of producers exporting to higher liability countries, as well as the interests of injured parties residing in a country with different liability standards (higher or lower) from that of the producer? See Recital (20). Does the change from "consent" in Art. 4 of the Proposal to "foresee" in Art. 3(1) (2nd paragraph) help? See also Art. 23, which, unlike the Proposal, now contains a definition of a company's "habitual residence." For a review

---

[33] See Note 1, supra.

of substantive product liability law, see Reimann, Harmony & Chaos in Products Liability: The Divergent Paths of Europe and the United States, in: F. Faust and G. Thüsing (eds.), Beyond Borders: Perspectives on International and Comparative Law 91 (2006).

5. For the rules relating to unfair competition (Art. 6), see Recitals (21–23).

6. Contrary to the Commission's original proposal, the Regulation does not contain rules for determining the law applicable to violations of privacy and rights relating to personality. Application of Art. 4, even when subject to exceptions, raises problems. A cumulation of applicable laws based on different places of injury was not acceptable to the Parliament, the press, and other media. They sought to identify a single law and to determine it from the perspective of the defendant's intended audience. Others sought a more plaintiff-oriented solution. See Hay, supra at I–147. When the impasse could not be resolved, these matters were excluded from the coverage of the present Regulation (Art. 1(2)(g)) and the EC Commission directed to submit a study by the end of 2008 (Art. 30(2)). Despite continued efforts, the matter still has not been resolved.

7. Several European countries provide specific conflicts rules for environmental damage.[34] Article 7 of the Regulation again uses the *lex loci*-focus of Art. 4(1) as the principal rule but gives the claimant the option to invoke the (presumably more favorable) law of the place of acting.[35] What is the purpose of this provision—will it raise standards of environmentally responsible conduct? A claimant may opt for higher compensation if injured by a defendant acting in a high-standard state; will that prompt the plaintiff's own state to raise standards? If not, plaintiffs will be compensated differently depending on whether the damage is caused by a foreign or a domestic defendant. If the defendant acts in a low-standard state and injures a high-standard-state plaintiff, will the latter be likely to opt for the law of the state of conduct? If not, will application of the law of the state of injury (under Art. 4) prompt the defendant's state to improve environmental standards? In the same vein: if an objective is to secure for EU-based plaintiffs the benefits of EU environmental standards as against polluters from non-member countries, would not Art. 4 by itself achieve that purpose?

8. *Damages—In General.* Art. 11(e) of the Proposal for the Regulation had provided that damages are covered by the applicable law, as determined by the Regulation, i.e., are "substantive," if "prescribed by law." Otherwise, presumably, they would be governed by forum law (as "procedural"). Separating the quantification of damages from the law applicable to the obligation makes no sense. Weintraub, Note 1, supra. The qualifying language has been dropped in Art. 15(c), as enacted. This had been urged: Weintraub, Note 1, supra. Does this mean that all damage issues, including

---

[34] See Art. 44 of the German Conflicts statute, expressly providing for the application of its Art. 40 to emissions from real property. To the same effect, Art. 138 of the Swiss Conflicts statute: see discussion by Siehr, Das Internationale Privatrecht der Schweiz 376–77 (2002).

[35] For the suggestion that generalizing such an option to invoke the more favorable law would advance conduct-regulating state interests, see Symeonides, supra, at 8.3,. See also id. at 9.3.

quantification, are now substantive? A literal reading of the provision would so suggest. However, there is some legislative history to indicate that, at all stages in the legislative process, the understanding was that damage quantification would be procedural. See Hay, supra at I–147 to I–149, I–151. Also noteworthy is that Art. 12(1)(c) of the Rome I Regulation again contains the qualifying language. Its Recital (7), as well as Recital (7) of the Rome II Regulation, call for the Regulations to be "consistent" with one another. How to resolve the question? Which way does Recital (33) point? Recital (32)? A final answer may need to await judicial clarification.

Punitive Damages. Art. 26—the public policy exception—no longer declares punitive damages to be against "Community public policy" (as the Commission's proposal would have provided). The previous language had been resisted by England and Ireland, perhaps in part because their domestic laws contain the concept of "exemplary damages," perhaps also because the award of such damages is not entirely unknown in Community law itself. See Hay, supra at I–150. The result was a compromise: Recital (32) clarifies in advance that the concept of "public policy" in Art. 26 permits a national court ("may . . . be regarded") to consider punitive damages to violate the forum's public policy.

9. Refer to the discussion of Mandatory Rules in the Notes following the Rome I Regulation, p. 1209, supra. The proposal for the Rome II Regulation had mirrored those rules. As enacted, the provision (Art. 16) addresses only overriding mandatory rules of the forum, dropping the reference to those of a third country. It is reported (Jan von Hein, in [2007] Versicherungsrecht 440, 443) that restricting the scope of Art. 16 as well as the compromise with respect to punitive damages, above, were the price for the participation of Ireland and the United Kingdom. Recall that Denmark opted out of the Rome I Regulation. For the application of Rome II rules in the United Kingdom after Brexit, see p. 1211, n. 31, supra.

10. *Renvoi.* States differ on whether a reference to foreign law, in cases other than contract, includes that law's conflicts rules. Some states provide for renvoi (e.g., Austria, Germany), others do not (e.g., Greece), while still others will consider foreign conflicts law only when it refers back to the forum (e.g., Japan). Russia, Belarus, and the Ukraine accept a reference back only in status matters. Art. 24 of the Regulation excludes renvoi for tort cases, as Art. 20 of Rome I does for contracts. If one function of renvoi is the desire to avoid the possible application of a law with little or no connection with the case, the provisions of the Regulation (Arts. 4(3) and others) for displacement of the otherwise applicable law by a law with a "manifestly closer connection," will serve that function. In states adhering to renvoi and not adopting other flexible rules, its application will be limited essentially to matters of family law and succession.

11. Art. 14 permits the parties, within limits, to choose the applicable law.[36] The provision raises some questions. Art. 14(1)(b) permits parties "pursuing

---

[36] Because of the special concern with the lex protectionis in the area of intellectual property rights (Art. 8), party autonomy does not extend to the infringement of those rights. EC Commission, supra n. 42, at 22–23 and 20.

a commercial activity" to stipulate the applicable law for potential tort claims in their contractual business arrangements. This makes sense; but what is "commercial activity"? With respect to jurisdiction (Brussels I Regulation and the Brussels Convention before it), the Court of Justice has interpreted "contract" narrowly and has not permitted specific jurisdiction in contract to pull in tort claims, lest the distinction between general and specific jurisdiction become diluted. See p. 1164, supra. What about a choice-of-law clause in a commercial contract: does it extend to tort claims between the parties? See the second paragraph of Art. 14(1)(b).

Art. 14(2) is an adaptation of Art. 3(3) of the original Rome Convention (now Rome I Regulation). The closest connection, in the case envisioned, is obviously with the state with which all elements—except the chosen law—are connected. In such circumstances, the rules of law of that state, "which cannot be derogated from," apply despite the parties' stipulation. The quoted language is a deliberate attempt to say "mandatory rules" without using those words; what is meant are those binding rules of that country's law that would have applied (under Art. 3(3)) but for the choice, even if they do not rise to the level of "mandatory laws" that would override a law made applicable by virtue of the Regulation's rules.[37]

Art. 14(3) clarifies that it refers to the law of a non-member state of the EC. Apart from this, Art. 14 does not say much about the conditions for a valid exercise of the right to make a choice. What is the intended difference between "reasonable certainty" in Art. 14(1), 2nd para., and "clearly demonstrated" in Art. 3(1) of the Rome I Regulation? What law does the court apply to make the determinations contemplated by the Recital? In particular, what governs the parties' "agreement?" See Art. 10 of the Rome I Regulation. For all of the above, see also Hartley, Choice of Law for Non-Contractual Liability: Selected Problems Under the Rome II Regulation, 57 Int'l & Comp.L.Q. 899 (2008).

12. Recall that the Court of Justice adopted a narrow definition of "contract" in the context of jurisdiction. See Case C-51/97, Réunion Europénne S.A. v. Spliethoff, [1998] ECR I-6511, paras. 17, 26. In addition to tort, the Rome II Regulation therefore provides specific treatment for each of three types of claims that civil law countries consider to be "non-contractual," simply because they do not arise from consensual undertakings. Arts. 10, 11, and 12 treat unjust enrichment, *negotiorum gestio*, and *culpa in contrahendo*, respectively. Of these, the last two are relatively unfamiliar to common lawyers. Negotiorum gestio, often translated as "agency without mandate," encompasses cases of discharging someone else's duty, but goes further than that. See D. Keehan, Negotiorum Gestio: A Civil Concept in the Common Law?, 55 Int'l & Comp.L.Q. 253 (2006). *Culpa in contrahendo* addresses pre-contractual liability, for instance, when violation of the pervasive good-faith-requirement in the negotiating process results in damage. See Arenas Garcia, La regulación de la responsabilidad precontractual en el Reglamento "Roma II," 7 Anuario Español de Derecho Internacional Privado 315 (2007).

---

[37] EC Commission, Explanatory Memorandum, supra n. 42, at 23.

See also Chong, Choice of Law for Unjust Enrichment/Restitution and the Rome II Regulation, 57 Int'l & Comp.L.Q. 863 (2008).

More often than not, these types of claims arise from some other, perhaps underlying, relationship between the parties. The three provisions therefore call for the application of the law applicable to that particular relationship, subject in all cases to an exception in favor of the "manifestly more closely connected" law.

In 2020, the European Court of Justice faced the question whether a claim involving the defendant's dominant market power arose in tort or in contract. While the parties' contract was "indispensable" for the decision, the consequences of defendant's conduct led to the conclusion that the action sounded in tort. Wikingerhof GmbH & Co. KG v. Booking.com BV, Case C-59/19, Grand Chamber Nov. 24, 2020, CELEX number: 62019CJ0059.

13. *United Kingdom*: Under Art. 25(2), cases arising as between two of the United Kingdom's three jurisdictions—England and Wales, Scotland and Northern Ireland, and Gibraltar—might lack the required internationality for the Regulation to apply. English implementing legislation—the *Law Applicable to Non-Contractual Obligations (England and Wales and Northern Ireland) Regulations 2008*, S.I., 2008, No. 2986—extends the Rome II Regulation's applicability to conflicts with respect to England and Wales, Northern Ireland, Scotland, and Gibraltar. Id., Regulation 6.[38]

---

3. CHOICE OF LAW FOR DIVORCE AND LEGAL SEPARATION: "ROME III"

Introduction

The Brussels IIa and IIa Recast Regulations provide for divorce jurisdiction in all EU member states (except Denmark) but do not address questions of the applicable law. As a result, national conflicts law determined the applicable law. National conflicts rules differed: some countries looked to the law of the parties' common nationality, to their (last common) habitual residence or, in the case of common law countries, to forum law. Substantive national law, to which conflicts rules might refer, likewise differed; some states provided for no-fault divorce, while others conditioned divorce on fault grounds or did not provide for divorce at all (Malta, at the time).

It appeared desirable to unify conflicts rules just as jurisdictional rules had been unified. An early proposal by the Commission may be found at COM/2006/0399–final—CNS 2006/0135. However, agreement was difficult to reach, particularly because of the considerable difference in substantive divorce law, which common conflicts rules might make applicable (see above).

The Treaty on the Functioning of the European Union (TFEU) provides that the European Council may authorize "enhanced

---

[38] See also the Note on "Brexit," p. 1134, supra.

cooperation" among a group of member states (Art. 326 et seq.). Fifteen members states requested the Council to authorize legislation, by way of "enhanced cooperation" among them, to provide rules on the law applicable to divorce and legal separations. Greece later withdrew; the remaining fourteen states are listed in Recital (6) of the Regulation below. The Council granted the request (Art. 328(2) TFEU), [2010] Official Journal L 189/12, the Commission and the participating member states drafted proposed legislation, and the Council, after complying with Treaty procedural requirements, approved the proposal and promulgated it as a Regulation on Dec. 20, 2010. Since that time, three additional states have opted in: Estonia, Greece, and Lithuania.

Council Regulation (EU) No 1259/2010 of 20 December 2010 Implementing Enhanced Cooperation In the Area of the Law Applicable to Divorce and Legal Separation
[2010] Official Journal L 343/10

. . .

Whereas:

. . .

(6)　Belgium, Bulgaria, Germany, . . . Spain, France, Italy, Latvia, Luxembourg, Hungary, Malta, Austria, Portugal, Romania and Slovenia . . . addressed a request to the Commission indicating that they intended to establish enhanced cooperation between themselves in the area of applicable law in matrimonial matters. . . .

(7)　On 12 July 2010 the Council adopted Decision 2010/405/EU authorising enhanced cooperation in the area of the law applicable to divorce and legal separation.

(8)　According to Article 328(1) of the Treaty on the Functioning of the European Union, when enhanced cooperation is being established, it is to be open to all Member States, subject to compliance with any conditions of participation laid down by the authorising decision. It is also to be open to them at any other time, subject to compliance with the acts already adopted within that framework, in addition to those conditions. . . .

(9)　This Regulation should create a clear, comprehensive legal framework in the area of the law applicable to divorce and legal separation in the participating Member States, provide citizens with appropriate outcomes in terms of legal certainty, predictability and flexibility, and prevent a situation from arising where one of the spouses applies for divorce before the other one does in order to ensure that the proceeding is governed by a given law which he or she considers more favourable to his or her own interests.

(10) The substantive scope and enacting terms of this Regulation should be consistent with Regulation (EC) No 2201/2003. However, it should not apply to marriage annulment.

This Regulation should apply only to the dissolution or loosening of marriage ties. The law determined by the conflict-of-laws rules of this Regulation should apply to the grounds for divorce and legal separation.

Preliminary questions such as legal capacity and the validity of the marriage, and matters such as the effects of divorce or legal separation on property, name, parental responsibility, maintenance obligations or any other ancillary measures should be determined by the conflict-of-laws rules applicable in the participating Member State concerned.

. . .

(12) This Regulation should be universal, i.e. it should be possible for its uniform conflict-of-laws rules to designate the law of a participating Member State, the law of a non-participating Member State or the law of a State which is not a member of the European Union.

(13) This Regulation should apply irrespective of the nature of the court or tribunal seized. Where applicable, a court should be deemed to be seized in accordance with Regulation (EC) No 2201/2003.

(14) In order to allow the spouses to choose an applicable law with which they have a close connection or, in the absence of such choice, in order that that law might apply to their divorce or legal separation, the law in question should apply even if it is not that of a participating Member State. Where the law of another Member State is designated, the network created by Council Decision 2001/470/EC of 28 May 2001 establishing a European Judicial Network in civil and commercial matters [2001 Official Journal L 174 —eds.], could play a part in assisting the courts with regard to the content of foreign law.

(15) Increasing the mobility of citizens calls for more flexibility and greater legal certainty. In order to achieve that objective, this Regulation should enhance the parties' autonomy in the areas of divorce and legal separation by giving them a limited possibility to choose the law applicable to their divorce or legal separation.

(16) Spouses should be able to choose the law of a country with which they have a special connection or the law of the forum as the law applicable to divorce and legal separation. The law chosen by the spouses must be consonant with the fundamental rights recognised by the Treaties and the Charter of Fundamental Rights of the European Union.

(17) Before designating the applicable law, it is important for spouses to have access to up-to-date information concerning the essential aspects of national and Union law and of the procedures governing divorce and legal separation. To guarantee such access to appropriate, good-quality information, the Commission regularly updates it in the Internet-based public information system set up by Council Decision 2001/470/EC.

(18) The informed choice of both spouses is a basic principle of this Regulation. Each spouse should know exactly what are the legal and social implications of the choice of applicable law. The possibility of choosing the applicable law by common agreement should be without prejudice to the rights of, and equal opportunities for, the two spouses. Hence judges in the participating Member States should be aware of the importance of an informed choice on the part of the two spouses concerning the legal implications of the choice-of-law agreement concluded.

(19) Rules on material and formal validity should be defined so that the informed choice of the spouses is facilitated and that their consent is respected with a view to ensuring legal certainty as well as better access to justice. As far as formal validity is concerned, certain safeguards should be introduced to ensure that spouses are aware of the implications of their choice. The agreement on the choice of applicable law should at least be expressed in writing, dated and signed by both parties. However, if the law of the participating Member State in which the two spouses have their habitual residence at the time the agreement is concluded lays down additional formal rules, those rules should be complied with. For example, such additional

formal rules may exist in a participating Member State where the agreement is inserted in a marriage contract. If, at the time the agreement is concluded, the spouses are habitually resident in different participating Member States which lay down different formal rules, compliance with the formal rules of one of these States would suffice. If, at the time the agreement is concluded, only one of the spouses is habitually resident in a participating Member State which lays down additional formal rules, these rules should be complied with.

(20) An agreement designating the applicable law should be able to be concluded and modified at the latest at the time the court is seized, and even during the course of the proceeding if the law of the forum so provides. In that event, it should be sufficient for such designation to be recorded in court in accordance with the law of the forum.

(21) Where no applicable law is chosen, and with a view to guaranteeing legal certainty and predictability and preventing a situation from arising in which one of the spouses applies for divorce before the other one does in order to ensure that the proceeding is governed by a given law which he considers more favourable to his own interests, this Regulation should introduce harmonised conflict-of-laws rules on the basis of a scale of successive connecting factors based on the existence of a close connection between the spouses and the law concerned. Such connecting factors should be chosen so as to ensure that proceedings relating to divorce or legal separation are governed by a law with which the spouses have a close connection.

(22) Where this Regulation refers to nationality as a connecting factor for the application of the law of a State, the question of how to deal with cases of multiple nationality should be left to national law, in full observance of the general principles of the European Union.

(23) If the court is seized in order to convert a legal separation into divorce, and where the parties have not made any choice as to the law applicable, the law which applied to the legal separation should also apply to the divorce. Such continuity would promote predictability for the parties and increase legal certainty. If the law applied to the legal separation does not provide for the conversion of legal separation into divorce, the divorce should be governed by the conflict-of-laws rules which apply in the absence of a choice by the parties. This should not prevent the spouses from seeking divorce on the basis of other rules in this Regulation.

(24) In certain situations, such as where the applicable law makes no provision for divorce or where it does not grant one of the spouses equal access to divorce or legal separation on grounds of their sex, the law of the court seized should nevertheless apply. This, however, should be without prejudice to the public policy clause.

(25) Considerations of public interest should allow courts in the Member States the opportunity in exceptional circumstances to disregard the application of a provision of foreign law in a given case where it would be manifestly contrary to the public policy of the forum. However, the courts should not be able to apply the public policy exception in order to disregard a provision of the law of another State when to do so would be contrary to the Charter of Fundamental Rights of the European Union, and in particular Article 21 thereof, which prohibits all forms of discrimination.

(26) Where this Regulation refers to the fact that the law of the participating Member State whose court is seized does not provide for divorce, this should be interpreted to mean that the law of this Member State does not have the institute of divorce. In such a case, the court should not be obliged to pronounce a divorce by virtue of this Regulation.

Where this Regulation refers to the fact that the law of the participating Member State whose court is seized does not deem the marriage in question valid for the purposes of divorce proceedings, this should be interpreted to mean, inter alia, that such a marriage does not exist in the law of that Member State. In such a case, the court should not be obliged to pronounce a divorce or a legal separation by virtue of this Regulation.

(27) Since there are States and participating Member States in which two or more systems of law or sets of rules concerning matters governed by this Regulation coexist, there should be a provision governing the extent to which this Regulation applies in the different territorial units of those States and participating Member States or to different categories of persons of those States and participating Member States.

(28) In the absence of rules designating the applicable law, parties choosing the law of the State of the nationality of one of them should at the same time indicate which territorial unit's law they have agreed upon in case the State whose law is chosen comprises several territorial units each of which has its own system of law or a set of rules in respect of divorce.

(29) Since the objectives of this Regulation, namely the enhancement of legal certainty, predictability and flexibility in international matrimonial proceedings and hence the facilitation of the free movement of persons within the Union, cannot be sufficiently achieved by the Member States and can therefore, by reasons of the scale and effects of this Regulation be better achieved at Union level, the Union may adopt measures, by means of enhanced cooperation where appropriate, in accordance with the principle of subsidiarity as set out in Article 5 of the Treaty on European Union. In accordance with the principle of proportionality, as set out in that Article, this Regulation does not go beyond what is necessary in order to achieve those objectives.

(30) This Regulation respects fundamental rights and observes the principles recognised by the Charter of Fundamental Rights of the European Union, and in particular by Article 21 thereof, which states that any discrimination based on any ground such as sex, race, colour, ethnic or social origin, genetic features, language, religion or belief, political or any other opinion, membership of a national minority, property, birth, disability, age or sexual orientation shall be prohibited. This Regulation should be applied by the courts of the participating Member States in observance of those rights and principles,

HAS ADOPTED THIS REGULATION:

CHAPTER I

SCOPE, RELATION WITH REGULATION (EC) No 2201/2003 ["Brussels IIa"[39], DEFINITIONS AND UNIVERSAL APPLICATION

Article 1

Scope

1. This Regulation shall apply, in situations involving a conflict of laws, to divorce and legal separation.

2. This Regulation shall not apply to the following matters, even if they arise merely as a preliminary question within the context of divorce or legal separation proceedings:

(a) the legal capacity of natural persons;

(b) the existence, validity or recognition of a marriage;

(c) the annulment of a marriage;

---

[39] P. 1167, supra.

(d)   the name of the spouses;

(e)   the property consequences of the marriage;

(f)   parental responsibility;

(g)   maintenance obligations;

(h)   trusts or successions.

Article 2

Relation with Regulation (EC) No 2201/2003

This Regulation shall not affect the application of Regulation (EC) No 2201/2003 ["Brussels-IIa," p. 1169, supra —eds.].

Article 3

Definitions

For the purposes of this Regulation:

1.   "participating Member State" means a Member State which participates in enhanced cooperation on the law applicable to divorce and legal separation by virtue of Decision 2010/405/EU, or by virtue of a decision adopted in accordance with the second or third subparagraph of Article 331(1) of the Treaty on the Functioning of the European Union;

2.   the term "court" shall cover all the authorities in the participating Member States with jurisdiction in the matters falling within the scope of this Regulation.

Article 4

Universal application

The law designated by this Regulation shall apply whether or not it is the law of a participating Member State.

CHAPTER II
UNIFORM RULES ON THE LAW APPLICABLE
TO DIVORCE AND LEGAL SEPARATION

Article 5
Choice of applicable law by the parties

1.   The spouses may agree to designate the law applicable to divorce and legal separation provided that it is one of the following laws:

(a)   the law of the State where the spouses are habitually resident at the time the agreement is concluded; or

(b)   the law of the State where the spouses were last habitually resident, in so far as one of them still resides there at the time the agreement is concluded; or

(c)   the law of the State of nationality of either spouse at the time the agreement is concluded; or

(d)   the law of the forum.

2.   Without prejudice to paragraph 3, an agreement designating the applicable law may be concluded and modified at any time, but at the latest at the time the court is seized.

3.   If the law of the forum so provides, the spouses may also designate the law applicable before the court during the course of the proceeding. In that event, such designation shall be recorded in court in accordance with the law of the forum.

Article 6
Consent and material validity

1.   The existence and validity of an agreement on choice of law or of any term thereof, shall be determined by the law which would govern it under this Regulation if the agreement or term were valid.

2.   Nevertheless, a spouse, in order to establish that he did not consent, may rely upon the law of the country in which he has his habitual residence at the time the court is seized if it appears from the circumstances that it would not be reasonable to determine the effect of his conduct in accordance with the law specified in paragraph 1.

Article 7
Formal validity

1.   The agreement referred to in Article 5(1) and (2), shall be expressed in writing, dated and signed by both spouses. Any communication by electronic means which provides a durable record of the agreement shall be deemed equivalent to writing.

2.   However, if the law of the participating Member State in which the two spouses have their habitual residence at the time the agreement is concluded lays down additional formal requirements for this type of agreement, those requirements shall apply.

3.   If the spouses are habitually resident in different participating Member States at the time the agreement is concluded and the laws of those States provide for different formal requirements, the agreement shall be formally valid if it satisfies the requirements of either of those laws.

4.   If only one of the spouses is habitually resident in a participating Member State at the time the agreement is concluded and that State lays down additional formal requirements for this type of agreement, those requirements shall apply.

Article 8
Applicable law in the absence of a choice by the parties

In the absence of a choice pursuant to Article 5, divorce and legal separation shall be subject to the law of the State:

(a)   where the spouses are habitually resident at the time the court is seized; or, failing that

(b)   where the spouses were last habitually resident, provided that the period of residence did not end more than 1 year before the court was seized, in so far as one of the spouses still resides in that State at the time the court is seized; or, failing that

(c)   of which both spouses are nationals at the time the court is seized; or, failing that

(d)   where the court is seized.

Article 9
Conversion of legal separation into divorce

1.   Where legal separation is converted into divorce, the law applicable to divorce shall be the law applied to the legal separation, unless the parties have agreed otherwise in accordance with Article 5.

2.   However, if the law applied to the legal separation does not provide for the conversion of legal separation into divorce, Article 8 shall apply, unless the parties have agreed otherwise in accordance with Article 5.

Article 10
Application of the law of the forum

Where the law applicable pursuant to Article 5 or Article 8 makes no provision for divorce or does not grant one of the spouses equal access to divorce or legal separation on grounds of their sex, the law of the forum shall apply.

Article 11
Exclusion of renvoi

Where this Regulation provides for the application of the law of a State, it refers to the rules of law in force in that State other than its rules of private international law.

Article 12
Public policy

Application of a provision of the law designated by virtue of this Regulation may be refused only if such application is manifestly incompatible with the public policy of the forum.

Article 13
Differences in national law

Nothing in this Regulation shall oblige the courts of a participating Member State whose law does not provide for divorce or does not deem the marriage in question valid for the purposes of divorce proceedings to pronounce a divorce by virtue of the application of this Regulation.

Article 14
States with two or more legal systems—territorial conflicts of laws

Where a State comprises several territorial units each of which has its own system of law or a set of rules concerning matters governed by this Regulation:

(a)   any reference to the law of such State shall be construed, for the purposes of determining the law applicable under this Regulation, as referring to the law in force in the relevant territorial unit;

(b)   any reference to habitual residence in that State shall be construed as referring to habitual residence in a territorial unit;

(c)   any reference to nationality shall refer to the territorial unit designated by the law of that State, or, in the absence of relevant rules, to the territorial unit chosen by the parties or, in absence of choice, to the territorial unit with which the spouse or spouses has or have the closest connection.

Article 15
States with two or more legal systems— inter-personal conflicts of laws

In relation to a State which has two or more systems of law or sets of rules applicable to different categories of persons concerning matters governed by this Regulation, any reference to the law of such a State shall be construed as referring to the legal system determined by the rules in force in that State. In the absence of such rules, the system of law or the set of rules with which the spouse or spouses has or have the closest connection applies.

Article 16
Non-application of this Regulation to internal conflicts of laws

A participating Member State in which different systems of law or sets of rules apply to matters governed by this Regulation shall not be required to apply this Regulation to conflicts of laws arising solely between such different systems of law or sets of rules.

. . .

NOTES

1. Jurisdiction for divorce and legal separation continues to be governed by the "Brussels IIa" Regulation (see its Art. 3, p. 1173, supra). Note how closely the Rome III Regulation's applicable law provisions (Arts. 5 and 8) track those of the Jurisdiction Regulation. Both Regulations, and especially Rome III, seek to identify a closely connected forum and law for the divorce. Note in particular that the options listed in Art. 8 of Rome III are in priority order (". . . Failing that . . ."), while the Brussels IIa Regulation does not prioritize among the various bases for jurisdiction. Whether the forum may assert jurisdiction as a last resort is left to national law by Brussels IIa (Art. 7(1), p. 1174, supra), while Rome III specifically lists forum law as the last option (Art. 8(d)).

2. In the United States, the applicable law in divorce is the lex fori. The suggestion by Judge Hastie in Alton v. Alton, p. 923 supra, to apply the law of the parties' domicile to guard against circumvention of the societal interests of their home state never took hold in this country. The provisions of Rome III seek to achieve Judge Hastie's objective, with forum law applicable only as a fall-back.

Neither in the United States nor in the national law of most other countries are parties free to stipulate the applicable law for divorce. In the United States, a change in applicable law can be effected only by a change in habitual residence (domicile). In other countries, changing the applicable law might even be harder, for instance, when the other country's law looks to the parties' nationality or last common habitual residence. The novel provision of Art. 5 of Rome III makes "the informed choice of both spouses . . . a basic principle of [the] Regulation" (Recital (18)). The parties' freedom of choice is not open-ended but is restricted to the exact same options that Art. 8 establishes for cases in which the parties made no choice. But, while Art. 8 prioritizes (see above), Art. 5 leaves the parties free (". . . or . . .") to choose from among the possible applicable laws offered. Whether the parties' choice-of-law agreement is valid (was there capacity, was there consent?) is governed by the chosen law (Art. 6). This provision parallels the solution adopted by Arts. 7(5) and 10 of the Rome I Regulation (pp. 1142, 1143, supra).

3. Rome III provides rules for the choice of the applicable law that are of "universal application" (Art. 4), the same as do the Rome I and II Regulations, i.e., they replace the national choice-of-law rules of participating states regardless of whether the law designated in this way is that of a participating or of a non-participating member state or third country. Thus, if Americans seek a divorce in France—satisfying the jurisdictional prerequisites of the Brussels IIa Regulation—the French court will now apply the law designated by Arts. 5 or 8, as the case may be. What if that inquiry points to the United States, e.g., because the spouses were last habitually resident there? After all, there is no "American" divorce law. Art. 14 envisions such a case. Applying that provision encounters the further difficulty that there is no "American" (federal) rule designating the applicable state law. Here, Art. 14(a) or the last part of Art. 14(c) will help: presumably, in the hypothetical given, it will be the law of the state of the spouses' last habitual residence in the United States. Prior to the adoption of Rome III, a national court in the European Union (or, today, a non-EU court) could reach the same result on the basis of American law: the U.S. Constitution provides in Amendment XIV (§ 1) that persons are "citizens of the United States and of the state wherein they reside." A reference to the law of American "nationality" thus contains a reference to a state of the Union as well. For early discussion in a different context (applicable law follows jurisdiction in American divorce law), see Hay, in [1988] IPRax 265 (in German). Note that Art. 15 envisions a different case of "more than one legal system," viz. the case in which there is secular and religious law in force in the *same* state. In the United States, this provision may also be relevant when the question concerns the applicability of state or Native American tribal law to parties residing in the same state.

4.   A hypothetical: until recently, Maltese law did not provide for divorce. Could (a) one or two Maltese nationals or former habitual residents obtain a divorce in France, and did Malta have to recognize such a divorce, if granted? (b) Could one or two German nationals or former habitual residents obtain a divorce in Malta?

(a)   Jurisdiction of the French court is determined by Art. 3 of Brussels IIa (assumed as satisfied in the hypothetical); the applicable law is that designated by Rome III. Here, the parties could choose the law of the French forum (Art. 5(c)) or, if they made no choice, seek application of French law under Art. 10 and obtain a divorce (no *renvoi* to Maltese law—Art. 11). Recognition of the divorce decree is again governed by Brussels IIa: Malta could not refuse recognition on the ground that its law did not provide for divorce—Art. 25.

(b)   Assuming that Malta had jurisdiction under Brussels IIa, a special provision—particularizing the general public-policy exception of Art. 12 of Rome III—permitted it to refuse to proceed and to grant a divorce: Art. 13.

Divorce legislation entered into force in Malta on October 1, 2011, implementing the result of a referendum of earlier in the year.

5.   *Further Reading:* Aude Fiorini, Rome III—Choice of Law in Divorce: Is the Europeanization of Family Going too Far?, 22 Int'l J.L. & Pol'y & Fam. 178 (2008); Linda Silberman, Rethinking Rules of Conflict of Laws in Marriage and Divorce: What Can We Learn from Europe?, 82 Tul.L.Rev. 1999 (2008). See also House of Lords, European Union Committee, Rome

III—Choice of Law in Divorce, 52nd Report of Session 2005–06, HL Paper 272 (2006). See also Kohler, Zur Gestaltung des europäischen Kollisionsrechts für Ehesachen: Der steinige Weg zu einheitlichen Vorschriften über das anwendbare Recht für Scheidung und Trennung, [2008] FamRZ 1673.

4.   MAINTENANCE OBLIGATIONS

Council Regulation (EC) No. 4/2009 on Jurisdiction, Applicable Law, and Enforcement of Decisions and Cooperation in Matters of Maintenance Obligations

[2009] Official Journal L 7/1

(Textual Note)

[The jurisdictional provisions of Regulation 4/2009 are considered at p. 1189, supra. The present Note concerns the law applicable to maintenance obligations.]

Art. 15 of EC Regulation No. 4/2009 makes the choice-of-law rules of the 2007 Hague Protocol applicable to interstate and international maintenance claims in member state courts (other than Denmark and the United Kingdom), presumably from June 18, 2010. The references in the following are to the provisions of the 2007 Hague Protocol. All references to a country's law are to its substantive law (to the exclusion of its conflicts law: Art. 12). As in the context of jurisdiction, supra, the concept of a "family relationship" (Art. 1) is meant to be open-ended and includes, depending on the applicable national law, maintenance obligations of unmarried partners. This last aspect has decreased somewhat in importance as a majority of EU member states now recognize same-sex marriages (14 in 2020)[40] or civil unions with partners enjoying spousal benefits (8 in 2020).[41]

Default Rules. The general default rule—in the absence of a valid choice of law by the parties themselves (below), but subject to some special exceptions—is to apply the law of the maintenance creditor's state of habitual residence. Art. 3(1). If the latter changes, so does the applicable law. Art. 3(2). Special default rules apply to the obligations of parents toward their children, of other persons toward children under the age of 21, and of children toward their parents: if the creditor cannot obtain support in application of Art. 3, the lex fori applies (Art. 4(2)); if the creditor sues at the debtor's habitual residence, that law applies before Art. 3 (Art. 4(3)); and, failing all of the foregoing, the law of the parties' common nationality applies. Another special rule (Art. 5) applies to obligation between spouses, ex-spouses, or parties to an annulled marriage: upon demand by either party, the law of the state with a closer relationship to the marriage than the law applicable under Art. 3 applies

---

[40]   Austria, Belgium, Denmark, Finland, France, Germany, Ireland, Luxembourg, Malta, Netherlands, Portugal, Spain, Sweden, United Kingdom.

[41]   Croatia, Cyprus, Czech Republic, Estonia, Greece, Hungary, Italy, Slovenia.

("particularly the [law of the] State of their last common habitual residence").

Defenses. The law applicable to the claim also extends to any defenses the debtor may have (see Art. 11(a)). In addition, Art. 6 permits the debtor to show (except in claims arising from a parent-child relationship or under Art. 5) that there is no obligation under both the laws of the debtor's habitual residence and the parties common nationality. This rule may at first seem strange. However, it protects a debtor who has no liability under the spouses' common citizenship law against liability solely on the ground that the creditor has taken up habitual residence in a liability-favoring country. If the debtor has also made such a move, the protection stops. But see under "Public Policy," infra.

While the applicable law also determines the extent of the obligation and the basis for the calculation of its amount (Art. 11(a) and (c)), Art. 14 directs that "the needs of the creditor and the resources of the debtor . . . shall be taken into account [by the forum] in determining the amount of the maintenance." This provision, looking toward individualizing the award on the basis of personal circumstances, bears some resemblance to the policy expressed in Recital (33) of the Rome II Regulation, p. 1214, supra.

Choice of Law by the Parties. The Protocol distinguishes between the action at hand and possible future litigation between the parties. For the former (". . . for the purpose only of a particular proceeding . . ."), the parties may agree—expressly and in a signed writing or a recorded (also: electronic) medium—on the law of the forum of their litigation. Art. 7.

For a general, not specific-proceeding-related choice of the applicable law, Art. 8(1) provides four permissible choices: the law of the country of (1) nationality or (2) habitual residence of either party at the time the choice is made; or the law the parties chose, or which in fact applies, to their (3) "property regime" or (4) divorce or legal separation. Note that suit in a particular forum, with jurisdiction over the defendant as provided by the Regulation does not result in the application of forum law even in the absence of any objection by the defendant to that effect: Art. 7, preceding paragraph, and its requirements as to formality apply.

The parties' ability to choose the applicable law is limited further in three respects. Two are designed to protect the obligee as the weaker party under either of the following circumstances: party choice of the applicable law is excluded altogether for obligations toward persons under age 18 or those mentally impaired; a maintenance creditor's renunciation of a claim must be permissible under his or her law of habitual residence, Art. 8(3–4).

The third limitation (Art. 8(5)) also protects the weaker party but recognizes that this may be either the obligee or the obligor: "Unless . . . the parties were fully informed and aware of the consequences" of their choice of law, the chosen law "shall not apply [(the default rules then do)] where [its] application ... would lead to manifestly unfair and unreasonable consequences for any of the parties." The provision directs the court to consider the effects of the parties' choice on the individual case. What if application of the default rule also leads to a harsh result for one of the parties? See text immediately following.

Public Policy. All applicable-law conventions (as, indeed, those dealing with the recognition of decisions) contemplate non-application of the instrument's norms on grounds of local (the forum's) public policy. In the case of a choice of law by the parties, the public-policy concerns of an involved state on behalf of one of the parties are addressed by the limitations established by Art. 5 (see text, previous paragraph). The general public policy exception of Art. 13 therefore applies mainly in other, more general contexts.

In the great majority of cases, no problems may be expected to arise: the reference to the claimant's law of habitual residence will more often than not mean that the forum will apply its own law. Even when place of suit and applicable law are different, it is unlikely that the latter will be so unfavorable to the claimant that the forum will be moved to disregard it on public policy grounds.

An exceptional case may be presented by the situation addressed by Art. 6 (supra): the law of the parties' common nationality and the debtor's law of habitual residence (for instance, because he remained in that country) do not provide for a maintenance obligation, but the claimant's new country of habitual residence (which is also the forum) does provide for such an obligation. Note that Art. 6, in turn, excludes parent-child and inter-spousal claims. Cases falling under Art. 6 and presenting a public policy problem under Art. 13 are thus hard to imagine. In any case, they will be few and far between. Art. 13 is a traditional and—for completeness' sake—useful provision, but cannot be expected to have much of a limiting effect.

Public Bodies. Interim (or even long-term) support is often provided by public agencies. Do they have a claim for reimbursement from the maintenance debtor once that person is located and amenable to jurisdiction? The Protocol divides the answer into two parts. It assigns to the law governing a public body (Art. 10) the question whether that public body has a claim for reimbursement of funds provided to the maintenance creditor. The extent of the debtor's obligation to reimburse a public body, in contrast, is governed by the law applicable to the maintenance obligation (Art. 11(f)).

NOTES

1.   Will an American court review the rendering EU court's choice of the applicable law? Will it have any concerns or objections if the court chose its own or that of another state (not the home state of the maintenance debtor)?

2. Should parties be able to stipulate the law applicable to maintenance obligations? Are the limits set by the new Regulation reasonable? Too lenient?

III. SUMMARY OF OTHER LEGISLATION

In addition to the legislative acts described in some detail in Parts I and II, above, the European Union has adopted a number of procedural measures to facilitate the enforcement of decisions and payment obligations in civil matters, thereby supplementing the Brussels I—now Ia—Regulation, supra, at p. 1137.[42] Furthermore, two further major substantive areas were the subject of EU legislation: jurisdiction and applicable law (a) in matters of succession and (b) with respect to the property regime of married couples and of members of registered partnerships. The following highlights a few major points of these two laws.

Succession

Regulation (EU) No. 650/2012 entered into force in August 2015 and deals with jurisdiction, recognition of decisions, and applicable law in matters of succession.[43] Denmark, Ireland, and the United Kingdom exercised their right to opt out. In contrast to American law, but in keeping with civil-law concepts, the Regulation treats a decedent's estate as a whole, not differentiating between moveable and immoveable assets: the court at the decedent's habitual residence at death has jurisdiction over all assets, regardless of where they are situated (Art. 4). There are two exceptions: the decedent may have made a choice of the applicable law (below), in which case the parties may agree that the court of that state (if an EU member state) shall exercise jurisdiction (Art. 5). It is also possible that a foreign court, where assets are located, might refuse to recognize the EU court's decision with respect to such assets (for instance, an American court with respect to local real property, over which it has exclusive jurisdiction by American standards). For such cases, the Regulation permits the EU court to refrain from ruling with respect to such assets (Art. 12).

The applicable law provision tracks the one on jurisdiction: the law of the decedent's habitual residence at death applies to "the succession as a whole" (Art. 21), but the decedent could have chosen the law of his nationality at the time of making the choice or at death (Art. 22). As in the Rome Regulations, the applicable law provisions are of "universal application" (Art. 20).

---

[42] These include, among others: Regulation (EC) No. 1393/2007, [2007] Official Journal L324/79; (Service of Documents); Regulation (EC) No. 1206/2001, [2001] Official Journal L174/1 (Taking Evidence Abroad); Council Directive 2002/8/EC, [2003] Official Journal 26/41 (Legal Aid for Access to Justice in Cross-Border Disputes); Regulation (EC) No. 805/2004, [2004] Official Journal L 143/15 (Enforcement Order for Uncontested Claims);Regulation (EC) No. 861/2007, [2007] Official Journal L 199/0 (Small Claims (up to Euro 2,000) Procedure).

[43] [2012] Official Journal L 201/107.

It might be, of course, that the applicable law contains something unknown to the forum, for instance when the hypothetically applicable American law provides for dower rights, but the European situs of the real property does not have that concept (nor does it for common-law types of future interests). Art. 31 calls on the forum court to "adapt" the foreign right "to the closest equivalent right in rem" under forum law.

The recognition and enforcement provisions closely mirror those of the Brussels Ia Regulation.

For further discussion, see Marongui Buonaiuti, The European Succession Convention and Third Country Courts, 12 J. Private Int'l L. 545 (2016); Pfeiffer, Legal Certainty and Predictability in International Succession Law, 12 J. Private Int'l L. 566 (2016); S.I. Strong, The European Succession Regulation and the Arbitration of Trust Disputes, 103 Iowa L. Rev. 2205, 2010 et seq. (2017–18); Zalucki, Attempts to Harmonize the Inheritance Law in Europe: Past, Present, Future, 103 Iowa L. Rev. 2317 (2017–18).

Matrimonial and Partnership Property Rights

A number of member states were eager to supplement the Brussels IIa and Rome III Regulations with provisions addressing matrimonial property rights upon death or divorce and, indeed, to make similar provisions for persons living in a registered partnership. In the absence of agreement among all members, the interested states, the Commission, and the Council again resorted to the "enhanced cooperation" procedure first used for the Rome III Regulation, supra, p. 1227. Two Regulations took effect in January 2019.

Regulation (EU) 2016/1103[44] concerns matrimonial property issues with respect to international married couples. The Regulation does not define "marriage," but leaves this to national law (Recital (17)), as it does questions concerning the existence, validity, or recognition of a foreign marriage (Art. 1(2)(b)). Jurisdiction in most cases tracks jurisdiction for succession (death of a spouse) or for divorce (Rome III) (Arts. 4–5). The applicable law provisions (of "universal application," Art. 20) apply to "all assets . . . regardless where located" (Art. 21), again not distinguishing between movables and immovable, the same as in the Succession Regulation, supra. The spouses as applicable law where they (or one of them) are habitually resident or the law of nationality of either of them (Art. 22). If they made no choice, Art. 26 provides—prioritized order—for the application of the law of habitual residence at the time of marriage, then that of their common nationality at that time, or of the state with which they were most closely connected at the time of marriage.

---

[44] [2016] Official Journal L 183/1. The Regulation applies to: Austria, Belgium, Bulgaria, Croatia, Czech Republic, Finland, France, Germany, Greece, Italy, Italy, Luxembourg, Malta, Netherlands, Portugal, Slovenia, Spain, and Sweden.

Recognition and enforcement of decrees again follow the scheme of the Brussels Ia Regulation, supra, p. 1151.

Regulation No. 2016/1104[45] makes essentially similar provisions for registered partnerships. It leaves the questions of the existence and validity of a registered partnership to national law (Recital (21) and Art. 1(2)(b)), but requires that to qualify the form of the living arrangement must be provided for by law and that its registration is mandatory (Art. 3). The jurisdictional provisions track those of Regulation 2016/1103, the parties may choose the law of their habitual residence or nationality as the applicable law (Art. 22), otherwise the law of the state where the partnership was created will ordinarily apply (Art. 26). Note, as mentioned at pp. 918, 920, supra, eight EU memberships provide for civil unions (as of 2020), while the number if member states providing for same-sex marriage has increased to fourteen.

---

[45]   [2016] Official Journal L 183/30.

INDEX

References are to Pages